ENVIRONMENTAL PROTECTION

ASPEN PUBLISHERS

ENVIRONMENTAL PROTECTION

Law and Policy

Fifth Edition

Robert L. Glicksman

Robert W. Wagstaff Professor of Law
University of Kansas

David L. Markell

Steven M. Goldstein Professor
Florida State University College of Law

William W. Buzbee

Professor and Director of the Emory Environmental and Natural Resources
Law Program
Emory University School of Law

Daniel R. Mandelker

Howard A. Stamper Professor of Law
Washington University

A. Dan Tarlock

Distinguished Professor of Law
IIT Chicago-Kent College of Law

 Wolters Kluwer
Law & Business

AUSTIN   BOSTON   CHICAGO   NEW YORK   THE NETHERLANDS

ISBN 978-0-7355-6348-3

Library of Congress Cataloging-in-Publication Data

Environmental protection : law and policy / Robert L. Glicksman . . . [et al.] – 5th ed.
   p. cm.
  ISBN 978-0-7355-6348-3 (hardcover : alk. paper)
1. Environmental law–United States–Cases. I. Glicksman, Robert L.

KF3775.A7A53 2007
344.7304′6–dc22

2007007420

About Wolters Kluwer Law & Business

Wolters Kluwer Law & Business is a leading provider of research information and workflow solutions in key specialty areas. The strengths of the individual brands of Aspen Publishers, CCH, Kluwer Law International and Loislaw are aligned within Wolters Kluwer Law & Business to provide comprehensive, in-depth solutions and expert-authored content for the legal, professional and education markets.

CCH was founded in 1913 and has served more than four generations of business professionals and their clients. The CCH products in the Wolters Kluwer Law & Business group are highly regarded electronic and print resources for legal, securities, antitrust and trade regulation, government contracting, banking, pension, payroll, employment and labor, and healthcare reimbursement and compliance professionals.

Aspen Publishers is a leading information provider for attorneys, business professionals and law students. Written by preeminent authorities, Aspen products offer analytical and practical information in a range of specialty practice areas from securities law and intellectual property to mergers and acquisitions and pension/benefits. Aspen's trusted legal education resources provide professors and students with high-quality, up-to-date and effective resources for successful instruction and study in all areas of the law.

Kluwer Law International supplies the global business community with comprehensive English-language international legal information. Legal practitioners, corporate counsel and business executives around the world rely on the Kluwer Law International journals, loose-leafs, books and electronic products for authoritative information in many areas of international legal practice.

Loislaw is a premier provider of digitized legal content to small law firm practitioners of various specializations. Loislaw provides attorneys with the ability to quickly and efficiently find the necessary legal information they need, when and where they need it, by facilitating access to primary law as well as state-specific law, records, forms and treatises.

Wolters Kluwer Law & Business, a unit of Wolters Kluwer, is headquartered in New York and Riverwoods, Illinois Wolters Kluwer is a leading multinational publisher and information services company.

To Emily, Erica, Jaclyn,
Zachary, and to Coppert and his "little girl", Bertie

R.L.G.

To Mona, Rebecca, Jenny, and Rachel,
and to my parents, William and Elaine Markell

D.L.M.

To Lisa, Tian, and Seana, and to my parents,
John and Ellen Buzbee

W.W.B.

To Marlene

D.R.M.

To Vivien, Robert, Katherine, and Marc

A.D.T.

SUMMARY OF CONTENTS

CONTENTS

CHAPTER II.   ENVIRONMENTAL FEDERALISM   83

CHAPTER III.   THE ADMINISTRATIVE LAW OF
                  ENVIRONMENTAL PROTECTION   137

CHAPTER IV.   THE NATIONAL ENVIRONMENTAL
                 POLICY ACT   229

CHAPTER VII.   PROTECTING THE WATER RESOURCE

CHAPTER IX.   LIABILITY FOR AND REMEDIATION
               OF HAZARDOUS SUBSTANCE
               CONTAMINATION   889

CHAPTER X.   ENFORCEMENT OF ENVIRONMENTAL LAW   983

PREFACE TO THE FIFTH EDITION

Environmental law continues to be characterized by political ferment and corresponding legal change. Although many central cases and statutory frameworks remain stable, environmental law demands attention to statutory and regulatory amendments, changes in agency policy, and the issuance of important new cases. Regular revision of environmental law casebooks is therefore warranted. The fifth edition of this casebook has been thoroughly updated to reflect recent and proposed changes in environmental law.

Some of the changes reflect the increased importance of discrete issues or environmental problems. Chapter 6, for example, has reorganized and significantly expanded on the materials that deal with new source review (NSR) under the Clean Air Act, in light of the judicial, administrative, and legislative activity that NSR issues have generated. Chapter 6 now also includes greatly expanded coverage of global climate change in recognition of the likelihood that it will become the defining environmental challenge of our time.

Other changes to the text are broader in focus. To reflect the continuing importance of issues concerning the allocation of federal and state authority to pursue environmental protection initiatives, we have added a new chapter to the casebook, Chapter 2, on environmental federalism. Similarly, the growth of international environmental law has persuaded us that the time has come to add another new chapter, Chapter 11, which is completely devoted to this area of environmental law. Despite these two new thematic treatments, both federalism and international environmental law issues continue to crop up throughout the text.

This edition of the casebook also reflects a reorganization and expansion of the introductory material in Chapter 1. Chapter 1 now includes more extensive treatment of the common law origins and component of environmental law, as well as a consolidated and slightly expanded discussion of economic perspectives on environmental harms and regulation. We have also expanded the coverage in Chapter 4 of biodiversity-related issues, including more extensive treatment of the Endangered Species Act. Chapter 7 continues to track the efforts of EPA, the Corps of Engineers, regulated entities, and the courts to define the scope of the Clean Water Act. The Supreme Court's 2006 decision in the *Rapanos* case takes center stage there. The chapter on CERCLA (which has become Chapter 9) devotes considerable attention to the right of potentially responsible parties to seek contribution, an area thrown into chaos as a result of the Supreme Court's 2004 decision in the *Aviall* case.

In addition, we have updated the materials throughout the book, adding new principal cases and other primary documents, revising note materials, creating new problems, and making an effort to enhance clarity through devices such as visual aids. We will continue to track recent developments and make our analyses available to casebook users both in the annual professors' updates made available by the publisher every summer and at the casebook's website, http://web.ku.edu/~rglicks/ envprot/, which is periodically updated.

Given the dynamic nature of environmental law, it is crucial to bring new perspectives to the subject. Beginning with the third edition, the original three senior authors—Professors Anderson, Mandelker, and Tarlock—have added outstanding new co-authors, starting with the current lead co-author, Professor Robert Glicksman, and continuing with Professor David Markell, and have gradually reduced their participation in the book. The transition to a new team is almost complete.

One of the most exciting changes we make in this edition is the addition of a new co-author, William W. Buzbee, Professor of Law and Director, Environmental and Natural Law Program, at the Emory University School of Law. Bill brings to the book, aside from his vast store of energy and enthusiasm, the expertise gained from his work on environmental, land use, and litigation matters both for public interest groups and in private practice. The groundbreaking scholarship Bill has produced as a faculty member at Emory spans an enormous terrain, but it makes him a natural choice to conceive and write the book's new chapter on environmental federalism. Bill is also responsible for the restructuring and expansion of Chapter 1.

We encourage users of this casebook to forward their thoughts on and suggestions for improvements on any future editions to any of us. Our e-mail addresses are available at the casebook's website.

Robert L. Glicksman
David L. Markell
William W. Buzbee
Daniel R. Mandelker
A. Dan Tarlock

Lawrence, Kansas
Tallahassee, Florida
Atlanta, Georgia
St. Louis, Missouri
Chicago, Illinois

January 2007

ACKNOWLEDGMENTS

Any casebook is a collaborative effort among many people. Professor Glicksman would like to thank Interim Dean Michael J. Davis and Dean Gail B. Agrawal for facilitating work on this project. Professor Markell would like to Julie Lemmer, FSU class of 2007, for assistance on Chapter 11, and Sarah Meyer, FSU class of 2007, for assistance on Chapters 7 and 10. The authors owe a particular debt of gratitude to Chris Wold and John Knox, who graciously reviewed drafts of the new chapter on international environmental law and provided useful feedback. With gratitude, we would like once again to acknowledge Carol McGeehan, our first editor, of Aspen Publishers for her support in bringing this edition to print. We also thank Eric Holt, Senior Developmental Editor at Aspen Publishers, and Katy Guimon, Project Manager at Publication Services, Inc., for helping us to navigate the publication process for the fifth edition.

The authors gratefully acknowledge the permissions granted to reproduce the following materials.

Ackerman, Observation of the Transformation of the U.S. Forest Service: The Effects of the National Environmental Policy Act on U.S. Forest Service Decision Making, 20 Envtl. L. 703, 708-713 (1990). Reprinted with permission of Environmental Law. Copyright © 1990.

Adler, Against "Individual Risk": A Sympathetic Critique of Risk Assessment, 153 U. Pa. L. Rev. 1121, 1133-1139, 1161-1162 (2005). Copyright © 2005 University of Pennsylvania Law Review, with the permission of William S. Hein & Co., Inc.

Bonine, The Evolution of Technology-Forcing in the Clean Air Act. Reprinted with permission from Environment Reporter, Vol. 6, Monograph No. 21, p.2 (July 25, 1975). Copyright © 1975 by The Bureau of National Affairs, Inc. (800-372-1033) http://www.bna.com.

Bosselman & Tarlock, The Influence of Ecological Science on American Law: An Introduction, 69 Chi.-Kent L. Rev. 847, 854-856, 861-862 (1994). Reprinted with permission of the authors. Copyright © 1994 by Chicago-Kent College of Law.

Botkin, Daniel, Discordant Harmonies: A New Ecology for the Twenty-first Century, 1991. Copyright © Oxford University Press. Used by permission from Oxford University Press.

Bryner, Gary, Blue Skies, Green Politics: The Clean Air Act of 1990. Reprinted with permission of Congressional Quarterly Press, 43, 71-73, 122. Copyright © 1993 by Congressional Quarterly Press.

Chambers & Green, Introduction: Toward an Effective Framework for Sustainable Development, in Reforming International Environmental Governance: From Institutional Limits to Innovative Reforms 1, 1-11 (W. Chambers & J. Green eds., 2005). Copyright © 2005 by the United Nations University. Reprinted with permission of the United Nations University Press.

Doremus, Patching the Ark: Improving Legal Protection of Biological Diversity, 18 Ecology L.Q. 265, 269-273 (1991). Reprinted with permission of the Regents of the University of California. Copyright © 1991 by Ecology Law Quarterly.

Eccleston, The NEPA Planning Process: A Comprehensive Guide with Emphasis on Efficiency (1999). John Wiley & Sons, Inc., Figure 2.1, p.52, and Figure C.8, p.383. Reprinted with permission of John Wiley & Sons, Inc. Copyright © 1999.

Garver, Geoffrey, CEC Mechanisms and Frameworks for Resolving Disputes over Transboundary Environmental Impacts, CBA-ABA Second Annual National Environmental, Energy and Resources Law Summit (28 Apr. 2006). Copyright © 2006 by the Canadian Bar Association. Reprinted with permission of Geoffrey Garver.

Greening NAFTA, The North American Commission for Environmental Cooperation (D. Markell & J. Knox eds.). Copyright © 2003 by the Board of Trustees of the Leland Stanford Jr. University.

Hardin, The Tragedy of the Commons, 162 Science 1243 (1968). Copyright © 1968 by the American Association of Sciences. Reprinted with permission of Science and Professor Garrett Hardin.

Heinzerling, Selling Pollution, Forcing Democracy, 14 Stan. Envtl. L.J. 300, 318, 323, 332, 342-343 (1995). Copyright © 1995 by the Board of Trustees of the Leland Stanford Junior University.

Karkkanian, Information as Environmental Regulation: TRI Performance Benchmarking, Precursor to a New Paradigm?, 89 Geo. L.J. 257 (2001). Copyright © 2001 by the Georgetown Law Journal. Reprinted with permission.

Knox, The Myth and Reality of Transboundary Environmental Impact Assessment, 96 Am. J. Int'l L. 291, 291-292 (2002). Copyright © 2002 by the American Society of International Law.

Lin, The Unifying Role of Harm, 2006 Wis. L. Rev. 897, 922-930, 945-946, 955-968, 984. Copyright © 2005 by The Board of Regents of the University of Wisconsin System. Reprinted by permission of the Wisconsin Law Review.

McGarity, The Courts and the Ossification of Rulemaking: A Response to Professor Seidenfeld. Published originally in 75 Tex. L. Rev. 525, 528, 533-535 (1997). Copyright © 1997 by the Texas Law Review Association. Reprinted by permission.

Noss, Reed F. & Allen Y. Cooperrider, Saving Nature's Legacy 32-33 (1994). Reprinted by permission of Island Press Environmental Sourcebook. Copyright © 1994 Defenders of Wildlife. Reprinted by permission of Island Press.

Page, A Generic View of Toxic Chemicals and Similar Risks, 7 Ecology L.Q. 207-223 (1978). Copyright © 1978 by the Regents of the University of California. Reprinted from the Ecology Law Quarterly, Vol. 7, No. 2, by permission of the Regents of the University of California.

Sunstein, Montreal versus Kyoto: A Tale of Two Protocols, _____ Harv. Envtl. L. Rev. _____ (forthcoming). Copyright © 2006 by the Harvard Environmental Law Review of the Harvard Law School.

Tarlock, The Non-Equilibrium Paradigm in Ecology and the Partial Unraveling of Environmental Law, 27 Loy. L.A. L. Rev. 1121 (1994). Copyright © 1994 by the Loyola of Los Angeles Law Review.

Wagner, Commons Ignorance: The Failure of Environmental Law to Produce Needed Information on Health and the Environment 1619, 1622, 1631-1634, 1639-1641, 1650-1651, 1653-1654, 1656-1657, 1663-1664, 1670, 1677-1679 (2004). Copyright © 2004 Duke University School of Law.

I

ENVIRONMENTAL LAW'S FOUNDATIONS

Problem 1-1

Leopold Forest is a private forest that was logged in the nineteenth century and is now a second-growth forest. The forest supports a wide variety of flora and fauna, none of which is subject to an immediate threat of extinction. Global Mining purchased the mineral rights necessary to open a mine in the forest. The mine will comply with all applicable federal, state, and local regulations, but there is substantial concern among local scientists and environmental groups that the mine may change the forest and its watershed. Some scientists think that the yellow mountain daisy community, which supports the purple-tailed hawk, will be eliminated, although no definitive scientific studies exist to support their concern. The plant and purple-tailed hawks are found throughout a four-state region, but the scientists are concerned that the local hawk community is a significant evolutionary unit because of its unique genetic composition, which has evolved over time in isolation from other hawk communities. In addition, the mine wastes will change the color of Rushing Creek from a deep blue to a gray-green and will increase the possibility of rapid algae growth near the banks. The mine will also be located between a widely used hiking trail and the Upper Rushing Creek Valley, a scenic vista that was extensively painted in the nineteenth century by the famous Saturday Painting Club, the first group of native-born romantic painters in the United States. A local environmental nongovernmental organization is contemplating a legal action to enjoin the operation of the mine and has asked you to assess the nonstatutory legal remedies and theories of relief that might be available to them. The organization also hopes that you will consider arguments that might persuade government decision-makers to modify the mine's plans, even if you, the courts, or regulators ultimately determine that legal victory is uncertain. Your client is concerned with success in minimizing or preventing harms from the mine, not just with victory in the courts. What is your advice?

A. ENVIRONMENTAL LAW'S ROOTS AND RATIONALES

The modern environmental law frameworks that will dominate your attention in this book are primarily statutory and regulatory, with most dating from the early 1970s

1

through 1990, and most passed by the federal government. These modern legislative frameworks did not, however, appear out of nowhere. Nor were environmental harms unknown as a legal problem before that time. Today's environmental laws did not supplant all that came before, but built on existing frameworks and often explicitly preserve state law and, of particular importance, state common law related to environmental harms and use of environmental amenities.

But a preliminary question should be asked. Is there a need for any legal intervention to deal with environmental harms? What rationales justify these modern regulatory statutes or the remedies provided by state statutes or state common law? When should an environmental lawyer or policymaker turn to statutes, regulations, common law, or perhaps arguments rooted in other disciplines, especially economics, political science, and ecology?

To set the stage for the rest of this book, this chapter introduces the reader to the foundations of environmental law. First, the chapter provides readings discussing classic rationales for why environmental harms occur, and why environmental harms should not be ignored or go unremedied by the legal system. This requires review of a handful of basic economic and political concepts that shed light on why environmental ills are so pervasive and why market actions alone are unlikely to deter or correct such harms. Economic and market factors, however, are far from the only justification for legal intervention. Of particular importance are ecological and philosophical justifications for addressing environmental harms, be they from pollution or other modifications of nature. Although less subject to easy categorization, broad-based changes in political and social perspectives also explain the increased focus during the twentieth century on conserving natural resources, discouraging waste, and addressing widespread harms associated with America's rapid industrialization. Especially since the late 1960s, polls consistently reveal broad citizen support for a cleaner environment. See Carlson, Public Priorities: Environment vs. Economic Growth: Age and Politics Influence Attitudes (Gallup, April 12, 2005); Dunlap & Scarce, Poll Trends: Environmental Problems and Protection, 55 Pub. Opinion Q. 651 (1991); Moore, Most Americans Say Government Is Doing Too Little for the Environment (Gallup News Service, April 6, 2006). The era when polluters might assume that they had a right to pollute is long past. The question now tends to be whether limited pollution or environmental harms should be allowed, along with the related question of how best to assess and limit those harms.

After exploring various rationales for legal intervention to address environmental harms, this chapter turns to long-established and still important common law means to address environmental ills. Despite the creation of the many environmental law statutes that you will study, common law remedies remain a significant part of the environmental lawyer's arsenal and a significant incentive for polluters to avoid causing environmental harms. Few environmental statutes provide monetary relief for those harmed by pollution; common law claims are a critical tool to provide redress, even if regulators fulfill their roles. Common law claims are a foundation of modern environmental law not only because of their continuing viability and importance but also because their limitations provided a key impetus for modern regulatory statutes.

B.   ENVIRONMENTALISM'S REJECTION OF EXPLOITATION EXPECTATIONS

Environmentalism can roughly be defined as the view that the unrestrained modification of natural systems through resource exploitation and development and the unchecked application of technology has substantial, accelerating, and potentially adverse consequences for humankind. Environmental protection has evolved to include three broad objectives: (1) the reduction of the use of air, soil, and water media as sinks for waste disposal; (2) the protection of the public from long-term health and ecosystem degradation risks associated with exposure to toxic and other harmful substances; and (3) the conservation of biodiversity. More recently, debates over "environmental justice" have increased sensitivity to the distributional impacts of environmental harms, as well as the distributional impacts of various environmental law regimes.

Environmentalism cuts against the grain of many central tenets and assumptions of Western civilization, which has consistently promoted material progress through the exploitation of nature's bounty. This change is described by the geographer Gilbert White, in Reflections on Changing Perceptions of the Earth, 19 Ann. Rev. Energy & Env't (1994):

> People around the world in the 1990s are perceiving the earth as more than a globe to be surveyed, or developed for the public good in the short term, or to be protected from threats to its well-being both human and natural. It is all of these to some degree, but has additional dimensions. People in many cultures accept its scientific description as a matter of belief. They recognize a commitment to care for it in perpetuity. They accept reluctantly the obligation to come to terms with problems posed by growth in numbers and appetites. This is not simply an analysis of economic and social consequences of political policies toward environmental matters. The roots are a growing solemn sense of the individual as part of one human family for whom the earth is its spiritual home.

Throughout history, almost all societies have characterized undeveloped nature as a storehouse of raw commodities to be exploited, manipulated, "improved," and transformed through the institutions of government or the market. In modern terms, they "commodified" nature. Undeveloped resources such as a clear stream, a rain or old-growth forest, or a mangrove swamp were not considered resource stocks because they lacked market value and society did not appreciate the functions they performed. Environmentalism teaches that we should value ecosystems either intrinsically or for the beneficial services, such as pollution reduction and flood control, that they provide society, although the relationship between ecosystem change and societally unacceptable consequences is much more complex than we thought some 30 years ago.

Environmental law professor Joseph Sax argues that judicial resistance to legal protection of the environment may spring from a refusal to see nature not as something to be transformed or exploited, but as something of value in its natural state. In critiquing recent Supreme Court "takings" jurisprudence, Professor Sax states that the anti-environmental animus of recent cases reflects fundamentally "different views of property rights." In the view of Sax, the "tranformative economy" perspective sees property as existing to be modified and reworked for human benefit. An "ecological view of property, the economy of nature," would perceive land and nature as "already at work, performing important services in its unaltered state." Sax, Property Rights and the Economy of Nature: Understanding *Lucas v. South Carolina Coastal Council*, 45 Stan. L. Rev. 1433, 1442 (1993). This collision of perspectives frequently divides the Supreme Court and continues to divide individuals in their views about legal efforts to protect the environment.

As argued in L. Milbrath, The World Is Relearning Its Story about How the World Works, in Environmental Politics in the International Arena 21, 24-27 (S. Kamieniecki ed., 1993), a "New Environmental Paradigm" (or NEP) rejects the assumption that economic growth, markets, and technological progress will address social ills and not unduly harm the environment:

> The vanguard advocates of the NEP . . . argue that the presumptions that economic growth, high consumption, and unrestrained growth in population can continue indefinitely are dangerously fallacious. Such life patterns will swiftly deplete resources and, more importantly, are likely to alter biogeo-chemical earth systems so that they behave unpredictably and injure life systems. Unpredictability of earth systems, such as the climate, would have devastating consequences for the society and economy; turbulent earth systems could not only spoil the dreams of the growth advocates but could also destroy much of our civilizational infrastructure, causing poverty and death around the globe. The vanguard argues further that unfettered markets do not protect ecosystems and that we must use foresight and planning to get to the future we want. Environmentalists . . . point out that life-styles with less material consumption can be equal in quality, if not actually superior, to life-styles seeking persistently to consume more and more.

The environmental paradigm described by Milbrath has it roots in an array of disciplines, but most important for students of environmental law and policy is an understanding of basic concepts and terminology of both economics and ecology, as well as ethically based arguments for environmental protection. The next three sections provide an introduction to these concepts.

C. ECONOMIC PERSPECTIVES ON ENVIRONMENTAL HARMS AND POLICY CHOICE

Problem 1-2

The Institute for Global Environmental Analysis has asked you to prepare a brief economic and legal analysis of global climate change. You are to take as a given that consumption of fossil fuels (coal, oil, and natural gas) emits CO_2 into the atmosphere and that during the twentieth century, the Earth's temperature increased by 0.5°C from these greenhouse gases. You are also to take as a given that the possible adverse impacts include temperature and rainfall changes from extreme flood to severe drought events, shifts in ecosystems, more severe storms, and sea level rise. As a result, energy demands may rise. How should the gases produced by energy generation and vehicle use be characterized? Does it follow from economic analysis that the emitters should be responsible for the reduction of CO_2 emissions to "safer" levels? Is the cost of curbing the emissions relevant to the first two questions? What economic arguments can you fashion for (a) why CO_2 emitters should cut back on their emissions and (b) why government intervention will likely be necessary but may be hard to prompt?

1. Introduction: Why We Pollute

When economists tried to find an explanation for the environmental problem, they looked at the same facts that philosopher Aldo Leopold did, but drew the opposite conclusion. To Leopold, whose writing is presented below, the Abrahamic concept of private property had to give way to a land ethic based on "love, respect, and admiration for land, and a high regard for its value." By "value," Leopold meant "something far broader than mere economic value; I mean value in the philosophic sense." A Sand County Almanac, at 223 (1949).

To economists, the problem is not the well-established phenomenon of private property but the opposite—the lack of clearly assigned property rights in common resources. Scarcity, and the discipline and market changes it provokes, may not even be perceived if environmental amenities and their destruction are off the ledger. Economics and ecology have provided us with powerful analyses of the roots and nature of environmental harms. Economists largely ignored adverse environmental impacts until the 1960s, but they quickly made up for lost time and have greatly influenced the public policy debate since the 1970s. The following article by biologist Garrett Hardin, which had its roots in debates over the problem of overpopulation, has substantially influenced economic and environmental thinking about the relationship between property and environmental problems. Many of its basic analytic insights also appeared in the earlier article by Scott Gordon, The Economic Theory of a Common-Property Resource: The Fishery, 62 J. Pol. Econ. 124 (1954). A number of key market imperfections that frequently are linked to environmental harms will be introduced after this classic work on the "tragedy of the commons."

HARDIN, THE TRAGEDY OF THE COMMONS
162 Science 1243, 1243-1248 (1968)

It is fair to say that most people who anguish over the population problem are trying to find a way to avoid the evils of overpopulation without relinquishing any privileges they now enjoy. They think that farming the seas or developing new strains of wheat will solve the problem—technologically. I try to show here that the solution they seek cannot be found. The population problem cannot be solved in a technical way, any more than can the problem of winning the game of tick-tack-toe.

What Shall We Maximize?

Population, as Malthus said, naturally tends to grow "geometrically," or, as we would now say, exponentially. In a finite world this means that the per capita share of the world's goods must steadily decrease. Is ours a finite world?

A fair defense can be put forward for the view that the world is infinite: or that we do not know that it is not. But, in terms of the practical problems that we must face in the next few generations with the foreseeable technology, it is clear that we will greatly increase human misery if we do not, during the immediate future, assume that the world available to the terrestrial human population is finite. "Space" is no escape.

A finite world can support only a finite population; therefore, population growth must eventually equal zero. (The case of perpetual wide fluctuations above and below zero is a trivial variant that need not be discussed.) When this condition is met, what will be the situation of mankind? Specifically, can Bentham's goal of "the greatest good for the greatest number" be realized?

No—for two reasons, each sufficient by itself. The first is a theoretical one. It is not mathematically possible to maximize for two (or more) variables at the same time. This was clearly stated by [two Princeton game theorists in 1947], but the principle is implicit in the theory of partial differential equations, dating back at least to D'Alembert (1717-1783).

The second reason springs directly from biological facts. To live, any organism must have a source of energy (for example, food). This energy is utilized for two purposes: mere maintenance and work. For man, maintenance of life requires about 1600 kilocalories a day ("maintenance calories"). Anything that he does over and above merely staying alive will be defined as work, and is supported by "work calories" which he takes in. Work calories are used not only for what we call work in common speech; they are also required for all forms of enjoyment, from swimming and automobile racing to playing music and writing poetry. If our goal is to maximize population it is obvious what we must do: We must make the work calories per person approach as close to zero as possible. No gourmet meals, no vacations, no sports, no music, no literature, no art. . . . I think that everyone will grant, without argument or proof, that maximizing population does not maximize goods. Bentham's goal is impossible.

In reaching this conclusion I have made the usual assumption that it is the acquisition of energy that is the problem. The appearance of atomic energy has led some to question this assumption. However, given an infinite source of energy, population growth still produces an inescapable problem. The problem of the acquisition of energy is replaced by the problem of its dissipation, as J. H. Fremlin has so wittily shown. The arithmetic signs in the analysis are, as it were, reversed; but Bentham's goal is still unobtainable.

The optimum population is, then, less than the maximum. The difficulty of defining the optimum is enormous; so far as I know, no one has seriously tackled this problem. Reaching an acceptable and stable solution will surely require more than one generation of hard analytical work—and much persuasion. . . .

We can make little progress in working toward optimum population size until we explicitly exorcize the spirit of Adam Smith in the field of practical demography. In economic affairs, The Wealth of Nations (1776) popularized the "invisible hand," the idea that an individual who "intends only his own gain," is, as it were, "led by an individual hand to promote . . . the public interest." . . .

The Tragedy of Freedom in a Commons

The rebuttal to the invisible hand in population control is to be found in a scenario first sketched in a little-known pamphlet in 1833 by a mathematical amateur named William Forster Lloyd (1794-1852). We may well call it "the tragedy of commons," using the word "tragedy" as the philosopher Whitehead used it: "The essence of dramatic tragedy is not unhappiness. It resides in the solemnity of the remorseless working of things." He then goes on to say, "This inevitableness of destiny can only be illustrated in terms of human life by incidents which in fact involve unhappiness. For it is only by them that the futility of escape can be made evident in the drama."

The tragedy of the commons develops in this way. Picture a pasture open to all. It is to be expected that each herdsman will try to keep as many cattle as possible on the commons. Such an arrangement may work reasonably satisfactorily for centuries because tribal wars, poaching, and disease keep the numbers of both man and beast well below the carrying capacity of the land. Finally, however, comes the day of reckoning, that is, the day when the long-desired goal of social stability becomes a reality. At this point, the inherent logic of the commons remorselessly generates tragedy.

As a rational being, each herdsman seeks to maximize his gain. Explicitly or implicitly, more or less consciously, he asks, "What is the utility to me of adding one more animal to my herd?" This utility has one negative and one positive component.

1. The positive component is a function of the increment of one animal. Since the herdsman receives all the proceeds from the sale of the additional animal the positive utility is nearly + 1.
2. The negative component is a function of the additional overgrazing created by one more animal. Since, however, the effects of overgrazing are shared by all the herdsmen, the negative utility for any particular decision-making herdsman is only a fraction of 1.

Adding together the component partial utilities, the rational herdsman con-cludes that the only sensible course for him to pursue is to add another animal to his herd. And another; and another. . . . But this is the conclusion reached by each and every rational herdsman sharing a commons. Therein is the tragedy. Each man is locked into a system that compels him to increase his herd without limit—in a world that is limited. Ruin is the destination toward which all men rush, each pursuing his own best interest in a society that believes in the freedom of the commons. Freedom in a commons brings ruin to all. . . .

What shall we do? We have several options. We might sell them off as private property. We might keep them as public property, but allocate the right to enter them. The allocation might be on the basis of wealth, by the use of an auction system. It might be on the basis of merit, as defined by some agreed upon standards. It might be by lottery. Or it might be on a first-come, first-served basis, administered to long queues. These, I think, are all the reasonable possibilities. They are objectionable. But we must choose—or acquiesce in the destruction of the commons that we call our National Parks.

Pollution

In a reverse way, the tragedy of the commons reappears in problems of pollution. Here it is not a question of taking out of the commons, but of putting something in—sewage, or chemical, radioactive, and heat wastes into water; noxious and dangerous fumes into the air; and distracting and unpleasant advertising signs into the line of sight. The calculations of utility are much the same as before. The rational man finds that his share of the cost of the wastes he discharges into the commons is less than the cost of purifying his wastes before releasing them. Since this is true for everyone, we are locked into a system of "fouling our own nest," so long as we behave only as independent, rational, free-enterprisers.

The tragedy of the commons as a food basket is averted by private property, or something formally like it. But the air and waters surrounding us cannot readily be fenced, and so the tragedy of the commons as a cesspool must be prevented by different means, by coercive laws or taxing devices that make it cheaper for the polluter to treat his pollutants than to discharge them untreated. We have not progressed as far with the solution of this problem as we have with the first. Indeed, our particular concept of private property, which deters us from exhausting the positive resources of the earth, favor pollution. The owner of a factory on the bank of a stream—whose property extends to the middle of the stream—often has difficulty seeing why it is not his natural right to muddy the waters flowing past his door. The law, always behind the times, requires elaborate stitching and fitting to adapt it to this newly perceived aspect of the commons. . . .

How to Legislate Temperance?

Analysis of the pollution problem as a function of population density uncovers a not generally recognized principle of morality, namely: the morality of an act is a function of the state of the system at the time it is performed. Using the commons as a cesspool does not harm the general public under frontier conditions, because there is no public; the same behavior in a metropolis is unbearable. A hundred and fifty years ago a plainsman could kill an American bison, cut out only the tongue for his dinner, and discard the rest of the animal. He was not in any important sense being wasteful. Today, with only a few thousand bison left, we would be appalled at such behavior.

NOTES ON THE TRAGEDY AND ENVIRONMENTAL POLICY

1. *Post-Hardin Thinking.* Along with Rachel Carson's Silent Spring, which is excerpted below, The Tragedy of the Commons is among the most powerful foundations of environmental law. Hardin's conclusion that commons will inevitably degrade has often been accepted as gospel by the environmental movement, but it has been challenged by political scientists and lawyers who have documented many instances of effective conservation cooperation among commons users, at least in more primitive cultures or small communities. The leading works are E. Ostrum, Governing the Commons: The Evolution of Institutions for Collective Action (1990); E. Ostrum, Rules, Games and Common Pool Resources (1994); National Research Council, Proceedings of a Conference on Common Property Resources Management (1988); and R. Ellickson, Order without Law: How Neighbors Settle Disputes (1991). Bosselman, Limitations Inherent in the Title to Wetlands at Common Law, 15 Stan. Envtl. L.J. 247 (1996), is an insightful case study of how the common law encouraged sustainable use of the fens of northeast England.

2. *Governance Issues.* The commons dilemma is often argued to provide the basis for severe government restrictions on the use of natural sinks for waste disposal or

ecosystems for commodity production. But, as Professor James E. Krier has pointed out, Hardin's argument contains a contradiction: "The public has to coerce the government to coerce it, and to do this the public must organize. Yet the inability to organize or coordinate is the problem to begin with." Krier, The Tragedy of the Commons Part Two, 15 Harv. J.L. & Pub. Pol'y 325, 338 (1992).

As revealed further in this chapter's tracing of the history of environmental protection and in Chapter 2's discussion of environmental federalism, environmental law is pervaded by complex and overlapping legal frameworks and divided regulatory turfs among federal, state, and local governments, and institutions such as legislatures, courts, and agencies. These forms of regulatory overlap, jurisdictional mismatch, and complexity can create a "regulatory commons" problem. Much as the herdsman in Hardin's work will fail to consider the actions of others and collective repercussions of excessive resource use, the existence of shared, overlapping, or conflicting regulatory turfs may lead both those desiring environmental protection and those who might supply it to fail to perceive the larger picture. Inaction or ineffective action may result. Hence, environmental lawyers and policymakers need to take into account not just unowned commons natural resources, but regulatory commons where no single regulator has clear primacy over a legal ill, and instead many share potential responsibility. See Buzbee, Recognizing the Regulatory Commons: A Theory of Regulatory Gaps, 89 Iowa L. Rev. 1 (2003).

3. *Is Congestion the Key Variable?* Professor Carol Rose has explored many facets of environmental policy through a law and economics perspective. In Rose, Rethinking Environmental Controls: Management Strategies for Common Resources, 1991 Duke L.J. 1., she suggests that a key variable is not just the "commons" problem, but that some "[c]ongestible resources such as fishing areas are typically the subjects of environmental problems. Their common use seems unproblematic under conditions of low consumption; under these circumstances there is plenty for everyone, and so no one tries to patrol additional fishing. But at some point, if increased fishing makes the resource perceptibly scarcer, and perhaps even threatens the resource with ruin, we collectively start to feel the pinch." Id. at 6-7.

4. *Commons, Property, and the Liberal Tradition.* Most environmental thinking adheres to the liberal tradition and seeks the least intrusive invasion of private property and individual liberty to remedy a scientifically defined problem. See Sagoff, Can Environmentalists Be Liberals? Jurisprudential Foundations of Environmentalism, 16 Envtl. L. 755 (1986); Wandesforde-Smith, Learning from Experience, Planning for the Future: Beyond the Parable (and Paradox) of Environmentalists as Pin-Striped Pantheists, 13 Ecology L.Q. 715 (1986); and Westbrook, Liberal Environmental Jurisprudence, 27 U.C. Davis L. Rev. 619 (1994). W. Ophuls, Ecology and the Politics of Scarcity (1977), dissented from this discourse by suggesting a Platonic alternative: "During the transition from any form of steady state one can envision it would be imperative to use physical resources as efficiently as possible, and this would probably mean greater centralization and expert control in the short term, even if the long-term goal is a technologically simple, decentralized society favorable to a democratic politics."

The second edition of the book, W. Ophuls & A. S. Boyan, Jr., Ecology and the Politics of Scarcity Revisited: The Unraveling of the American Dream 3 (1992), reiterated the book's original thesis that we must move to a steady-state society because "the external reality of ecological scarcity has cut the ground out from under our

political system, making reformist politics of ecological management all but useless."
But, in an afterword, Ophuls argued that this premise does not lead to the need for
antidemocratic solutions. He drew on De Tocqueville's distinction between government and administration and argued that we need more government but not administration. The book called for "[a] decentralized Jeffersonian policy of relatively small,
intimate, locally autonomous, and self-governing communities rooted in the land (or
other local ecological resource) and affiliated at the federal level only for a few clearly
defined purposes." Id. at 302-303.

    5. *Hardin and Pessimism.* As you will see in the succeeding chapters, the United
States has responded to the problem of environmental degradation primarily by regulating private choice through prohibitions on major types of pollution or landscape
degradation. It has not concentrated on the prohibition of small, cumulative consumer choices. In general, it has simply avoided the problem of population control
and any talk of limits. But see G. Hardin, Living within Limits: Ecology, Economics,
and Population Taboos (1993). Nonetheless, the environmental movement has often
had an apocalyptic tone to it. Kenneth Boulding's 1966 paper, The Economics of
the Coming Spaceship Earth, in Environmental Quality in a Growing Economy
(H. Jarrett ed., 1971), constructed two economic models—the cowboy and the
spaceman—and concluded that the present lay with the former but the future lay
with the latter:

> In the spaceman economy, what we are primarily concerned with is stock maintenance,
> and any technological change which results in the maintenance of a given total stock
> with a lessened throughput (that is, less production and consumption) is clearly a gain.
> This idea that both production and consumption are bad things rather than good things is
> very strange to economists, who have been obsessed with the income-flow concepts to the
> exclusion, almost, of capital-stock concepts. [Id. at 3.]

    Boulding's sketch of the future was followed by neo-Malthusian eco-disaster
scenarios, sponsored by the Club of Rome, a private international group concerned
with population and pollution. D. H. Meadows et al., The Limits to Growth (1972),
argue that the exponential growth rates of population and of industrial production
(and thus pollution) would soon press the finite limits of the planet Earth, with
catastrophic declines in the welfare of all. The models used in The Limits to Growth
were based on J. Forrester, World Dynamics (1971). The Limits to Growth produced
a spate of critical responses. See, e.g., Kaysen, The Computer That Printed Out
W*O*L*F, 50 Foreign Aff. 660 (1972), and P. Passell & L. Ross, The Retreat from
Riches: Affluence and Its Enemies (1973). (A similar document, A Blueprint for
Survival, appeared in the January 1972 issue of British Ecologist.) The collapse
thesis was thoroughly reevaluated in Thinking about the Future (1973), edited by
H. S. D. Cole, C. Freeman, M. Jahoda & K. L. R. Pavitt, an interdisciplinary team
from the University of Sussex, in England. Heller, Coming to Terms with Growth
and the Environment, in Energy, Economic Growth and the Environment 3
(S. Schurr ed., 1972), is a thoughtful examination of the positive relationship that
might exist between economic growth and pollution control. Krier & Gillette,
The Uneasy Case for Technological Optimism, 84 Mich. L. Rev. 405 (1985), present a thoughtful argument for reopening the debate about the ability of technology,
as promoted and constrained by markets and government intervention, to solve
environmental problems.

2.   The Classic Economics Model of Environmental Problems: Key Concepts

Lawyers think lawsuits and regulation. Hardin emerged from training as a biologist, but melded in his work both biological understanding and logic rooted in a focus on incentives and markets. Economists think markets, and analyze environmental ills by seeing how and why markets contribute to these ills and invariably influence efforts to find solutions. Early economists who turned their attention to environmental quality problems started from the premise that environmental quality was simply another example of a resource that had become scarce because demand exceeded supply. For economists, the demand (or taste) for clean air, clean water, minimal risks, or biodiversity is the same as the demand for any other resource, be it mountain bikes, blue corn chips, or Starbucks coffee: how much clean air, clean water, or wilderness should there be, compared with alternative possibilities such as industrial waste disposal sinks, mines, or ski resorts? Economists also generally agree that in an ideal world these resource allocation choices would be made most efficiently and fairly through the operation of the free-market economy. See H. Macaulay & B. Yandle, Environmental Use and the Market (1977). Consumers would vote with their dollars to allocate resources between biodiversity and ski resorts or between levels of risk exposure just as they decide between Coke and Pepsi. Few people, if any, assert that the market is currently capable of doing this.

Several sorts of market flaws contribute to environmental harms, as well as to efforts to impose remedial measures through political and legal means. Although many environmentalists criticize excessive faith in the power of markets to correct environmental harms, economic concepts actually both explain the pervasiveness of environmental harms and point toward legally based solutions.

a.   Key Terms

A key concept to grasp is that of *externalities*. If you imagine a typical pollution setting, where a factory's emissions cause harm to its neighbors, an externality is implicated. In this setting, we confront a "negative externality," which economists define "as a human-made, un-bargained-for, negative element of the environment. Pollution is termed an externality because it imposes costs on people who are external to the transaction between the producer and consumer of the polluting product." E. Goodstein, Economics and Environment 32-33 (1995). Hence, an economist would not regard the harm that a person caused to herself, or the harm that a person was exposed to as a result of a consensual, informed bargaining process, as an externality. If environmental goods such as air or water may be polluted or used without any cost to the user, economists predict that too much pollution or excessive use will follow. As Goodstein states, if such goods are "'underpriced,' . . . [b]ecause no one owns these resources, in the absence of government regulation or legal protection for pollution victims, businesses will use them up freely, neglecting the external costs imposed on others." In contrast, if such goods were priced such that a polluter had to pay for the harm caused, there might still be pollution, but the activity would no longer be imposing an externality on others. Economists speak of "negative" externalities, in the sense of uncompensated harms, and "positive" externalities, where someone may create a good enjoyed by many, but for which the creator is unpaid.

But externalities and the tragedy of the commons are far from the only key economic concepts important to understanding why environmental harms occur. Efficient markets also depend on market participants having *perfect information* about market choices. Perfect information is, of course, an aspiration and a near impossibility in the real world. Still, environmentally harmful activities are pervaded by information flaws and uncertainties. Pollution producers do not know who or what will be harmed, victims of pollution typically cannot even figure out who caused the harms, and the impacts of contact with environmental pollution are frequently nearly impossible to calculate. Scientific complexities and uncertainties make it very difficult to secure anything more than tentative information about environmental impacts. Deriving an appropriate price for environmental harms, let alone determining who should be part of such bargaining, is also rife with uncertainties.

Furthermore, markets will not function appropriately in allocating goods and services if *transaction costs* prevent people from getting together and coming to consensual solutions. Where pollution affects many people in uncertain ways, high transaction costs, such as costs of negotiation, figuring out appropriate solutions, and finding people who will cooperate, are a substantial hurdle to market solutions. As political economist Mancur Olson established in his renowned book The Logic of Collective Action (1965), the high costs of *collective action* explain both many environmental ills and political failures to provide redress. The many victims of pollution are unlikely to act together because they individually often experience small amounts of harm, and the costs of transacting with each other will dwarf any possible recovery. Pollution victims are thus unlikely to bargain for compensation through the market, but they are also unlikely to act collectively in political or legal arenas for the same reason. Relatedly, because environmentally harmful activity usually affects many, those affected will be tempted to hope that others will take the laboring oar and confront the actor causing the harm. This phenomenon is known as the *free rider* problem.

On the other hand, those with a concentrated interest in a particular approach, especially potential regulation, are likely to see both pollution and its regulation as creating substantial benefits and potential costs. Producers of risk also tend to be fewer in number and to have a shared interest. The net effect of collective action dynamics is that victims of pollution are far less likely to act effectively in political settings, while those creating risk will be nearly certain to act, due to the higher stakes and relatively small transaction costs associated with acting collectively. The disadvantage faced by victims of environmental harms is exacerbated by the free rider temptation to rely on others' efforts. Still, where an environmental ill is truly localized, is traceable, and causes determinate effects on a small number of actors, and both the causer of harms and the victims are known to each other, market solutions are possible. The problem is that such circumstances are rare.

Despite the market flaws that contribute to environmental ills and confound efforts to find political solutions, economics-oriented scholars and policymakers still tend to look at environmental problems through a market-based lens and seek solutions that use or mimic markets. Since markets cause most environmental harms, it would indeed be myopic to ignore the workings of markets in devising solutions. Still, some property rights advocates with a strong animus against regulatory or bureaucratic solutions to environmental ills advocate discarding much of modern environmental law in favor of reliance on markets, coupled with reliance on common law litigation. See Terry L. Anderson & Donald R. Leal, Free Market Environmentalism (2001).

The viability of such prescriptions has been strongly challenged but has nevertheless influenced public discourse. For a symposium issue presenting and critiquing such arguments, see Symposium—Free Market Environmentalism, 15 Harv. J.L. & Pub. Pol'y (1992).

Economic analysis of environmental problems is seductively powerful because it purports not only to explain the cause of the problems, but also to justify legislative and judicial intervention to solve the problems. Proponents also often see economic insights as useful in determining the means or instruments of intervention. Further, because welfare economics accepts the legitimacy of current patterns of production and consumption, neither its explanations nor its prescriptions for change are radical. Classic environmental regulation is well within the liberal political tradition because it seeks to restrict individual autonomy only when other individuals are seriously harmed by pollution. See Westbrook, Liberal Environmental Jurisprudence, 27 U.C. Davis L. Rev. 619 (1994).

Yet although the application of economic analysis is increasingly accepted and often legislatively mandated, economic analysis remains controversial, posing two distinct questions. First, how effectively can economic prescriptions be applied? No matter how elegant various explanations and models are, it is not always certain that the information necessary to utilize the models can be collected in order to produce resource allocations superior to those being made by means of messy political and administrative processes. See Cole & Grossman, When Is Command-and-Control Efficient? Institutions, Technology, and the Comparative Efficiency of Alternative Regulatory Regimes for Environmental Protection, 1999 Wis. L. Rev. 887. The second and broader question is, how relevant and helpful is economic analysis compared with other theories and approaches to environmental protection? See D. Driesen, The Economic Dynamics of Environmental Law (2003). For a recent work melding a critique of economic approaches to regulation and literature on commons regulation, see Sinden, The Tragedy of the Commons and the Myth of a Private Property Solution, 78 U. Colo. L. Rev. (forthcoming 2007).

b.   Coase's Insights and the "Polluter Pays" Principle

Can one conclude that if a negative environmental externality exists, the discharger must assume financial responsibility for all of the social costs of his activity? In short, is it clear that the polluter must pay? A few economists and many lawyers have drawn this conclusion from new-welfare economics, but this normative conclusion was challenged in 1960 in a seminal article that is central to economic analyses of environmental ills.

In The Problem of Social Cost, 3 J.L. & Econ. 1 (1960), Nobel Laureate Ronald Coase argued that it is wrong to think in terms of only one party causing harm to another. According to Coase, the "harmful effects" problem is "a problem of a reciprocal nature" rather than a unilateral one. In his view, "harmful effects" arise when two parties whose resource uses are incompatible compete for the right to use the same resource. Among his key insights is that if the government intervenes and prevents a polluter or cattle rancher (or other causer of harmful effects) from causing harm to a neighbor, then the polluter or cattle rancher is harmed. "The real question that has to be decided is: should A be allowed to harm B or should B be allowed to harm A." He recast the challenge as one about "avoid[ing] the more serious harm."

Coase contends that, viewed from a societal perspective, competing parties are likely to negotiate an efficient allocation of resources if there are "no costs in carrying out market transactions." Id. at 15. He then, however, devotes substantial attention to the reason transaction costs will always exist, and in fact will often be the key determinant in whether consensual bargaining will result in socially efficient outcomes. Especially in settings with numerous parties, difficult bargaining points, and an array of activities, bargaining solutions are unlikely. He does not concede that a governmental solution is invariably the answer. Anticipating, if not giving birth to, a more skeptical view of regulation that is prevalent today, as well as to later comparative institutional perspectives, Coase states that "[a]ll solutions have costs and there is no reason to suppose that government regulation is called for simply because the problem is not well handled by the market or the firm." Id. at 18. For an introduction to "comparative institutional analysis," which calls for comparison of how different institutions will address social ills, see N. Komesar, Imperfect Alternatives—Choosing Institutions in Law, Economics and Public Policy (1994).

Coase's insights have had a wide impact but have not gone unchallenged. Diverse lessons have been drawn from this work. Many advocates of market solutions to social ills focus on Coase's view that without transaction costs, parties will bargain to achieve efficient outcomes. Since some transaction costs will always exist, the question is how often bargaining outcomes will be reached without legal intervention. Coase himself appears to be of several minds about this, sometimes seeming to assume that consensual bargaining will typically occur and offer the best solution to the "harmful effects" problem, and in other settings claiming that economists have overlooked the magnitude of the transaction costs problem. He states in a recent book that "[t]he world of zero transaction costs has often been described as a Coasian world. Nothing could be further from the truth." R. H. Coase, The Firm, the Market, and the Law, 174-179 (1988). As Coase further explains,

> The reason why economists went wrong was their theoretical system did not take into account a factor which is essential if one wishes to analyze the effect of a change in the law on the allocation of resources. This missing factor is the existence of transaction costs. . . . Once we take transaction costs into account, the various parties have no incentive (or a reduced incentive) to disclose the information needed to formulate an optimal liability rule. Indeed, this information may not even be known to them, since those who have no incentive to disclose information have no reason for discovering what it is. Information needed for transactions which cannot be carried out will not be collected.

The law plays a critical role in determining the baseline situation and the transaction costs associated with efforts (if any) to reach a consensual solution. In Coase's words, "what incentives will be lacking depends on what the law is, since this determines what contractual arrangements will have to be made to bring about those actions which maximize the value of production. The result brought about by different legal rules is not intuitively obvious and depends on the facts of each particular case." For discussion of whether Coase has often been misconstrued, see Katz, The Strategic Structure of Offer and Acceptance: Game Theory and the Law of Contract Formation, 89 Mich. L. Rev. 215, 219 (1990).

The implications and soundness of Coase's insights remain the subject of considerable debate. Mishan, Pareto Optimality and the Law, 19 Oxford Econ. Papers (n.s.) 255 (1967), and Mishan, The Economics of Disamenity, 14 Nat. Resources J. 55 (1974), mount a detailed technical argument to show that an optimal allocation depends on the existing assignment of rights ("existing law") and that the costs of reaching an ideal solution also depend on the existing assignment of rights. The initial assignment of rights may not affect social welfare, but under this and related critiques of Coase, the initial endowments parties hold will influence how wealth is distributed. Jules Coleman has advanced the argument that Coase was wrong in denying the existence of nonreciprocal causal claims, but right in arguing that cause is not a per se justification for state intervention. J. Coleman, Markets, Morals and the Law 76-81 (1988). Thus, one should worry about who is liable.

However, the fundamental insight of Coase, that the presence of externalities does not automatically justify government regulation, has had a profound effect on environmental law. Perhaps for this reason, the principle that the polluter must pay "has not received the broad geographic and subject matter support over the long term accorded to the principle of preventive action, or attention accorded the precautionary principle in recent years." P. Sands, 1 Principles of International Environmental Law 213 (1995). Principle 16 of the 1992 Rio Declaration states only that national authorities should endeavor to promote the internalization of environmental costs and the use of economic instruments, taking into account the approach that the polluter should, in principle, bear the costs of pollution, with due regard to the public interest and without distorting international trade and investment.

If you are advising a federal or state policymaker about whether to regulate a new sort of environmental risk, how does Coase's analysis influence your approach to the problem? At a minimum, these economic concepts and Coase's arguments should lead you to see several potential policy pathways, rather than any single obvious answer. Identify the key variables you would want to examine.

c. Nonuse Values and Incommensurability: Are Some Values Extrinsic or Not Capable of Measurement?

Suppose that the primary external cost of an activity is that it forecloses enjoyment of a scenic vista. If no market exists to measure the opportunity cost of the activity, is the degradation of the vista an external cost that should be internalized? Traditionally, these costs were ignored because no market existed to value them. Is willingness to pay the only criterion for allocating resources? Neo-welfare economics assumes that consumers can measure their preferences rationally when confronted with a range of choices. Measurement is possible because properly established market prices will accurately reveal the value a consumer attaches to a product. Economists now accept the principle that the dichotomy between monetized and nonmonetized costs is not economically rational. The decision to develop or degrade a resource has an opportunity cost—the value forgone by resource development. This value can be reflected in individual preferences and thus is equivalent to preferences revealed through the market. The problem is the measurement of these costs, not whether or not they exist.

In a seminal article, Conservation Reconsidered, 57 Am. Econ. Rev. 777 (1967), John Krutilla advanced the argument that nonuse values exist and can and should be measured. He argued that public intervention to preserve unique natural environments, especially when development would produce irreversible change, was economically justified in order to prevent future shortages caused by a progressive change in taste favoring amenities. It was rational to "purchase" a present option for future use:

> Another reason for questioning the allocative efficiency of the market for the case in hand has been recognized only more recently. This involves the notion of option demand. This demand is characterized as a willingness to pay for retaining an option to use an area or facility that would be difficult or impossible to replace and for which no close substitute is available. Moreover, such a demand may exist even though there is no current intention to use the area or facility in question and the option may never be exercised. If an option value exists for rare or unique occurrences of nature, but there is no means by which a private resource owner can appropriate this value, the resulting allocation may be questioned. [Id. at 780.]

Krutilla subsequently explored the technical problems of developing a dynamic model of valuing option demand and tried to test it by applying it to several case studies.

Resource economists now generally argue that the appropriate measure of the value of a resource is its *total economic value*, which is the sum of its use and nonuse values. Many continue to debate whether these values are in fact "real" compared with pollution damage. However, the debate has shifted from the legitimacy of nonuse values to the comparative merits of different measurement techniques (see Chapter 9, section E). See M. Freeman III, The Measurement of Environmental Resource Values: Theory and Methods (1993).

d. Ethics or Economics?

Is willingess to pay the correct measure of the optimal level of environmental quality? In a fundamental attack on the adequacy of economic approaches to environmental protection, Sagoff, Economic Theory and Environmental Law, 79 Mich. L. Rev. 1393 (1985), argues that public and private preferences are two different logical categories. "The economist asks of objective beliefs a question that is appropriate only to subjective wants." In Principles of Federal Pollution Control Law, 71 Minn. L. Rev. 19 (1986), Sagoff attempts a synthesis of the moral and economic justifications for environmental law and argues that environmental statutes seek to eliminate moral evils but that economic values operate as a legitimate constraint, and the degree of the constraint is a function of the ethical duty. Thus, costs are less relevant when the government seeks to reduce severe toxic risks and more relevant when it seeks to reduce *de minimis* hazards and background risks.

Even if Sagoff is right, should economic considerations still play a role in addressing environmental harms? Can economic variables be considered without undercutting other justifications for environmental protection? How should policymakers balance economic considerations and other variables? Will policymakers ever be able to ignore markets and economic factors?

e. Cost-Benefit Analysis and Economic Perspectives

The role of economic analysis is especially controversial in the use of cost-benefit analysis (CBA) to evaluate risk minimization standards. Cost-benefit analysis is a formal method of comparing the costs and benefits of public action to determine if public actions or funds result in a net efficiency gain or represent an unjustified subsidy or dead-weight loss. Such analysis can be used either to advocate environmental protection or to stifle regulation. Its very underpinnings and supposed neutrality have been the subjects of fierce debate over the past 25 years. For an array of readings concerning CBA, see Chapter 3, section C. CBA analysis is rooted in economic perspectives on regulatory policy because of its focus on costs and market repercussions. Gunningham & Young, Toward Optimal Environmental Policy: The Case of Biodiversity Conservation, 24 Ecology L.Q. 243, 268 (1997), quote a study estimating that 90 cents of every dollar invested in biodiversity conservation protection is spent on undoing perverse incentives to destroy biodiversity. For further introduction to the topic, see Driesen, The Societal Cost of Environmental Regulation: Beyond Administrative Cost-Benefit Analysis, 24 Ecology L.Q. 545 (1997); Heinzerling, Regulatory Costs of Mythic Proportions, 107 Yale L.J. 1981 (1998); and Heinzerling, Environmental Law and the Present Future, 87 Geo. L.J. 2025 (1999).

D. THE ENVIRONMENTAL LESSONS OF ECOLOGY

All disciplines that approach environmental problems systematically have been greatly influenced by the science of ecology. The word "ecology," derived from the Greek word *oikos* ("house" or "place to live"), was not coined until 1869, and the science of ecology dates from only 1890. Ecology has to do with the structure and function of nature, considered in a grand perspective. Initially, the science was attractive to policymakers looking for a quick fix because it was thought to offer scientific laws, or a fairly certain promise of them, that would translate directly into moral and hence legal imperatives. In his introduction to a collection of essays, The Subversive Science: Essays Toward an Ecology of Man (P. Shepard & D. McKinley eds., 1969), Paul Shepard expressed this idea as follows: "Ecology may testify as often against our uses of the world, even against conservation techniques of control and management for sustained yield, as it does for them. Although ecology may be treated as a science, its greater and overriding wisdom is universal." Introduction: Ecology and Man—A Viewpoint, in The Subversive Science 1, at 4-5.

However, ecology as a science was ill prepared to realize its potential when the environmental decade began. Before then, ecology was a nonprestigious branch of learning. True, it boasted some brilliant scientists and some gifted, almost poetic, writers; but the state of its knowledge was crude because its path had diverged from that of pure science, led by reductionist physics—which, in the name of elegance and with the stated goal of obtaining directly useful knowledge—had gradually shifted its focus from nineteenth-century holistic views of nature to the application of smaller and smaller units of analysis. Odum, A New Ecology for the Coast, in Coastal Alert: Scientists Speak Out 145 (T. Jackson & D. Reische eds., 1981). Carpenter, The Scientific Basis of NEPA—Is It Adequate?, 6 Envtl. L. Rep. (ELI) 50,014 (1976); and Carpenter, Ecology in Court, and Other Disappointments of Environmental Science and Environmental Law, 15 Nat. Resources Law. 573 (1983), are useful summaries of the gap between the information demands of regulation and available research. Sagoff, Ethics, Ecology, and the Environment: Integrating Science and Law,

56 Tenn. L. Rev. 77 (1988), is a thorough review of the debates within ecology about its mission.

Law has a knack for adopting an idea from another discipline just as the idea is being questioned and rejected in the discipline. This happened with ecology. Ecology was attractive because the idea that ecosystems had a natural equilibrium state provided a normative basis for much of environmental law, from environmental impact assessment to pollution control. In his widely influential book, Fundamentals of Ecology 89 (2d ed. 1959), Eugene Odum warned that

> tinkering with basic ecosystems of the world can result either in a glorious future for mankind, or in his complete destruction if too many large-scale mistakes are made. Although nature has remarkable resilience, the limits of homeostatic mechanisms can easily be exceeded by the actions of man. When treated sewage is introduced into a stream at a moderate rate, the system is able to "purify itself" and return to the previous condition within a comparatively few miles downstream. If the pollution is great or if toxic substances for which no natural homeostatic mechanisms have been evolved are included, the stream may be permanently altered or even destroyed as far as usefulness to man is concerned.

However, the idea of a natural, static or equilibrium state of nature is no longer accepted in ecology. After providing an excerpt from Rachel Carson's hugely influential work that draws on ecological understandings to warn of the broad, systemic harms of chemicals such as DDT, used especially to control pests, we summarize the development of the idea that ecosystems were once naturally in equilibrium, and recent theories that substantially modify this idea.

RACHEL CARSON, SILENT SPRING
1-3, 277-278, 295-297 (1962) (Houghton Mifflin 1994 Ed.)

[As mentioned later in this chapter's tracing of the arc of this country's environmental protection efforts, virtually every historian and scholar of environmentalism mentions Carson's book as being one of several factors that led to a new and widespread concern with environmental protection during the 1960s and 1970s. This excerpt provides just a short portion of her dramatic presentation and clear message against the excessive use of pesticides.]

I. *A Fable for Tomorrow*

There was once a town in the heart of America where all life seemed to live in harmony with its surroundings. . . . Then a strange blight crept over the area and everything began to change. Some evil spell had settled on the community; mysterious maladies swept the flocks of chickens; the cattle and sheep sickened and died. Everywhere was a shadow of death. The farmers spoke of much illness among their families. In the town the doctors had become more and more puzzled by new kinds of sickness appearing among their patients. There had been several sudden and unexplained deaths, not only among adults but even among children, who would be stricken suddenly while at play and die within a few hours.

There was a strange stillness. The birds, for example—where had they gone? Many people spoke of them, puzzled and disturbed. The feeding stations in the backyards were deserted. The few birds seen anywhere were moribund; they trembled violently and could not fly. It was a spring without voices. . . .

No witchcraft, no enemy action had silenced the rebirth of new life in this stricken world. The people had done it themselves. . . . A grim specter has crept upon us almost unnoticed, and this imagined tragedy may easily become a stark reality we all shall know.

What has already silenced the voices of spring in countless towns in America? This book is an attempt to explain. . . .

17. THE OTHER ROAD

We stand now where two roads diverge. But unlike the roads in Robert Frost's familiar poem, they are not equally fair. The road we have long been traveling is deceptively easy, a smooth superhighway on which we progress with great speed, but at its end lies disaster. The other fork of the road—the one "less traveled by"—offers our last, our only chance to reach a destination that assures the preservation of our earth.

The choice, after all, is ours to make. If, having endured much, we have at last asserted our "right to know," and if, knowing, we have concluded that we are being asked to take senseless and frightening risks, then we should no longer accept the counsel of those who tell us that we must fill our world with poisonous chemicals; we should look about and see what other course is open to us.

A truly extraordinary variety of alternatives to the chemical control of insects is available. Some are already in use and have achieved brilliant success. Others are in the stage of laboratory testing. Still others are little more than ideas in the minds of imaginative scientists, waiting for the opportunity to put them to the test. All have this in common: they are biological solutions, based on understanding of the living organisms they seek to control, and of the whole fabric of life to which these organisms belong. . . .

Through all these new, imaginative, and creative approaches to the problem of sharing our earth with other creatures there runs a constant theme, the awareness that we are dealing with life—with living populations and all their pressures and counterpressures, their surges and recessions. Only by taking account of such life forces and by cautiously seeking to guide them into channels favorable to ourselves can we hope to achieve a reasonable accommodation between the insect hordes and ourselves.

NOTE

Carson's book forced citizens and policymakers to consider whether insects, often considered pests deserving of extirpation, needed to be protected, and whether measures to control insects posed equal or greater risks than the insects themselves. Although ecological understandings have radically changed in recent decades, Carson's call for caution and "taking into account such life forces" remains a central tenet of environmentalism today. As you read further into this textbook, note how many environmental amenities protected by the law were once viewed as nuisances worthy of destruction to improve the human condition. Take note as well how much judicial resistance to environmental protection measures may spring from judges who are reluctant to toss aside their preconceptions about what kind of natural environments provide value and deserve protection. See Chapter 5 (regarding endangered species protection), Chapter 7 (regarding wetlands protection), and Chapter 8 (regarding chemical, pesticide, and toxic waste regulation).

BOSSELMAN & TARLOCK, THE INFLUENCE OF ECOLOGICAL SCIENCE ON AMERICAN LAW: AN INTRODUCTION
69 Chi.-Kent L. Rev. 847, 854-856, 861-862 (1994)

[The vision of ecology embraced in the 1960s derives from the work of two botanists working in Nebraska during the progressive era: Roscoe Pound, who migrated into law and became one of the towering figures of American jurisprudence, and Frederick Clements. Pound and Clements pioneered the use of the "quadrant" method to survey vegetation patterns on the Nebraska prairie; this work led to a static concept of the landscape that influenced both ecology and the emerging discipline of city planning.]

Clements liked to label his theory of ecology as succession, and he wrote extensively about natural processes by which one plant community replaces another in successive waves. But the part of his theory that had the greatest influence on public policy was not succession itself, but his contention that succession eventually would end in a climax state, at which point succession would cease because the landscape had reached its natural condition of equilibrium. Each plant and animal species would then occupy its niche in perpetual harmony. Of course, fire, flood, or other natural event might disrupt such harmony, but in the long run it would not matter because the process of succession would begin again and eventually return to the climax condition.

The idea of climax and equilibrium fell on fertile ground. For centuries, many theologically inclined students of science had inferred a balance of nature, divinely provided until the disrupters of the Garden of Eden bungled things. They argued that humans should search to fit themselves into the framework of natural processes so that a condition of permanent stability could be re-established.

The initial building block of Clements' ecology was the plant community. He thought that each such community functioned as a separate unit in the ecological process. Other biologists of the period, such as Hart Merriam, fostered this idea of separate and independent communities through the popularization of maps showing the separation of the natural world into specific life zones, each adapted to certain climatic and geographic conditions. As Clements' thinking progressed, he increasingly began to think of such communities and their animal inhabitants as akin to individual organisms that possessed an identity greater than the sum of their parts. Such organismic theories were extremely controversial, but Clements' basic theory of succession and climax dominated American ecology throughout the first half of the twentieth century. The idea of climax coincided nicely with the field observations of those biological scientists who were increasingly taking up residence in the more newly settled regions of the country and who, because they could obtain little historical data about landscape changes in their areas, had to rely on snapshot observations, the value of which would be enhanced if it could be assumed that the natural areas that they observed were representative of a permanent climax condition. . . .

The idea that the plants and animals living in a particular area formed an interdependent community was a dramatic breakthrough at the beginning of the twentieth century when most people had been educated to differentiate elements of the biota only by the place of the individual species on the "great chain of being." By the 1930s, however, some ecologists began to question whether even Clements and the other community ecologists had been thinking on too small a scale. Still, the idea of a stable, functioning system remained.

The concept of an ecosystem as a functioning, holistic, and inherently stable system vulnerable to serious and long-term insults from a wide variety of human activities drives the biodiversity branch of modern environmental law as well as a substantial part of the case against toxic pollutants. This ecosystem focus defined the distinctiveness of ecology as a science and provided a concrete, visible rationale for environmental regulation. The story of the idea's triumph is a fascinating example of the power of paradigms which resonate with deeply held non-scientific values to capture the imagination of scientists. It is also a story of the strengths and weaknesses of tying regulatory justifications and resource management programs to science when the science is still in the theoretical and experimental stage.

The ecosystem paradigm replaced Clements' theory that plant communities were an organism rather than a system of individual plants responding to various stimuli. A British ecologist floated the ecosystem concept as a theory in 1935, and within fifteen years it became an established scientific paradigm. Sir Alfred George Tansley, a distinguished Oxbridge ecologist and longtime friend and follower of Clements, was impressed with the progress of physics at the Cavendish Laboratory in Cambridge and proposed a conception, the ecosystem, to focus the science on a system which permitted nonprogressive vegetational change. "From Tansley's new 'systematic' point of view, systems — not organisms — underwent evolution." An ecosystem was defined as the whole system (in the sense of physics), including not only the organism-complex, but also the whole complex of physical factors forming what we call the environment of the biome — the habitat factors in the widest sense. Succession became a process rather than an end-state.

Tansley's shift from an organism to a system also carried with it the longstanding scientific belief that systems tended toward equilibrium. The idea of a "holistic . . . ecological concept that combined living organisms and the physical environment into a system" was a theory in the grand scientific tradition: it was not based on field observations. Two American ecologists, Ralph Lindeman and Eugene Odum, took the next step and made Tansley's theory operational. In so doing, they paved the way for the shift in environmental discourse from the aesthetic and spiritual to the scientific. The two modes of analysis had long been intertwined, but the case for what we now call ecosystem preservation was primarily made on aesthetic or moral grounds. For example, in a 1930 article, Wilderness Esthetics, Robert Marshall, one of the major proponents of wilderness preservation, contrasted the "dynamic beauty" of primitive areas to the static beauty of a Gothic cathedral and argued that "wilderness furnishes perhaps the best opportunity for pure esthetic enjoyment."

The ecosystem concept was made operational in Madison, Wisconsin — a historic center of applied progressivism in the United States. A University of Wisconsin ecologist, Ralph Lindeman, applied the ecosystem concept to the study of a Wisconsin lake and developed the building blocks of modern ecology "such as food webs, food chains, trophic levels, productivity, metabolism, energy flow, and ecological succession."

_____

Ecologists now follow a nonequilibrium paradigm. In Discordant Harmonies: A New Ecology for the Twenty-first Century 189-190 (Oxford University Press 1990), Daniel Botkin, a leading proponent of the new ecology, captures well several key components of this new nonequilibrium paradigm:

> [W]e understand, in spite of our wishes, that nature moves and changes and involves risks and uncertainties and that our judgments of our own actions must be made against this moving image.
>
> There are ranges within which life can persist, and changes that living systems must undergo in order to persist. We can change structural aspects of life within the acceptable ranges. Those changes that are necessary to the continuation of life we must allow to occur, or substitute for them at huge cost the qualities that otherwise would have been achieved. We can engineer nature at nature's rate and in nature's ways; we must be wary when we engineer nature at an unnatural rate and in novel ways. To conserve well is to engineer within the rule of natural changes, patterns, and ambiguities; to engineer well is to conserve, to maintain the dynamics of the living systems. The answer to the question about the human role in nature depends on time, culture, technologies, and peoples. There is no simple, universal (external to all peoples, cultures, times) answer. However, the answer to this question for our time is very much influenced by the fact that we are changing nature at all levels from the local to the global—that we have the power to mold nature into what we want it to be or to destroy it completely, and that we know we have that power.

As Dan Tarlock observes in Slouching toward Eden: The Eco-Pragmatic Challenges of Ecosystem Revival, 87 Minn. L. Rev. 1173, 1184-1186 (2003), this new perspective calls into question the very concept of ecosystems:

> Some ecologists have drawn a startling conclusion from the new ecology: The current concept of an ecosystem may no longer be a meaningful construct. The reason is that the new ecology undermines the crucial assumptions of the concept. Ecology has traditionally assumed that an ecosystem has definable boundaries, that it has spatial homogeneity, that we may substitute different flora and fauna and still maintain a sustainable system, that natural selection is relatively unimportant, that we can identify stability levels at different scales, and that humans are not part of ecosystems. These simplistic assumptions are now being recast. . . .
>
> The first lesson of the new ecology and the deconstructed ecosystem for revival is that we can never return to a state of nature; we can only approximate it for an undetermined period of time. The idea that ecosystems are moving rather than fixed targets and must be "mapped" at larger scales will subject the relevant environmental sciences to even greater stress. Scientists must answer questions that require mixed scientific and policy judgments. In contrast, environmental law and policy still have a tendency to view degraded ecosystems as broken machines. We want to know the causal relationship between the installation of a new part, a management action (experiment), and improved performance, an ecologically beneficial outcome. Science can rarely answer the causal relationship with the expected confidence or comfort level because it requires unprecedented and costly levels of data assembly and synthesis and the need to endlessly revisit previous conclusions and judgments.

Professor Lee Breckinridge, in Can Fish Own Water? Envisioning Nonhuman Property in Ecosystems, 20 J. Land Use & Envtl. L. 293 (2005), relates these new perspectives to changing scientific efforts to anticipate effects in systems that must be understood as dynamic and complex:

> Modern understandings of ecosystems reveal dynamic biophysical systems in which organisms interact with each other and with the abiotic components of their environment in complex ways. Feedback mechanisms produce nonlinear results, magnifying some phenomena while minimizing others. Equilibrium conditions exist, but these are dynamic phenomena produced through self-reinforcing patterns of ongoing activity rather than permanent conditions or steady states. A system may shift suddenly from one equilibrium and into another. Much remains uncertain and unpredictable about ecological systems and the organisms within them, precisely because the interactions are so complex and because small events can trigger large changes through nonlinear processes.
>
> The fluid, dynamic, and uncertain characteristics of ecosystems do not mean that meaningful patterns and processes are indecipherable in the midst of the transformation and change. Ecosystems have become the focus of intensive research in complex systems analysis. A key goal is to discern patterns and processes of ecological organization within "chaotic" phenomena.

---

1. *Nonequilibrium Theory's Implications:* What are the legal and ethical implications of Botkin's thesis? Some have read the nonequilibrium paradigm as an argument for not trying to "save" nature. However, the most common reading of Botkin is an argument for the more intense, holistic, and experimental management of "natural" and modified large-scale ecosystems. See S. Budiansky, Nature's Keepers: The New Science of Nature Management (1995). Scientists endorse the concept of adaptive management, which is a decisionmaking process based on the establishment of ecological performance targets, ecological risk assessment policy, monitoring, feedback, and change or adaptation. More generally, the more holistic emphasis on dynamic large systems leads to a greater appreciation of the need for large-scale landscape management to conserve biodiversity. National Research Council—National Academy of Sciences, Restoration of Aquatic Ecosystems: Science, Technology and Public Policy 372 (1992). This management will take place at larger scales; see Bosselman, What Lawyers Can Learn From Large-Scale Ecology, 17 Land Use & Envtl. L. 207 (2002), which stresses the very concept of an ecosystem. See O'Neill, Is It Time to Bury the Ecosystem Concept? (With Full Military Honors of Course!), 82 Ecology 3275 (2001).

2. *Complexity and the Need for Flexibility:* In Panarchy: Understanding Transformations in Human and Natural Systems 9-14 (L. Gunderson & C. S. Holling eds., 2002), Gunderson and Hollings suggest that "there is growing evidence that the partial perspectives from [economics, ecology, and organizational or institutional analysis] generate actions that are unsustainable." After highlighting the shortcoming of each discipline standing on its own, and introducing a few "caricatures" of nature that they find inadequate (among them "Nature Flat," "Nature Balanced," "Nature Anarchic," and "Nature Resilient"), they introduce and advocate consideration of a perspective they label "Nature Evolving." Under this view, nature

> is evolutionary and adaptive. It has been given recent impetus by the paradoxes that have emerged in successfully applying the previous more limited views. Complex systems

behavior, discontinuous change, chaos and order, self-organization, nonlinear systems behavior, and adaptive evolving systems are all code words characterizing the more recent activities. They are leading to integrative studies that combine insights and people from developmental biology and genetics, evolutionary biology, physics, economics, ecology, and computer science. . . . Nature Evolving is a view of abrupt and transforming change. It is a view that exposes a need for understanding unpredictable dynamics in ecosystems and a corollary focus on institutional and political flexibility.

How are these more complex characterizations of nature, ecology, and governance efforts likely to play out in legal institutions such as legislatures, agencies, and courts? How might you distill these various ecological insights and new perspectives to make effective arguments in legal settings?

E.   THE ETHICAL LESSONS OF ECOLOGY

Science is positive, not normative; however, environmentalists generally have drawn normative conclusions from ecology, many of them traceable to the beautifully crafted reflections of Aldo Leopold, first published in 1949. Note that some of Leopold's perspectives are consistent with modern ecological views, but others are not. Despite changing ecological understandings, Leopold's writings, like Rachel Carson's, continue to influence the path of environmental law. In A Sand County Almanac and Sketches Here and There 202-204, 214-216, 220, 224-225 (Oxford University Press paperback ed. 1968), Leopold articulated an argument rooted in ethics for why humans should respect the environment and avoid causing harm. In his view, such an ethical perspective calls for more than arguments rooted merely in property or economics:

There is as yet no ethic dealing with man's relation to land and to the animals and plants which grow upon it. Land . . . is still property. The land-relation is still strictly economic, entailing privileges but not obligations. . . .

An ethic may be regarded as a mode of guidance for meeting ecological situations so new or intricate, or involving such deferred reactions, that the path of social expediency is not discernible to the average individual. . . . Ethics are possibly a kind of community instinct in-the-making. . . .

The land ethic simply enlarges the boundaries of the community to include soils, waters, plants, and animals, or collectively: the land.

This sounds simple: do we not already sing our love for and obligation to the land of the free and the home of the brave? Yes, but just what and whom do we love? Certainly not the soil, which we are sending helter-skelter downriver. Certainly not the waters, which we assume have no function except to turn turbines, float barges, and carry off sewage. Certainly not the plants, of which we exterminate whole communities without batting an eye. Certainly not the animals, of which we have already extirpated many of the largest and most beautiful species. A land ethic of course cannot prevent the alteration, management, and use of these "resources," but it does affirm their right to continued existence, and, at least in spots, their continued existence in a natural state. . . .

In short, a land ethic changes the role of Homo sapiens from conqueror of the land-community to plain member and citizen of it. It implies respect for his fellow-members, and also respect for the community as such. . . .

A thing is right when it tends to preserve the integrity, stability, and beauty of the biotic community. It is wrong when it tends otherwise. . . .

NOTES AND QUESTIONS

1. *Legal Implications of Stewardship.* What are the implications of A Sand County Almanac for environmental law? Despite Leopold's widespread influence, his direct, and perhaps indirect, legal influence is small. The most common use has been to bolster assertions of the police power to protect the environment. For example, in Application of Christensen, 417 N.W.2d 607, 615 (Minn. 1988), the Minnesota Supreme Court upheld the denial of a wetland drainage permit with this language:

> Over ten years ago this court cited the conservationist Aldo Leopold for his espousal of a "land ethic" which envisions a community of interdependent parts. "The land ethic simply enlarges the boundaries of the community to include soils, waters, plants, and animals, or collectively: the land." County of Freeborn v. Bryson, 243 N.W.2d at 322, citing Sand County Almanac (1949) p. 203. We reaffirm our statements that the state's environmental legislation had given this land ethic the force of law, and imposed on the courts a duty to support the legislative goal of protecting our state's environmental resources. Vanishing wetlands require, even more today than in 1976 when Bryson was decided, the protection and preservation that environmental legislation was intended to provide.

Leopold's thinking is also directly reflected in Department of Cmty. Affairs v. Moorman, 664 So. 2d 930, 932 (Fla. 1995). The court upheld a zoning ordinance that limited the construction of fences on a Florida Key to maintain the minimum viable population of the miniature Florida Key deer. The county was designated an area of "critical state concern," and in upholding the state's power to contest a variance under the county ordinance, the court wrote that "[t]he clear policy underlying Florida environmental regulation is that our society is to be a steward of the natural world, not its unreasoning overlord."

Leopold identifies the institution of private property as a primary stumbling block to environmental stewardship. The issue is critical to environmental law because the Fifth and Fourteenth Amendments to the United States Constitution prohibit the taking, which includes excess regulation, of property without just compensation. See pages 378-387 below. In the initial regulation of air, water, and land pollution, constitutional objections to environmental regulation were largely unsuccessful. First-generation environmental regulation by and large codified and extended common law prohibitions against the maintenance of nuisances. Thus, dischargers could not claim the taking of a previously recognized entitlement. As we focus on the preservation of terrestrial biodiversity, the tension between stewardship and private property increases.

Although actual judicial citation to Leopold remains scarce, his land ethic forms the basis for developing theories of "green property." Green property theory seeks to incorporate the principle of stewardship into the individualistic liberal theories of property. See Goldstein, Green Wood in the Bundle of Sticks: Fitting Environmental Ethics and Ecology into Real Property Law, 25 B.C. Envtl. Aff. L. Rev. 347 (1998). It stresses that the natural interconnectedness of the arbitrary divisions of land produced by the common law justify more stringent limitations on individual parcel use to protect the integrity of remnant ecosystems. However, Leopold himself seems to have intended his land ethic as a call for private landowners to internalize conservation practices. See Freyfogle, The Land Ethic and Pilgrim Leopold, 61 U. Colo. L. Rev. 217, 236 (1990).

2. *Can Ecosystems Have Rights?* Environmental philosophers and others read Leopold as creating a new system of ethics that breaks with the individualistic, anthropocentric bias in Western philosophy and the Anglo-American insistence on a strict separation of fact from value. Environmental ethics posit specific duties, not just a plea for the evolution of changed attitudes, toward nature, although Leopold himself held a dualistic view of the relationship between man and nature. Environmental protection law is a complex mix of scientific and economic consequences constructed on the assertion that we have a moral duty to respect "nature." The insight that human activities that modify natural systems have short- and long-run adverse consequences is a powerful one. However, the question is whether this insight can support new rights that run to natural systems. We usually define rights as relatively absolute entitlements to a consistent outcome, and we limit the competing interests that can be traded off against them.

The argument for new environmental or ecosystem rights starts from the premise that the prevailing theory of Western civilization, that man commands nature, should be replaced with the radical view that he is just a participant in the biotic community. As Roderick Nash has observed, "[I]f Darwin killed dualism, the ecologists presided over its burial." The Rights of Nature: A History of Environmental Ethics 70 (1989). Nash traces the gradual expansion of the circle of rights and speculates on the implication of this expansion for environmentalism. He observes that "environmental ethics created entirely new definitions of what liberty and justice mean on planet earth. It recognized that there can be no individual welfare (or liberty) apart from the ecological matrix in which individual life must exist. A biocentric ethical philosophy . . . can be understood . . . as both the end and a new beginning of the American liberal tradition." Id. at 160.

3. *Leopoldian Ethics and the Western Philosophical Tradition.* The effort to construct a theory of ecological rights faces at least four formidable conceptual hurdles. First, rights are generally limited to sentient beings. This affords some hope for animal rights advocates, but not for the protection of entire ecosystems or landscapes. The best articulations of the possibility of bringing animals within a modified rights framework remain the late R. Nozick's Anarchy, State and Utopia 35-42 (1974) and P. Singer's Animal Rights (1975). But this extension of sentiency offers no help for proponents of ecosystem rights. Second, the argument that moral duties flow from ecological awareness flies in the face of the dominant philosophical view, following Hume, that fact should be separated from value. The distinction is vigorously supported in C. Mann & M. Plummer, Noah's Choice: The Future of Endangered Species 204-208 (1995). Are the categories truly absolute? Why have we as a society decided to protect the environment? Can one avoid the problem by dissolving the categories and by adopting moral concern for the functioning of the entire ecological system as the value? See generally P. Wenz, Environmental Justice (1988).

4. *Duties to Future Generations.* Can the anthropocentric-nonanthropocentric problem also be avoided by imposing a duty on present generations to protect future generations? The question is central to environmental law because many conflicts revolve around pleas for the deferral, perhaps infinitely, of the consumption of resources to benefit future generations. A major justification for many environmental policies is that the present consumption of resources should be limited to protect the interests of future generations. Considerable controversy exists among philosophers about whether rights can be possessed by unidentifiable (unborn) individuals and thus

whether any duties or moral obligations are owed to those yet to come.* How should present as opposed to future consumption be valued? See Heal, Economics and Resources, in Economics of Environmental and Natural Resources Policy 62 (J. A. Butlin ed., 1981). Professor Edith Brown Weiss has argued that the public trust concept is a basis for intergenerational equity as a limitation on present resource consumption. She has expanded her argument in her widely influential book, In Fairness to Future Generations: International Law, Common Patrimony, and Intergenerational Equity (1989). See generally the exchange between professors Edith Brown Weiss and Anthony D'Amato in 84 Am. J. Int'l. L. 190 and 198 (1990). For more discussion of the public trust doctrine, see section F.5 below.

5. *Is There a Nonequilibrium Environmental Ethic?* Recall the excerpts from Botkin and others regarding nonequilibrium ecology. One of the major lessons of nonequilibrium ecology is that it is not enough to fence off nature from human contact because nature is too dynamic. Does this underline Leopoldian ethics? Callicott, Do Deconstructive Ecology and Sociobiology Undermine Leopold's Land Ethic?, 18 Envtl. Ethics 353, 372 (1996), offers the following revision of Leopold's ethic:

> The summary moral maxim of the land ethic, nevertheless, must be dynamized in light of developments in ecology since the mid-twentieth century. Although Leopold acknowledged the existence and land-ethical significance of natural environmental change, he seems to have thought of it primarily on a very slow evolutionary temporal scale. But even so, he thereby incorporates the concept of inherent environmental change and the crucial norm of scale into the land ethic. In light of more recent developments in ecology, we can add norms of scale to the land ethic for both climatic and ecological dynamics in land-ethically evaluating anthropogenic changes in nature. One hesitates to edit Leopold's elegant prose, but as a stab at formulating a dynamized summary moral maxim for the land ethic, I hazard the following: "A thing is right when it tends to disturb the biotic community only at normal spatial and temporal scales. It is wrong when it tends otherwise."

6. *Religion and Man's Place in Nature.* For a nuanced tracing of how various religious traditions perceive man's place in nature, as well as diverse perceptions regarding the relationship of nature to God, see J. Passmore, Man's Responsibility for Nature: Ecological Problems and Western Traditions 5-6, 10, 12-14 (1974). He points out that in addition to religious strains of thought that emphasize man's dominion over nature, there is a Western tradition of the stewardship of nature.

F. COMMON LAW, NONSTATUTORY, AND CONSTITUTIONAL REMEDIES FOR ENVIRONMENTAL HARMS

Economic and ecological perspectives on the roots and repercussions of environmental harms point to the same conclusion—environmental harms should be

---

*See Kavka, The Paradox of Future Individuals, 11 Phil. & Pub. Aff. 93 (1982); Parfit, Future Generations: Further Problems, 11 Phil. & Pub. Aff. 113 (1982); Farber & Hemmersbaugh, The Shadow of the Future: Discount Rates, Later Generations, and the Environment, 46 Vand. L. Rev. 267 (1993).

discouraged. From an economics perspective, harmful conduct that creates no liability for the agent of harm will be produced in excess. Such negative externalities need somehow to become internalized, be it through consensual bargaining (as Coase posited might occur in some settings), through regulation prohibiting or limiting the harm in the first instance (the answer adopted by most modern environmental laws), or through long-established common law frameworks that provide rights to injunctive or monetary relief. Such common law frameworks have their roots in English law predating America's independence, but continued on their own somewhat distinct path in the roughly two hundred years before the explosion of modern federal environmental laws starting around 1970. Constitutionally based arguments for a right to a clean environment never took root under the federal constitution, but under a few state constitutions, limited constitutional rights to a clean environment have been recognized.

This section introduces the reader to the most important common law causes of action for environmental harms, as well as the public trust doctrine, a judicially derived doctrine of somewhat indeterminate origin but with occasionally substantial influence. The section closes with brief review of constitutionally based arguments for rights to a clean environment. Many of the cases excerpted precede modern federal environmental laws, but, as will also be discussed, most common law causes of action remain viable, typically even when environmentally harmful activity is permitted by federal law. They remain a key foundation of our environmental law, influencing statutory strategies but also remaining a key alternative means to remedy environmental harms when political officials refuse to take action. Common law actions face many hurdles and are viewed by most policymakers and scholars as inadequate to deter most environmental harms, but they remain an important part of the environmental lawyer's arsenal. They are often the sole means for injured citizens to be compensated for their harms.

In working through the following materials, assess which claims, if any, might be effective in deterring or remedying harms from a mine in the circumstances set forth in Problem 1-1.

1. Negligence Claims

Where a private or public actor causes an environmental harm, citizens and possibly other governments can experience substantial harms. Although most upper-class law students have studied tort law at great length and immediately think "negligence" when someone is harmed, most environmental harms result from intentional activity that may be just like the activity of many other, similar producers of environmental harms. Harms may flow from ordinary, standard conduct, even conduct that reflects the technological state of the art. In addition, broad-based environmental harms likely to generate litigation tend to be caused by large producers of risk such as manufacturers, refineries, power plants, and chemical plants. Thus, for victims of pollution and their lawyers, trying to prove that negligent operations caused a harm presents formidable challenges. For this reason, negligence common law theories tend to be little used for environmental harms unless (a) the harm arises out of what is clearly an accident, such as a spill or facility malfunction; (b) the remedies sought are of a sort recognized only under negligence doctrine, which does tend to have a more nuanced array of recognized remedies and categories of recoverable damage; or (c) insurance held by the causer of harm will pay any recovery, and, as is typically the case, insurance does not cover "intentional" acts. 46 C.J.S. Insurance §1153 (2005).

2. Public and Private Nuisance Claims

Rather than negligence claims, public and private nuisance actions are the norm for remedying environmental harms. Such claims are typically rooted in allegations of intentional conduct, although not in the sense of a specific intent to cause harm of a particular sort to a particular victim. Instead, the only intent that the plaintiff must show is that the activity causing the harm was undertaken intentionally. A reduced foreseeability requirement is imposed for such claims, requiring only that harms of the sort caused could reasonably be foreseen by the polluter. In both public and private nuisance cases, the idea that externalized harms should be internalized through an award of damages and injunctive relief is often explicitly cited by courts. See Boomer v. Atlantic Cement Co., 26 N.Y.2d 219, 225-226 (1970). Key to both theories are concepts of unreasonable harm. As you read the following materials, seek to sort out when each sort of claim is most advantageous. When will both sorts of nuisance claims be available?

a. Public Nuisance Claims

Public nuisance claims are often brought by governments on behalf of citizens and to protect lands in the jurisdiction, but also now can be brought by individuals and nongovernmental organizations. Such public nuisance actions typically involve broad-based harms, especially to commonly enjoyed resources. Public nuisance actions allow plaintiffs to aggregate damages and enjoin polluting activities that produce serious cumulative harms, rather than focus merely on individual impacts. Originally, public nuisance claims were based on criminal violations, but the modern theory is that a public nuisance is an unreasonable interference with the rights of the public.

The substantive standards are the same as for a private nuisance, but private parties have historically had standing to sue for a public nuisance only if they suffer special damages. See Bryson & Macbeth, Public Nuisance, The Restatement (Second) of Torts, and Environmental Law, 2 Ecology L.Q. 241 (1972). There has been a limited expansion of the standing rules. In re The Exxon Valdez (Alaska Native Class v. Exxon Corp.), 104 F.3d 1196 (9th Cir. 1997), illustrates the limits of the common law in allowing private actions for many types of pollution, especially diffuse ones. The Restatement of Torts (Second) §821C has a liberal standing rule for injunctive relief and abatement actions. Representatives of the general public, "as a citizen in a citizen's action, or as a member of a class in a class action," have standing. But §821C(1) limits damage actions to those who suffer "harm of a different kind from that suffered by other members of the public exercising the right common to the general public that was the subject of the interference." The court recognized that Native Americans injured by the Exxon Valdez spill had a right to sue for economic damages from lost fishing opportunities, but refused to allow them to sue to recover "cultural damage—damage to the Class members' subsistence way of life"—because the damages were not special. All Alaska residents have a right to subsistence hunting and fishing, and thus "'the right to obtain and share wild food, enjoy uncontaminated nature, and cultivate traditional, cultural, spiritual, and physiological benefits in pristine natural surroundings' is shared by all Alaskans." Id. at 1198. Compare Miotke v. City of Spokane, 678 P.2d 803 (Wash. 1984) (riparian owners and environmental organization had standing to recover damages for stream pollution because individuals suffered nausea, headaches, and insomnia). See generally Hodas, Private Actions for Public Nuisance: Common Law Citizen Suits for Relief from Environmental Harm, 16 Ecology L.Q. 883 (1989). Antolini, Modernizing Public Nuisance: Solving the Paradox of the Special Injury Rule, 28 Ecology L.Q. 755 (2001), reviews the turbulent history of §821 and the courts' general neglect of it, and proposes a new common law standard consistent with the rise of public law litigation by environmental groups and other nongovernmental organizations (NGOs).

In 1906 the Supreme Court decided Missouri v. Illinois, 200 U.S. 496. The case arose out of Chicago's successful effort to reverse the flow of the Chicago River to shift pollution from Lake Michigan into the Mississippi watershed. The case is a classic example of the limits of the common law of nuisance to deal with diffuse injuries and risks rather than proven damage to person or property. Downstream Missouri sued Illinois for increasing the risk of illness to Mississippi River communities. Justice Holmes's opinion for the Court, however, revealed the difficulty of carrying proof burdens in a case involving multiple pollution sources, risks of harm, and complex questions of causation:

> As to the principle to be laid down, the caution necessary is manifest. It is a question of the first magnitude whether the destiny of the great rivers is to be the sewers of the cities along their banks or to be protected against everything which threatens their purity. To decide the whole matter at one blow by an irrevocable fiat would be at least premature. If we are to judge by what the plaintiff itself permits, the discharge of sewage into the Mississippi by cities and towns is to be expected. We believe that the practice of discharging into the river is general along its banks, except where the levees of Louisiana have led to a different course. The argument for the plaintiff asserts it to be proper within certain limits. These are facts to be considered. . . .
>
> . . . At the outset we cannot but be struck by the consideration that if this suit had been brought fifty years ago it almost necessarily would have failed. There is no pretense that there is a nuisance of the simple kind that was known to the older common law. There is nothing which can be detected by the unassisted senses,—no visible increase of filth, no new smell. On the contrary, it is proved that the great volume of pure water from Lake Michigan, which is mixed with the sewage at the start, has improved the Illinois river in these respects to a noticeable extent. Formerly it was sluggish and ill smelling. Now it is a comparatively clear stream to which edible fish have returned. Its water is drunk by the fishermen, it is said without evil results. The plaintiff's case depends upon an inference of the unseen. It draws the inference from two propositions. First, that typhoid fever has increased considerably since the change, and that other explanations have been disproved; and second, that the bacillus of typhoid can and does survive the journey and reach the intake of St. Louis in the Mississippi.
>
> We assume the now-prevailing scientific explanation of typhoid fever to be correct. But when we go beyond that assumption, everything is involved in doubt. The data upon which an increase in the deaths from typhoid fever in St. Louis is alleged are disputed. The elimination of other causes is denied. The experts differ as to the time and distance within which a stream would purify itself. No case of an epidemic caused by infection at so remote a source is brought forward and the cases which are produced are controverted. . . .

. . . [T]he defendant's evidence shows a reduction in the chemical and bacterial accompaniments of pollution in a given quantity of water, which would be natural in view of the mixture of nine parts to one from Lake Michigan. It affirms that the Illinois is better or no worse at its mouth than it was before, and makes it at least uncertain how much of the present pollution is due to Chicago and how much to sources further down, not complained of in the bill. It contends that if any bacilli should get through, they would be scattered and enfeebled and would do no harm. . . . The evidence is very strong that it is necessary for St. Louis to take preventive measures, by filtration or otherwise, against the dangers of the plaintiff's own creation or from other sources than Illinois. What will protect against one will protect against another. The presence of causes of infection from the plaintiff's action makes the case weaker in principle as well as harder to prove than one in which all came from a single source. . . .

We might go more into detail, but we believe that we have said enough to explain our point of view and our opinion of the evidence as it stands. What the future may develop, of course we cannot tell. But our conclusion upon the present evidence is that the case proved falls so far below the allegations of the bill that it is not brought within the principles heretofore established in the cause. [Id. at 521-523, 525-526.]

Fears that the dismissal of the *Missouri* case might be a harbinger of general resistance to environmental public nuisance claims quickly proved unfounded.

GEORGIA v. TENNESSEE COPPER CO.
206 U.S. 230 (1907)

HOLMES, J.

This is a bill in equity filed in this court by the state of Georgia, in pursuance of a resolution of the legislature and by direction of the governor of the state, to enjoin the defendant copper companies from discharging noxious gas from their works in Tennessee over the plaintiff's territory. It alleges that, in consequence of such discharge, a wholesale destruction of forests, orchards, and crops is going on, and other injuries are done and threatened in five counties of the state. It alleges also a vain application to the state of Tennessee for relief. A preliminary injunction was denied; but, as there was ground to fear that great and irreparable damage might be done, an early day was fixed for the final hearing, and the parties were given leave, if so minded, to try the case on affidavits. This has been done without objection, and, although the method would be unsatisfactory if our decision turned on any nice question of fact, in the view that we take we think it unlikely that either party has suffered harm.

The case has been argued largely as if it were one between two private parties; but it is not. The very elements that would be relied upon in a suit between fellow-citizens as a ground for equitable relief are wanting here. The state owns very little of the territory alleged to be affected, and the damage to it capable of estimate in money, possibly, at least, is small. This is a suit by a state for an injury to it in its capacity of quasi-sovereign. In that capacity the state has an interest independent of and behind the titles of its citizens, in all the earth and air within its domain. It has the last word as to whether its mountains shall be stripped of their forests and its inhabitants shall breathe pure air. It might have to pay individuals before it could utter that word, but with it remains the final power. The alleged damage to the state as a private owner is merely a makeweight, and we may lay on one side the dispute as to whether the destruction of forests has led to the gullying of its roads.

The caution with which demands of this sort, on the part of a State, for relief from injuries analogous to torts, must be examined is dwelt upon in Missouri v. Illinois, 200 U.S. 496, 520, 521. But it is plain that some such demands must be recognized, if the grounds alleged are proved. When the States by their union made the forcible abatement of outside nuisance impossible to each, they did not thereby agree to submit to whatever might be done. They did not renounce the possibility of making reasonable demands on the ground of their still remaining quasi-sovereign interests; and the alternative to force is a suit in this court. Missouri v. Illinois, 180 U.S. 208, 241. . . .

It is a fair and reasonable demand on the part of a sovereign that the air over its territory should not be polluted on a great scale by sulphurous acid gas, that the forests on its mountains, be they better or worse, and whatever domestic destruction they have suffered, should not be further destroyed or threatened by the act of persons beyond its control, that the crops and orchards on its hills should not be endangered from the same source. If any such demand is to be enforced this must be notwithstanding the hesitation that we might feel if the suit were between private parties, and the doubt whether, for the injuries which they might be suffering to their property, they should not be left to action at law.

The proof requires but a few words. It is not denied that the defendants generate in their works near the Georgia line large quantities of sulphur dioxid[e] which becomes sulphurous acid by its mixture with the air. It hardly is denied and cannot be denied with success that this gas often is carried by the wind great distances and over great tracts of Georgia land. On the evidence the pollution of the air and the magnitude of that pollution are not open to dispute. Without any attempt to go into details immaterial to the suit, it is proper to add that we are satisfied by a preponderance of evidence that the sulphurous fumes cause and threaten damage on so considerable a scale to the forest and vegetable life, if not to health, with the plaintiff State as to make out a case within the requirements of Missouri v. Illinois, 200 U.S. 496. Whether Georgia by insisting upon this claim is doing more harm than good to her own citizens is for her to determine. The possible disaster to those outside the State must be accepted as a consequence of her standing upon her extreme rights.

For another, more recent case affirming the right of governments to seek public nuisance relief, see Machipongo Land and Coal Co. v. Commonwealth, 799 A.2d 751 (Pa. 2002) (holding that the Commonwealth can prohibit coal mining by showing that it has a "high potential" to increase dissolved solids and metal concentrations in trout streams or has a significant potential to disrupt a stream's hydrologic balance by increasing net alkalinity).

b.   Private Nuisance Claims

Private nuisance claims remain the bread and butter of environmental common law litigation. Where a citizen's property has been injured by another's pollution or environmental degradation, private nuisance claims are often the answer. The sorts of harms found actionable in private nuisance actions vary greatly, but still are limited. Some jurisdictions, for example, do not recognize interference with aesthetic sensibilities as actionable. See Robie v. Lillis, 299 A.2d 155 (N.H. 1972). Cf. State v. Piemontese, 659 A.2d 1385 (N.J. Super. App. Div. 1995) (ordinance that prohibited "unsightly" hedges and lawns unconstitutionally vague). A few courts have recognized that such an interference can be a nuisance but have limited the tort to land use pariahs such as junkyards. Foley v. Harris, 286 S.E.2d 186 (Va. 1982); Town of Delafield v. Sharpley, 568 N.W.2d 779 (Wis. App. 1997). But cf. Prah v. Maretti, 321 N.W.2d 182 (Wis. 1982) (interference with solar access).

A private nuisance is a nontrespassory invasion of another's interest in the use and enjoyment of land. The plaintiff must prove that the defendant's conduct is unreasonable and causes a substantial interference with the use and enjoyment of land or causes bodily injury. Nuisance is a hybrid tort that has elements of strict liability and intentional tort. Nuisance differs from negligence. The focus is on the reasonableness of the activity's effects in a particular place, not on the general reasonableness of the defendant's conduct. Nuisance evaluates the reasonableness of the conduct and its effects by comparing it to the surrounding land uses. Private nuisance claims hence can be a form of judicial zoning, with courts assessing whether a use is environmentally incompatible with the surrounding area. For example, Penland v. Redwood Sanitary Sewer Serv. Dist., 965 P.2d 433 (Or. App. 1998), affirmed a trial court decision that a sewage composting facility, located in a rural residential area on the Rogue River in southern Oregon, and that stank like "500 outhouses at once," was a nuisance. The appellate court quoted the trial judge's remarks after viewing the site. "The day we were out there, there were osprey flying over the river. . . . It's a beautiful, very much a residential" area. The trial judge also noted that the District switched from a sewage treatment to a composting facility in 1990 and the change was not foreseeable and was "akin" to locating an industrial use in the area. Thus, the intentional act is focused not on a specific intent to cause harm, but on the location of intentional activity in an unsuitable place.

The issue of what must be unreasonable, and what should be balanced in making such an assessment, has long confounded courts and led to varying formulations in the Restatements of Torts. The following two case excerpts from Connecticut should give you a feel for arguments and counterarguments over "unreasonable harm."

WALSH v. TOWN OF STONINGTON WATER POLLUTION CONTROL AUTHORITY
250 Conn. 443, 736 A.2d 811 (1999)

[Citizen neighbors of a coastal town's sewage treatment plant sued for damages resulting from the plant's odors. After a jury awarded them damages, the town challenged the trial court's formulation for the jury of how "unreasonableness" should be determined. Only the relevant case discussion is excerpted below.]

NORCOTT, J.

An analysis of the defendants' claims requires us to review the contours of the unreasonable use element of a common-law private nuisance cause of action. As we previously have stated, "'the law will not interfere with a use that is reasonable.'

Hurlbut v. McKone, 55 Conn. 31, 42 [1887]. 'It is the duty of every person to make a reasonable use of his own property so as to occasion no unnecessary damage or annoyance to his neighbor.' Nailor v. C.W. Blakeslee & Sons, Inc., 117 Conn. 241, 245 [1933]. A fair test of whether a proposed use constitutes a nuisance is 'the reasonableness of the use of the property in the particular locality under the circumstances of the case.' Wetstone v. Cantor, 144 Conn. 77, 80 [1956]." Nicholson v. Connecticut Half-Way House, Inc., 153 Conn. 507, 510 (1966). The test of unreasonableness is "essentially a weighing process, involving a comparative evaluation of conflicting interests in various situations according to objective legal standards." O'Neill v. Carolina Freight Carriers Corp., 156 Conn. 613, 617-18 (1968), quoting 4 Restatement, Torts §826, comment (b) (1939); see Nair v. Thaw, 156 Conn. 445, 452 (1968). In Maykut v. Plasko, 170 Conn. 310, 314 (1976), we again referred to the weighing process described in the Restatement, in determining whether the trial court had applied the proper test to determine the reasonableness of the defendants' use of their land. We concluded that the trial court had applied the proper test where "[t]he facts outlined in [the] memorandum of decision and set out in the finding include a consideration not only of the interest of the plaintiff, but of the defendants also." Id., at 315.

The charge to the jury in the present case was consistent with our prior holdings on the element of unreasonable use. When viewed in the context of the charge as a whole, the jury instructions concerning unreasonable use conveyed to the jury that it was to take into consideration and weigh the conflicting interests involved. The trial court stated at the outset of the explanation of the unreasonable use element of the claim that the jury "must consider the location of the condition and any other circumstances that you find proven which indicate whether the defendants [were] making a reasonable use of the property." . . . This statement indicates that the jury must take into account a multiplicity of factors. Reference to the fact that the use of the property for a plant is a reasonable use makes clear that the use of the defendants' land to operate a plant is reasonable in and of itself. By then noting that the determination of reasonableness is to be made in the context of odors produced by the plant, the trial court underscored that the weighing process for the jury to conduct is of the reasonableness of use in light of the production of unreasonable odors that the jury had determined existed in its answers to the first four interrogatories. We disagree with the defendants, therefore, that the effect of the jury instruction was to remove the interests of the defendants from the jury's consideration. Rather, we conclude that the trial court's charge provided a reasonably clear instruction that the jury must consider many factors in determining the reasonableness of use, including the reasonableness of use as a plant that creates certain odors in the course of its operation.

Moreover, the defendants' arguments regarding the impropriety of the jury instructions necessarily are unpersuasive because they are based on an inaccurate construction of the concept of unreasonable use. We begin by noting that the defendants' reliance upon the state mandate concerning water pollution control is misplaced. As discussed further in part III of this opinion, the fact that operating a plant is permissible, or even necessary, on the land in question does not necessarily shield the defendants from liability for harm to the land of others that may result from that use. "A municipality which creates a nuisance causing damage to the land of another is not excused from liability on the ground that the act is lawful in itself if, under all the circumstances, it is unreasonable." Cyr v. Brookfield, 153 Conn. 261, 265 (1965). As a result, we reject the defendants' claim that "[w]here a town is undertaking an activity in furtherance of a state goal and pursuant to a state mandate, the charge to the jury should protect the town from liability for actions that are necessary to carry out the state's directives."

The defendants also place much emphasis on our prior statement in *Cyr* that "[a]n intentional invasion of another's interest in the use and enjoyment of land is unreasonable under the rule stated in §822 [of the Restatement of Torts],[1] unless the utility of the actor's conduct outweighs the gravity of the harm." Cyr v. Brookfield, *supra*, 153 Conn. at 265-66, quoting 4 Restatement, *supra*, §826. On the basis of this statement, the defendants assert that the element of unreasonable use cannot be met in this case unless the harm to the plaintiffs outweighs the social utility of a plant, that is, the harm outweighs the benefit to the residents of the town as a whole. The comments in the Restatement (Second) of Torts on utility versus gravity of harm do not, however, support the interpretation asserted by the defendants. The Restatement (Second) provides the example that "[e]ven though the noise and smoke from a factory cannot feasibly be eliminated, the utility of the factory is not weighed in the abstract. In a suit for damages, the legal utility of the activity may also be greatly reduced by the fact that the actor is operating the factory and producing the noise and smoke without compensating his neighbors for the harm done to them. The conduct for which the utility is being weighed includes both the general activity and what is done about its consequences." 4 Restatement (Second), Torts §826, comment (e) (1979). The defendants' understanding of the balancing requirement does not involve simply the weighing of factors to determine reasonableness as the law requires.[2] Instead, application of the defendants' approach would result in an all-or-nothing scenario wherein the plaintiffs could never prove unreasonable use because their harm could never trump the undisputed need for a town plant. In other words, the plaintiffs would be expected to bear all of the harm without compensation for their damages, while receiving no greater benefits from the continued operation of the plant than any other resident of the town. Such an interpretation goes far beyond the necessary weighing process to be undertaken by the jury.

We conclude that the jury instructions were adequate to guide the jury properly in the determination of the issues.

NOTE AND QUESTION

Clarity or Confusion? Does *Walsh* offer a satisfactory or clear explication of how this balancing is to occur? Note that the court cites several Restatement of Torts

1. Section 822 of the Restatement (Second) of Torts now provides in relevant part: "One is subject to liability for a private nuisance if, but only if, his conduct is a legal cause of an invasion of another's interest in the private use and enjoyment of land, and the invasion is . . . (a) intentional and unreasonable. . . ."

2. In a similar vein, the town also cites to 2 D. Wright & W. Ankerman, Connecticut Jury Instructions (4th ed.1993) §44, p. 886, for the proposition that "[i]f there was nothing which the defendant could reasonably have done to guard against the danger, it cannot be held to have created a nuisance." This proposed instruction, and the case law from which it was generated, applies to claims of public nuisance wherein the condition or conduct complained of interfered with a right common to the general public. State v. Tippetts-Abbett-McCarthy-Stratton, 204 Conn. 177, 183 (1987). Without addressing the question of whether there was anything further that the town could have done to reduce or eliminate the production of odors, we simply note that such a requirement is irrelevant in the context of the present case.

formulations of the balancing or assessment of harm that is part of the assessment of "unreasonable" use or harm. Note also how some formulations focus on the conduct of the source of the harm, while others focus on nature or magnitude of the harm experienced by the victims. After *Walsh*, in Connecticut, was sorting out the relative interests and harms for the court, or for a jury?

After Connecticut courts and litigants struggled to make sense of *Walsh*, the state's highest court revisited the issue, not literally overruling *Walsh* but substantially modifying what needs to be considered in assessing reasonableness. Note that in this short case excerpt, which arose out of a conflict between neighbors and a nearby dairy farm generating allegedly offensive odors, the court emphasizes a particular Restatement formulation, rather than throwing all of them into the mix.

PETSEY v. CUSHMAN
259 Conn. 345, 788 A.2d 496 (2002)

Vertefeuille, J.

. . . "There is perhaps no more impenetrable jungle in the entire law than that which surrounds the word 'nuisance.'" W. Prosser & W. Keeton, *supra*, §86, p. 616. This court has stated often that a plaintiff must prove four elements to succeed in a nuisance cause of action: "(1) the condition complained of had a natural tendency to create danger and inflict injury upon person or property; (2) the danger created was a continuing one; (3) the use of the land was unreasonable or unlawful; [and] (4) the existence of the nuisance was the proximate cause of the plaintiffs' injuries and damages." These elements developed through a long line of cases that can be described best as public nuisance cases.[3]

Despite its grounding in public nuisance law, this four factor analysis has since been applied without distinction to both public and private nuisance causes of action. Although there are some similarities between a public and a private nuisance, the two causes of action are distinct. Indeed, Professors Prosser and Keeton in their treatise on the law of torts have stated: "The two have almost nothing in common, except that each causes inconvenience to someone, and it would have been fortunate if they had been called from the beginning by different names." W. Prosser & W. Keeton, *supra*, §86, p. 618. Public nuisance law is concerned with the interference with a public right, and cases in this realm typically involve conduct that allegedly interferes with the public health and safety. . . . Private nuisance law, on the other hand, is concerned with conduct that interferes with an individual's private right to the use and enjoyment of his or her land. Showing the existence of a condition detrimental to

3. Section 821B of the Restatement (Second) of Torts defines a public nuisance as "an unreasonable interference with a right common to the general public." See State v. Tippetts-Abbett-McCarthy-Stratton, *supra*, 204 Conn. at 183. Whether an interference is unreasonable in the public nuisance context depends, according to the Restatement (Second), on "(a) [w]hether the conduct involves a significant interference with the public health, the public safety, the public peace, the public comfort or the public convenience, or (b) whether the conduct is proscribed by [law]. . . ." 4 Restatement (Second), *supra*, §821B. The rights common to the general public can include, but certainly are not limited to, such things as the right to use a public park, highway, river or lake. Id., §821D, comment (c).

the public safety, or, as the first two elements of the four factor analysis discussed previously require, showing that the condition complained of had a natural tendency to create a continuing danger, is often irrelevant to a private nuisance claim. In light of the fundamental differences between these two distinct causes of action, we conclude that further attempts to employ the four part test discussed previously herein in the assessment of private nuisance causes of action would be imprudent; private nuisance claims simply do not fit comfortably within the same analytical rubric as public nuisance claims. We must restate, therefore, the elements that a plaintiff must prove to prevail on a claim for damages in a common-law private nuisance action.

In prescribing these specific elements, we look to the leading authorities in the field of common-law private nuisance for guidance. According to the Restatement (Second) of Torts, a plaintiff must prove that: (1) there was an invasion of the plaintiff's use and enjoyment of his or her property; (2) the defendant's conduct was the proximate cause of the invasion; and (3) the invasion was either intentional and unreasonable, or unintentional and the defendant's conduct was negligent or reckless. 4 Restatement (Second), *supra*, §822. Although the language used in this third element does not make the point clearly, under this test, showing unreasonableness is an essential element of a private nuisance cause of action based on negligence or recklessness. See id., §822, comment (k). Professors Prosser and Keeton define the plaintiff's burden in a similar manner. According to their view, a plaintiff in a private nuisance action must demonstrate that: (1) the defendant acted with the intent of interfering with the plaintiff's use and enjoyment of his or her property; (2) the interference with the use and enjoyment of the land was of the kind intended; (3) the interference was substantial; and (4) the interference was unreasonable. W. Prosser & W. Keeton, *supra*, §87, p. 622-25. In the context of a private nuisance, they define a defendant's intent as meaning merely that "the defendant has created or continued the condition causing the interference with full knowledge that the harm to the plaintiff's interests are occurring or are substantially certain to follow." Id., at 625.

This requirement of unreasonableness, a part of the third element in the test set forth in the Restatement (Second) and the fourth element in the test enunciated by Professors Prosser and Keeton, often has been stated, not in terms of whether the interference was unreasonable, but, rather, in terms of whether the defendant's conduct was unreasonable. See, e.g., Walsh v. Stonington Water Pollution Control Authority, *supra*, 250 Conn. at 446 (determining whether defendants' operation of wastewater treatment plant was "'unreasonable use'"). In its charge to the jury, the trial court in the present case framed the inquiry in such a manner.

Although similar, "[t]he two concepts—unreasonable interference and unreasonable conduct—are not at all identical." W. Prosser & W. Keeton, *supra*, §87, p. 623. "Confusion has resulted from the fact that the . . . interference with the plaintiff's use of his property can be unreasonable even when the defendant's conduct is reasonable. . . . Courts have often found the existence of a nuisance on the basis of unreasonable use when what was meant is that the interference was unreasonable, i.e., it was unreasonable for the defendant to act as he did without paying for the harm that was knowingly inflicted on the plaintiff. Thus, an industrial enterprise who properly locates a cement plant or a coal-burning electric generator, who exercises utmost care in the utilization of known scientific techniques for minimizing the harm from the emission of noxious smoke, dust and gas and who is serving society well by engaging in the activity may yet be required to pay for the inevitable harm caused to neighbors."

Id., §88, p. 629. As this example amply demonstrates, while an unreasonable use and an unreasonable interference often coexist, the two concepts are not equivalent, and it is possible to prove that a defendant's use of his property, while reasonable, nonetheless constitutes a common-law private nuisance because it unreasonably interferes with the use of property by another person. That was the situation in *Walsh*.

In *Walsh*, this court rejected the defendants' argument on appeal that their operation of the wastewater treatment plant in question could not constitute a nuisance since the operation of such a plant was clearly a reasonable use of property. Id., at 457. This court held that the production of odors by the defendants' plant could constitute a nuisance, notwithstanding the fact that operating a wastewater treatment plant was clearly a reasonable use of the property in question. Although the proposition was not stated expressly in *Walsh*, our holding in that case demonstrates that, while the reasonableness of a defendant's conduct is a factor in determining whether an interference is unreasonable, it is not an independent element that must be proven in order to prevail in all private nuisance causes of action. The inquiry is cast more appropriately as whether the defendant's conduct unreasonably interfered with the plaintiff's use and enjoyment of his or her land rather than whether the defendant's conduct was itself unreasonable. Quinnett v. Newman, *supra*, 213 Conn. at 348 (nuisance refers to condition that exists and not to act that creates it). The proper focus of a private nuisance claim for damages, therefore, is whether a defendant's conduct, i.e., his or her use of his or her property, causes an unreasonable interference with the plaintiff's use and enjoyment of his or her property. Herbert v. Smyth, *supra*, 155 Conn. at 81-82; see also Scribner v. Summers, 84 F.3d 554, 559 (2d Cir. 1996); Copart Industries, Inc. v. Consolidated Edison Co. of New York, Inc., 41 N.Y.2d 564, 570 (1977).

On the basis of our reexamination of our case law and upon our review of private nuisance law as described by the leading authorities, we adopt the basic principles of §822 of the Restatement (Second) of Torts and conclude that in order to recover damages in a common-law private nuisance cause of action, a plaintiff must show that the defendant's conduct was the proximate cause of an unreasonable interference with the plaintiff's use and enjoyment of his or her property. The interference may be either intentional; Quinnett v. Newman, *supra*, 213 Conn. at 348 (nuisance is created intentionally if defendant intends act that brings about condition found to be nuisance); or the result of the defendant's negligence. Id., at 348-49. Whether the interference is unreasonable depends upon a balancing of the interests involved under the circumstances of each individual case. In balancing the interests, the fact finder must take into consideration all relevant factors, including the nature of both the interfering use and the use and enjoyment invaded, the nature, extent and duration of the interference, the suitability for the locality of both the interfering conduct and the particular use and enjoyment invaded, whether the defendant is taking all feasible precautions to avoid any unnecessary interference with the plaintiff's use and enjoyment of his or her property, and any other factors that the fact finder deems relevant to the question of whether the interference is unreasonable. No one factor should dominate this balancing of interests; all relevant factors must be considered in determining whether the interference is unreasonable.

The determination of whether the interference is unreasonable should be made in light of the fact that some level of interference is inherent in modern society. There are few, if any, places remaining where an individual may rest assured that he will be able to use and enjoy his property free from all interference. Accordingly, the interference must be substantial to be unreasonable. See 4 Restatement (Second), *supra*, §822, comment (g); W. Prosser & W. Keeton, *supra*, §88, p. 626.

Ultimately, the question of reasonableness is whether the interference is beyond that which the plaintiff should bear, under all of the circumstances of the particular case, without being compensated.

NOTES AND QUESTIONS

1. *Recasting the "Unreasonableness" Focus.* Although the *Petsey* court undoubtedly retains some balancing as part of the private nuisance formulation, where is the focus now placed? Is this focus different from that in *Walsh*?

2. *Balancing and Economic Vitality.* As most students already know from their first-year courses on property law, and the common coverage in many classes of Boomer v. Atlantic Cement Co., 257 N.E.2d 870 (N.Y. 1970) (excerpted in Chapter 10), a court's finding of a nuisance in many jurisidictions has historically led to issuance of an injunction against the conduct causing harm. Hence, the unreasonableness balancing and liability determination can lead to a court-imposed shutdown of manufacturers that may be important to economic vitality and employment. Some states fashioned their common law so that this liability-injunction linkage was severed, at least where damages could still be recovered, see Madison v. Ducktown Sulphur Copper & Iron Co., 113 Tenn. 331, 83 S.W. 658 (1904), but it also at times would lead courts to deny the existence of a nuisance even where it appeared solidly proven.

In *Boomer*, New York refashioned its law to issue a conditional injunction against a cement company's polluting operations until it paid court-set "permanent damages." This case and a few related cases led to publication of one of the law's most influential law review articles, Calabresi & Melamed, Property Rules, Liability Rules and Inalienability: One View of the Cathedral, 85 Harv. L. Rev. 1089 (1972). Dean Calabresi and his co-author looked at nuisance cases and saw in them four possible modes of resolution, with the key variables being how different resolutions would leave certain tasks either to the court or to private negotiation, and who held the "entitlement" to enjoy or undertake an activity. You have been introduced to all but one of these various resolutions. Can you articulate what they are?

For the case decided virtually simultaneously with this article, and utilizing the less intuitively obvious fourth potential resolution, see Spur Industries, Inc. v. Del E. Webb Dev. Co., 494 P.2d 700 (Ariz. 1972).

3. *The Holdout.* Key to understanding judicial refusal to issue injunctions, or embrace of conditional injunctions with judicially set damages, is the concept of the *holdout.* Just because a defendant might offer a market-priced damages remedy to a pollution victim does not mean the victim will budge and surrender her right to an injunction. Even if a defendant offers well above the actual market value of the damage or outright acquisition of the plaintiff victim's property, the plaintiff might hold out, refusing to sell. The injunction then could become a permanent closure order for a plant of great local value. This possibility has led numerous jurisdictions to abandon the previously mechanical linkage of the finding of a nuisance and the issuance of an injunction.

4. *Nuisance and the Risk of Future Injury.* Advocates of statutory and regulatory answers to environmental ills sometimes describe such public law approaches as

different from common law in their preventive focus, seeking to limit or prevent harms before they occur. Certainly they are more decidedly preventive or precautionary in focus, but they also often actually add up to "right to pollute" laws, limiting but allowing pollution.

The preventive versus after-the-fact distinction between regulatory and common law answers is more a difference of degree. Where a proposed land use will become a nuisance, courts may use the apprehended or anticipatory nuisance doctrine to enjoin the proposed use before it begins. 58 Am. Jur. 2d Nuisances §339 (2006). Anticipatory nuisance is a widely recognized cause of action. Smith, Re-validating the Doctrine of Anticipatory Nuisance, 29 Vt. L. Rev. 687, 688 (2005); see Rock Island and Pacific R.R. Co. v. Iowa Dep't of Transp., 756 F.2d 517, 521 (7th Cir. 1985) ("A land use that will create a nuisance can be enjoined in advance, as an alternative to abating the nuisance once it comes into being."); Roach v. Combined Util. Comm'n, 351 S.E.2d 168 (S.C. App. 1986) ("An antic-ipatory nuisance is an act, occupation or structure which is not a nuisance per se, but which may become a nuisance by reason of circumstances, location or sur-roundings."). Anticipatory nuisance requires a high burden of proof because it restricts a landowner's freedom to use his land before any harm occurs. Smith, supra, at 697. Generally, the plaintiff must demonstrate that "[t]he injury must be practically certain, rather than merely probable." 58 Am Jur. 2d Nuisances §342 (2006). Because of the high burden of proof, the anticipatory nuisance doc-trine is seldom used.

3. Trespass Claims

The use of trespass actions to remedy groundwater contamination or air pol-lution is another example of the limits of the common law to promote a high level of environmental protection. To maintain a trespass claim, a plaintiff must prove that the defendant intended to act in a manner that produced an unlawful invasion and had good reason to know that, for example, the subsurface geology would permit the contamination to migrate beneath plaintiff's land. The discharge of toxic pollutants that migrate beneath another's land can also be a trespass. E.g., Davey Compressor Co. v. City of Delray Beach, 613 So. 2d 60 (Fla. App. 1993), approved, 639 So. 2d 595 (Fla. 1994); Sterling v. Velsicol Chem. Corp., 647 F. Supp. 303, 317-319 (W.D. Tenn. 1986), aff'd, 855 F.2d 1188, 1198 (6th Cir. 1988). Air pollution historically was not a trespass because the particles did not amount to a direct physical invasion. Indirect injuries had to be redressed as nuisances. However, the "tangible" invasion requirement has been rejected as unscientific. Martin v. Reynolds Metals Co., 342 P.2d 790 (Or. 1959); Bradley v. American Smelting and Ref. Co., 709 P.2d 782 (Wash. 1985).

Environmental trespass remains, however, different from a simple unconsented entry onto the land of another. Courts have aligned trespass with negligence and nuisance liability. Bradley and other cases require proof of "actual and substantial damages." For example, Chance v. BP Chem., Inc., 670 N.E.2d 985 (Ohio 1996), upheld the dismissal of a trespass, negligence, and nuisance action for injected liquid wastes that allegedly migrated beneath plaintiff's land. The court held that plaintiffs must show an actual interference with a reasonable and foreseeable use of the sub-surface beneath their land.

4. Strict Liability Claims

Common law claims rooted in strict liability theory also can provide plaintiffs with significant relief, but typically plaintiffs must convince a court that the activity causing the harm was unusually dangerous, was inherently dangerous in the location in which it occurred, or involved materials that are always inherently dangerous. For example, strict liability is a possibility for the discharge of hazardous waste into aquifers, but the plaintiff must still establish that defendant's conduct in fact caused injury. A New Jersey case, State Dep't of Envtl. Protection v. Ventron Corp., 468 A.2d 150 (N.J. 1983), imposed common law strict liability on the purchasers of a 40-acre tract from which mercury pollution was seeping into the ground.

Such claims are far from automatic victories for plaintiffs. Section 520 of the Restatement (Second) of Torts and some case law appear to impose a foreseeability requirement for strict liability. A post-*Ventron* New Jersey case indicates that the issue is open, but found that the owner of an industrial site that had processed radium since 1917 was strictly liable because it should have known that radium has always been an abnormally dangerous substance and "the injudicious handling, processing, and disposal of radium has [sic] for decades caused concern. . . ." T & E Indus., Inc. v. Safety Light Corp., 587 A.2d 1249, 1261 (N.J. 1991). Compare Cambridge Water Co. v. Eastern Counties Laeher, PLC (1994), 2 App. Cas. 264 (1994) 1 All E.R. 53, which imposed a foreseeability requirement on strict liability claims for past industrial practices that cause pollution.

The following case not only illuminates how lawyers and judges will seek to push environmental cases into more typical negligence settings, but also illustrates the power of strict liability claims.

BRANCH v. WESTERN PETROLEUM INC.
657 P.2d 267 (Utah 1982)

STEWART, Justice.

The Branches, the plaintiff property owners, sued for damages for the pollution of their culinary water wells caused by percolation of defendant Western Petroleum Inc.'s formation waters (waste waters from oil wells containing various chemical contaminants) into the subterranean water system that feeds the wells. A jury answered questions to special interrogatories, finding, *inter alia*, that the formation waters had contaminated plaintiffs' two wells and awarded damages of $8,050 for pollution of the well water, $700 for trespass, $10,000 for "mental suffering, discomfort and annoyance," and $13,000 punitive damages. The jury, over objection, was instructed on the theory of negligence; however, the trial court entered judgment on the basis of strict liability for the above amounts, except that damages for mental suffering, discomfort, and annoyance were disallowed.

Western appeals, arguing that the trial court erred in awarding damages for pollution of the wells on the basis of strict liability. It contends that negligence is the only valid legal theory upon which the judgment can be sustained and that the trial court erred (1) in not instructing on proximate cause; and (2) in not directing the jury to find the percentage of negligence attributable to each party as required by the Utah Comparative Negligence Act, U.C.A., 1953, §78-27-38. . . .

I

In December 1975, Western purchased forty acres of land in a rural area north of Roosevelt, Utah, which had previously been used as a gravel pit. Western used the property solely for the disposal of formation water, a waste water produced by oil wells while drilling for oil. Formation water contains oil, gas and high concentrations of salt and chemicals, making it unfit for culinary or agricultural uses. The formation water was transported by truck from various oil-producing sites and emptied into the disposal pit with the intent that the toxic water would dissipate through evaporation into the air and percolation into the ground. Alternative sites for disposing of the water were available to Western, but at a greater expense.

In 1976, the Branches purchased a parcel of property immediately adjacent to, and at an elevation of approximately 200 to 300 feet lower than, Western's property. The twenty-one acre parcel had on it a "diligence" well, which had been in existence since 1929, some outbuildings, and a home. After acquiring the property, the Branches made some $60,000 worth of improvements to the home and premises. Prior owners of the property used the water from the well for a grade A dairy and later a grade B dairy. Both dairy operations required that the water be approved for fitness and purity by appropriate state agencies. The Branches, as had all prior owners since 1929, used water from the diligence well for culinary purposes. The water from the diligence well was described as being sweet to the taste and of a high quality until December of 1976.

Two months after purchasing the property, the Branches noticed that the well water began to take on a peculiar taste and had the distinctive smell of petroleum products. Soap added to the water would no longer form suds. They observed that polluted water from Western's disposal pit was running onto the surface of the Branches' property and, on one occasion, reached their basement, causing damage to food stored there. After testing the diligence well water and finding it unfit for human consumption, and after their rabbits and one hundred chickens had died, apparently from the polluted water, the Branches began trucking water to their property from outside sources. In November, 1977, the Branches dug an additional well south of their home. Water from the new well was tested and found safe for culinary purposes. But after a few months, the new well also ceased producing potable water, and on advice of the State Health Department, the Branches ceased using the new well for culinary purposes and hauled water to their property almost until the time of trial.

The Branches requested Western to cease dumping formation water in the disposal pit, but Western refused unless the Branches would post a bond to cover the costs. Western did, however, agree to build a pond on its property to contain the escaping surface water and prevent it from flowing onto the Branches' land. In doing so, Western failed to establish the proper boundary line and built part of the pond on the Branches' land. After the Branches hired a surveyor to establish that Western had built the pond on their land, Western built another containing pond on its own property. The pond, however, was only partially successful in preventing the run-off onto the Branches' land from the disposal pit. Western caused additional damage by permitting its trucks to enter the Branches' property for the purpose of pumping out the containment ponds. When the discharge nozzles on the trucks were left open, polluted water was sprayed directly onto the Branches' land.

As a consequence of the unavailability of culinary water in her home, plaintiff Jeanne Branch returned to her original home in Colorado for a three or four month period so that she could "pull herself together." During this time, Lloyd Branch made weekly trips to and from Colorado to be with his family and otherwise tried to keep in contact with his wife on the telephone while he maintained his contracting business in Roosevelt.

Western's agents admitted that they did not know, and made no attempt to ascertain, what state law was with respect to permitting formation waters to seep or percolate into subsurface waters. Even after Western became aware of the laws relative to dumping, it still took no affirmative action to obtain approval of its ponds. . . .

[The jury] found, in response to special interrogatories, that "defendant's use of the evaporation pit for the dumping of formation water [was] a cause of the pollution of the water in plaintiffs' [wells]," and that Western caused 66 percent of the pollution in Branches' original well and 52 percent of the pollution in the new well. The rest of the pollution was found to be caused by other unspecified "parties or conditions." The jury also found that Western was "negligent . . . in dumping formation waters in its evaporation pit," and had also committed a "trespass upon plaintiffs' land . . . other than the claimed pollution of [the] wells."

II

The major substantive dispute is whether the trial court erred in entering judgment against Western on the basis of strict liability for pollution of the Branches' wells. Western argues that other states have based liability for pollution of subterranean waters on either negligence, nuisance, or trespass, and that since the Branches failed to allege nuisance or trespass, "the only accepted theory upon which this case could be based is negligence." Therefore, according to Western, the trial court erred in entering judgment on the basis of strict liability. Western further submits that since the court did not instruct the jury on proximate cause and comparative negligence, the judgment cannot stand. The Branches, on the other hand, take the position that Western created an abnormally dangerous condition by collecting contaminated water on its land for the purpose of having it seep or percolate into the groundwater and that, therefore, the law of strict liability controls. . . .

Two doctrines have developed in the common law to provide a remedy to a private landowner for nontrespassory injuries caused by another. The landmark case of Rylands v. Fletcher, 3 H. & C. 774, 159 Eng. Rep. 737 (1865), rev'd in Fletcher v. Rylands, L.R. 1 Ex. 265 (1866), aff'd in Rylands v. Fletcher, L.R. 3 H.L. 330 (1868), held that one who uses his land in an unnatural way and thereby creates a dangerous condition or engages in an abnormal activity may be strictly liable for injuries resulting from that condition or activity. Whether a condition or activity is considered abnormal is defined in terms of whether the condition or activity is unduly dangerous or inappropriate to the place where it is maintained. W. Prosser, Law of Torts §78, at 506 (4th ed. 1971). That doctrine was the genesis of §519 of the Restatement of Torts (1939), which, however, limited strict liability to "ultrahazardous activities." Prosser, *supra*, at 512.

Although Rylands v. Fletcher was initially rejected by a number of states, its influence has been substantial in the United States. According to the latest edition of Dean Prosser's treatise on torts, only seven American jurisdictions have rejected the rule of that case, while some thirty jurisdictions have essentially approved the rule. Id. at 509. Indeed, the strict liability rule of the Restatement of Torts was broadened in §519 of the Restatement (Second) of Torts by making it applicable to "abnormally dangerous activities."

Nuisance law also protects property interests from nontrespassory invasions. Unlike most other torts, it is not centrally concerned with the nature of the conduct causing the damage, but with the nature and relative importance of the interests interfered with or invaded. The doctrine of nuisance "has reference to the interests invaded, to the damage or harm inflicted, and not to any particular kind of action or omission which has led to the invasion." W. Prosser, *supra*, §87 at 73-75. Since it is not the nature of one's conduct that generally is essential to an action for nuisance, a person whose interests have been invaded may have a claim for relief based both on nuisance and on the nature of the conduct producing the damage. See Cities Service Oil Co. v. Merritt, Okl., 332 P.2d 677, 684 (1958); Wood v. Picillo, R.I., 443 A.2d 1244 (1982). As the court in *Wood* stated:

> The essential element of an actionable nuisance is that persons have suffered harm or are threatened with injuries that they ought not have to bear. Citizens for Preservation of Waterman Lake v. Davis, R.I., 420 A.2d 53, 59 (1980). Distinguished from negligence liability, liability in nuisance is predicated upon unreasonable injury rather than upon unreasonable conduct. Braun v. Iannotti, 54 R.I. 469, 471, 175 A. 656, 657 (1934). Thus, plaintiffs may recover in nuisance despite the otherwise nontortious nature of the conduct which creates the injury. . . .

It is of no consequence that a business which causes a nuisance is a lawful business. Mowrer v. Ashland Oil & Refining Co., *supra*, at 661. The production of formation water is a natural and necessary incident to the business of producing oil and gas. A business such as Western, which collects and disposes of formation water, conducts a wholly legitimate business. But that does not give it a license to dispose of waste in a manner that for practical purposes appropriates the property of others by making it impossible for them to use water which they are entitled to use. North Point C.I. Co. v. Utah & Salt Lake Canal Co., 52 P. 168 (Utah 1898). . . .

There are two separate, although somewhat related, grounds for holding Western strictly liable for the pollution of the Branches' wells. First, the facts of the case support application of the rule of strict liability because the ponding of the toxic formation water in an area adjacent to the Branches' wells constituted an abnormally dangerous and inappropriate use of the land in light of its proximity to the Branches' property and was unduly dangerous to the Branches' use of their well water. Several cases on comparable facts have applied strict liability due to the abnormal danger of polluting activity. For example, Mowrer v. Ashland Oil & Refining Co., Inc., 518 F.2d 659 (7th Cir.1975), applied strict liability to the leakage of crude oil and salt water into a fresh water well; Yommer v. McKenzie, 257 A.2d 138 (Md. 1969), applied the same rule to the seepage of gasoline from an underground tank into an adjoining landowner's well; Cities Service Co. v. Florida, 312 So. 2d 799 (Fla. App. 1975), applied strict liability to the escape of phosphate slime into a creek and river. See also Bumbarger v. Walker, 164 A.2d 144 (Pa. Super.1960) (strict liability for well pollution caused by defendant's mine blasting). See generally Clark-Aiken Co. v. Cromwell-Wright Co., 323 N.E.2d 876 (Mass. 1975) (strict liability applied to escape of impounded water); Indiana Harbor Belt R.R. Co. v. American Cynamid Co., 517 F. Supp. 314 (N.D. Ill.1981) (strict liability applied to spillage of toxic chemical that resulted in property damage and pollution of water supply); W. Prosser, *supra*, §78 at 512-13 and cases there cited. See also Atlas Chem. Indus., Inc. v. Anderson, 514 S.W.2d 309 (Tex. Civ. App. 1974), aff'd, 524 S.W.2d 681 (1975), where the Texas court, distinguishing a case relied upon by Western, Turner v. Big Lake Oil Co., 96 S.W.2d 221 (Tex. 1936), held the defendant strictly liable for polluting surface streams with industrial wastes. The strict liability rule of Rylands v. Fletcher was held to apply to pollution cases "in which the defendant has set the substance in motion for escape, such as the discharge of the harmful effluent or the emission of a harmful gas or substance."[6] *Atlas Chemical, supra,* at 314.

In concluding that strict liability should govern in that case, the court in *Atlas Chemical* reasoned that the common law rules of tort liability in pollution cases "should be in conformity with the public policy of this state as declared by the Legislature in the Texas Water Code. . . ." Id. at 315. The court also found support for the rule of strict liability in the policy consideration that an industry should not be able to use its property in such a way as to inflict injury on the property of its neighbors because to do so would result in effect in appropriating the neighbor's property to one's own use. An industrial polluter can and should assume the costs of pollution as a cost of doing business rather than charge the loss to a wholly innocent party. The court in *Atlas Chemical* stated:

> We know of no acceptable rule of jurisprudence which permits those engaged in important and desirable enterprises to injure with impunity those who are engaged in enterprises of lesser economic significance. The costs of injuries resulting from pollution must be internalized by industry as a cost of production and borne by consumers or shareholders, or both, and not by the injured individual. Id. at 316.

We think these reasons adequately support application of the rule of strict liability in this case.

NOTES AND QUESTIONS

1. *Who Was There First?* Note that in this case, the defendant was in its location prior to the plaintiffs. That fact was not dispositive. Should it be? Why or why not?

2. *Economics in Action.* Quoting *Atlas Chemical,* the court brings in the concept of internalizing the costs associated with a harmful activity. Would Coase agree with this statement? Can you construct a more sophisticated argument for why Western Petroleum should pay?

3. *The Facts.* Be sensitive to all of the facts that plaintiffs' counsel gathered to make their case. What sorts of facts would you need to gather if you were to bring a similar case for a client?

5.   The Public Trust Doctrine

Since the late 1960s, environmentalists have been searching for a substantive theory of environmental protection. Statutory and nuisance claims are typically now the first place lawyers turn for environmental damages, but the public trust doctrine continues to provide a source of argument and relief when other claims might fail.

---

6. Even if Western did not know that the formation water would enter the aquifer and cause damage to plaintiffs' wells, it could have determined the likelihood of that consequence. . . .

The public trust doctrine was transformed through scholarship and cases starting in the 1960s, but arguably has its roots in antiquity. Briefly, Roman and English common law posited that the beds of navigable rivers were held in trust for the public to protect the public right of navigation and associated uses, such as fishing and, later, recreation. Note, The Public Trust in Tidal Areas: A Sometimes Submerged Traditional Doctrine, 79 Yale L.J. 762 (1970). The doctrine became important in the nineteenth century as large harbors were filled to build new cities. Most courts held that states could terminate the trust in some unspecified percentage of tideland areas, but in 1892 the U.S. Supreme Court, citing not a single precedent and refusing to explain whether its decision was based on the Constitution or state law, held that the Illinois state legislature could not convey the submerged lands along Chicago's lakefront to a railroad because the grant violated the public trust:

> Such abdication is not consistent with the exercise of that trust which requires the government of the State to preserve such waters for the use of the public. The trust devolving upon the State for the public, and which can only be discharged by the management and control of property in which the public has an interest, cannot be relinquished by a transfer of the property. The control of the State for the purposes of the trust can never be lost, except as to such parcels as are used in promoting the interests of the public therein, or can be disposed of without any substantial impairment of the public interest in the lands and waters remaining. It is only by observing the distinction between a grant of such parcels for the improvement of the public interest, or which when occupied do not substantially impair the public interest in the lands and waters remaining, and a grant of the whole property in which the public is interested, that the language of the adjudged cases can be reconciled. General language sometimes found in opinions of lands under navigable waters, irrespective of any trust as to their use and disposition, must be read and construed with reference to the special facts of the particular cases. A grant of all lands under the navigable waters of a State has never been adjudged to be within the legislative power; and any attempted grant of the kind would be held, if not absolutely void on its face, as subject to revocation. The State can no more abdicate its trust over property in which the whole people are interested, like navigable waters and soils under them, so as to leave them entirely under the use and control of private parties, except in the instance of parcels mentioned for the improvement of the navigation and use of the waters, or when parcels can be disposed of without impairment of the public interest in what remains, than it can abdicate its police powers in the administration of government and the preservation of the peace. [Illinois Central R. Co. v. Illinois, 146 U.S. 387 (1892).]

For a recent reexamination of the case that calls into question some of its key conclusions, see Kearney & Merrill, The Origins of the American Public Trust Doctrine: What Really Happened in *Illinois Central,* 71 U. Chi. L. Rev. 799 (2004).

Illinois Central, its progeny, and state public trust cases raise as many questions as they resolve. As you read the notes and cases that follow, try to answer the following questions. Does the doctrine really create an insurmountable substantive barrier against land dispositions as occurred in *Illinois Central?* When can governments allow the development or sale of natural resources previously held by the government? Can procedural steps allow what would otherwise be judicially rejected? The following paragraphs offer some answers to these questions, but because the public trust doctrine has developed differently in different states, only careful research in each state can reveal the restrictions imposed by the public trust doctrine.

Environmentalists have built on *Illinois Central* to argue that the trust imposes both domestic and international law stewardship duties to manage all resources, especially public ones. E. Weiss, In Fairness to Future Generations: International Law, Common Patrimony, and Intergenerational Equity (1989). There is some precedent to extend it to public lands, but precedent is slim. For example, during the progressive conservation era, the Supreme Court invoked the public trust doctrine to reject the perennial western states' argument that the federal government lacked the power to retain and manage public lands for national forests, parks, and other public use classifications. Light v. United States, 220 U.S. 523 (1911). The Court repeated an earlier statement that "[a]ll the public lands are held in trust for the people of the whole country, United States v. Trinidad Coal & Coking Co., 137 U.S. 160," but rejected any judicial role in policing the trust. "And it is not for the courts to say how the trust shall be administered. That is for Congress to determine."

Two environmental interpretations of *Illinois Central* have emerged. The first, articulated by Professor Joseph Sax, argues that the trust is a procedural doctrine that allows courts to (a) decide if political decisions to reallocate public resources were made after a reasonable consideration of all alternatives and (b) to remand to the legislature if the political process failed to do so for reasons such as undue special interest influence. Sax, The Public Trust Doctrine in Natural Resources Law: Effective Judicial Intervention, 68 Mich. L. Rev. 471 (1970). The second theory eschews the indirect procedural-process route and posits that the trust contains a hierarchy of values with ecosystem stability at the top.

California's Supreme Court first said in dictum that the trust included ecosystem stability and recreation, Marks v. Whitney, 491 P.2d 374 (Cal. 1971), and then it applied the public trust doctrine to reallocate a vested water right whose exercise disrupted a delicate ecosystem. As you read the following case excerpt, assess whether California is adopting one of these two theories or a hybrid.

NATIONAL AUDUBON SOCIETY v. SUPERIOR COURT OF ALPINE COUNTY
658 P.2d 709, (Cal. 1983)

[As the movie *Chinatown* graphically illustrates, to sustain its growth, Los Angeles turned to the eastern slope of the Sierra Nevada mountains in the early 1900s after it had exhausted local water supplies. The Los Angeles Department of Water and Power eventually perfected appropriations to the tributary creeks to Mono Lake, a unique closed basin. As the city exercised its rights, the diversions lowered the lake by some 44 feet, altering the lake ecosystem by increasing the salinity of the lake. These alterations threatened the brine shrimp population that fed the birds that gathered on islands in the lake, and they dried up the bed between islands in the lake so that predators could now reach these former refuges. California's highest court held that the public trust required a reallocation of water to raise the lake level, although no specific level was specified by the California Supreme Court's opinion. Its key articulation of California's formulation of the public trust doctrine follows.]

BROUSSARD, J.

. . . a. The state as sovereign retains continuing supervisory control over its navigable waters and the lands beneath those waters. This principle, fundamental to the concept of the public trust, applies to rights in flowing waters as well as to rights in tidelands and lakeshores; it prevents any party from acquiring a vested right to appropriate water in a manner harmful to the interest protected by the public trust.

b. As a matter of current and historical necessity, the Legislature, acting directly through an authorized agency such as the Water Board, has the power to grant usufructuary licenses that will permit an appropriator to take water from flowing streams and use that water in a distant part of the state, even though this taking does not promote, and may unavoidably harm, the trust uses at the source stream. The population and economy of this state depend upon the appropriation of vast quantities of water for uses unrelated to in-stream trust values. California's Constitution, its statutes, decisions, and commentators all emphasize the need to make efficient use of California's limited water resources: all recognize, at least implicitly, that efficient use requires diverting water from in-stream uses. Now that the economy and population centers of this state have developed in reliance upon appropriated water, it would be disingenuous to hold that such appropriations are and have always been improper to the extent that they harm public trust uses, and can be justified only upon theories of reliance or estoppel.

c. The state has an affirmative duty to take the public trust into account in the planning and allocation of water resources, and to protect public trust uses whenever feasible. Just as the history of this state shows that appropriation may be necessary for efficient use of water despite unavoidable harm to public trust values, it demonstrates that an appropriative water rights system administered without consideration of the public trust may cause unnecessary and unjustified harm to trust interests. As a matter of practical necessity the state may have to approve appropriations despite foreseeable harm to public trust uses. In so doing, however, the state must bear in mind its duty as trustee to consider the effect of taking on the public trust (see United Plainsmen v. N.D. State Water Con. Commission (N.D. 1976) 247 N.W.2d 457-463) and to preserve, so far as consistent with the public interest, the uses protected by the trust.

NOTE AND QUESTIONS

The Mono Lake Denouement. Ultimately, a trial court fixed the lake level at 2 feet above the level at the time the litigation was initiated. This new level is approximately 25 feet below the prediversion level, but is considered sufficient to restore the ecosystem to something close to its prediversion functions. See also In re Water Use Permit Applications, Petitions for Interim Instream Flow Standard Amendments, and Petitions for Water Reservations for the Waiahole Ditch, 9 P.3d 409 (Haw. 2000) (public trust requires state to allocate abandoned water to instream and ecosystem restoration purposes before reallocating the supply for consumptive uses and to adopt a conservative margin of safety in setting instream and ecosystem restoration requirements).

Questions still abound: Does the trust extend to dry land? One district court held that the government had a trust duty to acquire enough land to buffer the Redwood National Park, Sierra Club v. Department of Interior, 376 F. Supp. 90, 398 F. Supp. 284 (N.D. Cal. 1974); but subsequent courts have refused to extend the trust to public lands, and the decided cases have confined it to navigable waters and associated areas such as beaches and stream access. Can one derive an operational principle of ecosystem stability from the public trust doctrine? Is prehuman intervention background the trust standard? What is background? Is it the predevelopment ecosystem in the area? Is it the prehuman settlement landscape? If not, what is the standard? In the *Mono Lake* case, the California Supreme Court did not use the prediversion level of a navigable lake as the standard. Can you articulate a general standard other than pre-anthropocentric change background? For a case seeing a municipal park as subject to the public trust doctrine, but allowing open legislative action to modify the parkland's use to educational purposes, see Paepke v. Public Bldg. Comm'n, 263 N.E.2d 11 (Ill. 1970).

For additional discussion of the public trust doctrine, see generally Lazarus, Changing Conceptions of Property and Sovereignty in Natural Resources: Questioning the Public Trust Doctrine, 71 Iowa L. Rev. 631 (1986); and Araiza, Democracy, Distrust, and the Public Trust: Process-Based Constitutional Theory, the Public Trust Doctrine, and the Search for a Substantive Environmental Value, 45 UCLA L. Rev. 385 (1997).

6.   Constitutionally Rooted Environmental Claims

Environmental law has evolved and even flourished without judicial recognition of federal constitutional rights to a clean environment. Lazarus, Restoring What's Environmental about Environmental Law in the Supreme Court, 47 UCLA L. Rev. 703 (2000). Indeed, in recent years, constitutional law doctrines have been wielded by litigators and recognized in the courts to weaken environmental protections. Percival, "Greening" the Constitution—Harmonizing Environmental and Constitutional Values, 32 Envtl. L. 809 (2002).

The basic reason for the lack of constitutional footing for an affirmative constitutionally based right to a clean environment is that the Constitution is primarily a charter of negative rights, rather than of affirmative government duties and individual entitlements to government action. In addition, a right to a decent environment does not fit within the classic paradigm of a constitutional right. Proponents of environmental protection are typically not an isolated minority subject to serious, long-terms risks of severe discrimination by legislatures indifferent or hostile to their concerns, and effective access to the legislative process is not blocked.

For these reasons, persistent arguments that the Supreme Court should recognize an implied right to environmental quality have met the same fate as most calls for constitutional change. In 1965, the Supreme Court, in a concurrence by Mr. Justice Goldberg in Griswold v. Connecticut, 381 U.S. 479 (1965), suggested that the Ninth Amendment and its penumbra could be the source of new implied constitutional rights. Nonetheless, courts quickly rejected arguments that the Fifth, Ninth, and Fourteenth Amendments could be the basis of an implied constitutional right to environmental quality. In United States v. 247.37 Acres, 2 Envt. Rep. Cas. (BNA) 20154 (S.D. Ohio 1972), a landowner challenged the condemnation of his farm for a U.S. Army Corps of Engineers flood control reservoir, in part because the Ninth Amendment guarantees "the preservation of their property and its surrounding environs in its natural state." The court declined the invitation to make new constitutional law because that function, it stated, was the sole province of the Supreme Court. Other courts reached the same result because of the lack of textual support and precedent, Ely v. Velde, 451 F.2d 1130 (4th Cir. 1971), or because of separation of powers considerations. "Such a construction would be ahistorical and would represent essentially a policy decision. In effect, plaintiffs invite this Court to enact a law. Since our system reserves to the legislative branch the task of legislating, this Court must decline the invitation." Tanner v. Armco Steel, 340 F. Supp. 532 (S.D. Tex. 1972).

If a right existed, what would it look like? For example, what level of public health protection would it guarantee? Zero risk? Most proponents of environmental protection reject this approach as irrational because some degree of risk is inevitable. See C. Sunstein, After the Rights Revolution: Reconceiving the Regulatory State (1990); Farber, Playing the Baseline: Civil Rights, Environmental Law, and Statutory Interpretation, 91 Colum. L. Rev. 676 (1991).

Despite resistance to recognition of federal constitutional rights to a clean environment, several states have constitutional provisions that recognize environmental rights. The Constitution of the Commonwealth of Pennsylvania, Article 1, §27, provides that "[t]he people have a right to clean air, pure water, and to the preservation of the natural, scenic, historic and esthetic values of the environment." However, the state supreme court refused to enjoin a 300-foot tower overlooking the Gettysburg battlefield. The majority held that the amendment was not self-executing, but the opinions of two concurring justices indicate that the real concern was the lack of standards to guide courts in making aesthetic judgments and the resulting unfairness that the increased risk of litigation, which had no basis at common law, created for property owners. Pennsylvania subsequently held that the amendment was self-executing, Commonwealth v. National Gettysburg Battlefield Tower, Inc., 311 A.2d 588 (Pa. 1973); Payne v. Kassab, 312 A.2d 86 (Pa. Commw. 1973), aff'd, 361 A.2d 263 (Pa. 1976), but state environmental constitutional law has not flourished. But cf. Machipongo Land and Coal Co. v. Commonwealth, 799 A.2d 751 (Pa. 2002) (Commonwealth can defend against takings claim from prohibiting coal mining in watershed if it can prove that proposed mine plan has a high potential to increase dissolved solids and metal concentrations in stream). The story is the same in Illinois. Glisson v. City of Marion, 720 N.E.2d 1034 (Ill. 1999) (state constitutional provision is limited to protection against pollution only and thus does not extend to biodiversity conservation).

The leading case illustrating the potential of state constitutional law as a source of expanded environmental protection is Montana Envtl. Info. Ctr. v. Department of Envtl. Quality, 988 P.2d 1236 (Mont. 1999). The state supreme court held that Articles II and IX of the state constitution, which guarantee a right to a clean and healthful environment, rendered a state water quality statute that exempted well monitoring from nondegradation review unconstitutional. The issue was whether open-pit gold mining into shallow aquifers, which served as mixing zones, near two high-quality rivers was subject to nondegradation review because the state's arsenic levels in the river might be exceeded. The Department of Environmental Quality concluded that the water would be diluted below state levels when it reached the river. The court held that the right to a clean and healthful environmental was fundamental and that no demonstrated harm to public health had to be established by the plaintiffs because the right "is implicated based on Plaintiff's demonstration that pumping tests proposed by . . . [the mine] would have added a known carcinogen . . . to the environment in concentrations greater than the conditions present in the receiving water." Id. at 1249.

Despite the lack of recognition of affirmative constitutional rights under the federal Constitution, the student must be aware that there are three increasingly important constitutional dimensions to environmental law that serve as resistance to environmental protection. First, the Supreme Court's active redrawing of federalism doctrine in recent years has implications for the extent of federal environmental powers under statutory law. See Chapter 2. Second, environmental protection can clash with long-recognized property entitlements and lead to regulatory takings claims. See Chapter 5, section C. Finally, state efforts to protect state amenities and, especially, regulate and encourage safe handling of waste, can run afoul of Dormant Commerce Clause doctrine. See Chapter 8, section G. See also Percival, "Greening the Constitution"—Harmonizing Environmental and Constitutional Values, 32 Envtl. L. 809 (2002).

In contrast to the United States' view of a constitution as an eternal guide to the process of political organization, most other countries view constitutions as a reflection of contemporary political and social priorities. Many new constitutions contain affirmative environmental protection and ecologically sustainable development mandates that contemplate further legislative action. E.g., Constitution of the Federative Republic of Brazil, Article 225 (1988); Constitution of the Republic of South Africa, Section 24 (1996). What is the value of a constitutional provision that imposes a broad affirmative duty on the state to protect environmental quality? See Krier, The Environment, the Constitution, and the Coupling Policy, 32 Mich. L. Quadrangle Notes 35 (1988); Ruhl, The Metrics of Constitutional Amendments, and Why Proposed Environmental Quality Amendments Don't Measure Up, 74 Notre Dame L. Rev. 245 (1999).

Environmental law's focus has been on the protection of ecosystems and statistical victims, but at least in Europe, it has been found to have roots in the protection of human dignity. See Lopez Ostra v. Spain, European Court of Human Rights (A/303/C) 20 European Human Right Reports 277 (1994) (finding that the failure of a Spanish town to protect plaintiff from odors and emissions of a group of tanning plants violated Section 8 of the European Convention on Human Rights).

7.   *Environmental Justice Theories*

Over the past 15 years, lawyers, policymakers, environmentalists, and civil rights advocates have turned their focus to the distributional consequences of environmental protection efforts on minority, poor, and at-risk groups, such as those for whom existing pollution standards are insufficiently stringent or who live near pollution "hot spots." "Environmental justice" is now one of the standards against which environmental protection programs and policy instruments must be measured. Also known by the monikers of "environmental equity" and "environmental racism," this new area of policy ferment has changed from a problem going virtually unrecognized to an issue that has spawned dozens of books, articles, cases, and an important Executive Order. What it has not spawned, however, is any recasting of constitutional doctrine to recognize any rights to environmental justice. Claims of discrimination by recipients of federal funds have been found actionable under Title VI, but basic Equal Protection claims or affirmative constitutional claims have not met with success. The environmental justice body of law and activity remains today in part a political movement, in part a category of claims, and in part a sort of grievance to which a handful of effective legal theories have at times been applied.

Executive Order 12,898, 59 Fed. Reg. 7629 (1994), mandates that each federal agency "shall make achieving environmental justice part of its mission." Executive Orders do not impose duties outside the government and, as in this instance and in most such orders, do not create any judicially cognizable cause of actions. Instead, such orders establish internal rules and priorities for the executive branch. Any president can undo a previous president's order with a countermanding order, but many remain well-established law. Executive Order 12,898 is an important addition to federal environmental policy because it legitimizes the environmental justice movement and ensures that environmental justice will be a factor to be considered in the administration of existing programs and the development of new ones. The Executive Order was drafted and signed in direct response to the growing political strength of the environmental justice movement. It is informed by the belief that there are defined population groups and communities that are insufficiently protected by existing environmental programs. Thus, disproportionate impact is the only substantive standard the Order adopts to measure existing regulatory programs. All federal agencies must now develop agency-wide justice strategies that identify and address the "disproportionately high and adverse human health or environmental effects of its programs, policies, and activities on minority populations and low-income populations." Other theories have also been tested, meeting with notable success or failure in the courts and other political settings. See Foster, Justice from the Ground Up: Distributive Inequities, Grassroots Resistance, and the Transformative Politics of the Environmental Justice Movement, 86 Cal. L. Rev. 775 (1998); Rechtschaffen, Advancing Environmental Justice Norms, 37 U.C. Davis L. Rev. 95 (2003). For additional coverage of environmental justice issues, see Chapter 8, section F, covering siting battles.

G.   COMMON LAW AND OTHER THEORIES DURING THE STATUTORY ENVIRONMENTAL ERA

As will quickly become apparent to students, environmental law is pervaded by statutory and regulatory edicts. An issue with which lawyers, legislators, and judges must often grapple concerns what is left of common law and other claims in areas that are now overwhelmingly statutory. As a related matter, why not rely on common law and the other theories discussed above to rectify environmental harms?

Advocates of market-based approaches to environmental protection generally disfavor reliance on statutory, regulatory, and bureaucratic responses to environmental harms. Instead, they prefer private bargaining or, where necessary, common law claims, because they rely on individual initiative and monetary incentives, and they tend not to make radical changes in legal rules that can disrupt expectations and markets. Several such advocates have asserted that common law claims have been replaced, not supplemented, by statutory schemes. See R. Meiners & B. Yandle, Common Law and the Conceit of Modern Environmental Policy, 7 Geo. Mason L. Rev. 923 (1999); T. Anderson, Enviro-Capitalism v. Enviro-Socialism, 4 Kan. J.L. & Pub. Pol'y 35, 39 (1995) (describing public law as an impediment to private law remedies). While the law has taken some twists and turns, the proposition that statutory schemes have generally replaced common law claims is most definitely in error. Only rarely do federal environmental laws displace state common law claims.

Note that in *Western Petroleum*, and also in *Walsh* and *Petsey*, defendants argued that their conduct was lawful in all respects, yet the courts rejected the defense. Defendants frequently argue that activity that is lawful and often explicitly permitted under state or federal statutes should not give rise to common law liability. Perhaps counterintuitively for lawyers new to this field, such a defense is typically rejected. The reasons are several and are significant to understanding environmental common law claims as well as environmental federalism, which is covered primarily in Chapter 2.

First, most major federal environmental statutes contain explicit "savings" clauses that preserve common law claims. Thus, judicial elimination of a common law remedy would run counter to explicit statutory mandate. See, e.g., Ouellette v. International Paper Co., 666 F. Supp. 58, 60-62 (D. Vt. 1987) (holding that common law nuisance claim not preempted by Clean Air Act); Her Majesty the Queen v. City of Detroit, 874 F.2d 332, 342-343 (6th Cir. 1989) (Clean Air Act does not preempt claims under state pollution statute); Gutierrez v. Mobil Oil Corp., 789 F. Supp. 1280, 1285-1286 (W.D. Tex. 1992) (Clean Air Act does not preempt state common law claims).

Second, the fact that statutes allow an activity does not mean that victims of harm should go remediless. Note that the *Western Petroleum* and *Petsey* cases both refer to the need to provide remedies for unreasonable harm, regardless of the reasonableness of the activity causing harm.

Third, as noted in *Western Petroleum*, economic incentives for less harmful polluting conduct are created when previously externalized harms are "internalized."

Some of the confusion concerning the effect of federal statutory frameworks on common law claims arises out of a trio of Supreme Court cases, two of which dealt with *federal* common law claims, while the third dealt ultimately with the question of what common law to apply. Economists advocating common law and market-based approaches to deal with environmental harms have misconstrued these cases and perhaps statutes to preclude ongoing reliance on common law claims. As explored in Thompson, Free Market Environmentalism and the Common Law: Confusion, Nostalgia and Inconsistency, 45 Emory L.J. 1329, 1330 (1996), common law claims do remain viable under both statutory language and case law. Any shortage of such claims is not a result of statutory edict, but of other barriers to the efficacy of common law claims. See below. Thompson explains how confusion likely results from the following case, and cases cited therein. As you read, carefully note the distinctions drawn between federal common law, state common law from the source or affected state, and language regarding the effect of federal statutory law.

INTERNATIONAL PAPER CO. v. OUELLETTE
479 U.S. 481 (1987)

Justice POWELL delivered the opinion of the Court.

This case involves the pre-emptive scope of the Clean Water Act, 86 Stat. 816, as amended, 33 U.S.C. §1251 et seq. (CWA or Act). The question presented is whether the Act pre-empts a common-law nuisance suit filed in a Vermont court under Vermont law, when the source of the alleged injury is located in New York.

I

[Petitioner International Paper Company (IPC) operated a pulp and paper mill on the New York side of Lake Champlain. IPC discharged waste into the lake through a pipe that runs through the water and ends just before reaching the state border with

Vermont, which divides the lake. Respondents were a group of property owners who owned or leased land on the Vermont shore. In 1978, the owners filed a class action suit against IPC, claiming that the discharge constituted a "continuing nuisance" under Vermont common law. They alleged that the pollutants diminished both the quality of the water and the value of their property. The action was filed in State Superior Court and later removed to Federal District Court for the District of Vermont.]

II

A brief review of the regulatory framework is necessary to set the stage for this case. Until fairly recently, federal common law governed the use and misuse of interstate water. This principle was called into question in the context of water pollution in 1971, when the Court suggested in dicta that an interstate dispute between a State and a private company should be resolved by reference to state nuisance law. Ohio v. Wyandotte Chemicals Corp., 401 U.S. 493, 499, n. 3 (1971) ("[A]n action such as this, if otherwise cognizable in federal district court, would have to be adjudicated under state law") (citing Erie R. Co. v. Tompkins, 304 U.S. 64 (1938)).

We had occasion to address this issue in the first of two Supreme Court cases involving the dispute between Illinois and Milwaukee. In *Milwaukee I*, the State moved for leave to file an original action in this Court, seeking to enjoin the city from discharging sewage into Lake Michigan. Illinois v. Milwaukee, 406 U.S. 91 (1972). The Court's opinion in that case affirmed the view that the regulation of interstate water pollution is a matter of federal, not state, law, thus overruling the contrary suggestion in *Wyandotte*. The Court was concerned, however, that the existing version of the Act was not sufficiently comprehensive to resolve all interstate disputes that were likely to arise. *Milwaukee I* therefore held that these cases should be resolved by reference to federal common law; the implicit corollary of this ruling was that state common law was preempted.[8] The Court noted, though, that future action by Congress to regulate water pollution might pre-empt federal common law as well. 406 U.S., at 107.

Congress thereafter adopted comprehensive amendments to the Act. We considered the impact of the new legislation when Illinois and Milwaukee returned to the Court several years later. Milwaukee v. Illinois, 451 U.S. 304 (1981) (*Milwaukee II*). There the Court noted that the amendments were a "'complete rewriting'" of the statute considered in *Milwaukee I*, and that they were "'the most comprehensive and far reaching'" provisions that Congress ever had passed in this area. 451 U.S., at 317-318. Consequently, the Court held that federal legislation now occupied the field, preempting all federal common law. The Court left open the question of whether injured parties still had a cause of action under state law. Id., at 310, n.4. The case was remanded for further consideration; the result on remand was the decision of the Court of Appeals for the Seventh Circuit in *Milwaukee III*, discussed *supra*. . . .

While source States have a strong voice in regulating their own pollution, the CWA contemplates a much lesser role for States that share an interstate waterway with

8. Although the Court's opinion could be read as distinguishing rather than overruling that part of *Wyandotte*, a later decision made it clear that state common-law actions did not survive *Milwaukee I*. See *Milwaukee II*, 451 U.S., at 327, n. 19; see also Glicksman, [Federal Preemption and Private Legal Remedies for Pollution, 134 U. Penn. L. Rev.] 156, n.176 (1985).

the source (the affected States). Even though it may be harmed by the discharges, an affected State only has an advisory role in regulating pollution that originates beyond its borders. Before a federal permit may be issued, each affected State is given notice and the opportunity to object to the proposed standards at a public hearing. 33 U.S.C. §1341(a)(2); *Milwaukee III, supra,* at 412. An affected State has similar rights to be consulted before the source State issues its own permit; the source State must send notification, and must consider the objections and recommendations submitted by other States before taking action. §1342(b). Significantly, however, an affected State does not have the authority to block the issuance of the permit if it is dissatisfied with the proposed standards. An affected State's only recourse is to apply to the EPA Administrator, who then has the discretion to disapprove the permit if he concludes that the discharges will have an undue impact on interstate waters. §1342(d)(2). Also, an affected State may not establish a separate permit system to regulate an out-of-state source. Thus the Act makes it clear that affected States occupy a subordinate position to source States in the federal regulatory program. . . .

III

With this regulatory framework in mind, we turn to the question presented: whether the Act pre-empts Vermont common law to the extent that law may impose liability on a New York point source. . . .

Given that the Act itself does not speak directly to the issue, the Court must be guided by the goals and policies of the Act in determining whether it in fact pre-empts an action based on the law of an affected State. Cf. City of Rome v. United States, 446 U.S. 156, 199 (1980) (POWELL, J., dissenting) ("We resort to legislative materials only when the congressional mandate is unclear on its face"). After examining the CWA as a whole, its purposes and its history, we are convinced that if affected States were allowed to impose separate discharge standards on a single point source, the inevitable result would be a serious interference with the achievement of the "full purposes and objectives of Congress." See Hillsborough County v. Automated Medical Laboratories, Inc., *supra,* 471 U.S. at 713. Because we do not believe Congress intended to undermine this carefully drawn statute through a general saving clause, we conclude that the CWA precludes a court from applying the law of an affected State against an out-of-state source. . . .

In determining whether Vermont nuisance law "stands as an obstacle" to the full implementation of the CWA, it is not enough to say that the ultimate goal of both federal and state law is to eliminate water pollution. A state law also is pre-empted if it interferes with the methods by which the federal statute was designed to reach this goal. See Michigan Canners & Freezers Assn. v. Agricultural Marketing & Bargaining Bd., 467 U.S. 461, 477 (1984). In this case the application of Vermont law against IPC would allow respondents to circumvent the NPDES permit system, thereby upsetting the balance of public and private interests so carefully addressed by the Act. . . .

An interpretation of the saving clause that preserved actions brought under an affected State's law would disrupt this balance of interests. If a New York source were liable for violations of Vermont law, that law could effectively override both the permit requirements and the policy choices made by the source State. The affected State's nuisance laws would subject the point source to the threat of legal and equitable penalties if the permit standards were less stringent than those imposed by the affected

State. Such penalties would compel the source to adopt different control standards and a different compliance schedule from those approved by the EPA, even though the affected State had not engaged in the same weighing of the costs and benefits. This case illustrates the problems with such a rule. If the Vermont court ruled that respondents were entitled to the full amount of damages and injunctive relief sought in the complaint, at a minimum IPC would have to change its methods of doing business and controlling pollution to avoid the threat of ongoing liability. In suits such as this, an affected-state court also could require the source to cease operations by ordering immediate abatement. Critically, these liabilities would attach even though the source had complied fully with its state and federal permit obligations. The inevitable result of such suits would be that Vermont and other States could do indirectly what they could not do directly—regulate the conduct of out-of-state sources.

Application of an affected State's law to an out-of-state source also would undermine the important goals of efficiency and predictability in the permit system. The history of the 1972 amendments shows that Congress intended to establish "clear and identifiable" discharge standards. See S. Rep. No. 92-414, p. 81 (1971). As noted above, under the reading of the saving clause proposed by respondents, a source would be subject to a variety of common-law rules established by the different States along the interstate waterways. These nuisance standards often are "vague" and "indeterminate." The application of numerous States' laws would only exacerbate the vagueness and resulting uncertainty. The Court of Appeals in *Milwaukee III* identified the problem with such an irrational system of regulation:

> For a number of different states to have independent and plenary regulatory authority over a single discharge would lead to chaotic confrontation between sovereign states. Dischargers would be forced to meet not only the statutory limitations of all states potentially affected by their discharges but also the common law standards developed through case law of those states. It would be virtually impossible to predict the standard for a lawful discharge into an interstate body of water. Any permit issued under the Act would be rendered meaningless. 731 F.2d, at 414.

It is unlikely—to say the least—that Congress intended to establish such a chaotic regulatory structure.

Nothing in the Act gives each affected State this power to regulate discharges. The CWA carefully defines the role of both the source and affected States, and specifically provides for a process whereby their interests will be considered and balanced by the source State and the EPA. This delineation of authority represents Congress' considered judgment as to the best method of serving the public interest and reconciling the often competing concerns of those affected by the pollution. It would be extraordinary for Congress, after devising an elaborate permit system that sets clear standards, to tolerate common-law suits that have the potential to undermine this regulatory structure.

C.

Our conclusion that Vermont nuisance law is inapplicable to a New York point source does not leave respondents without a remedy. The CWA precludes only those suits that may require standards of effluent control that are incompatible with those established by the procedures set forth in the Act. The saving clause specifically preserves other state actions, and therefore nothing in the Act bars aggrieved individuals from bringing a nuisance claim pursuant to the law of the source State. By its terms the CWA allows States such as New York to impose higher standards on their own point sources, and in *Milwaukee II* we recognized that this authority may include the right to impose higher common-law as well as higher statutory restrictions. 451 U.S., at 328 (suggesting that "States may adopt more stringent limitations . . . through state nuisance law, and apply them to in-state dischargers"); see also Committee for Jones Falls Sewage System v. Train, 539 F.2d 1006, 1009, and n.9 (CA4 1976) (CWA preserves common-law suits filed in source State). . . .

An action brought against IPC under New York nuisance law would not frustrate the goals of the CWA as would a suit governed by Vermont law.[19] First, application of the source State's law does not disturb the balance among federal, source-state, and affected-state interests. Because the Act specifically allows source States to impose stricter standards, the imposition of source-state law does not disrupt the regulatory partnership established by the permit system. Second, the restriction of suits to those brought under source-State nuisance law prevents a source from being subject to an indeterminate number of potential regulations. Although New York nuisance law may impose separate standards and thus create some tension with the permit system, a source only is required to look to a single additional authority, whose rules should be relatively predictable. Moreover, States can be expected to take into account their own nuisance laws in setting permit requirements.

IV

The District Court correctly denied IPC's motion for summary judgment and judgment on the pleadings. Nothing in the Act prevents a court sitting in an affected State from hearing a common-law nuisance suit, provided that jurisdiction otherwise is proper. Both the District Court and the Court of Appeals erred, however, in

---

19. The District Court concluded that the interference with the Act is insignificant, in part because respondents are seeking to be compensated for a specific harm rather than trying to "regulate" IPC. 602 F. Supp. 264, 271-272 (Vt. 1985). The Solicitor General, on behalf of the United States as amicus curiae, adopts only a portion of this view. He acknowledges that suits seeking punitive or injunctive relief under affected-state law should be pre-empted because of the interference they cause with the CWA. The Government asserts that compensatory damages actions, however, may be brought under the law of the State where the injury occurred. The Solicitor General reasons that compensatory damages only require the source to pay for the external costs created by the pollution, and thus do not "regulate" in a way inconsistent with the Act. The Government cites Silkwood v. Kerr-McGee Corp., 464 U.S. 238 (1984), for the proposition that in certain circumstances a court may find pre-emption of some remedies and not others.

We decline the Government's invitation to draw a line between the types of relief sought. There is no suggestion of such a distinction in either the Act or the legislative history. As the Court noted in *Silkwood*, unless there is evidence that Congress meant to "split" a particular remedy for pre-emption purposes, it is assumed that the full cause of action under state law is available (or as in this case, pre-empted). Id., at 255, 104 S. Ct., at 625. We also think it would be unwise to treat compensatory damages differently under the facts of this case. If the Vermont court determined that respondents were entitled only to the requested compensatory relief, IPC might be compelled to adopt different or additional means of pollution control from those required by the Act, regardless of whether the purpose of the relief was compensatory or regulatory. See Perez v. Campbell, 402 U.S. 637, 651-652 (1971) (effect rather than purpose of a state statute governs pre-emption analysis). As discussed, this result would be irreconcilable with the CWA's exclusive grant of authority to the Federal Government and the source State. Cf. Chicago & North Western Transportation Co. v. Kalo Brick & Tile Co., 450 U.S. 311, 324-325 (1981).

concluding that Vermont law governs this litigation. The application of affected-State laws would be incompatible with the Act's delegation of authority and its comprehensive regulation of water pollution. The Act pre-empts state law to the extent that the state law is applied to an out-of-state point source.

The decision of the Court of Appeals is affirmed in part and reversed in part. The case is remanded for further proceedings consistent with this opinion.

For further discussion of savings clauses and common law and state law claims, see Chapter 2.

A NOTE REGARDING HURDLES TO COMMON LAW SUCCESS

Federal statutory provisions, Supreme Court case law, and state court decisions overwhelmingly confirm that state common law environmental claims remain part of the arsenal of the environmental lawyer. Such claims are so uncommon, however, that market-oriented economists writing about environmental law have apparently concluded that the shortage of such claims must reflect a legal prohibition. Why are these claims brought with such infrequency? Perhaps more important, what is lacking in common law regimes such that the massive modern array of federal environmental laws is needed?

Professors Sidney A. Shapiro & Robert L. Glicksman, in Risk Regulation at Risk: Restoring a Pragmatic Approach 5-6 (2003), capture well many of the hurdles faced by torts plaintiffs complaining of environmental injuries:

> The importance of protecting human life and the environment led the 1960s reformers to reject tort law as the basis of government regulation of technological risks. In a tort system, persons who have been injured by corporate behavior have the burden of initiating expensive legal action to prove that their injury was caused by the defendant's actions. Moreover, someone who anticipates a potential injury usually cannot obtain protection against that risk. Although injunctive relief is theoretically available in actions such as private nuisance to avoid harms alleged to be the imminent result of technological development, the courts are reluctant to enjoin such "anticipatory nuisances" on the basis of the plaintiff's speculation.
>
> In light of its evidentiary burdens, tort law starts with the baseline assumption that individuals and corporations that operate in private markets should be free from government regulation until and unless a plaintiff can compile convincing proof that their conduct has caused an injury to a person or that person's property. This baseline comports with traditional liberalism and its emphasis on limited government, private autonomy, and the protection of private markets.
>
> The impotence of tort law was vividly demonstrated in the 1960s by the various prominent accidents and environmental injuries that occurred. Tort law failed in part because of what Talbot Page has called "ignorance of mechanism." The tort system will not compensate an individual unless that person has convincing evidence that the defendant caused the plaintiff's injury. If, however, the injury is allegedly caused by exposure to chemicals or other by-products of technological activity, few plaintiffs will be able to meet their burden of proof because the mechanisms of cancer are still not very well understood. Scientists and policy-makers understood even less about how disease is caused and develops in the 1970s, when most risk-reduction statutes were adopted. The "ignorance of mechanism" is exacerbated by the long latency period that typically elapses

between exposure to the disease and its manifestation. By the time the disease appears it is often impossible to isolate its cause or causes; the long latency period means that years if not decades worth of exposure have already occurred by then. Plaintiffs who sue over environmental injuries face an even more difficult task. Scientific understanding of the manner in which the by-products of technological development adversely affect the ecosystems into which they are discharged is, if anything, even more inadequate than our understanding of cancer mechanisms.

Risk regulation was a paradigm shift from the common law because Congress authorized regulators to act on the basis of anticipated harm, which permitted regulators to reduce personal and environmental risks despite an "ignorance of mechanism."

Common law cases are certainly still brought, especially where a plaintiff has experienced a substantial personal or property injury and needs compensation. It will be the rare plaintiff, however, who can trace the source of injury and prove that contact with a pollutant caused the alleged injury. Even rarer will be the setting where plaintiffs experience sufficiently serious injuries that the transaction costs of bringing suit, especially in light of uncertainties about an ultimate victory, do not dwarf a possible recovery. The broader the harm, the more likely it is that no single plaintiff will find it worth litigating. The use of contingency arrangements or class action devices may make financing such litigation feasible, but in a highly polluted environment, proof burdens will often be insurmountable. In addition, use of a class action arrangement buys plaintiffs a virtually certain additional layer of intensive motion practice over the suitability of class treatment. For a concise cataloguing of barriers to such private common law suits, see Brunet, Debunking Wholesale Private Enforcement of Environmental Rights, 15 Harv. J.L. & Pub. Pol'y 311 (1992).

H.   THE HISTORICAL ARC OF ENVIRONMENTAL LAW

The succeeding chapters will toss readers into a large and complex body of primarily statutory law, with a fair bit of constitutional and some international law as well. Much of this complexity is due to the way our nation's environmental laws have developed and been recast repeatedly over the past three decades. But even today's modern environmental statutes were built on the foundation of earlier conservation movements and prior laws and provisions, many of which live on today, even if little utilized. The closing two sections of this chapter offer a quick historical sketch of the development of America's environmental laws. The chapter closes by reviewing the sorts of regulatory strategies utilized in the laws that will be studied in depth in the succeeding chapters.

1.   *Reconceiving Wilderness and Natural Resource Values*

From an environmental perspective, "[t]he problem for human societies has been to balance their various demands against the ability of ecosystems to withstand the resulting pressures." C. Ponting, A Green History of the World: The Environment and the Collapse of Great Civilizations 17 (1992). Thus, many societies ultimately rise or fall as a result of the choices they make about their stocks of natural resources.

Environmental history has emerged as a major historical area and has refocused attention on the role of landscape and climate in shaping societies, and in his book Landscape and Memory (1995), the historian Simon Schama sums up the dismal lessons of these new histories. Although environmental history offers some of the most original and challenging accounts now being written, it inevitably relates the same dismal tale — of land taken, exploited, and exhausted; of traditional cultures reportedly living in a relation of sacred reverence with the soil displaced by the reckless individualist, the capitalist aggressor. W. Cronon, Changes in the Land: Indians, Colonists and the Ecology of New England (1983), is a classic example of the genre.

The more interesting question is how a new, anti-exploitation or stewardship narrative arose. Until the early eighteenth century, wilderness was the opposite of paradise. "When Adam and Eve were driven from the garden, the world they entered was a wilderness that only their labor and pain could redeem. Wilderness, in short, was a place one came only against one's will, and always in fear and trembling." W. Cronon, The Trouble with Wilderness or, Getting Back to the Wrong Nature, in UnCommon Ground: Toward Reinventing Nature 69, 71 (W. Cronon ed., 1995). By the end of the eighteenth century, wilderness had become a sublime place where one could encounter the divine.

In the United States, the nineteenth-century New England Transcendentalists were among the first to voice romantic reactions to the social disruption caused by the Industrial Revolution. They blended the Jeffersonian pastoral ideal of self-sufficient yeomen with the claim that nature "enjoyed its own morality which, when understood, could lead the sympathetic and responsive human being to a new spiritual awareness of his own potential, his obligations to others, and his responsibilities to the life-supporting processes of his natural surroundings." T. O. Riordan, Environmentalism 3 (2d ed. 1980). L. Marx, The Machine in the Garden: Technology and the Pastoral Ideal in America (1967), is a full exploration of the tension between pastoral visions and the realities of an industrialized society. See also R. Tomalin, W. H. Hudson: A Biography (1982), and L. K. Thomas, Man and the Natural World: A History of Modern Sensibility (1983). Environmentalism has become progressively more science-based, but the romantic origins of environmentalism still occasionally surface.

2.   The Conservation and Preservation Movements

Environmentalism can be traced both to a changed perception of "nature" and to the production and dissemination of information about the consequences of the unrestrained exploitation of nature. Starting in the nineteenth century, industrialized societies began to appreciate the adverse consequences of unrestrained resource exploitation and set new limits on resource use. From the Transcendentalists' attempts to develop a theory of the relationship between democracy and nature came two major resource use philosophies or movements that have greatly influenced the modern environmental era: the conservation and preservation movements.

Initially, the preservation movement was primarily concerned with preserving large areas of public lands that remained wilderness areas as national parks, either to prove that America had scenic beauty comparable to that of Europe, or to allow individuals to find in the wilderness the spiritual fulfillment that no longer seemed attainable in modern society. See R. Nash, Wilderness and the American Mind (3d ed. 1982), and J. Sax, Mountains without Handrails: Reflections on the National Parks (1980).

Until the late 1960s, the preservation movement, based on ambiguous claims about the morality of nature and the beauty of undisturbed areas, was an influential but minor strain in the second, and dominant, resource use philosophy, conservationism.

The conservation movement was part of a deeper, progressive effort to make science compatible with democratic values and thus counter then-prevailing theories of social Darwinism. As historian Edward A. Purcell explains in The Crisis of Democratic Theory: Scientific Naturalism and the Problem of Value 10 (1973), this led progressives to the notion that all environments can be bettered by scientific resource use:

> First, they interpreted the struggle for survival in terms of the species against its environ-ment, pointing out that nature revealed mutual aid among all members of the same species. Sympathetic unity of the species implied equality and cooperation. Second, they destroyed fatalistic determinism by insisting that evolution had produced human intel-ligence, which enabled man to control his environment for the benefit of all members of the species. Intelligence suggested the possibility of the conscious creation of a more just social order. Pragmatism and instrumentalism thus commandeered evolutionary natu-ralism and argued that it was egalitarian in theory and humanitarian in practice.

The intellectual roots of the conservation movement are usually traced to a book written in 1864 by a lawyer, diplomat, and self-trained scientist, George Perkins Marsh, but they can also be traced to the scientific surveys of the West in the middle of the nineteenth century, which ultimately led to federal retention and management of much of the public domain:

> The geologists and topographers were members of a newer elite community which was fast replacing that informed by the old army. As such, they often saw the West in terms of the scientific rather than the military problems involved. And where they were called upon to apply their knowledge, they thought largely in terms of efficiency and waste. This was in sharp contrast to the ideas of Western legislators and the demands of Western citizens, who had always thought of the West as a place to live in and develop and exploit. To them the geologist was not much different from a fur trader's guide, or a wagon master. His job was to lead them to the promised land and show them the way to the riches.
>   There arose then in the 1860s still another West to be placed beside the passage to India, the imperial domain, the beaver kingdom, the Great American Desert, the par-adise of flocks and herds, the empty Algeria, Arcadia, Golconda, and the Creator's mighty firmament. These had been revealed by explorers in the past. The new West was, by implication, the "resource West," to be revealed by the scientific explorer, but also to be guarded when the occasion demanded against reckless exploitation and the rampant, often illicit speculation that came to characterize the Grant administration, both in the East and in the West. Thus it became clear that in an age which depended upon and demanded exploitation and speculation, the explorer was once again ahead of his time and even running counter to it. Out of his Western experience came conservation and the first great national agencies dedicated to that proposition. [W. Goetzman, Explora-tion and Empire 356 (1966).]

Marsh's Man and Nature, republished ten years later as The Earth Modified by Human Action, was the first popular book to use what we now call the ecological perspective to draw attention to the consequences of overusing resources and to reach the normative conclusion that natural resource use policy should be based on use — rather than abuse — of nature's "spontaneous arrangements."

Man and Nature contributed significantly to the growth of interest in conservation. Conservationism was and is concerned with moderating the rate of present resource use to ensure plentiful supplies of needed commodities in the foreseeable future. Preservationism and conservationism, like the Anglican and Roman communions, share certain principles, but the two movements have retained a fair degree of separation because of a historic split. In the 1880s the founding fathers of the two movements, John Muir of the preservation movement and Gifford Pinchot of the conservation movement, split over forest use and later over water use policy. The defining moment was the battle to stop the Hetch Hetchy dam. Hetch Hetchy Valley is located north of Yosemite Valley and was almost as spectacular. In 1913 President William Howard Taft made the decision to allow the city of San Francisco to flood the valley to develop a secure public water supply, which it enjoys today. As one of the leading new western historians explains, the controversy was actually a three-way battle:

> In the battle over Hetch Hetchy, Pinchot and the conservationists believed that they confronted two sets of enemies: preservationists such as Muir and western entrepreneurs and speculators who cared nothing about Hetch Hetchy but who sought to stop the creation of municipally owned water and power companies. Muir and his allies pointed out that there were other possible reservoir sites for San Francisco, but conservationists and most urban progressives rejected the sites because they were in the hands of private developers who could hold the city at ransom. Conservationists believed that for the public good, San Francisco had to develop Hetch Hetchy. One side made preserving Hetch Hetchy a symbol of ethical, spiritual, and aesthetic standards; the other made destroying it a symbol of the victory of the public goods—also a matter of ethics—over the greedy interests of private developers. Both sides phrased the issue in terms of a managed West. Utility and public development won; preservation of nature lost. [R. White, "It's Your Misfortune and None of My Own": A History of the American West 413 (1991).]

The conservation movement, which stressed the use of scientific principles to make rational resource use choices, established two once-controversial fundamental principles that have had a great influence on environmental law. First, resource management is a legitimate public function and should be based on science and promote the efficient allocation of resources. Second, the state may legitimately restrain the use of private property when private initiative wastes and degrades natural resources. Progressive conservationism was a powerful political force in the first two decades of the twentieth century and helped to shape the structure and thrust of federal and state resource use programs. Powerful government agencies were established to develop resources for the purpose of reclamation of arid lands, flood control, and public power. In the debate over how best to use natural resources, preservationists became dissenters who lobbied Congress on an ad hoc basis to block certain projects or federal actions. See generally J. Petulla, American Environmental History: The Exploitation and Conservation of Natural Resources (2d ed. 1987); Hargrove, The Historical Foundations of American Environmental Attitudes, 1 Envtl. Ethics 209 (1979). The standard history of the conservation movement is the superb S. Hays, Conservation and the Gospel of Efficiency: The Progressive Conservation Movement 1890-1920 (1959); see also D. Strong, The Conservationists (1971).

Under the leadership of John Muir, the preservation movement scored a number of important political successes in setting aside national parks and curbing excessive use of public lands, but it lacked the breadth of vision acceptable to the American mind to displace scientific conservation as the dominant resource use policy. John Muir's ecological vision was perhaps too advanced for his time:

> Hetch Hetchy was a part of the flow of Nature. It was filled with waterfalls, and was the path of the Tuolumne River. It was the path of ancient glaciers, and a path new life had taken as it entered the mountains. And damming it was an act by men which bespoke their arrogance. Men who built dams believed they could control and harness the flow of Nature. Hetch Hetchy was also a consummation, as all the inseparable sections of the flow were. It was not an "exceptional" creation, since none of God's gardens were. It was part of a larger whole, an edenic valley. Yet when men chose to stop its flowing life, and did so not for the farmers of the Central Valley, but for the businessmen of the City of San Francisco, Muir saw in this action civilization's willingness to kill Nature for its own convenience. In theory—for the young Muir certainly—all dams in all valleys were arrogant gestures by men.
>
>   . . . The entire idea behind Yosemite Park, an idea so long in taking shape, was to hold inviolate the whole watersheds of the Merced and Tuolumne rivers. To violate that precedent was to damage the concept of a national park as more than a collection of scenic features. So it was that the principle of a national park as an ecological whole was also at stake. [M. Cohen, The Pathless Way: John Muir and the American Wilderness 330-331 (1984).]

According to conventional wisdom, it was not until the twentieth century that the full consequences of man's powers over nature began to portend disaster. As a result of the factors enumerated above, by the 1970s concern over resource use had secured a prominent place on political agendas, and the notion of resource misman-agement had acquired a sense of urgency it had lacked previously. The working assumption of the modern environmental movement was set forth by Barbara Ward and René Dubos in their book Only One Earth (1972):

> What is certain is that our sudden, vast accelerations—in numbers, in the use of energy and new materials, in urbanization, in consumptive ideals, in consequent pollution— have set technological man on a course which could alter dangerously and perhaps irreversibly, the natural systems of his planet upon which his biological survival depends. [Only One Earth, at 11.]

3.   The Political Emergence of the Modern Environmental Era

The subordination of preservationism to conservationism continued until 1969-1970, when what is now referred to as the environmental decade began. Sud-denly, debates over environmental quality shifted from a near exclusive focus on public lands protection or reservoir construction issues, or a local air or water pollution problem, to a national political issue. Environmental protection became a sometimes diffuse, but typically broad-based and enduring, national political priority that trig-gered an unprecedented legislative response from Congress. Council on Environmen-tal Quality, Tenth Annual Report 1-15 (1979), offers several reasons for the sudden emergence of environmental quality as a major political priority. The first of the two most important long-range trends was the post-World War II growth of affluence, which allowed many people to relocate in suburban communities. Many of those who moved to the suburbs witnessed firsthand the degradation of the very amenities they had relocated to enjoy.

The second major long-range trend was the growth of the synthetic organic chemical industry. As the synthetic chemical industry grew, and as more sophisticated monitoring devices were developed, it became increasingly clear that pollution posed a serious threat to human health. In this connection, an event of signal importance was the 1962 publication of Rachel Carson's brief against DDT, Silent Spring, which was provided in excerpt form earlier in this chapter. Silent Spring "began an educational process by which ecological precepts entered the common vocabulary," S. Udall, The Quiet Crisis and the Next Generation 203 (1988), and a continuing effort to document the adverse health effects of exposure to chemicals released into the air, water, and soil. See S. Steingraber, Living Downstream: An Ecologist Looks at Cancer and the Environment (1997), for an example of Carson's legacy.

Many have observed that crises are necessary to trigger political responses, see B. Adam, Timescapes of Modernity: The Environment and Invisible Hazards (1988). Reactions to the Santa Barbara oil spill that immediately preceded Earth Day in April 1970 showed the breadth of the environmental movement. L. Dye, Blowout at Platform A: A Crisis That Awakened a Nation (1971), contains a useful account of the reactions of the citizens of Santa Barbara to the spill. The mood of the late 1960s is described in Editors of Fortune, The Environment: A National Mission for the Seventies (1970). It is paradoxical that this spill, which took no human lives, caused no permanent impairment of human health, and seems to have produced no long-range ecological damage, became a national crisis that "brought home to a great many Americans a feeling that protection would not simply happen, but required their active support and involvement," Council on Environmental Quality, Tenth Annual Report, at 12. Subsequent disasters such as the radiation fallout from the fire in the nuclear reactor at the Chernobyl plant near Kiev in Ukraine, spills on the Rhine and in Spain, and the Exxon Valdez oil spill in Alaska, as well as concerns about global climate change, helped to internationalize the environmental movement and to focus public attention on the need for better environmental protection.

Finally, a major catalyst for the birth of the environmental movement was the transfer of political energy from the bitterly controversial and often violent civil rights and anti-Vietnam War movements to a movement that was clean, enjoyed widespread support, and promised to transcend old ideological issues.

But the exact reasons modern environmental law frameworks emerged when they did remains subject to debate. Richard Lazarus acknowledges that the "original 1970 Earth Day looks very much like a 'republican moment,'" coming at a time of "such heightened civic-mindedness that it is possible to overcome substantial institutional and political obstacles to potentially radical social change." Lazarus, The Making of Environmental Law 43-44 (2004). Lazarus, however, suggests that a more incremental change actually occurred, with modern frameworks building on earlier social movements and changing federal and state environmental laws. Environmental historian Richard N. L. Andrews similarly suggests that a combination of galvanizing events and incrementally increasing state, local, and federal environmental roles set the stage for the environmental decade's emergence around 1970. In addition, he observes that as states and municipalities began to respond to citizen environmental unrest and enact their own early environmental laws, industry opposition to federal regulation softened. "[A]s a few leading states and cities began to toughen their air pollution control regulations—though only a few . . . —key industries themselves acquired a powerful new interest in obtaining moderate and uniform federal standards that would preempt more stringent and inconsistent state and local standards." R. Andrews, Managing the Environment, Managing Ourselves: A History of American Environmental Policy 209 (1999). As discussed further below and in Chapter 2, industry willingness to countenance federal regulation did not mean they controlled it; the modern environmental laws actually enacted often were stringent and also typically preserved state regulatory roles, especially the right to be more stringent than federal standards.

4. A Brief Chronology of the Development of Modern Environmental Laws and Political Trends

The previous sections provided a broad overview of social attitudes and linked political movements that led to modern environmental law frameworks. This closing historical section offers a slightly different focus, emphasizing the linkages between political trends and the particular forms of environmental laws that resulted. The eras of environmental protection are, like all historical lines, arbitrary, but we offer them as a rough guide to bracket the statutes, regulations, and cases that you will study in this course. As just covered at length earlier in this chapter, common law claims and background principles of environmental law exist and influence statutory frameworks, but environmental law is primarily positive law. The environmental law that you will study for most of the remainder of this book, and work with as an attorney or policy-maker, reflects legislative, regulatory, and judicial perceptions of the diverse environmental problems confronting this country. Recent environmental history can be roughly divided into the following phases.

A. *State and Federal Law before 1968.* Environmental law as we know it today did not exist before 1968. Pollution control legislation existed before the 1960s and momentum for the federalization of pollution control had been building since the 1930s, but the common law of nuisance was the principal legal method to force the internalization of environmental "insults." Environmental concerns, as we now define them, existed, but they were largely aesthetic or spiritual claims asserted to preserve public lands from more intensive use and commodity production (e.g., the National Parks and Wilderness systems) or were public health based. Pollution was perceived as a local or state problem, although there were exceptions. The Ohio Valley had an interstate program going back to the 1930s to stop untreated discharges into the Ohio River. In the main, environmental values were either ignored or clearly subordinate to economic development.

Scattered instances of federal regulation existed. The Refuse Act of 1899 prohibited the discharge of refuse in navigable waters because a clear federal interest—interstate and foreign navigation—was threatened by large debris discharges into harbors. Untreated sewage discharges were identified as a serious local and interstate problem in the 1930s, but the initial post–World War II federal involvement was limited to federal grants to states. Still, as environmental ills began to loom larger in the national consciousness, and some states and cities began to respond, national environmental politics began to change.

Some of that change was independent of activities in the courts, but a few key early cases provided a rough template for the enforcement structures that would later become a central element in modern environmental laws. It is perilous to describe any single case as "the" critical or defining moment leading to political change, yet the regulatory battles, legal challenges, and court decision in Scenic Hudson Pres. Conference v. FPC, 354 F.2d 608 (2d Cir. 1965), proved to be greatly influential. It has been called the first environmental law case. Rabin, Federal Regulation in Historical Perspective, 38 Stan. L. Rev. 1189, 1298 (1986). In the case, citizens successfully challenged a proposal to modify the landscape of the Hudson River's highlands to accommodate a power generation facility that would pump water from the Hudson to a huge reservoir, which then would be released to power turbines during times of high energy demand. The landscape's beauty and fishery resources were threatened by the plan. As the Second Circuit noted, the citizen plaintiffs' claims were based on statutory and agency language allowing the Federal Power Commission to issue a license only if it could find that

> a prospective project [met] the statutory test of being "best adapted to a comprehensive plan for improving or developing a waterway," Federal Power Act §10(a), 16 U.S.C. §803(a). In framing the issue before it, the Federal Power Commission properly noted:
>
>> We must compare the Cornwall project with any alternatives that are available. If on this record Con Edison has available an alternative source for meeting its power needs which is better adapted to the development of the Hudson River for all beneficial uses, including scenic beauty, this application should be denied. . . .
>
>> "Recreational purposes" are expressly included among the beneficial public uses to which the statute [§10(a)] refers. The phrase undoubtedly encompasses the conservation of natural resources, the maintenance of natural beauty, and the preservation of historic sites. See Namekagon Hydro Co. v. Federal Power Comm., 216 F.2d 509, 511-512 (7th Cir. 1954). All of these "beneficial uses," the Supreme Court has observed, "while unregulated, might well be contradictory rather than harmonious." Federal Power Comm. v. Union Electric Co., 381 U.S. 90, 98 (1965). In licensing a project, it is the duty of the Federal Power Commission properly to weigh each factor. . . .
>>   This role does not permit it to act as an umpire blandly calling balls and strikes for adversaries appearing before it; the right of the public must receive active and affirmative protection at the hands of the Commission.
>>   This court cannot and should not attempt to substitute its judgment for that of the Commission. But we must decide whether the Commission has correctly discharged its duties, including the proper fulfillment of its planning function in deciding that the "licensing of the project would be in the overall public interest." The Commission must see to it that the record is complete. The Commission has an affirmative duty to inquire into and consider all relevant facts. . . .

Although the *Scenic Hudson* case did not break new doctrinal ground or interpret a pathbreaking statute, its emphasis on citizen and court willingness to look at all of a statute's language, and enforce language focused on environmental quality, provided a virtual template for environmental actions that continue today. For the first time, a court remanded an agency decision because it failed to consider adequately a trio of interests—aesthetics, fish and wildlife, and recreation—that constituted "environmental quality" circa the mid-1960s, and suggested that agencies had an affirmative duty to take these interests into account in their decisions. In his memorial to Judge Hays, Judge Henry J. Friendly described the case as "Judge Hays' most influential opinion for the court." In Memoriam, 635 F.2d lxi (1981). In his article, The Most Creative Moments in Environmental Law, 2000 Ill. L. Rev. 1, Professor

William Rogers lists *Scenic Hudson* as the second most creative moment in environmental law, behind Rachel Carson's Silent Spring.

Scenic Hudson established the fundamental pattern of environmental litigation that continues to this day. The case is distinguished by five important characteristics. First, it was initiated by an ad hoc citizen's group, which was forced to use the judicial process after political and administrative avenues failed. Nongovernmental organization (NGO) participation in the development of environmental law and policy is a feature of U.S. environmental law that has been admired and emulated all over the world. Second, standing was a major barrier, but the Second Circuit's liberal understanding of the interests that qualified for standing was echoed, with no further analysis, in the foundational Supreme Court standing case Sierra Club v. Morton, excerpted in Chapter 3, section A. Third, the plaintiff association was faced with the problem that there were no constitutional, common law, or statutory substantive theories that would allow it to argue that the FPC's decision to license the pump storage plant violated a right possessed by it. Fourth, plaintiffs were thus forced to craft a primarily procedural rather than substantive administrative law theory that would convince a court at least to reverse and remand the administrative decision. Post–New Deal administrative law was not promising. Decisions such as those delegated to the FPC were seen as best made by agency experts with minimal judicial supervision. Plaintiffs crafted a strategy that built on the traditional criticism of the administrative state: the rule of law demands strict fidelity to congressional mandates. This principle was combined with the theory that the injury was not substantive, in the sense that there was no principled basis for a court to order the agency to prefer preservation of Storm King Mountain over the pump storage plant, but procedural. The crux of the injury was a procedural error caused by the agency's failure to afford plaintiffs a meaningful opportunity to present a wide range of evidence about environmental degradation and, more important, to argue that alternatives to the project existed. The limits of procedural theories and relief are illustrated by the fact that the FPC reissued the license and the decision was upheld. Scenic Hudson Pres. Conference v. FPC, 453 F.2d 463 (2d Cir. 1971). Fifth, *Scenic Hudson* illustrated the potential of more intrusive judicial review.

In the following years, both in legislative provisions and in battles over implementation of and compliance with environmental laws, NGOs came to rely heavily on courts to shape as well as enforce environmental law. *Scenic Hudson*'s lawyer, David Sive, one of the seminal figures in modern environmental law, drew on his experience in the case to articulate a more general theory of judicial supervision of mission agencies. Some Thoughts of an Environmental Lawyer in the Wilderness of Administrative Law, 70 Colum. L. Rev. 612 (1970). See also A. Talbot, Power along the Hudson: The Storm King Case and the Birth of Environmentalism (1972) (recounting the legal and political history of the Storm King battles).

B. *The Environmental Moment: 1968-1973.* This represents the formative period of environmental law. Pollution control through technology emerged as a national priority, and the idea of ecosystem stability became the guiding principle behind NEPA and environmental impact assessment generally. NEPA, the Clean Air Act and Clean Water Act, risk-based pesticide regulation, and the Endangered Species Act were passed during this period, and federal pesticide law was transformed from a consumer protection to a cancer risk prevention law.

This particular burst of activity and, especially, the stringency of the laws enacted, resulted from a brief period of time when the Democrat-controlled Congress, led by Senators Edmund Muskie of Maine and Henry Jackson of Washington State, competed with the Republican President Nixon to out-"green" each other. Elliott et al., Toward a Theory of Statutory Evolution: The Federalization of Environmental Law, 1 J.L. Econ. & Org. 313, 316, 327 (1985). M. Landy et al., The Environmental Protection Agency: Asking the Wrong Questions from Nixon to Clinton 22-33 (1994), explain the competition in the broader context of both major political parties' efforts to appeal to suburban voters who responded positively to the growing media accounts of middle-class victims of environmental degradation.

During this period, the control and prevention of gross nuisances shifted from the courts to the newly created EPA and state agencies. The assumption was that air and water pollution problems were attributable to (1) industrial and municipal discharges, (2) the emission of soot from factories, and (3) automobile emissions that caused smog. This era also saw the adoption of the idea of performing a comprehensive environmental assessment before public works and important regulatory activities were undertaken. NEPA and "little NEPAs" enacted by states and municipalities, coupled with active and sympathetic judicial review by courts, especially the D.C. Circuit Court of Appeals, became important tools to contest activities that were previously virtually immune from judicial review.

During the early years of this period, there was a widespread perception that the mission agencies such as the then Atomic Energy Commission, Federal Power Commission, the U.S. Army Corps of Engineers, the Bureau of Reclamation, the federal land management agencies, and the Federal Highway Administration were making decisions without any consideration of the "environmental consequences" of these decisions or alternative, less environmentally destructive ways of achieving the mission's objective. It was difficult to challenge these decisions in court. The resource management laws contained broad delegations of discretion that virtually immunized them from judicial control. Courts typically applied the bedrock principle of administrative law that courts should defer to the exercise of administrative expertise to uphold most of these challenged management decisions unless the action was outside the scope of the statute. Moreover, the underlying question, to develop or to preserve, had long been considered a political rather than a legal question. Thus, there were few legal standards to apply, and challengers faced difficult standing issues.

Nevertheless, building on the more skeptical and intrusive sort of review utilized in the Scenic Hudson case mentioned above, by the late 1960s courts had begun to manifest a far more rigorous attitude, scrutinizing the actions of governments and polluters and enforcing the often aspirational language of the many new and amended environmental laws.

C. Extension and Refinements: 1973-1980. The period between 1969 and 1980 is referred to as the environmental decade. The 1970s saw the extension of legislative protection to a wide range of public health risks and the completion of the environmental moment despite mounting arguments that environmental protection should be "traded off" against other social objectives such as energy security. Legislative regulation of pollutants continued, but the emphasis shifted from gross nuisances to the identification and minimization of toxic risks. Questions over the balance between environmental protection and continued development became more important. Cancer became a proxy for many human health–related environmental problems. Programs were enacted to control the entry of toxic substances in commerce (the Toxic Substances Control Act); to protect the human use of resources (the Safe Drinking Water Act); to regulate the transportation, treatment, storage, and disposal of hazardous wastes (the Resource Conservation and Recovery Act); and to clean up orphaned waste dumps, broadly defined (the Comprehensive Environmental Response, Compensation, and Liability Act (CERCLA or Superfund)).

The environmental movement weathered the energy crisis of the 1970s, and the principle that environmental protection is a core value seems to have become a widely accepted and perhaps permanent political reality. For example, after the 1973 Arab oil embargo, the executive and Congress tried to stimulate increased coal production at a time when there was great concern about the environmental impacts of surface mining. After intense controversy, Congress enacted the Surface Mining Control and Reclamation Act (SMRCA) in 1977. SMCRA preserves some environmentally sensitive public and private lands from mining and requires that mined lands be reclaimed. See L. McBride & J. Pendergrass, Coal, in Environmental Law from Resources to Recovery 635 (C. Campbell-Mohn ed., 1993).

D. *The Bipartisan Consensus Begins to Crumble: 1980-1988.* This period can be characterized domestically as the period when the environmentally oriented bipartisan consensus started crumbling, and internationally as the time when the globalization of environmental issues became apparent. Globalization led to two important ideas that influence both international and domestic law. The first is the concept of global commons, such as polluted or stressed airsheds—related to such phenomena as acid rain and global climate change—and rain forests, along with the older commons, the seas. Second is the rise of the idea that biodiversity preservation is a transcendent value that should be broadly pursued. Biodiversity conservation, which is not self-defining, has provided a new focus for programs such as the Endangered Species Act and public land management. This focus helped, along with the divided Congress and executive, preserve the 1970s programs from major congressional revision.

Domestically, the period from 1980 to1988 was a testing ground. Initially, the Reagan administration (1981-1989) sought to roll back many of the gains of the previous decade; however, this strategy failed, and many programs were actually strengthened. Despite the lack of success in the legislature, President Reagan did issue a strong Executive Order mandating that most major regulations be subjected to cost-benefit analysis. Overall, the idea of environmental protection became more contingent and contested.

E. *Little Progress, Attack and Gridlock: 1988-Present.* The period extending from 1988 into the twenty-first century is difficult to characterize because it is marked by several divergent but overlapping trends. Politically, there has been little innovation in environmental programs. We continue to live off the intellectual capital of the active first 15 years of the modern environmental movement. The Clean Air Act amendments of 1990 represent the last major federal legislative initiative. Congress has intervened in many specific controversies, but has done little more than reauthorize and make minor adjustments to the major federal laws.

CERCLA was amended both in the late 1990s and early in the presidency of George W. Bush, but in ways intended to reduce liability uncertainties for, respectively, the lending industry and those involved with "brownfields" properties. Apart from so far ill-fated efforts to enact new laws or amendments to deal with the issue of greenhouse gases, and sporadic amendments of agricultural laws to encourage sounder environmental conduct, there are no major new domestic environmental statutory programs on the political agenda.

The major international initiatives centered on the implementation of the 1992 Rio Biodiversity Convention and on finding ways for nations to share the burden of rolling back greenhouse gas emissions to implement the United Nations Framework Convention on Climate Change, but little tangible progress has been made in implementing them since the 1992 Rio Summit. The ten-year follow-up conference held in Johannesburg was a virtual non-event in the wake of September 11, 2001. See generally Stumbling toward Sustainability (J. Dernbach ed., 2002).

Public support for environmental protection is found in polls to be consistently strong, but some question the depth of that support. There is a growing consensus that we are entering the second generation of environmental law, which is characterized by a highly politicized atmosphere that makes rational assessment of first-generation approaches difficult. Richard Lazarus has traced the increasingly polarized nature of national legislative politics, finding few signs of any reemerging bipartisan environmental coalitions. Lazarus, A Different Kind of "Republican Moment" in Environmental Law, 87 Minn. L. Rev. 999 (2003). Environmental law in the 1980s became highly politicized because of the tension between the Reagan and Bush administrations and the Democratic Congress, and this politicization continued during the 1990s with the combination of a Democratic president and a Republican Congress.

In 1994 Republicans captured both houses of Congress for the first time since 1952. Republicans centered their campaign on their highly publicized "Contract with America." Claiming the public's approval for change, they advocated more rigorous cost-benefit analyses to roll back existing and proposed new regulations, reliance on "sound" as opposed to allegedly speculative science, the elimination of unfunded state and local mandates, and greater protection for private property. See Glicksman & Chapman, Regulatory Reform and (Breach of) the Contract with America, 5 Kan. J.L. & Pub. Pol'y 9 (1996). This initiative produced a substantial pro–environmental protection backlash; few substantive changes were made. For more extensive discussion of cost-benefit analysis and this period, see Chapter 3, sections B and C.

Since the second President Bush assumed office, environmental protection has remained an area of dispute. The era of federal bipartisan work to improve the environment and its laws is only a memory. The result has been an increasingly sterile debate, with each side reaching for a kill, only to be beaten back, as happened in 1995-1996. The Republican party's triumph in the 2002 midterm legislative elections broke the political deadlock, but one-party rule was delayed for a time by Vermont Senator James Jeffords's switch from Republican to Independent status, preserving a bare Democratic majority in the Senate. During the next elections, in 2004, the Republican party secured control of all three branches, with a Republican president, control of both houses, and a numerical majority of federal judges having been appointed by Republican presidents. Despite this period of exclusive rule by a party long dedicated to "reforming" federal environmental laws, major statutory rollbacks still have not occurred. Some of this may result from a post-9/11 focus on national security issues and the United States' war in Iraq, but it also appears that overt attacks on environmental laws remain a political risk. A sufficient number of Republicans oppose environmental rollbacks such that the narrow Republican majority is insufficient to overcome opposition from Democrats and the small number of allied Republicans. The Democrats' recapturing of the House and the Senate in the 2006 midterm elections likely has reduced the risk of environmental rollbacks. With the White House still in Republican control, however, strengthening of environmental laws is unlikely.

Still, despite the lack of major legislative activity in recent years, weakening of federal environmental laws has occurred, but through less overt means than direct statutory amendments. Instead, where statutory changes have been made, it has often been through language in appropriations riders that have been subject to little or no advance public awareness or legislative discussion. Through such riders, for example, the Information (or Data) Quality Act was passed, giving citizens, industry, and any other stakeholders the ability to challenge information utilized by administrative agencies. See Chapter 3, section B. Similarly, appropriations riders have exempted certain activities and sometimes particular geographic areas from the law's usual protections and requirements.

In decisions focusing on standing doctrine, federalism-influenced statutory interpretations limiting federal regulatory power, and administrative law doctrines preserving executive discretion not to act, the Supreme Court and lower courts have in a broad array of areas weakened environmental laws, or at least made their enforcement less likely.

The legislative and Republican-Democrat political gridlock has stimulated innovation in the shadow of existing regulatory programs. There is considerable vertical and horizontal power sharing through collaborative public-private stakeholder processes. See Freeman, Collaborative Governance in the Administrative State, 45 UCLA L. Rev. 1 (1997); Seidenfeld, Empowering Stakeholders: Limits on Collaboration as the Basis for Flexible Regulation, 41 Wm. & Mary L. Rev. 411 (2000). The pros and cons of collaborative decision making as well as the implications for environmental lawyers are perceptively discussed in Karkkanien, Environmental Lawyering in the Age of Collaboration, 2002 Wis. L. Rev. 555. See also C. Powers & M. Chertow, Industrial Ecology: Overcoming Policy Fragmentation, in Thinking Ecologically: The Next Generation of Environmental Policy 20, 23 (M. Chertow & D. Esty eds., 1997).

In addition, some states, often through their attorneys general, have become more active in challenging federal regulatory rollbacks and have also stepped more actively into enforcement roles. States have also innovated in such areas as brownfields policy after the federal government proved slow to amend hazardous waste laws to address widely perceived flaws. Buzbee, Contextual Environmental Federalism, 14 N.Y.U. Envtl. L.J. 108 (2005). In major policy areas, especially in dealing with the risks of greenhouse gases and climate change, several states have taken the lead. As discussed at greater length in Chapter 2's coverage of the "race to the bottom," the extent and nature of state environmental protection efforts remain subject to fierce debate.

F. *The Roots of Ongoing Policy Ferment.* The political deadlock of the 1990s to the present masks a major intellectual ferment among academics and other policy analysts aimed at taking stock of the first generation of environmental protection, assessing more rationally its strengths and weaknesses, and devising strategies to maintain a sound level of environmental quality. Federal legislative gridlock has also contributed to creative local and regional ad hoc environmental conservation and ecosystem restoration experiments. In 1994 the National Environmental Policy Act reached its twenty-fifth anniversary, and this event triggered much thoughtful reassessment of initial efforts. E.g., Symposium, Twenty-five Years of Environmental Regulation, 27 Loyola L.A. L. Rev. 3 (1994).

The fundamental tensions of environmentalism remain unresolved. We may be moving into a more consensus-based preventive era, but there is a great deal of frustration with the politics of environmentalism independent of narrow partisan politics. There are two principal strains of this frustration. The first is the traditional development opposition to all forms of government regulation—except subsidy— which is having a strong run, especially in the inner-mountain West. See J. Switzer, Green Backlash: The History and Politics of Environmental Opposition in the U.S. (1997), and W. Graf, Wilderness Preservation and the Sagebrush Rebellions (1990). This has been augmented by efforts of critics of environmental regulation to equate environmentalism and "Soviet style" governance. In this view, environmental regulation represents the inefficient and unconstitutional interference with the natural right to exploit resources; overly centralized regulations, critics contend, impose regulatory burdens that are inadequately attuned to local conditions. See Chapter 2. It is becoming almost acceptable to question the validity of the basic principle of environmental quality.

The second strain is a more general unease with the growing disconnect between environmentalism and traditional concepts of rationality and our modern technology-based civilization. This is the subject of M. Lewis, Green Delusions: An Environmentalist Critique of Radical Environmentalism (1992). G. Easterbrook's very controversial book. A Moment on Earth: The Coming Age of Environmental Optimism (1995), chastises the environmental movement for its efforts to maintain itself solely through arguments that environmental catastrophes are imminent and for not keeping up with scientific developments. See also the controversial B. Lomberg, The Skeptical Environmentalist: Measuring the Real State of the World (2001). For a critical response to Lomberg, see Kysar, Some Realism about Environmental Skepticism: The Implications of Bjorn Lomborg's The Skeptical Environmentalist for Environmental Law and Policy, 30 Ecology L.Q. 223 (2003).

On the environmentalist side, citizens and policymakers look at problems such as climate change and associated greenhouse gases, environmental inequities, ongoing struggles to clean America's many areas plagued by degraded rivers and substandard air quality, as well as widespread failure to enforce existing laws, and see unfinished business and unaddressed ills. Calls for greater energy conservation continue to fall mostly on deaf ears, and gaps between statutory aspirations and implemented reality persist.

In short, persistent, fundamental divides among the dominant political parties and among the nation's regions continue to complicate environmental law and politics. Little is certain at this point, other than a climate of ongoing ferment and resulting policy debate.

I. ENVIRONMENTAL POLICY AND REGULATORY DESIGN CHOICE

As you dig more deeply into this nation's environmental laws and regulations, you may find yourself puzzled. Little in the way of uniform goals or regulatory approaches will be evident. Even within a single law, you will find several different goals and regulatory strategies. This statutory diversity is the result of several factors. First, most laws have been amended on numerous occasions. Although assembled as a single law in the United States Code or a book of environmental statutes, most laws reflect the goals of different political coalitions, different states of knowledge about the efficacy of particular regulatory designs, and responses to different events prompting statutory enactment or amendment. Sometimes laws have been triggered by a galvanizing environmental catastrophe or by risks highlighted by a popular book. Each major statutory amendment tends to incorporate effective regulatory approaches utilized in other laws, but seldom are old statutory provisions jettisoned. At other times, laws have been amended in response to legal developments, such as an unexpected and environmentally destructive court decision, or regulatory failures to act during a time of divided government, or particular electoral cycles that prompted short-lived coalitions to enact a new law. Compromises and partial efforts to achieve goals are the norm. As the chapter on international law states, "sustainability" is becoming an increasingly influential goal in international law, but it neither explains the passage of this nation's laws nor justifies their particular schemes.

As will quickly become evident, this lack of a unifying goal or regulatory approach, coupled with their frequent amendment, means that these laws are both best explained and perhaps justified as the result of pragmatic, incremental adjustments. For such a defense, see S. Shapiro & R. Glicksman, Risk Regulation at Risk: Restoring a Pragmatic Approach (2003).

As discussed above, the rigor with which modern environmental laws were enacted starting in the late 1960s is attributable to an array of factors. Few, however, would dispute that this nation's environmental laws are in many respects a political economic miracle; today's laws, still largely reflecting the laws enacted during the "environmental decade," protect dispersed citizens and environmental interests, often to the detriment of industries with concentrated interests in avoiding substantial regulatory costs. See Farber, Politics and Procedure in Environmental Law, 8 J.L. Econ. & Org. 59 (1992); Schroeder, Rational Choice versus Republican Moment Explanation for Environmental Law, 1969-73, 9 Duke Envtl. L. & Pol'y F. 29 (1998).

Many of this nation's laws remain impressive and surprisingly effective, but they are often difficult work. Do not expect comprehensive coverage or consistency across statutes, but do be sensitive to the array of regulatory choices reflected in this nation's laws.

To highlight a few key aspects of the laws you will study, this chapter closes by highlighting in brief form several important statutory attributes. First, this section identifies the several sorts of *goals* evident in environmental laws. Second, it identifies key *triggers* that justify action under the statutes. Third, it identifies the most common *regulatory strategies or designs* utilized in the field we call environmental law. You have already been introduced to two strategies manifest in common law approaches to environmental ills—reliance on private bargaining to resolve conflicts, and the award of damages or injunctive relief following proof of environmental harm. Modern environmental statutes use a wider array of strategies.

1. *Environmental Law Goals, Triggers, and Strategies*

Environmental laws all share some sort of connection with the environment, but often have little focus on the environment in the sense of ecological health. Other laws are focused overwhelmingly on a cleaner environment. Sometimes the three statutory elements that we suggest require analysis—goals, triggers, and regulatory strategies or designs—are somewhat collapsed. Modern environmental laws share little other than a general rejection of the common law strategy of providing remedies after a harm has occurred, but even that generalization is only partly accurate. Several major statutes, chiefly laws dealing with spills and disposal of hazardous materials and oils, do utilize after-the-fact imposition of monetary liability both to pay for cleanups and discourage future mishandling of such wastes. Most of our environmental laws, however, share the goal of preventing or addressing risks before harm occurs. Most laws also rely on regulatory agencies to turn statutory aspirations and often broadly articulated mandates into implemented reality. Exactly what institutions play particular regulatory roles varies widely across statutes.

This brief catalogue of goals, triggers, and regulatory designs or strategies is not meant to provide a comprehensive identification of which statutes utilize which regulatory features. Instead, it highlights major salient features in laws by way of examples. The Clean Air Act could be used to illustrate virtually every paragraph that follows; in its cumbersome several hundred pages, it employs almost every feature described. The same is true of other laws. The provisions mentioned highlight major statutory features and strategies that you will encounter and must learn to recognize.

a. Goals

A *Clean Environment.* Several laws have as their overarching goal cleaning up the environment or preserving the natural environment's attributes, especially biological integrity or biodiversity. The Clean Water Act and Endangered Species Act share these goals, while the Clean Air Act is more focused on health, with a somewhat secondary focus on the environment. CERCLA, also known as the Superfund law, has the goal of cleaning up contaminated lands, but primarily for health reasons. Several of its provisions, however, also require assessment of environmental impacts.

The goal of a clean environment is itself an aspiration that will probably never be reached. Instead, a major question is assessing just "how clean is clean," and how far a statute requires movement toward a clean environment. Seldom is a pristine, prehuman environment the goal. Instead, most laws allow varying degrees of environmental degradation, with current or anticipated uses often influencing the requisite level of pollution control. In addition, other goals such as protection of health are often considered in conjunction with clean environment goals.

Public Health. The Clean Air Act and CERCLA share a focus on cleaning up pollution to prevent or minimize risks to health. Similarly, pesticide and food laws and chemicals regulation have as their focus public health, as does the Safe Drinking Water Act. As with cleanliness goals, the significant regulatory choice relates to the relevant proxies or measures for health, and at what level of protection standards should be set.

Fairness or Remedying of Damages. The central goal of common law schemes is provision of a remedy or award of damages. Perhaps surprisingly, little in statutory environmental law shares these goals. Most laws focus on reducing certain risks and preserve the right to bring common law actions, but do not include their own separate right to a damages remedy. CERCLA allows for cost recovery actions when governments or individuals undertake a cleanup of hazardous waste contributed to by others, as do several other laws related to spills and hazardous materials, but the relief provided does not actually amount to damages, but is a judicial award of some or all of the costs of cleanup. Frequently, monetary remedies are combined with rights to injunctive relief mandating action or cessation of harmful activity.

b.   Triggers

Triggers for regulatory actions and obligations vary in form. Some triggers create obligations for the government to act, whereas others call for polluters to take remedial steps or report a pollution incident.

No Threshold Risk Determination. Some laws, such as food regulation, contain provisions that authorize protective government action against certain additives without proof of any risk in their regulated use. Similarly, certain types of unreported releases of hazardous substances can justify government sanctions, even without proof of any resulting risk or harm. In addition, some laws require improved environmental performance for certain sources of risk based on what can be technologically achieved, with little or no focus on or proof of risk before or after regulation. Especially for known carcinogens, laws sometimes require actions without any prior proof of manifested harms.

Risk-Based Thresholds. More common are laws that allow government action only upon a determination that risk exceeds some statutory threshold, usually some sort of risk to health or the environment. The degree of risk that must be shown can vary from minimal risk to a high proof threshold. The quintessential example of such a law is the Clean Air Act. Its various provisions reflect dramatically different sorts of risk-based triggers. Pervasive ambient air pollutants threatening health must be regulated to preserve health, allowing an adequate margin of safety, while stationary sources of pollution, such as factories, can be regulated if they can be reasonably anticipated to endanger public health or welfare. The main law governing pesticides, in contrast, requires regulatory scrutiny to determine if pesticide use will cause unreasonable health effects. Note, however, that how regulatory burdens are allocated can differ, with some laws requiring government proof of risk and other laws requiring industry proof of safety before a product can be entered into commerce. Several laws that utilize technology-based standards with little or no regard to risk contain provisions that bring risk evaluations back into the picture in later assessments of whether technology-based standards and resulting pollution permits leave residual risk. Prime examples of such schemes are found in the Clean Water Act's water quality and total maximum daily load provisions, and in the Clean Air Act's new provisions regarding hazardous air pollutants.

c.   Regulatory Designs and Strategies

Regulatory designs and strategies are many, and they are often utilized in tandem in the same statute and sometimes even within the same programs. They nevertheless have distinct attributes.

Economic Incentives. Both the oldest environmental law schemes, namely common law approaches, and the most modern schemes, such as those found in the 1990 amendments to the Clean Air Act, use economic incentives. These can range from awards of damages to "internalize" otherwise externalized harms, to taxing of harmful activity to create an incentive for improved performance, to the subsidizing of desired conduct.

Technology-Based Standards. Since the early 1970s, both the Clean Air and Clean Water Acts have embraced strategies that require regulators to determine, against some carefully crafted benchmark, what level of pollution reduction or emission level is able to be accomplished through technological means. The age of the polluting facility, the nature of the pollutant, and assessments of cost all usually influence what must be accomplished. Other such provisions can require little more than meeting what are common performance measures for an industry. Despite often being derided as inefficient "command and control" regulation, technology-based standards typically do not mandate the use of any particular technology, but instead require achieving the performance level of the benchmark group. The standards are typically later rolled into source-specific permits. A risk-averse industry will often simply adopt the technology considered by federal regulators in setting the required standard, but this is seldom the result of any technology mandate.

Technology-Forcing Provisions. Technology-forcing provisions are a variant of technology-based provisions. Instead of looking at what has been achieved, regulators typically determine what can be accomplished through the use of innovative technologies. In some instances, especially those concerning motor vehicle pollution under the Clean Air Act, legislative provisions have required ambitious levels of pollution reduction without advance knowledge of the particular means to the legislative end. Such provisions force the development of new pollution control technologies.

Technology Mandates. Rarely, and typically only as a fallback mechanism, some laws do require agencies to determine what technology is best to achieve a specific goal, and then mandate its use. Such mandates usually require that pollution control obligations later be rolled into a permit specific to each pollution source.

Risk or Ambient Environment-Based Standard Setting. In both the Clean Air and Clean Water Acts, provisions require regulators to set standards for what constitutes an adequately clean or safe environment. Once this level of ambient environmental cleanliness or level of acceptable risk is determined, then regulators must, in effect, engage in a reverse engineering sort of calculation. Sources contributing to the particular ambient environment must meet levels of pollution so that the ambient environment will at least move toward the specified level of cleanliness or risk. The quintessential example of such provisions is in the Clean Air Act's state implementation plan provisions and their linkage to attainment of National Ambient Air Quality Standards.

Information-Based Schemes. In numerous laws, governments or private actors, or both, must prepare and make public information about their environmental activities or the environmental impacts of proposed activities. This is seen most prominently in the National Environmental Policy Act (NEPA) as well as in later amendments to CERCLA requiring industry revelation of toxic releases. As interpreted by the Supreme Court, NEPA does not require the adoption of any particular environmentally sound outcome. Other laws with analogous or simultaneously applicable provisions, such as the Endangered Species Act, create substantial regulatory risks if information about possible harms is ignored. Even standard permit-based schemes such as the Clean Water Act industrial discharge permit program require that all stages of the permit process, from application to periodic compliance reports, be publicly accessible. Failure to provide required information, or the provision of false information, is subject to potentially severe penalties. Information-based schemes are particularly favored by economists and market-oriented policymakers because they facilitate informed market choice.

Liability-Based Schemes. CERCLA, or the Superfund law, as it is colloquially known, is designed to deter future creation of dangerous hazardous waste sites, but it achieves this goal not through advance permitting but through the imposition of huge cleanup liabilities on contributors to such sites. It is much like common law schemes, using monetary incentives to encourage environmentally sound behavior. It also utilizes more standard regulatory procedures for the process of determining how to categorize and clean up particular sites.

Phase-outs. Less common, but still highly effective at times, are laws and regulatory actions that require the phasing out of risky products or activities.

Constrained Balancing Standards. Professors Shapiro and Glicksman, in their book, Risk Regulation at Risk, *supra,* identify a number of laws as utilizing a "constrained balancing standards" approach. Id. at 37. Such provisions may embrace a health or environmental goal, but then require consideration of regulatory repercussions such as cost, economic impacts, what can be achieved in a certain time frame, or what is technologically feasible. Many technology-based forms of regulation, which are described above, utilize a variant of constrained balancing.

Cost-Benefit–Influenced Standard Setting. Although championed by many vocal critics of the modern regulatory state, few laws at this time subject regulatory actions to a cost-benefit analysis test. An Executive Order does so when consistent with underlying statutory law, and one regulatory reform law focused on unfunded mandates imposes a limited requirement of cost-benefit analysis, but most environmental laws merely require attention to costs or economic impacts among many other variables. Portions of major laws, especially a key provision in the Clean Air Act focused on health, do not allow attention to costs or benefits. The ferment on whether to require greater attention to costs and benefits of regulatory action will surely continue.

2. *Implementation and Enforcement Design Choice*

The preceding paragraphs focus on what regulatory strategies are imposed on polluters and others who might harm the environment. A different sort of regulatory design choice focuses on what regulatory institutions will play implementation and enforcement roles. The exact mix of roles varies in the statutory schemes you will study, but you should be sensitive to the following regulatory design choices.

Are provisions self-implementing or delegated to agencies, and how are requirements imposed on polluters? Although some major environmental laws impose burdens directly on regulatory targets and hence are self-implementing, most delegate implementation tasks to governmental institutions. Typically, federal agencies such as the U.S. EPA are statutorily delegated initial implementation obligations, such as issuing regulations following notice and comment rulemakings. Some laws, however, hand presumptive implementation authority to state actors. Even then, a dense web of regulations usually exist to guide policymakers. The criteria to be applied in delegations to agencies are often the most important statutory language guiding government conduct and allowing for oversight and judicial challenge. A further layer of delegation and articulation of legal obligations is contained in government-issued permits. Under most major statutes, agencies roll regulatory obligations and specification of permitted activities into source-specific permits. Compliance with such permits is often the key to translating environmental aspirations into implemented reality. Due to the centrality of this multi-level delegation process, virtually every stage is subject to citizen participation rights, judicial challenge, and enforcement by all levels of government and by citizens as well.

Do key provisions provide for elective or mandatory action? Be sensitive to the language of mandate, such as the use of "shall" or the imposition of statutory deadlines for action. Note also when laws provide criteria or goals, but do not require action in specified circumstances. Statutes vary wildly in the specificity of their language, sometimes granting broad discretionary authority, and other times micro-managing all that will occur. As you will see in the administrative law chapter and in many cases that follow, courts respond very differently to language of mandate or statutes that leave agencies with a substantial range of discretionary choices. A statutory allocation of tasks may make clear what institution is to act, but whether the action is elective or required often determines whether the statutory language leads to actual implementation or to delay.

Who can enforce the law? Most environmental laws empower several enforcers, with federal authorities, states, and citizens all handed potential enforcement authority, at least if the other does not act. In addition, allegedly "arbitrary and capricious" agency action or allegedly erroneous statutory interpretations are subject to challenge under well-established administrative law doctrines.

What creates enforceable legal obligations? Enforceable obligations can arise at different points for different actors. For example, it is quite common for a federal agency to have an initial obligation to promulgate a regulation, with states then able to assume implementation or enforcement roles, either in lieu of or in addition to federal agencies. Next, legal obligations are rolled into permits that are themselves subject to challenge in regulatory proceedings or later in court. Finally, violations of permit obligations by a polluter are separately subject to challenge. Few laws or even sections of laws create anything close to a single clear obligation. The complex regulatory statutes you will study set a sequence of regulatory actions in motion, generating many settings where lawyers seek to influence outcomes. Hence, a public interest lawyer concerned about mercury air pollution, for example, will typically monitor national regulations regarding such pollution, implementation at the state or regional level, levels of pollution control imposed on pollution sources in their permits, and actual compliance with such permits. Each regulatory stage specifying legal requirements allows for participation and comment by interested entities, including citizens and public interest groups, as well as the possibility of challenge in the courts.

As is apparent in this review of regulatory strategies and designs, a critical element in all environmental laws is how federal and state governments fill their implementation and enforcement roles. Chapter 2 turns to that topic.

FURTHER READING

We offer some suggestions for further reading on the topics raised in this chapter.

A.   *The Environmental Classics*

H. Brown, The Challenge of Man's Future (1954)
R. Carson, Silent Spring (1963)
B. Commoner, The Closing Circle (1971)
P. Ehrlich, The Population Bomb (1968)
P. Ehrlich (with A. Ehrlich), Population, Resources, Environment (1972)

P. Ehrlich, The End of Affluence (1974)

L. Marx, The Machine in the Garden: Technology and the Pastoral Ideal (1964)

Meyers, An Introduction to Environmental Thought: Some Sources and Some Criticisms, 50 Ind. L.J. 426 (1975)

F. Osborn, Our Plundered Planet (1948)

T. O. Riordan, Environmentalism 37-84 (2d ed. 1980)

S. Udall, The Quiet Crisis (1963, rev. ed. The Quiet Crisis and the Next Generation (1988))

B. Environmental Ethics

R. Attfield, Environmental Philosophy: Principles and Prospects (1994)

R. Attfield, The Ethics of Environmental Concern (1983)

Callicott, Hume's Is/Ought Dichotomy and the Relation of Ecology to Leopold's Land Ethic, 4 Envtl. Ethics 163-174 (1982)

Callicott, Intrinsic Value, Quantum Theory, and Environmental Ethics, 7 Envtl. Ethics 257-275 (1985)

Callicott, Nonanthropocentric Value Theory and Environmental Ethics, 21 Am. Phil. Q. 229-309 (1984)

Callicott, On the Intrinsic Value of Nonhuman Species, in The Preservation of Species 38-172 (B. Norton ed., 1986)

B. Callicott ed., A Companion to A Sand County Almanac (1988)

L. Ferry, The New Ecological Order (C. Volk trans., 1995)

W. Gravberg-Michaelson, A Worldly Spirituality: The Call to Take Care of the Earth (1984)

E. C. Hargrove, Foundations of Environmental Ethics (1989)

J. Hart, The Spirit of the Earth: A Theology of the Law (1984)

Hefferman, The Land Ethic: A Critical Appraisal, 4 Envtl. Ethics 235 (1982)

C. Meine, Aldo Leopold: His Life and Work (1988)

C. Merchant, Earthcare: Women and the Environment (1996)

Norton, Environmental Ethics and Nonhuman Rights, 4 Envtl. Ethics 17 (1982)

C. Stone, Earth and Other Ethics: The Case for Moral Pluralism (1987)

Tarlock, Environmental Law: Ethics or Science?, 7 Duke Envtl. L. & Pol'y F. 193 (1996)

P. Taylor, Respect for Nature: A Theory of Environmental Ethics (1986)

Tribe, Ways Not to Think About Plastic Trees: New Foundations for Environmental Law, 83 Yale L.J. 1315 (1974)

M. Zimmerman, Contesting Earth's Future: Radical Ecology and Postmodernity 374-375 (1994)

C. Environmental History

R. Andrews, Managing the Environment, Managing Ourselves: A History of American Environmental Policy (1999)

J. Flippen, The Nixon Administration, Politics and the Environment (2002)

S. Fox, John Muir and His Legacy: The American Conservation Movement (1981)

S. P. Hays, A History of Environmental Politics since 1945 (2000)

J. Hughes, An Environmental History of the World: Humankind's Changing Role in the Community of Life (2001)

J. R. McNeill, Something New Under the Sun: An Environmental History of the Twentieth-Century World (2000)

I. G. Simmons, Environmental History: A Concise Introduction (1993)

F. Turner, Rediscovering America: John Muir in His Time and Ours (1985)

D.   Environmental Justice

Austin & Schill, Black, Brown, Poor & Poisoned: Minority Grassroots Environmentalism and the Quest for Eco-Justice, 1 Kan. J.L. & Pub. Pol'y 69 (1991)

Boyle, It's Not Easy Bein' Green: The Psychology of Racism, Environmental Discrimination, and the Argument for Modernizing Equal Protection Analysis, 46 Vand. L. Rev. 937 (1993)

B. Bryant & P. Mohai eds., Race and the Incidence of Environmental Hazards (1992)

R. Bullard, Dumping in Dixie (1990)

Bullard, Anatomy of Environmental Racism and the Environmental Justice Movement, in Confronting Environmental Racism: Voices from the Grassroots (R. Bullard ed., 1993)

Bullard, Overcoming Racism in Environmental Decisionmaking, 36 Environment 10 (1994)

Cole, Remedies for Environmental Racism: A View from the Field, 90 Mich. L. Rev. 1991 (1992)

J. Gaventa, B. Ellen Smith & A. Willingham eds., Communities in Economic Crisis: Appalachia and the South (1990)

Godsil, Note, Environmental Racism, 90 Mich. L. Rev. 394 (1991)

B. Goldman, The Truth about Where You Live (1991)

R. Gottlieb, Forcing the Spring: The Transformation of the American Environmental Movement 6 (1993)

Kaswan, Environmental Laws: Grist for the Equal Protection Mill, 70 U. Colo. L. Rev. 387 (1999)

Lazarus, Pursuing "Environmental Justice": The Distributional Effects of Environmental Protection, 87 Nw. U. L. Rev. 787 (1993)

C. Rechtshaffen & E. Gauna, Environmental Justice: Law, Policy and Regulation (2002)

Symposium, Urban Environmental Justice, 21 Fordham Urb. L.J. 425 (1994)

E.   Political Theory, Property Rights, and
    Environmentalism

S. Board, Ecological Relations: Towards an Inclusive Politics of the Earth (2002)

Bosselman, Four Land Ethics: Order, Reform, Responsibility, Opportunity, 24 Envtl. L. 1439 (1994)

A. Bramwell. The Fading of the Greens: The Decline of Environmental Politics in the West (1994)

P. F. Cramer, Environmental Politics: The Role of Radical Environmentalism in Crafting American Environmental Policy (1998)

J. S. Dryzek, The Politics of the Earth: Environmental Discourses (1997)

J. S. Dryzek & D. Schlosberg, Debating the Earth: The Environmental Politics Reader (1998)

R. Eckersley, Environmentalism and Political Theory: Toward an Ecocentric Approach (1992)

Frazier, The Green Alternative to Classical Liberal Property Theory, 20 Vt. L. Rev. 299 (1995)

Freyfogle, The Owning and Taking of Sensitive Lands, 43 UCLA L. Rev. 77 (1995)

G. C. Gaard, Economical Politics; Ecofeminists and the Greens (1998)

R. Goodin, Green Political Theory (1992)

O. L. Graham, Environmental Politics and Policy (2000)

A. Jamison, The Making of Green Knowledge: Environmental Politics and Cultural Transformation (2001)

M. E. Kraft, Environmental Policy and Politics (2001)

McDaniel, Physical Matter as Creative and Sentient, 5 Envtl. Ethics 291 (1983)

J. M. Meyer, Political Nature: Environmentalism and the Interpretation of Western Thought (2001)

Rolston, Nature and Possibility of an Environmental Ethics, 3 Envtl. Ethics 31 (1981)

Rolston, Is There an Ecological Ethic?, in Ethics and the Environment 41 (D. Shere & T. Attig eds., 1983)

Sax, Property Rights and the Economy of Nature: Understanding *Lucas v. South Carolina Coastal Council*, 45 Stan. L. Rev. 1433 (1993)

Taylor, The Ethics of Respect for Nature, 3 Envtl. Ethics 197 (1981)

Taylor, In Defense of Biocentrism, 5 Envtl. Ethics 237 (1983)

Weston, Beyond Intrinsic Value: Pragmatism in Environmental Ethics, 7 Envtl. Ethics 7 (1985)

R. Wilder, Listening to the Sea: The Politics of Improving Environmental Protection (1998)

F.   Green Theology

C. Birch & J. Cobb, Jr., The Liberation of Life: From the Cell to the Community (1981)

S. McFague, The Body of God: An Ecological Theology (1993)

R. Ruether, Gaia and God: An Ecofeminist Theology of Earth Healing (1992)

Schwarzschild, The Unnatural Jew, 6 Envtl. Ethics 347 (1984)

II

ENVIRONMENTAL FEDERALISM

Environmental laws seldom contain direct, clear mandates. Instead, modern environmental statutory schemes work within the complex constraints of our federalist form of government. Modern environmental laws preserve certain roles for federal agencies, seek to enlist state and local government actors to play assisting or perhaps primary delegated roles, and preserve the possibility of additional state and local environmental laws and common law regimes. In addition, background constitutional law doctrines influence how these laws are interpreted, implemented, and enforced. This layering of environmental laws, coupled with doctrines influencing the roles federal and state actors can play, pervades environmental law. At each level of government, administrative law doctrines, which are the subject of Chapter 3, further influence how statutory aspirations are implemented in practice.

This chapter focuses on environmental federalism. To work effectively as an environmental lawyer or policymaker, one must develop facility with environmental federalism's wrinkles and choices. Multilayered law, entailing the possibility of conflict, cooperation, overlap, and fundamental challenges to governmental actors' authority, is the norm, not the exception. Constitutional law courses provide most environmental law students with a solid grounding in federalism doctrine. Nevertheless, the Supreme Court's active recasting of federalism doctrine over the past decade, coupled with particular challenges likely to arise in connection with environmental protection, require the inclusion of a separate chapter highlighting environmental federalism's many facets. Some of the subjects covered are constitutional in nature, but many involve questions of regulatory choice within areas under the largely unquestioned authority of federal and state actors.

This chapter examines environmental federalism law in the following order. First, we will look at the *rationales* for federal environmental regulation. When should an environmental problem be addressed by the federal government or the states? This fundamental question remains a subject of active policy and scholarship debate. Even if the federal government has power to act, should it?

Next, we turn to the question of *federal power* to protect the environment. This question primarily involves analysis of federal power under the Commerce Clause of the U.S. Constitution. The Supreme Court's varying approaches and persistent analytical divisions leave the question of federal power open to challenge and certain litigation in the coming years. This debate over the reach of federal or state power also influences how courts will interpret legislation.

We then examine means by which the federal government can *enlist or encourage state assistance.* Building off of this analysis, we next look briefly at the ways statutes deal with the reality of federal and state actors and multilayered laws. Most significantly, this section examines *delegated program federalism* (a form of *cooperative federalism*) and *savings clauses* that preserve existing law, typically state common law and parallel or completely independent, nonconflicting bodies of state law.

Federalism doctrine also provides opportunities for challenges to federal or state regulatory power, particularly where federal and state actors collide. Although the Constitution's Supremacy Clause clearly provides that federal law will trump conflicting state law, the resolution of controversy over conflicting laws implicates several doctrines and can serve to undercut state or federal law. *Sovereign immunity doctrine* can potentially immunize states from monetary liabilities and has been an area of substantial Supreme Court activity since the 1990s. *State sovereign immunity doctrine* is rooted in language from the Tenth and Eleventh Amendments, although it is justified in large part on claimed pre-constitutional understandings. As you will see, even if private actions against states are barred, states are still subject to potential liability and litigation.

Dormant Commerce Clause doctrine can prohibit state actions that could impede interstate commerce, even in the absence of any expressly conflicting federal law. This topic is covered in depth in a later chapter but briefly discussed here. *Preemption doctrine* sets limits on what kinds of state actions are permitted in areas addressed by federal law; as you will see, its many facets make preemption a doctrine that is more easily stated than applied.

In short, environmental federalism law remains an area of great complexity and ongoing debate. Environmental federalism law is about much more than just power or lack of power. Federalism frameworks influence strategic decisions by public and private actors. Familiarity with the different doctrines, rationales, and common choices manifested in this nation's environmental laws is critical to working effectively in the field of environmental law.

Problem 2-1

You are counsel for Greenbuild Inc., a large, national company interested in developing abandoned and possibly moderately contaminated real property, often in urban areas. These sites, typically referred to as *brownfield sites*, have often been abandoned or underutilized due to liability fears, but also often due to tax liens, disputes over ownership, and perhaps other easements and covenants related to conservation limiting how these sites will be used. Furthermore, site-specific agreements and orders under federal, state, and local laws sometimes limit permitted land uses due to concerns about exposure to hazardous substances and other pollutants. Your company has found that these many sorts of title and use uncertainties are hindering redevelopment efforts and reducing profitability. State and local governments also would like to see such brownfield properties redeveloped. Following a visit from a U.S. senator interested in strengthening her environmental and business reputation, your company's president has sought your guidance. In particular, she and the visiting senator want to know if federal legislation could survive challenges if it required all levels of government to input information into a shared national database that would record all use limitations on parcels of property over ten acres in size. Sketch your analysis of the constitutionality of such a law, paying special attention to how it might best be structured to pass constitutional muster and also to work effectively.

A. RATIONALES FOR FEDERAL ENVIRONMENTAL REGULATION

Even if the federal assertion of regulatory power can survive a direct constitutional attack, and even if such an assertion is beyond dispute, the question remains whether federal regulatory power should be asserted. Despite the broad perception since the late 1960s that the federal government is the chief environmental innovator and the level of government responsible for most major environmental improvements, recent influential scholarship questions the accuracy of that perception. Scholarly reexamination of the rationales for federal environmental regulation, as well as related historical analysis, continues today, influencing the worlds of academe and policy. Presumptions against federal regulation, or in favor of the preservation of certain areas as primarily ruled by state law, surface periodically in court decisions. Familiarity with the rationales for federal or state regulatory primacy, or for overlapping implementation and enforcement regimes, can be essential to success as a lawyer or policymaker. The following readings and notes provide an introduction to these debates and competing rationales.

1. Interstate Externalities

Perhaps the most widely accepted rationale for federal over state environmental standard setting is the interstate movement of pollution externalities. Since many forms of pollution, especially air and water pollution, as well as environmental threats to animals, plants, or endangered species, and the species themselves, can and typically do move across state borders, the primacy of federal regulation is often accepted. Stewart, Pyramids of Sacrifice? Problems of Federalism in Mandating State Implementation of National Environmental Policy, 86 Yale L.J. 1210, 1215 (1977) (discussing how interstate "spillovers . . . generate conflicts and welfare losses not easily remedied under a decentralized regime"). Other influential analyses include Merrill, Golden Rules for Transboundary Pollution, 46 Duke L.J. 931 (1997); Revesz, Federalism and Interstate Externalities, 144 U. Pa. L. Rev. 2341 (1996). States have little incentive to abate their own interstate pollution or that caused by their industries unless some higher level of government imposes such a requirement. As seen in Chapter 1, states can pursue public nuisance claims, but they often face difficult proof hurdles and generally will not succeed if there are many polluters contributing to a pollution stream.

Some scholars focus almost exclusively on the physical location or nature of the pollution and hence advocate the "matching principle," arguing that the regulator with jurisdiction most commensurate with the pollution's effects should have regulatory primacy. Butler & Macey, Externalities and the Matching Principle: The Case for Reallocating Environmental Regulatory Authority, 14 Yale L. & Pol'y Rev. 23 (1996). Others suggest that interstate business dynamics, resources that exceed a single jurisdiction, or interjurisdictional competition all can weigh in favor of federal regulation. See Buzbee, Recognizing the Regulatory Commons: A Theory of Regulatory Gaps, 89 Iowa L. Rev. 1, 25 (2003); see also Adler, Jurisdictional Mismatch in Environmental Federalism, 14 N.Y.U. Envtl. L.J. 130 (2005) (exploring the problem of jurisdictional mismatch, with an emphasis on limiting federal regulation to areas of clear federal institutional advantage).

2.   *Economies of Scale*

Where effective regulation requires substantial investigation of technological capabilities, links between pollutants and health impacts, or comprehensive assessment of diverse jurisdictions' pollution control efforts, economies of scale and free rider concerns will favor a federal role. Otherwise, no individual state will have the incentive to gather these sorts of valuable statistics, and other states will be tempted to "free ride" at the expense of any state that does make such an investment. Federal leadership also reduces the risk of duplicative regulatory investigation, and placing research capabilities in a single institution's hands likely will help that institution develop experience and expertise. For this reason, federal gathering and dissemination of information about pollution impacts and pollution control has long been part of federal environmental law. Seldom, if ever, does one encounter calls for the federal government's surrender of these informational roles, due to the widely shared view that federal action benefits from economies of scale.

3.   *The Race to the Bottom*

One of the most common justifications for federalizing environmental regulation is the fear that, without federal standards, the states will engage in a game of competitive deregulation or lowering of regulatory standards—a phenomenon typically called the "race to the bottom." This argument surfaces in Judge Wilkinson's opinion in Gibbs v. Babbitt, excerpted below. He identifies this dynamic as a justification for federal regulation that influenced Congress to enact environmental laws such as the Endangered Species Act. Stated most basically, race-to-the-bottom theory posits that without federal regulation, states will relax their standards in order to attract industrial development, with its attendant employment and tax benefits. Under this theory, each jurisdiction will end up sacrificing its citizens' preferred level of environmental cleanliness. In short, this competition results in suboptimal levels of environmental protection. See Stewart, *supra*, at 1211-1212; Stewart, The Development of Administrative and Quasi-Constitutional Law in Judicial Review of Environmental Decisionmaking: Lessons from the Clean Air Act, 62 Iowa L. Rev. 713, 747 (1977).*

In a 1992 article, New York University law professor (and now dean) Richard Revesz challenged the theoretical underpinnings of race-to-the-bottom theory. Rehabilitating Interstate Competition: Rethinking the "Race to the Bottom" Rationale for Federal Environmental Regulation, 67 N.Y.U. L. Rev. 1210 (1992). Revesz asserts that there is no formal support for the conclusion that interstate competition tends to lead

---

*Literature on the dynamics of interjurisdictional competition and its benefits and costs is also prominent outside the environmental area. See, e.g., Cary, Federalism and Corporate Law: Reflections upon Delaware, 83 Yale L.J. 663 (1974) (corporate law); Butler & Macey, The Myth of Competition in the Dual Banking System, 73 Cornell L. Rev. 677 (1988) (banking law); Kaplow, Fiscal Federalism and the Deductibility of State and Local Taxes under the Federal Income Tax, 82 Va. L. Rev. 413, 458-560 (1996) (tax law); Brown, Competitive Federalism and the Legislative Incentives to Recognize Same-Sex Marriage, 68 S. Cal. L. Rev. 745, 816-818 (1995) (family law); Been, Exit as a Constraint on Land Use Exactions: Rethinking the Unconstitutional Conditions Doctrine, 91 Colum. L. Rev. 473 (1991) (land use); Esty & Geradin, Market Access, Competitiveness, and Harmonization: Environmental Protection in Regional Trade Agreements, 21 Harv. Envtl. L. Rev. 269 (1997) (environmental protection in the context of free trade); Zelinsky, Against a Federal Patients' Bill of Rights, 21 Yale L. & Pol'y Rev. 443 (2003) (health care law).

to a race to the bottom in social welfare. Rather, using neo-classical economic models to simulate the effects of interstate competition, he argues that competition among states, like competition within industry, tends to produce socially efficient outcomes. Revesz questions the assumption that federal minima in the area of environmental regulation will prevent a race to the bottom; even if constrained by federal environmental standards, states could still choose to compete by lowering standards in other areas that remain under their control. Though not intended "as a definitive refutation to race-to-the-bottom arguments," Revesz argues that the forces of interstate competition are at least "presumptively beneficial." Id. at 1253.

His examination of the issue touched off a lively debate among legal scholars. Several critics challenged Revesz's theoretical framework, charging that it rested on assumptions that do not closely reflect real-world conditions. See Esty, Revitalizing Environmental Federalism, 95 Mich. L. Rev. 570 (1996) ("In the end, Revesz's theoretical dismissal of the race to the bottom depends on heroic assumptions, including perfect government rationality"); Swire, The Race to Laxity and the Race to Undesirability: Explaining Failures in Competition among Jurisdictions in Environmental Law, 14 Yale J. on Reg. 67 (1996) ("Environmental law is largely defined by the very factors that are assumed away in the models, such as many interstate externalities, deep public choice problems, and intractable theoretical and practical obstacles to measuring the social utility of environmental regulations").

Others have taken a more empirical approach. Most notably, in 1996, Professor Kirsten Engel published the results of a study in which 400 state environmental, economic, and legislative officials, along with selected interest groups, were polled regarding the existence of race-to-the-bottom behavior. Engel, State Environmental Standard-Setting: Is There a "Race" and Is It "to the Bottom"?, 48 Hastings L.J. 271 (1997). Among her findings: 57 out of 65 state regulators stated that concern over industry relocation affected environmental decisionmaking in their state; 47 out of 80 regulators believed that the degree of environmental regulation was a fairly or a very important factor in determining industry location/relocation; and 48 percent of state regulators reported that their state or agency had done something to lower their environmental standards in response to concerns over industry relocation. Among those officials reporting that industry relocation had played no role whatsoever in environment policymaking, most attributed this to the presence of federal standards that limited their ability to deregulate. Engel's findings provide strong empirical support for race-to-the-bottom theorists, as well as renewed support for the rationale for federal standard setting. She also strongly questions Revesz's basic assumption that the world of environmental standard setting resembles an efficient market. She points out that competition among states for industrial siting is characterized by small numbers of states and corporations, and is rife with imperfect information.

Professor Jerome Organ in 1995 examined state willingness to enact environmental standards more stringent than the presumptive federal standard, as specifically allowed under most federal statutes. He discovered that many states have enacted laws either prohibiting or creating procedural or substantive hurdles constraining environmental regulators from exceeding federal standards. Organ, Limitation on State Agency Authority to Adopt Environmental Standards More Stringent than Federal Standards: Policy Considerations and Interpretive Problems, 54 Md. L. Rev. 1373 (1995). He observes that the pervasiveness of these enactments confirms the theory that fears of competitive disadvantage, a central tenet of race-to-the-bottom theory, remain important to states. Id. at 1393 n.91.

Revesz responded to many of these criticisms in The Race to the Bottom and Federal Environmental Regulation: A Response to Critics, 82 Minn. L. Rev. 535 (1997), distilling and sharpening some of his main points. The following statement makes clear that he is not necessarily disputing the claim that environmental standards may drop in response to competition, but is positing that federal standards might induce a reduction in social welfare:

> I argue that even if states systematically enacted suboptimally lax environmental standards, federal environmental regulation would not necessarily improve the situation. If states cannot compete over environmental regulation because it has been federalized, they will compete along other regulatory dimensions, leading to suboptimally lax standards in other areas, or along the fiscal dimension, leading to the underprovision of public goods. Thus, the reduction in social welfare implicit in race-to-the-bottom arguments would not be eliminated merely by federalizing environmental regulation: federalization of all regulatory and fiscal decisions would be necessary to solve the problem. [Id. at 541.]

4. Centralization versus Decentralization

The benefits or costs of centralized or decentralized regulatory standard setting and implementation is a fourth variable weighed in most federalism discussions. Here arguments cut both ways, with advocates of decentralization favoring state primacy and advocates of centralization favoring a federal role. As you will see, most environmental laws adopt hybrid schemes, with both centralized and decentralized elements. Most numerical standard setting, however, whether for ambient environmental levels or by category of industry, is federally set. As Dean Rubin and Professor Feeley argue forcefully, decentralization arguments and federalism arguments are not the same, although the two are often confused. Rubin & Feeley, Federalism: Some Notes on a National Neurosis, 41 UCLA L. Rev. 903 (1994).

Decentralization Arguments. Professor Stewart has articulated well the arguments in favor of decentralized environmental regulation:

> This presumption [in favor of decentralization] serves utilitarian values because decisionmaking by state and local governments can better reflect geographical variations in preferences for collective goods like environmental quality and similar variations in the costs of providing such goods. Noncentralized decisions also facilitate experimentation with differing governmental policies, and enhance individuals' capacities to satisfy their different tastes in conditions of work and residence by fostering environmental diversity.
>
> Important nonutilitarian values are also served by noncentralized decisionmaking. It encourages self-determination by fragmenting governmental power into local units of a scale conducive to active participation in or vicarious identification with the processes of public choice. This stimulus to individual and collective education and self-development is enriched by the wide range of social, cultural and physical environments which noncentralized decisionmaking encourages. [Stewart, Pyramids, *supra*, at 1210-1211.]

Stewart and others also point out that reliance on an overly large regulator can lead to "diseconomies of scale" because the regulator will not be sensitive to smaller-scale variations and differences in priorities. In addition, in literature overlapping with "race-to-the-bottom" analyses, theorists posit that with many jurisdictions in competition for citizens, businesses, and revenues, that competition will lead to more efficient delivery of government services.

Centralization Arguments. Without a more centralized regulatory authority that views environmental harms as internal costs, and that will answer to constituents both causing and harmed by pollution, these harms may go unaddressed. In addition, many environmental ills and citizen demands for a safe and clean environment are rooted in the concept of the right to a clean environment, or at least the argument that a certain degree of environmental protection should be uniformly guaranteed across the nation. Finally, centralized environmental regulation can reduce the number of venues in which policy and legal battles occur. This can be particularly advantageous for groups with scant resources. As Daniel Esty states, with a "centralized" regulatory structure, "environmental groups find it easier to reach critical mass and thereby to compete on more equal footing with industrial interests." Esty, *supra*, at 650 n.302. This is linked to "public choice" rationales for federal or state regulation, discussed below.

Of course, a multiplicity of potential regulators can lead to confusion over lines of responsibility and to dissipation or misdirection of demands for regulatory protection, see Buzbee, *supra*, but the more clearly responsible a single regulator is for an environmental ill, the more likely it is that action will be taken. As mentioned above, economies of scale in gathering or creating information also favor a centralized governmental role.

Mixed Regimes with Centralized and Decentralized Regulatory Roles. Because of the many varieties of environmental ills, scholars such as Daniel Esty advocate "multi-tier regulatory structure[s] capable of mixing and matching decision levels depending on the issue at hand." Esty, *supra*, at 652. The Clean Air Act represents such a mixed regime, with its reliance on federal information gathering, federal standard setting, local implementation, and overlapping enforcement roles. Given the risk of under-enforcement due to lack of resources or political will, shared enforcement roles can create a more credible deterrent to polluters. See Buzbee, Contextual Environmental Federalism, 14 N.Y.U. Envtl. L.J. 108, 121-126 (2005).

5. Political, Economic, and Historical Rationales for Federal (or State) Regulation

A separate rationale for federal regulation, or perhaps state regulation, is rooted in observations about political and economic dynamics at the federal or state level. This is sometimes characterized as a "public choice" rationale that uses economic "rational actor" assumptions to predict how political and market actors will behave in political settings to further their goals. Others look at the history of environmental law and politics and make normative arguments about which level of government can and should address environmental harms.

Based on empirical observations about environmental politics, in an argument closely linked to the centralization arguments discussed above, Professor Stewart in 1977 posited that environmental groups might fare better in national politics than in state venues:

> Much of the politics of pollution control involves conflict between environmental groups and industrial and union interests. There are persuasive grounds for believing that, on the whole, environmental groups have a comparatively greater impact on policy decisions at the national level, even disregarding "commons" factors that make state and local governments particularly vulnerable to industry and union pressures. It is therefore not

surprising that environmental groups should favor determination of environmental policies by the federal government, and that increased public support for environmental protection should translate into increased legislation and regulation at the federal level. [Stewart, Pyramids, *supra*, at 1213.]

Stewart further suggested that appeals to morals and self-sacrifice may work better in national politics. In such settings "there are effective assurances that others are making sacrifices too. National policies can provide such assurances and can also facilitate appeals to sublimate parochial interests in an embracing national crusade." Id. at 1217.

In recent years, the idea that the federal venue is the most advantageous for environmental interests has been debated on both theoretical and historical grounds. Professor Daniel Esty built on Stewart's argument, stating that

asymmetries in information and the concentration of regulatory costs and benefits may give rise to asymmetries of political activity and influence between polluters and pollutees or between common-resource users and the public owners of these resources. Because these asymmetries may be more significant at the state and local levels, decentralization may represent a strategy to advance deregulation for the benefit of certain special interests. [Esty, *supra*, at 598.]

The preference for national regulation is not invariably associated with the environmentalist side. Once states start regulating in an area, industry may prefer federal regulation either to promote a uniform approach that will facilitate compliance economies of scale, or perhaps to secure a weaker preemptive action. See id. at 602. Still, the general perception remains that the federal legislative venue has been more willing to confront environmental harms with laws that have teeth. This perception has perhaps led to a "first mover" advantage for federal leadership, with federal legislators having long been perceived as the place to turn for responses to environmental problems. See Buzbee, Brownfields, Environmental Federalism, and Institutional Determinism, 21 Wm. & Mary L. Rev. 1, 27-58 (1997) (developing the "first mover" hypothesis in analysis focused on hazardous waste policies). In addition, political science scholarship indicates that federal politics is characterized by greater attention to issues, more press coverage, and increased surveying of citizen preferences. Id. at 44-46. Local and state politics, in contrast, are marked by less attention to issues and reduced awareness of both politician and citizen views. Id.; see also P. Peterson, City Limits 116-130 (1981). With polls consistently revealing broad-based support for environmental protection, the federal level, where issues-based politics is prevalent, likely is a venue more favorable to environmental interests than state or local fora.

More recently, several scholars have begun to question the story of past federal environmental leadership. Professor Jonathan Adler suggests that states were more active in addressing environmental ills in the pre-1970 period than is commonly acknowledged. Adler, The Fable of Federal Environmental Regulation: Reconsidering the Federal Role in Environmental Protection, 55 Case W. Res. L. Rev. 93 (2004); Adler, Fables of the Cuyahoga: Reconstructing a History of Environmental Protection, 14 Fordham Envtl. L.J. 89 (2002). Dean Revesz, in a recent article exploring "public choice rationales" for federal regulation, points to areas of recent state environmental activism to challenge the assumption that the federal government is more environmentally protective. Revesz, Federalism and Environmental Regulation: A Public Choice Analysis, 115 Harv. L. Rev. 553 (2001). He also finds unconvincing arguments that environmental interests will be disadvantaged in regulatory schemes that are less federally dominated, disputing long-standing arguments by Stewart, Esty, and others, as well as legislative assumptions underlying environmental law frameworks created between 1969 and the present.

In partial response to these arguments against a leading federal role, others suggest that analysts look more closely at the context leading to state activity, pointing out that much state activity during the past eight years reflects efforts to enforce federal law or to deal with out-of-state pollution not yet adequately undertaken by federal actors. Much state environmental law also reflects imitation of federal regulatory approaches. Similarly, state innovations have often been prompted by pressures to attain federal standards. See Buzbee, Contextual Federalism, *supra*.

Still, it is indisputable that some states do, at times, innovate and take a more proactive role in protecting the environment. California, for example, in the fall of 2006 enacted a law designed to ratchet back greenhouse gases contributing to climate change, while the federal government continued to resist any such requirement. For a discussion of greenhouse gas regulation and California's new law, see Chapter 6. For a discussion of preemption implications and other assessment of the benefits of federal and state activity regarding greenhouse gases, see section E.4, note 4 below.

6.   Using Competing Federalism Rationales

Little is certain in the world of environmental federalism. Apart from widespread acceptance of a federal role in gathering and generating environmental information, federalism rationales tend to engender debate. Sensitivity to how these competing rationales apply in the settings of diverse environmental ills is part of effective legal advocacy, whether one is working in a legislative, regulatory, or judicial venue. These rationales do not provide answers, but provide important artillery for legal advocacy.

B.   THE QUESTION OF FEDERAL COMMERCE POWER

The federal government has limited, specified powers under the Constitution. The federal government's power to control federal land use is rooted in the Constitution's Property Clause. That power has been broadly construed and subject to little debate. Instead, this section focuses on an area of active revision and debate—the limits of power under the Commerce Clause. Most modern environmental laws were passed pursuant to federal authority claimed under the Commerce Clause to "regulate Commerce . . . among the several states." U.S. Constitution, art. I, §8, cl. 3. The Supreme Court long ago abandoned the dualist presumption that federal and state governments had no overlapping authority; it also long ago abandoned rigid and narrow definitions of commerce that rendered the federal government unable to deal with a complex national economy. Nevertheless, what counts as commerce and thus as potentially subject to federal regulation remains contested. Especially in environmental law areas such as efforts to preserve biodiversity, protect wetlands, and save endangered species, arguments over federal power continue.

The following case introduces Commerce Clause doctrine and a recent series of related Supreme Court cases as they apply to one of the hot-button areas of federal power, endangered species protection. Note in particular the analytical differences between the appellate court's opinion and the dissent.

GIBBS v. BABBITT
214 F.3d 483 (4th Cir. 2000)

WILKINSON, C.J.

In this case we ask whether the national government can act to conserve scarce natural resources of value to our entire country. Appellants challenge the constitutionality of a Fish and Wildlife Service regulation that limits the taking of red wolves on private land. The district court upheld the regulation as a valid exercise of federal power under the Commerce Clause. We now affirm because the regulated activity substantially affects interstate commerce and because the regulation is part of a comprehensive federal program for the protection of endangered species. Judicial deference to the judgment of the democratic branches is therefore appropriate. . . .

The red wolf, *Canis rufus*, is an endangered species whose protection is at issue in this case. The red wolf was originally found throughout the southeastern United States. It was once abundant in the "riverine habitats of the southeast," and was especially numerous near the "canebrakes" that harbored large populations of swamp and marsh rabbits, the primary prey of the red wolf. 51 Fed. Reg. 41,790, 41,791 (1986). The FWS found that "the demise of the red wolf was directly related to man's activities, especially land changes, such as the drainage of vast wetland areas for agricultural purposes . . . and predator control efforts at the private, State, and Federal levels." Id. . . .

In 1986, the FWS issued a final rule outlining a reintroduction plan for red wolves in the 120,000-acre Alligator River National Wildlife Refuge in eastern North Carolina. See 51 Fed. Reg. 41,790. This area was judged the ideal habitat within the red wolf's historic range. Between 1987 and 1992, a total of 42 wolves were released in the Refuge. In 1993, the reintroduction program was expanded to include the release of red wolves in the Pocosin Lakes National Wildlife Refuge in Tennessee. Since reintroduction, some red wolves have wandered from federal refuges onto private property. From available data, as of February 1998 it was estimated that about 41 of the approximately 75 wolves in the wild may now reside on private land.

This case raises a challenge to 50 C.F.R. §17.84(c), a regulation governing the experimental populations of red wolves reintroduced into North Carolina and Tennessee pursuant to section 10(j). The FWS has extended the takings prohibitions of section 9(a)(1) to the experimental red wolf populations with certain exceptions. See 50 C.F.R. §17.84(c) (1998). As noted above, the taking provision of section 9(a)(1) prevents landowners from harassing, harming, pursuing, hunting, shooting, wounding, killing, trapping, capturing, or collecting any endangered species. See 16 U.S.C. §1532(19). However, in order to insure that other agencies and the public would accept the proposed reintroduction, the FWS relaxed the taking standards for wolves found on private land under its authority over experimental populations. . . .

In October, 1990, plaintiff, Richard Lee Mann, shot a red wolf that he feared might threaten his cattle. The federal government prosecuted Mann under §17.84(c), and Mann pled guilty. Mann's prosecution triggered some opposition to the red wolf program in the surrounding communities. After the program was in place for several years, the FWS held meetings with local governments and the public to receive feedback about the reintroductions. The Service contended that most people who commented expressed support for the program and that the reintroductions were generally supported by local, state and federal agencies, and elected officials. See 58 Fed. Reg. 62,086, 62,088 (1993). In addition, owners of nearly 200,000 acres of private land have permitted red wolves onto their land through agreements with the FWS. Nonetheless, Hyde and Washington Counties, and the towns of Belhaven and Roper, passed resolutions opposing the reintroductions of the wolves. The resolutions appeared to be based on the farming community's fears of prohibitions on private land use.

In response to discontent with the reintroduction program, the North Carolina General Assembly passed a bill entitled "An Act to Allow the Trapping and Killing of Red Wolves by Owners of Private Land." The Act makes it lawful to kill a red wolf on private property if the landowner has previously requested the FWS to remove the red wolves from the property. See 1994 N.C. Sess. Laws Ch. 635, amended by 1995 N.C. Sess. Laws Ch. 83 (adding Beaufort and Craven Counties to the Act, which initially covered only Hyde and Washington Counties). This law facially conflicts with the federal regulation. . . .

Appellants Charles Gibbs, Richard Mann, Hyde County, and Washington County filed the instant action challenging the federal government's authority to protect red wolves on private land. They seek a declaration that the anti-taking regulation, 50 C.F.R. §17.84(c), as applied to the red wolves occupying private land in eastern North Carolina, exceeds Congress's power under the interstate Commerce Clause, U.S. Const. art. I, §8, cl. 3 ("Congress shall have Power . . . To regulate Commerce . . . among the several States . . ."). Appellants also seek an injunction against continued enforcement of the anti-taking regulation on non-federal land. Appellants claim that the red wolves have proven to be a "menace to citizens and animals in the Counties." They further allege that because of the federal regulatory protections surrounding the wolves, North Carolinians cannot effectively defend their property.

On cross-motions for summary judgment, the United States District Court for the Eastern District of North Carolina held that Congress's power to regulate interstate commerce includes the power to regulate conduct that might harm red wolves on private land. See Gibbs v. Babbitt, 31 F. Supp. 2d 531 (E.D.N.C., 1998). . . .

II.

We consider this case under the framework articulated by the Supreme Court in United States v. Lopez, 514 U.S. 549 (1995), and United States v. Morrison, 529 U.S. 598 (2000), aff'g Brzonkala v. Virginia Polytechnic Inst. and State Univ., 169 F.3d 820 (4th Cir. 1999). While Congress's power to pass laws under the Commerce Clause has been interpreted broadly, both Lopez and Morrison reestablish that the commerce power contains "judicially enforceable outer limits." . . . It is essential to our system of government that the commerce power not extend to effects on interstate commerce that are so remote that we "would effectually obliterate the distinction between what is national and what is local." National Labor Relations Bd. v. Jones & Laughlin Steel Corp., 301 U.S. 1, 37 (1937). . . .

While this is rational basis review with teeth, the courts may not simply tear through the considered judgments of Congress. Judicial restraint is a long and honored tradition and this restraint applies to Commerce Clause adjudications. "Due respect for the decisions of a coordinate branch of Government demands that we invalidate a congressional enactment only upon a plain showing that Congress has exceeded its constitutional bounds." *Morrison*, 529 U.S. at 607. In fact, "[t]he substantial element of political judgment in Commerce Clause matters leaves our institutional capacity more in doubt than when we decide cases, for instance, under the Bill of Rights." *Lopez*, 514 U.S. at 579 (Kennedy, J., concurring). . . .

The *Lopez* Court recognized three broad categories of activity that Congress may regulate under its commerce power. "First, Congress may regulate the use of the channels of interstate commerce. Second, Congress is empowered to regulate and protect the instrumentalities of interstate commerce, or persons or things in interstate commerce, even though the threat may come only from intrastate activities. Finally, Congress' commerce authority includes the power to regulate those activities having a substantial relation to interstate commerce, i.e., those activities that substantially affect interstate commerce." Id. at 558-59.

Section 17.84(c) is "not a regulation of the use of the channels of interstate commerce, nor is it an attempt to prohibit the interstate transportation of a commodity through the channels of commerce." *Lopez*, 514 U.S. at 559. The term "channel of interstate commerce" refers to, *inter alia*, "navigable rivers, lakes, and canals of the United States; the interstate railroad track system; the interstate highway system; . . . interstate telephone and telegraph lines; air traffic routes; television and radio broadcast frequencies." United States v. Miles, 122 F.3d 235, 245 (5th Cir. 1997). This regulation of red wolf takings on private land does not target the movement of wolves or wolf products in the channels of interstate commerce.

This case also does not implicate *Lopez*'s second prong, which protects things in interstate commerce. Although the Service has transported the red wolves interstate for the purposes of study and the reintroduction programs, this is not sufficient to make the red wolf a "thing" in interstate commerce. See, e.g., . . . National Assoc. of Home Builders v. Babbitt, 130 F.3d 1041, 1046 (D.C. Cir. 1997) ("NAHB") (rejecting notion that Delhi Sands Flower-Loving Fly was a "thing" in interstate commerce). Therefore, if 50 C.F.R. §17.84(c) is within the commerce power, it must be sustained under the third prong of *Lopez*.

Under the third *Lopez* test, regulations have been upheld when the regulated activities "arise out of or are connected with a commercial transaction, which viewed in the aggregate, substantially affects interstate commerce." *Lopez*, 514 U.S. at 561. . . .

Although the connection to economic or commercial activity plays a central role in whether a regulation will be upheld under the Commerce Clause, economic activity must be understood in broad terms. Indeed, a cramped view of commerce would cripple a foremost federal power and in so doing would eviscerate national authority. The *Lopez* Court's characterization of the regulation of homegrown wheat in Wickard v. Filburn, 317 U.S. 111 (1942), as a case involving economic activity makes clear the breadth of this concept. The Court explained that "[e]ven *Wickard*, which is perhaps the most far reaching example of Commerce Clause authority over intrastate activity, involved economic activity in a way that the possession of a gun in a school zone does not." *Lopez*, 514 U.S. at 560. . . .

III.

Appellants argue that the federal government cannot limit the taking of red wolves on private land because this activity cannot be squared with any of the three categories that Congress may regulate under its commerce power. Appellants assert that 50 C.F.R. §17.84(c) is therefore beyond the reach of congressional authority under the Commerce Clause.

We disagree. It was reasonable for Congress and the Fish and Wildlife Service to conclude that §17.84(c) regulates economic activity. The taking of red wolves implicates a variety of commercial activities and is closely connected to several interstate markets. The regulation in question is also an integral part of the overall federal scheme to protect, preserve, and rehabilitate endangered species, thereby conserving valuable wildlife resources important to the welfare of our country. Invalidating this provision would call into question the historic power of the federal government to preserve scarce resources in one locality for the future benefit of all Americans. . . .

Unlike the Violence Against Women Act (VAWA) in *Morrison* and the Gun-Free School Zones Act (GFSZA) in *Lopez*, §17.84(c) regulates what is in a meaningful sense economic activity. . . . The relationship between red wolf takings and interstate commerce is quite direct—with no red wolves, there will be no red wolf related tourism, no scientific research, and no commercial trade in pelts. We need not "pile inference upon inference," *Lopez*, 514 U.S. at 567, to reach this conclusion. While a beleaguered species may not presently have the economic impact of a large commercial enterprise, its eradication nonetheless would have a substantial effect on interstate commerce. And through preservation the impact of an endangered species on commerce will only increase.

Because the taking of red wolves can be seen as economic activity in the sense considered by *Lopez* and *Morrison*, the individual takings may be aggregated for the purpose of Commerce Clause analysis. See *Morrison*, 529 U.S. at 611, n.4. While the taking of one red wolf on private land may not be "substantial," the takings of red wolves in the aggregate have a sufficient impact on interstate commerce to uphold this regulation. This is especially so where, as here, the regulation is but one part of the broader scheme of endangered species legislation.

Further, §17.84(c) is closely connected to a variety of interstate economic activities. Whether the impact of red wolf takings on any one of these activities qualifies as a substantial effect on interstate commerce is something we need not address. We have no doubt that the effect of the takings on these varied activities in combination qualifies as a substantial one. The first nexus between the challenged regulation and interstate commerce is tourism. The red wolves are part of a $29.2 billion national wildlife-related recreational industry that involves tourism and interstate travel. . . . Many tourists travel to North Carolina from throughout the country for "howling events"—evenings of listening to wolf howls accompanied by educational programs. These howlings are a regular occurrence at the Alligator River National Wildlife Refuge. According to a study conducted by Dr. William E. Rosen of Cornell University, the recovery of the red wolf and increased visitor activities could result in a significant regional economic impact. Rosen estimates that northeastern

North Carolina could see an increase of between $39.61 and $183.65 million per year in tourism-related activities, and that the Great Smoky Mountains National Park could see an increase of between $132.09 and $354.50 million per year. This is hardly a trivial impact on interstate commerce. Appellants understandably seek to criticize the Rosen study, but concede that the howling events attract interstate tourism and that red wolf program volunteers come from all around the country.

Appellants argue that the tourism rationale relates only to howling events on national park land or wildlife refuges because people do not travel to private land. They reason that without tourism on private land the regulated activity does not substantially affect interstate commerce. Yet this argument misses the mark. Since reintroduction, red wolves have strayed from federal lands onto private lands. Indeed, wolves are known to be "great wanderers." See 60 Fed. Reg. 18,940, 18,943 (1995). In 1998, it was estimated that 41 of the 75 wolves in the wild now live on private land. Because so many members of this threatened species wander on private land, the regulation of takings on private land is essential to the entire program of reintroduction and eventual restoration of the species. Such regulation is necessary to conserve enough red wolves to sustain tourism. Appellants in fact seem unmindful of the history of endangered species regulation. The Endangered Species Acts of 1966 and 1969 initially targeted conservation efforts only on federal lands, but they met with limited success. See Note, Evolution of Wildlife Legislation in the United States: An Analysis of the Legal Efforts to Protect Endangered Species and the Prospects for the Future, 5 Geo. Int'l Envtl. L. Rev. 441, 449-53 (1993). The Endangered Species Act of 1973 was motivated in part by the need to extend takings regulation beyond the limited confines of federal land. The prohibition of takings on private land was critical to the overall success of the ESA in halting and reversing the near extinction of numerous species. See 16 U.S.C. §1538(a)(1). The success of many commercial enterprises depends on some regulation of activity on private land, and interstate tourism is no exception.

Tourism, however, is not the only interstate commercial activity affected by the taking of red wolves. The regulation of red wolf takings is also closely connected to a second interstate market—scientific research. Scientific research generates jobs. It also deepens our knowledge of the world in which we live. . . . Protection of the red wolves on private land thus encourages further research that may have inestimable future value, both for scientific knowledge as well as for commercial development of the red wolf. . . .

When enacting the ESA, various legislators expressed these exact concerns, namely that species be conserved for future scientific development:

> The value of this genetic heritage is, quite literally, incalculable. . . . From the most narrow possible point of view, it is in the best interests of mankind to minimize the losses of genetic variations. The reason is simple: they are potential resources. . . . Who knows, or can say, what potential cures for cancer or other scourges, present or future, may lie locked up in the structures of plants which may yet be undiscovered, much less analyzed? . . . Sheer self-interest impels us to be cautious. [H.R. Rep. No. 93-412, at 4-5 (1973).]

B.

This regulation is also sustainable as "an essential part of a larger regulation of economic activity, in which the regulatory scheme could be undercut unless the intrastate activity were regulated." *Lopez*, 514 U.S. at 561. The Supreme Court in Hodel v. Indiana stated: "A complex regulatory program . . . can survive a Commerce Clause challenge without a showing that every single facet of the program is independently and directly related to a valid congressional goal. It is enough that the challenged provisions are an integral part of the regulatory program and that the regulatory scheme when considered as a whole satisfies this test." 452 U.S. 314, 329 n.17 (1981). . . .

IV.

Upholding this regulation is consistent with the "first principles" of a Constitution that establishes a federal government of enumerated powers. See *Lopez*, 514 U.S. at 552. *Lopez* and *Morrison* properly emphasize that we must carefully evaluate legislation in light of our federal system of government. "The Constitution requires a distinction between what is truly national and what is truly local." *Morrison*, 529 U.S. at 617-18. We must particularly scrutinize regulated activity that "falls within an area of the law where States historically have been sovereign and countenance of the asserted federal power would blur the boundaries between the spheres of federal and state authority." *Brzonkala*, 169 F.3d at 837.

A.

It is imperative to set forth at the outset the historic roles of federal and state authority in this area. The regulated activity at issue here does not involve an "area of traditional state concern," one to which "States lay claim by right of history and expertise." *Lopez*, 514 U.S. at 580, 583 (Kennedy, J., concurring).

Appellants argue that the regulation infringes on the traditional state control over wildlife. We are cognizant that states play a most important role in regulating wildlife — many comprehensive state hunting and fishing laws attest to it. State control over wildlife, however, is circumscribed by federal regulatory power. In Minnesota v. Mille Lacs Band of Chippewa Indians, the Supreme Court recently reiterated that "[a]lthough States have important interests in regulating wildlife and natural resources within their borders, this authority is shared with the Federal Government when the Federal Government exercises one of its enumerated constitutional powers." 526 U.S. 172, 204 (1999). In *Mille Lacs*, the Court upheld Chippewa Indian rights under an 1837 treaty that allowed the Chippewa to hunt, fish, and gather free of territorial, and later state, regulation. These Indian treaty rights were found to be "reconcilable with state sovereignty over natural resources." Id. at 205.

It is true that in the nineteenth century courts followed the legal precept that wildlife was the property of the state. See Geer v. Connecticut, 161 U.S. 519 (1896) (upholding a Connecticut statute that prohibited the interstate transportation of game birds that had been killed within the state). But the principles in *Geer* were modified early in the twentieth century. See Hughes v. Oklahoma, 441 U.S. 322, 329 (1979) ("The erosion of *Geer* began only 15 years after it was decided."). *Geer* was finally overruled in 1979 by Hughes v. Oklahoma, which held that states do not own the wildlife within their borders and that state laws regulating wildlife are circumscribed by Congress's commerce power. 441 U.S. at 326, 335. In light of *Mille Lacs* and *Hughes*, the activity regulated by §17.84(c) — the taking of red wolves on private property—is not an area in which the states may assert an exclusive and traditional prerogative in derogation of an enumerated federal power.

Appellants next argue that the application of this regulation to private land intrudes on the state's traditional police power to regulate local land use. Of course, states and localities possess broad regulatory and zoning authority over land within their jurisdictions. See Village of Euclid v. Ambler Realty Co., 272 U.S. 365 (1926). It is well established, however, that Congress can regulate even private land use for environmental and wildlife conservation. Courts have consistently upheld Congress's authority to regulate private activities in order to conserve species and protect the environment. For example, in a post-*Lopez* challenge to CERCLA, the Eleventh Circuit held that the private, on-site, intrastate disposal of hazardous waste was within Congress's authority to regulate because such disposal "significantly impacts interstate commerce." United States v. Olin Corp., 107 F.3d 1506, 1510 (11th Cir. 1997). In *Sweet Home*, the Supreme Court upheld a FWS regulation defining "harm" in the Endangered Species Act to include "significant habitat modification." 515 U.S. at 697. The regulation applied equally to private and public land. See id. at 692 (challenge brought by small landowners and logging companies). Here, the FWS similarly acted within its authority in determining that conservation of the red wolf population requires prohibiting certain takings on private land surrounding the refuges. See 51 Fed. Reg. 41,790, 41,792-93 (1986). . . .

In contrast to gender-motivated violence or guns in school yards, the conservation of scarce natural resources is an appropriate and well-recognized area of federal regulation. The federal government has been involved in a variety of conservation efforts since the beginning of this century. In 1900, Congress passed the Lacey Act, which provided penalties for the taking of wildlife in violation of state laws. See 16 U.S.C. §701. The Migratory Bird Treaty Act of 1918 forbade all takings of numerous bird species and explicitly preempted state laws. See 16 U.S.C. §§703-12. Furthermore, Congress has regulated wildlife on nonfederal property through numerous statutes, including the Bald Eagle Protection Act of 1940, which prohibits, *inter alia*, the taking, possession, selling, or exporting of bald eagles or any of their parts. See 16 U.S.C. §§668-668d. Similarly, the Marine Mammal Protection Act of 1972 regulates the taking of marine mammals and restricts the importing of marine mammals and their products through an elaborate system of permits. See 16 U.S.C. §§1361-1421h. The Magnuson Fishery Conservation and Management Act of 1976 provides national standards for fishery conservation and management along with an elaborate system of enforcement. See 16 U.S.C. §§1801-1883.

The Supreme Court has repeatedly upheld these statutes and the conservation efforts of Congress with regard to a variety of animal species. In Missouri v. Holland, the Court upheld the Migratory Bird Treaty Act as a necessary and proper means of executing Congress's treaty power. The conservation of endangered wildlife, Justice Holmes stated, was a "matter[] of the sharpest exigency for national well being." 252 U.S. 416, 432-33 (1920). In 1977, the Supreme Court held that Congress had the power under the Commerce Clause to grant federal fishing licenses for use in state waters, thereby preempting conflicting state laws. See Douglas v. Seacoast Products, Inc., 431 U.S. 265 (1977). Later in Andrus v. Allard, the Court emphasized that the "assumption that the national commerce power does not reach migratory wildlife is clearly flawed." 444 U.S. 51, 63 n.19 (1979).

Post-*Lopez* cases addressing wildlife conservation statutes do not call these cases into question, but rather uphold the exercise of agency power over private land use in order to conserve endangered species. In *Sweet Home*, for example, the Court upheld the Service's broad definition of "harm" in the ESA as including "significant habitat modification." 515 U.S. at 708. The lower courts have followed suit, both before and after *Lopez*. For example, in United States v. Hartsell, this court reaffirmed that Congress retains authority to regulate even non-navigable waters under the Commerce Clause. 127 F.3d 343, 348 & n.1 (4th Cir. 1997). The Ninth Circuit reaffirmed that the Bald Eagle Protection Act is a valid exercise of the commerce power because Congress had a rational basis for concluding that "extinction of the eagle would have a substantial effect on interstate commerce." See *Bramble*, 103 F.3d at 1482. In sum, it is clear from our laws and precedent that federal regulation of endangered wildlife does not trench impermissibly upon state powers. Rather, the federal government possesses a historic interest in such regulation—an interest that has repeatedly been recognized by the federal courts.

B.

It is important not simply to point to the historic fact of federal efforts in the area of resource conservation. Courts have respected the justifications for these federal efforts as well.

The Supreme Court has recognized that protection of natural resources may require action from Congress. This general point holds true where endangered species are concerned. Species conservation may unfortunately impose additional costs on private concerns. States may decide to forgo or limit conservation efforts in order to lower these costs, and other states may be forced to follow suit in order to compete. The Supreme Court has held that Congress may take cognizance of this dynamic and arrest the "race to the bottom" in order to prevent interstate competition whose overall effect would damage the quality of the national environment. In Hodel v. Virginia Surface Mining and Reclamation Ass'n, the Court upheld provisions of the Surface Mining Control and Reclamation Act of 1977 that regulated intrastate mining activities. 452 U.S. 264 (1981). The Court deferred to a congressional finding that nationwide standards were "essential" to insuring that competition in interstate commerce among sellers of coal would not be used to undermine environmental standards. See id. at 281-82. Congress expressed concern that such competition would disable states from improving and maintaining "adequate standards on coal mining operations within their borders." Id. The Court emphasized, "The prevention of this sort of destructive interstate competition is a traditional role for congressional action under the commerce clause." . . .

[The majority then addresses the arguments of Judge Luttig's dissent, closing with the following statement.]

Of course natural resource conservation is economic and commercial. If we were to decide that this regulation lacked a substantial effect on commerce and therefore was invalid, we would open the door to standardless judicial rejection of democratic initiatives of all sorts. Courts need not side with one party or the other on the wisdom of this endangered species regulation. We hold only as a basic maxim of judicial restraint that Congress may constitutionally address the problem of protecting endangered species in the manner undertaken herein. The political, not the judicial, process is the appropriate arena for the resolution of this particular dispute. The judgment of the district court is accordingly

AFFIRMED.

LUTTIG, J., dissenting.

[After providing a recapitulation of the majority's arguments and his own distillation of the Supreme Court's major federalism decisions, the dissent continues as follows.]

That these [majority opinion] conclusions are not even arguably sustainable under *Lopez*, *Morrison*, and *Brzonkala*, much less for the reasons cobbled together by the majority, is evident from the mere recitation of the conclusions. The killing of even all 41 of the estimated red wolves that live on private property in North Carolina would not constitute an economic activity of the kind held by the Court in *Lopez* and in *Morrison* to be of central concern to the Commerce Clause, if it could be said to constitute an economic activity at all. *Morrison*, 529 U.S. at 610 ("[A] fair reading of *Lopez* shows that the noneconomic, criminal nature of the conduct at issue was central to our decision in that case."). It is for this reason that the majority's attempted aggregation is impermissible: "While we need not adopt a categorical rule against aggregating the effects of any noneconomic activity in order to decide these cases, thus far in our Nation's history our cases have upheld Commerce Clause regulation of intrastate activity only where that activity is economic in nature." *Id.* at 613. But even assuming that such is an economic activity, it certainly is not an activity that has a substantial effect on interstate commerce. The number of inferences (not even to mention the amount of speculation) necessary to discern in this activity a substantial effect on interstate commerce is exponentially greater than the number necessary in *Lopez* to show a substantial effect on interstate commerce from the sale of guns near schools or in *Morrison* to show a substantial effect on interstate commerce from domestic assault. The number (and the speculation) is even greater than that necessary in Wickard v. Filburn, 317 U.S. 111 (1942). And, it bears reminding, the regulated activity in *Lopez* and *Wickard* at least was in some sense economic in character.

In a word, the expansive view of the Commerce power expressed by the majority today is . . . a view far more expansive than that expressed by any of the dissenting Justices in either *Lopez* or *Morrison*—a fact confirmed by the dissents in *Morrison*, ironically the case for which the majority herein unnecessarily held this case in abeyance. See Order of April 21, 2000 (Luttig, J., dissenting from abeyance order). . . .

Indeed, if the Supreme Court were to render tomorrow the identical opinion that the majority does today (not necessarily the decision, but the opinion, worded capaciously as it is), both *Lopez* and *Morrison* would be consigned to aberration. . . .

Nor, in the wake of *Lopez* and *Morrison*, can I accept my colleagues' view of the appropriate role of the judiciary in Commerce Clause disputes. As Judge Wilkinson's view of *Lopez* mirrors that of the dissenters in *Lopez* and *Morrison*, so also does my colleagues' view of the judiciary's role in Commerce Clause conflicts mirror that of the *Lopez* and *Morrison* dissenters. The majority herein, like the dissents in both *Lopez* and *Morrison*, takes the view that the political processes are the safeguard against federal encroachment upon the states. . . . The majority of the Supreme Court in *Lopez* and *Morrison* has left no doubt, however, that the interpretation of this clause of the Constitution, no less so than any other, must ultimately rest not with the political branches, but with the judiciary. See *Lopez*, 514 U.S. 549, 557 n.2 ("[W]hether particular operations affect interstate commerce sufficiently to come under the constitutional power of Congress to regulate them is ultimately a judicial rather than a legislative question, and can be settled finally only by this Court.") (quoting Heart of Atlanta Motel v. United States, 379 U.S. 241, 273, 85 (1964) (Black, J., concurring)); *Morrison*, 529 U.S. at 616 n.7 ("Departing from their parliamentary past, the Framers adopted a written Constitution that further divided authority at the federal level so that the Constitution's provisions would not be defined solely by the political branches nor the scope of legislative power limited only by public opinion and the legislature's self-restraint. See, e.g., Marbury v. Madison, 1 Cranch 137, 176 (1803) (Marshall, C.J.).").

Accordingly, I would faithfully apply in this case the Supreme Court's landmark decisions in *Lopez* and *Morrison*, as I would in any other case. The affirmative reach and the negative limits of the Commerce Clause do not wax and wane depending upon the subject matter of the particular legislation under challenge.

NOTES AND QUESTIONS: POWER AND THE ANALYTICAL FRAMEWORK

1. *Is the ESA Constitutional?* For discussions of the constitutionality of the ESA, see Mank, Protecting Intrastate Threatened Species: Does the Endangered Species Act Encroach on Traditional State Authority and Exceed the Outer Limits of the Commerce Clause?, 36 Ga. L. Rev. 723 (2002); and Nagle, The Commerce Clause Meets the Delhi Sands Flower-Loving Fly, 97 Mich. L. Rev. 174 (1998).

2. *Analytical Frameworks and Perspectives in Commerce Clause Challenges.* Judges Wilkinson and Luttig are both renowned conservative judges. Both were mentioned as potential Supreme Court Justices when President George W. Bush filled vacancies with Chief Justice Roberts and Justice Alito. Nevertheless, they disagree about far more than just the conclusion in this case. How does each approach his Commerce Clause analysis? Do they each assume that the Commerce Clause requires judicial scrutiny of one sort of "activity," or numerous sorts of activities implicated by the law? Which sort of review empowers the courts, and which leads to a more deferential mode of review? See Schapiro & Buzbee, Unidimensional Federalism: Power and Perspective in Commerce Clause Adjudication, 88 Cornell L. Rev. 1199 (2003), arguing that the judicial search for the relevant "activity" should consider the "impetus" for the legislation, "political motivation" for the law, and the activity "targeted" by the legislation—typically activity that causes harm or requires modification to maximize social welfare—as well as benefits and other effects that would flow from regulation. Under this view, a law will usually implicate several sorts of activities that might suffice to pass Commerce Clause muster. Which judge adopts a similar approach?

A second major issue concerns whether judges should assess constitutionality under the Commerce Clause by looking at activities in the aggregate or as part of a comprehensive scheme of regulation or (at the other end of the spectrum) application by application. What difference do these two approaches make? See note 3 below for more regarding the "comprehensive scheme" rationale.

3. Raich *and the Issue of "Comprehensive Schemes" and Aggregation: Classes of Activities, or an Individualized Focus?* Since *Gibbs*, and several years after *Lopez* and *Morrison*, the Supreme Court decided Gonzales v. Raich, 545 U.S. 1 (2006), a case involving a challenge to the constitutionality of a federal law, the Controlled

Substances Act, criminalizing local and home-grown marijuana use for medicinal purposes, even where allowed by a California state law. In language that surely would have influenced the terms of the earlier *Gibbs* majority and dissenting opinions, the Court rejected the challenge, stating

> Our case law firmly establishes Congress' power to regulate purely local activities that are part of an economic "class of activities" that have a substantial effect on interstate commerce. See, e.g., *Perez*, 402 U.S., at 151; Wickard v. Filburn, 317 U.S. 111, 128-129 (1942). As we stated in *Wickard*, "even if appellee's activity be local and though it may not be regarded as commerce, it may still, whatever its nature, be reached by Congress if it exerts a substantial economic effect on interstate commerce." Id., at 125. We have never required Congress to legislate with scientific exactitude. When Congress decides that the "'total incidence'" of a practice poses a threat to a national market, it may regulate the entire class. See Perez v. United States, 402 U.S. [146], at 154-155 [1971]. . . . *Wickard* thus establishes that Congress can regulate purely intrastate activity that is not itself "commercial," in that it is not produced for sale, if it concludes that failure to regulate that class of activity would undercut the regulation of the interstate market in that commodity. . . . Here [as in *Wickard*], Congress had a rational basis for concluding that leaving home-consumed marijuana outside federal control would similarly affect price and market conditions. . . .
>
> In assessing the scope of Congress' authority under the Commerce Clause, we stress that the task before us is a modest one. We need not determine whether respondents' activities, taken in the aggregate, substantially affect interstate commerce in fact, but only whether a "rational basis" exists for so concluding. *Lopez*, 514 U.S., at 557. Given the enforcement difficulties that attend distinguishing between marijuana cultivated locally and marijuana grown elsewhere, 21 U.S.C. §801(5), and concerns about diversion into illicit channels, we have no difficulty concluding that Congress had a rational basis for believing that failure to regulate the intrastate manufacture and possession of marijuana would leave a gaping hole in the CSA. . . .
>
> . . . Here, respondents ask us to excise individual applications of a concededly valid statutory scheme. In contrast, in both *Lopez* and *Morrison*, the parties asserted that a particular statute or provision fell outside Congress' commerce power in its entirety. This distinction is pivotal for we have often reiterated that "[w]here the class of activities is regulated and that class is within the reach of federal power, the courts have no power 'to excise, as trivial, individual instances' of the class." *Perez*, 402 U.S., at 154. [*Raich*, 545 U.S. at 17-23.]

In light of *Raich*, do you think Judge Luttig or Chief Judge Wilkinson has the better argument? What are the implications of *Raich* for attacks on environmental laws viewed as being at the cusp of federal power? See Blumm & Kimbrell, Gonzales v. Raich, the "Comprehensive Scheme" Principle, and the Constitutionality of the Endangered Species Act, 35 Envtl. L. 491 (2005).

4. *The Unclear Role of Legislative Findings and a Supporting Legislative Record.* In *Raich*, the Court stated the following about the effect of legislative findings:

> Findings in the introductory sections of the CSA explain why Congress deemed it appropriate to encompass local activities within the scope of the CSA. The submissions of the parties and the numerous amici all seem to agree that the national, and international, market for marijuana has dimensions that are fully comparable to those defining the class of activities regulated by the Secretary pursuant to the 1938 statute. Respondents nonetheless insist that the CSA cannot be constitutionally applied to their activities because Congress did not make a specific finding that the

intrastate cultivation and possession of marijuana for medical purposes based on the recommendation of a physician would substantially affect the larger interstate marijuana market. Be that as it may, we have never required Congress to make particularized findings in order to legislate, see *Lopez*, 514 U.S., at 562; *Perez*, 402 U.S., at 156, absent a special concern such as the protection of free speech, see, e.g., Turner Broadcasting System, Inc. v. FCC, 512 U.S. 622, 664-668 (1994) (plurality opinion). While congressional findings are certainly helpful in reviewing the substance of a congressional statutory scheme, particularly when the connection to commerce is not self-evident, and while we will consider congressional findings in our analysis when they are available, the absence of particularized findings does not call into question Congress' authority to legislate. [545 U.S. at 20-21.]

This language about findings appears to be less a resolution than yet another salvo in an ongoing Court battle about how, if at all, Congress needs to create a record or include findings for its laws to satisfy constitutional scrutiny. This question has arisen in straightforward Commerce Clause attacks, as in *Lopez* and *Raich*, but also in cases involving claims of state discrimination and, therefore, constitutional scrutiny under §5 of the Fourteenth Amendment.* The lack of an adequate "record" has proved fatal in several recent cases, see, e.g., United States v. Morrison, 529 U.S. 598 (2000); Board of Trustees of the Univ. of Ala. v. Garrett, 531 U.S. 356 (2001); but in Nevada v. Hibbs, 538 U.S. at 721 (2003), over scathing dissents, the record was found adequate in an opinion authored by Chief Justice Rehnquist to justify holding states liable for violation of the Family Medical Leave Act. This vote and opinion were a surprise to many; Rehnquist had in numerous cases since *Lopez* joined four other justices in striking down federal laws.

While the Court has repeatedly said "findings" are not required, this new judicial scrutiny of the record has changed how courts review the basis for legislative action, especially in settings implicating federalism concerns. Numerous scholars have questioned the appropriateness of such record review in light of the realities of the legislative process and the capabilities of the courts:

Legislative record review . . . represents a novel mode of judicial review that limits congressional power in crucial respects. This kind of review threatens to impose procedural and substantive constraints on legislative action that have no support in precedent or in constitutional text or structure. Moreover, the Court's reliance on the concept of "the legislative record," in the sense of a comprehensive set of documents reflecting the full scope of congressional deliberations underlying a statute, is fundamentally flawed on the most basic level. This kind of "legislative record" simply does not exist. The entire concept of a legislative record constitutes an inappropriate importation from different institutional settings of the expectation that a written record will justify a legal judgment. Congress acts on the basis of a wide variety of information, concerns, and interests. Informal contacts and latent policy judgments serve as key determinants of legislative conduct. The Court's new legislative record review seeks to reduce the legislative crucible to a written, comprehensive record. Such a process will not be "legislative" as we currently understand that term. In short, "the legislative record" is fundamentally

---

*As you may recall from your constitutional law courses, where state sovereignty is implicated, especially where citizens seek damages from a state, federal power under the Commerce Clause is not the end of the necessary analysis. State sovereign immunity still must be overcome, requiring judicial scrutiny under §5 of the Fourteenth Amendment to see if Congress had an adequate basis for impinging on state sovereignty. City of Boerne v. Flores, 521 U.S. 507 (1997); Seminole Tribe v. Florida, 517 U.S. 44 (1996).

incoherent. To render the concept coherent would require a transformation of legislation. [Buzbee & Schapiro, Legislative Record Review, 54 Stan. L. Rev. 87, 90 (2001).]*

If the Court returns to engaging in close scrutiny of legislative findings and the so-called record, what might the implications be for challenges to environmental laws that were generally passed over a decade ago, many involving legislative judgments made despite great uncertainty about their underlying science?

5. *The Losing Track Record of Commerce Clause Challenges to Environmental Laws.* Despite the Supreme Court's federalism revival imposing new limits on federal power, Commerce Clause challenges to federal environmental laws have so far failed. For example, largely due to hazardous wastes' largely stationary state, the federal CERCLA law was challenged as being beyond federal power. The Eleventh Circuit rejected that argument, focusing on how on- or off-site disposal of hazardous wastes can substantially affect commerce. United States v. Olin, 107 F.3d 1506 (11th Cir. 1997). Other Endangered Species Act challenges have, as in *Gibbs*, met with little success. See Rancho Viejo v. Norton, 323 F.3d 1062 (D.C. Cir. 2003); National Ass'n of Homebuilders v. Babbitt, 130 F.3d 1041 (D.C. Cir. 1997). As covered in the next section, constitutional challenges to the reach of the Clean Water Act have also failed in direct attacks, but nevertheless changed the reach of the law by influencing statutory interpretation of the Act.

C. FEDERAL POWER AND INTERPRETATION: COMMERCE CONCERNS AS A TIEBREAKER

So far, direct attacks on the Commerce Clause basis for federal environmental legislation have generally failed to elicit judicial declarations of unconstitutionality. Even if this continues to happen, it would be a mistake to assume that Commerce Clause arguments are therefore of little importance. As you will see in the following short excerpts from two recent Supreme Court cases, Commerce Clause concerns and claims that federal power is at its limit have the potential to make a major difference. These two cases are excerpted and covered at greater length in Chapter 7, among materials about the Clean Water Act and §404 "dredge and fill" permits. Section 404's requirements greatly limit the circumstances when wetlands and other waters can be destroyed or impaired. Due to real estate industry and agricultural interest in developing or using areas classified as wetlands or "waters of the United States" under the Clean Water Act, §404 has been repeatedly subjected to constitutional attack.

---

*For other critiques of the Court's new scrutiny of findings and the record, see Bryant & Simeone, Remanding to Congress: The Supreme Court's New "On the Record" Constitutional Review of Federal Statutes, 86 Cornell L. Rev. 328 (2001); Colker & Brudney, Dissing Congress, 100 Mich. L. Rev. 80 (2001); Frickey, The Fool on the Hill: Congressional Findings, Constitutional Adjudication, and United States v. Lopez, 46 Case W. Res. L. Rev. 695 (1996); Frickey & Smith, Judicial Review, the Congressional Process, and the Federalism Cases: An Interdisciplinary Critique, 111 Yale L.J. 1707 (2002); Post & Siegel, Equal Protection by Law: Federal Antidiscrimination Legislation After *Morrison* and *Kimel*, 110 Yale L.J. 441, 461 (2000).

SOLID WASTE AGENCY OF NORTHERN COOK COUNTY v.
U.S. ARMY CORPS OF ENGINEERS
531 U.S. 159 (2001)

CHIEF JUSTICE REHNQUIST delivered the opinion of the Court.

. . . Respondents—relying upon all of the arguments addressed above—contend that, at the very least, it must be said that Congress did not address the precise question of §404(a)'s scope with regard to nonnavigable, isolated, intrastate waters, and that, therefore, we should give deference to the "Migratory Bird Rule." See, e.g., Chevron U.S.A. Inc. v. Natural Resources Defense Council, Inc., 467 U.S. 837 (1984). We find §404(a) to be clear, but even were we to agree with respondents, we would not extend *Chevron* deference here.

Where an administrative interpretation of a statute invokes the outer limits of Congress' power, we expect a clear indication that Congress intended that result. See Edward J. DeBartolo Corp. v. Florida Gulf Coast Building & Constr. Trades Council, 485 U.S. 568, 575 (1988). This requirement stems from our prudential desire not to needlessly reach constitutional issues and our assumption that Congress does not casually authorize administrative agencies to interpret a statute to push the limit of congressional authority. This concern is heightened where the administrative interpretation alters the federal-state framework by permitting federal encroachment upon a traditional state power. See United States v. Bass, 404 U.S. 336, 349 (1971) ("[U]nless Congress conveys its purpose clearly, it will not be deemed to have significantly changed the federal-state balance"). Thus, "where an otherwise acceptable construction of a statute would raise serious constitutional problems, the Court will construe the statute to avoid such problems unless such construction is plainly contrary to the intent of Congress." *DeBartolo, supra*, at 575.

Twice in the past six years we have reaffirmed the proposition that the grant of authority to Congress under the Commerce Clause, though broad, is not unlimited. See United States v. Morrison, 529 U.S. 598 (2000); United States v. Lopez, 514 U.S. 549 (1995). Respondents argue that the "Migratory Bird Rule" falls within Congress' power to regulate intrastate activities that "substantially affect" interstate commerce. They note that the protection of migratory birds is a "national interest of very nearly the first magnitude," Missouri v. Holland, 252 U.S. 416, 435 (1920), and that, as the Court of Appeals found, millions of people spend over a billion dollars annually on recreational pursuits relating to migratory birds. These arguments raise significant constitutional questions. For example, we would have to evaluate the precise object or activity that, in the aggregate, substantially affects interstate commerce. This is not clear, for although the Corps has claimed jurisdiction over petitioner's land because it contains water areas used as habitat by migratory birds, respondents now, *post litem motam*, focus upon the fact that the regulated activity is petitioner's municipal landfill, which is "plainly of a commercial nature." Brief for Federal Respondents 43. But this is a far cry, indeed, from the "navigable waters" and "waters of the United States" to which the statute by its terms extends.

These are significant constitutional questions raised by respondents' application of their regulations, and yet we find nothing approaching a clear statement from Congress that it intended §404(a) to reach an abandoned sand and gravel pit such as we have here. Permitting respondents to claim federal jurisdiction over ponds and mudflats falling within the "Migratory Bird Rule" would result in a significant impingement of the States' traditional and primary power over land and water use. See, e.g., Hess v. Port Auth. Trans-Hudson Corp., 513 U.S. 30, 44 (1994) ("[R]egulation of land use [is] a function traditionally performed by local governments"). Rather than expressing a desire to readjust the federal-state balance in this manner, Congress chose to "recognize, preserve, and protect the primary responsibilities and rights of States . . . to plan the development and use . . . of land and water resources. . . ." 33 U.S.C. §1251(b). We thus read the statute as written to avoid the significant constitutional and federalism questions raised by respondents' interpretation, and therefore reject the request for administrative deference.

RAPANOS v. UNITED STATES
126 S. Ct. 2208 (2006)

[*Rapanos* and its companion case, *Carabell*, also involve questions about the statutory and constitutional reach of the Clean Water Act. In these consolidated cases, the Court had to construe the statutory definition of "navigable waters" as "waters of the United States" in connection with federal claims of jurisdiction over tributaries and wetlands adjacent to tributaries feeding into navigable-in-fact waters. The Court ended up splitting into a confusing 4-1-4 grouping, with five justices agreeing to a judgment requiring the courts and likely agency below on remand to better establish its jurisdiction, but no opinion for the Court. The middle opinion, by Justice Kennedy, agreed with this judgment but disagreed with virtually all of Justice Scalia's opinion, instead repeatedly adopting logic and language from the four-justice dissenting opinion penned by Justice Stevens. For reasons that will be explored in greater depth in the Chapter 7 coverage of wetlands protection, Justice Kennedy's opinion is viewed by most as the key opinion for future application by agencies and lower courts. Still, the disagreement between Justices Scalia and Kennedy concerning how federalism concerns should drive certain interpretations provides a strong reminder of how federalism concerns can have great power, even without any declaration of unconstitutionality.]

JUSTICE SCALIA announced the judgment of the court, delivered an opinion, which the CHIEF JUSTICE, JUSTICE THOMAS and JUSTICE ALITO join.

. . . Even if the phrase "the waters of the United States" were ambiguous as applied to intermittent flows, our own canons of construction would establish that the Corps' interpretation of the statute is impermissible. As we noted in SWANCC, the Government's expansive interpretation would "result in a significant impingement of the States' traditional and primary power over land and water use." 531 U.S., at 174. Regulation of land use, as through the issuance of the development permits sought by petitioners in both of these cases, is a quintessential state and local power. See FERC v. Mississippi, 456 U.S. 742, 768, n.30 (1982); Hess v. Port Auth. Trans-Hudson Corp., 513 U.S. 30, 44 (1994). The extensive federal jurisdiction urged by the Government would authorize the Corps to function as a de facto regulator of immense stretches of intrastate land—an authority the agency has shown its willingness to exercise with the scope of discretion that would befit a local zoning board. See 33 CFR §320.4(a)(1) (2004). We ordinarily expect a "clear and manifest" statement from Congress to authorize an unprecedented intrusion into traditional state authority. See BFP v. Resolution Trust Corp., 511 U.S. 531, 544 (1994). The phrase "the waters of the United States" hardly qualifies.

Likewise, just as we noted in SWANCC, the Corps' interpretation stretches the outer limits of Congress's commerce power and raises difficult questions about the ultimate scope of that power. See 531 U.S., at 173. (In developing the current regulations, the Corps consciously sought to extend its authority to the farthest reaches of the commerce power. See 42 Fed. Reg. 37,127 (1977).) Even if the term "the waters of the United States" were ambiguous as applied to channels that sometimes host ephemeral flows of water (which it is not), we would expect a clearer statement from Congress to authorize an agency theory of jurisdiction that presses the envelope of constitutional validity. See Edward J. DeBartolo Corp. v. Florida Gulf Coast Building & Constr. Trades Council, 485 U.S. 568, 575 (1988).[9] . . .

JUSTICE KENNEDY, concurring in the judgment. . . .

. . . With these concerns in mind, the Corps' definition of adjacency is a reasonable one, for it may be the absence of an interchange of waters prior to the dredge and fill activity that makes protection of the wetlands critical to the statutory scheme.

In sum the plurality's opinion is inconsistent with the Act's text, structure, and purpose. As a fallback the plurality suggests that avoidance canons would compel its reading even if the text were unclear. . . . In SWANCC, as one reason for rejecting the Corps' assertion of jurisdiction over the isolated ponds at issue there, the Court observed that this "application of [the Corps'] regulations" would raise significant questions of Commerce Clause authority and encroach on traditional state land-use regulation. 531 U.S., at 174. As SWANCC observed, and as the plurality points out here, the Act states that "[i]t is the policy of the Congress to recognize, preserve, and protect the primary responsibilities and rights of States to prevent, reduce, and eliminate pollution, [and] to plan the development and use . . . of land and water resources," 33 U.S.C. §1251(b). The Court in SWANCC cited this provision as evidence that a clear statement supporting jurisdiction in applications raising constitutional and federalism difficulties was lacking. 531 U.S., at 174.

The concerns addressed in SWANCC do not support the plurality's interpretation of the Act. In SWANCC, by interpreting the Act to require a significant nexus with navigable waters, the Court avoided applications—those involving waters without a significant nexus—that appeared likely, as a category, to raise constitutional difficulties and federalism concerns. Here, in contrast, the plurality's interpretation does not fit the avoidance concerns it raises. On the one hand, when a surface-water connection is lacking, the plurality forecloses jurisdiction over wetlands that abut navigable-in-fact waters—even though such navigable waters were traditionally subject to federal authority. On the other hand, by saying the Act covers wetlands (however remote) possessing a surface-water connection with a continuously flowing stream (however small), the plurality's reading would permit applications of the statute

9. JUSTICE KENNEDY objects that our reliance on these two clear-statement rules is inappropriate because "the plurality's interpretation does not fit the avoidance concerns that it raises"—that is, because our resolution both eliminates some jurisdiction that is clearly constitutional and traditionally federal, and retains some that is questionably constitutional and traditionally local. But a clear-statement rule can carry one only so far as the statutory text permits. Our resolution, unlike JUSTICE KENNEDY's, keeps both the overinclusion and the underinclusion to the minimum consistent with the statutory text. JUSTICE KENNEDY's reading—despite disregarding the text—fares no better than ours as a precise "fit" for the "avoidance concerns" that he also acknowledges. He admits that "the significant nexus requirement may not align perfectly with the traditional extent of federal authority" over navigable waters—an admission that "tests the limits of understatement," Gonzales v. Oregon, 126 S. Ct. 904, 932 (2005) (SCALIA, J., dissenting)—and it aligns even worse with the preservation of traditional state land-use regulation.

as far from traditional federal authority as are the waters it deems beyond the statute's reach. Even assuming, then, that federal regulation of remote wetlands and nonnavigable waterways would raise a difficult Commerce Clause issue notwithstanding those waters' aggregate effects on national water quality, but cf. Wickard v. Filburn, 317 U.S. 111 (1942); . . . the plurality's reading is not responsive to this concern. As for States' "responsibilities and rights," §1251(b), it is noteworthy that 33 States plus the District of Columbia have filed an amici brief in this litigation asserting that the Clean Water Act is important to their own water policies. These amici note, among other things, that the Act protects downstream States from out-of-state pollution that they cannot themselves regulate. . . .

NOTE

In his SWANCC dissent, joined by three other justices, Justice Stevens disputed the majority's characterization of §404 as intruding on a traditional area of state regulation of land use. Instead, he characterized the Clean Water Act and §404 as targeting water pollution. Do you see any problems with the Supreme Court's interpretations of federal environmental laws hinging on how they characterize the nature of that law, as well as on how the Court characterizes related or overlapping areas of state law? How about the Court's use of provisions preserving state roles? Is this area of law predictable? What incentives does the SWANCC Court create for legislators eager to pass federal law but also willing to preserve state authority?

D. SECURING STATE COOPERATION

Even if the federal government has the power to enact federal law, a separate issue is how the federal government can secure state cooperation in achieving federal goals. As this section and the sections that follow establish, states stand in a special, privileged position under our Constitution. Especially during the past couple of decades, an array of Supreme Court decisions has solidified the states' special status and the federal government's limited ability to impinge on state interests. This section starts with one of the most important federalism cases, New York v. United States, 505 U.S. 144 (1992), and the Court's articulation of the means by which the federal government can secure state cooperation without running afoul of principles of state sovereignty and a federal government of limited power. We then, in notes, look at successor cases to New York, as well as undertaking a closer examination of these additional means through which the federal government can attempt to entice states to cooperate.

NEW YORK v. UNITED STATES
505 U.S. 144 (1992)

O'CONNOR, J., delivered the opinion of the Court.

These cases implicate one of our Nation's newest problems of public policy and perhaps our oldest question of constitutional law. The public policy issue involves the disposal of radioactive waste: In these cases, we address the constitutionality of three provisions of the Low-Level Radioactive Waste Policy Amendments Act of 1985, 42 U.S.C. §2021b et seq. The constitutional question is as old as the Constitution: It consists of discerning the proper division of authority between the Federal Government and the States. We conclude that while Congress has substantial power under the Constitution to encourage the States to provide for the disposal of the radioactive waste generated within their borders, the Constitution does not confer upon Congress the ability simply to compel the States to do so. We therefore find that only two of the Act's three provisions at issue are consistent with the Constitution's allocation of power to the Federal Government.

I.

[Concerned about the possibility of a shortage of disposal sites for low-level radioactive waste, Congress enacted the Low-Level Radioactive Waste Policy Amendments Act of 1985. In its provisions, states that had borne the brunt of the nation's disposal responsibilities agreed to continue to accept waste for seven more years. In exchange, states without their own disposal sites agreed to end their reliance on the other states by 1992. The Act provided three types of incentives to ensure that the unsited states met their obligations under the bargain. States that met the statutory deadlines received monetary rewards. States that failed to make progress by certain dates were subject to reduced access to disposal sites. States that failed to account for all the waste generated within their borders by 1996 were required, upon the request of the generator of the waste, "[to] take title to the waste, be obligated to take possession of the waste, and shall be liable for all damages directly or indirectly incurred by such generator or owner as a consequence of the failure of the State to take possession of the waste. . . ." §2021e(d)(2)(C). Petitioners argued that the Act was unconstitutional under the Tenth Amendment and the Guarantee Clause.]

. . . The Act provides three types of incentives to encourage the States to comply with their statutory obligation to provide for the disposal of waste generated within their borders.

1. *Monetary incentives.* One quarter of the surcharges collected by the sited States must be transferred to an escrow account held by the Secretary of Energy. §2021e(d)(2)(A). The Secretary then makes payments from this account to each State that has complied with a series of deadlines. . . . Each State that has not met the 1993 deadline must either take title to the waste generated within its borders or forfeit to the waste generators the incentive payments it has received. §2021e(d)(2)(C).

2. *Access incentives.* The second type of incentive involves the denial of access to disposal sites. States that fail to meet the July 1986 deadline may be charged twice the ordinary surcharge for the remainder of 1986 and may be denied access to disposal facilities thereafter. §2021e(e)(2)(A). States that fail to meet the 1988 deadline may be charged double surcharges for the first half of 1988 and quadruple surcharges for the second half of 1988, and may be denied access thereafter. §2021e(e)(2)(B). States that fail to meet the 1990 deadline may be denied access. §2021e(e)(2)(C). Finally, States that have not filed complete applications by January 1, 1992, for a license to operate a disposal facility, or States belonging to compacts that have not filed such applications, may be charged triple surcharges. §§2021e(e)(1)(D), 2021e(e)(2)(D).

3. *The take title provision.* The third type of incentive is the most severe. The Act provides:

> If a State (or, where applicable, a compact region) in which low-level radioactive waste is generated is unable to provide for the disposal of all such waste generated within such State or compact region by January 1, 1996, each State in which such waste is generated, upon the request of the generator or owner of the waste, shall take title to the waste, be obligated to take possession of the waste, and shall be liable for all damages directly or indirectly incurred by such generator or owner as a consequence of the failure of the State to take possession of the waste as soon after January 1, 1996, as the generator or owner notifies the State that the waste is available for shipment. §2021e(d)(2)(C).

These three incentives are the focus of petitioners' constitutional challenge. . . .

Petitioners have abandoned their due process and Eleventh Amendment claims on their way up the appellate ladder; as the cases stand before us, petitioners claim only that the Act is inconsistent with the Tenth Amendment and the Guarantee Clause.

II.

A.

In 1788, in the course of explaining to the citizens of New York why the recently drafted Constitution provided for federal courts, Alexander Hamilton observed: "The erection of a new government, whatever care or wisdom may distinguish the work, cannot fail to originate questions of intricacy and nicety; and these may, in a particular manner, be expected to flow from the establishment of a constitution founded upon the total or partial incorporation of a number of distinct sovereignties." The Federalist No. 82, p. 491 (C. Rossiter ed. 1961). Hamilton's prediction has proved quite accurate. While no one disputes the proposition that "[t]he Constitution created a Federal Government of limited powers," Gregory v. Ashcroft, 501 U.S. 452, 457 (1991); and while the Tenth Amendment makes explicit that "[t]he powers not delegated to the United States by the Constitution, nor prohibited by it to the States, are reserved to the States respectively, or to the people"; the task of ascertaining the constitutional line between federal and state power has given rise to many of the Court's most difficult and celebrated cases. . . .

It is in this sense that the Tenth Amendment "states but a truism that all is retained which has not been surrendered." United States v. Darby, 312 U.S. 100, 124 (1941). As Justice Story put it, "[t]his amendment is a mere affirmation of what, upon any just reasoning, is a necessary rule of interpreting the constitution. Being an instrument of limited and enumerated powers, it follows irresistibly, that what is not conferred, is withheld, and belongs to the state authorities." 3 J. Story, Commentaries on the Constitution of the United States 752 (1833). This has been the Court's consistent understanding: "The States unquestionably do retai[n] a significant measure of sovereign authority . . . to the extent that the Constitution has not divested them of their original powers and transferred those powers to the Federal Government." Garcia v. San Antonio Metropolitan Transit Authority, *supra*, 469 U.S., at 549.

Congress exercises its conferred powers subject to the limitations contained in the Constitution. Thus, for example, under the Commerce Clause Congress may regulate publishers engaged in interstate commerce, but Congress is constrained in the exercise of that power by the First Amendment. The Tenth Amendment likewise restrains the power of Congress, but this limit is not derived from the text of the Tenth Amendment itself, which, as we have discussed, is essentially a tautology.

Instead, the Tenth Amendment confirms that the power of the Federal Government is subject to limits that may, in a given instance, reserve power to the States. The Tenth Amendment thus directs us to determine, as in this case, whether an incident of state sovereignty is protected by a limitation on an Article I power. . . .

The Federal Government undertakes activities today that would have been unimaginable to the Framers in two senses; first, because the Framers would not have conceived that any government would conduct such activities; and second, because the Framers would not have believed that the Federal Government, rather than the States, would assume such responsibilities. Yet the powers conferred upon the Federal Government by the Constitution were phrased in language broad enough to allow for the expansion of the Federal Government's role. Among the provisions of the Constitution that have been particularly important in this regard, three concern us here.

First, the Constitution allocates to Congress the power "[t]o regulate Commerce . . . among the several States." Art. I, §8, cl. 3. . . .

Second, the Constitution authorizes Congress "to pay the Debts and provide for the . . . general Welfare of the United States." Art. I, §8, cl. 1. As conventional notions of the proper objects of government spending have changed over the years, so has the ability of Congress to "fix the terms on which it shall disburse federal money to the States." Pennhurst State School and Hospital v. Halderman, 451 U.S. 1, 17 (1981). Compare, e.g., United States v. Butler, *supra*, 297 U.S., at 72-75 (spending power does not authorize Congress to subsidize farmers), with South Dakota v. Dole, 483 U.S. 203 (1987) (spending power permits Congress to condition highway funds on States' adoption of minimum drinking age). While the spending power is "subject to several general restrictions articulated in our cases," id., at 207, these restrictions have not been so severe as to prevent the regulatory authority of Congress from generally keeping up with the growth of the federal budget.

The Court's broad construction of Congress' power under the Commerce and Spending Clauses has of course been guided, as it has with respect to Congress' power generally, by the Constitution's Necessary and Proper Clause, which authorizes Congress "[t]o make all Laws which shall be necessary and proper for carrying into Execution the foregoing Powers." U.S. Const., Art. I, §8, cl. 18. . . .

Finally, the Constitution provides that "the Laws of the United States . . . shall be the supreme Law of the Land . . . any Thing in the Constitution or Laws of any State to the Contrary notwithstanding." U.S. Const., Art. VI, cl. 2. As the Federal Government's willingness to exercise power within the confines of the Constitution has grown, the authority of the States has correspondingly diminished to the extent that federal and state policies have conflicted. See, e.g., Shaw v. Delta Air Lines, Inc., 463 U.S. 85 (1983). We have observed that the Supremacy Clause gives the Federal Government "a decided advantage in th[e] delicate balance" the Constitution strikes between state and federal power. Gregory v. Ashcroft, 501 U.S., at 460.

The actual scope of the Federal Government's authority with respect to the States has changed over the years, therefore, but the constitutional structure underlying and limiting that authority has not. In the end, just as a cup may be half empty or half full, it makes no difference whether one views the question at issue in these cases as one of ascertaining the limits of the power delegated to the Federal Government under the affirmative provisions of the Constitution or one of discerning the core of sovereignty retained by the States under the Tenth Amendment. Either way, we must determine whether any of the three challenged provisions of the Low-Level Radioactive Waste Policy Amendments Act of 1985 oversteps the boundary between federal and state authority.

B.

Petitioners do not contend that Congress lacks the power to regulate the disposal of low level radioactive waste. Space in radioactive waste disposal sites is frequently sold by residents of one State to residents of another. Regulation of the resulting interstate market in waste disposal is therefore well within Congress' authority under the Commerce Clause. Cf. Philadelphia v. New Jersey, 437 U.S. 617, 621-623 (1978); Fort Gratiot Sanitary Landfill, Inc. v. Michigan Dept. of Natural Resources, 504 U.S. 353, 359 (1992). Petitioners likewise do not dispute that under the Supremacy Clause Congress could, if it wished, pre-empt state radioactive waste regulation. Petitioners contend only that the Tenth Amendment limits the power of Congress to regulate in the way it has chosen. Rather than addressing the problem of waste disposal by directly regulating the generators and disposers of waste, petitioners argue, Congress has impermissibly directed the States to regulate in this field. . . .

This litigation instead concerns the circumstances under which Congress may use the States as implements of regulation; that is, whether Congress may direct or otherwise motivate the States to regulate in a particular field or a particular way. Our cases have established a few principles that guide our resolution of the issue.

1.

As an initial matter, Congress may not simply "commandee[r] the legislative processes of the States by directly compelling them to enact and enforce a federal regulatory program." Hodel v. Virginia Surface Mining & Reclamation Ass'n, Inc., 452 U.S. 264, 288 (1981). In *Hodel*, the Court upheld the Surface Mining Control and Reclamation Act of 1977 precisely because it did not "commandeer" the States into regulating mining. The Court found that "the States are not compelled to enforce the steep-slope standards, to expend any state funds, or to participate in the federal regulatory program in any manner whatsoever. If a State does not wish to submit a proposed permanent program that complies with the Act and implementing regulations, the full regulatory burden will be borne by the Federal Government." Ibid.

The Court reached the same conclusion the following year in FERC v. Mississippi, *supra*. At issue in *FERC* was the Public Utility Regulatory Policies Act of 1978, a federal statute encouraging the States in various ways to develop programs to combat the Nation's energy crisis. We observed that "this Court never has sanctioned explicitly a federal command to the States to promulgate and enforce laws and regulations." Id., 456 U.S., at 761-762. As in *Hodel*, the Court upheld the statute at issue because it did not view the statute as such a command. . . .

These statements in *FERC* and *Hodel* were not innovations. While Congress has substantial powers to govern the Nation directly, including in areas of intimate concern to the States, the Constitution has never been understood to confer upon Congress the ability to require the States to govern according to Congress' instructions.

In providing for a stronger central government, therefore, the Framers explicitly chose a Constitution that confers upon Congress the power to regulate individuals, not States. As we have seen, the Court has consistently respected this choice. We have always understood that even where Congress has the authority under the Constitution to pass laws requiring or prohibiting certain acts, it lacks the power directly to compel the States to require or prohibit those acts. . . . The allocation of power contained in the Commerce Clause, for example, authorizes Congress to regulate interstate commerce directly; it does not authorize Congress to regulate state governments' regulation of interstate commerce.

2.

This is not to say that Congress lacks the ability to encourage a State to regulate in a particular way, or that Congress may not hold out incentives to the States as a method of influencing a State's policy choices. Our cases have identified a variety of methods, short of outright coercion, by which Congress may urge a State to adopt a legislative program consistent with federal interests. Two of these methods are of particular relevance here.

First, under Congress' spending power, "Congress may attach conditions on the receipt of federal funds." South Dakota v. Dole, 483 U.S., at 206. Such conditions must (among other requirements) bear some relationship to the purpose of the federal spending, id., at 207-208, and n.3; otherwise, of course, the spending power could render academic the Constitution's other grants and limits of federal authority. Where the recipient of federal funds is a State, as is not unusual today, the conditions attached to the funds by Congress may influence a State's legislative choices. See Kaden, Politics, Money, and State Sovereignty: The Judicial Role, 79 Colum. L. Rev. 847, 874-881 (1979). Dole was one such case: The Court found no constitutional flaw in a federal statute directing the Secretary of Transportation to withhold federal highway funds from States failing to adopt Congress' choice of a minimum drinking age. Similar examples abound. . . .

Second, where Congress has the authority to regulate private activity under the Commerce Clause, we have recognized Congress' power to offer States the choice of regulating that activity according to federal standards or having state law pre-empted by federal regulation. Hodel v. Virginia Surface Mining & Reclamation Ass'n, Inc., supra, 452 U.S., at 288. See also FERC v. Mississippi, supra, 456 U.S., at 764-765. This arrangement, which has been termed "a program of cooperative federalism," Hodel, supra, 452 U.S., at 289, is replicated in numerous federal statutory schemes. These include the Clean Water Act, 33 U.S.C. §1251 et seq.; see Arkansas v. Oklahoma, 503 U.S. 91, 101 (1992) (Clean Water Act "anticipates a partnership between the States and the Federal Government, animated by a shared objective"); the Occupational Safety and Health Act of 1970, 29 U.S.C. §651 et seq.; see Gade v. National Solid Wastes Mgmt. Ass'n, 505 U.S. 88, 97 (1992); the Resource Conservation and Recovery Act of 1976, 42 U.S.C. §6901 et seq.; see Department of Energy v. Ohio, 503 U.S. 607, 611-612 (1992); and the Alaska National Interest Lands Conservation Act, 16 U.S.C. §3101 et seq.; see Kenaitze Indian Tribe v. Alaska, 860 F.2d 312, 314 (CA9 1988).

By either of these methods, as by any other permissible method of encouraging a State to conform to federal policy choices, the residents of the State retain the ultimate decision as to whether or not the State will comply. If a State's citizens view federal policy as sufficiently contrary to local interests, they may elect to decline a federal grant. If state residents would prefer their government to devote its attention and resources to problems other than those deemed important by Congress, they may choose to have the Federal Government rather than the State bear the expense of a federally mandated regulatory program, and they may continue to supplement that program to the extent state law is not pre-empted. Where Congress encourages state regulation rather than compelling it, state governments remain responsive to the local electorate's preferences; state officials remain accountable to the people.

By contrast, where the Federal Government compels States to regulate, the accountability of both state and federal officials is diminished. If the citizens of New York, for example, do not consider that making provision for the disposal of radioactive waste is in their best interest, they may elect state officials who share their view. That view can always be pre-empted under the Supremacy Clause if it is contrary to the national view, but in such a case it is the Federal Government that makes the decision in full view of the public, and it will be federal officials that suffer the consequences if the decision turns out to be detrimental or unpopular.

But where the Federal Government directs the States to regulate, it may be state officials who will bear the brunt of public disapproval, while the federal officials who devised the regulatory program may remain insulated from the electoral ramifications of their decision. Accountability is thus diminished when, due to federal coercion, elected state officials cannot regulate in accordance with the views of the local electorate in matters not pre-empted by federal regulation. See Merritt, 88 Colum. L. Rev., at 61-62; La Pierre, Political Accountability in the National Political Process—The Alternative to Judicial Review of Federalism Issues, 80 Nw. U. L. Rev. 577, 639-665 (1985).

With these principles in mind, we turn to the three challenged provisions of the Low-Level Radioactive Waste Policy Amendments Act of 1985.

III.

The parties in these cases advance two quite different views of the Act. . . .

Construed as a whole, the Act comprises three sets of "incentives" for the States to provide for the disposal of low level radioactive waste generated within their borders. We consider each in turn.

A.

The first set of incentives works in three steps. First, Congress has authorized States with disposal sites to impose a surcharge on radioactive waste received from other States. Second, the Secretary of Energy collects a portion of this surcharge and places the money in an escrow account. Third, States achieving a series of milestones receive portions of this fund.

The first of these steps is an unexceptionable exercise of Congress' power to authorize the States to burden interstate commerce. While the Commerce Clause has long been understood to limit the States' ability to discriminate against interstate commerce, see, e.g., Wyoming v. Oklahoma, 502 U.S. 437, 454-455 (1992); Cooley v. Board of Wardens of Port of Philadelphia ex rel. Society for Relief of Distressed Pilots, 12 How. 299 (1852), that limit may be lifted, as it has been here, by an expression of the "unambiguous intent" of Congress. *Wyoming, supra,* 502 U.S., at

458; Prudential Ins. Co. v. Benjamin, 328 U.S. 408, 427-431 (1946). Whether or not the States would be permitted to burden the interstate transport of low level radioactive waste in the absence of Congress' approval, the States can clearly do so with Congress' approval, which is what the Act gives them.

The second step, the Secretary's collection of a percentage of the surcharge, is no more than a federal tax on interstate commerce, which petitioners do not claim to be an invalid exercise of either Congress' commerce or taxing power. Cf. United States v. Sanchez, 340 U.S. 42, 44-45 (1950); Steward Machine Co. v. Davis, 301 U.S. 548, 581-583 (1937).

The third step is a conditional exercise of Congress' authority under the Spending Clause: Congress has placed conditions—the achievement of the milestones—on the receipt of federal funds. Petitioners do not contend that Congress has exceeded its authority in any of the four respects our cases have identified. See generally South Dakota v. Dole, 483 U.S., at 207-208. The expenditure is for the general welfare, Helvering v. Davis, 301 U.S. 619, 640-641 (1937); the States are required to use the money they receive for the purpose of assuring the safe disposal of radioactive waste. 42 U.S.C. §2021e(d)(2)(E). The conditions imposed are unambiguous, Pennhurst State School and Hospital v. Halderman, 451 U.S., at 17; the Act informs the States exactly what they must do and by when they must do it in order to obtain a share of the escrow account. The conditions imposed are reasonably related to the purpose of the expenditure, Massachusetts v. United States, 435 U.S., at 461; both the conditions and the payments embody Congress' efforts to address the pressing problem of radioactive waste disposal. Finally, petitioners do not claim that the conditions imposed by the Act violate any independent constitutional prohibition. Lawrence County v. Lead-Deadwood School Dist. No. 40-1, 469 U.S. 256, 269-270 (1985).

Petitioners contend nevertheless that the form of these expenditures removes them from the scope of Congress' spending power. . . . The Constitution's grant to Congress of the authority to "pay the Debts and provide for the . . . general Welfare" has never, however, been thought to mandate a particular form of accounting. A great deal of federal spending comes from segregated trust funds collected and spent for a particular purpose. . . . The Spending Clause has never been construed to deprive Congress of the power to structure federal spending in this manner. . . . That the States are able to choose whether they will receive federal funds does not make the resulting expenditures any less federal; indeed, the location of such choice in the States is an inherent element in any conditional exercise of Congress' spending power.

The Act's first set of incentives, in which Congress has conditioned grants to the States upon the States' attainment of a series of milestones, is thus well within the authority of Congress under the Commerce and Spending Clauses. Because the first set of incentives is supported by affirmative constitutional grants of power to Congress, it is not inconsistent with the Tenth Amendment.

B.

In the second set of incentives, Congress has authorized States and regional compacts with disposal sites gradually to increase the cost of access to the sites, and then to deny access altogether, to radioactive waste generated in States that do not meet federal deadlines. As a simple regulation, this provision would be within the power of Congress to authorize the States to discriminate against interstate commerce. See Northeast Bancorp, Inc. v. Board of Governors, FRS, 472 U.S. 159, 174-175

(1985). Where federal regulation of private activity is within the scope of the Commerce Clause, we have recognized the ability of Congress to offer States the choice of regulating that activity according to federal standards or having state law pre-empted by federal regulation. See Hodel v. Virginia Surface Mining & Reclamation Ass'n, Inc., 452 U.S., at 288; FERC v. Mississippi, 456 U.S., at 764-765.

This is the choice presented to nonsited States by the Act's second set of incentives: States may either regulate the disposal of radioactive waste according to federal standards by attaining local or regional self-sufficiency, or their residents who produce radioactive waste will be subject to federal regulation authorizing sited States and regions to deny access to their disposal sites. The affected States are not compelled by Congress to regulate, because any burden caused by a State's refusal to regulate will fall on those who generate waste and find no outlet for its disposal, rather than on the State as a sovereign. A State whose citizens do not wish it to attain the Act's milestones may devote its attention and its resources to issues its citizens deem more worthy; the choice remains at all times with the residents of the State, not with Congress. The State need not expend any funds, or participate in any federal program, if local residents do not view such expenditures or participation as worthwhile. Cf. *Hodel*, *supra*, 452 U.S., at 288. Nor must the State abandon the field if it does not accede to federal direction; the State may continue to regulate the generation and disposal of radioactive waste in any manner its citizens see fit.

The Act's second set of incentives thus represents a conditional exercise of Congress' commerce power, along the lines of those we have held to be within Congress' authority. As a result, the second set of incentives does not intrude on the sovereignty reserved to the States by the Tenth Amendment.

C.

The take title provision is of a different character. This third so-called "incentive" offers States, as an alternative to regulating pursuant to Congress' direction, the option of taking title to and possession of the low level radioactive waste generated within their borders and becoming liable for all damages waste generators suffer as a result of the States' failure to do so promptly. In this provision, Congress has crossed the line distinguishing encouragement from coercion. . . .

The take title provision offers state governments a "choice" of either accepting ownership of waste or regulating according to the instructions of Congress. Respondents do not claim that the Constitution would authorize Congress to impose either option as a freestanding requirement. On one hand, the Constitution would not permit Congress simply to transfer radioactive waste from generators to state governments. Such a forced transfer, standing alone, would in principle be no different than a congressionally compelled subsidy from state governments to radioactive waste producers. The same is true of the provision requiring the States to become liable for the generators' damages. Standing alone, this provision would be indistinguishable from an Act of Congress directing the States to assume the liabilities of certain state residents. Either type of federal action would "commandeer" state governments into the service of federal regulatory purposes, and would for this reason be inconsistent with the Constitution's division of authority between federal and state governments. On the other hand, the second alternative held out to state governments—regulating pursuant to Congress' direction—would, standing alone, present a simple command to state governments to implement legislation enacted by Congress. As we have seen, the Constitution does not empower Congress to subject state governments to this type of instruction.

Because an instruction to state governments to take title to waste, standing alone, would be beyond the authority of Congress, and because a direct order to regulate, standing alone, would also be beyond the authority of Congress, it follows that Congress lacks the power to offer the States a choice between the two. Unlike the first two sets of incentives, the take title incentive does not represent the conditional exercise of any congressional power enumerated in the Constitution. In this provision, Congress has not held out the threat of exercising its spending power or its commerce power; it has instead held out the threat, should the States not regulate according to one federal instruction, of simply forcing the States to submit to another federal instruction. A choice between two unconstitutionally coercive regulatory techniques is no choice at all. Either way, "the Act commandeers the legislative processes of the States by directly compelling them to enact and enforce a federal regulatory program," Hodel v. Virginia Surface Mining & Reclamation Ass'n, Inc., *supra*, 452 U.S., at 288, an outcome that has never been understood to lie within the authority conferred upon Congress by the Constitution.

Respondents emphasize the latitude given to the States to implement Congress' plan. The Act enables the States to regulate pursuant to Congress' instructions in any number of different ways. States may avoid taking title by contracting with sited regional compacts, by building a disposal site alone or as part of a compact, or by permitting private parties to build a disposal site. States that host sites may employ a wide range of designs and disposal methods, subject only to broad federal regulatory limits. This line of reasoning, however, only underscores the critical alternative a State lacks: A State may not decline to administer the federal program. No matter which path the State chooses, it must follow the direction of Congress.

The take title provision appears to be unique. No other federal statute has been cited which offers a state government no option other than that of implementing legislation enacted by Congress. Whether one views the take title provision as lying outside Congress' enumerated powers, or as infringing upon the core of state sovereignty reserved by the Tenth Amendment, the provision is inconsistent with the federal structure of our Government established by the Constitution.

IV.

Respondents raise a number of objections to this understanding of the limits of Congress' power. . . .

Respondents note that the Act embodies a bargain among the sited and unsited States, a compromise to which New York was a willing participant and from which New York has reaped much benefit. Respondents then pose what appears at first to be a troubling question: How can a federal statute be found an unconstitutional infringement of state sovereignty when state officials consented to the statute's enactment?

The answer follows from an understanding of the fundamental purpose served by our Government's federal structure. The Constitution does not protect the sovereignty of States for the benefit of the States or state governments as abstract political entities, or even for the benefit of the public officials governing the States. To the contrary, the Constitution divides authority between federal and state governments for the protection of individuals. State sovereignty is not just an end in itself: "Rather, federalism secures to citizens the liberties that derive from the diffusion of sovereign power." Coleman v. Thompson, 501 U.S. 722, 759 (1991) (Blackmun, J., dissenting). "Just as the separation and independence of the coordinate branches of the Federal Government serves to prevent the accumulation of excessive power in any one branch, a healthy balance of power between the States and the Federal Government will reduce the risk of tyranny and abuse from either front." Gregory v. Ashcroft, 501 U.S., at 458 (1991). See The Federalist No. 51, p. 323 (C. Rossiter ed. 1961). Where Congress exceeds its authority relative to the States, therefore, the departure from the constitutional plan cannot be ratified by the "consent" of state officials. An analogy to the separation of powers among the branches of the Federal Government clarifies this point. The Constitution's division of power among the three branches is violated where one branch invades the territory of another, whether or not the encroached-upon branch approves the encroachment. . . .

State officials thus cannot consent to the enlargement of the powers of Congress beyond those enumerated in the Constitution. . . .

VII.

States are not mere political subdivisions of the United States. State governments are neither regional offices nor administrative agencies of the Federal Government. The positions occupied by state officials appear nowhere on the Federal Government's most detailed organizational chart. The Constitution instead "leaves to the several States a residuary and inviolable sovereignty," The Federalist No. 39, p. 245 (C. Rossiter ed. 1961), reserved explicitly to the States by the Tenth Amendment.

Whatever the outer limits of that sovereignty may be, one thing is clear: The Federal Government may not compel the States to enact or administer a federal regulatory program. The Constitution permits both the Federal Government and the States to enact legislation regarding the disposal of low level radioactive waste. The Constitution enables the Federal Government to pre-empt state regulation contrary to federal interests, and it permits the Federal Government to hold out incentives to the States as a means of encouraging them to adopt suggested regulatory schemes. It does not, however, authorize Congress simply to direct the States to provide for the disposal of the radioactive waste generated within their borders. While there may be many constitutional methods of achieving regional self-sufficiency in radioactive waste disposal, the method Congress has chosen is not one of them. The judgment of the Court of Appeals is accordingly

Affirmed in part and reversed in part.

[The dissents of JUSTICE WHITE (joined by JUSTICES BLACKMUN and STEVENS) and JUSTICE STEVENS are omitted.]

NOTES AND QUESTIONS

1. *Enticement Techniques.* For a federal legislator eager to enlist the states' assistance, what techniques remain constitutional after *New York?*

2. *The Limits of* New York. After *New York,* courts and analysts wondered about the implications of the case. What sorts of actions, short of legislative action, might the

federal government order states to undertake? *New York* was quickly extended when a closely divided Court in Printz v. United States, 521 U.S. 898 (1997), declared unconstitutional a federal requirement under the Brady Handgun Violence Protection Act that state law enforcement officials perform statutorily required duties, including background checks and handling related forms. A unanimous Court limited the reach of *New York* and *Printz* in Reno v. Condon, 528 U.S. 141 (2000), where it upheld a federal law restricting the ability of states or others to market drivers' registration information without the consent of the driver. The Court distinguished the *Reno* setting from those in *New York* and *Printz* by stating it did not involve "commandeering" state governmental actors or processes, but regulated states among others, restricting all in the marketing of driver information.

How should courts assess federal laws that mandate certain conduct by states in providing public amenities such as water and sewage treatment?

A NOTE ON STATE SOVEREIGN IMMUNITY

States engage in numerous types of conduct subject to federal law, ranging from serving as an employer, to running public facilities such as universities, prisons, and sewage treatment plants, to building large infrastructure projects. Through these and many other activities, states and state agencies create an array of pollution streams that can violate the law. *New York* and its progeny make clear that states can be subjected to regulation as are other individuals, with the caveat that at least some sorts of governmental functions or actions, especially legislative functions, cannot be "commandeered" by the federal government. But that is not the end of required federalism analysis.

Since the Court in *Lopez* started recasting the lines of federalism doctrine, virtually all areas of federalism doctrine have undergone change. One significant area of change, or at least substantial refinement, has been the Supreme Court's sovereign immunity case law. The importance of the Eleventh Amendment as a key text for federalist revisionism emerged in Seminole Tribe v. Florida, 517 U.S. 44 (1996). The text of the Eleventh Amendment appears to be quite specific and limited:

> The judicial power of the United States shall not be construed to extend to any suit in law or equity, commenced or prosecuted against one of the United States by Citizens of another State, or by Citizens or Subjects of any Foreign State.

In *Seminole Tribe*, however, the Supreme Court overruled Pennsylvania v. Union Gas, 491 U.S. 1 (1989), a case that had upheld federal power by allowing citizens to sue states to compel payment for cleanup costs under CERCLA. Although *Seminole Tribe* involved Indian gaming and not environmental liability, five justices concurred in a result holding that "the Eleventh Amendment prevents congressional authorization of suit by private parties against unconsenting States" in federal court. 517 U.S. at 72. Although some language appeared broadly to immunize states from suits by private parties in federal court, other language focused on immunity from claims seeking monetary relief.

In 1999, the Court issued three opinions, often identified as the *Alden* trio, on interrelated questions of sovereign immunity doctrine. All three reflected ongoing federalism divisions on the Rehnquist Court, each garnering a narrow 5-4 majority.

Due to their somewhat limited impact on federal environmental law, they are summarized here, along with commentary explaining why their impact is likely to be limited.

In *Alden*, the Court held that Congress lacks the power under Article I to subject nonconsenting states to private suits for damages in state courts. Alden v. Maine, 527 U.S. 706, 712 (1999). In *Alden*, state probation officers filed suit against the state of Maine in federal court seeking compensation and liquidated damages, alleging that Maine had violated the overtime provisions of the Fair Labor Standards Act (FLSA). After the district court dismissed the suit based on *Seminole Tribe*, the probation officers refiled the suit in state court. Although the FLSA authorized private actions against states in their own courts, the trial court dismissed the suit on the ground that it was barred by sovereign immunity.

Writing for the Court, Justice Kennedy, over the dissent of four justices, concluded that the Constitution's structure and history, along with the Court's authoritative interpretations, demonstrate that states' sovereign immunity is rooted in the sovereignty they enjoyed before the Constitution's ratification and is retained today except as altered by certain amendments. Justice Kennedy explained that "the Eleventh Amendment confirmed, rather than established sovereign immunity as a constitutional principle; it follows that the scope of the States' immunity from suit is demarcated not by the text of the Amendment alone but by fundamental postulates inherent in the constitutional design." Id. at 728-729.

Justice Kennedy next addressed whether Congress has the power to abrogate states' sovereign immunity in state courts from suits by private parties based on federal law. He concluded that even though the words of the Eleventh Amendment do not apply to suits against states in state court, neither the Constitution's text nor the Court's recent sovereign immunity decisions suggest that Congress has the authority to abrogate state immunity in state courts under the Constitution. Id. at 754.

However, Justice Kennedy pointed out that state sovereign immunity in state courts "does not confer upon the state a concomitant right to disregard the Constitution or valid federal law." Id. at 754-755. Justice Kennedy proceeded to identify reasons states may still comply with federal law: the good faith of the states; voluntary state consent to suits for violations of federal law, including "consent" obtained by Congress's exercise of its spending power; suits by another state or the federal government in federal court; Congress's power to abrogate states' sovereign immunity pursuant to its Fourteenth Amendment §5 powers to enforce due process and equal protection; suits against municipal governments or another government entity that is not an arm of the state; and *Ex parte Young*–type suits for injunctive relief directed against individual state officials.

In two other cases decided on the same day, the Court restricted the scope of Congress's enforcement authority under the Fourteenth Amendment, limiting two of the mechanisms by which states could be sued for retrospective relief. The Court, in College Sav. Bank v. Florida Prepaid Postsecondary Educ. Expense Bd., 527 U.S. 666, 672-690 (1999), held that §5 of the Fourteenth Amendment does not give Congress the authority to abrogate states' sovereign immunity in federal court for violations of federal trademark statutes. Writing for the Court, Justice Scalia found that under *Seminole Tribe*, Congress cannot rely on its commerce power to abrogate Eleventh Amendment immunity and that, under City of Boerne v. Flores, 521 U.S. 507 (1997), §5 of the Fourteenth Amendment gives Congress the power to abrogate state immunity only to remedy or prevent constitutional violations. The Court rejected plaintiff's arguments that the right to be free from a business competitor's false advertising about its own product and a generalized right to be secure in one's business interests were constitutionally cognizable protected property rights. After determining that Congress did not abrogate Florida's right to sovereign immunity, the Court found that Florida did not voluntarily waive its sovereign immunity by actively engaging in interstate commerce. In doing so, the Court expressly overruled Parden v. Terminal RR. Co. of Alabama Docks Dep't, 377 U.S. 184 (1964), which had held that where Congress conditioned the right to operate a railroad in interstate commerce upon amenability to suit in federal court, the state of Alabama consented to suit by operating a railroad in interstate commerce. A state's consent to waive its sovereign immunity requires an unequivocal and express waiver. The Court also stated that Congress might be able to accomplish the same result using its spending power. Id. at 686-687 ("Congress has no obligation to use its Spending Clause power to disburse funds to the states; such funds are gifts. In the present case however, what Congress threatens if the state refuses to agree to its condition is not the denial of a gift or gratuity, but a sanction: exclusion of the state from otherwise permissible activity.").

Similarly, in Florida Prepaid Postsecondary Educ. Expense Bd. v. College Sav. Bd., 527 U.S. 627, 630 (1999), the Court held that Congress lacks the authority under §5 of the Fourteenth Amendment to abrogate states' Eleventh Amendment immunity from suit in federal court for alleged violations of federal patent statutes. Chief Justice Rehnquist, writing for the Court, held that Congress clearly made known its intent to abrogate a state's sovereign immunity in the Patent and Plant Variety Protection Remedy Clarification Act. The second inquiry, however, is whether Congress acted pursuant to a valid exercise of power. The Court found that Congress did not have the authority under the Commerce Clause or Article I patent authority because Congress may not abrogate state sovereign immunity pursuant to Article I powers. To invoke §5, the Court reiterated that under *City of Boerne*, Congress must identify conduct transgressing the Fourteenth Amendment's substantive provisions and must tailor its legislative scheme to remedying or preventing such conduct. In passing the Act, Congress failed to identify a pattern of such infringement, let alone a pattern of constitutional violations.

Recognizing that patents may well be considered "property" for Fourteenth Amendment purposes, the Court determined that Congress did not find state remedies inadequate, and the legislative record indicated that the Act did not respond to a history of widespread and persisting deprivation of constitutional rights—conditions that are required of Congress in enacting legislation under §5. Finally, the Court concluded that even if some abrogation of state immunity was appropriate in this context, the statutory provision before the Court was too broad to withstand constitutional scrutiny. Congress did not limit the Act's coverage to cases involving arguable constitutional violations or confine its reach by limiting the remedy to certain types of infringement. Thus, the Court held that in light of the historical record and scope of coverage of the Act, the law could not be sustained under §5 of the Fourteenth Amendment.

Taken together, the *Alden* trio and the earlier *Seminole Tribe* decision raise questions about Congress's ability to provide for reliable enforcement of federal environmental laws. Clearly, the rulings limit the ability of citizens to obtain monetary relief against nonconsenting states. As you will see in Chapters 3 and 10, on administrative law and enforcement, most environmental "citizen suit" provisions do not provide for damages relief, but generally provide causes of action for injunctive relief, penalties, and attorneys' fees and costs. Citizens have played a critical adjunct role in environmental enforcement, often stepping in to enforce the law when federal or state actors have declined to act. What is the impact of these cases on such actions? Professors McAllister and Glicksman, in State Liability for Environmental Violations: The U.S. Supreme Court's "New" Federalism, 29 Envtl. L. Rep. (ELI) 10665, 10667 (1999), conclude that

> a variety of enforcement mechanisms and options remain available. [T]he Court's recent federalism decisions may make implementation and the enforcement of federal environmental laws more complicated and difficult in some instances but the decisions do not ultimately appear to preclude Congress from regulating environmental matters in any significant measure.

For a somewhat more pessimistic appraisal, see Araiza, Alden v. Maine and the Web of Environmental Law, 33 Loy. L.A. L. Rev. 1513 (2000).

It is clear that as a result of the *Alden* trio, state violators of environmental laws have a substantially reduced risk of liability if the federal government lacks interest in punishing those violations. See Burnette v. Carothers, 192 F.3d 52 (2nd Cir. 1999) (applying these cases and dismissing citizen suit claims under three environmental statutes, finding monetary relief precluded by sovereign immunity doctrine). For scholarly critiques of the effect of the *Alden* trio, see Adler, Judicial Federalism and the Future of Federal Environmental Regulation, 90 Iowa L. Rev. 377, 397-402, 431-433 (2005); Babcock, The Effect of the United States Supreme Court's Eleventh Amendment Jurisprudence on Clean Water Act Citizen Suits: Muddied Waters, 83 Or. L. Rev. 47 (2004).

E.   THE POWER ALLOCATION CHOICE: SAVINGS CLAUSES, DELEGATED PROGRAMS, AND PREEMPTION

Validly enacted federal law can trump contrary state laws under the Constitution's Supremacy Clause, which states in Article VI, "This Constitution, and the Laws of the United States which shall be made in Pursuance thereof . . . shall be the supreme Law of the Land." The Court's abundant, although confusing, body of preemption doctrine sets forth how and when federal law will preempt state law. In federal environmental laws, however, most major statutes explicitly preserve state law and even welcome more stringent state laws. Lehner, Act Locally: Municipal Enforcement of Environmental Law, 12 Stan. Envtl. L.J. 50, 78-79 (1993); Spence & Murray, The Law, Economics, and Politics of Federal Preemption Jurisprudence: A Quantitative Analysis, 87 Cal. L. Rev. 1125, 1146-1150 (1999). This section briefly discusses these "savings" clauses as well as the less common preempting provisions in federal environmental laws. It also provides a brief introduction to "delegated program" provisions in federal environmental law, under which states can assume substantial implementation and enforcement roles. This part closes by examining the basics of preemption case law, looking at the Court's recent *Engine Manufacturers* and *Bates* decisions to illustrate preemption doctrine's importance to environmental law.

1. Savings Clauses

As covered in Chapter 1, especially in materials concerning the *Ouellette* case, federal environmental laws generally do not displace all state laws, but in various ways retain or dovetail with state law. Federal laws that retain state law do so in provisions that are often characterized as *savings clauses*. Although each new statute has its particular formulations, this section reviews a few paradigmatic savings clause provisions. Keep in mind that statutes with savings clauses often also contain preemptive provisions, and that courts can still find a preemptive effect even when a statute contains a savings clause.

The Clean Water Act arguably contains the greatest number of savings clauses; some were perhaps drafted to mollify legislators concerned with expanded federal power, but others contain direct, clear content. Section 1251, the law's opening "declaration of goals and policy," contains a broad statement of "the policy of Congress to recognize, preserve, and protect the primary responsibilities and rights of States to prevent, reduce, and eliminate pollution, to plan the development and use . . . of land and water resources, and to consult with" EPA's administrator. 33 U.S.C. §1251(b). This subsection goes on to state the legislative intent to have states administer construction grant and permit programs under the statute's chief provisions, and also to have the federal government provide assistance with research, technical services, and funding. These initial provisions are more broad statements of policy than operative clauses or provisions that will resolve conflicts, but they certainly serve as broad anti-preemption statements. Nevertheless, as is evident in the excerpts from SWANCC and *Rapanos* above, at times the Supreme Court has looked at broad declarations regarding intent to preserve state power as grounds for limiting federal power, even in massive new federal anti-pollution legislation such as the Clean Water Act. The intent not to displace state riparian rights law is made with unusual clarity (and a fair bit of repetition in clauses not quoted here); it is stated to be the "policy of Congress that the authority of each State to allocate quantities of water shall not be superseded, abrogated or otherwise impaired by this Chapter." §1251(g).

Section 1365(e) explicitly preserves "any right which any person . . . may have under any statute or common law to seek enforcement of any effluent standard or to seek any other relief." This provision, you may recall, was significant in the *Ouellette* opinion excerpted in Chapter 1.

Of equal importance is the typical savings clause specifying that federal anti-pollution standards are a floor, constituting the minimum level of stringency or protection that must be provided by states and political subdivisions. States can pass additional "standard[s] or limitation[s]," or "any requirement respecting control or abatement of pollution," as long as they are not "less stringent" than federal requirements. Id.

Other statutes have similar savings clauses, some containing both general statements about states' retained regulatory power, such as 42 U.S.C. §7401(a)(3) (the Clean Air Act) or 42 U.S.C. §6901(a)(4) (the Resource Conservation and Recovery Act (RCRA)), and provisions preserving states' rights to protect the environment with more stringent protections. Compare 42 U.S.C. §6929 (allowing "more stringent" regulation under RCRA) and 42 U.S.C. §7416 (allowing additional state regulation of air pollution, other than that related to "moving sources," as long as it is not "less stringent" than federal requirements). The net effect is that other than in the rare explicitly preempting provisions, federal law serves as a stringency floor, not a ceiling;

states can enact additional, parallel laws or more stringent protections. See Glicksman, From Cooperative to Inoperative Federalism: The Perverse Mutation of Environmental Law and Policy, 41 Wake Forest L. Rev. 719, 737-743 (2006); Percival, Environmental Federalism: Historical Roots and Contemporary Models, 54 Md. L. Rev. 1141, 1175 (1995).

2.   Delegated Programs

Intertwined with savings clauses are provisions that are perhaps of greatest importance to understanding this nation's environmental laws. These are the quintessential *cooperative federalism* provisions, providing that states or their subdivisions can retain or assume responsibility for implementing and enforcing federal programs. These are often described as *delegated programs* because they involve broad delegation of federal regulatory obligations to states. As you will see in Chapter 10's discussion of environmental law enforcement, statutes and court decisions vary in terms of how much federal enforcement or "overfiling" power is retained when a state takes over a federal program; this hot-button issue is covered separately below.

Most major programs of this nation's pollution control legislation provide for the delegated program option. Indeed, this is such a pervasive feature, often contained in numerous provisions of a law, that this introduction to federalism will cover only a few to emphasize their most significant features. Natural resource laws, however, less frequently incorporate such cooperative federalism structures. Fischman, Cooperative Federalism and Natural Resources Law, 14 N.Y.U. Envtl. L.J. 179 (2005).

You will learn in depth about the two most significant delegated programs in subsequent chapters on the Clean Air and Clean Water Acts (Chapters 6 and 7). However, a brief summary of these provisions' key attributes is provided here. Under the Clean Water Act, the industrial discharge permitting program (the National Pollution Discharge Elimination System, or NPDES), lies presumptively in the hands of federal agencies, but states can pass laws and make other commitments to establish that they are qualified to assume the permit implementation and enforcement roles. Under §1342(b) and (c), the governor and state attorney general can submit to the Administrator of EPA a description of the program they propose to implement, with evidence that it conforms to federal statutory and regulatory requirements regarding stringency, participatory rights, permit duration, sanctions, and an array of other requirements. 33 U.S.C. §1342(b). State programs need not duplicate what the federal government would choose to do or had been doing. The onus is on the EPA Administrator to find that a state's program is inadequate: "The Administrator shall approve each such submitted program unless he determines that adequate authority does not exist" to carry out the specified regulatory obligations. States can lose this authority if, after federal notification and an opportunity for state correction, EPA determines that the state program, as written or in actual implementation, is no longer consistent with federal law. 42 U.S.C. §1342(c).

The Clean Air Act's state implementation plan (SIP) provisions, especially §110, 42 U.S.C. §7410, are much like those of the Clean Water Act NPDES program in setting forth an array of criteria states must meet to be primarily responsible for implementation plans designed to bring regions into compliance with federally set ambient air quality standards. In contrast to the NPDES provisions, the authorization to adopt SIPs places initial regulatory power in the hands of the states. Only if federal regulators or a court determines that a state is failing to comply with this provision's requirements can the state lose that power. As with the NPDES program, loss of state implementation power can occur only following notice and an opportunity for cure.

As you delve into the intricacies of the Clean Air Act, be sensitive to the wide variety of ways in which states can fail to meet federal goals or requirements and the nuanced series of procedural steps and sanctions that can follow. As you will see, the Clean Air Act distinguishes among failure to plan, failure to attain ambient air quality levels, failure to implement plans, and failure to enforce the law and plan commitments.

Many delegated programs are linked to monetary incentives. Partial federal underwriting of state efforts is common, often as an enticement for state participation, as allowed for in *New York v. United States* under well-established "conditional federal spending" powers. In addition, when a state falls short in carrying out its regulatory obligations, it can lose federal funds. Under the Clean Air Act, for example, the fear of loss of federal highway funding is a substantial motivator for states that might otherwise give federal clean air goals low priority. 42 U.S.C. §7509(b). Under many statutes, especially the Clean Water Act NPDES program, federal monetary support seldom covers more than a fraction of state costs. States nevertheless jealously guard and seek to preserve their planning and permitting authority. Whether it involves highly discretionary Clean Air Act planning for air quality control regions or more technical negotiations over industrial water pollution permits, states fight to preserve their regulatory roles rather than surrender them to federal regulators, who are perceived to be less sensitive to state and local conditions and politics.

3. Preempting Clauses

Preemption doctrine generates a great deal of disagreement, although most courts, lawyers, and scholars readily agree that "[m]odern preemption jurisprudence is a muddle." Caleb Nelson, Preemption, 86 Va. L. Rev. 225, 233 (2000). Professor Nelson questions "the usefulness of dividing . . . into separate analytical categories . . . 'express' preemption, 'field' preemption, and 'conflict' preemption. The Supreme Court itself has been unable to keep these categories 'rigidly distinct,' and they only get in the way of its analysis." Id. at 262 (citing to English v. General Elec. Co., 496 U.S. 72, 79, n.5 (1990)). Despite the uncertainties associated with these imperfect categories, they remain the starting point for preemption argument. Before turning to recent cases and notes illuminating preemption's influence on environmental law, this section lays out the basics of preemption doctrine.

In Crosby v. National Foreign Trade Council, 530 U.S. 363 (2000), the Supreme Court reviewed many of the central tenets of preemption doctrine. Congress undoubtedly has the power to preempt state law under the Constitution, but a finding of preemption does not require an explicit legislative statement of such intent:

> Even without an express provision for preemption, we have found that state law must yield to a congressional Act in at least two circumstances. When Congress intends federal law to "occupy the field," state law in that area is preempted. . . . And even if Congress has not occupied the field, state law is naturally preempted to the extent of any conflict with a federal statute. . . . We will find preemption where it is impossible for a private party to comply with both state and federal law, see, e.g., Florida Lime & Avocado Growers, Inc. v. Paul, 373 U.S. 132, 142-143 (1963), and where "under the circumstances

of [a] particular case, [the challenged state law] stands as an obstacle to the accomplishment and execution of the full purposes and objectives of Congress." . . . What is a sufficient obstacle is a matter of judgment, to be informed by examining the federal statute as a whole and identifying its purpose and intended effects: "For when the question is whether a Federal act overrides a state law, the entire scheme of the statute must of course be considered and that which needs must be implied is of no less force than that which is expressed. If the purpose of the act cannot otherwise be accomplished—if its operation within its chosen field else must be frustrated and its provisions be refused their natural effect—the state law must yield to the regulation of Congress within the sphere of its delegated power." [Id. at 372-373 (2000).]

In Gade v. National Solid Wastes Mgmt. Ass'n, 505 U.S. 88 (1992), the Court articulated with a bit more specificity when preemption might be found, even in the absence of explicitly preemptive language: "Absent explicit pre-emptive language, we have recognized at least two types of implied pre-emption: field pre-emption, where the scheme of federal regulation is 'so pervasive as to make reasonable the inference that Congress left no room for the States to supplement it,' . . . and conflict pre-emption, where 'compliance with both federal and state regulations is a physical impossibility' . . . or where state law 'stands as an obstacle to the accomplishment and execution of the full purposes and objectives of Congress.' . . . Our ultimate task in any pre-emption case is to determine whether state regulation is consistent with the structure and purpose of the statute as a whole." Id. at 98.

In Louisiana Pub. Serv. Comm'n v. FCC, 476 U.S. 355, 368-369 (1986), the Court explained that "[p]re-emption may result not only from action taken by Congress itself; a federal agency acting within the scope of its congressionally delegated authority may pre-empt state regulation." As discussed in the notes below, the agency power to preempt has recently become of great importance.

Although it is uncommon, federal environmental laws do at times explicitly preempt state laws. This occurs most frequently when federal law imposes a design requirement or calls for major design investments by industry. In such settings, a uniform federal standard can provide stability and a fixed regulatory target. The most notable preemptive provisions in federal environmental law relate to automobile emissions. As is evident in the following case, even apparently clear preemption provisions can, due to linguistic uncertainties or other, related provisions, create uncertainty and thus generate litigation. As you read *Engine Manufacturers*, a decision garnering eight supporting justices, be sensitive to how different interpretive techniques might lead to different outcomes. Does this case result in a sensible policy?

ENGINE MANUFACTURERS ASSOCIATION v. SOUTH COAST AIR QUALITY MANAGEMENT DISTRICT
541 U.S. 246 (2004)

JUSTICE SCALIA delivered the opinion of the Court.

Respondent South Coast Air Quality Management District (District) is a political subdivision of California responsible for air pollution control in the Los Angeles metropolitan area and parts of surrounding counties that make up the South Coast Air Basin. It enacted six Fleet Rules that generally prohibit the purchase or lease by various public and private fleet operators of vehicles that do not comply with stringent emission requirements. The question in this case is whether these local Fleet Rules escape pre-emption under §209(a) of the Clean Air Act (CAA), 81 Stat. 502, as renumbered and amended, 42 U.S.C. §7543(a), because they address the purchase of vehicles, rather than their manufacture or sale. . . .

II.

Section 209(a) of the CAA states:

> No State or any political subdivision thereof shall adopt or attempt to enforce any standard relating to the control of emissions from new motor vehicles or new motor vehicle engines subject to this part. No State shall require certification, inspection, or any other approval relating to the control of emissions . . . as condition precedent to the initial retail sale, titling (if any), or registration of such motor vehicle, motor vehicle engine, or equipment. [42 U.S.C. §7543(a).]

The District Court's determination that this express pre-emption provision did not invalidate the Fleet Rules hinged on its interpretation of the word "standard" to include only regulations that compel manufacturers to meet specified emission limits. This interpretation of "standard" in turn caused the court to draw a distinction between purchase restrictions (not pre-empted) and sale restrictions (pre-empted). Neither the manufacturer-specific interpretation of "standard" nor the resulting distinction between purchase and sale restrictions finds support in the text of §209(a) or the structure of the CAA.

"Statutory construction must begin with the language employed by Congress and the assumption that the ordinary meaning of that language accurately expresses the legislative purpose." Park 'N Fly, Inc. v. Dollar Park & Fly, Inc., 469 U.S. 189, 194 (1985). Today, as in 1967 when §209(a) became law, "standard" is defined as that which "is established by authority, custom, or general consent, as a model or example; criterion; test." Webster's Second New International Dictionary 2455 (1945). The criteria referred to in §209(a) relate to the emission characteristics of a vehicle or engine. To meet them the vehicle or engine must not emit more than a certain amount of a given pollutant, must be equipped with a certain type of pollution-control device, or must have some other design feature related to the control of emissions. This interpretation is consistent with the use of "standard" throughout Title II of the CAA (which governs emissions from moving sources) to denote requirements such as numerical emission levels with which vehicles or engines must comply, e.g., 42 U.S.C. §7521(a)(3)(B)(ii), or emission-control technology with which they must be equipped, e.g., §7521(a)(6).

Respondents, like the courts below, engraft onto this meaning of "standard" a limiting component, defining it as only "[a] *production* mandat[e] that require[s] *manufacturers* to ensure that the vehicles they produce have particular emissions characteristics, whether individually or in the aggregate." Brief for Respondent South Coast Air Quality Management District 13 (emphases added). This confuses standards with the means of enforcing standards. Manufacturers (or purchasers) can be made responsible for ensuring that vehicles comply with emission standards, but the standards themselves are separate from those enforcement techniques. While standards target vehicles or engines, standard-enforcement efforts that are proscribed by §209 can be directed to manufacturers or purchasers.

The distinction between "standards," on the one hand, and methods of standard enforcement, on the other, is borne out in the provisions immediately following §202. These separate provisions enforce the emission criteria—i.e., the §202 standards. Section 203 prohibits manufacturers from selling any new motor vehicle that is not covered by a "certificate of conformity." 42 U.S.C. §7522(a). Section 206 enables manufacturers to obtain such a certificate by demonstrating to the Environmental Protection Agency that their vehicles or engines conform to the §202 standards. §7525. Sections 204 and 205 subject manufacturers, dealers, and others who violate the CAA to fines imposed in civil or administrative enforcement actions. §§7523-7524. By defining "standard" as a "production mandate directed toward manufacturers," respondents lump together §202 and these other distinct statutory provisions, acknowledging a standard to be such only when it is combined with a mandate that prevents manufacturers from selling noncomplying vehicles.

That a standard is a standard even when not enforced through manufacturer-directed regulation can be seen in Congress's use of the term in another portion of the CAA. As the District Court recognized, CAA §246 (in conjunction with its accompanying provisions) requires state-adopted and federally approved "restrictions on the purchase of fleet vehicles to *meet clean-air standards*." 158 F. Supp. 2d, at 1118 (emphasis added); see also 42 U.S.C. §§7581-7590. (Respondents do not defend the District's Fleet Rules as authorized by this provision; the Rules do not comply with all of the requirements that it contains.) Clearly, Congress contemplated the enforcement of emission standards through purchase requirements.

Respondents contend that their qualified meaning of "standard" is necessary to prevent §209(a) from pre-empting "far too much" by "encompass[ing] a broad range of state-level clean-air initiatives" such as voluntary incentive programs. But it is hard to see why limitation to mandates on manufacturers is necessary for this purpose; limitation to mandates on manufacturers and purchasers, or to mandates on anyone, would have the same salvific effect. We need not resolve application of §209(a) to voluntary incentive programs in this case, since all the Fleet Rules are mandates.

In addition to having no basis in the text of the statute, treating sales restrictions and purchase restrictions differently for pre-emption purposes would make no sense. The manufacturer's right to sell federally approved vehicles is meaningless in the absence of a purchaser's right to buy them. It is true that the Fleet Rules at issue here cover only certain purchasers and certain federally certified vehicles, and thus do not eliminate all demand for covered vehicles. But if one State or political subdivision may enact such rules, then so may any other; and the end result would undo Congress's carefully calibrated regulatory scheme.

A command, accompanied by sanctions, that certain purchasers may buy only vehicles with particular emission characteristics is as much an "attempt to enforce" a "standard" as a command, accompanied by sanctions, that a certain percentage of a manufacturer's sales volume must consist of such vehicles. We decline to read into §209(a) a purchase/sale distinction that is not to be found in the text of §209(a) or the structure of the CAA.

III.

The dissent expresses many areas of disagreement with our interpretation, but this should not obscure its agreement with our answer to the question "whether these local

Fleet Rules escape pre-emption . . . because they address the purchase of vehicles, rather than their manufacture or sale." The dissent joins us in answering "no." See opinion of SOUTER, J. It reaches a different outcome in the case because (1) it feels free to read into the unconditional words of the statute a requirement for the courts to determine which purchase restrictions in fact coerce manufacture and which do not; and (2) because it believes that Fleet Rules containing a "commercial availability" proviso do not coerce manufacture.

As to the first point: The language of §209(a) is categorical. It is (as we have discussed) impossible to find in it an exception for standards imposed through purchase restrictions rather than directly upon manufacturers; it is even more inventive to discover an exception for only that subcategory of standards-imposed-through-purchase-restrictions that does not coerce manufacture. But even if one accepts that invention, one cannot conclude that these "provisos" save the day. For if a vehicle of the mandated type were commercially available, thus eliminating application of the proviso, the need to sell vehicles to persons governed by the Rule would effectively coerce manufacturers into meeting the artificially created demand. To say, as the dissent does, that this would be merely the consequence of "market demand and free competition" is fanciful. The demand is a demand, not generated by the market but compelled by the Rules, which in turn effectively compels production. To think that the Rules are invalid until such time as one manufacturer makes a compliant vehicle available, whereupon they become binding, seems to us quite bizarre. . . .

Finally, the dissent says that we should "admit" that our opinion pre-empts voluntary incentive programs. Voluntary programs are not at issue in this case, and are significantly different from command-and-control regulation. Suffice it to say that nothing in the present opinion necessarily entails pre-emption of voluntary programs. It is at least arguable that the phrase "adopt or attempt to enforce any standard" refers only to standards that are enforceable—a possibility reinforced by the fact that the prohibition is imposed only on entities (States and political subdivisions) that have power to enforce. . . .

The judgment is vacated, and the case is remanded for further proceedings consistent with this opinion.

[JUSTICE SOUTER's dissenting opinion is omitted.]

NOTES AND QUESTIONS

1. *Manufacturing Economies of Scale.* In *Engine Manufacturers*, the Court sees little difference between a standard requiring particular engine designs or performance, and state or local regulation limiting what sorts of vehicles can be purchased. Given the Clean Air Act's goals and the frequent focus in preemption law on avoiding the imposition of impossible, conflicting requirements, how would you have argued for a contrary outcome?

2. *Textualism and Policy Repercussions.* Seven justices join the majority opinion, an opinion that focuses overwhelmingly on language, interrelated provisions, and dictionaries. First, is this outcome compelled by statutory language? Second, when one is facing a court or judge that tends to use textualist modes of interpretation, are there any means by which an attorney can bring policy repercussions and broader statutory goals into the argument without losing the textualist judge or justice?

Many recent cases have dealt with various forms of product and risk regulation, often in connection with federal design or labeling requirements. Typically, the question is whether room is left for related state regulation or state common law claims over the design or safety of the product. Many of the laws giving rise to these cases contain both savings clauses and pre-emption clauses. These provisions do not, however, explicitly address the status of state common law liabilities. As a result of the tension between savings and pre-emptive provisions, and the failure explicitly to address common law liabilities, as well as the often substantial injuries that can flow from regulated products, this has become a fertile area of litigation. *Bates* is among the most recent cases dealing with these questions. As you will see in citations within the decision and in the following notes, this particular line of cases leaves a great deal of legal uncertainty for future similar cases.

BATES v. DOW AGROSCIENCES LLC
544 U.S. 431 (2005)

JUSTICE STEVENS delivered the opinion of the Court.

[Petitioners contended that their peanut crops were damaged by the application of respondent's pesticide ("Strongarm"). Strongarm's label asserted that the pesticide would be safe for use "in all areas where peanuts are grown." The petitioners alleged fraud, breach of warranty, tort claims, as well as violations of the Texas Deceptive Trade Practices–Consumer Protection Act (DTPA). The question at issue in this case was whether the Federal Insecticide, Fungicide, and Rodenticide Act (FIFRA) pre-empted their state law claims.]

III.

Against this background, we consider whether petitioners' claims are pre-empted by §136v(b), which, again, reads as follows: "Such State shall not impose or continue in effect any requirements for labeling or packaging in addition to or different from those required under this subchapter."

The introductory words of §136v(b)—"Such State"—appear to limit the coverage of that subsection to the States that are described in the preceding subsection (a). Texas is such a State because it regulates the sale and use of federally registered pesticides and does not permit any sales or uses prohibited by FIFRA. It is therefore beyond dispute that subsection (b) is applicable to this case.

The prohibitions in §136v(b) apply only to "requirements." An occurrence that merely motivates an optional decision does not qualify as a requirement. The Court of Appeals was therefore quite wrong when it assumed that any event, such as a jury verdict, that might "induce" a pesticide manufacturer to change its label should be viewed as a requirement. The Court of Appeals did, however, correctly hold that the term "requirements" in §136v(b) reaches beyond positive enactments, such as statutes and regulations, to embrace common-law duties. Our decision in *Cipollone* supports this conclusion. See 505 U.S., at 521 (plurality opinion) ("The phrase '[n]o requirement or prohibition' sweeps broadly and suggests no distinction between positive enactments and common law; to the contrary, those words easily encompass obligations that take the form of common-law rules"); see also id., at 548-549 (Scalia, J., concurring in judgment in part and dissenting in part). While the use of "requirements" in a pre-emption clause may not invariably carry this meaning, we think this is the best reading of §136v(b).

That §136v(b) may pre-empt judge-made rules, as well as statutes and regulations, says nothing about the scope of that pre-emption. For a particular state rule to be pre-empted, it must satisfy two conditions. First, it must be a requirement "for labeling or packaging"; rules governing the design of a product, for example, are not pre-empted. Second, it must impose a labeling or packaging requirement that is "in addition to or different from those required under this subchapter." A state regulation requiring the word "poison" to appear in red letters, for instance, would not be pre-empted if an EPA regulation imposed the same requirement.

It is perfectly clear that many of the common-law rules upon which petitioners rely do not satisfy the first condition. Rules that require manufacturers to design reasonably safe products, to use due care in conducting appropriate testing of their products, to market products free of manufacturing defects, and to honor their express warranties or other contractual commitments plainly do not qualify as requirements for "labeling or packaging." None of these common-law rules requires that manufacturers label or package their products in any particular way. Thus, petitioners' claims for defective design, defective manufacture, negligent testing, and breach of express warranty are not pre-empted.

To be sure, Dow's express warranty was located on Strongarm's label. But a cause of action on an express warranty asks only that a manufacturer make good on the contractual commitment that it voluntarily undertook by placing that warranty on its product. Because this common-law rule does not require the manufacturer to make an express warranty, or in the event that the manufacturer elects to do so, to say anything in particular in that warranty, the rule does not impose a requirement "for labeling or packaging." See id., at 525-526 (plurality opinion).

In arriving at a different conclusion, the court below reasoned that a finding of liability on these claims would "induce Dow to alter [its] label." 332 F.3d, at 332. This effects-based test finds no support in the text of §136v(b), which speaks only of "requirements." A requirement is a rule of law that must be obeyed; an event, such as a jury verdict, that merely motivates an optional decision is not a requirement. The proper inquiry calls for an examination of the elements of the common-law duty at issue, see *Cipollone*, 505 U.S., at 524; it does not call for speculation as to whether a jury verdict will prompt the manufacturer to take any particular action (a question, in any event, that will depend on a variety of cost/benefit calculations best left to the manufacturer's accountants).

The inducement test is unquestionably overbroad because it would impeach many "genuine" design defect claims that Dow concedes are not pre-empted. A design defect claim, if successful, would surely induce a manufacturer to alter its label to reflect a change in the list of ingredients or a change in the instructions for use necessitated by the improvement in the product's design. Moreover, the inducement test is not entirely consistent with §136v(a), which confirms the State's broad authority to regulate the sale and use of pesticides. Under §136v(a), a state agency may ban the sale of a pesticide if it finds, for instance, that one of the pesticide's label-approved uses is unsafe. This ban might well induce the manufacturer to change its label to warn against this questioned use. Under the inducement test, however, such a restriction would anomalously qualify as a "labeling" requirement. It is highly unlikely that

Congress endeavored to draw a line between the type of indirect pressure caused by a State's power to impose sales and use restrictions and the even more attenuated pressure exerted by common-law suits. The inducement test is not supported by either the text or the structure of the statute.

Unlike their other claims, petitioners' fraud and negligent-failure-to-warn claims are premised on common-law rules that qualify as "requirements for labeling or packaging." These rules set a standard for a product's labeling that the Strongarm label is alleged to have violated by containing false statements and inadequate warnings. While the courts of appeal have rightly found guidance in *Cipollone*'s interpretation of "requirements," some of those courts too quickly concluded that failure-to-warn claims were pre-empted under FIFRA, as they were in *Cipollone*, without paying attention to the rather obvious textual differences between the two pre-emption clauses.

Unlike the pre-emption clause at issue in *Cipollone*, §136v(b) prohibits only state-law labeling and packaging requirements that are "in addition to or different from" the labeling and packaging requirements under FIFRA. Thus, a state-law labeling requirement is not pre-empted by §136v(b) if it is equivalent to, and fully consistent with, FIFRA's misbranding provisions. Petitioners argue that their claims based on fraud and failure-to-warn are not pre-empted because these common-law duties are equivalent to FIFRA's requirements that a pesticide label not contain "false or misleading" statements, §136(q)(1)(A), or inadequate instructions or warnings. §§136(q)(1)(F), (G). We agree with petitioners insofar as we hold that state law need not explicitly incorporate FIFRA's standards as an element of a cause of action in order to survive pre-emption. As we will discuss below, however, we leave it to the Court of Appeals to decide in the first instance whether these particular common-law duties are equivalent to FIFRA's misbranding standards.

The "parallel requirements" reading of §136v(b) that we adopt today finds strong support in Medtronic, Inc. v. Lohr, 518 U.S. 470 (1996). In addressing a similarly worded pre-emption provision in a statute regulating medical devices, we found that "[n]othing in [21 U.S.C.] §360k denies Florida the right to provide a traditional damages remedy for violations of common-law duties when those duties parallel federal requirements." Id., at 495. As Justice O'Connor explained in her separate opinion, a state cause of action that seeks to enforce a federal requirement "does not impose a requirement that is 'different from, or in addition to,' requirements under federal law. To be sure, the threat of a damages remedy will give manufacturers an additional cause to comply, but the requirements imposed on them under state and federal law do not differ. Section 360k does not preclude States from imposing different or additional remedies, but only different or additional requirements." Id., at 513 (opinion concurring in part and dissenting in part). Accordingly, although FIFRA does not provide a federal remedy to farmers and others who are injured as a result of a manufacturer's violation of FIFRA's labeling requirements, nothing in §136v(b) precludes States from providing such a remedy.

Dow, joined by the United States as amicus curiae, argues that the "parallel requirements" reading of §136v(b) would "give juries in 50 States the authority to give content to FIFRA's misbranding prohibition, establishing a crazy-quilt of anti-misbranding requirements different from the one defined by FIFRA itself and intended by Congress to be interpreted authoritatively by EPA." Brief for Respondent 16. In our view, however, the clear text of §136v(b) and the authority of *Medtronic* cannot be so easily avoided. Conspicuously absent from the submissions by Dow and the United States is any plausible alternative interpretation of "in addition to or different from" that would give that phrase meaning. Instead, they appear to favor reading those words out of the statute, which would leave the following: "Such State shall not impose or continue in effect any requirements for labeling or packaging." This amputated version of §136v(b) would no doubt have clearly and succinctly commanded the pre-emption of all state requirements concerning labeling. That Congress added the remainder of the provision is evidence of its intent to draw a distinction between state labeling requirements that are pre-empted and those that are not.

Even if Dow had offered us a plausible alternative reading of §136v(b)—indeed, even if its alternative were just as plausible as our reading of that text—we would nevertheless have a duty to accept the reading that disfavors pre-emption. "[B]ecause the States are independent sovereigns in our federal system, we have long presumed that Congress does not cavalierly pre-empt state-law causes of action." *Medtronic*, 518 U.S., at 485. In areas of traditional state regulation, we assume that a federal statute has not supplanted state law unless Congress has made such an intention "'clear and manifest.'" New York State Conf. of Blue Cross & Blue Shield Plans v. Travelers Ins. Co., 514 U.S. 645, 655 (1995) (quoting Rice v. Santa Fe Elevator Corp., 331 U.S. 218, 230 (1947)); see also *Medtronic*, 518 U.S., at 485. Our reading is at once the only one that makes sense of each phrase in §136v(b) and the one favored by our canons of interpretation. The notion that FIFRA contains a nonambiguous command to pre-empt the types of tort claims that parallel FIFRA's misbranding requirements is particularly dubious given that just five years ago the United States advocated the interpretation that we adopt today.

The long history of tort litigation against manufacturers of poisonous substances adds force to the basic presumption against pre-emption. If Congress had intended to deprive injured parties of a long available form of compensation, it surely would have expressed that intent more clearly. See Silkwood v. Kerr-McGee Corp., 464 U.S. 238, 251 (1984). Moreover, this history emphasizes the importance of providing an incentive to manufacturers to use the utmost care in the business of distributing inherently dangerous items. See *Mortier*, 501 U.S., at 613 (stating that the 1972 amendments' goal was to "strengthen existing labeling requirements and ensure that these requirements were followed in practice"). Particularly given that Congress amended FIFRA to allow EPA to waive efficacy review of newly registered pesticides (and in the course of those amendments made technical changes to §136v(b)), it seems unlikely that Congress considered a relatively obscure provision like §136v(b) to give pesticide manufacturers virtual immunity from certain forms of tort liability. Overenforcement of FIFRA's misbranding prohibition creates a risk of imposing unnecessary financial burdens on manufacturers; under-enforcement creates not only financial risks for consumers, but risks that affect their safety and the environment as well.

Finally, we find the policy objections raised against our reading of §136v(b) to be unpersuasive. . . .

In sum, under our interpretation, §136v(b) retains a narrow, but still important, role. In the main, it pre-empts competing state labeling standards—imagine 50 different labeling regimes prescribing the color, font size, and wording of warnings—that would create significant inefficiencies for manufacturers. The provision also pre-empts any statutory or common-law rule that would impose a labeling requirement that diverges from those set out in FIFRA and its implementing regulations. It does not, however, pre-empt any state rules that are fully consistent with federal requirements.

Having settled on our interpretation of §136v(b), it still remains to be decided whether that provision pre-empts petitioners' fraud and failure-to-warn claims.

Because we have not received sufficient briefing on this issue, which involves questions of Texas law, we remand it to the Court of Appeals. We emphasize that a state-law labeling requirement must in fact be equivalent to a requirement under FIFRA in order to survive pre-emption. For example, were the Court of Appeals to determine that the element of falsity in Texas' common-law definition of fraud imposed a broader obligation than FIFRA's requirement that labels not contain "false or misleading statements," that state-law cause of action would be pre-empted by §136v(b) to the extent of that difference. State-law requirements must also be measured against any relevant EPA regulations that give content to FIFRA's misbranding standards. For example, a failure-to-warn claim alleging that a given pesticide's label should have stated "DANGER" instead of the more subdued "CAUTION" would be pre-empted because it is inconsistent with 40 CFR §156.64 (2004), which specifically assigns these warnings to particular classes of pesticides based on their toxicity.

In undertaking a pre-emption analysis at the pleadings stage of a case, a court should bear in mind the concept of equivalence. To survive pre-emption, the state-law requirement need not be phrased in the identical language as its corresponding FIFRA requirement; indeed, it would be surprising if a common-law requirement used the same phraseology as FIFRA. If a case proceeds to trial, the court's jury instructions must ensure that nominally equivalent labeling requirements are genuinely equivalent. If a defendant so requests, a court should instruct the jury on the relevant FIFRA misbranding standards, as well as any regulations that add content to those standards. For a manufacturer should not be held liable under a state labeling requirement subject to §136v(b) unless the manufacturer is also liable for misbranding as defined by FIFRA.

The judgment of the Court of Appeals is vacated, and the case is remanded for further proceedings consistent with this opinion.

NOTES

Bates upholds the validity of the challenged state common law actions, but the Court's preemption jurisprudence has been far from a model of consistency or clarity. As is evident in the *Bates* Court's distinguishing of *Medtronic* and other cases, it has sometimes been willing to broadly preempt state law claims. See, e.g., Geier v. American Honda Motor Co., 529 U.S. 861 (2000) (narrowly construing a savings clause and finding that National Traffic and Motor Vehicle Safety Act of 1966 preempted a design defect state tort claim). For a thorough canvassing of recent cases involving preemption claims in the setting of risk, pesticide, and product safety, see Vladeck, Preemption and Regulatory Failure, 33 Pepp. L. Rev. 95 (2005).

4. *Preemption by Agency Declaration*

In *Engine Manufacturers* and *Bates*, the Court worked primarily with arguments made in briefs, as well as with close parsing of statutory language and structure. During the spring of 2006, several different agencies working in different areas broadly declared the view that their regulatory actions should preempt state regulation, including common law liabilities related to the agency action.

This sort of "preambular preemption" was unusual. First, the mode of declaration—in Federal Register regulatory preambles—was unusual in form, especially given the fact that there was little or no advance notice of the intent to make such a declaration. These declarations also appeared to follow no process of the sort anticipated by Executive Order 13,132, 64 Fed. Reg. 43,255 (1999), which calls on agencies to engage in consultation with affected states before preempting state regulation. Finally, the few somewhat similar Federal Register declarations regarding preemption have, in the past, tended to declare an intent to preserve, not preempt, state regulation or common law. These actions have engendered criticism, but as of the fall of 2006, no appellate court has ruled on the effect of these clauses. Trial-level courts have been divided on their effect. See Sharkey, Preemption by Preamble: Federal Agencies and the Federalization of Tort Law, DePaul L. Rev. (forthcoming 2007).

Similarly, several agencies, through the United States Department of Justice in briefs, have recently articulated a more strongly pro-preemption position than in previous cases or regulatory materials. See Vladeck, *supra*, at 122-126. In *Bates*, for example, the Court rejected a pro-preemption argument by the federal government.

NOTES AND QUESTIONS

1. *Deference and Federalism Rationales.* The recent actions cited above raise a variety of issues. Should agency declarations in briefs or regulatory preambles receive deference? What kind of deference? After reading Chapter 3's excerpts of key cases articulating how courts should review agency action, consider which cases should apply in this setting. Should often declared presumptions against preemption apply here, or should agencies receive some sort of deference when they declare their views on the preemptive impact of a law or regulation? Finally, think through basic federalism rationales and consider arguments for and against such preemption declarations. For a discussion of how preemption presumptions apply when an agency interprets a statute to have a preemptive effect, see Mendelson, *Chevron* and Preemption, 102 Mich. L. Rev. 737 (2004).

2. *Agency Inertia, Regulatory Failure, and Broad Preemption Declarations.* If agencies consistently had abundant resources and implementation and enforcement zeal, broad preemption might pose little problem. Professor David Vladeck and many other observers of risk and environmental regulation find that budgetary limitations, political pressures, interest group influence, and ideological leanings all can result in agency failure to act. If inaction is a pervasive problem, then broad preemption declarations can leave citizens unprotected. Supporters of these declarations, however, see the elimination of legal uncertainty created by additional potential state law liabilities as a means to facilitate commerce. As the Consumer Products Safety Commission recently explained about its mattress flammability regulation, "[s]tate requirements . . . have the potential to undercut the Commission's uniform national flammability standard, create impediments for manufacturers . . . , establish requirements that make dual state and federal compliance physically impossible, and cause confusion among consumers. . . ." 16 C.F.R. Part 1633, Section N, discussed and quoted in 71 Fed. Reg. 13,471, 13,496-13,497 (2006).

3. *Rights without Remedies? And Damages?* Where citizens have been harmed by a product, perhaps in violation of federal regulatory requirements or perhaps as a result of some other product problem not addressed by regulation, citizens will often seek common law damages relief. Most regulatory statutes provide no such damages remedy. If agency preemption declarations regarding state law and state common law

liabilities are given broad effect, then injured citizens may be left with no remedy, even in the face of underlying legal violations. As Professor Sharkey observes in the article cited above, the Supreme Court has made it quite clear that implied causes of action will rarely be recognized. See Alexander v. Sandoval, 532 U.S. 275 (2001). Because many laws regarding product safety and labeling do not contain "citizen suit" provisions, as do most environmental laws directed at pollution or protection of natural resources, as opposed to products like pesticides, this combination of agency declarations and Court precedent threatens to leave citizens with no remedy for legal violations causing harms.

4. *Greenhouse Gases and State Power.* As this book goes to press, several states are seeking to regulate greenhouse gases. Whether these efforts will be upheld or pre-empted will soon be determined. For reflections on these efforts and their prospects, see Carlson, Federalism, Preemption, and Greenhouse Gas Emissions, 37 U.C. Davis L. Rev. 281 (2003); Engel, Who's Afraid of Overlapping Federal and State Jurisdiction?: Harnessing the Benefits of Dynamic Federalism in Environmental Law, 56 Emory L.J. 159 (2006).

F. DORMANT COMMERCE CLAUSE LIMITATIONS ON STATE REGULATION

As noted in virtually all constitutional law classes, state regulatory activity can be blocked by arguments rooted in dormant Commerce Clause doctrine. A case and notes related to this doctrine are included in Chapter 8, but brief coverage is included here to clarify the place of this body of law in federalism doctrine.

Most Supreme Court dormant Commerce Clause cases in recent years arise from state or municipal efforts to control and handle waste, especially efforts to ensure the existence of markets adequate to finance local waste-handling facilities. The problem occurs when one jurisdiction's efforts have the effect of precluding interstate commerce, by limiting the movement of goods either into or out of the jurisdiction. Such efforts do not require federal law or regulations to create an express conflict. Instead, it is a court's finding of an undue burden on interstate commerce that leads to invalidation on dormant Commerce Clause grounds. See section G of Chapter 8. Thus, federalism concerns do not just cut against federal power, or arise only when federal statutes or regulations come into conflict with state law. State and local activities can be struck down as unconstitutional based solely on court determinations about their adverse impact on interstate commerce.

III

THE ADMINISTRATIVE LAW OF
ENVIRONMENTAL PROTECTION

Environmental law, like all administrative law, is heavily influenced by the process by which it is adopted. Accordingly, it is helpful to survey some of the important issues raised by the processes that govern environmental decisionmaking before addressing in the remainder of this book the substance of environmental law that emerges from those processes.

Administrative law is largely concerned with two great questions. First, it is concerned with the roles of the three branches of government established by the Constitution in the creation and implementation of law and policy. Second, it is concerned with the procedures followed by the executive or independent agencies to whom legislative and non–Article III judicial authority has been delegated. Because administrative agencies have no explicit constitutional footing, their legal status has always been ambiguous and subject to intense debate. Criticisms of the "headless fourth branch of government" have been raised since the explosion of the administrative state during the New Deal in the 1930s. More recently, the impetus toward deregulation among academics, economists, and legislators that began during the 1980s fueled a renewed interest in fundamental administrative law questions such as the constitutional legitimacy of agencies and the role of the courts, Congress, and the executive branch in promoting greater accountability by agency decisionmakers. This chapter focuses on selected examples of how these debates have played out in the context of environmental law.

Those who are dissatisfied with agency decisions concerning environmental matters often seek to invoke the aid of the courts in reversing decisions they perceive to deviate from legislative mandates. But judicial assistance is available only if litigants have access to the courts. Accordingly, this chapter begins with a survey of various doctrines, such as standing to sue, which serve to limit that access. The issue is particularly resonant in the environmental law area because it was in large part the skillful advocacy by environmental interests before newly sympathetic judges that was responsible for the root-and-branch alteration of American administrative law during the 1970s. Two Supreme Court decisions in the 1970s facilitated the access of these groups to the courts and essentially eliminated standing as a serious obstacle to judicial review of environmental matters in the federal courts for nearly two decades. Another pair of formalist Supreme Court decisions in the early 1990s reopened the issue of standing and threatened to restrict significantly judicial review at the behest of environmental groups as a constraint on agency decisionmaking.

Even if access to the courts is available, judicial review will not limit agency discretion unless the courts take seriously the task of reviewing the merits of agency decisions. Section A of this chapter is therefore also devoted to a study of the standards that govern judicial review of agency interpretation and implementation of statutes. The materials reflect the continuing conflict between judicial inclinations to defer to administrative expertise and to provide meaningful review of agency decisions to insure that they conform to legislative mandates.

Congress also plays an active role in confining administrative discretion. The agencies that make decisions that affect the environment are all creatures of statute. Congress, of course, has a variety of tools for placing limits on how those decisions are made, including drafting statutes that confine agency discretion through specific mandates and holding hearings to oversee agency performance. Congress also can cut appropriations to express dissatisfaction with agency decisions or place restrictions on the ability of agencies to expend appropriated funds for disfavored purposes or projects. Congress increasingly resorted to this power of the purse to achieve its environmental policy objectives in the 1990s. It also enacted a series of statutes, applicable to all or most administrative agencies, which either require that agencies engage in analytical processes or apply substantive standards that further restrict agency discretion. Section B of this chapter briefly surveys these congressional oversight techniques.

Finally, the discretion of independent regulatory agencies such as EPA can be reined in by the executive branch. Section C of this chapter covers executive review of administrative agency decisionmaking and touches upon the policy and legal issues raised by efforts within the White House to control implementation of statutes enacted by Congress.

Not surprisingly, agencies whose discretion has been narrowed have responded to these kinds of oversight (especially by the courts and the executive branch) by seeking to recapture some of their independence. The final section of this chapter illustrates a tendency on the part of the agencies to shift from decisionmaking through formal mechanisms (such as rulemaking) that are subject to judicial, legislative, and executive branch review to more informal processes not saddled by those review processes. Among the questions raised by that shift is whether the new methods of doing business threaten to reduce the ability of those affected by agency decisions to have meaningful input into the decisionmaking process, and therefore to weaken the legitimacy of those decisions.

A.   JUDICIAL CONTROL OF ADMINISTRATIVE ENVIRONMENTAL DECISIONMAKING

1.   Access to the Courts: Standing and Related Preclusion Doctrines

Quite frequently, an administrative decision that is claimed to have negative environmental impacts is challenged by organizations and individuals who did not initiate the agency decisionmaking process. For example, if the Interior Department enters into a lease with a private company for mining on public lands, both parties to the lease probably will be satisfied with this decision (unless, of course, the agency imposes environmentally protective or other conditions that are unacceptable to the lessee). In such a case, judicial review will be sought, if at all, only by third parties concerned about the adverse environmental consequences of the Department's action.

Third parties who seek judicial review of agency actions must have standing to sue or they will be denied access to the courts. These third-party plaintiffs traditionally have faced difficult standing problems because of the rule that a plaintiff must show injury to a common law or statutory legal interest. That theory of access left no room for the generally concerned citizen representing a broad public interest, such as a public policy concern that was ecological or even philosophical in nature. In the leading case of Associated Indus., Inc. v. Ickes, 134 F.2d 694 (2d Cir. 1943), however, Judge Frank held that Congress could constitutionally authorize "so to speak, private Attorney Generals" to bring suit to prevent an administrative official from acting in violation of statutory power. Some administrative law scholars endorsed such public actions as consistent with the fundamental principles of representative government. The major constitutional argument against the public action is that it violates the "case or controversy" requirement of Article III of the Constitution. See Berger, Standing to Sue in Public Actions: Is It a Constitutional Requirement?, 78 Yale L.J. 816 (1969). The decisions reproduced and discussed in this section illustrate how the courts have swung back and forth between the theory that administrative standing should be based on private rights, created by common law or statute, and the theory that public actions can legitimately be policed by members of the public, which were intended to be the beneficiaries of regulatory programs.

SIERRA CLUB v. MORTON
405 U.S. 727 (1972)

Mr. JUSTICE STEWART delivered the opinion of the Court.

I

The Mineral King Valley is an area of great natural beauty nestled in the Sierra Nevada Mountains in Tulare County, California, adjacent to Sequoia National Park. It has been part of the Sequoia National Forest since 1926, and is designated as a national game refuge by special Act of Congress. Though once the site of extensive mining activity, Mineral King is now used almost exclusively for recreational purposes. Its relative inaccessibility and lack of development have limited the number of visitors each year, and at the same time have preserved the valley's quality as a quasi-wilderness area largely uncluttered by the products of civilization.

[The United States Forest Service, responding to rapidly increasing demand for skiing facilities, invited bids from private developers for the construction and operation of a combination ski resort and summer recreation area in the national forest. In January 1969, it approved a plan by Walt Disney Enterprises for "a $35 million complex of motels, restaurants, swimming pools, parking lots, and other structures designed to accommodate 14,000 visitors daily. This complex is to be constructed on 80 acres of the valley floor under a 30-year use permit from the Forest Service." The agency issued another permit for construction of ski lifts, ski trails, a cog-assisted railway, and utility installations. Access to the resort required construction by California of a 20-mile highway, a section of which would traverse Sequoia National Park. A proposed high-voltage power line needed to provide electricity for the resort would also cut through the Park. Approval of the Department of the Interior, which administers the Park, was required for both the highway and the power line.

In June 1969, the Sierra Club, which opposed the development, filed suit in federal district court, seeking a declaratory judgment that the proposed development violated a series of federal statutes and regulations governing management of the national parks and forests. The Club also sought to enjoin the agencies involved from issuing the permits necessary for development. It sued as a membership corporation with "a special interest in the conservation and the sound maintenance of the national parks, game refuges and forests of the country." The district court issued a preliminary injunction, ruling that the Sierra Club had standing to sue. After the Ninth Circuit reversed, the Club appealed.]

II

The first question presented is whether the Sierra Club has alleged facts that entitle it to obtain judicial review of the challenged action. Whether a party has a sufficient stake in an otherwise justiciable controversy to obtain judicial resolution of that controversy is what has traditionally been referred to as the question of standing to sue. Where the party does not rely on any specific statute authorizing invocation of the judicial process, the question of standing depends upon whether the party has alleged such a "personal stake in the outcome of the controversy," Baker v. Carr, 369 U.S. 186, 204, as to ensure that "the dispute sought to be adjudicated will be presented in an adversary context and in a form historically viewed as capable of judicial resolution." Flast v. Cohen, 392 U.S. 83, 101. Where, however, Congress has authorized public officials to perform certain functions according to law, and has provided by statute for judicial review of those actions under certain circumstances, the inquiry as to standing must begin with a determination of whether the statute in question authorizes review at the behest of the plaintiff.

The Sierra Club relies upon §10 of the Administrative Procedure Act (APA), 5 U.S.C. §702, which provides: "A person suffering legal wrong because of agency action, or adversely affected or aggrieved by agency action within the meaning of a relevant statute, is entitled to judicial review thereof." Early decisions under this statute interpreted the language as adopting the various formulations of "legal interest" and "legal wrong" then prevailing as constitutional requirements of standing. But, in Association of Data Processing Service Organizations, Inc. v. Camp, 397 U.S. 150, and Barlow v. Collins, 397 U.S. 159, ... we held more broadly that persons had standing to obtain judicial review of federal agency action under §10 of the APA where they had alleged that the challenged action had caused them "injury in fact," and where the alleged injury was to an interest "arguably within the zone of interests to be protected or regulated" by the statutes that the agencies were claimed to have violated.[5]

_____

5. In deciding this case we do not reach any questions concerning the meaning of the "zone of interests" test or its possible application to the facts here presented.

. . . [P]alpable economic injuries [of the kind allegedly suffered by the plaintiffs in *Data Processing* and *Barlow*] have long been recognized as sufficient to lay the basis for standing, with or without a specific statutory provision for judicial review. [But] neither *Data Processing* nor *Barlow* addressed itself to the question . . . as to what must be alleged by persons who claim injury of a noneconomic nature to interests that are widely shared. That question is presented in this case.

III

The injury alleged by the Sierra Club will be incurred entirely by reason of the change in the uses to which Mineral King will be put, and the attendant change in the aesthetics and ecology of the area. Thus, in referring to the road to be built through Sequoia National Park, the complaint alleged that the development "would destroy or otherwise adversely affect the scenery, natural and historic objects and wildlife of the park and would impair the enjoyment of the park for future generations." We do not question that this type of harm may amount to an "injury in fact" sufficient to lay the basis for standing under §10 of the APA. Aesthetic and environmental well-being, like economic well-being, are important ingredients of the quality of life in our society, and the fact that particular environmental interests are shared by the many rather than the few does not make them less deserving of legal protection through the judicial process. But the "injury in fact" test requires more than an injury to a cognizable interest. It requires that the party seeking review be himself among the injured.

The impact of the proposed changes in the environment of Mineral King will not fall indiscriminately upon every citizen. The alleged injury will be felt directly only by those who use Mineral King and Sequoia National Park, and for whom the aesthetic and recreational values of the area will be lessened by the highway and ski resort. The Sierra Club failed to allege that it or its members would be affected in any of their activities or pastimes by the Disney development. Nowhere in the pleadings or affidavits did the Club state that its members use Mineral King for any purpose, much less that they use it in any way that would be significantly affected by the proposed actions of the respondents.[8]

---

8. The only reference in the pleadings to the Sierra Club's interest in the dispute is contained in paragraph 3 of the complaint, which reads in its entirety as follows:

> Plaintiff Sierra Club is a non-profit corporation organized and operating under the laws of the State of California, with its principal place of business in San Francisco, California since 1892. Membership of the club is approximately 78,000 nationally, with approximately 27,000 members residing in the San Francisco Bay Area. For many years the Sierra Club by its activities and conduct has exhibited a special interest in the conservation and the sound maintenance of the national parks, game refuges and forests of the country, regularly serving as a responsible representative of persons similarly interested. One of the principal purposes of the Sierra Club is to protect and conserve the national resources of the Sierra Nevada Mountains. Its interests would be vitally affected by the acts hereinafter described and would be aggrieved by those acts of the defendants as hereinafter more fully appears.

[An amicus brief asserted that the Sierra Club conducted regular camping trips into the Mineral King area and that its members continued to use the area for recreational purposes. The Court noted that these allegations were not presented to either court below.] Moreover, the Sierra Club in its reply brief specifically declines to rely on its individualized interest, as a basis for standing. See n.15, *infra*. Our decision does not, of course, bar the Sierra Club from seeking in the District Court to amend its complaint by a motion under Rule 15, Federal Rules of Civil Procedure.

The Club apparently regarded any allegations of individualized injury as superfluous, on the theory that this was a "public" action involving questions as to the use of natural resources, and that the Club's longstanding concern with and expertise in such matters were sufficient to give it standing as a "representative of the public."[9] This theory reflects a misunderstanding of our cases involving so-called "public actions" in the area of administrative law. . . .

Taken together, [the Court's previous decisions] established a dual proposition: the fact of economic injury is what gives a person standing to seek judicial review under the statute, but once review is properly invoked, that person may argue the public interest in support of his claim that the agency has failed to comply with its statutory mandate. It was in the latter sense that the "standing" of the appellant in [a previous case] existed only as a "representative of the public interest." It is in a similar sense that we have used the phrase "private attorney general" to describe the function performed by persons upon whom Congress has conferred the right to seek judicial review of agency action.

The trend of cases arising under the APA and other statutes authorizing judicial review of federal agency action has been toward recognizing that injuries other than economic harm are sufficient to bring a person within the meaning of the statutory language, and toward discarding the notion that an injury that is widely shared is ipso facto not an injury sufficient to provide the basis for judicial review. We noted this development with approval in *Data Processing*. . . . But broadening the categories of injury that may be alleged in support of standing is a different matter from abandoning the requirement that the party seeking review must himself have suffered an injury.

Some courts have indicated a willingness to take this latter step by conferring standing upon organizations that have demonstrated "an organizational interest in the problem" of environmental or consumer protection. It is clear that an organization whose members are injured may represent those members in a proceeding for judicial review. But a mere "interest in a problem," no matter how longstanding the interest and no matter how qualified the organization is in evaluating the problem, is not sufficient by itself to render the organization "adversely affected" or "aggrieved" within the meaning of the APA. The Sierra Club is a large and long-established organization, with a historic commitment to the cause of protecting our Nation's natural heritage from man's depredations. But if a "special interest" in this subject were enough to entitle the Sierra Club to commence this litigation, there would appear to be no objective basis upon which to disallow a suit by any other bona fide "special interest" organization however small or short-lived. And if any group with a bona fide "special interest" could initiate such litigation, it is difficult to perceive why any individual citizen with the same bona fide special interest would not also be entitled to do so.

The requirement that a party seeking review must allege facts showing that he is himself adversely affected does not insulate executive action from judicial review, nor does it prevent any public interests from being protected through the judicial

9. This approach to the question of standing was adopted by the Court of Appeals for the Second Circuit in Citizens Committee for Hudson Valley v. Volpe, 425 F.2d 97, 105:

> We hold, therefore, that the public interest in environmental resources—an interest created by statutes affecting the issuance of this permit—is a legally protected interest affording these plaintiffs, as responsible representatives of the public, standing to obtain judicial review of agency action alleged to be in contravention of that public interest.

process.[15] It does serve as at least a rough attempt to put the decision as to whether review will be sought in the hands of those who have a direct stake in the outcome. That goal would be undermined were we to construe the APA to authorize judicial review at the behest of organizations or individuals who seek to do no more than vindicate their own value preferences through the judicial process. The principle that the Sierra Club would have us establish in this case would do just that.

. . . [T]he Court of Appeals was correct in its holding that the Sierra Club lacked standing to maintain this action. . . .

[The dissenting opinions of JUSTICES BLACKMUN, BRENNAN, and DOUGLAS are omitted.]

NOTES AND QUESTIONS

1. Did the Court's "user standing" rule place any serious limitations on the standing of plaintiffs with ideological interests? Do you see why *Sierra Club* in retrospect may be viewed as a victory for environmental interests, even though the Club did not prevail? The Club had no difficulty amending its complaint to allege facts sufficient to confer standing. Sierra Club v. Morton, 348 F. Supp. 219 (N.D. Cal. 1972). Why do you think the Club chose not to assert individualized injury to itself or its members?*

According to one account, the Supreme Court's reluctance in *Sierra Club* to recognize standing based on the plaintiff's ideological interests is consistent with the jurisprudence of John Wesley Hohfeld, who posited that all legal relations are relations between persons. This view fails to accommodate not only "the idea of a non-person occupying a legal position," but also "the idea of a group of persons occupying a legal position to protect an interest in which they or other persons for whom they serve as agents do not hold individual personal stakes." Manus, One Hundred Years of Green: A Legal Perspective on Three Twentieth Century Nature Philosophers, 59 U. Pitt. L. Rev. 557, 603 (1998).

2. *Injury in Fact and* SCRAP. *Sierra Club*'s relaxed user standard appeared to afford access to the courts to environmental public interest groups on the basis of third party standing. But because the plaintiff in that case did not allege individualized injury to itself or its members, it was not clear at what point the link between the challenged project and the claimed environmental harm would become so attenuated

15. In its reply brief, after noting the fact that it might have chosen to assert individualized injury to itself or to its members as a basis for standing, the Sierra Club states:

> The Government seeks to create a "heads I win, tails you lose" situation in which either the courthouse door is barred for lack of assertion of a private, unique injury or a preliminary injunction is denied on the ground that the litigant has advanced private injury which does not warrant an injunction adverse to a competing public interest. Counsel have shaped their case to avoid this trap.

The short answer to this contention is that the "trap" does not exist. The test of injury in fact goes only to the question of standing to obtain judicial review. Once this standing is established, the party may assert the interests of the general public in support of his claims for equitable relief.

*For a critique of *Sierra Club*, see Sax, Standing to Sue: A Critical Review of the Mineral King Decision, 13 Nat. Resources J. 76 (1973). For discussion of the history of the standing doctrine in environmental law cases, see Weinberg, Unbarring the Bar of Justice: Standing in Environmental Suits and the Constitution, 21 Pace Envtl. L. Rev. 27 (2003).

as to defeat the plaintiff's standing. United States v. Students Challenging Regulatory Agency Procedures (*SCRAP I*), 412 U.S. 669 (1973), provided an answer. A student group and environmental organization brought suit challenging a rate increase by the Interstate Commerce Commission (ICC). They argued that the increase would discourage the use of recycled materials by subjecting them to higher transportation charges than those applicable to virgin materials, and they sought to compel the ICC to prepare an environmental impact statement. The Supreme Court held that the plaintiffs had standing:

> Unlike the specific and geographically limited federal action of which the petitioner complained in *Sierra Club*, the challenged agency action in this case is applicable to substantially all of the Nation's railroads, and thus allegedly has an adverse environmental impact on all the natural resources of the country. Rather than a limited group of persons who used a picturesque valley in California, all persons who utilize the scenic resources of the country, and indeed all who breathe its air, could claim harm similar to that alleged by the environmental groups here. But we have already made it clear that standing is not to be denied simply because many people suffer the same injury. . . . To deny standing to persons who are in fact injured simply because many others are also injured, would mean that the most injurious and widespread Government actions could be questioned by nobody. We cannot accept that conclusion.
>
> But the injury alleged here is also very different from that at issue in *Sierra Club* because here the alleged injury to the environment is far less direct and perceptible. The petitioner there complained about the construction of a specific project that would directly affect the Mineral King Valley. Here, the Court was asked to follow a far more attenuated line of causation to the eventual injury of which appellees complained—a general rate increase would allegedly cause increased use of nonrecyclable commodities as compared to recyclable goods, thus resulting in the need to use more natural resources to produce such goods, some of which resources might be taken from the Washington area, and resulting in more refuse that might be discarded in national parks in the Washington area. The railroads protest that the appellees could never prove that a general increase in rates would have this effect, and they contend that these allegations were a ploy to avoid the need to show some injury in fact.

Id. at 687-688. The Court responded that the pleadings alleged facts sufficient to show standing; if the railroads believed that the allegations in the pleadings were untrue, they should have moved for summary judgment.

   3. *The Fall of the Standing Barrier.* The *SCRAP I* decision appeared to reduce the injury in fact requirement to a fiction. Occasionally the government and other defendants attempted to disprove plaintiffs' allegations of injury, but such attempts generally did not succeed. Taken together, *Sierra Club* and *SCRAP* sent clear signals to the lower courts that those seeking to enforce federal environmental legislation should be afforded relatively unhindered access to the courts. See Glicksman, A Retreat from Judicial Activism: The Seventh Circuit and the Environment, 63 Chi.-Kent L. Rev. 209, 219-220 (1987). Eventually, the Justice Department stopped vigorously asserting lack of standing in environmental cases.

   4. *The Erection of New Standing Obstacles:* Lujan I. Nearly two decades after the *SCRAP* decision, statutory beneficiaries were abruptly confronted with a reinvigorated standing barrier as a result of two cases decided by the Supreme Court in 1990 and 1992. The first of the two decisions was Lujan v. National Wildlife Fed'n, 497 U.S. 871 (1990) (*Lujan I*). The NWF sued the Department of the Interior and the Bureau of

Land Management (BLM), alleging that the agencies violated the Federal Land Policy and Management Act (FLPMA) and the National Environmental Policy Act (NEPA) in implementing what the NWF called the "land withdrawal review program." The BLM had revoked some withdrawals of public lands from developmental uses such as mining and classified other lands for multiple use management or disposal. The government claimed that the plaintiff lacked standing. The district court refused to allow the NWF to introduce the affidavits of four of its members, finding them to be untimely, and dismissed. The D.C. Circuit reversed, holding that two affidavits filed by NWF members (in which they alleged adverse effects on recreational use and aesthetic enjoyment of federal lands in the vicinity of lands that had been opened to mining and oil and gas leasing) were sufficient to establish standing to challenge all decisions under the land withdrawal review program and that the district court abused its discretion in rejecting the additional four affidavits.

The NWF relied on §10 of the APA to establish a right to review because neither FLPMA nor NEPA provides a private right of action. The Court, in an opinion by Justice Scalia joined by four other Justices, began by dissecting the APA's requirements. A plaintiff invoking §10 must show that it is suffering legal wrong or has been adversely affected or aggrieved by "agency action." In addition, the agency action must be "final." 5 U.S.C. §704.

The affidavits appeared to satisfy the "user standing" requirements set forth in *Sierra Club*, as interpreted in *SCRAP I* and applied in subsequent lower court cases spanning almost two decades. The four dissenting Justices found them to be sufficient, too. But Justice Scalia asserted that the two affidavits admitted by the district court did not satisfy the requirements of Rule 56 of the Federal Rules of Civil Procedure, which governs summary judgment motions, because they stated only that the NWF's members had used

> unspecified portions of an immense tract of territory, on some portions of which mining activity has occurred or probably will occur by virtue of [the challenged] governmental action. It will not do to "presume" [as the Court of Appeals did] the missing facts because without them the affidavits would not establish the injury they generally allege.

497 U.S. at 889. Taking a swipe at *SCRAP I*, the Court averred that its "expansive expression of what would suffice for [review of agency action under §10 of the APA] under its particular facts has never since been emulated by this Court." Id. Further, *SCRAP I* was irrelevant because it arose in the context of a Rule 12(b) motion to dismiss rather than a Rule 56 motion for summary judgment.

Justice Scalia added that, even if the additional four affidavits had been admitted, they would not have sustained the NWF's challenge to the BLM's "land withdrawal review program" because the so-called program did not constitute agency action for purposes of the APA, much less final agency action. The Court characterized the BLM's 1250 or so individual withdrawal revocation and land classification decisions instead as "the continuing (and thus constantly changing) operations of the BLM" in carrying out its responsibilities under FLPMA of reviewing withdrawals and classifications and developing land use plans. Although the NWF alleged rampant violations of the law in the implementation of the program, the Court refused to permit it to "seek wholesale improvement of this program by court decree, rather than in the offices of the Department or the halls of Congress, where programmatic improvements are normally made." Id. at 891.

5. *The Significance of* Lujan I. What is the status of Sierra Club v. Morton and the *SCRAP* case after Lujan v. NWF? What would the NWF's members have had to allege to have survived a motion for summary judgment on the standing issue? Was the real defect in the NWF's case not that the organization lacked standing but that the case was not yet ripe for review? What is the likely effect of the Court's decision on the ability of environmental groups such as the NWF to challenge the BLM's implementation of FLPMA?

What role did the "case or controversy" requirement of Article III play in the Court's decision? Lujan v. NWF is often cited as precedent for the proper interpretation of that requirement. To what extent are separation-of-powers concerns reflected in Justice Scalia's majority opinion? See Sheldon, *Lujan v. NWF*: Justice Scalia Restricts Environmental Standing to Constrain the Courts, 20 Envtl. L. Rep. (ELI) 10557 (1990).

The Court's retrenchment of environmental standing continued in the following case.

LUJAN v. DEFENDERS OF WILDLIFE
504 U.S. 555 (1992)

Justice Scalia delivered the opinion of the Court with respect to Parts I, II, III-A, and IV, and an opinion with respect to Part III-B, in which The Chief Justice, Justice White, and Justice Thomas join.

[In 1978, the Fish and Wildlife Service (FWS) and the National Marine Fisheries Service (NMFS) issued a joint regulation stating that the obligations imposed by §7(a)(2) of the Endangered Species Act of 1973 (ESA) extend to actions taken in foreign nations. Section 7(a)(2) requires federal agencies, in consultation with the Secretary of the Interior, to ensure that their actions are not likely to jeopardize the continued existence of any endangered or threatened species or result in the destruction of critical habitat. In 1986, the regulation was revised to require consultation only for actions taken in the United States or on the high seas. The Defenders of Wildlife sued the Secretary, seeking a declaratory judgment that the new regulation was inconsistent with §7(a)(2) and an injunction requiring the Secretary to reissue the original regulation. The district court dismissed for lack of standing, but the Eighth Circuit reversed. On remand, the district court denied the Secretary's motion for summary judgment and granted Defenders' motion on the standing issue, concluding that the Eighth Circuit had already ruled on the question. The Secretary sought review.]

II

. . . [T]he Constitution of the United States . . . limits the jurisdiction of federal courts to "Cases" and "Controversies[.]" . . . One of [the Constitutional] landmarks, setting apart the "Cases" and "Controversies" that are of the justiciable sort referred to in Article III—"serv[ing] to identify those disputes which are appropriately resolved through the judicial process," Whitmore v. Arkansas, 495 U.S. 149 (1990)—is the doctrine of standing. Though some of its elements express merely prudential considerations that are part of judicial self-government, the core component of standing is an essential and unchanging part of the case-or-controversy requirement of Article III.

Over the years, our cases have established that the irreducible constitutional minimum of standing contains three elements. First, the plaintiff must have suffered an "injury in fact"—an invasion of a legally protected interest which is (a) concrete and particularized;[1] and (b) "actual or imminent, not 'conjectural' or 'hypothetical.'" Second, there must be a causal connection between the injury and the conduct complained of—the injury has to be "fairly . . . trace[able] to the challenged action of the defendant, and not . . . th[e] result [of] the independent action of some third party not before the court." Simon v. Eastern Ky. Welfare Rights Org., 426 U.S. 26, 41-42 (1976). Third, it must be "likely," as opposed to merely "speculative," that the injury will be "redressed by a favorable decision."

The party invoking federal jurisdiction bears the burden of establishing these elements. . . . [E]ach element must be supported in the same way as any other matter on which the plaintiff bears the burden of proof, i.e., with the manner and degree of evidence required at the successive stages of the litigation. At the pleading stage, general factual allegations of injury resulting from the defendant's conduct may suffice, for on a motion to dismiss we "presum[e] that general allegations embrace those specific facts that are necessary to support the claim." [Lujan v. National Wildlife Federation, 497 U.S. 871, 889 (1990).] In response to a summary judgment motion, however, the plaintiff can no longer rest on such "mere allegations," but must "set forth" by affidavit or other evidence "specific facts," Fed. Rule Civ. Proc. 56(e), which for purposes of the summary judgment motion will be taken to be true. And at the final stage, those facts (if controverted) must be "supported adequately by the evidence adduced at trial."

When the suit is one challenging the legality of government action or inaction, the nature and extent of facts that must be averred (at the summary judgment stage) or proved (at the trial stage) in order to establish standing depends considerably upon whether the plaintiff is himself an object of the action (or forgone action) at issue. If he is, there is ordinarily little question that the action or inaction has caused him injury, and that a judgment preventing or requiring the action will redress it. When, however, as in this case, a plaintiff's asserted injury arises from the government's allegedly unlawful regulation (or lack of regulation) of someone else, much more is needed. In that circumstance, causation and redressability ordinarily hinge on the response of the regulated (or regulable) third party to the government action or inaction—and perhaps on the response of others as well. The existence of one or more of the essential elements of standing "depends on the unfettered choices made by independent actors not before the courts and whose exercise of broad and legitimate discretion the courts cannot presume either to control or to predict," ASARCO Inc. v. Kadish, 490 U.S. 605, 615 (1989) (opinion of KENNEDY, J.); and it becomes the burden of the plaintiff to adduce facts showing that those choices have been or will be made in such manner as to produce causation and permit redressability of injury. Thus, when the plaintiff is not himself the object of the government action or inaction he challenges, standing is not precluded, but it is ordinarily "substantially more difficult" to establish.

1. By particularized, we mean that the injury must affect the plaintiff in a personal and individual way.

III

A

Respondents' claim to injury is that the lack of consultation with respect to certain funded activities abroad "increas[es] the rate of extinction of endangered and threatened species." Of course, the desire to use or observe an animal species, even for purely esthetic purposes, is undeniably a cognizable interest for purpose of standing. See, e.g., Sierra Club v. Morton, 405 U.S., at 734. "But the 'injury in fact' test requires more than an injury to a cognizable interest. It requires that the party seeking review be himself among the injured." Id. at 734-35. To survive the Secretary's summary judgment motion, respondents had to submit affidavits or other evidence showing, through specific facts, not only that listed species were in fact being threatened by funded activities abroad, but also that one or more of respondents' members would thereby be "directly" affected apart from their " 'special interest' in th[e] subject."

With respect to this aspect of the case, the Court of Appeals focused on the affidavits of two Defenders' members — Joyce Kelly and Amy Skilbred. Ms. Kelly stated that she traveled to Egypt in 1986 and "observed the traditional habitat of the endangered Nile crocodile there and intend[s] to do so again, and hope[s] to observe the crocodile directly," and that she "will suffer harm in fact as the result of [the] American . . . role . . . in overseeing the rehabilitation of the Aswan High Dam on the Nile. . . ." Ms. Skilbred averred that she traveled to Sri Lanka in 1981 and "observed th[e] habitat" of "endangered species such as the Asian elephant and the leopard" at what is now the site of the Mahaweli project funded by the Agency for International Development (AID). [Ms. Skilbred averred that, although she did not see any endangered species in 1981, the Mahaweli project "will seriously reduce" endangered species habitat in areas that she visited, which might accelerate the extinction of those species. She averred that this threat harmed her because she intended to return to Sri Lanka "in the future" and hoped to spot elephants and leopards on that trip. At a subsequent deposition, Ms. Skilbred claimed that "I intend to go back to Sri Lanka," but had no current plans to do so: "I don't know [when]. There is a civil war going on right now. I don't know. Not next year, I will say. In the future."]

We shall assume . . . that these affidavits contain facts showing that certain agency-funded projects threaten listed species — though that is questionable. They plainly contain no facts, however, showing how damage to the species will produce "imminent" injury to Mses. Kelly and Skilbred. That the women "had visited" the areas of the projects before the projects commenced proves nothing. As we have said in a related context, " 'Past exposure to illegal conduct does not in itself show a present case or controversy regarding injunctive relief . . . if unaccompanied by any continuing, present adverse effects.' " Los Angeles v. Lyons, 461 U.S. 95, 102 (1983). And the affiants' profession of an "inten[t]" to return to the places they had visited before — where they will presumably, this time, be deprived of the opportunity to observe animals of the endangered species — is simply not enough. Such "some day" intentions — without any description of concrete plans, or indeed even any specification of when the some day will be — do not support a finding of the "actual or imminent" injury that our cases require.

Besides relying upon the Kelly and Skilbred affidavits, respondents propose a series of novel standing theories. The first, inelegantly styled "ecosystem nexus," proposes that any person who uses any part of a "contiguous ecosystem" adversely affected by a funded activity has standing even if the activity is located a great distance away.

This approach, as the Court of Appeals correctly observed, is inconsistent with our opinion in *National Wildlife Federation*, which held that a plaintiff claiming injury from environmental damage must use the area affected by the challenged activity and not an area roughly "in the vicinity" of it. It makes no difference that the general-purpose section of the ESA states that the Act was intended in part "to provide a means whereby the ecosystems upon which endangered species and threatened species depend may be conserved," 16 U.S.C. §1531(b). To say that the Act protects ecosystems is not to say that the Act creates (if it were possible) rights of action in persons who have not been injured in fact, that is, persons who use portions of an ecosystem not perceptibly affected by the unlawful action in question.

Respondents' other theories are called, alas, the "animal nexus" approach, whereby anyone who has an interest in studying or seeing the endangered animals anywhere on the globe has standing; and the "vocational nexus" approach, under which anyone with a professional interest in such animals can sue. Under these theories, anyone who goes to see Asian elephants in the Bronx Zoo, and anyone who is a keeper of Asian elephants in the Bronx Zoo, has standing to sue because the Director of [AID] did not consult with the Secretary regarding the AID-funded project in Sri Lanka. This is beyond all reason. Standing is not "an ingenious academic exercise in the conceivable," United States v. Students Challenging Regulatory Agency Procedures (*SCRAP*), 412 U.S. 669, 688 (1973), but as we have said requires, at the summary judgment stage, a factual showing of perceptible harm. It is clear that the person who observes or works with a particular animal threatened by a federal decision is facing perceptible harm, since the very subject of his interest will no longer exist. It is even plausible—though it goes to the outermost limit of plausibility—to think that a person who observes or works with animals of a particular species in the very area of the world where that species is threatened by a federal decision is facing such harm, since some animals that might have been the subject of his interest will no longer exist. It goes beyond the limit, however, and into pure speculation and fantasy, to say that anyone who observes or works with an endangered species, anywhere in the world, is appreciably harmed by a single project affecting some portion of that species with which he has no more specific connection.

B

Besides failing to show injury, respondents failed to demonstrate redressability. Instead of attacking the separate decisions to fund particular projects allegedly causing them harm, respondents chose to challenge a more generalized level of Government action (rules regarding consultation), the invalidation of which would affect all overseas projects. This programmatic approach has obvious practical advantages, but also obvious difficulties insofar as proof of causation or redressability is concerned. . . .

The most obvious problem in the present case is redressability. Since the agencies funding the projects were not parties to the case, the District Court could accord relief only against the Secretary: He could be ordered to revise his regulation to require consultation for foreign projects. But this would not remedy respondents' alleged injury unless the funding agencies were bound by the Secretary's regulation, which is very much an open question. . . . When the Secretary promulgated the regulation at issue here, he thought it was binding on the agencies. The Solicitor General, however, has repudiated that position here, and the agencies themselves apparently deny the Secretary's authority. . . .

[Even if the district court had ruled in the course of its standing inquiry that the regulation did bind other federal agencies, such a decision] would not have remedied respondents' alleged injury anyway, because it would not have been binding upon the agencies. They were not parties to the suit, and there is no reason they should be obliged to honor an incidental legal determination the suit produced. . . . The short of the matter is that redress of the only injury in fact respondents complain of requires action (termination of funding until consultation) by the individual funding agencies; and any relief the District Court could have provided in this suit against the Secretary was not likely to produce that action.

A further impediment to redressability is the fact that the agencies generally supply only a fraction of the funding for a foreign project. AID, for example, has provided less than 10% of the funding for the Mahaweli project. Respondents have produced nothing to indicate that the projects they have named will either be suspended, or do less harm to listed species, if that fraction is eliminated. . . . [I]t is entirely conjectural whether the nonagency activity that affects respondents will be altered or affected by the agency activity they seek to achieve. There is no standing.

IV

The Court of Appeals found that respondents had standing for an additional reason: because they had suffered a "procedural injury." The so-called "citizen-suit" provision of the ESA provides, in pertinent part, that "any person may commence a civil suit on his own behalf (A) to enjoin any person, including the United States and any other governmental instrumentality or agency . . . who is alleged to be in violation of any provision of this chapter." 16 U.S.C. §1540(g). The court held that, because §7(a)(2) requires interagency consultation, the citizen-suit provision creates a "procedural righ[t]" to consultation in all "persons"—so that anyone can file suit in federal court to challenge the Secretary's (or presumably any other official's) failure to follow the assertedly correct consultative procedure, notwithstanding his or her inability to allege any discrete injury flowing from that failure. To understand the remarkable nature of this holding one must be clear about what it does not rest upon: This is not a case where plaintiffs are seeking to enforce a procedural requirement the disregard of which could impair a separate concrete interest of theirs (e.g., the procedural requirement for a hearing prior to denial of their license application, or the procedural requirement for an environmental impact statement before a federal facility is constructed next door to them).[7] Nor is it simply a case where concrete injury has been suffered by many persons, as in mass fraud or mass tort situations. Nor, finally, is it the

7. There is this much truth to the assertion that "procedural rights" are special: The person who has been accorded a procedural right to protect his concrete interests can assert that right without meeting all the normal standards for redressability and immediacy. Thus, under our case law, one living adjacent to the site for proposed construction of a federally licensed dam has standing to challenge the licensing agency's failure to prepare an environmental impact statement, even though he cannot establish with any certainty that the statement will cause the license to be withheld or altered, and even though the dam will not be completed for many years. (That is why we do not rely, in the present case, upon the Government's argument that, even if the other agencies were obliged to consult with the Secretary, they might not have followed his advice.) What respondents' "procedural rights" argument seeks, however, is quite different from this: standing for persons who have no concrete interests affected—persons who live (and propose to live) at the other end of the country from the dam.

unusual case in which Congress has created a concrete private interest in the outcome of a suit against a private party for the government's benefit, by providing a cash bounty for the victorious plaintiff. Rather, the court held that the injury-in-fact requirement had been satisfied by congressional conferral upon all persons of an abstract, self-contained, noninstrumental "right" to have the Executive observe the procedures required by law. We reject this view.

We have consistently held that a plaintiff raising only a generally available grievance about government—claiming only harm to his and every citizen's interest in proper application of the Constitution and laws, and seeking relief that no more directly and tangibly benefits him than it does the public at large—does not state an Article III case or controversy. . . .

. . . Whether the courts were to act on their own, or at the invitation of Congress, in ignoring the concrete injury requirement described in our cases, they would be discarding a principle fundamental to the separate and distinct constitutional role of the Third Branch—one of the essential elements that identifies those "Cases" and "Controversies" that are the business of the courts rather than of the political branches. "The province of the court," as Chief Justice Marshall said in Marbury v. Madison, 5 U.S. (1 Cranch) 137, 170 (1803), "is, solely, to decide on the rights of individuals." Vindicating the public interest (including the public interest in Government observance of the Constitution and laws) is the function of Congress and the Chief Executive. The question presented here is whether the public interest in proper administration of the laws (specifically, in agencies' observance of a particular, statutorily prescribed procedure) can be converted into an individual right by a statute that denominates it as such, and that permits all citizens (or, for that matter, a subclass of citizens who suffer no distinctive concrete harm) to sue. If the concrete injury requirement has the separation-of-powers significance we have always said, the answer must be obvious: To permit Congress to convert the undifferentiated public interest in executive officers' compliance with the law into an "individual right" vindicable in the courts is to permit Congress to transfer from the President to the courts the Chief Executive's most important constitutional duty, to "take Care that the Laws be faithfully executed," Art. II, §3. It would enable the courts, with the permission of Congress, "to assume a position of authority over the governmental acts of another and co-equal department," and to become "'virtually continuing monitors of the wisdom and soundness of Executive action.'" [Allen v. Wright, 468 U.S. 737, 760 (1984)]. We have always rejected that vision of our role. . . .

Nothing in this contradicts the principle that "[t]he . . . injury required by Art. III may exist solely by virtue of 'statutes creating legal rights, the invasion of which creates standing.'" Warth v. Seldin, 422 U.S. 490, 500 (1975). . . . As we said in *Sierra Club*, "[Statutory] broadening [of] the categories of injury that may be alleged in support of standing is a different matter from abandoning the requirement that the party seeking review must himself have suffered an injury." 405 U.S., at 738. Whether or not the principle set forth in *Warth* can be extended beyond that distinction, it is clear that in suits against the Government, at least, the concrete injury requirement must remain.

We hold that respondents lack standing to bring this action and that the Court of Appeals erred in denying the summary judgment motion filed by the United States. . . .

JUSTICE KENNEDY, with whom JUSTICE SOUTER joins, concurring in part and concurring in the judgment. . . .

I agree with the Court's conclusion in Part III-A that, on the record before us, respondents have failed to demonstrate that they themselves are "among the injured." . . .

While it may seem trivial to require that Mses. Kelly and Skilbred acquire airline tickets to the project sites or announce a date certain upon which they will return, this is not a case where it is reasonable to assume that the affiants will be using the sites on a regular basis, see Sierra Club v. Morton, *supra*, 405 U.S., at 735, n.8, nor do the affiants claim to have visited the sites since the projects commenced. With respect to the Court's discussion of respondents' "ecosystem nexus," "animal nexus," and "vocational nexus" theories, I agree that on this record respondents' showing is insufficient to establish standing on any of these bases. I am not willing to foreclose the possibility, however, that in different circumstances a nexus theory similar to those proffered here might support a claim to standing. See Japan Whaling Ass'n v. American Cetacean Soc'y, 478 U.S. 221, 231, n.4 (1986) ("[R]espondents . . . undoubtedly have alleged a sufficient 'injury in fact' in that the whale watching and studying of their members will be adversely affected by continued whale harvesting").

In light of the conclusion that respondents have not demonstrated a concrete injury here sufficient to support standing under our precedents, I would not reach the issue of redressability that is discussed by the plurality in Part III-B.

I also join Part IV of the Court's opinion with the following observations. As Government programs and policies become more complex and far reaching, we must be sensitive to the articulation of new rights of action that do not have clear analogs in our common-law tradition. . . . In my view, Congress has the power to define injuries and articulate chains of causation that will give rise to a case or controversy where none existed before, and I do not read the Court's opinion to suggest a contrary view. In exercising this power, however, Congress must at the very least identify the injury it seeks to vindicate and relate the injury to the class of persons entitled to bring suit. The citizen-suit provision of the Endangered Species Act does not meet these minimal requirements, because while the statute purports to confer a right on "any person . . . to enjoin . . . the United States and any other governmental instrumentality or agency . . . who is alleged to be in violation of any provision of this chapter," it does not of its own force establish that there is an injury in "any person" by virtue of any "violation." 16 U.S.C. §1540(g)(1)(A).

The Court's holding that there is an outer limit to the power of Congress to confer rights of action is a direct and necessary consequence of the case and controversy limitations found in Article III. I agree that it would exceed those limitations if, at the behest of Congress and in the absence of any showing of concrete injury, we were to entertain citizen suits to vindicate the public's nonconcrete interest in the proper administration of the laws. While it does not matter how many persons have been injured by the challenged action, the party bringing suit must show that the action injures him in a concrete and personal way. . . .

JUSTICE STEVENS, concurring in the judgment.

Because I am not persuaded that Congress intended the consultation requirement in §7(a)(2) of the Endangered Species Act to apply to activities in foreign countries, I concur in the judgment of reversal. I do not, however, agree with the Court's conclusion that respondents lack standing. . . .

. . . An injury to an individual's interest in studying or enjoying a species and its natural habitat occurs when someone (whether it be the Government or a private party) takes action that harms that species and habitat. . . .

[In responding to Part III-B of Justice Scalia's opinion, Justice Stevens asserted that the Court] must presume that if this Court holds that §7(a)(2) requires consultation, all affected agencies would abide by that interpretation and engage in the requisite consultations. Certainly the Executive Branch cannot be heard to argue that an authoritative construction of the governing statute by this Court may simply be ignored by any agency head. Moreover, if Congress has required consultation between agencies, we must presume that such consultation will have a serious purpose that is likely to produce tangible results. . . . [I]t is not mere speculation to think that foreign governments, when faced with the threatened withdrawal of United States assistance, will modify their projects to mitigate the harm to endangered species. . . .

JUSTICE BLACKMUN, with whom JUSTICE O'CONNOR joins, dissenting.

. . . I question the Court's breadth of language in rejecting standing for "procedural" injuries. I fear the Court seeks to impose fresh limitations on the constitutional authority of Congress to allow citizen suits in the federal courts for injuries deemed "procedural" in nature. . . .

The Court . . . concludes that injury is lacking, because respondents' allegations of "ecosystem nexus" failed to demonstrate sufficient proximity to the site of the environmental harm. To support that conclusion, the Court mischaracterizes our decision in Lujan v. National Wildlife Federation, 497 U.S. 871 (1990), as establishing a general rule that "a plaintiff claiming injury from environmental damage must use the area affected by the challenged activity." In *National Wildlife Federation*, the Court required specific geographical proximity because of the particular type of harm alleged in that case: harm to the plaintiff's visual enjoyment of nature from mining activities. One cannot suffer from the sight of a ruined landscape without being close enough to see the sites actually being mined. Many environmental injuries, however, cause harm distant from the area immediately affected by the challenged action. Environmental destruction may affect animals traveling over vast geographical ranges, see, e.g., Japan Whaling Ass'n v. American Cetacean Soc'y, 478 U.S. 221 (1986) (harm to American whale watchers from Japanese whaling activities), or rivers running long geographical courses. It cannot seriously be contended that a litigant's failure to use the precise or exact site where animals are slaughtered or where toxic waste is dumped into a river means he or she cannot show injury. . . .

I have difficulty imagining this Court applying its rigid principles of geographic formalism anywhere outside the context of environmental claims. As I understand it, environmental plaintiffs are under no special constitutional standing disabilities. Like other plaintiffs, they need show only that the action they challenge has injured them, without necessarily showing they happened to be physically near the location of the alleged wrong. . . .

The Court . . . rejects the view that the "injury-in-fact requirement [is] satisfied by congressional conferral upon all persons of an abstract, self-contained, noninstrumental 'right' to have the Executive observe the procedures required by law." Whatever the Court might mean with that very broad language, it cannot be saying that "procedural injuries" as a class are necessarily insufficient for purposes of Article III standing.

Most governmental conduct can be classified as "procedural." Many injuries caused by governmental conduct, therefore, are categorizable at some level of generality as "procedural" injuries. Yet, these injuries are not categorically beyond the pale of redress by the federal courts. When the Government, for example, "procedurally" issues a pollution permit, those affected by the permittee's pollutants are not without standing to sue. Only later cases will tell just what the Court means by its intimation that "procedural" injuries are not constitutionally cognizable injuries. In the meantime, I have the greatest of sympathy for the courts across the country that will struggle to understand the Court's standardless exposition of this concept today.

The Court expresses concern that allowing judicial enforcement of "agencies' observance of a particular, statutorily prescribed procedure" would "transfer from the President to the courts the Chief Executive's most important constitutional duty, to 'take Care that the Laws be faithfully executed,' Art. II, §3." In fact, the principal effect of foreclosing judicial enforcement of such procedures is to transfer power into the hands of the Executive at the expense—not of the courts—but of Congress, from which that power originates and emanates.

Under the Court's anachronistically formal view of the separation of powers, Congress legislates pure, substantive mandates and has no business structuring the procedural manner in which the Executive implements these mandates. . . . In complex regulatory areas, however, Congress often . . . sets forth substantive policy goals and provides for their attainment by requiring Executive Branch officials to follow certain procedures, for example, in the form of reporting, consultation, and certification requirements. . . .

. . . Just as Congress does not violate separation of powers by structuring the procedural manner in which the Executive shall carry out the laws, surely the federal courts do not violate separation of powers when, at the very instruction and command of Congress, they enforce these procedures. . . .

. . . [The] acknowledgment of an inextricable link between procedural and substantive harm does not reflect improper appellate factfinding. It reflects nothing more than the proper deference owed to the judgment of a coordinate branch—Congress— that certain procedures are directly tied to protection against a substantive harm. . . .

In conclusion, I cannot join the Court on what amounts to a slash-and-burn expedition through the law of environmental standing. In my view, "[t]he very essence of civil liberty certainly consists in the right of every individual to claim the protection of the laws, whenever he receives an injury." Marbury v. Madison, 1 Cranch 137, 163 (1803). . . .

NOTES AND QUESTIONS

1. *Interpreting* Defenders. Why is "much more" needed to demonstrate standing where the plaintiff's asserted injury arises from the government's allegedly unlawful regulation of a third party? Why did the Defenders of Wildlife fail to satisfy its burden? Is *Defenders of Wildlife*, like Sierra Club v. Morton, just another example of inartful drafting of pleadings and affidavits by the plaintiff's attorneys, and thus easily avoided in future cases? What, if anything, does *Defenders of Wildlife* add to *Lujan I*? What effect will the case have on the causation and redressability components of Article III standing? Why did Justice Scalia conclude that the plaintiff failed to satisfy these parts of the standing test?

In *Defenders of Wildlife*, the Court rejected the plaintiffs' attempt to base their showing of injury in fact on an "animal nexus" theory. In American Soc'y for the Prevention of Cruelty to Animals v. Ringling Bros. and Barnum & Bailey Circus, 317 F.3d 334 (D.C. Cir. 2003), however, the court held that a former elephant handler, who had left the circus because of its alleged mistreatment of Asian elephants to which he had become emotionally attached, made a sufficient showing of injury to support standing to bring a citizen suit against the circus for violation of the ESA.

On what basis did Justice Scalia reject the plaintiff's assertion of procedural injury? What role did the separation of powers doctrine play in Justice Scalia's resolution of this issue? What was the relevance of Article II's "take Care" clause to a case involving an inquiry into the parameters of the case-or-controversy requirement of Article III? What is "an abstract, self-contained, noninstrumental" right? In Federal Election Comm'n v. Akins, 524 U.S. 11 (1998), a group of voters with views opposed to those of the American Israel Public Affairs Committee (AIPAC) challenged the FEC's determination that AIPAC was not subject to statutory reporting requirements. The Supreme Court held that the group had standing under Article III. The group's members suffered injury in fact because they were unable to obtain information that would help them evaluate candidates for office. That alleged informational injury was not a generalized grievance inappropriate for judicial resolution because, even though it was widely shared, it was concrete and directly related to voting, "the most basic of political rights." The alleged harm was fairly traceable to the FEC's decision, despite the possibility that the FEC would have exercised its prosecutorial discretion and not required AIPAC to report even if the statute applied to it. Is Akins consistent with Defenders of Wildlife, or has the Court erected more burdensome obstacles to standing in environmental law cases than in other areas? A report by the Georgetown University Law Center's Environmental Policy Project, Barely Standing: The Erosion of Citizen "Standing" to Sue to Enforce Federal Environmental Law (J. Echeverria & J. Zeidler eds., 1999), asserts that the erosion of public access to enforce the environmental laws is "the result of an unusually focused and determined effort at jurisprudential reform, spearheaded by U.S. Supreme Court Justice Antonin Scalia."

Before 1940, the predominant approach to standing was the "legal right" doctrine. See generally Pierce et al., Administrative Law and Process 162-164 (4th ed. 2004). Under that doctrine, a plaintiff had standing only if agency action impaired a "legal right" specifically granted to it by statute or common law. A nineteenth-century private right was a predicate for judicial intervention. As a result, courts were unable to "redress the systemic or probabilistic harms that Congress intended regulatory schemes to prevent." Sunstein, Standing and the Privatization of Public Law, 88 Colum. L. Rev. 1432, 1433 (1988). The doctrine was abandoned when the courts began to grant standing to intended statutory beneficiaries as well as to regulated entities. See, e.g., Scenic Hudson Preservation Conf. v. FPC, 354 F.2d 608, 615-617 (2d Cir. 1965). Is the net effect of the two Lujan cases to return to a regime in which it will be more difficult for intended regulatory beneficiaries than for regulated entities to establish standing to sue? See Sunstein, supra, at 1435-1436, 1458, 1463; Weinberg, Are Standing Requirements Becoming a Great Barrier Reef against Environmental Actions?, 7 N.Y.U. Envtl. L.J. 1 (1999) (decrying "[a]rchaic standing rules that hearken back to the era of special pleading"). What appears to be Justice Kennedy's view of the legal right approach? In 1996, the D.C. Circuit declared the legal right test officially dead. Mountain States Legal Found. v. Glickman, 92 F.3d 1228, 1233 (D.C. Cir. 1996) (timber company had standing to challenge Forest Service timber harvesting plan that curtailed logging). See also Cantrell v. City of Long Beach, 241 F.3d 674, 681 (9th Cir. 2001) ("That the litigant's interest must be greater than that of the public at large does not imply that the interest must be a substantive right sounding in property or contract.").

2. *The Functions of the Standing Doctrine.* The courts use the concept of standing to serve more than one purpose. See generally Nichol, Rethinking Standing, 72 Cal. L. Rev. 68 (1984). They use it to ensure that litigants are truly adverse and thus likely to present the case effectively and that those most directly concerned are able to litigate the issues in a case. As late as 1968, the Supreme Court stated that standing law

> does not by its own force raise separation of powers problems related to improper judicial interference in areas committed to other branches of the Federal Government. . . . Thus, in terms of Article III limitations on federal court jurisdiction, the question of standing is related only to whether the dispute sought to be adjudicated will be presented in an adversary context and in a form historically viewed as capable of judicial resolution. It is for that reason that the emphasis in standing problems is on whether the party invoking federal court jurisdiction has "a personal stake in the outcome of the controversy," and whether the dispute touches upon "the legal relations of parties having adverse legal interests."

Flast v. Cohen, 392 U.S. 83, 100 (1968). By 1984, the Court had made a remarkable about-face, declaring that standing doctrine could be understood by reference to a "single basic idea—the idea of separation of powers." Allen v. Wright, 468 U.S. 737, 752 (1984). Since then, the Court's standing cases have been suffused with discussion of that idea. While the earlier, instrumental justifications are still advanced, they appear to have become secondary to some Justices. Poisner, Comment, Environmental Values and Judicial Review after *Lujan*: Two Critiques of the Separation of Powers Theory of Standing, 18 Ecology L.Q. 335, 345 n.78 (1991).

Commentators have surmised that "a belief that majoritarian politics accurately aggregates the private preferences of society's members underlies the separation of powers theory of standing." Id. at 358, citing Pierce, The Role of the Judiciary in Implementing an Agency Theory of Government, 64 N.Y.U. L. Rev. 1239, 1277 (1989). Justice Scalia has remarked that the standing requirement excludes from the courts interests that are likely to lose in the political process (such as potential hikers and campers who would be harmed by construction of a new ski resort). Scalia, Rulemaking as Politics, 34 Admin. L. Rev. v, vi (1982).* Is it possible that the standing obstacle to judicial review will actually interfere with majoritarian preference aggregation? See Poisner, *supra*, at 372 (judicial review may compensate for antidemocratic tendencies of the bureaucratic structure by lessening the danger of agency capture, equalizing bargaining power between regulated industries and public interest plaintiffs, and heightening public scrutiny of agency decisions).

3. *Standing Doctrine and Citizen Suits.* What effect will *Defenders of Wildlife* have on the ability of private citizens to seek redress of allegedly unlawful government activity under the citizen suit provisions of the environmental laws (which are analyzed more thoroughly in Chapter 10, section C.4)? Does the decision preclude Congress from creating legal rights whose deprivation by the government creates

---

*Cf. Community Nutrition Inst. v. Block, 698 F.2d 1239, 1256 (D.C. Cir. 1983) (Scalia, J., concurring in part and dissenting in part), rev'd, 467 U.S. 340 (1984) ("Governmental mischief whose effects are widely distributed is more readily remedied through the political process, and does not call into play the distinctive function of the courts as guardians against oppression of the few by the many."). Compare Northwest Envtl. Def. Ctr. v. Owens Corning Corp., 434 F. Supp. 2d 957, 966 (D. Or. 2006) (finding "illogical" the proposition that "[t]he greater the threatened harm, the less power the courts would have to intercede" and rejecting the notion that "widely shared injury is not justiciable").

the injury in fact necessary to satisfy Article III? See Buzbee, Expanding the Zone, Tilting the Field: Zone of Interests and Article III Standing Analysis after *Bennett v. Spear*, 49 Admin. L. Rev. 763, 798 (1997). Professor Sunstein has claimed that, "[r]ead for all it is worth," *Defenders of Wildlife* invalidated the citizen suit provisions as they apply to actions to force agencies to perform nondiscretionary duties. Sunstein, *supra*, 91 Mich. L. Rev. at 165. Does the Court's holding necessarily sweep that broadly? The lower courts have not interpreted the case that way and have continued to reach the merits in citizen suits against EPA. Fletcher, The Structure of Standing, 98 Yale L.J. 221, 223-224 (1988), argues that "[i]f a duty is statutory, Congress should have essentially unlimited power to define the class of persons entitled to enforce that duty, for congressional power to create the duty should include the power to define those who have standing to enforce it." Political processes may not afford adequate relief to dispersed regulatory beneficiaries. Furthermore, intended statutory beneficiaries have already taken advantage of and prevailed in the political process by convincing Congress to enact the regulatory program they are seeking to enforce. They should not be forced to fight anew a battle they have already won, just because an agency is allegedly subverting the legislative design.*

Justice Scalia based his analysis in *Defenders of Wildlife* on Article II as well as Article III. He has argued elsewhere that executive nonimplementation of statutes is part of a well-functioning democratic process, keeping law current with existing views. Scalia, The Doctrine of Standing as an Essential Element of the Separation of Powers, 17 Suffolk U. L. Rev. 881, 897 (1983). Professor Sunstein responds that the "take Care" clause does not authorize the executive to violate the law through insufficient action any more than it does so through overzealous enforcement. Sunstein, *supra*, 88 Colum. L. Rev. at 1471.

> If administrative action is legally inadequate or if the agency has violated the law by failing to act at all, there is no usurpation of executive prerogatives in a judicial decision to that effect. Such a decision is necessary in order to vindicate congressional directives, as part of the judicial function "to say what the law is." The "take Care" clause and concerns of separation of powers argue in favor of rather than against a judicial role when statutory beneficiaries challenge agency behavior as legally inadequate.

Id. at 1471-1472, citing Marbury v. Madison, 5 U.S. (1 Cranch) 137, 177 (1803). Judicial efforts to use standing to limit enforcement of legislatively created rights thus confine "the power of the legislature to articulate public values and choose the manner in which they may be enforced." Fletcher, *supra*, at 233.

4. *Standing to Sue in the Courts of Other Nations.* The United States was a world leader in the development of environmental law in the 1970s, and its legislation provided a model for the adoption of standards elsewhere. It is somewhat ironic that access to the courts in environmental law cases in some other countries has become more accommodating than it is in the United States. A decision by the Supreme Court of the Philippines, Oposa v. Secretary of the Dep't of Env't & Natural Res. Fulgencio Factoran, G.R. No. 101083, July 30, 1993, 33 I.L.M. 173 (1994),

---

*See also Van Cleve, Congressional Power to Confer Citizen Broad Standing in Environmental Cases, 29 Envtl. L. Rep. (ELI) 10,028 (1999); Poisner, *supra*, at 1401 ("[I]f one rejects private preference aggregation as the single goal of the political process, it follows that self-government includes enabling any citizen to enforce public rights in courts when Congress so intends. A citizen's legitimate interest in the law does not end with the law's passage.").

is illustrative. A group of Filipino minors sued on their own behalf and on behalf of unborn generations to halt destruction of the country's natural rain forest, claiming that, as citizens and taxpayers, they were entitled to the full benefit and use of those resources. They sought an order canceling existing timber licensing agreements. The Supreme Court reversed the trial court's dismissal, holding that the petitioners had a right to sue on behalf of future generations; that the complaint relied on the fundamental right to a balanced and healthful ecology explicitly recognized in the 1987 Constitution; that the government's duty to protect and advance that right was clear, giving rise to a cause of action; and that the case did not raise a political question because it involved enforcement of rights in light of existing policies rather than formulation of new policies by the executive. The constitutional right to a healthful ecology reflected the "well founded fears of [the Constitution's] framers" that unless that right were recognized and enforced, future generations would "stand to inherit nothing but parched earth incapable of sustaining life." Does the Filipino court's decision represent a sounder approach to environmental standing than that reflected in the U.S. Constitution, as interpreted by the U.S. Supreme Court?*

The High Court of Australia endorsed broad citizen access to its courts in Truth About Motorways Pty Ltd. v. Macquarie Infrastructure Mgmt. Ltd. [2000] HCA 11 (9 March 2000). The issue was whether a corporation claiming no special interest in the subject matter of the dispute and that had suffered no loss or damage as a result of the defendant's conduct could sue under the Trade Practices Act, which prohibits misleading or deceptive conduct in trade or commerce. The statute authorizes suits by "a person." The defendant argued, by analogy to cases of the United States Supreme Court interpreting Article III of the U.S. Constitution, that Ch. III of the Australian Constitution barred suit. That provision vests jurisdiction in the Australian court over certain "matters" arising under laws enacted by the Parliament. The Court concluded that the plaintiff had standing and that the provisions of the Act enabling the corporation to sue did not violate the Constitution. According to Gleeson., C.J., and McHugh, J., "Parliament, by conferring standing upon any person to invoke the jurisdiction of the court has, at one time, created the potential for a justiciable controversy and conferred jurisdiction to determine the controversy." According to Gummow, J., in Australia, "it is a prime function of the judicial branch . . . to secure execution of the laws of the Commonwealth according to their tenor." Similarly, Kirby, J., argued against using the constitutional notion of a "matter" to "erode significantly" federal legislative powers and "to import a serious and unnecessary inflexibility" into the Australian Constitution. The framers chose not to adopt a narrow approach to the jurisdiction of the courts, such as might be derived from the U.S. Constitution's Article III case or controversy requirement. Further, the separation of powers reasoning relied on in *Defenders of Wildlife* does not apply in Australia, where ministers of the executive branch sit in the Parliament. Finally, *Defenders of Wildlife* has been the subject of strong dissent and scholarly criticism as constituting an unwarranted departure from earlier holdings.

5. *Associational Standing.* An association may sue on behalf of its members if the members have standing to sue in their own right, the interests the association seeks to protect are germane to the association's purposes, and neither the claim asserted nor the relief requested requires the participation of individual members in the lawsuit.

---

*See generally Owens, Comparative Law and Standing to Sue: A Petition for Redress to the Environment, 7 Envtl. Law. 321 (2001); Allen, Note, The Philippine Children's Case: Recognizing Legal Standing for Future Generations, 6 Geo. Intl. Envtl. L. Rev. 713 (1994).

International Union, UAW v. Brock, 477 U.S. 274 (1986); Hunt v. Washington State Apple Advertising Comm'n, 432 U.S. 333, 343 (1977). What if an association has no formal members; is it precluded from suing? See Friends of the Earth, Inc. v. Chevron Chem. Co., 129 F.3d 826 (5th Cir. 1997). For a good discussion of the function of associational standing doctrine, see Coho Salmon v. Pacific Lumber Co., 30 F. Supp. 2d 1231 (N.D. Cal. 1998). In Building and Constr. Trades Council v. Downtown Dev., Inc., 448 F.3d 138 (2d Cir. 2006), the court explained that the "germaneness" condition requires a court to assess whether an association's lawsuit, if successful, would reasonably tend to further the general interests that individual members sought to vindicate in joining the association and whether the lawsuit bears a reasonable connection to the association's knowledge and experience. Applying that test, the court held that a labor union could sue to abate waste disposal practices that allegedly created health risks for its members.

6. *The Impact of* Lujan I *and* Defenders of Wildlife: *Analysis of Alleged Injury in Fact.* To some observers, *Lujan I* and *Defenders of Wildlife* seemed to erect significant new obstacles to access to the courts by environmental public interest groups. In most cases, however, environmental plaintiffs have had little difficulty distinguishing the two cases in their efforts to show sufficient injury in fact to satisfy Article III. E.g., Dubois v. United States Dep't of Agric., 102 F.3d 1273, 1281-1282 (1st Cir. 1996); Mausolf v. Babbitt, 85 F.3d 1295, 1301-1302 (8th Cir. 1996). See also Resources Ltd., Inc. v. Robertson, 35 F.3d 1300 (9th Cir. 1994) (denying that, as a result of *Lujan I*, plaintiffs must satisfy a new, stricter burden of establishing injury in fact). These cases may simply be the result of more careful drafting of pleading and affidavits. Environmental groups clearly must devote more time to finding appropriate members who use the relevant resources and drafting documents that will enable them to survive a motion to dismiss or a summary judgment motion.

On occasion, the government prevails on its claim that environmental groups failed to allege sufficient injury in fact. E.g., Grassroots Recycling Network, Inc. v. EPA, 429 F.3d 1109 (D.C. Cir. 2005) (plaintiffs challenging EPA regulation allowing states to issue variances from EPA's criteria for sanitary landfills lacked standing because alleged injury in fact was conjectural and not imminent); Texas Indep. Producers and Royalty Owners Ass'n v. EPA, 410 F.3d 964 (7th Cir. 2005) (environmental group lacked standing to challenge validity of general permit for storm water discharges under the Clean Water Act (CWA)); Legal Envtl. Assistance Found., Inc. v. EPA, 400 F.3d 1278 (11th Cir. 2005) (environmental group alleging that EPA violated the Clean Air Act (CAA) by refusing to issue a determination that state's permit program was deficient did not assert sufficient injury in fact).

7. *Injury in Fact and Risk.* Justice Scalia stated in *Defenders of Wildlife* that, to satisfy Article III, a plaintiff must allege injuries that are actual or imminent rather than conjectural or hypothetical. An issue that often arises in cases involving alleged violations of the environmental laws is whether a risk of future harm is sufficient under this standard. In NRDC v. EPA, 464 F.3d 1 (D.C. Cir. 2006), the court held that NRDC's members alleged sufficient injury in fact to support the group's standing to challenge an EPA regulation exempting emissions of methyl bromide from CAA provisions designed to protect the stratospheric ozone layer. NRDC claimed that its members would face increased health risks as a result of the regulation. The court confirmed that increases in risk can suffice to confer standing, noting that environmental and health injuries often are "purely probabilistic." To prevent this category of injury from becoming "too expansive," the court generally requires

plaintiffs to demonstrate a "substantial probability" that they will be injured. NRDC met that test based on expert testimony showing a lifetime risk of about 1 in 200,000 that an individual would develop nonfatal skin cancer as a result of EPA's rule.

Similarly, Northwest Envtl. Def. Ctr. v. Owens Corning Corp., 434 F. Supp. 2d 957 (D. Or. 2006), ruled that the plaintiff in a CAA citizen suit had standing. The plaintiff alleged that the defendant's emissions of HCFCs would contribute to ozone depletion (heightening the risk that its members would be exposed to damaging levels of ultraviolet radiation) and global warming (which would harm environmental resources used by the plaintiff's members). The court relied on Congress's decision to authorize EPA to control HCFC emissions to characterize the alleged threatened harm as not "entirely chimerical." *Defenders of Wildlife* was distinguishable because the emissions would have local adverse effects in the area in which the plaintiff's members lived, worked, and played. Even the alleged risk of adverse effects from global warming—such as higher sea levels due to the melting of the polar ice caps—might be felt by the plaintiff's members in Oregon, the site of the proposed plant.*

8. *Injury in Fact and Procedural or Informational Injury.* Some environmental plaintiffs have been able to show injury in fact based on allegations of procedural injury, even after *Defenders of Wildlife*. To what extent does footnote 7 of that case provide an opening for environmental groups to rely on procedural injury to satisfy Article III? In Sierra Club v. Johnson, 436 F.3d 1269 (11th Cir. 2006), the court held that an environmental group had standing to challenge EPA's failure to object to a state permit issued under the CAA that did not comply with statutory public partic-ipation requirements based on a member's allegation that additional public input could have led to improvements in the permit that could have reduced the harm caused by the permittee's air pollution. In Portland Audubon Soc'y v. Endangered Species Comm., 984 F.2d 1534, 1537 (9th Cir. 1993), the plaintiffs satisfied Article III "if for no other reason than they allege procedural violations [ex parte communica-tions in violation of the APA] in an agency process in which they participated."

Other courts have been more reluctant to credit claims of procedural injury. Florida Audubon Soc'y v. Bentsen, 94 F.3d 658 (D.C. Cir. 1996), rejected claims of procedural injury due to an agency's failure to prepare an EIS on the effects of issuing a tax credit for the use of alternative fuel additives because the plaintiffs failed to show a sufficient geographic nexus to any asserted environmental injury. Judge Buckley concurred, asserting that the majority "now requires that a litigant [in a NEPA case] be able to establish the nature and likelihood of the environmental injury that it is the purpose of the [EIS] to identify." Id. at 672. The result, he argued, is to "erode the effectiveness of one of the most important environmental measures of the past gen-eration." Id. Judge Rogers's lengthy dissenting opinion charged that the majority had effectively made it "impossible for anyone to bring a NEPA claim in the context of a rulemaking with diffuse impact." Id. at 673.

Some courts have been receptive to claims of informational injury. The court in American Canoe Ass'n v. City of Louisa Water & Sewer Comm'n, 389 F.3d 536 (6th Cir. 2004), for example, found that an environmental group had standing to bring a citizen suit for alleged violations of a CWA permit based on both its members' and its own alleged informational injuries. The groups alleged that the defendant had

---

*See also Covington v. Jefferson County, 358 F.3d 626, 638 (9th Cir. 2004) (evidence of a concrete risk of harm is sufficient to show injury in fact; credible threat of risks to plaintiffs' home yields a loss of enjoyment of property, which shows injury in fact).

violated the permit's monitoring and reporting requirements. The court found sufficient informational injury based on allegations that the lack of information deprived a group member of the ability to make choices about whether it was safe to use the river for recreational purposes. The group also alleged that the defendant's violations of the monitoring and reporting requirements deprived it of information it needed to meet its reporting obligations to its own members and to propose legislation and bring litigation.*

Suppose that an individual who used lands in a national forest in the past submitted comments on logging projects proposed by the Forest Service. The agency, in accordance with statutory and regulatory procedures for disposition of administrative appeals, mailed to the individual a copy of the agency's decision and informed him of his right to appeal it. The notice, however, provided the wrong due date for the appeal — it was one day too late. When the individual filed her appeal by the date set forth in the notice, the Forest Service dismissed it as untimely. The individual sues the Forest Service, claiming that it is estopped from dismissing her appeal. To support her standing, the plaintiff relies on both procedural injury (the denial of her right to participate in the appeals process) and informational injury (the right to have access to the additional information that would have been generated if the Forest Service had allowed the appeal). What result? See Bensman v. United States Forest Serv., 408 F.3d 945 (7th Cir. 2005).

Professor Sunstein argues that "whether someone has informational standing depends on what Congress has said." Sunstein, Informational Regulation and Informational Standing: *Akins* and Beyond, 147 U. Pa. L. Rev. 613, 617 (1999). If Congress creates a legal right to information and authorizes private citizens to vindicate that right in court, "the standing question is essentially resolved." Id. Professor Sunstein interprets *Akins, supra,* as clarifying that Congress can grant standing to someone suffering a generalized injury.

9. *Causation and Redressability.* In the vast majority of cases, environmental groups have survived challenges to their standing based on lack of causation or redressability. What kind of evidence does a plaintiff have to introduce to trace impaired water used by its members to an upstream point source? See Piney Run Preservation Ass'n v. County Comm'rs, 268 F.3d 255 (4th Cir. 2001) (plaintiff need not show to a scientific certainty that defendant's effluent caused its harm, but only that defendant discharges a pollutant that causes or contributes to the kinds of injuries alleged). Compare Friends of the Earth, Inc. v. Crown Central Petroleum Corp., 95 F.3d 358 (5th Cir. 1996), a case in which the plaintiff alleged that the defendant had discharged pollutants and failed to monitor compliance in violation of the CWA. The court concluded that the plaintiff, whose members used a body of water located three tributaries and 18 miles downstream from the defendant's refinery, failed to meet the causation requirement. See generally Coplan, Refracting the Spectrum of Clean Water Act Standing in Light of *Lujan v. Defenders of Wildlife*, 22 Colum. J. Envtl. L. 169 (1997).

---

*See also NRDC v. Abraham, 223 F. Supp. 2d 162, 179 (D.D.C. 2002) (assertions of denial of access to materials to which the plaintiffs had a legal right under the Federal Advisory Committee Act were sufficient to demonstrate procedural injury in fact). Compare Foundation on Economic Trends v. Lyng, 943 F.2d 79, 84 (D.C. Cir. 1991) (asserting that the court had never sustained standing based solely on damage to a group's interest in disseminating the data expected to appear in an EIS and that such a result would "potentially eliminate any standing requirement in NEPA cases").

Justice Scalia stated in *Defenders of Wildlife* that when the existence of one or more elements of standing depends on the decisions of "independent actors" who are not before the court, it is ordinarily "substantially more difficult" to establish standing. One court remarked, however, that "the mere fact that third parties would have to act before actual development could take place [on federal lands] is not dispositive" of the standing issue. Wilderness Soc'y v. Robertson, 824 F. Supp. 947, 951 (D. Mont. 1993). In National Parks Conservation Ass'n v. Manson, 414 F.3d 1 (D.C. Cir. 2005), the court rejected the government's contention that an environmental group lacked standing to challenge the Interior Department's decision that construction of a coal-fired power plant would not have an adverse impact on visibility in Yellowstone National Park, in violation of the CAA. A finding of adverse effect by Interior precludes the state pollution agency from issuing a permit under the Act. Given this "formal legal relationship" between Interior and the state agency, the court concluded that the state agency was "not the sort of truly independent actor who could destroy the causation required for standing." Id. at 6.

On occasion, however, a court will toss out environmental plaintiffs due to their failure to demonstrate causation or redressability. See, e.g., Wilderness Soc'y v. Norton, 434 F.3d 584 (D.C. Cir. 2006) (holding that plaintiff alleging decreased enjoyment of wilderness areas in national park lacked standing because the relief it sought—orders requiring the Park Service to complete wilderness recommendations to the president, a description of wilderness boundaries, and wilderness suitability assessments—would not necessarily change agency wilderness management practices); Center for Biological Diversity v. Lueckel, 417 F.3d 532 (6th Cir. 2005) (holding that plaintiffs lacked standing because they did not show that designation of river corridors or establishment of a management plan, as allegedly required by the Wild and Scenic Rivers Act, would have provided more protection against the adverse effects of logging).

In what regard does Justice Scalia's opinion in *Defenders of Wildlife* facilitate the ability of environmental groups alleging procedural injury to demonstrate causation and redressability? See Committee to Save the Rio Hondo v. Lucero, *supra*, at 452; Idaho v. ICC, 35 F.3d 585, 591 (D.C. Cir. 1994). Consider Ohio Forestry Ass'n, Inc. v. Sierra Club, 523 U.S. 726 (1998). In dismissing an environmental group's challenge to a Forest Service land and resource management plan as unripe, the Court noted that "a person with standing who is injured by a failure to comply with the NEPA procedure may complain of that failure at the time the failure takes place, for the claim can never get riper." Id. at 737. Is this statement an invitation for the lower courts to find that environmental groups alleging procedural injuries due to noncompliance with NEPA have satisfied Article III standing requirements?

10. *Developmental Plaintiffs and Standing.* Interestingly, developmental interests have fared at least as badly on the standing issue since 1992 as environmental groups. In Forest Conservation Council v. Espy, 835 F. Supp. 1202 (D. Idaho 1993), *aff'd*, 42 F.3d 1399 (9th Cir. 1994), for example, the court held that a timber company lacked standing to challenge a forest plan because it did not demonstrate any actual or threatened injury in fact. Given Justice Scalia's reference in *Defenders of Wildlife* to denial of a license application as a situation in which procedural injury would likely afford the unsuccessful applicant standing to sue, it is perhaps surprising that developmental interests also have foundered on the shoals of alleged procedural injuries. See, e.g., Region 8 Forest Serv. Timber Purchasers Council v. Alcock, 993 F.2d 800 (11th Cir. 1993) (procedural injuries allegedly suffered by two timber companies were generalized grievances unconnected to a separate, concrete environmental or

economic interest). Some developmental interests also have been tossed out on causa-tion or redressability grounds. E.g., Crete Carrier Corp. v. EPA, 363 F.3d 490 (D.C. Cir. 2004) (trucking companies failed to show that EPA's refusal to reconsider emis-sion controls for heavy-duty diesel engines caused them injury because they would be obliged to comply with the controls under a consent decree even if EPA repealed the regulations); Baca v. King, 92 F.3d 1031 (10th Cir. 1996) (rancher lacked standing to challenge land exchange because court lacked authority to award the relief requested).

Suppose that an environmental group brings a citizen suit, alleging violations of CWA permits. Assuming the plaintiff can show that its members are suffering actual harm as a result of the defendant's discharges, it would have standing to seek an injunction barring further discharges in violation of the CWA because that relief would redress the alleged injuries. Would it also have standing to sue for the impo-sition of civil penalties, which are payable to the government, rather than the plaintiff? Consider the following case.

FRIENDS OF THE EARTH, INC. v. LAIDLAW ENVIRONMENTAL SERVICES (TOC), INC.
528 U.S. 167 (2000)

GINSBURG, J., delivered the opinion of the Court, in which REHNQUIST, C. J., and STEVENS, O'CONNOR, KENNEDY, SOUTER, and BREYER, JJ., joined. STEVENS, J., and KENNEDY, J., filed concurring opinions. SCALIA, J., filed a dissenting opinion, in which THOMAS, J., joined.

JUSTICE GINSBURG delivered the opinion of the Court.

This case presents an important question concerning the operation of the citizen-suit provisions of the Clean Water Act. Congress authorized the federal district courts to entertain Clean Water Act suits initiated by "a person or persons having an interest which is or may be adversely affected." 33 U.S.C. §§1365(a), (g). To impel future compliance with the Act, a district court may prescribe injunctive relief in such a suit; additionally or alternatively, the court may impose civil penalties payable to the United States Treasury. §1365(a). In the Clean Water Act citizen suit now before us, the District Court determined that injunctive relief was inappropriate because the defendant, after the institution of the litigation, achieved substantial compliance with the terms of its discharge permit. The court did, however, assess a civil penalty of $405,800. The "total deterrent effect" of the penalty would be adequate to forestall future violations, the court reasoned, taking into account that the defendant "will be required to reimburse plaintiffs for a significant amount of legal fees and has, itself, incurred significant legal expenses."

The Court of Appeals vacated the District Court's order. The case became moot, the appellate court declared, once the defendant fully complied with the terms of its permit and the plaintiff failed to appeal the denial of equitable relief. "[C]ivil penalties payable to the government," the Court of Appeals stated, "would not redress any injury Plaintiffs have suffered." . . .

We reverse the judgment of the Court of Appeals. The appellate court erred in concluding that a citizen suitor's claim for civil penalties must be dismissed as moot when the defendant, albeit after commencement of the litigation, has come into compliance. In directing dismissal of the suit on grounds of mootness, the Court of

Appeals incorrectly conflated our case law on initial standing to bring suit, see, e.g., Steel Co. v. Citizens for Better Environment, 523 U.S. 83 (1998), with our case law on post-commencement mootness. A defendant's voluntary cessation of allegedly unlawful conduct ordinarily does not suffice to moot a case. The Court of Appeals also misperceived the remedial potential of civil penalties. Such penalties may serve, as an alternative to an injunction, to deter future violations and thereby redress the injuries that prompted a citizen suitor to commence litigation.

[Section 402 of the CWA, 33 U.S.C. §1342, provides for the issuance by EPA or authorized states of National Pollutant Discharge Elimination System (NPDES) permits. These permits limit the discharge of pollutants and establish related monitoring and reporting requirements. Noncompliance with a permit constitutes a violation of the Act.

The South Carolina environmental agency issued an NPDES permit to Laidlaw, which owned a wastewater treatment plant in the state. The permit authorized Laidlaw to discharge treated water into the North Tyger River but placed limits on Laidlaw's discharge of several pollutants, including mercury, "an extremely toxic pollutant." The permit also imposed monitoring and reporting obligations. Laidlaw's discharges exceeded the permit limits for mercury nearly 500 times between 1987 and 1995, when the last recorded mercury discharge violation occurred.

In June 1992, FOE filed a citizen suit against Laidlaw, alleging noncompliance with the discharge limitations in Laidlaw's permit, as well as the related monitoring and reporting obligations. It sought declaratory and injunctive relief and an award of civil penalties. Laidlaw moved for summary judgment on the ground that FOE lacked Article III standing. The district court denied the motion, finding "by the very slimmest of margins," that FOE had standing.

In January 1997, the district court imposed on Laidlaw a civil penalty of $405,800, finding that it would have an adequate deterrent effect, even though Laidlaw had gained a total economic benefit of $1,092,581 as a result of its extended period of noncompliance with the discharge limit in its permit. The court denied injunctive relief because Laidlaw had been in "substantial compliance" with its permit since at least August 1992.

FOE appealed the civil penalty judgment, arguing that it was inadequate, but not the denial of injunctive relief. Laidlaw cross-appealed, arguing that FOE lacked standing. The Fourth Circuit assumed without deciding that FOE initially had standing to bring the action, but held that the case had since become moot. Citing Steel Co., that court found the case moot because "the only remedy currently available to [FOE]— civil penalties payable to the government—would not redress any injury [FOE has] suffered." The court remanded with instructions to dismiss. After that decision, Laidlaw permanently closed the incinerator facility, dismantled it, and put it up for sale. According to Laidlaw, all discharges from the facility permanently ceased.]

II

A

The Constitution's case-or-controversy limitation on federal judicial authority, Art. III, §2, underpins both our standing and our mootness jurisprudence, but the two inquiries differ in respects critical to the proper resolution of this case, so we address them separately. Because the Court of Appeals was persuaded that the case had become moot and so held, it simply assumed without deciding that FOE had initial standing. But because we hold that the Court of Appeals erred in declaring the case moot, we have an obligation to assure ourselves that FOE had Article III standing at the outset of the litigation. . . .

Laidlaw contends first that FOE lacked standing from the outset even to seek injunctive relief, because the plaintiff organizations failed to show that any of their members had sustained or faced the threat of any "injury in fact" from Laidlaw's activities. In support of this contention Laidlaw points to the District Court's finding . . . that there had been "no demonstrated proof of harm to the environment" from Laidlaw's mercury discharge violations.

The relevant showing for purposes of Article III standing, however, is not injury to the environment but injury to the plaintiff. To insist upon the former rather than the latter as part of the standing inquiry (as the dissent in essence does) is to raise the standing hurdle higher than the necessary showing for success on the merits in an action alleging noncompliance with an NPDES permit. Focusing properly on injury to the plaintiff, the District Court found that FOE had demonstrated sufficient injury to establish standing. For example, FOE member Kenneth Lee Curtis averred in affidavits that he lived a half-mile from Laidlaw's facility; that he occasionally drove over the North Tyger River, and that it looked and smelled polluted; and that he would like to fish, camp, swim, and picnic in and near the river between 3 and 15 miles downstream from the facility, as he did when he was a teenager, but would not do so because he was concerned that the water was polluted by Laidlaw's discharges. . . .

These sworn statements, as the District Court determined, adequately documented injury in fact. We have held that environmental plaintiffs adequately allege injury in fact when they aver that they use the affected area and are persons "for whom the aesthetic and recreational values of the area will be lessened" by the challenged activity. Sierra Club v. Morton, 405 U.S. 727, 735 (1972). . . .

. . . [T]he affidavits and testimony presented by FOE in this case assert that Laidlaw's discharges, and the affiant members' reasonable concerns about the effects of those discharges, directly affected those affiants' recreational, aesthetic, and economic interests. These submissions present dispositively more than the mere "general averments" and "conclusory allegations" found inadequate in [*Lujan I*]. Nor can the affiants' conditional statements—that they would use the nearby North Tyger River for recreation if Laidlaw were not discharging pollutants into it—be equated with the speculative "'some day' intentions" to visit endangered species halfway around the world that we held insufficient to show injury in fact in [*Defenders of Wildlife*] . . .

Laidlaw argues next that even if FOE had standing to seek injunctive relief, it lacked standing to seek civil penalties. Here the asserted defect is not injury but redressability. Civil penalties offer no redress to private plaintiffs, Laidlaw argues, because they are paid to the government, and therefore a citizen plaintiff can never have standing to seek them.

Laidlaw is right to insist that a plaintiff must demonstrate standing separately for each form of relief sought. But it is wrong to maintain that citizen plaintiffs facing ongoing violations never have standing to seek civil penalties.

We have recognized on numerous occasions that "all civil penalties have some deterrent effect." Hudson v. United States, 522 U.S. 93, 102 (1997). More specifically, Congress has found that civil penalties in Clean Water Act cases do more than promote immediate compliance by limiting the defendant's economic incentive to delay its attainment of permit limits; they also deter future violations. This congressional determination warrants judicial attention and respect. "The legislative history of the Act reveals that Congress wanted the district court to consider the need for retribution and deterrence, in addition to restitution, when it imposed civil penalties. . . . [The district court may] seek to deter future violations by basing the penalty on its economic impact." Tull v. United States, 481 U.S. 412, 422-423 (1987).

It can scarcely be doubted that, for a plaintiff who is injured or faces the threat of future injury due to illegal conduct ongoing at the time of suit, a sanction that effectively abates that conduct and prevents its recurrence provides a form of redress. Civil penalties can fit that description. To the extent that they encourage defendants to discontinue current violations and deter them from committing future ones, they afford redress to citizen plaintiffs who are injured or threatened with injury as a consequence of ongoing unlawful conduct. . . .

We recognize that there may be a point at which the deterrent effect of a claim for civil penalties becomes so insubstantial or so remote that it cannot support citizen standing. The fact that this vanishing point is not easy to ascertain does not detract from the deterrent power of such penalties in the ordinary case. . . . In this case we need not explore the outer limits of the principle that civil penalties provide sufficient deterrence to support redressability. Here, the civil penalties sought by FOE carried with them a deterrent effect that made it likely, as opposed to merely speculative, that the penalties would redress FOE's injuries by abating current violations and preventing future ones—as the District Court reasonably found when it assessed a penalty of $405,800.

Laidlaw contends that the reasoning of our decision in *Steel Co.* directs the conclusion that citizen plaintiffs have no standing to seek civil penalties under the Act. We disagree. *Steel Co.* established that citizen suitors lack standing to seek civil penalties for violations that have abated by the time of suit. We specifically noted in that case that there was no allegation in the complaint of any continuing or imminent violation, and that no basis for such an allegation appeared to exist. In short, *Steel Co.* held that private plaintiffs, unlike the Federal Government, may not sue to assess penalties for wholly past violations, but our decision in that case did not reach the issue of standing to seek penalties for violations that are ongoing at the time of the complaint and that could continue into the future if undeterred.[4]

B

. . . [W]e turn to the question of mootness.

The only conceivable basis for a finding of mootness in this case is Laidlaw's voluntary conduct—either its achievement by August 1992 of substantial compliance with its NPDES permit or its more recent shutdown of the Roebuck facility. It is well

---

4. . . . The dissent's . . . charge that citizen suits for civil penalties under the Act carry "grave implications for democratic governance," seems to us overdrawn. Certainly the federal Executive Branch does not share the dissent's view that such suits dissipate its authority to enforce the law. In fact, the Department of Justice has endorsed this citizen suit from the outset, submitting amicus briefs in support of FOE in the District Court, the Court of Appeals, and this Court. As we have already noted, the Federal Government retains the power to foreclose a citizen suit by undertaking its own action. 33 U.S.C. §1365(b)(1)(B). And if the Executive Branch opposes a particular citizen suit, the statute allows the Administrator of the EPA to "intervene as a matter of right" and bring the Government's views to the attention of the court. §1365(c)(2).

settled that "a defendant's voluntary cessation of a challenged practice does not deprive a federal court of its power to determine the legality of the practice." *City of Mesquite*, 455 U.S., at 289. "[I]f it did, the courts would be compelled to leave '[t]he defendant . . . free to return to his old ways.'" Id., at 289, n.10. In accordance with this principle, the standard we have announced for determining whether a case has been mooted by the defendant's voluntary conduct is stringent: "A case might become moot if subsequent events made it absolutely clear that the allegedly wrongful behavior could not reasonably be expected to recur." United States v. Concentrated Phosphate Export Ass'n, Inc., 393 U.S. 199, 203 (1968). The "heavy burden of persua[ding]" the court that the challenged conduct cannot reasonably be expected to start up again lies with the party asserting mootness.

The Court of Appeals justified its mootness disposition by reference to *Steel Co.*, which held that citizen plaintiffs lack standing to seek civil penalties for wholly past violations. In relying on *Steel Co.*, the Court of Appeals confused mootness with standing. The confusion is understandable, given this Court's repeated statements that the doctrine of mootness can be described as "the doctrine of standing set in a time frame: The requisite personal interest that must exist at the commencement of the litigation (standing) must continue throughout its existence (mootness)." [Arizonans for Official English v. Arizona, 520 U.S. 43, 68 n.22 (1997)].

Careful reflection on the long-recognized exceptions to mootness, however, reveals that the description of mootness as "standing set in a time frame" is not comprehensive. As just noted, a defendant claiming that its voluntary compliance moots a case bears the formidable burden of showing that it is absolutely clear the allegedly wrongful behavior could not reasonably be expected to recur. By contrast, in a lawsuit brought to force compliance, it is the plaintiff's burden to establish standing by demonstrating that, if unchecked by the litigation, the defendant's allegedly wrongful behavior will likely occur or continue, and that the "threatened injury [is] certainly impending." Whitmore v. Arkansas, 495 U. S. 149, 158 (1990). . . . The plain lesson of these cases is that there are circumstances in which the prospect that a defendant will engage in (or resume) harmful conduct may be too speculative to support standing, but not too speculative to overcome mootness. . . .

Standing doctrine functions to ensure, among other things, that the scarce resources of the federal courts are devoted to those disputes in which the parties have a concrete stake. In contrast, by the time mootness is an issue, the case has been brought and litigated, often (as here) for years. To abandon the case at an advanced stage may prove more wasteful than frugal. This argument from sunk costs does not license courts to retain jurisdiction over cases in which one or both of the parties plainly lacks a continuing interest, as when the parties have settled or a plaintiff pursuing a nonsurviving claim has died. But the argument surely highlights an important difference between the two doctrines.

. . . Denial of injunctive relief does not necessarily mean that the district court has concluded there is no prospect of future violations for civil penalties to deter. Indeed, it meant no such thing in this case. The District Court denied injunctive relief, but expressly based its award of civil penalties on the need for deterrence. . . .

. . . The facility closure, like Laidlaw's earlier achievement of substantial compliance with its permit requirements, might moot the case, but—we once more reiterate—only if one or the other of these events made it absolutely clear that Laidlaw's permit violations could not reasonably be expected to recur. The effect of both Laidlaw's compliance and the facility closure on the prospect of future violations is a disputed factual matter. FOE points out, for example—and Laidlaw does not appear to contest—that Laidlaw retains its NPDES permit. These issues have not been aired in the lower courts; they remain open for consideration on remand. . . .

[JUSTICE STEVENS's concurring opinion is omitted.]

JUSTICE KENNEDY, concurring.

Difficult and fundamental questions are raised when we ask whether exactions of public fines by private litigants, and the delegation of Executive power which might be inferable from the authorization, are permissible in view of the responsibilities committed to the Executive by Article II of the Constitution of the United States. The questions presented in the petition for certiorari did not identify these issues with particularity; and neither the Court of Appeals in deciding the case nor the parties in their briefing before this Court devoted specific attention to the subject. In my view these matters are best reserved for a later case. With this observation, I join the opinion of the Court.

JUSTICE SCALIA, with whom JUSTICE THOMAS joins, dissenting.

The Court begins its analysis by finding injury in fact on the basis of vague affidavits that are undermined by the District Court's express finding that Laidlaw's discharges caused no demonstrable harm to the environment. It then proceeds to marry private wrong with public remedy in a union that violates traditional principles of federal standing—thereby permitting law enforcement to be placed in the hands of private individuals. Finally, the Court suggests that to avoid mootness one needs even less of a stake in the outcome than the Court's watered-down requirements for initial standing. I dissent from all of this. . . .

I . . .

Typically, an environmental plaintiff claiming injury due to discharges in violation of the Clean Water Act argues that the discharges harm the environment, and that the harm to the environment injures him. This route to injury is barred in the present case, however, since the District Court concluded after considering all the evidence that there had been "no demonstrated proof of harm to the environment," [and] that the "permit violations at issue in this citizen suit did not result in any health risk or environmental harm." . . .

The Court finds these conclusions unproblematic for standing, because "[t]he relevant showing for purposes of Article III standing . . . is not injury to the environment but injury to the plaintiff." This statement is correct, as far as it goes. We have certainly held that a demonstration of harm to the environment is not enough to satisfy the injury-in-fact requirement unless the plaintiff can demonstrate how he personally was harmed. E.g., [*Defenders of Wildlife*], *supra*, at 563. In the normal course, however, a lack of demonstrable harm to the environment will translate, as it plainly does here, into a lack of demonstrable harm to citizen plaintiffs. While it is perhaps possible that a plaintiff could be harmed even though the environment was not, such a plaintiff would have the burden of articulating and demonstrating the nature of that injury. . . . Plaintiffs here have made no attempt at such a showing, but rely entirely upon unsupported and unexplained affidavit allegations of "concern." . . .

Inexplicably, the Court is untroubled by this. . . . Although we have previously refused to find standing based on the "conclusory allegations of an affidavit" [*Lujan I*], the Court is content to do just that today. By accepting plaintiffs' vague, contradictory, and unsubstantiated allegations of "concern" about the environment as adequate to prove injury in fact, and accepting them even in the face of a finding that the environment was not demonstrably harmed, the Court makes the injury-in-fact requirement a sham. If there are permit violations, and a member of a plaintiff environmental organization lives near the offending plant, it would be difficult not to satisfy today's lenient standard.

II

The Court's treatment of the redressability requirement—which would have been unnecessary if it resolved the injury-in-fact question correctly—is equally cavalier. As discussed above, petitioners allege ongoing injury consisting of diminished enjoyment of the affected waterways and decreased property values. They allege that these injuries are caused by Laidlaw's continuing permit violations. But the remedy petitioners seek is neither recompense for their injuries nor an injunction against future violations. Instead, the remedy is a statutorily specified "penalty" for past violations, payable entirely to the United States Treasury. Only last Term, we held that such penalties do not redress any injury a citizen plaintiff has suffered from past violations. Steel Co. v. Citizens for Better Environment, 523 U.S. 83, 106-107 (1998). The Court nonetheless finds the redressability requirement satisfied here, [holding] that a penalty payable to the public "remedies" a threatened private harm, and suffices to sustain a private suit.

That holding has no precedent in our jurisprudence, and takes this Court beyond the "cases and controversies" that Article III of the Constitution has entrusted to its resolution. Even if it were appropriate, moreover, to allow Article III's remediation requirement to be satisfied by the indirect private consequences of a public penalty, those consequences are entirely too speculative in the present case. The new standing law that the Court makes—like all expansions of standing beyond the traditional constitutional limits—has grave implications for democratic governance. . . .

. . . [I]t is my view that a plaintiff's desire to benefit from the deterrent effect of a public penalty for past conduct can never suffice to establish a case or controversy of the sort known to our law. Such deterrent effect is, so to speak, "speculative as a matter of law." . . .

By permitting citizens to pursue civil penalties payable to the Federal Treasury, the Act does not provide a mechanism for individual relief in any traditional sense, but turns over to private citizens the function of enforcing the law. A Clean Water Act plaintiff pursuing civil penalties acts as a self-appointed mini-EPA. Where, as is often the case, the plaintiff is a national association, it has significant discretion in choosing enforcement targets. Once the association is aware of a reported violation, it need not look long for an injured member, at least under the theory of injury the Court applies today. And once the target is chosen, the suit goes forward without meaningful public control. The availability of civil penalties vastly disproportionate to the individual injury gives citizen plaintiffs massive bargaining power—which is often used to achieve settlements requiring the defendant to support environmental projects of the plaintiffs' choosing. Thus is a public fine diverted to a private interest.

To be sure, the EPA may foreclose the citizen suit by itself bringing suit. 33 U.S.C. §1365(b)(1)(B). This allows public authorities to avoid private enforcement only by accepting private direction as to when enforcement should be undertaken — which is no less constitutionally bizarre. Elected officials are entirely deprived of their discretion to decide that a given violation should not be the object of suit at all, or that the enforcement decision should be postponed. See §1365(b)(1)(A) (providing that citizen plaintiff need only wait 60 days after giving notice of the violation to the government before proceeding with action). This is the predictable and inevitable consequence of the Court's allowing the use of public remedies for private wrongs. . . .

NOTES AND QUESTIONS

1. *Injury in Fact.* How were the plaintiffs in *Laidlaw* able to prove injury in fact whereas the plaintiffs in *Defenders of Wildlife* were not? Was it simply a matter of providing more detailed affidavits? How did the plaintiffs demonstrate injury, given the district court's finding that the defendant's discharge did not harm the quality of the receiving water? After *Laidlaw,* has the injury-in-fact requirement indeed become "a sham," as Justice Scalia charged? Does standing once again amount to nothing more than "an ingenious academic exercise in the conceivable"? Cf. American Canoe Ass'n v. Murphy Farms, Inc., 326 F.3d 505 (4th Cir. 2003) (Luttig, J.) ("In the environmental litigation context, the standing requirements are not onerous."). For criticism of the "artificial" distinction between injury to the plaintiff and injury to the environment drawn in *Laidlaw,* see Cassuto, The Law of Words: Standing, Environment, and Other Contested Terms, 28 Harv. Envtl. L. Rev. 79 (2004).

2. *Causation and Redressability.* The plaintiffs did not appeal the district court's denial of injunctive relief. The CWA's citizen suit provision authorizes the payment of civil penalties exclusively to the government. How, then, were the plaintiffs able to demonstrate that the imposition of civil penalties would redress their alleged injury? Did the result turn on the availability of the penalty payment for environmental mitigation projects? According to the majority, what is the test for redressability of a "private attorney general's" alleged injury based on the payment of civil penalties to the government? How did the majority distinguish the *Steel Co.* case? If the penalty payment winds up in the public coffers, how can it be said that the result of *Laidlaw* is that "a public fine is diverted to a private interest"? Is a citizen suit plaintiff really "self-appointed," given that Congress has authorized individuals or groups with standing to bring citizen suits?

Even after *Laidlaw,* environmental plaintiffs may have difficulty establishing causation and redressability. American Petroleum Inst. v. EPA, 216 F.3d 50 (D.C. Cir. 2000), was a suit in which environmental groups filed a petition for review challenging EPA's decision not to classify unleaded gas storage tank sediment (UGSTS) as a hazardous waste under the Resource Conservation and Recovery Act. The court held that the groups lacked standing because they failed to establish either a substantial probability that the shipments to the landfills located near members' properties contained UGSTS or a link between such deposits and the specific harms alleged by their members. The petitioners failed on redressability as well as causation grounds because their failure to connect the alleged injuries to UGSTS precluded them from establishing a likelihood that the alleged injuries would be redressed by a favorable decision requiring listing. See also Pritikin v. DOE, 254 F.3d 791 (2001).

Suppose that a group of owners and operators of stationary sources of air pollution sue EPA to challenge the validity of EPA's approval of a state implementation plan for achieving the national ambient air quality standards under the CAA. EPA claims that the group lacks standing because any injuries that members of the group suffer will result from the specific control measures adopted by the state in the plan, and not from any action by EPA. What would be the result? See BCCA Appeal Group v. EPA, 355 F.3d 817 (5th Cir. 2003).

3. *Standing and Mootness.* Why wasn't the case moot given that the defendant had ceased discharging and shut down the offending facility? Suppose that a company violates its NPDES permit but sells the point source at which the violation occurred before the filing of a citizen suit seeking payment of civil penalties. Is the case moot? See San Francisco Baykeeper, Inc. v. Tosco Corp., 309 F.3d 1153 (9th Cir. 2002). Suppose an environmental group sues a point source for discharging without a permit. After the complaint is filed, the state pollution control agency issues a permit that covers the point source's discharges. Is the case moot? May the court assess civil penalties for the discharges that occurred before issuance of the permit? See Mississippi River Revival, Inc. v. City of Minneapolis, 319 F.3d 1013 (8th Cir. 2003).

According to the majority in *Laidlaw*, how do the inquiries into standing and mootness differ? Are the purposes of the two doctrines different? Would it be fair to a plaintiff able to show standing at the commencement of the suit and that spends money hiring attorneys, filing a lawsuit, and demonstrating a violation, to dismiss its suit right before judgment on the ground that the defendant has come into compliance? How can the possibility of future harm-producing conduct be too speculative to support standing but not too speculative "to overcome mootness"?

4. *The Impact of* Laidlaw. It did not take long for the lower courts to begin responding to the Court's decision in *Laidlaw*. In Friends of the Earth, Inc. v. Gaston Copper Recycling Corp., 179 F.3d 107 (4th Cir. 1999), a panel of the Fourth Circuit had held that an environmental group lacked standing to bring a CWA citizen suit. Six weeks after *Laidlaw* was handed down, the entire court, sitting en banc, reversed that decision. Friends of the Earth, Inc. v. Gaston Copper Recycling Corp., 204 F.3d 149 (4th Cir. 2000). The defendant in *Gaston Copper* was a metals smelting facility alleged to be violating its CWA permit by discharging metals in excess of permit limits. One of the plaintiff's members (Shealy) lived four miles downstream from the facility on property that included a 67-acre lake formed behind a dam on the creek into which the metals were discharged. Shealy alleged that the defendant's pollution adversely affected his use and enjoyment of the lake. Because of the discharges, he was concerned that the lake water was polluted and was afraid that the discharged metals had lodged in fish in the lake. He also alleged that the discharges caused a decline in the value of his property.

In concluding that the plaintiff had standing, the Fourth Circuit pointed out that Shealy produced evidence of actual or threatened injury to a waterway in which he had a legally protected interest, given that he was a property owner whose lake lay in the path of the defendant's discharge. He and his family fished and swam in the lake. Shealy thus alleged precisely the types of injuries that Congress intended to prevent when it adopted the CWA. The court noted that it is "well established that 'the injury required by Article III may exist solely by virtue of statutes creating legal rights, the invasion of which creates standing.'" Id. at 156. Furthermore, the plaintiff presented ample evidence that Shealy's fears were reasonable and not based on mere conjecture. The defendant's discharge limits were set at the level necessary to protect the designated uses of the receiving waterways. As a result, "their violation necessarily means that these uses may be harmed." Id. at 157. The court also indicated that threatened as well as actual injury can satisfy Article III's standing requirements. "Threats or increased risk thus constitutes cognizable harm. Threatened environmental injury is by nature probabilistic. And yet other circuits have had no trouble understanding the injurious nature of risk itself." Id. at 160. By demanding more than that by way of proof of injury, the district court engaged in "a judicial evisceration of the Clean Water Act's protections. And separation of powers will not countenance it." Id. at 161. One concurring judge called *Laidlaw*, upon which the majority relied, "a sea change in constitutional standing principles." Another, quoting Justice Scalia, charged that *Laidlaw* "has unnecessarily opened the standing floodgates, rendering our standing inquiry 'a sham.'" Id. at 165 (Hamilton, J., concurring in the judgment).

Was it essential to the result in *Gaston Copper* that the environmental group's member was a property owner whose lake allegedly had been polluted by the defendant's discharges? Would the analysis have been the same if the group's members merely submitted affidavits that they used public resources, such as a navigable stream? Cf. Hall v. Norton, 266 F.3d 969 (9th Cir. 2001) (addressing standing of litigant who alleged that BLM land exchange and resulting development would exacerbate air pollution problems in Las Vegas).

Suppose that an environmental group files suit alleging that EPA's approval of a state permit for stationary sources under the CAA creates uncertainty among the group's members, all of whom live in the vicinity of the permitted sources, as to whether the emissions from the permitted sources are harming their health. Are these allegations sufficient to demonstrate injury in fact under Article III? See New York Pub. Interest Research Group v. Whitman, 321 F.3d 316 (2d Cir. 2003).

What is the test for determining whether an individual's fear of harm attributable to a defendant's discharges is "reasonable"? In Ecological Rights Found. v. Pacific Lumber Co., 230 F.3d 1141 (9th Cir. 2000), the court ruled that two environmental organizations whose members used a polluted stream for recreational purposes had standing to pursue alleged CWA violations. The organization need not allege that one of its members lives in the vicinity of the injured resources. What is necessary is a showing of "a connection to the area of concern sufficient to make credible the contention that the person's future life will be less enjoyable—that he or she really has or will suffer in his or her degree of aesthetic or recreational satisfaction—if the area in question remains or becomes environmentally degraded." Id. at 1149. Repeated recreational use itself, even if infrequent, can demonstrate injurious environmental injury. The court verified that an increased risk of harm can satisfy Article III's injury in fact requirement.

Farber, Environmental Litigation after Laidlaw, 30 Envtl. L. Rep. (ELI) 10516 (2000), argues that the effect of *Laidlaw* is to shift the focus of standing analysis under Article III in citizen suits against polluters from the impact of the defendant's activities on the plaintiff alone to the disruption of the plaintiff's relationship with the affected natural resources.*

---

*Symposium, Citizen Suits and the Future of Standing in the 21st Century: From *Lujan* to *Laidlaw* and Beyond, 11 Duke Envtl. L. & Pol'y F. No. 2 (2001); 12 Duke Envtl. L. & Pol'y F. No. 1 (2001), analyzes the state of standing law after *Laidlaw* from a variety of perspectives.

NOTE ON PRUDENTIAL AND STATUTORY STANDING REQUIREMENTS

In addition to Article III standing tests, plaintiffs suing in federal court must meet the "prudential limitations" on standing created by the courts or the statutory requirements derived from legislation. First, the harm asserted by the plaintiff must not represent a "generalized grievance" shared in substantially equal measure by all or a large class of citizens. Suppose plaintiffs alleging a violation of the CAA's stratospheric ozone protection provisions claim that the defendant, the operator of a landfill, released CFCs into the environment because the landfill was improperly managed and that the release created an increased risk that the plaintiffs would get skin cancer because of the depletion of the ozone layer caused by the CFCs. Is this the kind of generalized grievance that the court should refuse to hear? See Covington v. Jefferson County, 358 F.3d 626, 649-655 (9th Cir. 2004) (Gould, J., concurring) (reading Supreme Court standing cases as rejecting the proposition that "injury to all is injury to none"); Northwest Envtl. Def. Ctr. v. Owens Corning Corp., 434 F. Supp. 2d 957, 969 (D. Or. 2006) (concluding that "issues such as global warming and ozone depletion may be of 'wide public significance' but they are neither 'abstract questions' nor mere 'generalized grievances' ").

Second, the plaintiff generally must assert his or her own legal rights and interests rather than those of third parties.

> Without such limitations — closely related to Art. III concerns but essentially matters of judicial self-governance — the courts would be called upon to decide abstract questions of wide public significance even though other governmental institutions may be more competent to address the questions and even though judicial intervention may be unnecessary to protect individual rights.

Warth v. Seldin, 422 U.S. 490, 500 (1975).

Third, the plaintiff's alleged injury must be within the zone of interest protected by the constitutional or statutory provision in question. When the plaintiff relies on the APA rather than a substantive statute for its right to seek review, the zone of interest test is a judicial gloss on §702 of the APA, which provides that a person "adversely affected or aggrieved by agency action *within the meaning of a relevant statute*" may seek review (emphasis added). The zone of interest test also applies to claims based on substantive statutes such as the ESA.

Environmental plaintiffs have had little difficulty satisfying the zone of interest test in post-*Lujan* cases. Is the zone of interest requirement likely to provide a significant obstacle to developmental interests? The Supreme Court addressed the issue in Bennett v. Spear, 520 U.S. 154 (1997). The Bureau of Reclamation (BoR), which administered the Klamath irrigation project, consulted under the ESA with the FWS after informing the FWS that the project's operation might affect two species of endangered fish. The FWS issued a biological opinion finding it likely that operation would jeopardize the fish and describing "reasonable and prudent alternatives" (RPAs) to avoid jeopardy, including maintenance of minimum water levels in some lakes and reservoirs. The BoR agreed to abide by these RPAs. Two irrigation districts that received water from the project and two ranches within those districts sued the FWS, but not the BoR, denying the existence of evidence that any decline in fish populations was attributable to the project or that minimum water levels would benefit the fish. The plaintiffs alleged that these deficiencies violated §7 of the ESA, which requires each federal agency to ensure that any action authorized, funded, or carried out by it is not likely to jeopardize the continued existence of any listed species or result in the destruction or adverse modification of its critical habitat. They also alleged that the FWS violated §4 of the ESA, which governs the listing and critical habitat designation process, by failing to consider the economic impact of critical habitat designation and that the agency acted in an arbitrary and capricious fashion in violation of the APA. The plaintiffs claimed that their use of Klamath project water for recreational, aesthetic, and commercial purposes (including irrigation) would be damaged by implementation of the RPAs through reduction of the amounts of water available to them. The lower courts found no standing because these purposes did not fall within the ESA's zone of interest, but the Supreme Court reversed.

The Court held first that, by adopting the ESA's broadly worded citizen suit provision, 16 U.S.C. §1540(g), which authorizes "any person" to sue to enforce the Act, Congress repealed the zone of interest limitation on standing. Justice Scalia read that provision literally because

> the overall subject matter of this legislation is the environment (a matter in which it is common to think all persons have an interest) and . . . the obvious purpose of the particular provision in question is to encourage enforcement by so-called "private attorneys general." . . . The statutory language . . . is . . . clear[ ], and "the subject of the legislation makes the intent to permit enforcement by everyman even more plausible.
>
> It is true that the plaintiffs here are seeking to prevent application of environmental restrictions rather than to implement them. But the "any person" formulation applies to all the causes of action authorized by §1540(g)—not only to actions against private violators of environmental restrictions, and not only to actions against the Secretary asserting underenforcement under §1533, but also to actions against the Secretary asserting overenforcement under §1533. . . . [Id. at 165-166.]

After finding that the plaintiffs had constitutional standing, the Court concluded that the ESA authorized review of the petitioners' claim that the FWS failed to take economic impact into account in designating critical habitat. It also held, however, that the ESA's citizen suit provision did not vest the district court with jurisdiction of claims alleging that the FWS violated §7 of the ESA by acting without adequate supporting data. Judicial review of those claims was nevertheless available under the APA, provided the plaintiffs had standing. In defining the zone of interests within which plaintiffs' interests had to fall, the Court looked to the substantive statutory provisions allegedly violated by the FWS, §7 of the ESA. The district court found no standing because the plaintiffs were not directly regulated by the ESA and did not seek to vindicate its "overarching purpose of species preservation." But the Court stated that the scope of the statutory zone of interests must be assessed by reference to the particular provision whose violation forms the basis for the complaint. Section 7 of the ESA requires that each agency "use the best scientific and commercial data available" in insuring that its actions not jeopardize listed species or adversely affect their critical habitat. The Court found that the purpose of that provision is

> to ensure that the ESA not be implemented haphazardly, on the basis of speculation or surmise. While this no doubt serves to advance the ESA's overall goal of species preservation, we think it readily apparent that another objective (if not indeed the primary one) is to avoid needless economic dislocation produced by agency officials zealously but

unintelligently pursuing their environmental objectives. That economic consequences are an explicit concern of the Act is evidenced by §1536(h), which provides exemption from §1536(a)(2)'s no-jeopardy mandate where there are no reasonable and prudent alternatives to the agency action and the benefits of the agency action clearly outweigh the benefits of any alternatives. We believe the "best scientific and commercial data" provision is similarly intended, at least in part, to prevent uneconomic (because erroneous) jeopardy determinations. Petitioners' claim that they are victims of such a mistake is plainly within the zone of interests that the provision protects. . . .

Id. at 176-177. Accordingly, the plaintiff's §4 claim was reviewable under the ESA's citizen-suit provision and its §7 claims were reviewable under the APA.

Do nonhuman environmental resources, such as animals, have standing to sue? In Cetacean Cmty. v. Bush, 386 F.3d 1169 (9th Cir. 2004), the court concluded that nothing in Article III prevents Congress from authorizing suits to be brought on behalf of animals. It also concluded, however, that Congress did not provide such authorization in the ESA, the Marine Mammal Protection Act, NEPA, or the APA.

Buzbee, Expanding the Zone, Tilting the Field: Zone of Interests and Article III Standing Analysis after *Bennett v. Spear*, 49 Admin. L. Rev. 763, 764-765 (1997), maintains that *Bennett* results in "skewed standing criteria, or what I refer to as a 'tilted standing playing field,' disfavoring claims brought by the beneficiaries of regulation." Pierce, Is Standing Law or Politics?, 77 N.C. L. Rev. 1741 (1999), argues that "[a]ny claim that the Constitution, the original intent of the Framers, or Anglo-American legal history and tradition compel modern standing law is undermined by historical studies on standing," id. at 1767, and that the only reliable predictor of the outcome of standing cases is the political ideology of the judges hearing the case.

Section 102(2)(C) of NEPA requires that federal agencies prepare environmental impact statements before proceeding with any major federal action significantly affecting the quality of the environment. Does a plaintiff asserting economic injury have standing to challenge an agency's noncompliance with this NEPA obligation? In Ashley Creek Phosphate Co. v. Norton, 420 F.3d 924 (9th Cir. 2005), the court held that a plaintiff whose interests are purely economic in nature is not within NEPA's zone of interests. Accordingly, the court ruled that Ashley Creek did not have standing to challenge the BLM's decision to issue a phosphate lease to a manufacturer of phosphate-based fertilizer. Ashley Creek had challenged the decision on the basis of an alleged NEPA violation, asserting that the BLM should have considered as an alternative to issuance of the lease the possibility that the lessee could get all the phosphate it needed by purchasing phosphate mined by Ashley Creek, 250 miles away from the lease site. See also Arizona Cattle Growers' Ass'n v. Cartwright, 29 F. Supp. 2d 1100, 1108-1110 (D. Ariz. 1998). Compare Friends of the Boundary Waters Wilderness v. Dombeck, 164 F.3d 1115, 1125-1127 (8th Cir. 1999).

Will regulated entities who complain that their competitors are being treated too leniently by EPA be able to satisfy the zone of interest test? See, e.g., Honeywell Int'l, Inc. v. EPA, 374 F.3d 1363 (D.C. Cir. 2004).

Problem 3-1

The Clean Air Act requires that each state achieve national ambient air quality standards (NAAQS) designed to protect the public health with an adequate margin of safety. EPA has established NAAQS for ozone, among other air pollutants. After finding that the states in the Northeast have not yet achieved the ozone NAAQS and are unlikely to do so under current regulatory requirements, EPA issued a regulation requiring each state in the Northeast to implement a low-emission vehicle (LEV) plan that was already being implemented in California. California's LEV plan requires that 25 percent of the new car sales by each car manufacturer selling cars in that state be composed of cars that meet California's emission controls for two precursors of ozone pollution, hydrocarbons and oxides of nitrogen. California's controls are more stringent than the vehicle emission standards otherwise applicable to the auto manufacturers under the statute.

The Hot Rod Club of New Jersey (Hot Rod), a group of car racing enthusiasts devoted to attending and participating in amateur car races, filed suit on May 1, 2002, in the appropriate federal Court of Appeals challenging the validity of EPA's regulation. For a variety of reasons, it charged that the regulation is beyond EPA's statutory authority. Several of Hot Rod's members filed affidavits claiming that, as a result of the LEV requirement, the car manufacturers will be required to market in New Jersey a certain percentage of cars that comply with the stringent LEV emission standards. These cars have higher sticker prices than cars built to conform to the normal EPA standards because the emission control technology they contain is expensive for the manufacturers to install. Further, according to the affidavits, the requirement that 25 percent of sales comprise LEV vehicles will increase consumer competition for the remaining, lower-priced 75 percent of the market, thus driving up the prices of non-LEV cars as well. For both of these reasons, it will be more difficult for Hot Rod's members to find the kinds of cars they want and to afford to purchase them if and when they find them.

The Justice Department, which is representing the United States and EPA in the litigation commenced by Hot Rod, has moved to dismiss the suit on the ground that Hot Rod lacks standing. As an attorney for the Justice Department, what arguments can you make to support that motion to dismiss?

NOTE ON EXHAUSTION OF ADMINISTRATIVE REMEDIES, PRIMARY JURISDICTION, AND RIPENESS

In addition to the standing doctrine, a number of other administrative law doctrines can defeat judicial review of administrative agency decisions and thus are important to environmental litigants. Generally, these doctrines require judicial deference to agency decisionmaking when agency action is considered necessary to establish a basis for judicial review.

Exhaustion of Administrative Remedies. Exhaustion is a defense to judicial review when the agency has not had an opportunity to consider the plaintiff's claim for relief. The exhaustion doctrine allows the agency to perform functions within its "special competence," such as specialized fact-finding, interpretations of disputed technical subject matter, and resolution of disputes concerning the meaning of agency regulations. Affording the agency the first opportunity to perform these functions promotes administrative autonomy and efficiency and facilitates judicial review. See Izaak Walton League of Am. v. St. Clair, 497 F.2d 849 (8th Cir. 1974) (remanding to allow the Forest Service to determine the extent of mining activity in a wilderness area and whether a permit with protective conditions should be issued).*

A court may not dismiss a claim for relief under the APA unless the enabling statute involved or agency regulations specifically mandate exhaustion as a prerequisite to judicial review. Darby v. Cisneros, 509 U.S. 137 (1993), interpreting 5 U.S.C. §704. Some statutes bar litigants from asserting arguments not specifically raised during informal rulemaking or other administrative proceedings. E.g., 42 U.S.C. §7607(d)(7)(B) (CAA). What if a litigant fails to raise an issue during the administrative proceedings but the agency considers the issue on its own initiative, or because another party raised it; may the litigant challenge the agency's disposition of the issue in court? See Engine Mfrs. Ass'n v. EPA, 88 F.3d 1075, 1084 (D.C. Cir. 1996). May an agency waive an otherwise available exhaustion defense? See Ciba-Geigy Corp. v. Sidamon-Eristoff, 3 F.3d 40, 46 (2d Cir. 1993). For claims not based on the APA, the doctrine applies as a matter of judicial discretion.

The courts have refused to apply the exhaustion doctrine when an agency acts in excess of its delegated powers, when administrative remedies are deemed to be inadequate, when it would be futile to require the litigants to pursue them, or when the question is a purely legal one. See, e.g., Western Radio Serv. Co. v. Espy, 79 F.3d 896 (9th Cir. 1996). Statutory review provisions, however, may limit the availability of these exceptions. E.g., Texas Mun. Power Agency v. EPA, 89 F.3d 858, 876 (D.C. Cir. 1996) (refusing to invoke the futility exception). Courts frequently have made exceptions to the doctrine in NEPA cases. See Jette v. Bergland, 579 F.2d 59, 62 (10th Cir. 1978) ("[e]xceptions to the requirement of exhaustion [may] outweigh the advantages in the circumstances of a particular case").

Primary Jurisdiction. The related defense of primary jurisdiction arises when a court has original jurisdiction of a claim requiring the resolution of issues also placed within the competence of an agency. If the court recognizes the agency's primary jurisdiction, it suspends the judicial process until the agency can resolve the issues. The relative competence of agency and court to decide complex technical issues often underlies application of this defense. As a result, the defense is less likely to be invoked successfully where the issue is a purely legal one. E.g., Environmental Tech. Council v. Sierra Club, 98 F.3d 774, 789 (4th Cir. 1996). The need for uniformity in the interpretation of regulatory legislation is another basis for the rule. See Massachusetts v. Blackstone Valley Elec. Co., 67 F.3d 981, 992-993 (1st Cir. 1995) (remanding to EPA question of whether substance qualified as hazardous under Superfund law).

Suppose that an individual exposed to pesticides registered by EPA brings a personal injury action under state law against the manufacturer, requesting damages but not injunctive relief. Should the court dismiss the action on primary jurisdiction grounds? See Ryan v. Chemlawn Corp., 935 F.2d 129 (7th Cir. 1991). Cf. Southern Utah Wilderness Alliance v. BLM, 425 F.3d 735 (10th Cir. 2005) (holding that the BLM does not have primary jurisdiction over determination of statutory rights-of-way over public lands); Interfaith Cmty. Org. v. Honeywell Int'l, Inc., 399 F.3d 248, 267-268 (3d Cir. 2005) (concluding that federal district court's issuance of injunction to abate imminent and substantial endangerment to health and the environment in citizen suit brought under the Resource Conservation and Recovery Act did not

---

*See generally Gelpe, Exhaustion of Administrative Remedies: Lessons from Environmental Cases, 53 Geo. Wash. L. Rev. 1 (1985).

improperly usurp EPA's power and that "particular types of injunctive relief may not be circumscribed by arguments as to what an agency might have done").

The existence of explicit statutory rights of action cuts against application of the primary jurisdiction defense. See, e.g., NRDC v. Outboard Marine Corp., 692 F. Supp. 801 (N.D. Ill. 1988) (refusing to apply the doctrine to a citizen suit alleging violations of CWA permits, even though the discharger was pursuing administrative permit modifications). Litigants also can argue that agency referrals should not be made when the agency is hostile to the environmental claim. Cf. United States Public Interest Research Group v. Atlantic Salmon of Maine, L.L.C., 257 F. Supp. 2d 407, 424-426 (D. Me. 2003) (refusing to invoke primary jurisdiction doctrine, despite agency's special expertise, due to its inexcusable delay in effectively addressing the issues raised by defendants' waste disposal practices).

Finality and Ripeness. We have already seen an example in *Lujan I* of a case in which the Supreme Court refused to reach the merits because the agency whose decisions were challenged had not yet engaged in the "final agency action" required by §704 of the APA. The "final action" rule also has been codified or implied in various environmental statutes. See, e.g., 42 U.S.C. §6976(a). The ripeness doctrine is also intended to prevent judicial consideration of controversies before the administrative agency has made a final decision that puts the case in a concrete context. Ripeness determinations turn on the fitness of the issues for judicial resolution and the hardship to the parties of withholding court consideration. In National Ass'n of Home Builders v. U.S. Army Corps of Eng'rs, 440 F.3d 459 (D.C. Cir. 2006), the court held that a challenge to an EPA regulation defining the circumstances in which the CWA's dredge and fill permit requirement applies was ripe because the issues were purely legal, and industry faced hardship if forced to apply for a permit despite believing it was not required to do so or to ignore permit requirements and face civil or criminal penalties.

If the agency has taken a final position on an issue but has not yet begun an enforcement action, is there any reason to deny pre-enforcement judicial review? Abbott Laboratories v. Gardner, 387 U.S. 136 (1967), answered this question no, substituting crystallization of the agency position for the "final order" rule. In General Motors Corp. v. EPA, 363 F.3d 442 (D.C. Cir. 2004), the court held that an EPA letter confirming that hazardous waste regulations applied to an industrial process and discussing the possibility of enforcement actions in the absence of settlement did not constitute final agency action, and that a challenge to EPA's position was not ripe. Cf. Independent Equipment Dealers Ass'n v. EPA, 372 F.3d 420 (D.C. Cir. 2004) (holding that EPA letter that did not announce a new interpretation of or change CAA regulations, that imposed no obligations, and that had no binding effect on EPA or the regulated community was not judicially reviewable final agency action). A statutory provision authorizing pre-enforcement review may tip the balance toward review when the agency's position is fully crystallized and the issues are purely legal ones.

Ripeness problems can arise when plaintiffs challenge agency policies that provide the basis for agency actions but do not challenge a specific decision by the agency. In NRDC v. EPA, 22 F.3d 1125, 1132-1133 (D.C. Cir. 1994), the court found a challenge to an EPA policy allowing conditional approval of state implementation plans under the CAA to be ripe, despite the absence of a final rule codifying the policy. In Texas Indep. Producers and Royalty Owners Ass'n v. EPA, 410 F.3d 964 (5th Cir. 2005), on the other hand, the court held that a challenge to a final rule deferring a

CWA permit requirement for oil and gas construction was not ripe because EPA had announced its intention to examine applicability of permit requirements during the deferral period, judicial review would inappropriately interfere with administrative action, and the court would benefit from further factual development of the issues presented. Cf. Commonwealth Edison Co. v. Train, 649 F.2d 481, 484 (7th Cir. 1980) (EPA regulations requiring states to prevent water quality degradation were not ripe because they were directed to the states, and it was "impossible to determine at this point with any degree of certainty whether the [petitioners] will be injured by future action by the states").

Can a statement by an agency that appears in the preamble to a regulation published in the Federal Register be unripe for review? In Central and South West Serv., Inc. v. EPA, 220 F.3d 683, 689 n.2 (5th Cir. 2000), the court stated that "[a]n EPA declaration in the preamble to a final rule setting forth the Agency's final and binding interpretation of the statute qualifies as a reviewable regulation for purposes of judicial review." Compare Clean Air Act Implementation Project v. EPA, 150 F.3d 1200, 1208 (D.C. Cir. 1998); Ohio v. EPA, 997 F.2d 1520, 1539 (D.C. Cir. 1993).

Does the ripeness doctrine bar judicial review of land use plans issued by the federal land management agencies? The Forest Service is obliged to issue land and resource management plans for individual forest units in accordance with regulations designed to ensure optimal forest management. Subsequent decisions, such as the issuance of permits or timber contracts, must conform to the plan. 16 U.S.C. §1604(i). What arguments are available to the government that the plans are not ripe for review? What contrary arguments are available to a litigant dissatisfied with the contents of a plan?

The Supreme Court tackled the issue in Ohio Forestry Ass'n v. Sierra Club, 523 U.S. 726 (1998). The plaintiffs challenged the validity of those portions of a Forest Service plan authorizing logging on 126,000 acres in an Ohio national forest. The Court held that the challenge was not yet ripe for review. The plan itself did not inflict significant practical harm on the plaintiffs because site-specific environmental assessment, which could be challenged by the plaintiffs later on, was a prerequisite to logging activity. Won't it be more difficult, time-consuming, and expensive for a group like the Sierra Club to attack a multitude of site-specific timber sales than to seek invalidation of the plan pursuant to which those sales may be implemented? The Court also concluded that immediate judicial review of the lawfulness of logging would hinder the efforts of the Forest Service to refine its policies through plan revisions and application of the plan in practice. Finally, judicial review would be more meaningful in the context of a particular logging proposal. Agency decisions to implement land use plans may be ripe for review even if a challenge to the plan itself is not.

Problem 3-2

Blueberry Hills Development Corporation (BHD) owns a 60-acre tract of land, which it purchased ten years ago. BHD developed a subdivision plan to build 150 single-family homes on the tract. The local government approved the plan, as did the state environmental department, which is responsible for reviewing water and sewer systems in subdivisions. BHD entered into a contract for site grading and road and utility construction, and construction of the internal roads has begun.

After being notified by neighbors that the project had commenced, the U.S. Army Corps of Engineers, which, along with EPA, is responsible for administering the dredge and fill permit program under the Clean Water Act, visited the site. That program requires the approval of the Corps for any discharge of dredged or fill material into navigable waters. 33 U.S.C. §1344. The Corps has interpreted navigable waters to include certain wetlands, and the courts have deferred to that interpretation. The Corps recently issued a cease and desist order to BHD informing BHD that the Corps has concluded that the subdivision site includes wetlands and that BHD therefore must seek a permit before any further excavation work on the subdivision may proceed.

BHD has filed suit against the United States in federal district court and sought a preliminary injunction to prevent the Corps from enforcing §1344 or the cease and desist order against it. BHD has argued that the site of its subdivision does not qualify as wetlands. In its order to BHD, the Corps supported its conclusion that the subdivision site includes wetlands by citing to guidance issued jointly by the Corps and EPA defining what constitutes wetlands for purposes of the §1344 program. BHD has argued that the Corps lacks the authority to rely on the guidance because it was issued without compliance with the APA's procedures for the issuance of rules. According to BHD, under the previous guidance document, none of BHD's property would have qualified as wetlands.

The United States has filed a motion to dismiss the action on the grounds that BHD failed to exhaust its administrative remedies, that the issue of whether BHD's property qualifies as wetlands is not ripe for review, and that any attempt by the court to resolve the issue of whether the property includes wetlands would infringe upon the Corps's primary jurisdiction. According to the government, the Corps's regulations authorize BHD to challenge its determination that the property qualifies as wetlands (and to challenge the validity of the guidance) in an administrative proceeding to enforce the cease and desist order, a proceeding which the Corps has not yet begun.

What arguments should the government make to support its motion to dismiss?

NOTE ON RECOVERY OF ATTORNEYS' FEES

Even if a plaintiff can satisfy the constitutional and prudential standing requirements and avoid dismissal on exhaustion, ripeness, and related grounds, it must have the wherewithal to finance the litigation. The costs of paying an attorney sometimes comprise a formidable obstacle, particularly to nonprofit public interest groups. Although attorneys' fees are not usually available to prevailing parties under the so-called American rule, some federal courts developed a "private attorney general" exception that permitted the recovery of attorneys' fees in public interest litigation, such as environmental litigation. The Supreme Court rejected this exception in Alyeska Pipeline Serv. Co. v. Wilderness Soc'y, 421 U.S. 240 (1975), but Congress has since authorized the award of attorneys' fees under most environmental statutes. E.g., Clean Air Act §304(d). The courts have not always been receptive to these fee-shifting provisions. In Ruckelshaus v. Sierra Club, 463 U.S. 680 (1983), the Supreme Court interpreted a similar provision of the CAA, which authorized the award of fees "whenever [the court] determines that such award is appropriate," to bar recovery by anyone other than a party who prevailed at least in part. At least one lower court refused to award fees to a financially able party whose economic interests motivated it to sue, particularly because its successful challenge to an EPA decision under the CAA did not promote statutory goals. Western States Petroleum Ass'n v. EPA, 87 F.3d 280 (9th Cir. 1996). Compare Florida Power & Light Co. v. Costle, 683 F.2d 941 (5th Cir. 1982). How can a successful challenge to agency action fail to promote statutory objectives?

Reimbursement for attorneys' fees may be available even under statutes that do not themselves authorize fee shifting. The Equal Access to Justice Act (EAJA), 28 U.S.C. §2412, authorizes the mandatory award of attorneys' fees and expenses to any party "prevailing" against the United States unless a court finds "that the position of the United States was substantially justified or that special circumstances make an award unjust." Can a party qualify as a "prevailing party" if the case is settled before a final judicial resolution? In Buckhannon Bd. and Care Home, Inc. v. West Virginia Dep't of Health and Human Res., 532 U.S. 598 (2001), the Supreme Court held that a party is a "prevailing party" for purposes of the Fair Housing Act Amendments of 1988 and the Americans with Disabilities Act only if it secures a judgment on the merits or a court-ordered consent decree. The Court disavowed the "catalyst theory," under which a plaintiff can qualify as "prevailing" if it achieves the desired result because a lawsuit brought about a voluntary change in the defendant's conduct. The Court concluded that the catalyst theory improperly allowed fee awards absent a "judicially sanctioned change in the legal relationship of the parties." Id. at 605.

The *Buckhannon* holding presumably applies to the EAJA, which also limits fee awards to "prevailing parties." See Bark v. Larsen, 423 F. Supp. 2d 1135, 1139-1140 (D. Or. 2006). Does it apply, however, to the numerous environmental statutes that allow courts to award fees without requiring that the fee recipient be a "prevailing party"? The ESA, like the CAA, authorizes fee awards "whenever [the court] determines that such award is appropriate." 16 U.S.C. §1540(g)(4). In Loggerhead Turtle v. County Council, 307 F.3d 1318 (11th Cir. 2002), the court held that the catalyst theory survived *Buckhannon* under the ESA's citizen suit provision. The court found clear evidence that Congress intended that a plaintiff whose suit furthers the goals of a "whenever . . . appropriate" statute be entitled to recover attorneys' fees. In addition, the Court in *Buckhannon* discounted the argument that, if the catalyst theory were rejected, "mischievous defendants" could avoid liability for attorneys' fees in a meritorious suit by voluntarily changing their conduct. That strategy would not work, the Court reasoned, because as long as the plaintiffs retain a cause of action for damages, the defendant's change in conduct would not moot the case. Under citizen suit provisions such as the ESA's, however, the only relief that may be sought is equitable relief; damages are not available. Accordingly, rejection of the catalyst theory would induce rational defendants to voluntarily change their conduct to avoid fee liability if defeat seemed imminent. Such an outcome would "cripple the citizen suit provision of the [ESA,] in derogation of Congress's 'abundantly clear' intent to 'afford[ ] endangered species the highest of priorities." Id. at 1327. Suppose a statute authorizes fee awards "to any prevailing or substantially prevailing party, whenever the court determines such award is appropriate." Does the catalyst theory apply? See Kasza v. Whitman, 325 F.3d 1178 (9th Cir. 2003); Amigos Bravos v. EPA, 324 F.3d 1166, 1171 (10th Cir. 2003).

NOTE ON THE FEDERAL ADVISORY COMMITTEE ACT

The exhaustion doctrine requires that potential litigants take advantage of available opportunities to participate in the administrative process as a prerequisite to bringing suit. The Federal Advisory Committee Act (FACA) of 1972, 5 U.S.C. app. 2, is intended to ensure that those opportunities are meaningful in situations in which committees are established to advise administrative agencies in their decisionmaking processes. The Act was adopted in response to concerns that advisory committees tended to be stacked with representatives of the industries whose activities the agency soliciting the committees' advice was responsible for regulating. Section 10 of the Act requires that advisory committee meetings be open to the public and that interested persons be permitted to attend, appear before, or file statements with the committee. Reports and other documents made available to or prepared by a committee must be made available for public inspection and copying.

An advisory committee is defined as a committee, board, task force, or similar group that is established by statute, the President, or an agency in the interest of obtaining advice or recommendations for the President or a federal agency. A group of industry representatives that submitted a proposal to EPA to avoid regulation was deemed not to be an advisory committee in Huron Envtl. Activist League v. EPA, 917 F. Supp. 34 (D.D.C. 1996), because EPA lacked control over the group. The court relied on the Supreme Court's warning against a broad interpretation of FACA in Public Citizen v. United States Dep't of Justice, 491 U.S. 440 (1989).*

In Miccosukee Tribe v. Southern Everglades Restoration Alliance, 304 F.3d 1076 (11th Cir. 2002), the court rejected the contention that advisory committees established by federal agencies are not covered by FACA unless the inclusion of private individuals or group members threatens to infect government proceedings with the influence of special interests. How hard is it for an agency to avoid FACA's strictures? Can a litigant challenge the composition of a FACA committee as not "fairly balanced," as required by §5(b)(2) of FACA? See Colorado Envtl. Coalition v. Wenker, 353 F.3d 1221 (10th Cir. 2004); Sanchez v. Pena, 17 F. Supp. 2d 1235 (D.N.M. 1998). At least one court has held that there is no private right of action to enforce FACA, but that litigants may enforce the statute under the judicial review provisions of the APA. International Brominated Solvents Ass'n v. American Conf. of Governmental Indus. Hygienists, Inc., 393 F. Supp. 2d 1362, 1377-1378 (M.D. Ga. 2005).

What is the consequence of violating FACA's procedural requirements? Northwest Forest Resource Council v. Espy, 846 F. Supp. 1009 (D.D.C. 1994), involved a report issued by a team of experts convened by President Clinton to develop a plan to save the northern spotted owl. When the forest products industry sued to enjoin use of the report, the court held that the team violated FACA, but it refused to enjoin

---

*For other cases finding that entities were not FACA advisory committees due to the absence of agency control or management, see Miccosukee Tribe v. United States, 420 F. Supp. 2d 1324, 1341-1342 (S.D. Fla. 2006); Washington Toxics Coalition v. EPA, 357 F. Supp. 2d 1266 (W.D. Wash. 2004); Physicians Comm. for Responsible Medicine v. Horinko, 285 F. Supp. 2d 430 (S.D.N.Y. 2003). Compare California Forestry Ass'n v. United States Forest Serv., 102 F.3d 609 (D.C. Cir. 1996) (Sierra Nevada Ecosystem Project was subject to FACA because, even though it prepared a study for submission to Congress, the Forest Service intended to use the study); NRDC v. Abraham, 223 F. Supp. 2d 162 (D.D.C. 2002) (group composed of federal employees and employees of federal contractors was subject to FACA where the contractors provided advice on a project that lay outside their contract).

reliance on the report because it would be "presumptuous" to dictate what the President may consider in his decisionmaking. In NRDC v. Pena, 147 F.3d 1012 (D.C. Cir. 1998), the court characterized an injunction against the use of the output of a committee whose activities violated FACA as a "remedy of last resort." Id. at 1025. In deciding whether to issue a use injunction, the courts should consider whether doing so would promote FACA's principal purposes—avoidance of wasteful expenditures and public accountability.

In Cargill v. United States, 173 F.3d 323 (5th Cir. 1999), the court reasoned that "[i]f the courts do not enforce FACA by enjoining the work product of improperly constituted committees, FACA will be toothless, merely aspirational legislation. . . . If FACA has no teeth, the work product of spuriously formed advisory groups may obtain political legitimacy that it does not deserve. Hence, some kind of injunctive relief is appropriate." Id. at 341. The court nevertheless agreed with *Pena* that a use injunction should be the remedy of last resort. Citing California Forestry Ass'n v. United States Forest Serv., 102 F.3d 609 (9th Cir. 1996), the Fifth Circuit concluded that an injunction for a FACA violation is appropriate if the unavailability of such relief "would effectively render FACA a nullity." 173 F.3d at 342. It remanded to the district court to determine the appropriate relief for violations of FACA's congressional filing requirements by the National Institute for Occupational Safety and Health.

Some litigants have relied more successfully on FACA violations. One court upheld an injunction prohibiting the FWS from using a report prepared in violation of FACA in connection with its efforts to list the Alabama sturgeon as endangered. Alabama-Tombigbee Rivers Coalition v. Department of the Interior, 26 F.3d 1103 (11th Cir. 1994).*

Aurelia, Comment, The Federal Advisory Committee Act and Its Failure to Work Effectively in the Environmental Context, 23 B.C. Envtl. Aff. L. Rev. 87 (1995), asserts that the courts' failure to enforce the statute have rendered it ineffective. Is it possible that, even if the Act has not succeeded in altering the manner in which the agencies make their decisions or the range of information they rely upon in doing so, it nevertheless has opened up the decisionmaking process to public scrutiny?

The constitutional questions raised by judicial enforcement of FACA are discussed in Bybee, Advising the President: Separation of Powers and the Federal Advisory Committee Act, 104 Yale L.J. 51 (1994) (contending that FACA violates separation of powers by regulating the President's use of advisory committees and "aggrandizes Congress' relative powers over the President"). For a thorough analysis of the history, implementation, and interpretation of FACA, see Croley & Funk, The Federal Advisory Committee Act and Good Government, 14 Yale J. on Reg. 451 (1997).

Problem 3-3

The administrator of EPA has invited nine of the nation's governors to convene a "governor's forum" to assist EPA in addressing the problem of state ability to carry out regulatory programs that EPA is authorized to delegate to the states under the federal

---

*Cf. Idaho Farm Bureau Fed'n v. Babbitt, 900 F. Supp. 1349 (D. Idaho 1995) (court can enjoin agency from using report prepared in violation of FACA to support listing under the ESA, but should not invalidate a completed listing that was based on information prepared in violation of FACA).

pollution control laws. Under these laws, each state has the choice of following mandatory EPA standards if it chooses to accept these delegations or of foregoing delegation in favor of continued EPA implementation of the statutes. EPA retains the power to enforce regulatory requirements that a state with delegated authority fails to enforce. The administrator has charged the forum with developing proposals for increasing funding for delegated state programs and decreasing the burdens imposed by federal legislation on states that choose to exercise delegated authority.

The EPA administrator selected the nine governors who will participate in the forum as well as the governor who will chair the forum's meetings. The chair is responsible for scheduling meetings and setting the agenda for each meeting. The forum is solely responsible for developing proposals, which it will present to the administrator after the members of the forum have adopted them by majority vote. It receives no federal funds.

Are the forum's activities subject to FACA?

2.   Standards of Review

Once environmental plaintiffs clear the standing and other threshold jurisdictional hurdles, the issue becomes how thoroughly the courts will review the outcome of the agency's decisionmaking process. As indicated below, the answer tends to be context-specific, varying in accordance with the nature of the decision being challenged and the procedural context in which the agency made it. This section first briefly describes the kinds of decisions administrative agencies make and then explores how the courts approach the task of reviewing those decisions.

a.   The Types of Reviewable Administrative Action

Generally speaking, administrative lawmaking oscillates between the two extremes represented by courts and legislators. If the existing rights of one or a few individuals are challenged, the judicial model usually applies and the agency acts more like a court, conducting a trial-type hearing on the record with cross-examination and other procedural formalities. If noncompetitive governmental permissions or broad policies that will apply prospectively to large numbers of organizations or individuals are in question, the freewheeling informality of the legislative model usually applies.

The nature of the restrictions imposed on agencies by the Due Process Clause depends largely on the kind of administrative proceeding involved. The Supreme Court has adhered to a distinction between quasi-judicial agency "adjudication" and quasi-legislative agency "rulemaking." In United States v. Florida East Coast Ry., 410 U.S. 224 (1973), the Court held that an agency did not have to hold an on-the-record, trial-type hearing before issuing a "rule" under a statute requiring that the decision be made "after hearing." The regulated parties had no constitutional right to a trial-type hearing because the factual inferences relied on by the agency were used in "the formulation of a basically legislative-type judgment, for prospective application only, rather than in adjudicating a particular set of disputed facts." Id. at 246. The Court explained the distinction between rulemaking and adjudication by referring to two seminal due process cases. Londoner v. Denver, 210 U.S. 373 (1908), held that a landowner challenging an assessment for street paving who was allowed to file written objections but not to be heard orally was denied due process. But in Bi-Metallic Inv. Co. v. State Bd. of Equalization, 239 U.S. 441 (1915), due process did not require any hearing before state tax officers increased the valuation of all taxable property. The Court distinguished *Londoner* as a case in which a small number of persons was affected on individual grounds. The two cases thus distinguished between "proceedings for the purpose of promulgating policy-type rules or standards, on the one hand, and proceedings designed to adjudicate disputed facts in particular cases, on the other." 410 U.S. at 245.

Today, most administrative actions fall into five categories: (1) formal adjudication, (2) formal rulemaking, (3) informal notice-and-comment rulemaking, (4) informal adjudication or other informal action (such as approval of the location and funding of an interstate highway, as the *Overton Park* case, reproduced below, indicates), and (5) informal actions that require minimal procedural formalities (e.g., nonbinding policy statements). As section D of this chapter reveals, the fifth category appears to be growing.

Still, much environmental decisionmaking involves informal rulemaking under statutes like those addressed in Chapters 6-8. Consider the following explanation of the process:

> Agency decision making in regulating to protect health, safety, and the environment is overwhelmingly of the legislative sort, with a frequent dash of extra formality. It involves selecting and implementing statute-like policies that will apply prospectively to large classes of manufacturers, employers, and polluters. In developing their policies through standards, guidelines, and regulations—or *rules*, as they are collectively called—agencies follow a more or less standard process that is often called notice-and-comment rule making. First, they provide notice about what they want to require regulatees to do by publishing their proposed rules in the Federal Register. A period for public comment and counterproposal follows, which may include informal public hearings. Oral or written rebuttal and cross-examination between proponents of antagonistic views may be permitted, especially if factual matters remain in dispute. If they are doing their jobs properly, agencies respond in detail to the public commentary in the Federal Register when they issue rules in formal form. Sometimes they propose significantly modified rules and reopen the comment period. . . .
>
> Rule making is the fastest, least expensive, and politically most expedient way for agencies to carry out these diverse imperatives. It leaves the agencies maximum freedom to act within minimum procedural, informational, and participational restraints. . . . [Anderson, Human Welfare and the Administered Society: Federal Regulation in the 1970s to Protect Health, Safety, and the Environment, in Environmental and Occupational Medicine 835, 856-857 (W. Rom ed., 1983).]

NOTES AND QUESTIONS

1. *The Hybrid Rulemaking Experiment.* For a time during the 1970s, some lower federal courts reacted favorably to requests by litigants to require agencies to abide by "hybrid" procedures that allowed cross-examination and explain their decisions more thoroughly—in short, to require a more trial-like record. See, e.g., International Harvester Co. v. Ruckelshaus, 478 F.2d 615 (D.C. Cir. 1973). The Supreme Court, however, took a dim view of this hybrid rulemaking experiment in Vermont Yankee Nuclear Power Corp. v. NRDC, 435 U.S. 519, 523 (1978). It explained that the APA "settled long-continued and hard-fought contentions, and enact[ed] a formula upon

which opposing social and political forces have come to rest." Section 553 established the informal, notice-and-comment rulemaking procedures described above.

> . . . [G]enerally speaking this section of the Act established the maximum procedural requirements which Congress was willing to have the courts impose upon agencies in conducting rulemaking procedures. Agencies are free to grant additional procedural rights in the exercise of their discretion, but reviewing courts are generally not free to impose them if the agencies have not chosen to grant them. This is not to say necessarily that there are no circumstances which would ever justify a court in overturning agency action because of a failure to employ procedures beyond those required by the statute. But such circumstances, if they exist, are extremely rare. [Id.]

2. *Hybrid Rulemaking and the Federal Pollution Control Laws. Vermont Yankee* precludes the courts from adding to the procedures specified in the APA, but it does not bar Congress from supplementing or supplanting those procedures in substantive legislation or the agencies themselves from voluntarily going beyond statutory procedural mandates, and Congress has exercised this authority. Section 307(d) of the CAA, for example, provides more formalized rulemaking procedures for the adoption of many of the rules authorized by the Act. It requires EPA to develop a decision record that includes a summary of the factual data on which the rule is based, as well as "the major legal interpretations and policy considerations underlying the proposed rule." The Toxic Substances Control Act is another statute that grafts some of the procedural requirements characteristic of formal rulemaking or adjudication onto the adoption of rules. See 15 U.S.C. §2605(c)(2)-(3).

3. *Comparing Informal and Hybrid Rulemaking.* Well before *Vermont Yankee,* Judge Bazelon, writing for the court in EDF v. Ruckelshaus, 439 F.2d 584, 598 (D.C. Cir. 1971), claimed that "[w]hen administrators provide a framework for principled decision-making, the result will be to diminish the importance of judicial review by enhancing the integrity of the administrative process, and to improve the quality of judicial review in those cases where judicial review is sought." Professor Joseph Sax characterized that view as a "dubious example of wishful thinking. I know of no solid evidence to support the belief that requiring articulation, detailed findings or reasoned opinions enhances the integrity or propriety of administrative decisions." Sax, The (Unhappy) Truth about NEPA, 26 Okla. L. Rev. 239, 239 (1973).

Professor McGarity has argued that, although "informal rulemaking is still an exceedingly effective tool for eliciting public participation in administrative policy-making, it has not evolved into the flexible and efficient process that its early supporters originally envisioned," and that it has become "increasingly rigid and burdensome." McGarity, Some Thoughts on "Deossifying" the Rulemaking Process, 41 Duke L.J. 1385, 1385 (1992). He attributes the "ossification" of the rulemaking process in large part to the imposition of analytical requirements by both the courts and Congress. Sections B and C of this chapter explore the requirements imposed on the agencies by Congress and the executive branch.

b. Judicial Review of Statutory Interpretation

A different standard of judicial review may apply if a litigant asserts that an agency misinterpreted its enabling legislation than if it claims that the agency improperly implemented that statute in a given situation. The first question is basically a question of law, while the second requires the application of law or policy to the fact .situation before the agency. During the 1960s, at the inception of modern environmental consciousness in the United States, the Supreme Court had noted the deference to which agency statutory interpretations were entitled and concluded that agency interpretations of their own regulations should be accorded even greater judicial deference. See Udall v. Tallman, 380 U.S. 1 (1965). Due to a combination of faith in the legislative process, suspicion that administrative agencies were susceptible to capture by the interests they were responsible for regulating, and a sense that environmental values were special, the courts in the 1970s were willing to engage in fairly rigorous review of both kinds of questions in cases involving environmental matters. See Glicksman & Schroeder, EPA and the Courts: Twenty Years of Law and Politics, 54 Law & Contemp. Probs. #4 (Autumn 1991), at 249.

The Supreme Court ushered in a new era of deference to agency statutory interpretations in the following case.

CHEVRON U.S.A., INC. v. NATURAL RESOURCES DEFENSE COUNCIL, INC.
467 U.S. 837 (1984)

JUSTICE STEVENS delivered the opinion of the Court. . . .

When a court reviews an agency's construction of the statute which it administers, it is confronted with two questions. First, always, is the question whether Congress has directly spoken to the precise question at issue. If the intent of Congress is clear, that is the end of the matter; for the court, as well as the agency, must give effect to the unambiguously expressed intent of Congress.[9] If, however, the court determines Congress has not directly addressed the precise question at issue, the court does not simply impose its own construction on the statute, as would be necessary in the absence of an administrative interpretation. Rather, if the statute is silent or ambiguous with respect to the specific issue, the question for the court is whether the agency's answer is based on a permissible construction of the statute.

"The power of an administrative agency to administer a congressionally created . . . program necessarily requires the formulation of policy and the making of rules to fill any gap left, implicitly or explicitly, by Congress." Morton v. Ruiz, 415 U.S. 199, 231 (1974). If Congress has explicitly left a gap for the agency to fill, there is an express delegation of authority to the agency to elucidate a specific provision of the statute by regulation. Such legislative regulations are given controlling weight unless they are arbitrary, capricious, or manifestly contrary to the statute. Sometimes the legislative delegation to an agency on a particular question is implicit rather than explicit. In such a case, a court may not substitute its own construction of a statutory provision for a reasonable interpretation made by the administrator of an agency.

We have long recognized that considerable weight should be accorded to an executive department's construction of a statutory scheme it is entrusted to administer, and the principle of deference to administrative interpretations

9. The judiciary is the final authority on issues of statutory construction and must reject administrative constructions which are contrary to clear congressional intent. If a court, employing traditional tools of statutory construction, ascertains that Congress had an intention on the precise question at issue, that intention is the law and must be given effect.

has been consistently followed by this Court whenever decision as to the meaning or reach of a statute has involved reconciling conflicting policies, and a full understanding of the force of the statutory policy in the given situation has depended upon more than ordinary knowledge respecting the matters subjected to agency regulations. . . . United States v. Shimer, 367 U.S. 374, 382 (1961) . . .

[The remainder of the *Chevron* opinion is reproduced in Chapter 6, section F.4.]

NOTES AND QUESTIONS

1. How is a court to tell whether the statute is clear on the "precise question at issue"? What are the "traditional tools of statutory construction"? Do they include reference to legislative history? Underlying statutory purposes? Maxims of statutory construction? Previous judicial decisions interpreting the statute? Or is the reviewing court confined to an analysis of statutory plain meaning?* In FDA v. Brown & Williamson Tobacco Corp., 529 U.S. 120, 132 (2000), the Supreme Court asserted that when a reviewing court determines whether Congress has directly spoken to the precise question at issue, it "should not confine itself to examining a particular statutory provision in isolation. The meaning—or ambiguity—of certain words or phrases may only become evident when placed in context." In that case, the "context" included the agency's past interpretations of the scope of its own authority, the adoption of other statutes concerning the regulation of tobacco products, and the economic and political magnitude of the policy decision at issue.

Assume that the "object and policy" of a statute are relevant in assessing the reasonableness of an agency's statutory construction under step two of *Chevron*. Is it reasonable for an agency to interpret a Clean Air Act provision that requires compliance with technology-based controls "as expeditiously as practicable" to require industries burning hazardous waste as fuels to cease using that waste within two years, even if the agency cannot demonstrate that compliance with the requirement will result in any air quality benefits? See Chemical Mfrs. Ass'n v. EPA, 217 F.3d 861 (D.C. Cir. 2000). See also NRDC v. Abraham, 355 F.3d 179, 195 (2d Cir. 2004).

2. *The Source of* Chevron *Deference.* Is *Chevron* compelled by separation of powers principles? Is the gap-filling function of agencies endorsed by the Court consistent with the constitutional law nondelegation doctrine, which forbids Congress from delegating authority to an administrative agency without ascertainable legislative standards to guide agency discretion? See United States v. Henry, 136 F.3d 12, 16-17 (1st Cir. 1998). Once Congress authorizes the exercise of broad agency discretion, has it authorized the executive to interpret the statute as it chooses? Compare Farina, Statutory Interpretation and the Balance of Power in the Administrative State, 89 Colum. L. Rev. 452 (1989) with Kmiec, Judicial Deference to Executive Agencies and the Decline of the Nondelegation Doctrine, 2 Admin. L.J. 269 (1988).

How does the impact of a statutory interpretation on the allocation of power between the federal government and the states affect the application of *Chevron*? Does a special version of *Chevron* apply in contexts with federalism implications? See Solid Waste Agency of N. Cook County v. U.S. Army Corp of Engineers, 531 U.S. 159

---

*Compare Kmart Corp. v. Cartier, Inc., 486 U.S. 281 (1988) with Neal v. United States, 516 U.S. 284 (1996); Dole v. United Steelworkers of Am., 494 U.S. 26 (1990).

(2001). Cf. Maine v. Norton, 257 F. Supp. 2d 357, 385 (D. Me. 2003) (affording *Chevron* deference to FWS's interpretation of the ESA because the interpretation did not alter the federal-state framework—one of shared federal-state authority to manage resident wildlife—any more than Congress had already done when it enacted the statute).

3. *The Scope of the* Chevron *Deference Doctrine.* Should the degree of deference afforded an agency's statutory interpretation differ depending upon whether the interpretation arises in the context of rulemaking, adjudication, or more informal contexts such as policy statements or agency manuals? In Christensen v. Harris County, 529 U.S. 576 (2000), the Court held that an interpretation contained in an opinion letter did not warrant *Chevron*-style deference. Similarly, in United States v. Mead Corp., 533 U.S. 218 (2001), the Court held that

> administrative implementation of a particular statutory provision qualifies for *Chevron* deference when it appears that Congress delegated authority to the agency generally to make rules carrying the force of law, and that the agency interpretation claiming deference was promulgated in the exercise of that authority. Delegation of such authority may be shown in a variety of ways, as by an agency's power to engage in adjudication or notice-and-comment rulemaking, or by some other indication of a comparable congressional intent. [Id. at 226-227.]

In Barnhart v. Walton, 535 U.S. 212 (2002), however, the Court concluded (arguably in dictum) that the fact that an agency's longstanding interpretation had been reached "through means less formal than 'notice and comment' rulemaking does not automatically deprive that interpretation of the judicial deference otherwise its due," citing *Chevron.* It added that, even if *Christensen* suggested an "absolute rule to the contrary," *Mead* denied the suggestion. Rather, *Mead* "indicated that whether a court should give such deference depends in significant part upon the interpretive method used and the nature of the question at issue." In *Barnhart*, "the interstitial nature of the legal question, the related expertise of the Agency, the importance of the question to administration of the statute, the complexity of that administration, and the careful consideration the Agency has given the question over a long period of time all indicate that *Chevron* provides the appropriate legal lens through which to view the legality of the Agency interpretation here at issue." Id. at 221-222.

An agency interpretation that does not qualify for *Chevron* deference may nevertheless be entitled to some deference. The *Mead* Court recognized that judicial deference may still be appropriate, depending on factors such as "the degree of the agency's care, its consistency, formality, and relative expertness, and . . . the persuasiveness of the agency's position." Id. at 228 (citing Skidmore v. Swift & Co., 323 U.S. 134, 139-140 (1944)).*

Limitations on the scope of an agency's power to promulgate rules may narrow the application of the *Chevron* doctrine. See, e.g., Gonzales v. Oregon, 126 S. Ct. 904 (2006) (holding that attorney general's interpretation of Controlled Substances Act was not entitled to *Chevron* deference because the Act does not authorize him to issue

---

*See also Vigil v. Leavitt, 366 F.3d 1025, 1033 (9th Cir. 2004) (affording *Skidmore* but not *Chevron* deference to "preliminary interpretation" contained in EPA's advance notice); NRDC v. Abraham, 355 F.3d 179, 200 (2d Cir. 2004) (agency's definition of statutory term was "in the nature of an interpretive rule" because it did not go through full notice-and-comment procedures specified in statute, and therefore was not entitled to *Chevron* deference)

a rule declaring illegitimate a medical standard for care and treatment of patients that is specifically authorized by law). One court remarked that, "[f]ollowing *Mead*, the continuum of agency deference has been fraught with ambiguity." United States v. W.R. Grace & Co., 429 F.3d 1224, 1235 (9th Cir. 2005). For discussion of when the *Chevron* approach to statutory interpretation applies, see Sunstein, Chevron Step Zero, 92 Va. L. Rev. 187 (2006).

Suppose that an agency publishes a draft policy statement in the Federal Register, upon which it solicits comments. Before the agency issues the statement in final form, the propriety of one of the legal issues addressed in the statement becomes the subject of judicial review. What degree of deference, if any, should a court afford to an interpretation reflected in the policy statement? See Southern Utah Wilderness Alliance v. Dabney, 222 F.3d 819 (10th Cir. 2000).

4. *The Influence of Public Choice Theory.* Lawsuits brought largely by public interest firms during the 1970s challenged the very foundations of administrative law. The administrative law of judicial review changed rapidly, and a new model of the administrative process emerged in response to judicial intervention. In his synthesis of these developments, Professor Richard Stewart argued that the "new" administrative law rejected the expertise model, which confined the courts to protecting unconstitutional and illegal agency intrusions on individual rights, and replaced it with a model of the agency as a forum for resolving conflicts between various antagonistic groups. In short, the courts stood on its head a classic corollary of the expertise model — that experts must be shielded from crass political influence:

> Faced with the seemingly intractable problem of agency discretion, courts have changed the focus of judicial review (in the process expanding and transforming traditional procedural devices) so that its dominant purpose is no longer the prevention of unauthorized intrusions on private autonomy, but the assurance of fair representation for all affected interests in the exercise of the legislative power delegated to agencies.
>
> Implicit in this development is the assumption that there is no ascertainable, transcendent "public interest," but only the distinct interests of various individuals and groups in society. Under this assumption, legislation represents no more than compromises struck between competing interest groups.[206] This analysis suggests that if agencies were to function as a forum for all interests affected by agency decisionmaking, bargaining leading to compromises generally acceptable to all might result, thus replicating the process of legislation. Agency decisions made after adequate consideration of all affected interests would have, in microcosm, legitimacy based on the same principle as legislation and therefore the fact that statutes cannot control agency discretion would become largely irrelevant. [Stewart, The Reformation of American Administration Law, 88 Harv. L. Rev. 1669, 1712 (1975).]

Professor Stewart's argument that legislatures typically are incapable of transforming discernible public values into law whose implementation the courts can oversee presaged a shift in political thought based on the application of public choice theory to the legislative process. That theory assumes that legislators, like everyone else, are motivated by self-interest. Scholars and judges influenced by public choice

---

206. See, e.g., A. Bentley, The Process of Government (1908); D. Truman, The Governmental Process (1951). In the extreme form of this view, there is no objective, independent yardstick by which one can measure the content of compromise; compromises are legitimated by the process of their negotiation. For criticism of such analysis, see T. Lowi, [The Poverty of Liberalism (1968)]; R. Wolff, [The End of Liberalism (1969)]. . . .

theory have stressed the need for judges to view legislative delegations as interest group bargains struck by Congress and further argued that courts should generally uphold such bargains by limiting their inquiry into the meaning of the statute.* Judge Starr, for example, opined that "statutes are rarely, if ever, unidimensionally directed towards achieving or vindicating a single public policy." NRDC v. EPA, 822 F.2d 104, 113 (D.C. Cir. 1987). Even if a broad policy goal "is the animating force driving the legislation, achievement of actual passage invariably requires compromise and accommodation." Id. Such compromises may entail agreeing to let the agency resolve disputed issues over which a consensus failed to emerge. See NRDC v. EPA, 859 F.2d 156, 199 (D.C. Cir. 1988) ("it falls to the agency to reconcile competing legislative goals"). As a result, the courts should be circumspect about relying on broadly stated objectives to overturn an agency's interpretation of the statute because doing so risks tearing apart the legislative compromise. See American Min. Congress v. EPA, 824 F.2d 1177, 1185 n.10 (D.C. Cir. 1987).

Underlying such arguments is a loss of faith in the ability of Congress to be other than a conduit for special interests. Does *Chevron* reflect this deferential review posture? Other proponents of strong executive control of administrative agencies have applauded the decision. E.g., Pierce, *Chevron* and Its Aftermath: Judicial Review of Agency Interpretations of Statutory Provisions, 41 Vand. L. Rev. 301 (1988).

Chevron has had more than its fair share of detractors. According to Professor Hirshman, "if . . . the opinion is taken to its full extent to prescribe a rule of agency law-making from congressional silence, then, I think *Chevron* is simply wrong." Hirshman, Postmodern Jurisprudence and the Problem of Administrative Discretion, 82 Nw. U. L. Rev. 646, 687-688 (1988). Alternative theories of judicial review hold that courts should articulate fundamental substantive standards, Sunstein, Constitutionalism after the New Deal, 101 Harv. L. Rev. 421 (1987), or play a more aggressive role in insisting on greater rationality between means and ends of regulatory programs, Rose-Ackerman, Progressive Law and Economics—and the New Administrative Law, 98 Yale L.J. 341 (1988), even though they also have been influenced by public choice theory.**

5. *Deference to Agency Statutory Interpretations since* Chevron. Has *Chevron* had any effect on the way in which courts review agency statutory interpretations? If so, has the case ushered in an era of greater judicial deference? Has it made it easier or harder than before for courts to overturn agency statutory interpretations? If a judge is determined to reverse an agency's interpretation, how should he or she characterize the clarity of the statute? A study of federal appellate court review during the 1990s of EPA decisions found that in cases decided under step one of *Chevron*, EPA lost 59.1 percent of the time. Schroeder & Glicksman, *Chevron, State Farm,* and EPA in the Courts of Appeals during the 1990s, 31 Envtl. L. Rep. (ELI) 10371 (2001). In some of the step one cases, the courts have been willing to peruse the legislative history to buttress their

---

*See Easterbrook, The Supreme Court, 1983 Term-Forward: The Court and the Economic System, 98 Harv. L. Rev. 4 (1984); Easterbrook, Statutes' Domains, 50 U. Chi. L. Rev. 533 (1983); Posner, Economics, Politics, and the Reading of Statutes and the Constitution, 49 U. Chi. L. Rev. 263 (1982).

**For further reading, see Farber & Frickey, The Jurisprudence of Public Choice, 65 Tex. L. Rev. 873 (1987); Macey, Promoting Public-Regarding Legislation through Statutory Interpretation: An Interest Group Model, 86 Colum L. Rev. 223 (1986); Pierce, The Role of Constitutional and Political Theory in Administrative Law, 64 Tex. L. Rev. 469 (1985); Reese, Bursting the Chevron Bubble: Clarifying the Scope of Judicial Review in Troubled Times, 73 Fordham L. Rev. 1103 (2004); Symposium on the Theory of Public Choice, 74 Va. L. Rev. 167 (1988).

readings of "plain" statutory meaning. E.g., Davis County Solid Waste Mgmt. v. EPA, 101 F.3d 1395 (D.C. Cir. 1996) (invalidating CAA regulations applicable to municipal solid waste combustion); Ethyl Corp. v. EPA, 51 F.3d 1053 (D.C. Cir. 1995) (legislative history supported conclusion that EPA's interpretation of provision governing manufacture of fuel additives conflicted with plain statutory meaning). During the same time period, courts resolving challenges to EPA statutory interpretations under the second step of *Chevron* ruled in favor of the agency more than 92 percent of the time. In some of those cases, the courts have looked to the legislative history to ascertain legislative purpose. See American Mun. Power-Ohio v. EPA, 98 F.3d 1372 (D.C. Cir. 1996).

A more recent study of administrative law decisions by both the Supreme Court and the Courts of Appeals concluded that "the application of the *Chevron* framework is greatly affected by the judges' own convictions," that "the data reveal a strong relationship between the justices' ideological predispositions and the probability that they will validate agency determinations," and that "[i]f judicial decisions under the *Chevron* framework are assessed in crudely political terms, the voting patterns of Supreme Court justices fit with the conventional groupings of the justices along political lines—a clear signal that the *Chevron* framework is not having the disciplining effect that it is supposed to have." Sunstein & Miles, Do Judges Make Regulatory Policy? An Empirical Investigation of *Chevron*, 73 U. Chi. L. Rev. 823, 826 (2006).*

c. Judicial Review of Statutory Implementation

Once an agency determines what a statute means, it must apply the statute, as so interpreted, to the particular factual situation before it. What is the role of the reviewing court in resolving challenges to such mixed determinations of fact, law, and policy? Is the court likely to be more or less deferential in this context than in the context of reviewing statutory interpretation questions? Does the nature of the agency action (rulemaking, adjudication, or other informal action) affect the standard of review? The next case addressed these and other questions.

CITIZENS TO PRESERVE OVERTON PARK, INC. v. VOLPE
401 U.S. 402 (1971)

Opinion of the Court by Mr. JUSTICE MARSHALL, announced by Mr. JUSTICE STEWART. . . .

[Overton Park was a 342-acre city-owned park located near the center of Memphis. It contained a zoo, a nine-hole golf course, an outdoor theater, nature trails, a bridle path, picnic areas, and 170 acres of forest. In April 1968, after Tennessee

---

*For further analysis of the impact of *Chevron*, see Kerr, Shedding Light on *Chevron*: An Empirical Study of the *Chevron* Doctrine in the U.S. Courts of Appeals, 15 Yale J. on Reg. 1 (1998); Levy & Glicksman, Judicial Activism and Restraint in the Supreme Court's Environmental Law Decisions, 42 Vand. L. Rev. 343 (1989) (charging that courts can manipulate *Chevron*'s two-part test in order to promote a pro-development bias that undermines congressional environmental objectives).

acquired a right-of-way on both sides of the Park, the Secretary of Transportation announced that he concurred in the judgment of local officials that a portion of I-40, a six-lane interstate highway,[10] should be built through the Park. In 1969, the state acquired the right-of-way inside the Park from the city. The Secretary announced final approval for both the route and design of the project later that year. The proposed highway would sever the zoo from the rest of the Park, destroying 26 acres of the Park even though the roadway would be largely depressed below ground level. When completed, I-40 would provide Memphis with a major east-west expressway that would allow easier access to downtown Memphis from the residential areas on the eastern edge of the city.

Section 4(f) of the Department of Transportation Act of 1966 and §18(a) of the Federal-Aid Highway Act of 1968, 23 U.S.C. §138, prohibited the Secretary of Transportation from authorizing the use of federal funds to finance the construction of highways through public parks if a "feasible and prudent" alternative route exists. Absent such a route, the statutes allowed the Secretary to approve construction through parks only if there had been "all possible planning to minimize harm" to the park. Section 4(f) barred distribution of federal funds for the part of the highway slated to go through Overton Park until the Secretary determined whether the statute's requirements had been met, but federal funds for the rest of the project were not so restricted. When the Secretary announced his approval of the route and design of I-40, he did not issue any factual findings under §§4(f) or 18(a) as to why he believed there were no feasible and prudent alternative routes or why design changes could not be made to reduce harm to the Park.

Local and national conservation organizations, as well as private citizens from the Overton Park area, sued the Secretary, asserting that he violated §§4(f) and 18(a) by authorizing the expenditure of federal funds for the construction of the highway through Overton Park. The district court granted the Secretary's motion for summary judgment; the Sixth Circuit affirmed.]

Petitioners contend that the Secretary's action is invalid without [formal findings under §4(f)] and that the Secretary did not make an independent determination but merely relied on the judgment of the Memphis City Council. They also contend that it would be "feasible and prudent" to route I-40 around Overton Park either to the north or to the south. And they argue that if these alternative routes are not "feasible and prudent," the present plan does not include "all possible" methods for reducing harm to the park. Petitioners claim that I-40 could be built under the park by using either of two possible tunneling methods,[18] and they claim that, at a minimum, by using advanced drainage techniques the expressway could be depressed below ground level along the entire route through the park. . . .

Respondents argue that it was unnecessary for the Secretary to make formal findings, and that he did, in fact, exercise his own independent judgment which was supported by the facts. In the District Court, respondents introduced affidavits, prepared specifically for this litigation, which indicated that the Secretary had made the decision and that the decision was supportable. These affidavits were contradicted by affidavits introduced by petitioners. . . .

10. The proposed right-of-way will be 250 to 450 feet wide. . . .
18. Petitioners argue that either a bored tunnel or a cut-and-cover tunnel, which is a fully depressed route covered after construction, could be built. Respondents contend that the construction of a tunnel by either method would greatly increase the cost of the project, would create safety hazards, and because of increases in air pollution would not reduce harm to the park.

A threshold question—whether petitioners are entitled to any judicial review—is easily answered. Section 701 of the Administrative Procedure Act [APA] provides that the action of "each authority of the Government of the United States," which includes the Department of Transportation, is subject to judicial review except where there is a statutory prohibition on review or where "agency action is committed to agency discretion by law." In this case, there is no indication that Congress sought to prohibit judicial review and there is most certainly no "showing of 'clear and convincing evidence' of a . . . legislative intent" to restrict access to judicial review. Abbott Laboratories v. Gardner, 387 U.S. 136, 141 (1967).

Similarly, the Secretary's decision here does not fall within the exception for action "committed to agency discretion." This is a very narrow exception. The legislative history of the [APA] indicates that it is applicable in those rare instances where "statutes are drawn in such broad terms that in a given case there is no law to apply." S. Rep. No. 752, 79th Cong., 1st Sess., 26 (1945).

[Referring to the "feasible and prudent" and "all possible planning" language of §4(f), the Court stated:] This language is a plain and explicit bar to the use of federal funds for construction of highways through parks—only the most unusual situations are exempted.

Despite the clarity of the statutory language, respondents argue that the Secretary has wide discretion. They recognize that the requirement that there be no "feasible" alternative route admits of little administrative discretion. For this exemption to apply the Secretary must find that as a matter of sound engineering it would not be feasible to build the highway along any other route. Respondents argue, however, that the requirement that there be no other "prudent" route requires the Secretary to engage in a wide-ranging balancing of competing interests. They contend that the Secretary should weigh the detriment resulting from the destruction of parkland against the cost of other routes, safety considerations, and other factors, and determine on the basis of the importance that he attaches to these other factors whether, on balance, alternative feasible routes would be "prudent."

[The Court denied that Congress intended such a "wide-ranging endeavor." Use of parkland for highway construction will almost always minimize cost (because the public already owns the land and there will be no need to pay for right-of-way) and community disruption (because if a highway is built through a parkland homes and businesses need not be moved).]

Congress clearly did not intend that cost and disruption of the community were to be ignored by the Secretary. But the very existence of the statutes indicates that protection of parkland was to be given paramount importance. The few green havens that are public parks were not to be lost unless there were truly unusual factors present in a particular case or the cost or community disruption resulting from alternative routes reached extraordinary magnitudes. If the statutes are to have any meaning, the Secretary cannot approve the destruction of parkland unless he finds that alternative routes present unique problems.

Plainly, there is "law to apply" and thus the exemption for action "committed to agency discretion" is inapplicable. But the existence of judicial review is only the start: the standard for review must also be determined. For that we must look to §706 of the [APA], which provides that a "reviewing court shall . . . hold unlawful and set aside agency action, findings, and conclusions found" not to meet six separate standards. . . .

[Petitioners argued that the Secretary's approval of the construction of I-40 was subject to §706(2)(E) or (F), which the Court characterized as "standards of limited applicability." The Court found neither standard to be applicable.]

Review under the substantial-evidence test is authorized only when the agency action is taken pursuant to a rulemaking provision of the [APA] itself, 5 U.S.C. §553, or when the agency action is based on a public adjudicatory hearing. See 5 U.S.C. §§556, 557. The Secretary's decision to allow the expenditure of federal funds to build I-40 through Overton Park was plainly not an exercise of a rulemaking function. And the only hearing that is required by either the [APA] or the statutes regulating the distribution of federal funds for highway construction is a public hearing conducted by local officials for the purpose of informing the community about the proposed project and eliciting community views on the design and route. 23 U.S.C. §128. The hearing is nonadjudicatory, quasi-legislative in nature. It is not designed to produce a record that is to be the basis of agency action — the basic requirement for substantial-evidence review.

Petitioners' alternative argument also fails. De novo review of whether the Secretary's decision was "unwarranted by the facts" is authorized by §706(2)(F) in only two circumstances. First, such de novo review is authorized when the action is adjudicatory in nature and the agency factfinding procedures are inadequate. And, there may be independent judicial factfinding when issues that were not before the agency are raised in a proceeding to enforce nonadjudicatory agency action. H.R. Rep. No. 1980, 79th Cong., 2d Sess. Neither situation exists here.

Even though there is no de novo review in this case and the Secretary's approval of the route of I-40 does not have ultimately to meet the substantial-evidence test, the generally applicable standards of §706 require the reviewing court to engage in a substantial inquiry. Certainly, the Secretary's decision is entitled to a presumption of regularity. See, e.g., Pacific States Box & Basket Co. v. White, 296 U.S. 176, 185 (1935). But that presumption is not to shield his action from a thorough, probing, in-depth review.

The court is first required to decide whether the Secretary acted within the scope of his authority. This determination naturally begins with a delineation of the scope of the Secretary's authority and discretion. As has been shown, Congress has specified only a small range of choices that the Secretary can make. Also involved in this initial inquiry is a determination of whether on the facts the Secretary's decision can reasonably be said to be within that range. The reviewing court must consider whether the Secretary properly construed his authority to approve the use of parkland as limited to situations where there are no feasible alternative routes or where feasible alternative routes involve uniquely difficult problems. And the reviewing court must be able to find that the Secretary could have reasonably believed that in this case there are no feasible alternatives or that alternatives do involve unique problems.

Scrutiny of the facts does not end, however, with the determination that the Secretary has acted within the scope of his statutory authority. Section 706(2)(A) requires a finding that the actual choice made was not "arbitrary, capricious, an abuse of discretion, or otherwise not in accordance with law." 5 U.S.C. §706(2)(A). To make this finding the court must consider whether the decision was based on a consideration of the relevant factors and whether there has been a clear error of judgment. Although this inquiry into the facts is to be searching and careful, the ultimate standard of review is a narrow one. The court is not empowered to substitute its judgment for that of the agency. . . .

[The Court then held that neither the APA nor §§4(f) or 18(a) required formal findings of fact by the Secretary. It noted that the administrative record in the case was not before it since the lower courts had based their review on litigation affidavits that were post hoc rationalizations. It then remanded the case to the district court for "plenary review of the Secretary's decision" based on the record before the Secretary at the time he made his decision. The district court could require "the administrative officials who participated in the decision to give testimony explaining their action," though "inquiry into the mental processes of administrative decisionmakers is usually to be avoided."]

NOTES AND QUESTIONS

1. *The Fate of Overton Park and §4(f).* I-40 was never built through Overton Park because, on remand from the district court, the Secretary refused to approve the route, based on the record then before him, and attempts by the state to force Volpe to specify an acceptable route were rebuffed. Citizens to Preserve Overton Park v. Volpe, 357 F. Supp. 846 (W.D. Tenn. 1973), *rev'd*, 494 F.2d 1212 (6th Cir. 1974).

Congress amended §4(f) in the Safe Accountable, Flexible, Efficient Transportation Equity Act: A Legacy for Users, adopted in 2005. The statute now provides that the alternative consideration and harm minimization requirements will be deemed satisfied if the Secretary determines that a transportation project or program will have a *de minimis* impact on historic properties or on parks, recreation areas, or wildlife or waterfowl refuges. The Secretary may make a finding of *de minimis* impact only by determining, after public notice and an opportunity for public review and comment, that the program or project will not adversely affect the activities, features, and attributes of the area, and the officials with jurisdiction over the park, recreation area, or refuge concur with that finding. 23 U.S.C. §138(b). Further, the Secretary must issue regulations clarifying the factors and standards relevant to determining the prudence and feasibility of alternatives for a project subject to §4(f). 23 U.S.C. §138 note.

2. *"Hard Look" Review.* The statement in *Overton Park* that courts applying the APA's arbitrary and capricious standard must engage in a "searching and careful" inquiry—"a thorough, probing, in-depth review" of the full administrative record— raised considerably the level of judicial review under that standard. Before *Overton Park*, the arbitrary and capricious standard was widely believed to be highly indulgent toward the exercise of administrative discretion. After this case, the "hard look" doctrine of judicial review became common in judicial review of environmental decisionmaking.

The phrase "hard look review" originated in an appellate court decision written by Judge Harold Leventhal the year before *Overton Park* was decided. He remarked that the supervisory function of the courts calls on them "to intervene not merely in case of procedural inadequacies, or bypassing of the mandate in the legislative charter, but more broadly if the court becomes aware . . . that the agency has not really taken a hard look at the salient problems, and has not genuinely engaged in reasoned decisionmaking." Greater Boston Television Corp. v. FCC, 444 F.2d 841, 851 (D.C. Cir. 1970). Judge Leventhal's "hard look" gloss on the arbitrary and capricious standard*

---

*Note that Judge Leventhal used the term to describe the agency's obligation to take a "hard look" at the issues before it. The "hard look" moniker, however, soon came to describe the relatively rigorous review that courts applied to agency decisions to ensure that these decisions were not arbitrary and capricious.

thrust courts into an examination of the methodology and substance of agency decisionmaking to ensure that the decision being reviewed had adequate factual support.

But what if complex scientific and technical matters arise, as they often do under the environmental statutes; are the courts competent to "second-guess" agency determinations under the rubric of arbitrary and capricious review? The judges of the D.C. Circuit engaged in a spirited debate in the 1970s about the proper role of the courts in environmental litigation. In Ethyl Corp. v. EPA, 541 F.2d 1 (D.C. Cir. 1976) (excerpted in Chapter 8, section C), Chief Judge Bazelon argued that the best way for the courts in highly technical cases to guard against erroneous agency decisions is not to scrutinize the technical merits of the decision. Instead, the courts should "establish a decisionmaking process that assures a reasoned decision that can be held up to the scrutiny of the scientific community and the public."* Id. at 66.

Two other judges endorsed substantive review of some sort. Judge Wright took the position that, although the arbitrary and capricious standard is "highly deferential" and presumes the validity of agency action, the courts should not merely "rubberstamp the agency decision." Careful perusal of the technical record enables the court "to satisfy itself that the agency has exercised a reasoned discretion, with reasons that do not deviate from or ignore ascertainable legislative intent." The court's task is to "understand enough about the problem confronting the agency to comprehend the meaning of the evidence," the questions addressed, and the choices made. But Judge Wright warned courts to defer to the agency's expertise, not supplant it. The judicial role is to exercise "our narrowly defined duty of holding agencies to certain minimal standards of rationality."** Id. at 35-36.

Judge Leventhal also supported substantive review, arguing that Congress delegated its legislative powers to agencies, and courts had upheld those delegations, only on the condition that judicial review is available to ensure that agencies rationally exercise the delegated power within statutory limits. The courts therefore had been delegated a responsibility to engage in substantive review. Warning against "a charade that gives the imprimatur without the substance of judicial confirmation that the agency is not acting unreasonably," Leventhal summarized his views as follows: "Restraint, yes, abdication, no."*** Id. at 69.

3. "Hard Look" Review and the Nondelegation Doctrine. In the Ethyl case, both Judges Wright and Leventhal justified "hard look" judicial review by noting the willingness of the federal courts to uphold broad delegations of legislative

*Bazelon asserted that judges who address the merits risk making "plausible-sounding, but simplistic judgments. . . . Because substantive review of mathematical and scientific evidence by technically illiterate judges is dangerously unreliable, I continue to believe we will do more to improve administrative decision-making by concentrating our efforts on strengthening administrative procedures." 541 F.2d at 66-67. How free are the courts to follow Judge Bazelon's recommendations after the Supreme Court's decision in the Vermont Yankee case, discussed in section A.2.a of this chapter?

**See also Shapiro & Levy, Heightened Scrutiny of the Fourth Branch: Separation of Powers and the Requirement of Adequate Reasons for Agency Decisions, 1987 Duke L.J. 387 (endorsing "rationalist" review, which requires agencies to provide adequate reasons for their decisions, as required by the separation of powers, and claiming that it has become the primary method of constraining agency discretion).

***See also Leventhal, Environmental Decision Making and the Role of the Courts, 122 U. Pa. L. Rev. 509, 555 (1974) (explaining that the central role of the courts in environmental cases is ensuring that "mission-oriented agencies . . . will take due cognizance of environmental matters" and that environmental protection agencies implement statutory mandates that "environmental concerns be reconciled with other social and economic objectives").

power to administrative agencies. During the 1930s, the Supreme Court invalidated congressional legislation as standardless and improper delegations of the legislature's core policymaking function, but it has not done so since then. See Whitman v. American Trucking Ass'ns, Inc., 531 U.S. 457 (2001), reproduced in Chapter 6, section D.1.b. Both the "hard look" doctrine and the nondelegation doctrine "are grounded upon similar insights about the deficiencies of broadly written regulatory legislation," such as lack of notice to affected parties, lack of opportunity to participate in rule formulation, and "legislative cowardice in handing over lawmaking power while retreating to the role of second-guessing opportunist." Rodgers, Judicial Review of Risk Assessments: The Role of Decision Theory in Unscrambling the *Benzene* Decision, 11 Envtl. L. 301, 317 (1981).

Does intensive judicial procedural review compensate for overbroad congressional delegation? Intensive substantive judicial review? Professor Rodgers asserts that invalidating vague delegations is most appealing to courts viewing legislation "as a stable expression of consensus." Id. at 301. Is consensus likely in the environmental field?

4. Overton Park, Vermont Yankee, *and Judicial Review of Deregulation.* Did the Court in *Overton Park* specify the type of procedure to be followed in compiling a decision record? Does it in effect require agencies to compile records of decision in informal rulemaking and adjudication that are just as detailed as they must be in formal proceedings? Can you reconcile *Overton Park* with the Supreme Court's later decision in *Vermont Yankee*, discussed in section A.2.a above? The Court in *Vermont Yankee* left open the possibility of a constitutional challenge to the adequacy of agency procedures.

Vermont Yankee preceded the deregulation movement in the 1980s. Does the fact that the agency is relaxing a previous regulatory burden have any influence on the standard of review? The issue raised in Motor Vehicle Mfrs. Ass'n v. State Farm Mut. Auto. Ins. Co., 463 U.S. 29 (1983), was whether the Department of Transportation could rescind a previously adopted rule requiring passive restraints (airbags) in new cars. The auto industry argued that the decision to rescind should be governed by the same standard of review that applies to a decision not to adopt a rule in the first instance. But the Court, unanimously holding that the rescission was arbitrary and capricious, took the position that rescission of a previously adopted rule is different from a decision not to adopt a rule because there is a presumption that congressional policies contained in the enabling statute will be served best by a settled rule. "Accordingly, an agency changing its course by rescinding a rule is obligated to supply a reasoned analysis for change beyond that which may be required when an agency does not act in the first instance." Id. at 42. DOT acted arbitrarily because it offered no reasons to reject airbags, given their safety benefits. Industry argued that requiring DOT to consider an airbags-only alternative in effect dictated the procedures DOT had to follow, contrary to *Vermont Yankee*. The Court replied that it was neither specifying procedures nor requiring consideration of all policy alternatives. The "airbag is more than a policy alternative to the passive restraint standard; it is a technological alternative within the ambit of the existing standard." Id. at 51.

More generally, *State Farm* provides guidance on the factors to be considered in determining whether an agency's statutory implementation is arbitrary and capricious:

> Normally, an agency rule would be arbitrary and capricious if the agency has relied on factors which Congress has not intended it to consider, entirely failed to consider an

important aspect of the problem, offered an explanation for its decision that runs counter to the evidence before the agency, or is so implausible that it could not be ascribed to a difference in view or the product of agency expertise. [Id. at 43.]

5. *Arbitrary and Capricious v. Substantial Evidence Review.* The two standards of review encountered most frequently in environmental cases are the substantial evidence and the arbitrary and capricious standards. The substantial evidence standard discussed in *Overton Park* was developed for review of formal adjudications, for which a trial-type hearing record was available to the reviewing court. The "arbitrary and capricious" standard applies to quasi-legislative or informal decisionmaking, for which a "proper" record and hearing were not required; thus the reviewing court was more permissive and deferential—at least until *Overton Park*. Congress has required application of the substantial evidence test to review of some EPA regulations. E.g., 15 U.S.C. §2618(c)(1)(B)(i) (Toxic Substances Control Act). Although the substantial evidence test has long been viewed as the more searching of the two standards, it is not clear what, if any, meaningful differences exist between the two. See, e.g., Pennaco Energy, Inc. v. United States Dep't of the Interior, 377 F.3d 1147, 1156 n.6 (10th Cir. 2004) (stating that "[w]hen the arbitrary and capricious test is performing [the] function of assuring factual support [for the agency's decision], there is no substantive difference between what it requires and what would be required by the substantial evidence test, since it is impossible to conceive of a nonarbitrary factual judgment supported only by evidence that is not insubstantial in the APA sense").

The strictest standards in §706(2) of the APA are those calling for de novo review. According to *Overton Park*, under what circumstances does §706(2)(F) apply? Why didn't that standard apply in *Overton Park* itself? Section 706(2)(F) rarely applies in environmental cases.

6. *Substantive Review in Practice.* In Schroeder & Glicksman, *Chevron, State Farm*, and EPA in the Courts of Appeals during the 1990s, 31 Envtl. L. Rep. (ELI) 10371 (2001), the authors analyze judicial review of statutory implementation in the federal Courts of Appeals during the 1990s. They conclude that although the courts often cite *Overton Park, State Farm*, or both, when engaged in review of EPA's statutory implementation decisions, neither case has achieved the "iconic status" that *Chevron* has in the context of judicial review of statutory interpretation. The study found that litigants attacking EPA's methodology for collecting and interpreting scientific data rarely succeed, perhaps largely due to the judges' awareness of the relatively greater competence that agency decision makers have to make such judgments. Attacks on EPA's reasoning process are more likely to succeed, particularly when a litigant convinces a court that the agency has failed to provide any evidence to support its technical determinations, relied on evidence that conflicts with the stated views of its own experts, relied on technical models or methodologies that are obviously ill-suited to the task for which they were employed, failed to explain in any way an apparently illogical conclusion, left a gap in logic in its explanation, or engaged in internally inconsistent reasoning.

7. *The Relationship between* Chevron *and* Overton Park/State Farm. How does the judicial function differ if the question is (1) whether an agency's interpretation of an ambiguous statute is reasonable (a *Chevron*, step two issue) and (2) whether an agency's statutory implementation is arbitrary and capricious (a question governed by the *Overton Park* standard, as modified by *State Farm*)? The answer is far from clear. In Arent v. Shalala, 70 F.3d 610 (D.C. Cir. 1995), a case involving a challenge by

consumer groups to FDA regulations governing nutritional labeling of raw produce and fish, the judges who wrote the majority and concurring opinions agreed that *Chevron* review and arbitrary and capricious review overlap "at the margins." They disagreed, however, on which standard of review applied in that case. See also American Petroleum Inst. v. EPA, 216 F.3d 50, 57 (D.C. Cir. 2000) ("The second step of *Chevron* analysis and *State Farm* arbitrary and capricious review overlap, but are not identical.").

NOTE ON REVIEWABILITY

Section 704 of the APA provides that "[a]gency action made reviewable by statute and final agency action for which there is no adequate remedy in a court are subject to judicial review." But §701(a) recognizes two exceptions to the reviewability of agency action to the extent that "(1) statutes preclude judicial review; or (2) agency action is committed to agency discretion by law." Justice Marshall had no trouble holding in *Overton Park* that neither of these two provisions made the Secretary of Transportation's decision unreviewable. There was no evidence that Congress sought to prohibit judicial review and the decision was not "committed to agency discretion" because §4(f) constituted "law to apply." The Secretary claimed that §4(f) had enacted a balancing test. Why is this relevant to the "committed to agency discretion" problem?

Has *Overton Park* been qualified by Block v. Community Nutrition Inst., 467 U.S. 340 (1984), where the Court held, without citing *Overton Park*, that the presumption of judicial review may be overcome "whenever the congressional intent to preclude review is 'fairly discernible in the statutory scheme'"?

Congress has rarely precluded review in the environmental statutes. "Clear and convincing evidence" is necessary to demonstrate such an intention. Friends of the Crystal River v. EPA, 794 F. Supp. 674 (W.D. Mich. 1992), *aff'd*, 35 F.3d 1073 (6th Cir. 1994). Occasionally, such evidence is available. In High Country Citizens Alliance v. Clarke, 454 F.3d 1177 (10th Cir. 2006), the court concluded that the General Mining Law of 1872 precludes a person not claiming a property interest in the affected land from attacking the validity of a mineral patent issued by the BLM. According to the court, allowing such a suit would conflict with Congress's intent, reflected in the legislative history, to provide finality in the patent process to induce miners to invest the necessary time and capital to develop the industry. In Oregon Natural Resources Council v. Thomas, 92 F.3d 792 (9th Cir. 1996), the court held that an appropriations rider barred review of timber sales by the Forest Service allegedly made in violation of several environmental laws.*

The mere existence of agency discretion is insufficient to invoke the second exception to judicial review. After all, §706(2)(A) of the APA authorizes courts to set aside agency action that is "arbitrary, capricious, an abuse of discretion, or otherwise not in accordance with law." See American Canoe Ass'n v. EPA, 30 F. Supp. 2d 908, 925 (E.D. Va. 1998) (discussing the "uneasy tension" that exists between §§701(a)(2) and 706(2)(A)). The courts typically have little difficulty finding

---

*See also NRDC v. Johnson, 461 F.3d 164 (2d Cir. 2006) (provision of Federal Food, Drug, and Cosmetic Act precluded review in federal district court of EPA decision to leave pesticide tolerances for pesticide residues on food in effect); Inter Tribal Council of Ariz., Inc. v. Babbitt, 51 F.3d 199 (9th Cir. 1995) (review of federal lands exchange barred by statute).

"law to apply" in the statutes delegating discretionary authority to an agency. The agency's own output, such as regulations or land use plans, also may constrain agency discretion sufficiently to furnish the necessary "law to apply." See Kola, Inc. v. United States, 882 F.2d 361 (9th Cir. 1989) (Forest Service special use permit decision reviewable).

The courts are most likely to refuse to reach the merits on the basis of §701(a)(2) where a litigant challenges an agency decision not to enforce a statute or regulation. See Heckler v. Chaney, 470 U.S. 821 (1985). See also Ohio Pub. Interest Research Group, Inc. v. Whitman, 386 F.3d 792 (6th Cir. 2004) (holding that EPA's refusal to issue a notice of deficiency to state under §502(i) of the CAA based on conceded deficiencies in its Title V permit program was committed to agency discretion by law, and thus unreviewable pursuant to §701(a)(2)). Should the reluctance the courts display in such cases extend to a challenge to an agency refusal to initiate rulemaking proceedings in response to a private party's petition to do so? See American Horse Protection Ass'n v. Lyng, 812 F.2d 1 (D.C. Cir. 1987); National Wildlife Fed'n v. Secretary of Health & Human Serv., 808 F.2d 12 (6th Cir. 1986). Cf. Sierra Club v. Yeutter, 911 F.2d 1405, 1414 (10th Cir. 1990) (Forest Service's decision not to assert federal reserved water rights in wilderness areas in state water rights adjudications was nonreviewable).

The reviewability of agency inaction was also at issue in the following case.

NORTON v. SOUTHERN UTAH WILDERNESS ALLIANCE
542 U.S. 55 (2004)

Justice Scalia delivered the opinion of the Court.

In this case, we must decide whether the authority of a federal court under the Administrative Procedure Act (APA) to "compel agency action unlawfully withheld or unreasonably delayed," 5 U.S.C. §706(1), extends to the review of the United States Bureau of Land Management's stewardship of public lands under certain statutory provisions and its own planning documents.

I

[The Federal Land Policy and Management Act of 1976 (FLPMA) delegates to the Bureau of Land Management (BLM) the authority to manage the public lands. FLPMA dictates that the BLM adhere to a multiple use, sustained yield management standard.] "Multiple use management" is a deceptively simple term that describes the enormously complicated task of striking a balance among the many competing uses to which land can be put, "including, but not limited to, recreation, range, timber, minerals, watershed, wildlife and fish, and [uses serving] natural scenic, scientific and historical values." 43 U.S.C. §1702(c). . . . "[S]ustained yield" requires BLM to control depleting uses over time, so as to ensure a high level of valuable uses in the future. §1702(h). To these ends, FLPMA establishes a dual regime of inventory and planning. Sections 1711 and 1712, respectively, provide for a comprehensive, ongoing inventory of federal lands, and for a land use planning process that "project[s]" "present and future use," §1701(a)(2), given the lands' inventoried characteristics.

Of course not all uses are compatible. Congress made the judgment that some lands should be set aside as wilderness at the expense of commercial and recreational uses. A pre-FLPMA enactment, the Wilderness Act of 1964, provides that designated wilderness areas, subject to certain exceptions, "shall [have] no commercial enterprise and no permanent road," no motorized vehicles, and no manmade structures. 16 U.S.C. §1133(c). The designation of a wilderness area can be made only by Act of Congress, see 43 U.S.C. §1782(b).

Pursuant to §1782, the Secretary of the Interior has identified so-called "wilderness study areas" (WSAs), roadless lands of 5,000 acres or more that possess "wilderness characteristics," as determined in the Secretary's land inventory. §1782(a); see 16 U.S.C. §1131(c). As the name suggests, WSAs . . . have been subjected to further examination and public comment in order to evaluate their suitability for designation as wilderness. In 1991, out of 3.3 million acres in Utah that had been identified for study, 2 million were recommended as suitable for wilderness designation. This recommendation was forwarded to Congress, which has not yet acted upon it. Until Congress acts one way or the other, FLPMA provides that "the Secretary shall continue to manage such lands . . . in a manner so as not to impair the suitability of such areas for preservation as wilderness." 43 U.S.C. §1782(c). This nonimpairment mandate applies to all WSAs identified under §1782, including lands considered unsuitable by the Secretary.

Aside from identification of WSAs, the main tool that BLM employs to balance wilderness protection against other uses is a land use plan—what BLM regulations call a "resource management plan." Land use plans, adopted after notice and comment, are "designed to guide and control future management actions," [43 C.F.R. §1601.0-2 (2003)]. Generally, a land use plan describes, for a particular area, allowable uses, goals for future condition of the land, and specific next steps. Under FLPMA, "[t]he Secretary shall manage the public lands under principles of multiple use and sustained yield, in accordance with the land use plans . . . when they are available." 43 U.S.C. §1732(a).

Protection of wilderness has come into increasing conflict with another element of multiple use, recreational use of so-called off-road vehicles (ORVs), which include vehicles primarily designed for off-road use, such as lightweight, four-wheel "all-terrain vehicles," and vehicles capable of such use, such as sport utility vehicles. According to the United States Forest Service's most recent estimates, some 42 million Americans participate in off-road travel each year, more than double the number two decades ago. . . . The use of ORVs on federal land has negative environmental consequences, including soil disruption and compaction, harassment of animals, and annoyance of wilderness lovers. Thus, BLM faces a classic land use dilemma of sharply inconsistent uses, in a context of scarce resources and congressional silence with respect to wilderness designation.

[Southern Utah Wilderness Alliance and other organizations (collectively SUWA) filed suit in federal district court in Utah against the BLM and the Secretary of the Interior, seeking] declaratory and injunctive relief for BLM's failure to act to protect public lands in Utah from damage caused by ORV use. SUWA made three claims that are relevant here: (1) that BLM had violated its nonimpairment obligation under §1782(a) by allowing degradation in certain WSAs; (2) that BLM had failed to implement provisions in its land use plans relating to ORV use; (3) that BLM had failed to take a "hard look" at whether, pursuant to the National Environmental Policy Act of 1969 (NEPA) it should undertake supplemental environmental analyses for areas in which ORV use had increased. SUWA contended that it could sue to remedy these three failures to act pursuant to the APA's provision of a cause of action to "compel agency action unlawfully withheld or unreasonably delayed." 5 U.S.C. §706(1).

[The district court dismissed all three claims, but a divided panel of the Tenth Circuit reversed, concluding that the plaintiffs had alleged the BLM's failure to perform nondiscretionary duties, including FLPMA's nonimpairment obligation.]

II

All three claims at issue here involve assertions that BLM failed to take action with respect to ORV use that it was required to take. Failures to act are sometimes remediable under the APA, but not always. We begin by considering what limits the APA places upon judicial review of agency inaction.

The APA authorizes suit by "[a] person suffering legal wrong because of agency action, or adversely affected or aggrieved by agency action within the meaning of a relevant statute." 5 U.S.C. §702. Where no other statute provides a private right of action, the "agency action" complained of must be "*final* agency action." §704 (emphasis added). "Agency action" is defined in §551(13) to include "the whole or a part of an agency rule, order, license, sanction, relief, or the equivalent or denial thereof, or *failure to act*." (Emphasis added.) The APA provides relief for a failure to act in §706(1): "The reviewing court shall . . . compel agency action unlawfully withheld or unreasonably delayed."

Sections 702, 704, and 706(1) all insist upon an "agency action," either as the action complained of (in §§702 and 704) or as the action to be compelled (in §706(1)). The definition of that term begins with a list of five categories of decisions made or outcomes implemented by an agency—"agency rule, order, license, sanction [or] relief." §551(13). All of those categories involve circumscribed, discrete agency actions, as their definitions make clear [citing 5 U.S.C. §§551(4), (6), (8), (10), (11)].

The terms following those five categories of agency action are not defined in the APA: "or the equivalent or denial thereof, or failure to act." §551(13). But an "equivalent . . . thereof" must also be discrete (or it would not be equivalent), and a "denial thereof" must be the denial of a discrete listed action (and perhaps denial of a discrete equivalent).

The final term in the definition, "failure to act," is in our view properly understood as a failure to take an *agency action*—that is, a failure to take one of the agency actions (including their equivalents) earlier defined in §551(13). Moreover, even without this equation of "act" with "agency action" the interpretive canon of *ejusdem generis* would attribute to the last item ("failure to act") the same characteristic of discreteness shared by all the preceding items. A "failure to act" is not the same thing as a "denial." The latter is the agency's act of saying no to a request; the former is simply the omission of an action without formally rejecting a request—for example, the failure to promulgate a rule or take some decision by a statutory deadline. The important point is that a "failure to act" is properly understood to be limited, as are the other items in §551(13), to a discrete action.

A second point central to the analysis of the present case is that the only agency action that can be compelled under the APA is action legally *required*. This limitation appears in §706(1)'s authorization for courts to "compel agency action *unlawfully* withheld." . . . As described in the Attorney General's Manual on the APA, a document whose reasoning we have often found persuasive, §706(1) empowers a court only to compel an agency "to perform a ministerial or non-discretionary act," or "to take action upon a matter, without directing *how* it shall act." Attorney General's Manual on the Administrative Procedure Act 108 (1947) (emphasis added).

Thus, a claim under §706(1) can proceed only where a plaintiff asserts that an agency failed to take a *discrete* agency action that it is *required to take*. These limitations rule out several kinds of challenges. The limitation to discrete agency action precludes the kind of broad programmatic attack we rejected in Lujan v. National Wildlife Federation, 497 U.S. 871 (1990). There we considered a challenge to BLM's land withdrawal review program, couched as unlawful agency "action" that the plaintiffs wished to have "set aside" under §706(2). We concluded that the program was not an "agency action":

> [R]espondent cannot seek *wholesale* improvement of this program by court decree, rather than in the offices of the Department or the halls of Congress, where programmatic improvements are normally made. Under the terms of the APA, respondent must direct its attack against some particular "agency action" that causes it harm. Id., at 891 (emphasis in original).

The plaintiffs in *National Wildlife Federation* would have fared no better if they had characterized the agency's alleged "failure to revise land use plans in proper fashion" and "failure to consider multiple use," in terms of "agency action unlawfully withheld" under §706(1), rather than agency action "not in accordance with law" under §706(2).

The limitation to *required* agency action rules out judicial direction of even discrete agency action that is not demanded by law (which includes, of course, agency regulations that have the force of law). Thus, when an agency is compelled by law to act within a certain time period, but the manner of its action is left to the agency's discretion, a court can compel the agency to act, but has no power to specify what the action must be. . . .

III

A

With these principles in mind, we turn to SUWA's first claim, that by permitting ORV use in certain WSAs, BLM violated its mandate to "continue to manage [WSAs] . . . in a manner so as not to impair the suitability of such areas for preservation as wilderness," 43 U.S.C. §1782(c). SUWA relies not only upon §1782(c) but also upon a provision of BLM's Interim Management Policy for Lands Under Wilderness Review, which interprets the nonimpairment mandate to require BLM to manage WSAs so as to prevent them from being "degraded so far, compared with the area's values for other purposes, as to significantly constrain the Congress's prerogative to either designate [it] as wilderness or release it for other uses."

Section 1782(c) is mandatory as to the object to be achieved, but it leaves BLM a great deal of discretion in deciding how to achieve it. It assuredly does not mandate, with the clarity necessary to support judicial action under §706(1), the total exclusion of ORV use.

SUWA argues that §1782 does contain a categorical imperative, namely the command to comply with the nonimpairment mandate. It contends that a federal court could simply enter a general order compelling compliance with that mandate, without suggesting any particular manner of compliance. [But g]eneral deficiencies in compliance . . . lack the specificity requisite for agency action.

The principal purpose of the APA limitations we have discussed—and of the traditional limitations upon mandamus from which they were derived—is to protect agencies from undue judicial interference with their lawful discretion, and to avoid judicial entanglement in abstract policy disagreements which courts lack both expertise and information to resolve. If courts were empowered to enter general orders compelling compliance with broad statutory mandates, they would necessarily be empowered, as well, to determine whether compliance was achieved—which would mean that it would ultimately become the task of the supervising court, rather than the agency, to work out compliance with the broad statutory mandate, injecting the judge into day-to-day agency management. . . . The prospect of pervasive oversight by federal courts over the manner and pace of agency compliance with such congressional directives is not contemplated by the APA.

B

SUWA's second claim is that BLM failed to comply with certain provisions in its land use plans, thus contravening the requirement that "[t]he Secretary shall manage the public lands . . . in accordance with the land use plans . . . when they are available." 43 U.S.C. §1732(a). . . .

[SUWA claimed that, "in light of damage from ORVs in the Factory Butte area," the applicable resource management plan obligated the BLM to conduct "an intensive ORV monitoring program." The plan stated that the area open to ORV use "will be monitored and closed if warranted."] SUWA does not contest BLM's assertion in the court below that informal monitoring has taken place for some years, but it demands continuing implementation of a monitoring *program*. By this it apparently means to insist upon adherence to [a plan provision stating that] "[r]esource damage will be documented and recommendations made for corrective action," "[m]onitoring in open areas will focus on determining damage which may necessitate a change in designation," and "emphasis on use supervision will be placed on [limited and closed areas]." . . .

The statutory directive that BLM manage "in accordance with" land use plans, and the regulatory requirement that authorizations and actions "conform to" those plans, prevent BLM from taking actions inconsistent with the provisions of a land use plan. Unless and until the plan is amended, such actions can be set aside as contrary to law pursuant to 5 U.S.C. §706(2). The claim presently under discussion, however, would have us go further, and conclude that a statement in a plan that BLM "will" take this, that, or the other action, is a binding commitment that can be compelled under §706(1). In our view it is not—at least absent clear indication of binding commitment in the terms of the plan.

FLPMA describes land use plans as tools by which "present and future use is *projected*." 43 U.S.C. §1701(a)(2) (emphasis added). The implementing regulations make clear that land use plans are a preliminary step in the overall process of managing public lands—"designed to guide and control future management actions and the development of subsequent, more detailed and limited scope plans for resources and uses." 43 CFR §1601.0-2 (2003). The statute and regulations confirm that a land use plan is not ordinarily the medium for affirmative decisions that implement the agency's "project[ions]." 43 U.S.C. §1712(e) provides that "[t]he Secretary may issue management decisions to implement land use plans"—the decisions, that is, are distinct from the plan itself. Picking up the same theme, . . . [t]he BLM's Land Use Planning Handbook specifies that land use plans are normally not used to make site-specific implementation decisions. . . .

Quite unlike a specific statutory command requiring an agency to promulgate regulations by a certain date, a land use plan is generally a statement of priorities; it guides and constrains actions, but does not (at least in the usual case) prescribe them. It would be unreasonable to think that either Congress or the agency intended otherwise, since land use plans nationwide would commit the agency to actions far in the future, for which funds have not yet been appropriated. Some plans make explicit that implementation of their programmatic content is subject to budgetary constraints. While the plan [in this case] does not contain such a specification, we think it must reasonably be implied. A statement by BLM about what it plans to do, at some point, provided it has the funds and there are not more pressing priorities, cannot be plucked out of context and made a basis for suit under §706(1).

Of course, an action called for in a plan may be compelled when the plan merely reiterates duties the agency is already obligated to perform, or perhaps when language in the plan itself creates a commitment binding on the agency. But allowing general enforcement of plan terms would lead to pervasive interference with BLM's own ordering of priorities. . . . And while such a decree might please the environmental plaintiffs in the present case, it would ultimately operate to the detriment of sound environmental management. Its predictable consequence would be much vaguer plans from BLM in the future—making coordination with other agencies more difficult, and depriving the public of important information concerning the agency's long-range intentions.

We therefore hold that the Henry Mountains plan's statements to the effect that BLM will conduct "use supervision and monitoring" in designated areas—like other "will do" projections of agency action set forth in land use plans—are not a legally binding commitment enforceable under §706(1). That being so, we find it unnecessary to consider whether the action envisioned by the statements is sufficiently discrete to be amenable to compulsion under the APA.

IV

Finally, we turn to SUWA's contention that BLM failed to fulfill certain obligations under NEPA. Before addressing whether a NEPA-required duty is actionable under the APA, we must decide whether NEPA creates an obligation in the first place. NEPA requires a federal agency to prepare an environmental impact statement (EIS) as part of any "proposals for legislation and other major Federal actions significantly affecting the quality of the human environment." 42 U.S.C. §4332(2)(C). Often an initial EIS is sufficient, but in certain circumstances an EIS must be supplemented. See Marsh v. Oregon Natural Resources Council, 490 U.S. 360, 370-374 (1989). A regulation of the Council on Environmental Quality requires supplementation where "[t]here are significant new circumstances or information relevant to environmental concerns and bearing on the proposed action or its impacts." 40 CFR §1502.9(c)(1)(ii) (2003). In *Marsh*, we interpreted §4332 in light of this regulation to require an agency to take a "hard look" at the new information to assess whether supplementation might be necessary.

SUWA argues that evidence of increased ORV use is "significant new circumstances or information" that requires a "hard look." We disagree. As we noted in *Marsh,* supplementation is necessary only if "there remains 'major Federal actio[n]' to occur," as that term is used in §4332(2)(C). 490 U.S., at 374. In *Marsh,* that condition was met: the dam construction project that gave rise to environmental review was not yet completed. Here, by contrast, although the "[*a*]*pproval* of a [land use plan]" is a "major Federal action" requiring an EIS, 43 CFR §1601.0-6 (2003) (emphasis added), that action is completed when the plan is approved. The land use plan is the "proposed action" contemplated by the regulation. There is no ongoing "major Federal action" that could require supplementation (though BLM *is* required to perform additional NEPA analyses if a plan is amended or revised).

The judgment of the Court of Appeals is reversed, and the case is remanded for further proceedings consistent with this opinion.

NOTES AND QUESTIONS

1. *The Nonimpairment Mandate.* Is the analysis in the *SUWA* case limited to situations involving claims of allegedly improper agency inaction, or does it apply more broadly to allegedly improper actions as well? What is the significance of the requirement that a suit seeking review under §706(1) of the APA allege failure to perform a "discrete" agency action? What is the source of the requirement that the action be discrete? Is there any other limitation on the kinds of inaction covered by §706(1)? Why wasn't SUWA's claim that the BLM failed to comply with FLPMA's nonimpairment mandate justiciable? What is a "general deficiency" in compliance? What is the policy rationale for limiting judicial supervision of compliance with "broad statutory mandates"?

2. *Land Use Plans: Scope of Review Questions.* Two authors have observed that, "[a]t a minimum, [BLM and Forest Service land use plans] should provide bases for judicial review requiring the agency to explain seeming departures from plan provisions." 2 G. Coggins & R. Glicksman, Public Natural Resources Law §10F:1 (1991). Does the *SUWA* case contradict that observation? Would the result in *SUWA* have been different if the BLM's plan had stated that the agency "must" monitor for the effects of ORV use, instead of stating that the agency "will" do so? Does SUWA affect judicial review of agency decisions to allow site-specific activities that are prohibited by land use plans?

3. *Land Use Plans: Incentives for Planning Specificity.* Professors Coggins and Glicksman feared that the federal land management agencies might "promulgate plans so general as to be meaningless as limitations on or guidelines for subsequent management decisions. Some evidence indicates that agencies may prefer to write motherhood generalities rather than blueprints for future resource allocation and protection." Id. The Court in *SUWA* argued that the "predictable consequence" of allowing general enforcement of BLM plans "would be much vaguer plans from BLM in the future—making coordination with other agencies more difficult, and depriving the public of important information concerning the agency's long-range intentions." Can't it be argued that the Court's decision in *SUWA* is likely to have precisely those consequences?

4. *Supplemental EISs.* Under the Court's decision, will federal agencies ever be obligated to prepare a supplemental EIS for a land use plan based on changed conditions?

5. For criticism of *SUWA*, see Glicksman, "Judicial Review of Agency Inaction (and Action) in the Wake of *Norton v. Southern Utah Wilderness Alliance*," in Strategies for Environmental Success in an Uncertain Judicial Climate 163 (M. Wolf ed., 2005); Flournoy, "Following the Court Off-Road in *Norton v. Southern Utah Wilderness Alliance*," id. at 215.

B. CONGRESSIONAL CONTROL OF ADMINISTRATIVE ENVIRONMENTAL DECISIONMAKING

The power of agencies like EPA to issue and enforce regulations and take other actions to protect the environment is derivative from Congress. These agencies have only the powers delegated to them by the legislature. Although Congress has been willing to vest in many agencies decisionmaking authority over environmental matters, it has a variety of techniques for limiting the scope of that authority.* One technique is to limit the authority of the President to appoint and remove agency decisionmakers. Such limitations may prevent the President from appointing officials whose positions conflict with congressionally adopted policies or from removing those faithfully implementing those policies in a manner unsatisfactory to the Chief Executive. The Senate has the constitutional authority to advise and consent to the appointment of the heads of federal departments such as Interior and Agriculture and of independent agencies such as EPA, but it may not impose its own selections on the President. See Buckley v. Valeo, 424 U.S. 1 (1976). Congress has substantially more authority to limit presidential removal of executive officials by restricting the conditions under which it may occur, but even that authority may not be exercised if its effect is to interfere with the core functions of the executive branch. E.g., Morrison v. Olson, 487 U.S. 654 (1988).

Of greater practical, day-to-day relevance are the use of the appropriations process and the imposition of substantive statutory decisionmaking criteria as means for Congress to confine agency discretion. Traditionally, an agency's authorizing legislation delineates the standards it must apply in making decisions. Appropriations legislation provides the funds that permit the agency to implement its substantive mandates. Recently, however, Congress has increasingly resorted to appropriations bills as an additional source of limitations on agency substantive authority. The first subsection below considers some examples of this technique for controlling agency discretion. The second subsection deals with the use of substantive legislation to constrain agency discretion. It focuses on a series of statutes that require agencies to engage in analytical processes and make findings in support of their decisions that supplement the limitations on agency authority found in substantive enabling legislation.

---

*See generally Beermann, Congressional Administration, 43 San Diego L. Rev. 61 (2006) (analyzing the influence over the execution of the laws that results from Congress's "intimate" involvement, both formal and informal, in that process); Lazarus, The Neglected Question of Congressional Oversight of EPA: *Quis Custodiet Ipsos Custodes* (Who Shall Watch the Watchers Themselves)?, 54 Law & Contemp. Probs. No. 4 (Autumn 1991), at 205.

1. Control through the Appropriations Process

Congress has always used the appropriations process to induce agencies to conform their decisions to desired legislative norms. Agencies that perform in a way that legislators deem acceptable may be rewarded with higher funding levels, while those whose performance is disappointing may wind up with slashed appropriations. But Congress also has used the appropriations process more directly to affect decisions by administrative agencies on environmental issues. It has incorporated into appropriations bills provisions that supplement or override agency enabling statutes and environmental legislation such as NEPA and the Endangered Species Act. These provisions can have the effect of either expanding or contracting the discretion otherwise available to the affected agency. Sometimes, the attempts to affect the scope of agency discretion raise serious constitutional questions.

The controversies over the environmental effects of timber harvesting in the Pacific Northwest provide the backdrop for some of the most prominent examples of the use of appropriations bills to control agency decisionmaking (and limit judicial authority to mandate agency compliance with previously enacted legislation). Environmentalists tried throughout the 1980s to prevent liquidation of the old growth forests in this region, claiming that timber contracts awarded by the Forest Service and the BLM were inconsistent with a host of environmental laws. Beginning in 1984, Congress passed a series of appropriations riders that restricted judicial review of timber harvest plans adopted by the two federal land management agencies. A rider enacted in 1989, for example, provided that management of thirteen national forests known to contain northern spotted owls* in accordance with standards set forth in the rider (such as the specification of the number of board feet of timber to be cut) would be deemed to satisfy requirements under statutes such as NEPA and the ESA. Pub. L. No. 101-121, §318, 103 Stat. 701, 745-750 (1989). Agency noncompliance with those statutes had been alleged in several suits still pending at the time the rider was passed. The rider also provided that the guidelines for timber management it contained would not be subject to judicial review. Environmental groups challenged the rider, claiming that congressional specification of the results of pending litigation violated the separation of powers by infringing on judicial authority. The Supreme Court in Robertson v. Seattle Audubon Soc'y, 503 U.S. 429 (1992), upheld the constitutionality of the rider on the ground that it affected a change in the underlying substantive law that governed timber harvesting rather than commanded the outcome of pending litigation. See also Mount Graham Coalition v. Thomas, 89 F.3d 554 (9th Cir. 1996) (exemption from NEPA and the ESA for construction of astrophysical observatory upheld).

After the rider expired in 1990, the Ninth Circuit virtually shut down timber harvesting on federal lands in Washington and Oregon due to Forest Service and BLM noncompliance with the ESA and NEPA. See Seattle Audubon Soc'y v. Espy, 998 F.2d 699 (9th Cir. 1993). In a 1995 supplemental appropriations bill, Congress again sought to restrict judicial review of the legality of timber sales with potentially serious environmental impacts. Pub. L. No. 104-19, §2001, 109 Stat. 194, 240 (1995). The bill authorized the land management agencies to award salvage timber sales** "notwithstanding any other provision of law, including a law under the authority of

---

*The northern spotted owl was listed as a threatened species under the ESA, under compulsion of court order, in 1990. 55 Fed. Reg. 26,114.

**Salvage timber sales are meant to remove dead or damaged trees or trees susceptible to fire or insect attack. The statute also defined salvage timber to include "associated trees lacking the

which any judicial order may be outstanding on or after the date of enactment of this Act." Id. §2001(b)(1). Finally, the bill precluded any court from enjoining certain categories of salvage timber sales and provided that timber sales conducted in accordance with specified procedures would "be deemed to satisfy" a series of laws, including NEPA, the ESA, the National Forest Management Act, the Federal Land Policy and Management Act, and "[a]ll other applicable Federal environmental and natural resources laws." Id. §2001(i). Constitutional attacks on the rider failed, e.g., Northwest Forest Resource Council v. Pilchuck Audubon Soc'y, 97 F.3d 1161, 1165 (9th Cir. 1996), as did attempts by environmental groups to halt salvage sales on the basis of alleged noncompliance with statutory environmental requirements. Idaho Conservation League v. Thomas, 91 F.3d 1345 (9th Cir. 1996) (approving sale that conflicted with established Forest Service policies for watershed protection); Inland Empire Pub. Lands Council v. Glickman, 88 F.3d 697 (9th Cir. 1996) (refusing to halt sale conducted in violation of grizzly bear management standards).

The appropriations process has been used to constrict as well as augment agency discretion. In 1994, for example, Congress adopted a moratorium (subsequently extended by other appropriations bills) on the issuance of new patents for hardrock minerals on the federal lands. Pub. L. No. 103-322, §§112-113, 108 Stat. 2499, 2519 (1994). Former EPA Administrator William Reilly described the use of the appropriations process to redirect EPA discretion as "a guaranteed recipe for disillusionment on the part of the public." Former EPA Chief Criticizes Congress's Methods for Changing Agency, Inside EPA, Sept. 15, 1995, at 2.

2. *Control through Substantive Standards and Analytical Requirements*

The traditional reliance on agency expertise prompted Congress to delegate broad powers to federal administrative agencies during the New Deal and in subsequent years. It was not uncommon for the enabling statute of an agency such as the Interstate Commerce Commission to state simply that the agency was to regulate in the "public interest, convenience, and necessity" or for the Federal Trade Commission to be charged with preventing "unfair trade practices." The environmental legislation of the 1970s, such as the Clean Air and Water Acts, was always more specific than that, due in part to the fear of agency capture that prompted Congress to rein in agency discretion. As a result of congressional dissatisfaction with EPA's implementation of the statutes governing hazardous waste management and remediation, the pollution control statutes became even more prescriptive in the 1980s, with a resulting reduction in the range of EPA's discretion. The imposition of deadlines for issuance of regulations limited the agency's discretion to forestall making decisions and the specification of detailed decisionmaking criteria curtailed the ability of the agency to craft the content of those regulations. See generally Shapiro & Glicksman, Congress, the Supreme Court, and the Quiet Revolution in Administrative Law, 1988 Duke L.J. 819. Nevertheless, statutes such as those requiring the federal land

---

characteristics of a healthy and viable ecosystem for the purpose of ecosystem improvement or rehabilitation." Pub. L. No. 104-19, §2001(a)(3). Environmentalists charged that this provision created a huge loophole that would enable large-scale timber harvesting free of environmental constraints.

management agencies to promote multiple uses of lands and resources within their jurisdiction left those agencies with considerable room to maneuver.

The election of conservative majorities in Congress during the 1990s ushered in a new wave of legislative limitations on agency discretion. Legislators convinced that the pendulum had swung too far in the direction of rigorous environmental controls on industrial activity and development, introduced bills to require agencies such as EPA and the Occupational Safety and Health Administration (OSHA) to temper the goal of enhanced protection of the environment and workplace health and safety with a greater consciousness of countervailing considerations such as cost. Some of these bills included analytical requirements that supplemented the factors that agencies such as EPA were authorized to consider under existing legislation, but others were designed to redirect agency priorities in response to what the bills' supporters perceived as misplaced regulatory emphasis. See generally S. Shapiro & R. Glicksman, Risk Regulation at Risk: Restoring a Pragmatic Approach ch. 7 (2003).

The first of these bills to be adopted was the **Unfunded Mandates Reform Act of 1994**, Pub. L. No. 104-4, 109 Stat. 48 (1995), which requires each federal agency, unless otherwise prohibited by law, to assess the effects of its regulatory actions on state, local, and tribal governments and the private sector. Before an agency issues a regulation that includes any "federal mandate" (defined as a regulatory provision that would impose an enforceable duty on state, local, or tribal governments, other than a condition of federal assistance) that may result in the expenditure by governments in the aggregate or by the private sector of $100 million or more in any one year, it must prepare a written statement that includes a qualitative and quantitative assessment of the anticipated costs and benefits of the mandate, estimates future compliance costs of the mandate, and estimates the effect of the rule on the national economy if it is feasible to do so. 2 U.S.C. §1532. The Act also requires that, before issuing such a rule, the agency consider a reasonable number of regulatory alternatives and select from among them "the least costly, most cost-effective or least burdensome alternative that achieves the objective of the rule" for state and local governments and the private sector. Id. §1535(a). An agency need not comply with this requirement if its head publishes an explanation of why the agency did not adopt the identified alternative or it is precluded from doing so by law. Id. §1535(b). Neither failure to prepare a regulatory impact statement nor preparation of an inadequate statement provides a basis for judicial invalidation of agency regulations. Id. §1571(a)(3), (b). Failure to prepare such a statement can render agency regulations arbitrary and capricious, but not if the substantive legislation precludes consideration of the costs of regulatory implementation.*

Other statutes also require analytical support for regulatory endeavors that go beyond what is normally required by the APA. The **Regulatory Flexibility Act**, adopted in 1980 and amended by the Small Business Regulatory Enforcement Fairness Act,

---

*See generally Adler, Unfunded Mandates and Fiscal Federalism: A Critique, 50 Vand. L. Rev. 1137 (1997) (arguing that the propriety of unfunded mandates should be determined on a case-by-case basis through the political process rather than through the creation of "procedural roadblocks" like those in the 1995 Act); Dana, The Case for Unfunded Environmental Mandates, 69 S. Cal. L. Rev. 1 (1995) (arguing that a prohibition on unfunded mandates is unlikely to promote political accountability); Steinzor, Unfunded Environmental Mandates and the "New (New) Federalism": Devolution, Revolution, or Reform?, 81 Minn. L. Rev. 97 (1996) (arguing that dismantling of federal bureaucracies and devolution of power to states and localities is unlikely to result in adequate protection of the environment).

Pub. L. No. 104-121, 110 Stat. 847, 857-874 (1996), requires agencies proposing rules other than ones that will not have a "significant economic impact on a substantial number" of small businesses or governments to prepare and make available to the public a regulatory flexibility analysis (RFA). The analysis must describe the projected reporting, recordkeeping, and other compliance requirements of the proposed rule; estimate the affected classes of small entities; describe the steps the agency has taken to minimize significant economic impact on small entities; and justify selecting the alternative chosen. 5 U.S.C. §§603-604. Although noncompliance with the statute initially was not judicially reviewable, the 1996 amendments provided that any small entity that is adversely affected or aggrieved by final agency action is entitled to judicial review of agency compliance with these requirements, and that courts may order a noncomplying agency to take "corrective action," including remanding the rule to the agency or deferring enforcement of the rule against small entities. 5 U.S.C. §611(a)(4).

The 1996 amendments also established a procedure for congressional disapproval of agency rules. No rule can take effect until the agency promulgating it has submitted to each House of Congress a report on the rule. Major rules take effect 60 days after Congress receives the report or the rule is published in the Federal Register, whichever is later, unless Congress passes a joint resolution of disapproval (which may be overridden by a presidential veto). A rule that is disapproved may not be reissued in substantially the same form unless it is specifically reauthorized by a law enacted after the date of the joint resolution of disapproval. 5 U.S.C. §801(a)(3), (b)(2). This set of procedures applies to major rules. An agency's determination that a rule is not major is not subject to judicial review. 5 U.S.C. §805; In re Operation of the Missouri River Sys. Litig., 363 F. Supp. 2d 1145, 1173 (D. Minn. 2004), aff'd in part and vacated in part on other grounds, 421 F.3d 618 (8th Cir. 2005).

Litigants have had little success derailing agency regulatory actions on the basis of failure to comply with the Regulatory Flexibility Act's analytical requirements. In some cases, the courts defer to an agency's certification that it need not prepare an RFA because its action would not have a significant economic impact on a substantial number of small entities. See, e.g., Washington v. Daley, 173 F.3d 1158, 1170 (9th Cir. 1999).*

The **Paperwork Reduction Act**, 44 U.S.C. §§3501-3520, requires that agencies seeking to impose reporting or recordkeeping requirements on the private sector justify the collection of information as necessary for the proper performance of agency functions and nonduplicative of information available from other sources, and demonstrate that they have taken steps to minimize the burden of collecting information through the use of automated collection techniques and other means.** Agency noncompliance with the Act does not prevent promulgation of a rule, but it may

---

*Cf. Cement Kiln Recycling Coalition v. EPA, 255 F.3d 855, 869 (D.C. Cir. 2001) (the Act does not apply to small businesses indirectly affected by the regulation of other entities). See also Michigan v. EPA, 213 F.3d 663, 689-690 (D.C. Cir. 2000) (EPA need not prepare RFA in connection with call for revision of state implementation plans under the CAA because the call did not establish "requirements" applicable to anyone, including small entities; instead, it required states to determine how to obtain reductions in emissions necessary to mitigate interstate pollution). But see Northwest Mining Ass'n v. Babbitt, 5 F. Supp. 2d 9 (D.D.C. 1998) (remanding regulation to the BLM for failure to prepare RFA).

**See generally Funk, The Paperwork Reduction Act: Paperwork Reduction Meets Administrative Law, 24 Harv. J. on Legis. 1 (1987).

prevent enforcement. Dithiocarbamate Task Force v. EPA, 98 F.3d 1394, 1405 (D.C. Cir. 1996).

The **Information Quality Act**, 44 U.S.C. §3516 note, requires the Office of Management and Budget (OMB) to issue guidelines that provide "policy and procedural guidance" to federal agencies "for ensuring and maximizing the quality, objectivity, utility, and integrity of information (including statistical information) disseminated by Federal agencies." The IQA requires federal agencies to issue their own guidelines patterned after OMB's and establish administrative mechanisms allowing affected persons to seek and obtain correction of information that does not comply with the OMB guidelines. Among the significant questions raised by the IQA are whether its requirements apply to agencies engaged in informal, notice-and-comment rulemaking. Relying on its authority to implement the IQA, OMB has required extensive peer review of regulatory information before its dissemination, including information used in rulemaking. Final Information Quality Bulletin for Peer Review, 70 Fed. Reg. 2664 (2005). According to one analysis of the proposed version of the Bulletin, "OMB's proposals would continue its previous efforts to build almost out of whole cloth a procedural apparatus that is likely to stifle the government's efforts to provide useful information to the public about their safety and health risks and about risks to the environment." Shapiro, OMB's Dubious Peer Review Procedures, 34 Envtl. L. Rep. (ELI) 10064 (2004).*

The availability of judicial review of an agency's rejection of individual complaints about data quality is also unclear. One court held that the IQA does not create a private cause of action and that the courts therefore may not review an agency's decision to deny a party's information quality complaint.** Another court held that a trade association of salt producers lacked standing to bring a suit under the IQA. The plaintiffs had alleged that the Department of Health and Human Services violated the IQA by reporting on its website and in medical journals the results of studies showing that decreased use of salt could lower blood pressure and by recommending that all Americans limit salt intake. Salt Inst. v. Thompson, 440 F.3d 156 (4th Cir. 2006). Although the court recognized that the injury in fact required to demonstrate constitutional standing may exist solely by virtue of violations of statutes that create legal rights, it concluded that the IQA does not create in any third parties a legal right of access to information or to the correctness of information relied upon by a federal agency. Accordingly, the business plaintiffs did not allege invasion of a legal right, and failed to establish injury in fact.***

---

*See generally Shapiro, The Information Quality Act and Environmental Protection: The Perils of Reform by Appropriations Rider, 28 Wm. & Mary Envtl. L. & Pol'y Rev. 3239 (2004); Clune, Ossifying Ossification: Why the Information Quality Act Should Not Provide for Judicial Review, 36 Envtl. L. Rep. (ELI) 10430 (2006); Johnson, Junking the "Junk Science" Law: Reforming the Information Quality Act, 58 Admin. L. Rev. 37 (2006); Shapiro, The Case against the IQA, 22 Envtl. F. No. 4 (July/August 2005), at 26; Lacko, Comment, The Data Quality Act: Prologue to a Farce or a Tragedy?, 53 Emory L.J. 305 (2004).

**See In re Operation of the Missouri River Sys. Litigation, 363 F. Supp. 2d 1145, 1174-1175 (D. Minn. 2004) (holding that agency compliance with the IQA is "committed to agency discretion by law," and therefore immune from judicial review under 5 U.S.C. §701(a)(2)), *aff'd in part and vacated in part on other grounds*, 421 F.3d 618 (8th Cir. 2005).

***See generally Bourdeau, Information Quality Act Challenges to Flawed Use of Science, 19 Nat. Resources & Env't No. 4 (Spring 2005), at 41; Pak, Comment, An IQ Test for Federal Agencies? Judicial Review of the Information Quality Act Under the APA, 80 Wash. L. Rev. 731 (2005) (arguing that judicial review of an agency's denial of a request for correction is barred under APA §701(a)(1) and (2)).

Other legislation requires the use of cost-benefit and risk assessment requirements. E.g., the **Accountable Pipeline Safety and Partnership Act of 1996**, 49 U.S.C. §60102 (requiring the use of these analytical techniques in connection with the adoption of standards designed to meet the need for gas pipeline safety or the safe transportation of hazardous liquids). The controversy surrounding these techniques is discussed further later in this chapter and in Chapter 8.

C.   EXECUTIVE CONTROL OF ADMINISTRATIVE ENVIRONMENTAL DECISIONMAKING

Like Congress, the president has an interest in putting his policy stamp on the implementation of the environmental protection and natural resource management statutes. It is conventional wisdom that, although the president can influence the decisions of administrative agencies such as EPA by removing high-level agency appointees, he cannot dictate substantive decisions entrusted to agencies by statute. See, e.g., Percival, Presidential Management of the Administrative State: The Not-So-Unitary Executive, 51 Duke L.J. 963 (2001).

A related way for the president to influence the substance of agency decisions is to require that agencies clear their regulatory proposals with an official responsible to the president. President Reagan's Executive Order No. 12,291, 3 C.F.R. 127 (1982), *reprinted in* 5 U.S.C. §601 note, required agencies to conduct cost-benefit analyses for major rules. The Order assigned the responsibility for overseeing agency compliance to the Office of Information and Regulatory Affairs (OIRA) within the OMB, a part of the Executive Office of the President. It prohibited agencies from issuing any regulation whose benefits did not exceed its costs, unless their substantive enabling statutes required otherwise. OIRA could block publication of a major rule pending review for compliance with the Order. Executive Order No. 12,498, 3 C.F.R. 323 (1986), *reprinted in* 5 U.S.C. §601 note, extended the scope of executive oversight by requiring that agencies submit an annual regulatory plan for OIRA review and restricting the agencies' ability to pursue actions not included on the agenda. President George H. W. Bush established an interagency task force called the Council on Competitiveness to coordinate regulatory policy and the resolution of disputes between agencies and OIRA.

President Clinton's Executive Order No. 12,866, 58 Fed. Reg. 51,735 (1993), *reprinted in* 5 U.S.C. §601 note, revoked the previous orders but continued to require federal agencies to engage in cost-benefit analysis. The Order requires that, in choosing among alternative regulatory approaches, agencies select those that maximize net benefits, unless a statute requires another regulatory approach. To the extent permitted by law, agencies should adhere to a series of "principles of regulation," including designing regulations in the most cost-effective manner, proposing and adopting only those regulations whose benefits are reasonably determined to justify their costs, and tailoring regulations to impose the least burden on society. Id. §1(b). Agencies must provide OIRA with a list of planned regulatory actions. If either the agency proposing the action or OIRA decides that a particular action is significant (because, for example, it may have an annual effect on the economy of $100 million or more or adversely affect in a material way the economy, productivity, jobs, the environment, or public health or safety), the proposing agency must furnish to OIRA a detailed explanation. The explanation must describe the need for the regulatory action, assess its potential costs and benefits, assess the costs and benefits of potentially effective and reasonably feasible alternatives, and explain why the planned action is preferable to the identified alternatives. OIRA must provide "meaningful guidance and oversight so that each agency's actions are consistent with applicable law, the President's priorities, and the principles set forth in [the] Executive Order." Id. §6(b). What if these sources of guidance conflict; which should prevail? To the extent permitted by law, conflicts between the agency and OIRA should be resolved by the president or the vice president. Id. §7. Compliance with the provisions of the Executive Order is not judicially reviewable. Id. §10. See Idaho Mining Ass'n, Inc. v. Browner, 90 F. Supp. 2d 1078, 1102 (D. Idaho 2000).

Presidential attempts to confine agency discretion in making regulatory decisions have not been confined to the imposition of cost-benefit analytical requirements. In 1988, President Reagan issued Executive Order No. 12,630, 53 Fed. Reg. 8859 (1988), which directed federal agencies to avoid regulatory actions that would amount to takings of property without just compensation. Compliance with the Order is not judicially reviewable, however. See Duval Ranching Co. v. Glickman, 965 F. Supp. 1427, 1446 (D. Nev. 1997). See generally Jackson & Albaugh, A Critique of the Takings Executive Order in the Context of Environmental Regulation, 18 Envtl. L. Rep. (ELI) 10463 (1988). See also Exec. Order No. 12,612, 52 Fed. Reg. 41,685 (1987) (requiring agencies to consider principles of federalism in regulatory decisionmaking processes). For brief discussion of these and other executive orders affecting environmental rulemaking, see Seidenfeld, A Table of Requirements for Federal Administrative Rulemaking, 27 Fla. St. U. L. Rev. 533 (2000).

These efforts to subject regulatory decisions by federal agencies to review by the president or by officials close to him raise both policy and legal questions. The ultimate policy issue is who should control the cabinet and independent regulatory agencies. Congress has objected to OMB oversight because it impedes agencies from swiftly executing congressional mandates. Professor Sidney Shapiro asserts that the effectiveness of regulatory policy deteriorated as a result of presidential and legislative oversight during the Reagan and Bush administrations that impaired political accountability and failed to take advantage of agency expertise and experience. Shapiro, Political Oversight and the Deterioration of Regulatory Policy, 46 Admin. L. Rev. 1 (1994). Shapiro recommends the establishment of disclosure requirements for both presidential and legislative oversight and joint oversight based on a regulatory agenda.* Professor Percival concluded that Executive Office oversight on EPA decisionmaking resulted in delays in rulemaking, imposed pressure to weaken environmental regulation, and reduced the public's ability to monitor the rulemaking process and influence regulatory decisions. Percival, Checks without Balance: Executive Office Oversight of the Environmental Protection Agency, 54 Law & Contemp. Probs. No. 4 (Autumn 1991), at 127. According to Percival, "regulatory review should be founded on the principle that fidelity to statutory requirements, rather than to the preferences of the president or the regulated community, should be the touchstone of regulatory decisionmaking" on environmental issues. Id. at 201.

---

*See also Seidenfeld, A Big Picture Approach to Presidential Influence on Agency Policymaking, 80 Iowa L. Rev. 1 (1994) (urging that presidential oversight avoid micromanagement and be restricted to "big picture management").

Other observers endorse the theory of executive oversight while recognizing the potential for abuse. Strauss & Sunstein, The Role of the President and OMB in Informal Rulemaking, 38 Admin. L. Rev. 181 (1986), assert that regulatory review can improve interagency coordination and increase accountability. See also Pildes & Sunstein, Reinventing the Regulatory State, 62 U. Chi. L. Rev. 1 (1995). Others claim that cost-benefit analysis and related techniques can improve the substance of agency decisionmaking on regulatory matters. See, e.g., DeMuth & Ginsburg, White House Review of Agency Rulemaking, 99 Harv. L. Rev. 1075 (1986). Finally, proponents of Executive Office review argue that it can serve as a palliative for agency capture by well-organized special interests such as environmental groups. Id. at 1081; Miller et al., A Note on Centralized Regulatory Review, 43 Pub. Choice 83 (1984).

The principal legal issue is whether executive branch oversight violates separation of power principles because Congress has delegated the rulemaking function to a specific agency rather than to the Executive Office. Olson, The Quiet Shift of Power: Office of Management and Budget Supervision of Environmental Protection Agency Rulemaking under Executive Order 12,291, 4 Va. J. Nat. Resources L. 1 (1984), argues that Executive Order 12,291 may have violated separation of powers principles and given the OMB unwarranted authority to encroach on discretion delegated to agencies by Congress.*

A few cases have addressed the impact of executive oversight on the implementation of EPA's statutory duties. Several courts have concluded that OMB lacks the power to delay the issuance of EPA regulations beyond congressionally established deadlines in order to complete the review processes dictated by executive order. In EDF v. Thomas, 627 F. Supp. 566, 570 (D.D.C. 1986), the district court held that, even though "[a] certain degree of deference must be given to the authority of the President to control and supervise executive policymaking," OMB lacks the power to delay compliance with congressional mandates because such delay "is incompatible with the will of Congress." See also NRDC v. EPA, 797 F. Supp. 194 (E.D.N.Y. 1992).** Cases involving challenges to the substantive impact of executive oversight have been rare. In one such case, New York v. Reilly, 969 F.2d 1147 (D.C. Cir. 1992), the court remanded to EPA for further explanation the decision, made under pressure from the Council on Competitiveness, not to impose a ban on the combustion of lead-acid batteries.

Executive branch officials also may try to influence agency regulatory decisions on a less formal basis. Such attempts may give rise to some of the same objections raised in response to the activities of OIRA and the Council on Competitiveness. The APA restricts ex parte communications*** between "interested persons" and agency

---

*See generally Herz, Imposing Unified Executive Branch Statutory Interpretation, 15 Cardozo L. Rev. 219 (1993) (arguing that the constitutional argument for executive oversight is strongest in relation to agency statutory interpretations); Percival, Presidential Management of the Administrative State: The Not-So-Unitary Executive, 51 Duke L.J. 963 (2001) (arguing that "the president may advise agency heads concerning his views on particular rules" but may not "dictate regulatory decisions entrusted to them by law"); Colloquium, The Council on Competitiveness: Executive Oversight of Agency Rulemaking, 7 Admin. L.J. Am. U. 297 (1993).

**Cf. American Lung Ass'n v. Browner, 884 F. Supp. 345, 349 (D. Ariz. 1994) (refusing to consider OMB review process in setting schedule for agency implementation of the CAA because such review "serves no congressional purpose and is wholly discretionary").

***The APA defines an ex parte communication as "an oral or written communication not on the public record with respect to which reasonable prior notice to all parties is not given, but it shall not include requests for status reports. . . ." 5 U.S.C. §551(14).

officials engaged in adjudication. 5 U.S.C. §557(d). What is the rationale for such restrictions? In Portland Audubon Soc'y v. Endangered Species Comm., 984 F.2d 1534 (9th Cir. 1993), environmental groups challenged a decision by the Endangered Species Committee to exempt a series of timber sales proposed by the BLM from the requirements of the ESA. They asserted that President Bush's domestic policy adviser engaged in ex parte contacts with Committee members, including the Interior Secretary and the EPA Administrator, before the Committee made its decision. Is the president or his domestic policy adviser an "interested person" subject to §557(d) of the APA? The government argued that if the APA's ex parte communications ban encompasses the president and his aides it violates the doctrine of separation of powers, but the court rejected the argument "out of hand." Id. at 1546. Congress's important objectives in restricting ex parte contacts outweighed any *de minimis* impact on presidential power. The court therefore held that the communications were improper and remanded for an evidentiary hearing to determine their nature, extent, and effect. The APA's restrictions on ex parte communications have little applicability, however, to rulemaking proceedings. See, e.g., Sierra Club v. Costle, 657 F.2d 298, 400 (D.C. Cir. 1981) ("the concept of ex parte contacts is of more questionable utility" as applied to policy decisions reflected in informal rulemaking).

NOTE ON COST-BENEFIT ANALYSIS

The Rationale for Cost-Benefit Analysis. Why might Congress or the president choose to require that regulatory agencies engage in cost-benefit analysis? The technique is premised on the belief that rational choice is impossible without a full awareness of the consequences of a decision. Cost-benefit analysis also builds on the central tenet of economic theory that society's resources are limited and that the allocation of resources to achieve one objective necessarily precludes other allocations. Cost-benefit analysis implies that regulatory tasks should be ranked and that those regulations that show the highest cost-benefit ratios should be undertaken first, on the theory that limited government resources should be applied first to tasks yielding the highest marginal return in public health and environmental protection. Putting it slightly differently, cost-benefit analysis seeks to replicate the result that would have occurred as a result of free market bargaining between those who generate and are adversely affected by environmental externalities in the absence of transaction costs by requiring a reduction in environmental damage up to the point at which the costs and benefits of such a reduction are equal.

The Methodology of Cost-Benefit Analysis. Formal cost-benefit analysis assumes that one can (1) identify correctly and put accurate money prices on the social benefits of an activity (e.g., producing a product, building a public works project, regulating a dangerous substance), and (2) identify and price the things ("costs") whose value or alternative uses must be reduced to produce the benefits (e.g., raw materials, the natural environment, capital, and labor), so that one can (3) predict quantitatively the net posture of the activity, which may be expressed either as a ratio of benefits to costs or as the net increase in social utility one hopes to maximize. In the context of environmental regulation, the agency must compute costs, including compliance costs (capital equipment, maintenance, monitoring, etc.), the social benefits lost as a result of constraints on regulated activities, and arguably the transaction costs incurred by the agency in promulgating the regulation. Then the agency must undertake the harder task of placing a money value on benefits, e.g., the health injuries averted (cancer, mutations, diseases, other systematic disorders) and environmental degradation avoided.* Because these harms obviously have no established market prices that can be inserted into the agency's computations, studies must be performed to develop surrogate prices by imputing to affected individuals their willingness to pay to avoid these costs (e.g., from the payments they make for medical treatment or to move away from a hazardous neighborhood) or their willingness to be paid to risk harm (e.g., hazardous duty pay, reduced rent). The "willingness-to-pay" criterion is used by economists to ensure that "priceless" items are valued in the same way as articles in everyday commerce.

Difficulties in Implementing Cost-Benefit Analysis; Identification of Costs and Benefits. Cost-benefit analysis is saddled with several limitations as a device for determining the appropriate amount of environmental regulation. These limitations highlight the basic policy conflicts that occur when a highly industrialized society attempts to understand systematically and control the environmental risks it creates. Preparation of a cost-benefit analysis requires identification of the prospective costs and benefits of the regulatory action contemplated. This preliminary step may present knotty problems. In inventorying relevant costs and benefits, the benefit of workdays saved by disease prevention should be counted. Likewise, the lives of children and other non–wage earners are indisputably valuable, although traditional cost-benefit analysis focused only on wage losses averted. Should the benefits also include a dollar estimate of the reduced need for special diets for patients? Transportation costs to obtain medical treatment? Should victims' anxieties, nervous system disorders, and genetic injury be "priced"? How? Important effects may be neglected or deliberately ignored, especially in light of the high administrative costs of identifying and computing "remote" effects, the possibility that quantifying a speculative but potentially disastrous factor might tip the scales against an activity with definite immediate economic benefits, and the reluctance to include factors for which a firm causal nexus with the harm regulated has not yet been established.

Difficulties of Quantification. Even if the costs and benefits have been identified adequately, they may be extremely difficult to quantify. Often the best one can say about the benefits of controlling carcinogenic substances at a given exposure level, for example, is that the number of cancers varies within a range of several orders of magnitude (factors of ten). If a quantitative risk assessment of numbers of deaths, diseases, injuries, and other impacts cannot be made, they cannot be assigned more than a range of dollar values (e.g., "the health injury averted by this regulation may be between $1 million and $10 billion"). More fundamentally, "[p]erhaps the most significant objection to cost-benefit analysis is the inability of economic analysis to reduce the benefits of regulation to dollar equivalents to compare with regulatory costs." McGarity, A Cost-Benefit State, 50 Admin. L. Rev. 1, 63 (1998).

A particularly sensitive area of risk quantification concerns the dollar value of losing (or saving) a human life as a consequence of regulation. The valuation problem is similar for loss of an endangered species or a symbolic or unique aesthetic resource. Agencies are understandably uneasy about overtly assigning a dollar value to human life in their cost-benefit analyses, but those that do not do so overtly do so impliedly

*Note that the words "benefit" and "cost" require that the context of their usage be clearly stated. Otherwise, the "benefits" of reduced health risks may be confused with the economic "costs" of abatement or the "benefits" of not regulating an activity may be entered on the "benefits" side of the analysis rather than on the "costs" side, where they belong.

because there is no other way to reduce the costs and benefits of life-saving regulation to a common money measure. See Sagoff, On Markets for Risk, 41 Md. L. Rev. 755, 767 (1982). OMB guidance has suggested monetizing reductions in fatality risks attributable to regulation according to the willingness-to-pay approach, which is meant to reflect opportunity cost by measuring what individuals are willing to forgo to enjoy a particular benefit (in this case, a reduction in the risk of premature death).

An alternative is to express all non-health-related costs and benefits in dollars, but reduce all health-related matters (e.g., cases of disease and injury, days of restricted activity) to the common unit of lives saved (or lost) (or portions of lives saved or lost) by regulating (or refusing to regulate), without ever assigning a dollar value to them. This approach would create two bases for cost-benefit comparisons: dollars and lives. Decisionmakers would then decide whether or how strictly to regulate by comparing both dollar costs averted and lives saved. To some, however, framing the lives to be protected by regulation in such "statistical" terms "dehumanize[s] the suffering and death that scientific risk assessments tell us will occur due to particular hazards." Heinzerling, The Rights of Statistical People, 24 Harv. Envtl. L. Rev. 189, 207 (2000).

Adler, Fear Assessment: Cost-Benefit Analysis and the Pricing of Fear and Anxiety, 79 Chi.-Kent L. Rev. 977 (2004), argues that the failure by agencies to enumerate and price distressing mental states (such as fear, anxiety, worry, panic, or dread) that are causally connected to environmental hazards when they perform cost-benefit analyses creates an inappropriate asymmetry and that fear assessment should be a component of cost-benefit analysis. Professor Adler discusses how best to measure fear and related kinds of psychological distress that could be averted through regulation on a monetary scale.

The Discounting Controversy and Equitable Considerations. The selection of an appropriate discount rate raises additional issues. In formal cost-benefit analysis, whenever a benefit of regulation is to be enjoyed in the future, its future value is deflated or "discounted" to its present value. The benefits of regulation may be worth a lot in the future to us or to persons yet unborn, but since our present enjoyment of a future benefit exists only as an expectation that may never be enjoyed, the theory is that we will want to value it less now. The issue is important to cost-benefit analysis of health and safety regulation because the injuries caused by some chemicals may not be realized for generations, or even centuries. As a National Academy of Sciences report pointed out, if the discount rate were 5 percent, one toxic poisoning case in 1975 would be valued the same as 1733 cases in 200 years, or the same as the world population in 450 years. Decision Making for Regulating Chemicals in the Environment 43 (1975).

Because the recipients of a regulatory benefit may not be the same persons who pay the costs, the discounting controversy involves distributional considerations, which may entail a balancing of the interests of the living and the unborn. See J. Rawls, A Theory of Justice 284 (1971). OMB has acknowledged that generally accepted principles are lacking for determining the relative equities of different distributive effects.

Professor Lisa Heinzerling has argued vigorously against the propriety of discounting regulatory benefits based on the proposition that harms prevented in the future are worth less than harms prevented today. She asserts that the tendency of the beneficial consequences of environmental regulation to range along a continuum stretching from the immediate present to the distant future makes discounting in general and the use of life-years saved as a measure of the benefits of life-saving rules in particular inappropriate. Discounting skews cost-benefit analysis because deflating life-saving benefits greatly inflates costs per life saved.* The concept of "quality-adjusted life years" (QALYs) has been proposed as a means of assessing the cost-effectiveness of regulatory (or nonregulatory) alternatives without the need to quantify the value of a human life. According to supporters of this approach, the goal ought to be to deliver the greatest number of QALYs at the lowest possible cost. Critics charge, however, that assessment of regulatory alternatives based on the QALYs each will yield discriminates against the elderly and the disabled, whose lives are valued lower than those who are young and healthy. See F. Ackerman & L. Heinzerling, Priceless: On Knowing the Price of Everything and the Value of Nothing 98-102 (2004).

According to some critics of cost-benefit analysis, the equitable concerns raised by discounting represent only one aspect of its exclusion or downgrading of equitable considerations:

> [C]ost-benefit analysis ignores the question of *who* suffers as a result of environmental problems and, therefore, threatens to reinforce existing patterns of economic and social inequality. Cost-benefit analysis treats questions about equity as, at best, side issues, contradicting the widely shared view that equity should count in public policy. Poor countries, communities, and individuals are likely to express less "willingness to pay" to avoid environmental harms simply because they have fewer resources. Therefore, cost-benefit analysis would justify imposing greater environmental burdens on them than on their wealthier counterparts. With this kind of analysis, the poor get poorer. [L. Heinzerling & F. Ackerman, Pricing the Priceless: Cost-Benefit Analysis of Environmental Protection 2 (2001).]

Cost-Benefit Analysis and Value Selection. Ultimately, the critics charge, consistent application of the economic view creates a tendency among policy analysts to view arms, health, life, and environmental resources as part of a smoothly interchangeable mix, in which dollar evaluations allow regulators to trade off hats, cars, and desserts against items that are entirely different in nature. Any tradeoffs based on a weighing of toxicant reduction and economic and technological considerations is "fundamentally flawed," in this view, because when applied to "matters of intense personal interest" such as risk to life and highly valued environmental amenities, such tradeoffs ignore the "almost universal recognition that citizens of this country have a 'right' to a healthy environment and workplace, at least insofar as the societal pursuit of that right is not technologically impossible or prohibitively expensive." McGarity, Media-Quality, Technology, and Cost-Benefit Balancing Strategies for Health and Environmental Regulation, 46 Law & Contemp. Probs. (Summer 1983), at 159, 161.

Similarly, Mark Sagoff argues in On Markets for Risk, *supra*, that environmental legislation reflects a desire to promote autonomy, not efficiency, in the sense that it seeks to control the conditions under which we live. Thus, an efficiency-based justification for the use of cost-benefit analysis in environmental decisionmaking is not persuasive. "People want to determine the background level of risk; they do not want the working conditions of their lives to be determined by others. It does not matter how

---

*See Heinzerling, Discounting Our Future, 34 Land & Water L. Rev. 39 (1999); Heinzerling, Environmental Law and the Present Future, 87 Geo. L.J. 2025 (1999). Gaba, Environmental Ethics and Our Moral Relationship to Future Generations: Future Rights and Present Virtue, 24 Colum. J. Envtl. L. 249 (1999), urges that the moral relationship of the present generation to future generations be viewed not in terms of rights and obligations, but in terms of "virtue ethics."

cost-beneficial risks are; it is a question, rather, of who controls them." Id. at 764. In short, "[v]irtues like altruism, dignity, equity, fairness (in both the procedural and substantive senses), decency, mutuality, tolerance, and empathy that are highly valued in a civilized society are belittled or ignored entirely in a cost-benefit regulatory regime in which allocative efficiency is the only goal." McGarity, A Cost-Benefit State, *supra*, at 72.

Michaelson, Note, Rethinking Regulatory Reform: Toxics, Politics, and Ethics, 105 Yale L.J. 1891, 1919 (1996), argues that "cost-benefit analysis reorders risk allocation" by "shift[ing] regulation from a proxy liability rule in which persons receive the entitlement to their body to a proxy property rule in which toxics producers receive the entitlement to produce a profitable amount of poison. . . . [C]ost-benefit risk determination gives toxic producers the right to kill until the entitlement price (that point at which it 'pays' not to kill) is paid by the number of injured people."

Although they acknowledge the limitations of cost-benefit analysis, Professors Pildes and Sunstein support its continued use, provided that disaggregated cost and benefit data are publicly disclosed. Agencies should use cost-benefit analysis to inform thoughtful decisionmaking rather than as an objective determinant of appropriate policy and should consider the possibility that it fails to capture relevant values. Pildes & Sunstein, Reinventing the Regulatory State, 62 U. Chi. L. Rev. 1, 72 (1995). Other supporters of the use of cost-benefit analysis claim that this kind of analysis measures the benefits of protecting the environment based on the willingness of individuals to pay for such protection, and that market prices reflect altruistic as well as self-interested concerns. Thus, cost-benefit analysis reflects more than just utilitarian values.

Are the Benefits of EPA Regulations Worth the Costs? The OMB issued a report in 2005 in which it concluded that 41 major regulations issued by EPA between 1994 and 2005 imposed annual compliance costs between $15.1 and $16.7 billion, but generated annual health and other benefits that ranged from $44.3 to $233.7 billion. According to the OMB, most of the health benefits were attributable to the reduction in public exposure to fine particulate matter in the air.*

Problem 3-4

You are an attorney and policy analyst in the office of a centrist member of the U.S. Senate who regards herself as an independent-thinking legislator interested in sound policy, not partisan politics. A prominent economics think tank has dropped a proposed piece of legislation pertaining to cost-benefit analysis at your senator's office. The bill, if passed into law, would subject all federal agencies responsible for implementing "a program designed to protect human health, safety, or the environment" to a statutory obligation to undertake cost-benefit analysis before adopting "major regulations" (defined as those likely to result in an annual increase in costs of $25 million or more). In particular, the bill, whose requirements would "supplement, not supersede" the provisions of preexisting regulatory statutes, would require the relevant agencies to determine whether the "identified benefits of the regulation are likely to exceed the identified costs of the regulation." Based on that analysis, the agency would have to certify before proceeding with a major regulation that the benefits of the

---

*See OMB, 2005 Report to Congress on the Costs and Benefits of Federal Regulations and Unfunded Mandates on State, Local and Tribal Entities, available at http://www.whitehouse.gov/omb/inforeg/2005_cb/final_2005_cb_report.pdf.

regulation "will be likely to justify, and be reasonably related to, the incremental costs incurred by State, local, and tribal governments, the Federal Government, and other public and private entities as a result of the regulation." In addition, the bill would require that the agency adopt the regulatory alternative that is both feasible and that would create the "greatest net benefits." The bill defines the term "costs" as "the direct and indirect costs to the United States Government, to State, local, and tribal governments, and to the private sector, wage earners, consumers, and the economy, of implementing and complying with a regulation or alternative strategy." It defines benefits to mean "the reasonably identifiable significant health, safety, environmental, social, and economic benefits that are expected to result directly or indirectly from implementation of a regulation or alternative strategy."

The senator has set up a meeting at which the two of you and the rest of her staff will discuss the implications of the proposed bill for federal agencies engaged in the promulgation of rules that are designed to protect health, safety, or the environment, as well as likely responses to the bill of industry, agencies, and environmentalists. Be prepared to advise the senator whether to oppose, support, or seek amendments to the bill. If you suggest amendments or clarifications, be prepared to explain the reasoning behind your suggestions.

D. AVOIDING CONTROL THROUGH INFORMAL DECISIONMAKING

Many of the techniques for controlling agency discretion described above apply to agency attempts to implement policy through rulemaking. The cost-benefit requirements of Executive Order 12,866, for example, are triggered whenever an agency issues a regulation with an annual effect on the economy of $100 million or more. The analytical procedures of the Unfunded Mandates Act apply to regulatory provisions that impose enforceable duties, and the Regulatory Flexibility Act's procedures govern rules with a significant impact on small business. Regulations issued by agencies such as EPA are, of course, subject to judicial review under the arbitrary and capricious or substantial evidence standards.

What has been the impact of this aggregation of analytical overlays on agency decisionmaking processes? Consider the following assessment by Professor McGarity.

McGARITY, THE COURTS AND THE OSSIFICATION OF RULEMAKING: A RESPONSE TO PROFESSOR SEIDENFELD
75 Texas L. Rev. 525, 528, 533-535 (1997)

By the end of the 1980s, it was becoming increasingly clear that the informal rulemaking model was not faring very well. Its great virtue had been the efficiency with which federal agencies could implement regulatory policy and the degree to which affected members of the public could participate in the policymaking process. Throughout the late 1970s and early 1980s, however, the executive branch and, to a more limited extent, Congress added analytical requirements and review procedures, often at the behest of the regulated industries. These initiatives and the continuing scrutiny of reviewing courts under the hard look doctrine caused the rulemaking process to "ossify" to a disturbing degree. By the mid-1990s, it has become so difficult for agencies to promulgate major rules that some regulatory programs have ground to a halt and others have succeeded only because agencies have resorted to alternative policymaking vehicles. . . .

In today's regulatory climate it is very difficult for an agency to promulgate a rule. The "program office" responsible for the rule must gather (by contract or otherwise) information, conduct technical and economic analyses, assemble decision packages and preambles, and convince skeptical agency employees in other offices of the desirability of the program office's preferred alternatives. The rulemaking exercise is often considerably complicated by the absence of information on relevant questions and the corresponding need to draw inferences from existing data. The program office staff often relies upon impenetrable computer models to make predictions about the probable beneficial and adverse consequences of the proposal. Large uncertainties becloud all of these analytical exercises. . . .

If the agency leadership is persuaded that the rule should go forward, it must be circulated to the Office of Management and Budget (OMB) for review by OMB economists, many of whom are well-known and persistent critics of existing regulatory regimes. The agency must then publish the proposed rule and preamble in the Federal Register and make supporting documents available for public review and comment. The program office staff must then review and respond to the voluminous comments, many of which are prepared by sophisticated employees or consultants of the regulated industries. The supporting documents and analyses must then be revised in light of the comments, and the package must be circulated again through the agency and sent to OMB for further review. For any rulemaking initiative that may have a substantial impact on small businesses, the final rule and supporting documentation must then be sent to the relevant congressional committees to give them an opportunity (potentially extending for several months) to enact legislation disapproving the rule. Finally, any adversely affected person may challenge in court the propriety of the agency's rulemaking procedures, the correctness of its interpretations of its statute, and the rationality of its factual and policy conclusions in light of the information and analysis in the record. . . .

. . . Uncertainty about how reviewing courts will view both agency reliance upon its own expertise and agency rejections of arguments raised by outside commentators unquestionably adds to the ossification of the rulemaking process. Because agency staffers have no way of knowing how reviewing judges will react to their responses to blunderbuss attacks, their tendency is to adopt the cautious approach of commissioning expensive quantitative modeling exercises to support predictions and of responding to every conceivable argument raised in blunderbuss attacks.

The ossification complaint, however, goes beyond uncertainty about how judges will react to agency rulemaking efforts. Far more troublesome, in my view, is the tendency of reviewing courts to demand too much by way of explanation and analysis from the regulatory agencies. An agency can be certain that some judges will demand more than the agency can reasonably produce under existing resource constraints. Many currently sitting judges were appointed by presidents who took great pains to ensure that the appellate judiciary was populated with judges who were not sympathetic to governmental intervention into private economic arrangements. Far from neutral civic republican arbiters of agreed-upon conceptions of rationality, these judges are not at all reluctant to impose demanding informational and analytical requirements on agencies before allowing them to impose costly regulations upon an unwilling private sector. Even judges who do not share this antigovernment ideological perspective are often attracted to the synoptic paradigm and are therefore unduly demanding of the agencies. The real problem with judicial review under the hard look doctrine is not uncertainty—it is the inability of agencies to meet judicial expectations while still providing the protections that Congress intended.

NOTES AND QUESTIONS

1. *The Impact of "Ossification."* In an earlier article, Professor McGarity argued that the "ossification" of the rulemaking process described in the preceding excerpt has had additional undesirable consequences, including inefficient regulation, reduced agency flexibility, and, ultimately, frustration of legislative policy objectives:

> Since most regulatory statutes were enacted to accomplish progressive public policy goals, the ossification of the informal rulemaking process hinders or defeats the agency's pursuit of those goals. To some extent, the fact that the air and waters of the United States are still polluted, workplaces still dangerous, motor vehicles still unsafe, and consumers still being deceived is attributable to the expense and burdensomeness of the informal rulemaking process. In addition to frustrating congressional policy goals, the ossification of the informal rulemaking process deprives it of one of its greatest virtues— administrative efficiency. When agencies expend twice as many resources to achieve the same results, the taxpayer is the ultimate loser. To be sure, other societal goals, such as fairness, allocative efficiency, and factual accuracy, may demand more deliberative rulemaking procedures, analytical exercises, and other quality control requirements. And the extent to which a more burdensome rulemaking process reflects an appropriate balance among these competing goals is a matter on which reasonable minds can differ. Nevertheless, the fact that the ossification of the informal rulemaking process frustrates statutory goals is a primary reason for inquiring into the causes of and cures for the ossification phenomenon.
>
> The ossification of the informal rulemaking process also reduces agency incentives to experiment with flexible or temporary rules. Experimentation is welcome in an atmosphere in which rules can be undone if they do not produce the anticipated changes or cause unanticipated side effects. But experimentation is riskier in an atmosphere in which any change is likely to be irreversible. This inflexibility is especially unfortunate in the context of programs in which agencies must regulate on the "frontiers of scientific knowledge" with particularly treacherous "facts." New scientific discoveries can erode the technical basis for a rule that was promulgated only a few years ago. New technologies can make available fresh alternatives that were not considered at the time the agency first examined the issues. However, the agencies are understandably reluctant to rock the boat when to do so requires an enormously expensive rulemaking in which a successful outcome is by no means assured. . . . [McGarity, Some Thoughts on "Deossifying" the Rulemaking Process, 41 Duke L.J. 1385, 1391-1392 (1992).]

Not all observers agree with Professor McGarity's evaluation of the relative merits and demerits of the judicial, congressional, and executive branch control techniques which, according to McGarity, have led to rulemaking "ossification." Professor Seidenfeld claims, for example, that easing up on the rigors of judicial review of agency decisions is likely to reduce the usefulness of this check on agency arbitrariness.

Greater judicial deference may fail to reduce agency incentives to engage in excessive data collection because the chances of a rule surviving judicial review will still be greater with a more extensive supporting record. Still worse, more deferential review might harm agency deliberative processes by making it easier for an agency to adopt rules to benefit narrow interest groups.* The materials in section C above summarize the arguments in defense of continued executive branch oversight.**

2. *Agency Response to Limits on Discretion.* How have agencies reacted to the analytical burdens that congressional, executive, and judicial oversight of informal rulemaking has produced? One way to avoid the need to engage in the analytical processes mandated by the executive orders and statutes reviewed in the previous two sections is to make policy through a form other than rulemaking. Some agencies, like the Forest Service, have for years used handbooks and manuals, sometimes developed without public input, to guide agency decisionmakers. The courts have struggled to ascertain the legal status of such documents.*** EPA routinely includes disclaimers in its guidance documents under statutes such as the Comprehensive Environmental Response, Compensation, and Liability Act to the effect that the documents are intended solely for internal agency use and create neither legal rights for those who rely upon them nor legal duties for the agency to follow. Nevertheless, the documents are typically available to the public (EPA often publishes notice of their availability in the Federal Register or posts them on its website) and the regulated community uses them to try to persuade the agency to make favorable decisions.

Another way to avoid the need to comply with the analytical procedures applicable to regulations is to adopt or implement policy through an interpretive rule or policy statement. If an agency issues an interpretive rule or a general statement of policy, as opposed to a substantive or legislative regulation, it need not even comply with APA notice-and-comment rulemaking procedures. 5 U.S.C. §553(b)(A). See Beazer East, Inc. v. EPA, 963 F.2d 603 (3d Cir. 1992). What, then, is the difference between an interpretive rule or a policy statement and a legislative rule? Interpretive rules are those which purport to "clarify" existing law or regulations, while policy statements announce how the agency hopes to implement policy in the future through subsequent rulemakings or adjudications. Phillips Petroleum Co. v. Johnson, 22 F.3d 616 (5th Cir. 1994).

In Appalachian Power Co. v. EPA, 208 F.3d 1015 (D.C. Cir. 2000), the court chastised the "familiar" agency practice of "making law" without notice and comment, public participation, or publication in the Federal Register through guidance

---

*Seidenfeld, Demystifying Deossification: Rethinking Recent Proposals to Modify Judicial Review of Notice and Comment Rulemaking, 75 Tex. L. Rev. 483 (1997). See also Seidenfeld, Cognitive Loafing, Social Conformity, and Judicial Review of Agency Rulemaking, 87 Cornell L. Rev. 486 (2002) (arguing that judicial review under the arbitrary and capricious standard encourages decisionmaking that reduces the probability of bias).

**Jordan, Ossification Revisited: Does Arbitrary and Capricious Review Significantly Interfere with Agency Ability to Achieve Regulatory Goals through Informal Rulemaking?, 94 Nw. U. L. Rev. 393 (2000), answers the question posed in the negative based on an empirical study of cases decided between 1985 and 1995 in which the courts remanded all or part of the product of informal rulemaking initiatives by federal agencies.

***Compare Western Radio Serv. Co. v. Espy, 79 F.3d 896 (9th Cir. 1996) (Forest Service manual provision lacked the independent force and effect of law) with Stone Forest Indus., Inc. v. United States, 973 F.2d 1548, 1551 (Fed. Cir. 1992) (manual provision is evidence of the custom and practice of the agency). See also Back Country Horsemen of Am. v. Johanns, 424 F. Supp. 2d 89 (D.D.C. 2006) (invalidating Forest Service handbook amendments due to failure to provide notice and solicit public comments).

documents, purported policy statements, and the like. It refused to allow this "lawmaking" practice to be immune from judicial review.*

3. *The "No Surprises" Policy.* Regulated entities have on occasion sought to block what they perceive to be an end run around statutory procedures or analytical requirements by disputing the agency's characterization of its actions. In 1994, the FWS and several other federal agencies issued a "no surprises" policy under their authority to implement the ESA. This policy was designed to promote Congress's goal of assuring developers who agree to abide by habitat conservation plans as a means of protecting endangered species that they will not be subject to additional land use restrictions or compensation requirements, even if unforeseen circumstances arise after issuance that makes the need for further mitigation efforts clear. The agencies incorporated the policy into a draft Handbook for Habitat Conservation Planning and Incidental Take Permitting Process. When they proposed to finalize the handbook, commenters complained that the policy should have been issued as a regulation, with all of the attendant procedural safeguards and opportunities for public input. The agencies disagreed, asserting that "it [was not] necessary to codify the 'No Surprises' policy as a specific regulation, because it is simply a statement of policy." 61 Fed. Reg. 63,854, 63,856 (1996). They nevertheless claimed that the policy had been subjected to procedures similar to those used in issuing regulations, including a public review process when a notice of availability was published in the Federal Register for the draft handbook.

The agencies were sued by litigants claiming that the policy was invalid because it did not qualify for the APA exemption for interpretive rules or general statements of policy. In 1997, the agencies relented and agreed in a settlement of that suit to codify the policy in a proposed rule. 62 Fed. Reg. 29,091. They issued the final rule the following year. 63 Fed. Reg. 8,859 (1998). In Spirit of the Sage Council v. Norton, 294 F. Supp. 2d 67 (D.D.C. 2003), the court vacated a rule specifying the circumstances in which the Interior Department may revoke an incidental take permit due to the agency's failure to comply with notice and comment informal rulemaking procedures. Because the agency had relied on the "no surprises" rule to defend the validity of the permit revocation rule, the court also remanded the "no surprises" rule for reconsideration as a whole with the permit revocation rule.**

For another example of an unsuccessful effort to make policy informally, see Kelley v. EPA, 15 F.3d 1100 (D.C. Cir.), *rehearing denied*, 25 F.3d 1088 (D.C. Cir. 1994) (holding that EPA lacked the authority to issue an interpretive rule to determine the scope of liability of lenders for response costs under the Comprehensive

---

*See also Croplife Am. v. EPA, 329 F.3d 876 (D.C. Cir. 2003) (holding that EPA press release announcing that it would not consider third-party studies in evaluating the safety of pesticides was a binding regulation, not a policy statement); Chamber of Commerce v. United States Dep't of Labor, 174 F.3d 206 (D.C. Cir. 1999) ("directive" subjecting employers to an inspection by OSHA was a legislative rule, not a procedural rule or a policy statement). See generally Anthony, "Interpretive" Rules, "Legislative" Rules and "Spurious" Rules: Lifting the Smog, 8 Admin. L.J. Am. U. 1 (1994); Saunders, Interpretive Rules with Legislative Effect: An Analysis and a Proposal for Public Participation, 1986 Duke L.J. 346 (1986).

**See generally Baur & Donovan, The No Surprises Policy: Contracts 101 Meets the Endangered Species Act, 27 Envtl. L. 767 (1997); Parenteau, Rearranging the Deck Chairs: Endangered Species Act Reforms in an Era of Mass Extinction, 22 Wm. & Mary Envtl. L. & Pol'y Rev. 227 (1998); Ruhl, While the Cat's Asleep: The Making of the "New" ESA, 12 Nat. Resources & Env't No. 3, at 187 (Winter 1998).

Environmental Response, Compensation, and Liability Act because Congress intended the courts, not EPA, to determine issues of liability).

May an agency rely on informal guidance documents in enforcement proceedings by alleging that the documents put regulated entities on notice of how the agency interpreted statutory provisions? See Appeals Court Ruling May Void Effect of Bevill Waste Guidance, Inside EPA, Dec. 24, 1999, at 15-16 (discussing Molycorp, Inc. v. EPA, 197 F.3d 543 (D.C. Cir. 1999)).

4. *Regulatory Negotiation.* Widespread dissatisfaction with existing processes for resolving environmental issues, including formal adjudication, informal rulemaking, and lawsuits, have prompted increased resort to mediation and arbitration to resolve resource allocation controversies.* These efforts involve consensus building among the interested parties through the use of "facilitators" and focus groups. In another form of collaborative governance, regulatory negotiation (or reg-neg), federal agencies and major stakeholders negotiate to develop a consensus on the shape of regulation. Stakeholders may then agree not to challenge the resulting solution. One observer described the process as follows:

> Negotiated rule making is a consensus-based process, usually convened by an agency, through which stakeholders negotiate the substance of a rule. It represents the importation of alternative dispute resolution principles and strategies into the public policy context. In 1982, Philip Harter, who worked with the now defunct Administrative Conference of the United States to develop negotiated rule making, published what has become the classic article describing the reg-neg process and advocating its use. Harter proposed reg-neg as a response to the failures of the adversarial rule-making process, arguing that direct stakeholder negotiation of rules would restore legitimacy to rule making. Harter's article initiated a debate over the legitimacy of the process itself. This debate now consists of two distinct sides: those who argue that reg-neg is preferable to traditional rule making in terms of the cost, implementability, and legitimacy of the rules produced, and those suspicious of its potential to subvert the public interest by granting inordinate power to unaccountable private groups. However, there is broad agreement even among ardent supporters on at least two limitations on the process. First, reg-neg should be used only under specific conditions when the incentives are conducive to producing agreement. Second, there should be plenty of safeguards against agency capture, including post-consensus notice and comment, and judicial review. [Freeman, Collaborative Governance in the Administrative State, 45 UCLA L. Rev. 1, 34-35 (1997).]**

Experiments in stakeholder collaboration raise substantial constitutional and statutory authority questions. Collaborative governance may be characterized as an unconstitutional delegation of public lawmaking authority to private parties under Carter v. Carter Coal Co., 298 U.S. 238 (1936). To work, these experiments require each side to take risks and for the public participants to exercise a kind of prosecutorial discretion not to seek full enforcement of existing laws.

---

*See, e.g., McCroy, Environmental Mediation—Another Piece for the Puzzle, 6 Vt. L. Rev. 49 (1981); Schoenbrod, Limits and Dangers of Environmental Mediation: A Review Essay, 58 N.Y.U. L. Rev. 1453 (1983).
**See also Rossi, Participation Run Amok: The Costs of Mass Participation in Deliberative Agency Decisionmaking, 92 Nw. U. L. Rev. 173 (1997); McKinney, Negotiated Rulemaking: Involving Citizens in Public Decisions, 60 Mont. L. Rev. 499 (1999).

5. *Decisionmaking by Inaction.* An agency may avoid judicial review by failing to take any "action" at all. As both the *Lujan I* and *Southern Utah Wilderness Alliance* cases discussed earlier in this chapter indicate, those dissatisfied with the agency's inaction may find it difficult to secure judicial review of the failure to act.

6. *Assessing the Informalization of Agency Policymaking.* Is the tendency of federal agencies to implement environmental policy through less and less formal means a laudable development? Professor McGarity contends that it is not:

> Frustrated agencies are beginning to explore techniques for avoiding notice-and-comment rulemaking altogether, such as establishing rules in adjudications. . . . To the extent that agencies establish rules in adjudications in order to avoid informal rule-making, regulatees are not put on notice of the standards of conduct that such agencies are applying to them. As a result, both regulatees and regulatory beneficiaries are deprived of the open opportunity that informal rulemaking provides to influence the agencies' thinking.
>
> Perhaps more troublesome to the goals of open government is the increasing tendency of agencies to engage in "nonrule rulemaking" through relatively less formal devices such as policy statements, interpretative rules, manuals, and other informal devices. Although informal guidance documents and technical manuals are a necessary part of a complex administrative regime, they are promulgated without the benefit of comments by an interested public. . . .
>
> If all this leads the frustrated potential regulatee to wonder whether "secret law" is at play here, those fears may be well founded. . . .

McGarity, Some Thoughts on "Deossifying" the Rulemaking Process, 41 Duke L.J. 1385, 1393-1395 (1992). See also Anthony, Interpretive Rules, Policy Statements, Guidances, Manuals, and the Like—Should Federal Agencies Use Them to Bind the Public?, 41 Duke L.J. 1311 (1992).

IV

THE NATIONAL ENVIRONMENTAL POLICY ACT

A. CONGRESSIONAL PURPOSE AND JUDICIAL ENFORCEMENT

1. *An Environmental Magna Carta*

Congressional Purpose and History. The National Environmental Policy Act of 1969 (NEPA), one of the earliest and most influential congressional environmental laws, is often called an environmental Magna Carta. By injecting environmental concerns into federal agency decisionmaking and by making possible federal litigation challenging federal actions affecting environmental quality, NEPA moved concern about environmental problems to a high level of public salience.

One of the authors of this casebook has summarized the reasons the late Senator Henry Jackson, chairman of the Senate Interior and Insular Affairs Committee, decided to legislate a national environmental policy:

> Federal legislation was necessary because the creation of program, mission-oriented agencies has insured that these environmental considerations have been systematically underrepresented, in most short- and long-range decision making. Existing agencies were established to supervise the development of our natural resources consistent with the ethic which has prevailed throughout this country's history and, thus, they tended to overstress the benefits of development and to explore insufficiently the less environmentally damaging alternatives to current methods of meeting their programmed objectives. [Tarlock, Balancing Environmental Considerations and Energy Demands: A Comment on Calvert Cliffs' Coordinating Committee, Inc. v. AEC, 47 Ind. L. Rev. 645, 658 (1972).]

Reformers bent on changing agency decisionmaking as it affects environmental values could have proceeded through a piecemeal amendment of federal legislation. Congress has since adopted this strategy and has introduced similar environmental criteria in a wide variety of other federal programs. See, e.g., the Ports and Waterways Safety Act, 33 U.S.C. §1224(a) (requiring consideration of environmental factors affecting marine environment); Wilderness Act, 16 U.S.C. §1131(a) (wilderness areas to be administered to leave them unimpaired for future use and enjoyment, and to provide for protection and preservation of wilderness character).

NEPA took a different course, described by the two authors quoted below, one of whom was close to the legislative drafting:

> The challenge was to approach environmental management in a comprehensive way. The new values of environmental policy had to intrude somehow into the most remote recesses of the federal administrative machinery and begin to influence the multitude of decisions being made by thousands of officials. [Dreyfus & Ingram, The National Environmental Policy Act: A View of Intent and Practice, 16 Nat. Resources J. 243, 246 (1976).]

This comment raises a fundamental question about NEPA and its purposes. Agency decisionmaking was modified to include environmental values, but how was this change to be accomplished? Congress was not clear on this point, but several explanations of congressional purpose are possible. One is that NEPA's environmental mandates would be self-enforcing. Federal agencies would take NEPA's environmental commands into account in their decisionmaking and would make the changes necessary to incorporate environmental values. The Senate report supports this interpretation. See S. Rep. No. 91-296, at 21 (1969). Another view suggests that Congress contemplated external pressures from the public and from agencies with environmental expertise. The statute expressly requires comments from these sources on environmental impact statements prepared by federal agencies.

The federal courts have become an important source of external pressure for agency reform. They have assumed the major role in policing NEPA's requirements, and this chapter concentrates on the court decisions interpreting the statute. The judicial role in NEPA's enforcement may have been accidental. NEPA does not expressly provide for judicial review, and commentators disagree about whether Congress contemplated judicial enforcement. See Dreyfus & Ingram, *supra*.

Whether NEPA has accomplished a significant change in agency decisionmaking on environmental problems is an important question, and we will return to this question at the conclusion of this chapter.

Legislative History. The environmental impact statement that federal agencies must prepare on major federal actions significantly affecting the environment is NEPA's key requirement, but the early drafts of NEPA did not include it. They merely authorized a research program on environmental problems and created an advisory Council on Environmental Quality (CEQ) within the executive branch, modeled on the President's Council of Economic Advisors. NEPA's environmental impact statement requirement is largely the creation of Professor Lynton K. Caldwell, then a professor of political science at Indiana University. At Caldwell's urging, and at the urging of others, Senator Jackson added a statement of policy and later the "action-forcing" provision, requiring the preparation of an environmental impact statement (EIS). Senator Jackson endorsed the action-forcing impact statement idea, and it became part of the law.

The bill that was to become NEPA was unanimously approved by the Senate, but not before the Senate adopted two major amendments. One stated in part that NEPA would not "in any way affect the specific statutory obligations of any federal agency." This amendment, the result of a compromise between Senator Jackson and Senator Edmund Muskie, was enacted unchanged as §104. Senator Muskie was concerned that NEPA would undercut the effectiveness of air and water quality standard-setting legislation he had sponsored. The amendment was intended to prohibit federal agencies from considering under NEPA the air or water quality impacts of projects that met air and water quality standards established under Muskie's legislation.

A second important change prior to conference committee consideration deleted a requirement for an agency "finding" on environmental impact and substituted language that required a "detailed statement" on major federal actions—the environmental impact statement requirement.

The House then approved its counterpart of the Senate NEPA bill without the impact statement requirement suggested by Caldwell. The conference committee reconciled this difference by retaining the impact statement requirement but adding language requiring federal agencies to follow this procedure "to the fullest extent possible." This language was considered a compromise between the view of the House sponsor that NEPA did not change agency statutory mandates and Senator Jackson's intention to ensure across-the-board compliance by federal agencies. Although the conference report stated that NEPA's duties were "qualified" by the phrase, a statement by the House conference committee managers contended that Senator Jackson's strict view of compliance was adopted. 115 Cong. Rec. 39,703 (1969).

Both Houses hurriedly approved the conference report, with most of the debate centering on the executive reorganization required by creation of the CEQ. Few Congress members understood the import of the action-forcing provisions. See R. Andrews, Environmental Policy and Administrative Change: Implementation of the National Environmental Policy Act ch. 2 (1976), for an analysis of NEPA's legislative history.

NOTES AND QUESTIONS

1. *Alternative Strategies.* Was NEPA the only legislative strategy available to protect environmental resources? One of the authors of this casebook suggested the following three alternatives in Tarlock, *supra*, at 659:

   a. Agency decisionmakers could be required to consider additional information, including information on environmental consequences. NEPA adopted this approach.
   b. Congress could withdraw designated natural resource areas from development or give environmentally sensitive agencies a veto over development. This technique has been adopted for resource areas such as floodplains and wetlands.
   c. Agencies could be authorized to adopt environmental standards and to prohibit developments that violate these standards. Congress adopted this approach in the Clean Air and Water and the Resource Conservation and Recovery (solid and toxic wastes) Acts.

The critical student will want to contrast the environmentally sensitive decisionmaking process mandated by NEPA with the alternative techniques suggested by Professor Tarlock.

2. *Judicial Enforcement.* An early draft of the bill that became NEPA stipulated that every person had a right to a healthful environment, but this language was deleted over the objection of Senator Jackson. The earlier version of NEPA clearly would have

created an environmental interest capable of judicial enforcement. The present form of NEPA could have been a basis for courts to refuse standing to those seeking to compel an agency to comply with NEPA, but courts have, with little analysis, found that NEPA creates protected interests capable of judicial enforcement. See the *Calvert Cliffs* case, discussed below. How does the legislative history bear on the role of NEPA as compared with the three alternatives outlined by Professor Tarlock?

3. *Assumptions.* NEPA appears to have been based on a number of assumptions. One assumption, noted earlier, was that federal agency decisionmaking could be modified without revising the enabling legislation that authorizes their programs. Senator Jackson stressed this function of NEPA during congressional hearings. The second assumption, related to the first, was that environmental values are sufficiently defined and the science of ecology can provide the environmental information necessary to permit the environmental evaluations NEPA requires. See L. K. Caldwell, Environment: A Challenge to Modern Society 101-102 (1970). Consider the following, which was written soon after NEPA was enacted:

> Ecology has not yet achieved a predictive capacity to the extent that other natural sciences such as chemistry and physics have. There are few established "principles" of ecology upon which to construct a prediction. Most importantly, ecology by its very definition involves such a broad and complex number of things and interactions that adequate knowledge for practical application is very difficult to obtain. [Carpenter, The Scientific Basis of NEPA—Is It Adequate? 6 Envtl. L. Rep. (ELI) 50,014, 50,017 (1976).]

Note also that NEPA, because it contains no standards, provides no "baseline" from which the environmental impacts of an agency's action can be measured. How does this limitation affect federal agency compliance, assuming that "[e]cology has not yet achieved a predictive capacity"?

4. *CEQ.* CEQ, housed in the executive office of the president, has emerged as the primary overseer of NEPA. By executive order, President Nixon extended the responsibilities of CEQ to include the adoption of guidelines for the preparation of impact statements. Although not binding, most federal agencies relied on these guidelines when establishing their own impact statement procedures. Federal courts also gave significant weight to the guidelines. See, e.g., Greene County Planning Bd. v. FPC, 455 F.2d 412, 421 (2d Cir. 1972).

To overcome the limitations inherent in guidelines that are merely advisory, and to extend CEQ's role in administering NEPA, President Carter issued an executive order delegating authority to CEQ to issue regulations covering the entire Act, Exec. Order No. 11,990, 42 Fed. Reg. 26,967 (1997). CEQ issued regulations pursuant to the order in late 1978. For discussion of these regulations, see Fisher, The CEQ Regulations: New Stage in the Evolution of NEPA, 3 Harv. Envtl. L. Rev. 347 (1979). The only change in the regulations occurred in the Reagan administration, when CEQ modified the "worst case" analysis regulation, discussed below.

The Supreme Court has deferred to CEQ's interpretation of the statute, as in Robertson v. Methow Valley Citizens Council, 490 U.S. 332 (1989), where it deferred to CEQ's revocation of its worst case analysis regulation. Note, however, that CEQ's position in the administration of NEPA is unique. Because NEPA is a cross-cutting statute that applies only to federal agencies that have program and project responsibilities, the authority conferred on CEQ to adopt regulations may be entitled to less respect because it is independent of the authority to administer and apply the law.

CEQ's oversight of NEPA has also weakened because of reductions in budget and staff. It is no longer a three-person council and instead is headed by a chairperson.

5. *Questions about NEPA.* As you read the cases and materials that follow, you should ask yourself the following questions: What was the objective of the drafters of NEPA? Did they expect that existing mission agencies would self-destruct? If the answer to this question is obviously no, what did the drafters reasonably expect would be gained by the passage of a general charter of environmental goals coupled with what Senate staff members have admitted was an undefined concept of the action-forcing impact statement? Note that NEPA creates no general extra-agency enforcement mechanism, except the CEQ. Thus, the reader of the impact statement will be the superior of the preparers. What assumptions did the drafters make about the reader's reaction to the information contained in the impact statement? Are these assumptions sufficient to support the rule of strict compliance announced in *Calvert Cliffs*? Would the Supreme Court at that time have reversed a circuit court decision holding that NEPA creates no enforceable private rights?

One commentator has identified six issues in the debate over NEPA's purposes. Perhaps most important, "rational systems analysts wished to reform so-called incrementalist agency behavior." Second, "environmental scientists believed resources decisions were made with little or no recognition of complex ecosystem relationships or state-of-the-art scientific understanding of those relationships." Third, "[k]ey staffers and members of the Senate Interior Committee were frustrated by the absence of alternatives in agency proposals presented to Congress." Fourth, "a group of reformers in the legal community wished to counteract the power conveyed in broad delegations of rulemaking authority to administrative agencies." Fifth, "environmental and citizens group leaders championed public participation in resources policy decision processes." Finally, agencies adopted public participation programs as a means of obtaining support for their decisions. Culhane, NEPA's Impacts on Federal Agencies, Anticipated and Unanticipated, 20 Envtl. L. 681, 684-687 (1990).

2. *The* Calvert Cliffs *Decision*

It is clear that the drafters of NEPA, especially Professor Caldwell, expected Congress and the executive branch of the government, especially the Office of Management and Budget, to be the primary enforcers of NEPA. There is some evidence, as noted earlier, that some judicial enforcement was contemplated, but Congress, lawyers, bureaucrats, and environmentalists did not anticipate that NEPA would become a judicial vehicle to force agencies to consider environmental values. Some of the credit for this development can go to the federal Court of Appeals for the D.C. Circuit, which was then an activist court, and which used NEPA as one of several occasions to tell agencies how they should interpret their duties toward the public.

The first major NEPA case to reach the courts was Calvert Cliffs' Coordinating Comm., Inc. v. United States Atomic Energy Comm'n, 449 F.2d 1109 (D.C. Cir. 1971). The case considered a conflict between the Atomic Energy Commission (AEC)—later the Nuclear Regulatory Commission (NRC)—and protestors over AEC rules that limited its duty to consider environmental impacts in the licensing of nuclear power plants. The court, in a forceful decision by Judge Skelly Wright, used this occasion to consider the judicial enforceability of NEPA. Implicit in Judge Wright's decision is consideration of the Commission's contention that "the vagueness of the NEPA mandate and delegation" exempted federal agency actions under NEPA from judicial review as agency decisions "committed to agency discretion by law." The following excerpts from Judge Wright's opinion give the flavor of his response:

NEPA, first of all, makes environmental protection a part of the mandate of every federal agency and department. The Atomic Energy Commission, for example, had continually asserted, prior to NEPA, that it had no statutory authority to concern itself with the adverse environmental effects of its actions. Now, however, its hands are no longer tied. It is not only permitted, but compelled, to take environmental values into account. Perhaps the greatest importance of NEPA is to require the Atomic Energy Commission to consider environmental issues just as they consider other matters within their mandates. . . . Senator Jackson, NEPA's principal sponsor, stated that "[n]o agency will [now] be able to maintain that it has no mandate or no requirement to consider the environmental consequences of its actions." He characterized the requirements of Section 102 as "action-forcing" and stated that "[o]therwise, these lofty declarations [in Section 101] are nothing more than that."

The sort of consideration of environmental values which NEPA compels is clarified in Section 102(2)(A) and (B). In general, all agencies must use a "systematic, interdisciplinary approach" to environmental planning and evaluation "in decisionmaking which may have an impact on man's environment." In order to include all possible environmental factors in the decisional equation, agencies must "identify and develop methods and procedures . . . which will insure that presently unquantifiable environmental amenities and values may be given appropriate consideration in decisionmaking along with economic and technical considerations." To "consider" the former "along with" the latter must involve a balancing process. In some instances environmental costs may outweigh economic and technical benefits and in other instances they may not. But NEPA mandates a rather finely tuned and "systematic" balancing analysis in each instance. . . .

[T]he procedural duties of Section 102 must be fulfilled to the fullest extent possible. . . . They must be complied with to the fullest extent, unless there is a clear conflict of statutory authority. Considerations of administrative difficulty, delay or economic cost will not suffice to strip the section of its fundamental importance. . . .

We conclude, then, that Section 102 of NEPA mandates a particular sort of careful and informed decisionmaking process and creates judicially enforceable duties. The reviewing courts probably cannot reverse a substantive decision on the merits, under Section 101, unless it be shown that the actual balance of costs and benefits that was struck was arbitrary or clearly gave insufficient weight to environmental values. But if the decision was reached procedurally without individualized consideration and balancing of environmental factors—conducted fully and in good faith—it is the responsibility of the courts to reverse. As one District Court has said of Section 102 requirements: "It is hard to imagine a clearer or stronger mandate to the Courts." [449 F.2d at 1112-1115.]

NOTES AND QUESTIONS

1. Judge Wright's decision in *Calvert Cliffs* is important for its holding that agency duties under NEPA are judicially enforceable. Reread the Supreme Court's *Overton Park* decision, reproduced in section 3.A.2.c above, which declined to apply the "committed to agency discretion" exemption to a somewhat different environmental statute. Does *Overton Park* support Judge Wright's holding on this point? Note that

an agency's compliance with NEPA is judicially reviewable even though its actions under its enabling legislation may be "committed to agency discretion." See Schiffler v. Schlesinger, 548 F.2d 96 (3d Cir. 1977).

Calvert Cliffs is also important for its interpretation of NEPA's statutory mandate. Judge Wright discusses the "procedural" duties imposed by NEPA. What are they? Do they refer to the duty to prepare an impact statement when one is required or to the rules courts are to apply when they determine whether an impact statement is adequate?

Judge Wright's dictum that NEPA requires a "balancing process" attracted much attention and suggested that NEPA imposes substantive responsibilities that courts can enforce. The courts since have not really required "balancing," and the Supreme Court has not found a substantive requirement in NEPA. This issue is discussed below.

2. *Independent NEPA Review.* Another issue the court considered in *Calvert Cliffs* was whether NEPA required the AEC to consider the water quality impacts of nuclear power plants. In brief, AEC interpreted the Muskie-Jackson compromise to allow it merely to incorporate water quality standards adopted by EPA into its license. The court adopted the argument of protestors, who argued that NEPA required an independent evaluation of water quality impacts above and beyond compliance with EPA-approved water quality standards. Congress overruled this part of the *Calvert Cliffs* decision in subsequent amendments to the Clean Water Act. See §511(c)(2), 33 U.S.C. §1371(c)(2).

3. *NEPA Today.* The *Calvert Cliffs* decision came in the early days of NEPA, when the statute had taken agencies by surprise and they were still struggling to interpret the statute and often resisted compliance with its requirements. Agencies today are more mature, and their NEPA documents are usually a good faith attempt to comply with the statute. For this reason the role of the courts is quite different, and the issue may be a disconnect between the environmental data and an agency's refusal to listen, rather than an attempt to avoid statutory environmental disclosure obligations. For a case in which the disconnect problem led to invalidation of an impact statement for a major west side highway along the Hudson River in New York City, see Sierra Club v. United States Army Corps of Eng'rs (I), 701 F.2d 1011 (2d Cir. 1983). The district court found, for example, "that the FEIS contained false statements depicting the interpier region as 'biologically impoverished' and as a 'biological wasteland,' when in fact the interpier area in winter harbored a concentration of juvenile striped bass." The highway was eventually abandoned. The case and its sequel are discussed in section D.1, below.

B.   THRESHOLD ISSUES: MUST AN IMPACT STATEMENT BE PREPARED?

Figure 4-1 provides a typical breakdown of the kinds of causes of action brought in NEPA cases. The first issue to consider under NEPA is what the courts have come to call the threshold issue: whether an environmental impact statement must be prepared at all. Courts asked to decide the threshold issue must consider questions of interpretation raised by NEPA's somewhat vague language in §102(2)(C), which

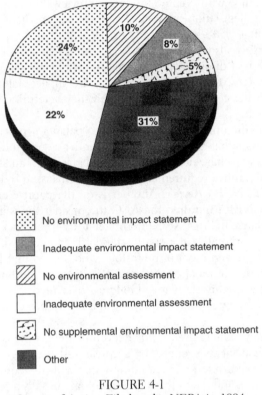

No environmental impact statement

Inadequate environmental impact statement

No environmental assessment

Inadequate environmental assessment

No supplemental environmental impact statement

Other

FIGURE 4-1
Causes of Action Filed under NEPA in 1994.

Source: Eccleston, The NEPA Planning Process: A Comprehensive Guide with Emphasis on Efficiency (1999). John Wiley and Sons, Inc., Figure C.8, p. 383. Reprinted with permission of John Wiley & Sons, Inc. Copyright © 1999.

requires an impact statement on "major federal actions significantly affecting the quality of the human environment." The materials that follow examine the meaning of these statutory terms as they govern the duty of federal agencies to prepare environmental impact statements.

Categorical Exclusions. This is an option, provided by CEQ regulations, that allows agencies to opt out of NEPA by excluding actions they believe are not covered by NEPA. CEQ regulations define a categorical exclusion, known as a CATX, as "a category of actions which do not individually or cumulatively have a significant effect on the human environment." 40 C.F.R. §1508.4. Federal agencies have adopted lists of actions they consider to be exempt as categorical exclusions. Agencies can also make decisions on categorical exclusions on much less documentation than when they prepare an impact statement, an approach CEQ has encouraged, but some agencies provide substantial documentation at this stage as a protective measure.

Agencies typically classify minor actions that are not expected to have significant environmental effects as categorical exclusions, and courts uphold these decisions if they are not arbitrary. See, e.g., Bicycle Trails of Marin v. Babbitt, 82 F.3d 1445 (9th Cir. 1996) (closing off-road areas in national parks to bicycle use). Unfortunately, the regulations create confusion because the criteria for adopting a categorical exclusion are similar to the criteria agencies must use when they decide whether to prepare an impact statement.

CEQ regulations also provide that an agency may not designate an action as a CATX if there are "extraordinary circumstances in which a normally excluded action may have a significant environmental effect." 40 C.F.R. §1508.4. Judicial challenges to a CATX often argue this exception to claim a CATX has improperly been made. See, e.g., Wilderness Watch v. Mainella, 375 F.3d 1085 (11th Cir. 2004) (decision to transport busloads of tourists through wilderness area not eligible as CATX for "routine and continuing government business").

Categorical exclusions have received a lot of attention because agencies see them as a way of escaping NEPA entirely. Following a task force report on NEPA implementation CEQ issued a detailed guidance on how a CATX should be designated. 74 Fed. Reg. 54,816 (2006) (requesting comments). Congress has also acted. In several statutes it expanded agency opportunities to adopt a CATX. In the Energy Policy Act of 2005, for example, it created a rebuttable presumption that certain oil or gas exploration and development activities qualify as a CATX. 42 U.S.C. §15942. The transportation act of 2005 authorizes the Department of Transportation to assign to a state the decision to designate a CATX under criteria established by the Department. 23 U.S.C. §326(a)(1). These statutes regressively entrust decisions on CATXs to "mission" agencies.

Environmental Assessments. If an agency decides an action is not categorically excluded, it may decide to prepare an impact statement or, as an alternative, conduct an environmental assessment to determine whether an impact statement is necessary. An environmental assessment is a "concise public document" which is to "[b]riefly provide sufficient analysis and evidence for determining" whether the agency should prepare an impact statement or make a Finding of No Significant Impact (FONSI) as the basis for a decision that an impact statement is not necessary. 40 C.F.R. §1508.9. See Figure 4-2. A FONSI is a document "briefly presenting the reasons" an impact statement is not necessary. 40 C.F.R. §1508.13. A FONSI is an example of informal agency decisionmaking. Note the importance of the FONSI. It allows the agency to escape the statute unless reversed in court.

An environmental assessment is to contain brief discussions of the need for the proposed action, alternatives to the proposed action, the environmental impacts of the proposed action and any alternatives, and a list of agencies and persons consulted during the assessment process. Id. Both short-term and long-term effects are relevant to a determination of significance. The regulations do not mandate public review of an environmental assessment, but the agency must include the public, any applicants, and other federal agencies in the environmental assessment process to the extent practicable. 40 C.F.R. §1501.4(b). Courts disagree on whether an EA must be put out for comment. See Defenders of Wildlife v. Hogarth, 330 F.3d 1358 (Fed. Cir. 2003) (public notice required). The environmental review process most often terminates without an impact statement being filed. Ten EAs are usually prepared by federal agencies for every EIS.

Comparison with the EIS. The Fifth Circuit has explained the difference between an EA and an EIS:

> An EIS must contain "a detailed statement of the expected adverse consequences of an action, the resource commitments involved in it, and the alternatives to it." An EA, on the other hand, is prepared in order to determine whether an EIS is required. An EA is a rough-cut, "low budget environmental impact statement" intended to determine

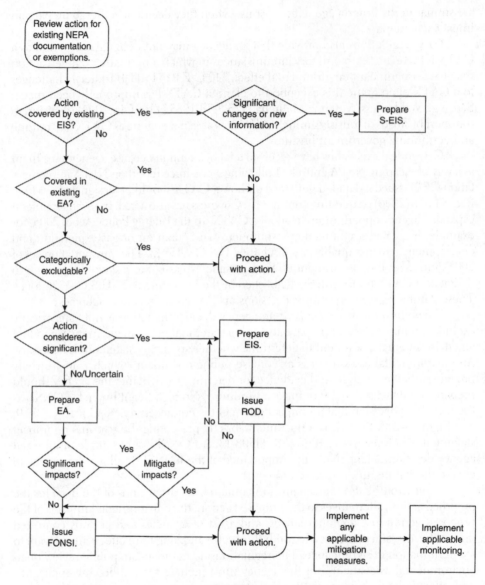

FIGURE 4-2

Eccleston, The NEPA Planning Process: A Comprehensive Guide with Emphasis on Efficiency (1999). John Wiley and Sons, Inc., Figure 2.1, p. 52. Reprinted with permission of John Wiley & Sons, Inc. Copyright © 1999.

whether effects are significant enough to warrant preparation of an EIS. An EA must include "brief discussions of the need for the proposal, of alternatives . . . , of the impacts of proposed action and alternatives, and a listing of agencies and persons consulted." 40 C.F.R. §1508.9(b). [Sierra Club v. Espy, 38 F.3d 792, 802-803 (5th Cir. 1994)].

The following problem will introduce you to the legal problems raised by NEPA, including the threshold environmental assessment issue. Transportation and highway projects make up one of the most numerous project groups that are subject to NEPA.

Problem 4-1

The state Department of Transportation has had a major limited-access highway connector, called the Outstate Connector, in the planning stages for over 20 years. A corridor map adopted by the Department shows the general location of the connector on the state's long-range transportation plan. The connector will go from Metro City, the capital city of the state, to River Junction, a smaller city. The hope is that building the new highway will open up economic opportunities in River Junction and in the area between that city and the capital.

The state has used federal funding to conduct preliminary planning and engineering studies for the Outstate Connector. To help with planning, the state Department of Transportation divided the highway into three segments. The first segment goes from the capital to an intersection with Interstate Highway 54, about 20 miles away. This segment crosses high-quality agricultural land. The second segment goes from this intersection another 50 miles to Wildlake, a small resort town. This segment crosses a major wildlife preserve, and bridges over the preserve are necessary at some points. The third and final segment goes from Wildlake another 100 miles to River Junction. This segment crosses numerous wetlands.

The Department has issued a FONSI on the first segment of the Outstate Connector based on an environmental assessment that the segment will not have significant environmental impacts. The environmental assessment considered a number of alternatives, including a "no-action" alternative and alternatives that would modify the design of the project but not its location. The Department has adopted the second segment as part of the state highway system, but does not plan to submit it to the Federal Highway Administration (FHWA) or to do an environmental assessment of this part of the highway. The status of the third segment is uncertain at this time.

An environmental organization, Save Our State (SOS), has opposed the Outstate Connector for some time. It especially opposes segments two and three because of the impact they will have on natural resource lands, and has suggested a number of alternatives. One alternative is an alternative route that would avoid prime agricultural and other natural resource lands. Another alternative would abandon the highway altogether in favor of a new rail line to River Junction.

As counsel to SOS, what would you advise? Would you advise litigation challenging the FONSI on the first segment? Would you include the other two segments in this lawsuit? If so, how? On what basis would you challenge the conclusion that the environmental effects of the connector are not significant? The failure to consider additional alternatives? As counsel to the Department of Transportation, what defenses would you suggest if this suit is brought?

1.   Is It Federal?

The first inquiry is whether an action that is claimed to need an impact statement is federal. Activities that federal agencies carry out, such as federal construction projects, are clearly federal. Federal agency decisions on projects carried out by private entities fall within NEPA as "federal" actions if there is the necessary federal nexus. An example is a federal permit for a project in wetlands. Projects carried out by state and local governments can also fall within NEPA as "federal" action if funded by federal assistance or if there is federal control or supervision. 40 C.F.R. §1508.18. See generally D. Mandelker, NEPA Law & Litigation §§8:18-8:22 (2d ed. 1992 & annual supplements).

Categories of Federal Actions. CEQ regulations do not define federal actions, but indicate the categories in which these actions "tend to fall." 40 C.F.R. §1508.18(b). These categories include:

1. The adoption of official policies, such as rules and regulations.
2. The adoption of "formal plans . . . which guide or prescribe alternative uses of federal resources, upon which future agency actions will be based."
3. The adoption of "programs, such as a group of concerted actions to implement a specific policy or plan" or "allocating agency resources to implement" a statutory program or executive directive.
4. The approval of specific projects such as "actions approved by permit or other regulatory decision as well as federal and federally assisted activities."

Can you think of examples that fit each of these categories? Federal approval can be minimal.

Projects Funded by Federal Assistance. Under the traditional federal assistance format, a state or local agency submits and the federal agency approves a specific project. NEPA clearly applies when a federal agency approves project assistance, but funding for preliminary studies is not usually enough because there is no final action. Macht v. Skinner, 916 F.2d 13 (D.C. Cir. 1990). Congress in recent years has adopted a new form of block grant assistance. In block grant programs, federal assistance is made available to states and local governments to use for a number of related programs in their discretion. Congress sometimes requires compliance with NEPA in block grant programs. See, e.g., Housing and Community Development Act of 1974, 42 U.S.C. §5304(g).

Whether NEPA applies if not expressly made applicable depends on the program and the extent of the federal commitment. In one case a court did not require an EIS on the construction of a new prison not funded with federal assistance. It rejected a claim that an EIS was required because the federal government provided general support for the state prison system. Citizens for a Better St. Clair County v. James, 648 F.2d 246 (5th Cir. 1981).

Federal Approvals, Permits, and Control. Federal permits and approvals, such as permits for development in wetlands, bring a proposed action under NEPA even if the project is to be carried out by a private or nonfederal entity:

> [T]here is "Federal action" within the meaning of the statute not only when an agency proposes to build a facility itself, but also whenever an agency makes a decision which permits action by other parties which will affect the quality of the environment. NEPA's impact statement procedure has been held to apply where a federal agency approves a lease of land to private parties, grants licenses and permits to private parties, or approves and funds state highway projects. In each of these instances the federal agency took action affecting the environment in the sense that the agency made a decision which permitted

some other party—private or governmental—to take action affecting the environment. [Scientists' Inst. for Pub. Info., Inc. v. AEC (SIPI), 481 F.2d 1079, 1088-1089 (D.C. Cir. 1973).]

The "Small Handle" Problem. In another class of cases, there may be a federal link with a private or governmental project, but it may not be sufficient in magnitude to bring the project within NEPA's requirements. These cases raise what is known as the "small handle" problem. For example, in Winnebago Tribe v. Ray, 621 F.2d 269 (8th Cir. 1980), a power company proposed to construct a 67-mile transmission line. The line required a permit from the U.S. Army Corps of Engineers for a 1.25-mile segment that crossed the Missouri River. An environmental assessment prepared by the Corps considered only the environmental impacts of the river crossing. The court rejected a "but for" argument by the tribe that NEPA applied to the entire transmission line because the line could not be constructed without the river crossing permit. Contra Colorado River Indian Tribes v. Marsh, 605 F. Supp. 1425 (C.D. Cal. 1985) (NEPA applies to 156-acre development project when the only federal action was a federal permit that was required for rip-rap to stabilize a river bank). Is this case consistent with *Winnebago Tribe*? See also 40 C.F.R. §1508.18.

State and local projects can also present this problem. In Maryland Conservation Council v. Gilchrist, 808 F.2d 1039 (4th Cir. 1986), the court held a state-funded highway project federalized. "[b]ecause of the inevitability of the need for at least one federal approval" allowing the highway to cross a park. See also Sierra Club v. Hodel, 848 F.2d 1068 (10th Cir. 1988) (Bureau of Land Management's approval of a county road improvement in a wilderness study area held federal because the Bureau had a duty to see that the improvements did not degrade the study area). Applying a narrower test, Southwest Williamson Cmty. Ass'n v. Slater, 243 F.3d 270 (6th Cir. 2001), found federal control insufficient when the federal agency had control over highway interchanges but not a connecting corridor. The court held the federal agency must be able to influence the outcome of a project through sufficient control and responsibility.

How important is it to extend NEPA to marginal situations? Is there a danger that the environmental mandate of the statute will be weakened through overextension? Consider, if you are inclined to narrow NEPA's reach, that a strict reading might exempt a series of small federal actions in a region even though their cumulative impact is significant. Does the policy underlying NEPA's enactment suggest a "cumulative federal impact" theory as the basis for applying the statute? Is this problem handled by the program impact statement requirement, discussed below? See Fitzgerald, Comment, Small Handles, Big Impacts: When Should the National Environmental Policy Act Require an Environmental Impact Statement?, 23 B.C. Envtl. Aff. L. Rev. 437 (1996).

2.   *Is It a Federal Action?*

Timing. An important problem involves determining whether a federal action has occurred. Section 102(2)(C) of NEPA requires an impact statement on "every recommendation or report on proposals for . . . major federal actions." The Supreme Court has emphasized the "proposal" requirement: "The committee report [on NEPA] made clear that the impact statement was required in conjunction with specific proposals for action." Kleppe v. Sierra Club, 427 U.S. 390, 401 n.12

(1976). The questions that arise are how specific a proposal must be, and when in the agency's decisionmaking process a proposal occurs that is subject to the impact statement requirement. CEQ has ambiguously defined a "proposal" as "that stage in the development of an action when an agency subject to the Act has a goal and is actively preparing to make a decision on one or more alternative means of accomplishing that goal and the effects can be meaningfully evaluated." 40 C.F.R. §1508.23. The *Kleppe* case is reproduced below, where the proposal requirement is discussed.

Nondiscretionary Actions. The courts have concluded that NEPA does not apply if agency action is nondiscretionary. In an early leading case, South Dakota v. Andrus, 614 F.2d 1190 (8th Cir. 1980), the court held NEPA did not apply to the Department of Interior's decision to issue a mineral patent for mining claims in a national forest. Reasoning that the primary purpose of NEPA is to aid agency decisionmaking, the court held the statute did not apply to ministerial acts. See also Citizens Against Rails-to-Trails v. Surface Transp. Bd., 267 F.3d 1144 (D.C. Cir. 2001) (issuance of Certificate of Interim Trail Use held ministerial).

The Supreme Court considered this problem in Department of Transportation v. Pub. Citizen, 541 U.S. 742 (2004). After the president lifted a moratorium on the operation of Mexican trucks in the United States, the Federal Motor Carrier Safety Administration (FMCSA) adopted regulations allowing Mexican trucks to operate. FMCSA prepared an environmental assessment on the regulations on the environmental effects of safety inspections of Mexican trucks in the United States. It did not consider the environmental effects of additional trade volume with Mexico because it concluded that any such increase would result from the president's lifting of the moratorium, not from the adoption of the regulations.

The Court held the agency did not have to consider the environmental effect of an increase in Mexican truck operations resulting from the adoption of the regulations. Plaintiff argued that the adoption of the regulations would "cause" an increase in truck volume as a reasonably foreseeable effect because the congressional rider prohibited the issuance of permits until the regulations were adopted. The Court rejected this argument because the agency had no authority to prevent the entry of Mexican trucks. It was required by statute to issue permits when applicants complied with statutory safety and financial responsibility requirements.

Inaction. Whether an impact statement is required for federal agency inaction presents another controversial issue. Consider the following problem: Although the states have primary authority for the management of wildlife on federal lands, the Department of the Interior "may" designate areas where no hunting is permitted. The state of Alaska decided to order a wolf kill in a substantial area of its federal lands. When requested to intervene, the Department refused to act and also refused to file an impact statement on its decision. Suit was then brought to require the preparation of an impact statement.

In Defenders of Wildlife v. Andrus, 627 F.2d 1238 (D.C. Cir. 1980), the court held that the Department's failure to act was federal "inaction" for which no impact statement was required. The court believed that because the federal statute did not compel the Department to act, it had no obligation to prepare an impact statement on its failure to act in a particular instance. As the court explained, "in no published opinion of which we have been made aware has a court held that there is 'federal action' where an agency has done nothing more than fail to prevent the other party's action from occurring." Id. at 1244. See also Aircraft Owners & Pilots Ass'n v. Hinson, 102 F.3d 1421 (7th Cir. 1996) (failure to enforce debatable legal claim to prevent closing of airport held inaction not subject to statute).

The inaction problem also arises when agencies are given statutory responsibilities they fail to carry out. In Norton v. Southern Utah Wilderness Alliance, 542 U.S. 55 (2004), reproduced in section 3.A.2.c, the Court held that NEPA does not apply to an agency's neglect of its statutory duties when it is other than a deliberate decision not to act. The Federal Land Policy and Management Act places a duty on the Secretary of Interior to manage federal lands identified as potential wilderness areas "so as not to impair the suitability of such areas for preservation as wilderness" while they are under review for designation and until Congress has determined otherwise. The Court held an action for judicial review under the Administrative Procedure Act did not lie for the agency's failure to carry out its statutory mandate to preserve potential wilderness areas from impairment. Though the Act defines an agency action subject to judicial review to include a "failure to act," the Court held the agency's refusal to carry out this statutory mandate was not judicially reviewable.

How should these issues be resolved? Federal agencies necessarily engage in a decisionmaking process in which they determine whether to take or authorize action that may have an environmental impact. If the agency decides not to undertake or authorize a project, has it necessarily engaged in "inaction" not subject to NEPA? See Fergenson, The Sin of Omission: Inaction as Action under Section 102(2)(C) of the National Environmental Policy Act of 1969, 53 Ind. L.J. 497 (1978).

3.   Is It a Major Federal Action Significantly Affecting the Environment?

An agency proposal may be an action sufficient to qualify under NEPA but may not be sufficiently "major" or "significant" to qualify under the statute. Many federal or federally authorized projects, such as federal dams or nuclear power plants, are sufficiently "major" to qualify under the statute. Indeed, CEQ regulations state that the word "major" "reinforces but does not have a meaning independent of significant." 40 C.F.R. §1508.18.

The "significance" requirement is more frequently contested and serves an important function under NEPA. It imposes a threshold test of environmental impact that must be met before a federal agency is required to prepare an impact statement on a major federal action. Objectors can challenge an agency finding of no significance, which is based on a FONSI, in court. A typical case follows.

ENVIRONMENTAL PROTECTION INFORMATION CENTER v. UNITED STATES FOREST SERVICE
451 F.3d 1005 (9th Cir. 2006)

HAWKINS, Circuit Judge:

The Environmental Protection Information Center ("EPIC") appeals from the district court's summary judgment in favor of the United States Forest Service

("USFS"). EPIC challenges USFS's failure to prepare an Environmental Impact Statement ("EIS") in connection with the proposed Knob Timber Sale in the Klamath National Forest and further argues that the Environmental Assessment ("EA") USFS did prepare was inadequate. EPIC also contends that the project violates the National Forest Management Act ("NFMA"). We affirm. [Only the discussion of the NEPA claim is reproduced.]

Facts and Procedural History

The Knob Timber Sale (the "Project") is a vegetation management project affecting the Salmon River Ranger District of the Klamath National Forest. The Project provides for harvesting timber from approximately 578 acres, scattered among twenty-seven units throughout the forest. The stated purpose of the Project "is to maintain stand health by leading stands into a resilient condition where they can provide a sustained yield of wood products and reduce their risk to potential catastrophic fire."

USFS issued an EA for the Project in October 2002. In preparing the EA, USFS relied on a number of documents, reports and studies, including biological assessments prepared by the National Marine Fisheries Service and the U.S. Fish and Wildlife Service ("FWS") in formal consultations required by Section 7 of the Endangered Species Act ("ESA"). The final EA identified and discussed in detail two key issues: (1) the Project's effect on the "critical habitat" of the northern spotted owl and (2) watershed effects, in which timber harvest, fuel reduction and road activities could potentially cause soil erosion or trigger slope failure, increasing sediment in streams.

Soon thereafter, USFS issued a decision notice and Finding of No Significant Impact ("FONSI") selecting the proposed action alternative. USFS explained that this alternative had the best potential to achieve the Project's purposes and that it would have long-term beneficial effects for the northern spotted owl and watershed health, with only minor or negligible short-term adverse effects.

EPIC filed suit in the district court, arguing that, under the National Environmental Policy Act ("NEPA"), USFS should have prepared a full EIS instead of an EA, and that the EA itself was inadequate. . . .

Standard of Review

We review the district court's grant of summary judgment de novo. Agency decisions that allegedly violate NEPA and NFMA are reviewed under the Administrative Procedure Act ("APA"), and may be set aside only if they are "arbitrary, capricious, an abuse of discretion, or otherwise not in accordance with law." [5 U.S.C. §706(2)(A).]

In reviewing an agency's decision not to prepare an EIS under NEPA, we employ an arbitrary and capricious standard that requires us to determine whether the agency has taken a "hard look" at the consequences of its actions, "based [its decision] on a consideration of the relevant factors," and provided a "convincing statement of reasons to explain why a project's impacts are insignificant." National Parks & Conservation Ass'n v. Babbitt, 241 F.3d 722, 730 (9th Cir. 2001).

Discussion

I. NEPA CLAIMS

A. STATUTORY BACKGROUND

An EIS is required for "major Federal actions significantly affecting the quality of the human environment. . . ." 42 U.S.C. §4332(2)(C). The agency first prepares an EA to determine whether an action will have a significant impact, thus requiring preparation of an EIS. 40 C.F.R.§1508.9. If the agency concludes there is no significant effect associated with the proposed project, it may issue a FONSI in lieu of preparing an EIS. 40 C.F.R. §1508.9(a)(1).

The critical term here is "significantly." Whether a project is "significant" depends on the project's "context" and its "intensity." 40 C.F.R. §1508.27. Context refers to the scope of the action, while intensity refers to the severity of the impact. The regulations include a list of ten intensity factors, four of which EPIC argues are applicable in this case:

> (1) Impacts that may be both beneficial and adverse. A significant effect may exist even if the Federal agency believes that on balance the effect will be beneficial.
> (5) The degree to which the possible effects on the human environment are highly uncertain or involve unique or unknown risks. . . .
> (7) Whether the action is related to other actions with individually insignificant but cumulatively significant impacts.
> (9) The degree to which the action may adversely affect an endangered or threatened species or its habitat that has been determined to be critical under the Endangered Species Act of 1973.

Id. at §1508.27(b). . . . [The discussion of only some of the objections to the EA are reproduced here.]

B. HARM TO THE NORTHERN SPOTTED OWL AND ITS CRITICAL HABITAT

One of EPIC's primary arguments is that the Project will harm the northern spotted owl, a threatened species, and its habitat that has been designated "critical habitat" under the ESA. To resolve EPIC's contentions, it is useful to examine the backdrop of the debate and the specific Project parameters. . . . [The owl was listed as an endangered species, critical habitat designated, and a Northwest Forest Plan (NFP) prepared.]

The NFP withdrew 8.8 million acres from potential timber harvesting, and designated approximately 7.4 million acres of forest land as "late successional reserves" ("LSRs"). LSRs overlap with about 70% of the owl's previously-defined critical habitat and are also generally off-limits to timber harvest, although thinning, salvage, and research activities are permitted under certain conditions. The remaining approximately 5.5 million acres were designated "matrix" lands or "adaptive management areas," and are potentially available for timber production, subject to standards in the NFP.

The Project involves logging on 578 acres scattered throughout the Klamath National Forest. Of this, 125 acres has been designated as "critical habitat" for the spotted owl. All of this critical habitat is outside the LSR and is thus in the "matrix" where timber production is permitted. However, within this 125 acres, only fourteen acres of nesting habitat would actually be removed (five acres from one unit and nine from another). In the third critical habitat unit, fifty-one acres of "high" quality nesting habitat would be degraded to "moderate" quality. The remaining sixty acres within the three critical habitat units is not considered suitable for nesting and roosting but is suitable for dispersal; according to the USFS EA and the FWS Biological Opinion ("BiOp"), all of the habitat units will maintain this dispersal function post-harvest.

1. Harm to the Species

Against this backdrop, EPIC alleges that a full EIS should have been performed or, alternatively, that the analysis of the issue in the EA is inadequate. The Project, EPIC asserts, is likely to affect the northern spotted owl and its critical habitat significantly. EPIC points to portions of the FWS BiOp in which the BiOp notes that "three nest sites could be destroyed" and that the logging will remove "most, if not all, of the small amount of existing nesting habitat" within the critical habitat units. [The BiOP is the Fish & Wildlife Service Biological Opinion on the owl issued under the ESA.]

These statements, however, must be read in context. For example, although the logging will remove existing nesting habitat from two critical habitat units, this amounts to a total of only fourteen acres. Similarly, the Project does not authorize the destruction of any existing nest sites, and surveys and seasonal restrictions operate to protect potentially occupied nest sites. The projected take of three nests or pairs of owls is based on extrapolations from nesting data, and FWS determined that this level of anticipated take was permissible under the ESA.

NEPA regulations direct the agency to consider the degree of adverse effect on a species, not the impact on individuals of that species. *See* Native Ecosystems [v. United States Forest Serv., 428 F.3d 1233,1240 (9th Cir. 2005)] ("[I]t does not follow that the presence of some negative effects necessarily rises to the level of demonstrating a significant effect on the environment."); see also Greater Yellowstone Coalition v. Flowers, 359 F.3d 1257, 1276 (10th Cir. 2004) ("[I]ssuance of an incidental take statement 'anticipating' the loss of some members of a threatened species does not automatically lead to the requirement to prepare a full EIS."). It was not arbitrary and capricious for USFS to determine that although there will be some effect on individual pairs, this will not cause a significant adverse effect on the species and require an EIS.

2. Uncertainty

Next, EPIC argues that an EIS was required because the effects on the spotted owl are too uncertain. EPIC focuses on a statement within the FWS BiOp in which FWS, after analyzing the Project's likely effects based on historic distributions of the spotted owl, notes that if activity centers and home ranges have changed, the effects may be distributed differently but cannot be "accurately described" without additional information. But EPIC fails to recite the remainder of the paragraph, in which FWS goes on to say:

> However, even if owl activity centers have changed in recent years, it is reasonable to assume that the density of owls in the project area should be roughly constant. . . . Therefore, the magnitude of the overall effect of habitat removal in home ranges and

core areas by the [Project] should not be substantially different from that estimated above.

Moreover, as this court has recently pointed out, the regulations do not antic- ipate the need for an EIS anytime there is *some* uncertainty, but only if the effects of the project are "highly" uncertain. See *Native Ecosystems,* 428 F.3d at 1240 ("Simply because a challenger can cherry pick information and data out of the administrative record to support its position does not mean that a project is highly controversial or highly uncertain."); see also 40 C.F.R. §1508.27(b)(5).

3. Increased Fire Risk in Critical Habitat

EPIC also alleges that the EA fails to disclose a concern of increased fire risk within critical habitat unit CA-22. However, the EA specifically acknowledges that in each critical habitat area, short-term fuel loading increases will occur but long-term loading will be reduced. It also recognizes that because fire risk is already low in CA-22, the overall benefit in this particular unit would be "minimal." USFS ultimately concludes that the proposed Project is still preferable to the no-action alternative because, without action, fuel loading would increase in the stand over the next five to ten years. The EA thus contains adequate disclosure of the risk and a reasoned evaluation of it, and does not reveal the need for an EIS on this ground. . . .

5. Reliance on FWS's "No Jeopardy" Opinion

EPIC also complains that USFS improperly relied on FWS's opinion that the Project would not "jeopardize" the northern spotted owl. EPIC argues that even if the Project does not violate the ESA by threatening the continued existence of a species, an EIS is still required if the Project "may adversely affect" the species. Clearly, NEPA and the ESA involve different standards, but this does not require USFS to disregard the findings made by FWS in connection with formal consultation mandated by the ESA. See, e.g., 40 C.F.R. §§1502.21, 1502.24.

Moreover, USFS did not rely solely on the "no jeopardy" conclusion, but on all of the analysis contained in the BiOp, as well as numerous other sources of informa- tion. In light of this information, USFS concluded in its FONSI that "[w]hile the Selected Alternative may affect habitat and has the potential to affect individual northern spotted owls, it will not be significant under [NEPA]." Although EPIC seems to urge that *any* impact to a listed species requires an EIS, USFS correctly argues that the regulation's "intensity" factor focuses on the "*degree* to which an action may adversely affect" a threatened species or critical habitat. See *Native Ecosystems,* 428 F.3d at 1240 (rejecting need for EIS despite FONSI's acknowledgment of pro- ject's impact on individual goshawks and their habitat, where USFS concluded impact on the species was not significant). . . .

C. IMPACTS TO WATERSHED

1. Uncertainty

EPIC contends that an EIS was also necessary because the Project is likely to have significant, short-term adverse impacts on the watershed and because the impacts are "uncertain." EPIC's allegation of "uncertainty" is based on the EA's use of the term "immeasurable" to describe increases in cumulative watershed effects. However, read in the proper context, this term reflects not uncertainty in projecting effects, but USFS's conclusion that any effects would be so negligible that they could not be measured: "These increases would be immeasurable and not likely to adversely affect water quality, anadromous fish habitat or species."

2. Short-Term Adverse Effects

EPIC also alleges that the EA's analysis of watershed impacts does not provide the "hard look" required by NEPA, that the agency did not use high-quality information, and that the agency focused disproportionately on the long-term benefits of the Project. Although EPIC alleges that the EA contains "very limited actual analysis of watershed impacts," in fact the EA contains fifteen pages devoted to the watershed issue, describing the existing status of the watershed and the projected impacts of the Project, and including precautions and methods that would be utilized to minimize impacts.

Although "[s]ignificance cannot be avoided by terming an action temporary," 40 C.F.R. §1508.27(b)(7), an adverse effect still must be significant to require an EIS. The EA does not ignore short-term adverse effects resulting from the Project. The EA addresses such effects throughout the analysis, concluding that both direct and indirect short-term effects will be "minor" or "negligible" for at least seven different, detailed reasons, including various protective measures incorporated into the Project parameters and the small and widely-dispersed nature of the areas affected. Although the EA expects beneficial long-term effects from the Project, it contains a reasoned evaluation of the short-term adverse impacts. Because these impacts are expected to be only "minor" or "negligible," an EIS was not required. . . .

E. RELIANCE ON MITIGATION MEASURES

EPIC also criticizes USFS's reliance on mitigation measures to downplay the adverse effects of the Project. It argues that the EA provides no data supporting the efficacy of its mitigation measures. *See National Parks,* 241 F.3d at 733-35 (EIS required where effectiveness of proposed mitigation measures was too uncertain).

This case differs from *National Parks,* however, because instead of analyzing potential impacts of a proposed action and then developing a plan to mitigate those adverse effects, the Project incorporates mitigation measures throughout the plan of action, so that the effects are analyzed with those measures in place. Thus, it cannot be said that the EA fails to analyze the effects of the mitigation measures; instead, the EA analyzes the Project under the enumerated constraints and concludes that any environmental impacts will not be significant.

The EA also contains very specific and detailed information on the ways that the timber harvest will be conducted in order to minimize effects on wildlife or watershed. In addition to these specifically identified measures, the EA also cross-references applicable Best Management Practices ("BMPs"), attached in an appendix, which are also quite detailed. Compare *wetlands* Action Network v. U.S. Army Corps of Eng'rs, 222 F.3d 1105, 1121 (9th Cir. 2000) (upholding mitigation measures where special permit conditions were "extremely detailed," even though all details of mitigation plan were not yet finalized) with Neighbors of Cuddy Mountain v. USFS, 137 F.3d 1372, 1380 (9th Cir. 1998) (holding that "perfunctory description" of mitigation measures was inadequate). The EA also explains that there will be concurrent monitoring of the implementation and effectiveness of these BMPs to aid in timely identification of threats and the need for preventative measures or project modifications. See Okanogan Highlands Alliance v. Williams, 236 F.3d 468, 476 (9th Cir. 2000) (upholding discussion of mitigation measures in an EIS where document provides methods for ensuring environmental problems do not develop).

In short, given the specificity of the protection measures, the analysis of the environmental impacts with these measures in place, and the provision for ongoing monitoring to ensure compliance, USFS has taken the requisite "hard look" at the Project's environmental consequences, and it was not arbitrary and capricious for it to determine that the impacts would not be significant with these mitigation measures in place. . . .

G. SHORT-TERM INCREASED FIRE RISK

EPIC further asserts that the EA contains inadequate disclosures about short-term increases in fire risk and that the EA does not demonstrate that the Project will meet the goal of reducing overall fire risk. In addition to the discussion noted above regarding fire risk within spotted owl critical habitat, the EA also contains a general section regarding fire risk and clearly discloses both the risk and the steps that will be taken to minimize that risk.

In a similar vein, EPIC contends USFS violated NEPA by failing to document that the Project will meet its stated purpose—i.e., reducing the risk of stand-replacing fires. EPIC asserts that USFS failed to address the "body of scientific literature that directly disputes Defendant's allegations that commercial logging in mature stands will decrease fire danger." USFS responds that all project logging will be accompanied by fuel treatment, citing studies that have, in the agency's view, shown thinning combined with prescribed fire/fuels treatment has yielded the best results in preventing catastrophic wildfires. When specialists express conflicting views, we defer to the informed discretion of the agency. See Earth Island Institute v. USFS, 442 F.3d 1147, 1160 (9th Cir. 2006).

Thus, we conclude that the EA adequately discloses and discusses the short-term increase of fire risk, and USFS's conclusion that the Project will meet the goal of long-term risk reduction is not arbitrary or capricious. . . .

Conclusion

While the Project will have at least some short-term adverse effects on the environment, the question is to what degree. Unfortunately, EPIC "seeks to capitalize on the Forest Service's thorough and candid environmental analysis by seizing on various bits of information and data . . . to claim that substantial questions exist as to whether the [Project] may have a significant effect on the environment." See *Native Ecosystems*, 428 F.3d at 1240. We find that the EA provided detailed and adequate consideration of information from a wide range of sources, and that USFS's conclusion that the adverse effects would not be "significant" with the meaning of NEPA was not arbitrary and capricious. We affirm the district court's grant of summary judgment on the NEPA claims. . . .

NOTES AND QUESTIONS

1. *Winning and Losing.* A count of the cases indicates federal agencies are more likely to win than to lose a case challenging a finding of no significance, despite the importance of the threshold decision. See the litigation survey on the CEQ website, http://www.NEPA.gov. The principal case is a typical case affirming a finding of no significance, and showing that when an agency conducts a comprehensive and thorough study of the environmental impacts of its action and decides an EIS is not necessary, a court is likely to agree. Earth Protector, Inc. v. Jacobs, 993 F. Supp. 701 (D. Minn. 2001), held an EIS was not necessary on a timber sale in a national forest and stressed the importance of comprehensive study:

> The administrative record of the Forest Service's decisionmaking process is voluminous. The process involved consultation with over 20 experts in various fields. The final EA demonstrates that the interdisciplinary team conducting the Environmental Assessment considered each of the concerns and values plaintiff raises before the Court, as well as many others, in a comprehensive and thorough manner. [Id. at 707.]

Idaho Sporting Cong. v. Thomas, 137 F.3d 1146 (9th Cir. 1998), another timber sale case, shows how a court can reach a different result when this kind of study is not done. It agreed with the plaintiff "that an EIS is necessary because there are substantial questions as to whether the timber sales will have a significant effect on the water quality of" two creeks, and that the report on which the EA relied "failed to conduct standard factual and scientific site specific analysis, and failed to provide the analytical data necessary for any public challenge to the proposed sale." Id. at 1150. The agency was not entitled to rely solely on expert opinion without hard data.

2. *The Standard of Judicial Review.* The principal case applied the arbitrary and capricious standard of judicial review to the significance decision adopted in Marsh v. Oregon Natural Res. Council, 490 U.S. 360 (1989), that settled a split in the circuits. The Court held this standard applied to the Corps of Engineers' decision that a supplemental impact statement was not necessary on a proposed dam at Elk Creek in the Rogue River Basin in Southwest Oregon, noting that the decision on whether to prepare a supplemental impact statement was similar to the decision on whether to prepare an impact statement in the first instance.

The Court held the arbitrary and capricious standard that requires deference to agency decisions was the appropriate judicial review standard because the significance decision "in this case is a classic example of a factual dispute." The dispute turned on whether new information undermined the conclusions contained in the impact statement, whether the information was accurate, and whether the review of the information by the agency's experts was incomplete, inconclusive, or inaccurate. Because the analysis of the relevant documents required a high level of expertise, the Court deferred to and upheld the agency's decision that a supplemental impact statement was not necessary.

The Court quoted and reaffirmed language from its *Overton Park* decision that judicial review must be searching and careful, but that the ultimate standard of review is narrow. When specialists express conflicting views, the Court noted, the agency must have discretion to rely on the "reasonable opinions of its own qualified experts" even if a court might find contrary views more persuasive as an original matter. Yet the Court added language that appeared to confirm the "hard look" doctrine:

> On the other hand, in the context of reviewing a decision not to supplement an EIS, courts should not automatically defer to the agency's express reliance on an interest in finality without carefully reviewing the record and satisfying themselves that the agency has made a reasoned decision based on its evaluation of the significance—or lack of significance—of the new information. A contrary approach would not simply render judicial review generally meaningless, but would be contrary to the demand that courts ensure that agency decisions are founded on a reasoned evaluation "of the relevant factors." [Id. at 378.]

Some circuits have elaborated on the arbitrary and capricious standard to require a more focused review:

> First, the agency [must have] accurately identified the relevant environmental concern. Second, once the agency has identified the problem it must have taken a "hard look" at the problem in preparing the EA. Third, if a finding of no significant impact is made, the agency must be able to make a convincing case for its finding. Last, if the agency does not find an impact of true significance, preparation of an EIS can be avoided only if the agency finds that the changes or safeguards in the project sufficiently reduce the impact to a minimum. [Native Ecosystems Council v. United States Forest Serv., 428 F.3d 1233 (9th Cir. 2005) (forest thinning project).]

Would this standard have required a different result in the principal case?

3. *Questions of Law.* In *Marsh* the Court noted that the significance decision in that case was not a question of law because it did not require a new interpretation of the statute or the application of the significance requirement to settled facts. In Goos v. Interstate Commerce Comm'n, 911 F.2d 1283 (8th Cir. 1990), the court held the reasonableness standard of judicial review it had adopted prior to *Marsh* applied to threshold questions that determine whether NEPA applies, such as whether the action is a major action. The court did not apply the *Marsh* arbitrary and capricious standard of judicial review because that case raised only factual questions and did not consider threshold issues. Do you agree?

As you go through this chapter, consider what questions are questions of law that require application of a de novo review standard. What about questions concerning the scope of, for example, the impact statement? See also National Trust for Historic Preserv. v. Dole, 828 F.2d 776 (D.C. Cir. 1987) (arbitrary and capricious standard applies to review of categorical exclusion of action from NEPA).

4. *The "Hard Look" Doctrine.* The "hard look" doctrine, discussed in section A.2.c of Chapter 3, figures prominently in NEPA cases, both cases reviewing a decision not to prepare an EIS and decisions reviewing impact statements. National Audubon Soc'y v. Department of the Navy, 422 F.3d 174 (4th Cir. 2005), provides an extensive discussion of the "hard look" doctrine in a decision holding an environmental impact statement inadequate:

> What constitutes a "hard look" cannot be outlined with rule-like precision. At the least, however, it encompasses a thorough investigation into the environmental impacts of an agency's action and a candid acknowledgment of the risks that those impacts entail.
>
> We may not, of course, use review of an agency's environmental analysis as a guise for second-guessing substantive decisions committed to the discretion of the agency.

However, this does not turn judicial review into a rubber stamp. "In conducting our NEPA inquiry, we must 'make a searching and careful inquiry into the facts and review whether the decision was based on consideration of the relevant factors and whether there has been a clear error of judgment.'" [Id. at 185-186.]

The court added that the inquiry was contextual and case specific, and that a court reviewing an impact statement for NEPA compliance "must take a holistic view of what the agency has done to assess environmental impact."

5. *CEQ Regulations for Significance.* The court in the principal case quoted from CEQ regulations that provide guidance to agencies in making the significance determination. As the case notes, the regulations base the significance decision on context and intensity and list several factors for determining intensity, some of which were in issue in the case. Some of these factors are discussed in the Note that follows. Notice that CEQ states that a finding of significance may be made even if an impact is beneficial. Most courts have also held or suggested that agencies must consider the beneficial effects of their actions. Catron County Bd. of Comm'rs v. United States Fish & Wildlife Serv., 75 F.3d 1429 (10th Cir. 1996) (suggesting beneficial effects require evaluation by NEPA); NRDC, Inc. v. Herrington, 768 F.2d 1355 (D.C. Cir. 1985) (both beneficial and adverse effects can be significant).

6. *What Does a Court Review?* Judicial review is complicated in NEPA cases because a district court proceeding intervenes between an agency's decision not to file an impact statement and an appeal to a court of appeals. As one court of appeals pointed out, it is not clear whether it is to review the agency's decision on the basis of the administrative record or to review the district court's decision under the usual "clearly erroneous" test. Sierra Club v. Marsh, 769 F.2d 868 (1st Cir. 1985). The court's pragmatic answer was to defer to district court findings of fact but to review more vigorously the district court's review of the agency's administrative record.

NOTE ON ENVIRONMENTAL IMPACTS
THAT MUST BE CONSIDERED

An agency must decide what type of impacts it will consider in addressing the significance of the potential environmental consequences of its proposal. The following discussion considers some of the impacts commonly involved, some of which were considered in the principal decision.

Uncertainty. An agency may argue it should not consider any environmental impacts that are uncertain, but CEQ regulations state that agencies are to consider "[t]he degree to which the effects on the quality of the human environment are highly uncertain." In National Parks & Conservation Ass'n v. Babbitt, 241 F.3d 722 (9th Cir. 2001), the agency was uncertain about the environmental impacts of an increase in the number of ships allowed in Glacier Bay in Alaska. The court held that the "[p]rep-aration of an EIS is mandated where uncertainty may be resolved by further collection of data." This decision seems consistent with the congressional purpose in adopting NEPA, but does it put the agency in an awkward dilemma? For discussion see Snowden, Judicial Review and Environmental Analysis under NEPA: "Timing Is Everything," 33 Envt. L. Rep. (ELI) 10050 (2002). May an agency then refuse to discuss an uncertain impact in an EIS?

Endangered Species. The principal case considered, in a NEPA context, the impact of the program on endangered species as required by CEQ regulations illustrating the interplay between NEPA and other statutes and the duty to comply with NEPA in addition to legislation that may govern the agency's decision. An action can have a significant effect on the environment even though the continued existence of an endangered species is not jeopardized, within the meaning of the Endangered Species Act. Greater Yellowstone Coalition v. Flowers, 359 F.3d 1257 (10th Cir. 2004).

The Urban Environment. NEPA is not limited to the natural environment:

> The Act must be construed to include protection of the quality of life for city residents. Noise, traffic, overburdened mass transportation systems, crime, congestion and even availability of drugs all affect the urban "environment" and are surely results of the "profound influences of . . . high-density urbanization [and] industrial expansion." [Hanley v. Mitchell, 460 F.2d 640, 647 (2d Cir. 1972) (*Hanly I*).]

What if a project complies with local zoning? In Maryland—National Capital Park & Planning Comm'n v. United States Postal Serv., 487 F.2d 1029 (D.C. Cir. 1973), the court noted an impact statement might not be necessary when a project, here a postal facility, was consistent with local zoning. The court viewed local approval of the development as a prior ratification through the political process of any environmental impacts that might occur. Is this view justified? See accord, Isle of Hope Historical Ass'n, Inc. v. Corps of Eng'rs, 646 F.2d 215 (5th Cir. 1981) (NEPA only requires consultation between federal and local officials on claimed violation of local planning and zoning). The courts have not required compliance with exclusionary zoning, Town of Groton v. Laird, 353 F. Supp. 344 (D. Conn. 1972) (Navy housing project did not comply with local zoning), but they require consideration of social and economic impacts only if they are associated with a primary physical impact. See Como-Falcon Coalition, Inc. v. Department of Labor, 465 F. Supp. 850 (D. Minn. 1978), *rev'd*, 609 F.2d 342 (8th Cir. 1979) (proposal to establish job corps center in buildings on former college campus); 40 C.F.R. §1508.14.

Indirect Impacts. CEQ regulations also require consideration of the indirect impacts of an action. 40 C.F.R. §1508.3(b). These are impacts that are "caused by the action and are later in time or further removed in distance." City of Davis v. Coleman, 521 F.2d 661 (9th Cir. 1975), is a leading case showing how this mandate can require consideration of the growth-inducing impacts of a project. A federally funded highway interchange was planned in a rural area near the city to service and stimulate new industrial development. The court rejected a decision not to prepare an impact statement because the agency did not discuss the inevitable industrial development and population increase that would have a potentially detrimental impact on the city's controlled growth policy, and create a demand for residential and commercial development and the beginning of urban sprawl.

City of Carmel-by-the-Sea v. United States Dep't of Transp., 123 F.3d 1142 (9th Cir. 1997), distinguished *City of Davis*. The court approved an impact statement for a freeway near Carmel. The court noted that Carmel was well developed, unlike Davis, and that existing development required the freeway even though it might also induce limited development. Is this a plausible distinction? Compare Sierra Club v. Cavanaugh, 447 F. Supp. 427 (D.S.D. 1978) (growth-inducing impacts of rural water system held negligible and would be solved by local zoning).

Risk and Psychological Stress. In Metropolitan Edison Co. v. People Against Nuclear Energy, 460 U.S. 766 (1983), the Nuclear Regulatory Commission (NRC) authorized a restart of TMI-1, one of the nuclear reactors located on the site of the Three Mile Island accident, but not the reactor that failed. People Against Nuclear Energy (PANE) was an association of residents in the area who opposed the operation of either reactor. It claimed that NEPA required NRC to consider the "severe psychological health damage to persons living in the vicinity" that would be caused by a restart of TMI-1, because the restart would remind residents of the nuclear accident and would raise the possibility that an accident could happen again. The Court disagreed. Holding that NEPA was limited to impacts on the physical environment, it added that the statute should "be read to include a requirement of a reasonably close causal relationship between a change in the physical environment and the effect at issue":

> PANE argues that the psychological health damage it alleges "will flow directly from the risk of [a nuclear] accident." But a risk of an accident is not an effect on the physical environment. A risk is, by definition, unrealized in the physical world. In a causal chain from renewed operation of TMI-1 to psychological health damage, the element of risk and its perception by PANE's members are necessary middle links. We believe that the element of risk lengthens the causal chain beyond the reach of NEPA. [Id. at 775.]

The Court also suggested that PANE's objections reflected a "policy disagreement" best resolved in the political process. For a case suggesting *PANE* means that agencies are no longer required to consider socioeconomic effects under NEPA, even when physical effects are present, see Olmsted Citizens for a Better Cmty. v. United States, 793 F.2d 201 (8th Cir. 1986). What is the basis for this holding?

   Causation. The Supreme Court in *Public Citizen*, discussed above, read *PANE* to mean a "but for" causal relationship is not sufficient to bring an action under NEPA, and held that the "rule of reason" inherent in NEPA likewise made this clear. Justice Brennan, concurring in *PANE*, distinguished cases in which a psychological injury arose "out of the direct sensory change in the environment." In most cases the environmental impact of an action will be direct and clear, as in the *Environmental Prot. Info. Ctr.* decision, reproduced above.

   Mitigation. The mitigated FONSI has become common in agency practice, as illustrated in that decision. Some states with laws based on NEPA, such as California, have provided for a mitigated finding of no significant impact by statute. CEQ regulations do not provide for mitigated FONSIs, but the CEQ indicated in a guidance document that federal agencies can include enforceable mitigation measures when they conclude an action is not significant. Council on Environmental Quality, "Forty Most Asked Questions Concerning CEQ's National Environmental Policy Act Regulations," Question 39, 46 Fed. Reg. 18,026, 18,037 (1981). The courts have held that agencies can take mitigation measures into account when deciding whether an action is significant. Cabinet Mountains Wilderness/Scotchman's Peak Grizzly Bears v. Peterson, 685 F.2d 678 (D.C. Cir. 1982) (exploratory mineral drilling in wilderness area).

   An environmental assessment does not require the full and "reasonably complete" discussion of mitigation measures that is required in an impact statement. However, a court must consider whether mitigation measures are an adequate buffer against negative impacts, and must decide whether they make these impacts so minor that an impact statement is not required. National Parks & Conservation Ass'n v. Babbitt, 241 F.3d 722 (9th Cir. 2001) (citing cases). The mere listing of mitigation measures without any analytical data is not enough. Klamath-Siskiyou Wildlands Ctr. v. United States Forest Serv., 373 F. Supp. 2d 1069 (D. Cal. 2004).

4.   Exemptions

CATRON COUNTY BOARD OF COMMISSIONERS v. UNITED STATES FISH AND WILDLIFE SERVICE
75 F.3d 1429 (10th Cir. 1996)

KELLY, Circuit Judge.

The United States Fish and Wildlife Service and various governmental officials (FWS, Secretary or Appellants) appeal the district court's order granting Catron County's (County or Appellee) motion for partial summary judgment in the County's action alleging that the Secretary of Interior (Secretary or Appellants), acting on behalf of the FWS, failed to comply with the National Environmental Policy Act of 1969 (NEPA), in designating certain lands within the County as critical habitat for the spikedace and loach minnow. In addition, the district court granted the County's motion for injunctive relief but stayed its order pending appeal. We exercise jurisdiction under 28 U.S.C. §1292(a)(1) and affirm.

I. Background

In 1985, the Secretary proposed listing the spikedace and loach minnow as threatened species and establishing a critical habitat for them. The Secretary's proposed designation comprised approximately 74 miles of river habitat in the County. The notice also provided for a sixty-day comment period, which was subsequently extended by an additional several weeks, and scheduled three public meetings to gather additional information and comments on the proposed actions. Also in his proposal, the Secretary determined that he was not required to comply with the documentation requirements of NEPA, claiming that Secretarial actions under §1533 of the Endangered Species Act (ESA), 16 U.S.C. §§1531-44, are exempt from NEPA as a matter of law. The Secretary received over one hundred written comments and over thirty oral comments. In 1986, pursuant to §1533(b)(6)(A) of the ESA, the Secretary adopted final regulations listing the species as threatened and extended the deadline for final designation of critical habitat. In June 1993, the County filed suit alleging that the Secretary failed to comply with the Administrative Procedure Act, the ESA and NEPA. In March 1994, the Secretary issued notice of final designation of critical habitat, which became effective on April 7, 1994. In April 1994, the County filed its motion for injunctive relief claiming that the Secretary had failed to comply with NEPA and seeking to prevent the Secretary from implementing and enforcing its designation of critical habitat. The district court granted Appellants' motion to consolidate for consideration both the County's motion for injunctive relief and the parties' motions for partial summary judgment.

On October 13, 1994, finding that the Secretary had failed to comply with NEPA in designating critical habitat, the district court granted the County's motions for partial summary judgment and injunctive relief.

II. Discussion . . .

B. STATUTORY FRAMEWORK . . .

[The court discussed NEPA and the Endangered Species Act.]

C. NEPA's APPLICABILITY TO ESA . . .

2. RELEVANT PRECEDENT

Compliance with NEPA is excused when there is a statutory conflict with the agency's authorizing legislation that prohibits or renders compliance impossible. See H.R. Conf. Rep. No. 91-765, 91st Cong., 1st Sess. (1969); see also Flint Ridge Dev. Co. v. Scenic Rivers Ass'n, 426 U.S. 776. Judicial interpretation of what constitutes a "conflict" with NEPA has varied, however. Courts have approved noncompliance with NEPA on the basis of statutory conflict after finding either (i) an unavoidable conflict between the two statutes that renders compliance with both impossible; or (ii) duplicative procedural requirements between the statutes that essentially constitute "functional equivalents," rendering compliance with both superfluous.

In *Flint Ridge*, the Supreme Court addressed a conflict between NEPA and the Interstate Land Sales Full Disclosure Act (Disclosure Act), which imposes a statutory duty upon the Secretary of Housing and Urban Development (HUD) to allow statements of record to go into effect within 30 days of filing unless the Secretary of HUD acts affirmatively within that time to suspend it for inadequate disclosure. See 15 U.S.C. §1706. Finding it "inconceivable that an environmental impact statement could, in 30 days, be drafted, circulated, commented upon, and then reviewed and revised," the Supreme Court held that a "clear and fundamental conflict of statutory duty" existed between NEPA and the Disclosure Act that prevented simultaneous compliance with both statutes. *Flint Ridge*, 426 U.S. at 788-91. In light of the "clear and unavoidable conflict in statutory authority," the Supreme Court held that "NEPA must give way . . . '[as] NEPA was not intended to repeal by implication any other statute.'" Id. at 788 (quoting United States v. SCRAP, 412 U.S. 669, 694).

NEPA compliance has also been excused by some courts where the particular action being undertaken is subject to rules and regulations that essentially duplicate the NEPA inquiry. See, e.g., Merrell v. Thomas, 807 F.2d 776, 778 (9th Cir. 1986) (holding that to require registration procedures under both NEPA and Federal Insecticide, Fungicide, and Rodenticide Act would be superfluous); Pacific Legal Foundation v. Andrus, 657 F.2d 829, 835 (6th Cir. 1981) (NEPA conflicts with ESA provisions regarding listing of species as endangered or threatened); Portland Cement Ass'n v. Ruckelshaus, 486 F.2d 375, 384 (D.C. Cir. 1973) (EPA not required to comply with NEPA when promulgating standards under §111 of the Clean Air Act). In view of the focus of the ESA critical habitat designation, we do not believe that the NEPA inquiry has been duplicated, nor do we believe the statutes are mutually exclusive. We rejected an analogous argument in Davis v. Morton, 469 F.2d 593 (10th Cir. 1972). We declined to find an unavoidable, irreconcilable conflict between NEPA and 25 U.S.C. §415, a statute that regulates secretarial approval of leases on Indian lands. Section 415 provided that "prior to approval of any lease [on Indian land] . . . the Secretary of Interior shall first satisfy himself that adequate consideration has been given to . . . the effect on the environment of the uses to which the leased lands will be subject." 25 U.S.C. §415. The government argued that NEPA did not apply to §415 because the latter statute required the Bureau of Indian Affairs (BIA) to consider the environmental ramifications of its authorization of leases. *Davis*, 469 F.2d at 598. We disagreed, noting that, unlike NEPA, §415 did not require substantive and in depth environmental consideration but rather a more focused analysis of issues concerning the lease of Indian land. We concluded that "unless the obligations of another statute are clearly mutually exclusive with the mandates of NEPA, the specific requirements of NEPA will remain in force." Id.

The Secretary relies upon Douglas County v. Babbitt, 48 F.3d 1495 (9th Cir. 1995), and urges us to adopt its holding. After careful consideration, we believe our precedent and analysis require a different result. In *Douglas County*, the Ninth Circuit addressed the precise issue before us. That case arose after the Secretary attempted to designate critical habitat for the Spotted Owl, a species he listed as threatened in June 1990 pursuant to the ESA. In May 1991, the Secretary issued a proposal designating over 11 million acres as critical habitat, asserting that he need not comply with NEPA's documentation requirements. See 48 Fed. Reg. 49,244 (1983) (letter from the Council on Environmental Quality (CEQ) indicating that the Secretary may cease complying with NEPA for actions under §1533 of ESA). After Douglas County filed suit claiming that the Secretary had failed to comply with NEPA, the Secretary issued a final habitat designation comprising almost 7 million acres of exclusively federal land. The district court held that Douglas County had standing to sue, granted Douglas' motion for summary judgment finding that NEPA did apply to the Secretary's decision to designate critical habitat under the ESA and, sua sponte, stayed the order pending appeal.

The Ninth Circuit affirmed in part and reversed in part, holding that while Douglas County did have standing, NEPA did not apply. *Douglas County*, 48 F.3d at 1507-08. We disagree with the panel's reasoning. First, given the focus of the ESA together with the rather cursory directive that the Secretary is to take into account "economic and other relevant impacts," we do not believe that the ESA procedures have displaced NEPA requirements. Secondly, we likewise disagree with the panel that no actual impact flows from the critical habitat designation. Merely because the Secretary says it does not make it so. The record in this case suggests that the impact will be immediate and the consequences could be disastrous. The preparation of an EA will enable all involved to determine what the effect will be. Finally, we believe that compliance with NEPA will further the goals of the ESA, and not vice versa as suggested by the Ninth Circuit panel. For these reasons and in view of our own circuit precedent, we conclude that the Secretary must comply with NEPA when designating critical habitat under ESA.

3. FACTUAL ANALYSIS

Appellants do not allege that compliance with both statutes is impossible due to an unavoidable, irreconcilable conflict between §1533 of ESA and NEPA's documentation requirements. Rather, Appellants argue that the similarity of the statutes' procedures, together with congressional failure to respond to judicial and executive announcements of NEPA noncompliance, evidence Congress' implicit intent to "displace[] NEPA's procedural and informational requirements."

It is clear that the provisions of the ESA governing the designation of critical habitat instruct the Secretary to follow procedures that to some extent parallel and perhaps overlap the requirements imposed by NEPA. Together, the ESA requirements for notice and environmental consideration partially fulfill the primary purposes of NEPA, namely, "to inject environmental consideration into the federal agency's decisionmaking . . . [and] inform the public that the agency" has considered the environment. [Weinberger v. Catholic Action of Hawaii, 454 U.S. 139, 143 (1981)].

Partial fulfillment of NEPA's requirements, however, is not enough. The plain language of NEPA makes clear that "to the fullest extent possible" federal agencies must comply with the act and prepare an impact statement for all major federal actions significantly affecting the environment. 42 U.S.C. §4332(2)(C). NEPA does not require particular results but rather a particular process. Robertson v. Methow Valley Citizens Council, 490 U.S. 332, 350 (1989). NEPA ensures that a federal agency makes informed, carefully calculated decisions when acting in such a way as to affect the environment and also enables dissemination of relevant information to external audiences potentially affected by the agency's decision.

By contrast, ESA's core purpose is to prevent the extinction of species by preserving and protecting the habitat upon which they depend from the intrusive activities of humans. See 16 U.S.C. §1531(b). While the protection of species through preservation of habitat may be an environmentally beneficial goal, Secretarial action under ESA is not inevitably beneficial or immune to improvement by compliance with NEPA procedure. The designation of critical habitat effectively prohibits all subsequent federal or federally funded or directed actions likely to affect the habitat. Id. at §1536(a)(2). The short- and long-term effects of the proposed governmental action (and even the governmental action prohibited under ESA designation) are often unknown or, more importantly, initially thought to be beneficial, but after closer analysis determined to be environmentally harmful. Furthermore, that the Secretary believes the effects of a particular designation to be beneficial is equally immaterial to his responsibility to comply with NEPA. "Even if the Federal agency believes that on balance the effect [of the action] will be beneficial," regulations promulgated by the Council on Environmental Quality (CEQ) nonetheless require an impact statement. 40 C.F.R. §1508.27(b)(1). NEPA's requirements are not solely designed to inform the Secretary of the environmental consequences of his action. NEPA documentation notifies the public and relevant government officials of the proposed action and its environmental consequences and informs the public that the acting agency has considered those consequences. A federal agency could not know the potential alternatives to a proposed federal action until it complies with NEPA and prepares at least an EA.

To interpret NEPA as merely requiring an assessment of detrimental impacts upon the environment would significantly diminish the act's fundamental purpose— to "help public officials make decisions that are based on understanding of environmental consequences, and take actions that protect, restore, and enhance the environment." 40 C.F.R. §1500.1(c). Appellants' theory would cast the judiciary as final arbiter of what federal actions protect or enhance the environment, a role for which the courts are not suited.

Here, the County alleges that the proposed designation will prevent continued governmental flood control efforts, thereby significantly affecting nearby farms and ranches, other privately owned land, local economies and public roadways and bridges. These claims, if proved, constitute a significant effect on the environment the impact of which and alternatives to which have not been adequately addressed by ESA. Furthermore, unlike the county in Douglas County, Catron County actually owns land potentially affected by the designation; the final designation in *Douglas County* included only federal land. It is true that after complying with NEPA's documentation requirements, the Secretary nonetheless may adhere to his proposed designation. Regardless, NEPA is clear: "to the fullest extent possible," federal agencies must comply with the act and prepare an impact statement for "major Federal actions significantly affecting the quality of the human environment." 42 U.S.C. §4332(2)(C), (E). . . .

[The court rejected an argument "that congressional failure to reverse or revise prior judicial and secretarial announcements of NEPA noncompliance evidences congressional endorsement of such noncompliance."]

AFFIRMED.

NOTES AND QUESTIONS

1. *NEPA's Reach.* NEPA's sweeping environmental mandate would seem to apply, without exemption, to the statutory obligations of all federal agencies. A basis for exemption can be found only in §104, discussed earlier, which states that NEPA is not to affect the "specific statutory obligations" of federal agencies. In *Calvert Cliffs*, the court held that §104 only relieves an agency of compliance with NEPA when its "specific statutory obligations" are clearly mutually exclusive of NEPA's requirements. *Calvert Cliffs* also held that §104 did not prohibit agencies from considering stricter water pollution controls than those required by EPA under the Clean Water Act. For a case mandating the preparation of an EIS on a critical habitat designation, see Middle Rio Grande Conservancy Dist. v. Norton, 294 F.3d 1220 (10th Cir. 2002).

The leading case on direct conflict is Flint Ridge Dev. Co. v. Scenic Rivers Ass'n, 426 U.S. 776 (1976), discussed in the principal decision. The Interstate Land Sales Full Disclosure Act, 15 U.S.C. §§1701-1720, requires developers to submit full disclosure statements on their land developments with the Department of Housing and Urban Development (HUD). A disclosure statement becomes effective 30 days after it is filed if it is complete and accurate on its face. The HUD Secretary may not substantively evaluate a developer's project but may only suspend the statement's effective date if the statement is procedurally defective.

HUD first claimed NEPA did not apply to its actions under the disclosure act because NEPA applies only to agencies "that have the ability to react to environmental consequences when taking action." Since HUD could not review the environmental impact of a proposed development, it claimed NEPA did not apply. The Court did not resolve this contention because it found HUD exempt under NEPA §102, requiring federal agencies to comply only "to the fullest extent possible." The disclosure act made the developer's statement effective 30 days after filing unless the HUD Secretary acted affirmatively to suspend the statement. It was inconceivable, the Court concluded, that an impact statement could be drafted, reviewed, and revised within that period. The Court found a "clear and fundamental conflict of a statutory duty." As an afterthought, the Court noted that the disclosure act authorized the HUD Secretary "to incorporate a wide range of environmental information into property reports." Is this a functional equivalence rule?

Compare Jones v. Gordon, 792 F.2d 821 (9th Cir. 1986). The court rejected an argument that statutory time limits imposed on the issuance of permits for the capture of whales precluded compliance with NEPA. The court distinguished *Flint Ridge* by holding that the statute authorized the agency to control the "triggering act for the statutory timetable" to allow compliance with NEPA. Accord: ASARCO Inc. v. Air Quality Coal., 601 P.2d 501 (Wash. 1979).

2. *Conflict in Statutory Purpose.* In *Catron County* the issue was a conflict in statutory purpose. How does the court use NEPA's legislative purpose to support a ruling that it applies to a habitat designation under the ESA, which is discussed in section 5.B? As the court notes, there is a conflict on this issue. Notice that the ESA does not confer the authority to consider the environmental impact of habitat designations under the statute, and that a habitat designation is arguably a benign environmental action. This did not trouble the court. For a different view, see Pacific Legal Found. v. Andrus, 657 F.2d 829 (6th Cir. 1981), where the court held an EIS is not required on the listing of an endangered species under the ESA. It held that the agency did not have discretion to consider environmental impacts, that the statutory criteria for listing endangered species precluded consideration of environmental impacts, and that the listing of an endangered species furthered NEPA's purposes.

3. *Statutory Exemptions.* Congress has frequently passed legislation exempting specific agency projects and programs from NEPA. Two of the projects exempted—the Alaska Pipeline and a San Antonio freeway—had been challenged in nationally publicized litigation under NEPA that had blocked both projects. See Earth Res. Co. v. Federal Energy Regulatory Comm'n, 617 F.2d 775 (D.C. Cir. 1980) (upholding Alaska pipeline exemption and applying it to plant that was not part of pipeline system). In one important case, the Supreme Court upheld a statute, passed in response to a pending lawsuit on northwest forests that are home to the spotted owl, that contained environmental management requirements intended to resolve the lawsuit. It held that the law "compelled changes in law" not tied to particular litigation. Robertson v. Seattle Audubon Soc'y, 503 U.S. 429 (1992).

Though Congress sometimes makes NEPA explicitly applicable to an agency program, see Energy Security Act, 16 U.S.C. §2705(b), it has also granted full or partial exemption from NEPA in several statutes, such as the National Forest Management Act, 16 U.S.C. §544o(f) (exempting certain actions under statute). For an argument that Congress is weakening NEPA through exemptions, see Sher & Hunting, Eroding the Landscape, Eroding the Laws: Congressional Exemption from Judicial Review of Environmental Laws, 15 Harv. Envtl. L. Rev. 435 (1991). See also the Surface Mining Control and Reclamation Act, 30 U.S.C. §1292(d).

Congress overruled *Calvert Cliffs* by prohibiting federal agencies from requiring stricter pollution controls than required by established water quality standards. Under §511(c)(1) of the Clean Water Act, only certain limited actions by EPA are subject to NEPA. This section provides that an impact statement is necessary only when federal funds are used in the construction of publicly owned treatment works or when EPA issues a permit for a new pollution source. An important example is the dredge and fill permit required by the Clean Water Act for development in wetlands. Congress also exempted EPA actions under the Clean Air Act from NEPA in the Energy Supply and Environmental Coordination Act of 1974, 15 U.S.C. §793(c)(1).

4. *Legislation and Appropriations.* The Supreme Court held that requests for appropriations were exempt from NEPA in Andrus v. Sierra Club, 442 U.S. 347 (1979). It noted, in part, that an EIS requirement at the appropriation stage would be redundant because it "would merely recapitulate the EIS's that should have accompanied the initial proposals of the programs." Andrus v. Sierra Club does not affect

NEPA's requirement that federal agencies prepare impact statements on legislative proposals submitted to Congress. Although potentially helpful as a means of providing Congress with information necessary to review the environmental impact of federal programs, the impact statement on legislative proposals is NEPA's neglected mandate. Very few have been submitted. Is a report on legislation a "proposal" for legislation? See Citizens for the Mgmt. of Alaska Lands v. Department of Agric., 447 F. Supp. 753 (D. Alaska 1978) (holding no, because to hold otherwise would violate political question doctrine).

The courts have differed on whether plaintiffs have standing to enforce the legislative impact statement requirement. Compare Chamber of Commerce v. Department of Interior, 439 F. Supp. 762 (D.D.C. 1977) (standing denied to challenge failure to prepare statement because proposal "in the lap of Congress" and injury was speculative) with Atchison, Topeka & Santa Fe Ry. Co. v. Callaway, 431 F. Supp. 722 (D.D.C. 1977) (standing granted to challenge impact statement on lock and dam proposal because inadequate impact statement denied plaintiffs important environmental information). For discussion, see Note, NEPA's Forgotten Clause: Impact Statements for Legislative Proposals, 58 B.U. L. Rev. 560 (1978).

5. *National Security Exemption.* In Weinberger v. Catholic Action of Hawaii, 454 U.S. 139 (1981), the U.S. Navy invoked the Freedom of Information Act (FOIA), 5 U.S.C. §552, to claim an impact statement was not required for the construction of new ammunition and weapons storage facilities in which the plaintiff claimed that nuclear weapons would be stored. The FOIA applies to NEPA, §102(2)(C).

The court of appeals required the preparation of a hypothetical EIS that would hypothesize but not concede that the facilities would be used for nuclear weapons storage. The Supreme Court reversed. It held that classified national defense matters were exempt from disclosure under the Act and that information on the storage of nuclear weapons fell in this category. For national security reasons, the Navy could neither admit nor deny that it proposed to store nuclear weapons, and so a court could not determine whether the Navy had taken an action to which NEPA applied. The Court added that if the Navy proposed to store nuclear weapons at the facility, the Defense Department regulations "can fairly be read to require that an EIS be prepared solely for internal purposes, even though such a document cannot be disclosed to the public." 454 U.S. at 146.

The cases have read *Catholic Action* to require preparation of an EIS when the Freedom of Information Act does not apply and have held that the application of NEPA to national security activities is a justiciable question. See No Gwen Alliance v. Aldridge, 855 F.2d 1380 (9th Cir. 1988) (but holding that nexus between radio emergency network and nuclear war was too tenuous to require discussion); Romer v. Carlucci, 847 F.2d 445 (8th Cir. 1988) (court can review EIS on MX missile deployment for compliance with NEPA). Reread §101. Are these decisions consistent with the statutory intent? See Dycus, NEPA's Secrets, 2 N.Y.U. Envtl. L.J. 300 (1993).

NOTE ON FUNCTIONAL EQUIVALENCE

The courts have also adopted an implied "functional equivalence" exemption from NEPA for agency actions that protect rather than harm the environment. They have applied the functional equivalence exemption only to actions taken by EPA in its environmental regulation programs.

The court stated the basis for the functional equivalence exemption in Portland Cement Ass'n v. Ruckelshaus, 486 F.2d 375 (D.C. Cir. 1973), which held that EPA need not prepare an impact statement prior to its adoption of air pollution emissions standards under §111 of the Clean Air Act. The court noted that §111 of the Clean Air Act required an emissions standard reflecting "the best system of emission reduction" and mandated the EPA Administrator to take "into account the cost of achieving such reduction." It interpreted these criteria to require the Administrator to consider both the adverse environmental effects and the costs to industry of a proposed standard, and to prepare a statement of reasons explaining EPA's environmental review to accompany the proposal through the remainder of the rulemaking process. The court found that although this procedure "may not import the complete advantages of the structured determinations of NEPA into the decisionmaking of EPA, it does . . . strike a workable balance between some of the advantages and disadvantages of full application of NEPA." The court continued:

> Without the problems of a NEPA delay conflicting with the constraints of the Clean Air Act, the ability of other agencies to make submissions to EPA concerning proposed rules, provides a channel for informed decisionmaking. These comments will be part of the record in the rulemaking proceeding that EPA must take into account.
>
> EPA's proposed rule, and reasons therefor, are inevitably on alert to environmental issues. The EPA's proposed rule and reasons may omit reference to adverse environmental consequences that another agency might discern, but a draft impact statement may likewise be marred by omissions that another agency identifies. To the extent that EPA is aware of significant adverse environmental consequences of its proposal, good faith requires appropriate reference in its reasons for the proposal and its underlying balancing analysis. [Id. at 386.]

Do you agree with the court's reasoning? Note that a federal agency exempted from NEPA under the functional equivalence rule is not required to meet all of the statutory impact statement requirements. It need not necessarily consider alternatives to its proposed action, for example. Judicial review of the agency's functional equivalence determination, such as an agency rule adopted in a formal rulemaking procedure, may also be narrower than judicial review of an impact statement.

What about the hazardous waste statutes? State of Alabama ex rel. Siegelman v. EPA, 911 F.2d 499 (11th Cir. 1990), held NEPA does not apply to EPA's permit procedure for hazardous waste landfills under RCRA. The court held that RCRA is intended to ensure that "EPA considers fully, with the assistance of meaningful public comment, environmental issues involved in the permitting of hazardous waste management facilities." Reconsider this decision when you study RCRA later in Chapter 8, section F.3.

Compare cases holding that the functional equivalence exemption does not apply. Jones v. Gordon, 621 F. Supp. 27 (D. Alaska 1985), aff'd on other grounds, 792 F.2d 821 (9th Cir. 1986) (National Marine Fisheries Service; not enough that agency given role of implementing environmental statute); Texas Comm. on Natural Res. v. Bergland, 573 F.2d 201 (5th Cir. 1978) (National Forest Management Act; National Forest Service not exclusively an environmental protection agency).

NOTE ON NEPA'S EXTRATERRITORIAL IMPACT AND ENVIRONMENTAL ASSESSMENT IN OTHER COUNTRIES

NEPA Abroad. Whether NEPA applies to the extraterritorial impacts of federal agency actions has produced a protracted controversy still not entirely resolved. NEPA does not expressly exclude or include extraterritorial environmental impacts, although the statute does require federal agencies to "recognize the worldwide . . . character of environmental problems." §102(2)(F). CEQ regulations do not address this problem, which was covered by an executive order issued by President Carter. Exec. Order No. 12,114, 44 Fed. Reg. 1957 (1979). The order, though not based on NEPA, requires environmental reviews of the extraterritorial environmental impacts of federal agency actions. The review is not as extensive as the environmental review covered by NEPA's impact statement. The order contains a number of exemptions, which relate primarily to national security actions.

The key principle that controls NEPA's extraterritorial application is the Supreme Court's decision in Equal Employment Opportunity Comm'n v. Arabian Am. Oil Co., 499 U.S. 244 (1991), which reaffirmed the rule establishing a presumption against extraterritorial application of statutes. However, Environmental Def. Fund, Inc., v. Massey, 986 F.2d 528 (D.C. Cir. 1993), later held NEPA applied to a decision by the National Science Foundation to incinerate wastes in Antarctica without preparing an impact statement. The court held NEPA applied to decision-making within this country, and also noted that the United States has "some measure of legislative control" in Antarctica through control over research installations and air transportation. The court also applied the exception in *Arabian Am. Oil* that the presumption against extraterritoriality applies with significantly less force when there is no potential for conflict with the laws of another country. This exception applied because Antarctica was a "sovereign-less" country. Compare Hirt v. Richardson, 127 F. Supp. 2d 833 (W.D. Mich. 1999) (NEPA applies to shipments of mixed oxide fuel intended for research power plant in Canada) with NEPA Coalition of Japan v. Aspin, 837 F. Supp. 466 (D.D.C. 1993) (impact statement not required on military bases in Japan subject to complex treaty arrangements).

Recent cases have not applied NEPA extraterritorially, noting that later Supreme Court decisions have placed the precedential importance of *Massey* in doubt. See Smith v. United States, 507 U.S. 197 (1993) (extraterritorial jurisdiction did not apply to tort claims in Antarctica). In Basel Action Network v. Maritime Admin., 370 F. Supp. 2d 57 (D.D.C. 2005), the court held that NEPA did not apply to the towing of vessels for scrapping to the United Kingdom. It distinguished *Massey*, because the United States does not have legislative control over the high seas, and because the presumption against extraterritoriality applies in "sovereignless" areas. See also Consejo de Desarrollo Economico de Mexicali v. United States, 438 F. Supp. 2d 1207 (D. Nev. 2006) (allocation of Colorado River water between United States and Mexico); Klick, Note, The Extraterritorial Effect of NEPA's EIS Requirement after *Environmental Defense Fund v. Massey*, 44 Am. U. L. Rev. 291 (1994).

Environmental Assessment in Other Countries. Should the question of NEPA's extraterritorial scope be informed by the knowledge that environmental impact assessment is now an environmental policy instrument widely used throughout the world to examine the likely adverse environmental impacts of a wide class of activities before they are undertaken? The European Economic Community adopted a Directive in 1985, which came into force in 1988, mandating environmental impact assessment

(EIA) throughout the EU. 85/337/EEC. The duty to conduct an assessment for covered projects is mandatory.

Unlike NEPA, the EU directive applies to projects rather than governmental agencies, and applies to both public and private projects "which are likely to have significant effects on the environment." Art. 1(1). Whether a project is likely to have a significant effect depends on its nature, size, and location. Art. 2(1). Annexes included in the Directive indicate what projects require a mandatory EIA and what projects require an EIA only when they have significant effects. The Directive authorizes member states to integrate EIA into procedures for the approval of development projects, into other procedures, or into procedures established to comply with the Directive. For discussion, see E. Wood, Environmental Impact Assessment: A Comparative Review (2d ed. 2003).

The Directive must be given a "direct effect" in member states. This means that legislation and regulations in member states must comply with it. See Regina v. North Yorkshire County Council, 1 All E.R. 969 (H.L.), an English House of Lords decision. England did not pass new complying legislation but integrated EIA into its planning and land use regulation procedures.

Environmental impact assessment was endorsed in Agenda 21 adopted by the 1992 Rio Conference. The Rio Declaration on Environment and Development, Principle 17, A/CONF.151.5/Rev.1, 31 I.L.M. 874 (1992). The practice has become so widespread that it can now be said to be customary international law.

C. IF AN IMPACT STATEMENT MUST BE PREPARED, WHAT IS ITS SCOPE?

When a federal agency decides or has been ordered by a court to prepare an impact statement, the next step is to determine its scope. This problem has several dimensions. One concerns the range of alternatives an agency must take into account. NEPA requires consideration of "alternatives" to the proposed action, a requirement that compels agencies to consider alternatives they would not otherwise consider. There is also a physical dimension. Agencies often divide proposed projects into more than one segment so they can minimize consideration of the environmental impacts by analyzing a project one part at a time.

Actions and projects that agencies consider may also be interrelated. A federal agency, for example, may authorize coal mining leases throughout a large area of public land. May the agency prepare an impact statement on each lease separately, or must it prepare an impact statement on all of the leases as a group? Another option is a program impact statement that can evaluate entire programs for their environmental impact before individual project decisions are made. The materials that follow first discuss the procedures in which an impact statement is prepared and then consider these issues.

1. How Environmental Impact Statements Are Prepared

It is useful here to review the process in which environmental impact statements are prepared. See Figure 4-3. If an agency decides to prepare an impact statement it

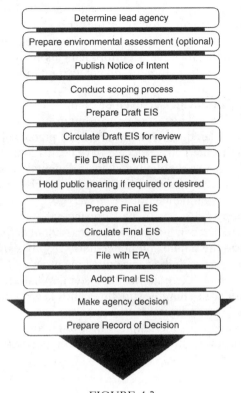

FIGURE 4-3
Steps in the EIS Preparation Process

Bass, Herson & Bogdan, The NEPA Book (2001). Solano Press Books. Figure 4-1, p.71.Reprinted with permission of Solano Press Books, copyright © 2001.

must file a Notice of Intent (NOI) in the Federal Register. 40 C.F.R. §1508.22. The NOI must briefly describe the proposed action, possible alternatives, and the proposed scoping process and provide the name of a lead agency contact.

The scoping process occurs next. Scoping determines the scope of the issues to be addressed in the impact statement and identifies the significant issues related to the proposed action. The process is to "eliminate from detailed study the issues which are not significant or which have been covered by prior environmental review." §1501.7(a)(3).

After the agency completes the scoping process it prepares a draft environmental impact statement (DEIS) "in accordance with the scope decided upon in the scoping process." §1502.09(a). NEPA requires circulation for comments, and CEQ has interpreted this requirement to apply to the draft impact statement. The commenting process is an important part of NEPA's full disclosure requirement. The statute requires circulation for comment to federal, state, and local agencies, and CEQ has extended the comment requirement by requiring comments from any agency that has requested copies of the DEIS, the applicant, the public, and "interested or affected" persons or organizations. §1503.1(a). Additional consultation with the federal wildlife agencies is required by the Fish and Wildlife Coordination Act, 16 U.S.C. §662(a).

The agency then prepares a final impact statement (FEIS) that must respond to comments on the draft statement in the following ways: modifying the proposed action or alternatives; proposing a new action or alternatives; developing or evaluating new alternatives; supplementing, modifying, or improving its analysis; making factual corrections; or explaining why the comments do not warrant further response. 40 C.F.R. §1503.4(a). The FEIS is circulated in the same manner as the draft EIS.

If the agency prepares an impact statement, it must also prepare a "concise public record of decision." §1505.2. The record of decision must state what the decision was, discuss alternatives considered, and state whether "all practicable means" to avoid or minimize harm from the alternative selected have been adopted and if not, why not.

Agencies must prepare a supplemental environmental impact statement (SEIS) when "significant" new circumstances or information or substantial changes affect the proposed action or its environmental impact. §1502.9(c). Scoping is not required if an agency decides to prepare a supplemental impact statement, but the statement is prepared, filed, and circulated in the same manner as a draft or final impact statement.

Go back and read the statute and notice how CEQ has amplified the statutory requirements. Do you agree with the decisionmaking process CEQ has created? Note also how many checkpoints there are in the system. What are they? Are there too many? Too few? Consider also how the structure of this decisionmaking process affects the way in which NEPA's requirements are applied to agency actions. How the alternatives requirement is applied, for example, will strongly affect the range and scope of the analysis and, by necessity, the "adequacy" of an impact statement. This requirement is considered next.

NOTES AND QUESTIONS

1. *Commenting.* Federal courts have been attentive to compliance with commenting procedures. They have invalidated an impact statement when the agency has modified its project subsequent to the draft statement but has not amended the statement to afford opportunity for comment. California v. Block, 690 F.2d 753 (9th Cir. 1982). Neither may responses to comments be perfunctory. A mere tabulation of comments is not enough. Id. at 773. A "mere admission of some impact" is not sufficient. National Wildlife Fed'n v. Andrus, 440 F. Supp. 1245, 1253 (D.D.C. 1977). See 40 C.F.R. §1503.4 (agency must explain why comments do not warrant further response).

The commenting procedure does not authorize a veto by the commenting agency. Sierra Club v. Callaway, 499 F.2d 982, 993 (5th Cir. 1974). Compare Warm Springs Dam Task Force v. Gribble, 565 F.2d 549, 554 (9th Cir. 1977): "[T]here is no requirement that the responsible agency alter its project or perform new studies in response to comments."

2. *EPA Review.* A potentially powerful supplementary environmental review requirement is contained in §309 of the Clean Air Act. It confers additional environmental review authority on EPA:

(a) The [EPA] Administrator shall review and comment in writing on the environmental impact of any matter relating to duties and responsibilities granted pursuant to . . . [the Clean Air] Act or other provisions of the authority of the Administrator, contained in any (1) legislation proposed by any Federal department or agency,

(2) newly authorized Federal projects for construction and any major Federal action (other than a project for construction) to which section 102(2)(C) of . . . [NEPA] applies and (3) proposed regulations published by any department or agency of the Federal Government. Such written comment shall be made public at the conclusion of any such review.

(b) In the event that the Administrator determines that any such legislation, action, or regulation is unsatisfactory from the standpoint of public health or welfare or environmental quality, he shall publish his determination and the matter shall be referred to the Council on Environmental Quality. [42 U.S.C. §7609.]

The breadth of §309 is apparent. It requires EPA to evaluate the merits of the agency proposal, not just the merits of the impact statement. Must the agency request EPA comment? Is EPA review limited solely to environmental matters? Is EPA review required only for matters subject to impact statements?

In most cases, the normal commenting process provides a substitute for a §309 intervention, and EPA has limited its §309 reviews to cases dealing with severe environmental problems. EPA carries out its reviews under guidelines that require an evaluation of the draft impact statement and the environmental merits of the action covered by the impact statement. EPA, Order 1640.1, Review of Federal Actions Impacting the Environment. It has also published a number of Guidance documents that govern its review responsibilities. They are available on its website. EPA's authority to declare a proposal environmentally unsatisfactory is discretionary. Sierra Club v. Morton, 379 F. Supp. 1254 (D. Colo. 1974) (reviewing legislative history of provision). A study of EPA compliance reviews showed little change in quality over the years. Tzoumis & Finegold, Looking at the Quality of Draft Environmental Impact Statements over Time: Have the Ratings Improved?, 29 Envtl. Impact Assess. Rev. 527 (2000).

What is the legal effect of an "unsatisfactory" environmental determination by EPA under §309? Note that §309(b) does not indicate what is to happen after an unsatisfactory determination is referred to the CEQ. In Alaska v. Andrus, 580 F.2d 465 (D.C. Cir. 1978), EPA's recommendation that an offshore oil and gas lease sale be delayed was held moot because the recommended delay had expired. In dictum, the court indicated that EPA's unsatisfactory determination "did give rise to a heightened obligation on [the Department of the] Interior's part to explain clearly and in detail its reasons for proceeding. It seems clear to us that §309 was intended to do something more than merely reiterate 102(2)(C) of NEPA." Id. at 475 n.44. The court added that an agency that decides to proceed in the face of an unsatisfactory EPA determination "must articulate clearly its reasons for doing so." Is this agency obligation procedural or substantive? How much weight did the court really give to an EPA §309 intervention?

3. *Delegation.* Federal agencies may delegate the preparation of an EIS. When this occurs there is a possibility for bias if the preparer is an applicant for a federal permit or wants to obtain work required by the project that is considered in the EIS. Do the following cases, regulations, and statutes adequately handle this problem?

Impact statements may not be prepared by applicants for a federal permit or other approval. Greene County Planning Bd. v. FPC, 455 F.2d 412 (2d Cir. 1972), held an EIS was self-serving because it was prepared by an applicant who applied for federal approval. However, an applicant may submit environmental information needed for an EIS or participate in environmental studies. Sierra Club v. Lynn, 502 F.2d 43 (5th Cir. 1974). See 40 C.F.R. §1506.5(b).

CEQ regulations also authorize the delegation of the preparation of impact statements to contractors. 40 C.F.R. §1506.5(c). Contractors are to "avoid" conflicts of interest and submit a disclosure that they have no financial or other interest in the project. The regulations also require the federal agency to furnish guidance, participate in EIS preparation, evaluate it independently, and take responsibility for its scope and content. See Associations Working for Aurora's Residential Env't v. Colorado Dep't of Transp., 153 F.3d 1122 (10th Cir. 1998) (federal oversight sufficient; contractor with enforceable promise or guarantee of work has conflict of interest, but not contractor who merely has expectation).

Congress authorized a delegation of impact statement preparation under §104(g) of the Housing and Community Development Act of 1974, 42 U.S.C. §5304(g). The courts have interpreted this provision as conferring only procedural responsibilities on the federal Department of Housing and Urban Development. It is not required to independently review impact statements submitted by local governments or prepare its own impact statement. See Brandon v. Pierce, 725 F.2d 555 (10th Cir. 1984). There is also a provision in NEPA, §102(2)(D), that authorizes the delegation of impact statements on federally funded highways to state highway agencies. For a discussion of delegation see Frank, Comment, Delegation of Environmental Impact Statement Preparation: A Critique of NEPA's Enforcement, 13 B.C. Envtl. Aff. L. Rev. 79 (1985).

4. *Lead and Cooperating Agencies.* In many cases in which NEPA applies, a single action or project may require approval from more than one agency. A lead agency must be designated in this situation. CEQ regulations adopted the lead agency approach and provide a number of factors to consider that are relevant to the lead agency designation. 40 C.F.R. §1501.5. See National Wildlife Fed'n v. Benn, 491 F. Supp. 1234 (S.D.N.Y. 1980). Where both the Corps and EPA had jurisdiction over ocean dumping, the court held the Corps could prepare the impact statement either in conjunction with or with partial reliance on EPA reports.

CEQ regulations provide a role for cooperating agencies when more than one agency has an interest in an action that requires environmental review. 40 C.F.R. §1501.6 (lead agency must request cooperation). Exclusion of cooperating agencies from the decisionmaking process can result in a violation of NEPA. International Snowmobile Mfrs. Ass'n v. Norton, 340 F. Supp. 2d 1249 (D. Wyo. 2004) (invalidating rule for which impact statement was prepared as prejudged political decision).

The lead and cooperating agency requirement clearly has problems. One agency may proceed with its action before the lead agency prepares the impact statement, thus frustrating the impact statement preparation process. See Upper Pecos Ass'n v. Stans, 452 F.2d 1233 (10th Cir. 1971), *vacated,* 409 U.S. 1021 (1972). Agencies also have different interests, and the lead agency may leave out a concern of interest to other agencies with jurisdiction over the project. Problems can also arise if the project approval process requires decisions by some agencies before other agencies can act. Designating the agency that must act first as the lead agency may not be appropriate. Multiple jurisdiction problems might best be solved by a revision of legislative authority for agency regulation and jurisdiction. Compare Cal. Pub. Resources Code §21067, which defines lead agency as "the public agency which has the principal responsibility for carrying out or approving a project," and §21165, providing for the preparation of impact reports by a lead agency.

CEQ's concern about collaboration among agencies led it to issue a memorandum on this subject in 2004. The 2003 NEPA Task Force Report to CEQ, Modernizing NEPA Implementation, recommended methods to increase collaboration among agencies, including guidance suggesting the elements of successful collaborative agreements. Id. at 33.

2.   *The Alternatives Requirement*

One of NEPA's major expectations was that federal agencies, directed by statute to carry out narrowly conceived missions, would consider less environmentally damaging alternatives they might not otherwise consider. Highway projects are a good example. The federal government funds state highways to meet expected highway needs. State transportation agencies usually meet these needs by selecting a location requiring the least expenditure of federal and state funds, even though less damaging alternative locations are available. Federal and state agencies are reluctant to consider alternatives to highway projects that interfere with their statutory mission to meet traffic needs through highway construction. Alternatives such as public transit, or even a change in highway location, can meet with substantial resistance.

NEPA provides a process through which agencies must consider alternatives. The section requiring the preparation of an environmental impact statement requires the discussion of "alternatives to the proposed action." §102(2)(C)(iii). Both the courts and CEQ have characterized this alternatives requirement as the "heart" of the impact statement process. Another section of NEPA provides independently for the consideration of alternatives. It requires agencies of the federal government to "study, develop, and describe appropriate alternatives to recommended courses of action in any proposal which involves unresolved conflicts concerning alternative uses of available resources." §102(2)(E). Most decisions interpreting the separate alternatives requirement have considered it in the context of the impact statement, but some decisions have given this requirement an independent effect.

The range of alternatives agencies can consider can be extensive. The most dramatic is the "no action" alternative, which requires the agency to abandon its project altogether. Other alternatives would keep but modify the proposed action. Consider the following classification:

> . . . [A] secondary alternative concede[s] that the agency action is necessary but suggest[s] that it be carried out in a different manner. . . . [A] secondary alternative . . . [may require] a different location for a project, or project changes that mitigate harmful environmental impacts. [D. Mandelker, Environment and Equity 120 (1981).]

Are agencies better equipped to evaluate primary or secondary alternatives? Which type of alternative is likely to lie outside the agency's jurisdiction to implement? Should this factor be considered by courts and agencies in the evaluation of alternatives?

The District of Columbia Court of Appeals expansively interpreted the alternatives requirement in an early and leading case. NRDC v. Morton, 458 F.2d 827 (D.C. Cir. 1972). The Secretary of the Interior announced a general sale of leases of oil and gas tracts on the Outer Continental Shelf of eastern Louisiana in response to an energy supply message by President Nixon. The impact statement prepared for the lease announcement stated that the elimination of then-existing oil import quotas might be an alternative to offshore leasing but that this determination required consideration of complex factors, including national security, that were beyond the scope of the impact statement. The court disagreed:

> [R]equired in the ensuing environmental impact statements would be the discussion by each department of the particular actions it could take as an alternative to the proposal underlying its impact statement.
>
> When the proposed action is an integral part of a coordinated plan to deal with a broad problem, the range of alternatives that must be evaluated is broadened. While the Department of the Interior does not have the authority to eliminate or reduce oil import quotas, such action is within the purview of both Congress and the President, to whom the impact statement goes. The impact statement is not only for the exposition of the thinking of the agency, but also for the guidance of these ultimate decision-makers, and must provide them with the environmental effects of both the proposal and the alternatives, for their consideration along with the various other elements of the public interest. [Id. at 834-835.]

The court also stated:

> The mere fact that an alternative requires legislative implementation does not automatically establish it as beyond the domain of what is required for discussion, particularly since NEPA was intended to provide a basis for consideration and choice by the decision-makers in the legislative as well as the executive branch. But the need for an overhaul of basic legislation certainly bears on the requirements of the Act. We do not suppose Congress intended an agency to devote itself to extended discussion of the environmental impact of alternatives so remote from reality as to depend on, say, the repeal of the antitrust laws. [Id. at 837.]

The Supreme Court had an opportunity to consider *Morton's* "reasonably available" rule in a nuclear power plant licensing case. The Court's decision follows.

VERMONT YANKEE NUCLEAR POWER CORP. v. NATURAL RESOURCES DEFENSE COUNCIL, INC.
435 U.S. 519 (1978)

JUSTICE REHNQUIST delivered the opinion of the Court.

[The Court consolidated for review two decisions by the now-superseded Atomic Energy Commission. Commission licensing procedures at this time were as follows: The utility first filed a preliminary safety analysis report, an environmental report, and information on antitrust implications. This information was reviewed by Commission staff, the Advisory Committee on Reactor Safeguards (ACRS), and a group of atomic energy experts. Both the ACRS and the experts submitted their evaluations to the Commission. A NEPA review was carried out by Commission staff, which prepared a draft and final impact statement. A three-member Atomic Safety and Licensing Board then held a public adjudicatory hearing, with the option of appeal to an appeal board and, in the board's discretion, to the Commission. The final agency decision was appealable to the federal Court of Appeals. Generally, the same procedure applied for an application for a license to operate a nuclear power plant.]

I . . .

C

In January 1969, petitioner Consumers Power Co. applied for a permit to construct two nuclear reactors in Midland, Mich. Consumers Power's application was examined by the Commission's staff and the ACRS. The ACRS issued reports which discussed specific problems and recommended solutions. It also made reference to "other problems" of a more generic nature and suggested that efforts should be made to resolve them with respect to these as well as all other projects. Two groups, one called Saginaw and another called Mapleton, intervened and opposed the application. Saginaw filed with the Board a number of environmental contentions, directed over 300 interrogatories to the ACRS, attempted to depose the chairman of the ACRS, and requested discovery of various ACRS documents. The Licensing Board denied the various discovery requests directed to the ACRS. Hearings were then held on numerous radiological health and safety issues. Thereafter, the Commission's staff issued a draft environmental impact statement. Saginaw submitted 119 environmental contentions which were both comments on the proposed draft statement and a statement of Saginaw's position in the upcoming hearings. The staff revised the statement and issued a final environmental statement in March 1972. Further hearings were then conducted during May and June 1972. Saginaw, however, choosing not to appear at or participate in these latter hearings, indicated that it had "no conventional findings of fact to set forth" and had not "chosen to search the record and respond to this proceeding by submitting citations of matters which we believe were proved or disproved." But the Licensing Board, recognizing its obligations to "independently consider the final balance among conflicting environmental factors in the record," nevertheless treated as contested those issues "as to which intervenors introduced affirmative evidence or engaged in substantial cross examination."

At issue now are 17 of those 119 contentions which are claimed to raise questions of "energy conservation." The Licensing Board indicated that as far as appeared from the record, the demand for the plant was made up of normal industrial and residential use. It went on to state that it was "beyond our province to inquire into whether the customary uses being made of electricity in our society are 'proper' or 'improper.'" With respect to claims that Consumers Power stimulated demand by its advertising the Licensing Board indicated that "[n]o evidence was offered on this point and absent some evidence that Applicant is creating abnormal demand, the Board did not consider the question." The Licensing Board also failed to consider the environmental effects of fuel reprocessing or disposal of radioactive wastes. The Appeal Board ultimately affirmed the Licensing Board's grant of a construction permit and the Commission declined to further review the matter.

At just about the same time, the Council on Environmental Quality revised its regulations governing the preparation of environmental impact statements. The regulations mentioned for the first time the necessity of considering in impact statements energy conservation as one of the alternatives to a proposed project. The new guidelines were to apply only to final impact statements filed after January 28, 1974. Thereafter, on November 6, 1973, more than a year after the record had been closed in the *Consumers Power* case and while that case was pending before the Court of Appeals, the Commission ruled in another case that while its statutory power to compel conservation was not clear, it did not follow that all evidence of energy conservation issues should therefore be barred at the threshold. In re Niagara Mohawk Power Corp., 6 A.E.C. 995 (1973). Saginaw then moved the Commission to clarify its ruling and reopen the *Consumers Power* proceedings.

In a lengthy opinion, the Commission declined to reopen the proceedings. The Commission first ruled it was required to consider only energy conservation alternatives which were "reasonably available," would in their aggregate effect curtail demand for electricity to a level at which the proposed facility would not be needed, and were susceptible of a reasonable degree of proof. It then determined, after a thorough examination of the record, that not all of Saginaw's contentions met these threshold tests. It further determined that the Board had been willing at all times to take evidence on the other contentions. Saginaw had simply failed to present any such evidence. The Commission further criticized Saginaw for its total disregard of even those minimal procedural formalities necessary to give the Board some idea of exactly what was at issue. The Commission emphasized that "[p]articularly in these circumstances, Saginaw's complaint that it was not granted a hearing on alleged energy conservation issues comes with ill grace." And in response to Saginaw's contention that regardless of whether it properly raised the issues, the Licensing Board must consider all environmental issues, the Commission basically agreed, as did the Board itself, but further reasoned that the Board must have some workable procedural rules and these rules

> in this setting must take into account that energy conservation is a novel and evolving concept. NEPA "does not require a 'crystal ball' inquiry." Natural Resources Defense Council v. Morton, 458 F.2d 827, 837 (1972). This consideration has led us to hold that we will not apply *Niagara* retroactively. As we gain experience on a case-by-case basis and hopefully, feasible energy conservation techniques emerge, the applicant, staff, and licensing boards will have obligations to develop an adequate record on these issues in appropriate cases, whether or not they are raised by intervenors.
>
> However, at this emergent stage of energy conservation principles, intervenors also have their responsibilities. They must state clear and reasonably specific energy conservation contentions in a timely fashion. Beyond that, they have a burden of coming forward with some affirmative showing if they wish to have these novel contentions explored further.

Respondents then challenged the granting of the construction permit in the Court of Appeals for the District of Columbia Circuit. . . .

We now turn to the Court of Appeals' holding "that rejection of energy conservation on the basis of the 'threshold test' was capricious and arbitrary," and again conclude the court was wrong.

The Court of Appeals ruled that the Commission's "threshold test" for the presentation of energy conservation contentions was inconsistent with NEPA's basic mandate to the Commission. The Commission, the court reasoned, is something more than an umpire who sits back and resolves adversary contentions at the hearing stage. 547 F.2d, at 627. And when an intervenor's comments "bring 'sufficient attention to the issue to stimulate the Commission's consideration of it,'" the Commission must "undertake its own preliminary investigation of the proffered alternative sufficient to reach a rational judgment whether it is worthy of detailed consideration in the EIS. Moreover, the Commission must explain the basis for each conclusion that further consideration of a suggested alternative is unwarranted." 547 F.2d, at 628, quoting from Indiana & Michigan Electric Co. v. FPC, 502 F.2d 336, 339 (1974).

While the court's rationale is not entirely unappealing as an abstract proposition, as applied to this case we think it basically misconceives not only the scope of the agency's statutory responsibility, but also the nature of the administrative process, the thrust of the agency's decision, and the type of issues the intervenors were trying to raise.

There is little doubt that under the Atomic Energy Act of 1954, state public utility commissions or similar bodies are empowered to make the initial decision regarding the need for power. The Commission's prime area of concern in the licensing context, on the other hand, is national security, public health, and safety. And it is clear that the need, as that term is conventionally used, for the power was thoroughly explored in the hearings. Even the Federal Power Commission, which regulates sales in interstate commerce, agreed with Consumers Power's analysis of projected need.

NEPA, of course, has altered slightly the statutory balance, requiring "a detailed statement by the responsible official on . . . alternatives to the proposed action." But, as should be obvious even upon a moment's reflection, the term "alternatives" is not self-defining. To make an impact statement something more than an exercise in frivolous boilerplate the concept of alternatives must be bounded by some notion of feasibility. As the Court of Appeals for the District of Columbia Circuit has itself recognized:

> There is reason for concluding that NEPA was not meant to require detailed discussion of the environmental effects of "alternatives" put forward in comments when these effects cannot be readily ascertained and the alternatives are deemed only remote and speculative possibilities, in view of basic changes required in statutes and policies of other agencies — making them available, if at all, only after protracted debate and litigation not meaningfully compatible with the timeframe of the needs to which the underlying proposal is addressed. [Natural Resources Defense Council v. Morton, 458 F.2d 827, 837-838 (1972).]

Common sense also teaches us that the "detailed statement of alternatives" cannot be found wanting simply because the agency failed to include every alternative device and thought conceivable by the mind of man. Time and resources are simply too limited to hold that an impact statement fails because the agency failed to ferret out every possible alternative, regardless of how uncommon or unknown that alternative may have been at the time the project was approved.

With these principles in mind we now turn to the notion of "energy conservation," an alternative the omission of which was thought by the Court of Appeals to have been "forcefully pointed out by Saginaw in its comments on the draft EIS." 547 F.2d, at 625. Again, as the Commission pointed out, "the phrase 'energy conservation' has a deceptively simple ring in this context. Taken literally, the phrase suggests a virtually limitless range of possible actions and developments that might, in one way or another, ultimately reduce projected demands for electricity from a particular proposed plant." Moreover, as a practical matter, it is hard to dispute the observation that it is largely the events of recent years that have emphasized not only the need but also a large variety of alternatives for energy conservation. Prior to the drastic oil shortages incurred by the United States in 1973, there was little serious thought in most Government circles of energy conservation alternatives. Indeed, the Council on Environmental Quality did not promulgate regulations which even remotely suggested the need to consider energy conservation in impact statements until August 1, 1973. And

even then the guidelines were not made applicable to draft and final statements filed
with the Council before January 28, 1974. The Federal Power Commission likewise
did not require consideration of energy conservation in applications to build hydroelectric facilities until June 19, 1973. And these regulations were not made retroactive
either. All this occurred over a year and a half after the draft environmental statement
for Midland had been prepared, and over a year after the final environmental statement had been prepared and the hearings completed.

We think these facts amply demonstrate that the concept of "alternatives" is an
evolving one, requiring the agency to explore more or fewer alternatives as they
become better known and understood. This was well understood by the Commission,
which, unlike the Court of Appeals, recognized that the Licensing Board's decision
had to be judged by the information then available to it. And judged in that light we
have little doubt the Board's actions were well within the proper bounds of its statutory
authority. Not only did the record before the agency give every indication that the
project was actually needed, but also there was nothing before the Board to indicate to
the contrary.

We also think the court's criticism of the Commission's "threshold test" displays
a lack of understanding of the historical setting within which the agency action took
place and of the nature of the test itself. In the first place, while it is true that NEPA
places upon an agency the obligation to consider every significant aspect of the environmental impact of a proposed action, it is still incumbent upon intervenors who
wish to participate to structure their participation so that it is meaningful, so that it
alerts the agency to the intervenors' position and contentions. This is especially true
when the intervenors are requesting the agency to embark upon an exploration of
uncharted territory, as was the question of energy conservation in the late 1960's and
early 1970's.

> [C]omments must be significant enough to step over a threshold requirement of mate-
> riality before any lack of agency response or consideration becomes of concern. The
> comment cannot merely state that a particular mistake was made . . . ; it must show why
> the mistake was of possible significance in the results. . . . Portland Cement Ass'n v.
> Ruckelshaus, 486 F.2d 375, 394 (1973).

Indeed, administrative proceedings should not be a game or a forum to engage in
unjustified obstructionism by making cryptic and obscure reference to matters that
"ought to be" considered and then, after failing to do more to bring the matter to
the agency's attention, seeking to have that agency determination vacated on the
ground that the agency failed to consider matters "forcefully presented." In fact,
here the agency continually invited further clarification of Saginaw's contentions.
Even without such clarification it indicated a willingness to receive evidence on the
matters. But not only did Saginaw decline to further focus its contentions, it virtually declined to participate, indicating that it had "no conventional findings of fact
to set forth" and that it had not "chosen to search the record and respond to this
proceeding by submitting citations of matter which we believe were proved or
disproved."

We also think the court seriously mischaracterized the Commission's "threshold
test" as placing "heavy substantive burdens . . . on intervenors. . . ." On the contrary,
the Commission explicitly stated: "We do not equate this burden with the civil litigation concept of a prima facie case, an unduly heavy burden in this setting. But the

showing should be sufficient to require reasonable minds to inquire further." We think this sort of agency procedure well within the agency's discretion.

In sum, to characterize the actions of the Commission as "arbitrary or capricious" in light of the facts then available to it as described at length above, is to deprive those words of any meaning. As we have said in the past:

> Administrative consideration of evidence . . . always creates a gap between the time the record is closed and the time the administrative decision is promulgated [and, we might add, the time the decision is judicially reviewed]. . . . If upon the coming down of the order litigants might demand rehearings as a matter of law because some new circumstance has arisen, some new trend has been observed, or some new fact discovered, there would be little hope that the administrative process could ever be consummated in an order that would not be subject to reopening. ICC v. Jersey City, 322 U.S. 503, 514 (1944).

We have also made it clear that the role of a court in reviewing the sufficiency of an agency's consideration of environmental factors is a limited one, limited both by the time at which the decision was made and by the statute mandating review. "Neither the statute nor its legislative history contemplates that a court should substitute its judgment for that of the agency as to the environmental consequences of its actions." Kleppe v. Sierra Club, 427 U.S., at 410 n.21. We think the Court of Appeals has forgotten that injunction here and accordingly its judgment in this respect must also be reversed.

NOTES AND QUESTIONS

1. *What* Vermont Yankee *Means.* Although the Supreme Court in *Vermont Yankee* quoted the "speculative alternative" language from *Morton*, it ignored *Morton's* more expansive reading of the alternatives requirement quoted above. Has the Supreme Court overruled *Morton*? Is the standard adopted by *Vermont Yankee* procedural or substantive? Did the Supreme Court mean to imply that an agency need not consider alternatives that would require amendment of its basic enabling legislation? Or does the case simply mean an agency need not consider remote and speculative alternatives?

For a critical view of *Vermont Yankee*, which takes the position that the Court misapplied the *Morton* decision, see Rodgers, A Hard Look at *Vermont Yankee*: Environmental Law under Strict Scrutiny, 67 Geo. L.J. 699 (1979). Professor Rodgers claims *Vermont Yankee* qualified the important "balls and strikes" doctrine. Under this doctrine, an agency does not sit as an umpire, calling balls and strikes, but must affirmatively seek out issues relevant to the case that may not have occurred to the parties. *Vermont Yankee* qualified this doctrine by holding that "the energy conservation alternative did not have to be addressed because the intervenors did not raise their objections with sufficient support and precision." Id. at 720. Rodgers argued that the burden placed on intervenors "means a great deal . . . in the case of arguable or partial alternatives, such as energy conservation, which is within a reasonable, albeit ambitious, range of policy options." Id. at 721. A panel of the District of Columbia Court of Appeals has since suggested that *Morton* is no longer good law because it is qualified by *Vermont Yankee*. City of Alexandria v. Slater, 198 F.3d 862, 869 n.4 (D.C. Cir. 1999).

CEQ regulations require federal agencies to consider the no-action alternative, other "reasonable courses of action," and mitigation measures not in the proposed action. 40 C.F.R. §1508.25(b). The regulations also require agencies to consider "reasonable alternatives" not within their jurisdiction. §1502.14(b). Are these regulations consistent with *Vermont Yankee*?

2. *Purpose, Need, and Statutory Objectives.* CEQ regulations require an impact statement to describe the "underlying purpose and need of the project for which it is responding in proposing alternatives." §1502.13. Courts have cautioned that agencies must take a middle ground when meeting this requirement:

> [A]n agency may not define the objectives of its action in terms so unreasonably narrow that only one alternative from among the environmentally benign ones in the agency's power would accomplish the goals of the agency's action, and the EIS would become a foreordained formality. Nor may an agency frame its goals in terms so unreasonably broad that an infinite number of alternatives would accomplish those goals and the project would collapse under the weight of the possibilities. [Citizens Against Burlington, Inc. v. Busey, 938 F.2d 190, 196 (D.C. Cir. 1991).]

Agencies will try the narrowing tack because narrowing the alternatives will narrow the scope of an action and help justify an agency's preferred alternative. The *Slater* decision, *supra*, is a good example. The court upheld an EIS on a replacement bridge across the Potomac in Washington, D.C., because it "seems rather obvious to us that it is not unreasonable in articulating its objectives for an agency to 'focus primarily on transportation and safety issues' when replacing a massively congested and structurally unsound bridge." The court then held the agency could use its estimate of future traffic need to reject a bridge with fewer lanes as an alternative. Is this self-serving?

Agencies do not always win these cases. In Davis v. Mineta, 302 F.3d 1104, 1119 (10th Cir. 2002), the court interpreted the statement of purpose for a highway project to foreclose limiting the purpose to the provision of a structure across a river, but commented that "if the Project did narrowly express its purposes and needs as requiring a new crossing across the Jordan River at 11400 South, we would conclude that such a narrow definition of Project needs would violate NEPA given the more general overarching objective of improving traffic flow in the area." Id. at 1119. Are the cases distinguishable?

3. *No-Action Alternative.* CEQ regulations also require consideration of a no-action alternative. 40 C.F.R. §1502.14(2). Though doing nothing may be preferable to an action or project that may have significant environmental impacts, the courts have been generous in approving agency decisions that reject no-action alternatives, though they have given little indication of when discussion of a no-action alternative is necessary. In some of these cases they rejected the no-action alternative because it would not meet project goals. For example, courts have rejected a no-action alternative in highway cases because it would not satisfy the purpose and need of the project, which is to provide highway improvements. See North Buckhead Civic Ass'n v. Skinner, 903 F.2d 1533 (11th Cir. 1990).

But see Van Abbema v. Fornell, 807 F.2d 633 (7th Cir. 1986). The court applied §102(2)(E) of NEPA and held the Corps had not properly considered a no-action alternative when it approved a dredge and fill permit for a coal-loading facility on the Mississippi River. The court noted that existing coal-loading facilities might well be adequate.

4. *Primary Alternatives.* The major questions in applying the alternatives require-ment are what kinds of alternatives agencies must discuss and whether the discussion of alternatives was adequate. In most cases, courts rejected arguments that an agency had failed to discuss a primary alternative or that a discussion of a primary alternative was inadequate.

South Carolina ex rel. Campbell v. O'Leary, 64 F.3d 892 (4th Cir. 1995), rejected an argument that the agency should have considered the reprocessing of spent nuclear fuel as an alternative to storage. It noted that "current national policy specifically seeks to avoid this possibility." Id. at 899. In another case the court upheld a refusal to consider mass transit as an alternative to a highway. North Buckhead Civic Ass'n v. Skinner, *supra.* Although admitting that agencies have an obligation to discuss an alternative that partially satisfies the need and purpose of a proposed project, the court held that "[t]here is no evidence here that heavy rail transit alone is a reasonable alternative to the construction of the Georgia 400 extension in the North Atlanta corridor. While mass transit lines would provide additional transportation capacity in the corridor, the problems of surface street congestion would remain completely unresolved." Id. at 1542. Has the court simply defined away the environmental problem? See also Coalition for Better Veterans Care, Inc. v. Veterans Admin., 16 Env't Rep. Cas. (BNA) 1685 (D. Or. 1981) (rejecting alternative of private treatment as alternative to hospital construction as "assault on basic policy"). But see *Van Abbema,* discussed *supra.*

Courts have also required agencies to consider primary alternatives. One court held, for example, that an agency had unreasonably refused to consider any alternative that included restoration of a burned forest area without salvage logging. League of Wilderness Defenders-Blue Mts. Biodiversity Project v. Marquis-Brong, 259 F. Supp. 2d 1115 (D. Or. 2003).

5. *Secondary Alternatives.* Courts are more willing to require a discussion of secondary alternatives that merely modify a proposed project. Some cases are contrary, see Citizens Against Burlington, Inc. v. Busey, *supra* (agency need not consider alter-natives that meet needs of airport expansion). When an agency has considered secondary alternatives the courts usually find the discussion adequate, sometimes holding that the alternative would be environmentally disruptive or would not be environmentally superior.

However, in Dubois v. United States Dep't of Agric., 103 F.3d 1273 (1st Cir. 1996), the court held that the federal agency did not adequately consider the alternative of using artificial water storage units instead of a natural pond as a source for snowmaking for a ski resort. The court noted that taking water from the pond would be environmentally devastating, that the agency had required construction of artificial ponds for another ski area, and that the resort owner held land on which it could feasibly construct artificial ponds.

Noting that several commenters had proposed artificial ponds as an alternative, the court held:

> Instead of "rigorously exploring" the alternative of using artificial water storage units instead of Loon Pond, the Forest Service's Final EIS did not respond to these comments at all. The agency did not in any way explain its reasoning or provide a factual basis for its refusal to consider, in general, the possibility of alternatives to using Loon Pond for snowmaking, or LCCC's reasonably thoughtful proposal in particular. This failure violated the Forest Service's EIS obligation under NEPA. [Id. at 1288.]

What prompted the court's decision in this case? Is there some threshold test objectors must meet to shift the burden to the agency to justify rejection of an alternative?

6. *Range of Alternatives Considered.* To what extent can agencies reduce the range of alternatives to limit the alternatives available? The courts will usually defer to an agency's decision on the range of alternatives considered if it appears sufficiently comprehensive and there is no attempt to eliminate alternatives that could be viable options. See, e.g., Friends of the Boundary Waters Wilderness v. Dombeck, 164 F.3d 1115 (8th Cir. 1999).

However, In California v. Block, 690 F.2d 753 (9th Cir. 1982), the Forest Service reviewed the future use of 62 million acres of roadless national forest land. All serious alternatives considered in its impact statement contemplated the development of some of this land, and no alternative would have retained more than 34 percent of the area in a wilderness condition. The court held that the alternatives considered were inadequate, noting that "it is puzzling why the Forest Service did not seriously consider an alternative that allocated more than a third of the . . . acreage to Wilderness." Id. at 768. What if the Forest Service had decided, as a matter of policy, that all of the wilderness area under consideration should be released for development? Could the agency then eliminate the wilderness alternative from consideration?

NOTE ON STATUTORY MODIFICATION
OF THE ALTERNATIVES REQUIREMENT

The alternatives requirement, as the "heart" of the environmental review required by NEPA, is one of the statute's most important contributions to environmental law. (The other is the requirement to consider the cumulative impact of an action.) Agencies have long been hostile to the alternatives requirement, however, as it can require them to abandon a preferred project or action. Congress has now responded by modifying this requirement as it applies to transportation projects, which make up a substantial number of projects reviewed under NEPA, and airport expansion.

In 2005 Congress enacted the Safe, Accountable, Flexible, Efficient Transportation Equity Act, which substantially modifies NEPA as it applies to highway and other transportation projects that require federal approval. Pub. L. No. 109-59, 119 Stat. 1144 (2005) (variously codified). For discussion see 36 Env't Rep. (BNA) 1627 (2005). The Department of Transportation is made the lead agency for NEPA compliance. It makes the purpose and need decision that determines what alternatives must be considered, which may include achieving a transportation objective identified in a statewide or metropolitan transportation plan or that supports "land use, economic development or growth objectives" established in federal, state, local, or tribal plans. 23 U.S.C. §139(f)(2-3). It also has the authority to determine the "range of alternatives" to be considered in any environmental document. §139(f)(4)(B). The lead agency is also to "determine" the methodologies to be used and the level of detail required to analyze alternatives, §139(f)(4)(c). The preferred alternative, at the discretion of the lead agency, can be developed at a higher level of detail than other alternatives if the lead agency determines that developing a higher level of detail will not prevent it from making an impartial decision on whether to accept another alternative that is being considered in the environmental review process. §139(f)(4)(D). This provision is apparently intended to avoid objections that consideration of a preferred alternative is proof of agency bias. Comparable provisions appear in the Aviation Streamlining Approval Process Act of 2003, 49 U.S.C. §47171. See Berger, False Promises: NEPA's Role in Airport Expansions and the Streamlining of the Environmental Review Process, 18 J. Envtl. L. & Litig. 279 (2003). The Federal Aviation Agency is made the lead agency for aviation projects. The definition of purpose and need by the Secretary of Transportation in any environmental review for these projects is binding on other agencies. 49 U.S.C. §47171(j). The statute also provides that the Secretary shall determine the reasonable alternatives for airport capacity enhancement projects. Other agencies participating in a coordinated environmental review process can consider only those alternatives to the project the Secretary determines to be reasonable. 49 U.S.C. §47171(k). Similar provisions appear in the Healthy Forests Restoration Act of 2003. See 16 U.S.C. §§6514, 9604. Additional discussion of new legislation that modifies NEPA is provided below.

3. Segmentation

The scope of an impact statement is defined by the geographic extent of the "action" covered, as well as by the environmental impacts that must be discussed. As noted earlier, many governmental projects are constructed in stages, and separating identifiable stages for coverage in an impact statement is often difficult. Highways are a good example. Major highways are divided into segments for purposes of federal funding. The question is whether these individual segments may be separated for impact statement purposes. Objectors may complain that this kind of "piecemealing" allows the highway agency to minimize environmental impacts by avoiding discussion of the cumulative impacts of the highway project. Agencies argue that widening the scope of the impact statement to include related projects is impractical and may compel the agency to consider the speculative impacts of projects not yet approved.

The following case considers a typical segmentation issue:

FLORIDA KEYS CITIZENS COALITION, INC. v. UNITED STATES ARMY CORPS OF ENGINEERS
374 F. Supp. 2d 1116 (S.D. Fla. 2005)

PAUL C. HUCK, District Judge.

[This case involves a highway safety improvement project for U.S. Highway 1, which is the principal highway in the Florida Keys. Originally the project was to be four lanes, but it was reduced to two lanes. The project also provides for the replacement of an existing bascule bridge with a high-level, fixed span bridge over a creek.] The [Federal Highway Administration (FHWA)] approved the bridge replacement portion of the 2LSP ("Bridge Replacement Project") over Jewfish Creek and Lake Surprise under NEPA by finding that it presented no impacts not known and scrutinized by the FEIS. The FHWA approved the remainder of the 2LSP, consisting primarily of roadway safety improvements ("Road Safety Improvements"), pursuant to a categorical exclusion under NEPA. Specifically, the FHWA found that the Road Safety Improvements are the type of safety improvements that are generally considered to be "categorically excluded" from detailed environmental review under NEPA, "such as shoulders for emergency use and bridge replacements and attendant environmental mitigation," which do not increase traffic capacity. . . .

[Plaintiffs contend] that the Project, and specifically the Bridge Replacement Project, has been improperly segmented from other projects or actions in order to limit the scope of the FEIS and the Reevaluation's environmental impact evaluation. The FHWA has promulgated regulations concerning environmental analysis of roadway systems "in order to ensure meaningful evaluation of alternatives and to avoid commitments to transportation improvements before they are fully evaluated. . . ." 23 C.F.R. §771.111(f). These regulations and the related judicial interpretations require a stand-alone project to: (1) connect logical termini and be of sufficient length to address environmental matters on a broad scope; (2) have independent utility or independent significance; and (3) not restrict consideration of alternatives for other reasonably foreseeable transportation improvements. The "independent utility" factor is the most important. Moreover, in determining whether these criteria are met, a central question is whether the project "will serve a significant purpose even if a second related project is not built. . . . Only when a given project effectively commits decisionmakers to a future course of action will this form of linkage argue strongly for joint environmental evaluation." Coalition on Sensible Transp., Inc. v. Dole, 826 F.2d 60, 69 (D.C. Cir. 1987). In turn, the question of whether a decision-maker is committed to a future course of action will largely turn upon whether the project irretrievably commits more public funding to other, future projects. Finally, courts have held that an agency's determination of the scope of a project is entitled to deference, and the regulations direct that an EIS's analysis of cumulative actions is required to cover only proposed actions rather than actions that are only a theoretical possibility. See 40 C.F.R. §1508.25(a)(2).

With the foregoing criteria in mind, the Court must determine whether the FHWA has impermissibly "segmented" the Bridge Replacement Project. To begin, the Bridge Replacement Project has independent utility, because it is designed to replace an obsolete bridge structure that is in need of replacement regardless of whether the Road Safety Improvements are also made. The record establishes that the existing bridge is more than 60 years old, in need of frequent repairs, subject to frequent mechanical failures, and considered "functionally obsolete," not to mention that standing alone it constitutes an identifiable major safety problem. Moreover, the Plaintiffs have not established that the completion of the Bridge Replacement Project will irretrievably commit the FHWA to the funding of other future projects identified in the Miller Study [of the project], which Plaintiffs contend should have been considered in the evaluation. Finally, the administrative record reflects that at least a portion of the projects recommended by the Miller Study are only in the planning stages and, therefore, do not qualify as proposed action.

Although, as indicated above, the Road Safety Improvements ultimately were approved pursuant to a categorical exclusion rather than by reliance upon the FEIS and Reevaluation, the extensive analysis of the Road Safety Improvements in these documents is sufficient for satisfying the cumulative impacts analysis required for the improved bridge. These documents do not, however, attempt to assess the full cumulative impacts from all future highway improvements that may eventually be completed to improve evacuation times out of the Florida Keys. Regardless, Plaintiffs have failed to establish that such a requirement falls within the NEPA requirements relating to cumulative impacts. See [Preserve Endangered Areas of Cobb's History v. United States Army Corps of Eng'rs, 87 F.3d 1242 (11th Cir. 1996)] ("Just because the project at issue connects existing highways does not mean that it must be considered as part of a larger highway project; all roads must begin and end somewhere."). Any attempt to assess the cumulative impacts from such future projects would be pure speculation and is not required. See 40 CFR §1508.25(a)(2). Accordingly, for all of the foregoing reasons, the Court concludes that the FHWA did not improperly segment the Bridge Replacement Project. See Village of Los Ranchos de Albuquerque v. Barnhart, 906 F.2d 1477, 1482-84 (10th Cir. 1990) (holding that a project for the construction of two highway bridges was properly deemed independent of the connecting highway interchange project because the bridges had logical termini, substantial independent utility, did not foreclose alternatives for future projects, and did not commit funds for any related projects). See also Conservation Law Found. v. FHWA, 24 F.3d 1465, 1472 (1st Cir. 1994) ("Two bridges on either side of an island appear to be perfectly logical termini. . . ."). Notwithstanding the foregoing, the record reflects that the FDOT and the FHWA recognized the reality that the Bridge Replacement Project was not designed in a vacuum, but rather is considered an "indivisible part" of the Road Safety Improvements. . . .

Accordingly, the Court will enter a final judgment against the Plaintiffs and in favor of all Defendants.

NOTES AND QUESTIONS

1. *The Segmentation Problem.* The segmentation problem is to define the action the agency must consider when carrying out its environmental review. It is closely tied to the question of when a comprehensive or "program" impact statement must be prepared for related projects, an issue considered in the *Kleppe* case, which is reproduced next. A decision prohibiting segmentation will increase the geographic scope of an action and, presumably, the extent of its possibly significant environmental impacts.

2. *Highway Segmentation.* The segmentation issue is especially troublesome in highway projects, which often are part of a comprehensive system difficult to disentangle, as in the principal case. The Federal Highway Administration regulation quoted in the principal case is longstanding, and is applied by the courts in deciding whether segmentation in a particular case is acceptable. Since U.S. 1 is the single highway through the narrow Florida Keys, the decision to segment the bridge seems difficult to accept, though the court's decision is consistent with other segmentation cases.

Highway segmentation is usually approved. In metropolitan areas, where highway systems are interdependent and interconnected, courts sometimes avoid segmentation problems by holding that the major issue to be considered is independent utility. See Save Barton Creek Ass'n v. Federal Highway Admin., 950 F.2d 1129 (5th Cir. 1992), finding independent utility, *inter alia*, because the highway connected two expressways and relieved transportation congestion. Is this correct?

Deciding on the "independent utility" of a proposed segment can be difficult. Assume a proposed and relatively short new segment of an interstate highway intended to provide a bypass around a small community. Can the segment be isolated for review in the impact statement because its primary purpose is to provide traffic relief for the community? Or is its primary purpose to provide a link in the interstate highway system? See Daly v. Volpe, 514 F.2d 1106 (9th Cir. 1975) (adopting the former view). Does this holding allow agencies to adopt any self-serving justification for a project segment?

Highway agencies sometimes lose segmentation cases, though not often. In Western N. Carolina Alliance v. North Carolina Dep't of Transp., 312 F. Supp. 2d 765 (E.D.N.C. 2003), the court rejected segmentation because there were no logical termini, connection with another highway would create congestion, there was an admission the highway had to be segmented to avoid environmental problems, segmentation would restrict consideration of alternatives, and all of the projects were under consideration at the same time.

3. *Interrelated Projects.* Segmentation problems also arise when a federal agency plans to develop or approves a project that contains several related but different components. In Hudson River Sloop Clearwater, Inc. v. Department of the Navy, 836 F.2d 760 (2d Cir. 1988), for example, the Navy planned to build a new port for its ships together with associated housing. The court held that the Navy could segment the port for purposes of preparing an EIS because the port would be operational if the Navy decided not to build the housing.

4. *Staged Projects.* Segmentation problems also arise when agencies plan to build projects in stages. County of Suffolk v. Secretary of Interior, 562 F.2d 1368 (2d Cir. 1977), is the leading case. The court held an impact statement on an offshore oil and gas lease sale did not have to discuss the environmental impacts of the onshore transportation routes, including onshore pipelines, that would transport any oil that might be found. Any discussion of these environmental effects was speculative because the building of the pipelines was at least three years away and transportation routes would not be known until oil was discovered.

4. *Regional and Program Impact Statements*

Discussion of the segmentation problem leads naturally to another alternative that can consider the interrelated impacts of a number of related projects: the program impact statement. The following Supreme Court case considers the circumstances under which program impact statements are required under NEPA.

KLEPPE v. SIERRA CLUB
427 U.S. 390 (1976)

Mr. JUSTICE POWELL delivered the opinion of the Court.

I

Respondents, several organizations concerned with the environment, brought this suit in July 1973 in the United States District Court for the District of Columbia. The defendants in the suit, petitioners here, were the officials of the Department and other federal agencies responsible for issuing coal leases, approving mining plans, granting rights-of-way, and taking the other actions necessary to enable private companies and public utilities to develop coal reserves on land owned or controlled by the Federal Government. Citing widespread interest in the reserves of a region identified as the

"Northern Great Plains region," and an alleged threat from coal-related operations to their members' enjoyment of the region's environment, respondents claimed that the federal officials could not allow further development without preparing a "comprehensive environmental impact statement under §102(2)(C) on the entire region. They sought declaratory and injunctive relief. . . .

[The district court, on the basis of extensive findings of fact and conclusions of law, granted petitioners' motions for summary judgment. On appeal, the Court of Appeals for the District of Columbia Circuit reversed and remanded for further proceedings. The Supreme Court then granted *certiorari*.]

II

The record and the opinions of the courts below contain extensive facts about coal development and the geographic area involved in this suit. The facts that we consider essential, however, can be stated briefly.

The Northern Great Plains region identified in respondents' complaint encompasses portions of four States—northeastern Wyoming, eastern Montana, western North Dakota, and western South Dakota. There is no dispute about its richness in coal, nor about the waxing interest in developing that coal, nor about the crucial role the federal petitioners will play due to the significant percentage of the coal to which they control access. The Department has initiated, in this decade, three studies in areas either inclusive of or included within this region. The North Central Power Study was addressed to the potential for coordinated development of electric power in an area encompassing all or part of 15 States in the North Central United States. It aborted in 1972 for lack of interest on the part of electric utilities. The Montana-Wyoming Aqueducts Study, intended to recommend the best use of water resources for coal development in southeastern Montana and northeastern Wyoming, was suspended in 1972 with the initiation of the third study, the Northern Great Plains Resources Program (NGPRP).

While the record does not reveal the degree of concern with environmental matters in the first two studies, it is clear that the NGPRP was devoted entirely to the environment. It was carried out by an interagency, federal-state task force with public participation, and was designed "to assess the potential social, economic and environmental impacts" from resource development in five States—Montana, Wyoming, South Dakota, North Dakota, and Nebraska. Its primary objective was "to provide an analytical and informational framework for policy and planning decisions at all levels of government" by formulating several "scenarios" showing the probable consequences for the area's environment and culture from the various possible techniques and levels of resource development. The final interim report of the NGPRP was issued August 1, 1975, shortly after the decision of the Court of Appeals in this case.

In addition, since 1973 the Department has engaged in a complete review of its coal-leasing program for the entire Nation. On February 17 of that year the Secretary announced the review and announced also that during study a "short-term leasing policy" would prevail, under which new leasing would be restricted to narrowly defined circumstances and even then allowed only when an environmental impact statement had been prepared if required under NEPA. The purpose of the program review was to study the environmental impact of the Department's entire range of coal-related activities and to develop a planning system to guide the national leasing program. The impact statement, known as the "Coal Programmatic EIS," went through several drafts before issuing in final form on September 19, 1975—shortly before the petitions for certiorari were filed in this case. The Coal Programmatic EIS proposed a new leasing program based on a complex planning system called the Energy Minerals Activity Recommendation System (EMARS), and assessed the prospective environmental impact of the new program as well as the alternatives to it. We have been informed by the parties to this litigation that the Secretary is in the process of implementing the new program.

Against this factual background, we turn now to consider the issues raised by this case in the status in which it reached this Court.

[In part III of its opinion the Court held that "there is no evidence in the record of an action or a proposal for an action of regional scope." It noted that the district court had found that "there was no existing or proposed plan or program on the part of the Federal Government for the regional development" of the Northern Great Plains area.]

IV

A

The Court of Appeals, in reversing the District Court, did not find that there was a regional plan or program for development of the Northern Great Plains region. It accepted all of the District Court's findings of fact, but concluded nevertheless that the petitioners "contemplated" a regional plan or program. The court thought that the North Central Power Study, the Montana-Wyoming Aqueducts Study, and the NGPRP all constituted "attempts to control development" by individual companies on a regional scale. It also concluded that the interim report of the NGPRP, then expected to be released at any time, would provide the petitioners with the information needed to formulate the regional plan they had been "contemplating." The Court therefore remanded with instructions to the petitioners to inform the District Court of their role in the further development of the region within 30 days after the NGPRP interim report issued; if they decided to control that development, an impact statement would be required.

We conclude that the Court of Appeals erred in both its factual assumptions and its interpretation of NEPA. We think the court was mistaken in concluding, on the record before it, that the petitioners were "contemplating" a regional development plan or program. It considered the several studies undertaken by the petitioners to represent attempts to control development on a regional scale. This conclusion was based on a finding by the District Court that those studies, as well as the new national coal-leasing policy, were "attempts to control development by individual companies in a manner consistent with the policies and procedures of the National Environmental Policy Act of 1969." But in context, that finding meant only that the named studies were efforts to gain background environmental information for subsequent application in the decisionmaking with respect to individual coal-related projects. This is the sense in which the District Court spoke of controlling development consistently with NEPA. Indeed, in the same paragraph containing the language relied upon by the Court of Appeals, the District Court expressly found that the studies were not part of a plan or program to develop or encourage development.

Moreover, at the time the Court of Appeals ruled there was no indication in the record that the NGPRP was aimed toward a regional plan or program, and subsequent events have shown that this was not its purpose. The interim report of the study, issued shortly after the Court of Appeals ruled, described the effects of several possible rates of coal development but stated in its preface that the alternatives "are for study and comparison only; they do not represent specific plans or proposals." All parties agreed in this Court that there still exists no proposal for a regional plan or program of development.

Even had the record justified a finding that a regional program was contemplated by the petitioners, the legal conclusion drawn by the Court of Appeals cannot be squared with the Act. The court recognized that the mere "contemplation" of certain action is not sufficient to require an impact statement. But it believed the statute nevertheless empowers a court to require the preparation of an impact statement to begin at some point prior to the formal recommendation or report on a proposal. The Court of Appeals accordingly devised its own four-part "balancing" test for determining when, during the contemplation of a plan or other type of federal action, an agency must begin a statement. The factors to be considered were identified as the likelihood and imminence of the program's coming to fruition, the extent to which information is available on the effects of implementing the expected program and on alternatives thereto, the extent to which irretrievable commitments are being made and options precluded "as refinement of the proposal progresses," and the severity of the environmental effects should the action be implemented.

The Court of Appeals thought that as to two of these factors—the availability of information on the effects of any regional development program, and the severity of those effects—the time already was "ripe" for an impact statement. It deemed the record unclear, however, as to the likelihood of the petitioners' actually producing a plan to control the development, and surmised that irretrievable commitments were being avoided because petitioners had ceased approving most coal-related projects while the NGPRP study was underway. The court also thought that the imminent release of the NGPRP interim report would provide the officials with sufficient information to define their role in development of the region, and it believed that as soon as the NGPRP was completed the petitioners would begin approving individual projects in the region, thus permitting irrevocable commitments of resources. It was for this reason that the court in its remand required the petitioners to report to the District Court their decision on the federal role with respect to the Northern Great Plains as a region within 30 days after issuance of the NGPRP report.

The Court's reasoning and action find no support in the language or legislative history of NEPA. The statute clearly states when an impact statement is required, and mentions nothing about a balancing of factors. Rather, as we noted last Term, under the first sentence of §102(2)(C) the moment at which an agency must have a final statement ready "is the time at which it makes a recommendation or report on a *proposal* for federal action." Aberdeen & Rockfish R. Co. v. SCRAP, 422 U.S. 289, 320 (1975) (*SCRAP II*) (emphasis in original). The procedural duty imposed upon agencies by this section is quite precise, and the role of the courts in enforcing that duty is similarly precise. A court has no authority to depart from the statutory language and, by a balancing of court-devised factors, determine a point during the germination process of a potential proposal at which an impact statement *should be prepared*. Such an assertion of judicial authority would leave the agencies uncertain as to their procedural duties under NEPA, would invite judicial involvement in the day-to-day decisionmaking process of the agencies, and would invite litigation. As the contemplation of a project and the accompanying study thereof do not necessarily result in a proposal for major federal action, it may be assumed that the balancing process devised by the Court of Appeals also would result in the preparation of a good many unnecessary impact statements. . . .

V

Our discussion thus far has been addressed primarily to the decision of the Court of Appeals. It remains, however, to consider the contention now urged by respondents. They have not attempted to support the Court of Appeals' decision. Instead, respondents renew an argument they appear to have made to the Court of Appeals, but which that court did not reach. Respondents insist that, even without a comprehensive federal plan for the development of the Northern Great Plains, a "regional" impact statement nevertheless is required on all coal-related projects in the region because they are intimately related.

There are two ways to view this contention. First, it amounts to an attack on the sufficiency of the impact statements already prepared by the petitioners on the coal-related projects that they have approved or stand ready to approve. As such, we cannot consider it in this proceeding, for the case was not brought as a challenge to a particular impact statement and there is no impact statement in the record. It also is possible to view the respondents' argument as an attack upon the decision of the petitioners not to prepare one comprehensive impact statement on all proposed projects in the region. This contention properly is before us, for the petitioners have made it clear they do not intend to prepare such a statement.

We begin by stating our general agreement with respondents' basic premise that §102(2)(C) may require a comprehensive impact statement in certain situations where several proposed actions are pending at the same time. NEPA announced a national policy of environmental protection and placed a responsibility upon the Federal Government to further specific environmental goals by "all practicable means, consistent with other essential considerations of national policy." §101(b). Section 102(2)(C) is one of the "action-forcing" provisions intended as a directive to "all agencies to assure consideration of the environmental impact of their actions in decisionmaking." Conference Report on NEPA, 115 Cong. Rec. 40416 (1969). By requiring an impact statement Congress intended to assure such consideration during the development of a proposal or—as in this case—during the formulation of a position on a proposal submitted by private parties. A comprehensive impact statement may be necessary in some cases for an agency to meet this duty. Thus, when several proposals for coal-related actions that will have cumulative or synergistic environmental impact upon a region are pending concurrently before an agency, their environmental consequences must be considered together. Only through comprehensive consideration of pending proposals can the agency evaluate different courses of action.[21]

21. Neither the statute nor its legislative history contemplates that a court should substitute its judgment for that of the agency as to the environmental consequences of its actions. See Scenic Hudson Preservation Conference v. FPC, 453 F.2d 463, 481 (2d Cir. 1971), cert. denied, 407 U.S. 926 (1972). The only role for a court is to insure that the agency has taken a "hard look" at environmental consequences; it cannot "interject itself within the area of discretion of the executive as to

Agreement to this extent with respondents' premise, however, does not require acceptance of their conclusion that all proposed coal-related actions in the Northern Great Plains region are so "related" as to require their analysis in a single comprehensive impact statement. Respondents informed us that the Secretary recently adopted an approach to impact statements on coal-related actions that provides:

> As a general proposition, and as determined by the Secretary, when action is proposed involving coal development such as issuing several coal leases or approving mining plans in the same region, such actions will be covered by a single EIS rather than by multiple statements. In such cases, the region covered will be determined by basin boundaries, drainage areas, areas of common reclamation problems, administrative boundaries, areas of economic interdependence, and other relevant factors.

At another point, the document containing the Secretary's approach states that a "regional EIS" will be prepared "if a series of proposed actions with interrelated impacts are involved . . . unless a previous EIS has sufficiently analyzed the impacts of the proposed action[s]." Thus, the Department has decided to prepare comprehensive impact statements of the type contemplated by §102(2)(C), although it has not deemed it appropriate to prepare such a statement on all proposed actions in the region identified by respondents.

Respondents conceded at oral argument that to prevail they must show that petitioners have acted arbitrarily in refusing to prepare one comprehensive statement on this entire region, and we agree. The determination of the region, if any, with respect to which a comprehensive statement is necessary requires the weighing of a number of relevant factors, including the extent of the interrelationship among proposed actions and practical considerations of feasibility. Resolving these issues requires a high level of technical expertise and is properly left to the informed discretion of the responsible federal agencies. Cf. *SCRAP II*, 422 U.S., at 325-26. Absent a showing of arbitrary action, we must assume that the agencies have exercised this discretion appropriately. Respondents have made no showing to the contrary.

Respondents' basic argument is that one comprehensive statement on the Northern Great Plains is required because all coal-related activity in that region is "programmatically," "geographically," and "environmentally" related. Both the alleged "programmatic" relationship and the alleged "geographic" relationship resolve, ultimately, into an argument that the region is proper for a comprehensive impact statement because the petitioners themselves have approached environmental study in this area on a regional basis. Respondents point primarily to the NGPRP, which they claim—and petitioners deny—focused on the region described in the complaint. The precise region of the NGPRP is unimportant, for its irrelevance to the delineation of an appropriate area for analysis in a comprehensive impact statement has been well stated by the Secretary:

> Resource studies [like the NGPRP] are one of many analytical tools employed by the Department to inform itself as to general resource availability, resource need and general environmental considerations so that it can intelligently determine the scope of environmental analysis and review specific actions it may take. Simply put, resource studies are a prelude to informed agency planning, and provide the data base on which the Department may decide to take specific actions for which impact statements are prepared. The scope of environmental impact statements seldom coincide[s] with

---

the choice of the action to be taken." Natural Resources Defense Council v. Morton, 458 F.2d 827, 838 (1972).

that of a given resource study, since the statements evolve from specific proposals for federal action while the studies simply provide an educational backdrop.

As for the alleged "environmental" relationship, respondents contend that the coal-related projects "will produce a wide variety of cumulative environmental impacts" throughout the Northern Great Plains region. They described them as follows: Diminished availability of water, air and water pollution, increases in population and industrial densities, and perhaps even climatic changes. Cumulative environmental impacts are, indeed, what require a comprehensive impact statement. But determination of the extent and effect of these factors, and particularly identification of the geographic area within which they may occur, is a task assigned to the special competency of the appropriate agencies. Petitioners dispute respondents' contentions that the interrelationship of environmental impacts is regionwide and, as respondents' own submissions indicate, petitioners appear to have determined that the appropriate scope of comprehensive statements should be based on basins, drainage areas, and other factors. We cannot say that petitioners' choices are arbitrary. Even if environmental interrelationships could be shown conclusively to extend across basins and drainage areas, practical considerations of feasibility might well necessitate restricting the scope of comprehensive statements.

In sum, respondents' contention as to the relationships between all proposed coal-related projects in the Northern Great Plains region does not require that petitioners prepare one comprehensive impact statement covering all before proceeding to approve specific pending applications. As we already have determined that there exists no proposal for regionwide action that could require a regional impact statement, the judgment of the Court of Appeals must be reversed, and the judgment of the District Court reinstated and affirmed. The case is remanded for proceedings consistent with this opinion. . . .

[JUSTICE MARSHALL wrote an opinion concurring in part and dissenting in part, in which he was joined by JUSTICE BRENNAN.]

NOTES AND QUESTIONS

1. *The Fragmentation Problem.* The *Kleppe* litigation was an attempt to overcome the limitation in NEPA that agencies are required to consider the environmental impacts of their actions one at a time. An earlier landmark NEPA case, Scientists' Inst. for Pub. Info., Inc. v. AEC (*SIPI*), 481 F.2d 1079 (D.C. Cir. 1973), seemed to support the plaintiff's case. There the Court of Appeals for the District of Columbia Circuit applied the fourfold balancing test rejected by the Supreme Court to require a programmatic impact statement on the technologic development program for the liquid fast metal nuclear breeder reactor. Though the development program was still in the research stage and no breeder reactors had been constructed, the court believed that the program constituted a "federal action." Judge Skelly Wright noted that the "[d]evelopment of the technology is a necessary precondition of construction of any plants" and added that "[t]o wait until a technology attains the stage of complete commercial feasibility before considering the possible adverse environmental effects attendant upon ultimate application of the technology will undoubtedly frustrate meaningful consideration and balancing of environmental costs against economic and other benefits." Id. at 1089.

The court then applied the fourfold balancing test to answer the timing question—"[w]hether a statement on the overall . . . [research] program should be issued now or at some uncertain date in the future." Id. at 1093. The court noted that the answer to the timing question required a finely tuned balancing because an impact statement could be prepared either too early, when it may be impossible to draft a meaningful impact statement, or too late, "when options will have been precluded without consideration of environmental effects."

> Thus we are pulled in two directions. Statements must be written late enough in the development process to contain meaningful information, but they must be written early enough so that whatever information is contained can practically serve as an input into the decision making process. [Id. at 1093-1094.]

The separate consideration of the federal action and the timing questions in *SIPI* seems in doubt after the more mechanical approach of *Kleppe*. The concurrent projects test adopted in *Kleppe* is of little help in evaluating the need for a program impact statement on technology development programs like the breeder reactor program, which has long been terminated. And, since *Kleppe* did not consider a multisegmented single project of the kind considered in the segmentation cases, the impact of *Kleppe* on segmentation doctrine also is unclear. For an extended discussion of *Kleppe*, see Johnston, *Kleppe v. Sierra Club*: An Environmental Planning Catch-22?, 1 Harv. Envtl. L. Rev. 182 (1976).

Some commentators consider *Kleppe* to be one of the "dirty dozen" (now 14) Supreme Court cases that have weakened NEPA. Based on your study of NEPA so far, do you agree?

2. *CEQ Regulations.* CEQ published what amounted to an official case note on the *Kleppe* opinion in the Federal Register. 42 Fed. Reg. 61,066, 61,069 (1977). CEQ stated that "the most useful principles for defining the scope of comprehensive environmental statements" were precedent-setting effect, interdependence, cumulation of impact, and availability of information. Id. at 61,071. Does this advice properly reflect the holding in *Kleppe*?

Present CEQ regulations covering impact statements on "broad actions" state that these actions are to be evaluated generically and geographically. 40 C.F.R. §1502.4(c). They add that statements on technological development programs are to be prepared "before the program has reached a stage of investment or commitment to implementation likely to determine subsequent development or restrict later alternatives." Id. §1502.4(c)(3). This regulation reflects *SIPI*. Does it meet the *Kleppe* tests?

3. *Applying* Kleppe. Ambiguities latent in the *Kleppe* decision make it difficult to predict its impact on the administration of NEPA. The Supreme Court's decision not to require an impact statement at the program planning stage, and the deference it paid to agency exercise of discretion, suggest that agencies may be able to avoid impact statement preparation until they are sufficiently comfortable with their plans to be able to formalize them in proposal form. See Texas Comm. on Natural Res. v. Bergland, 573 F.2d 201 (5th Cir. 1978) (upholding agency decision not to file program impact statement on timber management program).

Kleppe may confine the application of the impact statement requirement to incremental project decisions rather than to overall agency planning programs. As one commentator noted, "the less overall articulation of planning an agency undertakes (in the form of concrete proposals) the less actual environmental planning (in the form of impact statements) it can be compelled to perform." Johnston, *supra*, at 200. Recall the holding in Atlanta Coal. v. Atlanta Reg'l Comm'n, 599 F.2d 1333 (5th Cir. 1979), *supra*, that an impact statement was not necessary on the Atlanta regional transportation plan. That case relied heavily on *Kleppe*.

Compare NRDC, Inc. v. Hodel, 435 F. Supp. 590 (D. Or. 1977), *aff'd on other grounds sub nom*. Natural Resources Defense Council, Inc. v. Munro, 626 F.2d 134 (9th Cir. 1980). The federal Bonneville Power Administration and a number of private and public utilities entered into a cooperative program for the allocation of electric power throughout the Pacific Northwest. The court held that an impact statement was required on an extension of this program, which included plans for the construction of additional thermal power plants, as well as a number of agreements on purchasing and power allocation strategies. The court distinguished *Kleppe* and stated:

> [T]he Pacific Northwest is regarded as a distinct region for purposes of electrical power planning. . . . [The program contains] specific plans for regional development, hammered out after long negotiations and embodied in published documents. Individual projects undertaken by the federal government, by public and private utilities, and by industry are interrelated according to an integrated plan. [435 F. Supp. at 600.]

See also Port of Astoria v. Hodel, 595 F.2d 467 (9th Cir. 1979). The existence of the formally agreed-upon program distinguishes NRDC, Inc. v. Hodel from *Kleppe*. Compare *Atlanta Coal.*, in which the court noted that the plan did not commit the federal agency to a specific project. Is NRDC, Inc. v. Hodel distinguishable because a federal agency participated in the plan? More generally, should the courts rely on these formal distinctions in deciding whether to require the preparation of a programmatic impact statement? See Note, The Scope of the Program EIS Requirement: The Need for a Coherent Judicial Approach, 30 Stan. L. Rev. 767 (1978). See also Environmental Def. Fund, Inc. v. Andrus, 596 F.2d 848 (9th Cir. 1979) (programmatic impact statement required for Interior Department industrial water marketing plan for federally controlled reservoir).

4. *Post-Program Impact Statements*. Does the preparation of a programmatic impact statement eliminate the need to prepare an impact statement on a specific action included within the program when the programmatic impact statement is not sufficiently detailed to cover all aspects of the site-specific action? The decision on this issue is fact-specific and depends on the court's evaluation of whether site-related environmental impacts were covered in the program statement. Compare Ventling v. Bergland, 479 F. Supp. 174 (D.S.D. 1979) (no site-specific impact statement required) with NRDC v. Administrator, Energy Research & Dev. Admin., 451 F. Supp. 1245 (D.D.C. 1978) (contra). CEQ calls this process "tiering" and recommends that the site-specific impact statement refer back to applicable discussion contained in the program impact statement. See Comment, The Tiering of Impact Statements— Can the Process Be Stopped Halfway?, 20 Urb. L. Ann. 197 (1980).

If the issue in question is controversial enough, Congress may intervene directly in the scope issue. A Department of Interior appropriations act provided that any irrigation project in the Colorado River water system that is a multiphase project "shall proceed if a final environmental impact statement has been filed on such feature." When the Secretary of the Interior went ahead with a basinwide impact statement, a suit by the state of Utah and the Central Utah Water Conservancy District arguing that a basinwide impact statement was ultra vires was dismissed for lack of ripeness. Utah v. Andrus, 636 F.2d 276 (10th Cir. 1980).

5. *Connected, Cumulative, and Similar Actions.* Another CEQ regulation covers the problem of grouping related actions together for review. It requires consideration of connected, cumulative, and similar actions in the same impact statement. 40 C.F.R. §1508.25. Actions are "connected" if they "(i) Automatically trigger other actions which may require environmental impact statements. (ii) Cannot or will not proceed unless other actions are taken previously or simultaneously. (iii) Are interdependent parts of a larger action and depend on the larger action for their justification." §1508.25(a)(1). The regulation also requires a single impact statement for "cumulative actions, which when viewed with other proposed actions have cumulatively significant impacts and should therefore be discussed in the same impact statement." §1508.25(a)(2).

The Ninth Circuit applied these regulations in a leading case, Thomas v. Peterson, 753 F.2d 754 (9th Cir. 1985). The Forest Service prepared an environmental assessment on a road in a national forest and decided no impact statement was necessary because the road would not cause significant environmental impacts. Subsequently, the Service issued environmental assessments for proposed timber sales that would use the new road and concluded these sales also would not have significant environmental impact. The court decided these two projects had to be considered together. It held that "[t]he construction of the road and the sale of the timber in the Jersey Jack area meet the second and third, as well as perhaps the first of these [connected action] criteria. It is clear that the timber sales cannot proceed without the road, and the road would not be built but for the contemplated timber sales." The court also held the two projects had to be considered together as cumulative actions. "The record in this case contains considerable evidence to suggest that the road and the timber sales will have cumulatively significant impacts."

For an analysis that argues that *Peterson* expands on the *Kleppe* holding, see Hapke, *Thomas v. Peterson*: The Ninth Circuit Breathes New Life into CEQ's Cumulative and Connected Actions Regulations, 15 Envtl. L. Rep. (ELI) 10289, 10294 (1985) (court "crafted an approach that highlighted cumulative impacts as the controlling factor in determining EIS scope and timing"). Compare Headwaters, Inc. v. Bureau of Land Mgmt., 914 F.2d 1174 (9th Cir. 1990) (no need to consider cumulative impact of logging access road because road did not imply further development); Barnes v. Babbitt, 329 F. Supp. 2d 1141 (D. Ariz. 2004) (agency decisions interconnected).

A related regulation that requires the consideration of "similar" actions in the same impact statement has slightly different language that leads courts to accept agency decisions to separate projects. Klamath-Siskiyou Wildlands Ctr. v. Bureau of Land Mgmt., 387 F.3d 989 (9th Cir. 2004) (timber sales).

D. ADEQUACY

1. The Substantive versus Procedural Problem

The Problem. Once an agency has decided to prepare an environmental impact statement, it must meet the requirements for impact statements imposed by §102(2)(C). Ultimately, the courts must consider whether the impact statement is adequate, and the question they must resolve is this: Assuming that decisionmakers will seriously read and react to the information in the impact statement, is the statement likely to further the basic goal of NEPA, which is the promotion of more environmentally enlightened decisions? This question is troublesome for federal courts. At a minimum, as the decisions indicate, the impact statement is a full disclosure document, much like a Securities and Exchange Commission prospectus, and it must fully disclose the environmental impacts of the proposed action. But because the federal courts also take a "hard look" at agency decisions that have environmental consequences, more than mere disclosure may be required.

To understand the cases on the adequacy of an impact statement and the scope of judicial review, a basic distinction must be kept in mind, and that is the distinction between a challenge to the adequacy of an impact statement and a challenge to the merits of the decision. A NEPA plaintiff's first two challenges are to allege that an impact statement should have been prepared, if one has not been, and that if one was prepared, it is inadequate. The remedies for successful plaintiffs in these cases are the preparation of an initial, new, or supplemental impact statement. A challenge to the merits of the decision is based upon an unsatisfactory impact statement, but the impact statement is only one—although a very important—piece of evidence the decisionmaker must consider in making a final decision. The link between an unsatisfactory impact statement and the assertion that the final decision is arbitrary is the argument that, given the unsatisfactory impact statement, an informed decisionmaker could reach no other conclusion but that the proposed action should be rejected or modified. Recent Supreme Court decisions indicate that this is an impossible argument to win.

Courts and commentators usually refer to the duty to prepare an adequate impact statement as NEPA's "procedural" duty. They refer to the agency's responsibility to reject or modify a proposal for action because of an unsatisfactory impact statement as NEPA's "substantive" duty. The term "procedural duty" does not refer to the duty to observe hearing or other procedures in the preparation of an impact statement; it refers instead to the duty to comply sufficiently with the procedures mandated by NEPA for the preparation of an impact statement, so that the statement will contain a reasoned analysis on which the decisionmaker can base his decision. Courts ask whether an impact statement is "adequate" when they consider NEPA's procedural duty. The adequacy inquiry includes the following questions: Have all environmental impacts and alternatives been considered? If all alternatives and impacts have been considered, have they been adequately discussed and evaluated? What rules should the agency apply in discussing and evaluating alternatives and impacts?

Supreme Court Decisions. Whether NEPA should be given a substantive effect turns, in the words of *Overton Park*, on whether the statute has enacted "law to apply." Early court decisions concluded that NEPA had done just that. The leading case was Environmental Def. Fund, Inc. v. Corps of Eng'rs, 470 F.2d 289 (8th Cir. 1972), reviewing an impact statement prepared for Gillham Dam, a dam authorized to be constructed for flood control purposes in Arkansas. However, the Supreme Court soon laid to rest any expectancy that NEPA conferred substantive review.

At this point, reread the *Vermont Yankee* and *Kleppe* opinions, reproduced *supra*. Recall that in footnote 21 of *Kleppe* the Court observed that "[n]either the statute nor its legislative history contemplates that a court should substitute its judgment for that of the agency as to the environmental consequences of its actions." And in *Vermont Yankee* the Court observed that "NEPA does set forth significant substantive goals for the nation, but its mandate is essentially procedural."

Stryker's Bay Neighborhood Council v. Karlen, 444 U.S. 223 (1980), was another important early case. In proceedings challenging an urban renewal plan in New York City the Second Circuit had held that NEPA contained substantive standards that permitted the review of the merits of agency decisions, but the Supreme Court reversed. It held:

> *Vermont Yankee* cuts sharply against the Court of Appeals' conclusion that an agency, in selecting a course of action, must elevate environmental concerns over other appropriate considerations. On the contrary, once an agency has made a decision subject to NEPA's procedural requirements, the only role for a court is to insure that the agency has considered the environmental consequences; it cannot " 'Interject itself within the area of discretion of the executive as to the choice of the action to be taken.' " [Id. at 227-228, quoting the *Kleppe* footnote discussed above.]

The issue was finally settled in Robertson v. Methow Valley Citizens Council, reproduced below. The Supreme Court, citing *Strycker's Bay*, stated that although NEPA procedures are "almost certain" to affect substantive decisions, "it is now well settled that NEPA itself does not mandate particular results, but simply prescribes the necessary process."

NOTES AND QUESTIONS

1. *Understanding Judicial Review.* As the critical observer must have realized by now, "the procedural and substantive theories are interrelated, for a procedural requirement of a reasoned analysis, especially as applied to broad policies and programs, must ultimately lead to holdings that some justifications for an activity are acceptable while others are not. This is especially true if the standard of procedural adequacy is coupled with a detailed and probing analysis of the factual basis of the impact statement." C. Meyers & A. D. Tarlock, Water Resource Management 586 (2d ed. 1980). For a thoughtful analysis of judicial review problems by a late judge of the Court of Appeals for the District of Columbia Circuit who did much to bring about the "new" administrative law, see Leventhal, Environmental Decisionmaking and the Role of the Courts, 122 U. Pa. L. Rev. 509 (1974).

2. *Judicial Tests for the Review of Impact Statements.* The courts have expanded on the arbitrary and capricious standard of judicial review to elaborate more detailed tests for the review of impact statements. More particularly, they apply a "rule of reason" when reviewing the adequacy of impact statements, but supplement this general rule with more specific directives. Though the tests vary somewhat, their message is caught in the following quotation:

> [T]he . . . [EIS] must set forth sufficient information for the general public to make an informed evaluation, . . . and for the decisionmaker to "consider fully the environmental factors involved and to make a reasoned decision after balancing the risks of harm to the environment against the benefits to be derived from the proposed action." [The EIS gives] assurance that stubborn problems or serious criticism has not been "swept under the rug." [Sierra Club v. United States Army Corps of Eng'rs, 701 F.2d 1011, 1029 (2d Cir. 1983).]

The Supreme Court has also provided guidance. A court must conduct a review under the Administrative Procedure Act "to ensure that the agency has adequately considered and disclosed the environmental impact of its actions and that its decision is not arbitrary and capricious." Baltimore Gas & Elec. Co. v. NRDC, Inc., 462 U.S. 87, 97-98 (1983). A much-quoted early case, Sylva v. Linn, 482 F.2d 1282 (1st Cir. 1973), adopted a three-part test. The EIS must allow the court to determine whether the agency made a "good faith effort" to take environmental values into account. Second, the EIS must provide an "environmental full disclosure" to members of the public through an appropriate balance of nontechnical and scientific information. It may not contain vague, general, and conclusory reasoning. Finally, the EIS must ensure the integrity of the decision-making process by preventing problems and criticisms from being "swept under the rug," an admonition also contained in the previous quotation. All of this suggests more then minimal judicial attention.

3. *Injunctions.* Judicial intervention to ensure compliance with NEPA requires a remedy, and the traditional remedy in NEPA cases is a court-ordered injunction. NEPA plaintiffs usually seek a preliminary injunction to preserve the status quo in a case until the court can make a final decision. If the court does not issue a preliminary injunction, the plaintiff takes the risk that the defendant agency may proceed with its project, and may later convince the court that the case is moot because the project is substantially or entirely completed. Courts asked to order preliminary injunctions normally balance the equities, usually requiring the plaintiff to show probable success on the merits, irreparable injury, and that the injunction is in the public interest.

Some courts applied a "NEPA exception" and granted a preliminary injunction without considering the usual equity factors. Other courts relaxed the irreparable harm rule in NEPA cases and found irreparable harm in the damage that would be done to NEPA's statutory purposes if the court refused all injunctions. See NEPA Law & Litigation, *supra*, §§4:53-4:61. The Supreme Court's decisions in Weinberger v. Romero-Barcelo, 456 U.S. 305 (1982), and Amoco Prod. Co. v. Village of Gambell, 480 U.S. 531 (1987), may have changed this. The Court held that traditional equity principles apply to injunctions in environmental cases and that courts should not presume environmental harm, but added that the "balance of harms" will usually favor the issuance of an injunction.

The courts have applied *Weinberger* in NEPA cases. See Wisconsin v. Weinberger, 745 F.2d 412 (7th Cir. 1984). However, the First Circuit, in an extensive decision, held that *Amoco* does not modify the presumption in favor of preliminary injunctions it has applied in NEPA cases. Sierra Club v. Marsh, 872 F.2d 497 (1st Cir. 1989). See Rubinstein, Injunctions under NEPA after *Weinberger v. Romero-Barcelo* and *Amoco Production Co. v. Village of Gambell*, 5 Wis. Envtl. L.J. 1 (1998). See also Idaho Sporting Cong., Inc. v. Alexander, 222 F.3d 562 (9th Cir. 2000) (upholding decision to grant injunction).

2. What Is an "Adequate" Impact Statement?

Compliance with NEPA requires agencies to prepare an environmental impact statement that is an adequate "full disclosure" document. We will now consider what an impact statement must contain in order to meet the adequacy requirement. There are two issues in these cases. One is whether, as a matter of law, there are analytical requirements that agencies must satisfy before a court will hold an impact statement adequate. The second issue is whether a court believes that the environmental analysis in an impact statement satisfies the adequacy requirement. Both issues arise in the following case.

SIERRA CLUB v. MARITA
46 F.3d 606 (7th Cir. 1995)

FLAUM, Circuit Judge.

Plaintiffs Sierra Club, Wisconsin Forest Conservation Task Force, and Wisconsin Audubon Council, Inc. (collectively, "Sierra Club") brought suit against defendant United States Forest Service ("Service") seeking to enjoin timber harvesting, road construction or reconstruction, and the creation of wildlife openings at two national forests in northern Wisconsin. The Sierra Club claimed that the Service violated a number of environmental statutes and regulations in developing forest management plans for the two national forests by failing to consider properly certain ecological principles of biological diversity. The district court determined that the plaintiffs' claims were justiciable but then granted the Service summary judgment on the merits of those claims. We affirm.

I

The National Forest Management Act ("NFMA") requires the Secretary of Agriculture, who is responsible for the Forest Service, to develop "land and resource management plans" to guide the maintenance and use of resources within national forests. 16 U.S.C. §§1601-1604. In developing these plans the Secretary must determine the environmental impact these plans will have and discuss alternative plans, pursuant to the National Environmental Policy Act ("NEPA"), 42 U.S.C. §4321 et seq. The Secretary must also consider the "multiple use and sustained yield of the several products and services obtained" from the forests, pursuant to the Multiple-Use Sustained Yield Act ("MUSYA"), 16 U.S.C. §§528-531. . . . [The court described the planning process.]

The present case concerns management plans developed for two forests: Nicolet National Forest ("Nicolet") and Chequamegon (She-WA-me-gon) National Forest ("Chequamegon"). Nicolet spreads over 973,000 acres, of which 655,000 acres are National Forest Land, in northeastern Wisconsin, while Chequamegon encompasses 845,000 publicly-owned acres in northwestern and north-central Wisconsin.[1] Collectively, the Nicolet and the Chequamegon contain hundreds of lakes and streams, thousands of miles of roads and trails, and serve a wide variety of uses, including hiking, skiing, snowmobiling, logging, fishing, hunting, sightseeing, and scientific research. The forests are important for both the tourism and the forest product industries in northern Wisconsin.

In the late 1970s and early 1980s, the Nicolet and Chequamegon Forest Supervisors and interdisciplinary teams each began drafting a forest management plan for

1. Until the mid-1800s, both the Nicolet and Chequamegon were old-growth forests consisting primarily of northern hardwoods. Pine logging around 1900, hardwood logging in the 1920s, and forest fires (caused by clear cutting) significantly affected the landscape. Government replanting and forest-fire control efforts beginning in the 1930s have reclaimed much of the land as forest. The forests now contain a mixture of trees that markedly differs from the forests' pre-1800 "natural" conditions but is also more diverse in terms of tree type and age.

their respective forests. These plans were expected to guide forest management for ten to fifteen years beginning in 1986. . . . [Final drafts of both plans were issued, the plans were challenged in administrative appeals that were affirmed in part and remanded, and the Sierra Club then brought suit over both plans.]

II

[The court held the Sierra Club had standing and that the claims were ripe.]

III

The Sierra Club claims that the Service violated the NFMA and NEPA by using scientifically unsupported techniques to address diversity concerns in its management plans and by arbitrarily disregarding certain principles of conservation biology in developing those plans. The Sierra Club asserts that the Service abdicated its duty to take a "hard look" at the environmental impact of its decisions on biological diversity in the forests on the erroneous contentions that the Sierra Club's proposed theories and predictions were "uncertain" in application and that the Service's own methodology was more than adequate to meet all statutory requirements. According to the Sierra Club, the Service, rather than address the important ecological issues the plaintiffs raised, stuck its head in the sand. The result, the Sierra Club argues, was a plan with "predictions about diversity directly at odds with the prevailing scientific literature."

A

[The court discussed the NFMA statute and regulations that mandate consideration of diversity in preparing forest management plans.]

Several regulations under NEPA addressing the implementation of EISs also bear on the present case. First, the regulations require a "rigorous analysis" of alternatives to the proposed plan, including a "substantial treatment" of these alternatives in comparison to the proposed plan. 40 C.F.R. §1502.14 (1993). Second, the regulations require an agency undertaking an EIS to "insure the professional integrity, including scientific integrity, of the discussions and analyses in environmental impact statements." 40 C.F.R. §1502.24 (1993). Additionally, the regulations require that the analysis be undertaken with an "interdisciplinary approach" to "insure the integrated use of the natural and social sciences and the environmental design arts." 40 C.F.R. §1502.6 (1993). NEPA also requires consideration in an EIS of the "ecological" effects of a proposed action. 40 C.F.R. §1508.8 (1993). Ecological effects include "the effects on natural resources and on the components, structures, and functioning of affected ecosystems." Id. Finally, as a matter of general policy, NEPA is designed to ensure "that environmental information is available to public officials and citizens before decisions are made and before actions are taken. The information must be of high quality. Accurate scientific analysis, expert agency comments, and public scrutiny are essential to implementing NEPA." 40 C.F.R. §1500.1(b).

The regulations also specify what an agency should do in an EIS in the face of "incomplete or unavailable information." The regulation states in relevant part that where such information is not known, the EIS must include: (1) A statement that such information is incomplete or unavailable; (2) a statement of the relevance of the incomplete or unavailable information to evaluating reasonably foreseeable significant adverse impacts on the human environment; (3) a summary of existing credible scientific evidence which is relevant to evaluating the reasonably foreseeable significant adverse impacts on the human environment, and (4) the agency's evaluation of such impacts based upon theoretical approaches or research methods generally accepted in the scientific community. . . . 40 C.F.R. §1502.22(b) (1993).[7]

B

The Service addressed diversity concerns in the Nicolet and Chequamegon in largely similar ways, both of which are extensively detailed in the district court opinions issued below. The Service defined diversity as "the distribution and abundance of different plant and animal communities and species within the area covered by the Land and Resource Management Plan." The Service assumed that "an increase in the diversity of habitats increases the potential livelihood of diverse kinds of organisms."

The Service focused its attention first on vegetative diversity. Diversity of vegetation was measured within tree stands as well as throughout the forest, noting that such diversity is "desirable for diverse wildlife habitat, visual variety, and as an aid to protecting the area from wildfire, insects, and disease." The Service assessed vegetative diversity based on vegetative types, age class structure of timber types, within-stand diversity of tree species, and the spatial distribution pattern of all these elements across the particular forest. The Service also factored in other considerations, including the desirability of "large areas of low human disturbance" and amount of "old-growth" forest, into its evaluations. Using these guidelines, the Service gathered and analyzed data on the current and historical composition of the forests to project an optimal vegetative diversity.

The Service assessed animal diversity primarily on the basis of vegetative diversity. Pursuant to the regulations, the Service identified all rare and uncommon vertebrate wildlife species as well as those species identified with a particular habitat and subject to significant change through planning alternatives. The Service grouped these species with a particular habitat type, identifying 14 categories in the Nicolet and 25 (reduced to 10 similar types) in the Chequamegon. For each of these habitat types, the Service selected MIS [Management Indicator Species] (33 in the Nicolet and 18 in the Chequamegon) to determine the impact of management practices on these species in particular and, by proxy, on other species in general. For each MIS, the Service calculated the minimum viable population necessary in order to ensure the continued reproductive vitality of the species. Factors involved in this calculation included a determination of population size, the spatial distribution across the forest needed to ensure fitness and resilience, and the kinds, amounts and pattern of habitats needed to support the population.

Taking its diversity analysis into consideration, along with the [sic] its numerous other mandates, the Service developed a number of plan alternatives for each of the forests (eight in the Nicolet and nine in the Chequamegon). Each alternative emphasized a different aspect of forest management, including cost efficiency, wildlife

---

7. . . . [The court noted the regulations were amended in 1986 and assumed the amended regulation applied.] The primary amendment was the removal of the requirement that agencies include a "worst case analysis" if there is "information relevant to adverse impacts essential to a reasoned choice and is not known and the overall costs of obtaining it are exorbitant or . . . the means to obtain it are not known. . . . " . . .

habitat, recreation, and hunting, although all were considered to be "environmentally, technically, and legally feasible." In the Nicolet, the Service selected the alternative emphasizing resource outputs associated with large diameter hardwood and softwood vegetation; in the Chequamegon an alternative emphasizing recreational opportunities, quality sawtimber, and aspen management was chosen.

C

The Sierra Club argues that the diversity statute and regulations, as well as NEPA, required the Service to consider and apply certain principles of conservation biology in developing the forest plan. These principles, the Sierra Club asserts, dictate that diversity is not comprehensible solely through analysis of the numbers of plants and animals and the variety of species in a given area. Rather, diversity also requires an understanding of the relationships between differing landscape patterns and among various habitats. That understanding, the Sierra Club says, has led to the prediction that the size of a habitat—the "patch size"—tends to affect directly the survival of the habitat and the diversity of plant and animal species within that habitat.

A basic generalization of conservation biology is that smaller patches of habitat will not support life as well as one larger patch of that habitat, even if the total area of the smaller patches equals the total area of the large patch. This generalization derives from a number of observations and predictions. [The court noted that populations in a larger patch have a better chance of survival. Smaller patches can be destroyed by edge effects, which occur when one habitat's environment suffers because it is surrounded by different type of habitat. Distance between habitats makes it less likely that organisms can migrate from one habitat to another in the event of a local disturbance. Consequently, fewer organisms will survive such a disturbance and diversity will decline.] On the basis of these submissions, the Sierra Club desires us to rule that to perform a legally adequate hard look at the environmental consequences of landscape manipulation across the hundreds of thousands of hectares of a National Forest, a federal agency must apply in some reasonable fashion the ecological principles identified by well accepted conservation biology. Species-by-species techniques are simply no longer enough. Ecology must be applied in the analysis, and it will be used as a criterion for the substantive results.

As a way of putting conservation biology into practice, the Sierra Club suggested that large blocks of land (at least 30,000 to 50,000 acres per block), so-called "Diversity Maintenance Areas" ("DMAs"), be set aside in each of the forests. The Sierra Club proposed and mapped three DMAs for the Nicolet and two for the Chequamegon. In these areas, which would have included about 25 percent of each forest, habitats were to be undisturbed by new roads, timber sales, or wildlife openings. Neither forest plan, however, ultimately contained a DMA; the Chequamegon Forest Supervisor initially did include two DMAs, but the Regional Forester removed them from the final Chequamegon plan.

The Sierra Club contends that the Service ignored its submissions, noting that the FEISs and RODs for both the Nicolet and the Chequamegon are devoid of reference to population dynamics, species turnover, patch size, recolonization problems, fragmentation problems, edge effects, and island biogeography. According to the Sierra Club, the Service simply disregarded extensive documentary and expert testimony, including over 100 articles and 13 affidavits supporting the Sierra Club's assertions, and thereby shirked its legal duties.

The Service replies that it correctly considered the implications of conservation biology for both the Nicolet and Chequamegon and appropriately declined to apply the science. The Service asserts that it duly noted the "concern [of the Sierra Club and others] that fragmentation of the . . . forest canopy through timber harvesting and road building is detrimental to certain plant and animal species." The Service decided that the theory had "not been applied to forest management in the Lake States" and that the subject was worthy of further study. However, the Service found in both cases that while the theories of conservation biology in general and of island bioge-ography in particular were "of interest, . . . there is not sufficient justification at this time to make research of the theory a Forest Service priority." Given its otherwise extensive analysis of diversity, as well as the deference owed its interpretation of applicable statutory and regulatory requirements, the Service contends that it clearly met all the "diversity" obligations imposed on it.

IV

The case now turns to whether the Service was required to apply conservation biology in its analysis and whether the Service otherwise complied with its statutory mandates and regulatory prescriptions regarding diversity in national forests. We hold that the Service met all legal requirements in addressing the concerns the Sierra Club raises.

A

We note at the outset that the Sierra Club faces a high standard in challenging the Service's planning decisions. . . . [The court discussed the applicable "arbitrary and capricious" standard of judicial review and then noted:] Where an "agency has relied on factors which Congress has not intended it to consider, entirely failed to consider an important aspect of the problem, offered an explanation for its decision that runs counter to the evidence before the agency, or is so implausible that it could not be ascribed to a difference in view or the product of agency expertise," the agency has violated the standards of the APA. Motor Vehicle Mfrs. Ass'n v. State Farm Mut. Auto. Ins. Co., 463 U.S. 49 (1983).

B

. . . [The Sierra Club's NEPA claim was based on] NEPA's stipulations that environmental policy should focus on the "interrelations of all components of the natural environment," 42 U.S.C. §4331, and regulations which require an EIS to include an analysis of "ecological" effects. See 40 C.F.R. §1508.8. The Sierra Club concludes from these statutes and regulations that the Service was obligated to apply an ecological approach to forest management and failed to do so. In the Sierra Club's view, MISs and population viability analyses present only half the picture, a picture that the addition of conservation biology would make complete. . . . [The court held the NFMA was not violated.]

Third, the Sierra Club asserts that the Service failed in its responsibility under NEPA to utilize "high quality" science in preparing EISs and evaluating diversity in them. 40 C.F.R. §1500.1. The Sierra Club believes that it more than adequately demonstrated that conservation biology is (and was at the time the Service prepared its FEISs) an essential element of any proper scientific evaluation of diversity in the Nicolet and Chequamegon. The Sierra Club also points to a mountain of literature, as well as thirteen experts, that demonstrate its point. Indeed, the district court itself "safely assumed that the principles of conservation biology set forth by the plaintiffs represent sound ecological theory." The Sierra Club notes that the Service not only failed to apply these prevailing scientific views but drew conclusions directly at odds with them, especially in assuming that certain management activities, including cutting and creating wildlife openings, would help rather than hinder diversity. Consequently, the Service deserves no deference.

Again, we disagree. The Service is entitled to use its own methodology, unless it is irrational. The Service, as discussed at length in Section III, developed an appropriate method of analyzing diversity. The Sierra Club is correct that the Service did not employ conservation biology in its final analysis. However, the Service appropriately considered conservation biology and ultimately determined that science to be uncertain in application.[11] With regard to the Service's assumption that human intervention in the form of cuttings could aid diversity, the Service notes that it was precisely its intervention in the past fifty years that permitted the forests to rejuvenate after the logging and fires prior to the 1930s. Moreover, the Service proposes, without some intervention, the forests would return to their pre-1800s, climax hardwood composition, a composition less diverse than at present. We cannot conclude from the record and these explanations that the Service acted irrationally.

In supporting the Sierra Club's allegation that the Service used "bad" science, amici Society for Conservation Biology and the American Institute of Biological Sciences have suggested that we borrow the Supreme Court's test for admissibility of scientific expert testimony as set forth in Daubert v. Merrell Dow Pharmaceuticals, Inc., 509 U.S. 579 (1993),[12] as a way of determining whether the Service's scientific assertions are owed any deference under NEPA. We decline the suggestion. While such a proposal might assure better documentation of an agency's scientific decisions, we think that forcing an agency to make such a showing as a general rule is intrusive, undeferential, and not required. An EIS is designed to ensure open and honest debate of the environmental consequences of an agency action, not to prove admissibility of testimony in a court of law. Cf. 40 C.F.R. §1500.1(c) ("Ultimately, of course, it is not better documents but better decisions that count. NEPA's purpose is not to generate paperwork—even excellent paperwork—but to foster excellent action.").

Fourth, the Sierra Club contends that the rejection of its "high quality" science argument on the basis of "uncertainty" in the application of conservation biology was unscrupulous. The Sierra Club asserts that conservation biology represented well-accepted and well-respected science even at the time the Service developed its management plans in the mid-1980s and that this evidence was before the Service when it drafted the forest plans. Thus, if the Service's only argument against applying the "high quality" science of conservation biology was its uncertainty, the Service has utterly failed to respond to the challenge of conservation biology.

A brief look at available evidence suggests that the district court's understanding of uncertainty was correct and the Service's explanation principled. The Service, in

11. We thus do not have before us a case in which the Service "did not contain a significant discussion" of an environmental impact and thereby failed to take a "hard look" at an issue. Marble Mountain Audubon Soc'y v. Rice, 914 F.2d 179, 182 (9th Cir. 1990) (Service entirely ignored question of maintaining a biological corridor between two wilderness areas in drafting an EIS).

12. *Daubert* requires district courts to consider a number of factors in determining the admissibility of expert testimony regarding a scientific theory under F.R.E. 702, including (but not limited to) whether the theory can be or has been tested, whether the theory has been subjected to peer review and publication, the known or potential rate of error in applications of the theory, and the "general acceptance of the theory in the relevant scientific community." 509 U.S. at 591-94.

looking at island biogeography, noted that it had been developed as a result of research on actual islands or in the predominantly old-growth forests of the Pacific Northwest and therefore did not necessarily lend itself to application in the forests of Wisconsin. Literature submitted by the Sierra Club to the Service was not unequivocal in stipulating how to apply conservation biology principles in the Nicolet and Chequamegon. Likewise, a Sierra Club group member suggested during meetings regarding the Chequamegon that "the Forest Service should be a leader and incorporate this concept into the Plan. He indicated that it would set a precedent for other Forests and Regions." The Chequamegon Forest Supervisor also originally decided to include the DMAs in his forest plan not because science so compelled but as a way to research an as yet untested theory. Even recent literature has recognized that "new legislation may be necessary" in order to force the Service to adopt conservation biology. Robert B. Keiter, Conservation Biology and the Law: Assessing the Challenges Ahead, 69 Chi.-Kent L. Rev. 911, 916 (1994). Perhaps the Service "has the ability to reinterpret [its] own governing mandates to give species protection priority over visitor services and other concerns," id. at 921, but that is not and was not required.

The amici scientific societies suggest that the district court misunderstood the nature of scientific uncertainty. Their argument on this point boils down to the assertion that all scientific propositions are inherently unverifiable and at most falsifiable. Hence, amici argue, allowing the Service to ignore the theories of conservation biology because they are "uncertain" would, on the same logic, allow the Service to ignore the theory of gravity.

Amici, like the Sierra Club, misapprehend the "uncertainty" of which the Service and the district court spoke. We agree that an agency decision to avoid a science should not escape review merely because a theory is not certain. But, however valid a general theory may be, it does not translate into a management tool unless one can apply it to a concrete situation. The Service acknowledged the developments in conservation biology but did not think that they had been shown definitively applicable to forests like the Nicolet or the Chequamegon. Thus, circumstances did not warrant setting aside a large portion of these forests to study island biogeography and related theories at the expense of other forest-plan objectives. Given that uncertainty, we appropriately defer to the agency's method of measuring and maintaining diversity. See Baltimore Gas & Elec. Co. v. Natural Resources Defense Council, Inc., 462 U.S. 87 (1983).

Fifth and finally, the Sierra Club argues that even if the application of conservation biology was uncertain, the district court overlooked the dispositive NEPA regulation regarding scientific uncertainty, 40 C.F.R. §1502.22. The Sierra Club asserts that with regard to conservation biology, this regulation required the Service to "[state] the relevance of the incomplete or unavailable information to evaluating reasonably foreseeable significant adverse impacts on the human environment, . . . summarize existing credible scientific evidence which is relevant to evaluating the reasonably foreseeable significant adverse impacts on the human environment, and . . . evaluate such impacts based upon theoretical approaches or research methods generally accepted in the scientific community." 40 C.F.R. §1502.22(b). The Sierra Club contends that once the Service determined that the application of conservation biology was uncertain, §1502.22 obligated the agency to conduct and disclose its own evaluation of the effects of its management practices as predicted by conservation biology.

Regardless of whether the district court erred in ignoring §1502.22, the record clearly shows that the Service sufficiently complied with this regulation. The Service looked at and disclosed the foreseeable environmental effects of the proposed alternatives and discussed them at length. The fact that it did not adopt them is inconsequential, for "it is now well settled that NEPA itself does not mandate particular results, but simply prescribes the necessary process." *Methow Valley*, 490 U.S. at 350. Nor did §1502.22 require the Service to use a methodology it reasonably found lacking in certainty of application. "NEPA does not require that we decide whether an [EIS] is based on the best scientific methodology available, nor does NEPA require us to resolve disagreements among various scientists as to methodology." Friends of Endangered Species, Inc. v. Jantzen, 760 F.2d 976, 986 (9th Cir. 1985).

To the extent §1502.22 did mandate a discussion of conservation biology, the Service more than adequately complied. The Service specifically addressed the possibility of creating DMAs to study island biogeography. The Service concluded that setting aside the preferred alternative to establish this study area in Nicolet would likely cause "a reduction of services in the next ten years and in the long run." The Service did not, however, think that the setting aside of land in Chequamegon would impact goods and service there. Nonetheless, the Service determined that while the theory was "of interest," there was "conflicting scientific evidence regarding the necessity of providing large areas of old growth habitat," especially in a region like the Lake States area. Thus, "there is not sufficient justification available to make this study a priority for Forest Service research at this time." The Service allowed for the possibility that such a research proposal could be presented at a later date under the management plan as a site-specific proposal. This analysis of conservation biology appears to us to more than adequately meet whatever burden §1502.22 placed on the Service. The Supreme Court has noted that §1502.22 was designed to promote the functions of an EIS, "requiring agencies to take a 'hard look' at the consequences of the proposed action," by helping to "generate information and discussion on those consequences of greatest concern to the public and of greatest relevance to the agency's decision." *Methow Valley*, 490 U.S. at 356. The FEISs and RODs for both the Nicolet and the Chequamegon show that information and discussion was generated. . . .

For the foregoing reasons, we affirm the decisions of the district court.

NOTES AND QUESTIONS

1. *Reviewing Adequacy. Marita* is typical of the cases that consider the adequacy of an impact statement. The court first considered whether the agency used the correct analytic technique, and then considered whether the environmental assessment it carried out was adequate. The difference in *Marita* is the novelty of the biodiversity argument. Do you believe the court was correct in the way in which it handled this argument? As the *Marita* case also indicates, agencies that do a reasonable job with the state of the art in impact statement preparation can expect to survive a judicial challenge to the impact statement.

Marita applied the arbitrary and capricious standard of judicial review to its review of the impact statement's adequacy but did not apply any of the subordinate tests described in Note 2 in the previous Notes and Questions. Was this error? Would applying this test have made a difference?

2. *Uncertainty. Marita* also raises the uncertainty problem. The problem can arise, as in that case, when objectors claim the agency used the wrong analytic technique. Meeting this objection will require obtaining additional information. Uncertainty problems also arise when the environmental impacts of an action are unknown.

Objectors may argue that delay is needed to allow further study. The uncertainty problem is an important one; resolving it requires the court to balance the cost of delay to the agency against possible harm to the environment should commitments to the project be made before additional studies can be completed. This problem also arises at the environmental assessment stage, where CEQ regulations and the cases require the preparation of an EIS if the assessment shows that environmental effects are uncertain. See National Parks & Conservation Ass'n v. Babbit, discussed above in the Note on Environmental Impacts That Must Be Considered. Some courts do not require a discussion of uncertainty in an EIS if the gaps in information are identified, however. North Slope Borough v. Andrus, 642 F.2d 589 (D.C. Cir. 1980). Is there a reason for reaching a different result at the EIS stage? The uncertainty problem in impact statements is now handled by regulation, discussed in Note 3.

What if the agency weighs the uncertainties and decides that the probabilities indicate that no adverse environmental impacts will occur? In Baltimore Gas & Elec. Co. v. NRDC, cited in *Marita*, the Nuclear Regulatory Commission engaged in a generic rulemaking intended to provide guidelines for the licensing of nuclear power plants. As part of its evaluation of the environmental effects of the nuclear fuel cycle, the Commission determined that the permanent storage of nuclear wastes would have no significant environmental effects and should not be considered in nuclear power plant licensing decisions. Its conclusion was based on assumptions concerning the permanent disposal of wastes in a federal repository. The Commission adopted a "zero-release" assumption but conceded it could not be certain that no wastes would escape. The Court reviewed the Commission's assumption under the "arbitrary and capricious" standard of judicial review and concluded that the agency's assumption was acceptable under this deferential judicial review standard.

3. *Uncertainty and Worst Case.* CEQ originally had a "worst case" analysis rule, which *Marita* applied, as explained in footnote 7. The initial worst case analysis regulation was intended to deal with the uncertainty problem, such as an agency project or action whose impacts have a low probability of occurrence, but whose environmental consequences would be disastrous if they occurred. Agencies were supposed to analyze these consequences in view of this uncertainty. CEQ revoked the rule in 1986 because it was inconsistent with the rule of reason, and because it was an unproductive and inefficient technique that could breed endless hypothesis and speculation. The Supreme Court upheld CEQ's revocation of the worst case regulation in the *Robertson* case, which is reproduced below.

CEQ adopted a new rule to take the place of the worst case rule that requires a similar analysis. 40 C.F.R. §1502.22. Agencies must disclose that information is incomplete or unavailable and must obtain that information "if the incomplete information relevant to reasonably foreseeable significant adverse impacts is essential to a reasoned choice among alternatives and the overall costs of doing so are not exorbitant." If the costs of obtaining the information are exorbitant or the means of obtaining it are not known, agencies must:

(1) State that the information is incomplete or unavailable;
(2) State the relevance of this information to evaluating "reasonably foreseeable" significant environmental impacts;
(3) Summarize "credible scientific evidence" relevant to evaluating these impacts; and
(4) Evaluate these impacts "based upon theoretical approaches or research methods generally accepted in the scientific community."

A caveat to the fourth requirement states that the term "reasonably foreseeable" impacts shall include low-probability/catastrophic impacts if the analysis of the impact is supported by credible scientific evidence, is not based on pure conjecture, and is within the rule of reason.

The first step in the analysis is to determine whether the information is relevant to reasonably foreseeable significant environmental impacts. Lee v. United States Air Force, 354 F.3d 1229 (10th Cir. 2004) (noting rule applies only to "reasonably foreseeable significant adverse impacts"). If it is, the agency must then determine whether the information is "essential to a reasoned choice among alternatives." If so, the agency must make it available unless the cost of doing so is exorbitant or the means of doing so are not known. Courts review these decisions. Colorado Envtl. Coal. v. Dombeck, 185 F.3d 1162 (10th Cir. 1999) (upholding agency determination that data on lynx population were unavailable for diversity determination). Remember that agencies may have to prepare an impact statement if the effects of an action are uncertain. Does the regulation provide adequate safeguards to ensure that uncertain impacts will be discussed in impact statements?

4. *Biodiversity in NEPA Practice.* In *Marita*, the Sierra Club appeared to argue that the Forest Service should have considered habitat biodiversity in the management plans and avoided the habitat fragmentation the plans contemplated. CEQ has published a report on biodiversity, Incorporating Biodiversity Considerations into Environmental Impact Analysis under the National Environmental Policy Act (1993). The report does not recommend any specific environmental measures, but does make the following comments on NEPA practice:

> [T]he focus on a limited set of statute-driven or regulation-driven elements (e.g., endangered species) has significantly lessened the ability of NEPA analyses to consider the full range of biodiversity issues. . . . Current NEPA analyses often (1) focus on species, rather than ecosystems; (2) address the site scale, rather than the ecosystem or regional scale; and (3) concentrate on immediate short-term impacts rather than likely future impacts. [Id. at 18.]

Are these comments an implicit criticism of the *Marita* case? See also Noss, Some Principles of Conservation Biology, as They Apply to Environmental Law, 69 Chi.-Kent L. Rev. 893 (1994).

5. *Cost-Benefit Analysis.* It is by now reasonably settled that NEPA does not require a cost-benefit analysis. A strong statement rejecting a requirement for cost-benefit analysis under NEPA is found in Trout Unlimited v. Morton, 509 F.2d 1276 (9th Cir. 1974). CEQ does not require a cost-benefit analysis in impact statements and does not require that costs and benefits be given monetary values. 40 C.F.R. §1502.23. Cost-benefit analysis has been most extensively used in water resource and flood control projects, in which it has been institutionalized by congressional and administrative directives. For these and other projects for which cost-benefit analysis is used, this technique provides a rule of decision that contrasts with the open-ended review of costs and benefits that NEPA contemplates.

Courts will review a cost-benefit analysis if an agency decides to do one, however, though an agency analysis may be hard to rebut if it attempts a bona fide analysis. In Hughes River Watershed Conservancy v. Glickman, 81 F.3d 437 (4th Cir. 1996), for example, plaintiffs sought judicial review of a decision approving construction of a dam on the North Fork of the Hughes River in northwestern West Virginia.

A study commissioned for the dam estimated gross, rather than net, economic benefits, as required in the study contract. The court held that the agencies relied on the gross benefit calculation, and that this reliance impaired the environmental analysis of the project. The court also held that reliance on gross benefits prevented the public from obtaining accurate information about a project.

After remand, the agencies calculated benefits relying on net economic benefits and determined the project would have an overall positive net cost-benefit ratio. The court of appeals affirmed. Hughes River Watershed Conservancy v. Johnson, 165 F.3d 283 (4th Cir. 1999). See also Oregon Natural Res. Council v. Marsh, 832 F.2d 1489 (9th Cir. 1987) (agency used proper discount rate), and South Louisiana Envtl. Council, Inc. v. Sand, 629 F.2d 1005 (5th Cir. 1980) (inclusion of flood control benefits not erroneous because they were "wholly economic," had only a "peripheral relationship" to any environmental impact, and did not change the cost-benefit ratio to such an extent that the environmental analysis was distorted). Compare Texas Comm. on Natural Res. v. Marsh, 736 F.2d 262 (5th Cir. 1984) (economic values not weighted against environmental concerns). What makes this case different? See also Sierra Club v. Sigler, 695 F.2d 957 (5th Cir. 1983), in which the court found an impact statement faulty because the federal agency excluded a number of environmental costs from its cost-benefit analysis.

6. *Judicial Relief for Noncompliance.* What if an impact statement calls for environmentally protective measures that the agency does not follow when it completes its project, such as the measures adopted in *Marita*? Is judicial relief available? The courts have denied post-completion relief on a number of grounds, some holding that the case is moot because the project has been completed. Other courts refused to read into NEPA an implied cause of action to enforce an impact statement. See Noe v. Metropolitan Atlanta Rapid Transit Auth., 644 F.2d 434 (5th Cir. 1981) (noise from construction of rapid transit station exceeded noise levels predicted in impact statements). Commentators have been critical of these cases, suggesting that courts require agencies to file a supplemental impact statement when they deviate from an approved impact statement. See Note, EIS Supplements for Improperly Completed Projects: A Logical Extension of Judicial Review under NEPA, 81 Mich. L. Rev. 221 (1982).

NOTE ON "STATE OF THE ART" REVIEW

Cases such as *Marita* raise the broader question of the agency's duty to reflect the "state of the art" in the impact statement. It seems clear the agency cannot ignore respectable expert opinion contrary to its conclusions, but once the agency identifies a reasonable range of opinion, it need do little more than state that no consensus exists on the issue at hand. In fact, the more candid the agency is about adverse impacts, the better its chances are of successfully resisting a judicial ruling that the impact statement is inadequate. It is well settled that environmental analysis does not have to use the best methodology available. Neither are courts required to resolve disagreements among experts about methodology. Fund for Animals v. Norton, 294 F. Supp. 2d 92 (D.D.C. 2003). Agencies must explain the considerations they find persuasive when choosing one expert over another if there is conflicting evidence, however. National Wildlife Fed'n v. Adams, 629 F.2d 587 (9th Cir. 1980).

National Indian Youth Council v. Andrus, 501 F. Supp. 649 (D.N.M. 1980), *aff'd on other grounds sub nom.* National Indian Youth Council v. Watt, 664 F.2d 220

(10th Cir. 1981), illustrates the judicial approach. The court expressed a general unwillingness to probe deeply into state-of-the-art controversies on the very important issue of the efficacy of surface mine reclamation techniques:

> *Reclamation and Revegetation.* Plaintiffs first challenge the adequacy of the discussion of reclamation and revegetation in the FESs. Specifically, Plaintiffs contend (1) that there is a void of discussion as to the prevalent "state of the art" as to reclamation and revegetation; (2) that various essential elements of reclamation were omitted from the statements,—e.g., geology, soil and plant ecology, biogeography, and climactic history; (3) that there was insufficient observation of experimental reclamation plots on comparable lands; and (4) that the FESs fail to accurately depict the potential for failure of reclamation and revegetation.
>
> As for the "state of the art" contention, there simply is no requirement in Section 102(2)(C), or elsewhere in NEPA, that the "state of the art" of a scientific discipline be explicitly discussed in an EIS, especially as an autonomous category. It is implicit in the reclamation discussion in the FESs that there is a divergence of opinion as to what the "state of the art" of reclamation may be.
>
> It suffices that the diversity of thought within the reclamation community was reflected in the FESs and that the prevalent opinions, however contradictory one with another, were expressed. . . .
>
> Plaintiffs' second reclamation allegation that vital elements of reclamation were omitted from consideration in the statements met its demise during the presentation of Plaintiffs' own case. Plaintiffs' reclamation expert, Dr. Robert R. Curry, candidly admitted that there is an inability within the reclamation discipline to agree on a basic definition of reclamation or, indeed, its elements. Under the "rule of reason," a "controversy of experts" is beyond the scope of judicial review. A "controversy of experts" must remain free from judicial intervention where, as here, the experts within a particular scientific field are engaged in internal conflict to establish the parameters of their expertise. [501 F. Supp. at 668-669.]

However, a failure to disclose and discuss contrary scientific opinion can be fatal. Sierra Club v. Bosworth, 199 F. Supp. 2d 271 (N.D. Cal. 2002) (disapproving EIS for project to construct strategic fuel breaks and reduce fuels in areas burned by forest fires).

Catch-22? Despite cases like *National Wildlife Fed'n*, the preparation of an impact statement can pose an environmental catch-22 for the agency. No matter what the impact statement discloses, more will be required. Critics have complained that the impact statement process is wasteful and that statements are often bulky, trivial, and blurred in focus. See Bardach & Pugliaresi, The Environmental Impact Statement vs. the Real World, 49 Pub. Interest 22 (1977). CEQ responded to these criticisms in its regulations by requiring the scoping process, by placing a "normal" page limit of 150 pages on impact statements, and by urging that descriptions be "no longer than necessary." 40 C.F.R. §1501.7. The page limit is often broken in practice, and page limit problems continue to attract attention in calls for NEPA reform.

3. Cumulative Impacts

Problem 4-2

Review Problem 4-1. Now assume the Federal Highway Administration (FHWA) has considered all three segments of the highway in one EIS. Save Our

State now argues that FHWA should also have considered the improvement of a primary state highway in its EIS that provides access to the proposed Outstate Connector near Metro City. FHWA has refused to do so, claiming the highway is only in the planning stage. Save Our State also argues that FHWA should consider in its EIS the effect the Outstate Connector will have in encouraging new development at two interchanges along its route. FHWA again refuses, claiming the Connector is only intended to serve existing traffic needs, and that no additional population growth is expected in the area served by the highway. How would you evaluate these arguments?

The following case considers the cumulative impact problem in an environmental assessment, but the same issues arise in the preparation of environmental impact statements.

GRAND CANYON TRUST v. FEDERAL AVIATION ADMINISTRATION
290 F.3d 339 (D.C. Cir. 2002)

ROGERS, Circuit Judge:

The Grand Canyon Trust petitions for review of the decision of the Federal Aviation Administration ("FAA") approving the federal actions necessary to allow the city of St. George, Utah, to construct a replacement airport near Zion National Park. The Trust challenges the adequacy of the FAA's environmental assessment under §102(2)(C) of the National Environmental Policy Act of 1969 ("NEPA") and the FAA's conclusion that there would be no significant environmental impacts from the project necessitating preparation of an environmental impact statement under NEPA. Focusing on the noise impacts on the Park, the Trust principally contends that the FAA failed adequately to consider the cumulative impact on the natural quiet of the Park and instead addressed only the incremental impact of the replacement airport. We grant the petition.

I.

In 1995, the FAA began working with the City of St. George, Utah, to determine the feasibility of continuing use of the existing airport as compared to development of a new airport at a new site. A growing retirement community and projected air-traffic demand was outstripping the capacity of the existing airport, which could not be expanded due to geographic constraints. Three sites in addition to a no-action alternative were examined. In response to comments on a draft environmental assessment, the FAA conducted a Supplemental Noise Analysis on the potential noise impacts of the replacement airport on Zion National Park ("the Park"). The Park is located approximately 25 miles northeast of St. George and the preferred replacement airport alternative.

The FAA concluded that the noise impacts on the Park from the replacement airport would be negligible and insignificant. On January 30, 2001, the FAA approved the final environmental assessment, concluding that an environmental impact statement was unnecessary, and issued the record of decision, setting forth actions, determinations, and approvals that will allow St. George to construct the replacement airport. It is the determination underlying this record of decision, that the proposed action will not significantly affect the environment of the Park, that the Trust challenges.

II.

The essential disagreement between the parties is whether the FAA was required in its environmental assessment to address more than the incremental impact of the replacement airport as compared to the existing airport. NEPA requires federal agencies to prepare an environmental impact statement ("EIS") for "every . . . major Federal action[] significantly affecting the quality of the human environment." An environmental assessment ("EA") is made for the purpose of determining whether an EIS is required. See 40 C.F.R. §1508.9. "If *any* 'significant' environmental impacts might result from the proposed agency action then an EIS must be prepared *before* agency action is taken." Sierra Club v. Peterson, 717 F.2d 1409, 1415 (D.C. Cir. 1983) ("*Peterson*"). . . .

The Trust does not dispute that the FAA properly defined the relevant environmental concern of noise impacts from aircraft on the Park. Rather, the Trust contends that the FAA cannot be said to have taken a "hard look" at the problem when it considered only the incremental impacts of the replacement airport and not the total noise impact that will result from the relocated airport. The Trust notes that the EA does not address the cumulative impact in light of other air flights over the Park, air tours in or near the Park, and reasonably foreseeable future aircraft activity and airport expansions that will contribute to the cumulative noise impact on the Park. Indeed, the EA's statement on cumulative impact is, in full: "There are no known factors that could result in cumulative impacts as a result of the proposed St. George Replacement Airport." Further, the Trust notes, the FAA's Supplemental Noise Analysis disregards cumulative impacts. The FAA responds that it adequately considered the cumulative impact when it compared noise impacts associated with the replacement airport with the no-action alternative of continued use of the existing airport. It rejects the Trust's position that it was required in an EA to compare the project to an environmental baseline of natural quiet and to consider the total impact of aircraft noise on the Park.

The issue dividing the parties is settled by regulations promulgated by the Council on Environmental Quality ("CEQ") to implement NEPA and by case law applying those regulations. "The CEQ regulations, which . . . are entitled to substantial deference, impose a duty on all federal agencies." Marsh v. Oregon Natural Res. Council, 490 U.S. 360, 372 (1989). The CEQ regulations define each term within NEPA's requirement of an EIS for "every . . . major Federal action significantly affecting the quality of the human environment." The term "significantly" is defined as those actions "with individually insignificant but cumulatively significant impacts. Significance exists if it is reasonable to anticipate a cumulatively significant impact on the environment." 40 C.F.R. §1508.27(b)(7). "Cumulative impact," in turn, is defined as:

> the impact on the environment which results from the incremental impact of the action
> when added to other past, present, and reasonably foreseeable future actions regardless of

what agency (Federal or non-Federal) or person undertakes such other actions. Cumulative impacts can result from individually minor but collectively significant actions taking place over a period of time. 40 C.F.R. §1508.7. . . .

The courts, in reviewing whether a federal agency has acted arbitrarily and capriciously in finding no significant environmental impact, have given effect to the plain language of the regulations. While the factual settings differ in some respects from the instant case, the consistent position in the case law is that, depending on the environmental concern at issue, the agency's EA must give a realistic evaluation of the total impacts and cannot isolate a proposed project, viewing it in a vacuum. For example, in Coalition on Sensible Transportation v. Dole, 826 F.2d 60 (D.C. Cir. 1987) ("*Dole*"), this court stated that the CEQ regulations on cumulative impact "provide a distinct meaning to the concept" separate and apart from the notion of improper segmentation of agency action. Noting that the regulatory definition of cumulative impact specifies that the "'incremental impact of the action' [at issue]" must be considered "'when added to other past, present, and reasonably foreseeable future actions,'" id. (quoting 40 C.F.R. §1508.7), the court observed that, consistent with the regulation and purpose of NEPA, "it makes sense to consider the 'incremental impact' of a project for possible cumulative effects by incorporating the effects of other projects into the background 'data base' of the project at issue." The point, the court stated, was to provide in the EA "sufficient [information] to alert interested members of the public to any arguable cumulative impacts involving . . . other projects." Further, the court concluded that insofar as Kleppe v. Sierra Club, 427 U.S. 390 (1976), "may bear on an agency's duty to consider impacts in a context that realistically includes other pending projects, the [agency] fully complied by planning on the basis of . . . ultimate completion of the related projects." Id. Similarly, the court in *Peterson*, without regard to any particular NEPA regulation, reversed a finding of no significant impact and a decision to issue certain oil and gas leases in national forests without preparing an EIS, remanding the case because the agency had failed, as NEPA requires, to "fully assess . . . the possible environmental consequences" of activities "which have the potential for disturbing the environment." Natural Resources Defense Council, Inc. v. Hodel, 865 F.2d 288 (D.C. Cir. 1988), is to the same effect. There, the agency had failed to consider the cumulative impact, as defined in the CEQ regulations, of simultaneous development in the region on "species, particularly whales and salmon, that migrate through the different planning areas" when it considered only the effect on those species "within the Planning Area" rather than "the interregional effects." Id. at 297-99. Other circuits take a similar approach in applying the regulations. . . .

The FAA, in finding that the St. George replacement airport would have no significant impact on the environment of the Park, concluded that "there is little discernible increased noise intrusion to the Park" from the proposed replacement airport as compared to the existing airport, and that "the increase in noise levels that would result from the development of a replacement airport is negligible [because] aircraft traffic will increase even if the replacement airport is not constructed." The FAA's analysis appears principally in a Supplemental Noise Analysis attached to the EA, and proceeds on the basis of a comparison of the noise impacts from predicted air traffic at the existing airport and predicted air traffic at the larger replacement airport. . . . Comparing the predicted noise impact on the Park from the existing and replacement airports, the FAA found that Day-Night Noise Level

("DNL") would increase "due to the implementation of the replacement airport over the use of the existing airport" by no more than 3.5 dBA in 2008 and 3.2 dBA in 2018, which the FAA characterized as "extremely low" increases. The FAA concluded that "there will be little difference associated with the replacement airport, as compared with the existing airport, in the long-term based on the DNL metric."

The FAA also examined in the Supplemental Noise Analysis the peak hour Equivalent Noise Level ("LEQ") based on a threshold of 45 dBA, when aircraft would be clearly audible and noticeable in the Park. . . . Based on this data, the FAA found that while 2% to 7% of Park visitors would experience moderate to extreme annoyance due to aircraft noise from the existing St. George Airport, the number would only increase to 2% to 8% with the replacement airport using the 45 dBA threshold. Using a 35 dBA threshold, the FAA interpreted the data to mean that between 3% and 15% of Park visitors would be annoyed by aircraft noise from the existing airport, compared to 4% to 15% of visitors who would be annoyed by aircraft from the replacement airport, with a 3% increase (from 11% to 14%) of Park visitors experiencing moderate to extreme annoyance from the aircraft noise on the loudest flight path. The FAA concluded that "there will be little difference in noise between the existing and replacement airport."

In a section of the EA entitled "Impacts to Natural Quiet of the Park," the FAA did acknowledge the existence of "overflights" that pass over the Park. Noting that NPS had completed ambient noise monitoring in Zion National Park, the FAA stated that the results showed that "the background or ambient noise levels vary, but are often in the low 20 dBA." Finding that the typical peak or maximum noise levels from aircraft from either the existing or proposed St. George airport sites ranged from 45 to 65 dBA when passing directly overhead, the FAA concluded that, because "these aircraft are at or near cruise altitude, or in the case of jets [are] above 20,000 feet, the peak or maximum noise levels will remain the same for either airport site." While recognizing that these overflights constitute noise events that are higher than background natural quiet during periods when ambient noise levels are low, the FAA focused on the incremental impact, stating that it was "important to illustrate that the development of the St. George replacement airport has little effect on the overall aircraft noise levels in the Park." The FAA referred to the 250 overflights following established flight paths near or over the Park that are not associated with St. George Airport in concluding that "the replacement airport has very little contribution to the cumulative number of aircraft over flights over Zion National Park." The FAA observed that St. George Airport contributed only 31 flights using instrument flight rules over Zion, a number that was expected to increase to 48 in 2008 at the existing airport and 54 at the replacement airport, and to 67 in 2018 at the existing airport and 69 at the replacement airport. The FAA then found that the replacement airport would add only six additional flights using instrument flight rules per day in 2008 and only two additional such flights in 2018. In addition, the FAA predicted that less than four aircraft per day would fly over Zion using visual-flight-rules routes, a number the FAA predicted would remain the same for either the existing or the replacement site. The FAA concluded that the existing St. George airport would contribute only 11% of all existing flights using instrument flight rules over or near the Park, and that the increased flights from the replacement airport would represent only approximately 2% of the total aircraft flights using instrument flight rules over or near the Park.

The FAA's noise analysis in the EA, including the Supplemental Noise Analysis, may, in fact, be a splendid incremental analysis, but it fails to address what is crucial if the EA is to serve its function. While, as the FAA stresses, the EA is not intended to be a lengthy document, it must at a minimum address the considerations relevant to determining whether an EIS is required. NEPA regulations require that an agency consider cumulative impacts and the FAA's EA fails to address the total noise impact that will result from the replacement airport. Indeed, the FAA's own NEPA policy calls for consideration of cumulative impact, parroting the language of the NEPA regulations to include proposed projects and past, present, and reasonably foreseeable future actions. Comments on the draft EA called the FAA's attention to the need to consider mitigation measures in view of the results of the study of noise-annoyance to persons in the Park; the EA does not respond and provides no analysis of the 2% to 9% or the 4% to 15% level of annoyance shown in the NPS study. Yet, as the FAA was aware, the NPS had identified Zion National Park as among the nine national parks of "highest priority" for attention to noise impact on their natural quiet from overflights. Comments also expressed concern about the total impacts of noise on the Park and on Park visitors, yet the EA contains no analysis of the impact of 54 daily flights in 2008 and 69 in 2018 associated with St. George.

The Trust maintains that each flight may be responsible for a noise level of 45 to 65 dBA and points to expert testimony that an increase of 10 dBA correlates to a doubling of loudness such that a commercial jet overflight at the Park may be 4 to 23 times as loud as the natural soundscape. Even in the absence of the regulatory definitions it would be difficult to understand how an agency could determine that an EIS is not required if it had not evaluated existing noise impacts as well as those planned impacts that will exist by the time the new facility is constructed and in operation. As the Trust gleans from case law:

> a meaningful cumulative impact analysis must identify (1) the area in which the effects of the proposed project will be felt; (2) the impacts that are expected in that area from the proposed project; (3) other actions—past, present, and proposed, and reasonably foreseeable—that have had or are expected to have impacts in the same area; (4) the impacts or expected impacts from these other actions; and (5) the overall impact that can be expected if the individual impacts are allowed to accumulate. [Petitioner's Reply Br. at 3.]

The analysis in the EA, in other words, cannot treat the identified environmental concern in a vacuum, as an incremental approach attempts. Although the replacement airport may contribute only a 2% increase to the amount of overflights near or over the Park, there is no way to determine from the FAA's analysis in the EA whether, deferring to the FAA's expert calculations, a 2% increase, in addition to other noise impacts on the Park, will "significantly affect[]" the quality of the human environment in the Park. At no point does the FAA's EA aggregate the noise impacts on the Park. The analysis in the EA does not address the accumulated, or total, incremental impacts of various man-made noises, such as the 250 daily aircraft flights near or over the Park that originate at, or have as their destination, airports other than that in St. George. Neither does the EA consider in any manner the air tours near and over the Park originating from the St. George airport. Nor does the EA address the impact, much less the cumulative impact, of noise in the Park as a result of other activities, such as the planned expansions of other regional airports that have flights near or over the Park. Without analyzing the total noise impact on the Park as a result of the construction of the replacement airport, the FAA is not in a position to determine whether the additional noise that is projected to come from the expansion of the St. George airport facility at a new location would cause a significant environmental impact on the Park and, thus, to require preparation of an EIS. . . .

We remand the case because the record is insufficient for the court to determine whether an EIS is required. On remand, the FAA must evaluate the cumulative impact of noise pollution on the Park as a result of construction of the proposed replacement airport in light of air traffic near and over the Park, from whatever airport, air tours near or in the Park, and the acoustical data collected by NPS in the Park in 1995 and 1998 mentioned in comments on the draft EA. Other data may also prove relevant. . . .

NOTES AND QUESTIONS

1. *Considering Cumulative Impacts.* The principal case considered the discussion of cumulative impacts in an environmental assessment. Note the somewhat different role they play there, and note also that an agency must also consider other NEPA requirements, such as the alternatives requirement, in its EAs. For additional discussion of why an environmental assessment must discuss cumulative impacts, see Kern v. United States Bureau of Land Mgmt., 284 F.3d 1062 (9th Cir. 2002). *Kern* also summarizes the rules that apply when courts consider whether a discussion of cumulative impacts was adequate:

> Consideration of cumulative impacts requires "some quantified or detailed information; . . . general statements about 'possible' effects and 'some risk' do not constitute a 'hard look' absent a justification regarding why more definitive information could not be provided." The cumulative impact analysis must be more than perfunctory; it must provide a "useful analysis of the cumulative impacts of past, present, and future projects." Finally, cumulative impact analysis must be timely. It is not appropriate to defer consideration of cumulative impacts to a future date when meaningful consideration can be given now. When an agency's determination of what are "reasonably foreseeable future actions" and appropriate "component parts" is " 'fully informed and well-considered,' " we will defer to that determination. But we "need not forgive a 'clear error in judgment.' " [Id. at 1075.]

Courts frequently consider whether a discussion of cumulative impacts is adequate. See, e.g., Tomac v. Norton, 433 F.3d 852 (D.C. Cir. 2006) (discussion of potential for new business development held adequate). A Ninth Circuit case created problems concerning the level of detail required in the discussion of past cumulative impacts, but this problem has been addressed by a CEQ Guidance on the Consideration of Past Actions in Cumulative Impacts Analysis (2005).

2. *The CEQ Study.* CEQ has published another study, Considering Cumulative Impacts under the National Environmental Policy Act (1997), that provides guidance to agencies on cumulative impact analysis. The study adds that cumulative effects analysis can aggravate the uncertainty problem, but notes that "[w]here substantial uncertainties remain or multiple resource objectives exist, adaptive management provisions for flexible project implementation can be incorporated into the selected alternative." Id. at 3. How would you apply this advice to the impact statement in the *Grand Canyon Trust* case?

The study also recommends the delineation of "project impact zones" as the basis for studying cumulative impacts:

> Project impact zones for a proposed action are likely to vary for different resources and environmental media. For water, the project impact zone would be limited to the hydrologic system that would be affected by the proposed action. . . . Land-based effects may occur within some set distance from the proposed action. In addition, the boundaries for an individual resource should be related to the resource's dependence on different environmental media. [Id. at 15.]

3. *Extra-Record Evidence.* Is a NEPA case tried on the record the agency makes, or may the plaintiff introduce extra-record evidence at trial? Review the cases reproduced and discussed in this chapter and try to see where the record has been supplemented by evidence at trial. The decision on whether a plaintiff can supplement the record is critical in NEPA litigation. Without supplementation, the plaintiff will not be able to challenge an agency's conclusions with its own evidence.

In *Overton Park*, reproduced in Chapter 3, section A.2.c, the Supreme Court held that district courts should usually limit their review to the administrative record, and indicated a plaintiff may introduce extra-record evidence to supplement an agency's administrative record only when the record is incomplete or not clear. NEPA cases have applied these exceptions. County of Suffolk v. Secretary of the Interior, 562 F.2d 1368 (2d Cir. 1977), is a leading case for applying another exception allowing extra-record evidence when an agency fails to raise an important environmental issue in an impact statement. Other courts will allow evidence that is supplemental or cumulative, see North Slope Borough v. Andrus, 642 F.2d 589 (D.C. Cir. 1980), or when the record is not fully comprehensive. A court will always allow limited discovery to determine whether a record is complete. Bar MK Ranches v. Yeutter, 994 F.2d 735 (10th Cir. 1993).

4.   Mitigation

One very important problem that arises under NEPA is whether agencies have a responsibility to mitigate the environmental impacts of their actions, and if so, what that responsibility is. The following case considers this question:

ROBERTSON v. METHOW VALLEY CITIZENS COUNCIL
490 U.S. 332 (1989)

JUSTICE STEVENS delivered the opinion of the Court.

We granted certiorari to decide two questions of law. As framed by petitioners, they are:

1. Whether the National Environmental Policy Act requires federal agencies to include in each environmental impact statement: (a) a fully developed plan to mitigate environmental harm; and (b) a "worst case" analysis of potential environmental harm if relevant information concerning significant environmental effects is unavailable or too costly to obtain.

2. Whether the Forest Service may issue a special use permit for recreational use of national forest land in the absence of a fully developed plan to mitigate environmental harm.

Concluding that the Court of Appeals for the Ninth Circuit misapplied the National Environmental Policy Act of 1969 (NEPA), and gave inadequate deference to the Forest Service's interpretation of its own regulations, we reverse and remand for further proceedings.

I . . .

The Forest Service is authorized to manage the national forests for a number of purposes, including "outdoor recreation." It has issued approximately 170 special use permits pursuant to that authority for alpine and nordic ski areas. These permits are major federal actions that must be preceded by the preparation of an impact statement.

[Methow Recreation was awarded a special use permit to develop and operate a proposed Early Winters Ski Resort on Sandy Butte, a 6000-foot mountain in Okanogan National Forest, Washington, and on an adjacent 1,165-acre parcel. Sandy Butte, "like the Methow Valley it overlooks, is an unspoiled, sparsely populated area that the district court characterized as 'pristine.'" The Forest Service cooperated with state and county officials to prepare an impact statement known as the Early Winters Alpine Winter Sports Study.]

The Early Winters Study is a printed document containing almost 150 pages of text and 12 appendices. It evaluated five alternative levels of development of Sandy Butte that might be authorized, the lowest being a "no action" alternative and the highest being development of a 16-lift ski area able to accommodate 10,500 skiers at one time. The Study considered the effect of each level of development on water resources, soil, wildlife, air quality, vegetation and visual quality, as well as land use and transportation in the Methow Valley, probable demographic shifts, the economic market for skiing and other summer and winter recreational activities in the Valley, and the energy requirements for the ski area and related developments. The Study's discussion of possible impacts was not limited to on-site effects, but also, as required by Council on Environmental Quality (CEQ) regulations, see 40 CFR §1502.16(b) (1987), addressed "off-site impacts that each alternative might have on community facilities, socioeconomic and other environmental conditions in the Upper Methow Valley." As to off-site effects, the Study explained that "due to the uncertainty of where other public and private lands may become developed," it is difficult to evaluate offsite impacts, and thus the document's analysis is necessarily "not site-specific." Finally, the Study outlined certain steps that might be taken to mitigate adverse effects, both on Sandy Butte and in the neighboring Methow Valley, but indicated that these proposed steps are merely conceptual and "will be made more specific as part of the design and implementation stages of the planning process."

[The study concluded that although the ski resort would not have an adverse effect on air quality, off-site development that would accompany the resort would reduce air quality below state standards unless mitigation measures were taken. This impact would be created by increased automobile, fireplace, and wood stove use.]

[As mitigation measures t]he Study suggested that Okanogan County develop an air quality management plan, requiring weatherization of new buildings, limiting the number of wood stoves and fireplaces, and adopting monitoring and enforcement measures. In addition, the Study suggested that the Forest Service require that the master plan include procedures to control dust and to comply with smoke management practices.

In its discussion of adverse effects on area wildlife, the EIS concluded that no endangered or threatened species would be affected by the proposed development and that the only impact on sensitive species was the probable loss of a pair of spotted owls and their progeny. With regard to other wildlife, the Study considered the impact on 75 different indigenous species and predicted that within a decade after development vegetational change and increased human activity would lead to a decrease in population for 31 species, while causing an increase in population for another 24 species on Sandy Butte. Two species, the pine marten and nesting goshawk, would be eliminated altogether from the area of development.

In a comment in response to the draft EIS, the Washington Department of Game voiced a special concern about potential losses to the State's largest migratory deer herd, which uses the Methow Valley as a critical winter range and as its migration route. The state agency estimated that the total population of mule deer in the area most likely to be affected was "better than 30,000 animals" and that "the ultimate impact on the Methow deer herd could exceed a 50 percent reduction in numbers." The agency asserted that "Okanogan County residents place a great deal of importance on the area's deer herd." In addition, it explained that hunters had "harvested" 3,247 deer in the Methow Valley area in 1981, and that in 1980 hunters on average spent $1,980 for each deer killed in Washington, and they had contributed over $6 million to the State's economy. Because the deer harvest is apparently proportional to the size of the herd, the state agency predicted that "Washington business can expect to lose over $3 million annually from reduced recreational opportunity." The Forest Service's own analysis of the impact on the deer herd was more modest. It first concluded that the actual operation of the ski hill would have only a "minor" direct impact on the herd, but then recognized that the off-site effect of the development "would noticeably reduce numbers of deer in the Methow [Valley] with any alternative." Although its estimate indicated a possible 15 percent decrease in the size of the herd, it summarized the State's contrary view in the text of the EIS, and stressed that off-site effects are difficult to estimate due to uncertainty concerning private development.

As was true of its discussion of air quality, the EIS also described both on-site and off-site mitigation measures. Among possible on-site mitigation possibilities, the Study recommended locating runs, ski lifts, and roads so as to minimize interference with wildlife, restricting access to selected roads during fawning season, and further examination of the effect of the development on mule deer migration routes. Off-site options discussed in the Study included the use of zoning and tax incentives to limit development on deer winter range and migration routes, encouragement of conservation easements, and acquisition and management by local government of critical tracts of land. As with the measures suggested for mitigating the off-site effects on air quality, the proposed options were primarily directed to steps that might be taken by state and local government.

Ultimately, the Early Winters Study recommended the issuance of a permit for development at the second highest level considered—a 16-lift ski area able to accommodate 8,200 skiers at one time. On July 5, 1984, the Regional Forester decided to issue a special use permit as recommended by the Study. [To mitigate secondary impacts on air quality and a reduction in mule deer range the Forester directed the forest supervisor to implement mitigation measures "both independently and in cooperation with local officials."] . . .

[The plaintiffs appealed to the Chief Forester, who affirmed the Regional Forester's decision. They then brought suit claiming violations of NEPA. The suit was assigned to a Magistrate, who found that the impact statement was adequate.]

Concluding that the Early Winters Study was inadequate as a matter of law, the Court of Appeals reversed. Methow Valley Citizens Council v. Regional Forester, 833 F.2d 810 (CA9 1987). The court held that the Forest Service could not rely on "the implementation of mitigation measures" to support its conclusion that the impact on the mule deer would be minor "since not only has the effectiveness of these mitigation measures not yet been assessed, but the mitigation measures themselves have yet to be developed." It then added that if the agency had difficulty obtaining adequate information to make a reasoned assessment of the environmental impact on the herd, it had a duty to make a so-called "worst case analysis." Such an analysis is "formulated on the basis of available information, using reasonable projections of the worst possible consequences of a proposed action."

The court found a similar defect in the EIS's treatment of air quality. Since the EIS made it clear that commercial development in the Methow Valley will result in violations of state air quality standards unless effective mitigation measures are put in place by the local governments and the private developer, the Court of Appeals concluded that the Forest Service had an affirmative duty to "develop the necessary mitigation measures *before* the permit is granted" (emphasis in original). The court held that this duty was imposed by both the Forest Service's own regulations and §102 of NEPA. It read the statute as imposing a substantive requirement that "action be taken to mitigate the adverse effects of major federal actions." For this reason, it concluded that "an EIS must include a fair discussion of measures to mitigate the adverse environmental impacts of a proposed action." . . .

II

Section 101 of NEPA declares a broad national commitment to protecting and promoting environmental quality. To ensure that this commitment is "infused into the ongoing programs and actions of the Federal Government, the act also establishes some important 'action-forcing' procedures." 115 Cong. Rec. 40416 (remarks of Sen. Jackson). . . . [The Court then quoted §102.]

The statutory requirement that a federal agency contemplating a major action prepare such an environmental impact statement serves NEPA's "action-forcing" purpose in two important respects. It ensures that the agency, in reaching its decision, will have available and will carefully consider detailed information concerning significant environmental impacts; it also guarantees that the relevant information will be made available to the larger audience that may also play a role in both the decisionmaking process and the implementation of that decision.

Simply by focusing the agency's attention on the environmental consequences of a proposed project, NEPA ensures that important effects will not be overlooked or underestimated only to be discovered after resources have been committed or the die otherwise cast. Moreover the strong precatory language of §101 of the Act and the requirement that agencies prepare detailed impact statements inevitably bring pressure to bear on agencies "to respond to the needs of environmental quality." 115 Cong. Rec. 40425 (1969) (remarks of Sen. Muskie).

Publication of an EIS, both in draft and final form, also serves a larger informational role. It gives the public the assurance that the agency "has indeed considered environmental concerns in its decision making process," *Baltimore Gas & Electric* [Co. v. NRDC, Inc., 462 U.S. 87, 97 (1983)], and, perhaps more significantly, provides a springboard for public comment, see L. Caldwell, Science and the National Environmental Policy Act 72 (1982). Thus, in this case the final draft of the Early Winters Study reflects not only the work of the Forest Service itself, but also the critical views of the Washington State Department of Game, the Methow Valley Citizens Council, and Friends of the Earth, as well as many others, to whom copies of the draft Study were circulated. Moreover, with respect to a development such as Sandy Butte, where the adverse effects on air quality and the mule deer herd are primarily attributable to predicate off-site development that will be subject to regulation by other governmental bodies, the EIS serves the function of offering those bodies adequate notice of the expected consequences and the opportunity to plan and implement corrective measures in a timely manner.

The sweeping policy goals announced in §101 of NEPA are thus realized through a set of "action-forcing" procedures that require that agencies take a "'hard look' at environmental consequences," *Kleppe* [v. Sierra Club, 427 U.S. 390, 410 n.21 (1976)], and that provide for broad dissemination of relevant environmental information. Although these procedures are almost certain to affect the agency's substantive decision, it is now well settled that NEPA itself does not mandate particular results, but simply prescribes the necessary process. See Strycker's Bay Neighborhood Council, Inc. v. Karlen, 444 U.S. 223, 227-228 (1980) (per curiam); Vermont Yankee Nuclear Power Corp. v. Natural Resources Defense Council, Inc., 435 U.S. 519, 558 (1978). If the adverse environmental effects of the proposed action are adequately identified and evaluated, the agency is not constrained by NEPA from deciding that other values outweigh the environmental costs. See ibid.; *Stryker's Bay Neighborhood Council, Inc., supra,* at 227-228; *Kleppe,* 427 U.S., at 410, n.21. In this case, for example, it would not have violated NEPA if the Forest Service, after complying with the Act's procedural prerequisites, had decided that the benefits to be derived from downhill skiing at Sandy Butte justified the issuance of a special use permit, notwithstanding the loss of 15 percent, 50 percent, or even 100 percent of the mule deer herd. Other statutes may impose substantive environmental obligations on federal agencies, but NEPA merely prohibits uninformed—rather than unwise—agency action.

To be sure, one important ingredient of an EIS is the discussion of steps that can be taken to mitigate adverse environmental consequences. The requirement that an EIS contain a detailed discussion of possible mitigation measures flows from both the language of the Act and, more expressly, from CEQ's implementing regulations. Implicit in NEPA's demand that an agency prepare a detailed statement on "any adverse environmental effects which cannot be avoided should the proposal be implemented," 42 U.S.C. §4332[2](C)(ii), is an understanding that the EIS will discuss the extent to which adverse effects can be avoided. See D. Mandelker, NEPA Law and Litigation §10.38 (1984). More generally, omission of a reasonably complete discussion of possible mitigation measures would undermine the "action-forcing" function of NEPA. Without such a discussion, neither the agency nor other interested groups and individuals can properly evaluate the severity of the adverse effects. An adverse effect that can be fully remedied by, for example, an inconsequential public expenditure is certainly not as serious as a similar effect that can only be modestly ameliorated through the commitment of vast public and private resources. Recognizing the importance of such a discussion in guaranteeing that the agency has taken a "hard look" at the environmental consequences of proposed federal action, CEQ regulations require that the agency discuss possible mitigation measures in defining the scope of the EIS, 40 CFR §1508.25(b) (1987), in discussing alternatives to the proposed action, §1502.14(f), and consequences of that action, §1502.16(h), and in explaining its ultimate decision, §1505.2(c).

There is a fundamental distinction, however, between a requirement that mitigation be discussed in sufficient detail to ensure that environmental consequences have been fairly evaluated, on the one hand, and a substantive requirement that a complete mitigation plan be actually formulated and adopted, on the other. In this case, the off-site effects on air quality and on the mule deer herd cannot be mitigated unless nonfederal government agencies take appropriate action. Since it is those state and local governmental bodies that have jurisdiction over the area in which the adverse effects need be addressed and since they have the authority to mitigate them, it would be incongruous to conclude that the Forest Service has no power to act until the local agencies have reached a final conclusion on what mitigating measures they consider necessary. Even more significantly, it would be inconsistent with NEPA's reliance on procedural mechanisms—as opposed to substantive, result-based standards—to demand the presence of a fully developed plan that will mitigate environmental harm before an agency can act. Cf. *Baltimore Gas & Electric Co.*, 462 U.S., at 100 ("NEPA does not require agencies to adopt any particular internal decision making structure").

We thus conclude that the Court of Appeals erred, first, in assuming that "NEPA requires that 'action be taken to mitigate the adverse effects of major federal actions,'" and, second, in finding that this substantive requirement entails the further duty to include in every EIS "a detailed explanation of specific measures which will be employed to mitigate the adverse impacts of a proposed action."

III . . .

[The Court held that CEQ had properly amended its NEPA regulations to delete the requirement for a "worst case" analysis. The Court also held that the Forest Service's failure to develop a complete mitigation plan did not violate its own regulations.]

V

In sum, we conclude that NEPA does not require a fully developed plan detailing what steps will be taken to mitigate adverse environmental impacts. . . . The judgment of the Court of Appeals is accordingly reversed and the case is remanded for further proceedings consistent with this opinion.

It is so ordered.

NOTES AND QUESTIONS

1. *The Role of Mitigation.* Mitigation is important in the NEPA environmental assessment process. It gives the agency an opportunity to proceed with its action by modifying it, or by including additional measures that will prevent the action from having significant environmental effects. *Robertson* was willing to imply an obligation to consider mitigation measures but not an obligation actually to formulate and adopt them. The Court's holding on mitigation is a replay of the substantive v. procedural debate. Does this holding weaken the statute? See Rossmann, NEPA: Not So Well at Twenty, 20 Envtl. L. Rep. (ELI) 10174 (1990) (arguing yes).

2. *Adequacy of Mitigation Measures.* Courts since *Robertson* have reviewed discussions of mitigation measures in impact statements and have usually held them adequate. But judicial review is fact-specific. For example, in Neighbors of Cuddy Mountain v. United States Forest Serv., 137 F.3d 1372 (9th Cir. 1998), the Forest Service admitted a timber sale would negatively affect an endangered fish species because of increased sedimentation in three creeks, but provided only a perfunctory description of mitigation measures that could avoid this effect. The court held that the "broad generalizations and vague references to mitigation measures in relation to the streams affected" did not satisfy the "hard look" required by NEPA.

What if an impact statement discusses mitigation measures but admits they might not be successful? The court held that this discussion satisfied NEPA in Laguna Greenbelt, Inc. v. United States Dep't of Transp., 42 F.3d 517 (9th Cir. 1994). In an impact statement on a proposed tollway, the agency admitted that mitigation measures for habitat revegetation and wildlife corridor maintenance might not be successful. This did not make the discussion inadequate under the *Robertson* requirement:

> NEPA does not require a fully developed plan that will mitigate all environmental harm before an agency can act; NEPA requires only that mitigation be discussed in sufficient detail to ensure that environmental consequences have been fully evaluated. [Id. at 528, citing cases holding, *inter alia*, that an agency was not required to finish mitigation studies or execute mitigation plans before beginning a project.]

In a footnote, the court also rejected a suggestion that the impact statement was inadequate because it contained assurances not based on scientific evidence. It held there was no requirement that scientific uncertainties in mitigation measures must be discussed. Id. at 528 n.11. Is this holding consistent with the requirement that agencies must discuss scientific uncertainties that affect the evaluation of environmental impacts?

3. *Adaptive Management.* The enforcement or follow-up on a NEPA document after it has been accepted is a weak point in NEPA implementation. CEQ regulations encourage agencies to monitor compliance, and lead agencies must report monitoring and mitigation information "upon request." 40 C.F.R. §1505.3. This requirement applies, however, only if an agency commits to mitigation and other conditions in its decision. Id. §§1505.2(c), 1505.3. Agencies must decide whether post-decision monitoring and enforcement are "applicable for any mitigation."

The report of the NEPA task force called for the use of an adaptive management strategy as a means of monitoring decisions under NEPA. The task force report described the traditional environmental process as one involving prediction, mitigation, and implementation. It is a one-time process that does not provide for unanticipated change. Adaptive management is a term used since the 1970s to include post-decision responses to conditions and circumstances related to an action. It remedies this problem by adding a monitoring and adaptation element that allows agencies to address unanticipated results and adjust decisions accordingly. NEPA Task Force Report to the Council on Environmental Quality: Modernizing NEPA Implementation 47-49 (2003). This can be done without triggering the need for a supplemental EIS, discussed below in Note 5.

CEQ has also proposed incorporating the international environmental management system (EMS) based on ISO 1400 into the NEPA process. 71 Fed. Reg. 40,520 (2006) (requesting comments). CEQ states that "[t]he guide will be provided to all Federal agencies to help Federal agencies recognize the complementary relationship of EMS and NEPA and to assist them in aligning EMS elements with the NEPA statement of policy in Section 101 and the analysis and decision processes of Section 102 and incorporating the EMS approach into the NEPA process when establishing, implementing, and maintaining their EMS." The guide states that "it is conceivable that a well constructed EMS can include all the elements of the NEPA process and serve as the basis for complying with NEPA requirements. CEQ specifically solicits public comment on this idea."

For discussion see Ruhl, Regulation by Adaptive Management: Is It Possible?, 7 Minn. J.L. Sci. & Tech. 21 (2005); Karkkainen, Toward a Smarter NEPA: Monitoring and Managing Environmental Performance, 102 Colum. L. Rev. 903 (2002).

4. *Environmental Justice Executive Order.* An environmental justice Executive Order issued by President Clinton requires each federal agency, "to the greatest extent practicable," to make "achieving environmental justice part of its mission." Executive Order 12,898, 50 Fed. Reg. 7629 (1994). Agencies are to achieve this objective by identifying and addressing any disproportionately "high and adverse human health or environmental effects of its programs, policies, and activities on minority and low-income populations." A White House memorandum implementing the Order requires federal agencies to analyze the human health, economic, and social effects of their actions, including effects on minority and low income communities, when NEPA requires this analysis. Memorandum of Feb. 11, 1994.

CEQ Guidance states that the Executive Order "does not change the prevailing legal thresholds and statutory interpretations under NEPA and existing case law." Environmental Justice: Guidance under the National Environmental Policy Act 8 (1998). However, the guidance adds that the identification of disproportionately high and adverse effects on minority and low-income populations "should heighten agency attention to alternatives (including alternative sites), mitigation strategies, monitoring needs, and preferences expressed by the affected community or population." Id. For a case in which the Nuclear Regulatory Commission's Atomic Safety and Licensing Board rejected a uranium enrichment plant's application for a construction permit operating license due to the agency staff's inadequate consideration of environmental justice concerns, see In re Louisiana Energy Serv., L.P. (May 1, 1997). The Board ordered the staff to revise its final EIS to consider the effects of site selection on economically disadvantaged minority communities.

How does the Executive Order affect the analysis in the cases reproduced in this chapter? See Communities Against Runway Expansion, Inc. v. Federal Aviation Admin., 355 F.3d 678 (D.C. Cir. 2004) (correct comparison community selected for environmental justice analysis of noise from airport project). The court held the agency's environmental justice determination was subject to review under NEPA and the APA even though the Order expressly states that it does not provide for a private right of judicial review.

5. *Supplemental Environmental Impact Statements.* Even though an impact statement may adequately discuss the environmental impacts of a proposed action, circumstances may arise in which a supplemental impact statement is necessary. CEQ regulations require the preparation of supplemental statements when

 (i) The agency makes substantial changes in the proposed action that are relevant to environmental concerns; or
 (ii) There are significant new circumstances or information relevant to environmental concerns and bearing on the proposed action or its impacts. [40 C.F.R. §1502.9(c)(1).]

In Marsh v. Oregon Natural Res. Council, 490 U.S. 360 (1989), the Supreme Court upheld the regulation even though NEPA does not require supplemental statements, noting it would defeat the purpose of the statute if an action could escape additional review when new impacts were discovered. The Court held that agencies should apply a "rule of reason" to the decision on whether to prepare a supplemental statement and give a "hard look" to the environmental effects of an action even after they have given initial approval of a project. The Court also held it would apply the arbitrary and capricious standard of judicial review to an agency's decision that a supplemental impact statement was not necessary. It rejected a claim that new information required a supplemental statement because it held the information was neither new nor accurate.

Wisconsin v. Weinberger, 745 F.2d 412 (7th Cir. 1984), a pre-*Marsh* case, held that a supplemental statement is not necessary unless "new information provides a seriously different picture of the environmental landscape such that another hard look is necessary." What kinds of new information might trigger a supplemental statement in the cases reproduced in this chapter?

Most of the cases have rejected arguments that supplemental impact statements were necessary. They have held that supplemental statements are not necessary when the original impact statement adequately discussed the circumstances claimed to be new. E.g., Laguna Greenbelt, Inc. v. United States Dep't of Transp., 42 F.3d 517 (9th Cir. 1994) (effect of wildfires on area where tollway planned). Neither are supplemental statements required when the new circumstances are minor. Environmental Def. Fund v. Marsh, 651 F.2d 983 (5th Cir. 1981) (change in amount of soil disposal from new waterway). But see Commonwealth of Massachusetts v. Watt, 716 F.2d 946 (1st Cir. 1983) (agency reduced amount of oil expected to be discovered in offshore lease sale by 97 percent after original impact statement filed).

6. *What Does It Take to Win a NEPA Case?* The federal courts are the major enforcers of NEPA, so this is the place to ask what it takes to win a NEPA case. Because the courts defer to the agencies on many NEPA issues, and because agencies have matured in their compliance with NEPA, litigation may not seem useful. Distinctions must be made, however, between questions of law, questions of fact, and questions of mixed law and fact. Courts will intervene if an agency has not interpreted NEPA correctly. An example is a decision to segment projects that should be considered together, or to reject an alternative that should have been evaluated. Environmental assessments and EISs require the collection and evaluation of environmental information. Courts will not intervene if an agency has done this job well. They will

intervene, however, if an agency omits information or scientific opinion it should have considered or does not fully explain its conclusions. Review the issues discussed in this chapter and identify those that are most likely to receive careful judicial review.

NOTE ON STATE ENVIRONMENTAL POLICY LEGISLATION

Fifteen states, the District of Columbia, and Puerto Rico have state environmental policy acts (SEPAs) similar to NEPA, which require environmental assessments and the preparation of environmental impact statements. Most of these statutes are carbon copies of NEPA. However, the California Environmental Quality Act (CEQA) is unique as a lengthy, detailed prescription of how the environmental review process should be carried out.

Where SEPAs apply to local governments, a major innovation is the application of the environmental review process to local land use planning and land use decisions, such as rezonings and private project approvals. This is especially true in California, New York, and Washington, the most active SEPA states, where the environmental review process required by the state NEPA is as important as review under the traditional land use process.

Environmental reviews under SEPAs raise issues similar to those raised under NEPA. State judicial interpretations of SEPAs are usually comparable, although some of the state decisions have taken care to point out that the state law is to be more broadly applied. A few SEPAs specify a judicial review standard, e.g., Cal. Pub. Res. Code §21168.5 (prejudicial abuse of discretion).

Ministerial versus Discretionary. The distinction between ministerial and discretionary actions is more important under SEPAs when they apply to local actions, such as building permits, which do not appear to confer discretion on the permitting body. Applying the state environmental review process to a building permit clearly gives objectors leverage they would not otherwise have. An objection under the zoning ordinance is not possible if the project is a permitted use and no other discretionary zoning approvals are required.

The state cases have required an environmental review of building permits by holding that their approval was discretionary. Friends of Westwood, Inc. v. City of Los Angeles, 235 Cal. Rptr. 788 (Cal. App. 1987), for example, held a building permit approval for a high-rise office building subject to a special "plan-check" review was discretionary. Plan-check review was reserved for 100 to 150 of the 40,000 building permits the city considered annually. As part of the plan-check review the city had the opportunity to set and did set several standards concerning many aspects of the proposed building.

The court held that the term "ministerial" was limited to those approvals that can be legally compelled without modification or change. It applied this definition to hold that the plan-check building permit review in this case was not ministerial because the city had the discretion to require changes. Run-of-the-mill building permits that can be legally compelled are ministerial. See also Eastlake Cmty. Council v. Roanoke Assoc., Inc., 513 P.2d 36 (Wash. 1974).

Planning and Land Use Regulation Issues. In states where the SEPAs apply to planning and land use regulation, the overlap with SEPA reviews can be troublesome, and has been addressed through court decisions and remedial legislation. In Citizens of Goleta Valley v. Board of Supervisors, 801 P.2d 1161 (Cal. 1990), a county considered but rejected a number of alternatives for a shorefront hotel development. Objectors argued the county should have taken an optimal view of alternative sites throughout the region, but the court disagreed. It held the county's comprehensive land use and coastal plans addressed these issues, and added that an impact report "is not ordinarily an occasion for the reconsideration or overhaul of fundamental land use policy." Why didn't the federal court in *Marita* reach the same conclusion in considering the relationship between NEPA and the forest management plans?

California, New York, and Washington have now adopted reforms that attempt to integrate the planning and land use control process with SEPA environmental reviews. See Mandelker, Melding State Environmental Policy Acts with Land-Use Planning and Regulation, Land Use L. & Zoning Dig., Vol. 49, No. 3, at 3 (1997). One option provides that SEPA reviews are to rely on environmental analysis carried out in the land use planning process.

Socioeconomic Effects. In some states, the statutory definition of the "environment" to be considered in an impact statement is broad enough to support holdings, contrary to the federal view, that impact statements must consider socioeconomic effects even though a project does not have a separate physical impact on the environment. Chinese Staff & Workers Ass'n v. City of New York, 502 N.E.2d 176 (N.Y. 1986) (socioeconomic impacts of a high-rise luxury condominium in Chinatown section of New York City). Contra Wisconsin's Envtl. Decade, Inc. v. Wisconsin Dep't of Natural Res., 340 N.W.2d 722 (Wis. 1983). California's SEPA defines the term "environment" as "the physical conditions within the area which will be affected by a proposed project," including "objects of historic or aesthetic significance." Cal. Pub. Res. Code §21060.5

Substantive Effect. In a landmark opinion, the Washington Supreme Court gave a decisively substantive effect to its environmental policy act. Polygon Corp. v. City of Seattle, 578 P.2d 1309 (Wash. 1978), noted, 54 Wash. L. Rev. 693 (1979). A developer applied for a building permit to construct a high-rise condominium on one of Seattle's seven hills. The impact statement disclosed a number of adverse environmental effects, including view obstruction, excessive bulk and scale, and noise and shadow effects. The city building superintendent relied on these adverse effects to deny the building permit, and the court affirmed. Note that the court took this position even though the building was a permitted use under the city's zoning ordinance.

A subsequent legislative amendment qualified *Polygon* by authorizing denials only on the basis of "formally designated" local policies. Wash. Rev. Code §43.21C.060. Any such action also is appealable to the local legislative authority. Compare Save Our Rural Env't v. Snohomish County, 662 P.2d 816 (Wash. 1983), holding it was beyond the power of the court to disapprove a rezoning because the impact statement identified alternative sites. Is this consistent with *Polygon*?

California's SEPA allows agencies to approve impact reports only if they make findings that "changes or alterations have been required in, or incorporated into, the project which mitigate the significant effects on the environment." Cal. Pub. Res. Code §2181. The cases seem to have taken the position that the statute does not require selection of an environmentally superior alternative if modifications to a project mitigate its environmental impacts to an "acceptable" level. Laurel Hills Homeowners Ass'n v. City Council, 147 Cal. Rptr. 841 (Cal. App. 1978). For discussion of state environmental policy acts, see D. Mandelker, NEPA Law and Litigation ch. 12. For a comparison of these acts with NEPA see Mas, A Comparison of Three Elements of National and Select State Environmental Policy Acts, 5 Envt. Practice 349 (2003).

E.   WHERE IS NEPA TODAY? A CRITIQUE AND MEASURES FOR REFORM

1.   *Evaluation of the NEPA Process*

The Issues. Ultimately, the essential questions must be asked: Has NEPA worked? Has it made a difference in agency decisionmaking? Has it eliminated or at least mitigated the environmental impacts of agency projects and actions? As might be expected, the answers to these questions vary. Supporters of NEPA view it as having made a modest but important contribution to informed environmental decisionmaking. They report improvements in agency procedures for environmental evaluation and believe NEPA has brought about the mitigation if not the elimination of negative environmental impacts from agency actions. A recent study of eight agencies with major NEPA responsibilities, however, shows that funding for NEPA compliance has decreased at the same time that NEPA workload has increased, NEPA training and staff positions have been reduced, and "most agency headquarters NEPA offices lack an ongoing national tracking system to monitor the numbers or types of NEPA documents that their agency is preparing or has completed." Smythe & Isber, NEPA in the Agencies 1 (National Resources Council of America, 2002). Workload has increased because the number of federal actions subject to NEPA has increased, increasing emphasis on the role of nonfederal cooperating agencies. In addition, "[t]here is a pervasive tendency for senior policy officials to place more emphasis on reducing the time, costs, and paperwork associated with NEPA compliance than on assuring the quality and adequacy of the analysis." Id. at 2.

Critics see NEPA as a statute that requires unnecessary paperwork that delays or even eliminates beneficial projects. Impact statements are criticized as self-serving and bulky justifications for projects that agencies plan to undertake, whatever the environmental analysis reveals. Impact statements are also viewed as collections of irrelevant data with a blurred focus that do not contribute to informed evaluation. The past few years have seen increasing attention to the reform of NEPA through reports and guidance issued by CEQ, legislation modifying NEPA for selected programs, and a report by the House Resources Committee.

NEPA in Practice. A number of studies have been done on how agencies respond to and internalize their responsibilities under NEPA. Bardach & Pugliaresi, The Environmental-Impact Statement vs. the Real World, 49 Pub. Interest 22 (1977), is an early study of NEPA compliance in the Department of Interior that was critical of the impact statement process because the authors believe it is primarily a defensive agency activity. They note that the impact statement guarantees some sort of look at environmental issues, but not necessarily the "hard look" the courts require: "Indeed, the legal and institutional machinery that insures some look, inadvertently and most unfortunately precludes the *hard* look that could and should influence agency decisions. To put the case very baldly: Agencies cannot be penetrating or creative when their analyses are directed and mobilized for primarily defensive purposes." Id. at 24.

The authors provide a number of reasons for their conclusion. One is the "institutional pessimism" they find in agency impact statements. Too little pessimism, they believe, "can lead to charges of 'whitewashing' the proposed development and a court order requiring the department to go back and prepare an 'adequate' impact statement." Id. at 29. Neither do agencies "wish the impact statement to have the appearance of a 'balanced' document, lest environmental critics allege in a lawsuit that the balancing was incompetent or prejudicial to environmental interests." Id. at 34.

Bardach and Pugliaresi bring even more substantial charges against the effectiveness of NEPA. They claim, for example, that the legislation takes an unrealistic view of environmental impacts:

> The concept . . . [that an impact is any alteration in the state of the world] is not straightforward, of course. What it means depends in large measure on beliefs about what the world might look like in the absence of the project. The simplest and most legally and politically defensible belief is that the world would in no way look different than at present. Unfortunately, this view . . . is most unrealistic. There is constant change in human and natural environments all around us, but this endemic change is ordinarily not contemplated by the EIS. Nor does it ordinarily take into account how people, or other organizations, will adapt to change. [Id. at 30.]

The authors mix structural with empirically based criticism. Their criticism reflects a school of political thought that emphasizes the ability of political institutions to adapt to new obligations and responsibilities in a defensive manner that does not threaten or alter agency behavior. The following excerpt takes a more balanced view of NEPA's contribution to agency decisionmaking by looking at NEPA's effect on the United States Forest Service. After noting that NEPA has fostered an interdisciplinary approach to management and decisionmaking, the author comments:

> The Forest Service assimilation of NEPA and NFMA [the National Forest Management Act] has produced not only an expansion of Forest Service personnel and expertise beyond the traditional and limited forestry focus, but also better staffed and documented decisions. Until approximately twenty years ago, a majority of Forest Service professional employees were foresters. That has changed significantly. Now there is also a broad complement of engineers, landscape architects, wildlife biologists, computer analysts, sociologists, range conservationists, public involvement specialists, geologists, archaeologists, and even some lawyers. In response to the requirements of NEPA and NFMA (and the threat of challenge), these professionals have improved not only the information and analysis prepared for decisions, but also the documentation of those decisions in agency files and formal decision documents. . . .
>
> The Forest Service integration of NEPA is not without problems. One difficulty is that NEPA's procedures are frequently better suited to discrete projects than to the continuous and dynamic land management programs implemented by the Forest Service. Discrete projects involve a choice between whether or not to undertake specific action, and if so, how. If a decision on a project is delayed or invalidated, no action is taken and the status quo is maintained. As a land manager, however, the Forest Service must continuously manage the national forests. When programmatic change in this management is warranted, delay or failure to approve change means the continuation of unwarranted policies. Unlike the failure to act on a proposed project, which preserves the status quo, the failure to approve a new land management policy—even though it may not take affirmative action—can significantly affect national forest lands by continuing obsolete or undesirable practices. With Forest Service programs, failure to take new action is a decision to continue past action, which may be clearly unwarranted.
>
> Another problem with NEPA, as it is implemented by the Forest Service, involves the multiple layers of required analyses. . . . [P]roject level decisions may be tiered to one or more programmatic decisions made years earlier. As a result, conducting the multileveled analyses required to reach project level decisions often requires

extraordinary amounts of time, money, and manpower. Also, once decisions are made, their finality is suspect. [Ackerman, Observations on the Transformation of the Forest Service: The Effects of the National Environmental Policy Act on U.S. Forest Service Decision Making, 20 Envtl. L. 703, 709-712 (1990).

The author also notes difficulties with public participation in decisionmaking, which often has little impact because it is too limited, structured, and polarized. To what extent does the *Marita* case, reproduced above, illustrate the issues and problems Ackerman discusses? Smythe & Isber, *supra*, report the Forest Service "NEPA work-load is increasing because planning and management objectives are becoming more diverse, in part due to increasingly detailed direction from Congress and the courts." Id. at 7.

An earlier study of the Forest Service and the Corps of Engineers, S. Taylor, Making Bureaucracies Think: The Environmental Impact Statement Strategy of Administrative Reform (1984), answered with a "complicated and contingent" yes the question of whether the "average" agency project is better than it might have been before the impact statement process was introduced. See Book Review, 13 Ecology L.Q. 155 (1986). Taylor notes that project outcomes vary depending on whether a project can gain from incorporating environmental mitigation measures and on whether the project has enough "slack" to incorporate such measures, yet still be viable. Taylor notes that the uncertainties in the NEPA process give environmental groups additional leverage to challenge the adequacy of agency impact statements and compensate for CEQ's relatively weak oversight role. For an earlier study of the Corps, see D. Mazmanian & J. Nienaber, Can Organizations Change? Environmental Protection, Citizen Participation, and the Corps of Engineers (1979).

Notes on Reports on NEPA's Effectiveness and the Need for Reform

The CEQ NEPA Effectiveness Study. CEQ carried out an effectiveness study of NEPA's first 25 years that included organizations and individuals experienced in the application of NEPA. Council on Environmental Quality, The National Environmental Policy Act: A Study of Its Effectiveness after Twenty-five Years (1997). The report notes that NEPA helps agencies to make better decisions, produce better results, and build trust in communities, but often is triggered too late to be fully effective. It found problems in interagency coordination and suggested that agencies can improve environmental protection, get projects started earlier, and dramatically reduce NEPA compliance costs by monitoring and modifying project management rather than fully discussing environmental impacts before project approval. The report criticized the heavy reliance on environmental assessments, which creates a danger of diminished public participation, and means that individual minor actions may not require impact statements yet have major adverse cumulative effects.

The CEQ Task Force Report. CEQ later convened a task force whose report made a number of suggestions for improvements in NEPA practice.* It contains recommendations on several problems in the implementation of NEPA. These include technology and information management security, federal and intergovernmental collaboration, programmatic analysis and tiering, adaptive management and

---

*The NEPA Task Force Report to the Council of Environmental Quality: Modernizing NEPA Implementation (2003). The Report is available at http://ceq.eh.doe.gov/ntf/report/index.html.

monitoring, categorical exclusions, and environmental assessments. Some of these recommendations have already been implemented, as noted earlier.

The Council on Environmental Quality has completed its review of the Task Force recommendations, and the chair has issued a Memorandum including recommendations for improving the implementation of NEPA.* The memorandum suggests principles for modernizing NEPA implementation while recognizing the need to "[e]nsure timely and cost effective environmental reviews while maintaining environmentally sound decision-making that helps achieve the Nation's environmental, social and economic objectives" as well as maintaining "effective environmental impact assessment processes already in existence."

CEQ also released a Compendium of Useful Practices to improve the implementation of NEPA in September 2005. It defines a useful practice as "those processes, techniques, or innovative uses of resources that have either demonstrated actual improvements or have the potential to improve the cost, schedule, quality, performance, or some other factor that impacts [NEPA] implementation." It contains a discussion of adaptive management and monitoring, collaboration, environmental management systems, programmatic analysis, and tiering and technology. Case studies illustrate the recommendations for these topics. The compendium is available at http://ceq.eh.doe.gov/ntf/compendium/compendium.html.

House Resources Committee Task Force. Early in 2005 the House Resources Committee established a Task Force on Improving the National Environmental Policy Act that held hearings around the country and then published an interim report followed by a final staff report in July 2006 that was not adopted by the full committee. The election of a Democratic Congress casts doubt on its future. The report, Recommendations to Improve and Update the National Environmental Policy Act, recommends legislation on nine different topics: addressing delays in the process; enhancing public participation; better involvement for state, local, and tribal stakeholders; addressing litigation issues; clarifying alternatives analysis; better federal agency coordination; additional authority for CEQ; clarification of the meaning of "cumulative impacts"; and conducting studies. The recommendations are not a comprehensive and integrated approach to an amendment of NEPA, and to some extent are a hostile view of the statute.

NOTES AND QUESTIONS

1. *Which Way NEPA?* The contrast between the CEQ and House committee recommendations for NEPA is striking. CEQ recommends marginal improvement while the House committee report, though restricted, takes a generally hostile tone. Neither addresses the structural problems identified in the articles discussed earlier by Bardach and Pugliaresi and by Ackerman. What would you recommend?

2. *A Hostile Administration?* Observers claim the Bush administration has been hostile to NEPA.** Legislation has already been enacted, discussed below, that modifies NEPA for key federal agencies.

*Memorandum to Heads of Federal Agencies from James L. Connaughton on Implementing Recommendations to Modernize NEPA (May 2, 2005), available at http://ceq.eh.doe.gov/ntf/implementation.html. For discussion see 36 Envt. Rep. (BNA) 1355 (2005).

**R. Dreher, NEPA under Siege: The Political Assault on the National Environmental Policy Act (2005 Georgetown Environmental Law and Policy Institute), available at law.georgetown.edu/gelpi; Buccino, NEPA under Assault: Congressional and Administrative Proposals Would Weaken Environmental Review and Public Participation, 12 N.Y.U. Envtl. L.J. 50 (2003).

3. *The Litigation Record.* Has the success rate in NEPA litigation been affected by the increase in Republican appointments to federal courts? A recent study found that the political affiliation of the administration that appointed the judge deciding the case affected the outcome of NEPA cases. Between January 2001 and June 2004, there were 217 federal district court NEPA cases, with environmental plaintiffs achieving success 59.2 percent of the time when appearing before a Democrat-appointed judge, and only 28.4 percent of the time when appearing before a Republican-appointed judge. During the same period, only 107 NEPA cases were filed with the Circuit Courts of Appeals. Overall, environmental plaintiffs maintained their 44 percent historical success rate, but were nearly six times more likely to prevail before majority Democrat-appointed panels . . . than before majority Republican-appointed panels." Jay E. Austin et al., Judging NEPA: A "Hard Look" at Judicial Decision Making under the National Environmental Policy Act, Environmental Law Institute 8 (Nov. 2004), available at endangeredlaws.org.

A recent study of Forest Service litigation found the Service won nearly 58 percent of its cases and lost about 21 percent. Many of these cases involved NEPA. Keele et al., Forest Service Land Management Litigation 1989-2002, 104 J. Forestry 196 (2006). Seventeen percent of the cases reach a settlement, which the study finds to be an important dispute resolution tool.

4. *Recent Legislation.* Recent legislation covering the Department of Transportation, Department of Energy, and the Forest Service has significantly modified NEPA for these key agencies. Some parts of this legislation were discussed earlier. The most significant changes were made for Department of Transportation projects. The Safe, Accountable, Flexible, Efficient Transportation Equity Act of 2005 substantially modifies NEPA as it applies to environmental impact statements for these projects. Pub. L. No. 109-59, 119 Stat. 1144 (2005) (variously codified). For discussion see 36 Env't Rep. (BNA) 1627 (2005). It requires a modified NEPA review process for all highway projects, public transportation projects, and multimodal projects that require federal approval. 23 U.S.C. §139(a)(3)(B), (5). The Department is the lead agency for NEPA compliance; other agencies may be joint lead agencies, and any state or local government entity receiving federal funds for a project shall also serve as a joint lead agency. §139(c)(1-3). The lead agency is authorized to designate participating agencies. §139(d).

An important provision of the Act, discussed earlier, authorizes the Department to make the purpose and need decision necessary to a discussion of alternatives and to select the range of alternatives to be considered. The Act also contains provisions, discussed earlier, that delegate decisions on categorical exclusions to the Department.

The statute enacts a six-month statute of limitations for judicial review running from the publication of a Federal Register notice announcing that a permit, license, or approval is final. §139(l)(1). In addition, the Department as lead agency must consider new information after the close of a comment period on an EIS only if it satisfies requirements for a supplemental impact statement under departmental regulations, §139(l)(2), displacing CEQ regulations for this requirement. Similar legislation not quite as extensive was adopted for airport expansion projects funded by the Federal Aviation Administration. 49 U.S.C. §47171.

Make a list of the changes made to NEPA by the Transportation Act and decide whether they seriously disable the NEPA process for transportation projects. It is not clear whether this selective amendment of NEPA will continue in a Democratic Congress.

5. *References*. For evaluations of the role and future of NEPA, see L. Caldwell, The National Environmental Policy Act: An Agenda for the Future (1998); Caldwell, Beyond NEPA: Future Significance of the National Environmental Policy Act, 22 Harv. Envtl. L. Rev. 203 (1998); Pollack, Reimagining NEPA: Choices for Environmentalists, 9 Harv. Envtl. L. Rev. 359 (1985); Connaughton, Modernizing the National Environmental Policy Act: Back to the Future, 12 N.Y.U. Envtl. L.J. 1 (2003) (author is chair of CEQ); Trip & Alley, Streamlining NEPA's Environmental Review Process: Suggestions for Agency Reform, 12 N.Y.U. Envtl. L.J. 74 (2003). For studies of NEPA practices in federal agencies see Funk, NEPA at Energy: An Exercise in Legal Narrative, 20 Envtl. L. 759 (1990); Note, Federal Highways and Environmental Litigation: Toward a Theory of Public Choice and Administrative Reaction, 27 Harv. J. Legis. 229 (1990). For a Congressional Research Service report, see The National Environmental Policy Act: Streamlining NEPA (Feb. 8. 2006), available at www.opencrs.com/rpts/RL33267_20060208.pdf.

V

BIODIVERSITY CONSERVATION

Problem 5-1

The northern spitfire beetle lives on the edge of Ice Age Lake. It inhabits the Ice Age dunes, a 10,000-acre area of sand dunes and scrub forest land, and is found only in this ecosystem. One-half of the land is in a national forest, one-fourth lies in a state park, and the rest is privately owned. The beetle lives for three weeks in late August and then dies. There are over 290,000 varieties of beetles in the world, and the northern spitfire beetle is distinguished from similar species by a burnt-orange shell, which has been copied by jewelry designers in Budapest. The beetle does not support any other species in the ecosystem. Eco-tours has purchased 1,000 acres of private land to build a luxury eco-lodge. For $1,000 per night (food, but not alcohol, included), eco-tourists will be able to explore the Ice Age dunes, fish for Ice Age pike, and view wildlife in the area. Scientists are concerned that the lodge will shrink the beetle's habitat by about 15 percent and thus increase the risk of extinction. They are also concerned that global climate change may cause the beetle to migrate northward into areas where human-caused habitat fragmentation will make its survival more problematic in the coming decades. An entomologist at State University has proposed that the beetle be listed as a threatened or endangered species. The local lumber company has located a scientist who has published two papers arguing that the northern spitfire beetle is no more than a subspecies of the much more common northern orange stinging beetle. At a public hearing, local residents, who will have the opportunity to work in the lodge, ask representatives of the federal government why the beetle should be listed, what a listing would mean for the area, and, more generally, why they should be concerned about biodiversity. What is your answer?

A. INTRODUCTION TO BIODIVERSITY CONSERVATION

I keep waiting each day to make friends with the Forest Service. . . . The agency harbors, as a rotting log harbors nutrients and hope for the future, some of the country's best and most passionate hydrologists, entomologists, range managers, recreation specialists, ornithologists, wilderness specialists, and big game biologists. But the gears and levers of the agency are still pulled and fitted in Washington, in an agency run by a Congress . . . run . . . by the corporations that funded their election campaigns.

Rick Bass, Ecosystem Management, Wallace Stegner,
and the Yaak Valley of Northwestern Montana, in
Reclaiming the Native Home of Hope: Community,
Ecology and the American West 50 (R. Keiter ed., 1998).

Environmental law is subdividing into two major objectives: the prevention of pollution, especially toxic pollutants, and the conservation of biodiversity. The two objectives are, of course, related but they raise different ethical issues and often require different policy instruments. The objective of biodiversity protection is to conserve species richness. This can be done ex situ (via zoos and research facilities) or in situ (with the conservation of natural habitats). Biologist Edward O. Wilson in his book The Diversity of Life 333 (1992) argues that "ex situ methods will save a few species otherwise beyond hope, but the light and way for the world's biodiversity is the preservation of natural ecosystems." The general objective of biodiversity conservation may seem clear, but the scientific questions involved in deciding just what biodiversity we want to conserve and devising effective strategies to do so are extraordinarily, if not maddingly, complex. Fred Bosselman, A Dozen Biodiversity Puzzles, 12 N.Y.U. Envtl. L.J. 364 (2004), lays out the questions for lawyers.

Biodiversity protection did not emerge as a policy focus until the mid-1980s. For this reason, few laws expressly use the construct. Biodiversity is thus often a post hoc rationale for existing program objectives. In the 1990s, for example, the Endangered Species Act (ESA) evolved from a law designed to protect individual species that face extinction to regulations governing the protection of representative ecosystems. The ESA is the primary biodiversity protection mechanism in the United States. The conservation of biodiversity is also now an international concern. Article 8(d) of the Convention on Biological Diversity defines biodiversity conservation as "the protection of ecosystems, natural habitats and the maintenance of viable populations of species in natural surroundings."

Biodiversity conservation is an effort to preserve the dynamics of evolution, but immediate priorities are driven by efforts to arrest the loss of ecosystems and the extinction of flora and fauna. Biodiversity loss is ultimately a function of human population growth and resource consumption. The more immediate threats have been identified as habitat fragmentation, road building, the introduction of exotic species into ecosystems, and global climate change. R. Noss & A. Cooperrider, Saving Nature's Legacy: Protecting and Restoring Biodiversity 32-33 (1994), sets out the basis for the concern with habitat loss:

As usually happens in science, as ecologists learned more about fragmentation, the process turned out to be much more complex than once thought. Early fragmentation studies viewed the process as a species-area problem analogous to the formation of land-bridge islands as sea levels rose since the Pleistocene. Hence, island biogeographic theory was invoked to explain losses of species as the area of habitats declined and their isolation increased. Certainly, there are good analogies between real islands and caves, lakes, prairies in a forested landscape, or pieces of remnant forest in agricultural land. But there are differences, too. The water that surrounds real islands provides habitat for few terrestrial species. In contrast, the matrix surrounding habitat islands may be a rich source of colonists to the island, many of which are invasive weeds or predators on species inhabiting the island. Thus, species richness does not always decline on isolated habitat patches, as predicted by island biogeographic theory. Richness may even increase (at least temporarily) as species invade from adjacent disturbed areas. In such a case, species composition often shifts toward weedy, opportunistic species while sensitive species of habitat interiors are lost. The matrix in a fragmented landscape is also in a state of flux, as crops are planted and harvested, as tree plantations go through their rotations, as farming or silvicultural methods change, and as human settlements grow and decline. Thus the external environment of a habitat patch is not as constant or predictable as the water surrounding a real island.

Fragmentation is a process and ecological effects will change as the process unfolds. In the early stages of the process, the original landscape is perforated by human-created openings of various sizes, but the matrix remains natural habitat. At this stage, we would expect the abundance of native species of the original landscape to be affected little, although the access created by human trails or roads may reduce or extirpate large carnivores, furbearers, and the other species subject to human exploitation or persecution. Such losses are well documented historically. Also, a narrow endemic species whose sole habitat just happened to be in an area converted to human land use would also be lost. As human activity increases in the landscape, the gaps in the original matrix become larger, more numerous, or both, until eventually they occupy more than half of the landscape and therefore become the matrix. A highly fragmented landscape may consist of a few remnant patches of natural habitat in a sea of converted land. Many landscapes around the world have followed this pattern of change.

Fragmentation does not necessarily spell extinction. A species might persist in a highly fragmented landscape in three ways. First, it might be able to survive or even thrive in the matrix of human land use. A number of weedy plants, insects, fungi, microbes, and vertebrates such as European starlings and house mice fit this description. Second, it might be able to maintain viable populations within individual habitat fragments; this is an option only for plants, microbes, and small-bodied animals with modest area requirements. Or third, it might be highly mobile. A mobile species could integrate a number of habitat patches, either into individual home ranges or into an interbreeding population. Pileated woodpeckers, for example, have learned to fly among a number of small wood-lots to forage in landscapes that were formerly continuous forest.

Why do we value biodiversity?

DOREMUS, PATCHING THE ARK: IMPROVING LEGAL PROTECTION OF BIOLOGICAL DIVERSITY
18 Ecology L.Q. 265, 269-273 (1991)

1. The Utilitarian Basis for Preservation of Diversity

The utilitarian justification for the preservation of diversity rests on the direct and indirect usefulness of biological resources to humanity. Individual species provide us with a number of direct benefits. For example, we have domesticated our food crops, both plant and animal, from wild species. Other species can also provide a source of useful genetic traits. As breeding and genetic engineering technologies improve, such traits are becoming transferable across ever wider taxonomic distances.

Biological diversity is also a useful source of new medical drugs. Chemicals derived from higher plants form the major ingredient in about a quarter of all prescriptions written in the United States; chemicals derived from lower plants and microbes account for another eighth. Many of these drugs can be produced more cheaply by extraction than by chemical synthesis. Numerous species have yet to be examined for their medical properties. Thus, many useful chemicals may exist in the natural world. . . .

Nature may also serve more subtle needs. Human beings may have "a deep-rooted need" for contact with other living things. Such contact may promote both mental and physical health.

Besides the direct benefits above, ecosystems provide a number of indirect benefits to humanity. These "ecosystem services" include climate control, oxygen production, removal of carbon dioxide from the atmosphere, soil generation, nutrient cycling, and purification of freshwater supplies. Some of these functions could probably be performed by managed systems, at least on a small scale, but management of such systems on a global scale is presently beyond our technological capability. Moreover, some of these processes, such as nutrient cycling, are highly complex and not yet fully understood. . . .

2. The Esthetic Basis for Preservation of Diversity

Many people find beauty in the natural world, viewing natural objects, both living and nonliving, with a sense of admiration, wonder, or awe. Esthetic interest in nature is demonstrated in a variety of ways. For example, millions of Americans visit national parks and wildlife refuges every year. Some sixty million Americans participate in bird watching and millions more engage in other forms of wildlife-related recreation. Nature photography and gardening are enormously popular hobbies. A perennial audience exists for television nature documentaries.

Individual species and specific natural areas may also come, over time, to be imbued with powerful symbolic value. They may embody the cultural or political identity of a people. The bald eagle is one such symbolic species; Mt. Fuji is an example of a symbolic natural feature. This symbolism provides further evidence of the esthetic attractions of nature. . . .

3. The Ethical Basis for Preservation of Diversity

In 1949, Aldo Leopold advocated the extension of ethical obligations to the relations between man and nature, calling for the development of an "ecological conscience" reflecting "a conviction of individual responsibility for the health of the land." Since then, several commentators have argued that nonhuman organisms, and even non-living natural objects, have or should have rights based on their intrinsic value. Under such a view, human beings have an ethical obligation not to destroy these creatures and objects, at least in the absence of a strong countervailing value.

NOTE ON ECOSYSTEM SERVICES PROVISION AS A RATIONALE FOR BIODIVERSITY PROTECTION

The utilitarian rationale for biodiversity conservation has become the predominant one as a new concept—ecosystem services provision—has emerged to justify many biodiversity conservation initiatives.* A recent United Nations report links biodiversity conservation and ecosystem services. Millennium Ecosystem Assessment, Living Beyond Our Means: Natural Assets and Well Being 12 (Statement of the Board 2005). In brief, ecosystem service provision identifies services from which humans benefit, such as pollution filtering, species maintenance, flood protection, recreation, or just the pleasure that knowledge of the existence of a system gives. It then seeks to put a monetary value on these services, assuming that doing so is possible. The numbers can be huge. A widely cited article estimated the current value of 17 ecosystems as between 16 and 44 trillion dollars. Constanza et al., The Value of the World's Ecosystem Services and Natural Capital, 387 Nature 253 (May 15, 1997).

Two important legal consequences follow. First, if these numbers are included in decision analyses such as an EIS or a Forest Service plan, the relative values of ecosystem protection and exploitation can change dramatically. Thus, the traditional bias in favor of exploitation created by ignoring "off-balance-sheet values" can be partially reversed. Second, markets may be created in ecosystem service provision, which also reduces exploitation pressure.** This utilitarian rationale for ecosystem and biodiversity protection reflects the capture of much of the environmental policy discourse by science and welfare economics and has the potential to appeal to a wide variety of interests. Appeals to "hard" monetary dollar values are less polarizing than appeals to "soft" higher spiritual and aesthetic values.

Important questions remain. The first is whether the focus on monetizable services will cause society to ignore the conservation of biodiversity that currently provides no service to humanity. Operational and ethical questions follow. For example, it is not easy to connect service providers to beneficiaries. If an ecosystem owner has historically chosen to impair a service, is it fair now to compel her to provide the service or to overcome resistance, or should the government subsidize the service provision by paying her to forgo exploitation? See Salzman, Creating Markets for Ecosystem Services: Notes from the Field, 80 N.Y.U. L. Rev. 870 (2005). If markets are created, they will often be used to offset exploitation in a system. Hard questions may arise about whether the alleged service is in fact being provided and whether it justifies reducing the service capacity of an ecosystem. See Salzman & Ruhl, Currencies and the Commodification of Environmental Law, 53 Stan. L. Rev. 607 (2000). Finally, one can ponder the fact that one-quarter of all terrestrial species may be at risk of extinction from global climate and the related concern: "If we've changed our biological system to such an extent, then do we have to get worried about whether the services that are provided by natural ecosystems are going to continue?" E. Kolbett, Field Notes from a Catastrophe: Man, Nature, and Climate Change 87 (2006).

---

*See H. Monney & P. Ehrlich, Ecosystem Services: A Fragmentary History, in Nature's Services: Societal Dependence on Natural Systems (G. Daily ed., 1997).

**See G. Heal, Nature and the Market Place; Capturing the Value of Ecosystem Services (2000); G. Daily & K. Ellickson, The New Economy of Nature: The Quest to Make Conservation Profitable (2002).

SIERRA CLUB v. MARITA
46 F.3d 606 (7th Cir. 1995) (Reprinted, Chapter 4, p.000)

NOTES AND QUESTIONS

1. *Baselines and Adaptive Management.* Ecosystem management depends on the applied science of conservation biology because this is the source of substantive management principles such as the dedication of viable patches of habitat, linked by biological corridors, to biodiversity conservation rather than incompatible commodity production or intense development. National standards are often supplemented by experimental "place-driven" ones. In effect, these solutions often seek to restore a system's biological diversity by defining a baseline against which existing and future land uses will be measured.* Ecosystem management also increases the importance of adaptive management as the major resource management strategy. A National Research Council–National Academy of Sciences study captures the essence of adaptive management:

> Adaptive planning and management involve a decision making process based on trial, monitoring, and feedback. Rather than developing a fixed goal and an inflexible plan to achieve the goal, adaptive management recognizes the imperfect knowledge of interdependencies existing within and among natural and social systems, which requires plans to be modified as technical knowledge improves. [Committee on Restoration of Aquatic Ecosystems, National Research Council, Restoration of Aquatic Ecosystems: Science, Technology, and Public Policy 357 (1992).]

2. *The Scientific Case against* Marita. Just what was wrong with the Forest Service's decision to preserve indicator species? A professor of botany and environmental studies at the University of Wisconsin–Madison explains that students of conservation biology object to the decision because it is not only inappropriate but threatening to biodiversity. A decision to manage lands for a few select species may result in the conversion of lands to habitats favored by these species at the expense of other flora and fauna that contribute to biodiversity. "Such restricted approaches to conserving 'wildlife' or boosting quite local 'alpha' diversity have led us to chop up many managed landscapes into small fragments with abundant edge." Waller, Biodiversity as the Basis for Conservation Efforts, in Biodiversity and the Law 16, 22 (W. Snape III ed., 1996). He specifically objects to the Forest Service's measurement of forest diversity by the number of age classes represented within each area of the forest:

> This notion has the perverse (and perhaps intentional) effect of promoting clearcutting as a means to promote a variety of early age classes. In the Chequamegon and Nicolet National Forests in Wisconsin, the Forest Service explicitly defended high rates of clearcutting in their plans as a technique to enhance the 0-10 and 1-20-year-old age classes of various forest types. This policy is sadly ironic, as clearcuts in this area produce young aspen, a forest type already abundant in the surrounding landscape and one that is usually not allowed to mature into older and more diverse mixed forest. Selective cutting, particularly the harvest of individual trees, works far better to regenerate the mixed

---

*For a lucid discussion of the problems of defining ecological baselines, see Patten, Restoration as the Order of the 21st Century: An Ecologist's Perspective, 18 J. Land Resources & Envtl. L. 31 (1998). See also Symposium, 42 Ariz. L. Rev. No. 2 (2000).

hardwood forest that once dominated northern Wisconsin, as demonstrated by forestry practices on the nearby Menominee Indian reservation.

For these reasons, it is inappropriate to favor any single community type to the exclusion of others, even when the favored community has higher local diversity. This danger of relying on local (alpha) diversity as a criterion for conservation is evident in the comparison of the plant diversity among ten woodlands of varying size in northern Ireland. The two sites with the lowest local diversity turn out to be nature reserves chosen for their characteristic vegetation. [Id. at 23.]

Is Professor Waller's proposed management objective legally mandated under any of the statutes considered in the case? What baseline did the court implicitly adopt in *Marita*? Pre-human intervention? The forest as it existed after the lumber booms of the mid-nineteenth century? A computer model of the ecosystem? What is the relevance of non-equilibrium ecology for the establishment of baselines? Glisson v. United States Forest Serv., 138 F.3d 1181 (7th Cir. 1998), involved the issue of how to define the baseline in ecosystems that have been substantially modified over time. The Forest Service proposed to restore 10,500 acres in the Shawnee National Forest in southern Illinois. The ecological restoration project plan required the removal of stands of shortleaf pines, a listed endangered species under state law. The removal of the pines, planted in the project area in the 1930s, would also impact the pine warblers, but the Forest Service defined "natural" as "native to the project area." In a terse opinion, Judge Posner concluded that the pines were "too recent to satisfy the Service's conception of what it means for a plant or animal to be 'native' to an area." Id. at 1183.

NOTE ON SOURCES OF BIODIVERSITY CONSERVATION LAW

Biodiversity is a new concept and is not yet an accepted legal construct. "Biodiversity" law draws primarily from various sources of preexisting laws with related objectives. Society has long worried about the extinction of commercially valuable species. Fish and game laws have historically aimed at maintaining viable populations of species that are hunted or fished commercially and for sport by restricting hunting and fishing. See T. Lund, American Wildlife Law (1980). Biodiversity conservation builds on the tradition of state regulation of wildlife. Roman law classified wildlife as part of the negative community, a legal category whose members were deemed unowned until an individual acquired ownership through capture. In nineteenth-century America, the same reasoning was used to justify state regulation of capture. Courts accepted the fiction, at a time when assertions of the police power were suspect, that the state "owned" wildlife in trust for the benefit of its citizens. Geer v. Connecticut, 161 U.S. 519 (1896); Hughes v. Oklahoma, 441 U.S. 322 (1979). In the process, taking wildlife was transformed from a right to a privilege. McCready v. Virginia, 94 U.S. 391 (1876). Thus, property owners have no expectation of ownership of wildlife found on their land even if they have invested in reliance on hunting and fishing. A California case summarizes the modern law of wildlife ownership:

California wildlife is publicly owned and is not held by owners of private land where wildlife is present. . . . It is this state's policy to conserve and maintain wildlife for citizens' use and enjoyment, for their intrinsic and ecological values, and for aesthetic, education and nonappropriative uses. [Betchart v. California State Dep't of Fish and Game, 205 Cal. Rptr. 135, 136 (1984).]

In contrast to fauna, flora is treated as part of the land subject to private ownership.

The primary thrust of modern biodiversity law is to promote species survival through habitat conservation. This goal moves beyond the traditional rationale for state wildlife regulation because it both seeks to impose new management mandates on public land managers and to regulate the use of "ecologically sensitive" private land. Biodiversity conservation strategies generally use existing federal and state laws to create public and mixed public and private institutions to manage large areas of functionally connected habitat as a single ecosystem.* As the *Marita* case illustrates, a major legal problem is that ecosystem management is a scientific rather than a legal construct that must be superimposed over existing political jurisdictions and specific federal and state agency mandates. Public land management statutes date from an era when commodity production was the preeminent public land use. Modern statutes often permit biodiversity conservation on public lands, but they provide little guidance as to how this objective is to be integrated with older, commodity production mandates. Ecosystem protection strategies must overcome the fragmented, incomplete, and shared regulatory authority that exists both among the three levels of government and within these levels and the lack of integration among water and land management regulatory programs that impact biodiversity. The wetlands protection program created pursuant to §404 of the Clean Water Act, for example, is not necessarily an ecosystem management program as currently structured and administered because of the narrow geographic focus on individual wetlands. Other programs have the same problem.**

Domestic biodiversity conservation efforts are supported by the emerging international biodiversity conservation regime. The international biodiversity conservation regime is based on the Convention on International Trade in Endangered Species (CITES) and the 1992 Convention on Biological Diversity. CITES is an international treaty that seeks to preserve species, but not their habitats, threatened by trade. The major focus has been on elephants, tropical birds, and reptiles. For example, the CITES ban on ivory products from southern African elephants has been implemented in the United States by the ESA and by the African Elephant Conservation Act, 16 U.S.C. §§1361-1407, which bans the sale of most ivory products derived from these animals. See Favre, The Risk of Extinction: A Risk Analysis of the Endangered Species Act as Compared to CITES, 6 N.Y.U. Envtl. L.J. 341 (1998).

The Convention on Biological Diversity adopted at the 1992 Rio de Janeiro Conference on Environment and Economic Development entered into force at the end of 1993. The Convention is acceptable to the international community because it attempts to blend the pro-preservation view of the North with the pro-development views of the South. Efforts to "balance" these concerns diluted the Convention. For example, the Preamble affirms that "the conservation of biological diversity is a common concern of mankind" rather than a common (and thus shared) heritage

---

*See Thomson, Ecosystem Management: Great Idea, But What Is It, Will It Work, and Who Will Pay?, 9 Nat. Resources & Env't 42 (1995); Note, Saving an Endangered Act: The Case for a Biodiversity Approach to ESA Conservation Efforts, 45 Case W. Res. L. Rev. 553 (1995).

**See generally Keiter, Beyond the Boundary Line: Constructing a Law of Ecosystem Management, 65 U. Colo. L. Rev. 293 (1994); Tarlock, Biodiversity Federalism, 54 Md. L. Rev. 1315 (1995).

of mankind, as some nations advocated, and conservation duties are tempered by a capacity defense. But Article 6 posits that biological conservation is a national mandate. Article 8 reflects a preference for in situ (*e.g.*, reserves) rather than ex situ conservation, and it provides a set of benchmarks against which national programs can be measured. This preference is reinforced by recent criticisms of the effectiveness of captive breeding programs. Articles 23-27 create a potential enforcement and information dissemination scheme. A Convention Secretariat and Conference are created, and the possibility of international disputes is recognized.

   What are the primary lessons of conservation biology that can be applied to the design of habitat reserves?

> [There are] two major criteria for assessing the conservation value of sites: species richness (or diversity) and endemism. Other criteria commonly employed in conservation evaluations include naturalness, rarity, area (extent of habitat), threat of human interface, amenity value, educational value, scientific value, and representativeness. . . . [R]epresentation [is] perhaps the most comprehensive of all conservation criteria. Representation is based on a simple but compelling idea: a prerequisite for preserving maximum biological diversity in a given biological domain is to identify a reserve network which includes every possible species. Representation is subtly different from the criterion of representativeness.
>
>   Under the latter concept, sites are sought that represent archetypal communities. Once represented as a specimen in the collection, a community type is considered protected. In contrast, representation, as we see it, means capturing the full spectrum of biological and environmental variation with the understanding that this variation is dynamic and not easily classified. Because diversity occurs at multiple levels of organization, conservation programs ideally should seek to represent all genotypes, species, ecosystems, and landscapes in protected areas. In practice, vegetation usually provides a good surrogate for the rest of biodiversity in the short term, so long as variation within classified types is recognized and sensitive and endemic species are given the extra attention they deserve. [R. Noss & A. Cooperrider, Saving Nature's Legacy, *supra*, at 104-105.]

Over time, the Forest Service has adapted the manner in which it uses management indicator species as surrogates for biodiversity. Consider the following case.

NATIVE ECOSYSTEMS COUNCIL v. U.S. FOREST SERVICE
428 F.3d 1233 (9th Cir. 2005)

McKeown, Circuit Judge.

   [The Forest Service approved the Jimtown Vegetation Project in the Helena National Forest, whose objective was to lower the risk of a catastrophic fire by thinning, prescribed burning, and weed management. Parts of the forest consisted of dry ponderosa pine stands, within what the Forest Service characterized as "fire dependent ecosystems." Past efforts by the agency to prevent low-intensity, periodic fires had led to an increase in the likelihood of large, stand-replacing fires. The proposed project was located very close to a nest area used by a pair of northern goshawks. The Forest Service had designated goshawks as a sensitive species, which required that it prepare a Biological Evaluation to consider the potential impact of proposed forest management actions on the goshawks. The Forest Service's Evaluation concluded that the project might impact individual goshawks or their habitat, but was unlikely to contribute to a loss of species viability. It also concluded that the primary threat to goshawks is loss of habitat due to logging and fire.

The Helena National Forest Plan also designated goshawks as a management indicator species (MIS) for old-growth forest in the Helena National Forest. Forest Service planning regulations required the Forest Service to select MIS for the purpose of monitoring the effects of management activities in various types of habitat. Although the project did not include any old growth, the Forest Service took the position that the project would contribute to the development of a sustainable old-growth forest in the project area.

Native Ecosystems challenged the project, alleging that the Forest Service violated the National Forest Management Act (NFMA) because it threatened the forest-wide viability of the goshawk. The district court granted the Forest Service's motion for summary judgment, finding that the agency did not act arbitrarily and capriciously in concluding that the project would not impact goshawk viability under the NFMA.]

NFMA creates a two-step process for the management of our national forests. The Forest Service must first develop a Land Resource Management Plan ("Forest Plan") for each unit of the National Forest System. 16 U.S.C. §1604(f)(1). For individual management actions within a forest unit, all relevant plans, contracts, or permits must be consistent with each forest's overall management plan. Id. §1604(i).

In addition, NFMA imposes substantive requirements on the Forest Service's management of the national forests. NFMA requires that forest plans "provide for diversity of plant and animal communities based on the suitability and capability of the specific land area." 16 U.S.C. §1604(g)(3)(B). The Forest Service's NFMA regulations further require:

> Fish and wildlife habitat shall be managed to maintain viable populations of existing native and desired non-native vertebrate species in the planning area. For planning purposes, a viable population shall be regarded as one which has the estimated numbers and distribution of reproductive individuals to insure its continued existence is well distributed in the planning area. In order to insure that viable populations will be maintained, habitat must be provided to support, at least, a minimum number of reproductive individuals and that habitat must be well distributed so that those individuals can interact with others in the planning area.

36 C.F.R. §219.19 (2000). The duty to ensure viable populations "applies with special force" to sensitive species. Inland Empire Pub. Lands Council v. U.S. Forest Serv., 88 F.3d 754, 759 (9th Cir. 1996).

Native Ecosystems claims the Forest Service failed to comply with the substantive wildlife requirements of the NFMA. Specifically, Native Ecosystems claims the Forest Service failed to ensure goshawk viability, in violation of the NFMA, by failing to discuss forest-wide goshawk population trends and the impacts the Jimtown Project would have on goshawk viability and population trends. The 1986 Helena National Forest Plan designated goshawks as a management indicator species, and the Forest Service considers the goshawk to be a "sensitive species." As a result, Native

Ecosystems contends the Forest Service had a substantive duty under NFMA to ensure forest-wide goshawk viability before approving a project that would impact goshawk habitat.

Although Native Ecosystems admits that the Forest Service has monitored goshawks in the Helena National Forest for more than eight years, Native Ecosystems claims this monitoring fails to establish the existence of a viable population of goshawks. The record contains a 2002 Goshawk Nest Monitoring Report that chronicles goshawk sightings and goshawk nests from 1995 through 2002 in the Helena National Forest. The record also contains a 2003 chart listing goshawk sightings and nests from 1992 through 2003. On the basis of these reports, Native Ecosystems claims that there is not a viable population of goshawks in the Helena National Forest, or at least that goshawk viability cannot be presumed based on these charts. According to Native Ecosystems, the Forest Service must positively demonstrate forest-wide goshawk viability before proceeding with the Jimtown Project.

In contrast, the Forest Service views its responsibility under NFMA to ensure the viability of animal species as a duty to ensure adequate habitat for wildlife species, not an obligation to ensure the actual viability of a species in every locale. See 36 C.F.R. §219.19 (2000) ("[H]abitat shall be managed to maintain viable populations. . . ."); see also id. §219.19(a)(6) ("Population trends of the management indicator species will be monitored and relationships to habitat changes determined."). Because the Forest Service concluded that the Jimtown Project will not have a significant effect on goshawk habitat, the Forest Service concludes that the project meets NFMA's species viability requirement by preserving goshawk habitat. In addition, the Forest Service contends Native Ecosystems misinterpreted the two goshawk observation charts and argues that the charts demonstrate a nearly fifty percent occupancy rate of potential goshawk home ranges.

Our case law permits the Forest Service to meet the wildlife species viability requirements by preserving habitat, but only where both the Forest Service's knowledge of what quality and quantity of habitat is necessary to support the species and the Forest Service's method for measuring the existing amount of that habitat are reasonably reliable and accurate. Compare Idaho Sporting Cong. v. Thomas, 137 F.3d 1146, 1154 (9th Cir. 1998) (holding that under the circumstances of that case the Forest Service could use habitat as a proxy for population if the Forest Service performed further analysis and showed that "no appreciable habitat disturbance" would result from the planned activity), and Idaho Sporting Cong. v. Rittenhouse, 305 F.3d 957, 967-68, 972-73 (9th Cir. 2002) (holding that use of habitat as a proxy for population monitoring of the management indicator species was arbitrary and capricious where record indicated that the Forest Service's habitat standard and measurements were erroneous).

We recently explained the proxy-on-proxy approach to ensuring species viability under the NFMA:

> We have, in appropriate cases, allowed the Forest Service to avoid studying the population trends of the Indicator Species by using Indicator Species habitat as a proxy for Indicator Species population trends in a so-called "proxy on proxy" approach. Crucial to this approach, however, is that the methodology for identifying the habitat proxy be sound. If the habitat trend data is flawed, the proxy on proxy result, here population trends, will be equally flawed. [Lands Council v. Powell, 395 F.3d 1019, 1036 (9th Cir. 2005).]

The record does not demonstrate any flaws in the methodology used by the Forest Service to identify goshawk habitat. . . . The Forest Service's habitat analysis revealed that even if the Jimtown Project thinning area is not used by the nearby goshawk pair, there will be ample habitat available to them. A goshawk home range should contain approximately 5,400 acres of foraging habitat. The Jimtown Project will diminish the goshawk foraging habitat in the goshawk home range by approximately 480 acres (720 acres prior to the Jimtown Fire), leaving at least 6,780 acres of suitable foraging habitat in the relevant goshawk home range. The remaining foraging habitat exceeds the [scientific experts'] recommendation of 5,400 acres of foraging habitat per goshawk home range. Given that the Jimtown Project area does not contain old-growth forest and is designed to create an ecosystem that can support old growth in the long-term, and given that the NEPA documents incorporate the [experts'] habitat recommendations, we conclude that the Forest Service satisfied NFMA's species viability requirements by demonstrating that adequate goshawk habitat is preserved.

While the Forest Service experts predict that goshawks will use the thinned area of the Jimtown Project for foraging, there will still be sufficient foraging habitat even if the goshawks avoid the project area after thinning. The long-term benefit of preventing stand-replacing fires, which completely destroy goshawk habitat, is preferable over any short-term benefit the goshawks might receive from retaining the dense forest structure in the project area. The Forest Service considered the relevant factors and there has not been a clear error of judgment.

Consequently, we uphold the agency action under the APA's arbitrary and capricious standard.

NOTES AND QUESTIONS

1. What did the NFMA and the Forest Service planning regulations require the agency to do to preserve diversity within the national forests? In what sense was the Forest Service's approach in this case a "proxy-on-proxy" approach? Why did the court approve it? Corbin, Comment, The United States Forest Service's Response to Biodiversity Science, 29 Envtl. L. 377, 397 (1999), explains the agency's motivation for using MIS as surrogates for biodiversity:

> The advantages are obvious. In an age of budgetary and personnel constraints, land management agencies like the Forest Service cannot afford outlays of resources necessary to individually manage each species in an ecosystem. The ability to meet a seemingly impossible obligation to maintain viable populations of all wildlife by simply monitoring a handful of species is to move from the impossible to the probable.

See also id. (stating that the MIS approach to protecting biodiversity proceeds on the premise "that a single species can act as a bellwether for environmental change. According to this concept, the species is so closely tied to its environment that fluctuations in its population directly reflect environmental changes that impact other species as well.").

2. *The "Proxy-on-Proxy" Approach in Other Jurisdictions.* Other courts have refused to allow the Forest Service to rely on the proxy-on-proxy approach at all. In Sierra Club v. Martin, 168 F.3d 1 (11th Cir. 1999), for example, the court concluded that habitat analysis did not comply with the regulatory requirement that the Forest Service monitor population trends of MIS and their relationships to habitat changes. It

held that the agency's approval of timber sales was arbitrary and capricious because it failed to gather quantitative data on MIS and use that data to measure the impact of habitat changes on the forest's diversity. Other courts agreed with the Eleventh Circuit that the 1982 regulations did not permit the Forest Service to substitute habitat information for actual, quantitative population data. See, e.g., Utah Envtl. Cong. v. Bosworth, 439 F.3d 1184, 1191 (10th Cir. 2006).

3. *The 2005 Planning Regulations.* In 2005 the Forest Service amended its planning regulations. The amended regulations no longer require that the Forest Service provide for viable populations of plant and animal species. The agency provided three principal explanations for this omission. First, the Forest Service concluded, based on experience, "that ensuring species viability is not always possible" due to problems such as species-specific distribution problems, declines in species due to factors beyond the agency's control, or the inability of available land to support species. Second, individual forests contain "very large" numbers of recognized species, and the Forest Service found it "clearly impractical" to analyze all those species. Further, previous attempts to analyze the full suite of species via groups, surrogates, and representatives had mixed success in practice. Third, the agency's past focus on the viability requirement diverted attention and resources away from an ecosystem-based approach to land management, which the Forest Service now considers to be "the most efficient and effective way to manage for the broadest range of species with the limited resources available for the task." National Forest System Land and Resource Management Planning; Final Rule, 70 Fed. Reg. 1023 (2005). The regulations also eliminated the requirement that land use plans require population monitoring of MIS because "recent scientific evidence identified flaws in the MIS concept." Id. at 1048. Instead, "[t]he types and amount of data needed will be determined by [planning officials] taking into account best available science." National Forest System Land Management Planning Directives; Notice, 71 Fed. Reg. 5124, 5137 (2006). See generally Glicksman, Bridging Data Gaps through Modeling and Evaluation of Surrogates: Use of the Best Available Science to Protect Biological Diversity under the National Forest Management Act, __ Ind. L.J. _____ (forthcoming).

4. *Biodiversity and the Federal Land Management Agencies.* Congress has sought to protect biological diversity in the management of other categories of federal lands. See, e.g., 16 U.S.C. §460aaa (national monument establishment); 16 U.S.C. §460bbb-3(a)(6) (national recreation area). Karkkainen, Biodiversity and Land, 83 Cornell L. Rev. 1 (1997), urges federal acquisition of privately owned lands as the centerpiece of a federal biodiversity protection strategy, supplemented by federal regulation of private lands adjacent to core federal reserves. The article surveys efforts by each of the federal land management agencies to protect biodiversity and finds all of them wanting.

B.   THE ENDANGERED SPECIES ACT

The centerpiece of U.S. biodiversity conservation law is the Endangered Species Act (ESA). Its primary focus is the prevention of individual species extinction, but such prevention often requires habitat reserves. The presence of an endangered species on public or private land is often necessary to trigger efforts not only to preserve the species but to protect other species as well. The ESA is administered by the Fish and Wildlife Service (FWS), in the Department of the Interior, and the National Marine Fisheries Service (NMFS, sometimes referred to as the NOAA Fisheries), in the Department of Commerce. The latter has jurisdiction over ocean and anadromous fisheries.* For purposes of simplicity, most references in this chapter are to the FWS, but the statutory duties of the two agencies are the same.

1. An Overview of the Endangered Species Act

The first ESA case to reach the Supreme Court addressed how the Act balances the obligations of federal agencies under the ESA with the responsibilities they derive from their organic statutes. It also addressed the scope of judicial discretion to fashion remedies for violations of the ESA by those agencies.

TENNESSEE VALLEY AUTHORITY v. HILL
437 U.S. 153 (1978)

Mr. CHIEF JUSTICE BURGER delivered the opinion of the Court.

[The case is a classic story of an effort to stop an economically dubious public works project in the face of strong regional political support. In 1967, TVA began constructing the Tellico Dam on the Little Tennessee River, a shallow, fast-moving river, for hydroelectric power generation, flood control, recreation, and regional development. Opponents first succeeded in preventing the dam's opening because the EIS was inadequate, but this injunction was subsequently lifted when TVA filed an adequate statement. Shortly before the NEPA injunction was lifted, a University of Tennessee scientist discovered a three-inch, previously unknown species of perch, the snail darter. In 1975, the Secretary of the Interior listed the snail darter as an endangered species, noting that "the snail darter is a living entity which is genetically distinct and reproductively isolated from other fishes," and that it was unique to the reach of the Little Tennessee, which would be inundated by the dam. The fish would be adversely affected by the dam because it requires a swift-flowing aquatic habitat.

Tennessee's representatives in Congress made sure that funding for the dam continued. A month after the listing of the snail darter, Congress appropriated funds for the dam's completion. A House Appropriations Committee report in 1975 recommended that an additional $29 million be appropriated for the dam, stating: "The Committee directs that the project, for which an environmental impact statement has been completed and provided [to] the Committee, should be completed as promptly as possible." After the president signed the appropriations legislation, the plaintiffs filed a citizen suit under the ESA. The district court found that completion of the dam would result in adverse modification or destruction of the snail darter's habitat, but it refused to enjoin a substantially completed project. The Sixth Circuit reversed, holding that the Act did not permit a court to balance the equities. Congress nevertheless continued to fund the project after members of TVA's Board of Directors testified at hearings that TVA was successfully relocating the species and after the

---

*Anadromous fish are those that migrate from fresh- to saltwater sources and then back so that they may swim upstream to their birth waters to spawn.

House Appropriations Committee concluded that the ESA did not apply to substantially completed projects. TVA's general budget, which included funds for Tellico, was passed, and the president signed the bill on August 7, 1977.]

I . . .

Until recently the finding of a new species of animal life would hardly generate a cause célèbre. This is particularly so in the case of darters, of which there are approximately 130 known species, 8 to 10 of these having been identified only in the last five years. The moving force behind the snail darter's sudden fame came some four months after its discovery, when the Congress passed the Endangered Species Act of 1973 (Act), 16 U.S.C. §1531 et seq. This legislation, among other things, authorizes the Secretary of the Interior to declare species of animal life "endangered"[8] and to identify the "critical habitat" of these creatures.[9] When a species or its habitat is so listed, the following portion of the Act—relevant here—becomes effective:

> The Secretary [of the Interior] shall review other programs administered by him and utilize such programs in furtherance of the purposes of this chapter. All other Federal departments and agencies shall, in consultation with and with the assistance of the Secretary, utilize their authorities in furtherance of the purposes of this chapter by carrying out programs for the conservation of endangered species and threatened species listed pursuant to section 1533 of this title and *by taking such action necessary to insure that actions authorized, funded, or carried out by them do not jeopardize the continued existence of such endangered species and threatened species or result in the destruction or modification of habitat of such species* which is determined by the Secretary, after consultation as appropriate with the affected States, to be critical. 16 U.S.C. §1536 (1976 ed.) (emphasis added). . . .

II

We begin with the premise that operation of the Tellico Dam will either eradicate the known population of snail darters or destroy their critical habitat. Petitioner does not

---

8. An "endangered species" is defined by the Act to mean "any species which is in danger of extinction throughout all or a significant portion of its range other than a species of the Class Insecta determined by the Secretary to constitute a pest whose protection under the provisions of this chapter would present an overwhelming and overriding risk to man." 16 U.S.C. §1532(4). [The Court noted that the ESA covers animal and plant species, subspecies, and populations throughout the world needing protection, that about 1.4 million animal species and 600,000 plant species existed, and that as many as 10 percent of them—some 200,000—might qualify as endangered or threatened. That number could increase by three to five times if subspecies and populations were counted.]

9. The Act does not define "critical habitat," but the Secretary of the Interior has administratively construed the term:

> "Critical habitat" means any air, land, or water area (exclusive of those existing man-made structures or settlements which are not necessary to the survival and recovery of a listed species) and constituent elements thereof, the loss of which would appreciably decrease the likelihood of the survival and recovery of a listed species or a distinct segment of its population. The constituent elements of critical habitat include, but are not limited to: physical structures and topography, biota, climate, human activity, and the quality and chemical content of land, water, and air. Critical habitat may represent any portion of the present habitat of a listed species and may include additional areas for reasonable population expansion. 43 Fed. Reg. 874 (1978) (to be codified as 50 CFR §402.02).

now seriously dispute this fact. In any event, under §4(a)(1) of the Act, 16 U.S.C. §1533(a)(1), the Secretary of the Interior is vested with exclusive authority to determine whether a species such as the snail darter is "endangered" or "threatened" and to ascertain the factors which have led to such a precarious existence. By §4(d) Congress has authorized—indeed commanded—the Secretary to "issue such regulations as he deems necessary and advisable to provide for the conservation of such species." 16 U.S.C. §1533(d). . . .

. . . [T]wo questions are presented: (a) Would TVA be in violation of the Act if it completed and operated the Tellico Dam as planned? (b) If TVA's actions would offend the Act, is an injunction the appropriate remedy for the violation? For the reasons stated hereinafter, we hold that both questions must be answered in the affirmative.

(A)

It may seem curious to some that the survival of a relatively small number of three-inch fish among all the countless millions of species extant would require the permanent halting of a virtually completed dam for which Congress has expended more than $100 million. The paradox is not minimized by the fact that Congress continued to appropriate large sums of public money for the project, even after congressional Appropriations Committees were apprised of its apparent impact upon the survival of the snail darter. We conclude, however, that the explicit provisions of the Endangered Species Act require precisely that result.

One would be hard pressed to find a statutory provision whose terms were any plainer than those in §7 of the Endangered Species Act. Its very words affirmatively command all federal agencies "to *insure* that *actions authorized, funded, or carried out* by them do not jeopardize the continued existence" of an endangered species or "*result* in the destruction or modification of habitat of such species. . . ." 16 U.S.C. §1536. (Emphasis added.) This language admits of no exception. Nonetheless, petitioner urges, as do the dissenters, that the Act cannot reasonably be interpreted as applying to a federal project which was well under way when Congress passed the Endangered Species Act of 1973. To sustain that position, however, we would be forced to ignore the ordinary meaning of plain language. It has not been shown, for example, how TVA can close the gates of the Tellico Dam without "carrying out" an action that has been "authorized" and "funded" by a federal agency. Nor can we understand how such action will "*insure*" that the snail darter's habitat is not disrupted. Accepting the Secretary's determinations, as we must, it is clear that TVA's proposed operation of the dam will have precisely the opposite effect, namely the *eradication* of an endangered species.

Concededly, this view of the Act will produce results requiring the sacrifice of the anticipated benefits of the project and of many millions of dollars in public funds. But examination of the language, history, and structure of the legislation under review here indicates beyond doubt that Congress intended endangered species to be afforded the highest of priorities. . . .

The dominant theme pervading all Congressional discussion of the proposed [Endangered Species Act of 1973] was the overriding need *to devote whatever effort and resources were necessary* to avoid further diminution of national and worldwide wildlife resources. Much of the testimony at the hearings and much debate was devoted to the biological problem of extinction. Senators and Congressmen uniformly deplored the irreplaceable loss to aesthetics, science, ecology, and the national heritage should more species disappear. Coggins, Conserving Wildlife Resources: An Overview of the Endangered Species Act of 1973, 51 N.D. L. Rev. 315, 321 (1975). (Emphasis added.)

The legislative proceedings in 1973 are, in fact, replete with expressions of concern over the risk that might lie in the loss of *any* endangered species. . . .

In shaping legislation to deal with the problem thus presented, Congress started from the finding that "[t]he two major causes of extinction are hunting and destruction of natural habitat." S. Rep. No. 93-307, p. 2 (1973). Of these twin threats, Congress was informed that the greatest was destruction of natural habitats. . . . Witnesses recommended, among other things, that Congress require all land-managing agencies "to avoid damaging critical habitat for endangered species and to take positive steps to improve such habitat." Virtually every bill introduced in Congress during the 1973 session responded to this concern by incorporating language similar, if not identical, to that found in the present §7 of the Act. These provisions were designed, in the words of an administration witness, "for the first time [to] *prohibit* [a] federal agency from taking action which does jeopardize the status of endangered species" [Hearings on S. 1592 and S. 1983, 93d Cong., 1st Sess., 68 (1973) (emphasis added)]. . . .

As it was finally passed, the [ESA] represented the most comprehensive legislation for the preservation of endangered species ever enacted by any nation. Its stated purposes were "to provide a means whereby the ecosystems upon which endangered species and threatened species depend may be conserved," and "to provide a program for the conservation of such . . . species. . . ." 16 U.S.C. §1531(b). In furtherance of these goals, Congress expressly stated in §2(c) that "all Federal departments and agencies *shall* seek to *conserve endangered species* and threatened species. . . ." 16 U.S.C. §1531(c). (Emphasis added.) Lest there be any ambiguity as to the meaning of this statutory directive, the Act specifically defined "conserve" as meaning "to use and the use of *all methods and procedures which are necessary to bring any endangered species* or threatened species to the point at which the measures provided pursuant to this chapter are no longer necessary." §1532(2). (Emphasis added.) Aside from §7, other provisions indicated the seriousness with which Congress viewed this issue: Virtually all dealings with endangered species, including taking, possession, transportation, and sale, were prohibited, 16 U.S.C. §1538, except in extremely narrow circumstances, see §1539(b). The Secretary was also given extensive power to develop regulations and programs for the preservation of endangered and threatened species.[25] §1533(d). Citizen involvement was encouraged by the Act, with provisions allowing interested persons to petition the Secretary to list a species as endangered or threatened, §1533(c)(2), and bring civil suits in United States district courts to force compliance with any provision of the Act, §§1540(c) and (g).

Section 7 of the Act . . . provides a particularly good gauge of congressional intent. . . . [T]his provision had its genesis in the Endangered Species Act of 1966, but that legislation qualified the obligation of federal agencies by stating that they should seek to preserve endangered species only "*insofar as is practicable and*

---

25. A further indication of the comprehensive scope of the 1973 Act lies in Congress' inclusion of "threatened species" as a class deserving federal protection. Threatened species are defined as those which are "likely to become an endangered species within the foreseeable future throughout all or a significant portion of [their] range." 16 U.S.C. §1532(15).

consistent with the[ir] primary purposes. . . ." Likewise, every bill introduced in 1973 contained a qualification similar to that found in the earlier statutes. . . .

What is very significant in this sequence is that the final version of the 1973 Act carefully omitted all of the reservations described above. . . .

It is against this legislative background that we must measure TVA's claim that the Act was not intended to stop operation of a project which, like Tellico Dam, was near completion when an endangered species was discovered in its path. While there is no discussion in the legislative history of precisely this problem, the totality of congressional action makes it abundantly clear that the result we reach today is wholly in accord with both the words of the statute and the intent of Congress. The plain intent of Congress in enacting this statute was to halt and reverse the trend toward species extinction, whatever the cost. This is reflected not only in the stated policies of the Act, but in literally every section of the statute. . . .

Furthermore, it is clear Congress foresaw that §7 would, on occasion, require agencies to alter ongoing projects in order to fulfill the goals of the Act. . . .

One might [argue] that in this case the burden on the public through the loss of millions of unrecoverable dollars would greatly outweigh the loss of the snail darter. But neither the Endangered Species Act nor Art. III of the Constitution provides federal courts with authority to make such fine utilitarian calculations. On the contrary, the plain language of the Act, buttressed by its legislative history, shows clearly that Congress viewed the value of endangered species as "incalculable." Quite obviously, it would be difficult for a court to balance the loss of a sum certain—even $100 million—against a congressionally declared "incalculable" value, even assuming we had the power to engage in such a weighing process, which we emphatically do not.

[The Court next concluded that the continuing appropriations for the dam did not expressly repeal the ESA, and repeals by implication are not favored, especially for appropriations. "When voting on appropriations measures, legislators are entitled to operate under the assumption that the funds will be devoted to purposes which are lawful and not for any purpose forbidden. Without such an assurance, every appropriations measure would be pregnant with prospects of altering substantive legislation, repealing by implication any prior statute which might prohibit the expenditure."]

(B)

Having determined that there is an irreconcilable conflict between operation of the Tellico Dam and the explicit provisions of §7 of the [ESA], we must now consider what remedy, if any, is appropriate. It is correct, of course, that a federal judge sitting as a chancellor is not mechanically obligated to grant an injunction for every violation of law. This Court made plain in Hecht Co. v. Bowles, 321 U.S. 321, 329 (1944), that "[a] grant of jurisdiction to issue compliance orders hardly suggests an absolute duty to do so under any and all circumstances." As a general matter it may be said that "[s]ince all or almost all equitable remedies are discretionary, the balancing of equities and hardships is appropriate in almost any case as a guide to the chancellor's discretion." D. Dobbs, Remedies 52 (1973). . . .

But these principles take a court only so far. Our system of government is, after all, a tripartite one, with each branch having certain defined functions delegated to it by the Constitution. While "[i]t is emphatically the province and duty of the judicial department to say what the law is," Marbury v. Madison, 1 Cranch 137, 177 (1803), it is equally—and emphatically—the exclusive province of the Congress not only to formulate legislative policies and mandate programs and projects, but also to establish their relative priority for the Nation. Once Congress, exercising its delegated powers, has decided the order of priorities in a given area, it is for the Executive to administer the laws and for the courts to enforce them when enforcement is sought.

Here we are urged to view the Endangered Species Act "reasonably," and hence shape a remedy "that accords with some modicum of common sense and the public weal." But is that our function? We have no expert knowledge on the subject of endangered species, much less do we have a mandate from the people to strike a balance of equities on the side of the Tellico Dam. Congress has spoken in the plainest of words, making it abundantly clear that the balance has been struck in favor of affording endangered species the highest of priorities, thereby adopting a policy which it described as "institutionalized caution."

Our individual appraisal of the wisdom or unwisdom of a particular course consciously selected by the Congress is to be put aside in the process of interpreting a statute. Once the meaning of an enactment is discerned and its constitutionality determined, the judicial process comes to an end. We do not sit as a committee of review, nor are we vested with the power of veto. . . .

We agree with the Court of Appeals that in our constitutional system the commitment to the separation of powers is too fundamental for us to pre-empt congressional action by judicially decreeing what accords with "common sense and the public weal." Our Constitution vests such responsibilities in the political branches.

NOTES

The ESA has long been the subject of frequent political attacks, and efforts to weaken it through statutory amendments routinely occur. Property owners subject to the Act's constraints and other litigants have also attacked the constitutionality of the Act, alleging primarily that the statute exceeds the scope of Congress's authority to regulate interstate commerce. The judicial response to those attacks is discussed in Chapter 2's coverage of Gibbs v. Babbitt, 214 F.3d 483 (4th Cir. 2000), and the accompanying notes.*

2.   Listing and Critical Habitat Designation

CAPE HATTERAS ACCESS PRESERVATION ALLIANCE v. U.S. DEPARTMENT OF INTERIOR
344 F. Supp. 2d 108 (D.D.C. 2004)

LAMBERTH, District Judge.

This case concerns the piping plover, a small, sand-colored shorebird, and the designation of its critical habitat under the Endangered Species Act. Defendants, the

---

*For further discussions of the constitutionality of the ESA, see Mank, Protecting Intrastate Threatened Species: Does the Endangered Species Act Encroach on Traditional State Authority and Exceed the Outer Limits of the Commerce Clause?, 36 Geo. L. Rev. 723 (2002); Nagle, The Commerce Clause Meets the Delhi Sands Flower-Loving Fly, 97 Mich. L. Rev. 174 (1998).

Department of the Interior and its Fish and Wildlife Service (collectively the "Service"), designated 137 coastal areas to serve as the wintering plovers' critical habitat. Plaintiffs, a business association and two North Carolina counties, challenge numerous aspects of the Service's designation. . . .

I. Background

A. ESA, NEPA, AND DESIGNATION OF CRITICAL HABITAT

. . . [T]he congressionally identified purposes of the [Endangered Species Act (the ESA)] are "to provide a means whereby the ecosystems upon which endangered species and threatened species depend may be conserved" and "to provide a program for the conservation of such endangered species and threatened species." 16 U.S.C. §1531(b). An endangered species is a species that is "in danger of extinction throughout all or a significant portion of its range," id. §1532(6), while a threatened species is a species that is "likely to become an endangered species within the foreseeable future throughout all or a significant portion of its range," id. §1532(20). Congress conferred partial responsibility for implementing the ESA on the Secretary of the Interior, id. §1532(15), who, in turn conferred her responsibilities to the Service.

The ESA authorizes the Service to protect a species by listing it as threatened or endangered, id. §1533(a)(1), and then requires the Service to designate that species's critical habitat, id. §1533(a)(3), those lands that are essential to its conservation, id. §1532(5)(A). While determinations as to whether or not a species is endangered or threatened must be made "solely on the basis of the best scientific and commercial data available," id. §1533(b)(1)(A), designation of critical habitat additionally requires consideration of economic and other impacts, id. §1533(b)(2).

A critical habitat designation provides protection for threatened and endangered species by triggering what is termed a Section 7 consultation in response to actions proposed by or with a nexus to a federal agency. Id. §1536(a)(2). Section 7(a)(2) of the ESA requires each federal agency, in consultation with the Service, to "insure that any action authorized, funded, or carried out by such agency . . . is not likely to jeopardize the continued existence of any endangered species or threatened species or result in the destruction or adverse modification of habitat of such species . . . which is . . . critical." . . .

If an agency action may adversely affect a listed species's critical habitat, the action agency and the Service enter into a formal consultation process, at the conclusion of which the Service issues a biological opinion as to the effect of the federal agency action. If the Service concludes that the action will likely result in adverse modification of critical habitat, the Service shall set forth any reasonable and prudent alternatives to the action. See id. §1536(b)(3)(A). . . .

[In 2001, the Service designated critical habitat for the wintering plover, an endangered species, in North Carolina. The plaintiff was a business organization whose goals included "preserving and protecting a lifestyle and way of life historically prevalent on the Outer Banks of North Carolina, specifically, Cape Hatteras National Seashore." Its members regularly operated off-road vehicles (ORVs) on the beaches of North Carolina for recreational and commercial purposes. ORVs provide recreational access to seashore beaches that is essential for the area's tourism-based economy. Fearing that the designation would adversely affect the tourism industry by restricting use of the beaches due to beach closures, the plaintiff filed suit challenging the designation. Several environmental groups intervened as defendants in support of the designations.]

IV. Analysis of ESA Compliance ...

E. ECONOMIC ANALYSIS

Economics must play a role in critical habitat designation. "The Secretary shall designate critical habitat . . . on the basis of the best scientific data available and after taking into consideration the economic impact . . . of specifying any particular area as critical habitat." 16 U.S.C. §1533(b)(2). While economics must play a role, the Service has discretion when it comes time to decide whether to exclude areas from a critical habitat designation. "The Secretary may exclude any area from critical habitat if he determines that the benefits of such exclusion outweigh the benefits of specifying such area as part of the critical habitat, unless he determines, based on the best scientific and commercial data available, that the failure to designate such area as critical habitat will result in the extinction of the species concerned." Id.

The parties have focused their attention on the analysis of economic impacts flowing from predicted Section 7 consultations. Certain federal actions trigger consultations: those that are "likely to jeopardize the continued existence of any endangered species or threatened species or result in the destruction or adverse modification of habitat of such species." Id. §1536(a)(2). A Service regulation defines "[j]eopardize" as "an action that reasonably would be expected . . . to reduce appreciably the likelihood of both the survival and recovery of a listed species." 50 C.F.R. §402.02. The same regulation defines "[d]estruction or adverse modification" as an "alteration that appreciably diminishes the value of critical habitat for both the survival and recovery of a listed species." Id.

The Service concluded in its final rule that "no significant economic impacts are expected from critical habitat designation above and beyond those already imposed by the listing of wintering piping plovers."

Plaintiffs raise two closely related challenges to the Service's economic analysis. First, plaintiffs accuse the Service of following the functional equivalence approach. Second, plaintiffs challenge the Service's baseline approach to ascertaining the costs of designation.

Functional equivalence is the theory that the designation of critical habitat serves a minimal additional function separate from the listing [of] a species—that the effects of designation are mainly a subset of the effects of listing. In the words of the Service:

> on occupied critical habitat, a project that is unlikely to jeopardize the continued existence of a species is not likely to destroy or adversely modify critical habitat. Therefore, on occupied critical habitat, consultations and project modifications are likely to flow from the listing of the species, and no additional consultations or project modifications are likely to result as a "but for" effect of the critical habitat designation.

The baseline approach to calculating the economic impact of proposed critical habitat designations involves comparing the state of the world without or before the designation, the baseline, with the state of the world with or after the designation.

When the Service employs functional equivalence and baseline analysis in tandem to predict the economic impact of future Section 7 consultations, the result is syllogistic: no additional consultations or project modifications are likely to result from designations, the world before and after designations will likely have the same number of consultations and modifications, therefore, designations have no incremental economic impact related to these consultations and modifications.

Circuit courts are uncomfortable with this syllogism that threatens to, as a practical matter, remove from consideration the economic analysis required by statute. The Circuit Courts have reacted in, mainly, two ways. While the Fifth and Ninth Circuits take issue with the functional equivalence doctrine, Sierra Club v. U.S. Fish & Wildlife Serv., 245 F.3d 434 (5th Cir. 2001); Gifford Pinchot Task Force v. U.S. Fish & Wildlife Serv., 378 F.3d 1059 (9th Cir. 2004), the Tenth Circuit takes issue with the baseline approach, [N.M. Cattle Growers Ass'n v. U.S. Fish & Wildlife Serv., 248 F.3d 1277, 1285 (10th Cir. 2001)]. . . .

1. THE APPROACHES OF THE CIRCUIT COURTS

The Fifth and Ninth Circuits have rejected functional equivalence, and the Service regulation supporting it, as inconsistent with the express language of the ESA. It is the Tenth Circuit, though, that best lays out the origins and problems with the functional equivalence doctrine:

> The root of the problem lies in the [Service]'s long held policy position that [critical habitat designations] are unhelpful, duplicative, and unnecessary. . . .
> [T]he policy position of the [Service] finds its root in the regulations promulgated by the [Service] in 1986 defining the meaning of both the "jeopardy standard" (applied in the context of listing) and the "adverse modification standard" (applied in the context of designated critical habitat). . . . [T]he standards are defined as virtually identical, or, if not identical, one (adverse modification) is subsumed by the other (jeopardy). [N.M. Cattle Growers Ass'n, 248 F.3d at 1283.]

While the Tenth Circuit did not consider the validity of the regulation it discussed, the Fifth and Ninth Circuits both invalidated the regulation's definition of the adverse modification standard. These courts did not strike the definition because it was entirely identical to the definition of the jeopardy standard, but rather struck the adverse modification definition because it was blatantly inconsistent with the ESA's recovery goal and had largely been subsumed by the definition of the jeopardy standard.

One regulatory definition subsumes a second definition blatantly inconsistent with the ESA: this, the courts pointed out, made possible the doctrine of functional equivalence. These courts noted that the ESA requires costly Section 7 consultations in two distinct circumstances: when an activity will jeopardize a listed species and when an activity will result in destruction or adverse modification of critical habitat. See 16 U.S.C. §1536(a)(2). A Service regulation defines "[j]eopardize" as "an action that reasonably would be expected . . . to reduce appreciably the likelihood of *both the survival and recovery* of a listed species." 50 C.F.R. §402.02 (emphasis added). The same regulation defines "[d]estruction or adverse modification" as an "alteration that appreciably diminishes the value of critical habitat for *both the survival and recovery* of a listed species." Id. (emphasis added). Under the Service's regulation, by virtue of the "and"s, both listing and designation result in consultations only when a species's survival is at stake, which makes it impossible for an action to bring about a consultation if only recovery is at stake. The definition of the adverse modification standard, then, fails to account for the ESA's command that critical habitat be designated for "conservation," and not merely survival. 16 U.S.C. §1532(5)(A). In effect, the definition of the adverse modification standard, with its impetus on survival, is all but subsumed by the jeopardy standard. The regulation, then, is the root of the Service's doctrine of functional equivalence: the regulation permits the Service to assert that actions meeting the adverse modification standard almost always meet the jeopardy standard, making consideration of jeopardy a proxy for consideration of adverse modification.

The effect of functional equivalence on economic impact analysis and on conservation efforts quickly follows. The doctrine and regulation hold that actions interfering with conservation but not survival are not adverse modification or destruction. Thus, the Service's own regulation causes it to undercut the importance of critical habitat, to underestimate the number of Section 7 consultations, and thus, to undercount the economic impact of its regulations while simultaneously underprotecting the species it is statutorily charged with protecting.

Unlike the Fifth and Ninth Circuits that rejected the Service's functional equivalence doctrine and regulation, the Tenth Circuit has rejected the Service's baseline economic analysis. *N.M. Cattle Growers Ass'n*, 248 F.3d at 1285. The Tenth Circuit saw the same problem: it saw the same flaws in the functional equivalence regulation that the other circuits found repugnant, id. ("[E]conomic analysis done using the [Service's] baseline model is rendered essentially without meaning by 50 C.F.R. §402.02."), and it recognized that the "root of the problem lies in the [Service's] long held policy position that [critical habitat designations] are unhelpful, duplicative, and unnecessary," id. at 1283. The Tenth Circuit, however, could not decide the validity of the regulation because it was not before the court. Rather than stifle Congress's intent "that the [Service] conduct a full analysis of all the economic impacts of a critical habitat designation," the court held that the Service must consider all impacts, "regardless of whether those impacts are attributable co-extensively to other causes" and therefore held that "the baseline approach to economic analysis is not in accord with the language or intent of the ESA." Id. at 1285.

While the Tenth Circuit is correct that the ESA requires some economic analysis, it is wrong when it holds the baseline approach violates the language of the statute. Apparently hamstrung by its inability to consider the validity of 50 C.F.R. §402.02, the Tenth Circuit found another way to require the Service to perform a more rigorous economic analysis. This is an instance of a hard case making bad law. . . .

The baseline approach is a reasonable method for assessing the actual costs of a particular critical habitat designation. To find the true cost of a designation, the world with the designation must be compared to the world without it. This is precisely the advice that the Office of Management and Budget gives to federal agencies conducting impact analysis: "Identify a baseline. Benefits and costs are defined in comparison with a clearly stated alternative. This normally will be a 'no action' baseline: what the world will be like if the proposed rule is not adopted." Office of Management and Budget, Circular A-4: Regulatory Analysis 2 (Sept. 17, 2003). In order to calculate the costs above the baseline, those that are the "but for" result of designation, the agency may need to consider the economic impact of listing or other events that contribute to and fall below the baseline. The Service, however, must not allow the costs below the baseline to influence its decision to designate or not designate areas as critical habitat. That would be inconsistent with the ESA's prohibition on considering economic impacts during the species listing process.

Therefore, this Court concludes that while the Tenth Circuit's rejection of the baseline approach is unfounded, the Fifth and Ninth Circuits' rejection of the regulation supporting the Service's functional equivalence doctrine is well reasoned. . . .

2. FUNCTIONAL EQUIVALENCE AND THE REGULATORY DEFINITIONS

When designating habitat for the plover, the Service did not adhere to strictest functional equivalence approach. In other critical habitat designations, the Service has claimed that there will be no additional impact due to the designation. Here, the Service recognizes that some, albeit minimal, additional impacts will result. The Service acknowledges some potential economic impacts to consultation costs related to the designation: first, some completed consultations for projects still underway may need to be updated; second, future consultations may take longer due to the need to consider critical habitat concerns.

Based on these statements, the Court cannot conclude that the Service treated the jeopardy and adverse modification consultation triggers as identical; however, the Service appears to have minimized the economic impact of designation through its application of the invalid regulatory definition of adverse modification. In response to one comment, the Service approvingly cites its prior statement that "[a]ccording to our interpretations of the regulations, by definition, the adverse modification of critical habitat consultation standard is nearly identical to the jeopardy consultation standard." Further, an agency's actions get a presumption of regularity: in this case, the Service is presumed to have followed its definition of the adverse modification consultation trigger. Use of that definition created an "impropriety in the process." . . .

. . . [The court] asks the Service to clarify or modify its position on remand. The Service's regulations and practices that embrace functional equivalence have been confusing for too long. . . .

F. BEST SCIENTIFIC DATA AVAILABLE

Interveners make the broad argument that the Service's designation must stand despite any shortcomings because it was based on the "best scientific data available." 16 U.S.C. §1533(b)(2). Whether the service used the best science available as a basis for its designation is a red herring issue. The Service's need to use only the best science available, as opposed to perfect science, does not excuse any failure by the Service to comply with statutes. Simply put, the Service may not designate habitat, regardless of the quality of underlying scientific data, unless it follows statutory and regulatory requirements. . . .

NOTES AND QUESTIONS

1. How did the FWS distinguish between the terms "jeopardize" and "destruction or adverse modification"? What is the difference between the functional equivalence theory and the baseline approach, and what was the relationship between the two? On what basis did the court find the definition of "adverse modification" to be

flawed? In what way did that definition simultaneously underestimate the economic impact of critical habitat designation and "under-protect" listed species? How did the court's view of the validity of the baseline approach differ from that of the Tenth Circuit?

2. *To List or Not to List.* The first step in the protection of a species is the FWS's decision to list it as threatened or endangered. The difference between the two classifications is the degree and immediacy of the risk of extinction. Compare §§3(6) and 3(20). Section 4(b)(1)(A) requires that listing decisions be based on "the best scientific and commercial data available." Economic considerations are not relevant. The listing decision is crucial because once a species is listed, *TVA v. Hill* teaches that the government has a mandatory duty to protect the species if federal actions put it in jeopardy. The FWS's decision to list or to refuse to list is reviewable because it is based on a scientific record, but courts generally intervene only when the agency departs substantially from the scientific mandate of the statute or violates statutory procedures.[*] The FWS may resolve questions of scientific uncertainty with the same margin of safety accorded EPA in setting water and air pollution standards. See, e.g., City of Las Vegas v. Lujan, 891 F.2d 927 (D.C. Cir. 1989).

How much spatial risk must exist before a species can be listed? The Act provides that a species is endangered if it "is in danger of extinction throughout all or a significant portion of its range." §3(6). Defenders of Wildlife v. Norton, 258 F.3d 1136 (9th Cir. 2001), held that the Department of the Interior cannot categorically withdraw a listing for an endangered species at risk on both private and public land because sufficient public land is available for its survival. A species can become extinct if there are major geographical areas where it once existed but now no longer does. Thus, if the area in which the species is projected to survive is smaller than its historical range, the Secretary must explain his or her decision that this area is not "a significant portion of its range."

3. *What Is a Species?* The issue of how to define the species that qualify for protection is an increasingly critical one as the FWS tries to protect species specific to a stressed ecosystem. Section 3(16) of the ESA extends the definition of species to subspecies and distinct populations, even though the latter is not a scientific term. See Doremus, Listing Decisions under the Endangered Species Act: Why Better Science Isn't Always Better Policy, 75 Wash. U. L.Q. 1029 (1997). Biologists now have a much more complex view of species than they did in 1973. We tend to think of the classification of a species as a universal decision, but this is not always the case. In National Ass'n of Home Builders v. Norton, 340 F.3d 835 (9th Cir. 2003), the court held that the FWS improperly designated a population of cactus ferruginous pygmy-owls in Arizona as a distinct population segment. The court found that the agency failed to support its finding that the gap created by the loss of the Arizona owl population would be significant to the taxon as a whole.

4. *Critical Habitat Designation.* Must the Interior Secretary designate critical habitat whenever a species is listed as endangered or threatened? Section 4 seems to

---

[*]See, e.g., Idaho Farm Bureau Fed'n v. Babbitt, 58 F.3d 1392 (9th Cir. 1995) (concluding that the FWS was not barred from listing because it missed a statutory deadline for doing so and that the agency's failure to make available to the public a crucial study on the candidate species violated the APA); Southwest Ctr. for Biological Diversity v. Babbitt, 926 F. Supp. 920 (D. Ariz. 1996) (failure to take into account the latest scientific information). See 2 G. Coggins & R. Glicksman, Public Natural Resources Law §15C:3 (1990), for a full discussion of the cases reviewing the FWS's listing discretion. See also Bogert, That's My Story and I'm Stickin' to It: Is the "Best Available" Science Any Available Science under the Endangered Species Act?, 31 Idaho L. Rev. 85 (1994).

mandate that designation occur concurrently with a listing "to the maximum extent prudent and determinable." Only about 16 percent of listings are in fact accompanied by critical habitat designation, however. Some courts have accepted as a justification for the Secretary's refusal to designate critical habitat the likelihood that designation will encourage species destruction. See, e.g., Fund for Animals v. Babbitt, 903 F. Supp. 96 (D.D.C. 1995), amended, 967 F. Supp. 6 (D.D.C. 1997).

Other cases suggest that it will be difficult to justify a refusal to designate. NRDC v. United States Dep't of Interior, 113 F.3d 1121 (9th Cir. 1997), is illustrative. The FWS defended its failure to designate critical habitat for the coastal California gnatcatcher on two grounds. First, it argued that designation would increase the threat to the gnatcatcher because the publication of critical habitat descriptions and maps would enable landowners to identify gnatcatcher sites and develop them before designation resulted in restrictions on development potential. The court found this "increased threat" rationale to be inconsistent with the FWS's obligation under §4(b)(2) to balance the pros and cons of designation. Section 4(b)(2) allows the FWS to exclude portions of habitat from critical habitat designation only if it "determines that the benefits of such exclusion outweigh the benefits of specifying such area as part of the critical habitat." The FWS never weighed the benefits and risks of designation and did not show that designation would cause more landowners to destroy, rather than protect, gnatcatcher sites. Second, the FWS asserted that designation would not appreciably benefit the species because most populations of gnatcatchers were found on private lands, to which the §7 consultation requirement would not apply. According to the FWS, designation may be deemed beneficial to the species and therefore "prudent" only if it would result in the application of §7 to the majority of land-use activities occurring within critical habitat. The court characterized this position as an improper expansion of the "rare" statutory exception for imprudent designations into a broad exemption for imperfect designations. The record demonstrated that about 80,000 out of 400,000 acres of gnatcatcher habitat were publicly owned and therefore subject to §7 requirements. The FWS did not explain why a designation that would benefit such a large portion of critical habitat would not be "prudent." Center for Biological Diversity v. U.S. Fish and Wildlife Serv., 450 F.3d 930 (9th Cir. 2006), distinguished NDRC v. Department of Interior, because 1982 amendments to the ESA preserve the FWS's discretion not to designate habitat for species listed prior to 1982.

Nondesignation does not excuse noncompliance with §7 of the ESA. Jeopardy can still be found if there is no designation. United States v. Glenn-Colusa Irrigation Dist., 788 F. Supp. 1126 (E.D. Cal. 1992). But the failure to designate makes it somewhat easier to find no jeopardy. Pyramid Lake Paiute Tribe v. United States Dep't of the Navy, 898 F.2d 1410 (9th Cir. 1990).

Section 3(5) limits the extent of land that can be designated as "critical habitat." The term is defined as "the specific areas within the geographical area occupied by the species, at the time it is listed." Specific areas outside of this area may also be designated if they are "essential for the conservation of the species," but the statute warns that "[e]xcept in those circumstances determined by the Secretary, critical habitat shall not include the entire geographical area which can be occupied by the threatened or endangered species."*

*See generally Darin, Designating Critical Habitat under the Endangered Species Act: Habitat Protection versus Agency Discretion, 24 Harv. Envtl. L. Rev. 209 (2000).

3. Substantive and Procedural Duties for Federal Agencies under Section 7

DEFENDERS OF WILDLIFE v. EPA
420 F.3d 946 (9th Cir. 2005)

BERZON, Circuit Judge:

Under federal law, a state may take over the Clean Water Act pollution permit-ting program in its state from the federal Environmental Protection Agency (EPA) if it applies to do so and meets the applicable standards. This case concerns Arizona's application to run the Clean Water Act pollution permitting program in Arizona. When deciding whether to transfer permitting authority, the Fish and Wildlife Service (FWS) issued, and the EPA relied on, a Biological Opinion premised on the proposition that the EPA lacked the authority to take into account the impact of that decision on endangered species and their habitat.

The plaintiffs in this case challenge the EPA's transfer decision, particularly its reliance on the Biological Opinion's proposition regarding the EPA's limited author-ity. This case thus largely boils down to consideration of one fundamental issue: Does the Endangered Species Act authorize—indeed, require—the EPA to consider the impact on endangered and threatened species and their habitat when it decides whether to transfer water pollution permitting authority to state governments? For the reasons explained below, we hold that the EPA did have the authority to consider jeopardy to listed species in making the transfer decision, and erred in determining otherwise. For that reason among others, the EPA's decision was arbitrary and capricious. . . .

[The Clean Water Act ("the Act") established the National Pollution Discharge Elimination System (NPDES) permit program, which authorizes EPA to issue per-mits for the discharge of pollutants into navigable waters. See §402(a). The Act allows a state to apply to EPA to administer the NPDES program regarding waters within its borders. EPA "shall approve" any state proposal that meets nine specified statutory criteria. Once EPA transfers permitting authority to a state, EPA maintains an over-sight role to assure that the state follows the Act's standards. §402(c)(2). If EPA deter-mines that the state is not complying with those standards, it must demand corrective action. If the state does not take such action, EPA must withdraw approval of the state program. §402(c)(3). Section 7(a)(2) of the ESA requires that each federal agency insure that "any action authorized, funded, or carried out by such agency" is "not likely to jeopardize the continued existence of any endangered species or threatened species or result in the destruction or adverse modification of [critical] habitat of such species."]. Agencies must use the "best scientific and commercial data available" to make such decisions, and must do so "in consultation with and with the assistance of the Secretary [of the Interior]." Id. . . . An agency must determine if a proposed action "may affect" either endangered or threatened species (denominated "listed species," §402.02) or those species' critical habitat, and, if so, must seek formal consultation with the FWS, or, for marine species, the National Marine Fisheries Service. §402.14(a). During such consultations, the FWS issues a Biological Opinion analyz-ing whether the action is likely to jeopardize any listed species or its habitat. §402.14(h). The federal agency then makes a final decision regarding whether and how to pursue the proposed action.

A Biological Opinion must include a "summary of the information on which the opinion is based," a "detailed discussion of the effects of the action on listed species or critical habitat," and "[t]he Service's opinion on whether the action is likely to jeopardize the continued existence of a listed species or result in the destruction or adverse modification of critical habitat." §402.14(h). . . .

By its terms, section 7(a)(2) applies only to "federal agenc[ies]," not to state governmental bodies. Accordingly, the EPA's pollution permitting decisions are subject to section 7(a)(2), but state pollution permitting decisions are not.

Noting that the "EPA now consults with the [FWS and National Marine Fisheries Service] under section 7 of the [Endangered Species Act] on . . . approval of State National Pollutant Discharge Elimination (NPDES) permitting programs" but recognizing that after transfer, section 7 will not apply to the state's permitting decisions, the EPA signed a Memorandum of Agreement with the FWS governing the two agencies' involvement with transferred pollution permitting programs. Asserting that the "EPA's oversight includes consideration of the impact of permitted discharges on waters and species that depend on those waters," the Memorandum lists several procedures that the EPA and FWS will establish to ensure that they communicate federal endangered species concerns to state water pollution permitting agencies. The Memorandum is not, however, binding on states. Rather, the EPA will "*encourage* the State . . . to facilitate the involvement of permittees in the described processes." . . .

[Arizona applied in 2002 for the authority to administer the NPDES program within the state. Because EPA determined that the transfer could affect listed species in Arizona, it initiated formal §7 consultation with the FWS.] During the course of the consultation, FWS field office staff in Arizona expressed serious reservations about the proposed transfer. FWS staff noted that section 7 consultations regarding past pollution permits in Arizona had led to mitigating measures to protect species' critical habitat, and feared that, without such mandatory consultation, Arizona would issue permits without mitigating measures. As a result, there could be harm to certain listed species and habitat. . . . The staff concluded "that the transfer of this program from EPA to the State causes the loss of protections to species resulting from the section 7 process, and the impact of this loss must be taken into account in the effects analysis in the biological opinion." In response, EPA staff opined that the EPA lacked the legal authority to base its transfer decision on these concerns, because the agency does "not have the legal authority to regulate the non-water-quality-related impacts associated with State NPDES-permitted projects that are of concern to FWS, including the authority to object to such permits based on non-water-quality-related impacts to listed species."

[The FWS issued a Biological Opinion recommending approval of the transfer of permitting authority to Arizona. Noting the loss of §7 consultation, the Opinion recognized that, after the transfer, no federal agency would have the legal authority to consult with developers concerning the potential impact on listed species of NPDES permits. Even though Arizona could voluntarily consult with FWS, neither EPA nor the FWS could require that it do so. The Opinion nevertheless took the position that the loss "of any conservation benefit is not caused by EPA's decision to approve the State of Arizona's program. Rather, the absence of the section 7 process that exists with respect to [NPDES] permits reflects Congress' decision to grant States the right to administer these programs under state law provided the State's program meets the requirements of §402(b) of the Clean Water Act." The Opinion found that "the assumption of the program by the State of Arizona will not cause development, and concur that EPA's [Clean Water Act]-mandated approval of the program has only an attenuated causal link to the reduction in Federal [Endangered Species Act] conservation responsibilities." The Opinion also stated that other federal and state laws, including §9 of the ESA (which prohibits the taking of listed species) would sufficiently protect endangered species, so that transfer of permitting authority would not likely jeopardize such species or their critical habitat, in violation of §7(a)(2). EPA approved the permitting authority transfer two days after the FWS issued the Biological Opinion.]

III. The Merits . . .

B. COHERENT REASONING?

As an initial matter, the EPA's approval of Arizona's transfer application cannot survive arbitrary and capricious review because the EPA relied during the administrative proceedings on legally contradictory positions regarding its section 7 obligations. . . .

The EPA definitively stated several times during the decisionmaking process, including when announcing its final decision, that section 7 requires consultation regarding the effect of a permitting transfer on listed species. . . . [In addition, before deciding that consultation was necessary, EPA determined that transferring pollution permitting authority to Arizona "may affect" listed species and their critical habitat.]

Despite the lucidity and consistency of its position on the consultation point in the administrative proceedings, in litigation the EPA's lawyers have taken varying stances on the same issue. Before the Fifth Circuit, the EPA "suggest[ed]" that section 7 compelled consultation regarding pollution permitting transfers and, when necessary to protect species, allowed conditioning such transfers on formal agreements requiring states to follow section 7 procedures when issuing permits. Am. Forest & Paper Ass'n v. EPA, 137 F.3d 291, 297 (5th Cir. 1998). The Fifth Circuit rejected the latter position and did not address the former.

The EPA's brief in this case states that *American Forest* "supports a finding that EPA lacks" authority to protect endangered species when considering pollution permitting approvals. The same brief, however, maintains that we need not decide the question because the agency did not rely on this position in its decision in this case. . . .

. . . [W]e conclude that the obligation to consult—which, under the regulations, applies only to federal agency actions that "may affect" listed species, 50 C.F.R. §402.14(a)—and the reasons given in the Biological Opinion for concluding that the transfer decision would not have an indirect effect on endangered species cannot coexist under section 7(a)(2). The Biological Opinion reasoned that there could be no such effect, because (1) the EPA has no authority to disapprove transfer applications because of an impact on listed species, section 7(a)(2) of the Endangered Species Act notwithstanding; (2) any impact on the post-transfer protection of listed species was the result of Congress' determination that states have no consultation or mitigation obligations, not of the transfer decision; and (3) the potential future impact on listed species would be caused entirely by new private development, and the transfer decision would not cause such development. By relying on this line of reasoning after determining that it did have a consultation obligation, the EPA decided that it had to consult but had no authority to do anything concerning the matter about which it had to consult. One would not expect that Congress would set up such a nonsensical regime. Not surprisingly, it did not.

Section 7(a)(2) makes no legal distinction between the trigger for its requirement that agencies consult with FWS and the trigger for its requirement that agencies shape their actions so as not to jeopardize endangered species. An agency's obligation to consult is . . . in aid of its obligation to shape its own actions so as not to jeopardize listed species, not independent of it. Both the consultation obligation and the obligation to "insure" against jeopardizing listed species are triggered by "any action authorized, funded, or carried out by such agency," and both apply if such an "action" is under consideration.

This being the case, the two propositions that underlie the EPA's action—that (1) it must, under the Endangered Species Act, consult concerning transfers of CWA permitting authority, but (2) it is not permitted, as a matter of law, to take into account the impact on listed species in making the transfer decision—cannot both be true. Because the agency's decisionmaking was based on contradictory views of the same words in the same statutory provision, the ultimate decision was not the result of reasoned decisionmaking.

Additionally, the third prong of the Biological Opinion's reasoning—that it is private development, not the EPA's transfer decision, that would cause any impact on listed species—suffers from an independent lack of plausibility. Events can, of course, have more than one cause. Events can be caused by several actions in a "but-for" causal chain. If any one of the necessary actions does not take place, the ultimate event does not occur. Obviously, without private decisions to construct new developments, there will be no Clean Water Act construction permits and no impact from the issuance of such permits on listed species or their habitats. Just as obviously, without the transfer of permitting authority from the federal to the state government, developers could be required, as they were before the transfer decision, to mitigate any impact from their development on listed species. So the impact of private development will be different depending upon whether the federal or state government does the permitting. In other words, the two sets of decisions together—the private development decisions and the governmental transfer decision—but not either one independently, have the potential to affect listed species and their habitat. The Biological Opinion's determination to the contrary disregards the obvious cause analysis and thus fails the reasoned decisionmaking standard. . . .

C. Statutory Power to Protect Species?

Even viewed in isolation, the first explanation for the EPA's no impact conclusion—that the loss of section 7 consultation was not an effect of its transfer decision because the agency had no authority to base its transfer decision on the loss of consultation—fares no better.

Under the statutory regime, the statutory obligation is to "insure" against likely jeopardy of listed species. The two critical factors triggering this obligation are (1) that the "action" be one for which the agency can fairly be ascribed responsibility, namely, an action "authorized, funded or carried out" by the agency; and (2) that there is the requisite nexus to an impact on listed species, namely, a direct or indirect effect "likely to jeopardize the continued existence of any endangered species or threatened species or result in the destruction or adverse modification of [critical habitat]." 16 U.S.C. §1536(a)(2). There are, consequently, three relevant statutory concepts governing the reach of section 7(a)(2): the nexus to any impact on listed species, the nature of the obligation to "insure" against jeopardizing listed species, and the actions covered.

1. NEXUS

The case law indicates that a negative impact on listed species is the likely direct or indirect effect of an agency's action only if the agency has some control over that result. Otherwise, the requisite nexus is absent. . . .

[In Department of Transportation v. Public Citizen, 541 U.S. 752 (2004), a case decided under NEPA rather than the ESA, the question was whether the federal Department of Transportation] was required under NEPA to develop an environmental impact statement with regard to the pollution caused by the entry of Mexican trucks onto United States highways under the North American Free Trade Agreement. The Court held "that where an agency has *no ability to prevent a certain effect due to its limited statutory authority over the relevant actions,* the agency cannot be considered a legally relevant 'cause' of the effect." Id. at 770 (emphasis added); see also id. at 767 (analogizing "cause" inquiry for purpose of defining "indirect effects" to proximate cause inquiry in tort law).

Given the similarity in the applicable regulations, we adopt the *Public Citizen* standard for purposes of determining the likely effects of agency action under section 7(a)(2) of the Endangered Species Act. Accordingly, deciding whether the Biological Opinion followed Endangered Species Act regulations defining "indirect effects" requires us to determine whether the EPA can consider and act upon the loss of section 7 consultation benefits in deciding whether to transfer pollution permitting authority to Arizona. If so, then the EPA's transfer decision can be a cause of the loss of section 7 consultation benefits; the loss of those benefits should have been included in the Biological Opinion as an indirect effect of the potential transfer decision; and the loss of those benefits should have been considered and acted upon by the EPA.

2. "INSURE THAT ANY ACTION . . . IS NOT LIKELY TO JEOPARDIZE THE CONTINUED EXISTENCE OF ANY [LISTED] SPECIES"

. . . [W]e focus on whether the obligation in section 7(a)(2) to "insure" against jeopardizing listed species empowers the EPA to make decisions to preserve listed species and their habitat even if the Clean Water Act does not so specify. If so, then the EPA has the authority—indeed, because section 7(a)(2) speaks in mandatory terms, the duty—to deny a pollution permitting transfer application that meets Clean Water Act standards but would jeopardize protected species.

The language in section 7(a)(2) providing that each federal agency "shall . . . insure that any action authorized, funded or carried out by such agency" will not jeopardize listed species or their critical habitat is addressed to each agency, without exception. Our question is: what does it require each agency to do?

The ordinary meaning of "insure" as used in this context requires agencies to take action, as dictionary definitions make clear. . . .

The Supreme Court's seminal section 7 case, TVA v. Hill, 437 U.S. 153, 180 (1978), confirms this textual interpretation:

One would be hard pressed to find a statutory provision whose terms were any plainer than those in §7 of the Endangered Species Act. Its very words affirmatively command all federal agencies "to insure that actions authorized, funded, or carried out by them do not jeopardize the continued existence" of an endangered species or "result in the destruction or modification of habitat of such species. . . ." This language admits of no exception.

Id. at 173. An "affirmative command" by a superior authority—here, Congress—ordinarily carries with it both the obligation and the authority to obey that command. For example, despite policy arguments in favor of continuing construction of the dam, the Court in *Hill* relied on Congress's use of "the plainest of words" and section 7's equally plain legislative history to hold that further construction was in "irreconcilable conflict" with section 7. . . .

Another aspect of the statute's structure and history, not directly at issue in *Hill*, bolsters the conclusion that section 7 includes an affirmative grant of authority to attend to protection of listed species within agencies' authority when they take actions covered by section 7(a)(2). Section 7(a)(1) of the Endangered Species Act directs agencies to "utilize their authorities in furtherance of the purposes of this chapter by carrying out programs for the conservation of [listed] species." Section 7(a)(2), in contrast, does not refer to agencies' existing "authorities," but instead directs agencies that, when considering covered "actions," they are to proceed in a manner not likely to jeopardize listed species.

The House Report indicates that this distinction between the two sections was, as one would expect, deliberate. The Report noted the requirement of present section 7(a)(2) as imposing a "further require[ment]" beyond that of section 7(a)(1). H.R. Rep. No. 93-412, at 14 (1973). The contrasting language of the two sections indicates that the "further requirement" imposed by section 7(a)(2) turns on the distinction between using existing authority to promote conservation of species and conferring an additional, do-no-harm obligation—and reciprocal authority—applicable when the agency's own actions could cause harm to endangered species. . . .

We conclude that the obligation of each agency to "insure" that its covered actions are not likely to jeopardize listed species is an obligation in addition to those created by the agencies' own governing statute. The next question we must decide is whether the EPA's transfer decision is the kind of agency action to which that obligation applies.

3. ACTIONS "AUTHORIZED, FUNDED, OR CARRIED OUT" BY AN AGENCY

As we interpret section 7(a)(2) in light of the case law, the Endangered Species Act confers authority and responsibility on agencies to protect listed species when the agency engages in an affirmative action that is both within its decisionmaking authority and unconstrained by earlier agency commitments. The decision to approve a state's pollution permitting transfer application meets these criteria and is thus the sort of decision to which section 7(a)(2) applies. The Biological Opinion's reasoning that the EPA had no choice but to disregard the impact of the transfer on listed species in Arizona was therefore inconsistent with the statute.

Section 7(a)(2) applies to all agency actions "authorized, funded, or carried out" by the agency in question. This language does indicate that some agency actions are not covered—those the agency does not "authorize[ ], fund[ ], or carr[y] out." Our determination as to whether the transfer decision is covered thus depends on the meaning of those terms.

The regulatory provision that delineates the actions covered by section 7(a)(2) reads: "Section 7 and the requirements of this Part apply to all actions in which there is discretionary Federal involvement or control." 50 C.F.R. §402.03. Although there is no statutory reference to "discretionary involvement or control," there is the limitation, just noted, to actions "authorized, funded, or carried out" by the agency. As that limiting language is the only possible source for the regulation's "discretionary" qualification of "all actions," we take the regulation as a gloss on what the statutory limitation means and interpret the term "discretionary" accordingly.

Arizona and the Chamber note that the Clean Water Act specifies that the EPA "shall approve" state applications that meet certain enumerated factors. 33 U.S.C. §1342(b). They argue that this language precludes EPA "discretion" to act on behalf of listed species, and that, applying 50 C.F.R. §402.03, section 7 does not apply. However, "an agency cannot escape its obligation to comply with the [Endangered Species Act] merely because it is bound to comply with another statute that has consistent, complementary objectives." [Washington Toxics Coalition v. EPA, 413 F.3d 1024, 1032 (9th Cir. 2005)]. Applying this principle, we reject, for two reasons, Arizona and the Chamber's argument that §1342(b) of the Clean Water Act eliminates any obligation to follow section 7(a)(2) of the Endangered Species Act.

First, the EPA makes no argument that its transfer decision was not a "discretionary" one within the meaning of 50 C.F.R. §402.03. Indeed, it could not so argue for, as we have seen, the agency recognizes that it had a duty to consult, a duty the regulations would preclude if the federal involvement in or control of the transfer decision was not sufficiently "discretionary." . . .

Second, cases applying §402.03 are consistent with our understanding that the regulation's reference to "discretionary . . . involvement" is congruent with the statutory reference to actions "authorized, funded, or carried out" by the agency. Put another way, imposing section 7(a)(2)'s substantive requirements in those cases would have gone beyond the limited command of the statute.

Our §402.03 "discretionary . . . involvement or control" cases hold section 7(a)(2) inapplicable if the agency in question had "no ongoing regulatory authority" and thus was not an entity responsible for decisionmaking with respect to the particular action in question. For example, we have relied on the "discretionary . . . involvement" regulation to find section 7(a)(2) inapplicable where the agency lacked any decisionmaking authority over the action of the kind challenged. See Ground Zero Ctr. for Non-Violent Action v. U.S. Dep't of the Navy, 383 F.3d 1082, 1092 (9th Cir. 2004) (holding that the action at issue fell outside the agency's authority because the risk of harm to listed species arose from the President's decision regarding the Navy's nuclear submarine force, not the Navy's obedience to that order). Other cases have found section 7(a)(2) inapplicable where the challenged action was legally foreordained by an earlier decision, such as where the agency lacked the ability to amend an already-issued permit "to address the needs of endangered or threatened species." Envtl. Prot. Info. Ctr. v. Simpson Timber Co., 255 F.3d 1073, 1082 (9th Cir. 2001).

In contrast, we have held that section 7(a)(2) does apply where the agency in question had continuing decisionmaking authority over the challenged action. See *Wash. Toxics*, 413 F.3d at 1032 (holding that section 7(a)(2) applies to the EPA's registration of pesticides because of its "ongoing discretion to register pesticides, alter pesticide registrations, and cancel pesticide registrations).

In sum, we understand our cases applying the "discretionary . . . involvement" regulation to interpret that regulation to be coterminous with the statutory phrase limiting section 7(a)(2)'s application to those cases "authorized, funded, or carried out" by a federal agency. Where a challenged action has not been "authorized, funded, or carried out" by the defendant agency, we have held that section 7(a)(2) does not apply. Where the challenged action comes within the agency's decisionmaking authority and remains so, it falls within section 7(a)(2)'s scope.

. . . EPA had exclusive decisionmaking authority over Arizona's pollution permitting transfer application. The EPA's decision authorized the transfer, thus triggering section 7(a)(2)'s consultation and action requirements.

4. OTHER CIRCUITS

. . . [T]his case is the first in which we have specifically addressed the question whether section 7(a)(2) of the Endangered Species Act provides a modicum of additional authority to agencies, beyond that conferred by their governing statutes, to protect listed species from the impact of affirmative federal actions. Other circuits, however, have considered the question. The reasoning of those opinions reflects an existing intercircuit conflict on the question before us, with two circuits reading section 7(a)(2) as we do and two concluding that section 7 does not itself authorize agencies to protect listed species even when it is their own action that is jeopardizing then. Compare Defenders of Wildlife v. Administrator, EPA, 882 F.2d 1294, 1299 (8th Cir. 1989), and Conservation Law Found. v. Andrus, 623 F.2d 712, 715 (1st Cir. 1979) with Am. Forest & Paper Ass'n v. EPA, 137 F.3d 291, 294, 298-99 (5th Cir. 1998), and Platte River Whooping Crane Critical Habitat Maint. Trust v. FERC, 962 F.2d 27, 34 (D.C. Cir. 1992). We do not find the D.C. Circuit and Fifth Circuit cases persuasive, as they do not reflect a full consideration of the text and history of section 7(a)(2). . . .

In sum, the better reasoned out-of-circuit authority, as well as our own precedent, supports our conclusion that section 7(a)(2) independently empowers EPA to make pollution permitting transfer decisions on behalf of listed species and their habitat when undertaking covered actions.

5. SUMMARY

We hold that approving Arizona's pollution permitting transfer application was an agency action "authorized" by the EPA, thus triggering both section 7(a)(2)'s consultation requirement and its mandate that agencies not affirmatively take actions that are likely to jeopardize listed species. The EPA may have complied with its obligations under the Clean Water Act, but compliance with a "complementary" statute cannot relieve the EPA of its independent obligations under section 7(a)(2). Section 7(a)(2) imposes a duty on the EPA to "insure" its transfer decision is not likely to jeopardize protected species or adversely modify their habitat, and this duty exists alongside Clean Water Act provisions as the agency's "first priority." *Hill*, 437 U.S. at 185.

We therefore conclude that, under *Public Citizen*, the EPA's transfer decision will cause whatever harm may flow from the loss of section 7 consultation on the many projects subject to a water pollution permit, and that harm constitutes an indirect effect of the transfer. The Biological Opinion, which ignored this effect while recognizing that section 7 consultations concerning pollution permitting permits have saved species' critical habitat in the past, was therefore deficient. The EPA erred by relying on this fatally deficient Biological Opinion.

D. Other Bases for the EPA's Transfer Decision

Having concluded that the Biological Opinion upon which the EPA relied was flawed in its basic legal premise, we now consider whether that Opinion's other analyses, or any analysis outside the Biological Opinion that the EPA relied upon, saves the validity of the EPA's transfer decision. . . .

The Endangered Species Act makes it a crime to "take" any species listed as endangered, defining "take" as "harass, harm, pursue, hunt, shoot, wound, kill, trap, capture, or collect, or to attempt to engage in any such conduct." 16 U.S.C. §1538(a); 16 U.S.C. §1532(19). . . . Section 10 of the Endangered Species Act creates an "incidental take" permit program pursuant to which the Secretary of Interior may grant permits for activity—such as some construction projects—that may incidentally "take" an endangered species specimen, so long as the permittee sufficiently mitigates the risk of a take. See 16 U.S.C. §1539. These anti-take provisions apply to all actors, not only the federal government. §1538(a)(1). Accordingly, private developers are subject to sections 9 and 10 regardless of whether the EPA or a state government issues the developers' water pollution permits.

Sections 9 and 10 are important provisions, but they are not substitutes for section 7 coverage. Section 7 covers any federal agency action that could threaten species or their critical habitat. While the anti-take provisions prohibit "[e]liminating a threatened species' habitat," *Envtl. Prot. Info. Ctr.*, 255 F.3d at 1075, or "signifi-cant . . . modification or degradation where it actually kills or injures wildlife," 50 C.F.R. §17.3, the effectiveness of these prohibitions depends on their enforcement by the appropriate authorities. . . . [A]fter-the-fact enforcement cannot prevent threats to listed species the way section 7 can. Prevention of takings may come from the section 10 permitting process, but private parties choose whether to pursue a section 10 incidental take permit. Private parties only have an incentive to do so if there is a meaningful threat of section 9 enforcement.

On this record, there is no indication that section 9 is or will be enforced meaningfully enough to provide a sufficient substitute for section 7. The record reflects no instances in which FWS has initiated a section 9 enforcement action with regard to listed species in Arizona. Additionally, FWS staff stated . . . that they did "not believe that section 9 enforcement is an acceptable substitute for section 7 consultation." This opinion reflected staff concerns, expressed in internal emails, that section 9 is ill-suited to protect species such as the pygmy owl, whose numbers are so low that section 9 enforcement may come too late to prevent extinction. The Biological Opinion contains no indication the FWS will increase section 9 enforce-ment nor any other analysis alleviating FWS staff concerns. . . .

IV. Remedy

Typically, when an agency violates the Administrative Procedure Act and the Endangered Species Act, we vacate the agency's action and remand to the agency to act in compliance with its statutory obligations. In certain instances, however, "when equity demands, the [challenged action] can be left in place while the agency follows the necessary proce-dures." Idaho Farm Bureau Fed'n v. Babbitt, 58 F.3d 1392, 1405 (9th Cir. 1995). . . .

. . . Arizona annually issues tens of thousands of pollution permits pursuant to the EPA's action. We have concluded that, absent section 7 coverage, we have no strong assurances that these permits will not allow development projects that are likely to jeopardize listed species or adversely modify their habitat. The purpose of the Endangered Species Act—to conserve endangered and threatened species rather than allow them to go extinct, see 16 U.S.C. §1531—renders the risk of harm to listed species too great. . . . Our concern with the risk of extinction comports with our understanding of the Endangered Species Act's "institutionalized caution mandate." *Wash. Toxics*, 413 F.3d at 1030. Without greater assurances that harm to listed species would not occur, our "institutionalized caution" makes us unwilling on the present record to order any remedy other than vacation of the EPA's approval of Arizona's transfer application.

For the just-stated reasons, we vacate the EPA's decision to approve Arizona's pollution permitting application. . . .

NOTES AND QUESTIONS

1. On what grounds did EPA conclude that its decision to approve the transfer of NPDES permitting authority to Arizona would not have "indirect effects" on listed species? Why did the court disagree? What were the steps in the court's reasoning in support of its conclusion that EPA has the authority to base its transfer decision on the loss of consultation requirements under the ESA? What are the three "statutory concepts governing the reach of section 7(a)(2)" and how did they apply to this case? The Ninth Circuit denied a petition for rehearing of the case en banc, but six judges dissented, accusing the majority of "trampl[ing] all over the FWS's reasonable interpretation of the ESA, deliberately creat[ing] a square inter-circuit conflict with the Fifth and D.C. Circuits, and ignor[ing] at least six prior opinions of our own court." Defenders of Wildlife v. EPA, 450 F.3d 394, 395 (9th Cir. 2006) (Kozinski, J., dissenting).

2. *Substantive and Procedural Protection Duties.* Section 7(a)(2) requires federal agencies to insure that "any action" they fund, authorize, or carry out not be likely to jeopardize listed species or result in the destruction or adverse modification of critical habitat. "Actions" are broadly defined and include management plans prepared prior to a listing, for example. Pacific Rivers Council v. Thomas, 30 F.3d 1050 (9th Cir. 1994). But cf. Marbled Murrelet v. Babbitt, 83 F.3d 1068 (9th Cir. 1996) (advice to state agencies on endangered species enforcement efforts did not trigger FWS consultation requirements).

Assuming that an agency "action" is involved, the substantive protection duties are primarily implemented through the procedural obligation to consult with the FWS. An agency whose actions may jeopardize a listed species must consult with the FWS on ways to avoid the jeopardy. The FWS must determine whether listed species are present in the area and whether the proposed action is likely to affect a species or its habitat. If the answers to these questions are negative, the FWS can end informal consultation and the acting agency's ESA duties are satisfied. If the answer is affirmative, the FWS must begin a formal consultation process and prepare a biological opinion assessing whether the proposed action is likely to jeopardize listed species. An affirmative answer requires that the opinion include reasonable and prudent alternatives (RPAs) to avoid jeopardy. Although the acting agency is not bound to implement the RPAs contained in a biological opinion, deviation from the terms of the opinion increases the risk that the agency will be deemed in violation of the no-jeopardy prohibition. E.g., Tribal Village of Akutan v. Hodel, 869 F.2d 1185, 1193 (9th Cir. 1988).

3. *Judicial Review of Biological Opinions.* Biological opinions are subject to judicial review under the "arbitrary and capricious" standard. The court rejected a NMFS biological opinion in Idaho Dep't of Fish & Game v. National Marine Fisheries Serv., 850 F. Supp. 886, 891-893 (D. Or. 1994), *remanded as moot*, 56 F.3d 1071 (9th Cir. 1995). The opinion dealt with the potential effects of hydropower operations on a listed species of salmon. The NMFS inquired whether hydropower operations would result in a "significant" reduction in mortality relative to a 1986-1990 base period. The NMFS chose that particular base period because it represented the most recent series of years before consideration of the species for listing, it was long enough to encompass a full life cycle, and it reflected relatively consistent management practices. The court found the base period chosen by the NMFS to be unreasonable. The agency's focus on "consistent management practices" focused more on system capability than on the salmon's needs. In addition, the baseline was significantly shorter than base periods used in prior years; a longer base period that included years of higher abundance levels would have resulted in a higher species protection goal. The period 1986-1990 constituted record-low years for the species due to drought conditions in the area. Finally, the NMFS failed to consider alternative baselines.

Gifford Pinchot Task Force v. U.S. Fish and Wildlife Serv., 378 F.3d 1059 (9th Cir. 2004), was a challenge to a series of biological opinions that allowed incidental takes of spotted owls in the Pacific Northwest. Plaintiffs objected to the use of habitat proxies to determine jeopardy and argued that the FWS had to conduct on-the-ground population surveys. The court responded as follows:

> The test for whether the habitat proxy is permissible in this case is whether it "reasonably ensures" that the proxy results mirror reality. See Idaho Sporting Cong., Inc. v. Rittenhouse, 305 F.3d 957, 972-73 (9th Cir. 2002) (holding that deference to proxy on proxy approaches is not warranted when the proxy method does not "reasonably ensure" accurate results). . . . Though it is a close case, we conclude that the habitat models used here reasonably ensure that owl population projections from the habitat proxy are accurate.
>
> Based on a consideration of the entire record, the use of habitat as a proxy for species in this case makes sense. The habitat analysis here is not just a simplistic "x number acres = y number of owls" type of equation. Rather, the habitat proxy takes into account type of land, extent of degradation of the habitat, relationship between different habitats, the owls' distribution, and the owls' range. The jeopardy analysis also takes into account non-habitat factors, including competition from other species, forest insects, and disease. This detailed model for owl population is sufficient to ensure that the FWS's habitat proxy reasonably correlates to the actual population of owls. Finally, the habitat proxy does not exist in a vacuum: The FWS has a program of demographic studies that supplements and verifies the habitat results. . . .
>
> Second, Appellants argue that the statutory scheme does not allow a habitat proxy method for jeopardy assessment even if habitat proxy is a sound method. The ESA is concerned with two variables in the context of species preservation, the amount of species and the amount of species habitat. See, e.g., 16 U.S.C. §1536(a)(2). Appellants argue that because "habitat" is already accounted for in the adverse modification prong of Section 7 analysis, any analysis of jeopardy to species must look to the actual species themselves instead of simply analyzing habitat, or at the very least, must continually verify habitat models by on-the-ground population verifications.

> We reject this argument. Focus on actual species count is an overly narrow interpretation of what is required under the jeopardy prong. The FWS asserts that it uses different methodologies when it analyzes habitat under jeopardy and adverse modification, limiting potential overlap. Importantly, if the habitat proxy is used correctly, it can evaluate a species's habitat that has not been designated as "critical habitat," and thus is indirectly evaluating species that live outside the critical habitat. In the ordinary course, any endangered or threatened species may have some habitat that is not deemed critical habitat. See 16 U.S.C. §1532(5)(C) (noting that, except for circumstances established by the Secretary of the Interior, "critical habitat shall not include the entire geographical area which can be occupied by the threatened or endangered species"). Further, if habitat models are sufficiently accurate and are robust, in the sense that the results are accurate in many cases, then the models function as if the FWS were counting spotted owls. Because the ESA does not prescribe how the jeopardy prong is to be determined, nor how species populations are to be estimated, we hold that it is a permissible interpretation of the statute to rest the jeopardy analysis on a habitat proxy. [Id. at 1066-1067.]

Compare the court's treatment of the "proxy-on-proxy" issue in the context of national forest management in the *Northwest Ecosystem Council* case earlier in this chapter.

4. *The "Affirmative Conservation" Duty.* The court in the principal case referred to the obligation of federal agencies under §7(a)(1) to conserve listed species. This "affirmative conservation" duty is separate from the duty to avoid jeopardy or adverse impacts on critical habitat. The §7(a)(1) duty is the subject of much less litigation than the §7(a)(2) duty. Defenders of Wildlife v. Secretary, U.S. Dep't of the Interior, 354 F. Supp. 2d 1156 (D. Or. 2005), illustrates the potential impact of §7(a)(1). Environmental groups challenged the FWS's decision to downlist (and thereby provide less protection to) two distinct population segments of the gray wolf. They argued that the downlisting constituted a violation of the affirmative conservation duty because the FWS was not using all methods necessary to conserve the wolf. The FWS responded that §7(a)(1) does not apply to the FWS because the agency's implementation of the ESA is a program, in and of itself, that is designed to effectuate the conservation of listed species. The court found the argument to be inconsistent with the plain language of §7(a)(1), which makes "all" federal agencies subject to the affirmative conservation duty. The court also held, however, that the FWS did not violate the duty because it had implemented specific and concrete conservation and recovery programs for the gray wolf. The court in Defenders of Wildlife v. Andrus, 428 F. Supp. 167 (D.D.C. 1977), found that the FWS violated the duty by failing to determine, before it issued regulations governing the sport hunting of migratory game birds, whether misidentification due to poor visibility would result in the mistaken killing of listed bird species.

4.   The Section 9 Taking Prohibition

TVA v. Hill and *Defenders of Wildlife* involved §7 of the ESA, which applies only to the federal government. Section 9 prohibits "any person," which includes both federal agencies and private individuals, from "taking" an endangered species. §9(a)(1)(B). The killing of a listed species clearly qualifies as a "take," but what about habitat destruction? The following case addresses this issue.

BABBITT v. SWEET HOME CHAPTER OF COMMUNITIES FOR A GREAT OREGON
515 U.S. 687 (1995)

STEVENS, J., delivered the opinion of the Court, in which O'CONNOR, KENNEDY, SOUTER, GINSBURG, and BREYER, JJ., joined. O'CONNOR, J., filed a concurring opinion. SCALIA, J., filed a dissenting opinion, in which REHNQUIST, C.J., and THOMAS, J., joined.

JUSTICE STEVENS delivered the opinion of the Court.

. . . Section 9 of the Act makes it unlawful for any person to "take" any endangered or threatened species. The Secretary has promulgated a regulation that defines the statute's prohibition on takings to include "significant habitat modification or degradation where it actually kills or injures wildlife." This case presents the question whether the Secretary exceeded his authority under the Act by promulgating that regulation.

I

Section 9(a)(1) of the Endangered Species Act provides the following protection for endangered species:

> Except as provided in sections 1535(g)(2) and 1539 of this title, with respect to any endangered species of fish or wildlife listed pursuant to section 1533 of this title it is unlawful for any person subject to the jurisdiction of the United States to— . . .
>   (B) take any such species within the United States or the territorial sea of the United States[.] 16 U.S.C. §1538(a)(1).

Section 3(19) of the Act defines the statutory term "take":

> The term "take" means to harass, harm, pursue, hunt, shoot, wound, kill, trap, capture, or collect, or to attempt to engage in any such conduct. 16 U.S.C. §1532(19).

The Act does not further define the terms it uses to define "take." The Interior Department regulations that implement the statute, however, define the statutory term "harm":

> Harm in the definition of "take" in the Act means an act which actually kills or injures wildlife. Such act may include significant habitat modification or degradation where it actually kills or injures wildlife by significantly impairing essential behavioral patterns, including breeding, feeding, or sheltering. 50 CFR §17.3 (1994).

This regulation has been in place since 1975.

A limitation on the §9 "take" prohibition appears in §10(a)(1)(B) of the Act, which Congress added by amendment in 1982. That section authorizes the Secretary to grant a permit for any taking otherwise prohibited by §9(a)(1)(B) "if such taking is incidental to, and not the purpose of, the carrying out of an otherwise lawful activity." 16 U.S.C. §1539(a)(1)(B). . . .

Respondents advanced three arguments to support their submission that Congress did not intend the word "take" in §9 to include habitat modification, as the Secretary's "harm" regulation provides. First, they correctly noted that language in the Senate's original version of the ESA would have defined "take" to include "destruction, modification, or curtailment of [the] habitat or range" of fish or wildlife, but the Senate deleted that language from the bill before enacting it. Second, respondents argued that Congress intended the Act's express authorization for the Federal Government to buy private land in order to prevent habitat degradation in §5 to be the exclusive check against habitat modification on private property. Third, because the Senate added the term "harm" to the definition of "take" in a floor amendment without debate, respondents argued that the court should not interpret the term so expansively as to include habitat modification.

[The district court dismissed plaintiffs' complaint. A divided panel of the D.C. Circuit initially affirmed, but on rehearing, it reversed. The majority concluded that, like the other words in the definition of "take," the word "harm" is limited to the direct application of force against the animal taken. That decision created a split among the circuits, the Ninth Circuit having previously held that "take" may include habitat modification. Palila v. Hawaii Dep't of Land and Natural Res., 852 F.2d 1106 (9th Cir. 1988) (*Palila II*).] We granted certiorari to resolve the conflict. Our consideration of the text and structure of the Act, its legislative history, and the significance of the 1982 amendment persuades us that the Court of Appeals' judgment should be reversed.

II

Because this case was decided on motions for summary judgment, we may appropriately make certain factual assumptions in order to frame the legal issue. First, we assume respondents have no desire to harm either the red-cockaded woodpecker or the spotted owl; they merely wish to continue logging activities that would be entirely proper if not prohibited by the ESA. On the other hand, we must assume, *arguendo*, that those activities will have the effect, even though unintended, of detrimentally changing the natural habitat of both listed species and that, as a consequence, members of those species will be killed or injured. Under respondents' view of the law, the Secretary's only means of forestalling that grave result—even when the actor knows it is certain to occur[9]—is to use his §5 authority to purchase the lands on which the survival of the species depends. The Secretary, on the other hand, submits that the §9 prohibition on takings, which Congress defined to include "harm," places on respondents a duty to avoid harm that habitat alteration will cause the birds unless respondents first obtain a permit pursuant to §10.

The text of the Act provides three reasons for concluding that the Secretary's interpretation is reasonable. First, an ordinary understanding of the word "harm" supports it. The dictionary definition of the verb form of "harm" is "to cause hurt

---

9. . . . [T]he Secretary's definition of "harm" is limited to "act[s] which actually kil[l] or injur[e] wildlife." 50 CFR §17.3 (1994). . . . We do not agree with the dissent that the regulation covers results that are not "even foreseeable . . . no matter how long the chain of causality between modification and injury." Respondents have suggested no reason why . . . the "harm" regulation itself . . . should not be read to incorporate ordinary requirements of proximate causation and foreseeability. . . .

or damage to: injure." Webster's Third New International Dictionary 1034 (1966). In the context of the ESA, that definition naturally encompasses habitat modification that results in actual injury or death to members of an endangered or threatened species.

Respondents argue that the Secretary should have limited the purview of "harm" to direct applications of force against protected species, but the dictionary definition does not include the word "directly" or suggest in any way that only direct or willful action that leads to injury constitutes "harm."[10] Moreover, unless the statutory term "harm" encompasses indirect as well as direct injuries, the word has no meaning that does not duplicate the meaning of other words that §3 uses to define "take." A reluctance to treat statutory terms as surplusage supports the reasonableness of the Secretary's interpretation.[11]

Second, the broad purpose of the ESA supports the Secretary's decision to extend protection against activities that cause the precise harms Congress enacted the statute to avoid. In TVA v. Hill, 437 U.S. 153 (1978), we described the Act as "the most comprehensive legislation for the preservation of endangered species ever enacted by any nation." . . .

Third, the fact that Congress in 1982 authorized the Secretary to issue permits for takings that §9(a)(1)(B) would otherwise prohibit, "if such taking is incidental to, and not the purpose of, the carrying out of an otherwise lawful activity," strongly suggests that Congress understood §9(a)(1)(B) to prohibit indirect as well as deliberate takings. The permit process requires the applicant to prepare a "conservation plan" that specifies how he intends to "minimize and mitigate" the "impact" of his activity on endangered and threatened species, §10(a)(2)(A), making clear that Congress had in mind foreseeable rather than merely accidental effects on listed species. No one could seriously request an "incidental" take permit to avert §9 liability for direct, deliberate action against a member of an endangered or threatened species, but respondents would read "harm" so narrowly that the permit procedure would have little more than that absurd purpose. . . . Congress' addition of the §10 permit provision supports the Secretary's conclusion that activities not intended to harm

---

10. Respondents and the dissent emphasize what they portray as the "established meaning" of "take" in the sense of a "wildlife take," a meaning respondents argue extends only to "the effort to exercise dominion over some creature, and the concrete effect of [sic] that creature." This limitation ill serves the statutory text, which forbids not taking "some creature" but "tak[ing] any [endangered] species" — a formidable task for even the most rapacious feudal lord. More importantly, Congress explicitly defined the operative term "take" in the ESA, no matter how much the dissent wishes otherwise, thereby obviating the need for us to probe its meaning as we must probe the meaning of the undefined subsidiary term "harm." Finally, Congress' definition of "take" includes several words — most obviously "harass," "pursue," and "wound," in addition to "harm" itself — that fit respondents' and the dissent's definition of "take" no better than does "significant habitat modification or degradation."

11. In contrast, if the statutory term "harm" encompasses such indirect means of killing and injuring wildlife as habitat modification, the other terms listed in §3 — "harass," "pursue," "hunt," "shoot," "wound," "kill," "trap," "capture," and "collect" — generally retain independent meanings. Most of those terms refer to deliberate actions more frequently than does "harm," and they therefore do not duplicate the sense of indirect causation that "harm" adds to the statute. In addition, most of the other words in the definition describe either actions from which habitat modification does not usually result (e.g., "pursue," "harass") or effects to which activities that modify habitat do not usually lead (e.g., "trap," "collect"). To the extent the Secretary's definition of "harm" may have applications that overlap with other words in the definition, that overlap reflects the broad purpose of the Act.

an endangered species, such as habitat modification, may constitute unlawful takings under the ESA unless the Secretary permits them.

The Court of Appeals made three errors in asserting that "harm" must refer to a direct application of force because the words around it do.[15] First, the court's premise was flawed. Several of the words that accompany "harm" in the §3 definition of "take," especially "harass," "pursue," "wound," and "kill," refer to actions or effects that do not require direct applications of force. Second, to the extent the court read a requirement of intent or purpose into the words used to define "take," it ignored §9's express provision that a "knowing" action is enough to violate the Act. Third, the court employed *noscitur a sociis* to give "harm" essentially the same function as other words in the definition, thereby denying it independent meaning. The canon, to the contrary, counsels that a word "gathers meaning from the words around it." Jarecki v. G. D. Searle & Co., 367 U.S. 303, 307 (1961). The statutory context of "harm" suggests that Congress meant that term to serve a particular function in the ESA, consistent with but distinct from the functions of the other verbs used to define "take." The Secretary's interpretation of "harm" to include indirectly injuring endangered animals through habitat modification permissibly interprets "harm" to have "a character of its own not to be submerged by its association." Russell Motor Car Co. v. United States, 261 U.S. 514, 519 (1923).

Nor does the Act's inclusion of the §5 land acquisition authority and the §7 directive to federal agencies to avoid destruction or adverse modification of critical habitat alter our conclusion. Respondents' argument that the Government lacks any incentive to purchase land under §5 when it can simply prohibit takings under §9 ignores the practical considerations that attend enforcement of the ESA. Purchasing habitat lands may well cost the Government less in many circumstances than pursuing civil or criminal penalties. In addition, the §5 procedure allows for protection of habitat before the seller's activity has harmed any endangered animal, whereas the Government cannot enforce the §9 prohibition until an animal has actually been killed or injured. . . . [17]

We need not decide whether the statutory definition of "take" compels the Secretary's interpretation of "harm," because our conclusions that Congress did not unambiguously manifest its intent to adopt respondents' view and that the Secretary's interpretation is reasonable suffice to decide this case. See generally Chevron U.S.A. Inc. v. Natural Resources Defense Council, Inc., 467 U.S. 837 (1984). The latitude the ESA gives the Secretary in enforcing the statute, together with the degree of

15. The dissent makes no effort to defend the Court of Appeals' reading of the statutory definition as requiring a direct application of force. Instead, it tries to impose on §9 a limitation of liability to "affirmative conduct intentionally directed against a particular animal or animals." Under the dissent's interpretation of the Act, a developer could drain a pond, knowing that the act would extinguish an endangered species of turtles, without even proposing a conservation plan or applying for a permit under §9(a)(1)(B); unless the developer was motivated by a desire "to get at a turtle," no statutory taking could occur. Because such conduct would not constitute a taking at common law, the dissent would shield it from §9 liability, even though the words "kill" and "harm" in the statutory definition could apply to such deliberate conduct. We cannot accept that limitation. In any event, our reasons for rejecting the Court of Appeals' interpretation apply as well to the dissent's novel construction.

17. Congress recognized that §§7 and 9 are not coextensive as to federal agencies when, in the wake of our decision in *Hill* in 1978, it added §7(o), 16 U.S.C. §1536(o), to the Act. That section provides that any federal project subject to exemption from §7, 16 U.S.C. §1536(h), will also be exempt from §9.

regulatory expertise necessary to its enforcement, establishes that we owe some degree of deference to the Secretary's reasonable interpretation.[18] . . .

IV

When it enacted the ESA, Congress delegated broad administrative and interpretive power to the Secretary. See 16 U.S.C. §§1533, 1540(f). . . . The proper interpretation of a term such as "harm" involves a complex policy choice. When Congress has entrusted the Secretary with broad discretion, we are especially reluctant to substitute our views of wise policy for his. See *Chevron*, 467 U.S., at 865-866. In this case, that reluctance accords with our conclusion, based on the text, structure, and legislative history of the ESA, that the Secretary reasonably construed the intent of Congress when he defined "harm" to include "significant habitat modification or degradation that actually kills or injures wildlife."

In the elaboration and enforcement of the ESA, the Secretary and all persons who must comply with the law will confront difficult questions of proximity and degree; for, as all recognize, the Act encompasses a vast range of economic and social enterprises and endeavors. These questions must be addressed in the usual course of the law, through case-by-case resolution and adjudication.

The judgment of the Court of Appeals is reversed. . . .

JUSTICE O'CONNOR, concurring.

My agreement with the Court is founded on two understandings. First, the challenged regulation is limited to significant habitat modification that causes actual, as opposed to hypothetical or speculative, death or injury to identifiable protected animals. Second, even setting aside difficult questions of scienter, the regulation's application is limited by ordinary principles of proximate causation, which introduce notions of foreseeability. These limitations, in my view, call into question . . . many of the applications derided by the dissent. Because there is no need to strike a regulation on a facial challenge out of concern that it is susceptible of erroneous application, however, and because there are many habitat-related circumstances in which the regulation might validly apply, I join the opinion of the Court.

In my view, the regulation is limited by its terms to actions that actually kill or injure individual animals. Justice Scalia disagrees, arguing that the harm regulation "encompasses injury inflicted, not only upon individual animals, but upon populations of the protected species." At one level, I could not reasonably quarrel with this observation; death to an individual animal always reduces the size of the population in which it lives, and in that sense, "injures" that population. But by its insight, the dissent

18. Respondents also argue that the rule of lenity should foreclose any deference to the Secretary's interpretation of the ESA because the statute includes criminal penalties. The rule of lenity is premised on two ideas: first, " 'a fair warning should be given to the world in language that the common world will understand, of what the law intends to do if a certain line is passed' "; second, "legislatures and not courts should define criminal activity." United States v. Bass, 404 U.S. 336, 347-350 (1971) (quoting McBoyle v. United States, 283 U.S. 25, 27 (1931)). . . . We have never suggested that the rule of lenity should provide the standard for reviewing facial challenges to administrative regulations whenever the governing statute authorizes criminal enforcement. Even if there exist regulations whose interpretations of statutory criminal penalties provide such inadequate notice of potential liability as to offend the rule of lenity, the "harm" regulation, which has existed for two decades and gives a fair warning of its consequences, cannot be one of them.

means something else. Building upon the regulation's use of the word "breeding," Justice Scalia suggests that the regulation facially bars significant habitat modification that actually kills or injures hypothetical animals (or, perhaps more aptly, causes potential additions to the population not to come into being). Because "[i]mpairment of breeding does not 'injure' living creatures," Justice Scalia reasons, the regulation must contemplate application to "a population of animals which would otherwise have maintained or increased its numbers."

I disagree. As an initial matter, I do not find it as easy as Justice Scalia does to dismiss the notion that significant impairment of breeding injures living creatures. To raze the last remaining ground on which the piping plover currently breeds, thereby making it impossible for any piping plovers to reproduce, would obviously injure the population (causing the species' extinction in a generation). But by completely preventing breeding, it would also injure the individual living bird, in the same way that sterilizing the creature injures the individual living bird. . . .

. . . I see no indication that Congress, in enacting [§9(a)(1)], intended to dispense with ordinary principles of proximate causation. Strict liability means liability without regard to fault; it does not normally mean liability for every consequence, however remote, of one's conduct. See generally W. Keeton et al., Prosser and Keeton on The Law of Torts 559-560 (5th ed. 1984) (describing "practical necessity for the restriction of liability within some reasonable bounds" in the strict liability context). . . .

Proximate causation is not a concept susceptible of precise definition. It is easy enough, of course, to identify the extremes. The farmer whose fertilizer is lifted by tornado from tilled fields and deposited miles away in a wildlife refuge cannot, by any stretch of the term, be considered the proximate cause of death or injury to protected species occasioned thereby. At the same time, the landowner who drains a pond on his property, killing endangered fish in the process, would likely satisfy any formulation of the principle. . . . I note, at the least, that proximate cause principles inject a foreseeability element into the statute, and hence, the regulation, that would appear to alleviate some of the problems noted by the dissent. . . .

NOTES AND QUESTIONS

1. *What Habitat Modification Is a §9 Taking?* What limitations does the majority opinion impose on defining habitat destruction or modification as a §9 taking? Does *Sweet Home* require proof that the species' habitat has previously been harmed? The issue arose in Marbled Murrelet v. Babbitt, 83 F.3d 1060 (9th Cir. 1996). The marbled murrelet is a stealthy seabird that ranges between old-growth forests in northern California and the Pacific Ocean. They are difficult to sight and do not nest; instead the female lays eggs in depressions in moss-covered limbs of large old growth trees. A lumber company, whose activities had been enjoined as a threat to the bird, argued that *Sweet Home* requires proof that a species has been killed or injured before a §9 injunction can issue, but the court rejected this reading: "A reasonably certain threat of imminent harm to a protected species is sufficient for issuance of an injunction." Id. at 1066. *Marbled Murrelet* adopts a risk-margin of safety analysis similar to that adopted by courts in air and water pollution cases. See also Forest Conservation Council v. Rosboro Lumber Co., 50 F.3d 781, 784 (9th Cir. 1995). But cf. NWF v. Burlington N. R.R., 23 F.3d 1508, 1512 n.8 (9th Cir. 1994); American Bald Eagle v. Bhatti, 9 F.3d 163, 165-167 (1st Cir. 1993).

The potential scope and limits of the term "harm" are illustrated by the *Marbled Murrelet* court's treatment of the argument that impaired breeding constitutes harm to a population, not a species, and thus cannot be the basis for a §9 injunction. The regulation upheld in *Sweet Home* defines harm to include "significant habitat modification or degradation where it actually kills or injures wildlife by significantly impairing essential behavioral patterns, including breeding, feeding or sheltering." 50 C.F.R. §17.3. According to the Ninth Circuit, under *Sweet Home*, a habitat modification that significantly impairs the breeding and sheltering of a protected species amounts to "harm." Harm therefore includes the threat of future harm. In *Marbled Murrelet*, the evidence supported the finding that implementation of a lumber company's harvesting plan would likely harm the birds by impairing their breeding and increasing the likelihood of attack by predators on both young and adult murrelets.

2. *Incidental Take Permits.* The majority opinion in *Sweet Home* refers to the FWS's authority under §10(a)(1)(B) to issue incidental take permits. Must an incidental take permit specify the number of animals killed that will trigger a take determination? Arizona Cattle Growers' Ass'n v. U.S. Fish and Wildlife Serv., 273 F.3d 1229 (9th Cir. 2001), held that the FWS may use ecological conditions rather than numbers to define the take trigger only if it establishes that "no such numerical value could be practically obtained." Can the FWS issue an incidental take permit when its own findings indicate that species losses need to be mitigated, the developer has rejected a key mitigation alternative, and no map of the developer's mitigation habitat dedication is available? See Gerber v. Norton, 294 F.3d 173 (D.C. Cir. 2002).

3. *So What?* The ultimate question is whether the ESA is effective in preventing species extinction. The Act's effectiveness is a source of continuing scientific and political controversy. The basic scientific criticism is that the species-by-species approach neither prevents extinction nor promotes biodiversity conservation.* S. Budiansky, Nature's Keepers 171 (1995), sets out the oft-repeated criticism of the Act.

> Of the more than fourteen hundred species listed as endangered or threatened since . . . 1966, only twenty-two have ever been "delisted." Of those, eight were removed from the list because it was found that the original data used to justify the listing was in error, usually when additional populations were discovered; seven were removed from the list because of extinction. That leaves seven supposedly bone fide success stories: the Pacific grey whale, the American alligator, the Arctic peregrine falcon, the Rydberg milk vetch (a plant found in Utah), and three birds found on a single Pacific island. But even here the evidence is not clear-cut. The milk vetch and alligator were thought to have been listed in error and never to have been truly endangered; grey whale populations have been increasing steadily since the nineteenth century, as demand for whale products evaporated; and the birds of Palau Islands may have recovered largely due to the (unassisted) regrowth of vegetation wiped out in bombing during World War II.

NOTE ON MULTIPLE SPECIES HABITAT CONSERVATION PLANS

Section 9 is the most controversial section of the ESA because it has the potential to stop a great deal of private real estate development in biodiversity hot spots such as California, Florida, and Texas. Any land clearing could be a "taking."** The ESA was

---

*See C. Mann & M. Plummer, Noah's Choice: The Future of Endangered Species (1995).

**See Houck, Why Do We Protect Endangered Species, and What Does That Say about Whether Restrictions on Private Property to Protect Them Constitute Takings?, 80 Iowa L. Rev. 297 (1995).

amended in 1982 to deal with this problem. In that year, a controversy over an endangered butterfly population on San Bruno Mountain south of San Francisco led to the adoption of §10. Section 10 allows the creation of Department of Interior–approved Habitat Conservation Plans (HCPs). An HCP was originally a single species land reserve program funded by developer exactions and public funds. An approved HCP is the basis for the issuance of an incidental take permit. The permit allows a development to proceed on the theory that "the taking will not appreciably reduce the likelihood of the survival and recovery of the species" because of efficacy of the HCP. §10(a)(2)(B)(iv).*

Habitat planning is becoming more proactive and moving toward large-scale bio-regional ecosystem management experiments. Plans cover multiple species and require cooperation among federal agencies, state and local governments, and private landowners.** Second-generation HCPs in southern California illustrate the evolution of §10 and the legal problems that have arisen from efforts to extend the ESA to long-term ecosystem adaptive management. To avoid listing a threatened songbird in southern California, the state enacted a statute in 1991 that encourages voluntary local government and private landowner participation in the preparation of Natural Community Conservation Plans (NCCPs) to protect natural areas that provide habitat for a variety of rare species. The statute authorizes any person or governmental agency to prepare an NCCP pursuant to an agreement with, and guidelines written by, the state Department of Fish and Game. Each plan must promote "protection and perpetuation of natural wildlife diversity while allowing compatible and appropriate development and growth." Once the state agency approves an NCCP, it may authorize developments that might otherwise be found to have an adverse impact on listed or candidate species if they are consistent with the NCCP. These plans are to be large-scale, multi-species equivalents of existing HCPs authorized under the federal ESA.

The Department of Interior responded to California's initiative by protecting the California gnatcatcher under a special rule. The Department interpreted §4(d) of the ESA to allow it to conclude that any destruction of gnatcatcher habitat or actual killing of the bird will not be an illegal "take," provided that the actions are consistent with local land use plans prepared pursuant to a state ecosystem protection planning act. In 1996 Orange County created a substantial reserve system encompassing large core blocks of prime habitat connected by migration corridors. In 1997 the city of San Diego approved an even more ambitious multi-species HCP.

HCP creation and management raise substantial taking issues discussed in the notes following Lucas v. South Carolina Coastal Council, *infra*,*** and it is not surprising that the federal government has sought to create incentives for voluntary land and financial contributions to create reserve systems. The major incentive for landowner participation in these voluntary species protection efforts is the assurance that participation will be the extent of his or her ESA obligations. Can the federal

---

*See Ruhl, How to Kill Endangered Species, Legally: The Nuts and Bolts of Endangered Species Act "HCP" Permits for Real Estate Development, 5 Envtl. Law. 345 (1999).

**See Lin, Participants' Experiences with Habitat Conservation Plans and Suggestions for Streamlining the Process, 23 Ecology L.Q. 369 (1996); Karkkainen, Collaborative Ecosystem Governance: Scale, Complexity, and Dynamism, 21 Va. Envtl. L.J. (2002); Ruhl, Biodiversity Conservation and the Ever-Expanding Web of Federal Laws Regulating Nonfederal Lands: Time for Something Completely Different?, 66 U. Colo. L. Rev. 555 (1995); Symposium, The Ecosystem Approach: New Departures for Land and Water, 24 Ecology L.Q. 619 (1997).

***See Thompson, The Endangered Species Act: A Case Study in Takings and Incentives, 49 Stan. L. Rev. 305 (1997).

government provide this assurance, however, if new species are discovered or the HCP does not work? In 1994 the Department of the Interior promulgated its "no surprises" policy, which promises that once an HCP is approved, no new reserve additions for subsequently listed species will be required except in extraordinary circumstances.* Does this policy conflict with the principle that the government can never be estopped from exercising its regulatory powers? Can the government in effect promise not to "prosecute" future ESA violations? Bosselman, The Statutory and Constitutional Mandate for a No Surprises Policy, 24 Ecology L.Q. 707 (1997), argues that §10 authorizes the policy and that United States v. Winstar Corp., 518 U.S. 839 (1996), supports the proposition that the federal government may bind itself to assume the costs of changes in future regulations.

The southern California model multi-species HCP depends on a high degree of cooperation and collaboration among traditionally noncooperative units of government and between public and private parties. One form of cooperation is reliance on state and local protection initiatives to meet federal objectives. Environmental advocates, schooled in the success of demanding judicial enforcement of the letter of environmental statutes, often object because the federal government defers full enforcement of the law. This tension is illustrated by Oregon Natural Resources Council v. Daley, 6 F. Supp. 2d 1139 (D. Or. 1998). The NMFS initially recommended listing species of coho salmon as threatened. It ultimately chose instead to rely on the Oregon Coastal Salmon Restoration Initiative (OCSRI), which was intended to address the multiple causes of the species' decline through a coordinated voluntary and regulatory restoration program and the use of adaptive management. The NMFS concluded that implementation of the OCSRI would prevent the salmon from becoming endangered within the next two years. The district court found that the NMFS lacks the authority under the ESA to defer a listing decision indefinitely while waiting for some possible future event. The NMFS's decision not to list amounted to deferral of a final listing decision to allow Oregon "to perhaps take some action." The ESA requires the NMFS to consider five factors in making listing decisions, one of which is "the adequacy of existing regulatory mechanisms." §4(a)(1)(D). The statute also requires the agency to consider these factors based on the best available data "after taking into account those efforts, if any, being made by any State . . . to protect such species, whether by predator control, protection of habitat and food supply, or other conservation practices." §4(b)(1)(B).

The court concluded that the plain language of these provisions bars the NMFS from relying on plans for future actions to reduce threats and protect a species as a basis for deciding that listing is not currently warranted. "The NMFS may only consider conservation efforts that are currently operational, not those promised to be implemented in the future." 6 F. Supp. 2d at 1154. The "more difficult issue," according to the court, was whether the ESA permits consideration of voluntary, as opposed to regulatory, actions. The court concluded that "for the same reason that the Secretary may not rely on future actions, he should not be able to rely on unenforceable efforts. Absent some method of enforcing compliance, protection of a species can never be assured. Voluntary actions, like those planned in the future, are necessarily speculative." As a result, "voluntary or future conservation efforts by a state should be given no weight in the listing decision. Instead, the NMFS must base its decision on current,

---

*The subsequent procedural history was discussed in Chapter 3, page 000.

enforceable measures." Id. at 1155. The court held that the NMFS improperly relied on future and voluntary measures contained in the OCSRI.

C. THE REGULATORY TAKING PROBLEM

LUCAS v. SOUTH CAROLINA COASTAL COUNCIL
505 U.S. 1003 (1992)

JUSTICE SCALIA delivered the opinion of the Court.

In 1986, petitioner David H. Lucas paid $975,000 for two residential lots on the Isle of Palms in Charleston County, South Carolina, on which he intended to build single-family homes. In 1988, however, the South Carolina Legislature enacted the Beachfront Management Act, which had the direct effect of barring petitioner from erecting any permanent habitable structures on his two parcels. . . .

. . . In its original form, the South Carolina Act required owners of coastal zone land that qualified as a "critical area" (defined in the legislation to include beaches and immediately adjacent sand dunes) to obtain a permit from the newly created South Carolina Coastal Council (Council) (respondent here) prior to committing the land to a "use other than the use the critical area was devoted to on [September 28, 1977]." . . .

. . . No portion of the lots, which were located approximately 300 feet from the beach, qualified as a "critical area" under the 1977 Act; accordingly, at the time Lucas acquired these parcels, he was not legally obliged to obtain a permit from the Council in advance of any development activity. . . .

Under that 1988 legislation, the Council was directed to establish a "baseline" connecting the landward-most "point[s] of erosion . . . during the past forty years" in the region of the Isle of Palms that includes Lucas's lots. . . . In action not challenged here, the Council fixed this baseline landward of Lucas's parcels. That was significant, for under the Act construction of occupiable improvements was flatly prohibited seaward of a line drawn 20 feet landward of, and parallel to, the baseline. . . . The Act provided no exceptions. . . .

[Lucas sued, charging that the statutory ban on construction amounted to a taking of his property without just compensation.]

Prior to Justice Holmes's exposition in Pennsylvania Coal Co. v. Mahon, 260 U.S. 393 (1922), it was generally thought that the Takings Clause reached only a "direct appropriation" of property, Legal Tender Cases, 12 Wall. 457, 551 (1871), or the functional equivalent of a "practical ouster of [the owner's] possession." . . . Justice Holmes recognized in Mahon, however, that if the protection against physical appropriations of private property was to be meaningfully enforced, the government's power to redefine the range of interests included in the ownership of property was necessarily constrained by constitutional limits. . . . These considerations gave birth in that case to the oft-cited maxim that "while property may be regulated to a certain extent, if regulation goes too far it will be recognized as a taking." . . .

The trial court found Lucas's two beachfront lots to have been rendered valueless by respondent's enforcement of the coastal-zone construction ban. Under Lucas's theory of the case, . . . that finding entitled him to compensation. Lucas believed it unnecessary to take issue with either the purposes behind the Beachfront Management Act, or the means chosen by the South Carolina Legislature to effectuate those purposes. [According to the South Carolina Supreme Court, however, the statute represented an exercise of the state's police powers to mitigate the harm to the public interest that Lucas's use of his land might cause. The court treated Lucas's failure to challenge the statute's purposes as a concession that the beach/dune area along the South Carolina coast is a valuable public resource, that the erection of new construction contributes to the destruction of that resource, and that discouraging new construction near the beach/dune area was necessary to prevent great public harm. It held that these concessions triggered a line of cases holding that regulation of property uses that are akin to public nuisances are not compensable takings.]

. . . The "harmful or noxious uses" principle was the Court's early attempt to describe in theoretical terms why government may, consistent with the Takings Clause, affect property values by regulation without incurring an obligation to compensate — a reality we nowadays acknowledge explicitly with respect to the full scope of the State's police power. . . .

Where the State seeks to sustain regulation that deprives land of all economically beneficial use, we think it may resist compensation only if the logically antecedent inquiry into the nature of the owner's estate shows that the proscribed use interests were not part of his title to begin with. This accords, we think, with our "takings" jurisprudence, which has traditionally been guided by the understandings of our citizens regarding the content of, and the State's power over, the "bundle of rights" that they acquire when they obtain title to property. It seems to us that the property owner necessarily expects the uses of his property to be restricted, from time to time, by various measures newly enacted by the State in legitimate exercise of its police powers; "[a]s long recognized, some values are enjoyed under an implied limitation and must yield to the police power." Pennsylvania Coal Co. v. Mahon, 260 U.S., at 413. . . . In the case of land, however, we think the notion pressed by the Council that title is somehow held subject to the "implied limitation" that the State may subsequently eliminate all economically valuable use is inconsistent with the historical compact recorded in the Takings Clause that has become part of our constitutional culture. . . .

. . . We believe similar treatment must be accorded confiscatory regulations, i.e., regulations that prohibit all economically beneficial use of land: Any limitation so severe cannot be newly legislated or decreed (without compensation), but must inhere in the title itself, in the restrictions that background principles of the State's law of property and nuisance already place upon land ownership. A law or decree with such an effect must, in other words, do no more than duplicate the result that could have been achieved in the courts — by adjacent landowners (or other uniquely affected persons) under the State's law of private nuisance, or by the State under its complementary power to abate nuisances that affect the public generally, or otherwise.

On this analysis, the owner of a lake-bed, for example, would not be entitled to compensation when he is denied the requisite permit to engage in a landfilling operation that would have the effect of flooding others' land. Nor the corporate owner of a nuclear generating plant, when it is directed to remove all improvements from its land upon discovery that the plant sits astride an earthquake fault. Such regulatory action may well have the effect of eliminating the land's only economically productive use, but it does not proscribe a productive use that was previously permissible under relevant property and nuisance principles. The use of these properties for what are now expressly prohibited purposes was always unlawful, and (subject to other constitutional limitations) it was open to the State at any point to make the implication of those background principles of nuisance and property law explicit. In light of our traditional resort to "existing rules or understandings that stem from an independent source such as state law" to define the range of interests that qualify for protection as "property" under the Fifth and Fourteenth Amendments, Board of Regents of State Colleges v. Roth, 408 U.S. 564, 577 (1972), this recognition that the Takings Clause does not require compensation when an owner is barred from putting land to a use that is proscribed by those "existing rules or understandings" is surely unexceptional. When, however, a regulation that declares "off-limits" all economically productive or beneficial uses of land goes beyond what the relevant background principles would dictate, compensation must be paid to sustain it.

The "total taking" inquiry we require today will ordinarily entail (as the application of state nuisance law ordinarily entails) analysis of, among other things, the degree of harm to public lands and resources, or adjacent private property, posed by the claimant's proposed activities, see, e.g., Restatement (Second) of Torts §§826, 827, the social value of the claimant's activities and their suitability to the locality in question, see, e.g., id., §§828(a) and (b), 831, and the relative ease with which the alleged harm can be avoided through measures taken by the claimant and the government (or adjacent private landowners) alike, see, e.g., id., §§827(e), 828(c), 830. The fact that a particular use has long been engaged in by similarly situated owners ordinarily imports a lack of any common-law prohibition (though changed circumstances or new knowledge may make what was previously permissible no longer so), see id., §827, Comment g. So also does the fact that other landowners, similarly situated, are permitted to continue the use denied to the claimant. . . .

[To avoid a taking on remand,] South Carolina must identify background principles of nuisance and property law that prohibit the uses [Lucas] now intends in the circumstances in which the property is presently found. . . .

JUSTICE BLACKMUN, dissenting.

Today the Court launches a missile to kill a mouse. . . .

If the state legislature is correct that the prohibition on building in front of the setback line prevents serious harm, then, under this Court's prior cases, the Act is constitutional. "Long ago it was recognized that all property in this country is held under the implied obligation that the owner's use of it shall not be injurious to the community, and the Takings Clause did not transform that principle to one that requires compensation whenever the State asserts its power to enforce it." Keystone Bituminous Coal Assn. v. DeBenedictis, 480 U.S. 470, 491-492 [(1987)]. . . .

. . . In determining what is a nuisance at common law, state courts make exactly the decision that the Court finds so troubling when made by the South Carolina General Assembly today: They determine whether the use is harmful. Common-law public and private nuisance law is simply a determination whether a particular use causes harm. There is nothing magical in the reasoning of judges long dead. They determined a harm in the same way as state judges and legislatures do today. If judges in the 18th and 19th centuries can distinguish a harm from a benefit, why not judges in the 20th century, and if judges can, why not legislators? . . .

. . . Nothing in the discussions in Congress concerning the Takings Clause indicates that the Clause was limited by the common-law nuisance doctrine.

Common-law courts themselves rejected such an understanding. They regularly recognized that it is "for the legislature to interpose, and by positive enactment to prohibit a use of property which would be injurious to the public." [Commonwealth v. Tewksbury, 11 Metc., at 57 (Mass. 1846)]. . . . Commonwealth v. Parks, 155 Mass. 531, 532 (1892) (Holmes, J.) ("[T]he legislature may change the common law as to nuisances, and may move the line either way, so as to make things nuisances which were not so, or to make things lawful which were nuisances").

In short, I find no clear and accepted "historical compact" or "understanding of our citizens" justifying the Court's new takings doctrine. Instead, the Court seems to treat history as a grab bag of principles, to be adopted where they support the Court's theory, and ignored where they do not. If the Court decided that the early common law provides the background principles for interpreting the Takings Clause, then regulation, as opposed to physical confiscation, would not be compensable. If the Court decided that the law of a later period provides the background principles, then regulation might be compensable, but the Court would have to confront the fact that legislatures regularly determined which uses were prohibited, independent of the common law, and independent of whether the uses were lawful when the owner purchased. What makes the Court's analysis unworkable is its attempt to package the law of two incompatible eras and peddle it as historical fact.

NOTES AND QUESTIONS

1. *What Happened to Mr. Lucas's Exposed House?* After the case, the state of South Carolina purchased the lot from Lucas. The Coastal Council then sold the lot to new owners, who constructed a house. One of the original lawyers for the state indicates that erosion has accelerated since 1994 and the house is in danger of falling into the inlet. The owners applied to the Coastal Council for an exception (variance) to the coastal preservation law to put large sand bags in front of the house in an attempt to save it; the state allowed them to do this, but not to put up a retaining wall.

2. *The Historical Basis for Physical and Regulatory Takings.* Takings jurisprudence involves several levels of questions. The first is historical: Is a regulatory taking consistent with the original intent of the drafters of the Constitution? Most students of takings history argue that the Fifth Amendment was intended to apply only to physical appropriations.* Proponents of Justice Scalia's approach in *Lucas* agree that the history of the Fifth Amendment is thin but argue that it reflects Lockean respect for private property.**

3. *Is a Coherent Takings Doctrine Possible?* Assuming that regulation that does not involve physical expropriation may amount to a taking, when does it do so? Academic commentators have tried to guide courts on how to decide when regulations that severely diminish the economic value of a tract of land constitute a taking either by looking at the purpose of the regulation or by applying criteria to evaluate the

---

*F. Bosselman et al., The Taking Issue: A Study of the Constitutional Limits of Governmental Authority to Regulate the Use of Privately Owned Land without Paying Compensation to the Owners (1973); Hart, Colonial Land Use Law and Its Significance for Modern Takings Doctrine, 109 Harv. L. Rev. 1252 (1996); Treanor, The Original Understanding of the Takings Clause and the Political Process, 95 Colum. L. Rev. 782 (1995); Treanor, The Origins and Significance of the Just Compensation Clause of the Fifth Amendment, 94 Yale L.J. 694 (1985).

**R. Epstein, Takings: Private Property and the Power of Eminent Domain (1985).

fairness of not compensating an impacted property owner. The late Professor Allison Dunham contributed an influential answer by distinguishing between government activities designed to prevent a landowner from undertaking an activity that harms other landowners and those intended to force a landowner to benefit others. Dunham, A Legal and Economic Basis for City Planning, 58 Colum. L. Rev. 650, 664 (1958). Much subsequent commentary is a variation on this theme.* How would you classify a land use regulation intended to conserve biodiversity under each of these dichotomies? The relationship between the harm-benefit approach and the *Lucas* analytical framework has been described as follows:

> Although *Lucas* purported to reject the harm-benefit test as neither "objective" nor "value-free," *Lucas* itself incorporated common law nuisance into takings law.** Both the harm-benefit test and the approach adopted in *Lucas* share the notion of harm as socially defined. The critical difference between the two approaches is that the *Lucas* inquiry attempts to enshrine common law historical understandings of harm into the takings doctrine, whereas the harm-benefit test looks to contemporary community norms, which are influenced but not dictated by historical allocations of rights. [Lin, The Unifying Role of Harm in Environmental Law, 2006 Wis. L. Rev. 897, 934.]

Commentators who find the harm-benefit distinction to be too indeterminate to decide whether a compensable taking has occurred have sought to ascertain when compensation is justly due as a result of governmental interference with recognized property relationships. Some have invoked Jeremy Bentham, who defined property as a settled expectation of undisturbed use and enjoyment, and then asked the question, When can the government legitimately claim that a regulation does not frustrate legitimate expectations? Relying both on utilitarian and Rawlsian justifications for property and the legitimacy of state regulation, in a classic article Professor Frank Michelman framed the critical issue as whether the state gave fair prior notice that it would not recognize individual claims to exploit the resource. Michelman, Property, Utility, and Fairness: Comments on the Ethical Foundations of Just Compensation Law, 80 Harv. L. Rev. 1165 (1967).

---

*Professor Sax recast the harm-benefit test as an arbitration-enterprise versus appropriation and then as a conflict resolution versus expropriation test. Sax, Takings and the Police Power, 74 Yale L.J. 36, 67 (1964); Sax, Takings: Private Property and Public Rights, 81 Yale L.J. 149, 172 (1971).

**In rejecting the harm-benefit test as a viable means of determining when land use regulation amounts to a taking, Justice Scalia asserted that "the distinction between 'harm-preventing' and 'benefit-conferring' regulation is often in the eye of the beholder. It is quite possible, for example, to describe in either fashion the ecological, economic, and esthetic concerns that inspired the South Carolina Legislature in the present case. One could say that imposing a servitude on Lucas's land is necessary in order to prevent his use of it from 'harming' South Carolina's ecological resources; or, instead, in order to achieve the 'benefits' of an ecological preserve." *Lucas*, 505 U.S. at 1024. He added that "[a] given restraint will be seen as mitigating 'harm' to the adjacent parcels or securing a 'benefit' for them, depending upon the observer's evaluation of the relative importance of the use that the restraint favors." Id. at 1025. According to Scalia, the constitutionality of land use regulations should not depend on whether statutes like the South Carolina law contain findings that the targets of regulation are inflicting harm on the community. "Since such a justification can be formulated in practically every case, this amounts to a test of whether the legislature has a stupid staff. We think the Takings Clause requires courts to do more than insist upon artful harm-preventing characterizations." Id. at 1025 n.12.

4. *The Green Critique.* Another level of analysis focuses on the nature of private property and the role that it should play in society. The conventional view is that strong, exclusive property rights are the keystone of commerce and nonarbitrary government. See Rose, Property as a Keystone Right, 71 Notre Dame L. Rev. 329 (1996). In contrast, the basic environmental critique of *Lucas* is that the Court's concept of property is too individualistic and insufficiently communitarian. In A Sand County Almanac, Aldo Leopold identified the institution of private property as a primary stumbling block to environmental stewardship. This argument and his land ethic form the basis for developing theories of "green property." Green property theory seeks to incorporate the principle of stewardship into the individualistic liberal theories of property. It stresses that the natural interconnectedness of the arbitrary divisions of land produced by the common law justify more stringent limitations on individual parcel use to protect the integrity of remnant ecosystems.*

5. Lucas *Defenses.* Are there any justifications for not requiring compensation for a regulation whose application results in a deprivation of all economically viable use? The *Lucas* majority offers such a justification. Most of the attention has been focused on Justice Scalia's statement that a landowner has no right to compensation if the regulation duplicates a restriction that inheres "in the title itself, in the restrictions that background principles of the State's law of property or nuisance already place on land ownership." In his concurring opinion, Justice Kennedy suggested that the background principles justification was intended by Justice Scalia to be a very narrow justification because it looks backward to a natural-law Blackstonian vision of the common law, which imposes minimal restraints on land development and thus excludes contemporary biodiversity regulation. He suggested, however, that the state could recognize other limitations through legislation.** The background principles test may be broader than Justice Scalia envisions because there are many common law doctrines (such as the public trust doctrine) that limit legitimate investment-backed expectations.

6. *Timing Questions.* Suppose that a property owner asserting a regulatory takings claim purchased the property after the adoption of the regulatory scheme being challenged. Should that fact alone preclude the owner from demonstrating a sufficient interference with investment-backed expectations to support a claim for compensation? In Palazzolo v. Rhode Island, 533 U.S. 606 (2001), Rhode Island defended a constitutional challenge by the owner of a wetland parcel to the state's denial of a development permit on the ground that the property was acquired after

---

*See Goldstein, Green Wood in the Bundle of Sticks: Fitting Environmental Ethics and Ecology into Real Property Law, 25 B.C. Envtl. Aff. L. Rev. 347 (1998); Frazier, The Green Alternative to Classical Liberal Property Theory, 20 Vt. L. Rev. 299, 357-363 (1995); Frazier, Protecting Ecological Integrity within the Balancing Function of Property Law, 28 Envtl. L. 53 (1998); Freyfogle, The Construction of Ownership, 1996 U. Ill. L. Rev. 173 (1996); Freyfogle, The Owning and Taking of Sensitive Lands, 43 UCLA L. Rev. 77 (1995); Sax, Property Rights and the Economy of Nature: Understanding Lucas v. South Carolina Coastal Council, 45 Stan. L. Rev. 1433, 1447-1448 (1993); Bosselman, Four Land Ethics: Order, Reform, Responsibility, Opportunity, 24 Envtl. L. 1439 (1994).

**For discussion of cases recognizing statutory or regulatory enactments as "background principles" for purposes of the *Lucas* exception, see Glicksman, Making a Nuisance of Takings Law, 3 Wash. U. J.L. & Pol'y 149 (2000). Blumm & Ritchie, Lucas's Unlikely Legacy: The Rise of Background Principles as Categorical Takings Defenses, 29 Harv. Envtl. L. Rev. 321 (2005), argue that courts have recognized a wide variety of categorical nuisance defenses to takings claims.

the state enacted its regulatory program. Justice Kennedy's majority opinion rejected the contention that those who purchase after the regulation goes into effect are automatically barred from asserting a successful takings claim under *Lucas* based on adverse economic impact, concluding that "the state may not put so potent a Hobbesian stick into the Lockean bundle." Justice O'Connor's concurring opinion, however, posited that the timing of the purchase may be relevant under the multi-factor balancing test enunciated in Penn Central Transp. Co. v. New York City, 438 U.S. 104 (1978). That test applies when an owner has suffered adverse economic impact that does not amount to a complete denial of all economically viable use. It requires courts to assess the economic effect of the regulation on the parcel as a whole, the extent to which the regulation interferes with reasonable investment-backed expectations, and the character of the government action. A person who acquires property knowing that it is already regulated may have a difficult time convincing a court that the regulation interferes with his or her legitimate expectations at the time of purchase.

The Court in *Palazzolo* remanded so that the state courts could determine if the permit denial was a taking. On remand, the superior court found no taking because one-half of the waters were subject to the public trust and thus could not be filled, and development of the site would constitute a public nuisance. Palazzolo v. Rhode Island, 2005 WL 1645974 (R.I. Super. July 5, 2005).

7. *Defining the Regulated Parcel. Lucas* establishes that a regulation that deprives property of all economically viable use is a per se taking. In order to apply that test, one must ascertain what the regulated "property" is. Similarly, courts applying the *Penn Central* balancing test must ascertain, among other things, the degree of the economic impact that the regulation has on the property of the takings claimant. Again, how should courts define the "property"? At least as far back as *Penn Central*, the Supreme Court has directed courts to base takings analysis on the impact of regulation on the "parcel as a whole." The Court reaffirmed that approach in Tahoe-Sierra Preservation Council, Inc. v. Tahoe-Sierra Regional Planning Agency, 535 U.S. 302 (2002). The issue was whether a moratorium on development imposed during the process of devising a comprehensive land use plan triggered takings liability under the *Lucas* per se test. The Tahoe Regional Planning Agency (TRPA) imposed the moratorium for 32 months in order to maintain the status quo pending completion of a study on the impact of development on Lake Tahoe, which Mark Twain described as "not merely transparent, but dazzlingly, brilliantly so," and the adoption of a strategy for environmentally sound growth around the Lake.

The owners of property subject to the moratorium initiated a facial attack on the moratorium. They claimed that the enactment of a temporary regulation that, while in effect, denies a property owner all viable economic use amounts to a per se taking under *Lucas*, requiring the payment of compensation equal to the use value of the property for the period the moratorium is in effect. The Court had stated in *Penn Central* that takings jurisprudence

> does not divide a single parcel into discrete segments and attempt to determine whether rights in a particular segment have been entirely abrogated. In deciding whether a particular governmental action has effected a taking, this Court focuses rather both on the character of the action and on the nature and extent of the interference with rights in the parcel as a whole.

438 U.S. at 130-131. In *Tahoe-Sierra*, the Court applied that principle to reject the *Lucas* claim as follows:

> Certainly, our holding that the permanent "obliteration of the value" of a fee simple estate constitutes a categorical taking does not answer the question whether a regulation prohibiting any economic use of land for a 32-month period has the same legal effect. Petitioners seek to bring this case under the rule announced in *Lucas* by arguing that we can effectively sever a 32-month segment from the remainder of each landowner's fee simple estate, and then ask whether that segment has been taken in its entirety by the moratoria. Of course, defining the property interest taken in terms of the very regulation being challenged is circular. With property so divided, every delay would become a total ban; the moratorium and the normal permit process alike would constitute categorical takings. Petitioners' "conceptual severance" argument is unavailing because it ignores *Penn Central*'s admonition that in regulatory takings cases we must focus on "the parcel as a whole." We have consistently rejected such an approach to the "denominator" question. See [Keystone Bituminous Coal Ass'n v. DeBenedictis, 480 U.S. 470, 495 (1987).] The starting point for the court's analysis should have been to ask whether there was a total taking of the entire parcel; if not, then *Penn Central* was the proper framework.
>
> An interest in real property is defined by the metes and bounds that describe its geographic dimensions and the term of years that describes the temporal aspect of the owner's interest. Both dimensions must be considered if the interest is to be viewed in its entirety. Hence, a permanent deprivation of the owner's use of the entire area is a taking of "the parcel as a whole," whereas a temporary restriction that merely causes a diminution in value is not. Logically, a fee simple estate cannot be rendered valueless by a temporary prohibition on economic use, because the property will recover value as soon as the prohibition is lifted.
>
> Neither *Lucas* . . . nor any of our other regulatory takings cases compels us to accept petitioners' categorical submission. In fact, these cases make clear that the categorical rule in *Lucas* was carved out for the "extraordinary case" in which a regulation permanently deprives property of all value; the default rule remains that, in the regulatory taking context, we require a more fact specific inquiry. [535 U.S. at 330-332.]

In Lingle v. Chevron U.S.A., Inc., 544 U.S. 528 (2005), the Court described both permanent physical invasions and total economic wipeouts as "two relatively narrow categories" and reaffirmed the applicability of the *Penn Central* balancing test when a regulation involves neither of these kinds of categorical takings.

8. *The Relevance of Ends-Means Fit.* In *Lingle*, a unanimous Court eliminated one method of demonstrating a regulatory taking. It repudiated oft-cited dicta that originated in Agins v. City of Tiburon, 447 U.S. 255 (1981), and squarely held that a regulation that does not substantially advance the purported government interest does not amount to a taking. The absence of such a fit between the ends sought and the means chosen to achieve them is irrelevant to the takings inquiry because it provides no information about the magnitude or distribution of the regulatory burden.

9. *Takings and the ESA.* In 1992-1993, California and the federal Bureau of Reclamation (BoR) reduced water deliveries to state permit holders and federal contractees to comply with a NMFS biological opinion. Tulare Lake Basin Water Storage Dist. v. United States, 49 Fed. Cl. 313 (2001), held that a 3 percent reduction of federal contract entitlements over a two-year period constituted a per se physical taking, rather than a regulatory taking, because the government substituted itself

for the contract project beneficiary. Previous ESA cases held that a state water rights claim conferred no immunity from ESA compliance duties, *e.g.*, Kandra v. United States, 145 F. Supp. 2d 1192 (D. Or. 2001), but *Tulare Lake* rejected the argument that the state's public trust doctrine was a background title limitation.

Another Court of Federal Claims judge reached the opposite result. Irrigators in the Klamath Project, located in California and Oregon, sued the federal government for $1 billion after irrigation deliveries were substantially cut off during a drought in 2001 to conserve listed fish and birds. Klamath Irrigation Dist. v. United States, 67 Fed. Cl. 504 (2005), found no physical taking and held that individual farmers had only contract and not property rights in unappropriated water. In addition, many reclamation contracts, including those in the Klamath, absolved the government of liability for "water shortages—hydrological, regulatory, or hybrid—that may occur within the system." The court also suggested that even if the contracts did not specifically provide for delivery interruptions, the ESA could be characterized as a sovereign act that overrode the BoR's duties under the Reclamation Act.*

10. *State Takings Legislation.* In recent years, some state legislatures have sought to provide a level of protection for regulated property owners that exceeds that provided by the takings clause of the 14th Amendment. Oregon provides a particularly dramatic example. During the 2004 general election, Oregon voters approved Ballot Measure 37, codified at Or. Rev. Stat. Ann. §197.352. The statute requires the state and local governments within the state to either provide just compensation to landowners for reductions in the fair market value of private property whose use is restricted by "land use regulations" or modify, remove, or not apply those regulations. It defines "land use regulations" broadly to include any statute regulating the use of land or any interest in land; administrative rules and goals of the Land Conservation and Development Commission; local government comprehensive plans, zoning ordinances, land division ordinances, and transportation ordinances; and statutes and administrative rules regulating farming and forest practices. Property owners whose neighbors were exempted from land use regulation as a result of the adoption of Ballot Measure 37 filed a declaratory judgment action, alleging, among other things, that the statute improperly intruded on the plenary power of the legislature, violated the separation-of-powers principles of the state constitution, and violated the due process clause of the 14th amendment to the U.S. Constitution. The trial court declared Measure 37 to be unconstitutional on five grounds. It concluded, for example, that the people, acting through the initiative process, had improperly limited the legislature's plenary power to regulate to protect the public health, safety, and welfare, stating that "a government cannot be forced to choose between exercising its plenary power to regulate for [these purposes] or paying private parties to comply with the law."

The Oregon Supreme Court reversed, upholding the statute. MacPherson v. Department of Admin. Serv., 130 P.3d 308 (Or. 2006). It reasoned:

> Oregon's legislative bodies have not divested themselves of the right to enact new land use regulations in the future. Nothing in Measure 37 forbids the Legislative Assembly or the people from enacting new land use statutes, from repealing all land use statutes, or

*Cf. Benson, The *Tulare* Case: Water Rights, The Endangered Species Act, and the Fifth Amendment, 32 Envtl. L. 551 (2002). The author argues that the court in *Tulare Lake* should have applied the *Penn Central* balancing test because the taking was regulatory, and denied taking liability because there was evidence of neither economic damage nor a loss of reasonable investment-backed expectations, given that water rights are subject to the public trust and the reasonable use doctrine.

from amending or repealing Measure 37 itself. Simply stated, Measure 37 is an exercise of the plenary power, not a limitation on it. The measure does not impair the plenary power of the Legislative Assembly or the people's exercise of their initiative power. The trial court's contrary conclusion was error.

Id. at 315. The court also held that Measure 37 did not violate the state constitution's "equal privileges and immunities" provision by limiting the compensation obligation to landowners who acquired their property prior to enactment of the land use regulations that they wish to avoid, or its separation-of-powers provision, either by intruding on the executive power or by failing to provide adequate safeguards to prevent improper use of the power conferred. The trial court also held that the statute violated both procedural and substantive due process guaranteed by the U.S. Constitution. The Supreme Court disagreed, rejecting the plaintiffs' argument that Measure 37 allows claimants to demand payment for the economic impact of a regulatory scheme that did not rise to the level of a taking under the Fifth Amendment to the United States Constitution, thereby giving rise to "reverse extortion." It added:

> The people, in exercising their initiative power, were free to enact Measure 37 in furtherance of policy objectives such as compensating landowners for a diminution in property value resulting from certain land use regulations or otherwise relieving landowners from some of the financial burden of certain land use regulations. Neither policy is irrational; no one seriously can assert that Measure 37 is not reasonably related to those policy objectives. [Id. at 322.]

What are the likely effects of Ballot Measure 37 on land use and environmental regulation? According to one critic of the measure, "In the face of Measure 37, there is a tangible threat of a regulation rollback on a property-by-property basis, leading to an incoherent patchwork of land use regulations and reluctance by state, regional, or local governments to undertake most new land use regulations because of the Measure." Sullivan, Year Zero: The Aftermath of Measure 37, 38 Urb. Law. 237, 272 (2006).*

---

*See also Clune, Government Hardly Could Go On: Oregon's Measure 37, Implications for Land Use Planning and a More Rational Means of Compensation, 38 Urb. Law. 275 (2006) (asserting that, due to the Measure's failure to provide a source for compensation, the statute "threatens to void the state's entire land use planning system," and warning that "similar initiatives will likely be proposed elsewhere"). See generally Symposium, Ballot Measure 37: The Redrafting of Oregon's Landscape, 36 Envtl. L. 1 (2006).

VI

PROTECTING THE AIR RESOURCE

It isn't pollution that's harming the environment. It's the impurities in our air and water that are doing it.

Former Vice President Dan Quayle, quoted in New Orleans Times-Picayune, June 14, 1998, at E1

The problem of air pollution prompted Congress, after 15 years of study, to enact a complex, expensive, and pervasive federal regulatory statute, the Clean Air Act of 1970 (CAA). The Act, the first of the many pollution statutes enacted during the environmental decade, regulates all new vehicles and hundreds of thousands of large and small stationary sources throughout the nation. It is appropriate for several reasons to select the CAA as the first major pollution control legislation to be analyzed in this casebook. First, the Act was the model for other federal environmental programs. Second, it relies on a variety of regulatory techniques (including ambient, performance, and design standards), allowing us to assess the strengths and weaknesses of the regulatory approaches used throughout environmental law.

Third, the CAA was the first federal pollution control statute to incorporate economic incentive–based approaches, such as marketable permits, as an important component of the arsenal Congress chose to achieve its environmental protection goals. In his classic book Pollution, Property and Prices (1968), the Canadian economist John Dales argued that the most efficient way to control pollution is to charge for the right to emit amounts up to a government-established ceiling and to create markets in pollution rights. Supporters of this approach assert that it minimizes the costs involved in controlling pollution. The tradable SO_2 permit program adopted by Congress in the 1990 CAA amendments, which many believe has efficiently mitigated the adverse effects of acid rain, has led to other experiments in market environmentalism, under the CAA and elsewhere.

Fourth, the CAA provides an opportunity to examine the evolution of an environmental regulatory program as it responds to unanticipated implementation obstacles and the discovery of previously unknown environmental risks. Despite the considerable improvement in air quality that has been achieved in response to the Act's mandates, the CAA has not eliminated air pollution in urban centers, particularly in the most intractable areas, such as the Los Angeles basin. The persistence of these pockets of air pollution has raised difficult policy questions about the most efficient and equitable means of achieving the CAA's health-related goals by bringing the nation into compliance with the statute's fundamental feature, the national ambient air quality standards. In addition, the nation has faced air quality issues that were unforeseen at the time of the Act's adoption in 1970 and that were thus unaddressed in the original version of the statute. These include acid rain, stratospheric ozone depletion, and global climate change. Congress tackled the first two problems in the 1990 amendments to the CAA, but it has yet to take meaningful action to address climate change and, indeed, the very question of whether the statute vests in EPA the authority to regulate important greenhouse gases such as CO_2 remains unsettled.

Fifth, the CAA provides an example of a regulatory program whose implementation requires deciding how to provide equitable treatment of the different kinds of sources that contribute to an environmental problem. The Act has prompted significant emissions reductions from stationary sources such as industrial facilities. It has been less successful at combating pollution from automobiles. Should the focus of future emission reduction efforts shift from stationary to mobile sources? The pursuit of rigorous efforts to reduce pollution from cars and trucks has the potential to affect individual lifestyle choices by constraining, for example, the use of automobiles for commuting. Is the American public willing to adjust to such changes? See, e.g., Kentucky Res. Council, Inc. v. EPA, 304 F. Supp. 2d 920, 923 (W.D. Ky. 2004) (stating that "many believe that [an automobile vehicle emission testing program] was 'intrusive and wasteful'"). As the materials in this chapter indicate, the fate of several provisions of the 1990 CAA amendments designed to crack down on mobile source emissions casts serious doubt on this point.

Sixth, the CAA raises difficult questions of environmental federalism involving the choice of the level of government to which the responsibility for formulating pollution control policies should be allocated. Many of these questions are addressed in Chapter 2, which covers the topic of federalism and environmental law in a variety of contexts. Federalism questions arising under the CAA are noted throughout this chapter.

Finally, air pollution creates trans-boundary disputes (both interstate and international) that have posed difficult technical and political problems. For example, even if emissions reduction in a polluted area requires aggressive steps, ambient concentrations of pollution in the area may remain higher than the levels mandated by the national ambient air quality standards because of emissions in upwind states and cities. Is it fair to require costly further reductions in upwind sources when the benefits of those reductions will not be enjoyed by those who bear the costs? Is it fair to require those living in the affected areas to bear the brunt of eliminating pollution attributable to activities from which they do not benefit? Policymakers responsible for implementing the CAA continue to grapple with these and similar dilemmas.

A. AIR POLLUTION: TYPES, SOURCES, IMPACTS, AND CONTROL TECHNIQUES

1. Pollutants and Their Sources

Like much of environmental law, air pollution control law relies on a factual foundation that is more scientifically sophisticated than those underpinning other legal regimes with which you may be familiar. Chemistry, engineering, medicine, and meteorology interact with law in the production of modern air quality control policies. Scientific understanding of air pollution is constantly in flux, which challenges air quality management schemes to remain ever ready for change. See Pedersen, Why the Clean Air Act Works Badly, 129 U. Pa. L. Rev. 1059, 1062 (1981).

Air pollution consists of particles and gases in the air that, for various reasons, are viewed as undesirable. Whether a substance is a pollutant necessarily involves a social judgment; an air pollutant may be a valuable resource that is simply out of place in the air. Urban air pollutants include carbon monoxide, oxides of sulfur and nitrogen, a great variety of hydrocarbon compounds, and trace amounts of industrial materials such as lead, mercury, asbestos, and chlorine.

Not all pollution is man-made. For example, hydrocarbons and hydrogen sulfide (later becoming sulfur oxides) form when organic materials decompose; forest fires and volcanoes release tons of carbon monoxide, hydrocarbons, and particulate matter into the air; naturally occurring "background" radiation augments that caused by human activities; and the introduction of lead into the environment by humans adds to levels occurring naturally. Although widely derided, President Reagan's assertion that trees cause pollution has some validity, 19 Env't Rep. (BNA) 1086 (1988); the story is not nearly that simple, however. Plants emit gaseous volatile organic compounds (VOCs) called terpenes. Although these substances were not a problem a century ago, today they react with oxides of nitrogen from car exhaust to generate ground-level ozone. See, e.g., Di Carlo et al., Missing OH Reactivity in a Forest: Evidence for Unknown Reactive Biogenic VOCs, 304 Science 722 (2004). See also Virginia v. EPA, 108 F.3d 1397, 1400 n.1 (D.C. Cir. 1997) (citing the "heightened appreciation of the importance of reactive [VOCs] emitted by vegetation"). Trees, of course, are also beneficial to the environment, both directly and indirectly. They produce oxygen; help move carbon dioxide from the air to the soil, where it can be dissolved in water; and filter airborne particulates that settle on their leaves and are washed to the ground by rain. They also lower the temperature on hot days, which can reduce the demand for electricity-dependent air conditioning, whose generation causes air pollution.

Major Conventional Pollutants. Several air pollutants appear in such quantities or cause such serious harm that they have received major regulatory attention over the past several decades. Table 6-1 summarizes the adverse effects of air pollutants currently regulated as so-called criteria pollutants under the CAA. The odorless and colorless gas carbon monoxide (CO) forms when fossil fuels do not burn completely. Vehicles are its major source, and because of its weight, CO tends to collect in city street "canyons." CO bonds strongly with hemoglobin in the blood, and as a result impairs mental functions and fetal development, and aggravates cardiovascular diseases. Controls on motor vehicles require proper engine tuning and catalytic or thermal exhaust gas conversion to form combustible compounds.

Nitrogen oxides form when air is heated, principally in motor vehicle engines and high-temperature power plant furnaces. Nitrogen dioxide (NO_2) is a pungent, brownish-red gas that aggravates respiratory and cardiovascular diseases, causes kidney inflammation, impairs visibility, and retards plant growth. Abatement techniques, which are less effective than those for other pollutants, include catalytic control of motor vehicle emissions and "scrubbing" of stack gases with caustic substances or urea.

Like CO, gaseous and particulate hydrocarbon compounds (HCs) form when fuels or other carbon-bearing substances are burned. Vehicle engines and fuel evaporation are the major sources of these VOCs, but they can also escape during the

TABLE 6-1

Effects of Ambient Air Pollutants Regulated by the Clean Air Act

Pollutant	Effects
Ozone	Respiratory tract problems such as difficulty in breathing, reduced lung function, possible premature aging of lung tissue, and asthma; eye irritation; nasal congestion; reduced resistance to infection; damage to trees and crops
Particulate matter	Eye and throat irritation, bronchitis, lung damage; impaired visibility; cancer
Carbon monoxide	Impairment of blood's ability to carry oxygen; damage to cardiovascular, nervous, and pulmonary systems
Sulfur dioxide	Respiratory tract problems, including diminished lung capacity and permanent damage to lung tissue; primary component of "killer fogs"; precursor of acid rain, which damages trees, vegetation, and aquatic life
Nitrogen dioxide	Respiratory illnesses and lung damage, damage to immune system; precursor of acid rain
Lead	Brain damage and retardation, especially in children

Source: G. Bryner, Blue Skies, Green Politics: The Clean Air Act of 1990, 43 (1993).

manufacture or handling of asphalt, rubber, and petroleum products. Rotting organic materials, home fireplaces, and forest fires also generate HCs. VOCs contribute to the health problems and visibility impairment associated with smog because they are major precursors in the formation of photochemical oxidants through atmospheric reactions. HC control techniques are analogous to those for CO emissions.

Photochemical oxidants are formed when precursor pollutants such as HCs and NO_x react with each other and with atmospheric gases in the presence of sunlight. In combination, they appear to produce smog, whose principal oxidant component is ozone (O_3).* Photochemical oxidants aggravate respiratory and cardiovascular illnesses. Exposure to ozone for six to seven hours at relatively low concentrations can significantly reduce lung function and induce respiratory inflammation in healthy individuals during periods of moderate exercise. EPA, National Air Quality and Emissions Trend Report, 1993 Executive Summary. A 1998 study found a correlation between elevated ozone levels and lung cancer in nonsmoking men. 29 Env't Rep. (BNA) 1634 (1998). A later study covering 95 large U.S. urban communities that include about 40 percent of the total U.S. population found a statistically significant association between short-term (daily or weekly) changes in ozone and mortality, and concluded that exposure to short-term spikes in ground-level ozone concentrations may be linked to thousands of deaths a year in the United States. Bell et al., Ozone and Short-Term Mortality in 95 US Urban Communities, 1987-2000, 292 J. Am. Med. Ass'n 2372 (2004). Similarly, researchers at the Yale School of Forestry and Environmental Studies concluded that reductions in ozone pollution by about 35 percent

* "Although ozone in the lower atmosphere harms ambient (breathable) air quality, ozone in the stratosphere prevents cancers caused by overexposure to the sun's ultraviolet radiation. Ironically, destruction of stratospheric ozone tends to increase ambient ozone levels by permitting more ultraviolet radiation to reach the surface of the Earth." Virginia v. United States, 74 F.3d 517, 519 n.1 (4th Cir. 1996).

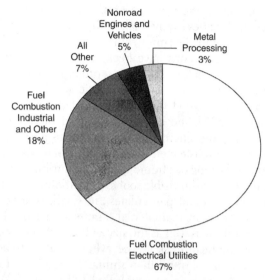

FIGURE 6-1
SO_2: What Is It? Where Does It Come From?

Source: www.epa.gov/air/urbaniar/SO_2/what1.html

could save about 4,000 deaths annually in the United States.[*] Study Links Smog Increase, Urban Deaths, http://www.cnn.com/2004/HEALTH/11/16/smog.study.reut.index.html. Ozone also contributes to visibility impairment; damages rubber, textiles, and paints; and causes plants to drop their leaves and fruit prematurely. Controls require reductions in NO_x, HC, and possibly sulfur dioxide emissions.

Lead, a ubiquitous, naturally occurring element, appears in the air as an oxide aerosol or dust. The principal source of ambient lead used to be emissions from motor vehicles that burned leaded gasoline. Today, lead smelting and processing, the manufacture of lead products, the combustion of coal and refuse, and the use of pesticides containing lead continue to contribute to ambient lead pollution. Lead accumulates in body organs and impairs bone growth and the development and functioning of the nervous, circulatory, and renal systems. Exposure has been reduced by eliminating lead additives from gasoline and paint and lead soldering from tin cans and by instituting dietary controls.

A colorless gas with a pungent odor, sulfur dioxide (SO_2) forms when coal and oil are burned in power plants or space heaters or when sulfur-bearing metal ores such as lead and copper are smelted (see Figure 6-1). Electric utilities produce a major

[*] A series of studies published in the July 2005 issue of Epidemiology concluded that for every 10 parts per billion increase in daily ozone levels, the death rate over the next three days goes up about 0.85-0.87 percent. One study found a strong short-term association between ozone and mortality, particularly cardiovascular and respiratory mortality. Older people and people living in cities without air conditioning seem to be at particular risk. See, e.g., Bell et al., A Meta-Analysis of Time-Series Studies of Ozone and Mortality with Comparison to the National Morbidity, Mortality, and Air Pollution Study, 16 Epidemiology 436 (2005); Levy et al., Ozone Exposure and Mortality: An Empiric Bayes Metaregression Analysis, 16 Epidemiology 458 (2005); Ito et al., Associations between Ozone and Daily Mortality: Analysis and Meta-Analysis, 16 Epidemiology 446 (2005). For further information, see EPA, Air Quality Criteria for Ozone and Related Photochemical Oxidants (Final 2006), http://cfpub.epa.gov/ncea/cfm/recordisplay.cfm?deid=149923.

portion of the SO_2 emitted in the United States. SO_2 aggravates respiratory diseases and irritates the eyes. Asthmatics, individuals with cardiovascular disease or chronic lung disease (such as bronchitis or emphysema), children,[*] and the elderly are particularly susceptible. SO_2 emissions have been successfully reduced by using low-sulfur fuels, removing sulfur before fuel use, scrubbing stack gases with lime, and using catalytic technology to convert SO_2 to sulfuric acid.

The public has a fairly good understanding of the polluting nature of total suspended particulates (TSPs), the collection of solid or liquid particles such as dust, pollen, soot, metals, and chemical compounds dispersed in the atmosphere. Cinders and soot from urban waste incinerators are common sources, but any burning or abrasion of a solid or splashing of a liquid typically contributes to TSPs. Particle size and weight vary dramatically, from visible soot to air particles detectable only under an electron microscope. Power plant particulates are small, spherical, glassy particles usually less than 50 microns in diameter, the same as a typical human hair (see Figure 6-2). The composition as well as the size of the particle may be determinative of the degree of the public health risk it poses when inhaled. In addition, soot from certain sources may be more harmful than similarly sized particles from a different source. See Revkin, E.P.A. Finds Some Soot Is Bad, Other Soot Is Worse, N.Y. Times, Sept. 11, 2001, at D1.

Particulates exacerbate asthma and other respiratory or cardiovascular symptoms, sully and damage building materials, impair visibility, contribute to cloud formation, and interfere with plant growth.[**] Researchers believe that settleable particles (50 microns and larger) present few health risks compared with aerosols (smaller than 50 microns) and fine particulates (less than 3 microns in diameter). Fine particulates, which can penetrate deeply into the lungs, may be carcinogenic, while many of the larger particulates now regulated are caught in the nose and pulmonary mucous membranes and eventually excreted. A study of 500,000 people in 116 U.S. cities indicated that long-term exposure to microscopic soot particles significantly increases the risk of lung cancer and heart disease. Revkin, Soot Particles Strongly Tied to Lung Cancer, Study Finds, N.Y. Times, Mar. 6, 2002, at A14. Studies also have found that minor increases in fine particle concentrations are associated with higher hospital admission rates for cardiovascular and respiratory problems, especially heart failure. Dominici et al., Fine Particulate Air Pollution and Hospital Admission for Cardiovascular and Respiratory Diseases, 295 J. Am. Med. Ass'n 1127 (2006).[***] TSPs are reduced by up to 99.75 percent by cleaning stack gases with electrostatic precipitators,

---

[*]Researchers have linked increased concentrations of particulate matter, carbon dioxide, and nitrogen dioxide to a greater incidence of death among infants from respiratory causes and sudden infant death syndrome. Ritz et al., Air Pollution and Infant Death in Southern California, 1989-2000, 118 Pediatrics 493 (August 2006).

[**]Exposure to particulate matter also may cause heritable mutations in DNA. See Somers et al., Reductions in Particulate Air Pollution Lowers the Risk of Heritable Mutations in Mice, 304 Science 1008 (2004).

[***]In 2004 EPA reported that soot-filled air caused 15,000 premature deaths, 95,000 cases of chronic or acute bronchitis, and thousands of hospital admissions for respiratory or cardiovascular illnesses. EPA, Particulate Matter Research Program: Five Years of Progress (2004), available at http://www.epa.gov/pmresearch/pm_research_accomplishments/pdf/pm_resrach_program_five_years_of_progress.pdf. Another study found an association between exposure to vehicular traffic in urban areas and onset of myocardial infarction within one hour afterward, although the study did not attempt to determine whether the association relates primarily to traffic-related air pollution or also included stress and noise. Peters et al., Exposure to Traffic and the Onset of Myocardial Infarction, 351 New Eng. J. Med. 1721 (2004).

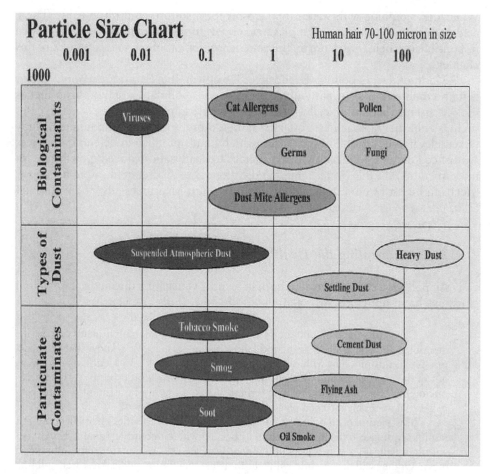

FIGURE 6-2
Particle Size Chart

Source: www.healthyairusa.com/kb_part_chart.html

scrubbers, or fabric filters. "Fugitive" emissions can be controlled by spraying construction and demolition sites with water.

The foregoing discussion suggests a natural distinction between primary pollutants, which are directly emitted as a result of human activities, and secondary pollutants, which form when human emissions combine with naturally occurring atmospheric gases, water vapor, and each other, with sunlight usually powering the chemical reactions. Although regulators' main concern may be the harm caused by secondary pollutants such as photochemical oxidants, they have to reduce them by controlling primary pollutants such as HC and NO_x.

Evidence now suggests that sulfates, very small secondary particulates derived from gaseous SO_2, may be primarily responsible for the health effects originally attributed to SO_2 and large primary particulates. Similarly, fine nitrate particles formed from NO_2 may cause many of the health effects once attributed to NO_2. Sulfate and nitrate aerosols are formed when chemical reactions occur in the atmosphere, sometimes days after the aerosols' emission from smokestacks or motor vehicles.

When they combine with water, the aerosols form sulfuric and nitric acids. These acids may then show up as acid rain, snow, or dew hundreds of miles from the source responsible for them. For more on the acid deposition problem, see section I.2 of this chapter.

Many other air pollutants endanger health or the environment only under certain conditions and in particular locales. These pollutants include toxic metals such as arsenic, beryllium, cadmium, and mercury; minerals such as asbestos; gases such as chlorine; radioactive substances; and scores of organic compounds. A study linked elevated levels of phytochelatins, which plants produce to defend themselves against cell damage induced by heavy metals, to deaths and reduced growth rates of red spruce trees in the United States and Europe. See Gawel et al., Role for Heavy Metals in Forest Decline Indicated by Phytochelatin Measurements, 381 Nature 64 (2002).

2.   Documenting the Health Effects of Air Pollution

Air pollution chiefly threatens human health. Marshaling the medical proof that emissions harm human health often defies the best efforts of scientists:

> Describing the direct physiological effects of air pollution on humans can be like describing the shape of an iceberg floating in the sea. . . . [W]e know that the most massive health problem with air pollution is not associated with identifiable episodes but in the gradual erosion of health by frequent and long-term exposures. Hypotheses linking this type of exposure with specific illness require murky assumptions and estimates that are easily attacked piecemeal by dissenters. . . .
>
> Most victims of air pollution will not die during an air episode. They will contract a respiratory disease or another symptom associated with air pollution, gradually weaken, and then typically die from pneumonia, a heart attack, or failure of some other vital organ. Or they will bear a child with a birth defect that future medical research will link to an air pollutant. Or perhaps they will develop a disease, such as cancer, caused by a dimly understood set of factors with air pollution as only one possible component. [G. Sewell, Environmental Quality Management 168-170 (1975).]

Despite these uncertainties, many studies describe the benefits of controlling air pollution. One study released in 2006, for example, found that a reduction of one microgram of soot per cubic meter of air is associated with a 3 percent decline in death rates from cardiovascular disease, respiratory illness, and lung cancer. Each such decrease may extend the lives of 75,000 Americans per year. Laden et al., Reduction in Fine Particulate Air Pollution and Mortality, 173 Am. J. Respiratory & Critical Care Med. 667 (2006). Figure 6-3 presents a continuum of risks associated with various forms of air pollution.

3.   The Evolving Mix of Emissions Sources

The contributions of various emissions sources to air pollution have shifted since the adoption of the CAA in 1970. In that year, transportation sources accounted for 46.7 percent of VOC emissions in the United States, while industrial sources contributed 32.5 percent of the total. By 1991 transportation sources contributed

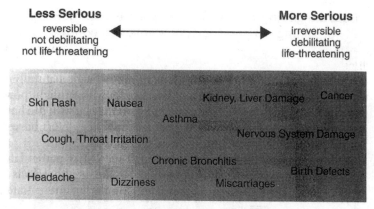

FIGURE 6-3
Which Risks Are of Greatest Concern?

Source: www.epa.gov/oar/oaqps/air_risc/3_90_022.html

only 30.1 percent of VOC emissions, with industrial sources responsible for 46.6 percent of the total. Similarly, the contribution by transportation sources to lead pollution fell dramatically, from 82.2 to 32.6 percent, between 1970 and 1991. Industrial contributions to lead pollution increased from 12.0 to 44.5 percent of the total during that same period. Statistical Abstract of the United States 1993, at 225. The Commission for Environmental Cooperation reported in 2005 that lead compounds, which are linked to cancer and birth defects, are the leading developmental toxicant released by industrial facilities in North America. Although lead emissions from mobile sources have declined dramatically due to the removal of lead from gasoline, primary metal smelters and electric utilities continue to emit large quantities of lead.* Emissions of sulfur oxides due to fuel combustion at electric utilities fell between 1970 and 1998 (from 15.8 million tons to 13.2 million tons), but emissions of nitrogen oxides from those sources increased during the same period from 4.4 million to 6.1 million tons a year. Statistical Abstract of the United States 1996, at 234; Statistical Abstract of the United States 1991, at 216.

The relative contributions of mobile sources must be examined against the backdrop of growth in the number of motor vehicles in use and vehicle miles traveled. In 1980 there were 155 million vehicles (automobiles, buses, and trucks) registered in the United States. By 1999 the number had risen to 231 million. In 1970 vehicle miles traveled in the United States totaled 1.1 billion; by 2003 that figure had increased to nearly 2.9 billion. In 1970 automobiles consumed 92.3 billion gallons of fuel in the United States; in 2003 the figure was 169.6 billion gallons. Statistical Abstract of the United States 2006, Tables 1078, 1084, 1085. Compare Figure 6-4. The number of Americans who commuted to work by automobile rose from 62 million to 97 million between 1980 and 2000, and the number of people who commuted 90 minutes or more to work rose between 1990 and 2000 from 1.8 to 3.4 million. Among the tasks

---

*See Commission for Environmental Cooperation, Taking Stock (2005), available at http://www.cec.org/takingstock/index.cfm?varlan=english.

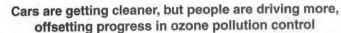

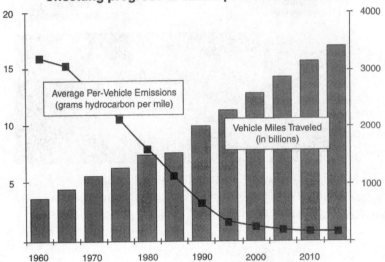

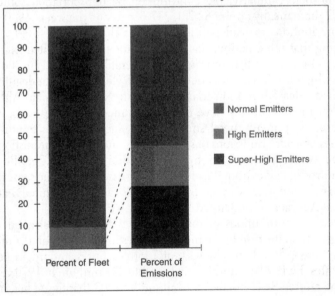

FIGURE 6-4

Source: www.epa.gov/oms/04-ozone.htm

facing air pollution control policymakers is to determine the impact of existing regulation on this mix of emissions and the future regulatory responses necessary to reduce emissions in problem areas still further.

4. The State of Air Quality and Its Improvement

Pollution levels for the six major conventional air pollutants have declined in recent years. EPA reported that ambient levels of the criteria pollutants declined by the following percentages between 1983 and 2002: lead, 94 percent; CO, 65 percent; SO_2, 54 percent; NO_2, 21 percent; and ozone, 22 percent based on one-hour data and 14 percent based on eight-hour data. EPA, Six Principal Pollutants, http://www.epa.gov/airtrends/sixpoll.html. Emissions of all of the criteria pollutants fell between 1970 and 2005.[*] EPA's Air Emissions Trend Report, http://www.epa.gov/airtrends/econ-emissions.html, shows that aggregate emissions of the six criteria pollutants have fallen by more than 50 percent since 1970, from 301.5 million tons in 1970 to 147.8 million tons in 2003. This decline occurred despite economic growth of more than 150 percent during the same period. Despite these improvements, the American Lung Association (ALA) reported in 2006 that nearly 151 million Americans (more than 51 percent of the population) lived in 369 counties with unhealthy levels of ozone and particulate pollution.[**]

5. The Economic Impact and Distributional Effects of Air Pollution and Air Pollution Control

The relationship between the economic costs and benefits of air pollution control is a matter of sharp controversy. L. Lave & E. Seskin, Air Pollution and Human Health (1977), found that the initial benefits of the CAA ($23 billion) exceeded its costs ($15 billion). An EPA report released in October 1997 asserted that benefits resulting from the statute during the period 1970-1990 were anywhere from 10 to 94 times greater than the costs it imposed, even without taking into account nonquantifiable health and environmental benefits. See Shapiro & Glicksman, Risk Regulation at Risk: Restoring A Pragmatic Approach 77-78 (2003). The agency's figures have not gone unchallenged. Crandall et al., Clearing the Air: EPA's Self-Assessment of Clean-Air Policy, 1996 Regulation #4, at 35, claim that a draft version of the EPA study failed to show that the marginal benefits of most clean-air policies are equal to or greater than the marginal costs, that the true health benefits attributable to reduced pollution levels are much less than EPA claims, and that the true costs of control are much higher than EPA's figures indicate.

---

[*]Emissions of CO fell from 197.3 million tons in 1970 to 89 million tons in 2005. The numbers (in millions of tons per year) for the other criteria pollutants and their precursors are as follows: NO_x (26.9 to 19), PM_{10} (12.2 to 2), SO_2 (31.2 to 15), VOCs (33.7 to 16), and lead (0.221 to 0.003). EPA, Air Emissions Trends—Continued Progress through 2005, http://www.epa.gov/airtrends/2006/econ-emissions.html.

[**]Cook, Most Americans Live with Unhealthy Air, Lung Association Says, but Quality Improving, 37 Env't Rep. (BNA) 941 (2006). The ALA also reported that seven of the ten cities with the worst smog pollution are in California (with Los Angeles leading the list); Houston, Dallas–Fort Worth, and Knoxville were the others. Five of the cites with the highest levels of particle pollution are also in California, along with Pittsburgh (PA), Detroit, Atlanta, Cleveland, Birmingham (AL), and Cincinnati. In an earlier report, EPA found that 243 counties in 21 states and the District of Columbia, with a total population of nearly 100 million, do not meet national ambient air quality standards for fine particulate matter. Former EPA Administrator Mike Leavitt predicted that partial conformance by 2010 would prevent at least 15,000 premature deaths and 75,000 cases of chronic bronchitis each year. 35 Env't Rep. (BNA) 1405 (2004).

The burdens and benefits of air quality control policies are almost certainly unevenly distributed among classes of emitters and receptors. Some studies indicate that the poor benefit more than the rich from these policies. See, e.g., Gianessi et al., The Distributional Effects of Uniform Air Pollution Policy, 93 Q.J. Econ. 281 (1979). Other researchers have found that residents of low- and middle-income areas in the South Coast Air Basin of California were exposed to higher levels of ozone and particulate pollution than residents of wealthier districts. Brajer & Hall, Recent Evidence on the Distribution of Air Pollution Effects, 10 Contemp. Pol. Issues 2, at 63 (April 1992). Another study concluded that racial minority groups tend to live in counties with higher emissions levels than those to which whites are exposed. Perlin et al., Distribution of Industrial Air Emissions by Income and Race in the United States: An Approach Using the Toxic Release Inventory, 29 Envtl. Sci. & Tech. 1, at 69 (January 1995).

B.   THE HISTORY OF AIR POLLUTION: FROM COMMON LAW NUISANCE TO THE CLEAN AIR ACT

Although air pollution was scarcely acknowledged as a national problem before World War II and did not move to the top of the public agenda until the end of the 1960s, the legal foundations of air pollution control were laid centuries earlier in England. The earliest relief from air pollution was provided through private common law nuisance actions; a public nuisance broadly affecting the community was subject to abatement following a jury trial. The common law crime of public nuisance is the earliest example of quasi-statutory intervention by local government to protect environmental quality.

1. Beginnings

The first smoke abatement ordinance appears to have been enacted in 1273 in London. Smoke ordinances enacted in the United States in the late nineteenth century required the manufacture of furnaces that could consume their own smoke, or forbade the burning of high-sulfur coal. Laitos, Legal Institutions and Pollution: Some Intersections between Law and History, 15 Nat. Resources J. 423, 434 (1975). The more sophisticated ordinances empowered municipal health officials and the courts to specify performance levels for air pollution controls and, occasionally, to specify the equipment needed to achieve them. They also authorized action even in the absence of proof of actual harm. Indicators such as dense smoke or the burning of soft coal became legal surrogates for actual harm. As a result, the legislature could adopt controls as a precaution without having to wait for scientific evidence to accumulate. Modern pollution control laws make extensive use of devices that foreclose inquiry into the extent and nature of the injury on which regulatory programs are predicated.

2. Early Legislation

After World War II, state and city governments expanded their arsenals of pollution control techniques, yet air pollution slowly increased, as did congressional frustration with ineffectual state efforts to combat the problem. In 1955, the federal government entered the field for the first time with a modest program of research and technical assistance directed primarily at the causes and effects of air pollution, which had not been established. Air Pollution Control Act, Pub. L. No. 84-159, 69 Stat. 322. In the 1950s, the smog in Los Angeles was linked to automobile emissions; after that the motor vehicle became the central focus of air pollution legislation. In 1960, Congress enacted a research and technical assistance program for motor vehicles. Motor Vehicle Act of 1960, Pub. L. No. 86-493, 74 Stat. 162.

Congress expanded the federal role throughout the 1960s. In 1963, it required the Department of Health, Education, and Welfare (HEW) (now called the Department of Health and Human Services) to provide the states with scientific information, called "criteria documents," on the effects of various air pollutants. Clean Air Act, Pub. L. No. 88-206, 77 Stat. 392. These studies would eventually provide the technical basis for HEW's establishment of mandatory uniform national ambient air quality standards. The 1963 legislation also empowered the secretary of HEW to initiate enforcement proceedings if pollution "endangered the health or welfare of persons." Responsibility was so diffused, however, that no effective enforcement actions were ever mounted under the 1963 Act. The Motor Vehicle Air Pollution Control Act, Pub. L. No. 89-272, 79 Stat. 992 (1965), authorized HEW to establish emissions standards for new motor vehicles and engines based on "technological feasibility and economic costs." The Air Quality Act, Pub. L. No. 90-148, 81 Stat. 485 (1967), authorized HEW to designate geographic air quality control regions. The states were to adopt ambient air quality standards for each major pollutant, subject to HEW approval, which would define the maximum levels of pollution necessary to maintain health and welfare in each region. Each state also had to adopt an implementation plan, again subject to HEW approval, specifying emissions limitations for individual sources necessary to enable the state to achieve the standards.

The 1967 Act failed completely in practice, partly because of the difficult scientific and institutional problems the federal and state agencies faced in preparing implementation plans and enforcing standards. The states lacked adequate resources for these tasks, and federal subsidies did not make up the difference. The states nevertheless accumulated considerable experience in using technology-based standards. They pioneered the use of permits that enabled regulators to obtain a specific, written agreement in advance that sources would comply with abatement requirements. See generally Currie, State Pollution Statutes, 48 U. Chi. L. Rev. 27 (1981).

3. The 1970 Act

In 1970, Congress overhauled federal air pollution control with vote margins that rivaled those on declarations of war (Senate 73-0; House of Representatives 374-1). Yet just beneath the surface of this apparent unanimity, deep conflicts lurked:

> The prevailing wisdom is that the current federal air pollution policy was chosen irrationally. . . . Scientists argue that the [Clean Air Act] is based on misconceptions about biological and physical systems. Atmospheric chemists suggest that the notion of threshold levels of emissions that are damaging to health is not supported by research. Physicists believe that the diffusion of pollutants and their chemical interaction are much more complex than can be appropriately handled by the simple standards in

the 1970 act. Engineers claim that the deadlines set by the legislation are not technically realistic. Economists, the most outspoken of critics, condemn federal regulations as inefficient, inequitable, and ineffectual. [Ingram, The Political Rationality of Innovation: The Clean Air Act Amendments of 1970, in Approaches to Controlling Air Pollution 12, 12-13 (A. Friedlaender ed., 1978).]

As the materials throughout this chapter indicate, many of these same charges continue to be raised.

4.   Conflicting Goals

The apparent "irrationality" of federal air pollution control begins with the failure at the outset to concur on what the term "air pollution" means. Its meaning hinges on which of two major pollution reduction goals is adopted. The conservation goal defines air pollution as any concentration that degrades air below the "background" levels of substances in the ambient air as a result of natural processes; pollution is any change produced artificially. The economic goal defines pollution in terms of the costs of degradation; any proposed reduction of damages from pollution must yield tangible benefits in excess of the tangible costs of cleaner air. This chapter will use the term "air pollution" to refer to air quality levels below those allowed by a legislature, agency, or court. The conflict between the conservation and economic strategies remains intense. The conservation strategy is based in part on moral and philosophical grounds. Conservationists argue that natural environments should be preserved or restored for aesthetic or moral reasons. The rational imperative of the economic goal suggests that, in a society of limited resources, the objective should be to adopt efficient pollution control levels and cost-effective reduction strategies. This can be done by converting the benefits of air pollution control, to the greatest extent possible, to monetary values, after which it becomes possible to compare at the margin the costs of emission reduction with the benefits achieved.

Proponents of the economic approach were singularly ineffectual in 1970 in convincing the public that costly air pollution controls would sacrifice other valuable social benefits that the money spent on air pollution control might bring. Most members of Congress seemed uninterested in calculating the opportunity costs of emission reductions. Further, Congress apparently ignored the likelihood that air pollution control costs vary among regions and that an efficient policy would correlate regional reduction levels and control costs.

5.   The 1977 Amendments

Private stationary sources did a passable job under the 1970 version of the CAA in reducing total emissions of some air pollutants (notably TSP, SO_2, and HC) nationwide. At the same time, the clean-air program threatened to hamper economic growth in the more developed regions of the country by making it difficult to build new sources. The 1970 Act itself gave few hints as to how new industrial facilities were to be rationally accommodated with the goal of reducing air pollution.

The initial effort by states to control mobile-source pollutants was less successful. The deadlines for achieving national ambient air quality standards were too optimistic in light of the serious oxidant and CO problems in some urban areas. In addition, the emissions standards for new vehicles did not fulfill the central abatement function expected of them because vehicle manufacturers were able to delay compliance deadlines. The manufacturers' failures forced the states to rely on transportation control strategies such as dispersing traffic, providing incentives for people to take mass transit or not to drive, instituting inspection and maintenance programs, and setting standards for older vehicles. These techniques directly affected the driving public, sometimes in ways that were viewed as exceedingly restrictive and intrusive. When states and cities balked at secondary controls, EPA tried to force them to implement transportation control plans (TCPs). The results were a political disaster. A series of lawsuits and congressional amendments to the Act quickly brought the EPA initiatives to a standstill. See, e.g., EPA v. Brown, 431 U.S. 99 (1977) (declaring challenges to TCPs moot because EPA agreed to eliminate the requirement that states adopt TCPs).

In 1977 Congress adopted a pragmatic set of "midcourse corrections" in recognition of the shortcomings of its original approach. By then Congress's proenvironmental ardor had cooled somewhat, the opposition to strong air pollution controls had rallied, the Arab oil embargo had occurred, certain components of air pollution programs had foundered on political shoals, and industry and consumers had begun to absorb the costs of controlling air pollution. On the one hand, industry secured delays in meeting the 1970 vehicle emissions standards along with concessions for coal-burning power plants and other industries. Congress endorsed extensions of the deadlines for meeting the national ambient air quality standards and provided relief from the burdensome traffic management strategies EPA had imposed to control smog. On the other hand, Congress established controls over new construction in both clean- and dirty-air areas (through a process called new source review) and took steps to prevent the erosion of existing high air quality, protect visibility, and strengthen enforcement provisions.

The 1970 Act did not include a program specifically designed to protect the pristine air quality of places like the American Southwest, where the relatively common 80-mile scenic vistas were being threatened by the growing number of coal-fired power plants in the region. The Act did state that its purpose was to "protect and enhance" the nation's air resources, a phrase the courts interpreted as requiring EPA to produce a plan for maintaining air quality in clean-air areas. In 1977, Congress endorsed the program developed by EPA in response to judicial decree by mandating a detailed pre-construction review procedure for major new stationary sources seeking to locate in clean-air areas.

6. The 1990 Amendments

Following the adoption of the 1977 amendments, the localization of air quality problems gave rise to increasing regional conflict. The northeastern states supported legislation on acid rain, but it was stalled by congressional representatives of states that were sources of high-sulfur coal, whose mining jobs would be threatened by acid rain control measures. Detroit automakers fought the enactment of more stringent controls necessary to deal with smog problems in cities like Los Angeles and Houston.

A series of factors combined to produce a set of statutory amendments in 1990 that greatly increased the length, specificity, and scope of the Act. These factors included the failure of industrial critics of the Act to accommodate their often conflicting interests; concerns that the Act failed to ensure that the costs of emission controls were justified by the benefits of cleaner air, and that the laborious process of obtaining permits for new construction hampered economic growth; and charges that EPA's implementation of the statute in the 1980s was overly solicitous of industry wish lists and insufficiently protective of the public health. See G. Bryner, Blue Skies, Green Politics: The Clean Air Act of 1990, at 88 (1993). The 1990 amendments imposed new deadlines for compliance with the national ambient air quality standards and prescribed in greater detail the means to which the states had to resort to achieve compliance, including the imposition of limits on vehicle use. The amendments transformed the mechanism for controlling hazardous air pollutants from a health-based to a primarily technology-based model in recognition of EPA's inability or unwillingness to limit emissions under the original approach. Congress adopted a new set of controls on precursors of acid deposition, which included an innovative emissions trading program. Congress phased out the production and use of ozone-depleting chemicals in an effort to protect the integrity of the stratospheric ozone layer. Finally, Congress created a federal permit program to facilitate both compliance with and enforcement of the Act's multifarious obligations.

The amended Act almost immediately came under attack as being too costly, insufficiently attentive to state and local concerns, and overly intrusive into the everyday affairs of businesses and vehicle users. Beginning in 1995, a series of minor amendments to the Act were adopted that eliminated some of the more objectionable provisions regarding automobile inspection and maintenance and mandatory employer van pooling.

C.   A SUMMARY OF THE CLEAN AIR ACT TODAY

The Clean Air Act, as amended in 1970, 1977,* and 1990,** provides the basic framework for modern air pollution control. The summary that follows highlights the key elements of this massive and complex Act. You may want to consult this summary from time to time to maintain your perspective as you move through the remaining materials in this chapter.

The Regulatory Provisions: A Preview. The CAA depends on two very different types of regulatory standards (ambient and technology-based) and two very different governmental roles (federal standard setting and state implementation). The paramount goals of the Act are to clean up dirty air to an acceptable level and to maintain high air quality where it still exists. See §101(b)(1). The federal ambient standards and state implementation plans are shaped to accomplish these goals. Other provisions, however, are keyed to the ability of air pollution control technology to reduce emissions from stationary or mobile sources at an acceptable cost. Standards and implementation procedures vary depending on two additional

---

*Pub. L. No. 95-95, 91 Stat. 685.
**Pub. L. No. 101-549, 104 Stat. 2399.

TABLE 6-2
National Ambient Air Quality Standards

Pollutant	Standard Value*	Standards Type
Carbon monoxide (CO)		
8-hour average	9 ppm (10 mg/m^3)	Primary
1-hour average	35 ppm (40 mg/m^3)	Primary
Nitrogen dioxide		
Annual arithmetic mean	0.053 ppm (100 μg/m^3)	Primary and secondary
Ozone (O$_3$)		
8-hour average	0.08 ppm	Primary and secondary
1-hour average	0.12 ppm (applies only in limited areas)	Primary and secondary
Lead (Pb)		
Quarterly average	1.5 μg/m^3	Primary and secondary
Particulate (PM$_{10}$)**		
Annual arithmetic mean	Revoked	Primary and secondary
24-hour average	150 μg/m^3	Primary and secondary
Particulate (PM$_{2.5}$)***		
Annual arithmetic mean	15 μg/m^3	Primary and secondary
24-hour average	35 μg/m^3	Primary and secondary
Sulfur dioxide (SO$_2$)		
Annual arithmetic mean	0.03 ppm (80 μ/m^3)	Primary
24-hour average	0.14 ppm (365 μg/m^3)	Primary
3-hour average	0.50 ppm (1,300 μg/m^3)	Secondary

 * Parenthetical value is approximately equivalent concentration.
 ** Particle diameter of 10 microns or less.
 *** Particle diameter of 2.5 microns or less.
 Source: www.epa.gov/air/criteria.html

factors: whether sources are stationary or mobile, and whether sources are located in clean-air or dirty-air areas of the country. When you fully understand the interaction of these four pairs of components (ambient versus technology-based standards, federal versus state implementation, stationary versus mobile sources, clean-air versus dirty-air areas), you will have a firm grasp on the bulk of the regulatory programs established by the Act.

Ambient Air Quality Standards. Ambient standards specify maximum pollutant concentrations deemed to be safe for exposure over various time periods. Because they do not specify limitations that must be placed on actual sources, ambient standards cannot constitute a complete basis for air pollution control; they must be coupled with measures limiting individual source emissions. Sections 108 and 109 of the CAA authorize EPA to promulgate national ambient air quality standards (NAAQS) by regulation after the agency has gathered the necessary scientific information in the criteria documents first required by the 1963 legislation. EPA must set primary NAAQS to protect human health with an adequate margin of safety; secondary standards are designed to protect additional environmental values such as plant and animal life, property, and aesthetic sensibilities. Standards currently exist for six "criteria pollutants." See Table 6-2.*

*For additional information on the NAAQS, see http://www.epa.gov/ttn/naaqs/.

The primary emphasis of the CAA is on the "attainment" of these ambient standards. The Act requires states to select and implement the combination of emissions limitations on stationary and mobile sources necessary to ensure that they meet and maintain the ambient standards. The states make these choices through the adoption (subject to EPA approval) of a separate state implementation plan (SIP) for each of the criteria pollutants.

Emissions Standards. Technology-based uniform national emissions standards specify the pollution control performance levels expected from particular types of air pollution sources. The Act contains four types of federally uniform emissions standards.* First, it includes technology-based standards for vehicle emissions. The 1970 Act set deadlines of five years for vehicle manufacturers to reduce CO, HC, and NO_x emissions by 90 percent from 1970 levels; the deadlines, however, were extended through a series of administrative and congressional actions. The statute currently requires that EPA issue and periodically revise standards for vehicle emissions that, in the agency's judgment, cause or contribute to a level of air pollution that may reasonably be anticipated to endanger public health or welfare. §202(a)(1). The 1990 amendments required EPA for the first time to control vehicle emissions of hazardous air pollutants such as benzene and formaldehyde. §202(*l*). The statute prevents states (except California) from setting standards for new vehicles different from those set by Congress. §209. It also regulates the use of fuels whose emissions cause or contribute to public health or welfare risks (§211(c)(1)), and prohibits the use of leaded gasoline (§211(g)) and the sale of diesel fuel with excessive sulfur content (§211(i)). State vehicle inspections and traffic management plans supplement these mechanisms.

Second, the Act requires nationally uniform new source performance standards (NSPS) for various categories of stationary sources. The NSPS require the application of the best system of emissions reduction that, taking into account such factors as cost, EPA determines has been adequately demonstrated. §111(a)(1). The NSPS cover all types of emissions that "may reasonably be anticipated to endanger public health or welfare." §111(b)(1)(A).

Third, §112 of the Act provides uniform national emission standards for hazardous air pollutants (NESHAP). Originally, EPA was to issue standards for those pollutants at the level that would provide "an ample margin of safety to protect the public health." Although hundreds of hazardous substances appeared to qualify for regulation, EPA listed only a handful of substances between 1970 and 1990 for NESHAPs preparation. The 1990 amendments completely overhauled the program for regulating hazardous air pollutants. Congress itself has established a list of 189 hazardous air pollutants. §112(b)(1). EPA must determine which source categories pose a threat of adverse human health or environmental effects through their emissions of a listed pollutant and establish emission standards for each such category. §112(c)(2). The statute authorizes two rounds of standards. The first round consists of technology-based standards that require the maximum degree of reduction that EPA determines is achievable. §112(d)(2). The standards for new sources are designed to be more stringent than those for existing sources. EPA must assess and report to Congress on any risks to the public health that remain after application of the round 1 standards. If Congress fails to act on the agency's recommendations for further legislation to

---

*Three additional emissions standards that have been combined, somewhat untidily, with the ambient standards approach will emerge later in this discussion.

address those risks, EPA must issue a second round of controls if necessary to provide an ample margin of safety to protect the public health or prevent adverse environmental effects. The statute requires the issuance of round 2 standards for any source category of carcinogenic emissions if the round 1 standards do not reduce the lifetime excess cancer risk to the most exposed individual to less than one in a million. §112(f)(2)(A).

Fourth, the statute requires that existing sources in nonattainment areas (those that have not yet achieved the NAAQS) install, at a minimum, "reasonably available control technology" (RACT). §172(c)(1).

State Implementation Plans. The nationally applicable emission standards for new vehicles and stationary sources described above constitute a principal line of attack against air pollution, but achievement of the NAAQS remains the CAA's paramount objective. The states have the primary responsibility for designing and implementing plans to achieve the ambient standards. §§107(a), 110(a)(2). In designing a SIP, state officials make many controversial decisions detailing the steps industrial plants, businesses, mobile-source owners, airports, highway departments, and local traffic control officials must take to bring the state's air quality control regions (of which the nation has been divided into more than 200) into compliance with the NAAQS. Once approved by EPA, SIPs are enforceable by both state and federal authorities. §113.

The 1977 amendments distinguished for the first time "clean-air" and "dirty-air" areas of the nation. Since then, the CAA has applied different requirements to regions that have yet to attain the NAAQS and regions that have relatively clean or even pristine air quality. The Act's nonattainment program provisions spell out SIP requirements for the former, while Congress addressed clean-air regions in the provisions dealing with the prevention of significant deterioration (PSD) of air quality. §§160-169A. The different SIP requirements for PSD and nonattainment regions apply to each SIP-controlled pollutant individually. In effect, a separate "sub-SIP" applies to each pollutant depending on its PSD or nonattainment status. Thus, the statute now divides, or "zones," the United States into PSD and nonattainment areas on a pollutant-by-pollutant basis, with overlapping designations when an area has attained the NAAQS for one pollutant but not for another.

The Nonattainment Provisions. Because many areas had still not met the NAAQS by the time it adopted the 1990 amendments, Congress tackled the nonattainment program more vigorously than it had previously. In doing so, it removed some of the discretion the states had to develop whatever mix of controls they deemed best suited to achieving the NAAQS. The amendments crafted a new set of NAAQS deadlines that differ depending on the degree to which pollutant concentrations exceed the NAAQS. See §§181(a)(1) (ozone), 186(a)(1) (CO), 188(c) (PM_{10}), 192(a) (other criteria pollutants). Los Angeles, for example, now has until 2010 to comply with the NAAQS for ozone.

The statute now imposes on states with nonattainment areas a set of general requirements and a series of pollutant-specific requirements whose stringency varies in relation to the severity of the nonattainment problem. The general requirements, set forth in §172(c) of the Act, include the RACT requirement for existing sources mentioned above and a requirement that SIPs make reasonable further progress (defined as annual incremental reductions in emissions) toward compliance with the relevant NAAQS. In addition, the SIP of a state with a nonattainment area must require a permit for the construction and operation of any new or modified major stationary source in the area. To qualify for a permit, the applicant must comply with a strict technology-based emissions standard defined by the "lowest achievable emissions rate" (LAER) for the applying facility. If the state's SIP does not require existing sources to reduce emissions enough to accommodate new construction without exceeding the NAAQS, the applicant itself must purchase or secure from existing sources a reduction in emissions more than sufficient to offset new emissions from the proposed facility. §173(a).

The pollutant-specific requirements supplement or increase the severity of these general requirements. The statute categorizes nonattainment areas based on the degree to which ambient concentrations exceed the NAAQS. Ozone nonattainment areas, for example, are divided into marginal, moderate, serious, severe, and extreme classifications. The stringency of the required controls (such as the amount of offset needed to qualify for a new source permit) increases with pollutant concentrations. SIPs for ozone nonattainment areas must provide for reductions in emissions of VOCs and NO_x by specified amounts.

As for controls on mobile sources, the 1990 amendments reversed a trend begun in the mid-1970s. In 1974 and 1975, Congress prohibited EPA from imposing parking surcharges and from spending federal funds to tax or regulate parking facilities. The 1977 amendments further restricted federal authority. They prohibited, for example, federal controls on indirect sources that attract large numbers of vehicles, including shopping centers, sports complexes, and airports. The 1990 amendments, on the other hand, appeared to recognize that additional reductions in stationary-source emissions would be more expensive and difficult to achieve, and that mobile-source reductions were necessary if the NAAQS for ozone and CO were ever going to be satisfied. Accordingly, the 1990 amendments cracked down on vehicle usage in nonattainment areas. Gasoline vapor recovery systems, clean-fuel vehicle programs, transportation controls, and traffic control measures are all required in certain ozone nonattainment areas. The requirements for CO nonattainment areas are similar.

The 1990 amendments subject states that fail to comply with their nonattainment area obligations to a variety of sanctions. These include the withholding of federal grants in support of air pollution planning and control programs and highway construction, and the imposition of multiple offset requirements that will make it harder to construct new or modified major stationary sources that may be important to a state's economic development. §179. The 1990 amendments contain a series of additional pollutant-specific sanctions that include the imposition of penalty fees calculated on the basis of the level of emissions of VOCs. §185.

Prevention of Significant Deterioration. The 1990 amendments did not affect the PSD program. Under that program, major emitting facilities must install the "best available control technology" (BACT), to be determined for each facility, and demonstrate that plant operation will not cause ambient air to be "significantly" degraded. §§165(a)(4), 169(3). What constitutes a significant increment depends on the exact location of the proposed facility. §163. All clean-air areas of the country are placed in one of three classes. The increment of deterioration in ambient concentrations allowed within Class I areas, which mainly consist of major national parks and wilderness areas, is quite small, necessarily constricting new industrial development near the southwestern parklands. Class III increments were set generously at approximately half the NAAQS levels, and Class II increments fall in between. Visibility is protected separately, with "best available retrofit technology" (BART) to be applied as needed to existing sources that impair visibility. §169A.

The Act's "Hybrid" Emission Standards. The three emission standards applicable to sources that are required to apply for permits under the nonattainment, PSD, and visibility protection programs—LAER, BACT, and BART—are not technology based in the same sense as the mobile-source standards, the NSPS, and RACT for existing sources. These three standards are not applied uniformly, but on a case-by-case basis. In setting them, the states are supposed to play a larger role than EPA, depending on PSD and nonattainment SIP needs. Perhaps these hybrid standards—partly ambient quality oriented and partly technology oriented—can best be viewed as technical guidelines for officials as they negotiate with source operators on the extent of abatement necessary to achieve local air quality goals. In this process NSPS have provided a benchmark; ordinarily BACT and even the stricter LAER are set close to the NSPS baseline.

Acid Deposition Control. Under a program added in 1990, Congress set a goal of reducing annual emissions of SO_2 by 10 million tons and emissions of NO_x by 2 million tons from 1980 levels. Beginning in 2000, annual emissions of SO_2 were capped nationwide at 8.9 million tons. Title IV of the Act requires that EPA allocate SO_2 emission allowances to electric utility plants with fossil fuel–fired combustion devices. It is unlawful for any regulated source to emit SO_2 in excess of the allowances it holds. Each allowance entitles its holder to emit one ton of SO_2. However, the statute authorizes the transfer of allowances among regulated sources as well as among nonregulated persons. A regulated utility, therefore, may purchase additional allowances instead of reducing its emissions, and environmental groups may purchase allowances and retire them from the system. Industrial sources of SO_2 may opt into the program.

Stratospheric Ozone Protection. Based on evidence of an ever-expanding hole in the stratospheric ozone layer (initially detected over Antarctica but now present in the Northern Hemisphere as well), Congress adopted a new Title VI in 1990 aimed at eliminating ozone-depleting chemicals. The statute required a gradual phasing out of the production of chlorofluorocarbons by 2001. EPA was obliged to phase out use of these substances during the same period. Beginning in 2015, the statute will limit the production and use of hydrochlorofluorocarbons. EPA may accelerate these schedules if practicable or if necessary to prevent harmful effects on the ozone layer. §606(a).

Permits. Title V of the statute, adopted in 1990, establishes for the first time a federal CAA permit program that covers sources regulated under the acid deposition control provisions of the statute, sources subject to NSPS or NESHAPs, sources required to have either a nonattainment or a PSD permit, and other major sources. The states must develop permit programs that conform to minimum EPA requirements and are subject to sanctions for failure to do so. EPA may establish and administer a permit program for a state that fails to submit an acceptable program of its own. Permit applicants must submit plans detailing how they will comply with applicable regulatory requirements. Permits must include enforceable emission limitations and schedules of compliance with applicable requirements, including those derived from the SIP. EPA may veto state-issued permits.

Enforcement. The statute provides an array of enforcement mechanisms to redress noncompliance with its various obligations. Section 113 allows the federal government to seek civil or criminal penalties for statutory or regulatory violations. Section 304 allows private citizens to step in if neither the federal government nor the states are adequately enforcing the law. If adequate statutory notice has been given, §304 allows "any person" to commence a civil action on his own behalf against emitters alleged to be in violation of emissions standards or limitations or alleged to have failed to obtain the necessary permits for new facility construction under the Act's nonattainment and PSD provisions. Citizens may sue to compel EPA to perform nondiscretionary duties.

Upon receiving evidence that air pollution is presenting "an imminent and substantial endangerment to the health of persons" and that local government has not acted to remedy the problem, EPA may issue administrative orders or sue in federal district court to abate the dangerous condition under §303. This authority allows EPA to secure prompt relief from a dangerous condition before the Act's primary but more cumbersome regulatory programs take effect.

Judicial Review. Judicial review of EPA's actions under the CAA is available under §307 in the federal courts of appeals. Section 307(d) establishes special procedures for EPA rulemaking that supplant the provisions of the Administrative Procedure Act.

NOTE ON PROTECTION OF INDOOR AIR QUALITY

Recent research has revealed that the air within homes and other "weatherized" and "energy-efficient" structures contains significantly higher concentrations of many pollutants than does outdoor air. The sources of these pollutants are items and products very common in the home or office: asbestos (from insulation); formaldehyde and other toxic compounds (from cleaning products and chemical processes such as dry cleaning); tobacco smoke (which contains over 2,000 chemicals, many known carcinogens); heating fuels; pesticides; volatile organic compounds from such varied sources as hot water, deodorizers, and paints; plastics; biological contaminants such as microorganisms, molds, and mildews; and outdoor air pollutants that enter buildings through ventilation. These substances may cause human health problems ranging from allergies to asthma to cancer. See Reitze & Carof, The Legal Control of Indoor Air Pollution, 25 B.C. Envtl. Aff. L. Rev. 247, 248-251 (1998). A particularly troublesome indoor air pollutant is radon, a decay product of uranium that is found in many homes and that has been a known cancer-causing agent for centuries. According to EPA, radon is the leading cause of lung cancer among nonsmokers and the second leading cause of lung cancer overall. The combination of radon exposure and smoking appears to be particularly lethal. See EPA, Health Risks, http://www.epa.gov/iaq/radon/healthrisks.html.

EPA has long interpreted the CAA as vesting it with the power to regulate only outdoor air pollution. See 40 C.F.R. §50.1(e). This position has never been definitively confirmed or refuted. Congress has delegated authority to various federal agencies—including EPA under other laws, the Consumer Product Safety Commission, and the Occupational Safety and Health Administration—to take steps to limit exposure to particular kinds of indoor air pollution threats. But no statute gives any agency the broad regulatory authority to address indoor air pollution across the board that the CAA vests in EPA for outdoor air pollution.

D. UNIFORM NATIONAL PRIMARY AND SECONDARY AMBIENT AIR QUALITY STANDARDS

In developing uniform primary and secondary national ambient air quality standards (NAAQS), EPA faces the formidable task of determining, for each of the major air pollutants, separate numerical, time-limited ambient concentration levels that can be tolerated without endangering health and welfare anywhere in the nation. The following subsection introduces the problem of setting numerical standards to protect public health under conditions of scientific uncertainty.

Once EPA has promulgated ambient standards, responsibility under the CAA shifts from the federal government to the states. Each state must submit a SIP that specifies emission limitations and other measures necessary to attain the standards by the various statutory deadlines contained in the Act. Subsection 2 below addresses the constraints that apply to the states in carrying out that task.

1. Establishment of the NAAQS

a. Listing of Criteria Pollutants

As the preceding discussion indicates, the only air pollutants for which NAAQS currently exist are those listed in Table 6-2. What is the scope of EPA's discretion in selecting pollutants for promulgation of the NAAQS? In NRDC v. Train, 411 F. Supp. 864 (S.D.N.Y. 1976), NRDC brought a citizen suit under §304(a)(2) to force EPA to list lead as a criteria pollutant under §108 of the Act. NRDC argued that the agency had a mandatory duty to list lead once it determined that the pollutant "has an adverse effect on public health or welfare"* and comes from the requisite numerous or diverse sources. EPA conceded that lead met both tests, but claimed that §108(a)(1)(C), which requires that EPA "plan[] to issue air quality criteria," left the decision to list or not list within the Administrator's sole discretion. According to EPA, discretion was necessary because the choice of regulating lead under different sections of the Act involved "complex considerations." In particular, EPA had to consider whether to list lead as a criteria pollutant under §108 or establish standards restricting the lead content of gasoline under §211(c)(1). EPA chose §211 because it would be simpler and more efficient and would not add to the burdens imposed on the states by the obligation to adopt SIPs for the other criteria pollutants.

EPA's choices were not easy ones. On the one hand, at the time EPA was considering the optimal strategy for limiting exposure to lead, gasoline combustion accounted for about 88 percent of airborne lead; smelters contributed just under 4 percent. Smelters are not very numerous and usually are located in less populous regions. EPA observed that some lead and copper smelters might be "severely strained economically" if regulated under SIPs as a means of meeting any NAAQS ultimately adopted. 43 Fed. Reg. 46,256 (1978). Do these facts support the policy of concentrating on mobile-source lead pollution and letting the smelters go? On the other hand,

---

*The statute has since been amended; EPA must now list a pollutant under §108 if, among other things, its emissions, "in [EPA's] judgment, cause or contribute to air pollution which may reasonably be anticipated to endanger public health or welfare." §108(a)(1)(A).

under the ambient approach, nothing would have to be done in the vast regions of the country where lead is not a problem, whereas the §211(c)(1) approach required the imposition of costly controls on lead in gasoline throughout the nation. The ambient approach theoretically permitted selective land use planning to regulate the spacing and timing of lead emissions as needed, whereas fuel controls blanketed the nation. Was regulation of lead under §111 an additional available alternative? See §111(b)(1)(A), (d).

The court in *NRDC* ruled for the plaintiff. It interpreted §108 as requiring EPA to list a pollutant under the two enumerated conditions in §108(a)(1)(A)-(B), "one factual and one judgmental." According to the court, §§108 and 211(c) are "neither mutually exclusive nor alternative provisions." The court pointed out that any reductions in lead resulting from §211(c) regulations would make the states' task of achieving the NAAQS for lead easier. On appeal, the district court's judgment was affirmed in NRDC v. Train, 545 F.2d 320 (2d Cir. 1976). The court agreed that Congress did not give EPA the discretion to list only the pollutants for which the Administrator thought ambient standards were the most appropriate strategy. It concluded that Congress intended the ambient standard and SIP strategy to be the linchpin of the Act and built safeguards into the Act (such as citizen suits) to prevent delays: "Congress sought to eliminate, not perpetuate, opportunity for administrative foot-dragging." Id. at 328.

Despite being forced to promulgate an ambient standard for lead, EPA continued to place primary reliance on its regulations limiting the lead content of gasoline. Congress ultimately banned all lead in gasoline as of December 31, 1995. §211(g)(1), (n). Ambient lead concentrations declined by 78 percent between 1986 and 1995. 27 Env't Rep. (BNA) 1803 (1996).

Americans nevertheless continue to be exposed to lead from many sources, as indicated in Figure 6-5. Even though lead may no longer be used in gasoline, it can remain in streets or soil long after it was emitted, and children playing outside may be exposed to it. In addition, lead paint is found in many older homes; renovation of those homes can release lead into the air, as can wind blowing through open windows. Many homes have contaminated water that leaches from lead pipes when ammonia is added to the water to strengthen the purification capability of chlorine. Lead can also leach into food and drinks from utensils or containers made with lead. Lead solder is still used in the cans for some imported goods. The Consumer Product Safety Commission in 2004 recalled more than 150 million pieces of toy jewelry found to contain lead. Children could ingest unsafe levels of lead by sucking on or swallowing the toys. About one-quarter of the nation's children are exposed to lead at home, and more than 400,000 each year are found to have unsafe levels of lead in their blood. Scientists have not detected any safe level of lead in blood, so exposure to any amount poses a risk of adverse health effects. Adults can experience such effects (including cardiovascular disease, tooth decay, miscarriage, kidney disease, cognitive problems, and cataracts) decades after being exposed to lead. See Brody, Dally No Longer: Get the Lead Out, N.Y. Times, Jan. 17, 2006, at D6. NRDC v. Train forced a basic change in EPA's air quality management strategy for lead. Other important CAA policy changes also began with a §304 suit challenging EPA's failure to perform a nondiscretionary duty.*

Why haven't more pollutants been listed as criteria pollutants under §108 since the forced listing of lead?

*For further discussion of the use of citizen suits, both to force EPA to perform nondiscretionary duties and to force polluters to comply with statutory and regulatory emission limitations, see Chapter 10, section C.4.

1970 Lead Emissions Sources
221,000 tons

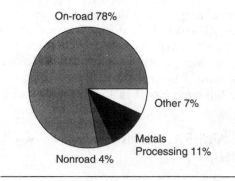

1997 Lead Emissions Sources
3,915 tons

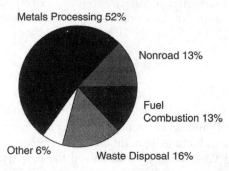

FIGURE 6-5

Source: http://www.epa.gov/air/urbanair/lead/what.html

b. The NAAQS for Ozone and Particulate Matter

The second step, after listing, in promulgating an ambient standard is the preparation of a criteria document. Section 108(a)(2) makes clear that the "criteria" are descriptive rather than prescriptive and refer not to standards or guidelines that sources must meet, but rather to the latest scientific knowledge concerning the injury to public health or welfare that the pollutant may cause. The third step, required by §109(a)(2), to occur simultaneously with the publication of the criteria document, is for EPA to issue proposed numerical primary and secondary NAAQS and, after soliciting and considering public input, final standards. The NAAQS must be based on the criteria document. Section 7409(d)(1) requires EPA to review the existing air quality criteria and NAAQS at least once every five years.

What factors must EPA consider in determining the appropriate levels for the NAAQS? Section 109(b)(1) provides that the primary standards are those that, "allowing an adequate margin of safety, are requisite to protect the public health." Under §109(b)(2), the secondary standards are those that are "requisite to protect the public welfare from any known or anticipated adverse effects associated with the presence of such pollutant in the ambient air." After EPA promulgated NAAQS for lead in 1978, the Lead Industries Association challenged the standards in Lead Indus. Ass'n, Inc. v. EPA, 647 F.2d 1130 (D.C. Cir. 1980). One of the issues was whether EPA erred by refusing to consider economic and technological feasibility in setting the standards. The court held that it did not, because "the statute and its legislative history make clear that economic considerations play no part in the promulgation of ambient air quality standards under Section 109." Id. at 1148. That ruling went undisturbed for more than 20 years, after which time the same issue arose before the Supreme Court in the following case.

WHITMAN v. AMERICAN TRUCKING ASSOCIATIONS, INC.
531 U.S. 457 (2001)

JUSTICE SCALIA delivered the opinion of the Court.

These cases present the following questions: (1) Whether §109(b)(1) of the Clean Air Act (CAA) delegates legislative power to [EPA]. (2) Whether the [EPA] Administrator may consider the costs of implementation in setting national ambient air quality standards (NAAQS) under §109(b)(1). . . .

I

. . . These cases arose when, on July 18, 1997, the Administrator revised the NAAQS for particulate matter (PM) and ozone. American Trucking Associations, Inc., and its co-respondents . . . —which include, in addition to other private companies, the States of Michigan, Ohio, and West Virginia—challenged the new standards in the Court of Appeals for the District of Columbia Circuit, pursuant to 42 U.S.C. §7607(b)(1).

The District of Columbia Circuit accepted some of the challenges and rejected others. It agreed with [the respondents] that §109(b)(1) delegated legislative power to the Administrator in contravention of the United States Constitution, Art. I, §1, because it found that the EPA had interpreted the statute to provide no "intelligible principle" to guide the agency's exercise of authority. American Trucking Ass'ns, Inc. v. EPA, 175 F.3d 1027, 1034 (1999). The court thought, however, that the EPA could perhaps avoid the unconstitutional delegation by adopting a restrictive construction of §109(b)(1), so instead of declaring the section unconstitutional the court remanded the NAAQS to the agency. . . . The Court of Appeals [also] unanimously rejected respondents' argument that the court should depart from the rule of Lead Industries Ass'n, Inc. v. EPA, 647 F.2d 1130, 1148 (CADC 1980), that the EPA may not consider the cost of implementing a NAAQS in setting the initial standard. . . .

The Administrator and the EPA petitioned this Court for review of the first . . . question[] described in the first paragraph of this opinion. Respondents conditionally cross-petitioned for review of the second question. . . .

II

In *Lead Industries*, the [D.C.] Circuit held that "economic considerations [may] play no part in the promulgation of ambient air quality standards under Section 109" of the

CAA. In the present cases, the court adhered to that holding, as it had done on many other occasions. See, e.g., American Lung Ass'n v. EPA, 134 F.3d 388, 389 (1998); NRDC v. EPA, 902 F.2d 962, 973 (1990); American Petroleum Inst. v. Costle, 665 F.2d 1176, 1185 (CADC 1981). Respondents argue that these decisions are incorrect. We disagree; and since the first step in assessing whether a statute delegates legislative power is to determine what authority the statute confers, we address that issue of interpretation first and reach respondents' constitutional arguments in Part III, *infra*.

Section 109(b)(1) instructs the EPA to set primary ambient air quality standards "the attainment and maintenance of which . . . are requisite to protect the public health" with "an adequate margin of safety." 42 U.S.C. §7409(b)(1). Were it not for the hundreds of pages of briefing respondents have submitted on the issue, one would have thought it fairly clear that this text does not permit the EPA to consider costs in setting the standards. The language, as one scholar has noted, "is absolute." D. Currie, Air Pollution: Federal Law and Analysis 4-15 (1981). The EPA, "based on" the information about health effects contained in the technical "criteria" documents compiled under §108(a)(2), is to identify the maximum airborne concentration of a pollutant that the public health can tolerate, decrease the concentration to provide an "adequate" margin of safety, and set the standard at that level. Nowhere are the costs of achieving such a standard made part of that initial calculation.

Against this most natural of readings, respondents make a lengthy, spirited, but ultimately unsuccessful attack. They begin with the object of §109(b)(1)'s focus, the "public health." When the term first appeared in federal clean air legislation—in the [1955 Air Pollution Control Act]—which expressed "recognition of the dangers to the public health" from air pollution—its ordinary meaning was "[t]he health of the community." Webster's New International Dictionary 2005 (2d ed. 1950). Respondents argue, however, that §109(b)(1), as added by the [1970 Act], meant to use the term's secondary meaning: "[t]he ways and means of conserving the health of the members of a community, as by preventive medicine, organized care of the sick, etc." Words that can have more than one meaning are given content, however, by their surroundings, and in the context of §109(b)(1) this second definition makes no sense. Congress could not have meant to instruct the Administrator to set NAAQS at a level "requisite to protect" "the art and science dealing with the protection and improvement of community health." Webster's Third New International Dictionary 1836 (1981). We therefore revert to the primary definition of the term: the health of the public.

Even so, respondents argue, many more factors than air pollution affect public health. In particular, the economic cost of implementing a very stringent standard might produce health losses sufficient to offset the health gains achieved in cleaning the air—for example, by closing down whole industries and thereby impoverishing the workers and consumers dependent upon those industries. That is unquestionably true, and Congress was unquestionably aware of it. . . . The 1970 Congress . . . not only anticipated that compliance costs could injure the public health, but provided for that precise exigency. Section 110(f)(1) of the CAA permitted the Administrator to waive the compliance deadline for stationary sources if, *inter alia*, sufficient control measures were simply unavailable and "the continued operation of such sources is *essential . . . to the public health or welfare*." 84 Stat. 1683 (emphasis added). Other provisions explicitly permitted or required economic costs to be taken into account in implementing the air quality standards. Section 111(b)(1)(B), for example, commanded the Administrator to set "standards of performance" for certain new sources of emissions that as specified in §111(a)(1) were to "reflec[t] the degree of emission limitation achievable through the application of the best system of emission reduction which (taking into account the cost of achieving such reduction) the Administrator determines has been adequately demonstrated." Section 202(a)(2) prescribed that emissions standards for automobiles could take effect only "after such period as the Administrator finds necessary to permit the development and application of the requisite technology, giving appropriate consideration to the cost of compliance within such period." See also . . . §211(c)(2) (similar limitation for fuel additives). . . . Subsequent amendments to the CAA have added many more provisions directing, in explicit language, that the Administrator consider costs in performing various duties. See, e.g., 42 U.S.C. §7545(k)(1) (reformulate gasoline to "require the greatest reduction in emissions . . . taking into consideration the cost of achieving such emissions reductions"); §7547(a)(3) (emission reduction for nonroad vehicles to be set "giving appropriate consideration to the cost" of the standards). We have therefore refused to find implicit in ambiguous sections of the CAA an authorization to consider costs that has elsewhere, and so often, been expressly granted. See Union Elec. Co. v. EPA, 427 U.S. 246, 257 n.5 (1976).

Accordingly, to prevail in their present challenge, respondents must show a textual commitment of authority to the EPA to consider costs in setting NAAQS under §109(b)(1). And because §109(b)(1) and the NAAQS for which it provides are the engine that drives nearly all of Title I of the CAA, 42 U.S.C. §§7401-7515, that textual commitment must be a clear one. Congress, we have held, does not alter the fundamental details of a regulatory scheme in vague terms or ancillary provisions—it does not, one might say, hide elephants in mouseholes. Respondents' textual arguments ultimately founder upon this principle.

Their first claim is that §109(b)(1)'s terms "adequate margin" and "requisite" leave room to pad health effects with cost concerns. . . . [W]e find it implausible that Congress would give to the EPA through these modest words the power to determine whether implementation costs should moderate national air quality standards.

The same defect inheres in respondents' next two arguments: that while the Administrator's judgment about what is requisite to protect the public health must be "based on [the] criteria" documents developed under §108(a)(2), see §109(b)(1), it need not be based *solely* on those criteria; and that those criteria themselves, while they must include "effects on public health or welfare which may be expected from the presence of such pollutant in the ambient air," are not necessarily *limited* to those effects. Even if we were to concede those premises, we still would not conclude that one of the unenumerated factors that the agency can consider in developing and applying the criteria is cost of implementation. That factor is *both* so indirectly related to public health and so full of potential for canceling the conclusions drawn from direct health effects that it would surely have been expressly mentioned in §§108 and 109 had Congress meant it to be considered. Yet while those provisions describe in detail how the health effects of pollutants in the ambient air are to be calculated and given effect, see §108(a)(2), they say not a word about costs.

Respondents point, finally, to a number of provisions in the CAA that *do* require attainment cost data to be generated. Section 108(b)(1), for example, instructs the Administrator to "issue to the States," simultaneously with the criteria documents, "information on air pollution control techniques, which information shall include data relating to the cost of installation and operation." And §109(d)(2)(C)(iv) requires the Clean Air Scientific Advisory Committee to "advise the Administrator of any adverse public health, welfare, social, economic, or energy effects which may result from various strategies for attainment and maintenance" of NAAQS. Respondents argue that these provisions make no sense unless costs are to be considered in setting the NAAQS. That is not so. These provisions enable the Administrator to assist the States in carrying out their statutory role as primary *implementers* of the NAAQS. It is to the States that the Act assigns initial and primary responsibility for deciding what emissions reductions will be required from which sources. See 42 U.S.C. §§7407(a), 7410 (giving States the duty of developing implementation plans). It would be impossible to perform that task intelligently without considering which abatement technologies are most efficient, and most economically feasible—which is why we have said that "the most important forum for consideration of claims of economic and technological infeasibility is before the state agency formulating the implementation plan," Union Elec. Co. v. EPA, 427 U.S., at 266. Thus, federal clean air legislation has, from the very beginning, directed federal agencies to develop and transmit implementation data, including cost data, to the States. That Congress chose to carry forward this research program to assist States in choosing the means through which they would implement the standards is perfectly sensible, and has no bearing upon whether cost considerations are to be taken into account in formulating the standards.[3]

. . . The text of §109(b), interpreted in its statutory and historical context and with appreciation for its importance to the CAA as a whole, unambiguously bars cost considerations from the NAAQS-setting process. . . . [4] We therefore affirm the judgment of the Court of Appeals on this point.

III

Section 109(b)(1) of the CAA instructs the EPA to set "ambient air quality standards the attainment and maintenance of which in the judgment of the Administrator, based on [the] criteria [documents of §108] and allowing an adequate margin of safety, are requisite to protect the public health." The Court of Appeals held that this section as interpreted by the Administrator did not provide an "intelligible principle" to guide the EPA's exercise of authority in setting NAAQS. "[The] EPA," it said, "lack[ed] any determinate criteria for drawing lines. It has failed to state intelligibly how much is too much." 175 F.3d, at 1034. The court hence found that the EPA's interpretation (but not the statute itself) violated the nondelegation doctrine. We disagree.

In a delegation challenge, the constitutional question is whether the statute has delegated legislative power to the agency. Article I, §1, of the Constitution vests "[a]ll legislative Powers herein granted . . . in a Congress of the United States." This text permits no delegation of those powers, and so we repeatedly have said that when Congress confers decisionmaking authority upon agencies *Congress* must "lay down by legislative act an intelligible principle to which the person or body authorized to [act] is directed to conform." J. W. Hampton, Jr., & Co. v. United States, 276 U.S.

---

3. . . . For many of the same reasons described in the body of the opinion, as well as the text of §109(b)(2), . . . we conclude that the EPA may not consider implementation costs in setting the secondary NAAQS.

4. Respondents' speculation that the EPA is secretly considering the costs of attainment without telling anyone is irrelevant to our interpretive inquiry. If such an allegation could be proved, it would be grounds for vacating the NAAQS, because the Administrator had not followed the law. See, e.g., Chevron U.S.A. Inc. v. Natural Resources Defense Council, Inc., 467 U.S. 837, 842-843 (1984). It would not, however, be grounds for this Court's changing the law.

394, 409 (1928). We have never suggested that an agency can cure an unlawful delegation of legislative power by adopting in its discretion a limiting construction of the statute. . . . The idea that an agency can cure an unconstitutionally standardless delegation of power by declining to exercise some of that power seems to us internally contradictory. The very choice of which portion of the power to exercise—that is to say, the prescription of the standard that Congress had omitted—would *itself* be an exercise of the forbidden legislative authority. Whether the statute delegates legislative power is a question for the courts, and an agency's voluntary self-denial has no bearing upon the answer.

We agree with the Solicitor General that the text of §109(b)(1) of the CAA at a minimum requires that "[f]or a discrete set of pollutants and based on published air quality criteria that reflect the latest scientific knowledge, [the] EPA must establish uniform national standards at a level that is requisite to protect public health from the adverse effects of the pollutant in the ambient air." Requisite, in turn, "mean[s] sufficient, but not more than necessary." These limits on the EPA's discretion are strikingly similar to the ones we approved in [previous cases].

The scope of discretion §109(b)(1) allows is in fact well within the outer limits of our nondelegation precedents. In the history of the Court we have found the requisite "intelligible principle" lacking in only two statutes, one of which provided literally no guidance for the exercise of discretion, and the other of which conferred authority to regulate the entire economy on the basis of no more precise a standard than stimulating the economy by assuring "fair competition." See Panama Refining Co. v. Ryan, 293 U.S. 388 (1935); A.L.A. Schechter Poultry Corp. v. United States, 295 U.S. 495 (1935). We have, on the other hand, upheld the validity of §11(b)(2) of the Public Utility Holding Company Act of 1935, which gave the Securities and Exchange Commission authority to modify the structure of holding company systems so as to ensure that they are not "unduly or unnecessarily complicate[d]" and do not "unfairly or inequitably distribute voting power among security holders." American Power & Light Co. v. SEC, 329 U.S. 90, 104 (1946). We have approved the wartime conferral of agency power to fix the prices of commodities at a level that " 'will be generally fair and equitable and will effectuate the [in some respects conflicting] purposes of th[e] Act.' " Yakus v. United States, 321 U.S. 414, 420, 423-426 (1944). And we have found an "intelligible principle" in various statutes authorizing regulation in the "public interest." See, e.g., National Broadcasting Co. v. United States, 319 U.S. 190, 225-226 (1943) (FCC's power to regulate airwaves); New York Central Securities Corp. v. United States, 287 U.S. 12, 24-25 (1932) (ICC's power to approve railroad consolidations). In short, we have "almost never felt qualified to second-guess Congress regarding the permissible degree of policy judgment that can be left to those executing or applying the law." Mistretta v. United States, 488 U.S. 361, 416 (1989) (Scalia, J., dissenting).

It is true enough that the degree of agency discretion that is acceptable varies according to the scope of the power congressionally conferred. While Congress need not provide any direction to the EPA regarding the manner in which it is to define "country elevators," which are to be exempt from new-stationary-source regulations governing grain elevators, see §7411(i), it must provide substantial guidance on setting air standards that affect the entire national economy. But even in sweeping regulatory schemes we have never demanded, as the Court of Appeals did here, that statutes provide a "determinate criterion" for saying "how much [of the regulated harm] is too much." 175 F.3d, at 1034. . . . It is therefore not conclusive for delegation purposes that, as respondents argue, ozone and particulate matter are "nonthreshold" pollutants that inflict a continuum of adverse health effects at any airborne concentration greater than zero, and hence require the EPA to make judgments of degree. "[A] certain degree of discretion, and thus of lawmaking, inheres in most executive or judicial action." Mistretta v. United States, *supra*, at 417 (Scalia, J., dissenting). Section 109(b)(1) of the CAA, which to repeat we interpret as requiring the EPA to set air quality standards at the level that is "requisite"—that is, not lower or higher than is necessary—to protect the public health with an adequate margin of safety, fits comfortably within the scope of discretion permitted by our precedent.

We therefore reverse the judgment of the Court of Appeals remanding for reinterpretation that would avoid a supposed delegation of legislative power. It will remain for the Court of Appeals—on the remand that we direct for other reasons—to dispose of any other preserved challenge to the NAAQS under the judicial-review provisions contained in 42 U.S.C. §7607(d)(9). . . .

JUSTICE THOMAS, concurring. . . .

The parties to this case who briefed the constitutional issue wrangled over constitutional doctrine with barely a nod to the text of the Constitution. Although this Court since 1928 has treated the "intelligible principle" requirement as the only constitutional limit on congressional grants of power to administrative agencies, the Constitution does not speak of "intelligible principles." Rather, it speaks in much simpler terms: "*All* legislative Powers herein granted shall be vested in a Congress." U.S. Const., Art. 1, §1 (emphasis added). I am not convinced that the intelligible principle doctrine serves to prevent all cessions of legislative power. I believe that there are cases in which the principle is intelligible and yet the significance of the delegated decision is simply too great for the decision to be called anything other than "legislative."

As it is, none of the parties to this case has examined the text of the Constitution or asked us to reconsider our precedents on cessions of legislative power. On a future day, however, I would be willing to address the question whether our delegation jurisprudence has strayed too far from our Founders' understanding of separation of powers.

JUSTICE STEVENS, with whom JUSTICE SOUTER joins, concurring in part and concurring in the judgment.

. . . I wholeheartedly endorse the Court's result [on the nondelegation issue] and endorse its explanation of its reasons, albeit with the following caveat.

The Court has two choices. We could choose to articulate our ultimate disposition of this issue by frankly acknowledging that the power delegated to the EPA is "legislative" but nevertheless conclude that the delegation is constitutional because adequately limited by the terms of the authorizing statute. Alternatively, we could pretend, as the Court does, that the authority delegated to the EPA is somehow not "legislative power." Despite the fact that there is language in our opinions that supports the Court's articulation of our holding, I am persuaded that it would be both wiser and more faithful to what we have actually done in delegation cases to admit that agency rulemaking authority is "legislative power."

The proper characterization of governmental power should generally depend on the nature of the power, not on the identity of the person exercising it. . . . If the NAAQS that the EPA promulgated had been prescribed by Congress, everyone would agree that those rules would be the product of an exercise of "legislative power." The same characterization is appropriate when an agency exercises rulemaking authority pursuant to a permissible delegation from Congress.

My view is not only more faithful to normal English usage, but is also fully consistent with the text of the Constitution. In Article I, the Framers vested "All legislative Powers" in the Congress, Art. I, §1, just as in Article II they vested the "executive Power" in the President, Art. II, §1. Those provisions do not purport to limit the authority of either recipient of power to delegate authority to others. . . . Surely the authority granted to members of the Cabinet and federal law enforcement agents is properly characterized as "Executive" even though not exercised by the President.

It seems clear that an executive agency's exercise of rulemaking authority pursuant to a valid delegation from Congress is "legislative." As long as the delegation provides a sufficiently intelligible principle, there is nothing inherently unconstitutional about it. . . . I would hold that when Congress enacted §109, it effected a constitutional delegation of legislative power to the EPA.

JUSTICE BREYER, concurring in part and concurring in the judgment.

. . . I . . . agree with the Court's determination in Part II that the [CAA] does not permit [EPA] to consider the economic costs of implementation when setting national ambient air quality standards under §109(b)(1) of the Act. But I would not rest this conclusion solely upon §109's language or upon a presumption, such as the Court's presumption that any authority the Act grants the EPA to consider costs must flow from a "textual commitment" that is "clear." In order better to achieve regulatory goals—for example, to allocate resources so that they save more lives or produce a cleaner environment—regulators must often take account of all of a proposed regulation's adverse effects, at least where those adverse effects clearly threaten serious and disproportionate public harm. Hence, I believe that, other things being equal, we should read silences or ambiguities in the language of regulatory statutes as permitting, not forbidding, this type of rational regulation.

In this case, however, other things are not equal. Here, legislative history, along with the statute's structure, indicates that §109's language reflects a congressional decision not to delegate to the agency the legal authority to consider economic costs of compliance.

For one thing, the legislative history shows that Congress intended the statute to be "technology forcing." Senator Edmund Muskie, the primary sponsor of the 1970 amendments to the Act, introduced them by saying that Congress' primary responsibility in drafting the Act was not "to be limited by what is or appears to be technologically or economically feasible," but "to establish what the public interest requires to protect the health of persons," even if that means that *industries will be asked to do what seems to be impossible at the present time.*" 116 Cong. Rec. 32901-32902 (1970) (emphasis added). . . .

Indeed, this Court, after reviewing the entire legislative history, concluded that the 1970 amendments were "expressly designed to force regulated sources to develop pollution control devices that *might at the time appear to be economically or technologically infeasible.*" Union Elec. Co. v. EPA, 427 U.S. 246, 257 (1976) (emphasis added). . . .

To read this legislative history as meaning what it says does not impute to Congress an irrational intent. Technology-forcing hopes can prove realistic. Those persons, for example, who opposed the 1970 Act's insistence on a 90% reduction in auto emission pollutants, on the ground of excessive cost, saw the development of catalytic converter technology that helped achieve substantial reductions without the economic catastrophe that some had feared. . . .

At the same time, the statute's technology-forcing objective makes regulatory efforts to determine the costs of implementation both less important and more difficult. It means that the relevant economic costs are speculative, for they include the cost of unknown future technologies. It also means that efforts to take costs into account can breed time-consuming and potentially unresolvable arguments about the accuracy and significance of cost estimates. Congress could have thought such efforts not worth the delays and uncertainties that would accompany them. . . .

Moreover, the Act does not, on this reading, wholly ignore cost and feasibility. As the majority points out, the Act allows regulators to take those concerns into account when they determine how to implement ambient air quality standards. . . .

The Act also permits the EPA, within certain limits, to consider costs when it sets deadlines by which areas must attain the ambient air quality standards. . . . And Congress can change those statutory limits if necessary. . . .

Finally, contrary to the suggestion of the Court of Appeals and of some parties, this interpretation of §109 does not require the EPA to eliminate every health risk, however slight, at any economic cost, however great, to the point of "hurtling" industry over "the brink of ruin," or even forcing "deindustrialization." American Trucking Assns., Inc. v. EPA, 175 F.3d 1027, 1037, 1038 n.4 (CADC 1999). The statute, by its express terms, does not compel the elimination of all risk; and it grants the Administrator sufficient flexibility to avoid setting ambient air quality standards ruinous to industry.

Section 109(b)(1) directs the Administrator to set standards that are "requisite to protect the public health" with "an adequate margin of safety." But these words do not describe a world that is free of all risk—an impossible and undesirable objective. See Industrial Union Dept., AFL-CIO v. American Petroleum Inst., 448 U.S. 607, 642 (1980) (plurality opinion) (the word "safe" does not mean "risk-free"). Nor are the words "requisite" and "public health" to be understood independent of context. . . . And what counts as "requisite" to protecting the public health will similarly vary with background circumstances, such as the public's ordinary tolerance of the particular health risk in the particular context at issue. The Administrator can consider such background circumstances when "decid[ing] what risks are acceptable in the world in which we live." NRDC v. EPA, 824 F.2d 1146, 1165 (CADC 1987).

The statute also permits the Administrator to take account of comparative health risks. That is to say, she may consider whether a proposed rule promotes safety overall. A rule likely to cause more harm to health than it prevents is not a rule that is "requisite to protect the public health." For example, as the Court of Appeals held and the parties do not contest, the Administrator has the authority to determine to what extent possible health risks stemming from reductions in tropospheric ozone (which, it is claimed, helps prevent cataracts and skin cancer) should be taken into account in setting the ambient air quality standard for ozone. See 175 F.3d, at 1050-1053 (remanding for the Administrator to make that determination). . . .

NOTES AND QUESTIONS

1. *The Role of Cost in Standard Setting.* What factors govern EPA's decision about the degree of strictness with which to set the primary NAAQS? In particular, what roles

do economic impact and feasibility play in that determination? According to the respondents in *American Trucking*, what was the intended "secondary meaning" of the term "public health" in §109(b)(1)? Why did the Court conclude that such a meaning does not require that EPA consider cost in establishing the primary NAAQS? According to the respondents, what words in §109(b)(1) are broad enough to encompass cost concerns? On what grounds did the Court disagree? How did the Court interpret the provision requiring that the primary NAAQS be based on criteria documents issued under §108(a)(2)? Why doesn't EPA's obligation to supply to the states information relating to the cost of air pollution control support respondents' claim that EPA must consider cost in setting the primary NAAQS? How could the ambient air quality standards be set through an analysis that takes costs into account? As Union Elec. Co. v. EPA, excerpted at page 437, demonstrates, the statute permits consideration of economic impact at various stages of the implementation of the standards. Compare Sierra Club v. EPA, 375 F.3d 537, 541 (7th Cir. 2004) ("when the statute is ambiguous the EPA is free to take costs into account"). Oren, The Supreme Court Forces a U-Turn: The Fate of *American Trucking*, 34 Envtl. L. Rep. (Envtl. L. Inst.) 10687 (2004), argues that the Court reached the correct result using unpersuasive reasoning.

Sinden, In Defense of Absolutes: Combating the Politics of Power in Environmental Law, 90 Iowa L. Rev. 1405 (2005), argues that "absolute" standards are preferable to the use of cost-benefit analysis as a means of determining appropriate levels of environmental protection, at least in certain circumstances. Professor Sinden defines absolute (or cost-blind) standards as those that are gauged only to the protection of human health or the environment and that prohibit any consideration of economic costs, such as the CAA's NAAQS. She claims that absolute standards, by treating environmental interests as trumps that override cost considerations except in extraordinary circumstances, perform a crucial "power-shifting function" by helping to counteract the power imbalance between diffuse citizen interests and moneyed corporate interests that tend to distort agency decisions on environmental issues.

2. *The Benefits of Ozone Pollution.* Can ozone pollution be good for public health and the environment? That issue was raised in a portion of the D.C. Circuit's decision in *American Trucking* that was not appealed to the Supreme Court. Industry argued that, in setting the primary NAAQS for ozone, EPA improperly ignored the health benefits of tropospheric ozone in acting as a shield from the harmful effects of the sun's ultraviolet rays, including cataracts and skin cancers. The court addressed industry's contention as follows:

> Petitioners presented evidence that according to them shows the health benefits of tropospheric ozone as a shield from the harmful effects of the sun's ultraviolet rays—including cataracts and both melanoma and nonmelanoma skin cancers. In estimating the effects of ozone concentrations, EPA explicitly disregarded these alleged benefits.
>
> EPA explained its decision first as a matter of statutory interpretation. Under the Clean Air Act, EPA's ambient standards for any pollutant are to be "based on [the] criteria" that EPA has published for that pollutant. 42 U.S.C. §7409(b)(1) & (2). The "criteria," in turn, are to "reflect the latest scientific knowledge useful in indicating the kind and extent of all identifiable effects on public health or welfare which may be expected from the presence of such pollutant in the ambient air, in varying quantities." Id. §7408(a)(2). The reference to "all identifiable effects" would seem on its face to include beneficent effects.
>
> EPA attempts to avoid this straightforward reading in several ways. First, it points to the term "such pollutant," arguing that the statute requires it to focus exclusively on the

characteristics that make the substance a "pollutant." But the phrase "pollutant" is simply a label used to identify a substance to be listed and controlled by the statute. While it is perfectly true that a substance known to be utterly without adverse effects could not make it onto the list, this fact of nomenclature does not visibly manifest a congressional intent to banish consideration of whole classes of "identifiable effects."

EPA also relies on the fact that two of the three specified considerations under §108(a)(2)'s general mandate refer to "adverse effect[s]." . . . EPA's argument would be of uncertain force even if all three types of effects specifically required to be considered were spoken of as "adverse effects"; there is no reason to read "adverse" back into the "all identifiable effects" of §108(a)(2). But as one of the three specified classes refers to "effects" unmodified, id. §7408(a)(2)(A), we can reject EPA's argument without even reaching that issue. That Congress qualified "effects" in clauses (B) and (C) with "adverse" seems only to strengthen the supposition that in (A)—and in the general mandate—it intended to cover all health or welfare effects. Therefore if petitioners' contentions are right, clause (A) applies to ozone: the presence of ultraviolet radiation at various levels "alter[s] the effects [of ozone] on public health or welfare" by making them on the whole less malign—perhaps even beneficial.

EPA next argues that Title VI of the Clean Air Act, id. §§7671-7671q, which mandates certain measures to preserve stratospheric ozone, represents a complete consideration of ozone's beneficial role as a UV shield. Petitioners' claim, however, is that ground-level (tropospheric) ozone—the subject of this rule—has a UV-screening function independent of the ozone higher in the atmosphere. EPA points to nothing in the statute that purports to address tropospheric ozone.

[The court concluded that the statute is not ambiguous, but even it is, EPA's interpretation of it was unreasonable.] [I]t seems bizarre that a statute intended to improve human health would, as EPA claimed at argument, lock the agency into looking at only one half of a substance's health effects in determining the maximum level for that substance. At oral argument even EPA counsel seemed reluctant to claim that the statute justified disregard of the beneficent effects of a pollutant bearing directly on the health symptoms that accounted for its being thought a pollutant at all (suppose, for example, a chemical that both impedes and enhances breathing, depending on the person or circumstances); he also seemed unable to distinguish that case from the one here—where the chemical evidently impedes breathing but provides defense against various cancers.

Legally, then, EPA must consider positive identifiable effects of a pollutant's presence in the ambient air in formulating air quality criteria under §108 and NAAQS under §109. . . .

As we said above, we are remanding to EPA to formulate adequate decision criteria for its ordinary object of analysis—ill effects. We leave it to the agency on remand to determine whether, using the same approach as it does for those, tropospheric ozone has a beneficent effect, and if so, then to assess ozone's net adverse health effect by whatever criteria it adopts. [American Trucking Ass'ns, Inc. v. EPA, 175 F.3d 1027, 1051-1052 (D.C. Cir. 1999).

On remand, EPA concluded that the alleged health benefits of ground-level ozone in reducing exposure to ultraviolet radiation are too uncertain to justify any relaxation in the ozone NAAQS. 67 Fed. Reg. 614 (2003).

3. *The Nondelegation Issue.* What is the source of the nondelegation doctrine? How did the Court react to the D.C. Circuit's position that EPA could cure the absence of a determinate criterion by specifying on remand the test for determining the appropriate stopping point for primary NAAQS that is "requisite" to protect the public health? What intelligible principle did the Court discern in §109(b)(1)? How does the scope of the regulatory program bear on application of the nondelegation

doctrine? What position did the concurring Justices take on the nondelegation issue? For another environmental law case implicating the nondelegation doctrine, see the *Industrial Union Dep't* case, excerpted in Chapter 8, section D.2.*

4. *Risk-Based and Precautionary Regulation.* In the *Lead Industries Ass'n* case, industry argued that Congress intended that the NAAQS protect the public health only against effects known to be "clearly harmful to health" as a means to ensure that EPA would not adopt excessively stringent standards. The court disagreed that EPA's authority was limited in that manner, emphasizing "the preventive or precautionary nature" of the CAA's mandate to establish ambient quality standards.

> It may be . . . LIA's view that the Administrator must show that there is a "medical consensus that (the effects on which the standards were based) are harmful. . . . If so, LIA is seriously mistaken. This court has previously noted that some uncertainty about the health effects of air pollution is inevitable. And we pointed out that "[a]waiting certainty will often allow for only reactive, not preventive regulat[ory action]." Ethyl Corp. v. EPA, [541 F.2d 1, 25 (D.C. Cir. 1976)]. Congress apparently shares this view; it specifically directed the Administrator to allow an adequate margin of safety to protect against effects which have not yet been uncovered by research and effects whose medical significance is a matter of disagreement. . . . Congress' directive to the Administrator to allow an "adequate margin of safety" alone plainly refutes any suggestion that the Administrator is only authorized to set primary air quality standards which are designed to protect against health effects that are known to be clearly harmful.
>
> Furthermore, we agree with the Administrator that requiring EPA to wait until it can conclusively demonstrate that a particular effect is adverse to health before it acts is inconsistent with both the Act's precautionary and preventive orientation and the nature of the Administrator's statutory responsibilities. Congress provided that the Administrator is to use his judgment in setting air quality standards precisely to permit him to act in the face of uncertainty. And as we read the statutory provisions and the legislative history, Congress directed the Administrator to err on the side of caution in making the necessary decisions. We see no reason why this court should put a gloss on Congress' scheme by requiring the Administrator to show that there is a medical consensus that the effects on which the lead standards were based are "clearly harmful to health." All that is required by the statutory scheme is evidence in the record which substantiates his conclusions about the health effects on which the standards were based. Accordingly, we reject LIA's claim that the Administrator exceeded his statutory authority. . . . [647 F.2d at 1154-1157.]

In effect, then, the court concluded that Congress intended to vest EPA with the authority to protect the public "against effects that research has not yet uncovered" (i.e., against risk).

The scope of agency authority to protect against risk was at issue in a series of early cases involving efforts to suspend or cancel the registration of DDT, an herbicide whose use allegedly was toxic to humans, animals, and nontarget plants, under the

---

*See also South Dakota v. United States Dep't of the Interior, 423 F.3d 790 (8th Cir. 2005) (holding that a statute that delegated to the Secretary of the Interior the authority to acquire land "for the purpose of providing land for Indians" did not violate the nondelegation doctrine). For more on the nondelegation doctrine, see Heinzerling, The Clean Air Act and the Constitution, 20 St. Louis U. Pub. L. Rev. 121 (2001); McGarity, The Clean Air Act at a Crossroads: Statutory Interpretation and Longstanding Administrative Practice in the Shadow of the Delegation Doctrine, 9 N.Y.U. Envtl. L.J. 1 (2000); Symposium, The Phoenix Rises Again: The Nondelegation Doctrine from Constitutional and Policy Perspectives, 20 Cardozo L. Rev. 731-1018 (1999).

Federal Insecticide, Fungicide, and Rodenticide Act (FIFRA), 7 U.S.C. §§136-136y. In *EDF v. Ruckelshaus*, 465 F.2d 528 (D.C. Cir. 1973), the court remanded EPA's decision not to suspend the registration pending resolution of cancellation proceedings, under a statutory provision authorizing suspension if "such action is necessary to prevent an imminent hazard." The court found that evidence of "a substantial likelihood that serious harm will be experienced" during the cancellation proceedings would justify suspension. The same year, *EDF v. EPA*, 489 F.2d 1247 (D.C. Cir. 1973), endorsed EPA's cancellation of DDT's registration for most uses. The court upheld EPA's conclusion that continued use of the herbicide posed unreasonable risks to health and the environment.

The precautionary approach to regulation was fully articulated in two landmark decisions, *Reserve Mining Co. v. EPA*, 514 F.2d 492 (8th Cir. 1975), and *Ethyl Corp. v. EPA*, 541 F.2d 1 (D.C. Cir. 1976), which are discussed further in Chapter 8. These opinions posit that whenever a statute instructs a regulator to protect the public from exposure to the danger (risk) of possible harm, as opposed to harm certain to occur unless exposure is prevented, Congress intended for the regulator to weigh subjectively the magnitude of the harm (if it did occur) against the probability that it will occur at all and then decide what regulatory action is warranted in light of the seriousness of the risk presented. In *Ethyl*, the court upheld EPA's adoption of standards under §211(c)(1)(A) of the CAA that phased out the use of lead in gasoline. The statute authorized EPA to regulate the lead content if it determined that emissions "will endanger" public health, without providing any guidance on how strict the standard had to be. Similarly, *Lead Industries* reveals that the precautionary standard in §109 gives EPA great leeway to set standards despite scientific uncertainty.

5. *Peer Review of the NAAQS.* The Environmental Research, Development, and Demonstration Authorization Act of 1978, 42 U.S.C. §4365, authorizes the creation of a Scientific Advisory Board (SAB) to render advice on a wide range of environmental issues and assess the integrity of EPA research. The 1977 CAA amendments established the Clean Air Scientific Advisory Committee (CASAC), a seven-member independent advisory committee authorized to review ambient standards and criteria documents every five years. CASAC must publicly review any proposed EPA standard under §§109, 111, or 112. §109(d)(2).

6. *Risk-Based Regulation of Hazardous Air Pollutants.* Risk-based and precautionary regulation has not always been successful. Before 1990 the CAA required that EPA issue national emission standards for hazardous air pollutants, which were defined as pollutants that "may reasonably be anticipated to result in an increase" in serious illness or mortality. The standards had to be set "at the level which in [the Administrator's] judgment provides an ample margin of safety to protect the public health." Most of the pollutants that EPA considered regulating under this authority were known or suspected carcinogens. EPA struggled with the proper analytical methodology for setting standards for these substances in light of its view that it was impossible to establish a safe threshold level of exposure to them and its obligation to provide "an ample margin of safety." In *NRDC v. EPA*, 824 F.2d 1146 (D.C. Cir. 1987), the court rejected NRDC's argument that the statute required a complete prohibition on emissions whenever EPA was incapable of establishing a safe threshold level. According to Judge Bork, "Congress' use of the word 'safety' . . . is significant evidence that it did not intend to require the Administrator to prohibit all emissions of non-threshold pollutants. . . . '[S]afe' does not mean 'risk-free.' Instead, something is 'unsafe' only when it threatens humans with 'a significant risk of harm.'" Id. at 1152. The court also

held, however, that EPA's chosen methodology for setting emission levels for non-threshold pollutants was improper because the agency substituted technological feasibility for health protection as the primary consideration. Precluded from placing significant emphasis on cost, EPA virtually abandoned efforts to regulate hazardous air pollutants. In 1990 Congress amended the statute by authorizing EPA in §112 to adopt a technology-based approach to regulation of hazardous air pollutants. It retained risk-based standards as a backup in the event that technology-based controls did not reduce the risks of exposure to acceptable levels.

7. *Unanswered Questions.* The Court in *American Trucking* remanded the case to the Court of Appeals "to dispose of any preserved challenge to the NAAQS" under §307(d)(9). That provision authorizes judicial reversal of any decision by EPA that is "arbitrary, capricious, an abuse of discretion, or otherwise not in accordance with law." In the following decision the D.C. Circuit addressed claims by industry and a group of states that the particulate matter and ozone standards were arbitrary and capricious.

AMERICAN TRUCKING ASSOCIATIONS, INC. v. EPA
283 F.3d 355 (D.C. Cir. 2002)

TATEL, Circuit Judge: . . .

III . . .

State and Business Petitioners urge us to vacate the primary NAAQS [for PM2.5] because EPA "did not apply *any* legal standard, much less the correct standard." In support of this argument, they cite two passages in the final PM2.5 rule. In one, Petitioners claim, EPA asserted that it had no obligation to determine a "safe level" of PM2.5 prior to adopting a primary NAAQS. In the other, EPA allegedly acknowledged that "its approach 'might result in regulatory programs that go *beyond* those that are *needed* to effectively reduce risks to public health.'" 62 Fed. Reg. at 38,675 (emphasis added). As Petitioners see it, these "concessions" prove that EPA failed to set the primary NAAQS at levels "'requisite'—that is, not lower or higher than . . . necessary—to protect the public health with an adequate margin of safety," as mandated by *Whitman*, 531 U.S. at 475-76.

Petitioners' argument suffers from two significant flaws. First, the final PM rule makes neither alleged concession. In the first passage, which Petitioners cite as evidence that EPA failed to identify a "safe level" of PM2.5, the Agency merely disclaimed any obligation to set primary NAAQS by means of a two-step process, identifying a "safe level" and then applying an additional margin of safety. Instead, EPA stated, it "may take into account margin of safety considerations throughout the process as long as such considerations are fully explained and supported by the record." Nothing in this statement implies that EPA failed to determine "safe levels" for fine particulate matter; indeed, the Agency's establishment of new primary NAAQS demonstrates that it did reach a conclusion regarding "safe" daily and annual-average PM2.5 levels. . . .

Viewed in its proper context, EPA's other alleged "concession"—that the new NAAQS "go beyond" what is necessary to protect public health—proves equally chimerical. In the final PM2.5 rule, EPA said only that "a number of . . . commenters [to the proposed NAAQS] strongly supported standard levels more stringent than those proposed by" the Agency, but that "setting such [lower] standards . . . *might result in regulatory programs that go beyond those that are needed to effectively reduce risks to public health.*" Id. at 38,675 (emphasis added). This passage in no way supports Petitioners' argument that EPA failed to set the primary PM2.5 NAAQS at levels " 'requisite' . . . to protect the public health with an adequate margin of safety." *Whitman*, 531 U.S. at 475-76. Instead, the passage documents EPA's rejection of lower standards, demonstrating that the Agency not only recognized, but acted upon, its statutory obligation to set the primary NAAQS at levels no lower than necessary to reduce public health risks.

Petitioners' argument that EPA neither identified nor applied the proper legal standard also exaggerates the Agency's obligation to quantify its decisionmaking. The argument relies on two statements from the rulemaking and one from [the D.C. Circuit's initial decision in *American Trucking* (ATA I)]: EPA's assertion that it need not "determine a 'safe level' " of PM2.5 before calculating a margin of safety; the Agency's "disavow[al]" of certain "specific risk estimates"; and finally, the Agency's claim that "there is no threshold 'amount of scientific information or degree of certainty' required to promulgate or revise a NAAQS." [The court rejected the Petitioners' contention that American Lung Ass'n v. EPA, 134 F.3d 388 (D.C. Cir. 1998), requires EPA "to identify perfectly safe levels of pollutants, to rely on specific risk estimates, or to specify threshold amounts of scientific information."]

Although we recognize that the Clean Air Act and circuit precedent require EPA qualitatively to describe the standard governing its selection of particular NAAQS, we have expressly rejected the notion that the Agency must "establish a measure of the risk to safety it considers adequate to protect public health every time it establishes a [NAAQS]." NRDC v. EPA, 902 F.2d 962, 973 (D.C. Cir. 1990), *vacated in part*, 921 F.2d 326 (D.C. Cir. 1991). Such a rule would compel EPA to leave hazardous pollutants unregulated unless and until it completely understands every risk they pose, thus thwarting the Clean Air Act's requirement that the Agency err on the side of caution by setting primary NAAQS that "allow[] an adequate margin of safety[.]" 42 U.S.C. §7409(b)(1). The Act requires EPA to promulgate protective primary NAAQS even where, as here, the pollutant's risks cannot be quantified or "precisely identified as to nature or degree," 62 Fed. Reg. at 38,653. For its part, *American Lung Ass'n* requires only that EPA "engage in reasoned decision-making," not that it definitively identify pollutant levels below which risks to public health are negligible.

Thus, EPA's inability to guarantee the accuracy or increase the precision of the PM2.5 NAAQS in no way undermines the standards' validity. Rather, these limitations indicate only that significant scientific uncertainty remains about the health effects of fine particulate matter at low atmospheric concentrations. As the exhaustive rulemaking process makes clear, EPA set the primary NAAQS notwithstanding that uncertainty, just as the Act requires.

We are equally unpersuaded by State and Business Petitioners' argument that EPA should have considered whether reducing atmospheric concentrations of fine particles would increase levels of " 'ozone or . . . a different fine particle component,' potentially *increasing* [overall] health risk[s]." 61 Fed. Reg. at 65,768. Petitioners apparently believe EPA may not regulate one pollutant without determining how that regulation would affect the levels of all other pollutants with which the first could react. Given the complexity of atmospheric chemistry, however, imposing such a requirement would hamstring the Agency, preventing it from complying with the Clean Air Act's mandate to set protective primary NAAQS. We might feel differently about EPA's obligations in this regard had Petitioners pointed to clear evidence that lowering atmospheric PM2.5 levels will necessarily increase levels of other pollutants. Petitioners cite no such evidence, however. . . .

IV . . .

American Trucking Associations and the other Ozone Petitioners challenge the NAAQS [for ozone] along several lines. To begin with, just as State and Business Petitioners argued with respect to the NAAQS for particulate matter, Ozone Petitioners contend that EPA neither identified nor applied "*any* legal standard" in setting the ozone NAAQS. . . . As we discussed earlier, however, EPA has no obligation either to identify an accurate "safe level" of a pollutant or to quantify precisely the pollutant's risks prior to setting primary NAAQS. Rather, EPA must err on the side of caution, just as it did here—setting the NAAQS at whatever level it deems necessary and sufficient to protect the public health with an adequate margin of safety, taking into account both the available evidence and the inevitable scientific uncertainties.

Petitioners raise two specific arguments regarding the primary ozone NAAQS. First, they assert that EPA "failed to determine whether attainment of the [old, one-hour-average, primary ozone] standard would leave unacceptable public health risk," and relatedly, that "none of the alternative [eight]-hour standards [considered by EPA] is significantly more protective of the public health than the [old] [one]-hour NAAQS." We disagree. As noted earlier, not only is the record replete with references to studies demonstrating the inadequacies of the old one-hour standard, but EPA discussed at length the advantages of a longer averaging time, including reduced risk of prolonged exposures to unhealthy ozone levels and increased uniformity of protection across different urban areas. Moreover, EPA specifically cited CASAC's "consensus . . . that an [eight]-hour standard [is] more appropriate for a human health-based standard than a [one]-hour standard" and its recommendation that "the present . . . standard be eliminated and replaced with an [eight]-hour standard." Given this record evidence, our deferential standard of review, and the Clean Air Act's requirement that EPA must either follow CASAC's advice or explain why the proposed rule "differs . . . from . . . [CASAC's] recommendations," 42 U.S.C. §7607(d)(3), Petitioners cannot seriously expect us to second-guess EPA's conclusion regarding the inadequacy of the old, one-hour-average standard.

Though somewhat more persuasive, Petitioners' second specific challenge also falls short. They argue that in selecting a level of 0.08 ppm rather than 0.09 or 0.07, EPA reached "inconsistent conclusions regarding specific health risks," thus "demonstrat[ing] that [the Agency's] decision to revise the NAAQS lacks a rational basis and therefore is arbitrary and capricious." In support of this point, Petitioners challenge EPA's three justifications for selecting 0.08 rather than 0.07: that no CASAC member supported a standard below 0.08; that health effects at ozone levels below 0.08 are transient and reversible; and that 0.07 would be too close to peak background levels. As to the first point, Petitioners observe that "most members of the CASAC panel who expressed an opinion on standard level supported a level *above* . . . 0.08 ppm." . . . In addition, Petitioners point out, *ATA I* expressly discredits the contention that ozone health effects are more transient and reversible at concentrations below 0.08 ppm than at concentrations between 0.08 and 0.09. 175 F.3d at 1035 (. . . "it is far from apparent that any health effects existing above [0.08 ppm] are permanent or irreversible"). Petitioners finally note that proximity to peak background levels is an indeterminate standard that points to no particular level for the primary NAAQS.

Although we think Petitioners' individual criticisms have some force, we are satisfied that in selecting a level of 0.08 rather than 0.07 (or, for that matter, 0.09), EPA "engage[d] in reasoned decision-making." *American Lung Ass'n*, 134 F.3d at 392. For one thing, CASAC's inability to reach consensus is hardly dispositive; EPA is entitled to give "significant weight" to the fact that no committee member advocated a level of 0.07 ppm, particularly as eight of the ten panel members who expressed opinions advocated a level of 0.08 ppm or greater, while the remaining two simply "endorsed the [0.07-0.09 ppm] range presented by the Agency . . . and stated that the [final] selection should be a policy decision." Also, although relative proximity to peak background ozone concentrations did not, in itself, necessitate a level of 0.08, EPA could consider that factor when choosing among the three alternative levels. Most convincing, though, is the absence of *any* human clinical studies at ozone concentrations below 0.08. This lack of data amply supports EPA's assertion that the most serious health effects of ozone are "less certain" at low concentrations, providing an eminently rational reason to set the primary standard at a somewhat higher level, at least until additional studies become available. Overall, therefore, we disagree with Petitioners that in selecting 0.08 ppm rather than a lower or higher level, EPA reached "inconsistent conclusions." The Agency could reasonably conclude that existing data support a standard below 0.09 but do not yet justify a standard below 0.08.

This brings us, finally, to Petitioners' challenges to the secondary ozone NAAQS. According to Petitioners, the secondary NAAQS are unlawful because EPA failed to account for factors other than ozone — including "temperature, rainfall, and pests" — that affect crop-yield. This is unreasonable. EPA had no more obligation to consider climatic conditions and pests in "evaluat[ing] whether its new [secondary] standard would measurably improve crop yield," than to consider automobile accidents and malnutrition in evaluating whether its new primary standard would measurably improve public health. The Clean Air Act directs EPA to protect public welfare from adverse effects of ozone and other pollutants; the Agency cannot escape that directive simply because ozone wreaks less havoc than temperature, rainfall, and pests. . . .

NOTES AND QUESTIONS

1. *The PM$_{2.5}$ Standard.* To what extent is EPA required to quantify the level of exposure to a criteria pollutant that is "safe"? What would such a quantification requirement mean in the context of efforts to regulate non-threshold pollutants? In what way did the court use the cautionary nature of the statute to reject the petitioners' attacks on the PM$_{2.5}$ standard? Does the statute mandate that EPA tack on the required "margin of safety" in any particular fashion? The D.C. Circuit decided in *Lead Indus. Ass'n* that the CAA does not require that EPA add on one margin of safety at the end of its effort to ascertain the "requisite" level of public health protection, instead of building in multiple margins of safety into the standards at various points of analysis. Why didn't EPA err in failing to consider whether reduction of PM$_{2.5}$ would increase overall health risks by exacerbating other forms of air pollution?

In 2006, EPA revised the NAAQS for PM again. It lowered the primary standard for particles smaller than 2.5 microns ($PM_{2.5}$) from 65 to 35 $\mu g/m^3$ averaged over 24 hours. The agency rejected the recommendation of CASAC, however, that it adopt even more stringent standards. It refused to tighten the standard for $PM_{2.5}$ averaged on an annual basis (which remained at 15 $\mu g/m^3$, but which CASAC recommended be reduced to 13 or 14 $\mu g/m^3$) or the short-term standard for PM_{10}. It also revoked the annual standard for coarse particles. EPA set the secondary PM standards equal in all respects to the primary standards, as revised. 71 Fed. Reg. 61,144, 61,144 (2006).

2. *The Ozone Standard.* On what basis did EPA justify selection of a level of 0.08 ppm rather than 0.07 or 0.09? What was the basis for Petitioners' attack on the secondary NAAQS for ozone? Why did the court reject the attack?

3. *The Environmental Petitioners' Claims.* Environmental groups in the 2002 ATA case attacked the $PM_{2.5}$ standard as being too lenient. The court disagreed with their contention that EPA should have set a stricter daily standard rather than relying almost exclusively on an annual standard, and that the secondary standard was inadequate to improve visibility in much of the western United States.

4. *Judicial Consideration of the SO_2 NAAQS.* In 1996 EPA decided not to revise the annual and 24-hour primary standards for SO_2. It admitted that a substantial portion (at least 20 percent) of mild to moderate asthmatics were being exposed to SO_2 concentrations that could be expected to cause adverse respiratory symptoms, and that repeated occurrences of such effects should be regarded as a significant health issue. But the agency also concluded that the problem was not a "broad public health problem when viewed from a national perspective." Rather, the localized, infrequent, and site-specific risks involved would be better addressed at the state level. Instead of revising the NAAQS, therefore, EPA announced that it would rely largely on state control of short-term peak SO_2 levels. If a state had reason to believe that ambient levels of SO_2 may constitute an imminent and substantial endangerment, it could consider taking immediate action to protect the public health. EPA reserved the right to act in the event the state failed to address an imminent and substantial endangerment or if EPA had evidence that SO_2 levels caused an endangerment due to their frequency, magnitude, and reported health impacts.

Is this approach to public health protection authorized by §109? By any other provision of the CAA? See §303. Consider American Lung Ass'n v. EPA, 134 F.3d 388 (D.C. Cir. 1998), which remanded EPA's decision not to revise the primary SO_2 standard to control exposure to high-level SO_2 bursts of five or more minutes for lack of an adequate explanation. The Administrator concluded that no national public health problem had been identified because the bursts were infrequent and site-specific. The bursts affect asthmatics, who are subject to bronchoconstriction, but the effects range from short-term discomfort to rare instances of death when individuals are exposed to SO_2 concentrations below 1.0 ppm while they are engaged in strenuous activity. The medical community is split regarding the medical significance of the effects, and research studies on the number of asthmatics who suffer stress from repeated bursts were inconclusive:

> . . . [W]e think the Administrator has failed to explain [her conclusion] that SO_2 bursts do not amount to a "public health" problem within the meaning of the Act. The link between this conclusion and the factual record as interpreted by EPA—that "repeated" exposure is "significant" and that thousands of asthmatics are exposed more than once a year—is missing. Why is the fact that thousands of asthmatics can be expected to suffer

atypical physical effects from repeated five-minute bursts of high-level sulfur dioxide not a public health problem? Why are from 180,000 to 395,000 annual "exposure events" . . . so "infrequent" as to warrant no regulatory action? Why are disruptions of ongoing activities, use of medication, and hospitalization not "adverse health effects" for asthmatics? Answers to these questions appear nowhere in the administrative record.

In her only statement resembling an explanation for her conclusion that peak SO_2 bursts present no public health hazard, the Administrator characterizes the bursts as "localized, infrequent and site-specific." But nothing in the Final Decision explains why "localized," "site-specific" or even "infrequent" events might nevertheless create a public health problem, particularly since, in some sense, all pollution is local and site-specific, whether spewing from the tailpipes of millions of cars or a few offending smoke stacks. From the record, we know that at least six communities experience "repeated high 5-minute peaks greater than 0.60 ppm SO_2," and agency counsel told us at oral argument that these so-called "hot spots" are not the only places where repeated exposure occurs. Nowhere, however, does the Administrator explain why these data amount to no more than a "local" problem.

Without answers to these questions, the Administrator cannot fulfill her responsibility under the Clean Air Act to establish NAAQS "requisite to protect the public health," 42 U.S.C. §7409(b)(1), nor can we review her decision. Judicial deference to decisions of administrative agencies like EPA rests on the fundamental premise that agencies engage in reasoned decision-making. . . . Where, as here, Congress has delegated to an administrative agency the critical task of assessing the public health and the power to make decisions of national import in which individuals' lives and welfare hang in the balance, that agency has the heaviest of obligations to explain and expose every step of its reasoning. [Id. at 392.]

Suppose the agency had found that SO_2 bursts caused adverse health effects for asthmatics. Would it have been required to amend the NAAQS? How does the "margin of safety" requirement of §109(b)(1) bear on this question? What obligations does the statute impose on the agency to protect sensitive individuals? In another portion of the opinion, the court stated that

Congress defined the public health broadly. NAAQS must protect not only average healthy individuals, but also "sensitive citizens"—children, for example, or people with asthma, emphysema, or other conditions rendering them particularly vulnerable to air pollution. If a pollutant adversely affects the health of these sensitive individuals, EPA must strengthen the entire national standard. [Id. at 389.]

Does EPA have the same discretion to refuse to set a margin of safety that it has to set one? Given the lack of scientific consensus and the fact that most adverse effects of SO_2 bursts appear to be reversible, was it not reasonable for the Administrator to defer the setting of a more stringent standard until further research resolved some of the uncertainties?

5. *More on Cost Considerations.* Another case cited by the D.C. Circuit in *American Trucking* is NRDC v. EPA, 902 F.2d 962 (D.C. Cir. 1990). In that case the court rejected a challenge by the American Iron & Steel Institute (AISI) to EPA's 24-hour and annual primary standards for SO_2. Among other things, AISI argued that EPA violated §109(b)(1) by failing to consider the adverse consequences to the public health that would result from the unemployment attributable to efforts to comply with the standard. But the court found the argument to be meritless. "Consideration of costs associated with alleged health risks from unemployment

would be flatly inconsistent with the statute, legislative history, and case law on this point." Id. at 973.

NOTE ON THE CONCEPT OF TECHNOLOGY FORCING

Technology-Based and Technology-Forcing Standards. The Supreme Court in *American Trucking* described the CAA as "technology forcing" in character. The Court had previously found that the Act was "expressly designed to force regulated sources to develop pollution control devices that might at the time appear to be economically or technologically infeasible." Union Elec. Co. v. EPA, 427 U.S. 246, 257 (1976). The concept of technology forcing emerged most clearly in the context of the statutory provisions designed to reduce emissions from mobile sources—cars, trucks, and buses. As enacted in 1970, the CAA required automobile manufacturers to curtail new vehicle emissions of pollutants such as HC, CO, and NO_x by 90 percent within five or six years. The manufacturers claimed that the technology necessary to meet these vehicle emission standards did not yet exist and could not be developed by the statutory deadline. Congress adopted the standards anyway, in the hope that they would provide industry with a strong incentive to invest in research and development, thus forcing an acceleration in the pace of technological innovation. When industry failed to comply and EPA failed to extend the deadlines, the court in International Harvester Co. v. Ruckelshaus, 478 F.2d 615 (D.C. Cir. 1973), remanded for further consideration given its "grave doubts" as to the soundness of EPA's prediction that the necessary technology would be available in time to meet the standards. Id. at 648. EPA eventually backed down, and Congress subsequently provided additional extensions.

Debate over the propriety of applying technology forcing to vehicle emission controls has since reemerged. The scope of EPA's discretion to force the development of new technologies was at issue in NRDC v. Thomas, 805 F.2d 410 (D.C. Cir. 1986). NRDC challenged EPA's 1985 regulations to reduce heavy-duty motor vehicle emissions of particulate matter (some of it coated with carcinogenic compounds) and NO_x as too lenient, and the Engine Manufacturers Association attacked them as too stringent. Congress did not establish emission standards for heavy-duty engines. Instead, it ordered EPA to set "standards which reflect the greatest degree of emission reduction achievable through the application of technology which the Administrator determines will be available for the model year to which such standards apply." §202(a)(3)(A)(iii). In issuing those standards, EPA was to give "appropriate consideration to the cost of applying such technology within the period of time available to manufacturers and to noise, energy, and safety factors associated with the application of such technology." Id.

NRDC claimed that EPA improperly failed to set the standards at levels based on what the most advanced engine, the technological leader in the industry, was capable of achieving. EPA instead devised its regulations on the basis of what the engine manufacturing industry as a whole could accomplish. The court sided with EPA, concluding that the statute did not mandate "a leader-specific balancing" process. Industry fared no better in its attack on the particulate standards as being too stringent. Section 202(a)(3)(A)(iii) required EPA to set standards based on technology that "will be available" for the applicable model year. Industry argued that the statute did not envision technology forcing and that, as a result, EPA was confined to the adoption of standards reflecting technology that was adequately demonstrated. But the court held that the statute did indeed envision technology forcing:

> The agency describes technology-forcing standards as those that "are to be based upon that technology which the Administrator determines will be available, and not necessarily that technology which is *already available*. The adoption of such standards helps to encourage and hasten the development of new technology." 49 Fed. Reg. 40,258, 40,258 (1984). On the other hand, an adequately demonstrated technology "is one which has been *shown* to be reasonably reliable, reasonably efficient, and which can reasonably be expected to serve the interests of pollution control without becoming exorbitantly costly in an economic or environmental way." Essex Chem. Corp. v. Ruckelshaus, 486 F.2d 427, 433 (D.C. Cir. 1973). That the provisions at issue in this case seek to promote technological advances while also accounting for cost does not detract from their categorization as technology-forcing standards. As we pointed out in NRDC v. EPA, 655 F.2d 318, 328 (D.C. Cir. 1981):
>
> > The legislative history of both the 1970 and the 1977 amendments demonstrates that Congress intended the agency to project future advances in pollution control capability. It was "expected to press for the development and application of improved technology rather than be limited by that which exists today." S. Rep. No. 1196, 91st Cong., 2d Sess. 24 (1970). . . . [Id. at 429 n.30.]

The CAA "level[ed its] sights on the future, permitting the agency to set standards based on projections of technology that is not currently available." Id. at 429. Compare Bluewater Network v. EPA, 370 F.3d 1 (D.C. Cir. 2004), where the court rejected an environmental group's claim that §213(a)(3) requires EPA to set emission standards for snowmobiles at a level of stringency that would require discontinuation of all vehicles other than those satisfying "basic demand." The court concluded that EPA may rely on cost and other statutory factors to set standards at a level less stringent than reflected by across-the-fleet implementation of advanced technologies.

The court in NRDC v. Thomas distinguished between technology-forcing standards and those based on adequately demonstrated technology, concluding that Congress intended in the context of heavy-duty vehicle emission controls to authorize the imposition of the former. In a subsequent·case, NRDC v. Reilly, 983 F.2d 259 (D.C. Cir. 1993), the same court characterized this distinction as one between "absolute" and technology-based standards. The discussion arose in the context of a challenge to EPA's failure to issue regulations under §202(a)(6) to control vehicle refueling emissions through on-board devices. EPA regarded on-board refueling vapor recovery (ORVR) as inherently and unreasonably unsafe.

> We have previously noted a distinction between provisions in the [CAA] that are "technology-based" and those that are "absolute." See NRDC v. EPA, 655 F.2d 318, 322 & 332 n.25 (D.C. Cir. 1981). Technology-based provisions require EPA to promulgate standards only after finding that the requisite technology exists or may be feasibly developed. Absolute standards, on the other hand, require compliance with statutorily prescribed standards and time tables, irrespective of present technologies. Absolute standards presume that industry can be driven to develop the requisite technologies.[12] In this case, the

---

12. This results in the so-called "technology-forcing" character of the CAA. See Union Elec. Co. v. EPA, 427 U.S. 246, 257 (1976); NRDC v. Thomas, 805 F.2d 410, 429 (D.C. Cir. 1986); see also 116 Cong. Rec. 42,381, 42,382 (1970) (claims of technological impossibility not sufficient to avoid standards under the CAA) (comments of Senator Muskie). It is the nature of technology-forcing sections that technical problems, including those involving safety, are ironed out in the

use of the word "systems" in section 202(a)(6), in combination with the statutorily fixed time table, indicates that this provision falls into the "absolute" category and, hence, is technology-forcing. There is nothing in the section warranting EPA's decision to limit its consideration of ORVR to a single existing technology. Moreover, this statutory command was not, EPA's protestations to the contrary notwithstanding, unrealistic. While it is true that alternative control methods are not production-ready, several are beyond the conceptualization stage and should have been amenable to engineering evaluation. [Id. at 268-269.]

The court found it significant that EPA did not conclude that ORVR systems were incapable of being made safe, and held that the agency's failure to issue the regulations conflicted with the technology-forcing intent of §202(a)(6). What is the role of technology forcing under a statute that orders EPA to adopt emission control standards that "achieve the greatest degree of emission reduction achievable through the application of technology which [EPA] determines will be available," but also requires that EPA consider "the lead time necessary to permit the development and application of the requisite technology"? See *Bluewater Network, supra* (upholding regulations issued under §213(a)(3), (b)).

How is EPA supposed to distinguish between an "absolute" and a more modest technology-based statutory mandate? How revealing is the statutory language likely to be? What were the statutory terms that led the courts in the two *NRDC* cases to conclude that Congress intended to force the development of vehicle emission control technology? Which of the following vehicle emission control provisions appear to be technology forcing in nature: §§202(a)(3)(A)(i), 202(a)(3)(D), 202(a)(4)(A)-(B), 202(a)(6), 202(g)(1), 202(i)(3)(B)?

The Basis for Forcing Technology. EPA frequently is required to set standards based on the agency's assessment of the likely future course of technological development. The court in *Thomas* held that EPA could impose a technology-forcing standard. Does the court's emphasis lie on merely projecting and predicting future development or on pressing and motivating the manufacturers to do better? Consider the following:

> Early federal efforts in the field of air pollution tried to attack the engineering problem through public funding of research and development projects. It was assumed that equipment would be used if it were available. But as it became recognized that the owner of a pollution source did not have a natural incentive to install abatement equipment even when available, federal legislation moved into a second phase, requiring installation by federal enforcement. In this second phase, however, it was still assumed that the responsibility to develop new equipment lay with the Government rather than the polluter. Thus, federal laws requiring installation of available equipment were accompanied by a stepped-up effort to solve the engineering problem through federal research and development.
>
> Eventually it was recognized that government resources alone could not solve the engineering problem, nor was the problem being solved by other means. In fact, there was every incentive for a polluter *not* to solve it, just as there was every incentive not to install pollution control equipment already in existence. This led to the third phase of legislation, which directly confronted the policy problem of who bears the responsibility, and endorsed the concept of "technology-forcing." The polluter, it was decided, has the

---

course of the statutorily spurred process of research and development. It is not necessary, or even anticipated, that required systems will be absolutely safe at the prototype stage of development.

responsibility not only to install needed equipment, but also to invent it. This makes sense for a number of reasons. The polluter is likely to have far greater knowledge of the cause of the problem, the best ways to abate it, and the most efficient ways of integrating the potential solutions into normal business practices. The competitive system normally discourages any individual polluter from voluntarily undertaking additional expenses for the sake of pollution control. But this new approach can be used to encourage individuals (whether owners of pollution sources or independent entrepreneurs) to search for solutions. If a government-imposed emission limit is scheduled to take effect on a certain date, the one who finds a solution has a ready-made market for his invention. [J. Bonine, The Evolution of Technology-Forcing in the Clean Air Act, 6 Env't Rep. (BNA) Monograph No. 21, at 2 (July 25, 1975).]

The Role of Risk Reduction in Technology Forcing. What is the relationship between the health protection goals of a statute like the CAA and the objective of technology forcing? If a technology-forcing mandate is based on a decision to press industry to perform better, the question remains how hard to press for improved emission controls. Assessing the importance of rapid developments requires considering the health risks that technology is being "forced" to reduce. A precise formulation of this point appeared in Sierra Club v. Costle, 657 F.2d 298 (D.C. Cir. 1981), in which Judge Wald speculated that EPA cannot decide meaningfully how much marginal pollution reduction to require at very high levels of control—at which each new increment of pollution control secures much less pollution reduction than the preceding one—without examining whether the small pollution control gain is worth its high cost in terms of health protection "purchased." Thus marginal investment in pollution control becomes a surrogate dollar measure of the marginal health gains that progressively stricter regulation might "buy." Even if a statute does not explicitly require that health be considered in setting technology-based standards, it may be impossible for EPA to exclude it entirely from the judgment process. For more on technology forcing, see generally La Pierre, Technology-Forcing and Federal Environmental Protection Statutes, 62 Iowa L. Rev. 771 (1977).

2.   Achievement of the NAAQS through State Implementation Plans

The CAA makes the states primarily responsible for ensuring adequate air quality within their geographic areas. Each state must submit for EPA approval a state implementation plan (SIP) that specifies the manner in which the NAAQS will be achieved and maintained within each air quality control region (AQCR) within the state. §107(a). This section describes how states designate AQCRs and develop, submit for EPA approval, and revise their SIPs.

a.   Designation of Air Quality Control Regions

Although different problems face "clean-air" and "dirty-air" areas, the 1970 Act made no distinction among types of AQCR based on the severity of air pollution. The 1977 amendments divided the country into nonattainment areas, where the NAAQS have not been met, and attainment areas (also known as clean-air or nondegradation or PSD areas), where the quality of the air is better than the ambient standards require.

Sections F and G below elaborate on the different control strategies for these two types of regions and describe how the broad discretion initially vested in the states to achieve the NAAQS has been circumscribed by the provisions of the 1977 and 1990 amendments that govern nonattainment or PSD areas. For now, the essential point is that each state is responsible for meeting the ambient standards for its AQCRs, and the SIPs detail the means the state will use to do so.

The Act requires that, within one year of issuance or revision of a NAAQS, each state submit to EPA a list of AQCRs within the state divided into three categories: nonattainment, attainment, and unclassifiable. §107(d)(1)(A). EPA must review these submissions and approve them (with whatever modifications EPA deems necessary) within two years of issuance or revision of the NAAQS. §107(d)(1)(B). In determining whether to modify a state's choice of boundary lines for AQCRs, EPA tends to defer to the governor's recommendations. See, e.g., Pennsylvania v. EPA, 429 F.3d 1125 (D.C. Cir. 2005). EPA may also initiate the process of redesignation on the basis of planning and control considerations or air quality–related considerations. §107(d)(3).

The category into which an AQCR falls is important because the controls that apply to air pollution sources within the area, the nature of the state's obligations in formulating its SIP, and the sanctions available to the government for noncompliance with the NAAQS all differ depending on the status of an AQCR. The extent to which new stationary sources must apply for a construction and operating permit, for example, differs between nonattainment and attainment areas, as do the substantive criteria for permit issuance. Some states have attempted to upgrade nonattainment areas to attainment status to avoid the constraints and sanctions that apply exclusively to the former. Ohio v. Ruckelshaus, 776 F.2d 1333 (6th Cir. 1985), upheld EPA's refusal to allow the state to carve out and redesignate as an attainment area an upwind county that was part of the Cleveland nonattainment area. The state argued that the county qualified as an attainment area because air quality monitoring data indicated that the relevant NAAQS (for ozone) was being achieved in the county. At the time, §171(2) of the statute defined a nonattainment area as "an area which is shown by monitored data or which is calculated by air quality modeling . . . to exceed any [NAAQS] for such pollutant." EPA refused the state's request for redesignation because nearly 20 percent of ozone precursors in Cleveland, where the ozone NAAQS was not being achieved, originated in the upwind county. Compare Illinois State Chamber of Commerce v. EPA, 775 F.2d 1141 (7th Cir. 1985) (reversing as inconsistent with prior implementation policy EPA's refusal to allow redesignation of two ozone nonattainment areas because they contributed to nonattainment in nearby Chicago). How would these two cases be decided under the current statute? See §§171(2), 107(d)(1), (3)(E), (4)(A)(iv)-(v). How does the presence of interstate pollution affect the ability of the states to redesignate AQCRs? See §107(d)(3)(A), (e)(2).

Section 107(d)(3)(E) sets forth the requirements for redesignation of an AQCR. These include the approval of a maintenance plan for the area that complies with §175A. The plan must provide for the maintenance of the NAAQS for at least ten years after the redesignation and contain "such additional measures, if any, as may be necessary to ensure such maintenance." §175A(a). A state seeking redesignation also must submit a SIP revision that contains contingency measures, including a requirement that the state implement "all measures with respect to the control of the air pollutant concerned which were contained in the [SIP] for the area before redesignation of the area as an attainment area." §175A(d). Suppose that EPA had never approved a new source review (NSR) permit program under §§172(c)(5) and

173 while the area was classified as nonattainment. Must EPA include NSR as a contingency measure before it can redesignate the area as attainment? See Greenbaum v. EPA, 370 F.3d 527 (6th Cir. 2004) (deferring to EPA's negative answer). How specific must the description of the contingency measures in the maintenance plan be? See Sierra Club v. EPA, 375 F.3d 537 (7th Cir. 2004).

b.   Formulation, Approval, and Revision of SIPs

Section 110(a)(1) requires each state to adopt and submit a SIP to EPA within three years (or any shorter period prescribed by EPA) of EPA's issuance of the NAAQS. SIPs must contain "enforceable emission limitations and other control measures, means, or techniques . . . as may be necessary or appropriate" to meet and maintain the NAAQS. §110(a)(2)(A). Although SIPs and SIP revisions do not take effect as federal law until EPA approves them, §110(k)(3), the Supreme Court made it clear early on that Congress meant to leave the choice of emissions limitations for existing air pollution sources to the states, as long as the combination of measures selected were sufficient to achieve compliance with the NAAQS:

> The Act gives . . . [EPA] no authority to question the wisdom of a State's choices of emissions limitations if they are part of a plan which satisfies the standards of §110(a)(2). . . . Thus, so long as the ultimate effect of a State's choice of emission limitations is compliance with the national standards for ambient air, the state is at liberty to adopt whatever mix of emission limitations it deems best suited to its particular situation. [Train v. NRDC, Inc., 421 U.S. 60, 79 (1975).]

The following case, decided a year later, confirms this initial understanding of the relationship between federal and state authority to craft an emission control strategy and also addresses the scope of state discretion to push harder than the statute requires in controlling emissions. The failure of some states to comply with the NAAQS induced Congress in both the 1977 and 1990 amendments to remove some of the states' discretion. As you study the CAA in this chapter, take note of how the statute and EPA's implementation of it strike a balance between expeditious pursuit of acceptable air quality and a distaste for intruding too heavily on state prerogatives or on the ability of individuals to choose how, when, and where they may drive their cars and trucks.

UNION ELECTRIC COMPANY v. EPA
427 U.S. 246 (1976)

Mr. JUSTICE MARSHALL delivered the opinion of the Court.

[After the expiration of variances issued by Missouri to Union Electric for three of its coal-fired generating plants, EPA notified the company that its SO_2 emissions violated the state's SIP. Section 307(b)(1) allowed petitions for review of EPA's approval of a SIP to be filed in the federal courts of appeals more than 30 days after such approval only if the petition was "based solely on grounds arising after such 30th day." Union Electric claimed that economic and technological difficulties that had arisen more than 30 days after EPA's approval made compliance with the emission limitations impossible. . . . The Eighth Circuit held that it lacked jurisdiction because only matters which would justify setting aside EPA's initial approval of a SIP are properly reviewable after the initial 30-day review period. Since EPA lacked the power to reject a SIP based on claims of economic and technological infeasibility, such claims could not serve at any time as the basis for a court's overturning an approved plan.]

I

[T]he Clean Air Amendments of 1970 . . . reflect congressional dissatisfaction with the progress of existing air pollution programs and a determination to "tak[e] a stick to the States" [Train v. NRDC, Inc., 421 U.S. 60, 64 (1975)], in order to guarantee the prompt attainment and maintenance of specified air quality standards. The heart of the Amendments is the requirement that each State formulate, subject to EPA approval, an implementation plan designed to achieve national primary ambient air quality standards—those necessary to protect the public health—"as expeditiously as practicable but . . . in no case later than three years from the date of approval of such plan." §110(a)(2)(A). The plan must also provide for the attainment of national secondary ambient air quality standards—those necessary to protect the public welfare—within a "reasonable time." Each State is given wide discretion in formulating its plan, and the Act provides that the Administrator "shall approve" the proposed plan if it has been adopted after public notice and hearing and if it meets eight specified criteria. §110(a)(2). . . .

II

[The Court held that if "new grounds" are alleged for an appeal more than 30 days after the approval or promulgation of a SIP, "they must be such that, had they been known at the time the plan was presented to the Administrator for approval, it would have been an abuse of discretion for the Administrator to approve the plan."]

   Since a reviewing court—regardless of when the petition for review is filed—may consider claims of economic and technological infeasibility only if the Administrator may consider such claims in approving or rejecting a state implementation plan, we must address ourselves to the scope of the Administrator's responsibility. The Administrator's position is that he has no power whatsoever to reject a state implementation plan on the ground that it is economically or technologically infeasible. . . . [W]e agree that Congress intended claims of economic and technological infeasibility to be wholly foreign to the Administrator's consideration of a state implementation plan.

   As we have previously recognized, the 1970 Amendments to the Clean Air Act were a drastic remedy to what was perceived as a serious and otherwise uncheckable problem of air pollution. The Amendments place the primary responsibility for formulating pollution control strategies on the States, but nonetheless subject the States to strict minimum compliance requirements. These requirements are of a "technology-forcing character," and are expressly designed to force regulated sources to develop pollution control devices that might at the time appear to be economically or technologically infeasible.

This approach is apparent on the face of §110(a)(2). The provision sets out eight criteria that an implementation plan must satisfy, and provides that if these criteria are met, . . . the Administrator "shall approve" the proposed state plan. The mandatory "shall" makes it quite clear that the Administrator is not to be concerned with factors other than those specified, and none of the eight factors appears to permit consideration of technological or economic infeasibility.[5] . . .

It is suggested that consideration of claims of technological and economic infeasibility is required by the first criterion that the primary air quality standards be met "as expeditiously as practicable but . . . in no case later than three years . . ." and that the secondary air quality standards be met within a "reasonable time." §110(a)(2)(A). The argument is that what is "practicable" or "reasonable" cannot be determined without assessing whether what is proposed is possible. This argument does not survive analysis.

Section 110(a)(2)(A)'s three-year deadline for achieving primary air quality standards . . . leaves no room for claims of technological or economic infeasibility. The 1970 congressional debate . . . centered on whether technology forcing was necessary and desirable in framing and attaining air quality standards sufficient to protect the public health, standards later termed primary standards. . . . The Senate bill . . . flatly required that, possible or not, health-related standards be met "within three years."

The Senate's stiff requirement was intended to foreclose the claims of emission sources that it would be economically or technologically infeasible for them to achieve emission limitations sufficient to protect the public health within the specified time. As Senator Muskie, manager of the Senate bill, explained to his chamber:

> The first responsibility of Congress is not the making of technological or economic judgments or even to be limited by what is or appears to be technologically or economically feasible. Our responsibility is to establish what the public interest requires to protect the health of persons. This may mean that people and industries will be asked to do what seems to be impossible at the present time. [116 Cong. Rec. 32901-32902 (1970).]

This position reflected that of the Senate committee:

> In the Committee discussions, considerable concern was expressed regarding the use of the concept of technical feasibility as the basis of ambient air standards. The Committee determined that 1) the health of people is more important than the question of whether the early achievement of ambient air quality standards protective of health is technically feasible; and 2) the growth of pollution load in many areas, even with application of available technology, would still be deleterious to public health.
>
> Therefore, the Committee determined that existing sources of pollutants either should meet the standard of the law or be closed down. . . . [S. Rep. No. 91-1196, at 2-3 (1970).]

The Conference Committee and, ultimately, the entire Congress accepted the Senate's three-year mandate for the achievement of primary air quality standards, and

---

5. Comparison of the eight criteria of §110(a)(2) with other provisions of the [Act] bolsters this conclusion. Where Congress intended the Administrator to be concerned about economic and technological infeasibility, it expressly so provided. Thus, §§110(a), 110(f), 111(a)(1), 202(a), 211(c)(2)(A), and 231(b) of the Amendments all expressly permit consideration [of the cost of compliance]. Section 110(a)(2) contains no such language.

the clear import of that decision is that the Administrator must approve a plan that provides for attainment of the primary standards in three years even if attainment does not appear feasible. [H]owever, the conferees strengthened the Senate version. The Conference Committee made clear that the States could not procrastinate until the deadline approached. Rather, the primary standards had to be met in less than three years if possible; they had to be met "as expeditiously as practicable." §110(a)(2)(A). Whatever room there is for considering claims of infeasibility in the attainment of primary standards must lie in this phrase, which is, of course, relevant only in evaluating those implementation plans that attempt to achieve the primary standard in less than three years.

It is argued that when such a state plan calls for proceeding more rapidly than economics and the available technology appear to allow, the plan must be rejected as not "practicable." . . . Since the arguments supporting [the] theory [that EPA may reject a SIP for being too strict as well as for being too lax] are also made to show that the Administrator must reject a state plan that provides for achieving more than the secondary air quality standards require, we defer consideration of this question in order to outline the development and content of the secondary standards provision of §110(a)(2)(A).

Secondary air quality standards . . . were subject to far less legislative debate than the primary standards. . . . The final Amendments . . . adopted the House's requirement that [the secondary standards] be met within a "reasonable time." §§109(b), 110(a)(2)(A). Thus, technology forcing is not expressly required in achieving standards to protect the public welfare.

It does not necessarily follow, however, that the Administrator may consider claims of impossibility in assessing a state plan for achieving secondary standards. . . . [T]he scope of the Administrator's power to reject a plan depends on whether the State itself may decide to engage in technology forcing and adopt a plan more stringent than federal law demands.[7]

Amici Appalachian Power Co. et al. argue . . . that the States are precluded from submitting implementation plans more stringent than federal law demands by §110(a)(2)'s second criterion that the plan contain such control devices "as may be necessary" to achieve the primary and secondary air quality standards. §110(a)(2)(B). The contention is that an overly restrictive plan is not "necessary" for attainment of the national standards and so must be rejected by the Administrator.

The principal support for this theory of amici lies in the fact that while the House and Senate versions of §110(a)(2) both expressly provided that the States could submit for the Administrator's approval plans that were stricter than the national standards required, the section as enacted contains no such express language. . . . [W]hile the final language of §110(a)(2)(B) may be less explicit than the versions originally approved by the House and the Senate, the most natural reading of the "as may be necessary" phrase in context is simply that the Administrator must assure that the minimal, or "necessary" requirements are met, not that he detect and reject any state plan more demanding than federal law requires. . . .

We read the "as may be necessary" requirement of §110(a)(2)(B) to demand only that the implementation plan submitted by the State meet the "minimum conditions"

---

7. A different question would be presented if the Administrator drafted the plan himself pursuant to §110(c). Whether claims of economic or technical infeasibility must be considered by the Administrator in drafting an implementation plan is a question we do not reach.

of the Amendments.[13] Beyond that, if a State makes the legislative determination that it desires a particular air quality by a certain date and that it is willing to force technology to attain it or lose a certain industry if attainment is not possible such a determination is fully consistent with the structure and purpose of the Amendments, and §110(a)(2)(B) provides no basis for the EPA Administrator to object to the determination on the ground of infeasibility.[14]

In sum, we have concluded that claims of economic or technological infeasibility may not be considered by the Administrator in evaluating a state requirement that primary ambient air quality standards be met in the mandatory three years. And, since we further conclude that the States may submit implementation plans more stringent than federal law requires and that the Administrator must approve such plans if they meet the minimum requirements of §110(a)(2), it follows that the language of §110(a)(2)(B) provides no basis for the Administrator ever to reject a state implementation plan on the ground that it is economically or technologically infeasible. Accordingly, a court of appeals reviewing an approved plan under §307(b)(1) cannot set it aside on those grounds, no matter when they are raised.

III

Our conclusion is bolstered by recognition that the Amendments do allow claims of technological and economic infeasibility to be raised in situations where consideration of such claims will not substantially interfere with the primary congressional purpose of prompt attainment of the national air quality standards. Thus, we do not hold that . . . sources unable to comply with emission limitations must inevitably be shut down.

Perhaps the most important forum for consideration of claims of economic and technological infeasibility is before the state agency formulating the implementation plan. So long as the national standards are met, the State may select whatever mix of control devices it desires, and industries with particular economic or technological problems may seek special treatment in the plan itself. Moreover, if the industry is not exempted from, or accommodated by, the original plan, it may obtain a variance, as petitioner did in this case; and the variance, if granted after notice and a hearing, may be submitted to the EPA as a revision of the plan. Lastly, an industry denied an exemption from the implementation plan, or denied a subsequent variance, may be able to take its claims of economic or technological infeasibility to the state courts.[16] . . .

13. Economic and technological factors may be relevant in determining whether the minimum conditions are met. Thus, the Administrator may consider whether it is economically or technologically possible for the state plan to require more rapid progress than it does. If he determines that it is, he may reject the plan as not meeting the requirement that primary standards be achieved "as expeditiously as practicable" or as failing to provide for attaining secondary standards within "a reasonable time."

14. In a literal sense, of course, no plan is infeasible since offending sources always have the option of shutting down if they cannot otherwise comply with the standard of the law. Thus, there is no need for the Administrator to reject an economically or technologically "infeasible" state plan on the ground that anticipated noncompliance will cause the State to fall short of the national standards. Sources objecting to such a state scheme must seek their relief from the State.

16. Of course, the [Act does] not require the States to formulate their implementation plans with deference to claims of technological or economic infeasibility, to grant variances on those grounds, or to provide judicial review of such actions. Consistent with Congress' recognition of the primary role of the States in controlling air pollution, the [Act leaves] all such decisions to the States. . . .

Even if the State does not intervene on behalf of an emission source, techno-logical and economic factors may be considered in at least one other circumstance. When a source is found to be in violation of the state implementation plan, the Administrator may, after a conference with the operator, issue a compliance order rather than seek civil or criminal enforcement. Such an order must specify a "reason-able" time for compliance with the relevant standard, taking into account the seri-ousness of the violation and "any good faith efforts to comply with applicable requirements." §113(a)(4). Claims of technological or economic infeasibility, the Administrator agrees, are relevant to fashioning an appropriate compliance order under §113(a)(4).[18]

In short, the Amendments offer ample opportunity for consideration of claims of technological and economic infeasibility. Always, however, care is taken that consid-eration of such claims will not interfere substantially with the primary goal of prompt attainment of the national standards. Allowing such claims to be raised by appealing the Administrator's approval of an implementation plan, as petitioner suggests, would frustrate congressional intent. It would permit a proposed plan to be struck down as infeasible before it is given a chance to work, even though Congress clearly contem-plated that some plans would be infeasible when proposed. And it would permit the Administrator or a federal court to reject a State's legislative choices in regulating air pollution, even though Congress plainly left with the States, so long as the national standards were met, the power to determine which sources would be burdened by regulation and to what extent. Technology forcing is a concept somewhat new to our national experience and it necessarily entails certain risks. But Congress considered those risks in passing the 1970 [Act] and decided that the dangers posed by uncon-trolled air pollution made them worth taking. Petitioner's theory would render that considered legislative judgment a nullity, and that is a result we refuse to reach.

Affirmed.

[JUSTICE POWELL, concurring, agreed with the majority's interpretation of the Act but believed that it might lead to economically disastrous consequences. He found it "difficult to believe that Congress would adhere to its absolute position if faced with the potentially devastating consequences to the public" that might arise from the shutdown of a public utility, and asserted the belief that "Congress, if fully aware of this Draconian possibility, would strike a different balance."]

NOTES AND QUESTIONS

1. *Statutory Interpretation.* Why didn't the references in the version of §110(a)(2) in effect at the time of *Union Elec.* to achievement of the primary standards as "expe-ditiously as practicable" and to the secondary standards within a "reasonable time" authorize EPA to reject a SIP on feasibility grounds? What other provisions of the Act helped the Court to reach the result it did? Several of the provisions referred to in *Union Elec.* have since been amended. Section 110(a)(2) no longer specifies the

---

18. If he chooses not to seek a compliance order, or if an order is issued and violated, the Administrator may institute a civil enforcement proceeding. §113(b). Additionally, violators of an implementation plan are subject to criminal penalties under §113(c) and citizen enforcement suits under §304. Some courts have suggested that in criminal or civil enforcement proceedings the violator may in certain circumstances raise a defense of economic or technological infeasibility. We do not address this question here.

deadlines for compliance with the primary and secondary NAAQS. Those deadlines now appear at several places in the statute. AQCRs not designated as nonattainment areas must achieve the primary NAAQS within three years after adoption of the 1990 amendments or within five years of issuance of a finding by EPA that a SIP was substantially inadequate under the pre-1990 version of §110(a)(2). §110(n)(2). A nonattainment area is obliged to comply with the primary NAAQS "as expeditiously as practicable," but no later than five years from the date the area was designated nonattainment (or ten years, if EPA so provides, based on the severity of nonattainment and the feasibility of control measures). §172(a)(2)(A). A nonattainment area must comply with the secondary NAAQS "as expeditiously as practicable" after the date it was designated nonattainment. §172(a)(2)(B). These deadlines do not apply if the statute provides other dates for compliance in nonattainment areas, §172(a)(2)(D). See §§181(a), 186(a), 188(c), 192. The list of mandatory SIP requirements in §110(a)(2) now includes 13 rather than 8 elements, and the "as may be necessary" phrase is now a part of §110(a)(2)(A) instead of §110(a)(2)(B). EPA's obligation to approve a SIP containing each of these elements now appears in §110(k)(3) rather than in §110(a)(2). Finally, the time limit for seeking judicial review of EPA's approval of a SIP under §307(b)(1) has been extended to 60 days. Do any of these changes alter the result in *Union Elec.*?

2. *Other Contexts for Consideration of Feasibility.* The Court in *Union Elec.* discussed the various contexts in which regulated entities could raise claims of "technological and economic infeasibility." What is the relationship between those two different kinds of feasibility? See Honeywell Int'l, Inc. v. EPA, 374 F.3d 1363, 1372-1373 (D.C. Cir. 2004). The availability of other forums for raising feasibility concerns obviously made the Court more comfortable with its holding. As the Court indicated, several options exist for individual polluters to elude or delay compliance with stringent emissions limitations contained in state plans. The earliest and strategically most effective opportunity, of course, is when the state selects the regionwide combination of emissions limitations for all sources that will achieve the SIP goals within the statutory deadlines.

If a source fails to obtain an emissions limitation acceptable to it when the SIP is first prepared, it may seek a variance from the state pollution control agency if applicable state legislation authorizes variances. A state variance usually operates as an amendment to the SIP. In Train v. NRDC, 421 U.S. 60 (1975), the Supreme Court held that a variance could be approved only if it did not cause a violation of the NAAQS or prevent a state from meeting the SIP compliance deadline. EPA review of SIP revisions is now governed by §110(k)(3) and (*l*). What approach do those provisions take to the conditions under which variances may be approved as SIP revisions? See Hall v. EPA, 273 F.3d 1146 (9th Cir. 2001) (considering whether §110(*l*) permits approval of SIP amendments based simply on a showing that the amendments do not relax preexisting SIP rules). As *Union Elec.* points out, a party also may take its claim of infeasibility to a state court.

3. *More on SIP Revisions.* A state may not revise an EPA-approved SIP without further EPA approval. Kentucky Res. Council, Inc. v. EPA, 304 F. Supp. 2d 920 (W.D. Ky. 2004) (holding that state statute repealing vehicle emission testing program that was part of EPA-approved SIP was preempted by the CAA); Sweat v. Hull, 200 F. Supp. 2d 1162 (D. Ariz. 2001) (finding that state's repeal and nonenforcement of program for detecting excess vehicle emissions through remote sensing devices constituted a violation of the CAA). In General Motors Corp. v. United States, 496 U.S. 530 (1990), the

Supreme Court held that EPA may enforce a SIP provision that has been amended by a state if EPA has not yet approved the amendment. A source subject to such an amended provision may be able to rely on EPA's delay as a mitigating factor in an enforcement action. See also Sierra Club v. TVA, 430 F.3d 1337, 1346-1350 (11th Cir. 2005) (holding that §110(i) of the CAA prevents a state from unilaterally modifying SIP provisions, and that defendant was liable for violating unmodified provision).

4. *Feasibility as a Defense in Enforcement Proceedings.* Although the Supreme Court left the issue open in *Union Elec.,* it now seems clear that a noncomplying source may not raise a defense of economic and technological infeasibility in an enforcement action. Navistar Int'l Transp. Corp. v. EPA, 858 F.2d 282 (6th Cir. 1988); NRDC v. Thomas, 705 F. Supp. 1 (D.D.C. 1988). But cf. Union Elec. Co. v. EPA, 593 F.2d 299 (8th Cir. 1979) (leaving the question open). Can Congress constitutionally foreclose all consideration of economic and technological feasibility? In Michigan Dep't of Envtl. Quality v. Browner, 230 F.3d 181 (6th Cir. 2000), the court upheld EPA's disapproval of SIP revisions that automatically exempted from enforcement actions violations of emission standards occurring during periods of abnormal conditions, startup, shutdown, or malfunctions.

5. *Conditional Approval of SIPs.* What if EPA deems certain provisions of a SIP acceptable but regards others as insufficient; may it approve part of the plan or approve the entire plan subject to the condition that the state remedy the defective provisions? See §110(k)(3)-(4). McCarthy v. Thomas, 27 F.3d 1363 (9th Cir. 1994), was a citizen suit intended to force Tucson and Phoenix to enlarge their mass transit systems in compliance with SIPs for CO nonattainment areas. EPA conditionally approved the SIPs despite the absence of measures that would ensure timely attainment of the NAAQS. The court concluded that a part of a state's proposal that EPA approves conditionally (with only minor deficiencies to be remedied) becomes part of the SIP. Accordingly, the mass transit provisions were binding on the two cities. Compare Bethlehem Steel Corp. v. Gorsuch, 742 F.2d 1028 (7th Cir. 1984) (EPA cannot approve a SIP in part if the effect is to render the plan more stringent than the one adopted by the state).

May EPA approve a SIP on the condition that the state adopt measures specified by EPA, rather than simply require that the state take whatever steps it desires to achieve the NAAQS? In Virginia v. EPA, 108 F.3d 1397 (D.C. Cir. 1997), EPA, acting under §110(k)(5), declared the SIPs of 12 states to be substantially inadequate to attain the NAAQS for ozone. EPA required these states to revise their SIPs by adopting a low-emission vehicle (LEV) program (already in effect in California) to reduce motor vehicle emissions of NO_x and VOCs. Several states challenged the conditional approval, claiming that EPA may not condition approval of a SIP on the state's adoption of control measures chosen by EPA. The court agreed, concluding that the 1990 amendments did not eliminate a state's "liberty to 'adopt whatever mix of emission limitations it deems best suited to its particular situation.' Train v. NRDC, 421 U.S. at 79." 108 F.3d at 1408-1409. EPA argued that §110(k)(5) authorizes it, upon a finding of inadequacy, to require the states to include in their SIPs whatever measures EPA deems "necessary" to correct the inadequacy. But the court found that the "as necessary" language of §110(k)(5) is meant to restrict rather than broaden EPA's authority: EPA may only call for the revisions that are necessary to correct the problem rather than require that a state adopt a "wholesale revision of its entire plan." Id. at 1409-1410. Does this interpretation of §110(k)(5) conform to the thrust of the 1990 amendments, which was to reduce the discretion of states with nonattainment areas to select applicable control measures? Is §110(*l*) relevant? The court also held that §184(c)(5) provides EPA with the authority to condition SIP approval on the adoption of particular control measures, but that §§177 and 202 forbid EPA from conditioning approval on the adoption of California's LEV program. Is the court's interpretation of §110(k) unnecessary dictum?

May EPA conditionally approve SIPs that contain no specific remedial measures but that promise to adopt such measures within a year? See NRDC v. EPA, 22 F.3d 1125 (D.C. Cir. 1994). See also Sierra Club v. EPA, 356 F.3d 296 (D.C. Cir. 2004) (rejecting the contention that all a state needs to do to qualify for conditional approval is commit to adopting specific enforceable measures by a certain date, even if the state does not tell EPA what those measures are, or even know what they are). BCCA Appeal Group v. EPA, 355 F.3d 817 (5th Cir. 2004), however, upheld EPA's determination that a state's enforceable commitment to adopt unspecified control measures on a fixed schedule as part of an overall control strategy was an "appropriate" means, technique, schedule, or timetable for compliance under §110(a)(2)(A). Environmental Def. v. EPA, 369 F.3d 193 (2d Cir. 2004), endorsed EPA's test for determining whether a commitment is appropriate: (1) whether it addresses a limited portion of the reductions needed for attainment, (2) whether the state can fulfill it, and (3) whether it is for a reasonable time. The court distinguished the 1994 NRDC decision because in this case, the state's SIP included a comprehensive and detailed plan for attainment.

6. *Formulation of Implementation Plans by EPA.* EPA's authority to issue an implementation plan for a state that has not complied with its statutory obligations is still derived from §110(c). Under what circumstances is EPA obliged to issue a federal implementation plan (FIP)? For the definition of a FIP, see §302(y). The Court, in footnote 7 of *Union Elec.,* left open the question of whether EPA must consider claims of economic or technological infeasibility when it is formulating a FIP. What arguments support such an obligation? Are there contrary arguments?

7. *Justice Powell Triumphant.* Justice Powell's views in *Union Elec.* essentially prevailed in Sierra Club v. Georgia Power Co., 180 F.3d 1309 (11th Cir. 1999). For extensive discussion of the SIP process, including suggestions for why it has failed to lead to achievement of the NAAQS in many areas, see Reitze, Air Quality Protection Using State Implementation Plans—Thirty-seven Years of Increasing Complexity, 15 Vill. Envtl. L.J. 209 (2004).

NOTE ON TALL STACKS AND OTHER DISPERSION TECHNIQUES

Although the CAA requires SIPs to contain enforceable emission limitations, it also authorizes such other measures, means, or techniques "as may be necessary." §110(a)(2)(A). Must a state rely primarily on emissions limitations on existing sources, or may it rely on other techniques to meet the NAAQS? Are any techniques forbidden under the CAA scheme? Can a facility disperse pollution by constructing tall stacks? The court in NRDC v. EPA, 489 F.2d 390 (5th Cir. 1974), *rev'd on other grounds,* Train v. NRDC, Inc., 421 U.S. 60 (1975), invalidated this technique because it did not reduce emissions; instead, it merely distributed them over a wider area. Two other courts extended that rationale to "intermittent" controls (which distribute emissions temporally instead of geographically), disapproving the strategies of reducing operations at the source or switching to less-polluting fuel when atmospheric conditions cause high pollution levels. Kennecott Copper Corp. v. Train, 526 F.2d 1149 (9th Cir. 1975); Big Rivers Elec. Corp. v. EPA, 523 F.2d 16 (6th Cir. 1975).

The legislative history of the 1990 amendments includes the following discussion of the tall stacks issue:

> The [1970] Act was written at a time when the interstate transport of air pollution was not widely acknowledged. Indeed, it was the implementation of the Clean Air Act which created a substantial number of the interstate pollution problems. Rather than reducing their emissions of sulfur dioxide, electric utilities proposed the use of "tall stacks" to inject pollution into the upper atmosphere where it could be diluted and transported over long distances. Although illegal, this policy was expressly approved by the first Administrator of the Environmental Protection Agency, William D. Ruckelshaus, and quickly led to the widespread use of super-tall smokestacks.
>
> Although the Congress enacted curbs on the use of tall stacks in [1977, and enacted provisions] to control interstate air pollution[, these provisions] largely failed to achieve the congressionally intended goal of curbing and controlling interstate air pollution. Thus, the law remains today largely what it was when written in 1970, keyed almost entirely to achieving local ambient air quality standards. [S. Rep. No. 101-228, at 553 (1989).]

The 1977 amendments addressed the dispersion techniques controversy in §123, which provides that the "degree of emission limitation" is not to be affected by stack height in excess of "good engineering practice" or by any dispersion technique. "Dispersion technique" is defined to mean "any intermittent or supplemental control of air pollutants varying with atmospheric conditions." In addition, §302(k) defines an emission limitation as a requirement that "limits the quantity, rate, or concentration of emissions of air pollutants on a continuous basis." Section 123 does not prohibit the building of tall stacks. It merely limits the extent to which a polluter can take credit for tall stacks in meeting its emission limitations.

Section 123 defines "good engineering practice" as that height "necessary" to ensure that emissions will not cause local "excessive concentration" due to atmospheric downwash from "nearby" structures or terrain. This is an attempt to resolve the tension between prohibiting dispersion that causes pollution outside the local region and at the same time prohibiting "downwash" locally from terrain and structures that can create unhealthy local "hot spots." Sierra Club v. EPA, 719 F.2d 436 (D.C. Cir. 1983), affirmed most of the regulations but held that EPA must adopt an absolute, health-based standard in defining excessive concentrations. EPA issued revisions to the stack height regulations in response to Sierra Club in 1985. Among other things, the revisions redefined "excessive concentrations" and modified the methods for determining good-engineering-practice stack height credit. NRDC v. Thomas, 838 F.2d 1224, 1234 (D.C. Cir. 1988), upheld the amended regulations.

Some plant operators have argued that the statute allows them to avoid air quality violations by means of strategies (rejected by the courts in the mid-1970s) that include closing the plant or switching to less-polluting fuels. Do the 1977 amendments prohibit these intermittent control technique strategies? Are there circumstances when the "dilution is not the solution to pollution" maxim is wrong?

c. Monitoring and Modeling

As the preceding discussion indicates, the CAA requires each state to determine whether its AQCRs should be classified as nonattainment or attainment. To achieve the NAAQS in a nonattainment area, a state must impose emissions controls on individual sources of the nonattainment pollutant or its precursors that are sufficient to reduce ambient concentrations by the necessary amounts. Once a state has set individual emission limitations, it must enforce them. EPA has developed air quality monitoring and modeling techniques to assist in each of these tasks. The accuracy and reliability of the models have been challenged in several cases. Although the courts generally defer to EPA's selection of modeling techniques, in a few cases they have set aside EPA's application of these models.

Monitoring, Modeling, and AQCR Designation. The statute authorizes EPA to use monitoring or modeling in the designation of AQCRs. The agency need not base its designation on actual rather than model-predicted air quality. PPG Indus., Inc. v. Costle, 630 F.2d 462 (6th Cir. 1980) (but holding that modeling was based on erroneous data). Because of the uncertainties inherent in air quality modeling, EPA allows the use of supplemental analysis to demonstrate attainment in cases where modeling shows ambient concentration levels in excess of the NAAQS. See 1000 Friends of Maryland v. Browner, 265 F.3d 216, 234 (4th Cir. 2001). See also Sierra Club v. EPA, 356 F.3d 296 (D.C. Cir. 2004) (construing §182(c)(2)(A) to allow EPA to adjust results of photochemical grid modeling to ensure consistency with real-world observations as a means of demonstrating attainment of ozone NAAQS).

May EPA base an AQCR designation on predicted growth in pollution as well as on present air quality? See *PPG Indus., supra,* which upheld EPA's view that §107(d)(1) (before it was amended in 1990) allows consideration of "projected future violations" as the basis for a nonattainment area designation. Is this result still appropriate under the current version of §107(d)(1)? See generally Kramer, Air Quality Modeling: Judicial, Legislative and Administrative Reactions, 5 Colum. J. Envtl. L. 236 (1979).

Monitoring, Modeling, and SIP Formulation. EPA at first used the "rollback" model, approved in Texas v. EPA, 499 F.2d 289 (5th Cir. 1974), to review SIPs. The court held that the rollback model was "neutral" because "it establishes as a starting point the commonsensical proposition that pollutants will be reduced proportionally to reductions in their chemical precursors." Id. at 301. The contribution of different sources to pollution varies, however, and a simplistic uniform proportionate rollback is hardly "neutral."

EPA later adopted more sophisticated diffusion models. In Cleveland Elec. Illuminating Co. v. EPA, 572 F.2d 1150 (6th Cir. 1978), the court reviewed a FIP drafted by EPA for Ohio under §110(c) after the state refused to prepare its own. The court refused to find that the model EPA used was arbitrary or capricious, despite the availability of more advanced models, the existence of monitoring data inconsistent with the model's predictions, and evidence that the model systematically overpredicted emissions. In Environmental Def. v. EPA, 369 F.3d 193 (2d Cir. 2004), the issue was whether EPA's approval of New York's SIP complied with §182(c)(2)(A), which requires that attainment demonstrations for ozone nonattainment areas be "based on photochemical grid modeling." The court upheld EPA's approval of the SIP, even though New York demonstrated attainment through a "weight of the evidence" approach that adjusted the results of the grid modeling to correct for inaccuracies. The court interpreted the statute as requiring only that grid modeling form the "foundation and principal component of the attainment demonstration." See also BCCA Appeal Group v. EPA, 355 F.3d 817 (5th Cir. 2004) (upholding EPA's reliance on photochemical grid model in approving Texas's demonstration that Houston's SIP would attain NAAQS, despite the model's inability to replicate the city's unique meteorological conditions).

In other cases, the courts have rejected EPA models when severe weaknesses have been identified. E.g., Columbus & Southern Ohio Elec. Co. v. Costle, 638 F.2d 910 (6th Cir. 1980) (invalid assumptions concerning weather stability conditions); Ohio v. EPA, 784 F.2d 224 (6th Cir. 1986) (arbitrary reliance on model for stack emissions without testing it against actual monitoring data).

Monitoring and Enforcement. Finally, disputes over the appropriate kind and extent of monitoring can arise in enforcement proceedings. In United States v. Louisiana Pac. Corp., 925 F. Supp. 1484 (D. Colo. 1996), the state issued a permit requiring the defendants to install continuous opacity monitoring (COM) systems. The defendant argued that §110(a)(2)(F) does not require that every source install and use monitoring devices and that, absent EPA-issued emissions monitoring guidance for a source category, the state lacked the power to require monitoring. The court held that §§110(a)(2)(A) and (F) and 114 allow the states to implement and enforce emission monitoring requirements not prescribed by EPA to ensure the enforceability of emissions limitations. See also Grand Canyon Trust v. Public Serv. Co., 294 F. Supp. 2d 1246 (D.N.M. 2003) (COM is relevant but not necessarily determinative evidence of CAA violations); United States v. Comunidades Unidas Contra La Contaminacion, 106 F. Supp. 2d 216 (D.P.R. 2000) (upholding EPA finding that utility violated monitoring requirements because it used improper methodology in conducting opacity readings).

NOTE ON CONTINUOUS EMISSIONS MONITORING AND "ALL CREDIBLE EVIDENCE"

Although EPA has taken the position that the CAA does not limit its authority to use any type of information to prove a violation, some courts have interpreted EPA regulations that refer to specific test methods for determining compliance as precluding the agency's reliance on evidence obtained through other methods. EPA sought to broaden the evidentiary basis for proving violations when it adopted the "all credible evidence" rule. 62 Fed. Reg. 8,314 (1997). The agency eliminated a regulation barring reliance on data derived from anything other than reference test methods to demonstrate noncompliance. In particular, it clarified that the inclusion in a SIP of enforceable test methods for SIP emissions limits does not preclude enforcement based on other credible evidence relevant to whether a source would have satisfied applicable requirements if the appropriate compliance test procedures or methods had been performed. EPA cited as authority for the new rule §113(a) and (e)(1) of the CAA. What language in these two provisions supports EPA's interpretation? See also §§114(a)(3), 504(b); S. Rep. No. 101-228, at 358 (1989).

EPA emphasized that the rule addressed an evidentiary issue and neither was intended to increase nor would have the effect of increasing the stringency of underlying emission standards. It simply removed what had been construed as a regulatory bar to the admission of non–reference test data to prove the violation of an emission standard, regardless of the credibility and probative value of those data. Thus, according to the agency, the rule did not affect whether emission standards require intermittent or continuous compliance.* The rule would benefit EPA and the states, which would be able to use a wider range of evidence to assess a source's compliance status and respond to noncompliance. Regulated sources also would benefit by being able to use the same, broader range of evidence to contest allegations of noncompliance in enforcement actions. The "all credible evidence" rule is not available, however, in citizen suits to enforce the emission limitations in a SIP. Sierra Club v. TVA, 430 F.3d 1337, 1351-1353 (11th Cir. 2005).

EPA explained the advantage of the non–reference test data made available by the rule to those seeking to enforce CAA obligations:

> Reference tests may not yield a representative emissions picture because the sources typically schedule, set up and run the tests themselves. This allows sources to "fine tune" their operations and emissions control processes prior to the tests, and generate results that may not be typical of day-to-day source operations. Reference tests can also be expensive and burdensome: They can cost up to $100,000, and take a week or more to complete. . . .
>
> Where available, continuous emission monitoring (CEM) data** and well-chosen parametric monitoring data . . . generally provide accurate data regarding a source's compliance with emission limits and standards. These data also generally cover a greater percentage of a source's time in operation and are more representative of a source's ongoing compliance status than sporadic performance testing. [62 Fed. Reg. at 8,315.]

Industry representatives were not nearly as sanguine about the purpose or potential impact of the "all credible evidence" rule. They asserted that CEM distorts a source's compliance status due to the inevitability of occasional violations despite the source's having average emissions levels that comply fully with applicable limitations. As a result, companies will have to take steps to ensure that emissions always fall below those limitations. The practical effect will be a 50 percent tightening of standards.

NRDC v. EPA, 194 F.3d 130 (D.C. Cir. 1999), found a set of industry challenges to the 1997 rule to be unripe. In the same case, the court rejected NRDC's challenges to EPA's Compliance Assurance Monitoring rules. Based on §114(a)(3), these rules require major sources to use parametric monitoring. The court held that §114(a)(3) does not require EPA to find direct emissions monitoring to be impractical before it may authorize the monitoring of major source control parameters. The court did invalidate the portion of the regulations requiring that major sources certify whether *data* are continuous or intermittent because the statute requires that sources certify whether *compliance* is continuous or intermittent. EPA amended the regulations on remand to make it clear that a source must certify that it has been in continuous or intermittent compliance. 68 Fed. Reg. 38,518 (2003). See also Sierra Club v. EPA, 353 F.3d 976, 991-992 (D.C. Cir. 2004) (upholding EPA's decision to allow control device operating parameter monitoring instead of CEM for smelters).

---

*The notion that monitoring requirements do not affect the substance of the emission standards to which they relate was rejected in Appalachian Power Co. v. EPA, 208 F.3d 1015 (D.C. Cir. 2000). Regulations that specify test methods and frequency of testing for compliance are substantive in nature in that they impose duties on regulated entities. Changes in monitoring methods can affect the stringency of the relevant emission limitation. Monitoring requirements also impose significant compliance costs.

**Continuous emission monitors measure and record the chemical composition of a waste stream at regular intervals within smokestacks.

In another case, the court found that EPA violated the Administrative Procedure Act (APA) by issuing a final regulation that repudiated its proposed interpretation of CAA monitoring requirements and adopted instead the opposite interpretation without first providing an additional opportunity for notice and comment. In the proposal, EPA took the position that state permitting authorities may impose periodic monitoring requirements beyond those imposed by EPA if additional requirements are necessary to ensure permit compliance. In the final rule, EPA concluded that state permitting authorities are *prohibited* from adding new monitoring requirements if the Title V permit already contains some periodic monitoring requirements, even if they are insufficient. The court refused to allow EPA "to pull a surprise switcheroo" of this sort. Environmental Integrity Project v. EPA, 425 F.3d 992, 996 (D.C. Cir. 2005).

E. NATIONALLY UNIFORM EMISSION STANDARDS FOR NEW SOURCES

Although Congress enshrined attainment of the NAAQS as the overall goal of the CAA, it subjected a variety of mobile and stationary sources to uniform federal emissions standards. Emissions standards are direct limitations on the emissions that regulated sources can discharge. In contrast to the health-based ambient air quality approach, most CAA emissions standards issued by EPA are "technology based" or "technology limited" because they require EPA to determine the technical and engineering feasibility of pollution control by sources that use similar production processes. Based on its feasibility studies, EPA sets performance-oriented standards that specify the quantity of pollutant that may be emitted per unit of product, raw material, or fuel input. At least in theory, the standards pressure regulated sources to make improvements in pollution control by installing control technologies and by changing to fuels, raw materials, and manufacturing processes that emit less pollution. The new source performance standards (NSPS) authorized by §111 are one example of a technology-based standard.

   The Scope of the New Source Performance Standards. The Act requires compliance with technology-based NSPS applicable to new and modified stationary sources. See §111(e). A "new source" is defined in §111(a)(2). What factors may EPA consider in establishing NSPS? See §111(a)(1). For purposes of §111, EPA has defined modification as "any physical or operational change to an existing facility which results in an increase in the emission rate to the atmosphere of any pollutant to which a standard applies." 40 C.F.R. §60.14(a). The extension of "new source" review to modified sources is critical because it sweeps changes in operation in existing sources into new source review (NSR) programs (discussed in section F below). The addition or use of any system or device whose primary function is the reduction of air pollutants does not constitute a modification, except when an emission control system is removed or is replaced by a system which EPA determines to be less environmentally beneficial. Id. §60.14(e)(5). How far does this definition stretch? See National-Southwire Aluminum Co. v. EPA, 838 F.2d 835 (6th Cir. 1988) (turning off pollution control equipment is modification); Hawaiian Elec. Co. v. EPA, 723 F.2d 1440 (9th Cir. 1984) (change to fuel containing more sulfur than allowed by existing permit is modification for purposes of NSR).

Read §111(b)-(c), (g). For what categories of sources is EPA supposed to issue NSPS? What role do the states play in the implementation of the NSPS? What do you suppose is the function of §111(f)?

The Rationale for the NSPS. The idea of imposing uniform national emissions standards dates back to the hearings on the 1967 amendments. The reasons offered in support of uniform emissions standards for new sources included (1) the unreliability of ambient standards, (2) the elimination of regional pollution havens and "hot spots," (3) the inability of states to take necessary action, (4) the rapidity with which emissions standards could be adopted, (5) simplicity of enforcement, (6) due consideration of economic and technical factors, and (7) the reduction of atmospheric transport of pollutants to distant polluted areas that would result. The wisdom of the CAA's reliance on nationally uniform new source emissions controls, however, has since been called into question. The Act arguably creates an incentive for sources to keep older, dirtier plants in operation as long as possible in order to avoid triggering the more rigorous controls applicable to new plants. The result is arguably bad not only for the environment, but also for the economy, as the construction of newer, more efficient and productive plants is delayed. See Ackerman & Stewart, Reforming Environmental Law, 37 Stan. L. Rev. 1333, 1335-1336 (1985).

Technology Forcing and NSPS. Are §111 NSPS technology forcing? The §111 requirement that technology be "adequately demonstrated," taking various costs into account, seems on its face to preclude technology forcing that would require a higher level of performance than current technology is capable of producing. Cf. §111(j). Portland Cement Ass'n v. Ruckelshaus, 486 F.2d 375 (D.C. Cir. 1973), indicated that Congress did not require a technology to be in routine use before it can be adopted. To be "adequately demonstrated" means to be "available" at a future date when the technology may reasonably be expected to be installed and to work: "Section 111 looks toward what may fairly be projected for the regulated future, rather than the state of the art at present." Id. at 391-392. But the cases do not seem to allow EPA to add a "margin for striving" on top of its forecast of routine technological development. See National Lime Ass'n v. EPA, 627 F.2d 416 (D.C. Cir. 1980) (remand of NSPS because EPA failed to show that the standard was "achievable" for the industry as a whole). EPA may compensate for a shortage of data, however, by extrapolating a technology's performance in one industry in determining its availability in another. Lignite Energy Council v. EPA, 198 F.3d 930 (D.C. Cir. 1999) (upholding NSPS for coal-fired industrial boilers based on extrapolation from studies of utility boilers).

NSPS and Existing Sources. What gap in the CAA scheme is §111(d) designed to plug? Does it give EPA added flexibility to choose among the ambient, hazardous (§112), nondeterioration, and new source standards? See D. Currie, Air Pollution §§3.19-3.25 (1981).

NSPS for Coal-Fired Electricity-Generating Facilities. Sierra Club v. Costle, 657 F.2d 298 (D.C. Cir. 1981), sustained a controversial NSPS for electric utilities. The standard required utilities to employ some form of flue gas desulfurization (or "scrubbing") technology, a relatively expensive means of reducing emissions, instead of simply increasing their use of low-sulfur coal. EPA enacted the NSPS sustained in *Sierra Club* in response to amendments to §111(a)(1) adopted in 1977. Those amendments defined a "standard of performance" applicable to any air pollutant emitted from fossil fuel–fired stationary sources as a standard that (1) established allowable emission limitations and (2) required "the achievement of a percentage reduction in the emissions from [those categories] of sources from the emissions which would have resulted from the use of fuels which are not subject to treatment prior to combustion." Thus, utilities could not meet the standards by limiting the hours or levels of plant operation or by burning untreated low-sulfur coal. The amended standard thus pitted West against East because it required that the emissions from low-sulfur western coal be scrubbed despite the relatively low SO_2 levels produced by the burning of that coal.

Critics charged that the scrubber-based NSPS for coal-fired power plants would cost billions more than standards that could be achieved primarily through coal washing and with the burning of low-sulfur coal. See, e.g., B. Ackerman & W. Hassler, Clean Coal/Dirty Air or How The Clean Air Act Became a Multibillion-Dollar Bailout for High-Sulfur Coal Producers and What Should Be Done about It (1981). Ackerman and Hassler viewed the amended §111(a)(1) as an unwarranted subsidy to eastern high-sulfur coal interests.*

The issue was put to rest when Congress amended §111(a)(1) again in 1990. A Senate report on the amendments explained that "[t]he original intention of the provision was to prevent western low sulfur coal from shutting eastern high sulfur coal out of the fuel market," but that this subsidy was no longer necessary because the provisions of the 1990 amendments that limited SO_2 emissions to abate acid deposition would induce new utility sources to reduce their emissions as much as possible. The report added that the amendments would remain in effect only as long as acid rain control provisions remain in effect. S. Rep. No. 101-228, at 656 (1989). For further discussion of the acid deposition control provisions adopted in 1990, see section I.2, below. What has been the fate of the percentage reduction requirement? Have the views of Ackerman and Hassler prevailed?

Multiple Emissions Points, Bubbles, and Efficiency. A power *plant* may consist of several boiler *units*, each of which emits pollutants and is presently subject to NSPS. Other industrial subcategories subject to NSPS also may emit pollutants from several locations within a plant. For NSPS purposes, should the entire plant be considered the source, or should each piece of emissions-generating equipment within the plant be considered a separate source? See §111(a)(3). The same question has arisen under the NSR provisions discussed in sections F and G below.

The issue of how to define a "source" that is subject to NSPS or NSR is crucial because a broader definition of the term allows plant operators more leeway in deciding the level of control at individual units, thus promoting economic efficiency. The critical point is that marginal emissions control costs vary widely among pieces of plant equipment that emit the same pollutants. Substantial cost savings may be possible if plant operators are allowed to reduce emissions the most in the units for which control is the cheapest, until the marginal investment for every pound of emissions controlled at all units is equal. Hahn & Hester, Where Did All the Markets Go? An Analysis of EPA's Emissions Trading Program, 6 Yale J. on Reg. 109 (1989).

In 1975, EPA authorized regulators and plant operators to consider the entire plant to be the source subject to NSPS. 40 Fed. Reg. 58,416. EPA imagined the plant to be covered by a "bubble," with only one emissions point at the top. Under this "plantwide" definition of a source, NSPS would apply only if a physical or operational change resulted in an increase in emissions from that point; increases in individual

---

*See also Ackerman & Hassler, Beyond the New Deal: Coal and the Clean Air Act, 89 Yale L.J. 1466 (1980). For EPA's criticism of Ackerman and Hassler, see Smith & Randle, Comment on Beyond the New Deal, 90 Yale L.J. 1398 (1981). See also the authors' reply, Beyond the New Deal: Reply, 90 Yale L.J. 1412 (1981). For a defense of the standard, see Trisko, Universal Scrubbing: Cleaning the Air, 84 W. Va. L. Rev. 983 (1982).

contributing units beneath the bubble would not trigger NSPS if they were offset by emissions reductions elsewhere under the bubble. The court in ASARCO Inc. v. EPA, 578 F.2d 319 (D.C. Cir. 1978), invalidated the NSPS bubble policy. It concluded that the plantwide definition, by permitting in-plant modifications that did not increase overall plantwide emissions to elude or "net out" of the NSPS requirements, might retard the application of new technology that met the strict NSPS criteria and therefore delay the improvement in air quality that §111 was designed to achieve.

The same court accepted the plantwide definition for purposes of the PSD program in Alabama Power Co. v. Costle, 636 F.2d 323 (D.C. Cir. 1980). Later, in the *Chevron* case, reproduced below in section F.4 (where the merits and disadvantages of the bubble concept and similar regulatory techniques are discussed in greater detail), the Supreme Court upheld the use of the bubble for modified sources in nonattainment areas, indicated its disapproval of *ASARCO*, and refused to overturn *Alabama Power*.

EPA subsequently reinstated the bubble under certain circumstances for the NSPS program. See 17 Env't Rep. (BNA) 2151 (1987); 58 Fed. Reg. 28,780 (1993) (discussing "compliance bubbles"). For a discussion of compliance bubbles, see R. Liroff, Reforming Air Pollution Regulation: The Toil and Trouble of EPA's Bubble 110-117 (1986).

F. NONATTAINMENT AREAS: THE SPECIAL PROBLEMS OF DIRTY-AIR AREAS

1. *The Scope of the Nonattainment Problem*

Many areas of the country, particularly industrialized urban areas, were not able to meet the deadlines for achieving the NAAQS established in the 1970 version of the CAA for one or more criteria pollutants. Problems included the technical and economic challenge of effective pollution control, the inadequacy of some SIPs, the intransigence of some sources, inadequate enforcement, and litigation that delayed the implementation of some state regulations.

The problems differed from pollutant to pollutant. For sulfur oxides or TSP, the primary causes of missed deadlines were high concentrations of sources in industrialized eastern and midwestern areas (requiring a larger percentage reduction by each source) and the difficulties of adequately controlling emissions at large smelters and electricity-generating facilities located primarily in the West. "Dirty-air" areas therefore feared that the CAA would foreclose most new growth.

The main reasons for missing the deadlines for mobile-source pollutant ambient standards were more complex. First, the deadlines were hopelessly optimistic in view of the magnitude of the ozone and CO problem in some urban areas. Second, Congress extended the deadlines for achieving the 1975 and 1976 emissions standards for new vehicles into the late 1970s. Even if the states had the will, the Act allowed only California to set more stringent emissions standards for new vehicles. Instead, to control mobile source emissions, the statute thrust the states back to secondary strategies such as dispersing traffic, providing incentives not to drive or to take mass transit, policing the performance of new car emissions control systems through inspection and maintenance programs, and (in theory more than in practice) setting retrofit standards for older vehicles. Third, the secondary techniques directly affected the driving public, sometimes in ways that drivers viewed as exceedingly restrictive. As a result, these non-technological control alternatives crumbled one by one under the political reality of the average American's daily dependence on the automobile.

Against this backdrop, EPA attempted to provide for new industrial growth with its 1975 "offset" program. This program allowed new sources to build in nonattainment areas if they could offset their new emissions by cutting back emissions at other existing facilities or by paying other existing sources to reduce emissions. EPA also confronted the automobile head-on. For example, it promulgated, and the Ninth Circuit approved, Draconian gas rationing regulations for Los Angeles, explaining that NAAQS attainment for some mobile-source pollutants would require an 82 percent reduction in summer automobile traffic in the city. City of Santa Rosa v. EPA, 534 F.2d 150 (9th Cir. 1976). The rules were subsequently withdrawn.

To avoid the need for such strategies, EPA sought direct legislative relief. Congress responded by amending the CAA in 1977. On the one hand, the amendments gave EPA and regulated sources the delays they sought; states now had until 1982 or 1987 (in the case of some areas that were designated nonattainment for ozone or CO) to meet the NAAQS. On the other hand, Congress imposed new constraints on the states in the implementation and enforcement of SIPs in nonattainment areas to facilitate compliance. The amendments established a permit program for the construction of major stationary sources in nonattainment areas, for example, including a codification of the offset policy.

These constraints notwithstanding, many urban areas were still not in compliance with the NAAQS by the end of the 1980s. More than 90 percent of these areas, for example, had failed to attain the NAAQS for ozone by 1989. Virginia v. United States, 74 F.3d 517, 520 (4th Cir. 1996). Congress responded by amending the Act in 1990. The 1990 amendments extended the deadlines again and imposed still more rigorous obligations on states containing nonattainment areas, with the effect of reducing still further the initial flexibility afforded the states to design whatever mix of emission controls they desired to achieve the NAAQS. As indicated below, the obligations, the deadlines for compliance with the NAAQS, and the sanctions for noncompliance differ depending on the severity of the nonattainment problem.

As you study the nonattainment coverage, consider what steps should be taken in the event that implementation of the 1990 amendments fails to result in compliance with the NAAQS. Should Congress impose further restrictions on the discretion of the states in selecting how to reduce emissions, or should it move in an entirely different direction? Should it continue moving, as it did in the 1990 amendments, toward increased reliance on economic incentives as a supplement to or substitute for more traditional command-and-control regulatory techniques? How much of the burden of reducing emissions still further should come from stationary and from mobile sources?

NOTE ON THE OZONE AND CARBON MONOXIDE NONATTAINMENT PROBLEM

Excessive concentrations of ozone (smog) and carbon monoxide are the major nonattainment problems in urban areas. As shown in Figure 6-6, VOCs and NO_x are

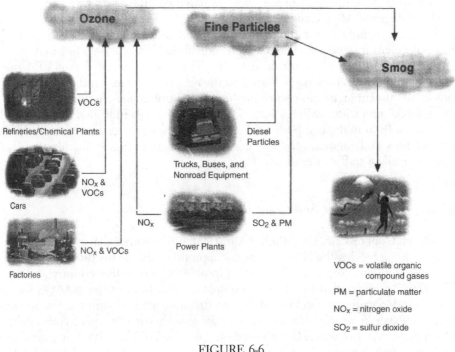

FIGURE 6-6
Smog Sources

Source: http://www.epa.gov/oar/oaqps/regusmog/smog.html

both important precursors to ozone formation in the atmosphere. The major sources of VOCs include industrial processes, transportation, and solvent uses, while NO_x are generated largely by transportation sources and utility and industrial boilers. Hydrocarbons (HCs) are an important type of VOC.

The multiple sources of ozone precursors make control difficult:

> Reducing emission of VOCs or NO_x may or may not produce a decrease in ozone concentrations, depending on the mix of pollutants that is present. Reducing NO_x can even increase ozone concentrations, in some instances. The effect of emission control on ozone concentrations depends on meteorological conditions, the absolute and relative amounts of VOCs and NO_x emitted in a particular area, and the background concentrations of ozone and its precursors that are present. Every urban area has a different balance between VOCs and NO_x. Furthermore, day-to-day variability in emissions levels, background VOC and NO_x concentrations, and wind patterns leads to day-to-day variations in the balance between VOCs and NO_x in each area. [U.S. Office of Technology Assessment, Urban Ozone and the Clean Air Act 58 (1988).]

Consumer and commercial products also contribute to ozone pollution through emissions of VOCs. In fact, EPA concluded in 1995 that 28 percent of all man-made VOC emissions emanate from those products. Section 183(e) of the CAA authorizes EPA to regulate VOC emissions from categories of consumer and commercial products through application of the "best available controls." §183(e)(3)(A). Allied Local and Regional Mfrs. Caucus v. EPA, 215 F.3d 61 (D.C. Cir. 2000), held that, in regulating the manufacture and distribution of paints and architectural coatings, EPA need not determine the reactivity of each individual VOC species, but may assess reactivity on the basis of industrial category. The court also ruled that EPA may regulate product sales nationwide based on the agency's conclusion that VOC emissions in attainment areas can contribute to nonattainment elsewhere.

Carbon monoxide, unlike ozone, is directly emitted. As indicated in section A.1 above, it results from the combustion of carbon-containing materials in power plants, furnaces, fires, and engines. Most CO exceedances occur in high-concentration "hot spots" near major traffic arteries.

2. Deadlines for Achieving the NAAQS

When Congress amended the CAA in 1990, it recognized that a uniform set of deadlines for achieving the NAAQS was not appropriate due to the differences in the nature, extent, and sources of pollution problems across the country. Section 172(a)(2)(A) provides that the date for complying with the primary NAAQS for an area that is designated nonattainment for the first time after adoption of the amendments is the date by which attainment can be achieved as expeditiously as practicable, but not more than five years after designation. See also §192(a). EPA may extend the deadline for up to ten years based on the severity of nonattainment and the availability and feasibility of control measures. The secondary standards must be achieved in such areas as expeditiously as practicable. §172(a)(2)(B). These same deadline provisions apply to nonattainment areas for pollutants newly added to the §108(a) list of criteria pollutants, and to criteria pollutants for which EPA revises the NAAQS after adoption of the 1990 amendments. The deadlines contained in §172(a) apply only if the CAA does not specifically provide different attainment dates. §172(a)(2)(D).

The scheme for compliance in areas that were already designated as nonattainment before the 1990 amendments is considerably more complex. The deadlines depend on the criteria pollutant involved and the severity of the nonattainment problem. The statute divides ozone nonattainment areas, for example, into five classifications based on increasing "design values," or ambient concentrations, of that pollutant. Marginal areas were required to comply with the primary NAAQS as expeditiously as practicable, but no later than 1993. Moderate areas had to comply no later than 1996, serious areas by 1999, severe areas by 2005 or 2007, and extreme areas by 2010.* §181(a)(1), Table 1. One-year extensions are available under limited circumstances. §181(a)(5). What deadlines apply to areas that, although once designated as attainment or unclassifiable, subsequently fall out of attainment status? See §§181(b), 192(c); Association of Irritated Residents v. EPA, 423 F.3d 989 (9th Cir. 2005) (holding that §188(e), which allows a state to request a five-year extension of the NAAQS deadline for a serious PM_{10} area, does not preclude EPA from approving deadline extensions under §179(d) after finding that a PM_{10} area has failed to attain

*When Congress was considering the adoption of the 1990 amendments, the Los Angeles area was the only one that qualified as an extreme ozone nonattainment area. Based on ozone concentrations that existed at that time, severe areas included Baltimore, Chicago, Houston-Galveston, Milwaukee-Racine, Muskegon, Michigan, New York–New Jersey–Long Island, Philadelphia-Wilmington-Trenton, and San Diego. S. Rep. No. 101-228, at 35 (1989).

the NAAQS). The statute establishes a similar range of deadlines for CO (§186) and particulate matter (§188(c)). The states must achieve the primary NAAQS for the other criteria pollutants as expeditiously as practicable, but not later than 1995. See §192(b).

WHITMAN v. AMERICAN TRUCKING ASSOCIATIONS, INC.
531 U.S. 457 (2001)

JUSTICE SCALIA delivered the opinion of the Court. . . .

[The facts of this case and other portions of the Supreme Court's opinion are reproduced at page 414 above.]

IV

[The final two issues addressed by the Court dealt with EPA's authority to implement the revised ozone NAAQS in nonattainment areas. The CAA imposes on these areas additional restrictions beyond those imposed generally by §110 on all SIPs.] These additional restrictions are found in the five substantive subparts of Part D of Title I, 42 U.S.C. §§7501-7515. Subpart 1, §§7501-7509a, contains general nonattainment regulations that pertain to every pollutant for which a NAAQS exists. Subparts 2 through 5, §§7511-7514a, contain rules tailored to specific individual pollutants. Subpart 2, added by the Clean Air Act Amendments of 1990, addresses ozone. 42 U.S.C. §§7511-7511f. The dispute before us here, in a nutshell, is whether Subpart 1 alone (as the agency determined), or rather Subpart 2 or some combination of Subparts 1 and 2, controls the implementation of the revised ozone NAAQS in non-attainment areas. . . .

  . . . We cannot agree with the Court of Appeals that Subpart 2 clearly controls the implementation of revised ozone NAAQS, because we find the statute to some extent ambiguous. We conclude, however, that the agency's interpretation goes beyond the limits of what is ambiguous and contradicts what in our view is quite clear. We therefore hold the implementation policy unlawful.

  The text of Subpart 1 at first seems to point the way to a clear answer to the question, which Subpart controls? Two sections of Subpart 1, 7502(a)(1)(C) and 7502(a)(2)(D), contain switching provisions stating that if the classification of ozone nonattainment areas is "specifically provided [for] under other provisions of [Part D]," then those provisions will control instead of Subpart 1's. Thus it is true but incomplete to note, as the Administrator does, that the substantive language of Subpart 1 is broad enough to apply to revised ozone standards. See, e.g., §7502(a)(1)(A) (instructing the Administrator to classify nonattainment areas according to "any revised standard, including a revision of any standard in effect on November 15, 1990"); §7502(a)(2)(A) (setting attainment deadlines). To determine whether that language *does* apply one must resolve the further textual issue whether some *other* provision, namely Subpart 2, provides for the classification of ozone nonattainment areas. If it does, then according to the switching provisions of Subpart 1 it will control.

  So, does Subpart 2 provide for classifying nonattainment ozone areas under the revised standard? It unquestionably does. The backbone of the subpart is Table 1, printed in §7511(a)(1) . . . , which defines five categories of ozone nonattainment areas and prescribes attainment deadlines for each. Section 7511(a)(1) funnels all nonattainment areas into the table for classification, declaring that "[e]ach area designated nonattainment for ozone . . . shall be classified at the time of such designation, under Table 1, by operation of law." And once an area has been classified, "the primary standard attainment date for ozone shall be as expeditiously as practicable but not later than the date provided in table 1." The EPA argues that this text is not as clear or comprehensive as it seems, because the title of §7511(a) reads "Classification and attainment dates for 1989 nonattainment areas," which suggests that Subpart 2 applies only to areas that were in nonattainment in 1989, and not to areas later designated nonattainment under a revised ozone standard. The suggestion must be rejected, however, because §7511(b)(1) specifically provides for the classification of areas that *were* in attainment in 1989 but have subsequently slipped into nonattainment. It thus makes clear that Subpart 2 is *not* limited solely to 1989 nonattainment areas. This eliminates the interpretive role of the title, which may only "she[d] light on some ambiguous word or phrase in the statute itself," Carter v. United States, 530 U.S. 255, 267 (2000).

It may well be, as the EPA argues . . . that some provisions of Subpart 2 are ill fitted to implementation of the revised standard. Using the old 1-hour averages of ozone levels, for example, as Subpart 2 requires, see §7511(a)(1), would produce at best an inexact estimate of the new 8-hour averages. Also, to the extent that the new ozone standard is stricter than the old one, the classification system of Subpart 2 contains a gap, because it fails to classify areas whose ozone levels are greater than the new standard (and thus nonattaining) but less than the approximation of the old standard codified by Table 1. And finally, Subpart 2's method for calculating attainment dates—which is simply to count forward a certain number of years from November 15, 1990 (the date the 1990 CAA Amendments took force), depending on how far out of attainment the area started—seems to make no sense for areas that are first classified under a new standard after November 15, 1990. If, for example, areas were classified in the year 2000, many of the deadlines would already have expired at the time of classification.

These gaps in Subpart 2's scheme prevent us from concluding that Congress clearly intended Subpart 2 to be the exclusive, permanent means of enforcing a revised ozone standard in nonattainment areas. The statute is in our view ambiguous concerning the manner in which Subpart 1 and Subpart 2 interact with regard to revised ozone standards, and we would defer to the EPA's reasonable resolution of that ambiguity. We cannot defer, however, to the interpretation the EPA has given.

Whatever effect may be accorded the gaps in Subpart 2 as implying some limited applicability of Subpart 1, they cannot be thought to render Subpart 2's carefully designed restrictions on EPA discretion utterly nugatory once a new standard has been promulgated, as the EPA has concluded. The principal distinction between Subpart 1 and Subpart 2 is that the latter eliminates regulatory discretion that the former allowed. While Subpart 1 permits the EPA to establish classifications for nonattainment areas, Subpart 2 classifies areas as a matter of law based on a table. Compare §7502(a)(1) with §7511(a)(1) (Table 1). . . . Whereas Subpart 1 gives the EPA considerable discretion to shape nonattainment programs, Subpart 2 prescribes large parts of them by law. Compare §7502(c) and (d) with §7511a. Yet according to the EPA, Subpart 2 was simply Congress's "approach to the implementation of the [old] 1-hour" standard, and so there was no reason that "the new standard could not simultaneously be implemented under . . . subpart 1." 62 Fed. Reg. 38,856, 38,885 (1997). To use a few apparent gaps in Subpart 2 to render its textually explicit applicability to nonattainment areas under the new standard utterly inoperative is to go over the edge of reasonable interpretation. The EPA may not construe the statute in a way that completely nullifies textually applicable provisions meant to limit its discretion.

The EPA's interpretation making Subpart 2 abruptly obsolete is all the more astonishing because Subpart 2 was obviously written to govern implementation for some time. Some of the elements required to be included in SIP's under Subpart 2 were not to take effect until many years after the passage of the Act. See [§§7511a(e)(3); 7511a(c)(5)(A); 7511a(g)(1)]. A plan reaching so far into the future was not enacted to be abandoned the next time the EPA reviewed the ozone standard—which Congress knew could happen at any time, since the technical staff papers had already been completed in late 1989. Yet nothing in the EPA's interpretation would have prevented the agency from aborting Subpart 2 the day after it was enacted. Even now, if the EPA's interpretation were correct, some areas of the country could be required to meet the new, more stringent ozone standard in *at most* the same time that Subpart 2 had allowed them to meet the old standard. Compare §7502(a)(2) (Subpart 1 attainment dates) with §7511(a) (Subpart 2 attainment dates). . . . An interpretation of Subpart 2 so at odds with its structure and manifest purpose cannot be sustained.

We therefore find the EPA's implementation policy to be unlawful. . . . After our remand, and the Court of Appeals' final disposition of this case, it is left to the EPA to develop a reasonable interpretation of the nonattainment implementation provisions insofar as they apply to revised ozone NAAQS. . . .

NOTES AND QUESTIONS

1. Did the Court find the statute to be clear or ambiguous on whether Subpart 1 or 2 of the nonattainment provisions applies to the revised ozone NAAQS? According to the Court, what is the principal distinction between Subparts 1 and 2? Why did the Court reject EPA's argument that the Subpart 2 deadlines clearly do not apply to areas designated as nonattainment under a revised ozone standard adopted after 1989? What "gaps" result from the conclusion that the Subpart 2 deadlines apply to such areas? What made EPA's interpretation of the statute unreasonable? What must the agency do on remand?*

2. *EPA Regulations on Remand.* In 2004, EPA issued final regulations to implement the 8-hour ozone NAAQS. 69 Fed. Reg. 23,951. Under the regulations, each area with a current 1-hour design value at or above 0.121 ppm (the lowest 1-hour design value in Table 1 of §181(a)(1)) will be classified under Subpart 2 of Part D based on its 8-hour design value and will be subject to the control obligations associated with its classification. All other areas will be covered under Subpart 1 using their 8-hour design values and will be subject to the control obligations in §172. Subpart 2 areas will be classified as marginal, moderate, serious, severe, or extreme based on the area's 8-hour design value. Because Table 1 is based on 1-hour design values, and application of the table as written would produce absurd results, EPA promulgated a

---

*See generally Luneberg, Clean Air Act Implementation and the Impact of Whitman v. American Trucking Associations, Inc., 63 U. Pitt. L. Rev. 1 (2001); Oren, The Supreme Court Forces a U-Turn: The Fate of American Trucking, 34 Envtl. L. Rep. (ELI) 10687 (2004).

regulation translating the thresholds in Table 1 from 1-hour to 8-hour values. EPA also decided to establish an "overwhelming transport" classification that will be available to Subpart 1 areas demonstrating that they are affected by overwhelming transport of ozone and its precursors and that they meet the definition of a rural transport area in §182(h). Areas would not have to demonstrate that transport was due solely to sources outside the state. EPA deferred the decision on what controls would be applicable to overwhelming transport areas. It indicated that it would revoke the 1-hour standard, including the associated designations and classifications, one year after the effective date of the designations for the 8-hour NAAQS. According to EPA, 474 counties in 32 states failed to meet the new ozone NAAQS. See also 70 Fed. Reg. 39,413 (2005) (affirming 2004 final rules in denying petitions for reconsideration); 70 Fed. Reg. 71,612 (2005) (final rule implementing the 8-hour ozone NAAQS, which covers issues such as how to apply the RACT, RACM, and RFP requirements, discussed below, and how to apply new source review in ozone nonattainment areas).

The D.C. Circuit struck down and remanded the 2004 regulations implementing the 8-hour ozone standard in part in South Coast Air Quality Mgmt. Dist. v. EPA, 472 F.3d 882 (D.C. Cir. 2006). The court held that, to the extent the 2004 regulations subject areas with an 8-hour design value exceeding 0.09 ppm to Subpart 1 instead of Subpart 2, EPA misinterpreted the statute and "trespassed into areas where Subpart 2 unquestionably applies." Id. at 892. Under the Supreme Court's decision in Whitman, EPA has the discretion to apply Subpart 1 only to the extent that an area is not attaining the NAAQS but its air quality is not as dangerous as the level addressed by the 1990 amendments (0.09 ppm on an 8-hour scale). "[T]he regulation of the eight-hour standard is to be independent of the one-hour standard. Eight-hour nonattainment areas must be subject to Subpart 2 wherever they have air at least as unhealthful as Congress contemplated when enacting the 1990 Amendments." Id. at 893. The court rejected industry's claim that, in creating an updated version of Table 1 of §181 to account for the new 8-hour version of the ozone NAAQS, EPA failed to recognize that 8-hour ozone is more difficult to reduce than 1-hour ozone. The court also held that EPA has the authority to revoke the 1-hour standard, as long as adequate anti-backsliding provisions are introduced pursuant to §172(e). But it invalidated EPA's decision not to continue to apply the NSR program, §185 penalties, and contingency plans to areas not meeting the 1-hour standard, rejecting EPA's contention that none of these requirements would qualify as "controls" for purposes of §172(e).

3.   General State Implementation Plan Requirements for Nonattainment Areas

Specifying new deadlines for achieving the NAAQS is one thing; actually achieving them is another. Under §107(a), the primary responsibility for achieving the NAAQS remains with the states, but the CAA constrains the discretion of the states in developing control strategies to allocate required reductions among sources. Some of the constraints apply to all states with AQCRs designated as nonattainment. A plethora of others vary, like the amended NAAQS deadlines, in accordance with the criteria pollutant for which an AQCR is classified as nonattainment and the severity of the nonattainment problem. States with nonattainment areas were required to revise their SIPs to conform to the requirements of the 1990 amendments. §172(b). The amended SIPs had to comply not only with the minimal requirements for all SIPs set forth in §110(a)(2), but also with plan provisions unique to nonattainment areas.

The general nonattainment area provisions are described in §172(c). Each state with a nonattainment area must include in its SIP an updated inventory of actual emissions from all sources of the nonattainment pollutant. §172(c)(3). The SIP must provide for reasonable further progress (RFP), defined as annual incremental reductions in emissions for the purpose of ensuring timely attainment of the NAAQS. §§172(c)(2), 171(1). Nonattainment states must implement all reasonably available control measures (RACM) as expeditiously as practicable, including emissions reductions from existing sources obtainable through the application of reasonably available control technology (RACT). §172(c)(1). May EPA define RACM as limited to those measures that would advance the date at which an area reaches attainment? See BCCA Appeal Group v. EPA, 355 F.3d 817, 847-848 (5th Cir. 2004); Sierra Club v. EPA, 314 F.3d 735 (5th Cir. 2002); Sierra Club v. EPA, 294 F.3d 155, 162 (D.C. Cir. 2002). The court in Ober v. Whitman, 243 F.3d 1190 (9th Cir. 2001), upheld EPA's decision to exempt *de minimis* sources from transportation control measures.

The SIP for a state with nonattainment areas also must require permits for the construction and operation of new or modified major stationary sources in the area. §172(c)(5). This permit program, along with a similar permit program for PSD areas, is referred to as new source review (NSR). It is the focus of the next subsection. Nonattainment SIPs must include other enforceable emission limitations and control techniques, including economic incentives such as emission fees and marketable permits, as well as compliance timetables. §172(c)(6). They also must include contingency measures that go into effect automatically in the event that a nonattainment area fails to make RFP or attain the NAAQS by the applicable deadline. §172(c)(9). May a state designate as contingency measures emission controls that originated before EPA found the SIP to be deficient under the nonattainment provisions, but that continue to manifest an effect after the plan fails? See Louisiana Envtl. Action Network v. EPA, 382 F.3d 575, 582-584 (5th Cir. 2004) (finding EPA's affirmative answer to be consistent with the purposes of the CAA).

The statutory provisions dealing with specific criteria pollutants may supplement or supplant these more general requirements. SIPs for ozone nonattainment areas must include measures that become more stringent as ambient concentrations increase. Thus, for example, SIPs that cover moderate ozone nonattainment areas must require reductions in emissions of VOCs of at least 15 percent from amounts emitted in 1990. §182(b)(1)(A). In serious ozone nonattainment areas, compliance with the RFP mandate entails annual reductions in emissions of VOCs of 3 percent from 1990 levels, with some exceptions. §182(c)(2)(B). Not surprisingly, most of the special SIP provisions for carbon monoxide nonattainment areas deal with the use of automobiles. See §187. The provisions applicable to both CO and particulate matter nonattainment areas contain annual emission reductions (called milestones) that elaborate on the RFP requirement for those areas. See, e.g., §§187(d), 189(c).

The 1990 amendments divided nonattainment areas for particulate matter into two categories, moderate and serious. SIPs for moderate areas must include provisions to ensure implementation of "reasonably available control measures." §189(a)(1)(C). SIPs for serious areas also must include provisions to ensure implementation of the "best available control measures." §189(b)(1)(B). Although the statute does not define either term, EPA has defined the latter as the maximum degree of emissions reduction of PM, determined on a case-by-case basis, taking into account economic impacts and other costs. Vigil v. Leavitt, 381 F.3d 826 (9th Cir. 2004), upheld EPA's approval of an Arizona SIP that required farmers to adopt one of a group of best management practices (BMPs) designed to reduce PM emissions. The court concluded that the "best" measures did not require farmers to adopt more than one form of BMPs. But the court also concluded that EPA failed to explain adequately its rejection of reformulated diesel fuel required by the California Air Resources Board since 1993 as a best available control measure.

Problem 6-1

In a report issued before the adoption of the 1990 amendments, the U.S. Office of Technology Assessment (OTA) described a series of source-specific control strategies for reducing emissions in nonattainment areas. These strategies included: the adoption of RACT for stationary sources; the establishment of federally regulated controls on selected stationary sources of VOCs; onboard technology on motor vehicles to capture gasoline vapor during refueling; advanced "Stage II" control devices on gas pumps to capture gasoline vapor during motor vehicle refueling; inspection and maintenance (I&M) programs for motor vehicles to test the performance of catalytic converters; more stringent exhaust emissions standards for gasoline highway vehicles; new restrictions on fuel volatility; and the use of methanol instead of gasoline as a fuel for vehicles in centrally owned fleets.*

Suppose you are responsible for developing the first draft of the SIP revisions for all of the ozone nonattainment areas located in your state (which include moderate, serious, and severe areas). How much discretion do you have in relying on each of these control strategies? Which ones does the statute mandate? Are any precluded? Does the statute require any strategies not listed in the OTA report? Can you think of any other techniques or strategies that the state might want to include in its SIP?

Problem 6-2

Suppose a county that was designated as a moderate nonattainment area for ozone in 1977 demonstrates that, for each of the last three years, it has been in compliance with the NAAQS. The county has filed a petition with EPA to be redesignated as an attainment area under §107(d)(3)(E), but EPA has not yet ruled on the petition. EPA nevertheless issues a rule in which it declares that the county need not comply with the 15 percent RFP and attainment demonstration requirements of §182(b)(1)(A)(i) or the contingency measures requirement of §172(c)(9). In addition, EPA rules that the state will not be subject to sanctions for failure to submit SIP revisions that address these requirements. A local environmental group challenges the validity of the rule, asserting that it is inconsistent with the statutory language and purposes and with EPA's decision to continue to require the county to adhere to some nonattainment area requirements (including RACT and a vehicle I&M program). The complaint also alleges that §107(d)(3)(E) provides the exclusive means of

---

*The provisions of the statute that are designed to control emissions from mobile sources in nonattainment areas are addressed in more detail in section F.5.

redesignating an area from nonattainment to attainment. What arguments can EPA make to support its rule?

4. Controlling Emissions from Stationary Sources in Nonattainment Areas

a. The Scope of the New Source Review Permit Program

One of the mandatory components of a SIP that covers nonattainment areas is a permit program for the construction and operation of new or modified major stationary sources. §172(c)(5). The CAA contains a similar program for PSD areas, which is covered in section G.2 below. Together, the two permit programs are often referred to as the new source review (NSR) program. The *Chevron* case, reproduced immediately below, and the notes that follow it deal with the scope of the nonattainment portion of the NSR program. *Chevron* also focuses on the bubble concept, to which you were introduced in section E in connection with the new source performance standards of §111. The two *New York* cases and accompanying notes that follow also deal with the scope of NSR, in both the nonattainment and PSD contexts. The next subsection, which includes the *CARE* case, addresses the substantive requirements of the nonattainment area permit program. Because one of those, the offset requirement, raises issues similar to those that relate to the bubble concept, detailed consideration of the merits of the bubble concept and of incorporating other economic incentives into the CAA's regulatory scheme is deferred until after the *CARE* case.

CHEVRON U.S.A., INC. v. NATURAL RESOURCES DEFENSE COUNCIL, INC.
467 U.S. 837 (1984)

JUSTICE STEVENS delivered the opinion of the Court.

In the Clean Air Act Amendments of 1977, Congress enacted certain requirements applicable to States that had not achieved the national air quality standards established by the Environmental Protection Agency (EPA) pursuant to earlier legislation. [Section 172(c)(5)* of the] amended Clean Air Act required these "nonattainment" States to establish a permit program regulating "new or modified major stationary sources" of air pollution. . . . The EPA regulation promulgated to implement this permit requirement allows a State to adopt a plantwide definition of the term "stationary source."[2] Under this definition, an existing plant that contains several pollution-emitting devices may install or modify one piece of equipment without meeting the permit conditions if the alteration will not increase the total emissions

---

*[EDS.: At the time of this case, the relevant provision was §172(b)(6).]

2. "(i) 'Stationary source' means any building, structure, facility, or installation which emits or may emit any air pollutant subject to regulation under the Act.

"(ii) 'Building, structure, facility, or installation' means all of the pollutant-emitting activities which belong to the same industrial grouping, are located on one or more contiguous or adjacent properties, and are under the control of the same person (or persons under common control) except the activities of any vessel." 40 C.F.R. §§51.18(j)(1)(i) and (ii) (1983).

from the plant. The question presented by these cases is whether EPA's decision to allow States to treat all of the pollution-emitting devices within the same industrial grouping as though they were encased within a single "bubble" is based on a reasonable construction of the statutory term "stationary source."

[The Court of Appeals set aside the 1981 regulations containing the plantwide definition of the term "stationary source" in NRDC v. Gorsuch, 685 F.2d 718 (D.C. Cir. 1982). Finding neither the statutory language nor the legislative history dispositive, that court resorted to "the purposes of the nonattainment program." Id. at 276 n.39. The court had addressed the applicability of the bubble concept to other CAA programs twice before in Alabama Power Co. v. Costle, 636 F.2d 323 (D.C. Cir. 1979), and ASARCO Inc. v. EPA, 578 F.2d 319 (D.C. Cir. 1978), both of which were discussed above in connection with the NSPS bubble. Based on these precedents, the court reasoned that the bubble concept was "mandatory" in programs designed merely to maintain existing air quality, but "inappropriate" in programs whose purpose was to improve air quality. Because the purpose of the nonattainment provisions is to improve air quality, the court held that the bubble concept was prohibited.]

II . . .

. . . [T]he Court of Appeals misconceived the nature of its role in reviewing the regulations at issue. Once it determined . . . that Congress did not actually have an intent regarding the applicability of the bubble concept to the permit program, the question before it was not whether in its view the concept is "inappropriate" in the general context of a program designed to improve air quality, but whether the Administrator's view that it is appropriate in the context of this particular program is a reasonable one. . . . [W]e agree with the Court of Appeals that Congress did not have a specific intention on the applicability of the bubble concept in these cases, and conclude that the EPA's use of that concept here is a reasonable policy choice for the agency to make. . . .

V

The legislative history of the portion of the 1977 Amendments dealing with nonattainment areas does not contain any specific comment on the "bubble concept" or the question whether a plantwide definition of a stationary source is permissible under the permit program. It does, however, plainly disclose that in the permit program Congress sought to accommodate the conflict between the economic interest in permitting capital improvements to continue and the environmental interest in improving air quality. Indeed, the House Committee Report identified the economic interest as one of the "two main purposes" of this section of the bill. It stated:

> Section 117 of the bill, adopted during full committee markup, establishes a new section 127 of the Clean Air Act. The section has two main purposes: (1) to allow reasonable economic growth to continue in an area while making reasonable further

progress to assure attainment of the standards by a fixed date; and (2) to allow States greater flexibility for the former purpose than EPA's present interpretative regulations afford. . . . [25] [H.R. Rep. No. 95-294, at 211 (1977), 1977 U.S. Code Cong. & Admin. News 1077, 1290.]

VI

As previously noted, prior to the 1977 Amendments, the EPA had adhered to a plant-wide definition of the term "source" under a NSPS program. . . .

In August 1980, however, the EPA adopted a regulation that, in essence, applied the basic reasoning of the Court of Appeals in these cases. The EPA took particular note of the two then-recent Court of Appeals decisions, which had created the bright-line rule that the "bubble concept" should be employed in a program designed to maintain air quality but not in one designed to enhance air quality. Relying heavily on those cases, EPA adopted a dual definition of "source" for nonattainment areas that required a permit whenever a change in either the entire plant, or one of its components, would result in a significant increase in emissions even if the increase was completely offset by reductions elsewhere in the plant. The EPA expressed the opinion that this interpretation was "more consistent with congressional intent" than the plantwide definition because it "would bring in more sources or modifications for review," 45 Fed. Reg. 52,697 (1980), but its primary legal analysis was predicated on the two Court of Appeals decisions.

In 1981 a new administration took office and initiated a "Government-wide reexamination of regulatory burdens and complexities." 46 Fed. Reg. 16,281. In the context of that review, the EPA reevaluated the various arguments that had been advanced in connection with the proper definition of the term "source." . . .

In explaining its conclusion, the EPA first noted that the definitional issue was not squarely addressed in either the statute or its legislative history and therefore that the issue involved an agency "judgment as how to best carry out the Act." Ibid. It then set forth several reasons for concluding that the plantwide definition was more appropriate. It pointed out that the dual definition "can act as a disincentive to new investment and modernization by discouraging modifications to existing facilities" and "can actually retard progress in air pollution control by discouraging replacement of older, dirtier processes or pieces of equipment with new, cleaner ones." Ibid. Moreover, the new definition "would simplify EPA's rules by using the same definition of 'source' for PSD, nonattainment new source review and the construction moratorium. This reduces confusion and inconsistency." Ibid. Finally, the agency explained that additional requirements that remained in place would accomplish the fundamental purposes of achieving attainment with NAAQS's as expeditiously as possible. . . .

---

25. . . . [T]he second "main purpose" of the provision—allowing the States "greater flexibility" than the EPA's interpretative Ruling— . . . is entirely consistent with the view that Congress did not intend to freeze the definition of "source" contained in the existing regulation into a rigid statutory requirement.

VII

In this Court respondents expressly reject the basic rationale of the Court of Appeals' decision. That court . . . interpreted the policies of the statute . . . to mandate the plantwide definition in programs designed to maintain clean air and to forbid it in programs designed to improve air quality. Respondents . . . contend that the text of the Act requires the EPA to use a dual definition [in the context of both the PSD and nonattainment area permit programs].

STATUTORY LANGUAGE

The definition of the term "stationary source" in §111(a)(3) refers to "any building, structure, facility, or installation" which emits air pollution. This definition is applicable only to the NSPS program by the express terms of the statute; the text of the statute does not make this definition applicable to the permit program. Petitioners therefore maintain that there is no statutory language even relevant to ascertaining the meaning of stationary source in the permit program aside from §302(j), which defines the term "major stationary source." We disagree. . . .

The definition in §302(j) tells us what the word "major" means—a source must emit at least 100 tons of pollution to qualify—but it sheds virtually no light on the meaning of the term "stationary source." It does equate a source with a facility—a "major emitting facility" and a "major stationary source" are synonymous under §302(j). The ordinary meaning of the term "facility" is some collection of integrated elements which has been designed and constructed to achieve some purpose. Moreover, it is certainly no affront to common English usage to take a reference to a major facility or a major source to connote an entire plant as opposed to its constituent parts. Basically, however, the language of §302(j) simply does not compel any given interpretation of the term "source."

Respondents recognize that, and hence point to §111(a)(3). Although the definition in that section is not literally applicable to the permit program, it sheds as much light on the meaning of the word "source" as anything in the statute. As respondents point out, use of the words "building, structure, facility, or installation," as the definition of source, could be read to impose the permit conditions on an individual building that is a part of a plant. . . . The language may reasonably be interpreted to impose the requirement on any discrete, but integrated, operation which pollutes. This gives meaning to all of the terms—a single building, not part of a larger operation, would be covered if it emits more than 100 tons of pollution, as would any facility, structure, or installation. Indeed, the language itself implies a "bubble concept" of sorts: each enumerated item would seem to be treated as if it were encased in a bubble. While respondents insist that each of these terms must be given a discrete meaning, they also argue that §111(a)(3) defines "source" as that term is used in §302(j). The latter section, however, equates a source with a facility, whereas the former defines "source" as a facility, among other items.

We are not persuaded that parsing of general terms in the text of the statute will reveal an actual intent of Congress. We know full well that this language is not dispositive; the terms are overlapping and the language is not precisely directed to the question of the applicability of a given term in the context of a larger operation. To the extent any congressional "intent" can be discerned from this language, it would appear that the listing of overlapping, illustrative terms was intended to enlarge, rather than to confine, the scope of the agency's power to regulate particular sources in order to effectuate the policies of the Act.

LEGISLATIVE HISTORY . . .

. . . We find that the legislative history as a whole is silent on the precise issue before us. It is, however, consistent with the view that the EPA should have broad discretion in implementing the policies of the 1977 Amendments.

More importantly, that history plainly identifies the policy concerns that motivated the enactment; the plantwide definition is fully consistent with one of those concerns—the allowance of reasonable economic growth—and, whether or not we believe it most effectively implements the other, we must recognize that the EPA has advanced a reasonable explanation for its conclusion that the regulations serve the environmental objectives as well. Indeed, its reasoning is supported by the public record developed in the rulemaking process, as well as by certain private studies.[37]

Our review of the EPA's varying interpretations of the word "source"—both before and after the 1977 Amendments—convinces us that the agency primarily responsible for administering this important legislation has consistently interpreted it flexibly—not in a sterile textual vacuum, but in the context of implementing policy decisions in a technical and complex arena. The fact that the agency has from time to time changed its interpretation of the term "source" does not, as respondents argue, lead us to conclude that no deference should be accorded the agency's interpretation of the statute. An initial agency interpretation is not instantly carved in stone. On the contrary, the agency, to engage in informed rulemaking, must consider varying interpretations and the wisdom of its policy on a continuing basis. Moreover, the fact that the agency has adopted different definitions in different contexts adds force to the argument that the definition itself is flexible, particularly since Congress has never indicated any disapproval of a flexible reading of the statute. . . .

POLICY

The arguments over policy that are advanced in the parties' briefs create the impression that respondents are now waging in a judicial forum a specific policy battle which they ultimately lost in the agency and in the 32 jurisdictions opting for the "bubble concept," but one which was never waged in the Congress. Such policy arguments are more properly addressed to legislators or administrators, not to judges.[38]

37. "Economists have proposed that economic incentives be substituted for the cumbersome administrative-legal framework. The objective is to make the profit and cost incentives that work so well in the marketplace work for pollution control. . . . [The 'bubble' or 'netting' concept] is a first attempt in this direction. By giving a plant manager flexibility to find the places and processes within a plant that control emissions most cheaply, pollution control can be achieved more quickly and cheaply." L. Lave & G. Omenn, Cleaning Air: Reforming the Clean Air Act 28 (1981).

38. Respondents point out if a brand new factory that will emit over 100 tons of pollutants is constructed in a nonattainment area, that plant must obtain a permit pursuant to [§172(c)(5)] and in order to do so, it must satisfy the §173 conditions. . . . Respondents argue if an old plant containing several large emitting units is to be modernized by the replacement of one or more units emitting over 100 tons of pollutant with a new unit emitting less—but still more than 100 tons—the result should be no different simply because "it happens to be built not at a new site, but within a pre-existing plant." Brief for Respondents 4.

In these cases, the Administrator's interpretation represents a reasonable accommodation of manifestly competing interests and is entitled to deference: the regulatory scheme is technical and complex, the agency considered the matter in a detailed and reasoned fashion, and the decision involves reconciling conflicting policies. Congress intended to accommodate both interests, but did not do so itself on the level of specificity presented by these cases. Perhaps that body consciously desired the Administrator to strike the balance at this level, thinking that those with great expertise and charged with responsibility for administering the provision would be in a better position to do so; perhaps it simply did not consider the question at this level; and perhaps Congress was unable to forge a coalition on either side of the question, and those on each side decided to take their chances with the scheme devised by the agency. For judicial purposes, it matters not which of these things occurred.

Judges are not experts in the field, and are not part of either political branch of the Government. Courts must, in some cases, reconcile competing political interests, but not on the basis of the judges' personal policy preferences. In contrast, an agency to which Congress has delegated policy-making responsibilities may, within the limits of that delegation, properly rely upon the incumbent administration's views of wise policy to inform its judgments. While agencies are not directly accountable to the people, the Chief Executive is, and it is entirely appropriate for this political branch of the Government to make such policy choices—resolving the competing interests which Congress itself either inadvertently did not resolve, or intentionally left to be resolved by the agency charged with the administration of the statute in light of everyday realities.

When a challenge to an agency construction of a statutory provision, fairly conceptualized, really centers on the wisdom of the agency's policy, rather than whether it is a reasonable choice within a gap left open by Congress, the challenge must fail. In such a case, federal judges—who have no constituency—have a duty to respect legitimate policy choices made by those who do. The responsibilities for assessing the wisdom of such policy choices and resolving the struggle between competing views of the public interest are not judicial ones: "Our Constitution vests such responsibilities in the political branches." TVA v. Hill, 437 U.S. 153, 195 (1978).

We hold that the EPA's definition of the term "source" is a permissible construction of the statute which seeks to accommodate progress in reducing air pollution with economic growth. . . .

The judgment of the Court of Appeals is reversed.

NOTES AND QUESTIONS

1. *Chevron* stands as a strong statement on the need for deference to agency interpretations of statutes. For additional discussion of the administrative law aspects of *Chevron*, see Chapter 3, section A.2.b.

2. Why did the Court of Appeals hold that the bubble concept was inappropriate in the context of the nonattainment area program? What was the source of the "bright line" distinction upon which it relied? How do you think NRDC tried to take advantage of that distinction before the Court of Appeals? Why did NRDC change its argument when the case reached the Supreme Court? How had EPA approached the bubble concept before it issued the regulations reviewed in this case? What was

EPA's explanation for its endorsement of the bubble concept in 1981? What do you make of the Court's contention that each of the four components of the definition of a stationary source in §111(a)(3) can be viewed "as if it were encased in a bubble"?

How convincing is the Court's reading of the legislative history of the nonattainment area permit program? Would Congress have enacted a stringent new source review program if it had been aware that the cleanup required by the program could be dodged with ease through application of the bubble concept?

3. *The Bubble after 1990.* The 1990 amendments to the CAA explicitly endorse the bubble concept but make it more difficult to "bubble out" of NSR in certain nonattainment areas. A stationary source located in a serious ozone nonattainment area that emits or has the potential to emit less than 100 tons per year of VOCs, for example, may not use the bubble concept to avoid the permit program unless the increase in emissions that results from a physical change or change in the method of operation of any discrete operation, unit, or other pollutant-emitting activity at the source is offset by emissions reductions of at least 1.3 times that amount. §182(c)(7). If such a source emits or has the potential to emit 100 tons per year or more of VOCs, it may not use the bubble at all to avoid the permit program, although it may be able to avoid the stringent technology-based requirements of the permit program (described below) by achieving an internal offset ratio of at least 1.3:1. §182(c)(8). See also §182(e)(2).

4. *"Major" Sources. Chevron* focused on the issue of whether a major stationary source had been modified, thereby becoming subject to the permit requirement of §172(c)(5). But what constitutes a major stationary source for purposes of the non-attainment area permit program? The answer differs depending on the criteria pollutant for which the area is designated nonattainment and the severity of the nonattainment problem. In a serious ozone nonattainment area, for example, a major stationary source is one that emits or has the potential to emit at least 50 tons of VOCs per year. §182(c). In a severe ozone nonattainment area, the threshold for a major stationary source is 25 tons of VOCs per year, §182(d), while in an extreme area the threshold is 10 tons per year. §182(e). Why did Congress choose to lower the threshold qualifications for a major stationary source as the concentration of ozone in nonattainment areas increased?

Suppose that a business is considering constructing a warehouse that will not emit any pollutants, but will be serviced by trucks that emit CO and ozone precursors (oxides of nitrogen). The warehouse will be located in a region categorized as a moderate nonattainment area for both CO and ozone. Assuming that the emissions from the trucks will exceed the 100-ton threshold of §302(j), will the business have to apply for a nonattainment area permit? See Village of Oconomowoc Lake v. Dayton Hudson Corp., 24 F.3d 962 (7th Cir. 1994).

In 2002, EPA adopted a package of NSR reforms. The validity of those reforms was at issue in the following case.

NEW YORK v. EPA
413 F.3d 3 (D.C. Cir. 2005)

Before: ROGERS and TATEL, Circuit Judges, and WILLIAMS, Senior Circuit Judge. PER CURIAM.

[The 1977 CAA amendments] directed that major stationary sources undertaking modifications must obtain preconstruction permits, as must major new sources, through a process known as "New Source Review" ("NSR"). According to a preexisting definition referenced in the 1977 amendments, a source undertakes a modification when "any physical change . . . or change in the method of operation . . . which increases the amount of any air pollutant emitted by such source" occurs. 42 U.S.C. §7411(a)(4). EPA has interpreted this rather terse definition in [rules issued in 1980, 1992, and 2002. Industry petitioners argued that the 2002 rule interpreted "modification" too broadly, while government and environmental petitioners argued that the rule's interpretation was too narrow.]

I. Background . . .

The [1970 CAA] required new or modified sources to conform to emissions limits, known as "New Source Performance Standards" ("NSPS"), set by EPA. See id. §7411. Because "[t]he Act contemplated" that these criteria would be "more stringent than those needed to meet . . . NAAQS," Alabama Power Co. v. Castle, 636 F.2d 323, 346 (D.C. Cir. 1979), the meaning of "modified sources" took on particular significance: if an existing source made a "modification," it needed to conform its change to NSPS, whereas an unmodified source only needed to meet whatever lesser requirements (if any) the SIP imposed for attaining NAAQS.

[The 1977 amendments added a preconstruction review process for new or modified major sources located in either "nonattainment" areas or PSD areas (i.e., areas which meet the NAAQS or where there is insufficient information to evaluate whether NAAQS are being met). The court referred to the first as "Nonattainment New Source Review" (NNSR), to the second as "Prevention of Significant Deterioration" (PSD), and to the two collectively as "New Source Review" (NSR).]

In sum, the 1977 amendments carved out a significant difference between existing sources on the one hand and new or modified sources on the other. The former faced no NSR obligations—in the common phrase, they were "grandfathered"—while the latter were subject to strict standards. Limiting NSR to new or modified sources was one method of accomplishing the amendments' goal of "a proper balance between environmental controls and economic growth" (statement of Rep. Waxman).

[EPA issued NSR regulations in 1978 and again in 1980 to conform to interpretations of the CAA set forth in Alabama Power v. Castle, 636 F.2d 323 (D.C. Cir. 1979). The 1980 regulations changed EPA's definition of modification. The 1980 regulations defined a "major modification" as "any physical change in or change in the method of operation of a major stationary source that would result in a significant net emissions increase of any pollutant subject to regulation under the Act." It also defined "[n]et emissions increase" as "any increase in actual emissions from a particular physical change or change in method of operation" that occurred after taking into account, through a process known as "netting," "any other increases and decreases in actual emissions at the source that are contemporaneous with the particular change and are otherwise creditable."]

In the proceedings before us today, industry petitioners and EPA dispute what the 1980 rule meant. Both agree that for a source to undertake a modification, it must first make a physical or operational change other than an increase in the hours of operation. They disagree over how to measure an "increase" in emitted pollutants once a change has occurred. According to industry petitioners, the 1980 regulation provided that an emissions "increase" occurs only if the maximum hourly emissions rate goes up as a result of the physical or operational change. According to EPA, however, an increase occurs under the 1980 regulations if, after netting, a source's past annual emissions (typically measured by averaging out the two "baseline" years prior to the change) are less than future annual emissions (measured by calculating the source's potential to emit after the change). EPA proffered this interpretation, which quickly became known as the "actual-to-potential" test, in proceedings leading up to Puerto Rican Cement Co. v. EPA, 889 F.2d 292 (1st Cir. 1989), and Wisconsin Electric Power Co. v. Reilly, 893 F.2d 901 (7th Cir. 1990) ("WEPCo"). . . .

Puerto Rican Cement's facts illustrate the practical difference between industry's and EPA's interpretations. In that case, a factory sought to make a physical change: it would replace old cement kilns that operated 60% of the time with a new kiln that would emit fewer pollutants per hour. "If operated to achieve about the same level of production [as the old ones], the new kiln will pollute far less than the older kilns; but, if the Company operates the new kiln at significantly higher production levels, it will emit more pollutants than did the older kilns." 889 F.2d at 293. Under the actual-to-potential test, the company "increased" its emissions after the change, making it subject to NSR: operated at full potential, the new kiln would emit more pollutants than the old kilns had emitted when actually in operation. Under the interpretation urged by industry petitioners, however, the company had not undergone an "increase" in emissions—and thus would not trigger NSR—since the new kiln would have a lower hourly emissions rate than the old ones. Siding with EPA, the First Circuit agreed that the company had to obtain an NSR permit to make the intended change.

WEPCo, which is important because of EPA's response to it, addressed whether EPA could apply the actual-to-potential test to utility plants undergoing extensive renovations. The petitioner argued that given the particular nature of the utility market, it was unfair to compare a utility's past actual emissions with its future potential emissions. Instead, the petitioner argued—and the Seventh Circuit agreed—that EPA should measure future emissions by projecting future actual emissions rather than by assuming, as it had done under the actual-to-potential test, that the source would operate at full capacity in the future. . . .

EPA dealt with *WEPCo* by issuing a 1992 rule that changed the test utilities used for measuring emissions increases. Under the new test, known as the "actual-to-projected-actual test," utilities would determine whether they had post-change increases in emissions—and thus whether they needed NSR permits—by comparing actual emissions before the change to their projections of actual post-change emissions. . . .

[EPA's 2002 regulations] departed from the prior rules in several significant respects relevant to this litigation. First, it adopted the actual-to-projected-actual test for all existing sources, though leaving sources the option to continue using the actual-to-potential test if they preferred. Second, it altered the method for measuring past actual emissions. Under the 1980 rule, sources determined past actual emissions by averaging their annual emissions during the two years immediately prior to the change, though they could use either different, more representative periods or source-specific allowable emissions levels, if they could convince the permitting authorities. In contrast, under the 2002 rule, sources other than electric utilities determine past actual emissions by averaging annual emissions of any two consecutive years during the ten years prior to the change. EPA determined that this change eliminated the need for case-specific alternatives. . . . Fourth, the rule provided that sources that saw no reasonable possibility that post-change emissions would prove higher than past actual emissions need keep no records of actual post-change emissions. Fifth, the rule [allowed sources to make changes that might otherwise have constituted modifications if they comply with the requirements of the so-called Clean Unit option.] Under [that] option, sources that install technology "comparable to" [best available control technology (BACT)] (if in PSD regions) or [lowest achievable emission rates (LAER)] (if in NNSR regions) may make whatever changes they want over the next ten years without triggering NSR, provided that these changes do not cause them to exceed the "emissions limitations" set by their comparable technology. . . .

III. Baseline Emissions

[NSR applies to a "modification" of a major stationary source. To determine whether a physical or operational change results in an "increase" in emissions, a source must calculate its baseline level of "actual emissions." The 1980 rule defined that term as "the average rate, in tons per year, at which the unit actually emitted the pollutant during a two-year period which precedes the [change] and which is representative of normal source operation," but it allowed reference to a different time period upon a determination that it was "more representative of normal source operation."]

The 2002 rule reinterprets the term "increases" by adopting a new method for calculating baseline actual emissions. For sources other than electric utilities, "baseline actual emissions" are defined as "the average rate, in tons per year, at which the emissions unit actually emitted the pollutant during any consecutive 24-month period selected by the [source] within the 10-year period immediately preceding [the change]." A source must adjust its baseline downward to reflect any legally enforceable emissions limitations that have been imposed since the baseline period, and it may not use a more "representative" baseline period outside the ten-year "lookback period." A source may use a different baseline period for each regulated pollutant. . . .

Government and environmental petitioners raise two sets of challenges to the ten-year lookback period. First, they contend that the ten-year lookback period reflects an impermissible interpretation of the statutory term "increases" because it allows sources to increase their emissions beyond their most recent levels without triggering NSR. Second, they contend that EPA's selection of a ten-year lookback period is arbitrary and capricious because it contravenes the statutory purpose of protecting and enhancing air quality. . . . [W]e conclude that petitioners' challenges to the ten-year lookback period fail to overcome the presumption of validity afforded to EPA regulations under the CAA.

A.

Statutory Interpretation. While the CAA defines a "modification" as any physical or operational change that "increases" emissions, it is silent on how to calculate such "increases" in emissions. 42 U.S.C. §7411(a)(4). According to government petitioners, the lack of a statutory definition does not render the term "increases" ambiguous, but merely compels the court to give the term its "ordinary meaning." . . . [G]overnment petitioners contend that the ordinary meaning of "increases" requires the baseline to be calculated from a period immediately preceding the change. They maintain, for example, that in determining whether a high-pressure weather system "increases" the local temperature, the relevant baseline is the temperature immediately preceding the arrival of the weather system, not the temperature five or ten years ago. . . .

EPA maintains that its choice of the ten-year lookback period is entitled to deference under *Chevron* Step 2 because it is based on a permissible construction of the ambiguous term "increases." EPA [points out] that if the weather system arrives in the evening, it is inappropriate to compare the nighttime temperature immediately following the arrival of the system to the daytime temperature immediately preceding the arrival of the system. The important point is that the period immediately preceding a change may not be analogous to the period following the change and thus may not yield a meaningful comparison for the purpose of determining whether the change "increases" emissions. Hence, government petitioners' reliance on the "ordinary meaning" of "increases" fails to address a practical reality. . . .

It is EPA's position that the ten-year lookback period is based on a permissible interpretation of the CAA because it "fulfills the statutory goal of balancing economic growth with the need to protect air quality." According to EPA, the ten-year lookback period promotes economic growth and administrative efficiency by affording sources the flexibility to respond rapidly to market changes, focusing limited regulatory resources on changes most likely to harm the environment, and eliminating conflicts over whether a proposed baseline period is "more representative of normal source operations." At the same time, EPA believes that the ten-year lookback period protects air quality by eliminating the regulatory disincentive to make physical or operational changes that improve efficiency and reduce emissions rates. We conclude that EPA supports these conclusions with "detailed and reasoned" analysis based on its experience and expertise.

In explaining the benefits of the ten-year lookback period, EPA appropriately refers to the problems experienced under the 1980 rule. EPA notes that under the 1980 rule, establishing a representative baseline period other than the two-year period immediately preceding the change was "complex and time-consuming" and often involved "disputed judgment calls." EPA further notes that under the 1980 rule, sources experiencing periods of low production faced the unwelcome choice of either "surrendering capacity" by capping emissions at unrepresentative low levels or incurring the time and expense of securing NSR permits "for even small, non-excluded changes to a portion of the plant." According to industry comments on the ten-year lookback period, this dilemma discourages sources from making economically efficient and environmentally beneficial changes during periods of low production. Similarly, as EPA points out[,] . . . the 1980 rule "results in a baseline that decreases each time production decreases. In other words, if economic downturn temporarily slows production at a facility for a few years, the facility's baseline actually decreases and the facility loses operational flexibility. It also discourages facilities from voluntarily implementing pollution prevention measures." . . .

Environmental petitioners further contend that the ten-year lookback period does not ensure a representative baseline because it allows sources with shorter business cycles to choose among two or three peaks, not just the most recent one. . . .

EPA recognizes that "business cycles differ markedly by industry," as [indicated by a study commissioned by EPA of several industries' business cycles from peak to peak and from trough to trough]. But in an effort to promote operational flexibility and administrative efficiency, EPA chose to apply a fixed ten-year look-back period to all sources in order to lend "clarity and certainty to the process" and to avoid the administrative burden of determining "representative" baselines on a case-by-case basis. This policy choice, which reconciles conflicting interests in accuracy and efficiency, based on years of regulatory experience, is entitled to deference under *Chevron* Step 2. . . .

B.

Environmental Impact. Government and environmental petitioners contend that EPA's choice of a ten-year lookback period is arbitrary and capricious because it allows sources to increase their emissions to historic levels without triggering NSR, thereby harming air quality and public health. . . . Government petitioners emphasize that NSR is a "critical tool" for attaining and maintaining CAA air quality standards, and that the 2002 rule "severely undermines this tool by requiring States to allow older, poorly controlled sources to continue operating without pollution controls well into the future." In *Alabama Power*, the court recognized that the "statutory scheme intends to 'grandfather' existing industries; but the provisions concerning modifications indicate that this is not to constitute perpetual immunity from all standards under the PSD program. If these plants increase pollution, they will generally need a permit."

Government petitioners maintain that the ten-year lookback period frustrates the purpose of the modification provision by allowing sources to restore their emissions capacities to historic levels without obtaining NSR permits. Likewise, environmental petitioners contend that the ten-year lookback period unlawfully seeks "to preserve a unit's historical operating levels and associated emissions." They explain that as sources age, their operating capacities diminish "by roughly one percentage point for each year of age." Therefore, they conclude, "physical or operational changes that restore an existing source to its original capacity significantly increase the amount of pollution emitted by that source as compared to its emissions level during the period immediately preceding the change."

EPA acknowledges that fewer changes will trigger NSR under the 2002 rule than under the 1980 rule. However, based on its experience and its Environmental Impact Analysis [EIA], EPA "believe[s] that the environment will not be adversely affected" by the ten-year lookback period "and in some respects will benefit" from it. As noted, it is EPA's position that the ten-year lookback period eliminates the regulatory disincentive for sources to implement changes that improve operating efficiency and reduce emissions rates. EPA further believes that the ten-year lookback period will not hinder states from achieving CAA air quality standards because NSR is not the primary mechanism for reducing emissions from existing sources. EPA explains in its Report to the President:

> The NSR program is by no means the primary regulatory tool to address air pollution from existing sources. The Clean Air Act provides for several other public health–driven and visibility-related control efforts: for example, the National Ambient Air Quality Standards Program implemented through enforceable State Implementation Plans, the NO_x SIP Call, the Acid Rain Program, the Regional Haze Program, etc. Thus, while NSR was designed by Congress to focus particularly on sources that are newly

constructed or that make major modifications, Congress provided numerous other tools for assuring that emissions from existing sources are adequately controlled.

EPA, New Source Review: Report to the President 3-4 (2002). According to EPA, "these programs have achieved, and will continue to achieve, tens of millions of tons per year of [emissions] reductions which are completely unaffected by the [2002] rule." . . .

EPA concluded in its [EIA] that the "overall consequences" of the ten-year lookback period are "negligible" because it affects only "a very small number of facilities." . . .

Still, as government petitioners point out, even "small" increases in emissions can harm public health. Government petitioners cite several studies demonstrating the relationship between increases in emissions of particulate matter and increases in mortality rates, especially among diabetics, asthmatics, and children. Similarly, the American Thoracic Society and other amici curiae point to studies indicating that emissions of particulate matter significantly increase mortality rates, especially among infants of poor families; increase lung cancer rates; aggravate asthma and other respiratory diseases; and impose significant social welfare costs. Again, relying on its [EIA], EPA believes that the 2002 rule "will result in health and welfare benefits from reduced concentrations of pollutants."

. . . EPA acknowledges that its [EIA] is based on incomplete data and thus cannot reasonably quantify the 2002 rule's impact on public health. Indeed, a General Accounting Office ("GAO") Report to Congress stated that the economic and environmental impacts of the 2002 rule are "uncertain because of limited data and difficulty in determining how industrial companies will respond to the rule." GAO noted, for example, that because EPA lacked comprehensive data, it relied on industry anecdotes in concluding that NSR discourages sources from making changes that improve operating efficiency. GAO further pointed out that EPA's projection that these efficient changes will decrease actual emissions is based on the unverified assumption that sources will not increase their production levels after implementing the changes. Nevertheless, GAO did not conclude that the 2002 rule lacked adequate evidentiary support. Rather, GAO recommended that EPA "monitor the emissions impacts of the rule" and "use the monitoring results to determine whether the rule has created adverse effects that the agency needs to address." In light of our vacatur of the Clean Unit . . . portions of the 2002 rule, on which EPA relied in concluding that "collectively, the five NSR [provisions in the 2002 rule] will improve air quality," there is a heightened need for EPA to have sufficient data to confirm that the remaining portions of the 2002 rule do not result in increased emissions that harm air quality and public health. . . .

For now, it suffices to conclude that EPA's predictive judgment is entitled to deference. Incomplete data does not necessarily render an agency decision arbitrary and capricious, for "[i]t is not infrequent that the available data do not settle a regulatory issue, and the agency must then exercise its judgment in moving from the facts and probabilities on the record to a policy conclusion." EPA explained the available evidence and offered a "rational connection between the facts found and the choice made." Petitioners do not provide a basis for the court to conclude that EPA's choice of a ten-year lookback period is "arbitrary, capricious, an abuse of discretion, or otherwise not in accordance with law."

IV. Methodology and Enforceability . . .

Recordkeeping and Reporting Requirements. Sources making physical or operational changes under the 2002 rule need not keep records unless they meet three criteria. First, sources must choose to project post-change emissions, instead of using the actual-to-potential test. Second, under the actual-to-projected-actual test, sources must determine they will not trigger NSR by significantly increasing their emissions. Third, sources must nonetheless believe that there is a "reasonable possibility that [the] project . . . may result in a significant emissions increase." [Sources satisfying all three criteria must record information about the change, including a description of the project, identification of the emissions unit(s) whose emissions of a regulated NSR pollutant could be affected by the project, and a description of the applicability test used to determine that the project is not a major modification for any regulated NSR pollutant.]

By contrast, sources believing no reasonable possibility of a significant emissions increase exists need keep no records at all—neither the data on which they based their projections nor records of actual emissions going forward. Government petitioners argue that by allowing sources to decide whether to keep records relating to a particular change, EPA has rendered the actual-to-projected-actual methodology unenforceable. How, they ask, will EPA ensure that sources are not escaping NSR if they are allowed to destroy the data crucial to that determination?

Insisting that no enforceability problem exists, EPA argues that the 2002 rule increases recordkeeping requirements for non-utilities. Although it is technically correct that non-utilities were subject to less stringent recordkeeping requirements pre-2002, EPA's position ignores the major differences between the current and former methods. Prior to 2002, sources other than utilities evaluated post-change emissions under the more onerous actual-to-potential test, which presumed that sources would operate at their maximum post-change potential to emit. Given that assumption, sources' actual post-change emissions could not, by definition, exceed their potential-to-emit, making records of these actual emissions unnecessary for the purpose of ascertaining whether post-change emissions increased beyond expectations. Moreover, to avoid NSR, which is easily triggered under the actual-to-potential test, sources could opt to establish an enforceable emissions cap based on projected post-change actual emissions. Thus, under the pre-2002 regime, non-utilities either accepted the rigors of the actual-to-potential test, eliminating the need for recordkeeping, or subjected their actual emissions to monitoring by state permitting authorities. . . .

Of course, one might wonder why sources with no "reasonable possibility" of significantly increased emissions should keep records at all. If EPA actually knew which sources had no "reasonable possibility" of triggering NSR, these sources would obviously have no need to keep records. The problem is that EPA has failed to explain how, absent recordkeeping, it will be able to determine whether sources have accurately concluded that they have no "reasonable possibility" of significantly increased emissions. . . .

At oral argument, EPA counsel asserted that under the reasonable possibility standard, enforcement authorities could conduct inspections and request information. Although conceding that nothing in the record addressed how authorities could access data through these mechanisms once a source had failed to keep records, counsel maintained that the methodology is enforceable simply because such actions are "inherent" in EPA's enforcement authority. EPA certainly has such inherent enforcement authority, but even inherent authority depends on evidence. . . .

Because EPA has failed to explain how it can ensure NSR compliance without the relevant data, we will remand for it either to provide an acceptable explanation for its "reasonable possibility" standard or to devise an appropriately supported alternative. . . .

VI.   Clean Units

To maximize source flexibility and to encourage sources to install state-of-the-art pollution control technology, the 2002 rule establishes "an innovative approach to NSR applicability" that measures "increases" in terms of "Clean Unit" status instead of actual emissions. Under this approach, a change does not "increase" emissions and thus does not trigger NSR as long as it does not alter the unit's Clean Unit status, even if the change increases the source's net actual emissions. A unit automatically qualifies for Clean Unit status if it has installed "state-of-the-art" pollution control technology (LAER or BACT) as a result of major NSR within the last ten years. A unit that has not undergone major NSR can also qualify for Clean Unit status if it demonstrates that its pollution control technology is "comparable" to LAER or BACT and that its allowable emissions will not violate national ambient air quality standards or new source performance standards. A unit retains its Clean Unit status for ten years, and may renew its Clean Unit status upon expiration, as long as it complies with the emissions limitations and work practice requirements in its NSR permit. . . .

In the 1977 amendments to the CAA, Congress defined "major emitting facilit[ies]" as "stationary sources of air pollutants which *emit*, or have the *potential to emit*, one hundred tons per year or more of any air pollutant." 42 U.S.C. §7479(1) (emphasis added). The juxtaposition of the terms "emit" and "potential to emit" indicates that when Congress enacted the NSR program in 1977, it was conscious of the distinction between actual and potential emissions, using the term "emit" to refer to actual emissions and the term "potential to emit" to refer to potential emissions. . . .

Similarly, in the same section of the 1977 amendments to the CAA, Congress defined "best available control technology" as "an *emission limitation* based on the maximum degree of reduction of each pollutant . . . *emitted* from any major emitting facility." 42 U.S.C. §7479(3) (emphasis added). Again, the juxtaposition of the terms "emission limitation" and "emitted" indicates that Congress was conscious of the distinction between actual and allowable emissions, using the term "emitted" to refer to actual emissions and the term "emission limitation" to refer to allowable emissions.

In the same section of the 1977 amendments to the CAA, Congress applied NSR to "the modification (as defined in section 7411(a) of this title) of any source or facility." 42 U.S.C. §7479(2)(C). Section 7411(a) defines a "modification" as any physical or operational change that "increases the amount of any air pollutant *emitted* by [the] source." 42 U.S.C. §7411(a)(4) (emphasis added). As noted, when Congress enacted the 1977 amendments to the CAA, it distinguished between actual, potential, and allowable emissions. If Congress had intended for "increases" in emissions to be measured in terms of potential or allowable emissions, it would have added a reference to "potential to emit" or "emission limitations." The absence of such a reference must be given effect. Moreover, even if the word "emitted" does not by itself refer to actual emissions, the phrase "the *amount* of any air pollutant *emitted* by [the] source" plainly refers to actual emissions. 42 U.S.C. §7411(a)(4) (emphasis added). . . .

Therefore, because the plain language of the CAA indicates that Congress intended to apply NSR to changes that increase actual emissions instead of potential or allowable emissions, we hold that EPA lacks authority to promulgate the Clean Unit provision, and we vacate that portion of the 2002 rule, as contrary to the statute under *Chevron* Step 1. . . .

WILLIAMS, Senior Circuit Judge, concurring.

I join the opinion for the court. We remand the recordkeeping and reporting elements of the 2002 rule because of EPA's failure to explain its decisions on these elements. As I understand the remand, the agency's obligation is to analyze the trade-off between compliance improvement and the burdens of data collection and reporting. In making its choice on some specific degree and type of collection and reporting, it must articulate a reasoned judgment as to why any proposed additional burden would not be justifiable in terms of the likely enhancement of compliance. It need not show that the system chosen will achieve perfect NSR compliance—a showing that I do not believe we could lawfully demand. Perfection is often too costly to be sensible.

On a broader note, this case illustrates some of the painful consequences of reliance on command-and-control regulation in a world where emission control is typically far more expensive, per unit of pollution, when accomplished by retrofitting old plants than by including state-of-the-art control technology in new ones. In the interests of reasonable thrift, such regulation inevitably imposes more demanding standards on the new. But that provides an incentive for firms to string out the life of old plants. Indefinite plant life is impossible without modifications, however, so the statute conditions modifications on the firm's use of technological improvements. This in turn replicates the original dilemma: a broad concept of modification extends both the scope of the mandate for improved technology and the incentive to keep the old. By contrast, emissions charges or marketable pollution entitlements provide incentives for firms to use—at any and every plant—all pollution control methods that cost less per unit than the emissions charge or the market price of an entitlement, as the case may be.

NOTES AND QUESTIONS

1. What were the differences between the 1980 and 2002 versions of EPA's NSR rules? What practical differences did these changes make? How did the court respond to each of the challenges to the 2002 regulations? Why did the court uphold EPA's new approach to determining baseline actual emissions, including the ten-year look-back period? How did EPA and the court respond to the charge that the ten-year lookback period would harm air quality and the public health, even though EPA conceded that its analysis was based on incomplete data and that it could not reasonably quantify the impact of the 2002 rule on public health? What was the flaw the court found in the NSR recordkeeping and reporting requirements? Why did the court invalidate the Clean Unit provision?

2. What Is an "Increase"? NSR applies in the event of a "modification" of a major stationary source. A modification occurs if there is a physical or operational change that results in an increase in emissions. How does one calculate whether such an increase has taken place? The courts have disagreed on this issue. In United States v. Duke Energy Corp., 278 F. Supp. 2d 619 (W.D.N.C. 2003), the court concluded that an increase in emissions occurs for these purposes only if a physical or operational change increases the *hourly rate* of emissions. EPA had argued that an increase may occur even if the hourly rate of emissions does not change if, following the change, there is an increase in the *hours of operation*. See also United States v. Alabama Power Co., 372 F. Supp. 2d 1283 (N.D. Ala. 2005). On appeal from the district court's decision in *Duke Power*, the Fourth Circuit affirmed, although on different grounds. It reasoned that the CAA requires that EPA use the same definition of "modification" for purposes of both the NSPS and PSD programs. Because EPA's NSPS regulations, promulgated before enactment by Congress of the PSD provisions in 1977, defined a modification as a physical change that increases a plant's hourly rate of emissions, EPA was bound to interpret the term "modification" the same way in the context of the PSD program. United States v. Duke Energy Corp., 411 F.3d 539 (4th Cir. 2005). But in United States v. Cinergy Corp., 458 F.3d 705 (7th Cir. 2006), the court denied that the CAA requires EPA to define the "vague" statutory term "modification" in an identical way for purposes of both the nonattainment and PSD NSR programs. The court deferred to EPA's interpretation (i.e., that the proper test for a modification in the context of the PSD NSR program is whether a physical or operational change causes an increase in annual emissions). The court reasoned that using an hourly rate test would

> give a company that had a choice between making a physical modification that increased the hourly emissions rate and one that enabled an increase in the number of hours of operation an incentive to make the latter change even if that would produce a higher annual level of emissions, because it would elude the permit requirement.
>
> [The use of an hourly rate test] would also distort the choice between rebuilding an old plant and replacing it with a new one. The [CAA] treats old plants more leniently than new ones because of the expense of retrofitting pollution-control equipment. But there is an expectation that old plants will wear out and be replaced by new ones that will be subject to the more stringent pollution controls that the [CAA] imposes on new plants. One thing that stimulates replacement of an old plant is that aging produces more frequent breakdowns and so reduces a plant's hours of operation and hence its output. [Industry's] interpretation would give the company an artificial incentive to renovate a plant and by so doing increase the plant's hours of operation, rather than to replace the plant. For by going the first route it could increase the plant's output without having to invest in preventing the enhanced output from generating increased pollution.

Id. at 709. The court added, however, that industry's interpretation was not necessarily incorrect on the ground that it would inevitably produce outlandish results.

> Under [a total annual emissions test], Cinergy, rather than having to choose between repair and replacement to enhance output, might decide to buy electricity from other electric utilities, and their plants might pollute more than Cinergy's do. And while Cinergy can determine a plant's hourly rate of emissions easily enough just by observing

the plant in operation, it cannot predict the plant's annual emissions rate because that depends on the number of hours of operation; and who knows in advance how many hours a plant will operate? Of course the company can always curtail those hours if it sees itself approaching the ceiling. But that might complicate its customer relations, as well as sacrificing significant revenue. True, what is required for determining whether a construction permit must be sought for a planned physical change in the plant is not pre-science, but merely a reasonable estimate of the amount of additional emissions that the change will cause; yet it may be a very difficult estimate to make.

Id. The Supreme Court granted *certiorari* in *Duke Energy* in 2006.

3. *What Is a Physical Change?* For years EPA has exempted from NSR physical or operational changes that qualify as "routine maintenance, repair, and replacement." In 2003, EPA adopted regulations that expanded the scope of the exemption. The following case addressed the legality of the changes.

NEW YORK v. EPA
443 F.3d 880 (D.C. Cir. 2006)

ROGERS, Circuit Judge.

In New York v. EPA, 413 F.3d 3 (D.C. Cir. 2005) ("*New York I*"), the court addressed the first of two rules promulgated by the Environmental Protection Agency providing ways for stationary sources of air pollution to avoid triggering New Source Review ("NSR"). . . . We now address the second rule, the Equipment Replacement Provision ("ERP"), which amends the Routine Maintenance, Repair, and Replacement Exclusion ("RMRR") from NSR requirements. Under [§111(a)(4) of the CAA], sources that undergo "any physical change" that increases emissions are required to undergo the NSR permitting process [under both the nonattainment and PSD permit programs]. The exclusion has historically provided that routine maintenance, repair, and replacement do not constitute changes triggering NSR. The ERP both defined and expanded that exclusion. EPA explained:

> [The] rule states categorically that the replacement of components with identical or functionally equivalent components that do not exceed 20% of the replacement value of the process unit and does not change its basic design parameters is not a change and is within the RMRR exclusion.

Hence, the ERP would allow sources to avoid NSR when replacing equipment under the twenty-percent cap notwithstanding a resulting increase in emissions. . . . We now vacate the ERP because it is contrary to the plain language of section 111(a)(4) of the Act.

. . . Since the inception of NSR, RMRR has been excluded from the definition of "modification." Heretofore, EPA applied the RMRR exclusion through "a case-by-case determination by weighing the nature, extent, purpose, frequency, and cost of the work as well as other factors to arrive at a common sense finding." Consistent with Alabama Power Co. v. Costle, 636 F.2d 323 (D.C. Cir. 1979), which recognized EPA's discretion to exempt from NSR "some emission increases on grounds of *de minimis* or administrative necessity," EPA has for over two decades defined the RMRR exclusion as limited to "*de minimis* circumstances." The ERP provides a bright-line rule and expands the traditional scope of the RMRR by exempting certain equipment replacements from NSR. See, e.g., 40 C.F.R. §52.21(cc) (2005).[2]

The government and environmental petitioners contend that the ERP is contrary to the plain text of the Act because the statutory definition of "modification" applies unambiguously to any physical change that increases emissions, necessarily including the emission-increasing equipment replacements excused from NSR by the rule. They maintain that the word "any," when given its natural meaning, requires that the phrase "physical change" be read broadly, such that EPA's attempt to read "physical change" narrowly would relegate the word "any" to an insignificant role. . . .

The petitioners and EPA agree that the phrase "physical change" is susceptible to multiple meanings, each citing dictionary definitions. However, "the sort of ambiguity giving rise to *Chevron* deference 'is a creature not of definitional possibilities, but of statutory context.'" American Bar Ass'n v. FTC, 430 F.3d 457, 469 (D.C. Cir. 2005). As the parties point out, the ordinary meaning of "physical change" includes activities that "make different in some particular," "make over to a radically different form," or "replace with another or others of the same kind or class." Webster's Third New International Dictionary 373 (1981). To say that it is "physical," in this context, indicates that the change must be "natural or material," rather than "mental, moral, spiritual, or imaginary." The parties agree that in "[r]eal-world, common-sense usage," "physical change" includes equipment replacements. They further agree that the ERP would excuse from NSR requirements certain emission-increasing activities that EPA has historically considered to be "physical changes."

The parties' essential disagreement, then, centers on the effect of Congress's decision in defining "modification" to insert the word "any" before "physical change." According to the petitioners, the word "any" means that the phrase "physical change" covers any activity at a source that could be considered a physical change that increases emissions. According to EPA, "any" does nothing to resolve ambiguity in the phrase it modifies. EPA maintains that because "physical change" is "susceptible to multiple meanings," "identifying activities that are 'changes' for NSR purposes . . . requires an exercise of Agency expertise," "the classic situation in which an agency is accorded deference under *Chevron*." Under this approach, once EPA has identified an activity as a "physical change," the word "any" requires that the activity be subject to NSR. We conclude that the differences between the parties' interpretations of the role of the word "any" are resolved by recognizing that "[r]ead naturally, the word 'any' has an expansive meaning, that is, 'one or some indiscriminately of whatever kind,'" United States v. Gonzales, 520 U.S. 1, 5 (1997), and that courts must give effect to each word of a statute. Because Congress used the word "any," EPA must apply NSR

---

2. The ERP provides:

Without regard to other considerations, routine maintenance, repair and replacement includes, but is not limited to, the replacement of any component of a process unit with an identical or functionally equivalent component(s), and maintenance and repair activities that are part of the replacement activity, provided that all of the requirements in paragraphs (cc)(1) through (cc)(3)of this section are met.

40 C.F.R. §52.21(cc). Paragraph (cc)(1) establishes that the fixed capital cost of the replacement component cannot exceed twenty percent of the replacement value of the process unit. Paragraph (cc)(2) states that the replacement cannot change the basic design parameters of the process unit. Paragraph (cc)(3) requires that the replacement activity not cause the process unit to exceed any independent, legally enforceable emission limitation.

whenever a source conducts an emission-increasing activity that fits within one of the ordinary meanings of "physical change." . . .

Although EPA is correct that the meaning of "any" can differ depending upon the statutory setting, the context of the Clean Air Act warrants no departure from the word's customary effect. . . . [T]he question of statutory interpretation here does not arise in a setting in which the Supreme Court has required heightened standards of clarity to avoid upsetting fundamental policies. EPA points to no "strange and indeterminate results" that would emerge from adopting the natural meaning of "any" in section 111(a)(4) of the Act. Given Congress's goal in adopting the 1977 amendments of establishing a balance between economic and environmental interests, see Wisconsin Elec. Power Co. v. Reilly, 893 F.2d 901, 909-10 (7th Cir. 1990) ("WEPCo"), it is hardly "farfetched" for Congress to have intended NSR to apply to any type of physical change that increases emissions. In this context, there is no reason the usual tools of statutory construction should not apply and hence no reason why "any" should not mean "any." Indeed, EPA's interpretation would produce a "strange," if not an "indeterminate," result: a law intended to limit increases in air pollution would allow sources operating below applicable emission limits to increase significantly the pollution they emit without government review.

Even without specific reliance on the effect of "any," this court has construed the definition of "modification" broadly. In *Alabama Power*, the court explained that "the term 'modification' [in section 111(a)(4)] is nowhere limited to physical changes exceeding a certain magnitude." 636 F.2d at 400. . . . More recently, in *New York I*, the court looked to the plain meaning of section 111(a)(4) and the absence of contrary legislative history in holding that even pollution control projects constituted "physical changes." Likewise, the Seventh Circuit concluded in *WEPCo* that the purposes of the 1977 amendments to the Act required an expansive reading of the plain language of section 111(a)(4). . . .

. . . EPA's approach to interpreting "physical change," as well as a similar approach by industry intervenors that focuses on the thirty-nine words following "any," contravenes several rules of statutory interpretation. EPA's position is that the word "any" does not affect the expansiveness of the phrase "physical change"; it only means that, once the agency defines "change" as broadly or as narrowly as it deems appropriate, everything in the agency-defined category is subject to NSR. To begin, that reading, contrary to "a cardinal principle of statutory construction," would make Congress's use of the word "any" "insignificant" if not "superfluous." Reading the definition in this way makes the definition function as if the word "any" had been excised from section 111(a)(4); there is virtually no role for "any" to play. Additionally, the approaches of EPA and industry would require Congress to spell out all the applications covered by a definition before a court could conclude that Congress had directly spoken regarding a particular application, ignoring the fact that a definition, like a general rule, need not list everything it covers. EPA's approach would ostensibly require that the definition of "modification" include a phrase such as "regardless of size, cost, frequency, effect," or other distinguishing characteristic. Only in a Humpty Dumpty world[3] would Congress be required to use superfluous words while an agency could ignore an expansive word that Congress did use. We decline to adopt such a world-view.

_____

3. See TVA v. Hill, 437 U.S. 153, 173 n.18 (1978) (quoting Through the Looking Glass, in The Complete Works of Lewis Carroll 196 (1939)).

In contrast, the petitioners' approach, by adopting an expansive reading of the phrase "any physical change," gives natural effect to all the words used by Congress and reflects both their common meanings and Congress's purpose in enacting the 1970 and 1977 amendments. To improve pollution control programs in a manner consistent with the balance struck by Congress in 1977 between "the economic interest in permitting capital improvements to continue and the environmental interest in improving air quality," *Chevron*, 467 U.S. at 851, Congress defined the phrase "physical change" in terms of increases in emissions. After using the word "any" to indicate that "physical change" covered all such activities, and was not left to agency interpretation, Congress limited the scope of "any physical change" to changes that "increase [ ] the amount of any air pollutant emitted by such source or which result [ ] in the emission of any air pollutant not previously emitted." 42 U.S.C. §7411(a)(4). Thus, only physical changes that do not result in emission increases are excused from NSR. Because Congress expressly included one limitation, the court must presume that Congress acted "intentionally and purposely," Barnhart v. Sigmon Coal Co., 534 U.S. 438, 452 (2002), when it did not include others. So construed, each word in the phrase "any physical change" has a meaning consonant with congressional intent and the scope of the definitional phrase is limited only by Congress's determination that such changes be linked to emission increases.

. . . EPA, through its historical practice and its words, has acknowledged that the equipment replacements covered by the ERP are "physical changes" under one of the ordinary meanings of the phrase. EPA may not choose to exclude that "[r]eal-world, common-sense usage of the word 'change.'" Moreover, a physical change is not the sole criterion for triggering NSR under the definition of "modification." The expansive meaning of "any physical change" is strictly limited by the requirement that the change increase emissions. See 42 U.S.C. §7411(a)(4).[4]

The fact that EPA, through the RMRR exclusion, has historically interpreted "any physical change" to exclude changes of trivial regulatory concern on a *de minimis* rationale, does not demonstrate that the meaning of "physical change" is ambiguous. Rather, it reflects an agency's inherent power to overlook "trifling matters." . . . Reliance on the *de minimis* doctrine invokes congressional intent that agencies diverge from the plain meaning of a statute only so far as is necessary to avoid its futile application. . . . [T]he court [in *Alabama Power*] explained that *de minimis* standards served to alleviate "severe" administrative and economic burdens by lifting requirements on "minuscule" emission increases. While the court today expresses no opinion regarding EPA's application of the *de minimis* exception, given the limits on the scope of the *de minimis* doctrine, EPA appropriately has not attempted to justify the ERP as an exercise of *de minimis* discretion. As EPA has disclaimed the assertion that its prior expansive interpretations of "any physical change" were "absurd or futile," it is in no position to claim that the ERP is necessary to avoid absurdity. . . .

. . . EPA cannot show that historical fact prevents a broad reading of "any physical change" inasmuch as EPA for decades has interpreted that phrase to mean "virtually all changes, even trivial ones, . . . generally interpret[ing] the [RMRR] exclusion as being limited to *de minimis* circumstances." 68 Fed. Reg. at 61,272.

As for logic, EPA cannot show any incoherence in Congress requiring NSR for equipment replacements that increase emissions while allowing replacements that do

---

4. The court has no occasion to decide whether part replacements or repairs necessarily constitute a "modification" under the definition taken as a whole.

not increase emissions to avoid NSR. EPA acknowledges the reasonableness of its past expansive interpretation of "any physical change." To the extent that EPA relies on the argument that allowing ERP projects has the potential to lower overall emissions through increased efficiency even if emissions increase at a source, the court in *New York I* rejected EPA's similar argument in support of an exemption from NSR for pollution control projects. The court stated that "Congress could reasonably conclude, for example, that tradeoffs between pollutants are difficult to measure, and thus any significant increase in emissions of any pollutant should be subject to NSR." *New York I*, 413 F.3d at 41. Absent a showing that the policy demanded by the text borders on the irrational, EPA may not "avoid the Congressional intent clearly expressed in the text simply by asserting that its preferred approach would be better policy." *Engine Mfrs.*, 88 F.3d at 1089.

Likewise, EPA offers no reason to conclude that the structure of the Act supports the conclusion that "any physical change" does not mean what it says. EPA does not address the Act's structure except in defending the reasonableness of the ERP as a policy choice. In that context, EPA points to the Act's "many other systematic air programs," particularly "model market-based programs," as support for its view that economic and environmental interests can be effectively balanced while limiting the application of NSR to existing sources. Although EPA might prefer market-based methods of controlling pollution, Congress has chosen a different course with NSR.

Accordingly, we hold that the ERP violates section 111(a)(4) of the Clean Air Act in two respects. First, Congress's use of the word "any" in defining a "modification" means that all types of "physical changes" are covered. Although the phrase "physical change" is susceptible to multiple meanings, the word "any" makes clear that activities within each of the common meanings of the phrase are subject to NSR when the activity results in an emission increase. As Congress limited the broad meaning of "any physical change," directing that only changes that increase emissions will trigger NSR, no other limitation (other than to avoid absurd results) can be implied. The definition of "modification," therefore, does not include only physical changes that are costly or major. Second, Congress defined "modification" in terms of emission increases, but the ERP would allow equipment replacements resulting in non–*de minimis* emission increases to avoid NSR. Therefore, because it violates the Act, we vacate the ERP.

NOTES AND QUESTIONS

1. Which portion of the D.C. Circuit's opinion in *New York I* provided the strongest support for the court's holding in *New York II* (the principal case)? According to the court, how would its acceptance of EPA's approach have required Congress to alter its statutory drafting? Why didn't *Alabama Power's* recognition of EPA's inherent authority to exempt *de minimis* effects from regulation support EPA's approach?

2. The courts have grappled with other aspects of the RMRR exemption. One issue is whether to assess what is "routine" by reference to a particular plant or to the entire industry of which it is a part. In the district court decision in *Duke Power*, discussed in the notes following *New York I*, the court held that what is routine maintenance must be decided on an industry-wide basis as opposed to looking only at the history of the individual plant at issue, because EPA has historically taken that approach. But in United States v. Ohio Edison Co., 276 F. Supp. 2d 829 (S.D. Ohio 2003), the court deferred to EPA's view that the determination of what is routine

should be made on a plant-by-plant basis, taking into account the nature, extent, purpose, frequency, and cost of the activity. Among the factors that convinced the court that Ohio Edison's changes were not routine were the large scale and extent of the activities at issue; the fact that Ohio Edison funded the projects using its capital improvement budget and that the projects were capitalized for accounting purposes; the purpose of the activities, which was to extend the lives of the generating units; the fact that almost all of the major component and equipment replacements at the plant had never been performed before on the particular unit; and the major capital expenditures associated with each of the activities. Cf. United States v. Southern Indiana Gas and Elec. Co., 258 F. Supp. 2d 884, 886 (S.D. Ind. 2003) ("[a]lthough the routine maintenance exemption does not turn on whether a certain type of project is prevalent within industry as a whole, the frequency with which similar projects take place throughout industry" is relevant to whether the RMMR exemption applies).

3. *The Impact of the 2002 and 2003 Changes to NSR.* EPA's Office of the Inspector General reported that the regulations amending the NSR program "seriously hampered" enforcement cases filed against utilities during the Clinton administration and weakened EPA's ability to negotiate settlements.[*] The National Research Council of the National Academy of Sciences issued a report in 2006 including a comprehensive review of the likely effects of EPA's 2002 and 2003 revisions to the NSR program. The report found, for example, that the ERP provisions at issue in the principal case would be expected to result in a moderate decrease in SO_2 emissions for the first 6 years, followed by about 6 years of little change. After 12 years, the ERP rule would likely result in higher emissions, perhaps substantially so, compared with what would result if pre-revision rules continued. In addition, the report found that ERP would be expected to cause an increase in emissions of nitrogen oxides, perhaps in substantial amounts, after the first few years. These increases could be mitigated if EPA implements its 2005 Clean Air Interstate Rule (CAIR), a "cap-and-trade" program aimed at lowering emissions from power plants in eastern and midwestern states, which is discussed below in the context of interstate pollution. But the report also suggests that a cap-and-trade program with caps below those specified by the CAIR would be a more cost-effective approach to lowering emissions than aggressive regulation under NSR.[**]

The Harvard University School of Public Health reported in early 2001 that nine coal-burning power plants located near Chicago and grandfathered out of NSR compliance requirements were responsible for 300 premature deaths and thousands of illnesses each year. See 32 Env't Rep. (BNA) 77 (2001).

4. *"Clear Skies."* The Bush administration and its congressional allies sponsored legislation several times, beginning in 2002, dubbed the "Clear Skies Act." The bill would eliminate NSR for power plants (which would be excluded from the definition of "major stationary sources") and replace it with a market-based cap-and-trade program applicable to emissions of SO_2, NO_x, and mercury (but not CO_2). The bill would shrink the scope of NSR by limiting the term "modifications" to plant changes that increase a facility's hourly emissions rate. The bill would also limit EPA's ability to mandate reductions in emissions contributing to interstate pollution.

---

[*]New Source Review Rule Change Harms EPA's Ability to Enforce against Coal-Fired Electric Utilities, Report No. 2004-P-00034, available at http://www.epa.gov/oigearth/reports/2004/20040930-2004-P-00034.pdf.

[**]See National Research Council, New Source Review for Stationary Sources of Air Pollution (2006), available at http://www.nap.edu/catalog/11701.html.

Administration spokespersons claimed that the changes would lead to greater and more efficient reductions in pollutant emissions. See Kriz, Burning Questions, Nat'l J. (April 6, 2002) at 976. In a study by a research firm commissioned by the Bush administration to analyze its plan, however, Abt Associates concluded that Clear Skies would cost industry significantly less than would two competing legislative proposals (introduced by Senators Carper and Jeffords), but would provide billions of dollars less in health benefits and cause thousands fewer premature deaths to be averted annually. Janofsky, Study Ranks Bush Plan to Cut Air Pollution as Weakest of 3, N.Y. Times, April 10, 2004. An interim report released by the National Research Council concluded that Clear Skies probably would not result in lower emissions at individual sources compared with those required under the existing NSR program: "It is therefore unlikely that Clear Skies would result in emission limits at individual sources that are tighter than those achieved when NSR is triggered at the same sources."*

Problem 6-3

An electric power plant owned and operated by National Electric Company (NECO) consists of five coal-fired steam-generating units that were placed in operation between 1935 and 1950. Over the years, the performance of some of the units has declined due to age-related deterioration. NECO proposes to repair and replace the turbine-generators, boilers, mechanical and electrical auxiliaries, and the common plant support facilities. Under EPA's regulations, routine maintenance, repair, and replacement do not constitute modifications for purposes of determining the applicability of NSR. EPA's NSPS for coal-fired electric power plants have been in effect for some time. NECO's proposed repair and replacement program would cause emissions of SO_2 to increase from the deteriorated plant's current levels, but only if the plant were operated at full capacity, 24 hours a day. NECO has never operated its plant at full capacity on a round-the-clock basis in the past.

If NECO decides to proceed with its proposed repair and replacement program, will the renovated plant be subject to NSR for coal-fired electric power plants?

b.   The Substantive Requirements of the Nonattainment Area Permit Program

The owner of a major stationary source whose construction or operation in a nonattainment area is subject to the permit program under §172(c)(5) must satisfy the program's substantive requirements to qualify for a permit. Those requirements are described in §173. Under §173(a)(2), the permit applicant will have to comply with the lowest achievable emission rate (LAER), as defined in §171(3). This technology-based requirement is determined by the states on a case-by-case basis for each permit. LAER was intended to be the strictest of the CAA's technology-based standards — stricter than the "best available control technology" (BACT), which is applicable to

---

* The Interim Report of the Committee on Changes in New Source Review Programs for Stationary Sources of Air Pollution (2005), available at http://www.nap.edu/books/0309095786/html/.

sources applying for PSD permits, and which in turn is stricter than the NSPS under §111.

A permit applicant also must demonstrate that all major stationary sources owned or operated by it (or by an affiliated company) are in compliance or on a schedule of compliance with all applicable emission limitations under the CAA. §173(a)(3). See Sierra Club v. Leavitt, 368 F.3d 1300 (11th Cir. 2004) (remanding to EPA to consider whether it was appropriate for state to approve nonattainment permit of partial owner of noncompliant major stationary source, where the part owned by the applicant was in compliance). A permit must be denied if EPA finds that the applicable SIP is not being properly implemented for the nonattainment area that includes the proposed source. §173(a)(4). Under §173(a)(5), the proposed source must be justified on cost-benefit grounds.

The potential economic benefits of the construction of new or modified major stationary sources make it easy to understand why states may want to encourage industry to undertake such projects. But how can authorization to construct and operate a major new or modified source of the nonattainment pollutant avoid exacerbating the existing nonattainment problem? How is it possible to accommodate the dual economic growth and environmental improvement objectives of the nonattainment program to which the Supreme Court referred in *Chevron*? EPA's response took the form of its offset policy, initially formulated in 1976, 41 Fed. Reg. 55,524, and later incorporated into the 1977 amendments. The statute authorizes two ways of permitting the construction and operation of major stationary sources without jeopardizing the air quality improvement objectives of the nonattainment provisions. Under §173(a)(1)(B), the so-called growth allowance provision, the state can extract from existing stationary sources and mobile sources enforceable emissions reductions greater than those that would otherwise be required by the "reasonable further progress" requirements and that would be projected as necessary to achieve timely compliance with the NAAQS deadlines. The excess reductions can then be doled out to new sources seeking permission to operate in the nonattainment area.

If the state does not build this kind of growth allowance into its SIP, then it is up to the source seeking a permit to accommodate the economic growth and air quality improvement objectives. Section 173(a)(1)(A) authorizes it to do so by securing, from whatever currently emitting sources it can, an enforceable reduction in emissions more than sufficient to offset the new emissions from the proposed facility. This type of emissions trading is called an *extra-source offset*, to distinguish it from the "bubbles," or intra-source offsets, that enable existing sources to avoid NSR altogether. EPA has explained the extra-source offset as follows:

> In *nonattainment* areas, major new stationary sources and major modifications are subject to a preconstruction permit requirement that they secure sufficient surplus emission reductions to more than "offset" their emissions. This requirement is designed to allow industrial growth in nonattainment areas without interfering with attainment and maintenance of ambient air quality standards. [51 Fed. Reg. 43,814, 43,830 (1986).]

Generally speaking, a permit applicant must secure its offset from an existing plant located in the same nonattainment area. §173(c)(1). What is the purpose of this limitation? The pollutant-specific nonattainment area provisions impose special offset requirements in certain instances. Permit applicants whose plants will be located in marginal ozone nonattainment areas, for example, must extract 1.1 pounds of reductions from existing sources for each pound of VOCs they will emit. §182(a)(4). The ratio of reductions from existing sources to emissions from the newly permitted source is 1.15:1 for moderate ozone nonattainment areas (§182(b)(5)), 1.2:1 for serious areas (§182(c)(10)), 1.3:1 for severe areas (§182(d)(2)), and 1.5:1 for extreme areas (§182(e)(1)), with some exceptions.

One of the issues raised by extra-source offsets is whether they represent real reductions in emissions or are spurious "paper" reductions with no beneficial impact. Section 173(c)(2) addresses this issue by prohibiting the use of emissions reductions that are already required by the statute or by federal or state regulations to satisfy the offset requirement. The next case also considers this issue. A citizens group opposed plans to locate a large oil refinery in Portsmouth, Virginia, due to the anticipated increase in HC emissions. The area already violated the since-repealed NAAQS for HC. Local officials, on the other hand, welcomed the prospect of new jobs and a significant annual increase in property tax income. The case arose under an Interpretive Ruling that preceded the adoption of the 1990 amendments, but the issues it presents continue to be relevant.

CITIZENS AGAINST THE REFINERY'S EFFECTS, INC. v. EPA
643 F.2d 183 (4th Cir. 1981)

K. K. HALL, Circuit Judge. . . .

[Before the 1977 amendments, the CAA] created a no-growth environment in areas where the clean air requirements had not been attained. EPA recognized the need to develop a program that encouraged attainment of clean air standards without discouraging economic growth. Thus the agency proposed an Interpretive Ruling in 1976 which allowed the states to develop an "offset program" within the State Implementation Plans. 41 Fed. Reg. 55,524 (1976). The offset program, later codified by Congress in the 1977 Amendments to the Clean Air Act, permits the states to develop plans which allow construction of new pollution sources where accompanied by a corresponding reduction in an existing pollution source. 42 U.S.C. §7502(b)(6)* and §7503. In effect, a new emitting facility can be built if an existing pollution source decreases its emissions or ceases operations as long as a positive net air quality benefit occurs. [The 1976 ruling required calculation of a base time period to determine how much reduction is needed in existing pollutants to offset the new source. The ruling defined the base period as the first year of the SIP or, where the state has not yet developed a SIP, as the year in which a construction permit application is filed.]

If the proposed factory will emit carbon monoxide, sulfur dioxide, or particulates, the EPA requires that the offsetting pollution source be within the immediate vicinity of the new plant. The other two pollutants, hydrocarbons and nitrogen oxide, are less "site-specific," and thus the ruling permits the offsetting source to locate anywhere within a broad vicinity of the new source.

*[The current provision is §172(c)(5).—EDS.]

The Refinery

[Hampton Roads Energy Company (HREC)] proposes to build a petroleum refinery and offloading facility in Portsmouth, Virginia. Portsmouth has been unable to reduce air pollution enough to attain the national standard for one pollutant, photochemical oxidants, which is created when hydrocarbons are released into the atmosphere and react with other substances. Since a refinery is a major source of hydrocarbons, the Clean Air Act prevents construction of the HREC plant until the area attains the national standard.

[In 1975, HREC applied to a state agency (the Virginia Board, or the Board) for a refinery construction permit. The agency issued the permit in 1975 and later extended it. In an effort to facilitate its ruling for HREC, the Board proposed to use the offset ruling to comply with the CAA. In 1977, the Board submitted a SIP to EPA that included the HREC permit. The Board] proposed to offset the new HREC hydrocarbon pollution by reducing the amount of cutback asphalt[5] used for road paving operations in three highway districts by the Virginia Department of Highways. By switching from "cutback" to "emulsified" asphalt, the state can reduce hydrocarbon pollutants by the amount necessary to offset the pollutants from the proposed refinery.[6] [EPA approved the Virginia offset plan, with some modifications, despite critical comments by Citizens Against the Refinery's Effects (CARE).] . . .

The Geographic Area

CARE contends that the state plan should not have been approved by EPA since the three—highway-district area where cutback usage will be reduced to offset refinery emissions was artificially developed by the state. The ruling permits a broad area (usually within one AQCR) to be used as the offset basis. . . .

The agency action in approving the use of three highway districts was neither arbitrary, capricious, nor outside the statute. First, Congress intended that the states and the EPA be given flexibility in designing and implementing SIPs. Such flexibility allows the states to make reasoned choices as to which areas may be used to offset new pollution and how the plan is to be implemented. Second, the offset program was initiated to encourage economic growth in the state. Thus a state plan designed to reduce highway department pollution in order to attract another industry is a reasonable contribution to economic growth without a corresponding increase in pollution. Third, to be sensibly administered the offset plan had to be divided into districts which could be monitored by the highway department. Use of any areas other than highway districts would be unwieldy and difficult to administer. Fourth, the scientific understanding of ozone pollution is not advanced to the point where exact air transport may be predicted. Designation of the broad area in which hydrocarbons may be transported is well within the discretion and expertise of the agency.

---

5. "Cutback" asphalt has a petroleum base which gives off great amounts of hydrocarbons. "Emulsified" asphalt uses a water base which evaporates, giving off no hydrocarbons.

6. The three highway districts so designated comprise almost the entire eastern one-third of the state. This area cuts across four of the seven Virginia Air Quality Control Regions (AQCR).

The Legally Binding Plan

For several years, Virginia has pursued a policy of shifting from cutback asphalt to the less expensive emulsified asphalt in road-paving operations. The policy was initiated in an effort to save money, and was totally unrelated to a State Implementation Plan. Because of this policy, CARE argues that hydrocarbon emissions were decreasing independent of this SIP and therefore are not a proper offset against the refinery. They argue that there is not, in effect, an actual reduction in pollution.

The Virginia voluntary plan is not enforceable and therefore is not in compliance with the 1976 Interpretive Ruling which requires that the offset program be enforceable. The EPA, in approving the state plan, obtained a letter from the Deputy Attorney General of Virginia in which he stated that the requisites had been satisfied for establishing and enforcing the plan with the Department of Highways. Without such authority, no decrease in asphalt-produced pollution is guaranteed.[8] In contrast to the voluntary plan, the offset plan guarantees a reduction in pollution resulting from road-paving operations. . . . [The court affirmed EPA's approval of the SIP.]

NOTES AND QUESTIONS

1. *Subsequent Developments.* In 1997, EPA approved a request by Virginia's congressional delegation to redesignate Hampton Roads to attainment status for ozone. The area had not violated the NAAQS for three years. The delegation feared that continuing the area's nonattainment status would disrupt the Navy's plan to move jet fighter squadrons from closed bases in California and Florida to bases in the Hampton Roads area. To what extent should national security considerations factor into implementation of environmental statutes such as the Clean Air Act? See §173(e)(3). See also §§112(i)(4), 604(f); Kasza v. Browner, 133 F.3d 1159 (9th Cir. 1998); Center for Biological Diversity v. Pirie, 201 F. Supp. 2d 113 (D.D.C. 2002).*

2. *Creating Emission Reduction Credits.* EPA's 1986 Emission Trading Policy Statement addressed concerns about spurious offsets. It limited emissions trading in nonattainment areas that lack a demonstrated plan to achieve attainment to trades that would produce a net air quality benefit resulting in interim progress toward attaining the NAAQS. According to EPA:

> Emission reduction credits (ERCs) are the common currency of all trading activity. ERCs may be created by reductions from either stationary, area, or mobile sources. To assure that emissions trades do not contravene relevant requirements of the Clean Air Act, only reductions which are *surplus, enforceable, permanent,* and *quantifiable* can qualify as ERCs and be banked or used in an emissions trade. [51 Fed. Reg. 43,814, 43,831 (1986).]

Did the emissions trade in CARE meet these requirements? EPA studies in the early 1970s revealed that water-based paving asphalt was rapidly replacing petroleum-based

---

8. Despite the fact that the voluntary plan has been in force for several years, 1977 was the year of the highest consumption of cutback asphalt.

*See generally Bethurem, Environmental Destruction in the Name of National Security: Will the Old Paradigm Return in the Wake of September 11?, 8 Hastings W.-Nw. J. Envtl. L. & Pol'y 109 (2002); Truban, Comment, Military Exemptions from Environmental Regulations: Unwarranted Special Treatment or Necessary Relief?, 15 Vill. Envtl. L.J. 139 (2004).

asphalt for energy conservation and cost reasons. By 1977, EPA had recognized water-based asphalt as a minimum "reasonably available control technology" (RACT) that existing sources of air pollution might adopt, yet EPA did not require states to impose RACT in nonattainment areas until 1979. Under the CARE decision, Virginia and other resourceful states could generously offer as "legally binding" offsets reduced petroleum-based asphalt use between 1976 and 1979 even though water-based asphalt was cheaper; offered a better energy conservation strategy; was a readily available, soon-to-be-required emission control technology; and was destined for highway use whether or not CAA offsets were created.

Sierra Club v. Georgia Power Co., 365 F. Supp. 2d 1287 (N.D. Ga. 2004), rejected a challenge to a state agency's issuance of a Title V CAA permit to a power company, concluding that the offsets met the state agency's requirement that they be "real, permanent, quantifiable, enforceable, and surplus." Under the state's regulations, offsets were real if they resulted in a reduction in actual emissions. They were enforceable if the state agency could enforce them as operating permit conditions. They were permanent if they were guaranteed for the life of the corresponding emission reduction credit through an enforceable mechanism such as a permit condition. They were surplus if they were not required by local, state, or federal regulations and were in excess of reductions used by the state agency in issuing other permits or to demonstrate attainment of the NAAQS or reasonable further progress towards achieving the NAAQS.

Can a source use emission reduction credits created by the shutdown of another plant? The 1986 policy statement allowed credits for shutdowns subject to "stringent qualitative review" to ensure consistency with SIP planning goals, such as avoidance of double counting and shifting demand. Motivation was not a factor, but it had to be shown that there was an application to make the shutdown state enforceable through a banking mechanism prior to the time the shutdown occurred. The same rules applied to curtailments.

3. *The Offset Area.* The court allowed Virginia to include in the offset highways selected from any area into which HC might in time be transported, rather than confining the offsets to the urban area around the new source. Yet the Interpretive Ruling favored keeping offsets at least within the same AQCR as the proposed source. How would the Hampton Refinery offset fare after the 1990 amendments? See §173(c)(1).

4. *Establishing a Dependable and Fair Supply of Marketable Offsets.* Without a fixed, dependable base of allowable emissions, emitters will be reluctant to purchase offsets at high prices, only to be faced with the possibility of finding them plentiful and cheap the next day. Sources that can provide relatively cheap offsets (i.e., sources with inherently low emission control costs) will not want to part with their emissions rights if they believe that they will need them themselves imminently or because offsets may increase greatly in value. An EPA-approved SIP relaxation would automatically create new offset possibilities, and a SIP constriction would potentially extinguish them. In markets in which the government prints new money or restricts money supply, prices fluctuate and the outcomes of economic transactions become less predictable. Offset transactions are sensitive to the same risks. See T. Tietenberg, Emissions Trading ch. 6 (1985).

5. *The Relationship between LAER and the Offset Requirement.* If the offset policy is in effect, why should LAER be required? Recall that NSPS would also apply. With the offset policy in effect, are NSPS necessary? In fact, if total areawide

annual emissions quotas are set at levels adequate to ensure "reasonable further progress" and eventual attainment of the NAAQS, and if offsets within the quota can be freely bought and sold, is there a need for additional regulatory controls at all?

NOTES AND QUESTIONS ON BUBBLES, OFFSETS, AND OTHER ECONOMIC INCENTIVE–BASED REGULATORY TECHNIQUES

1. *Kinds of Economic Incentive–Based Techniques for Controlling Pollution.* Before addressing the relative merits and disadvantages, theoretical and practical, of the use of economic incentives instead of or in addition to traditional command-and-control regulation to achieve reductions in emissions, it is helpful to review the various types of incentive-based mechanisms that have been or may be authorized under the CAA.

EPA's Emission Trading Policy Statement, 51 Fed. Reg. 43,814 (1986), endorsed the use of several kinds of emission trading. The first kind, to which you were introduced in connection with the *Chevron* case, is called netting. This form of trading enables the owner or operator of an existing source to avoid having to comply with the requirements of a permit program applicable to modifications of major stationary sources by compensating for increased emissions at some points within a source by reducing emissions elsewhere within the source to produce emission reduction credits (ERCs). R. Liroff, Reforming Air Pollution Regulation: The Toil and Trouble of EPA's Bubble 6 (1986). A source that nets out of NSR must still comply with NSPS requirements.

A related mechanism is the bubble concept. In *Chevron*, the Supreme Court deferred to EPA's view that the bubble concept was an appropriate device to escape the nonattainment area permit program. But use of the bubble is not limited to avoidance of NSR. Existing firms can offset emissions increases and decreases in a similar manner. See Goldschein, Going Mobile: Emissions Trading Gets a Boost from Mobile Source Emission Reduction Credits, 13 UCLA J. Envtl. L. & Pol'y 225, 229 n.30 (1994/1995). EPA's bubble policy for existing sources, first published in 1979, allowed a source with multiple emission points (e.g., stacks or vents), each of which is subject to specific emissions limitation requirements in an EPA-approved SIP, to meet its total SIP emissions control requirements for a given criteria pollutant with a mix of controls different from the combination mandated by its existing SIP obligations.

The nonattainment area permit program relies on a third kind of emission trading. The offset mechanism of §173(a)(1)(A), which was the subject of the *CARE* case, requires new or modified major stationary sources to extract from existing sources enforceable emission reductions that more than offset the increased emissions attributable to the permitted source.

A fourth concept, emission credit banking, "encompasses the processes of creating, certifying and storing ERCs" for later use in trading transactions. Dudek & Palmisano, Emissions Trading: Why Is This Thoroughbred Hobbled?, 13 Colum. J. Envtl. L. 217, 227 (1988). The bank purchases offsets or other emission reduction credits and holds them until an applicant needs them.

EPA's Tier 2 rules establishing limits on the sulfur content of gasoline, issued under §211(c) of the Act, include a program for banking and selling sulfur reduction credits. 64 Fed. Reg. 6,698 (2000). EPA regulations require crude oil refiners to meet a corporate average gasoline sulfur cap. A refinery may generate bankable credits by reducing sulfur at least 10 percent below its 1990 baseline level.

2. *The Theoretical Advantages of Emission Trading.* The primary theoretical advantage of emission trading is that it holds out the prospect for more economically efficient control of pollution than does a pure command-and-control system of regulation. Emission trading affords plant managers greater choice in deciding how to reduce emissions so that they can take advantage of the fact that the marginal costs of reducing emissions vary considerably among different types of installations and plants. Economists argue that, if left alone, plant managers will choose to reduce emissions the most in plant components with the lowest marginal emissions control costs. This strategy allows them to reduce emissions at the lowest possible cost, freeing the money saved from less efficient approaches for income-producing investment elsewhere. The application of different legal requirements to different units in a plant deprives managers of the opportunity to make these cost-minimizing choices. As EPA has recognized, the problem with traditional source-specific emission standards, such as RACT, is that

> [e]ven though set as performance standards, these regulations have a tendency to treat all sources within a category the same and to be oriented toward the lowest common denominator, that is, toward sources within the class that have the greatest difficulty and/or greatest cost of control. Such standards simultaneously miss substantial opportunities for cheap emissions controls by "better" sources, and impose a disproportionately high cost (per ton of pollutant reduced) on a smaller group of sources. Government frequently lacks information on untapped but cost-effective control options, and sources have no incentive to be forthcoming. Government also tends to overlook smaller or unconventional sources. [Open Market Trading Rule for Ozone Smog Precursors, 60 Fed. Reg. 39,668, 39,670 (1995).]

The bubble concept and offsets may allow efficient emission reductions within a plant and an area, respectively. If the total emissions allowed to escape through one imaginary vent at the top of the hypothetical bubble over a plant were projected to be equal to or less than the total approved emissions from all emissions points within the plant, the plant's operator might be able to achieve the level of control at less expense by placing relatively more control on emissions points with low marginal costs of control and less on points with high costs. With respect to offsets:

> The offset price is set by the parties. . . . [E]ach polluter will hold his rights until the offset price is greater than his costs of emission abatement. If the price of an offset is more than the cost of abatement, the rational profit-motivated decision would be to abate emissions and sell an offset. Theoretically, trading would continue until each polluter's cost of an additional reduction would equal the cost of an additional offset right. Prices would reach this equilibrium because each polluter would reduce pollution by purchasing abatement equipment until the next (marginal) reduction would be equally as costly as purchasing the right to emit pollutants. Limiting the amount of offsets through control of the supply of pollution rights would ensure that the equilibrium price would be relatively high, stimulating voluntary reductions. The allocation of rights would be economically efficient when no source could benefit from a trade without greater cost to another source. [Mendrick, Note, Regulating with a Carrot: Experimenting with Incentives for Clean Air, 31 Buff. L. Rev. 193, 204-205 (1982).]

In the case of either internal trading through bubbles or external trading through offsets, emission trading "'encourages those who know most about control opportunities, environmental managers for the industries, to use that knowledge to achieve environmental objectives at minimum cost.'" Goldschein, *supra*, at 230.

3. *Open-Market v. Cap-and-Trade Programs.* The advocates of emission trading do not agree on the optimal form that trading programs should assume. In particular, there is disagreement on whether it is preferable to establish an open-market or a cap-and-trade (or emission budget) system. While the former "allows sources to create tradable reduction credits by reducing their emissions below levels required by [SIPs],* cap-and-trade systems set an overall cap on the amount of emissions permitted as a whole. Emissions are then quantified and apportioned to sources, which can use them for compliance or sell them to other sources. This approach is used in EPA's acid rain program," which is discussed in section I.2 below. Zacaroli, Greater Role Sought for Emissions Trading in Environmental Regulation, 26 Env't Rep. (BNA) 331, 333 (1995).**

Proponents of cap-and-trade systems criticize open-market schemes because they lack baselines against which emission reductions can be measured. Zacaroli, *supra*, at 333. But cap-and-trade systems tend to have lengthy startup periods because they require agreement on matters such as baseline emissions levels, the size of the cap, and the allocation of allowances. These programs tend to be limited to well-measured pollutants from relatively uniform industrial sectors with a relatively small number of sources. 60 Fed. Reg. at 39,670. EPA has urged the use of the open-market approach on a transitional basis, until more comprehensive cap-and-trade programs can be established. Open-market programs "have the potential to reach more diverse and numerous types of sources (including mobile sources) than have been covered to date by emissions budget programs." Id. at 39,671. Open-market trading is flexible and imposes low transaction costs because trades can occur without prior government approval. In addition, EPA has indicated that, while allowing credits for reductions from shutdowns and curtailments is not compatible with an open-market system, such credits can be accommodated under a cap-and-trade program. The agency envisions the two kinds of trading programs as being complementary.

*How does an open market system differ, if at all, from the forms of emission trading (such as netting, bubbles, and offsets) described above? Consider EPA's explanation:

The open market system differs both in concept and execution from the traditional emissions reduction credit (ERC) programs, "bubbles," "netting," and "offsets." These programs involve trading of contemporaneous emissions rates that extend indefinitely into the future. The open market, on the other hand, involves trading of discrete quantities (tons) of emission reductions already made. The discrete reductions are measured from an emissions baseline that is generally defined as the lower of actual or legally allowable emissions at the source. Retrospective quantification of discrete reductions offers the potential for achieving greater certainty and verifiability for all parties regarding reductions already accomplished. [Open Market Trading Rule for Ozone Smog Precursors, 60 Fed. Reg. 39,668, 39,671 (1995).]

**For other examples of CAA cap-and-trade programs, see Standards of Performance for New and Existing Stationary Sources: Electric Utility Steam Generating Units, 70 Fed. Reg. 28,606 (2005) (nationwide cap-and-trade program for mercury emissions from power plants); Rule to Reduce Interstate Transport of Fine Particulate Matter and Ozone (Clean Air Interstate Rule); Revisions to Acid Rain Program, 70 Fed. Reg. 25,162 (2005) (establishing model rules for multistate cap-and-trade programs for annual SO_2 and NO_x emissions for $PM_{2.5}$ and seasonal NO_x emissions for ozone available for use in states that contribute significantly to nonattainment of the NAAQS for fine particles and ozone in downwind states).

4. *Economic Incentive Programs.* In addition to establishing a cap-and-trade program to assist in achieving reductions in the emission of pollutants that contribute to acid rain, the 1990 amendments also endorsed the use of economic incentives in the nonattainment provisions. One of the sanctions available if a state fails to achieve RFP or comply with an applicable emission reduction milestone is the requirement that the state adopt an economic incentive program (EIP), which may authorize the use of emissions fees and marketable permits. §182(g)(3). Similar requirements apply to CO nonattainment areas. See §187(d)(3). In 1994, EPA issued rules to govern the content of EIPs. Economic Incentive Program Rules, 59 Fed. Reg. 16,690. A well-designed EIP, according to EPA, will allow emission sources facing differential costs of control to lower overall control costs through emission trading and will encourage sources already able to meet their emission caps to find ways to reduce emissions beyond what traditional regulatory programs would otherwise require.

The EIP rules authorize emission trading between stationary sources subject to the RACT requirement and any sources (stationary, mobile, or area) not subject to RACT if trading will result in an "exceptional environmental benefit," defined as a level of reductions that is significantly greater than RACT-level amounts. Is this authorization consistent with §172(c)(1) of the Act? Does that provision require each existing source subject to RACT to itself make the reductions achievable by the application of RACT? Or may a source subject to RACT comply with its obligations under a SIP by making no reductions itself, but instead purchasing excess emission reductions from other sources, including mobile sources? Which interpretation of §172(c)(1) is more consistent with the concept of technology forcing? Which is more consistent with the economically efficient reduction of emissions? If these two goals conflict, which should take precedence?

Suppose a state qualifies for emission reduction credits by limiting emissions from state-operated sources to levels below those required by the statute and applicable regulations. May the state use those credits as a lure for new businesses contemplating incorporation within the state by offering to grant them credits for free? See Hernandez, New York Offers Pollution Permits to Lure Companies, N.Y. Times, May 19, 1997, at A1.

5. *Objections to Emission Trading.* Despite its potential for achieving emission reductions more efficiently than more traditional command-and-control regulation can, emission trading has not been universally lauded.

> Environmentalists have tended to be skeptical of emissions trading policy, arguing that environmental quality objectives have been sacrificed in the name of economic efficiency. They assert that the program merely serves as another loophole for industry to evade regulations. However, there is a deeper sense in which environmentalists oppose reforms of this type. A fundamental premise underlying emissions trading is that explicit trading of emissions rights is an acceptable activity. This is not a premise which many environmentalists will accept, even if it can be shown that such activity will lead to substantial improvements in environmental quality. The reasons for this resistance are complex. For some, it is an issue of morality — clean air is viewed as a basic inalienable right which is not for sale at any price. Even for those who do not view this moral position as absolute, there is an important symbolic issue at stake: Allowing firms to trade emission rights sends a message that decisions about tradeoffs between economics and environmental quality can be left to the polluters. [Hahn, Regulatory Reform at EPA: Separating Fact from Illusion, 4 Yale J. on Reg. 173, 179-180 (1986).]

Trading proposals have been attacked on both economic and environmental grounds. Since avoiding NSPS or NSR would allow an existing plant to continue to pollute at the same level while expanding or rebuilding, the bubble and kindred schemes create an incentive to keep an old plant in operation long past its optimal lifetime and discourage the opening of new plants. See Judge Williams's opinion in *New York II* above. Thus, two very important national goals—one environmental and one economic—are frustrated: (1) as a general rule, new plants emit less pollution than existing ones; and (2) new plants are more productive because they are built to reflect changing markets, population shifts, fluctuations in resources and labor supplies, and competitive opportunity.

Another environmental objection to emissions trading is based on the possibility that trades will result in the development of "hot spots" of pollution, where concentrations of the traded pollutant are dangerously high or otherwise interfere with statutory ambient quality objectives. Nash & Revesz, Markets and Geography: Designing Marketable Permit Schemes to Control Local and Regional Pollutants, 28 Ecology L.Q. 569 (2001), propose a model marketable permit program that, according to the authors, will avoid these problems. The program would require governmental approval of emissions permits trading. The reviewer would use atmospheric dispersion models to assess whether a particular trade would result in unacceptable pollutant concentrations.

The use of economic incentives as a substitute for or supplement to command-and-control regulation has been hailed as a means of increasing governmental accountability. Professors Ackerman, Stewart, and Sunstein all have argued that trading programs are preferable to traditional regulation because they require as a starting point an explicit decision concerning what levels of pollution are acceptable. Debate over appropriate levels of pollution control rather than over appropriate control technologies will be more accessible, and for that reason will inspire broader public participation and promote reasoned governmental decisionmaking regarding environmental goals. The effect will be to shift responsibility for pollution control decisions from bureaucrats and self-interested factions to the affected public.* But this claim has prompted skepticism as well.

> [The history of the adoption of the acid rain provisions of the 1990 amendments to the CAA] challenges the view that establishing a system of marketable pollution permits will promote . . . democratic values, such as deliberation, decentralization, and freedom from faction. . . . In reality, Congress paid little attention to the overall limit on sulfur dioxide emissions set by the 1990 Amendments. . . . Moreover, the market system created by the 1990 Amendments owes much of its content to the influence of special interest groups. . . . Thus, the legislative process that created this new market system appears to have been exactly the kind of process which proponents of market-based regulation had hoped to move beyond. . . .
>
> [Professor Heinzerling argues that "the history of the 1990 Amendments reveals that reasoned deliberation did not occur." Moreover, she claims that it is unlikely to occur if other pollution trading schemes are debated. "Because such regulation would likely apply to existing pollution sources, political attention will fix on permit allocation rather than pollution levels, thus virtually ensuring a repeat of the interest-group struggles of 1990."]

*See, e.g., Ackerman & Stewart, Reforming Environmental Law: The Democratic Case for Market Incentives, 13 Colum. J. Envtl. L. 171 (1988); Sunstein, Administrative Substance, 1991 Duke L.J. 607; Sunstein, Democratizing America through Law, 25 Suffolk L. Rev. 949 (1991).

. . . [T]he elimination of democracy-based justifications for pollution trading requires us to face squarely the distributional objections to pollution trading. Although they do not say so explicitly, the projects of legal scholars like Stewart, Ackerman, and Sunstein seem to be designed, in part, to address concerns that pollution trading programs will distribute pollution unevenly, or that they will at least do so unfairly, by basing decisions about the distribution of pollution solely on firms' costs of control. If pollution trading programs are indeed more democratic, the argument might go, then the distributional objection is of little moment because one might assume that citizens effectively agreed to the distributional mechanism through their participation in the decisionmaking process. However, if pollution trading programs do not assure meaningful citizen participation in decisions about the environment, then the distributional objection goes unmet: some unconsenting citizens must endure greater pollution, in the service of reducing the overall costs of environmental compliance. [Heinzerling, Selling Pollution, Forcing Democracy, 14 Stan. Envtl. L.J. 300, 318, 323, 332, 342-343 (1995).]

Johnson, Economics v. Equity: Do Market-Based Environmental Reforms Exacerbate Environmental Injustice?, 56 Wash. & Lee L. Rev. 111 (1999), claims that market-based reforms will probably exacerbate environmental justice problems.*

6. *Emissions Trading in Practice.* Some reports indicate that early source bubbles did not decrease emissions and resulted in little technological innovation. Driesen, The Economic Dynamics of Environmental Law: Cost-Benefit Analysis, Emissions Trading, and Priority-Setting, 31 B.C. Envtl. Aff. L. Rev. 501, 519 (2004), argues that "[t]rading reduces the incentive for high-cost sources to apply new technology. In theory, emissions trading probably weakens net incentives for innovation." Others have concluded that "paper trades" of emission credits that never really existed or that would have happened anyway (such as a credit resulting from a plant shutdown or a credit resulting from plant-controlled emissions that are lower than RACT) in some cases may have actually increased rather than lowered emissions. See Liroff, *supra*, at ch. 4. Similarly, despite its theoretical promise, the offset mechanism is rarely used. See Reitze, A Century of Air Pollution Control Law: What's Worked; What's Failed; What Might Work, 21 Envtl. L. 1549, 1628 (1991).

Netting out to avoid NSR has been a more popular form of emission trading and seems to have produced substantial cost savings. Hahn & Hester, *supra*, at 132-136. Netting does not appear to have had much of an effect on environmental quality, primarily because the nonattainment problem in the areas in which netting has occurred is due principally to mobile sources. Liroff, *supra*, at 132. Because netting is an internal trade, it may actually dampen the market for external trades if a source can accomplish the same objective internally.

Why has industry not embraced emission trading to the extent that its proponents predicted? Uncertainties in the process may have inhibited trading. Professor Reitze asserts, for example, that information is often lacking about both baseline and actual current emissions. Banking, which allows businesses to save emission reduction credits for future use, has been "almost nonexistent." Reitze, *supra*, at 1628-1629. The failure to take advantage of available banking mechanisms is due in large part to fears that regulators will tighten emission control requirements and thus effectively eliminate what once was an emission surplus. Goldschein, *supra*, at 234. High transaction

*See also Chinn, Comment, Can the Market Be Fair and Efficient? An Environmental Justice Critique of Emissions Trading, 26 Ecology L.Q. 80 (1999); Drury et al., Pollution Trading and Environmental Injustice: Los Angeles' Failed Experiment in Air Quality Policy, 9 Duke Envtl. L. & Pol'y F. 231 (1999).

costs attributable to the need of potential traders to negotiate trade terms and to secure the approval of regulators also discourage trading. Inertia and concerns over the legality of particular trades are additional culprits.

Some state emission trading programs have not fared well. New Jersey environmental officials announced plans in 2002 to end a highly touted open-market trading program, characterizing it as "an experiment that failed." The program's critics had complained that it resulted in a shifting of emissions from one source to another but not in emissions reductions. See DeMarco, The Origin and Demise of New Jersey's Open Market Emissions Trading Program, 35 Envtl. L. Rep. (ELI) 10032 (2005) (arguing that the program was plagued by an "absence of real safeguards and numerical targets essential to achieving substantiated environmental improvements"). A California trading program has been called "an unmitigated disaster from both a public health and an administrative perspective." Steinzor, "You Just Don't Understand!"—The Right and Left in Conversation, 32 Envtl. L. Rep. (ELI) 11109 (2002).*

7. *Emission Trading and the Constitution.* Does the government risk incurring liability under the taking clause if it authorizes emission trading, such as the banking of emission reduction credits, and subsequently renders such banked credits worthless by reducing permissible emission levels? What are the arguments for and against the conclusion that a compensable regulatory taking has occurred in those circumstances? Consider §403(f) of the CAA, which deals with the trading scheme that forms a part of the acid deposition control provisions of the statute.**

8. *Beyond Emission Trading.* The incentive-based techniques discussed above all involve the engrafting of trading schemes onto more traditional regulatory programs. Would it be possible to scrap those programs altogether and substitute a new strategy that relies wholly on the economics-based approach? One such strategy would rely on emissions fees or taxes instead of regulatory restrictions. See W. Baumol & W. Oates, The Theory of Environmental Policy 135 (1975); J. Dales, Pollution, Property, and Prices (1968).

A pure emissions fee would not be based on achieving predetermined levels of ambient air quality; rather, it would be set by comparing the dollar value of the *marginal* (additional or incremental) damage to health and welfare caused by the last unit of pollutant emitted with the emitter's *marginal* investment in emissions control equipment that will abate that additional unit of pollution. The fee for each unit of pollutant emitted should be set equal to the dollar amount at which the marginal damage and marginal abatement costs are equal. In Figure 6-7, for example, as Plant 1's SO_x emissions increase (right to left) to hypothetical maximum uncontrolled emissions of 100 tons, the marginal health and other environmental injury, expressed in dollars, increases with each marginal ton of emissions (MD). But as Plant 1 installs more emissions control equipment or otherwise reduces sulfur emissions, its marginal costs of controlling each additional ton rise (MC, left to right). The MC curve becomes especially steep as it approaches very low emissions levels. Abatement may proceed in phases, as large units of pollution control equipment are added, one after the other, so that the MC curve becomes a staircase. The MD curve

---

*For a discussion of emissions trading programs in a variety of air pollution and other contexts, see Environmental Trading, 20 Nat. Resources & Env't 1 (Summer 2005) (entire issue devoted to analysis of emissions trading).

**See generally Austin, Comment, Tradable Emissions Programs: Implications under the Takings Clause, 26 Envtl. L. 323 (1996); Savage, Note, Confiscation of Emission Reduction Credits: The Case for Compensation under the Takings Clause, 16 Va. Envtl. L.J. 227 (1997).

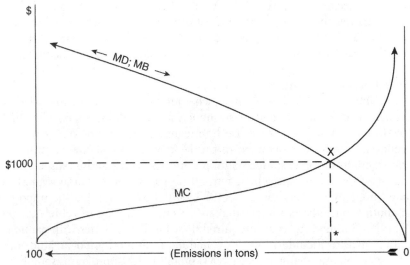

*Tenth ton emitted; ninetieth ton controlled.

FIGURE 6-7
Plant 1: SO$_x$ Emissions

also plots the marginal benefits (MB) of increased abatement, read as reduced damages from left to right. It arguably represents the willingness of receptors to "bribe" Plant 1 to reduce emissions or the amount receptors should be willing to invest to avoid injury to themselves.

At X, marginal damage equals marginal abatement cost. The emissions fee should be set equal to $1,000 per ton—no more, no less. A higher fee would reduce emissions and cause more to be spent on pollution control, but the additional pollution control costs would exceed the additional benefits (in terms of reduced damage) from the increased abatement. A lower fee would not stimulate Plant 1 to control all possible emissions of pollutant for which abatement is cheaper than the injury the emissions inflict.

The practical problems of calculating the dollar value of marginal damage and abatement costs for individual sources in thousands of specific settings are overwhelming. The pure emissions fee, therefore, remains more of an ideal than a concrete proposal for legislative action. A more practical variant, *averaging* marginal abatement costs across entire categories of emitters, has attracted numerous proponents. On the injury side, even the most serious fee system advocates concede the difficulty of computing regional or national environmental injury costs associated with varying pollution levels.

5.   Controlling Emissions from Mobile Sources in Nonattainment Areas

Given that emissions from cars, trucks, and buses are a major component of the nonattainment problem for ozone and CO, one might expect to see EPA aggressively seeking to limit those emissions. EPA has indeed tried to crack down on emissions from mobile sources as a means of accelerating attainment of the NAAQS, but those efforts have a checkered history at best. A critical element in EPA's pre-1977 mobile-source strategy was the Transportation Control Plan (TCP), through which it sought in some areas to impose dramatic controls on automobile usage. The TCP aimed at reducing the use of automobiles through controls ranging from the encouragement of car pooling to improvements in public mass transit. These measures are known as Transportation Control Measures (TCMs).

The American public likes to drive, whether it be to commute to work or to take to the open road for a weekend or summer vacation. Public opposition to EPA's attempts to control car and truck use by means of TCPs and TCMs was prompt and vociferous. Congress responded in the 1977 amendments by curtailing federal authority to control mobile-source pollution through TCPs and by suspending existing TCP provisions for private vehicle retrofitting, gas rationing, parking supply reduction, and bridge tolls. In addition, the 1977 legislation prohibited the imposition of federal controls on indirect sources that attract large numbers of vehicles.

The 1977 amendments also required that the SIPs of states with ozone or CO nonattainment areas include a "specific schedule" for imposition of an auto emissions control inspection and maintenance (I&M) program. I&M programs soon became a key TCP strategy. The states persuaded EPA that in meeting the extended NAAQS deadlines they should be allowed to rely heavily on the emissions reductions the federal vehicle emissions standards were supposed to achieve under Title II of the CAA. Title II authorized EPA to certify, test, and recall vehicles; enforce warranty provisions; and prosecute persons who tamper with pollution control devices or use leaded fuels. But the effectiveness of emissions controls declines rapidly soon after vehicles are put into service, and the number of vehicles on the road increased even as the pollutant amounts emitted by each vehicle fell. As a result, the vehicle emission standards proved just as ineffective in eliminating ozone and CO nonattainment problems after 1977 as they had before.

When Congress amended the CAA again in 1990, it restored some of EPA's authority to require measures in ozone and CO nonattainment areas that, if implemented, would restrict vehicle use. The worse the nonattainment problem, the greater is EPA's authority to require significant changes in activities with the potential to generate mobile-source emissions of ozone precursors or CO. The existence of that authority on paper, however, does not necessarily translate into effective controls in the real world. EPA and any states seeking to constrain mobile source emissions must still deal with the love affair between the average American and his or her car(s). As you will see in the following discussion, Congress has backtracked on several of the mandates included in the 1990 amendments to limit mobile source emissions. It remains to be seen whether meaningful measures to control these emissions are feasible, but experience provides little cause for optimism.

The remainder of this subsection explores some of the provisions of the 1990 amendments that relate to mobile-source emissions in nonattainment areas and the legal and practical issues that the application of those provisions have raised or may present in the future.

a. Vehicle Inspection and Maintenance Programs

I&M programs have been at the center of political and legal controversy over the implementation of nonattainment plans. Although they are capable of reducing automotive pollution, they are costly to implement and tend to be regarded as intrusive. Kentucky's vehicle emission testing program, for example, "has always generated more than its share of controversy. By necessity, it imposes a certain amount of inconvenience and expense upon citizens whose vehicles regularly meet its standards. Not surprisingly, many people find the testing requirements intrusive and wasteful." Kentucky Res. Council, Inc. v. EPA, 304 F. Supp. 2d 920, 923 (W.D. Ky. 2004).

The 1990 amendments require states with marginal or moderate ozone nonattainment areas to implement a basic I&M program that conforms to EPA guidance. §182(a)(2)(B)(i), (b)(4). A basic program involves visual inspection of pollution control devices and measurement of exhaust during engine idling. States with serious, severe, or extreme areas must establish more costly enhanced I&M programs to reduce HC and NO_x emissions, which include computerized on-road testing devices, denial of registration for noncomplying vehicles, and operation of the program on a centralized basis instead of through local gasoline service stations. E.g., §182(c)(3)(A), (C).

EPA favored the centralized operation of I&M facilities that lack the authority to make repairs in deficient vehicles because it regarded centralized testing as more accurate and less likely to result in the issuance of undeserved waivers based on the high cost of repairs. State officials tended to support decentralized programs run by local service station operators, claiming that centralization would provide car owners with fewer testing stations to choose from, require that they wait in longer lines, and impose on them the inconvenience of having to fix noncomplying cars elsewhere before returning for retesting. The states also wanted to protect the investments that service station owners had made in testing equipment. See Dwyer, The Practice of Federalism under the Clean Air Act, 54 Md. L. Rev. 1183, 1212 (1995).

EPA's I&M regulations under the 1990 amendments required testing at centralized facilities unless a state could demonstrate that a decentralized program was equally effective. A program in which service stations could both test and repair was presumed not to be equally effective. Several state legislatures refused to establish centralized, test-only programs. Ultimately, Congress adopted the National Highway System Designation Act of 1995, Pub. L. No. 104-59, §348, 109 Stat. 568. That statute bars EPA from requiring states with ozone nonattainment areas to establish centralized emissions testing facilities and authorizes states to resort to test-and-repair facilities. Following adoption of that 1995 legislation, EPA took additional steps "to provide greater flexibility to states to tailor their I/M programs to better meet local needs." 65 Fed. Reg. 45,526, 45,527 (2000).

What does this tale indicate about Congress's willingness to adhere to vigorous requirements to reduce vehicle exhaust? See Reitze, Federalism and the Inspection and Maintenance Program under the Clean Air Act, 27 Pac. L.J. 1461, 1515 (1996) (listing "excessive waivers, motorist noncompliance, inadequate quality control, outdated test procedures, insufficient enforcement . . . , inadequate data collection and analysis, inadequate resources, and improper testing" as problems that plague the I&M program). What does the fate of the I&M program suggest about the prospects of devolving additional authority to state and local governments to implement pollution control legislation? See McGarity, Regulating Commuters to Clear the Air: Some Difficulties in Implementing a National Program at the Local Level, 27 Pac. L.J. 1521, 1620 (1996) ("The history of federal I/M programs plainly demonstrates that the states are entirely unwilling to implement such programs voluntarily," couching opposition in the "rhetoric of state sovereignty").

Mandatory I&M programs may one day be replaced by the use of remote sensing devices that can be set up at roadsides for random testing. The process involves shooting an infrared beam across the road and measuring CO and hydrocarbon emissions from passing vehicles. A video camera photographs the license plates of the cars so that citations can be issued to polluters. Wildavsky, Remote Sensors, Common Sense, Nat'l J., Feb. 24, 1996, at 445.

b. Gasoline Vapor Recovery

Another control strategy is the recovery of gasoline vapor hydrocarbon VOCs that escape during refueling. The entry of gasoline vapor into the atmosphere during refueling can be limited by reducing the gasoline's volatility, capturing gasoline vapors in a container "on board" the vehicle, or capturing gasoline vapors by routing them back to the station's main tank.

In 1990, Congress ordered EPA to issue standards requiring new cars to be equipped with onboard controls. §202(a)(6). EPA refused to issue the standards, concluding that the safety risks were unreasonable, given the availability of alternative means of controlling vapor emissions. Although the agency claimed that it had discretion to pursue this option, the court in NRDC v. Reilly, 983 F.2d 259 (D.C. Cir. 1993), found EPA's duty to issue the standards to be mandatory. On remand, EPA phased in onboard controls that are designed to achieve a minimum emission capture efficiency of 95 percent. 59 Fed. Reg. 16,262 (1994). Congress also required SIPs in all but marginal ozone nonattainment areas to require controls at the pump. §182(b)(3).

c. Alternative Fuels

The 1990 amendments sought to encourage or mandate the use of alternative fuels with lower pollution potential than motor gasoline derived from crude oil. See, e.g., §211(h), (m). Exxon Mobil Corp. v. EPA, 217 F.3d 1246 (9th Cir. 2000), upheld EPA's approval of a Nevada SIP revision requiring that all gasoline sold in the winter have an oxygen content of at least 3.5 percent. The court interpreted §211(m)(2) as creating a federal floor, but not a ceiling.

The 1990 amendments also sought to encourage the use of ethanol as an oxygenate to reduce emissions of CO, but Congress repealed the oxygenate requirements in the Energy Policy Act of 2005, Pub. L. No. 109-58, §1504, 119 Stat. 594, 1077.[*] The primary oxygenates added to reformulated gasoline (RFG) to increase its oxygen content are ethanol, which is primarily made from corn, and methyl tertiary butyl ether (MTBE), which is derived primarily from nonrenewable resources such as natural gas and petroleum. See Figure 6-8. Unfortunately, the use of ethanol in RFG increases volatility and emissions of VOCs, especially in the summer. MTBE does not have that effect, but it generated other environmental concerns. MTBE is the second most common VOC (behind chloroform, a by-product of chlorine

---

[*]See Regulation of Fuels and Fuel Additives: Removal of Reformulated Gasoline Oxygen Content Requirement, 71 Fed. Reg. 26,691 (2006).

FUEL	ADVANTAGES	DISADVANTAGES
ELECTRICITY	• Potential for zero vehicle emissions • Power plant emissions easier to control • Can recharge at night when power demand is low	• Current technology is limited • Higher vehicle cost; lower vehicle range, performance • Less convenient refueling
ETHANOL	• Excellent automotive fuel • Very low emissions of ozone-forming hydrocarbons and toxics • Made from renewable sources • Can be domestically produced	• High fuel cost • Somewhat lower vehicle range
METHANOL	• Excellent automotive fuel • Very low emissions of ozone-forming hydrocarbons, and toxics • Can be made from a variety of feedstocks, including renewables	• Fuel could initially be imported • Somewhat lower vehicle range
NATURAL GAS (METHANE)	• Very low emissions of ozone-forming hydrocarbons, toxics and carbon monoxide • Can be made from a variety of feedstocks, including renewables • Excellent fuel, especially for fleet vehicles	• Higher vehicle cost • Lower vehicle range • Less convenient refueling
PROPANE	• Cheaper than gasoline today • Most widely available clean fuel today • Somewhat lower emissions of ozone-forming hydrocarbons and toxics • Excellent fuel, especially for fleet vehicles	• Cost will rise with demand • Limited supply • No energy security or trade balance benefits
REFORMULATED GASOLINE	• Can be used in all cars without changing vehicles or fuel distribution system • Somewhat lower emissions of ozone-forming hydrocarbons, nitrogen oxides, and toxics	• Somewhat higher fuel cost • Few energy security or trade balance benefits

FIGURE 6-8
Summary Table of Alternative Fuel Advantages & Disadvantages

Source: http://www.epa.gov/otaq/06-clean.htm

disinfection) found in municipal drinking water sources. See generally Al-Bahish et al., Emerging Toxic Torts: MTBE and Mold, 17 Nat. Resources & Env't 219 (Spring 2003).

Before the 2005 amendments, several states took steps to ban the use of MTBE as a fuel additive to prevent groundwater pollution. MTBE producers attacked those initiatives on preemption grounds. Oxygenated Fuels Ass'n, Inc. v. Davis, 331 F.3d 665 (9th Cir. 2003), held that the CAA did not implicitly preempt California's ban on MTBE. OFA argued that Congress intended to give gasoline producers an unrestricted choice among oxygenate fuel additives and the state's ban conflicted with that goal. The court found no evidence that Congress sought to achieve "oxygenate neutrality." OFA also argued that the ban conflicted with the CAA because it would substantially disrupt the gasoline market and cause an increase in prices, but the court found no evidence that the CAA's goals included a smoothly functioning market and cheap gasoline.

The public reaction to MTBE indicates that the alternative fuels program, like the I&M requirements of the CAA, has the potential to induce a backlash. Even if alternative fuels are proven to be safe, will their use be feasible, given the difficulty of finding fueling stations?

d. Clean-Fuel Vehicles

Under the 1990 amendments, states with specified ozone or CO nonattainment areas must revise their SIPs to establish a clean-fuel vehicle program for covered fleets. §246(a)(1). See also §182(c)(4) (serious ozone nonattainment areas). Clean-fuel vehicles must meet standards issued by EPA under §242. Revised SIPs must require an increasing percentage of all new covered fleet vehicles (ten or more vehicles owned or operated by a single person) to use clean alternative fuels when operating in a covered nonattainment area. §246(b). The SIP also must require fuel providers to make clean alternative fuels available to covered fleet operators at central fueling locations. §246(e). See generally Bale, The Newest Frontier in Motor Vehicle Emission Control: The Clean Fuel Vehicle, 15 Va. Envtl. L.J. 213 (1995-1996).

e. Transportation Controls and Related Measures

Stung by its experience during the mid-1970s, EPA was reluctant to require transportation control measures (TCMs) of the sort described in §108(f)(1) after the 1977 amendments. E.g., Delaney v. EPA, 898 F.2d 687 (9th Cir. 1990) (EPA's refusal to require reasonably available TCMs was arbitrary). The states resisted implementing them even when they were required. The 1990 amendments enhanced EPA's authority to require states to include TCMs in their SIPs. States with serious and severe ozone nonattainment areas must submit to EPA periodic demonstrations that aggregate vehicle mileage, vehicle emissions, and congestion levels are consistent with projections in the SIP for attaining the NAAQS. See Figure 6-9. If current figures exceed the projections, the state must revise its SIP to include a TCM program to reduce emissions of ozone precursors. §182(c)(5). See also §§182(e)(4), 187(b)(2).

Will EPA have the fortitude to press the states to adopt control measures they have strongly resisted in the past? Will the driving public abide by these measures? Does it make sense for Congress to shift the burden of reducing ozone and CO pollution from businesses and governments to individual drivers?

The fate of the employee trip reduction program under the 1990 amendments may help answer these questions. The amendments required states with ozone non-attainment areas to require each employer of 100 or more persons to increase average passenger occupancy per vehicle commuting between home and the office during peak travel periods by at least 25 percent. Congress anticipated that employers would either provide van pools for their employees or provide incentives for employees to carpool or take public transportation to work. But businesses subject to these requirements resented their new obligations, complaining that they should not be forced to redress past state failures to achieve the NAAQS. In 1995, Congress barred EPA from financing the program. Pub. L. No. 104-19, 109 Stat. 194. It later amended the Act to give states the *discretion* to revise their SIPs to require employers to implement

Clean-Fueled Vehicles and Potential Ozone Reductions in a Typical City

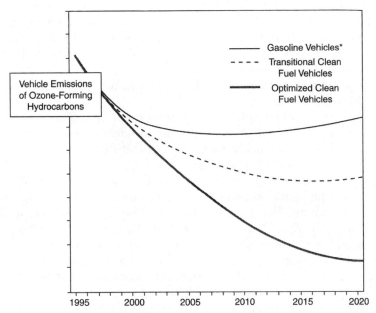

FIGURE 6-9

Source: http://www.epa.gov/oms/04-ozone.htm

programs to reduce work-related vehicle trips and miles traveled by employees. §182(d)(1)(B).*

The Safe Accountable, Flexible, Efficient Transportation Equity Act: A Legacy for Users (SAFETEA-LU), Pub. L. No. 109-59, §6001(a), 119 Stat. 1144 (2005), requires that large, urbanized areas located in nonattainment AQCRs prepare transportation plans. Among other things, a plan must include strategies to improve the performance of existing transportation facilities to relieve vehicle congestion. The statute prohibits the use of federal funds on any highway project in an urbanized area with a population of over 200,000 people that is classified as nonattainment for either ozone or CO if the project would significantly increase carrying capacity for single-occupant vehicles, unless the project is subject to a process designed to manage traffic congestion through travel demand reduction and operational management strategies. 49 U.S.C. §5303(m)(1).

---

*For a discussion of the reasons for the failure of the trip reduction program, see Professor Oren's trilogy, Getting Commuters out of Their Cars: What Went Wrong?, 17 Stan. Envtl. L.J. 141 (1998); Detail and Implementation: The Example of Employee Trip Reduction, 17 Va. Envtl. L.J. 123 (1998); How a Mandate Came from Hell: The Makings of the Federal Employee Trip Reduction Plan, 28 Envtl. L. 267 (1998).

f. Indirect Source Review

The 1977 amendments eliminated federal measures for improving air quality through land use controls on the spacing and location of facilities that attract large numbers of vehicles. These "indirect sources" include highways, airports, parking garages and lots, shopping centers, and large office and apartment buildings. States are free to adopt indirect source review (ISR) requirements, but EPA may not require that they be included in SIPs.

All facilities that could be subjected to parking supply reductions—parking lots, garages, and other existing off-street facilities—are clearly excluded from EPA-imposed control. But the Act makes it equally clear that EPA could impose controls on new or existing on-street parking and other TCMs. §110(a)(5)(C), (E). Do exclusive bus and carpool lanes and other traffic flow improvement strategies that involve modifying highways or highway use (e.g., bike lanes) fit the definition of indirect sources? Suppose that a major city located on a river proposes to build a tunnel underneath the river. The city will vent CO from the tunnel through a ventilation building located nearby. The city is part of a nonattainment area for CO. Is the ventilation building a major stationary source for which the city must file a permit under §172(c)(5), or is it an indirect source whose regulation is left to the discretion of the state? See Sierra Club v. Larson, 2 F.3d 462 (1st Cir. 1993).

The ISR provisions of the Act were not amended in 1990. ISR apparently is even more abhorrent than the extremely unpopular TCMs. In prohibiting ISR in 1977, Congress sought to avoid effectively divesting control over land use siting decisions from the local governments that had traditionally exercised them. H.R. Rep. No. 95-294, at 1301 (1977).

6. *Sanctions for Failure to Comply with Nonattainment Area Requirements*

The issue of what steps to take against states failing to comply with the obligations imposed on them to achieve the NAAQS has long been a troublesome one. The 1977 amendments imposed a ban on new construction of major stationary sources in nonattainment areas if the state did not attain the standards by 1983. EPA also could withhold the state's sewage treatment funding if SIP submission and compliance deadlines were not met. §316.

EPA interpreted its obligation to impose sanctions narrowly. It refused to impose construction bans on new sources solely for failure to achieve standards by the statutory attainment dates. EPA was equally unenthusiastic about the funding cutoff provisions, but the courts imposed sanctions in citizen suits seeking to force compliance with the nonattainment plan provisions in states that had not adopted required control strategies. See American Lung Ass'n v. Kean, 871 F.2d 319 (3d Cir. 1989).

The 1990 amendments represented both a loosening and a tightening of the screws on states with persistent nonattainment problems. Congress repealed EPA's authority to impose the most dreaded sanction, the moratorium on the construction of major stationary sources, although in some instances moratoria imposed before 1990 remained in effect. §110(n)(3). But §179(a) of the amended Act confirmed EPA's power to impose sanctions on states that fail to submit required SIP revisions, submit unacceptable revisions, or fail to implement approved SIP provisions, absent timely corrective action by the state within 18 months. In these circumstances, EPA may withhold federal grants for air pollution planning and control programs, prohibit the award of federal highway construction funds, or increase the ratio of emission reductions from existing sources to emission increases from new or modified major stationary sources needed to satisfy the offset requirement of §173(a)(1). How much sense does the first of these sanctions make? Compare §179(b)(1)(B).

In addition to these general sanctions, the statute provides for special sanctions that apply to noncompliance with the ozone, CO, and particulate matter nonattainment provisions. If a severe ozone nonattainment area fails to achieve the primary NAAQS on time, major stationary sources of VOCs within the area become subject to penalty fees for each ton emitted. §185(a)-(b). For the worst-polluted severe areas, the new source review provisions for extreme areas go into effect upon noncompliance with RFP milestones or the ultimate NAAQS deadline. §181(b)(4)(B). What are those requirements and how do they compare with the requirements that otherwise apply in severe areas? See §182(c)(7)-(8), (e)(1)-(2). The statute requires that, under certain circumstances, EPA reclassify nonattainment areas that do not meet the NAAQS attainment deadlines (e.g., from serious to severe). §181(b)(2)(A). EPA may adjust statutory deadlines (other than attainment dates) when it reclassifies an ozone nonattainment area. §182(i). Suppose that a serious ozone nonattainment area fails to meet the applicable compliance deadline because of emissions that originate in another state. May EPA extend the deadline for compliance without reclassifying the area as severe? See Southern Organizing Comm. for Econ. and Soc. Justice v. EPA, 333 F.3d 1288 (11th Cir. 2003); Sierra Club v. EPA, 311 F.3d 853 (7th Cir. 2002); Sierra Club v. EPA, 294 F.3d 159, 160-162 (D.C. Cir. 2002). In those cases, the courts struck down EPA's policy of allowing extensions of compliance deadlines for nonattainment areas adversely affected by upwind emissions of ozone precursors. Cf. Sierra Club v. EPA, 356 F.3d 296 (D.C. Cir. 2004) (approving EPA's decision to extend deadline for submitting revised SIP for severe area). The sanctions for defaulting CO and particulate matter nonattainment areas are similar to those for ozone. See §§186(b)(2)(A), 187(d)(3), (g), 188(b)(2), 189(d).

G.   PREVENTION OF SIGNIFICANT DETERIORATION

1.   Origins and Purposes of the PSD Program

The Origins of PSD. Lurking in the background in the early 1970s was the issue of whether air quality in areas of the nation that already enjoyed air cleaner than that required by the NAAQS should be allowed to deteriorate to the ambient standards. Congress did not address the nondegradation issue until 1977. In the meantime, motivated primarily to protect the unique vistas in the western national parks, the Sierra Club sued EPA in 1972 to force it to do so. It adopted a simple legal argument: Congress plainly stated in §101 that a purpose of the CAA was to "protect" as well as "enhance" air resources. The Club thought that EPA had to take Congress at its cryptic word.

Relying on §101, legislative history from the 1960s, and prior federal commitments to maintain existing air quality, a federal district court held that EPA had a nondiscretionary duty to adopt measures that would improve air quality and prevent all but nonsignificant deterioration of existing high air quality levels. The circuit court affirmed without issuing an opinion, and the Supreme Court also affirmed, without opinion, dividing 4-4 on the issue. Sierra Club v. Ruckelshaus, 344 F. Supp. 253 (D.D.C. 1972), *aff'd per curiam without opinion*, 2 Envtl. L. Rep. (ELI) 20656 (D.C. Cir. 1972), *aff'd by an equally divided Court*, 412 U.S. 541 (1973). Congress endorsed that result in the 1977 amendments.

The Purposes of PSD. The PSD program, §§160-169A, was designed to achieve several goals. One justification was health-based: the primary NAAQS might turn out to be insufficient to protect against known or suspected adverse effects of ambient concentrations of the criteria pollutants. Limiting pollutant concentrations in so-called clean-air areas might also reduce adverse health and welfare effects, such as acid rain and visibility impairment, resulting from long-range transport of air pollutants. The PSD program sought to provide special protection to scenic vistas in pristine areas of the West. It also responded to fears that, absent protection of air quality better than that required by the NAAQS, states with clean air could compete for industrial expansion using the ability to degrade air quality as a bargaining chip. Thus, a PSD program would equalize the burden of air pollution controls among more and less industrialized areas. See H.R. Rep. No. 95-294, at 103-141 (1977).

The leading study of the justifications for a nondegradation policy is still Hines, A Decade of Nondegradation Policy in Congress and the Courts: The Erratic Pursuit of Clean Air and Clean Water, 62 Iowa L. Rev. 643 (1977). According to Professor Hines, the policy responds to "the historical evidence that, unless restrained by some external force or internal command, mankind incessantly exploits and ultimately despoils or destroys natural environments" and recognizes that "it is morally necessary to think about what kind of world will be passed along to future generations." Id. at 649. Thus, "[w]hile the nondegradation principle does not rely solely on philosophical grounds for its justification, . . . the ethical force of the idea best explains the action taken." Id.

Development of the Regulatory Program for PSD. EPA issued its first set of PSD regulations in 1974. After adoption of the 1977 amendments to the CAA, EPA issued a second set of PSD guidelines (43 Fed. Reg. 26,380), which was immediately challenged in court. The reviewing court's decision in Alabama Power Co. v. Costle, 636 F.2d 323 (D.C. Cir. 1979), provided a kind of environmental lawyer's PSD hornbook. *Alabama Power* reshaped the PSD program to an appreciable extent. To implement the decision, EPA revised its regulations again. 45 Fed. Reg. 52,676 (1980).

2. The Current PSD Program: An Overview

The following excerpt describes the highlights of the current PSD program.* Keep in mind that an AQCR can be a PSD area for one or more pollutants even though it is a nonattainment area for other pollutants, and no part of the country is nonattainment for all pollutants. The PSD regulations are at 40 C.F.R. §52.21.

---

*For a thorough review of the program see Oren, Prevention of Significant Deterioration: Control-Compelling v. Site-Shifting, 74 Iowa L. Rev. 1 (1988); Oren, The Protection of Parklands from Air Pollution: A Look at Current Policy, 13 Harv. Envtl. L. Rev. 313 (1989); Glicksman, Pollution on the Federal Lands I: Air Pollution Law, 12 UCLA J. Envtl. L. & Pol'y 1, 29-59 (1993).

NATIONAL RESEARCH COUNCIL OF THE NATIONAL
ACADEMY OF SCIENCES, ON PREVENTION OF
SIGNIFICANT DETERIORATION OF AIR QUALITY
5-18 (1981)

In the Clean Air Act Amendments of 1977, Congress specified the initial clas-sification of the lands for PSD purposes. [Under §162(a),] [c]ertain lands, where existing good air quality is deemed to be of national importance, were designated Class I and may not be reclassified. These mandatory Class I areas include all international parks, national wilderness areas larger than 5,000 acres, national memorial parks larger than 5,000 acres, and national parks larger than 6,000 acres that were in existence when the amendments were passed. [Under §162(b), a]ll other areas to which the PSD provisions apply were initially designated Class II. . . . [The Act provides procedures for reclassification to Class I or III.]*

Defining Significant Deterioration

[Section 163 of] [t]he Act defines significant deterioration due to the presence of sulfur dioxide (SO_2) and total suspended particulate matter (TSP) by setting maximum allow-able increases over baseline concentrations (increments) for these pollutants for each of three classes of land, subject to the restriction that the allowed increases may not result in concentrations that exceed either the primary or the secondary NAAQS. Increments for SO_2 and TSP called Set I pollutants are defined for both a long-term (annual) average concentration and maximum concentrations over short periods of time. . . .

As a result of the decision in Alabama Power v. Castle, the baseline concentra-tion includes (a) the ambient concentration resulting from actual emissions from existing sources at the time of the first application for a permit to construct a major emitting facility in a PSD area, and (b) the projected emissions from major stationary sources that began construction before January 6, 1975, but had not begun operation by the time of the first permit application. [See §169(4).] . . .

The 1977 Amendments also require EPA to devise means for preventing significant deterioration of air quality from other pollutants regulated under the Act. [These are called the Set II pollutants; see §166.]

Preconstruction Review

To assess the potential consequences of emissions from new sources for ambient air quality and the consumption of increments, proposed sources of pollution must be reviewed before construction [under §165(a)]. However, not all sources are subject to preconstruction review for PSD purposes. Only major stationary sources or major modifications to existing stationary sources in areas in which the PSD provisions apply are subject to review. As a result of the decision in Alabama Power v. Castle, a major source located in a nonattainment area is not subject to PSD review even if

---

*Congress intended that the federal government play a limited role in reviewing decisions by state governments or Indian tribes to redesignate areas as Class I or Class III on social, economic, or environmental grounds. See, e.g., Arizona v. EPA, 151 F.3d 1205 (9th Cir. 1998), amended, 170 F.3d 870 (9th Cir. 1999). No state has redesignated a PSD area to Class III.

TABLE 6-3
NAAQSs for SO_2 and TSP and Maximum Allowable Increases in Concentrations
over the Baseline in PSD Areas ($\mu g/m^3$)

Pollutant	Maximum Allowable Increases			NAAQS	
	Class I	Class II	Class III	Primary	Secondary
Particulate Matter					
Annual geometric mean	5	19	37	75	60
24-hour maximum*	10	37	75	260	150
Sulfur Dioxide					
Annual arithmetic mean	2	20	40	80	—
24-hour maximum*	5	91	182	365	—
3-hour maximum*	25	512	700	—	1300

* Short-term maxima may be exceeded no more than once per year.

emissions from the source adversely affect air quality in a PSD area, unless the affected PSD area and the source are in different states.

There are two classes of major stationary sources. In one class are all stationary sources that emit or have the potential to emit 250 or more tons per year of any pollutant regulated under the Act. In the other class are any stationary sources from a list of 28 types of industrial facilities that emit or have the potential to emit 100 tons or more per year of any regulated pollutant. . . . [Section 169(1) contains the list.]

In EPA's earlier regulations, the potential for a source to emit pollutants was to be judged without taking into account any air pollution control equipment. The decision in *Alabama Power* overturned this interpretation, and thus potential to emit now means the maximum capacity of a source to emit pollutants under its actual physical and operational design, which includes any air pollution control equipment. . . .

Major modifications of existing sources are defined as physical or operational changes that result in a significant net increase in emissions of any pollutant regulated under the Act. Regulations specify what a significant increase is for each pollutant. . . .

Stationary point sources that are not large enough to be classified as major sources and distributed sources such as urban growth . . . , including emissions from mobile sources that accompany this growth, are not subject to preconstruction review; however, changes in air quality due to emissions from such sources are to be counted against the increments. It is up to the permitting authorities to maintain inventories of the nonmajor sources as well as the major sources and to assess the effects of emissions from both major and nonmajor sources. . . .

The AQRV [Air Quality-Related Values] Test for Class I Areas

To represent the national interest in Class I areas that encompass federal lands, federal officials have been given special roles in the preconstruction review of proposed facilities that may affect those lands. Under the Act, the federal land manager and the federal official who is directly responsible for managing federal land in a Class I area have an affirmative responsibility to protect AQRVs in that land. One way of discharging that responsibility is to determine whether a proposed major source will adversely affect those values. The federal land manager is the secretary of the department with authority over the federal land in question. Other than visibility, the Act does not specify what AQRVs are.

Even if Class I increments have not been consumed and a proposed new source would not cause or contribute to concentrations of pollutants that exceed the increments, a construction permit cannot be issued if the federal land manager demonstrates to the satisfaction of the state that the proposed facility would nonetheless have adverse consequences for AQRVs on the federal lands in question.

Conversely, when Class I increments have been consumed or when a proposed source would cause or contribute to concentrations of pollutants that do exceed the increments, a permit may still be issued if the applicant can demonstrate to the satisfaction of the federal land manager that the emissions from the facility will not have adverse consequences for AQRVs on federal lands in the Class I area. The burden of proof in these circumstances is on the applicant. When such waivers of the Class I increments are granted, the Act specifies new maximum allowable increases over ambient concentrations, which are the same as the increments for Class II areas. . . .

Neither the AQRV test nor waivers and variances are applicable to Class II and III areas.

Visibility Protection in Mandatory Class I Areas

Section 169A of the Act established as part of the PSD provisions a national goal of both preventing future impairment of visibility in mandatory Class I areas and remedying existing impairment due to man-made pollution. Visibility protection against degradation in the future is to be accomplished through the PSD provisions for review of new sources. Remedying existing impairment requires retrofitting emission control equipment to existing sources that adversely affect visibility.

Regulations to implement Section 169A require the 36 states containing mandatory Class I areas where visibility has been identified as an important value to revise their SIPs in three ways: they must add provisions for using the best available retrofit technology (BART) on certain installations of existing major sources; they must adopt certain measures to supplement new source review programs regarding visibility; and they must identify and evaluate long-term strategies for achieving the national goal.

Under the visibility regulations, the state authority is required to make a determination of BART for each existing major stationary source that may reasonably be suspected of causing or contributing to visibility impairment in a mandatory Class I area. The state is required to consult with the appropriate federal land manager in identifying sources and determining BART. The determination of BART is to take into account the costs of compliance, the energy and (nonatmospheric) environmental impacts of retrofitting existing control equipment, the remaining useful life of the facility, and the degree of improvement in visibility that may be expected to result from the application of the technology. Sources 15 years old or older at the time of passage of the 1977 amendments are exempted from the retrofit program. . . .

ALASKA DEPARTMENT OF ENVIRONMENTAL CONSERVATION v. EPA
540 U.S. 461 (2004)

JUSTICE GINSBURG delivered the opinion of the Court.

[The issue in this case was whether EPA could block construction of a new major pollutant-emitting facility to which the Alaska Department of Environmental

Conservation (ADEC) had issued a PSD permit on the ground that ADEC's best available control technology (BACT) determination was unreasonable in light of §169(3).

Under §165(a)(1) of the CAA, no "major emitting facility" may be constructed or modified unless a permit prescribing emission limitations has been issued for the facility. Alaska's SIP imposed an analogous requirement, and in particular, it required a PSD permit for a modification that increased nitrogen oxide (NO_x) emissions by more than 40 tons per year. Among other things, §165(a)(4) bars issuance of a PSD permit unless "the proposed facility is subject to the best available control technology" (BACT), as defined in §169(a)(3), for each pollutant subject to regulation that is emitted from the facility. Alaska regulations defined BACT in similar terms as "the emission limitation that represents the maximum reduction achievable for each regulated air contaminant, taking into account energy, environmental and economic impacts, and other costs."

Cominco operated a zinc mine, the Red Dog Mine, in northwest Alaska. The mine was the region's largest private employer and it supplied a quarter of the area's wage base. In 1988, ADEC issued a PSD permit to Cominco to operate the mine, which qualified as a "major emitting facility" under the CAA and Alaska's SIP. In 1996, Cominco initiated a project that would expand zinc production by 40 percent and increase NO_x emissions by more than 40 tons per year. It applied to ADEC for a PSD permit to allow increased electricity generation by one of its standby generators, MG-5. On March 3, 1999, ADEC proposed to define BACT for MG-5 as an emission control technology known as selective catalytic reduction (SCR),[5] which reduces NO_x emissions by 90 percent. Cominco responded by proposing as BACT an alternative control technology—Low NO_x[6]—that achieves a 30 percent reduction in NO_x pollutants.

ADEC staff initially concluded that SCR was BACT for MG-5. It found that SCR "is the most stringent" technology and that it was technically and economically feasible. It also pointed out that "SCR has been installed on similar diesel-fired engines throughout the world." Despite the staff's conclusion that SCR was "technologically, environmentally, and economically feasible" for Cominco, ADEC endorsed the use of Low NO_x in a draft PSD permit. EPA objected to ADEC's failure to designate SCR as BACT. In response, ADEC issued a second draft permit on September 1, 1999, again finding Low NO_x to be BACT. Contradicting the staff's previous conclusion that SCR was "technically and economically feasible," ADEC found that SCR imposed "a disproportionate cost" on the mine. According to ADEC, requiring SCR for a rural Alaska utility would lead to a 20 percent price increase, and, in comparison with other BACT technologies, SCR came at a "significantly higher" cost. ADEC's technical analysis contained no economic basis for a comparison between the mine and a rural utility.

EPA protested again, stating in a letter to ADEC that "Cominco has not adequately demonstrated any site-specific factors to support their claim that the installation of [SCR] is economically infeasible" at the mine, and that ADEC's refusal to

---

5. SCR requires injections of "ammonia or urea into the exhaust before the exhaust enters a catalyst bed made with vanadium, titanium, or platinum. The reduction reaction occurs when the flue gas passes over the catalyst bed where the NO_x and ammonia combine to become nitrogen, oxygen, and water. . . ."

6. In Low NO_x, changes are made to a generator to improve fuel atomization and modify the combustion space to enhance the mixing of air and fuel.

designate SCR as BACT on cost-effectiveness grounds was erroneous. EPA suggested that ADEC analyze whether requiring SCR would have adverse economic impacts on Cominco. Cominco declined to submit financial data to ADEC, stating that such an inquiry was unnecessary and expressing "concerns related to confidentiality." Cominco asserted that its debt was high despite continuing profits and invoked the need for "[i]ndustrial development in rural Alaska."

On December 10, 1999, ADEC issued the final permit, approving Low NO_x as BACT. ADEC failed to include the economic analysis EPA had suggested, conceding that it had made "no judgment . . . as to the impact of . . . [SCR's] cost on the operation, profitability, and competitiveness of the Red Dog Mine." ADEC relied on SCR's adverse effect on the mine's "impact on the economic diversity" of the region and on the venture's "world competitiveness." ADEC did not explain how it could assess adverse effects on the region's economy or the mine's "world competitiveness" without financial information showing SCR's impact on the operation of the mine.

EPA issued two orders to ADEC under §§113(a)(5) and 167. The first prohibited ADEC from issuing a PSD permit to Cominco "unless ADEC satisfactorily documents why SCR is not BACT." The second prohibited Cominco from commencing construction or modification at the mine. ADEC and Cominco sought review of EPA's orders in the Ninth Circuit, which held that §§113(a)(5) and 167 authorized EPA to issue the orders and that it had properly exercised its discretion in doing so. It stated that EPA had "authority to determine the reasonableness or adequacy of the state's justification for its decision." EPA did not abuse its discretion because (1) Cominco failed to "demonstrat[e] that SCR was economically infeasible" and (2) "ADEC failed to provide a reasoned justification for its elimination of SCR as a control option."]

III

Centrally at issue in this case is the question whether EPA's oversight role, described by Congress in CAA §§113(a)(5) and 167, extends to ensuring that a state permitting authority's BACT determination is reasonable in light of the statutory guides. . . . In notably capacious terms, Congress armed EPA with authority to issue orders stopping construction when "a State is not acting in compliance with any [CAA] requirement or prohibition . . . relating to the construction of new sources or the modification of existing sources," §7413(a)(5), or when "construction or modification of a major emitting facility . . . does not conform to the requirements of [the PSD program]," §7477. . . .

All parties agree that one of the "many requirements in the PSD provisions that the EPA may enforce" is "that a [PSD] permit contain a BACT limitation." It is therefore undisputed that the Agency may issue an order to stop a facility's construction if a PSD permit contains no BACT designation.

EPA reads the Act's definition of BACT, together with CAA's explicit listing of BACT as a "[p]reconstruction requiremen[t]," to mandate not simply a BACT designation, but a determination of BACT faithful to the statute's definition. In keeping with the broad oversight role §§113(a)(5) and 167 vest in EPA, the Agency maintains, it may review permits to ensure that a State's BACT determination is reasonably moored to the Act's provisions. We hold . . . that the Agency has rationally construed the Act's text and that EPA's construction warrants our respect and approbation.

BACT's statutory definition requires selection of an emission control technology that results in the "maximum" reduction of a pollutant "achievable for [a] facility" in view of "energy, environmental, and economic impacts, and other costs." 42 U.S.C. §7479(3). This instruction, EPA submits, cabins state permitting authorities' discretion by granting only "authority to make *reasonable* BACT determinations," i.e., decisions made with fidelity to the Act's purpose "to insure that economic growth will occur in a manner consistent with the preservation of existing clean air resources," 42 U.S.C. §7470(3). Noting that state permitting authorities' statutory discretion is constrained by CAA's strong, normative terms "maximum" and "achievable," §7479(3), EPA reads §§113(a)(5) and 167 to empower the federal Agency to check a state agency's unreasonably lax BACT designation.

EPA stresses Congress' reason for enacting the PSD program—to prevent significant deterioration of air quality in clean-air areas within a State and in neighboring States. §§7470(3), (4). That aim, EPA urges, is unlikely to be realized absent an EPA surveillance role that extends to BACT determinations. The Agency notes in this regard a House Report observation:

> Without national guidelines for the prevention of significant deterioration a State deciding to protect its clean air resources will face a double threat. The prospect is very real that such a State would lose existing industrial plants to more permissive States. But additionally the State will likely become the target of "economic-environmental blackmail" from new industrial plants that will play one State off against another with threats to locate in whichever State adopts the most permissive pollution controls. [H.R. Rep. No. 95-294, p. 134 (1977).]

. . . Federal agency surveillance of a State's BACT designation is needed, EPA asserts, to restrain the interjurisdictional pressures to which Congress was alert. . . .

ADEC argues that the statutory definition of BACT, §7479(3), unambiguously assigns to "the permitting authority" alone determination of the control technology qualifying as "best available." Because the Act places responsibility for determining BACT with "the permitting authority," ADEC urges, CAA excludes federal Agency surveillance reaching the substance of the BACT decision. EPA's enforcement role, ADEC maintains, is restricted to the requirement "that the permit contain a BACT limitation."

Understandably, Congress entrusted state permitting authorities with initial responsibility to make BACT determinations "case-by-case." §7479(3). A state agency, no doubt, is best positioned to adjust for local differences in raw materials or plant configurations, differences that might make a technology "unavailable" in a particular area. But the fact that the relevant statutory guides—"maximum" pollution reduction, considerations of energy, environmental, and economic impacts—may not yield a "single, objectively 'correct' BACT determination," surely does not signify that there can be no unreasonable determinations. Nor does Congress' sensitivity to site-specific factors necessarily imply a design to preclude in this context meaningful EPA oversight under §§113(a)(5) and 167. EPA claims no prerogative to designate the correct BACT; the Agency asserts only the authority to guard against unreasonable designations.

Under ADEC's interpretation, EPA properly inquires whether a BACT determination appears in a PSD permit, but not whether that BACT determination "was made on reasonable grounds properly supported on the record." Congress, however, vested EPA with explicit and sweeping authority to enforce CAA "requirements" relating to the construction and modification of sources under the PSD program, including BACT. We fail to see why Congress, having expressly endorsed an expansive surveillance role for EPA in two independent CAA provisions, would then implicitly preclude the Agency from verifying substantive compliance with the BACT provisions and, instead, limit EPA's superintendence to the insubstantial question whether the state permitting authority had uttered the key words "BACT." . . . [7]

Even if the Act imposes a requirement of reasoned justification for a BACT determination, ADEC ultimately argues, such a requirement may be enforced only through state administrative and judicial processes. . . .

It would be unusual, to say the least, for Congress to remit a federal agency enforcing federal law solely to state court. We decline to read such an uncommon regime into the Act's silence. EPA, the expert federal agency charged with enforcing the Act, has interpreted the BACT provisions and its own §§113(a)(5) and 167 enforcement powers not to require recourse to state processes before stopping a facility's construction. That rational interpretation, we agree, is surely permissible. . . .

In sum, EPA interprets the Act to allow substantive federal Agency surveillance of state permitting authorities' BACT determinations subject to federal court review. We credit EPA's longstanding construction of the Act and confirm EPA's authority, pursuant to §§113(a)(5) and 167, to rule on the reasonableness of BACT decisions by state permitting authorities.

IV . . .

We turn finally, and more particularly, to the reasons why we conclude that EPA properly exercised its statutory authority in this case. . . .

We do not see how ADEC, having acknowledged that no determination "[could] be made as to the impact of [SCR's] cost on the operation . . . and competitiveness of the [mine]," could simultaneously proffer threats to the mine's operation or competitiveness as reasons for declaring SCR economically infeasible. ADEC, indeed, forthrightly explained why it was disarmed from reaching any judgment on whether, or to what extent, implementation of SCR would adversely affect the mine's operation or profitability: Cominco had declined to provide the relevant financial data, disputing the need for such information and citing "confidentiality" concerns. No record evidence suggests that the mine, were it to use SCR for its new generator, would be obliged to cut personnel, or raise zinc prices. Absent evidence of that order, ADEC lacked cause for selecting Low NO_x as BACT based on the more stringent control's impact on the mine's operation or competitiveness.

[The Court found that ADEC provided no other valid justification for its choice of Low NO_x. ADEC itself had previously found that SCR's control costs per ton were "well within what ADEC and EPA considers economically feasible."]

7. According to the Agency, "[i]t has proven to be relatively rare that a state agency has put EPA in the position of having to exercise [its] authority," noting that only two other reported judicial decisions concern EPA orders occasioned by States' faulty BACT determinations [Allsteel, Inc. v. EPA, 25 F.3d 312 (CA6 1994); Solar Turbines Inc. v. Seif, 879 F.2d 1073 (3d Cir. 1989)]. EPA's restrained and moderate use of its authority hardly supports the dissent's speculation that the federal Agency will "displac[e]" or "degrad[e]" state agencies or relegate them to the performance of "ministerial" functions. Nor has EPA ever asserted authority to override a state-court judgment. . . .

EPA appropriately rejected ADEC's comparison between the mine and a rural utility because there was no evidence to suggest that the economic impact of the cost of SCR on a large and profitable zinc producer "would be anything like its impact on a rural, non-profit utility that must pass costs on to a small base of individual consumers." ADEC's readiness to support Cominco's project for increasing mine production and Cominco's "contributions to the region" did not satisfy ADEC's own standards of a "source-specific . . . economic impac[t]" that demonstrated SCR to be inappropriate as BACT. In short,] . . . EPA validly issued stop orders because ADEC's BACT designation simply did not qualify as reasonable in light of the statutory guides. . . .

Affirmed.

JUSTICE KENNEDY, with whom THE CHIEF JUSTICE, JUSTICE SCALIA, and JUSTICE THOMAS join, dissenting.

The majority, in my respectful view, rests its holding on mistaken premises, for its reasoning conflicts with the express language of the [CAA], with sound rules of administrative law, and with principles that preserve the integrity of States in our federal system. . . . [EPA] sought to overturn the State's decision, not by the process of judicial review, but by administrative fiat. The Court errs, in my judgment, by failing to hold that EPA, based on nothing more than its substantive disagreement with the State's discretionary judgment, exceeded its powers in setting aside Alaska's BACT determination. . . .

The majority holds that, under the CAA, state agencies are vested with "initial responsibility for identifying BACT in line with the Act's definition of that term" and that EPA has a "broad oversight role" to ensure that a State's BACT determination is "reasonably moored to the Act's provisions." The statute, however, contemplates no such arrangement. It directs the "permitting authority"—here, the Alaska Department of Environmental Conservation (ADEC)—to "determine" what constitutes BACT. To "determine" is not simply to make an initial recommendation that can later be overturned. It is "[t]o decide or settle . . . conclusively and authoritatively." American Heritage Dictionary 495 (4th ed. 2000). . . .

To be sure, §§113(a) and 167 authorize EPA to enforce requirements of the Act. These provisions, however, do not limit the States' latitude and responsibility to balance all the statutory factors in making their discretionary judgments. If a State has complied with the Act's requirements, §§113(a)(5) and 167 are not implicated and can supply no separate basis for EPA to exercise a supervisory role over a State's discretionary decision. . . . When the statute is read as a whole, it is clear that the CAA commits BACT determinations to the discretion of the relevant permitting authorities. Unless an objecting party, including EPA, prevails on judicial review, the determinations are conclusive. . . .

EPA insists it needs oversight authority to prevent a "race to the bottom," where jurisdictions compete with each other to lower environmental standards to attract new industries and keep existing businesses within their borders. Whatever the merits of these arguments as a general matter, EPA's distrust of state agencies is inconsistent with the Act's clear mandate that States bear the primary role in controlling pollution and, here, the exclusive role in making BACT determinations. In "cho[osing] not to dictate a Federal response to balancing sometimes conflicting goals" at the expense of "[m]aximum flexibility and State discretion," H.R. Rep. No. 95-294, p. 146 (1977), Congress made the overriding judgment that States are more responsive to local conditions and can strike the right balance between preserving environmental quality and advancing competing objectives. By assigning certain functions to the States, Congress assumed they would have a stake in implementing the environmental objectives of the Act. . . .

The presumption that state agencies are not to be trusted to do their part is unwarranted in another respect: EPA itself said so. As EPA concedes, States, by and large, take their statutory responsibility seriously, and EPA sees no reason to intervene in the vast majority of cases. In light of this concession, EPA and amici not only fail to overcome the established presumption that States act in good faith, but also admit that their fears about a race to the bottom bear little relation to the real-world experience under the statute. . . .

[The dissent pointed out that the CAA contains "safeguards to correct arbitrary and capricious BACT decisions when they do occur." EPA may not approve a State's PSD permit program unless the program provides an opportunity for state judicial review. Before issuing an individual permit, the state must allow all "interested persons," including EPA, to submit comments, including comments on the state's BACT determination. §165(a)(2). The state must inform EPA of "every action" taken in the course of the permit approval process, §175(d), and any person who participated in the comment process, including EPA, can pursue an administrative appeal and judicial review in state court of the state's decision. According to the dissent, the availability of that judicial review negated the argument that, "absent EPA's oversight, there is a legal vacuum where BACT decisions are not subject to review." Moreover, "EPA followed none of the normal procedures here."]

There is a further, and serious, flaw in the Court's ruling. Suppose, before EPA issued its orders setting aside the State's BACT determination, an Alaska state court had reviewed the matter and found no error of law or abuse of discretion in ADEC's determination. The majority's interpretation of the statute would allow EPA to intervene at this point for the first time, announce that ADEC's determination is unreasoned under the CAA, and issue its own orders nullifying the state court's ruling. This reworking of the balance between State and Federal Governments, not to mention the reallocation of authority between the Executive and Judicial Branches, shows the implausibility of the majority's reasoning. . . .

. . . Under the majority's holding, decisions by state courts would be subject to being overturned, not just by any agency, but by an agency established by a different sovereign. We should be reluctant to interpret a congressional statute to deny to States the judicial independence guaranteed by their own constitutions. . . . The Federal Government is free, within its vast legislative authority, to impose federal standards. For States to have a role, however, their own governing processes must be respected. New York v. United States, 505 U.S. 144 (1992). . . .

The broader implication of today's decision is more unfortunate still. The CAA is not the only statute that relies on a close and equal partnership between federal and state authorities to accomplish congressional objectives. Under the majority's reasoning, these other statutes, too, could be said to confer on federal agencies ultimate decisionmaking authority, relegating States to the role of mere provinces or political corporations, instead of coequal sovereigns entitled to the same dignity and respect. If cooperative federalism is to achieve Congress' goal of allowing state governments to be accountable to the democratic process in implementing environmental policies, federal agencies cannot consign States to the ministerial tasks of information gathering and making initial recommendations, while reserving to themselves the authority to make final judgments under the guise of surveillance and oversight. . . .

NOTES AND QUESTIONS

1. What was the statutory basis for EPA's issuance of the two orders to ADEC and Cominco? What "requirement" of the CAA did ADEC and Cominco violate, according to EPA? What is the scope of EPA's review of state PSD permitting decisions, according to EPA and ADEC? Why did the Court approve of EPA's interpretation? Why did the dissent adopt ADEC's view? Does the dissenting opinion present an accurate depiction of the allocation of decisionmaking authority between EPA and the states that Congress intended? Is there really an "equal partnership between federal and state authorities"? According to the dissenters, does the majority opinion present Tenth Amendment problems?

2. The NRC excerpt that precedes the *ADEC* case stated that BACT "is at least as stringent as an applicable NSPS, but in general is not as stringent as the LAER requirement to which the new source would be subject in a nonattainment area." New or modified non-major stationary sources in PSD areas are not subject to NSR (or BACT), but may be subject to NSPS under §111.

NOTES AND QUESTIONS ON THE PSD NSR PERMIT PROGRAM

The PSD permit program applies to any "major emitting facility on which construction is commenced after August 7, 1977 [the effective date of the 1977 amendments] in any area to which this part applies." §165(a)(1). This deceptively simple phrase gives rise to a host of questions concerning the scope of the PSD permit program. The first part of the notes and questions that follow fleshes out some of these threshold questions. If the permit program applies, a permit applicant must satisfy the substantive requirements of §165(a) in order to qualify for a permit. The second part below addresses exactly what those requirements are.

The Scope of the PSD Permit Program

1. *"Major" Facilities and "Potential to Emit."* What is a "major emitting facility"? See §169(1). A facility may escape being classified as "major" "if either of two different forces limits its rate of emission of air pollutants to below a specified amount: first, physical or mechanical limits constraining its rate of emission; and second, legal limits, in the form of legal restrictions on its rate of emission or hours of operation. 40 C.F.R. §51.166(b)(4)." United States v. Marine Shale Processors, 81 F.3d 1329, 1352 (5th Cir. 1996).

Suppose that a proposed new facility would engage in two different kinds of industrial activities, one of which (chemical processing) is among the kinds of activities subject to the 100-ton-per-year threshold for a "major emitting facility" in §169(1), and the other of which (waste processing) is subject to the default 250-ton-per-year threshold. If the facility emits more than 100 tons but less than 250 tons per year of air pollutants, is it a major emitting facility subject to the PSD permit program? See LaFleur v. Whitman, 300 F.3d 256 (2d Cir. 2002).

Is a facility's "potential to emit" assessed on the basis of uncontrolled or controlled emission levels? According to the NRC excerpt, how did the *Alabama Power* case dispose of this issue? See 636 F.2d at 352-355; United States v. Louisiana-Pacific Corp., 682 F. Supp. 1122, 1141 (D. Colo. 1987) (EPA may not base "potential to emit" on operation not contemplated by design of plant).

Suppose an electric utility decides to replace an old, inefficient peak load generator that operates only a few days each year with a modern generator. It could operate the new generator every day but almost certainly will not. Only if the generator were operated every day would emissions of SO_2 exceed 100 tons annually. The utility is hesitant to promise EPA that it will never increase actual emissions above the levels emitted from the existing generator because of uncertainties about the precise nature of future electricity demand. Must the utility apply for a PSD permit? Is it fair for EPA to compare actual emissions from existing operations with potential emissions from proposed replacement operations in determining the applicability of the PSD permit program? See Puerto Rican Cement Co. v. EPA, 889 F.2d 292 (1st Cir. 1989).

Suppose that a proposed plant will emit less than 100 tons per year of particulates from its smokestack but will release more than that amount in fugitive emissions. Fugitive emissions are derived primarily from traffic on unpaved roads and from wind erosion. They account for most of the air pollution generated at certain kinds of industrial operations. Will the plant have to apply for a PSD permit? In 1984, EPA issued a list of 27 categories of industrial stationary sources for which fugitive emissions must be included in determining whether a source is major for purposes of the PSD permit program. Surface coal mining was excluded from the list because, according to EPA, the costs of regulation would exceed the benefits. NRDC challenged that determination on the grounds that cost-benefit analysis is not the correct standard. In NRDC v. EPA, 937 F.2d 641 (D.C. Cir. 1991), the court concluded that §302(j) vests sufficiently broad discretion in EPA that it may decide whether to include fugitive emissions on cost-benefit grounds. Why did §302(j) apply instead of §169(1)?

2. *The Definition of a "Modification" in the PSD Permit Program.* When is a proposed plant modification subject to PSD permit review? See §§165(a)(1), 169(2)(C). What level of emissions from a unit added to an existing plant will trigger PSD review? *Alabama Power* held that a modification that increases emissions to *any* extent (except for *de minimis* increases) requires PSD review, invalidating an EPA regulation limiting PSD review to the same 100- or 250-ton-per-year threshold Congress established in defining a "major emitting facility." 636 F.2d at 400. In Great Basin Mine Watch v. EPA, 401 F.3d 1094 (9th Cir. 2005), the court ruled that EPA did not act arbitrarily in refusing to aggregate the increases caused by three modifications to the same facility in a single year and in concluding that no permit was necessary because no single modification caused a 40-ton-per-year increase in emissions.

3. *Plant Location.* Suppose that a proposed major particulate-emitting facility will be located in a nonattainment area for particulates, but its emissions will adversely affect air quality in a nearby attainment area for particulates; may the facility be constructed without a PSD permit? As a result of *Alabama Power*, unless a facility is located in a PSD or unclassifiable area in the same state as the area in which it will degrade air quality, it need not apply for a PSD permit. If both the nonattainment and PSD areas are located in the same state, there may be other mechanisms in the statute

by which adverse impacts on the air quality in the PSD area can be avoided. See, e.g., §161. The problem is more serious, however, if the two areas are located in different states. *Alabama Power* blocks reaching over a state boundary to apply the PSD requirements, no matter how severely the proposed facility impairs air quality in a neighboring state. The problem is not confined to short distances. Even distant new sources 200 to 300 miles away could be linked to local loss of air quality.

Because both PSD and nonattainment requirements apply on the basis of individual pollutants, a major new plant may want to locate in an area that is nonattainment for one pollutant but is PSD for others. Even a dense urban area can be a Class II PSD area, despite serious nonattainment problems, if ambient levels of a single criteria pollutant fall under the NAAQS. As a result, a plant seeking to locate in an industrialized zone often must undergo nonattainment review for ozone and PSD review for pollutants such as CO and NO_x.

The Substantive Requirements of the PSD Permit Program

4. *The Baselines and Increment Consumption.* Section 165(a)(3) requires a PSD permit applicant to demonstrate that emissions from the proposed major emitting facility will neither cause nor contribute to violations of maximum allowable increases, maximum allowable concentrations, the NAAQS, or any other applicable emission standard. Congress established the maximum allowable increases, or PSD increments, for SO_2 and particulates in §163(b). The PSD increments for Class I areas are the smallest and those for Class III areas are the largest.

The maximum allowable concentrations are determined by adding the maximum allowable increases to the baseline concentration of either SO_2 or particulates. See §163(b)(4). How is the baseline concentration calculated? See §169(4). What purpose is served by allowing baseline determinations to be postponed until the time of the first PSD permit application? The EPA could see none and tried to fix the baseline determination date at August 7, 1977, the date of enactment of the 1977 amendments. The *Alabama Power* court disagreed with EPA's reading of the statute and mandated the "first applicant" policy. 636 F.2d at 374-376. Is it possible that the PSD increment may be consumed before the first PSD permit application for a particular PSD area is even filed? What incentives does this situation create for those considering the construction of a major emitting facility in a PSD area? EPA and most states allocate the available PSD increments on a first-come, first-served basis.

5. *Monitoring, Modeling, and the Rationality of the PSD Baseline Increment Analysis.* To determine the projected impact of a proposed major emitting facility, it is necessary to gauge the air quality in the affected PSD area before construction is permitted to begin. Section 165(a)(2), (e) requires an analysis that includes at least one year of preconstruction air quality monitoring to determine whether emissions from the proposed facility will result in violations of the maximum allowable increases or maximum allowable concentrations.

The administration of the PSD increment system is anything but straightforward.* As the NRC excerpt explains, under the 1977 amendments the

* See generally Stensvaag, Preventing Significant Deterioration under the Clean Air Act: Baselines, Increments, and Ceilings—Part I, 35 Envtl. L. Rep. (ELI) 10807 (2005); Part II, 36 Envtl. L. Rep. (ELI) 10017 (2006).

baseline and the increments are computed from a mishmash of monitoring data and regulatory fiats about hypothetical and actual emissions that must be (or cannot be) counted. The result is that actual air quality in PSD areas may bear little resemblance to what the regulatory accounting system says it is.

EPA has attempted to overcome these problems through modeling. But modeling capability is far from perfect and tends to be least successful in situations where increment exceedance is likely. The courts nevertheless have been deferential to the efforts of EPA and the states to address the shortcomings of models. See Sur Contra La Contaminacion v. EPA, 202 F.3d 443 (1st Cir. 2000); *Alabama Power*, 636 F.2d at 381-388. PSD permit holders also may be required to conduct post-construction monitoring, presumably to correct errors in the predicted level of increment consumption and to help EPA refine its models. §165(a)(7). The court in *Alabama Power* held that EPA has the discretion not to require post-construction monitoring. 636 F.3d at 373.

6. *The BACT Determination.* Suppose that a proposed facility, to be located in a PSD area for particulates, will emit not only particulates, but also SO_2 and NO_x. To which of these pollutants will the BACT requirement at issue in the *ADEC* case apply? See §165(a)(4). What if the plant will emit heavy metals listed as hazardous air pollutants under §112 in amounts less than 10 tons per year; will those pollutants also be subject to BACT?

A source comes under nonattainment review only for the particular pollutants for which nonattainment violations exist and only if the proposed plant exceeds the size cutoff for each of those pollutants. But PSD review occurs for all pollutants subject to regulation under the CAA that will be emitted by a major facility in any amount, so long as one pollutant exceeds the 100/250-ton PSD trigger emissions level. According to *Alabama Power*, EPA must apply BACT to each pollutant regulated for any purpose under any provision of the CAA, 636 F.2d at 403, although the agency may exempt *de minimis* amounts.

The *ADEC* case provides some insights into how BACT is determined. Does §169(3) rule out switching fuel or reducing or interrupting operations to meet BACT? Compare NSPS under §111. Administration of the BACT requirement historically has been lenient, as in *ADEC*. Critics have charged that BACT determinations exacerbate a basic flaw of the CAA by putting the heaviest cleanup burden on the newest sources and that they yield inefficient controls by restricting emissions control options, leading to wide discrepancies between the marginal costs of control among sources.

NOTE ON THE APPLICATION OF PSD TO THE SET II POLLUTANTS

The Clean Air Act establishes PSD increments only for SO_2 and particulates. Section 166 of the statute required EPA to issue PSD regulations for the other criteria pollutants (referred to as the Set II pollutants) by 1979. Those regulations were to "provide specific numerical measures against which a permit application may be evaluated," as well as protect air quality values and "fulfill the goals" of §§101 and 160 of the Act. §166(c). The statute also requires that these regulations "provide specific measures at least as effective as the increments in [§163] to fulfill such goals and purposes." §166(d).

EPA issued PSD regulations for NO_x in 1988. It adopted the same three-tiered classification of PSD areas reflected in §§162 and 164. It also relied on the same

increment consumption mechanism that the statute established for the Set I pollutants, with calculation of the permissible increments based on the NAAQS. As a result,
EPA adopted PSD regulations only for nitrogen dioxide (NO_2), the only oxide of
nitrogen for which EPA had established a NAAQS. Finally, it set the increments at
the same percentage of the NO_2 NAAQS as that of the Set I increments relative to their
annual NAAQS.

In EDF v. EPA, 898 F.2d 183 (D.C. Cir. 1990), the Environmental Defense
Fund challenged the regulations. The court struck down the regulations, holding that
EPA did not provide a plausible explanation of the relationship between §166(c) and
(d). The problem with EPA's exclusive reliance on the NAAQS for NO_2 was that there
might be other NO_x pollutants with minimal effects on public health (the focus of the
primary NAAQS for NO_2) but with significant adverse effects on natural, recreational,
scenic, or historic values, all of which are to be protected under the PSD program. See
§160(2). The court remanded the regulations to EPA for further consideration of
whether its Set II increments promoted the goals and purposes referred to in §166(c).

In 2005, EPA finally responded to the court's remand. After 15 years of analysis,
the agency decided to retain the NO_2 increments reviewed in EDF. 70 Fed. Reg.
59,582 (2005). EPA amended the regulations, however, to afford states the option of
seeking approval of alternative approaches that do not rely on increments, as long as
those approaches satisfy the requirements of §166(c) and (d). 40 C.F.R. §51.166(c)(2).
EPA suggested implementation of the model cap-and-trade program under the Clean
Air Act Interstate Rule, discussed below, as a possibility.

3.   Control of Visibility Impairment

The Values at Stake. The spacious western sky is a striking natural and cultural
asset that has played an important role in mobilizing public support for the national
park system. The annual median visual range in the Rocky Mountain states exceeds
100 miles in most areas, as opposed to 9 to 25 miles in regions east of the Mississippi
River and south of the Great Lakes. National Park Service, Air Quality in the National
Parks 2-10, 2-12 (1988). Visibility has increased in some areas of the West, such as the
Grand Canyon, Las Vegas, and Phoenix, since 1970, apparently as a result of measures
required by the CAA. Grand Canyon Visibility Transport Commission, Options for
Improving Western Vistas (Draft Contractor's Report) (Nov. 4, 1995), at I-8, IV-6. On
the other hand, visibility has declined in some parts of the East, such as the Great
Smoky Mountains National Park, largely due to increased emissions of man-made fine
sulfur particulate matter. National Park Service, Air Pollution Issues: Great Smoky
Mountains National Park 2 (Oct. 1996).

Causes of Visibility Impairment. Particles and gases impair visibility by scattering
or absorbing light. The chief light-absorbing aerosol is soot, which often is the cause of
plume blight or general visibility reduction in urban areas. Light scattering depends
on particle size; the best scatterers are the smaller particles, which present more
surface area per unit of weight. The only gaseous pollutant that is a significant absorber
of light is NO_2, which by absorbing blue light produces a brownish discoloration in
smokestack plumes.

Types of Visibility Impairment. Pollution impairs visibility in three ways, each of
which presents a different regulatory challenge. The first—plume blight from a single
source, such as a coal-fired power plant—is the most obvious. In areas closest to a

plant, light scattering by fly ash and discoloration by NO_2 are the dominant processes. Further away, after colorless SO_2 has been transformed to sulfate particles, sulfates and NO_2 determine the visible character of the plume. The first astronauts reported that the plume from the Four Corners Power Plant in northeastern New Mexico, which stretched for over 1,000 miles, was the most striking human artifact visible from space.

At the opposite extreme, thoroughly diffused "older" pollutants may cause a second form of visibility-impairing pollution: large-scale regional haze. Sulfates are the chief culprit, although a myriad of other pollutants also contribute to haze. In the southwestern national parks, 90 percent of regional sulfate haze originates hundreds of miles away, chiefly at copper smelters in Arizona, New Mexico, Texas, and possibly the Los Angeles area. A third visibility-impairing phenomenon, intermediate between plumes and regional haze, consists of small pockets of haze that form in valleys or around other land forms, usually in layered bands of discoloration. Urban smog, eastern high-humidity haze, and pollution pockets generated by unique western geo-logical features (especially high terrain) are examples.

Visibility and the PSD Permit Program. The CAA protects visibility through a two-tier scheme. A state must deny a PSD permit to a major new emitting facility even though Class I increments are not violated if the facility is expected to have an "adverse impact" on "air quality-related values" (AQRVs). See §165(d)(2). Neither of these phrases is defined in the Act. Conversely, a source that would violate the increments may obtain a permit if it can show that AQRVs are not violated. Visibility is the principal air quality-related value that must be reviewed under §165 before a major new source can be sited near a Class I area. In Montana Envtl. Info. Ctr. v. Montana Dep't of Envtl. Quality, 112 P.3d 964 (Mont. 2005), the court held that the state agency had an independent responsibility to determine whether a proposed power plant would adversely affect visibility in Class I areas, and could not simply defer to the federal land manager's conclusion that it would not. The AQRV provision has had little effect. By one account, the Class I increments are a poor indicator of park damage because they assume that all damage comes from new sources of pollution rather than from the cumulative impact of new and existing sources. Oren, The Protection of Parklands from Air Pollution: A Look at Current Policy, 13 Harv. Envtl. L. Rev. 313 (1989).

Visibility Protection for Mandatory Class I PSD Areas. A separate visibility protection program not technically part of PSD is provided by §169A for mandatory Class I areas in which EPA designates visibility as an important value. All but two of the mandatory Class I areas are on the EPA list. See 40 C.F.R. §§81.401-81.437. Section 169A requires states to adopt long-term strategies for making "reasonable progress" toward a national goal of remedying and preventing impairment of visibility from air pollution in mandatory Class I areas. §169A(b)(2)(B). The affected states must revise their SIPs to identify existing major stationary sources whose emissions cause or contribute to visibility impairment. Each such source must install the "best available retrofit technology" (BART) if built after 1962. §169A(b)(2)(A).

Regulation of "Reasonably Attributable" Visibility Impairment. In 1980, EPA issued regulations under §169A to control visibility impairment reasonably attribut-able to a single existing stationary source or a small group of such sources. EPA deferred addressing regional haze because of the difficulty of identifying, measuring, and controlling that kind of visibility impairment. In Central Ariz. Water Conserva-tion Dist. v. EPA, 990 F.3d 1531 (9th Cir. 1993), the court approved a federal imple-mentation plan requiring a 90 percent reduction in SO_2 emissions at an Arizona power plant that, according to EPA, was contributing to visibility impairment at the Grand Canyon. The plan represented the first time that an existing source was forced to reduce its emissions as a result of the 1980 regulations. Cordan, Lost in the Haze? *Central Arizona* Fulfills Congress's Promise to Protect Visibility in the National Parks, 24 Envtl. L. 1371, 1372 (1994). The scrubbers that the utility installed to reduce visibility impairment resulted in reductions in SO_2 emissions, which provided the utility with surplus allowances under the acid deposition control program discussed in section I.2 below. In 1994, the utility agreed to trade 25,000 SO_2 allowances, worth about $3.75 million, to a utility in Syracuse, New York, in exchange for 1.75 million CO_2 allowances so that the Arizona utility could meet its voluntary commitment to the Department of Energy to limit its emissions of greenhouse gases. The New York utility donated the SO_2 allowances to nonprofit groups, which planned to retire them from the allowance system. The New York utility would receive a tax credit for the donation. See L.A. Times, Nov. 18, 1994, at 1; Passell, For Utilities, New Clean-Air Plan, N.Y. Times, Nov. 18, 1994, at C1.

Regulation of Regional Haze. In 1999, EPA issued regulations that required all states to submit regional haze SIP revisions. 64 Fed. Reg. 35,714 (1999). American Corn Growers Ass'n v. EPA, 291 F.3d 1 (D.C. Cir. 2002), upheld in part and vacated in part the 1999 regional haze regulations. The court held that EPA violated the statute by requiring the states to consider the degree of improvement in visibility anticipated to result from the use of BART on a group or areawide basis instead of a source-specific basis. It rejected industry's claim, however, that EPA exceeded its authority by adopting the achievement of "natural visibility" as the goal of the regional haze program. Finding the same flaw in a plan for reducing visibility impairment in the Grand Canyon region, the court in Center for Energy and Econ. Dev. v. EPA, 398 F.3d 653 (D.C. Cir. 2005), invalidated EPA's approval of the plan. The plan calculated the degree by which BART would improve visibility (so that it could establish milestones that were equivalent to that degree of improvement) by reference to all sources affecting an area, rather than by reference to individual plants. The court regarded this methodology as inconsistent with the definition of BART in §169A(g)(2).

EPA responded to *American Corn Growers* by issuing revised regional haze regulations. The regulations provide several approaches by which the states may determine which stationary sources cause or contribute to visibility impairment, and thus are subject to BART. In deciding on the appropriate type and level of control for reducing emissions for individual sources, the states may take into account the degree of improvement in visibility that may result from the use of BART on a source-by-source basis. 70 Fed. Reg. 39,104 (2005).

Transport Commissions. The 1990 amendments require EPA to report periodically to Congress on existing visibility problems and to address whether other provisions of the statute are likely to redress them. §169B. If EPA finds that current or projected interstate transport of air pollutants contributes significantly to visibility impairment in Class I PSD areas, it may establish a visibility transport commission to recommend measures for remedying adverse effects on visibility. These may include the creation of clean air corridors in which additional emissions restrictions would apply, the imposition of nonattainment area permit requirements on nonmajor sources in those areas, and the issuance of regional haze regulations. §169B(d)(2). EPA need not abide by a commission's recommendations, however. Congress ordered EPA to establish a commission for the region affecting visibility in the Grand Canyon. §169B(f).

H. MOTOR VEHICLE EMISSION STANDARDS

[The materials in this section are located at the casebook's website.]

I. CONTROL OF OTHER POLLUTANTS

1. *Hazardous Air Pollutants*

[The materials in this section are located at the casebook's website.]

2. *Interstate Pollution and Acid Deposition*

a. The Difficulty of Controlling Interstate Pollution

The Localized Nature of the 1970 Act. The 1970 CAA reflected the assumption that local, easily identifiable sources cause most air pollution problems and that an adequate SIP will enable a state to achieve the NAAQS within its own borders. But it soon became apparent that air pollution does not respect political boundaries. Emissions from out-of-state sources may prevent a downwind state from designing a SIP that achieves the NAAQS through controls on its own sources at a reasonable cost. Interstate air pollution problems occur, for example, where state boundaries pass through or near urban areas, creating intergovernmental conflicts over the responsibility for pollution abatement.

The 1970 Petitions Process in Theory. Only two sections of the pre-1990 CAA directly addressed interstate air pollution. Section 110(a)(2)(E) (recodified as amended at §110(a)(2)(D))* required that every SIP contain adequate provisions

> (i) prohibiting any stationary source within the State from emitting any air pollutant in amounts which will (I) prevent attainment or maintenance by any other State of such national primary or secondary ambient air quality standard, or (II) interfere with measures required to be included in the applicable implementation plan for any other State under [the PSD and visibility protection provisions], and (ii) insuring compliance with the requirements of §126. . . .

Section 126(a) mandated that every SIP require that each major proposed new or modified source subject to the PSD provisions of the Act or "which may significantly contribute to levels of air pollution in excess of the [NAAQS] in an air quality control region outside the State in which such source intends to locate" notify states whose air quality might be affected by the source at least 60 days before commencement of construction. Under §126(b), any state had the right to petition

---

*The cross-reference in §126(b) should be to §110(a)(2)(D)(i), not §110(a)(2)(D)(ii). Congress inadvertently substituted (ii) for (i) in the course of a routine renumbering process occasioned by the adoption of the 1990 amendments. See Appalachian Power Co. v. EPA, 249 F.3d 1032, 1043 (D.C. Cir. 2001).

EPA for a finding that "any major source emits or would emit any air pollutant in violation of the prohibition of §110(a)(2)(E)(i)." EPA was required to rule on the petition within 60 days. If EPA issued the requested finding, it would be a violation of the applicable SIP of the state in which the major source was located for it to be constructed or to operate in violation of the prohibition of §110(a)(2)(E)(i). In other words, notwithstanding the issuance of a construction and operating permit by the state in which the source was located, it was a violation of that very state's SIP to construct or operate a major source in the face of EPA's finding that the source was causing or would cause a violation of the statute's interstate pollution prohibitions. Even if the source state did not enforce that SIP violation, EPA or a private citizen could.

The 1970 Petitions Process in Practice. The petitions process created by the 1970 statute was an abject failure as a means of mitigating interstate pollution.

> EPA failed to act against any sources of interstate pollution under either of the two relevant provisions [§110(a)(2)(E) or §126]. The most formidable obstacle for affected states seeking the agency's assistance against out-of-state air pollution was . . . the need to prove that source state polluters caused air quality violations in an affected state. EPA interpreted the statute to require the affected state petitioner to prove that source state pollution was "significantly contributing" to air quality standard violations in the petitioning state, and the courts deferred to that interpretation. In addition, the statute required affected states to trace the violation to a specific source. EPA exacerbated these difficulties when it refused to accept the mathematical and meteorological models that affected states employed for ranges longer than fifty kilometers, despite the fact that long-range transport of pollution is the basis for a large share of interstate pollution. [Glicksman, Watching the River Flow: The Prospects for Improved Interstate Water Pollution Control, 43 Wash. U. J. Urb. & Contemp. L. 119, 167-168 (1993).]

The courts also read the "significant contribution" test that appeared in §110(a)(2)(E) as applying to §126(a). See, e.g., Air Pollution Control Dist. of Jefferson County v. EPA, 739 F.2d 1071 (6th Cir. 1984). Several downwind states petitioned unsuccessfully to halt interstate pollution. See, e.g., New York v. EPA, 852 F.2d 574 (D.C. Cir. 1988); Connecticut v. EPA, 696 F.2d 147 (2d Cir. 1982).

Assume that State A believes that SO_2 emissions from an aggregate of several sources in upwind State B are preventing it from attaining the SO_2 NAAQS. Under the 1970 version of the statute, as interpreted by EPA and the courts, could State A successfully bring a §126 petition against State B? Did the 1990 amendments (reflected in the current versions of §§110(a)(2)(D) and 126) alleviate State A's burden of proof? See Glicksman, *supra*, at 168-169.

NAAQS Violations and Growth Issues. The interstate pollution sections apply only to NAAQS attainment and maintenance. What does this do to local "margins of growth," such as those created under §173(a)(1)(B)? The leading case is *Jefferson County, supra.* The Jefferson County District, which includes Louisville, Kentucky, petitioned EPA under §126. It argued that SO_2 emission limits approved by EPA for a power plant across the Ohio River in Indiana prevented the attainment and maintenance of the SO_2 NAAQS, which had not yet been attained in the county. The district also claimed that the power plant's emission limits would interfere with the county's efforts to prevent significant deterioration of air quality once the SO_2 NAAQS were attained. These limits were several times higher than the emission limits approved for a power plant that was the major producer of SO_2 in Jefferson County. The court upheld EPA's decision to reject the §126 petition, concluding that the county's margin of growth established a local air quality standard more stringent than was demanded by the CAA. EPA argued that the interstate pollution provisions only prohibited attainment or maintenance of national air quality standards. The court found that national uniformity in the interpretation of the Act was especially important in applying the interstate pollution provisions.

Is the court's result subject to attack on equity grounds? See Silverstein, Interstate Air Pollution: Unresolved Issues, 3 Harv. Envtl. L. Rev. 291, 292 (1979) (contending that interstate equity requires a fair allocation of the burden of reducing interstate pollution, based on factors such as whether the upwind state's SIP contains stringent or lax emission standards, whether emission standards are being violated in that state, and the extent to which sources in the downwind state contribute to the nonattainment problem).

Interstate Pollution and the PSD Provisions. Assume downwind State A has attained the NAAQS for SO_2 and so is subject to the PSD program for that pollutant. Now assume that no applications for new or modified sources that emit SO_2 have been filed in State A. May upwind State B approve a SIP that will cause increased emissions of SO_2 sufficient to negate State A's PSD status? Recall that a duty to conduct a PSD analysis is not triggered until an application is filed. Connecticut v. EPA, 656 F.2d 902 (2d Cir. 1981), did not decide this issue, but noted that a downwind state could protect its PSD status through the interstate pollution sections if it adopted voluntary measures to reinforce its PSD designation. But see New York v. EPA, 716 F.2d 440 (7th Cir. 1983). Does *Jefferson County, supra,* bear on this problem?

Interstate Transport Regions. In addition to the revisions it adopted to §§110(a)(2)(D) and 126, Congress in 1990 authorized the creation of interstate transport regions to address transboundary air pollution. Under what circumstances may EPA establish a transport commission to deal with interstate pollution? What are the powers of such a commission? See §176A. Congress itself established a transport region for ozone that encompasses 11 states in the Northeast and the District of Columbia. §184. What obligations does the statute impose on states within that region? How does the authority of the ozone transport commission compare with the powers of a commission established under §176A? Given EPA's historic reluctance to grant petitions filed under §126, are the provisions of the 1990 amendments concerning transport regions likely to create an effective mechanism for dealing with interstate pollution?

The CAA and Control of Interstate Externalities. Professor Revesz attributes the CAA's failures to control interstate pollution to a variety of factors. Revesz, Federalism and Interstate Environmental Externalities, 144 U. Pa. L. Rev. 2341 (1996). The technology-based provisions, such as the NSPS, fail to regulate the number or location of sources within a particular state. The NAAQS do not bar a state meeting those standards from exporting pollution to downwind states from stationary sources located near the border. The acid rain provisions discussed below are limited in scope: they deal with only two pollutants and, for the most part, one kind of facility (electric utilities). The effectiveness of the provisions designed to deal with interstate pollution, §§110(a)(2)(D) and 126, has been impaired by EPA's refusal to acknowledge predictions of the effects of emissions beyond a range of 50 kilometers, its refusal to establish NAAQS for sulfates, and its refusal to recognize the cumulative impacts of upwind sources. Revesz urges the adoption of tougher controls on activities generating interstate externalities through a marketable permit system allowing interstate coordination that would be difficult to accomplish through non-market-based federal regulation.*

MICHIGAN v. EPA
213 F.3d 663 (D.C. Cir. 2000)

Before: WILLIAMS, SENTELLE, and ROGERS, Circuit Judges.

Opinion PER CURIAM.**

Dissenting opinion filed by Circuit Judge SENTELLE . . .

[The CAA authorizes EPA to call for SIP revisions if it finds that a SIP is inadequate to attain or maintain the NAAQS, to meet requirements imposed by pollutant transport commissions, or "to otherwise comply with any requirement of this chapter." §110(k)(5). In October 1998, EPA issued a final rule, based on violations of §110(a)(2)(D)(i)(I), mandating that 22 states and the District of Columbia revise their SIPs to mitigate the interstate transport of ozone. 63 Fed. Reg. 57,356 (1998). EPA required that each state reduce NO_x—an ozone precursor—by the amount accomplishable by "highly cost-effective controls," which the agency defined as those capable of removing NO_x at a cost of $2,000 or less per ton.]

I.   General Claims . . .

C.   DETERMINING "SIGNIFICANT" CONTRIBUTION

Section 110(a)(2)(D)(i)(I) applies only to states that "contribute significantly" to nonattainment in a downwind state. Petitioners . . . challeng[e] EPA's determination of "significance." . . .

2.   CONSIDERATION OF COSTS

Petitioners claim §110(a)(2)(D)(i)(I) does not permit EPA to take into consideration the cost of reducing ozone. . . .

Before reviewing the petitioners' attacks we must first describe how EPA went about the business at hand. It first determined that 23 jurisdictions are "significant" contributors to downwind nonattainment. In making this listing EPA drew lines based on the magnitude, frequency, and relative amount of each state's ozone contribution to a nonattainment area. For example, in one calculation it looked at the number of NO_x parts per billion ("ppb") that a candidate state's emissions made to exceedances in specific downwind locations (examined as a proportion of those exceedances). . . . Although EPA looked at other measures, e.g., the percentage contribution of a state's emissions to total concentrations in a specified area, no one quarrels either with its use of multiple measures, or with the way it drew the line at this stage.

Although the dividing line was a very low threshold of contribution, in the end EPA's rule called for termination of only a subset of each state's contribution. EPA

---

*On the ineffectiveness of transboundary pollution control regimes generally, see Merrill, Golden Rules for Transboundary Pollution, 46 Duke L.J. 931 (1997).

**Judge Williams wrote Parts I.B-C and II.B; Judge Sentelle wrote Parts I.A, II.A, II.C, and III.A. . . .

decided that the 23 "significant contributors" need only reduce their ozone by the amount achievable with "highly cost-effective controls." Thus, once a state had been nominally marked a "significant contributor," it could satisfy the statute, i.e., reduce its contribution to a point where it would not be "significant" within the meaning of §110(a)(2)(D)(i)(I), by cutting back the amount that could be eliminated with "highly cost-effective controls." EPA's design was to have a lot of states make what it considered modest NO_x reductions, uniformly limited to ones that could be achieved (in EPA's estimate) for less than $2000 a ton. As a result, naturally, the ultimate line of "significance," whether measured in volume of NO_x emitted or arriving in nonattainment areas, would vary from state to state depending on variations in cutback costs.

State and Industry/Labor petitioners argue that this approach runs afoul of §110(a)(2)(D), which they read as prohibiting any consideration of costs or cost-effectiveness in determining what contributions are "significant." So far as appears, none of the states proposes that EPA, if reversed, must require complete extirpation of their NO_x emissions. Rather, the gamble—at least of the small contributors—is evidently that if EPA were barred from considering costs, it would never have included such states. . . . We note that no party makes any claim that EPA was either confined to adopting rules whose benefits exceeded their costs, or permitted to use that criterion in selecting its final rule. Nor has it been argued that the term "significant" required consideration of costs.

State petitioners initially argued that it was "arbitrary and unlawful" for EPA to make cost effectiveness a "controlling factor" or "linchpin" in the determination of significant contribution under §110(a)(2)(D). Thus EPA's error, as the states would have it, was in considering costs too much: "Petitioning States do not claim that there is no role for cost considerations; Petitioning States simply stress that EPA must establish a definition of significance that is dominated by air quality factors, as air quality is the sole factor mentioned in the statute." In support of this position, State petitioners cited our en banc decision in NRDC v. EPA, 824 F.2d 1146, 1163 (D.C. Cir. 1987), where we held that a statutory mandate for EPA to set a standard with an "ample margin of safety to protect the public health" did not preclude the consideration of costs and technological feasibility, but that these concerns could not be the "primary consideration."

At oral argument, counsel for the states abandoned this position and decided that the statute flatly prohibits EPA from considering costs at all. Indeed, counsel eventually went so far as to claim that if faced with two states, one of which could eliminate all relevant emissions at a trivial cost, while the other could eliminate none at a cost of less than $5000 a ton, EPA must mandate the same cutback for each. . . .

. . . In its opening and reply brief Industry/Labor argued that "§110(a)(2)(D) requires consideration of only air quality impacts in determining the significance of any contribution." However, at oral argument Industry/Labor offered a construction of the statute that seemed to restore to EPA via §110(k)(5) what it would take away via §110(a)(2)(D). Industry/Labor claimed that costs could be considered when EPA determines if a SIP is "adequate" under §110(k)(5). . . .

. . . By its terms [§110(a)(2)(D)(i)(I)] is focused on "amounts" of "emissions activity" that "contribute significantly to nonattainment." The fundamental dispute is over the clarity of the phrase "contribute significantly." Must EPA simply pick some flat "amount" of contribution, based exclusively on health concerns, such that any excess would put a state in the forbidden zone of "significance"? Or was it permissible for EPA to consider differences in cutback costs, so that, after reduction of all that could be cost-effectively eliminated, any remaining "contribution" would not be considered "significant"? In deciding on the permissible ceiling, EPA used "significant" in the second way.

The term "significant" does not in itself convey a thought that significance should be measured in only one dimension—here, in the petitioners' view, health alone. Indeed, "significant" is a very odd choice to express unidimensionality; consider the phrase "significant other." In some contexts, "significant" begs a consideration of costs. In finding a threshold requirement of "significant risk" in §3(8) of the Occupational Health and Safety Act, 29 U.S.C. §652(8), a plurality of the Supreme Court understood a "significant" risk as something more than a "mathematical straitjacket," and held that "[s]ome risks are plainly acceptable and others are plainly unacceptable." Industrial Union Dept., AFL-CIO v. American Petroleum Institute ("*Benzene*"), 448 U.S. 607, 655 (1980) (plurality opinion). The plurality withheld judgment on whether the Act required a "reasonable correlation between costs and benefits," but the upshot of inserting the adjective "significant" was a consideration of which risks are worth the cost of elimination. . . . OSHA's reaction to the term "significant" seems to confirm what some commentators have asked rhetorically: "[C]an an agency sensibly decide whether a risk is 'significant' without also examining the cost of eliminating it?" S. Breyer et al., Administrative Law and Regulatory Policy 65 (4th ed. 1999).

Petitioners conspicuously fail to describe the intellectual process by which EPA would determine "significance" if it may consider only health. EPA has determined that ozone has some adverse health effects—however slight—at every level. Without consideration of cost it is hard to see why any ozone-creating emissions should not be regarded as fatally "significant" under §110(a)(2)(D)(i)(I). Perhaps EPA might (under such a rule) let the upwind states off at the stringency level of the programs imposed on nonattainment areas, but petitioners do not explain how "significance" can exclude cost but admit equity. . . .

In *NRDC* we considered §112 of the Clean Air Act, requiring EPA to set an air quality standard for hazardous pollutants with an "ample margin of safety" to protect the public health. We held that this phrase did not preclude a consideration of costs. [The court next discussed other cases reaching similar results under other CAA provisions.]

These cases are unexceptional in their general view that preclusion of cost consideration requires a rather express congressional direction. Three of the cases, moreover, . . . involve statutory language with just the same structure as here. A mandate directed to some environmental benefit is phrased in general quantitative terms ("ample margin of safety," "substantial restoration," and "major"), and contains not a word alluding to non-health tradeoffs; in each case we found that in making its judgments of degree the agency was free to consider the costs of demanding higher levels of environmental benefit. So too here.

Petitioners point to no evidence of the requisite "clear congressional intent to preclude consideration of cost." *NRDC*, 824 F.2d at 1163. The text, we have already seen, works no such preclusion. As for the statutory structure, petitioners willingly concede that costs may be considered under §110(k)(5) in determining the adequacy of a state plan. Why would a Congress intent on precluding cost considerations allow such an escape hatch? The petitioners cite no legislative history suggesting that cost considerations should be barred.

In sum, there is nothing in the text, structure, or history of §110(a)(2)(D) that bars EPA from considering cost in its application.

3. UNIFORM CONTROLS

As we have seen, EPA required that all of the covered jurisdictions, regardless of amount of contribution, reduce their NO_x by an amount achievable with "highly cost-effective controls." Petitioners claim that EPA's uniform control strategy is irrational in two distinct ways. First, they observe that where two states differ considerably in the amount of their respective NO_x contributions to downwind nonattainment, under the EPA rule even the small contributors must make reductions equivalent to those achievable by highly cost-effective measures. This of course flows ineluctably from the EPA's decision to draw the "significant contribution" line on a basis of cost differentials. Our upholding of that decision logically entails upholding this consequence.

The second objection is that because of distance and the vagaries of pollutant migration and ozone formation, a molecule of NO_x emitted in Indiana (for example) may cause far less adverse health impact than a molecule emitted in eastern Pennsylvania. EPA acknowledges that "[s]ources that are closer to the nonattainment area tend to have much larger effects on air quality than sources that are far away." 63 Fed. Reg. at 25,919. While EPA's cost-effectiveness standard and emissions trading seem to mean that EPA will secure the resulting aggregate NO_x reduction at roughly the lowest possible cost, they do not necessarily mean that it will have secured the resulting aggregate health benefits at the lowest cost. Petitioners ask, in effect, why EPA did not, by one means or another (e.g., in the emissions trading system), make reductions from sources near the nonattainment areas (or otherwise more damaging, molecule for molecule) more valuable than ones from distant sources?

EPA considered this approach, modeling the efficacy of regional alternatives compared to its uniform strategy. Its researchers found that non-uniform regional approaches by comparison did not "provide either a significant improvement in air quality or a substantial reduction in cost." The complaining states offer no material critique of EPA's methodology in reaching this answer, which in fact some independent investigators have confirmed. . . . We have no basis to upset EPA's judgment. . . .

III. Federalism . . .

[Based on the work on solutions to interstate ozone pollution conducted by the Ozone Transport Assessment Group (OTAG), a body composed of representatives of EPA, the states, industry, and environmental groups,] EPA ordered the challenged SIP call under the authority of section 110(k)(5) in order to address significant contribution to 1-hour ozone nonattainment as described under section 110(a)(2)(D). In fashioning the SIP call, EPA focused on OTAG's determination that "[r]egional NO_x emissions reductions are effective in producing ozone benefits." EPA also took into consideration OTAG's conclusion that while NO_x controls are effective in addressing regional ozone problems, VOC controls are most effective locally and are most advantageous to urban nonattainment areas. Because OTAG concluded that NO_x reductions provide the key to addressing regional ozone problems, EPA's SIP call addresses regional ozone nonattainment through NO_x emissions "budgets" established by the agency for each covered state. The budgets represent the amount of allowable NO_x emissions remaining after a covered state prohibits the NO_x amount contributing significantly to downwind nonattainment. While EPA calculated the budgets using highly cost-effective emission controls, the agency allows the states to choose the control measures necessary to bring their emissions within the budget requirements. Under EPA's budget plan, a state "may choose from a broader menu of cost-effective, reasonable alternatives" including alternatives that "may even be more advantageous in light of local concerns." In fact, EPA has stated that the states have "full discretion in selecting the controls, so that [the states] may choose any set of controls that would assure achievement of the budget." [63 Fed. Reg.] at 57,378. In addition, each state has the option of adopting an interstate trading program that allows it to purchase NO_x "allowances" from sources that have elected to over-control. The SIP call also gives the states the option in some circumstances to use "banked" allowances (i.e. allowances from prior years) to comply with emissions limits.

Petitioners assert that EPA's NO_x budget program impermissibly intrudes on the statutory right of the states to fashion their SIP submissions in the first instance. In support of this position, the petitioners primarily rely on our decision in Virginia v. EPA, 108 F.3d 1397 (D.C. Cir.), *modified on other grounds*, 116 F.3d 499 (D.C. Cir. 1997), where we held that EPA may not use a section 110(k)(5) SIP call to order states to adopt a particular approach to achieving the SIP requirements listed in section 110. Under the rule at issue in *Virginia*, EPA required states to adopt California's vehicle emission program and in effect set the numerical emissions limitations and mandated the means for the states to achieve the necessary emissions reductions.... We held that EPA's approach exceeded its authority under section 110 because each state retains the authority to determine in the first instance the necessary and appropriate control measures needed to satisfy section 110's standards.

Our holding in *Virginia* was mandated by the Supreme Court's decision in Train v. NRDC, 421 U.S. 60 (1975).... The *Train* decision and subsequent precedent make clear that section 110 left to the states "the power to [initially] determine *which sources* would be burdened by regulation and to *what extent.*" Union Elec. Co. v. EPA, 427 U.S. 246, 269 (1976) (emphasis added). As we elaborated in *Virginia*, "the Supreme Court decided . . . that [section 110] did not confer upon EPA the authority to condition approval of [a state's] implementation plan . . . on the state's adoption of a specific control measure." *Virginia*, 108 F.3d at 1408. For the reasons set forth below, we conclude that the NO_x budgets do not fall within the realm of impermissible SIP call regulation as defined in *Virginia* and *Train*.

Given the *Train* and *Virginia* precedent, the validity of the NO_x budget program underlying the SIP call depends in part on whether the program in effect constitutes an EPA-imposed control measure or emission limitation triggering the *Train/Virginia* federalism bar: in other words, on whether the program constitutes an impermissible source-specific means rather than a permissible end goal. However, the program's validity also depends on whether EPA's budgets allow the covered states real choice with regard to the control measure options available to them to meet the budget requirements.

Section 110(a)(2)(D) requires SIPs to contain adequate provisions prohibiting emissions from "any source or other type of emissions activity within the State" that "contribute significantly" to NAAQS nonattainment in another state. Here, EPA mandates that 22 states and the District of Columbia implement section

110(a)(2)(D) using its NO$_x$ budget system. In essence, the NO$_x$ budget in question is an EPA mandate prohibiting NO$_x$ emissions in the 23 jurisdictions from exceeding a tonnage specific to that jurisdiction. Of concern to petitioners, the budget rule prohibits states from seeking compliance, in whole or part, by controlling VOC emissions even though VOCs as well as NO$_x$ emissions contribute to ozone problems.

Yet, the budget plan's defining aspects do not necessarily cause the program to conflict with the limiting principles contained in *Train* and *Virginia*. Analyzing the budget rule together with the relevant precedent, we hold that based on section 110's silence, EPA reasonably interpreted section 110 as providing it with the authority to determine a state's NO$_x$ significant contribution level and agree with EPA that the NO$_x$ budget plan does no more than project whether states have reduced emissions sufficiently to mitigate interstate transport.

Under section 110, EPA must "approve a [SIP] submittal as a whole if it meets all of the applicable requirements of [the Act]." §110(k)(3). While the states have considerable latitude in fashioning SIPs, the CAA "nonetheless subject[s] the States to strict minimum compliance requirements" and gives EPA the authority to determine a state's compliance with the requirements. *Union Elec. Co.*, 427 U.S. at 256-57 (referring to the requirements contained in the statute). . . .

Moreover, EPA does not tell the states how to achieve SIP compliance. Rather, EPA looks to section 110(a)(2)(D) and merely provides the levels to be achieved by state-determined compliance mechanisms. Specifically, EPA set NO$_x$ reduction levels based, in part, on assumptions about reductions obtainable through highly cost-effective controls. However, EPA made clear that states do not have to adopt the control scheme that EPA assumed for budget-setting purposes. States can choose from a myriad of reasonably cost-effective options to achieve the assigned reduction levels. While EPA bases the budgets here on "highly cost-effective" control measures, the states remain free to implement other "cost-effective" or "reasonably cost-effective" measures in place of the ones identified by EPA. More importantly, EPA went so far as to give the states "full discretion in selecting . . . controls," 63 Fed. Reg. at 57,378, thereby allowing states to attain their budgets by imposing even quite unreasonable, very cost-ineffective controls. . . .

Regarding EPA's decision not to rely on VOC reductions, EPA reasonably concluded that long-range ozone transport can only be addressed adequately through NO$_x$ reductions. Petitioners' reliance and emphasis on VOC reductions in lieu of NO$_x$ reductions ignores the scientific basis for EPA's rule. OTAG and EPA concluded that VOC controls would not effectively address interstate ozone transport. Furthermore, states can cure any NO$_x$ reduction "disbenefits" with corresponding optional VOC controls. Thus, the SIP call cannot be invalidated merely because EPA reasonably chose not to regulate VOCs.

In sum, we conclude that EPA's NO$_x$ budget program reasonably establishes reduction levels and leaves the control measure selection decision to the states. . . . Since the challenged budget program does not mandate a "specific, source-by-source emission limitation[]," the NO$_x$ budget plan does not run afoul of *Train* or *Virginia*. . . .

SENTELLE, Circuit Judge, dissenting:

Unlike the majority's journey through this regulatory scheme, mine is neither lengthy nor complex, because I get off at the first stop. . . . It would appear to me that

Congress clearly empowered EPA [in §110(a)(2)(D)(i)(I)] to base its actions on amounts of pollutants, those amounts to be measured in terms of significance of contribution to downwind nonattainment. Instead, EPA has chosen, doubtless in the pursuit of beneficent ends, to assert authority to require the SIPs to contain provisions based not on the amounts of pollutants, nor even on the relative significance of the contributions of such pollutants to downwind nonattainment, but on the relative cost-effectiveness of alleviation. I agree with the State petitioners that it is undeniable that EPA has exceeded its statutory authority. . . .

    . . . By focusing on "significance" or what it means to be "significant," the majority ignores the fact that the statute permits EPA to address that which is "*contribut[ed]* significantly." §110(a)(2)(D)(i)(I) (emphasis added). And what should EPA look for as being contributed significantly? Congress clearly answered that question for the agency as being an "amount" of an "air pollutant." Considering that Congress expressly gave EPA authority with regard to "any *air pollutant* in *amounts* which will . . . *contribute* significantly to nonattainment . . . ," id. (emphasis added), I marvel at an interpretation that permits cost-effectiveness to find a place in a statutory provision addressing amounts of air pollutant contribution. While the contribution must affect nonattainment significantly, no reasonable reading of the statutory provision in its entirety allows the term significantly to springboard costs of alleviation into EPA's statutorily defined authority. . . .

    I see nothing in Chevron U.S.A., Inc. v. NRDC, Inc., 467 U.S. 837 (1984), that either compels or counsels the majority's result. EPA argues that Congress did not define significant contribution. True, it did not. Neither did it define amount. But neither EPA nor the majority have offered any reasonable interpretation of those words which makes them depend upon or even relate to the cost-effectiveness of alleviation.[1] EPA comes close to arguing: Congress has not expressly forbidden us to use this criterion, therefore we may use it. . . .

NOTES AND QUESTIONS

    1. *What Is a "Significant Contribution"?* What do the 1990 amendments to the CAA seem to have been designed to accomplish with respect to EPA's burden of proving that emissions activity in one state is contributing significantly to nonattainment in another? What positions did the states and the industry/labor petitioners take with regard to the role that the costs of reducing ozone pollution plays in the implementation of §110(a)(2)(D)(i)(I)? What two interpretive choices did the majority consider in determining what that role is? Which did EPA select? How did the majority think that the *Benzene* case was relevant to assessing the propriety of EPA's choice? How did Judge Sentelle interpret that case? Is it impossible to identify a "sensible" basis for determining whether a risk is significant without examining the cost of eliminating it?

    2. NO_x *Budgets.* What is an NO_x "budget"? What was EPA's purpose in computing such a budget for the state subject to the SIP call? Why did the court find that the NO_x budget program did not impermissibly infringe on state prerogatives under

---

    1. [Judge Sentelle distinguished the *Benzene* case, stating that] "[o]bviously, the "significance" of the risk deals with its importance, not the cost of its alleviation. . . ."

the CAA, as sketched out in cases such as *Union Elec.* (reproduced at page 437 of the casebook) and *Train* (quoted at page 437)?*

3. *Successful §126 Ozone Petitions.* In 2000, in response to petitions filed by a group of northeastern states under §126, EPA found that certain large electric utilities and industrial boilers and turbines located in upwind states violated the §110(a)(2)(D) provision barring one state from significantly contributing to air pollution in other states. As a result, it ordered nearly 400 facilities in 12 states (including some of the petitioning states) and the District of Columbia to reduce annual emissions by more than 500,000 tons from 2007 levels. In addition, EPA established a cap-and-trade program as the remedy for the violations of §110(a)(2)(D) that it found. 65 Fed. Reg. 2,674, 2,686 (2000).

The validity of EPA's disposition of the §126 petitions was addressed in Appalachian Power Co. v. EPA, 249 F.3d 1032 (D.C. Cir. 2001). A group of states from the Midwest and the Southeast and operators of electric generating facilities argued that the CAA precluded EPA from making any findings in response to the northeastern states' §126 petition while the NO_x call at issue in the *Michigan* case was pending. According to the petitioners, principles of cooperative federalism dictate that the states be allowed the opportunity to decide how to reduce NO_x emissions without direction from EPA. The court disagreed, holding that the statute does not require that proceedings under either §110 or §126 be completed before the agency may proceed with action under the other provision. In the alternative, the petitioners argued that although EPA may act under either §110 or §126, it may not impose §126 findings and a SIP call simultaneously. The court deferred, however, to EPA's determination that the two provisions operate independently. The industry petitioners also challenged the methodology by which EPA supported its findings that the upwind states significantly contributed to nonattainment of the ozone NAAQS in downwind states. According to the petitioners, §126 requires that EPA find a significant independent contribution from a major source or group of stationary sources in the upwind state. The court found, however, that it was reasonable for EPA to link its stationary-source findings to the significance of a state's total NO_x emissions. The court nevertheless remanded to EPA to explain further the manner in which it allocated NO_x allowances to the upwind states. See also Appalachian Power Co. v. EPA, 251 F.3d 1026 (D.C. Cir. 2001) (reaching the same result in a challenge to technical amendments to NO_x call). On remand from the decisions in the two *Appalachian Power* cases, EPA decided to retain the previously determined results but to provide a fuller explanation. The court in West Virginia v. EPA, 362 F.3d 861 (D.C. Cir. 2004), accepted EPA's explanation as reasonable.

4. *The Clean Air Act Interstate Rule (CAIR).* In 2005 EPA adopted the Clean Air Interstate Rule based on its finding that 28 states and the District of Columbia contribute significantly to nonattainment of the NAAQS for either $PM_{2.5}$, ozone, or both in downwind states. 70 Fed. Reg. 25,162. EPA required these states to amend their SIPs' statewide emissions reduction requirements for SO_2 (a precursor to $PM_{2.5}$ formation) and NO_x (a precursor to both ozone and $PM_{2.5}$ formation). The states must phase in the controls between 2009 and 2015. EPA also established a model multistate cap-and-trade program for SO_2 and NO_x that states could choose to adopt to meet the

---

*EPA issued a final rule on remand from the court's decision in *Michigan*, in which it established the final NO_x budget for states subject to the SIP call. 69 Fed. Reg. 21,604 (2004). For commentary on the *Michigan* case, see McCubbin, *Michigan v. EPA:* Interstate Ozone Pollution and EPA's "NO_x SIP Call," 20 St. Louis U. Pub. L. Rev. 47 (2001).

proposed emissions reductions "in a flexible and cost-effective manner." The CAIR ozone season NO_x trading program will replace the current NO_x call at issue in *Michigan*. The CAIR also allows transfer of allowances among sources covered by the acid rain program and the model cap-and-trade program under the CAIR, but precludes multiple uses of a single allowance. See also 71 Fed. Reg. 25,304 (2006) (denying petitions for reconsideration of CAIR). EPA subsequently promulgated federal implementation plans to control interstate transport of SO_2 and NO_x to apply in states that do not have timely, approved SIPs that meet the requirements of the CAIR. EPA adopted as the control requirements for these federal plans the model trading rules that states may use under the CAIR, with minor changes to account for federal implementation.

     5. *International Air Pollution*. Section 179B exempts from some of the statute's enforcement mechanisms for nonattainment areas those states that are able to establish that they would have attained the NAAQS but for emissions of ozone, CO, or PM_{10} emanating from outside the United States. See Sierra Club v. EPA, 346 F.3d 955 (9th Cir. 2003) (California unable to establish that it would have attained the NAAQS for PM_{10} but for emissions generated in Mexico).

b.   The Acid Deposition Controversy

CLEAN AIR ACT AMENDMENTS OF 1990, REPORT OF THE COMMITTEE ON ENERGY AND COMMERCE, U.S. HOUSE OF REPRESENTATIVES, ON H.R. 3030
H.R. Rep. No. 101-490, pt. 1, at 157-158 (1990)

The Clean Air Act was originally designed mainly to reduce high pollution levels that tend to occur near major pollution sources. It did not contemplate that long-distance transport of air pollutants could cause widespread adverse impacts.

     Scientists have since learned that SO_2 and NO_x pollution from power plants, factories, and other sources can be carried hundreds or even thousands of miles through the atmosphere, chemically transformed in the process, and eventually returned to earth as sulfuric and nitric acids. These acids often [are] picked up in droplets of rain or snow, but sometimes the particles simply fall back as "dry deposition." . . . [S]uch acid pollution has been associated with a variety of harmful effects, on health, especially to those with respiratory ailments; lakes; forests; and man-made materials, such as buildings, bridges, statuary, and car finishes. . . .

     The small acidic sulfate and nitrate particles (acid aerosols) which form in the atmosphere from SO_2 and NO_x pollution irritate the lungs, causing constricted breathing. They pose risks to asthmatics and others with already impaired breathing abilities. Some epidemiological studies have suggested that acid aerosols increase the incidence of chronic cough and bronchitis and death rates.

     Acidification of lakes and streams in the U.S. is another widespread effect of acid deposition. Although there are some natural acidic water bodies, "most of the acidity comes from acid deposition," according to findings of [the National Acid Precipitation Assessment Program (NAPAP)]. Nationally, acid deposition has reportedly acidified over one thousand large lakes (greater than 10 acres) and thousands of miles of streams. According to [the Office of Technology Assessment], thousands more lakes and streams are "extremely vulnerable" to further acidification. . . .

Acid deposition has been implicated in the damage of some forests. Contact with highly acidified rain or fog can directly injure leaves and needles. And over the long term, acid deposition may stunt tree growth by altering soil chemistry, both by washing away vital nutrients, such as magnesium and calcium, and by contaminating the soil with heavy metals like aluminum, that are freed from soil particles.

The red spruce forests along the crest of the Appalachian Mountains, which stretch from Maine to Georgia, have been the most damaged. These forests have suffered widespread decline, including the death of 40-70 percent of the spruce on some mountaintops in Vermont, New York, and North Carolina. NAPAP has found that regular exposure to extremely acidic clouds (average pH of 3.6) is contributing to the decline, along with exposure to ozone, disease, insects, and unusual weather conditions.

The pollutants that create acid deposition also have a major impact on visibility. The sulfate particles that form from SO_2 emissions scatter light and reduce visibility. The problem is particularly great during summer months, because high humidity and temperatures promote sulfate formation. . . .

Finally, acid deposition causes substantial economic impacts by eroding man-made building materials, such as steel, stones, and paint. According to some estimates, the cost of damage in 17 Eastern States alone could be as high as $2 billion per year.

NOTES AND QUESTIONS

1. *Scientific Uncertainty.* This excerpt from the legislative history of the 1990 amendments fails to disclose the controversy that surrounded the debate over whether—and if so, how—to control emissions of the precursors of acid deposition. Uncertainty attended the questions of whether there is a linear relationship between precursor gases and sulfate or nitrate formation and the nature of the relationship between sources and receptors. The Office of Technology Assessment (OTA) remarked that "the uncertainties are so large that it is difficult to describe the patterns or magnitude of risk." U.S. Office of Technology Assessment, Acid Rain and Transported Air Pollutants 32 (1984).

Research conducted since the adoption of the acid deposition control provisions of the 1990 amendments has reduced this uncertainty and confirmed the severity of the problem. In 1996, researchers found that the Hubbard Brook Experimental Forest in the White Mountains of New Hampshire essentially stopped growing about ten years before and would probably not recover for a long time due to soil chemistry alteration attributable to acid rain. Stevens, The Forest that Stopped Growing: Trail Is Traced to Acid Rain, N.Y. Times, Apr. 16, 1996, at B6. The study concluded that increased acidity deprived the soil of alkaline chemicals such as calcium that are essential for plant growth. These chemicals, or cations, are leached from the soil by acid precipitation and carried away in runoff. The researchers stopped short of asserting a firm cause-and-effect relationship, however, between the depletion of cations in the soil and the slowing of forest growth.

A 1999 report by NAPAP concluded that soil in high-elevation forests in the Colorado Front Range, the Allegheny Mountains in West Virginia, the Great Smoky Mountains in Tennessee, and the San Gabriel Mountains near Los Angeles was becoming more acidic due to excess nitrogen; that excess nitrogen in the Chesapeake Bay is causing algae blooms that suffocate other life forms; and that lakes and streams in the Sierra Nevada, Cascade, Rocky, and Adirondack mountains are suffering from chronically high acidity. Dao, Study Sees Acid Rain Threat in Adirondacks and Beyond, N.Y. Times, Apr. 5, 1999, at A19. A report by the General Accounting Office indicated that, ten years after the adoption of the 1990 amendments, sulfur levels had declined in most lakes tested in the Adirondack Mountains, but that nitrogen levels had increased in twice as many lakes as those in which it had declined. Dao, Acid Rain Law Found to Fail in Adirondacks, N.Y. Times, Mar. 27, 2000, at A1.

   2. *Political Obstacles to Control of Acid Deposition.* Perhaps as much as any other issue, acid rain control highlights the important distributive judgments that often accompany air pollution control efforts. The fact that acid deposition is a long-range phenomenon meant that efforts to control it would have different impacts in various regions of the country. Much of the problem was focused in New York's Adirondack Mountains and New England, where the evidence of acidified lakes was strong. Northeastern states, which supported efforts to control emissions of acid rain precursors, charged that the predominant cause of the problem was the concentration of old electric power plants in the Midwest. In addition, the impact of controls on utility rates and thus on state and regional economies raises serious distributive problems. Some observers estimated, for example, that forcing coal-fired power plants to control acid rain precursors would significantly increase electric rates in Ohio. One way for power plants to reduce SO_2 emissions and the resulting formation of sulfates is to switch from coal with a high sulfur content to coal with a low sulfur content or to other low-sulfur fuels. States with large deposits of high-sulfur coal, such as West Virginia and Kentucky, therefore feared that requirements to reduce SO_2 emissions would translate into economic ruin for the local coal mining industry. States further west with thriving low-sulfur coal industries anticipated reaping the benefits of a new acid rain control program.

   These divisive regional conflicts prevented an agreement over acid deposition control amendments to the CAA throughout the 1980s. The logjam broke when Congress amended the CAA in 1990. Based on a proposal by the George H. W. Bush administration, the solution was politically attractive because, by that time, the public viewed acid rain as a serious problem. In addition, the new program was relatively narrow, subjecting only coal-fired power plants, the very industry that had long opposed any compromises, to regulation.

   Another factor that smoothed the way for the acid rain program was its "reliance on a market-like scheme of emissions trading [that] made it the kind of initiative that industry-oriented and conservative members of Congress could accept. It was based on an argument that critics of regulation had been making for decades—that government intervention needed to be more decentralized, flexible, and efficient." [Bryner, Blue Skies, Green Politics: The Clean Air Act of 1990, at 95-96 (1993).]

   3. *The Costs and Benefits of Control.* In 1995, EPA reported that the health benefits (primarily reductions in premature deaths and new cases of chronic bronchitis) of controlling emissions of SO_2 under the acid rain provisions of the 1990 amendments in the 31 eastern states would amount to between $3 and $11 billion in 1997. These benefits would far exceed the estimated costs of control, which were substantially lower than the earlier worst-case estimates: $1.2 billion in 1997 and $2.4 billion in 2010. EPA Press Advisory, 1995 WL 740253 (Dec. 15, 1995). EPA estimated that by 2010, annual health benefits should fall within a range of $12 to $40 billion, which

would be 5 to 17 times the costs of implementing SO_2 controls. Orange County (Cal.) Reg., Dec. 16, 1995, at A34.

Fears that acid rain control would adversely affect the high-sulfur coal mining industry proved justified. Many mines in Appalachia and other coal-mining areas east of the Mississippi closed. The result was a precipitous decline in coal mine employment in states such as Illinois, Indiana, Ohio, Pennsylvania, Kentucky, and West Virginia. While coal production in the east fell, production in the west increased markedly. Loss of jobs in mining communities also causes harm to companies that equip mines and service their gear. The 1990 amendments authorized the payment of limited unemployment compensation and retraining benefits to miners thrown out of work as a result of the amendments, but hard-hit mining communities tended to regard these efforts as insufficient. Kilborn, East's Coal Towns Wither in the Name of Cleaner Air, N.Y. Times, Feb. 15, 1996, at A1.

c. Emissions Trading and the Control of Acid Deposition

INDIANAPOLIS POWER & LIGHT CO. v. EPA
58 F.3d 643 (D.C. Cir. 1995)

Title IV of the Clean Air Act establishes an acid rain program to reduce emissions of sulfur dioxide and nitrogen oxides, the primary precursors of acid rain. See 42 U.S.C. §§7651-7651o. Title IV imposes a national cap of 8.90 million tons of sulfur dioxide emissions per year on electric utilities. 42 U.S.C. §§7651b(a)(1), 7651d(a)(3). The emissions reductions are to occur in two phases. [See Figure 6-10.] In Phase I, . . . 110 utilities with the largest coal-fired utility electric generating units must reduce their emissions to 2.50 pounds of sulfur dioxide per million British thermal units (Btus) of fuel consumed by each power-generating unit in the "baseline" years of 1985, 1986 and 1987. 42 U.S.C. §7651c. Each utility unit is allocated a number of fully marketable pollution allowances so that it may emit sulfur dioxide at this level. 42 U.S.C. §7651c. Each allowance authorizes the emission of one ton of sulfur dioxide during one calendar year and may be bought, sold, traded or banked for future use or resale. 42 U.S.C. §§7651a(3), 7651b(b).

Beginning in 1995, the emissions from each Phase I unit may not exceed the number of allowances that unit holds. 42 U.S.C. §7651c(a). Emissions from a Phase I unit that exceed the number of allowances allocated to it are unlawful and are subject to various fines and penalties. 42 U.S.C. §§7651b(g), 7651j. To comply with Title IV requirements and ensure that its emissions do not exceed its allowances, a utility has three options. A utility can switch from coal with a high sulfur content to low-sulfur coal, purchase allowances from other utilities or install costly sulfur dioxide control technology known as "scrubbers." Congress encouraged the installation of scrubbers by establishing an extension allowance program. 42 U.S.C. §7651c(d).

MADISON GAS & ELECTRIC CO. v. EPA
25 F.3d 526 (7th Cir. 1994)

Under Phase II of the statutory program, . . . the EPA is required to award, effective in the year 2000, SO_2 emission allowances to each of the nation's 2,200 electric

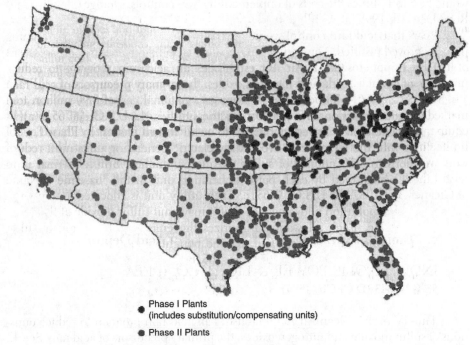

Phase I Plants
(includes substitution/compensating units)

Phase II Plants

FIGURE 6-10
Affected Sources under the Acid Rain Program

Source: http://www.epa.gov/airmarkets/cmap/mapgallery/mg_affected_sources.html

utilities. §7651d. Each allowance permits the emission of one ton of SO_2 per year. The allowances can be bought and sold. §7651b(b). This is the novel feature of the acid rain program. A market in pollution is created. Clean utilities can make money selling their excess allowances and dirty utilities that do not want to expend the resources necessary to become clean can instead buy allowances from the clean utilities.

NOTES AND QUESTIONS

1. *Statutory Purposes.* Congress sought in the 1990 amendments to reduce the adverse effects of acid deposition through reductions in annual emissions of SO_2 by 10 million tons and of NO_x by about 2 million tons from 1980 emission levels. The program was also designed to encourage energy conservation, the use of renewable and clean alternative technologies, and pollution prevention. §401(a). How might the program accomplish these goals? According to the statute, the allowance program described in the *Indianapolis Power & Light Co.* excerpt "allocates the costs of achieving the required reductions in emissions . . . among sources in the United States. Broad-based taxes and emissions fees that would provide for payment of the costs of achieving required emissions reductions by any party or parties other than the sources required to achieve the reductions are undesirable." Pub. L. No. 101-549, §407, 104 Stat. 2399 (1990). Undesirable from an economic or a political perspective?

2. *The Potential Inequities of an Allowance System Based on Historical Usage.* How were the allowances that authorize emissions of SO_2 by electric power plants initially allocated? See §§404 (Phase I), 405 (Phase II). The use of a historical "baseline" to determine regulatory rights creates the potential for inequity. Given that allowances were doled out primarily on the basis of historical operating practice and that the statute prohibits SO_2 emissions in excess of the allowances held by a power plant, for example, how will a new utility procure the allowances sufficient to cover its emissions? See Dennis, Comment, Smoke for Sale: Paradoxes and Problems of the Emissions Trading Program of the Clean Air Act Amendments of 1990, 40 UCLA L. Rev. 1101, 1116-1117 (1993). See also Texas Mun. Power Agency v. EPA, 89 F.3d 858 (D.C. Cir. 1996) (EPA acted properly in relying on an emission rate calculated from a statewide average in determining the allowances to be received by a utility unit whose emission rate was not included in the relied-upon database).

EPA must establish a pool of reserve allowances to use for the grant of extension allowances and other purposes, but such allowances are capped at 3.5 million. §404(a)(2). How should EPA dole out these allowances? By lottery? On a first-come, first-served basis? See Monongahela Power Co. v. Reilly, 980 F.2d 272 (4th Cir. 1992) (refusing to require EPA to process requests for extension allowances filed before EPA issued implementing regulations). What if disputes arise concerning the allocation of allowances to an affected unit with multiple owners; in what forum should such a dispute be resolved? See §408g(i); *Madison Gas & Elec. Co., supra* (eligibility for Phase II bonus allowances under §405(c) turned on whether utility's aggregate capacity included two plants in which it held only a 22 percent interest).

3. *Allowances and Property Rights.* The statute describes an allowance as "a limited authorization to emit SO_2," which "does not constitute a property right." §403(f). What do you suppose was the rationale behind this provision? Might it be advisable to reduce the number of available allowances? What legal problems might be caused by an attempt to do so by EPA? See Dennis, *supra,* at 1126-1127.

4. *Allowance Trading in Practice.* Several years after adoption of the 1990 amendments, the General Accounting Office reported that utilities had tended to take advantage of cost-saving opportunities within their own plants (such as switching from high- to low-sulfur coal) rather than to use trading to meet requirements.[*] At the same time, the price of an allowance was far below what utility lobbyists had predicted. One explanation was that the market was not working. But another was that industry lobbyists had engaged in "gaming"—intentionally overestimating the costs of control (and the price of an allowance) in an attempt to dissuade Congress from adopting stringent controls. As a result, the regulatory burden Congress thought it was imposing on utilities was far less than originally predicted. To put it another way, Congress could have purchased far more pollution control for the amount it was willing to force industry to commit to the problem than the statute actually accomplished. A third explanation involved the low price of coal. How is that price relevant? As the deadline for Phase II limits approached, creating more potential buyers, the market heated up and sales of allowances increased.

5. *State Efforts to Control Acid Deposition.* Is it possible that the trading of allowances will make the acid rain problem worse rather than better, at least in some areas? What is the likely result of a trade of allowances from a New York utility to a power plant in the Midwest? In 2000, the New York legislature adopted the Air Pollution Mitigation Law, which assessed an "air pollution mitigation offset" equal to

---

[*]U.S. General Accounting Office, Air Pollution—Allowance Trading Offers an Opportunity to Reduce Emissions at Less Cost, GAO/RCED 95-30, 1994 WL 792389 (Dec. 16, 1994).

any sum received for the sale or trade of SO_2 allowances to a unit in an upwind state. Any amount received by a regulated unit for such an allowance was forfeited to the state public utility commission. The offset could be avoided only with the attachment of a restrictive covenant to a transfer of SO_2 allowances prohibiting their later transfer to and usage in an upwind state. When the facial constitutionality of the law was challenged, the court in Clean Air Markets Group v. Pataki, 338 F.3d 82 (2d Cir. 2003), held that the CAA preempted New York's law because the latter interfered with the method selected by Congress for regulating SO_2 emissions, including a nationwide allowance transfer system. The state statute effectively banned allowance sales to utilities in upwind states. The court did not reach the issue of whether the state statute violated the dormant Commerce Clause.

6. *Industrial SO_2 Emissions.* Industrial, fossil fuel–fired combustion sources that emit SO_2 may opt into the emission allowance system. §410. Why would a facility voluntarily subject itself to the conditions of the system? According to EPA, "only combustion sources that would profit by selling excess allowances are expected to participate in the program. . . . [R]evenue generated by selling excess allowances could help sources to offset costs of compliance with other programs." 60 Fed. Reg. 17,100 (1995).

7. *Limits on Emissions of NO_x by Utilities.* The acid deposition control provisions limit emissions of NO_x as well as SO_2. §407. A utility may avoid the prescribed emission limits by requesting from EPA an alternative emission limit on the basis of its inability to meet the regulatory limit through the use of low NO_x burner technology. §407(d).

8. *The Effect of the 1990 Amendments on Acid Deposition.* Despite the potential obstacles to a well-functioning market in SO_2 allowances, EPA has reported that the acid rain emissions trading program has reduced SO_2 emissions from power plants by 32 percent and emissions of NO_x by 37 percent.[*] An increase during 2002-2003 may have been due in part to the use of "banked" emissions allowances. Spike in Utility SO_2 Emissions Prompts Criticism of Trading Programs, Inside E.P.A. Weekly, Sept. 24, 2004, at 13. A 2005 White House report to Congress[**] indicated that sulfate deposition dropped by 40 percent in the Northeast between 1990 and 2002. The report also indicated, however, that many water bodies in the region (except in the Adirondack Mountains) had not shown signs of recovery from acidic conditions. See Figure 6-11. Wet nitrate deposition did not decline during the same period.[***]

NOTE ON THE INTERNATIONAL IMPLICATIONS OF ACID DEPOSITION

The Nature of the Problem. Canada has long been seriously concerned about the impact of acid rain on its lakes and forests. Before the adoption of the 1990 amendments, Canadian officials estimated that one out of ten Canadian jobs depends on its

---

[*]EPA's Air Emissions Trend Report, available at http://www.epa.gov/airtrends/econ-emissions.html.

[**]The National Acid Precipitation Assessment Program Report to Congress: An Integrated Assessment, available at http://www.cleartheair.org/documents/NAPAP_FINAL_print.pdf.

[***]See 36 Env't Rep. (BNA) 1759 (2005). See also http://www.epa.gov/airmarkets/cmprpt/arp04/index.html (reporting that, as of 2004, electric power plants reduced their annual emissions of SO_2 by about 34 percent compared with 1990 levels, and that NO_x emissions fell during that time to about half the level anticipated without the acid rain program).

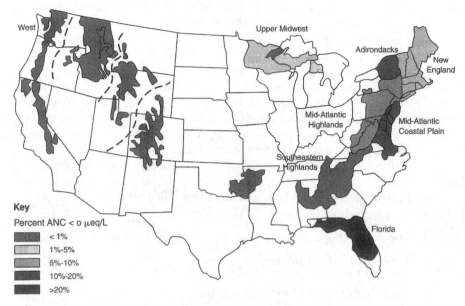

Key

Percent ANC < o μeq/L

    < 1%

    1%-5%

    5%-10%

    10%-20%

    >20%

Source: NAPAP 1991, 1990 Integrated Assessment Report

FIGURE 6-11
Acidic Surface Waters in Surveyed Regions

Source: http://www.epa.gov/airmarkets/cmap/mapgallery/mg_acidic_waters.html.

forests, that about 60 percent of the acid rain that falls on Canada comes from the United States, and that U.S. sources contribute 4 times as much SO_2 and 11 times as much NO_x to Canada's eastern provinces as the United States receives from Canada. 12 Env't Rep. (BNA) 648 (1981).

The Legal Approach. Section 115 of the CAA addresses international air pollution. Paradoxically, it affords Canada a somewhat stronger ground to attack Ohio River Valley sulfate pollution than it affords New York. Do you see why? Canadian legislation satisfies the section's requirement that the foreign country give the United States equal treatment.

EPA Administrator Douglas Costle attempted to invoke §115 in 1980, but his successor rejected his findings. See Thomas v. New York, 802 F.2d 1443 (D.C. Cir. 1986). After the decision in *Thomas*, the province of Ontario and several states and environmental groups petitioned EPA for a rulemaking under §115 that would result in the issuance of endangerment and reciprocity findings with respect to U.S. emissions that allegedly result in harmful levels of acid deposition in Canada. EPA argued that it need not make an endangerment finding until it was able to identify the sources of pollution. Because EPA could not trace pollutants adversely affecting Canada to specific sources in the United States, it was not obliged to do anything. The petitioners claimed that §115 mandated abatement measures even if EPA could not pinpoint particular sources, and that Costle's 1981 letters effectively made both the endangerment and reciprocity findings required by §115. In Her Majesty the Queen in Right of Ontario v. EPA, 912 F.2d 1525 (D.C. Cir. 1990), the court concluded that judicial review was premature. EPA had neither made a final decision on whether endangerment and reciprocity findings could be made, nor conclusively determined whether it could adequately trace pollutants to specific sources.

The Diplomatic Approach. The Canada–United States Air Quality Agreement, 30 I.L.M. 676 (1991), committed the two nations to reductions of both SO_2 and NO_x. Canada fully implemented its treaty commitments by 1994, reducing SO_2 emissions by more than 50 percent in the seven eastern provinces. The United States would comply with its obligations primarily by implementing the 1990 CAA amendments. The treaty set up an International Joint Commission to conduct five-year reviews of progress in reducing transboundary air pollution. In 1996, the first such review concluded that the two countries had generally succeeded in meeting their obligations to reduce acid deposition. The progress report issued in 2004 found that both countries had significantly reduced their SO_2 emission levels; Canada's emissions had fallen 50 percent since the 1980s and U.S. emissions had fallen 40 percent. Hunter et al., International Environmental Law and Policy 556 (3d ed. 2007).*

3.   *Protection of Stratospheric Ozone*

a.   The Problem of Ozone Depletion

CLEAN AIR ACT AMENDMENTS OF 1989
S. Rep. No. 101-228, at 383-385 (1989)

In 1985, scientists discovered a significant loss of ozone over a portion of the southern hemisphere that was about the size of North America. The collapse of the ozone layer was not predicted by any of the scientific theories or models. Measurements of what has become a seasonal phenomenon have revealed losses greater than 50 percent in the total column and greater than 95 percent [for] an altitude of 15 to 20 kilometers (9 to 12 miles). The discovery of this "Hole" in the stratospheric ozone layer over Antarctica gave renewed impetus to international efforts to understand and protect the ozone layer.

In September 1987, the Montreal Protocol on Substances That Deplete the Ozone Layer (the Protocol) [26 I.L.M. 1550 (1987); amended by 32 I.L.M. 874 (1992)] was negotiated and signed by more than two dozen nations. The Protocol entered into force in January 1989 and approximately 50 nations are now Parties to the Protocol.

Signatories to the Protocol, including the United States, agreed to respond to this threat by imposing limits on consumption (defined as production plus imports minus exports of bulk quantities) of [chlorofluorcarbons (CFCs)] and halons. Production and use of CFCs and halons are being curtailed worldwide because of the risks that current production levels and use patterns pose to human health and the

---

*For additional discussion of transboundary pollution problems, see Menz, Transborder Emissions Trading between Canada and the United States, 35 Nat. Resources J. 803 (1995); Roelofs, Note, United States–Canada Air Quality Agreement: A Framework for Addressing Transboundary Air Pollution Problems, 26 Cornell Int'l L.J. 421 (1993); Transboundary Conflicts, 21 Nat. Resources & Env't 1 (Summer 2006). Transboundary pollution between Mexico and the United States also has been an issue. See, e.g., The Border Smog Reduction Act, Pub. L. No. 105-286 (1999) (requiring cars to have properly serviced pollution control systems before entering California from Mexico).

environment. The current version of the Protocol requires industrialized countries such as the United States to (1) limit CFC consumption, beginning in 1989, (2) reduce CFC consumption 50 percent by 1998, and (3) limit halon consumption, beginning in 1992.

Since the Montreal Protocol was negotiated and signed in 1987, the causal link between CFCs and the Antarctic ozone "Hole" has been substantiated. In addition, recent scientific studies have demonstrated that destruction of the ozone layer is not limited to remote, uninhabited portions of Antarctica. Scientists have observed and measured losses of ozone on a global scale. Losses of ozone since 1970 have been measured during the winter months on a worldwide basis, including losses ranging from 2.3 percent to 6.2 percent over densely-populated portions of the Northern Hemisphere. . . .

These measurements of actual ozone loss are significantly greater than computer models had predicted and raise serious questions about the adequacy of the control measures set forth in the Montreal Protocol and existing EPA regulations. Recent reports from Antarctica showing that this year's "Hole" has grown and now covers 10 *million* square miles, in addition to reports from the Arctic indicating the possible formation of a Northern Hemisphere "Hole," lend a new sense of urgency to ongoing negotiations to amend and strengthen the Montreal Protocol.

By waiting for measurements of actual ozone loss, by failing to take appropriate action on the basis of credible scientific theory, governments around the world allowed a manageable environmental threat to become an environmental crisis. As a result of atmospheric lag time and the persistence of CFCs and similar ozone-depleting and greenhouse-forcing gases, it is too late to prevent additional damage to the ozone layer or human-induced global climate change. Our challenge is to take action as rapidly as possible that will, to the greatest extent possible, (1) reduce the threat of additional damage to the ozone layer and (2) reduce the rate and magnitude of human-induced global climate change.

NOTES AND QUESTIONS

1. *How Much Is Gone?* Between 1980 and 1995, more than 6 percent of global ozone was destroyed. 17 Discover (Jan. 1996), at 78. In 1995 ozone levels were about 40 percent of what they were in the 1960s, and 2000 witnessed the largest hole ever measured (more than 11 million square miles, or three times larger than the United States), appearing earlier in the season than usual. Ozone Hole Is Largest Ever Seen, Lawrence J.-World, Sept. 9, 2000, at 9A. National Oceanic and Atmospheric Administration (NOAA) scientists measured the second-largest hole in the ozone layer over Antarctica in 2003. 34 Env't Rep. (BNA) 2239 (2003).

2. *How Do CFCs and Other Chemicals Attack the Ozone Layer?* Before 1990 CFCs were widely used in the United States as coolants for air conditioners and refrigerators, as propellants for aerosol sprays, and as cleansers for computer micro-chips and other electronic parts. In Covington v. Jefferson County, 358 F.3d 626, 649 (9th Cir. 2004) (Gould, J., concurring), one federal judge explained that CFCs can have an atmospheric lifetime of 45-100 years:

In that extensive time span, each CFC, converted to chlorine monoxide (ClO) after reactions with sunlight, can destroy hundreds of molecules of stratospheric ozone

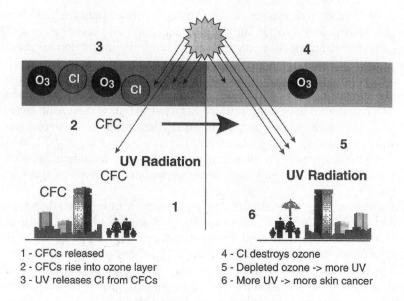

FIGURE 6-12
The Process of Ozone Depletion

Source: http://www.epa.gov/ozone/science/process.html

because the ClO is a catalyst. ClO first reacts with an oxygen atom (O) to form a chlorine atom (Cl) and an oxygen molecule (O_2). The chlorine atom (Cl) reacts with an ozone molecule (O_3) to re-form ClO along with an oxygen molecule (O_2). The ClO, then, is ready to begin the ozone-depletion cycle once more. Once released, CFCs by natural processes create ClO, which is an unrelenting destroyer of ozone. Because this process occurs at the molecular level, it is difficult for us to fathom the cumulative impact of repetitive small destructions of ozone, but science knows that the impact of this process, if unrestrained, will be devastating to all life on earth.

See Figure 6-12.

3. *What Difference Does It Make?* The stratospheric ozone layer shields the Earth's surface from ultraviolet radiation. Exposure to ultraviolet radiation can cause skin cancer and cataracts and impair the functioning of the human immune system. NASA scientists confirmed that levels of harmful ultraviolet radiation on Earth increased steadily from 1979 to 1992. Daily Env't Rep. 150 (BNA), Aug. 5, 1996, at A-7. According to EPA, each 1 percent decline in atmospheric ozone is capable of increasing nonmalignant skin cancer rates by 5 percent and malignant skin cancer rates by 2 percent. Dutch researchers concluded that in the absence of controls on chemicals that deplete stratospheric ozone, skin cancer rates in the United States and northwest Europe would more than triple by 2100. 27 Env't Rep. (BNA) 1590 (1996).

4. *The Montreal Protocol.* In light of evidence of a worsening of the ozone depletion problem, the signatories to the Montreal Protocol agreed in 1990 to eliminate production and use of CFCs by 2000. Developing countries were afforded an extra ten years to comply, with the possibility of further extensions for halons. What justification

might there be for providing this kind of leeway to developing countries? See also CAA §604c(e). In 1992, the parties to the Protocol again accelerated the phase-out deadline for developed countries for CFCs, methyl chloroform, and carbon tetrachloride and established a schedule for phasing out hydrochlorofluorocarbons (HCFCs) by 2030. The Montreal protocol is discussed further in Chapter 11, section C.

5. *Tropospheric and Stratospheric Ozone.* Is it possible that the reduction of ground-level (or tropospheric) ozone will have some of the same adverse effects on the environment as depletion of stratospheric ozone? The Department of Energy and the Office of Management and Budget have raised concerns that reducing ozone levels pursuant to a tightening of the NAAQS would increase the public's exposure to ultraviolet radiation by lowering levels of tropospheric ozone, which blocks ultraviolet radiation. What criteria should govern a decision to trade off risks for one group of the population against risks for another population segment?

In American Trucking Ass'ns, Inc. v. EPA, 175 F.3d 1027 (D.C. Cir. 1999), *rev'd on other grounds*, 531 U.S. 457 (2001), the court remanded EPA's 1997 revisions to the NAAQS for ozone in part because EPA disregarded evidence that tropospheric ozone blocks ultraviolet radiation from the sun. The agency therefore failed to consider whether a more stringent primary standard for ozone might have harmful effects on the public health. EPA found on remand that the beneficial effects of increased ground-level ozone do not justify the adoption of a less stringent ozone NAAQS. 67 Fed. Reg. 614 (2003).

NOTE ON THE TRAIL SMELTER CASE

Although international efforts to abate transboundary pollution, such as the Montreal Protocol, have accelerated in recent years, the problem is not a new one. The absence of a centralized legislative or executive body makes it significantly more difficult both to develop and to enforce international legal obligations compared with domestic laws. See generally Levy, International Law and the Chernobyl Accident: Reflections on an Important but Imperfect System, 36 U. Kan. L. Rev. 81 (1987). The signatories to a treaty can overcome some of these difficulties by agreeing to a system of dispute resolution and enforcement mechanisms. An early example is the Trail Smelter Arbitration (United States v. Canada) (1941), 3 U.N.R.I.A.A. 1938 (1949), in which the United States alleged that SO_2 emissions from a Canadian smelting plant caused damage in the United States. An Arbitral Tribunal established by a 1935 convention concluded that "no State has the right to use or permit the use of its territory in such a manner as to cause injury by fumes in or to the territory of another or the properties or persons therein, when the case is of serious consequence and the injury is established by clear and convincing evidence." It concluded that Canada was responsible for the conduct of the smelter and had to indemnify the United States for $78,000 in damage. The Tribunal also enjoined the smelter from causing further damage in the United States and provided that further indemnification would be due if such damage occurred.* The *Trail Smelter* case is discussed further in Chapter 11, section A.

---

*For further litigation involving pollution generated by the Trail Smelter plant, see Pakootas v. Teck Cominco Metals, Ltd., 452 F.3d 1066 (9th Cir. 2006) (relating to transboundary hazardous substance contamination).

How often is a remedy such as the one provided in the *Trail Smelter* decision likely to be available to a nation suffering the effects of transboundary pollution? Given the difficulties experienced by states in abating interstate pollution under §126 of the CAA, is it realistic to expect a typical nation to be able to prove that activities in another country have caused it harm? Could Canada have convinced a tribunal operating under the same convention to abate damage caused by acid rain alleged to have originated in the United States?

b.   The Phase-out of Ozone-Depleting Substances

The 1990 CAA amendments include provisions that correspond to the responsibilities of the United States under the Montreal Protocol. The statute phased out the production of Class I ozone-depleting substances (including CFCs, halons, carbon tetrachloride, and methyl chloroform) by 2000. §604(a). Effective January 1, 2000 (January 1, 2002, for methyl chloroform), it was unlawful for any person to produce any amount of a Class I substance. §604(b). What exceptions does the statute provide? See §604(e)-(g); NRDC v. EPA, 464 F.3d 1 (D.C. Cir. 2006) (rejecting a challenge to EPA regulation implementing the "critical use" exemption because side agreement to the Montreal Protocol that was not ratified by Congress was not "the law of the land," enforceable in the federal courts). The statute required EPA to issue regulations to ensure that the consumption of Class I substances is phased out in accordance with the same schedule. §604(c).

Beginning January 1, 2015, it is unlawful to introduce into interstate commerce any Class II ozone-depleting substances (HCFCs) that have not been recycled, used, and entirely consumed in the production of other chemicals or used as a refrigerant in appliances manufactured before January 1, 2020. §605(a). The production of Class II substances will be banned effective January 1, 2030, §605(b)(2), and EPA must issue regulations phasing out consumption on the same schedule. §605(c). EPA may accelerate the production or consumption phase-out schedules for Class I or Class II substances if necessary to protect health and the environment against harmful effects on stratospheric ozone, if an accelerated phase-out is practicable (taking into account factors such as technological achievability and safety), or if the Montreal Protocol is modified to speed up the ban on production, consumption, or use of ozone-depleting chemicals. §606(a). President George H. W. Bush accelerated the phase-out of the production of Class I substances to January 1, 1996. 58 Fed. Reg. 65,018 (1993).

The statute requires EPA to issue regulations governing the issuance of transferable allowances for the production of Class I and II substances. What conditions does the statute impose on "emission trading" of ozone-depleting substances? See §607.

To the maximum extent practicable, Class I and II substances must be replaced by chemicals, product substitutes, or alternative manufacturing processes that reduce overall risks to human health and the environment. §612(a). EPA must issue rules making it unlawful to replace any Class I or II substances with any substitute substance EPA determines may present adverse effects to human health or the environment, where EPA has identified an alternative to that replacement that reduces overall risk and is currently or potentially available. §612(c). See Honeywell Int'l, Inc. v. EPA, 374 F.3d 1363 (D.C. Cir. 2004) (vacating EPA's decision to allow limited use of ozone-depleting chemicals if technical constraints prevented use of approved substitute that did not deplete ozone), *opinion withdrawn in part on reconsideration*, 393 F.3d 1315 (D.C. Cir. 2005).

Is It Working? Scientists at the NOAA found in 1996 that the amount of ozone-depleting chemicals in the lower atmosphere had declined for the first time since measurements began. They credited the Montreal Protocol for the improvement. Daily Env't Rep. (BNA) 105, May 31, 1996, at D4. The United Nations Environment Program reported in 2002 that levels of ozone-depleting gases were at or near their projected peak in the stratosphere and had begun a slow decline in the troposphere. Scientists again attributed the improvement to the Montreal Protocol, but warned that noncompliance could result in increased threats to the integrity of the ozone layer. They also warned that persistent levels of ozone-depleting substances in the atmosphere would continue to threaten the ozone layer for years. 33 Env't Rep. (BNA) 2082 (2002). Scientists reported in 2005 that the recovery of the ozone layer over Antarctica is likely to take as much as 20-25 years longer than previously anticipated—until about 2065—due to the continuing releases of ozone-depleting chemicals from older-model refrigerators and air conditioners. Chang, Scientists: Ozone Hole Recovery May Take Longer than Expected, Lawrence J.-World, Dec. 7, 2005, at 6A.

Researchers reported in 2006 that it is unclear whether recent improvements in ozone levels are due to the decline in the amount of ozone-depleting substances in the atmosphere. Rather, natural variability in ozone abundance caused by factors such as the solar cycle and changes in transport and temperature may override the relatively small changes expected from recent decreases in ozone-depleting substances. Weatherhead & Anderson, The Search for Signs of Recovery of the Ozone Layer, 411 Nature 39 (2006).*

4. Global Climate Change

MASSACHUSETTS v. EPA
415 F.3d 50 (D.C. Cir. 2005)

[The portions of the opinions in this case that address EPA's authority to regulate greenhouse gas (GHG) emissions from new motor vehicles appear at page 564 of the casebook. The following excerpts from Judge Tatel's dissenting opinion describe scientific information concerning the causes, extent, and impact of global climate change.]

"Greenhouse gases are accumulating in Earth's atmosphere as a result of human activities, causing surface air temperatures and subsurface ocean temperatures to rise." So begins page one of the National Research Council's 2001 report, *Climate Change Science: An Analysis of Some of the Key Questions* ("NRC Rep."). . . .

As the NRC Rep. explains, [GHGs] trap heat radiated from earth, and their atmospheric concentrations are increasing "as a result of human activities." [See Figure 6-13.] For example, "[h]uman activities . . . responsible for the increase" in atmospheric concentrations of carbon dioxide (CO_2)—the chief GHG—include "[t]he primary source, fossil fuel burning," as well as "[t]ropical deforestation." The resulting increases are striking. In the 400,000 years prior to the Industrial Revolution,

*For an assessment of the impact of the Montreal Protocol and the 1990 CAA provisions relating to ozone depletion, see Hufford & Horwitz, 19 Nat. Resources & Env't 4 (Spring 2005), at 8.

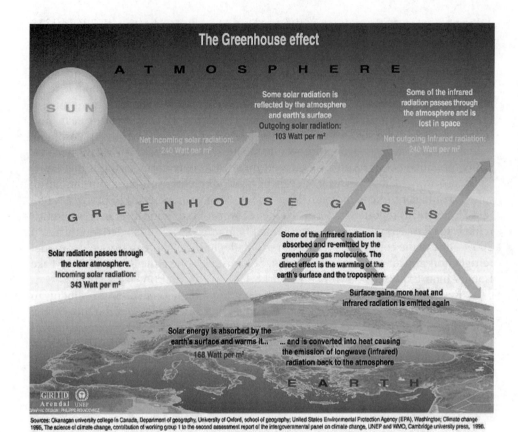

FIGURE 6-13
The Greenhouse Effect

Source: http:/yosemite.epa.gov/oar/globalwarming.nsf/content/Climate.html

atmospheric CO_2 concentrations "typically ranged between 190" parts per million by volume (ppmv) "during the ice ages to near 280 ppmv during the warmer 'interglacial' periods." By 1958, atmospheric concentrations were 315 ppmv (12.5% above the pre-Industrial-Revolution high of 280 ppmv), and by 2000 they had risen to 370 ppmv (17% above the 1958 level). Similarly, prior to the Industrial Revolution, atmospheric concentrations of methane (CH_4), another GHG, ranged from .3 ppmv to .7 ppmv; now, "current values are around 1.77 ppmv." Atmospheric concentrations of other GHGs like nitrous oxide (N_2O) have also risen. Notably, GHGs not only disperse throughout the lower atmosphere, but also linger there at length: "Reductions in the atmospheric concentrations of these gases following possible lowered emissions rates in the future will stretch out over decades for methane, and centuries and longer for carbon dioxide and nitrous oxide."

Increased GHG atmospheric concentrations are causing "climate forcings"— "imposed perturbation[s] of Earth's energy balance" measured in terms of units of watts per square meter (W/m^2). Drawing from another report—an Intergovernmental Panel on Climate Change (IPCC) report with which the NRC "generally agrees"— the NRC Report quantifies these climate forcings. CO_2, "probably the most important climate forcing agent today," has "caus[ed] an increased forcing of about 1.4 W/m^2" between 1750 and 2000. More lies ahead:

> CO_2 climate forcing is likely to become more dominant in the future as fossil fuel use continues. If fossil fuels continue to be used at the current rate, the added CO_2 forcing in 50 years will be about 1 W/m^2. If fossil fuel use increases by 1-1.5% per year for 50 years, the added CO_2 forcing instead will be about 2 W/m^2.

Thus, by 2050, the total CO_2 forcing since 1750 could be . . . 2.4-3.4 W/m^2. The other GHGs "together cause a climate forcing approximately equal to that of CO_2," or more if one includes certain indirect effects of increased CH_4 emissions. While atmospheric GHG increases are not the only causes of climate forcings—for example, changes in solar irradiance and in concentrations of tropospheric ozone also appear to have caused climate forcings, and atmospheric concentration changes in aerosols like sulphates appear to have caused negative (cooling) climate forcings—all other forcings are less certain and appear less substantial than those caused by GHGs.

The extent to which these forcings affect average global temperatures depends on the climate's sensitivity, a condition that is not precisely known. "Well-documented climate changes . . . imply that the climate sensitivity is near . . . 3°C" (5.4°F) for a 4 W/m^2 forcing—a number a bit above the total CO_2 forcing predicted by 2050—"but with a range from 1.5°C to 4.5°C (2.7 to 8.1°F)."

Turning to the practical effects of GHG climate forcings, the NRC Rep. observes that a "diverse array of evidence points to a warming of global surface temperatures." Though the "rate of warming has not been uniform," measurements "indicate that global mean surface air temperature warmed by about .4-.8°C (.7-1.5°F) during the 20th century." The report notes that "[t]he Northern Hemisphere as a whole experienced a slight cooling [during] 1946-75," . . . possibly due to the widespread burning of high sulfur coal and resultant sulfate emissions or to changes in ocean circulation in the Atlantic. The report also observes that, as the IPCC report points out, the "warming of the Northern Hemisphere during the 20th century is likely to have been the largest of any century in the past thousand years."

In evaluating the relationship between GHG atmospheric increases and twentieth-century temperature increases, the NRC Report states that due to the

> large and still uncertain level of natural variability inherent in the climate record and the uncertainties in the time histories of various forcing agents (and particularly aerosols), a causal linkage between the buildup of greenhouse gases in the atmosphere and the observed climate changes during the 20th century cannot be unequivocally established.

. . . [R]ead in context, [this statement] appears little more than an application of the principle that, as the NRC Rep. later puts it, "[c]onfidence limits and probabilistic information, with their basis, should always be considered as an integral part of the information that climate scientists provide to policy and decision makers." Indeed, the NRC Rep. goes on to state that the "fact that the magnitude of the observed warming is large compared to natural variability as simulated in climate models is suggestive of such a linkage" between GHG atmospheric concentration increases and twentieth-century temperature increases, though not "proof" of it.

The NRC Rep. further suggests that uncertainties about future warming relate chiefly to its scope.

Climate change simulations for the period of 1990 to 2100 based on IPCC emissions scenarios yield a globally averaged surface temperature increase by the end of the century of 1.4 to 5.8°C (2.5 to 10.4°F) relative to 1990. The wide range of uncertainty in these estimates reflects both the different assumptions about future concentrations of greenhouse gases and aerosols in the various scenarios considered by the IPCC and the differing climate sensitivities of the various climate models used in the simulations. The range of climate sensitivities implied by these predictions is generally consistent with previously reported values.

These numbers, of course, are averages: the "predicted warming is higher over higher latitudes than low latitudes, especially during winter and spring, and larger over land than over sea."

With this warming will come secondary effects. Predicted impacts in the United States include increased likelihood of drought, greater heat stress in urban areas, rising sea levels, and disruption to many U.S. ecosystems. The likelihood and scope of these impacts vary depending on the magnitude of future temperature increases. Because the "predicted temperature increase is sensitive to assumptions concerning future concentrations of greenhouse gases and aerosols," which in turn depend on future emissions, "national policy decisions made now and in the longer-term future will influence the extent of any damage suffered by vulnerable human populations and ecosystems later in this century." . . .

[Judge Tatel then quoted at length from the NRC's discussion of the consequences of increased climate change of various magnitudes:]

The U.S. National Assessment of Climate Change Impacts . . . directly addresses the importance of climate change of various magnitudes by considering climate scenarios from two well-regarded models. . . . These two models have very different globally-averaged temperature increases (2.7 and 4.4°C (4.9 and 7.9°F), respectively) by the year 2100. A key conclusion from the National Assessment is that U.S. society is likely to be able to adapt to most of the climate change impacts on human systems, but these adaptations may come with substantial cost. The primary conclusions from these reports are summarized for agriculture and forestry, water, human health, and coastal regions.

In the near term, agriculture and forestry are likely to benefit from CO_2 fertilization effects and the increased water efficiency of many plants at higher atmospheric CO_2 concentrations. Many crop distributions will change, thus requiring significant regional adaptations. Given their resource base, the Assessment concludes that such changes will be costlier for small farmers than for large corporate farms. However, the combination of the geographic and climatic breadth of the United States, possibly augmented by advances in genetics, increases the nation's robustness to climate change. These conclusions depend on the climate scenario, with hotter and drier conditions increasing the potential for declines in both agriculture and forestry. In addition, the response of insects and plant diseases to warming is poorly understood. On the regional scale and in the longer term, there is much more uncertainty.

Increased tendency towards drought, as projected by some models, is an important concern in every region of the United States even though it is unlikely to be realized everywhere in the nation. Decreased snow pack and/or earlier season melting are expected in response to warming because the freeze line will be moving to higher elevations. The western part of the nation is highly dependent on the amount of snow pack and the timing of the runoff. The noted increased rainfall rates have implications for pollution runoff, flood control, and changes to plant and animal habitat. Any significant climate change is likely to result in increased costs because the nation's investment in water supply infrastructure is largely tuned to the current climate.

Health outcomes in response to climate change are the subject of intense debate. Climate change has the potential to influence the frequency and transmission of infectious disease, alter heat- and cold-related mortality and morbidity, and influence air and water quality. Climate change is just one of the factors that influence the frequency and transmission of infectious disease, and hence the assessments view such changes as highly uncertain. This said, changes in agents that transport infectious diseases (e.g., mosquitoes, ticks, rodents) are likely to occur with any significant change in precipitation and temperature. Increases in mean temperatures are expected to result in new record high temperatures and warm nights and an increase in the number of warm days compared to the present. Cold-related stress is likely to decline whereas heat stress in major urban areas is projected to increase if no adaptation occurs. The National Assessment ties increases in adverse air quality to higher temperatures and other air mass characteristics. . . . Children, the elderly, and the poor are considered to be the most vulnerable to adverse health outcomes. The understanding of the relationships between weather/climate and human health is in its infancy and therefore the health consequences of climate change are poorly understood. The costs, benefits, and availability of resources for adaptation are also uncertain.

Fifty-three percent of the U.S. population lives within the coastal regions, along with billions of dollars in associated infrastructure. Because of this, coastal areas are more vulnerable to increases in severe weather and sea level rise. Changes in storm frequency and intensity are one of the more uncertain elements of future climate change prediction. However, sea level rise increases the potential damage to coastal regions even under conditions of current storm intensities and can endanger coastal ecosystems if human systems or other barriers limit the opportunities for migration.

In contrast to human systems, the U.S. National Assessment makes a strong case that ecosystems are the most vulnerable to the projected rate and magnitude of climate change, in part because the available adaptation options are very limited. Significant climate change will cause disruption to many U.S. ecosystems, including wetlands, forests, grasslands, rivers, and lakes. . . .

The impacts of these climate changes will be significant, but their nature and intensity will depend strongly on the region and timing of the occurrence. At a national level, the direct economic impacts are likely to be modest. However, on a regional basis the level and extent of both beneficial and harmful impacts will grow. Some economic sectors may be transformed substantially and there may be significant regional transitions associated with shifts in agriculture and forestry. . . . The possibility of abrupt or unexpected changes could pose greater challenges for adaptation.

Even the mid-range scenarios considered in the IPCC result in temperatures that continue to increase well beyond the end of this century, suggesting that assessments that examine only the next 100 years may well underestimate the magnitude of the eventual impacts. For example a sustained and progressive drying of the land surface, if it occurred, would eventually lead to desertification of regions that are now marginally arable, and any substantial melting or breaking up of the Greenland and Antarctic ice caps could cause widespread coastal inundation. [NRC Rep. at 19-20.]

NOTES AND QUESTIONS

1. *Global Temperature Trends.* According to the NOAA's National Climatic Data Center, as of early 2006, the five warmest years since 1890 were 2005, 1998, 2002, 2003, and 2004. Of the 20 hottest years on record, 19 have occurred since 1980. See Figure 6-14. Global temperature increased by about 0.6°C during the twentieth

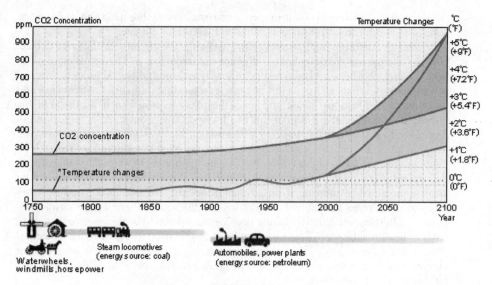

FIGURE 6-14
Energy Consumption and Global Warming

Source: http://www.omsolar.net/en/omsolar1/img/graph1.gif

century, and some scientists predict it will increase by another 2.6°C over this century.[*]

2. *CO₂ Concentrations.* The NRC Report quoted in Judge Tatel's opinion in the *Massachusetts* case provides information on atmospheric concentrations of greenhouse gases such as CO_2, indicating that they rose from 280 parts per million by volume (ppmv) before the Industrial Revolution to 315 ppmv in 1958 and to 370 ppmv in 2000. As of 2006, CO_2 concentrations had risen still further to 380 ppmv, the highest concentration in at least the past 10 million years. Kennedy & Hanson, Ice and History, 311 Science 1673 (2006). Some scientists predict that CO_2 concentrations will increase to 500 ppmv by 2050, a level that last occurred during the Eocene epoch, 55 to 60 million years ago. At that time there were palm trees in Wyoming, crocodiles in the Arctic, and a coniferous forest in Antarctica. Shaw, Fueling Our Future, Harv. Mag., May-June 2006, at 40, 43.

Where do GHGs such as CO_2 come from? They come from human activity, at least in part, and from activities that involve the burning of fossil fuels in particular. Carbon emissions in the United States almost doubled between 1960 and 2001. U.S. emissions of CO_2 from cars and trucks increased by 25 percent between 1990 and 2003, largely because of the increased sales of sport-utility vehicles. Cook, Carbon Dioxide from Cars Rises 25 Percent in 13 years, Environmental Defense Reports, 36 Env't Rep. (BNA) 1655 (2005). U.S. emissions of GHGs reached an all-time high in

---

[*]See Board on Atmospheric Sciences and Climate, Surface Temperature Reconstructions for the Last 2,000 Years (2006). See also Hansen et al., Global Temperature Change, 103 Proc. Nat'l Acad. Sci. 14,288 (2006) (finding that global temperature has increased about 0.2°C per decade over the last 30 years, that the planet is probably within 1°C of the maximum temperature of the past million years, and that a further increase of 1°C relative to 2000 will constitute "dangerous" climate change).

2004, when they were almost twice as high as the average annual rate since 1990. Revkin, Gas Emissions Reached High in U.S. in '04, N.Y. Times. Dec. 21, 2005, at A20.

3. *The Link between GHGs and Climate Change.* The Congressional Research Service stated in a 1996 report that IPCC scientists had acknowledged a "discernible" human impact on the global climate system, but that "the question is now raised whether scientists can affirm a 'smoking gun,' which would indicate that humans are indeed the cause of recent climatic change and would be responsible for future global warming." Congressional Research Service, Global Climate Change (March 18, 1996). Most scientists now agree that the smoking gun has been found. In 2002 the United States released US Climate Action Report 2002: The United States of America's Third National Communication Under the United Nations Framework Convention on Climate Change.* The Report stated that "[g]reenhouse gases are accumulating in the Earth's atmosphere as a result of human activities, causing global mean surface air temperature and subsurface ocean temperature to rise." The report added, however, that "[w]hile the changes observed over the last several decades are likely due mostly to human activities, we cannot rule out that some significant part is also a reflection of natural variability."

The Climate Change Science Program, which coordinates and integrates scientific research on climate change supported by 13 federal departments and agencies, found in 2004 that although temperature changes in North America from 1900 to 1949 were probably due to natural climate variation, changes between 1950 and 1999 were unlikely to be due only to such variation. "Observed trends over this period are consistent with simulations that include anthropogenic forcing from increasing atmospheric greenhouse gases and sulfate aerosols."**

In 2005 the International Climate Change Taskforce (ICCT) concluded that "[t]he international consensus of scientific opinion, led by the [IPCC], is agreed that global temperature is increasing and that the main cause is the accumulation of carbon dioxide and other greenhouse gases in the atmosphere as a result of human activities. Scientific opinion is also agreed that the threat posed will become more severe over coming decades." The report asserted that the cost of failing to mobilize to address this threat is likely to be extremely high, both in economic and in social and human terms. "Impacts on ecosystems and biodiversity are likely to be devastating. Preventing dangerous climate change, therefore, must be seen as a precondition for prosperity and a public good, like national security and public health."***

As long ago as 1989, a Senate committee considering the 1990 CAA amendments reached similar conclusions about the "smoking gun" issue and the risks of failing to address the causes of global climate change:

> It is easy to overstate the uncertainty that surrounds this issue. It is true that scientists disagree about matters such as whether the greenhouse effect has already

---

*The report is available at http://yosemite.epa.gov/oar/globalwarming.nsf/content/ResourceCenterPublicationsUSClimateActionReport.html).

**Our Changing Planet: The U.S. Climate Change Science Program for Fiscal Years 2004 and 2005, available at http://www.usgcrp.gov/usgcrp/Library/ocp2004-5/default.htm.

***Meeting the Climate Challenge: Recommendations of the International Climate Change Taskforce, available at http://72.14.203.104/search?q=cache:JyXsrQKZ-b0J:www.tai.org.au/Publications_Files/Papers%26Sub_Files/Meeting%2520the%2520Climate%2520Challenge%2520FV.pdf+meeting+the+climate+change&hl=en&gl=us&ct=clnk&cd=3.

begun. Similarly, there is no scientific consensus about the precise timing or magnitude of the predicted changes.

Nevertheless, there is a remarkable degree of scientific consensus concerning the threat of massive, uncontrolled global climate change. Specifically, most experts agree that if we do not change our pattern of polluting the atmosphere, many of us, our children, and our grandchildren will experience devastating climate changes of a magnitude and at a rate that will preclude natural evolutionary responses.

There appears to be consensus on another critical point. That is: by the time there is scientific proof for every detail of the problem, it will be too late to avoid the most devastating impacts of an intensified greenhouse effect and global climate change. We can ill-afford to wait for 5 or 10 years of research before we take action to (1) limit the rate and extent of future climate change by reducing atmospheric emissions and concentrations of greenhouse gases, and (2) implement adaptation strategies for coping with the changes to which we are already committed. [S. Rep. No. 101-228, at 379-80 (1989).]

On the last point, Australian biologist Tim Flannery has warned that "[i]f humans pursue a business-as-usual course for the first half of this century, I believe that the collapse of civilization due to climate change becomes inevitable." Zimmer, Sweating It, N.Y. Times Book Review, Mar. 12, 2006, at 8.

4. *Climate Change and the Public Health.* The IPCC has projected a significant temperature increase over the next century, although the degree of increase is uncertain. See Figure 6-15. What kinds of effects would such an increase have on human health? Among the possible consequences is a rise in heat-related deaths due to cardiovascular, cerebrovascular, and respiratory disease (especially among the elderly). If increased temperature results in reduced agricultural output, malnutrition might rise, particularly in developing countries. The World Health Organization reported in 2005 that global warming during the previous 30 years directly contributed to 150,000 deaths annually worldwide. It traced the deaths to events such as heat waves that can cause heart failure or trigger crop failures leading to malnutrition, or to climate fluctuations that alter the transmission of infectious diseases.* Rising temperatures may facilitate the growth of molds and other allergens that cause respiratory problems; rising CO_2 has been shown to increase the timing and release of bioallergens such as ragweed. The incidence of malaria and other infectious diseases may worsen due to the proliferation of mosquitoes, ticks, and fleas, all of which are sensitive to subtle changes in temperature and humidity. The physical changes in the environment (such as rising sea levels that threaten to flood coastal properties) also may lead to increases in psychiatric disorders such as anxiety, depression, and even suicide. See Haines & Patz, Health Effects of Climate Change, 291 J. Am. Med. Ass'n 99 (2004). A build-up of GHGs in the atmosphere is also expected to result in an increase in ground-level ozone pollution. The number of "red alert" days in the summer, when air quality is deemed unhealthy for everyone, could nearly double by mid-century in large U.S. cities.** Temperature increases may also facilitate the growth of poison ivy.

*See Impact of Regional Climate Change on Human Health, available at http://www. nature.com/nature/journal/v438/n7066/abs/nature04188.html.
**See http://www.cnn.com/2004/TECH/science/08/04/environment.smog.reut/index.html. Southern California recorded 86 "red alert" days between May 1 and October 1, 2005, due to ozone pollution. Greenwire, Sept. 29, 2006.

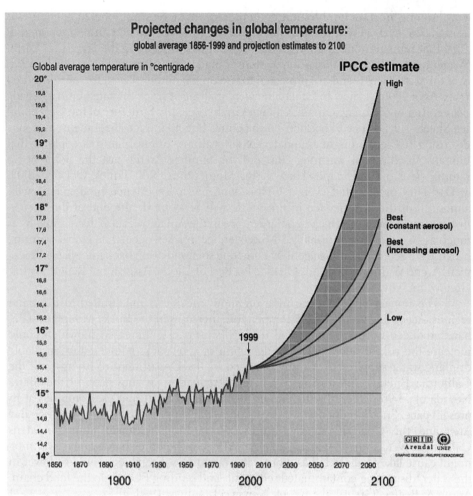

FIGURE 6-15
Projected Changes in Global Temperatures

Source: http://www.grida.no/climate/vital/graphics/large/22.jpg

5. *Climate Change, Climate Events, and the Physical Environment.* Global climate change has already begun to alter the weather and the Earth's physical attributes, and more such changes are likely in the offing. Traditional seasonal rhythms have been disrupted in parts of the United States, including earlier arrivals of birds, insects, and plants in the spring.* Some scientists claim that rising sea temperatures may already be resulting in hurricanes of increasing intensity, although others assert that recent increases in hurricane strength are part of long-term cycles unrelated to climate change.**

*See Clear the Air, Season Creep: How Global Warming Is Already Affecting the World Around Us, available at http://www.cleartheair.org/seasoncreep/index.vtml.
**See, e.g., Trenberth & Shea, Atlantic Hurricanes and Natural Variability in 2005, 33 Geophysical Res. Letters L12704 (2006); Santer et al., Forced and Unforced Ocean Temperature Changes in Atlantic and Pacific Tropical Cyclogenesis Regions, 103 Proc. Nat'l Acad. Sci. 13,905

Among the most troublesome consequences of increasing global temperatures is a rise in sea level, a process which has already begun. The Arctic Council reported in 2004 that human-induced changes in arctic climate are among the largest on Earth. Winter temperatures in Alaska and western Canada have increased by as much as 7°F over the past 50 years and are projected to rise up to another 9°F in the next hundred years. As of 2006, glaciers in Greenland were melting at twice the rate of just a decade before. Rignot & Kanagaratnam, Changes in the Velocity Structure of the Greenland Ice Sheet, 311 Science 986 (2006). If the entire Greenland ice sheet melts, as it may do, rising sea levels might inundate coastal nations. Some scientists contend that human-caused global warming "has put the familiar Arctic past the point of no return." Revkin, No Escape: Thaw Gains Momentum, N.Y. Times, Oct. 25, 2005, at D1. They predict that even if GHGs continue to experience moderate growth, almost all of the summer ice in the Arctic will be gone by the end of the twenty-first century, producing an open polar sea. Ice in the Antarctic is also decreasing, by as much as 36 cubic miles annually.* Moreover, ice loss will accelerate global warming because ice acts as a cooling agent by reflecting solar radiation back into space. Freedman, Arctic Warming Portends Change for Rest of Globe, Assessment Report Warns, Greenwire, Nov. 18, 2004.

The impact of global warming on snow and ice is not limited to the polar regions. According to one report, temperature increases in the Rocky Mountain states have produced warmer winters and reduced snowpacks. Increased snowmelt could increase the risk of flooding, while depletion of snowpacks could reduce available drinking water supplies.** A study financed by the Department of Energy and the California Energy Commission predicted a reduction in snowpack in the Sierra Nevada of 73-90 percent by the end of the century if fossil fuel use continues at its present pace. Such a reduction would disrupt water supplies to the San Francisco Bay Area and the Central Valley. Murphy, Study Finds Climate Shift Threatens California, N.Y. Times, Aug. 17, 2004, at A19. On the other hand, global warming might cause lake levels to fall as more water evaporates. Freighters would sit lower in the water, disturbing contaminated sediments and sending PCBs into the food chain. Annin & Begley, Great Lake Effect, Newsweek, July 5, 1999, at 52.

Researchers at the Scripps Institute for Oceanography at the University of California–San Diego reported in 2006 that climate change caused by anthropogenic activity is the primary driver behind the sudden and dramatic increase in large wild-fires in the western United States beginning in the 1980s. They found a strong asso-ciation between early spring snowmelts in the mountains and the incidence of large wildfires. Earlier snowmelts can lead to an earlier and longer dry season, which creates greater opportunities for severe wildfires. Aside from creating risks to persons and property, these fires may change forest composition and reduce forest density, decreas-ing the capacity of western forests to serve as storage sinks for carbon.***

(2006). See generally Glicksman, Global Climate Change and the Risks to Coastal Areas from Hurricanes and Rising Sea Levels: The Costs of Doing Nothing, 53 Loy. L. Rev. (forthcoming 2007).

*See Velicogna & Wahr, Measurements of Time-Variable Gravity Show Mass Loss in Antarctica, 311 Science 1754 (2006); Eilperin, Antarctic Ice Sheet Is Melting Rapidly, Wash. Post, March 3, 2006, at A1.

**See Rocky Mt. Climate Org., Less Snow, Less Water: Climate Disruption in the West (Sept. 2005). The report is available at http://www.rockymountainclimate.org/website%20pictures/Less%20Snow%20Less%20Water.pdf.

***See Westerling et al., Warming and Earlier Spring Increases Western U.S. Forest Wildfire Activity, available at www.sciencexpress.org/6July 2006/Page1/10.1126/science.1128834.

6. *Climate Change and Wildlife.* Global climate change is already creating problems for wildlife. CO_2, for example, is changing the world's oceans at a rate at least 100 times greater than during the 650,000 years that preceded the Industrial Revolution. Between 1800 and 1994, the oceans absorbed about 476 billion tons of CO_2, causing an increase in concentrations of CO_2 in the upper layers of the oceans from 280 ppm to nearly 380 ppm. Researchers report that this absorption is causing changes in water chemistry that could adversely affect corals, mollusks, and plankton and disrupt marine food webs. Warmer water killed about one-third of the coral reefs at official monitoring sites in the Caribbean during 2005. Furthermore, the changes appear to be occurring at faster rates than are attributable to natural fluctuations.[*]

The melting of the polar ice caps is destroying the habitat of the polar bear. In early 2007, the Fish and Wildlife Service proposed to list the animal as threatened under the Endangered Species Act, noting that models of the impact of future warming project disappearance of most of the sea ice cover in the Arctic region. 72 Fed. Reg. 1064 (2007).[**] Similarly, the melting of permafrost in Alaska is causing mud to pour into rivers, threatening resident salmon populations. Kluger, Polar Ice Caps Are Melting Faster than Ever, Time, March 26, 2006.

Researchers reported in 2006 that the extinction of harlequin frogs and golden toads in Costa Rica is tied to global warming. They asserted that rising sea surface and air temperatures caused by human-induced global warming facilitated the growth and spread of a pathogenic chytrid fungus, which killed the amphibians. Pounds et al., Widespread Amphibian Extinctions from Epidemic Disease Driven by Global Warming, 439 Science 161 (2006). Scientists fear that the fungus threatens to lead to the first loss of an entire taxonomic class (amphibians) since the dinosaurs became extinct. See Mendelson et al., Confronting Amphibian Declines and Extinctions, 313 Science 48 (2006) (stating that "[g]lobal climate change may be encouraging local conditions ideal for" the persistence and spread of fungus that kills amphibians).[***]

The manner in which human activities may affect global climate conditions is often surprising. Some scientists have argued that overfishing of sardines is contributing to global warming. Sardines eat phytoplankton. If those plants are not eaten, they sink to the bottom of the ocean, decompose, and produce methane and hydrogen sulfide gas that rises to the surface. Methane traps 21 times as much heat as does carbon dioxide. According to one researcher, the study showed that "overfishing of one species of fish, such as sardines, can profoundly alter an entire marine ecosystem." Dean, Earth's Uncanned Crusaders: Will Sardines Save Our Skin?, N.Y. Times, Nov. 23, 2004, at D1. Increasing water temperatures due to global climate change may also facilitate the invasion of bodies of water such as the Great Lakes by exotic species (such as zebra mussels) that cannot survive in colder waters. These species could squeeze out native species, changing the entire lake ecosystem. A warming of lake waters also could cause plankton to descend further in the lakes, where temperatures are cooler.

[*]See Feely et al., Carbon Dioxide and Our Ocean Legacy (April 2006), available at http://www.net.org/documents/ocean_acidification_4-5-06.pdf; Kleypas et al., Impacts of Ocean Acidification on Coral Reefs and Other Marine Calcifiers: A Guide for Future Research (June 2006), available at http://www.ucar.edu/news/releases/2006/report.shtml.

[**]See also Center for Biological Diversity, Endangered Species Act Listing Process for Polar Bears Underway, available at http://www.biologicaldiversity.org/swcbd/SPECIES/polarbear/index.html.

[***]See also Impact of Climate Change on Arctic Ecosystems: A Snapshot of Mammals and Forests, available at http://www.ametsoc.org/atmospolicy/documents/061407ArticEcosytems.pdf (describing how warmer temperatures allow parasites harmful to wildlife to proliferate).

Because less light penetrates to those depths, plankton will grow more slowly, producing less food at the base of the lakes' food chain. Annin & Begley, Great Lake
Effect, Newsweek, July 5, 1999, at 52.

7. *Climate Change and Social Dislocation.* Climate change has the potential to
cause serious social and economic dislocation. If temperature increases lead to
drought that reduces crop yields, food shortages may result. If the melting of the
polar ice caps causes sea levels to rise significantly, coastal areas may be flooded
and massive migrations of those who live in the affected areas may be necessary.
Some of these problems may already be occurring. The Inuit Circumpolar Conference, a coalition that represents the indigenous populations of the Arctic Circle, has
filed a petition with the Inter-American Conference on Human Rights, an arm of the
Organization of the American States. The petition seeks a declaration that inaction by
the United States on GHG emissions amounts to a human rights violation against the
Inuit people. Rising sea levels, deteriorating permafrost, and unusually violent storms
have made some of the Alaskan barrier islands long populated by the Inuit uninha-
bitable. The petition seeks a recommendation that the U.S. adopt mandatory limits on
GHG emissions. See Choo, Feeling the Heat, ABA J., July 2006, at 29, 33. Increasing
surface temperatures also may destroy or adversely affect certain recreational industries, such as the skiing industry.*

8. *Global Warming and Other Air Pollution Problems.* A complicating factor in
crafting strategies to mitigate global warming is the possibility that efforts to abate other
kinds of air pollution will exacerbate global warming. The depletion of stratospheric
ozone due to emissions of CFCs has had a cooling effect in the lower stratosphere, at
least in some areas. Particles contained in aerosols attributable to urban and industrial
pollution mitigate global warming by making clouds brighter and capable of reflecting
more light. Schwartz & Buseck, Atmospheric Science: Absorbing Phenomena, 288
Science 989 (2000). Efforts to control acid rain may exacerbate global warming by
removing sulfur in the air that reflects the sun's heat and slows global warming.

9. *Redressing Global Warming.* The greenhouse effect and global warming are
worldwide problems. Fuel consumption and deforestation, including the destruction
of the rain forests, in other countries are major contributors. Even if one accepts as
facts that the climate is warming and that human activity is responsible, uncertainties
remain in predicting the effects of human activity on global climate change. In light of
those uncertainties, what steps, if any, should governments take now? An obvious
strategy is reducing the use of fuels, such as coal, that are high CO_2 producers through
the development of products and processes that increase energy efficiency and the use
of alternative energy sources such as natural gas and nuclear power. Among the
technologies being pursued to reduce GHG emissions are integrated gasification
combined cycle, a form of electricity generation that involves converting coal to a
gaseous fuel before igniting it and that allows separation of CO_2 emissions for capture
and storage. See Kriz, No Silver Bullet, Nat'l J., Aug. 5, 2006, at 16.

Consider the following discussion of the appropriate remedies for global
warming:

> How real is the human-induced global warming threat? Another 10-15 years of
> continued warming would add certainty to the scientific projections, but waiting for this

---

*See, e.g., Aspen Global Change Institute, Aspen Climate Study Finds Serious Risk to the
Future of Skiing (July 26, 2006), available at http://www.agci.org/pdf/ACIA_Press_
Release07.26.doc.pdf.

added assurance might put society at risk for a larger dose of climate change than if actions to curb or slow the buildup of greenhouse gases were implemented now. But actions on what scale? Moreover, in times of fiscal restraint and deficit reduction, many policymakers, here and abroad, are counseling cautious courses of action to address potential climate change. They wish to avoid committing their governments and private sectors to the expenditure of major resources in support of remedial, perhaps expedient actions for consequences that are theoretical and cannot be foreseen with confidence.

Given uncertainties about the timing, pace, and magnitude of global warming projections . . . the question is posed: What policy responses, if any, are appropriate, now, or in the future? Some have suggested that collectively, a number of anticipatory, yet flexible policy responses might be likened to the purchase of an "insurance policy" to hedge against the risks of potential climate change in the future. . . .

Broader national responses could range from engineering countermeasures, to passive adaptation, to prevention, and an international law of the atmosphere. . . . Policy options that stress energy efficiency and conservation, renewable energy, planting trees to enhance CO_2 sequestration from the atmosphere, and fuel substitution are important examples. Many scientists also stress that such actions might buy time to gain a better understanding of global climate change, by forestalling the onset of potential global warming or, at least, slowing the rate of climate change that may be human-induced. [Congressional Research Service, Global Climate Change (March 18, 1996).]

Some scientists endorse taking steps in the short term to reduce emissions of substances other than CO_2 that contribute to global warming, such as methane, ozone, and black carbon soot. Those substances contribute to other forms of air pollution as well, and therefore the public is more likely to accept steps to curtail their emissions. Moreover, it may be easier to reduce those emissions with the use of existing and developing technologies than it would be to curtail the burning of fossil fuels to reduce CO_2 emissions. Some scientists respond that the manner in which these other pollutants interact and influence climate is so poorly understood that focusing on cutting their emissions is a risky endeavor. See Revkin, Debate Rises over a Quick(er) Climate Fix, N.Y. Times, Oct. 3, 2000, at D1.

As indicated above, tree planting is one way to remove CO_2 from the atmosphere. How far should this idea be taken? Some congressional Republicans endorsed a plan in 1998 of *expanded* logging on public lands as a means of combating global warming. The plan would involve cutting down mature forests, which have slowed their growth, and replacing them with farms of more rapidly growing tree species. Skeptics claim that the adverse environmental consequences of such a simplistic plan would far outweigh any benefits it might bring. Removing the existing forest would lead to the immediate dissipation of carbon in the soil, and to decades of CO_2 emissions. Cutting down existing forests also would have adverse consequences on watershed protection and species diversity. See Cushman, Scientists Are Turning to Trees to Repair the Greenhouse, N.Y. Times, Mar. 3, 1998, at B15.

Carbon sequestration is receiving increasing attention as a means of mitigating global warming. This technique involves storing carbon by removing it from the air so that it cannot trap heat. Some possibilities appear to be more fanciful than others. Aside from planting new forests, scientists have proposed capturing CO_2 from power plants and factories and injecting it into underground geologic formations such as depleted oil wells, injecting CO_2 into the ocean, spiking the oceans with iron sulfate to spur the growth of algae that consume CO_2, creating microbes to boost plant consumption of CO_2, and reintroducing animals such as bison and musk oxen to Siberia to restore the carbon-rich grasslands that existed there eons ago. Some of these schemes have actually been tried: oil producers have been shooting CO_2 into wells as a means of enhancing petroleum recovery, and Norway's state-owned oil company has injected CO_2 into aquifers beneath the North Sea. See Solomon, A Radical Approach to Global Warming, Nat'l J., Oct. 2, 1999, at 2828-2829. By one estimate, the cost of compressing CO_2, shipping it to offshore platforms, and pumping it into sediments that have accumulated on the ocean floor would be about 1 percent of the U.S. gross domestic product, an amount equal to annual government spending on the Iraq war. Shaw, Fueling Our Future, Harv. Mag., May-June 2006, at 40, 47-48. Dissolution of CO_2 in the oceans, however, would make the water more acidic, creating potentially adverse consequences for aquatic life. See Chang, Strategy Has a "Greenhouse" Gas Bottled up under Land and Sea, N.Y. Times, June 17, 2001, at A1 (nat'l ed.).[*]

Proposed remedies like carbon sequestration fall under the heading of geoengineering, which involves altering the earth's environment on a large scale to promote habitability. Among the possibilities scientists have proposed are putting trillions of small lenses in orbit around the earth to reflect light away from the planet, injecting sulfur into the stratosphere to cool it, and laying reflective films over deserts or placing plastic islands in the oceans to reflect more sunlight into space. These ideas have yet to generate broad enthusiasm among scientists specializing in climate control. See Broad, How to Cool a Planet (Maybe), N.Y. Times, June 27, 2006, at D1.

10. *The FCCC.* More than 150 nations signed the Framework Convention on Climate Change (FCCC), 31 I.L.M. 849 (1992), at the June 1992 Rio Earth Summit. The FCCC's objective is "to achieve . . . stabilization of greenhouse gas concentrations in the atmosphere at a level that would prevent dangerous anthropogenic interference with the climate system" within a time frame that permits ecosystems to adapt naturally to climate change, avoids threats to food production, and enables sustainable economic development. Id. at 854. The Convention acknowledges that change in the Earth's climate and its adverse effects are a common international concern, expresses concern that human activities have enhanced the natural greenhouse effect, notes the uncertainties in predicting climate change, and calls for cooperation among nations, "in accordance with their common but differentiated responsibilities and respective capabilities and their social and economic conditions." Id. at 851. The FCCC states that "[t]he Parties should protect the climate system for the benefit of present and future generations of humankind, on the basis of equity," and take "precautionary measures to anticipate, prevent or minimize the causes of climate change and mitigate its adverse effects." Id. at 854. Although it calls on signatories to "[t]ake climate change considerations into account, to the extent feasible, in their relevant social, economic and environmental policies and actions," it commits no one to specific reductions of greenhouse gases. Id. at 855. The United States Senate ratified the FCCC in October 1992, but took the position that the Convention does not require any implementing legislation.

11. *The Kyoto Protocol.* In 1997, a tentative agreement called the Kyoto Protocol was reached in which the industrialized nations agreed to reduce emissions of CO_2 and other global warming gases by 2012. Not all nations committed to the same percentage reductions. The United States agreed to cut emissions by an average of

---

[*]See also House et al., Permanent Carbon Dioxide Storage in Deep-Sea Sediments, 103 Proc. Nat'l Acad. Sci. 12,291 (Aug. 15, 2006) (discussing strategies for preventing escape of CO_2 injected into the ocean).

7 percent below 1990 levels between 2008 and 2012. The European Union agreed to an 8 percent reduction, while Japan committed to a 6 percent cut. To spur reductions in developing countries, the Protocol established a Clean Development Mechanism designed to transfer energy-efficient technologies and nonpolluting forms of energy production from developed to developing nations by providing emission reduction credits for the transferor nations. Opposition by developing nations to a broader emissions trading scheme, however, prevented agreement on this feature. The United States signed the Protocol in November 1998. Members of the U.S. Senate denounced the Protocol for not extracting commitments from developing countries, however, and President George W. Bush repudiated the Kyoto Protocol early in his administration. He subsequently explained that cutting CO_2 emissions below 1990 levels "would have meant I would have presided over massive layoffs and economic destruction."[*]

In July 2001, representatives of 178 nations convened in Bonn, Germany, to sign an agreement requiring reductions in emissions of gases linked to global warming. Thirty-eight industrialized nations committed to reducing combined emissions of GHGs by 2012 to a level 5.2 percent below that measured in 1990. The treaty established the first global system for buying and selling CO_2 emission reduction credits. Countries will be able to earn credits for human-induced carbon "sinks" that extract CO_2 from the air. Industrialized nations may earn additional credits for investing in projects in developing countries that will reduce GHG emissions. The United States refused to sign the agreement. The Kyoto Protocol nevertheless entered into force on February 16, 2005. See 36 Env't Rep. (BNA) 320 (2005). Russia ratified the treaty on November 18, 2004, becoming the 128th nation to do so. These signatories account for more than 55 percent of the world's CO_2 emissions. Only four industrialized nations have not ratified the treaty: the United States, Australia, Liechtenstein, and Monaco.

The Bonn negotiations failed to resolve several important issues, including the nature of the mechanisms for ensuring compliance with treaty obligations and the composition of a board to oversee compliance. At the 2005 annual UN Climate Change Conference in Montreal, 157 countries agreed to require developing countries to move toward voluntary reductions. Parties that fail to meet the emissions reduction targets established at Kyoto during the 2008-2012 period will have to make those reductions as well as pay an additional 30 percent penalty during the following period.[**] An ad hoc working group of the Kyoto Protocol's signatories agreed after additional meetings in Bonn in 2006 that industrial nations will need to agree to additional cuts in GHG emissions after 2012. 37 Env't Rep. (BNA) 1154 (2006). Wiener, On the Political Economy of Global Environmental Regulation, 87 Geo. L.J. 749 (1999), explores the role of parochial rent seeking by national governments and interest groups in global environmental regulation, using the climate change negotiations as an example.

The Chicago Climate Exchange (CCX) has created a voluntary market in GHG emission credits. Members agree to reduce emissions by a certain percentage each year. If they exceed the target, they may sell credits to other CCX members. Those who have sold credits include dairy farmers who use manure as fuel to generate electricity and farmers engaged in no-till farming. Breslau, It Can Pay to Be Green, Newsweek,

---

[*]News Release, President Discusses Democracy in Iraq with Freedom House, March 30, 2006, available at http://www.whitehouse.gov/news/releases/2006/03/print/20060329-6.html.

[**]See http://unfccc.int/meetings/cop_11/items/3394.php.

May 22, 2006, at 45. By May 2006, the CCX had more than 175 participants (including one state and several cities), more than 6 million carbon allowances had been traded, and the price for an allowance ranged from $3 to $5 per metric ton of CO_2. Goodell, Capital Pollution Solution?, N.Y. Times Mag., July 30, 2006, at 34, 36. Driesen, Free Lunch or Cheap Fix? The Emissions Trading Idea and the Climate Change Convention, 26 B.C. Envtl. Aff. L. Rev. 1 (1998), argues that emissions trading will reduce short-term costs but lessen innovation and democratic accountability.

12. *Intergenerational and International Equity.* The FCCC's reference to the interests of future generations raises the issue of intergenerational equity. One writer asserts that the norm of intergenerational equity "encompasses both the moral principle that no generation has priority over another and the legal standard that there is equality among generations." Wood, Intergenerational Equity and Climate Change, 8 Geo. Int'l Envtl. L. Rev. 293, 295 (1996). Does this norm place an obligation on the present generation to take action to prevent global climate change? According to Wood, the FCCC "begins the process of defining that obligation." Id.

Do all nations share equally in whatever responsibilities intergenerational equity norms create to mitigate the adverse effects of global climate change? The FCCC refers to "differentiated responsibilities" in accordance with "social and economic conditions." It also recognizes the need for "developed countries" to take immediate action as "a first step towards comprehensive response strategies" and takes account of "the special difficulties of those countries, especially developing countries, whose economies are particularly dependent on fossil fuel production, use and exportation." 31 I.L.M. at 851. Finally, it recognizes that "all countries, especially developing countries, need access to resources required to achieve sustainable social and economic development, and that, in order for developing countries to progress towards that goal, their energy consumption will need to grow. . . ." Id. at 852.

Does the CAA provide EPA with the authority to address global climate change? The following case addresses that issue.

MASSACHUSETTS v. EPA
415 F.3d 50 (D.C. Cir. 2005)

Judgment of the Court filed by Circuit Judge RANDOLPH.

[Twelve states, three cities, and numerous environmental organizations appealed EPA's denial of a petition requesting that it regulate emissions of carbon dioxide (CO_2), methane (CH_4), nitrous oxide (N_2O), and hydrofluorocarbons (HFCs) from new motor vehicles under §202(a)(1) of the CAA. EPA concluded that it did not have statutory authority to regulate GHG emissions from motor vehicles and that, even if it did, it would not exercise the authority at this time. Ten other states and several trade associations intervened in support of EPA. In denying the petition, EPA found that the scientific information submitted in support of the petition did not add significantly to the knowledge already provided by the National Research Council (NRC), part of the National Academy of Sciences (NAS). The White House had requested that the NAS assist it in reviewing climate change policy. The NAS is authorized by statute to advise the federal government on scientific and technical matters when requested.]

The [NRC] concluded that "a causal linkage" between greenhouse gas emissions and global warming "cannot be unequivocally established." [National Research Council, Climate Change Science: An Analysis of Some of the Key Questions (2001), at 17.] The earth regularly experiences climate cycles of global cooling, such as an ice age, followed by periods of global warming. Global temperatures have risen since the industrial revolution, as have atmospheric levels of carbon dioxide. But an increase in carbon dioxide levels is not always accompanied by a corresponding rise in global temperatures. For example, although carbon dioxide levels increased steadily during the twentieth century, global temperatures decreased between 1946 and 1975. Considering this and other data, the [NRC] concluded that "there is considerable uncertainty in current understanding of how the climate system varies naturally and reacts to emissions of greenhouse gases." . . . And, as the [NRC] noted, past assumptions about effects of future greenhouse gas emissions have proven to be erroneously high.

Relying on Ethyl Corp. v. EPA, 541 F.2d 1 (D.C. Cir. 1976), petitioners challenge EPA's decision to forgo rulemaking "[u]ntil more is understood about the causes, extent and significance of climate change and the potential options for addressing it." In our view *Ethyl* supports EPA, not petitioners. . . . In requiring the EPA Administrator to make a threshold "judgment" about whether to regulate, §202(a)(1) gives the Administrator considerable discretion. Congress does not require the Administrator to exercise his discretion solely on the basis of his assessment of scientific evidence. What the *Ethyl* court called "policy judgments" also may be taken into account. By this the court meant the sort of policy judgments Congress makes when it decides whether to enact legislation regulating a particular area.

The EPA Administrator's analysis, although it did not mention *Ethyl*, is entirely consistent with the case. In addition to the scientific uncertainty about the causal effects of greenhouse gases on the future climate of the earth, the Administrator relied upon many "policy" considerations that, in his judgment, warranted regulatory forbearance at this time. New motor vehicles are but one of many sources of greenhouse gas emissions; promulgating regulations under §202 would "result in an inefficient, piecemeal approach to the climate change issue." The Administrator expressed concern that unilateral regulation of U.S. motor vehicle emissions could weaken efforts to persuade developing countries to reduce the intensity of greenhouse gases thrown off by their economies. Ongoing research into scientific uncertainties and the Administration's programs to address climate change—including voluntary emission reduction programs and initiatives with private entities to develop new technology—also played a role in the Administrator's decision not to regulate. The Administrator pointed to efforts to promote "fuel cell and hybrid vehicles" and ongoing efforts to develop "hydrogen as a primary fuel for cars and trucks." The Administrator also addressed the matter of remedies. Petitioners offered two ways to reduce CO_2 from new motor vehicles: reduce gasoline consumption and improve tire performance. As to the first, the Department of Transportation—the agency in charge of fuel efficiency standards—recently issued new standards requiring greater fuel economy, as a result of which millions of metric tons of CO_2 will never reach the stratosphere. As to tire efficiency, EPA doubted its authority to regulate this subject as an "emission" of an air pollutant. "With respect to the other [greenhouse gases]—CH_4, N_2O, and HFCs—petitioners make no suggestion as to how those emissions might be reduced from motor vehicles."

It is therefore not accurate to say, as petitioners do, that the EPA Administrator's refusal to regulate rested entirely on scientific uncertainty, or that EPA's decision represented an "open-ended invocation of scientific uncertainty to justify refusing to regulate." A "determination of endangerment to public health," the court said in *Ethyl*, "is necessarily a question of policy that is to be based on an assessment of risks and that should not be bound by either the procedural or the substantive rigor proper for questions of fact." *Ethyl*, 541 F.2d at 24. And as we have held, a reviewing court "will uphold agency conclusions based on policy judgments" "when an agency must resolve issues 'on the frontiers of scientific knowledge.'" Envtl. Def. Fund v. EPA, 598 F.2d 62, 82 (D.C. Cir. 1978).

We thus hold that the EPA Administrator properly exercised his discretion under §202(a)(1) in denying the petition for rulemaking. . . .

TATEL, Circuit Judge, dissenting. . . .

. . . Unlike Judge Randolph, I think EPA's order cannot be sustained on the merits. EPA's first given reason—that it lacks statutory authority to regulate emissions based on their contribution to welfare-endangering climate change—fails, as I explain in Part III, because the statute clearly gives EPA authority to regulate "any air pollutant" that may endanger welfare, 42 U.S.C. §7521(a)(1), with "air pollutant" defined elsewhere in the statute as "including any physical, chemical, biological, radioactive . . . substance or matter which is emitted into or otherwise enters the ambient air," id. §7602(g). EPA's second given reason—the one accepted by Judge Randolph—is that even if it has statutory authority, it nonetheless "believes" that "it is inappropriate to regulate [greenhouse gas] emissions from motor vehicles" due to various policy reasons. As I explain in Part IV, however, none of these policy reasons relates to the statutory standard—"cause, or contribute to, air pollution which may reasonably be anticipated to endanger public health or welfare," §7521(a)(1)—and the Clean Air Act gives the Administrator no discretion to withhold regulation for such reasons. . . .

III . . .

. . . [T]he threshold question is this: does the Clean Air Act authorize EPA to regulate emissions based on their effects on global climate? . . .

[Section 202(a)(1) of the CAA] plainly authorizes regulation of (1) any air pollutants emitted from motor vehicles that (2) in the Administrator's judgment cause, or contribute to, air pollution which may reasonably be anticipated to endanger public health or welfare. EPA's claimed lack of authority relates to the first of these two elements. According to EPA, GHGs like CO_2, CH_4, N_2O, and hydrofluorocarbons (HFCs) "are not air pollutants."

Congress, however, left EPA little discretion in determining what are "air pollutants." Added in 1970 and amended in 1977, CAA section 302(g) defines the term as follows:

> The term "air pollutant" means any air pollution agent or combination of such agents, including any physical, chemical, biological, radioactive . . . substance or matter which is emitted into or otherwise enters the ambient air.

42 U.S.C. §7602(g). This exceedingly broad language plainly covers GHGs emitted from motor vehicles: they are "physical [and] chemical . . . substance[s] or matter . . . emitted into . . . the ambient air." Indeed, in one CAA provision, added in 1990, Congress explicitly included CO_2 in a partial list of "air pollutants."

Section 103(g) instructs the Administrator to research "nonregulatory strategies and technologies for preventing or reducing multiple air pollutants, including sulfur oxides, nitrogen oxides, heavy metals, PM-10 (particulate matter), carbon monoxide, and *carbon dioxide*." Id. §7403(g) (emphasis added). . . .

Unswayed by what it calls "narrow semantic analyses"—but what courts typically call *Chevron* step one—EPA claims that a "more holistic analysis . . . [of] the text, structure, and history of the CAA as a whole, as well as the context provided by other legislation that is specific to climate change," justifies its conclusion that it cannot regulate GHGs like CO_2 for their effects on climate change. . . .

EPA first suggests that because the 1965, 1970, and 1977 Congresses showed little concern about the specific problem of global warming, reading the CAA's language to cover such problems would be like finding "an elephant in a mousehole." EPA is correct that those Congresses spilled little ink on the issue of global warming: while the legislative history contains a few stray references to human-forced climate change, in those years the scientific understanding of the issue was nascent at best. But EPA errs in suggesting that because Congress may not have precisely foreseen global warming, the Act provides no authorization for GHG regulation. Hardly a mousehole, the definition of "air pollutants" . . . enables the Act to apply to new air pollution problems as well as existing ones. . . . Indeed, Congress expressly instructed EPA to be on the lookout for climate-related problems in evaluating risks to "welfare." Section 302(h), added in 1970, explains that "[a]ll language referring to effects on welfare includes, but is not limited to, effects on soils, water, crops, vegetation, manmade materials, animals, wildlife, weather, visibility, *and climate*." 42 U.S.C. §7602(h) (emphasis added).

EPA's second reason for its interpretation—that for practical and policy reasons global warming should be dealt with through specifically tailored statutes—likewise fails to trump Congress's plain language. It may well be that a statute aimed solely at global warming would deal with the problem more effectively than one aimed generally at air pollution. But an agency may not "avoid the Congressional intent clearly expressed in the [statutory] text simply by asserting that its preferred approach would be better policy." [Engine Mfrs. Ass'n v. EPA, 88 F.3d 1075, 1089 (D.C. Cir. 1996).] Perhaps recognizing this point, EPA attempts to link its policy arguments to the statute by claiming that because the 1977 and 1990 Congresses enacted provisions specific to another global pollution problem—depletion of stratospheric ozone—we must infer that the Act's general provisions do not cover such global problems. Once again, EPA makes much of very little. While the 1977 Congress did add provisions aimed specifically at ozone depletion, it also made clear that "[n]othing in this [ozone-specific] part shall be construed to alter or affect the authority of the Administrator under . . . any other provision of this Act." Pub. L. No. 95-95, §58, 91 Stat. 685, 730 (1977). Similarly, I see nothing in the 1990 Congress's enactment of other provisions specific to stratospheric ozone protection, see 42 U.S.C. §§7671 to 7671q, indicating it thought EPA lacked authority under general provisions like section 202 to regulate emissions contributing to global pollution. This is particularly true since that Congress also enacted provisions specific to certain regional pollutants, see, e.g., id. §§7651 to 7651o (acid rain control), which, pursuant to general CAA provisions, EPA already had authority to regulate.

EPA also attempts an unworkability argument. Its argument goes like this: another part of the CAA provides that the Administrator shall maintain a list of air pollutants that, among other things, "in [the Administrator's] judgment, cause or contribute to air pollution which may reasonably be anticipated to endanger public health or welfare." Id. §7408(a)(1)(A). Once pollutants go on this list, the Administrator must set national ambient air quality standards (NAAQS) for them. . . . According to EPA, these provisions would be unworkable if applied to CO_2: because CO_2 disperses relatively evenly throughout the lower atmosphere, states would have only minimal control over their atmospheric CO_2 concentrations and thus over whether they meet the CO_2 NAAQS. EPA then concludes that because CO_2 regulation would be unworkable in the NAAQS context, no general CAA provisions, including section 202(a)(1), authorize it to regulate any GHGs.

This unwieldy argument fails. Even assuming that states' limited ability to meet CO_2 NAAQS renders these provisions unworkable as to CO_2, but see id. §7509a(a) (providing a safe harbor for states that fail to meet NAAQS due to emissions emanating from outside the country), the absurd-results canon would justify at most an exception limited to the particular unworkable provision, i.e., the NAAQS provision. As EPA acknowledges, regulating CO_2 emissions from automobiles is perfectly feasible. . . .

In sum, GHGs plainly fall within the meaning of "air pollutant" in section 302(g) and therefore in section 202(a)(1). If "in [the Administrator's] judgment" they "cause, or contribute to, air pollution which may reasonably be anticipated to endanger public health or welfare," 42 U.S.C. §7521(a)(1), then EPA has authority—indeed, the obligation—to regulate their emissions from motor vehicles.

IV.

EPA's . . . "fallback argument" . . . is that even if GHGs are air pollutants, the agency gave appropriate reasons and acted within its discretion in denying the petition for rulemaking. . . .

. . . I find it difficult even to grasp the basis for EPA's action. . . .

EPA's Discretion to Make an Endangerment Finding

In the petition denial, EPA states:

> [T]he CAA provision authorizing regulation of motor vehicle emissions does not impose a mandatory duty on the Administrator to exercise her judgment. Instead, section 202(a)(1) provides the Administrator with discretionary authority to address emissions. . . . While section 202(a)(1) uses the word "shall," it does not require the Administrator to act by a specified deadline and it conditions authority to act on a discretionary exercise of the Administrator's judgment regarding whether motor vehicle emissions cause or contribute to air pollution that may reasonably be anticipated to endanger public health or welfare.

. . . In EPA's view, "the Agency's authority to make the threshold finding is discretionary" and petitioners err in suggesting that "if the statutory test for making the finding is met, EPA has no choice but to set standards."

EPA's brief also turns several policy concerns raised in other portions of its petition denial into rationales for holding off examining endangerment. . . .

EPA's reasoning is simply wrong. In effect, EPA has transformed the limited discretion given to the Administrator under section 202—the discretion to determine whether or not an air pollutant causes or contributes to pollution which may reasonably be anticipated to endanger public health or welfare—into the discretion to withhold regulation because it thinks such regulation bad policy. But Congress did not give EPA this broader authority, and the agency may not usurp it.

Section 202(a)(1)'s language . . . establishes the limits of EPA's discretion. This section gives the Administrator the discretion only to "judg[e]," within the bounds of substantial evidence, whether pollutants "cause, or contribute to, air pollution which may reasonably be anticipated to endanger public health or welfare." If conflicting credible evidence exists, e.g., some evidence suggesting that GHGs may reasonably be anticipated to endanger welfare and other evidence suggesting the opposite, then the Administrator has discretion in weighing this evidence. If the facts are known but require no single conclusion as to whether a pollutant "may reasonably be anticipated to endanger public health or welfare"—such as in a case where there exists a small-to-moderate risk that a pollutant will cause a small-to-moderate amount of harm—then the Administrator has discretion in assessing whether these facts amount to endangerment. If the Administrator concludes based on substantial evidence that more research is needed before he can judge whether GHGs may reasonably be anticipated to endanger welfare, then he has discretion to hold off making a finding.

But section 202(a)(1) plainly limits the Administrator's discretion—his judgment—to determining whether the statutory standard for endangerment has been met. The Administrator has no discretion either to base that judgment on reasons unrelated to this standard or to withhold judgment for such reasons. In claiming otherwise, EPA not only ignores the statute's language, but also fails to reckon with this circuit's related precedent. . . .

In short, EPA may withhold an endangerment finding only if it needs more information to determine whether the statutory standard has been met. Similarly, for EPA to find no endangerment (as Judge Randolph, going beyond the agency's own arguments, appears to claim happened here), it must ground that conclusion in the statutory standard and may not rely on unrelated policy considerations.

The statutory standard, moreover, is precautionary. At the time we decided *Ethyl*, section 202(a)(1) and similar CAA provisions either authorized or required the Administrator to act on finding that emissions led to "air pollution *which endangers* the public health or welfare." See 42 U.S.C. §1857f-1(a)(1) (1976) (emphasis added). After *Ethyl* found that "the statutes and common sense *demand* regulatory action to prevent harm, even if the regulator is less than certain that harm is otherwise inevitable," *Ethyl*, 541 F.2d at 25 (emphasis added), the 1977 Congress not only approved of this conclusion, but also wrote it into the CAA. Section 202(a)(1) . . . now requires regulation to precede certainty. It requires regulation where, in the Administrator's judgment, emissions "contribute to air pollution *which may reasonably be anticipated to endanger public health or welfare.*" 42 U.S.C. §7521(a)(1) (emphasis added). As the House Report explained: "In order to emphasize the precautionary or preventative purpose of the act (and, therefore, the Administrator's *duty* to assess risks rather than wait for proof of actual harm), the committee not only retained the concept of endangerment to health; the committee also added the words 'may reasonably be anticipated to.'" H.R. Rep. No. 95-294, at 51 (emphasis added).

Given this framework, it is obvious that none of EPA's proffered policy reasons justifies its refusal to find that GHG emissions "contribute to air pollution which may reasonably be anticipated to endanger public health or welfare." . . .

First, EPA claims that global warming still has many scientific uncertainties associated with it. In this regard, EPA makes much of the NRC's statements that a link between human-caused atmospheric GHG concentration increases and this past century's warming "cannot be unequivocally established." But the CAA nowhere calls for proof. It nowhere calls for "unequivocal" evidence. Instead, it calls for the Administrator to determine whether GHGs "contribute to air pollution which may reasonably be anticipated to endanger" welfare. EPA never suggests that the uncertainties identified by the NRC Report prevent it from determining that GHGs "may reasonably be anticipated to endanger" welfare. In other words, . . . the agency has failed here to explain its refusal to find endangerment in light of the statutory standard.

EPA's silence on this point is telling. Indeed, looking at the NRC Report as a whole, I doubt EPA could credibly conclude that it needs more research to determine whether GHG-caused global warming "may reasonably be anticipated to endanger" welfare. Though not offering certainty, the report demonstrates that matters are well within the "frontiers of scientific knowledge." The report also indicates that the projected consequences of global warming are serious. . . .

EPA similarly fails to link its second policy justification—that setting fuel economy standards represents the only currently available way to regulate CO_2 emissions and petitioners "make no suggestion[s]" for how to reduce CH_4, N_2O, and HFC emissions—with the statutory standard. As discussed earlier, the fact that DOT sets fuel economy standards pursuant to the [Energy Policy and Conservation Act] in no way prevents EPA from setting standards pursuant to the CAA. It is true that DOT has recently increased fuel economy standards for light trucks—a fact EPA didn't even bother to mention in its brief—but unless DOT's action affects whether GHGs "contribute to air pollution which may reasonably be anticipated to endanger public health or welfare," it provides no support for EPA's decision.

As to EPA's point about other GHGs, it may well be that no current technologies exist for reducing their emissions. But once again, this has nothing at all to do with the statutory endangerment standard. Indeed, in section 202(a)(2), Congress has made it crystal clear that endangerment findings must not wait on technology.

> Any regulation prescribed under paragraph (1) of this subsection (and any revision thereof) shall take effect after such period as the Administrator finds necessary to permit the development and application of the requisite technology, giving appropriate consideration to the cost of compliance within such period.

42 U.S.C. §7521(a)(2). As the Senate Report explained, EPA "is expected to press for the development and application of improved technology rather than be limited by that which exists." S. Rep. No. 91-1196, at 24 (1970). In refusing to make an endangerment finding because it lacks currently available technology for controlling these emissions, EPA goes well beyond the bounds of its statutory discretion.

EPA's final policy reasons likewise fail. Because other domestic and foreign sources contribute to atmospheric GHG concentrations, GHG regulation might well "result in an inefficient, piecemeal approach to addressing the climate change issue." But again, Congress has expressly demanded such an approach. Section 202(a)(1) requires EPA to regulate if it judges that U.S. motor vehicle emissions "cause, or *contribute to*, air pollution," 42 U.S.C. §7521(a)(1) (emphasis added). EPA (understandably) offers no basis for thinking that U.S. automobile emissions are not contributing to global warming. Indeed, why would the "Administration's global climate change policy plan support[] increasing automobile fuel economy," if motor vehicle emissions were contributing nothing to global warming? Similarly, EPA's concern that regulation could weaken U.S. negotiating power with other nations has nothing at all to do with whether GHGs contribute to welfare-endangering air pollution. Finally, while EPA obviously prefers nonregulatory approaches to regulatory ones, Congress gave the Administrator discretion only in assessing whether global warming "may reasonably be anticipated to endanger" welfare, not "free[dom] to set policy on his own terms," *Ethyl*, 541 F.2d at 29.

In short, EPA has utterly failed to relate its policy reasons to section 202(a)(1)'s standard. Indeed, nowhere in its policy discussion does EPA so much as mention this standard—"may reasonably be anticipated to endanger public health or welfare." EPA apparently dislikes the fact that section 202(a)(1) says the Administrator "shall" regulate—rather than "may" regulate—on making an endangerment finding. But EPA cannot duck Congress's express directive by declining to evaluate endangerment on the basis of policy reasons unrelated to the statutory standard. Although EPA is free to take its policy concerns to Congress and seek a change in the Clean Air Act, it must obey the law in the meantime.

EPA's DISCRETION AFTER MAKING AN ENDANGERMENT FINDING

Alternatively, EPA may have believed that even if it made an endangerment finding, it had no obligation to regulate GHG emissions. . . . Refusing to regulate following an endangerment finding would violate the law. Indeed, EPA appears to have abandoned this argument. In a (rare) concession to the Act's text, EPA counsel acknowledged at oral argument, "I don't think that we would contest that if the agency had made an endangerment finding, that then you would have to give some significance to the term 'shall' in [section] 202(a)." . . .

NOTES AND QUESTIONS

1. How did Judge Randolph interpret the scope of EPA's discretion under §202(a)(1)? Aside from the alleged scientific uncertainty surrounding the causes of global climate change, what was the basis for EPA's decision not to regulate the emissions of greenhouse gases from new motor vehicles? Is the decision in NRDC v. Train, 545 F.2d 320 (2d Cir. 1976), discussed at pages 411-412 above, relevant to whether the CAA requires EPA to regulate GHG emissions?

2. What was Judge Tatel's response to EPA's contention that it lacks the statutory authority to regulate greenhouse gas emissions based on their contribution to climate change? How did he respond to EPA's reasons for "ignoring" the statutory text? On what basis would Judge Tatel have rejected EPA's fallback argument—that it acted within its statutory discretion in denying the petition for rulemaking to regulate greenhouse gas emissions from new motor vehicles?

3. The court denied various states' petition for rehearing en banc. Massachusetts v. EPA, 433 F.3d 66 (D.C. Cir. 2005). Judge Tatel dissented, contending that the initial panel decision "has no precedential effect" because the panel never considered the question of whether EPA has authority under the CAA to regulate greenhouse gas emissions and that Judge Randolph's views on whether EPA's refusal to regulate

greenhouse gases was arbitrary and capricious were his alone. The Supreme Court granted *certiorari* on June 26, 2006.

4. *Coordination of Federal Climate Change Activities Relating to Technology Development.* The Energy Policy Act of 2005, Pub. L. No. 109-58, §1601, 119 Stat. 594, 1109-13, adopted several "[GHG] intensity reducing strategies." The Act requires the president to establish a Committee on Climate Change Technology to coordinate federal climate change technology activities and programs. 42 U.S.C. §13389(b)(1). The Committee must submit to the president a national strategy to promote the deployment and commercialization of GHG intensity-reducing technologies and practices. Id. §13389(c)(1). The Secretary of Energy, in consultation with the Committee, may establish an advisory committee to identify statutory, regulatory, economic, and other barriers to the commercialization and deployment of those technologies and practices in the United States, id. §13389(f)(1), and to develop recommendations for removing those barriers. Id. §13389(g)(1).

5. *State and Local Action.* In the absence of meaningful federal action to limit the emission of GHGs, some states have tackled the global warming problem.[*] California has taken the lead. In 2002, the state adopted a law setting limits on CO_2 emissions from new cars. Several automakers sued the state, arguing that its GHG emission regulations are preempted by the federal government's authority to regulate fuel economy. See Central Valley Chrysler-Jeep, Inc. v. Witherspoon, 456 F. Supp. 2d. 1160 (E.D. Cal. 2006). In 2006 the state adopted the California Global Warming Solutions Act of 2006, Cal. Health & Safety Code §§38501-38599. The Act requires the State Air Resources Board to adopt a statewide GHG emissions limit, to be achieved by 2020, that is equivalent to the statewide level in 1990. The Board also must adopt regulations to achieve the maximum technologically feasible and cost-effective emission reductions of GHGs (which include CO_2, methane, nitrous oxide, and HCFCs) from categories of sources. Among the options available to the Board is a system of market-based declining annual aggregate emissions limits for categories of sources that emit GHGs. The Act also authorizes the Board to allow the use of market-based compliance mechanisms. In addition, Massachusetts and Connecticut committed to reducing GHG emissions to 1990 levels by 2010 and to 10 percent below those levels by 2020. 35 Env't Rep. (BNA) 1051 (2004).

In late 2005, seven states in the northeastern and mid-Atlantic regions of the United States signed an agreement to establish binding caps on CO_2 emissions by electric utilities. Under the Regional Greenhouse Gas Initiative (RGGI), the states agreed to reduce emissions by 2.5 percent each year beginning in 2015. By 2019, each state must reduce its annual emissions to 10 percent below baseline levels established in the agreement. The program will operate in a manner similar to the CAA's acid deposition trading program. Each state will issue an allowance for each ton of CO_2 emitted by electric utilities. Covered utilities will have to hold enough allowances to cover their emissions, and total emissions will be capped. Plants with excess allowances may sell them, and plants needing extra emissions may buy them. Each state would retain 25 percent of its total allowances and sell them to utilities. The revenue

---

[*]For analysis of the constitutionality of state and local actions to address global warming, see Hodas, State Law Responses to Global Warming: Is It Constitutional to Think Globally and Act Locally?, 21 Pace Envtl. L. Rev. 53 (2003); Note, Foreign Affairs Preemption and State Regulation of Greenhouse Gas Emissions, 119 Harv. L. Rev. 1877 (2006).

would be used to promote energy efficiency and home energy conservation efforts, and to provide rebates for utility consumers.*

Efforts to control air pollution that contributes to global warming have also moved into the courts. In Friends of the Earth, Inc. v. Watson, 35 Envtl. L. Rep. (ELI) 20,179, 2005 WL 2035596 (N.D. Cal. 2005), several environmental groups and local governments brought suit under NEPA against the Overseas Private Investment Corporation (OPIC) and the Export-Import Bank of the United States, claiming that the two agencies had provided assistance to particular projects that contribute to climate change without complying with NEPA. The court denied the defendants' motion for summary judgment, concluding that the plaintiffs demonstrated standing, the plaintiffs challenged final agency actions under the APA, OPIC's substantive statute did not bar judicial review, and procedures in that statute do not displace NEPA procedures. But in Connecticut v. American Elec. Power Co., 406 F. Supp. 2d 265 (D. Conn. 2005), the court dismissed as a non-justiciable political question a public nuisance action to abate the defendant electric utilities' contribution to global warming.

6. *Climate Change and Tort Law.* Could plaintiffs suffering harm as a result of global climate change seek redress through the tort system? Some observers contend that viable tort claims may be available. One possibility is a product liability action against automobile manufacturers based on the contention that they could and should have manufactured cars that emit fewer GHGs. See Choo, Feeling the Heat, ABA J., July 2006, at 29, 33. California's attorney general sued six U.S. and Japanese automakers for damages on this theory in 2006. Plaintiffs in such tort actions obviously would have to show that the defendants' acts (or failures to act) caused their harm.

7. For further reading, see Healy & Tapick, Climate Change: It's Not Just a Policy Issue for Corporate Counsel—It's a Legal Problem, 29 Colum. J. Envtl. L. 89 (2004) (discussing existing regulatory programs relating to emissions of greenhouse gases).

J.   FACILITATING ENFORCEMENT: CLEAN AIR ACT PERMITS

As the materials on water pollution in Chapter 7 indicate, the federal Clean Water Act (CWA) centers around a comprehensive permit program for all point sources of water pollution. The 1970 version of the CAA lacked a similar broad-reaching national operating permit mechanism. Most changes in emission limits for individual sources had to be processed by the states as SIP revisions, subject to EPA approval. This led to delays as minor revisions tended to pile up in EPA regional offices. The 1990 amendments created a new permit program. §§501-507. The Senate Report on the amendments explained that the program would facilitate enforcement by clarifying the obligations of individual sources and making it easier to track compliance, and by

*In 2006, the states participating in RGGI issued a model rule that will form the basis of individual state statutory or regulatory proposals to implement the program. http://www.rggi.org/modelrule.htm. See generally Regional Greenhouse Gas Initiative, http://www.rggi.org/; Note, State Collective Action, 119 Harv. L. Rev. 1855, 1863 (2006).

expediting implementation of new control requirements. A source's pollution control obligations were often scattered throughout "numerous, often hard-to-find provisions of the SIP or other Federal regulations," and often it was never made clear in a SIP how its general regulation applied to a specific source. The new permit program would collect all of a source's CAA obligations in one permit document and clarify how the SIP's general rules apply to the permit holder. EPA, the states, and the public would benefit because they would find it easier to identify the requirements applicable to a source and determine its compliance status. Regulated sources would benefit from the greater certainty provided by the permit's identification of relevant obligations. By identifying the baseline requirements for each source, permits would also facilitate emissions trading. Regulated sources also would benefit because the permit program would simplify and expedite procedures for modifying a source's pollution obligations. Before 1990, most such changes took the form of SIP amendments, subject to lengthy EPA review. The new permit program placed time limits on EPA review of state permit decisions. Finally, the permit program would assist states in implementing their CAA programs by imposing fees on permit applicants to offset program administration costs. See S. Rep. No. 101-228, at 346-348 (1989).

COMMONWEALTH OF VIRGINIA v. BROWNER
80 F.3d 869 (4th Cir. 1996)

MICHAEL, Circuit Judge:

[Virginia sought review of EPA's disapproval of the state's proposed program for issuing air pollution permits. It contested EPA's finding that the state failed to comply with Title V of the CAA, §§501-507, because the proposal lacked adequate provisions for judicial review of the state's permitting decisions. Virginia also charged that the Act's sanctions provisions, CAA §§179(b) & 502(d), violated the Tenth Amendment and the spending clause of the Constitution.]

I.

Title V's key provision, CAA §502, prohibits major stationary sources of air pollution from operating either without a valid permit or in violation of the terms of a permit. The permit is crucial to the implementation of the Act: it contains, in a single, comprehensive set of documents, all CAA requirements relevant to the particular polluting source. In a sense, a permit is a source-specific bible for Clean Air Act compliance. . . .

States are directed to submit for EPA approval their own programs for issuing permits. CAA §502(d)(1). EPA may not approve a proposed permit program unless it meets certain minimum criteria set out in CAA §502(b). Among other things, states must . . . provide for review in state courts of permitting decisions (§502(b)(6)).

If a state fails to submit a permit program, or submits a permit program that EPA disapproves for failure to comply with CAA §502(b), the state becomes subject to sanctions designed to encourage compliance. CAA §502(d).

One sanction deprives states of certain federal highway funds. CAA §179(b)(1). However, the state loses no funds that would be spent in regions that are in "attainment" within the meaning of the Act. CAA §179(b)(1)(A). . . . CAA §179(b)(1)(B).

A second sanction increases the pollution offset requirements already imposed on private polluters within ozone nonattainment areas. Normally, new [or modified] major stationary sources of pollution may not be operated within nonattainment areas . . . unless pollution from other sources is reduced to offset increased pollution from the new or modified source. [§182(a)(4), (b)(5), (c)(10), (d)(2), (e)(1).] . . . The sanction supersedes these normal ratios by increasing the ratio in all ozone nonattainment areas to 2:1, requiring 200 tons of old pollutants to be eliminated for every 100 tons of new pollutants allowed. CAA §179(b)(2). The offset sanction, therefore, could slow the rate of industrial development within a noncomplying state.

A third sanction eliminates the state's ability to manage its own pollution control regime. If the state does not gain approval for its permit program, EPA develops and implements its own Title V permitting program within the noncomplying state. CAA §502(d)(3). . . .

III.

Virginia claims that EPA erroneously determined that Virginia's permit program contained inadequate judicial review provisions. . . . We find that EPA correctly determined that Virginia's proposed judicial review provisions do not comply with the Act. . . .

. . . [Under §502(b)(6), a] state permit program will be disapproved unless the state submits a legal opinion stating that the proposed Title V program allows state court review of permitting decisions upon the request of "the [permit] applicant, any person who participated in the public participation process . . . and any other person who could obtain judicial review of such actions under State laws." 40 C.F.R. §70.4(b)(3)(x). EPA interprets the statute and regulation to require, at a minimum, that states provide judicial review of permitting decisions to any person who would have standing under Article III of the United States Constitution.

Virginia law grants standing to seek judicial review of permitting decisions to "[a]ny owner aggrieved by" such decisions. Va. Code §10.1-1318(A). This provision satisfies CAA §502(b)(6)'s requirement that the permit "applicant" be allowed to seek judicial review. But §502(b)(6) also requires that states grant certain standing rights to members of the public, and here is where Virginia's judicial review provision falls short of the mark. Under Virginia's provision, a member of the public "who is aggrieved by a final [permitting decision] who participated, in person or by submittal of written comments, in the public comment process" may only seek judicial review of a permitting decision if he can establish that

> (i) [he] has suffered an actual, threatened, or imminent injury; (ii) such injury is an invasion of an immediate, legally protected, *pecuniary and substantial* interest which is concrete and particularized; (iii) such injury is fairly traceable to the [permitting decision] and not the result of the action of some third party not before the court; and (iv) such injury will likely be redressed by a favorable decision of the court.

Va. Code §10.1-1318(B) (emphasis supplied).

According to EPA, this provision is too restrictive: limiting availability of review to those persons with "pecuniary and substantial" interests violates CAA §502(b)(6). We agree with EPA. . . .

As Virginia reads the statute, the final clause, "who could obtain judicial review of that action under applicable [state] law," modifies all three categories of persons earlier described as being allowed to seek judicial review: "the applicant," "any person who participated in the public comment process," and "any other person." Thus, according to Virginia, §506(b)(6) requires states to grant standing to participants in the public comment process only if those persons would otherwise have standing under existing state law.

Virginia's proposed reading is contrary to ordinary principles of statutory construction and to the rules of English usage. The clause, "who could obtain judicial review of that action under applicable law," modifies only the immediately preceding category, "any other person." . . .

Properly read, the final clause simply allows the states to grant broader standing rights than those otherwise required under federal law. . . .

[The court next rejected Virginia's contention that its "pecuniary and substantial interest" requirement satisfied the statute.]

IV.

Having determined that EPA had a valid reason to disapprove Virginia's permit program, we now examine whether Title V and its sanctions provisions are constitutional. Virginia claims that Title V and its sanctions provisions are unconstitutional because they impinge upon a fundamental element of state sovereignty, the state's right to articulate its own rules of judicial standing. . . .

We agree that Congress lacks power to impinge upon "the core of sovereignty retained by the States." New York v. United States, 505 U.S. 144, 158-60 (1992). We also agree that an important aspect of a state's sovereignty is the administration of its judicial system. Thus, a state cannot be required to create a court with power to decide federal claims, if no court otherwise exists. Similarly, a state may apply neutral venue rules to require that federal claims be brought in a particular state court. But the Supremacy Clause compels state judges to apply federal law, if such law is applicable. U.S. Const. art. VI, cl. 2. Furthermore, to require an existing state administrative body to adjudicate a dispute arising under federal law does not unreasonably interfere with state sovereignty. Testa v. Katt, 330 U.S. 386 (1947) (state court must entertain civil action arising under federal Emergency Price Control Act).

. . . [W]e find that the CAA does not compel the states to modify their standing rules; it merely induces them to do so. The CAA is constitutional because although its sanctions provisions potentially burden the states, those sanctions amount to inducement rather than "outright coercion." See *New York*, 505 U.S. at 165-67. . . .

Two sources of Congressional power allow use of the highway sanction. Because the elimination of air pollution promotes the general welfare, Congress may tie the award of federal funds to the states' efforts to eliminate air pollution. . . . U.S. Const. art. I, §8, cl. 1. Furthermore, the Commerce Clause, U.S. Const. art. I, §8, cl. 3, gives Congress the power to regulate "activities causing air or water pollution, or other environmental hazards that may have effects in more than one State." Hodel v. Virginia Surface Mining & Reclamation Ass'n, 452 U.S. 264, 282 (1981).

Generally, Congress may use the power of the purse to encourage states to enact particular legislation. This power, however, is not limitless. Exercise of the power to the point of "outright coercion" violates the Constitution. . . . Also, it has been suggested that federal funds may be subject to conditions "only in ways reasonably related to the purpose for which the funds are expended." [South Dakota v. Dole, 483 U.S. 203, 213 (1987) (O'Connor, J., dissenting).] No court, however, has ever struck down a federal statute on grounds that it exceeded the Spending Power.

The highway sanction here does not rise to the level of "outright coercion." First, a state does not lose any highway funds that would be spent in areas of the state that are in attainment. CAA §179(b)(1)(A). Second, even within nonattainment areas, federal highway funds may be spent on projects designed to promote safety or designed to reduce air pollution. CAA §179(b)(1). More severe funding restrictions than those at issue here have been upheld. . . .

And contrary to what Virginia claims, the conditions on spending are reasonably related to the goal of reducing air pollution. The CAA as a whole is a comprehensive scheme to cope with the problem of air pollution from all sources. Congress may ensure that funds it allocates are not used to exacerbate the overall problem of air pollution. It is therefore of no consequence that a highway sanction, which will have the effect of reducing emissions from mobile pollution sources, is being used to induce compliance with a portion of the Act designed to reduce emissions from stationary sources.

We hold that the highway sanction, CAA §179(b)(1), is a valid exercise of the Spending Power. As a valid exercise of that power, it also comports with the requirements of the Tenth Amendment. Congress has not overstepped its bounds here. . . .

The offset sanction, CAA §179(b)(2), which limits new construction or modification of major stationary sources of air pollution, is constitutional because it regulates private pollution sources, not states.

The burden of the offset sanction falls on private parties. The more stringent offset requirements will likely make it more difficult for individual pollution sources (manufacturers, utilities, and the like) to upgrade or modify existing plants and equipment or to open new plants. Thus, although the sanction may burden some Virginia citizens, it does not burden Virginia as a governmental unit. For this reason, the sanction does not violate the principles of federalism embodied in the Tenth Amendment. . . .

The final sanction, federal permit program implementation, CAA §502(d)(3), also is constitutional. The essence of a Tenth Amendment violation is that the state is commanded to regulate. Here, Virginia is not commanded to regulate; the Commonwealth may choose to do nothing and let the federal government promulgate and enforce its own permit program within Virginia. Because "the full regulatory burden will be borne by the Federal Government," the sanction is constitutional. *Hodel*, 452 U.S. at 288.

. . . If anything, the CAA's method—to give the states a chance first to avoid imposition of any federal plan by promulgating satisfactory regulations—seems less coercive than [a statute upheld in a previous case; that statute adopted an environmental regulatory program but allowed each state to opt out of federal regulation by establishing its own program that met federal standards]. The CAA simply "establishes a program of cooperative federalism that allows the States, within limits established by federal minimum standards, to enact and administer their own regulatory programs, structured to meet their own particular needs." *Hodel*, 452 U.S. at 289.

Because Congress may choose to preempt state law completely, it may also take the less drastic step of allowing the states the ability to avoid preemption by adopting and implementing their own plans that sufficiently address congressional concerns. . . .

Finally, the CAA's sanctions provisions maintain unity between regulation and political accountability. If sanctions are imposed, it will be "the Federal Government that makes the decision in full view of the public, and it will be federal officials that suffer the consequences if the decision turns out to be detrimental or unpopular." *New York*, 505 U.S. at 168. The sanctions provisions are constitutional.

NOTES AND QUESTIONS

1. Why did Virginia's permit program provide insufficient access to the state courts for review of permitting decisions? How did the Virginia statute depart from the constitutional standing requirements discussed in Chapter 3, section A.1? What are the potential consequences of a state's failure to establish an operating permit program that complies with the minimal statutory requirements? Why did the court reject Virginia's constitutional attacks on each of the three applicable sanctions? Why doesn't the CAA coerce the states into opening their courts to litigants seeking to challenge implementation of the state's permit program?

2. *Scope of the Title V Permit Program.* After the effective date of an approved state permit program, it is unlawful for any person required to apply for a permit issued under Title V to operate except in compliance with such a permit. §502(a). To whom does the permit requirement apply? See id. EPA may exempt categories of non-major sources from the permit program if it finds that compliance is impracticable, infeasible, or unnecessarily burdensome. See also Western States Petroleum Ass'n v. EPA, 87 F.3d 280 (9th Cir. 1996) (overturning EPA's disapproval of state's attempt to exempt insignificant emissions units from Title V monitoring, reporting, and record-keeping requirements).

3. *Substantive Permit Requirements.* What must a source do to qualify for a permit? See §503. What requirements must a permit impose on the applicant? See §504(a)-(c). May EPA issue a permit despite noncompliance with the requirements of Title V on the ground that the defects amounted to "harmless error"? See §505(b)(2); New York Pub. Interest Research Group, Inc. v. Whitman, 321 F.3d 316 (2d Cir. 2003). In New York Pub. Research Interest Group, Inc. v. Johnson, 427 F.3d 172 (2d Cir. 2005), the plaintiff challenged EPA's failure to object, pursuant to §505(b)(1), to New York's issuance of operating permits to two coal-fired power plants that had previously received notices of violation from the state environmental agency. The court held that EPA erred in approving the permits despite the fact that they failed to include compliance schedules. The court also held that the imposition of quarterly reporting requirements relating to opacity standards did not comply with the requirement in §503(b)(2) that permittees "promptly report any deviations from permit requirements." Cf. Sierra Club v. Johnson, 436 F.3d 1269 (11th Cir. 2006) (holding that EPA improperly failed to object to state permit that did not comply with public participation requirements of §505(b)(2)).

What effect will the new permit program have on citizen suits brought under §304 of the Clean Air Act? See Macfarlane & Terry, Citizen Suits: Impacts on Permitting and Agency Enforcement, 11 Nat. Resources & Env't (Spring 1997), at 20. What is the effect of compliance with a properly issued permit? See §504(f). According to EPA, this "permit shield" is not available for noncompliance with applicable requirements that occurred before or continue after submission of a permit application. Inside EPA Weekly, June 23, 1995, at 9. Under what circumstances may EPA veto a state permit? See §505(b).

VII

PROTECTING THE WATER RESOURCE

The river must have been wonderful when he was young. The shad would run up it in the spring and there was a run of salmon also. Now it had an oily odor from the cotton mills upstream.

> J. P. Marquand, Wickford Point 92-93 (1939)

The availability of safe, secure, and sustainable water is essential for public health and the environment—here in the U.S. and throughout the world.

> EPA Administrator Johnson, Water Environment Federation's
> 78th Annual Conference & Exhibition, Washington, D.C. (Oct. 31, 2005),
> http://yosemite.epa.gov/opa/admpress.nsf

INTRODUCTION

This chapter reviews the legal framework of the Clean Water Act (CWA) for controlling water pollution and the efforts that EPA and others have made to implement this framework. While the CWA is the centerpiece of the nation's efforts to protect our waters, numerous other federal, state, and local laws are intended to protect these waters as well. These include the statutes covered in Chapters 8 and 9, such as the Safe Drinking Water Act (intended to protect U.S. water supplies), the Resource Conservation and Recovery Act (RCRA) (intended to prevent the release of hazardous wastes into our waters in certain cases), and various cleanup authorities, such as the Oil Pollution Act of 1990 and CERCLA, as well as RCRA (which create remediation-type approaches to environmental law), among others.

A. THE STATE OF THE NATION'S WATERS, AND THE MAJOR SOURCES AND IMPACTS OF WATER POLLUTION

A Look at the Quality of Our Nation's Waters. Statistics abound about the quality of our nation's waters. More than 30 years of regulatory efforts under the CWA to reduce water pollution have (at significant cost) achieved considerable progress, but substantial deficiencies in water quality and regulatory challenges remain. A 2002 EPA publication summarizes the progress made and funds expended:

> The application of technology-based requirements through the National Pollutant Discharge Elimination System (NPDES) permit program has achieved tremendous success in controlling point source pollution and restoring the nation's waters. By 1990 over 87% of the major municipal facilities and 93% of major industrial facilities were in compliance with NPDES permit limits. EPA has estimated that in 1997, annual private point source control costs were about $14 billion and public point source costs were about $34 billion. [EPA, Office of Water, Proposed Water Quality Trading Policy (April 25, 2002).]

Oliver Houck, certainly no apologist for the Act or efforts at implementation over the past 30 years, lauds its accomplishments:

> The 1972 Amendments [to the CWA] worked. Industrial pollution plummeted; rates of wetland loss slowed, and in some regions even reversed; and municipal loadings . . . dropped by nearly 50% while their populations served were doubling in size . . . [T]he unavoidable fact is that the Act's fixed deadlines, best-you-can-do technology standards, individual permits, and multiple enforcement mechanisms generated widespread compliance, new and improved technologies, source reduction, waste recycling, and a growing number of voluntary, quasi-voluntary, and alternative abatement schemes. By any measure—number of dischargers on permit, pounds of pollution abated, stream segments improved, fisheries restored to waters where they had not been seen for decades—the Act has made its case in court and, by its imitation, to the world. [O. Houck, The Clean Water Act TMDL Program: Law, Policy, and Implementation 3-4 (2d ed. 2002).]

Despite this progress, however, a significant proportion of our waters remain impaired and unavailable for the uses designated for them under federal law (including swimming and fishing). Based on the 2000 inventory of our nation's waters, only about 60 percent of assessed stream miles, 55 percent of assessed lake acres, and 50 percent of assessed estuarine square miles fully support the uses set for them. EPA's inventory notes that even for these waters, "significant proportions . . . were threatened and might degrade in the future." EPA, National Water Quality Inventory: 2000 Report (Aug. 2002). Figure 7-1 is a summary of the quality of assessed rivers, lakes, and estuaries.

EPA's inventory is much less comprehensive in reviewing the quality of our nation's waters than one might expect. As Figure 7-1 reflects, it covers less—in some cases considerably less—than 50 percent of our nation's stream miles, lakes, ponds, reservoir acres, and estuaries. EPA suggests that non-assessed waters are actually more likely than assessed waters to meet designated uses because states tend to focus their assessments on "known problem areas." EPA, Office of Water, Proposed Water Quality Trading Policy (April 25, 2002). Oliver Houck offers a somewhat more critical gloss concerning the incompleteness of the inventory; he notes that "[w]e have been spared knowing how polluted our waters are by the simple fact that we have not made a serious effort to find out." Houck, The Clean Water Act TMDL Program: Law, Policy, and Implementation, supra, at 4. There are, of course, many reasons for the incompleteness of the inventory. In defense of EPA and the states, water systems are expansive and complex. It also is difficult in some cases to distinguish chronic from transient impairment. Obtaining credible data that meet QA/QC (quality assurance/quality control) requirements, with properly calibrated equipment operated appropriately, requires substantial resources.

Water Body Type	Total Size	Amount Assessed* (% of Total)	Good (% of Assessed)	Good but Threatened (% of Assessed)	Polluted (% of Assessed)
Rivers (miles)	3,692,830	699,946 (19)	367,129 (53)	59,504 (8)	269,258 (39)
Lakes (acres)	40,603,893	17,339,080 (43)	8,026,988 (47)	1,348,903 (8)	7,702,370 (45)
Estuaries (sq. miles)	87,369	31,072 (36)	13,850 (45)	1,023 (<4)	15,676 (51)

*Includes water bodies assessed as not attainable for one or more uses.
Note: Percentages may not add up to 100 due to rounding.
Source: EPA, National Water Quality Inventory: 2000 Report Profile (Aug. 2002).

FIGURE 7-1
Summary of Quality of Assessed Rivers, Lakes, and Estuaries

Causes and Sources of Impairment. EPA reports that siltation, nutrients, bacteria, metals (primarily mercury), and oxygen-depleting substances are among the top causes of impairment of our waters, and that nonpoint source (or NPS) pollution (i.e., pollution from urban and agricultural land that is transported by precipitation and runoff) is the leading source. EPA, National Water Quality Inventory: 2000 Report ES-3 (Aug. 2002). The Agency's chart depicting the major causes and sources of impairment is reproduced as Figure 7-2.

	Rivers and Streams	Lakes, Ponds, and Reservoirs	Estuaries
Causes	Pathogens (bacteria)	Nutrients	Metals (primarily mercury)
Causes	Siltation (sedimentation)	Metals (primarily mercury)	Pesticides
Causes	Habitat alterations	Siltation (sedimentation)	Oxygen depletion
Sources	Agriculture	Agriculture	Municipal point sources
Sources	Hydrological modifications	Hydrologic modifications	Urban runoff, storm sewers
Sources	Habitat modifications	Urban runoff, storm sewers	Industrial discharges

Source: U.S. EPA, National Water Quality Inventory: 2000 Report Profile (Aug. 2002).

FIGURE 7-2
Leading Causes and Sources* of Impairment in Assessed Rivers, Lakes, and Estuaries
*Excluding unknown, natural, and "other" sources.

There are significant gaps in knowledge concerning the causes and sources of water pollution as well, with EPA noting that "[i]t is important to understand the difficulties in identifying causes and, in particular, sources of pollution in impaired waters. For many waters, states and other jurisdictions classify the causes and sources as unknown." Id.

Impacts. EPA describes the impacts of water pollution on public and environmental health as follows:

> Water pollution threatens public health both directly through the consumption of contaminated food or drinking water, and indirectly through skin exposure to contaminants present in recreational or bathing waters. Contaminants that threaten human health include toxic chemicals and waterborne disease-causing pathogens such as viruses, bacteria, and protozoans.
>
> Some of the problems caused by toxic and pathogen contamination include fish, wildlife, and shellfish consumption advisories, drinking water closures, and recreational (e.g., swimming) restrictions. [Id. at ES-4.]

More on Data Quality and Quantity: Issues Concerning the Information Infrastructure. The 2000 National Water Quality Inventory Report and its predecessors have been subject to considerable criticism.* An obvious deficiency is the incompleteness of the reports, notably the paucity of data concerning the majority of our waters. In a 2002 report, for example, the GAO reported that "states have little of the information they need to assess the quality of their waters and, in particular, to identify those that are impaired." U.S. GAO, Water Quality: Inconsistent State Approaches Complicate Nation's Efforts to Identify Its Most Polluted Waters 1, GAO-02-186 (Jan. 2002); see also U.S. GAO, Water Quality: Key EPA and State Decisions Limited by Inconsistent and Incomplete Data, GAO/RCED-00-54 (March 2000).

EPA has made efforts to upgrade the inventory reports. It has strongly encouraged states and other front-line reporters to submit "integrated water quality monitoring and assessment reports" that satisfy the requirements of §303(d) of the CWA as well as §305(b). The former requires states to identify impaired waters and to "develop allocations of the maximum amount of a pollutant each impaired water can receive and still meet water quality standards." §303(d). EPA "anticipates that the development of an *Integrated Report* will benefit the public by providing a clearer summary of the water quality status of the nation's waters and the management actions necessary to protect and restore them." EPA, National Water Quality Inventory: 2000 Report Profile (Aug. 2002). EPA indicates in its Guidance for 2006 Assessment, Listing and Reporting Requirements Pursuant to Sections 303(d), 305(b) and 314 of the Clean Water Act, 70 Fed. Reg. 47,200 (2005), that its goal is that all 50 states will use the integrated reporting format by 2008.

NOTES AND QUESTIONS ON THE QUALITY OF OUR NATION'S WATERS

1. October 18, 2002, marked the thirtieth anniversary of the CWA. Different retrospectives have been published that provide varied perspectives on the progress

*The 2000 report is the thirteenth in a series published since 1975 under CWA §305(b), which requires the states to assess their water quality biennially and report their findings to EPA, and directs EPA to collect these data and summarize the findings in a national report known as the National Water Quality Inventory.

that has been made and the challenges that remain. See, e.g., Symposium: The Clean Water Act at Thirty: Progress, Problems, and Potential, 55 Ala. L. Rev. 537-881 (2004).

2. Data gathering concerning the quality of our nation's waters extends far beyond the §§303(d) and 305(b) reports. For example, EPA issued a "report card" on the quality of the nation's coastal waters in December 2004, finding that the nation's estuaries are in "fair condition," with poor conditions in the Northeast Coast and Puerto Rico regions and fair conditions in the Southeast Coast, Gulf Coast, Great Lakes, and West Coast regions. EPA National Coastal Condition Report II, ES.3 (Dec. 2004), EPA-620/R-03/002. EPA's April 2006 Wadeable Streams Assessment assessed 1,392 streams throughout the contiguous states, finding that 42 percent of stream miles are in poor condition, 28 percent are in good condition, and 25 percent are in fair condition. http://www.epa.gov/owow/streamsurvey/. The USGS concluded in a 2006 report that pesticides in groundwater wells, streams, and rivers do not exceed water quality standards for human health, but could pose a risk to aquatic life or fish-eating wildlife. USGS, Pesticides in the Nation's Streams and Ground Water, 1992-2001, http://pubs.usgs.gov/circ/2005/1291/.

Numerous other efforts have been undertaken to investigate the state of our nation's waters and to correct current problems and prevent new ones from emerging. The H. John Heinz III Center for Science, Economics and the Environment, for example, issued a report in 2002 entitled The State of the Nation's Ecosystems: Measuring the Lands, Waters, and Living Resources of the United States. The Center characterizes the report as an effort to strengthen the empirical foundation for informed decisionmaking, but acknowledges that more work is needed:

> The report emerging from this process presents a unique system of indicators that is simultaneously relevant to contemporary policy and decision making, balanced and unbiased in what it chooses to report on, and scientifically credible in the data it presents. We hope and believe that The State of the Nation's Ecosystems and its planned successors will help to strengthen the empirical foundation for American environmental policymaking in the same way that the emergence of solid data about changes in GDP, employment, and inflation helped to strengthen the country's economic policymaking in the last half-century. . . .
>   . . . We believe that the articulation of a coherent framework for reporting, a clear-eyed assessment of the strengths and weaknesses of available data, and the identification of data gaps are important advances. [The report's] strengths notwithstanding, however, we are well aware that this report is at best an early step on a long path toward realization of the comprehensive, mature, and well-grounded system of ecosystem and environmental reporting that the nation deserves.
>   . . . [W]e believe that a multisector effort is needed to address key gaps identified in this report. For almost half the indicators identified in this report as necessary to characterize the state of the nation's ecosystems, gaps in scientific understanding, operational monitoring, or data coordination have made it impossible to produce useful national data. [Id. at viii.]

The Center's 2003 and 2005 updates to this report are available at http://www.heinzctr.org/ecosystems/intro/updates.shtml.

3. *The Costs of Water Pollution Control and Protection of Our Water Supplies Are Substantial.* Total public and private spending on water pollution control between 1972 and 1996 is estimated at $700 billion. Davies & Mazurek, Pollution Control in the United States: Evaluating the System 70 (1998). Signaling the potentially large

sums involved in protecting our waters, EPA estimates a "funding gap" of up to $536 billion for wastewater infrastructure between 2000 and 2019, although it suggests that this gap "largely disappears if municipalities increase clean water and drinking water spending at a real rate of growth of three percent per year." EPA, Clean Water and Drinking Water Gap Analysis, Executive Summary (Sept. 2002). EPA's June 2005 survey, Drinking Water Infrastructure Needs Survey and Assessment: Third Report to Congress (2005), indicates that drinking water utilities will require about $277 billion over the next 20 years for infrastructure-related needs. The American Society of Civil Engineers gave wastewater and drinking water infrastructure each a grade of D–. Condition of U.S. Infrastructure Given Poor Grade by Engineering Group in Report, 46 Daily Env't A-12 (BNA) (March 10, 2005). EPA reports in its Clean Water State Revolving Fund Programs/2005 Annual Report that, since its inception in 1987, the Clean Water State Revolving Fund (SRF) has loaned more than $50 billion for projects to help repair and upgrade wastewater treatment plants, along with other water quality–related initiatives. http://www.epa.gov/owm/cwfinance/cwsrf/annreport2005.htm.

4. *Is It Worth It?* Determining the benefits, and costs, of various pollution control strategies often is complex. The challenges associated with evaluating the appropriateness of expenditures are illustrated by a 1994 EPA study aimed at calculating the marginal costs and benefits of improvements in water pollution control, such as control of urban sewer and stormwater overflow and the reduction of toxic pollutants. The study found that quantified benefits did not exceed the costs but that reduction initiatives should proceed because of cost calculation uncertainties and the number of benefits for which monetary estimates have not been developed. Davies & Mazurek, Pollution Control in the United States: Evaluating the System 132-133 (1998).

5. *Where Are We Going?* The first generation of CWA administration assumed that the major sources of pollution were industrial and municipal discharges and that pollution could be substantially reduced through technology. The CWA combined with market shifts in industrial production have substantially removed many pollutants from streams, but we now recognize that a more integrated pollution control approach is necessary to achieve "healthy" aquatic ecosystems because other sources of pollution, including land use practices, continue to frustrate attainment of the CWA's goals. We are now moving toward a more holistic view of stream systems as we recognize the close relationship between land use practices and water quality. EPA is extending its focus from the control of point sources of pollution to watershed management. This shift reflects the efforts of William Reilly, Administrator of the EPA in the George H. W. Bush administration (1988-1992), to reorient EPA to more scientifically based pollution prevention and ecosystem protection and restoration strategies. M. Landy et al., The Environmental Protection Agency: Asking the Wrong Questions from Nixon to Clinton 279-301 (1994). New objectives include restoring degraded aquatic ecosystems, establishing baselines for the maintenance of ecologically functioning systems, and controlling nonpoint source pollution. See National Research Council, The Restoration of Aquatic Ecosystems: Science, Technology and Public Policy (1992). Whether these objectives can be achieved is another question. S. Davidson et al., Chesapeake Waters: Four Centuries of Controversy, Concern, and Legislation (1997), surveyed the continued degradation of the world-famous bay and pessimistically concluded that public agencies lack the capability to manage the resources because nature is too complex, scientific information is too limited, and public choice is too reactive. The GAO provided an update on the

Chesapeake Bay in July 2006, noting that despite the significant investment in resto-ration (the Bay received about $5.6 billion in funding from 1995 to 2004), resource constraints continue to challenge the completion of these efforts. U.S. GAO, Chesa-peake Bay Program: Improved Strategies Needed to Better Guide Restoration Efforts, GAO-06-614T (July 13, 2006). See also EPA OIG, Evaluation Report: Saving the Chesapeake Bay Watershed Requires Better Coordination of Environmental and Agricultural Resources (Nov. 20, 2006).

6. *Security Issues.* As one might expect, the attacks on September 11, 2001, and their aftermath have focused attention on the security of the nation's water infrastruc-ture. The Council on Foreign Relations, for example, has concluded that "drinking water remains vulnerable to mass destruction." Drinking Water: U.S. Water Supply Vulnerable to Attacks, Council on Foreign Relations Says, Daily Env't Rep. (BNA) A-9 (Nov. 5, 2002). Congress enacted the Public Health Security and Bioterrorism Pre-paredness and Response Act of 2002, which, among other things, amends the Safe Drinking Water Act to require larger utilities to assess the vulnerability of their systems to terrorism and to file those assessments with EPA. In 2003, EPA established a "permanent homeland security office" to be housed in the Office of the Administrator.* A 2006 survey of the U.S. Conference of Mayors found that security relating to drinking water and wastewater facilities, as well as the need to update the aging infrastructure of such facilities, are major concerns. Mayors List Aged Infrastructure, Supply, Security among Chief Water Priorities, Daily Env't Rep. (BNA) (Jan. 26, 2006), at A-12.

B. BACKGROUND OF WATER POLLUTION REGULATION

In 1607, the first English colonists in the Chesapeake Bay region drew their drinking water from the often-brackish James River estuary, which ebbed and flowed past the shores of the swampy island that was to be called Jamestown. In doing so, they exposed themselves to disease-carrying bacteria from their own wastes (according to a theory of a twentieth century historian) and subjected themselves to gradual salt poisoning from the brackish water. Those who sickened and died may have been the first recorded victims of water pollution in the Bay. [F. Capper et al., Governing Chesapeake Waters: A History of Water Quality Controls on Chesapeake Bay, 1607-1972 (1983), citing C. Earle, Envi-ronment, Disease and Mortality in Early Virginia, in The Chesapeake in the Seven-teenth Century 96 (T. Tate & D. Ammorman eds., 1979).]

1. *Nineteenth-Century Water Pollution Problems and Legal Responses*

Until the nineteenth century, the major water pollution problem was fecal contamination. Cities relied on the natural waste–assimilative capacity of oceans,

---

*For more on EPA's activities, see http://cfpub.epa.gov/safewater/watersecurity/index.cfm. ELI's 2003 report, Homeland Security and Drinking Water: An Opportunity for Comprehensive Protection of a Vital Natural Resource (2003), discusses the protection of drinking water in light of security concerns.

lakes, and rivers or on cesspools, privy vaults, and scavenger systems. As a seventeenth-century English visitor to Venice observed, "Though the flood or ebb of salt water bee [sic] small, yet with that motion it carried away the filth of the city." C. Hibbert, Venice: The Biography of a City 131 (1989). Other cities, such as London, were not so lucky, experiencing virulent cholera epidemics as a result of contamination of drinking water supplies by human waste. Eventually the discovery of the relationship between germs and illness, and specifically the role of polluted water in spreading infections, led to widespread sanitation efforts to eliminate germs or to avoid contact with their sources. By 1920 most large public drinking water supplies were using chlorination to kill disease-causing microbes. See J. Tarr, The Search for the Ultimate Sink: Urban Pollution in Historical Perspective (1996). Disinfection was a great public health advance, although in recent years there have been concerns about the cancer risks of chlorination by-products. See S. Putnam & J. Wiener, Seeking Safe Drinking Water, in Risk versus Risk: Tradeoffs in Protecting Health and the Environment 124 (J. Graham & J. Wiener eds., 1995). Until the mid-twentieth century industrial waste practices were virtually unrestrained because industrial pollution was not seen as a major public health threat.

2. The Twentieth-Century Evolution of Federal Water Pollution Control Policy

Until after World War II, pollution control was assumed to be a local and state responsibility. Chapter 6 traced the evolution of the shift from local and state to federal responsibility in air pollution regulation. The shift is similar for water pollution, although the federal interest in the quality of navigable waters antedates its interest in air pollution.

Federal water pollution control policy has moved through three stages and is moving into a fourth. The first three stages were (1) post hoc federal actions against those who have discharged substances into navigable waters; (2) a federal-state effort to dedicate different waters to varying levels of waste assimilation, with federal enforcement as a last resort; and (3) a federal effort to reduce pollution by imposing technology-based standards on effluents discharged, as opposed to setting standards for the quality of receiving waters, with state enforcement of federal policy. The technology-based effluent limitations strategy to substantially reduce waste discharges, put in place in 1972, represents the third stage and remains the heart of the program. This strategy remains a fundamental feature of the CWA, but increasing emphasis is being given to ambient-based strategies and to the protection of healthy ecosystems. See Adler, Integrated Approaches to Water Pollution: Lessons from the Clean Air Act, 23 Harv. Envtl. L. Rev. 203 (1999).

a. Post Hoc Actions against Discharges

Because of the federal government's traditional interest in the protection of navigation, federal water pollution control legislation existed long before air pollution control legislation. The oldest surviving statute of current interest is §13 of the Rivers and Harbors Act of 1899. This simple statute, which grew out of efforts to regulate potential obstructions to navigation, prohibits the discharge of "any refuse matter of any kind or description whatever other than that flowing from streets and sewers and passing therefrom in a liquid state," without a permit from the Secretary of the Army, 33 U.S.C. §407. The measurement and control of water pollution have become much more scientific and technical, but the Rivers and Harbors Act's legacy establishing pollution as any discharge of a foreign substance into a body of water had a profound influence on CWA jurisprudence.

b.   Water Use Zoning

Until 1948, the federal government's role in pollution control was limited to special problems, such as refuse discharged into navigable waters and oil spills. The Federal Water Pollution Control Act of 1948 modestly but significantly expanded the federal government's role. The surgeon general was authorized to conduct investigations; make grants to state and local agencies for research; make loans for the construction of treatment works; and declare interstate pollution a public nuisance, although the necessary investigation to determine if a nuisance in fact existed could not begin unless the local agency authorized it. In 1956 federal efforts were strengthened when Congress began to subsidize the construction of sewage treatment works. See Wilson, Legal Aspects of Water Pollution Control, in U.S. Department of Health, Education, and Welfare, Proceedings: The National Conference on Water Pollution 354, 364-369 (1961).

By the end of the 1950s, a consensus was emerging among key legislators that would expand the federal role. See Federal-State Relations in Transition: Implications for Environmental Policy, A Report Prepared by the Congressional Research Service of the Library of Congress for the Committee on Environment and Public Works, S. Rep. No. 87-52, at 3-32 (1962). Northern states, which had so-so track records for cleaning up their waters, became increasingly concerned that southern and western states were trying to lure industry with their low water quality standards, and thus the industrialized states began to support the idea of minimum standards for federal water quality. See D. Carr, Death of the Sweet Waters: The Politics of Pollution (1966). The idea also found some support among industry. A similar tolerance—or even preference—among the large firms in an industry for federal regulation as a means of eliminating competition from smaller firms was first noted in G. Kolko, The Triumph of Conservatism (1960), and this observation was applied to the pollution field in W. Tucker, Progress and Privilege: America in the Age of Environmentalism (1982).

At an important National Conference on Water Pollution in 1959, the assistant surgeon general offered the following reason for the emergence of water pollution as a national problem:

> Prior to 1940, there was a somewhat orderly transition from a rural to an industrial economy. Cities were still separate entities, generally with appreciable distances between shocks of pollution. Industries were in or near cities. Pollution, for the most part, was natural organic materials with concentrations of biological contaminants. Improvements in water treatment and extension of waste treatment kept the scales reasonably in balance. Excessive pollution, where it occurred, was still largely localized and over short stretches of streams.

Since 1940, three major influences aggravate the pollution situation. All three are World War II related:

1. There was a fantastically increased tempo in the transition to metropolitan and industrial development—the formation of gigantic metropolitan complexes extending hundreds of miles generally following major watercourses. Industries go where there is water and populations build up where there is industry.
2. There was practically no construction of municipal or industrial waste treatment works over the period 1940 to 1947. Men and materials were needed for the war effort.
3. The avalanche of technological progress brought with it a whole array of new-type contaminants, such as synthetic chemicals and radioactive wastes. Production and use of such materials continue upward at substantial rates. [Hollis, The Water Pollution Image, in Proceedings of the National Conference on Water Pollution 30, 32 (1961).]

The Water Quality Act of 1965 required all states to enact water quality standards for interstate navigable waters, although many states already had such standards in place. It empowered the federal government to convene a conference and to investigate pollution problems and remedies, if the pollution substantially endangered the health of citizens in another state or if substantial injury would result in those attempting to market shellfish in interstate commerce. The governor of an injured state could request and thereby trigger a federal government conference. If the pollution was wholly intrastate, the governor had the exclusive right to determine if a federal conference would be convened. Amendments in 1966 increased the federal contribution to sewage treatment plants and initiated funding of water quality planning programs.

Professor N. William Hines described the 1965 Act's "water quality standards zone" approach of allocating assimilative uses for different reaches of a stream.

The water quality standards . . . involve three essential components: First, a determination is made concerning the present and future uses to be made of each body or stretch of interstate water. . . . Second, the specific water quality characteristics allowed or required for such uses must be identified and descriptive or numerical values established for each of them. . . . The third component of the standards is a precise, detailed plan for achieving and preserving the criteria established, including such ingredients as preventive steps, construction schedules, enforcement actions, surveillance and monitoring. [Hines, Controlling Industrial Water Pollution: Color the Problem Green, 9 B.C. Indus. & Com. L. Rev. 553, 585-586 (1968).]

Professor Hines has written the definitive history of the evolution of federal water pollution control policy prior to the Clean Water Act of 1972, Nor Any Drop to Drink: Public Regulation of Water Quality; Part I: State Pollution Control Programs, 52 Iowa L. Rev. 186 (1966); Part II: Interstate Arrangements for Pollution Control, 52 Iowa L. Rev. 432 (1966); Part III: The Federal Effort, 52 Iowa L. Rev. 799 (1967).

c.   The Clean Water Act: An Overview

(1)   Goals

In 1972 Congress concluded that the water quality approach was not working. The amendments it adopted that year departed from the 1965-1966 legislation in three major ways. First, Congress substituted the goal of no pollution discharges for the goal of calibrating discharges to water use. Second, a two-tiered system of progressively higher technology-based effluent limitations supplemented existing water quality standards. Third, the federal role in setting water pollution policy was expanded substantially, though states were assigned a significant role as well if they enacted qualifying programs.

In the Senate debate, Senator Edmund Muskie likened water pollution to cancer and offered the following explanation for a control-at-any-cost strategy:

> Can we afford clean water? Can we afford rivers and lakes and streams and life itself? Those questions were never asked as we destroyed the waters of our Nation, and they deserve no answers as we finally move to restore and renew them. These questions answer themselves. [Senate Consideration of the Report of the Conference Comm., Oct. 4, 1972, reprinted in Senate Comm. on Public Works, 1 Legislative History of the Water Pollution Control Act Amendments of 1972, S. Rep. No. 93-1, at 164 (1973) (hereinafter cited as 1972 Legislative History).]

The structure of the CWA can be analyzed in terms of multiple levels of commands. First, the lofty objective of CWA §101(a) is "to restore and maintain the chemical, physical, and biological integrity of the Nation's waters." Only slightly less lofty are the national goal in CWA §101(a)(1) "that the discharge of pollutants into the navigable waters be eliminated by 1985" and the §101(a)(2) interim goal that by 1983, "wherever attainable," waters be made fishable and swimmable. The national objective and the interim goal, however, are not directly enforceable. Rather, Congress chose to further achievement of these goals indirectly, in part through creation of technology-based effluent limitation standards. These standards also were to serve as objectives in and of themselves:

> The Congressional debate makes it clear that supporters of the 1972 amendments saw them as an explicit rejection of ambient water quality standards, either as a feasible basis for determining effluent reduction or as a basis for enforcement. Rather, if technology allows an effluent limitation to be achieved, it should be done. [Freeman, Air and Water Pollution Policy, in Current Issues in U.S. Environmental Policy 12, 48 (1978).]

Was it a good idea for Congress to establish unenforceable and unachievable objectives and goals? The major environmentalist argument for unenforceable goals has been that they help to hold Congress's and regulators' feet to the fire. The contrary case is that symbolic legislation obscures the difficult policy choices that must be made to achieve the objective and delays the rational resolution of regulatory problems. Dwyer, The Pathology of Symbolic Legislation, 17 Ecology L.Q. 233 (1990). See also Lazarus, The Tragedy of Distrust in the Implementation of Federal Environmental Law, 54 Law & Contemp. Probs. 311 (1991).

(2) Structure

The CWA divides pollution into two fundamental categories: pollution emanating from point and from nonpoint sources. The legal definition of a point source is complicated (see pages 594-603), but for our immediate purposes it can be defined as a confined discharge. Point sources are subjected to a two-level reduction standard that initially relies on the adoption of effluent reduction technology, with limited consideration of the costs versus the benefits of effluent reduction. In addition to "technology-based controls," point sources also may be subject to water quality—based controls if that is necessary for the receiving waters to meet water quality standards.

Point sources are regulated under the National Pollutant Discharge Elimination System (NPDES) permit program. Under the "new federalism" in vogue in the early 1970s, states were permitted to administer their own programs if they met federal standards. As indicated in the following table, which summarizes the status of approved NPDES and several other CWA programs, the vast majority of states now are authorized to administer the NPDES permit program.

NPDES permits establish the effluent limitations a discharger must meet and the deadline for meeting them. The issuance of an NPDES permit by EPA is resolved through a quasi-judicial proceeding. Federal regulations for federally issued NPDES permits can be found at 40 C.F.R. §122.

State	Approved State NPDES Permit Program	Approved to Regulate Federal Facilities	Approved State Pretreatment Program	Approved General Permits Program	Approved Biosolids (Sludge) Program
Alabama	✓	✓	✓	✓	
Alaska					
American Samoa					
Arizona	✓	✓	✓	✓	✓
Arkansas	✓	✓	✓	✓	
California	✓	✓	✓	✓	
Colorado	✓			✓	
Connecticut	✓	✓	✓	✓	
Delaware	✓			✓	
District of Columbia					
Florida	✓	✓	✓	✓	
Georgia	✓	✓	✓	✓	
Guam					
Hawaii	✓	✓	✓	✓	
Idaho					
Illinois	✓	✓		✓	
Indiana	✓	✓		✓	

State	Approved State NPDES Permit Program	Approved to Regulate Federal Facilities	Approved State Pretreatment Program	Approved General Permits Program	Approved Biosolids (Sludge) Program
Iowa	✓	✓	✓	✓	
Kansas	✓	✓		✓	
Kentucky	✓	✓	✓	✓	
Louisiana	✓	✓	✓	✓	
Maine	✓	✓	✓	✓	
Maryland	✓	✓	✓	✓	
Massachusetts					
Michigan	✓	✓	✓	✓	
Minnesota	✓	✓	✓	✓	
Mississippi	✓	✓	✓	✓	
Missouri	✓	✓	✓	✓	
Montana	✓	✓		✓	
Nebraska	✓	✓	✓	✓	
Nevada	✓	✓		✓	
New Hampshire					
New Jersey	✓	✓	✓	✓	
New Mexico					
New York	✓	✓		✓	
North Carolina	✓	✓	✓	✓	
North Dakota	✓	✓	✓	✓	
Northern Mariana Islands					
Ohio	✓	✓	✓	✓	✓
Oklahoma	✓	✓	✓	✓	✓
Oregon	✓	✓	✓	✓	
Pennsylvania	✓	✓		✓	
Puerto Rico					
Rhode Island	✓	✓	✓	✓	

State	Approved State NPDES Permit Program	Approved to Regulate Federal Facilities	Approved State Pretreatment Program	Approved General Permits Program	Approved Biosolids (Sludge) Program
South Carolina	✓	✓	✓	✓	
South Dakota	✓	✓	✓	✓	✓
Tennessee	✓	✓	✓	✓	
Texas	✓	✓	✓	✓	✓
Trust Territories					
Utah	✓	✓	✓	✓	✓
Vermont	✓		✓	✓	
Virgin Islands	✓				
Virginia	✓	✓	✓	✓	
Washington	✓		✓	✓	
West Virginia	✓	✓	✓	✓	
Wisconsin	✓	✓	✓	✓	✓
Wyoming	✓	✓		✓	

Source: http://cfpub.epa.gov/npdes/statestats.cfm.

The CWA focuses primarily on two classes of point sources, municipal sewage treatment plants and industrial discharges. Both types of point sources must apply for, and operate in compliance with, an NPDES permit issued by either the federal government or a qualified state program. Sewage treatment plants are subject to technology-based standards known as "primary" and "secondary" treatment. CWA §301(b)(1)(B). Publicly owned sewage treatment plants (POTWs) at first were eligible for grants to upgrade their treatment systems, but these grants have given way to a revolving loan program initially funded by federal grants and loans. POTWs accept wastewater from industries as well as households; industries that discharge pollutants into POTWs are known as "indirect dischargers" (because the industrial entity is not discharging its effluent directly into a navigable water, but is instead sending the effluent to a POTW for treatment before it is discharged). Indirect industrial dischargers may be required to treat ("pretreat") their effluent before sending it to a POTW. Indirect dischargers are to control their effluent discharges into the POTWs so that they do not interfere with the operation of the POTW or contribute to or cause the exceedance of the POTW's permit limits. CWA §307(b)(1); 40 C.F.R. §403.5.

Direct industrial dischargers have been subject to various levels of technology-based controls and treatment over the years. The minimum level of treatment required is known as best practicable control technology currently available (BPT). Dischargers initially were to be in compliance with limits based on such technologies by 1977. Dischargers then were to meet limits based on more stringent technology-based standards, known as best available technology economically achievable (BAT or BATEA), by 1983 (§301(b)(2)(A)). These deadlines have been extended over the years.

The 1977 amendments divided pollutants into three classes: conventional, nonconventional, and toxic. BAT is still required for nonconventional and toxic pollutants, but conventional pollutants are subject to a less rigorous treatment standard, BCT (best conventional pollutant control technology). EPA categorizes "conventional" pollutants as biochemical oxygen-demanding substances (BOD), total suspended solids, fecal coliform bacteria, pH, and oil and grease. The BCT limitations for pollutants must be at least as stringent as BPT limits. In addition to BPT, BAT, and BCT, there are new source performance standards known as BADT (best available demonstrated control technology), which are similar in some ways to those in the Clean Air Act (described in Chapter 6). CWA §306. Determining the technology (or technologies) qualifying as BPT, BAT, and so on often is no easy matter. Congress has provided somewhat different methodologies for EPA to use in making these determinations, and EPA's judgments often are subject to legal challenge, as discussed in more detail below.

The CWA establishes a second line of defense to water pollution, known as "water quality standards," to complement technology-based standards. Water quality–based controls are known as the "safety net" feature of the CWA regulatory scheme because the Act requires that permits be based on more stringent water quality–based standards when technology-based standards fail to achieve applicable water quality standards. CWA §301(b)(1)(C). Water quality standards are discussed in more detail in section E below. Many observers expect water quality–based controls to play an increasingly important role in managing discharges to address the remaining deficiencies in water quality. Implementing a water quality–based approach will not be simple or fast. As indicated at the outset, Congress focused on implementation of a technology-based approach in 1972 in part because of the failure of the ambient-based approach that had been used up to that point. Two of the outstanding questions at this point are (1) whether we have learned enough over the past 30 years to produce better results with an ambient-based approach than we achieved the last time, and (2) whether the tools the CWA provides are adequate to enable us to achieve our goals.

Nonpoint sources have long been considered less amenable to add-on technologies because they require changes in land use activities—such as agriculture, mining, forestry, and construction—that cause runoff into streams. The CWA traditionally has subjected nonpoint source controls to softer, state-run planning and management programs and best practice standards.

While our primary focus in this chapter is the CWA's NPDES permitting scheme for direct dischargers, with secondary emphasis on the §404 permitting scheme covering discharges of dredge and fill material and on the Act's strategies for addressing nonpoint source pollution, the Act's coverage extends beyond these areas. In particular, oil spills are treated in a separate section of the Act, §311, 33 U.S.C. §1321. A series of spills in 1989 revived interest in this section and in the natural resources damage assessment standards developed under Superfund. See pages 957-960. In response to the *Exxon Valdez* and other spectacular oil spills, Congress enacted the Oil Pollution Act of 1990, Pub. L. No. 101-380, 104 Stat. 484. The Oil Pollution Act retains prior federal legislation, but liability is now determined by the Act. Liability- or remediation-based approaches to environmental regulation of the sort embodied by §311 and OPA are covered in detail in Chapter 9.

C. THE CWA'S NPDES PERMIT PROGRAM FOR POINT SOURCES: JURISDICTIONAL BOUNDARIES

Section 301 of the Clean Water Act generally makes unlawful the discharge of any pollutant. This general proscription, however, is subject to several qualifications. This section focuses on one of the most significant exceptions, notably that a party may discharge pollutants if it has obtained an NPDES permit under CWA §402 that authorizes the discharge.

NPDES permitting jurisdiction extends to discharges that satisfy the following four elements: (1) addition (2) of a pollutant (3) from a point source (4) into a navigable water. See CWA §502(7), (12), (14). The rest of this section explores all four elements, with a particular focus on point sources and navigable waters. The definition of "navigable waters" in particular has raised significant issues concerning the scope of congressional power under the Commerce Clause.

1. Definition of a Point Source

As noted earlier, the CWA divides pollution sources into two categories: point and nonpoint. There is no biological rationale for this division. Pesticide residues, for example, are just as harmful whether they enter a drinking water supply from a chemical company's outfall or as the result of agricultural runoff. The reason for the distinction is technological and political. Congress expressed great faith in the ability of engineers to limit what came out of pipes but less faith in their ability to control nonpoint source pollution:

> There is no effective way as yet, other than land use control, by which you can intercept that runoff and control it in the way that you do a point source. We have not yet developed technology to deal with that kind of problem. We need to find ways to deal with it, because a great quantity of pollutants is discharged by runoff, not only from agriculture but from construction sites, from streets, from parking lots, and so on, and we have to be concerned with developing controls for them. [Senate Debate on S. 2770, Nov. 2, 1971, reported in 1972 Legislative History, at 1315.]

Further, to move aggressively against nonpoint sources of pollution, the federal government would have had to mandate new local land use control and agricultural practices standards. In 1972 Congress was unwilling to do this directly, so it attempted to address local land use and agricultural management by shifting the responsibility for nonpoint source pollution control to the states, subject to federal planning standards.

The legal consequence of characterizing water pollution as "point source" pollution is significant. If a source is a point source, an NPDES permit must be obtained and the discharger is subject to the applicable technology-based effluent limitations. CWA §502(14) defines "point source" as follows (it does not define the term "non-point source"):

> any discernible, confined and discrete conveyance, including but not limited to any pipe, ditch, channel, tunnel, conduit, well, discrete fissure, container, rolling stock, concentrated animal feeding operation, or vessel or other floating craft, from which pollutants are or may be discharged. This term does not include agricultural stormwater discharges and return flows from irrigated agriculture.

EPA perceived from the beginning that what came out of a pipe did not exhaust the definition of point source, but it chose not to specify the extent of "non-outfall" point sources. Initially, EPA sought to exempt the most controversial, potential non-pipe point sources from the NPDES permit program. These sources include all silvicultural point sources, all confined animal feedlots, and all irrigation return flows from less than 3,000 acres. NRDC v. Costle, 568 F.2d 1369 (D.C. Cir. 1977), rejected EPA's argument that it could avoid regulation of these sources because such regulation would be administratively infeasible. The court did hold, however, that EPA could introduce flexibility into its program by issuing general areawide permits for classes of point source dischargers.

The question of what kinds of activities qualify as point sources has arisen in a wide variety of contexts, as the following case reflects.

UNITED STATES v. PLAZA HEALTH LABORATORIES, INC.
3 F.3d 643 (2d Cir. 1993)

GEORGE C. PRATT, Circuit Judge: . . .

Facts and Background

[Defendant Villegas co-owned and served as vice president of Plaza Health Laboratories, Inc., a blood-testing laboratory in Brooklyn, New York. Between April and September 1988, Villegas loaded containers of numerous vials of human blood generated from his business into his personal car and drove to his residence at the Admirals Walk Condominium in Edgewater, New Jersey. Once at his condominium complex, Villegas removed the containers from his car and carried them to the edge of the Hudson River. On one occasion he carried two containers of the vials to the bulkhead that separates his condominium complex from the river, and placed them at low tide within a crevice in the bulkhead that was below the high-water line. Numerous vials subsequently were discovered in the water and along the shore. Ten of the retrieved vials contained blood infected with the hepatitis-B virus. All of the vials recovered were eventually traced to Plaza Health Laboratories.

Based on the discovery of the vials, Plaza Health Laboratories and Villegas were indicted on counts of violating §309(c)(2) and (3) of the CWA. Villegas contended that one element of the CWA crime, knowingly discharging pollutants from a "point source," was not established in his case because the CWA §502(14) definition of "point source" does not include discharges that result from the individual acts of human beings.]

Discussion . . .

A.   Navigating the Clean Water Act

The basic prohibition on discharge of pollutants is in 33 U.S.C. §1311(a), which states:

> Except as in compliance with this section and sections 1312, 1316, 1317, 1328, 1342, and 1344 of this title, the *discharge* of any *pollutant* by any person shall be unlawful.

Id. (emphasis added).

The largest exception to this seemingly absolute rule is found in 33 U.S.C. §1342, which establishes the CWA's national pollutant discharge elimination system, or NPDES:

> (a) Permits for discharge of pollutants
>   (1) Except as provided in sections 1328 [aquaculture] and 1344 [dredge and fill permits] of this title, the Administrator may, after opportunity for public hearing, issue a permit for the discharge of any pollutant . . . *notwithstanding section 1311(a) of this title,* upon condition that such discharge will meet . . . all applicable requirements under sections 1311, 1312, 1316, 1317, 1318, and 1343 of this title. . . .

33 U.S.C. §1342(a) (emphasis added).

Reading §1311(a), the basic prohibition, and §1342(a)(1), the permit section, together, we can identify the basic rule, our rhumb line to clean waters, that, absent a permit, "the discharge of any pollutant by any person" is unlawful. 33 U.S.C. §1311(a).

We must then adjust our rhumb line by reference to two key definitions — "pollutant" and "discharge." "Pollutant" is defined, in part, as "biological materials . . . *discharged* into water." 33 U.S.C. §1362(6) (emphasis added). "Discharge," in turn, is "any addition of any pollutant to navigable waters *from any point source . . .*" (emphasis added). 33 U.S.C. §1362(12).

As applied to the facts of this case, then, the defendant "added" a "pollutant" (human blood in glass vials) to "navigable waters" (the Hudson River), and he did so without a permit. The issue, therefore, is whether his conduct constituted a "discharge," and that in turn depends on whether the addition of the blood to the Hudson River waters was "from any point source." For this final course adjustment in our navigation, we look again to the statute.

> The term "point source" means any discernible, confined and discrete conveyance, including but not limited to any pipe, ditch, channel, tunnel, conduit, well, discrete fissure, container, rolling stock, concentrated animal feeding operation, or vessel or other floating craft, from which pollutants are or may be discharged. This term does not include agricultural stormwater discharges and return flows from irrigated agriculture.

33 U.S.C. §1362(14). . . .

As the parties have presented the issue to us in their briefs and at oral argument, the question is "whether a human being can be a point source." Both sides focus on the district court's conclusion in its *rule 29* memorandum that, among other things, the requisite "point source" here could be Villegas himself. . . .

. . . [T]he problem [is] highlighted by the district court's analytical struggle to find somewhere in the Villegas transaction a "discernible, confined and discrete conveyance." Simply put, that problem is that this statute was never designed to address the random, individual polluter like Villegas.

To determine the scope of the CWA's "point source" definition, we first consider the language and structure of the act itself. If the language is not plain, an excursion into legislative history and context may prove fruitful. Judicial interpretations of the term can be instructive as well, as may be interpretive statements by the agency in charge of implementing the statute. If we conclude after this analysis that the statute is ambiguous as applied to Villegas, then the rule of lenity may apply. Moskal v. United States, 498 U.S. 103, 107 (1990); United States v. Concepcion, 983 F.2d 369, 380 (2d Cir. 1992).

1. LANGUAGE AND STRUCTURE OF ACT.

Human beings are not among the enumerated items that may be a "point source." Although by its terms the definition of "point source" is nonexclusive, the words used to define the term and the examples given ("pipe, ditch, channel, tunnel, conduit, well, discrete fissure," etc.) evoke images of physical structures and instrumentalities that systematically act as a means of conveying pollutants from an industrial source to navigable waterways.

In addition, if every discharge involving humans were to be considered a "discharge from a point source," the statute's lengthy definition of "point source" would have been unnecessary. It is elemental that Congress does not add unnecessary words to statutes. Had Congress intended to punish any human being who polluted navigational waters, it could readily have said: "any person who places pollutants in navigable waters without a permit is guilty of a crime."

The Clean Water Act generally targets industrial and municipal sources of pollutants, as is evident from a perusal of its many sections. Consistent with this focus, the term "point source" is used throughout the statute, but invariably in sentences referencing industrial or municipal discharges. See, e.g., 33 U.S.C. §1311 (referring to "owner or operator" of point source); §1311(g)(2) (allows an "owner or operator of a point source" to apply to EPA for modification of its limitations requirements); §1342(f) (referring to classes, categories, types, and sizes of point sources); and §1314(b)(4)(B) (denoting "best conventional pollutant control technology measures and practices" applicable to any point source within particular category or class).

This emphasis was sensible, as "[i]ndustrial and municipal point sources were the worst and most obvious offenders of surface water quality. They were also the easiest to address because their loadings emerge from a discrete point such as the end of a pipe." David Letson, Point/Nonpoint Source Pollution Reduction Trading: An Interpretive Survey, 32 Nat. Resources J. 219, 221 (1992).

Finally on this point, we assume that Congress did not intend the awkward meaning that would result if we were to read "human being" into the definition of "point source." Section 1362(12)(A) defines "discharge of a pollutant" as "any addition of any pollutant to navigable waters from any point source." Enhanced by this definition, §1311(a) reads in effect "the addition of any pollutant to navigable waters *from any point source by any person* shall be unlawful" (emphasis added). But were a human being to be included within the definition of "point source," the prohibition would then read: "the addition of any pollutant to navigable waters *from any person by any person* shall be unlawful," and this simply makes no sense. As the statute stands today, the term "point source" is comprehensible only if it is held to the context of industrial and municipal discharges.

2. LEGISLATIVE HISTORY AND CONTEXT. . . .

The legislative history of the CWA, while providing little insight into the meaning of "point source," confirms the act's focus on industrial polluters. Congress required NPDES permits of those who discharge from a "point source." The term "point source," introduced to the act in 1972, was intended to function as a means of identifying industrial polluters—generally a difficult task because pollutants quickly disperse throughout the subject waters. The Senate report for the 1972 amendments explains:

> In order to further clarify the scope of the regulatory procedures in the Act the Committee had added a definition of point source to distinguish between control requirements where there are *specific confined Conveyances, such as pipes,* and control requirements which are imposed to control runoff. The control of pollutants from runoff is applied pursuant to section 209 and the authority resides in the State or other local agency. [S. Rep. No. 92-414, reprinted in 1972 U.S.C.C.A.N. 3668, 3744.]

Senator Robert Dole added his comments to the committee report:

> Most of the problems of agricultural pollution deal with non-point sources. Very simply, a non-point source of pollution is one that does not confine its polluting discharge to one fairly specific outlet, such as a sewer pipe, a drainage ditch or a conduit; thus, a feedlot would be considered to be a nonpoint source as would pesticides and fertilizers. [Id. at 3760 (supplemental views).]

We find no suggestion either in the act itself or in the history of its passage that Congress intended the CWA to impose criminal liability on an individual for the myriad, random acts of human waste disposal, for example, a passerby who flings a candy wrapper into the Hudson River, or a urinating swimmer. Discussions during the passage of the 1972 amendments indicate that Congress had bigger fish to fry. . . .

[The court here compared the CWA to the permitting scheme in the Rivers and Harbors Act of 1899.]

3. CASELAW.

Our search for the meaning of "point source" brings us next to judicial constructions of the term.

The "point source" element was clearly established in the few CWA criminal decisions under §1319(c) that are reported.

With the exception of *Oxford Royal Mushroom, supra,* the cases that have interpreted "point source" have done so in civil-penalty or licensing settings, where greater flexibility of interpretation to further remedial legislative purposes is permitted, and the rule of lenity does not protect a defendant against statutory ambiguities. See, e.g., Avoyelles Sportsmen's League, Inc. v. Marsh, 715 F.2d 897, 922 (5th Cir.1983) ("point source" includes bulldozing equipment that discharged dredged materials onto wetland).

For example, our circuit recently held in Dague v. City of Burlington, a civil-penalty case, that a discharge of pollutant-laden leachate into a culvert leading to navigable waters was through a "point source." 935 F.2d 1343, 1354-55 (2d Cir. 1991), *rev'd in part on other grounds*, 505 U.S. 557 (1992). But in *Dague*, unlike in this case, the city's discharge involved a culvert, one of the specifically enumerated examples of a "point source" set forth in §1362(14). *Dague*, 935 F.2d at 1354. *Dague* thus presented a classic "point source" discharge.

The government relies on broad dicta in another civil case, United States v. Earth Sciences, Inc., 599 F.2d 368, 373 (10th Cir. 1979), in which the court held "[t]he concept of a point source was designed to further this [permit regulatory] scheme by embracing the broadest possible definition of any identifiable conveyance from which pollutants might enter the waters of the United States." We do not find this *Earth Sciences* dicta persuasive here, however, because that court found a "point source" in a ditch used in the mining operation—certainly not a far leap when "ditch" also is an expressly listed example of a "point source." We cannot, however, make the further leap of writing "human being" into the statutory language without doing violence to the language and structure of the CWA.

4.   REGULATORY STRUCTURE.

Finally, not even the EPA's regulations support the government's broad assertion that a human being may be a "point source." The EPA stresses that the discharge be "through pipes, sewers, or other conveyances."
Discharge of a pollutant means:

(a) Any addition of any "pollutant" or combination of pollutants to "waters of the United States" from any "point source" . . .

This definition includes additions of pollutants into waters of the United States from:
surface runoff which is collected or channelled by man; *discharges through pipes, sewers, or other conveyances* owned by a State, municipality, or other person which do not lead to a treatment works; and discharges through pipes, sewers, or other conveyances, leading into privately owned treatment works. This term does not include an addition of pollu-tants by any "indirect discharger." [40 C.F.R. §122.2 (1992) (emphasis supplied).]

In sum, although Congress had the ability to so provide, §1362(14) of the CWA does not expressly recognize a human being as a "point source"; nor does the act make structural sense when one incorporates a human being into that definition. The legislative history of the act adds no light to the muddy depths of this issue, and cases urging a broad interpretation of the definition in the civil-penalty context do not persuade us to do so here, where Congress has imposed heavy criminal sanctions. Adopting the government's suggested flexibility for the definition would effectively read the "point source" element of the crime out of the statute, and not even the EPA has extended the term "point source" as far as is urged here.

We accordingly conclude that the term "point source" as applied to a human being is at best ambiguous.

B. RULE OF LENITY. . . .

[The court concluded that, because it was not clear that a human being is a "point source" under the CWA, the criminal provisions of the CWA did not clearly proscribe Villegas's conduct and did not accord him fair warning of the sanctions the law placed on that conduct. As a result, under the rule of lenity, it dismissed the prosecutions against him.]

OAKES, Circuit Judge, dissenting:

. . . [B]ecause I do not agree that a person can never be a point source, and because I believe that Mr. Villegas' actions, as the jury found them, fell well within the bounds of activity proscribed by the Clean Water Act's bar on discharge of pollutants into navigable waters, I am required to dissent. . . .

I begin with the obvious, in hopes that it will illuminate the less obvious: the classic point source is something like a pipe. This is, at least in part, because pipes and similar conduits are needed to carry large quantities of waste water, which represents a large proportion of the point source pollution problem. Thus, devices designed to convey large quantities of waste water from a factory or municipal sewage treatment facility are readily classified as point sources. Because not all pollutants are liquids, however, the statute and the cases make clear that means of conveying solid wastes to be dumped in navigable waters are also point sources. See, e.g., 33 U.S.C. §1362(14) ("rolling stock," or railroad cars, listed as an example of a point source); Avoyelles Sportsmen's League, Inc. v. Marsh, 715 F.2d 897, 922 (5th Cir. 1983) (backhoes and bulldozers used to gather fill and deposit it on wetlands are point sources).

What I take from this look at classic point sources is that, at the least, an organized means of channeling and conveying industrial waste in quantity to navigable waters is a "discernible, confined and discrete conveyance." The case law is in accord: courts have deemed a broad range of means of depositing pollutants in the country's navigable waters to be point sources. See, e.g., Rybachek v. EPA, 904 F.2d 1276 (9th Cir. 1990) (placer mining; sluice box from which discharge water is redeposited in stream is point source, despite provisions protecting some mining activities); United States v. M.C.C. of Fla., Inc., 772 F.2d 1501, 1505-06 (11th Cir. 1985) (tugs redepositing dirt from bottom of water body onto beds of water grass are point sources discharging the dirt), *vacated on other grounds*, 481 U.S. 1034 (1987) (defendants' right to jury trial); Sierra Club v. Abston Constr. Co., 620 F.2d 41, 45 (5th Cir. 1980) (spill of contaminated runoff from strip mine, if collected or channeled by the operator, is point source discharge). . . .

In short, the term "point source" has been broadly construed to apply to a wide range of polluting techniques, so long as the pollutants involved are not just human-made, but reach the navigable waters by human effort or by leaking from a clear point at which waste water was collected by human effort. From these cases, the writers of one respected treatise have concluded that such a "man-induced gathering mechanism plainly is the essential characteristic of a point source" and that a point source, "[p]ut simply, . . . is an identifiable conveyance of pollutants." 5 Robert E. Beck, Waters & Water Rights §53.01(b)(3) at 216-17 (1991). . . . See . . . Appalachian Power Co. v. Train, 545 F.2d 1351, 1373 (EPA may regulate channeled runoff, but not unchanneled runoff). In explaining why a broad definition was needed, the *Kennecott Copper* court, quoting American Petroleum Inst. v. EPA, 540 F.2d 1023, 1032 (10th Cir. 1976) noted that the statute sets as its goal the "attainment of the no discharge objective," and that this objective could not be achieved if the term "point source" were read narrowly. 612 F.2d at 1243.

This broad reading of the term "point source" is essential to fulfill the mandate of the Clean Water Act, in that

> [t]he touchstone of the regulatory scheme is that those needing to use the waters for waste distribution must seek and obtain a permit to discharge that waste, with the quantity and quality of the discharge regulated. The concept of a point source was designed to further this scheme by embracing the broadest possible definition of any identifiable conveyance from which pollutants might enter the waters of the United States. . . .
>
> We believe it contravenes the intent of FWPCA and the structure of the statute to exempt from regulation any activity that emits pollution from an identifiable point. [*Earth Sciences*, 599 F.2d 368, 373.]

Nonetheless, the term "point source" sets significant definitional limits on the reach of the Clean Water Act. Fifty percent or more of all water pollution is thought to come from nonpoint sources. . . . So, to further refine the definition of "point source," I consider what it is that the Act does not cover: nonpoint source discharges.

Nonpoint source pollution is, generally, runoff: salt from roads, agricultural chemicals from farmlands, oil from parking lots, and other substances washed by rain, in diffuse patterns, over the land and into navigable waters.[3] The sources are many, difficult to identify and difficult to control. Indeed, an effort to greatly reduce nonpoint source pollution could require radical changes in land use patterns which Congress evidently was unwilling to mandate without further study. The structure of the statute—which regulates point source pollution closely, while leaving nonpoint source regulation to the states under the Section 208 program—indicates that the term "point source" was included in the definition of discharge so as to ensure that nonpoint source pollution would *not* be covered. Instead, Congress chose to regulate first that which could easily be regulated: direct discharges by identifiable parties, or point sources. . . .

While Villegas' activities were not prototypical point source discharges—in part because he was disposing of waste that could have been disposed of on land, and so did not need a permit or a pipe—they much more closely resembled a point source discharge than a nonpoint source discharge. First, Villegas and his lab were perfectly capable of avoiding discharging their waste into water: they were . . . a "controllable" source.

Furthermore, the discharge was directly into water, and came from an identifiable point, Villegas. Villegas did not dispose of the materials on land, where they could be washed into water as nonpoint source pollution. Rather, he carried them,

---

3. According to the EPA, nonpoint source pollution is caused by diffuse sources that are not regulated as point sources and normally is associated with agricultural, silvicultural, and urban runoff, runoff from construction activities, etc. Such pollution results in the human-made or human-induced alteration of the chemical, physical, biological, and radiological integrity of water. In practical terms, nonpoint source pollution does not result from a discharge at a specific, single location (such as a single pipe) but generally results from land runoff, precipitation, atmospheric deposition, or percolation. EPA Office of Water, Office of Water Regulations and Standards, Nonpoint Source Guidance 3 (1987).

from his firm's laboratory, in his car, to his apartment complex, where he placed them in a bulkhead below the high tide line. I do not think it is necessary to determine whether it was Mr. Villegas himself who was the point source, or whether it was his car, the vials, or the bulkhead: in a sense, the entire stream of Mr. Villegas' activity functioned as a "discrete conveyance" or point source. The point is that the source of the pollution was clear, and would have been easy to control. Indeed, Villegas was well aware that there were methods of controlling the discharge (and that the materials were too dangerous for casual disposal): his laboratory had hired a professional medical waste handler. He simply chose not to use an appropriate waste disposal mechanism.

Villegas' method may have been an unusual one for a corporate officer, but it would undermine the statute—which, after all, sets as its goal the elimination of discharges, 33 U.S.C. §1311(a)—to regard as "ambiguous" a Congressional failure to list an unusual method of disposing of waste. I doubt that Congress would have regarded an army of men and women throwing industrial waste from trucks into a stream as exempt from the statute. Since the Act contains no exemption for de minimus [sic] violations—since, indeed, many Clean Water Act prosecutions are for a series of small discharges, each of which is treated as a single violation—I cannot see that one man throwing one day's worth of medical waste into the ocean differs (and indeed, with this type of pollution, it might be that only a few days' violations could be proven even if the laboratory regularly relied on Villegas to dispose of its waste by throwing it into the ocean). A different reading would encourage corporations perfectly capable of abiding by the Clean Water Act's requirements to ask their employees to stand between the company trucks and the sea, thereby transforming point source pollution (dumping from trucks) into nonpoint source pollution (dumping by hand). Such a method is controllable, easily identifiable, and inexcusable. To call it nonpoint source pollution is to read a technical exception into a statute which attempts to define in broad terms an activity which may be conducted in many different ways. . . .

My colleagues suggest that a person can never be a point source, relying heavily on the supposed redundancy produced when the Act's language barring the "discharge of any pollutant by any person" is read with the definitional terms placed in terms of the linguistic variables, as follows: "any addition of any pollutant to navigable waters from a person by a person." Granted, this sounds odd. But I believe the oddity is an artifact of assuming that the term "person" means the same thing in both parts of the sentence, and that in both cases it means what it means in everyday language.

The apparent oddness disappears when one grasps that the first term "person" in the peculiar sentence means "a person acting as a point source"[6] and that the second term "person" has been defined, typically for statutes imposing responsibility on a variety of parties, but not typically for ordinary speech, as a responsible party. As the linguistic hint "any" before both "person" and "point source" suggests, the terms are to be construed broadly. . . .

Having resorted to the language and structure, legislative history and motivating policies of the Clean Water Act, I think it plain enough that Congress intended the

6. In my view, persons can be both point and nonpoint sources of pollution. They may be point sources when they deposit waste directly into water; they may be nonpoint sources when they, for example, spread fertilizer on the ground or deposit oil in a driveway, leaving it to be washed into nearby rivers. Thus, to say that the Clean Water Act bars persons polluting, rather than point sources polluting, would be too broad.

statute to bar corporate officers from disposing of corporate waste into navigable waters by hand as well as by pipe. . . .

2. The Concept of "Navigable Waters"

A second major element required to trigger NPDES jurisdiction is that a discharge be to "navigable waters," defined in CWA §502(7) as "waters of the United States. . . ." Issues of constitutional as well as statutory interpretation have been in the forefront of efforts to determine the types of waters that Congress intended, and is empowered, to reach in the exercise of its regulatory powers.

a. Constitutional Power to Regulate Water Pollution

All federal environmental regulation must be grounded in an enumerated power of the Constitution. The most obvious source of federal power to regulate water pollution is the Commerce Clause, art. 1, §8. For several decades the constitutional power of Congress to regulate any form of point or nonpoint pollution of surface water, wetlands, and groundwater under the Commerce Clause was assumed to rest on Wickard v. Filburn, 317 U.S. 111 (1942), which upheld regulation of intrastate activities that cumulatively had a substantial effect on interstate commerce, and the Court's post–New Deal era deference to congressional conclusions about the nexus between a regulated activity and interstate commerce. However, in 1995 the Court refused to defer to Congress for the first time in 59 years. United States v. Lopez, 514 U.S. 549 (1995), held that Congress lacked the authority under the Commerce Clause to enact the Gun-Free School Zones Act, which made it a federal crime to possess a firearm in a school zone. This question of whether there is the requisite constitutional nexus to support regulation of particular types of water pollution has attracted considerable attention concerning the definition of "navigable waters" under the CWA, one of the key elements for establishing NPDES (as well as §404) permit jurisdiction under the Act. It is impossible to separate entirely questions of constitutional interpretation from issues of statutory construction; thus, while we introduce the former here, we address them to some extent below as well.

b. Statutory Boundaries on the Regulation of Water Pollution

A second question is whether Congress has exercised the full extent of its regulatory power over water under the Commerce Clause. The CWA speaks of preventing the discharge of pollutants into "navigable waters," and §402 speaks of permits for the discharge of pollutants into navigable waters. Navigable waters are defined in CWA §502(7) as "the waters of the United States, including the territorial seas." Does this definition expand the historic definition of navigability, and does Congress have the constitutional power to do so?

This issue has received attention from the Supreme Court in its 1985 *Riverside Bayview*, 2001 SWANCC, and 2006 *Rapanos* decisions, from which we provide excerpts below. Each case considered the definition of navigable waters in the context of the CWA §404 program, discussed below, but this definition also is relevant to the scope of the NPDES permit program, as well as the TMDL program, and water quality certifications. Advance Notice of Proposed Rulemaking on the Clean Water Act Regulatory Definition of "Waters of the United States," 68 Fed. Reg. 1993 (2003). The Corps of Engineers and EPA have promulgated various definitions of wetlands in recent years under the CWA, and the scope of these regulations, as well as Congress's authority under the CWA to regulate activities in wetlands, have been subject to numerous court challenges. We provide the text of the current regulations in our discussion of CWA §404 jurisdiction at pages 687-692. The Supreme Court considered this issue in the following case.

UNITED STATES v. RIVERSIDE BAYVIEW HOMES, INC.
474 U.S. 121 (1985)

JUSTICE WHITE delivered the opinion of the Court.

This case presents the question whether the Clean Water Act (CWA), . . . together with certain regulations promulgated under its authority by the Army Corps of Engineers, authorizes the Corps to require landowners to obtain permits from the Corps before discharging fill material into wetlands adjacent to navigable bodies of water and their tributaries.

I

The relevant provisions of the Clean Water Act originated in the Federal Water Pollution Control Act Amendments of 1972, and have remained essentially unchanged since that time. Under §§301 and 502 of the Act, . . . any discharge of dredged or fill materials into "navigable waters"—defined as the "waters of the United States"—is forbidden unless authorized by a permit issued by the Corps of Engineers pursuant to §404. . . . After initially construing the Act to cover only waters navigable in fact, in 1975 the Corps issued interim final regulations redefining "the waters of the United States" to include not only actually navigable waters but also tributaries of such waters, interstate waters and their tributaries, and nonnavigable intrastate waters whose use or misuse could affect interstate commerce. 40 Fed. Reg. 31,320 (1975). More importantly for present purposes, the Corps construed the Act to cover all "freshwater wetlands" that were adjacent to other covered waters. . . . In 1977, the Corps refined its definition of wetlands . . . [to] read as follows:

> The term "wetlands" means those areas that are inundated or saturated by surface or ground water at a frequency and duration sufficient to support, and that under normal circumstances do support, a prevalence of vegetation typically adapted for life in saturated soil conditions. Wetlands generally include swamps, marshes, bogs and similar areas. 33 C.F.R. §323.2(c) (1978).

In 1982, the 1977 regulations were replaced by substantively identical regulations that remain in force today. See 33 C.F.R. §323.2 (1985).

Respondent Riverside Bayview Homes, Inc. (hereafter respondent), owns 80 acres of low-lying, marshy land near the shores of Lake St. Clair in Macomb County, Michigan. In 1976, respondent began to place fill materials on its property as part of its preparations for construction of a housing development. The Corps of Engineers, believing that the property was an "adjacent wetland" under the 1975 regulation defining "waters of the United States," filed suit in the United States District Court for the Eastern District of Michigan, seeking to enjoin respondent from filling the property without the permission of the Corps.

[The district court initially held that some of Riverside's property below 575.5 feet above sea level was a wetland, and the Court of Appeals remanded for consideration of the effect of the intervening 1977 amendments on the regulation. On remand, the district court again held the property to be a wetland subject to the Corps' permit authority, but the Sixth Circuit construed the Corps' regulations to exclude from the category of adjacent wetlands—and hence from that of "waters of the United States"—wetlands that were not subject to flooding by adjacent navigable waters at a frequency sufficient to support the growth of aquatic vegetation. . . . We now reverse.

II

The question whether the Corps of Engineers may demand that respondent obtain a permit before placing fill material on its property is primarily one of regulatory and statutory interpretation: we must determine whether respondent's property is an "adjacent wetland" within the meaning of the applicable regulation, and, if so, whether the Corps' jurisdiction over "navigable waters" gives it statutory authority to regulate discharges of fill material into such a wetland. . . .

III

. . . [T]he question whether the regulation at issue requires respondent to obtain a permit before filling its property is an easy one. The regulation extends the Corps' authority under §404 to all wetlands adjacent to navigable or interstate waters and their tributaries. Wetlands, in turn, are defined as lands that are "inundated *or saturated* by surface *or ground water* at a frequency and duration sufficient to support, and that under normal circumstances do support, a prevalence of vegetation typically adapted for life in saturated soil conditions." 33 C.F.R. §323.2(c) (1985) (emphasis added). The plain language of the regulation refutes the Court of Appeals' conclusion that inundation or "frequent flooding" by the adjacent body of water is a *sine qua non* of a wetland under the regulation. Indeed, the regulation could hardly state more clearly that saturation by either surface or ground water is sufficient to bring an area within the category of wetlands, provided that the saturation is sufficient to and does support wetland vegetation. . . .

Without the nonexistent requirement of frequent flooding, the regulatory definition of adjacent wetlands covers the property here. The District Court found that respondent's property was "characterized by the presence of vegetation that requires saturated soil conditions for growth and reproduction," and that the source of the saturated soil conditions on the property was ground water. There is no plausible suggestion that these findings are clearly erroneous, and they plainly bring the property within the category of wetlands as defined by the current regulation. In addition, the court found that the wetland located on respondent's property was adjacent to a body of navigable water, since the area characterized by saturated soil conditions and wetland vegetation extended beyond the boundary of respondent's property to Black Creek, a navigable waterway. Again, the court's finding is not clearly erroneous. Together, these findings establish that respondent's property is a wetland adjacent to a navigable waterway. Hence, it is part of the "waters of the United States" as defined by 33 C.F.R. §323.2 (1985), and if the regulation itself is valid as a construction of the term "waters of the United States" as used in the Clean Water Act, a question which we now address, the property falls within the scope of the Corps' jurisdiction over "navigable waters" under §404 of the Act.

IV

A

An agency's construction of a statute it is charged with enforcing is entitled to deference if it is reasonable and not in conflict with the expressed intent of Congress. . . . Accordingly, our review is limited to the question whether it is reasonable, in light of the language, policies, and legislative history of the Act, for the Corps to exercise jurisdiction over wetlands adjacent to but not regularly flooded by rivers, streams, and other hydrographic features more conventionally identifiable as "waters."

On a purely linguistic level, it may appear unreasonable to classify "lands," wet or otherwise, as "waters." Such a simplistic response, however, does justice neither to the problem faced by the Corps in defining the scope of its authority under §404(a) nor to the realities of the problem of water pollution that the Clean Water Act was intended to combat. In determining the limits of its power to regulate discharges under the Act, the Corps must necessarily choose some point at which water ends and land begins. Our common experience tells us that this is often no easy task: the transition from water to solid ground is not necessarily or even typically an abrupt one. Rather, between open waters and dry land may lie shallows, marshes, mudflats, swamps, bogs—in short, a huge array of areas that are not wholly aquatic but nevertheless fall far short of being dry land. Where on this continuum to find the limit of "waters" is far from obvious.

Faced with such a problem of defining the bounds of its regulatory authority, an agency may appropriately look to the legislative history and underlying policies of its statutory grants of authority. Neither of these sources provides unambiguous guidance for the Corps in this case, but together they do support the reasonableness of the Corps' approach of defining adjacent wetlands as "waters" within the meaning of §404(a). Section 404 originated as part of the Federal Water Pollution Control Act Amendments of 1972, which constituted a comprehensive legislative attempt "to restore and maintain the chemical, physical, and biological integrity of the Nation's waters." CWA §101, 33 U.S.C. §1251. This objective incorporated a broad, systemic view of the goal of maintaining and improving water quality: as the House Report on the legislation put it, "the word 'integrity' . . . refers to a condition in which the natural structure and function of ecosystems is [are] maintained." H.R. Rep. No. 92-911, p. 76 (1972). Protection of aquatic ecosystems, Congress recognized, demanded broad federal authority to control pollution, for "[w]ater moves in hydrologic cycles and it is essential that discharge of pollutants be controlled at the source." . . .

We cannot say that the Corps' conclusion that adjacent wetlands are inseparably bound up with the "waters" of the United States—based as it is on the Corps' and

EPA's technical expertise—is unreasonable. In view of the breadth of federal regulatory authority contemplated by the Act itself and the inherent difficulties of defining precise bounds to regulable waters, the Corps' ecological judgment about the relationship between waters and their adjacent wetlands provides an adequate basis for a legal judgment that adjacent wetlands may be defined as waters under the Act. . . .

Following its decision in *Riverside Bayview*, in 2001 the Supreme Court again had occasion to consider the scope of the term "navigable waters," this time in the context of the Corps' definition of such waters to include habitat for migratory birds.

SOLID WASTE AGENCY OF NORTHERN COOK COUNTY v. UNITED STATES ARMY CORP OF ENGINEERS
531 U.S. 159 (2001)

CHIEF JUSTICE REHNQUIST delivered the opinion of the Court.

. . . The United States Army Corps of Engineers (Corps) has interpreted §404(a) to confer federal authority over an abandoned sand and gravel pit in northern Illinois which provides habitat for migratory birds. We are asked to decide whether the provisions of §404(a) may be fairly extended to these waters, and, if so, whether Congress could exercise such authority consistent with the Commerce Clause, U.S. Const., Art. I, §8, cl. 3. We answer the first question in the negative and therefore do not reach the second.

Petitioner, the Solid Waste Agency of Northern Cook County (SWANCC), is a consortium of 23 suburban Chicago cities and villages that united in an effort to locate and develop a disposal site for baled nonhazardous solid waste. The Chicago Gravel Company informed the municipalities of the availability of a 533-acre parcel, . . . which had been the site of a sand and gravel pit mining operation for three decades up until about 1960. Long since abandoned, the old mining site eventually gave way to a successional stage forest, with its remnant excavation trenches evolving into a scattering of permanent and seasonal ponds of varying size (from under one-tenth of an acre to several acres) and depth (from several inches to several feet).

The municipalities decided to purchase the site for disposal of their baled nonhazardous solid waste. . . . [B]ecause the operation called for the filling of some of the permanent and seasonal ponds, SWANCC contacted federal respondents (hereinafter respondents), including the Corps, to determine if a federal landfill permit was required under §404(a) of the CWA.

Section 404(a) grants the Corps authority to issue permits "for the discharge of dredged or fill material into the navigable waters at specified disposal sites." The term "navigable waters" is defined under the Act as "the waters of the United States, including the territorial seas." §1362(7). The Corps has issued regulations defining the term "waters of the United States" to include

> waters such as intrastate lakes, rivers, streams (including intermittent streams), mudflats, sandflats, wetlands, sloughs, prairie potholes, wet meadows, playa lakes, or natural ponds, the use, degradation, or destruction of which could affect interstate or foreign commerce. . . . 33 CFR §328.3(a)(3) (1999).

In 1986, in an attempt to "clarify" the reach of its jurisdiction, the Corps stated that §404(a) extends to instrastate waters:

    a. Which are or would be used as habitat by birds protected by Migratory Bird Treaties; or

    b. Which are or would be used as habitat by other migratory birds which cross state lines. . . . 51 Fed. Reg. 41217.

This last promulgation has been dubbed the "Migratory Bird Rule."

    The Corps . . . ultimately asserted jurisdiction over the balefill site pursuant to subpart (b) of the "Migratory Bird Rule." The Corps found that approximately 121 bird species had been observed at the site, including several known to depend upon aquatic environments for a significant portion of their life requirements. Thus, . . . the Corps formally "determined that the seasonally ponded, abandoned gravel mining depressions located on the project site, while not wetlands, did qualify as 'waters of the United States' . . . based upon the following criteria: (1) the proposed site had been abandoned as a gravel mining operation; (2) the water areas and spoil piles had developed a natural character; and (3) the water areas are used as habitat by migratory bird [sic] which cross state lines." . . .

    [The Corps ultimately refused to issue a §404 permit. Petitioner filed suit challenging the Corps' jurisdiction over the site. The District Court granted summary judgment to respondents on the jurisdictional issue. On appeal to the Court of Appeals, petitioner argued that respondents had exceeded their statutory authority in interpreting the CWA to cover nonnavigable, isolated, intrastate waters based upon the presence of migratory birds and, in the alternative, that Congress lacked the power under the Commerce Clause to grant such regulatory jurisdiction.

    The Court of Appeals held that Congress has the authority to regulate such waters based upon "the cumulative impact doctrine, under which a single activity that itself has no discernible effect on interstate commerce may still be regulated if the aggregate effect of that class of activity has a substantial impact on interstate commerce." . . . The aggregate effect of the "destruction of the natural habitat of migratory birds" on interstate commerce, the court held, was substantial because each year millions of Americans cross state lines and spend over a billion dollars to hunt and observe migratory birds. The Court of Appeals then turned to the regulatory question. The court held that the CWA reaches as many waters as the Commerce Clause allows and, given its earlier Commerce Clause ruling, it therefore followed that respondents' "Migratory Bird Rule" was a reasonable interpretation of the Act.]

    We granted certiorari . . . and now reverse.

    Congress passed the CWA for the stated purpose of "restor[ing] and maintain-[ing] the chemical, physical, and biological integrity of the Nation's waters." 33 U.S.C. §1251(a). . . . Relevant here, §404(a) authorizes respondents to regulate the discharge of fill material into "navigable waters," which the statute defines as "the waters of the United States, including the territorial seas." Respondents have interpreted these words to cover the abandoned gravel pit at issue here because it is used as habitat for migratory birds. We conclude that the "Migratory Bird Rule" is not fairly supported by the CWA.

    This is not the first time we have been called upon to evaluate the meaning of §404(a). In United States v. Riverside Bayview Homes, Inc., . . . we held that the Corps had §404(a) jurisdiction over wetlands that actually abutted on a navigable waterway. In so doing, we noted that the term "navigable" is of "limited import" and that Congress evidenced its intent to "regulate at least some waters that would not be deemed 'navigable' under the classical understanding of that term." ... But our holding was based in large measure upon Congress' unequivocal acquiescence to, and approval of, the Corps' regulations interpreting the CWA to cover wetlands adjacent to navigable waters. ... We found that Congress' concern for the protection of water quality and aquatic ecosystems indicated its intent to regulate wetlands "inseparably bound up with the 'waters' of the United States. ..."

It was the significant nexus between the wetlands and "navigable waters" that informed our reading of the CWA in *Riverside Bayview Homes*. Indeed, we did not "express any opinion" on the "question of the authority of the Corps to regulate discharges of fill material into wetlands that are not adjacent to bodies of open water. ..." In order to rule for respondents here, we would have to hold that the jurisdiction of the Corps extends to ponds that are *not* adjacent to open water. But we conclude that the text of the statute will not allow this. ...

We ... decline respondents' invitation to take what they see as the next ineluctable step after *Riverside Bayview Homes*: holding that isolated ponds, some only seasonal, wholly located within two Illinois counties, fall under §404(a)'s definition of "navigable waters" because they serve as habitat for migratory birds. As counsel for respondents conceded at oral argument, such a ruling would assume that "the use of the word navigable in the statute ... does not have any independent significance." ... We cannot agree that Congress' separate definitional use of the phrase "waters of the United States" constitutes a basis for reading the term "navigable waters" out of the statute. We said in *Riverside Bayview Homes* that the word "navigable" in the statute was of "limited effect" and went on to hold that §404(a) extended to nonnavigable wetlands adjacent to open waters. But it is one thing to give a word limited effect and quite another to give it no effect whatever. The term "navigable" has at least the import of showing us what Congress had in mind as its authority for enacting the CWA: its traditional jurisdiction over waters that were or had been navigable in fact or which could reasonably be so made. ...

Respondents contend that ... at the very least, it must be said that Congress did not address the precise question of §404(a)'s scope with regard to nonnavigable, isolated, intrastate waters, and that, therefore, we should give deference to the "Migratory Bird Rule." See, e.g., Chevron U.S.A., Inc. v. Natural Resources Defense Council, Inc., 467 U.S. 837 (1984). We find §404(a) to be clear, but even were we to agree with respondents, we would not extend *Chevron* deference here.

Where an administrative interpretation of a statute invokes the outer limits of Congress' power, we expect a clear indication that Congress intended that result. This requirement stems from our prudential desire not to needlessly reach constitutional issues and our assumption that Congress does not casually authorize administrative agencies to interpret a statute to push the limit of congressional authority. This concern is heightened where the administrative interpretation alters the federal-state framework by permitting federal encroachment upon a traditional state power. ... Thus, "where an otherwise acceptable construction of a statute would raise serious constitutional problems, the Court will construe the statute to avoid such problems unless such construction is plainly contrary to the intent of Congress." ...

These are significant constitutional questions raised by respondents' application of their regulations, and yet we find nothing approaching a clear statement from

Congress that it intended §404(a) to reach an abandoned sand and gravel pit such as we have here. Permitting respondents to claim federal jurisdiction over ponds and mudflats falling within the "Migratory Bird Rule" would result in a significant impingement of the States' traditional and primary power over land and water use. . . . Rather than expressing a desire to readjust the federal-state balance in this manner, Congress chose to "recognize, preserve, and protect the primary responsibilities and rights of States . . . to plan the development and use . . . of land and water resources. . . ." 33 U.S.C. §1251(b). We thus read the statute as written to avoid the significant constitutional and federalism questions raised by respondents' interpretation, and therefore reject the request for administrative deference.

We hold that 33 CFR §328.3(a)(3) (1999), as clarified and applied to petitioner's balefill site pursuant to the "Migratory Bird Rule," exceeds the authority granted to respondents under §404(a) of the CWA. The judgment of the Court of Appeals for the Seventh Circuit is therefore

Reversed.

JUSTICE STEVENS, with whom JUSTICE SOUTER, JUSTICE GINSBURG, and JUSTICE BREYER join, dissenting. . . .

The Court has previously held that the Corps' broadened jurisdiction under the CWA properly included an 80-acre parcel of low-lying marshy land that was not itself navigable, directly adjacent to navigable water, or even hydrologically connected to navigable water, but which was part of a larger area, characterized by poor drainage, that ultimately abutted a navigable creek. United States v. Riverside Bayview Homes, Inc. . . . Our broad finding in *Riverside Bayview* that the 1977 Congress had acquiesced in the Corps' understanding of its jurisdiction applies equally to the 410-acre parcel at issue here. Moreover, once Congress crossed the legal watershed that separates navigable streams of commerce from marshes and inland lakes, there is no principled reason for limiting the statute's protection to those waters or wetlands that happen to lie near a navigable stream. . . .

I . . .

As we recognized in *Riverside Bayview*, the interests served by the statute embrace the protection of " 'significant natural biological functions, including food chain production, general habitat, and nesting, spawning, rearing and resting sites' " for various species of aquatic wildlife. . . . For wetlands and "isolated" inland lakes, that interest is equally powerful, regardless of the proximity of the swamp or the water to a navigable stream. . . .

The majority accuses respondents of reading the term "navigable" out of the statute. But that was accomplished by Congress when it deleted the word from the §502(7) definition. . . .

II . . .

In 1975, the Corps . . . adopted the interim regulations that we upheld in *Riverside Bayview*. As we noted in that case, the new regulations understood "the waters of the United States" to include, not only navigable waters and their tributaries, but also "nonnavigable intrastate waters whose use or misuse could affect interstate commerce." . . .

Even if the majority were correct that Congress did not extend the Corps' jurisdiction in the 1972 CWA to reach beyond navigable waters and their nonnavigable tributaries, Congress' rejection of the House's efforts in 1977 to cut back on the Corps' 1975 assertion of jurisdiction clearly indicates congressional acquiescence in that assertion. Indeed, our broad determination in *Riverside Bayview* that the 1977 Congress acquiesced in the very regulations at issue in this case should foreclose petitioner's present urgings to the contrary. . . . [13] . . .

III . . .

Contrary to the Court's suggestion, the Corps' interpretation of the statute does not "encroac[h]" upon "traditional state power" over land use. "Land use planning in essence chooses particular uses for the land; environmental regulation, at its core, does not mandate particular uses of the land but requires only that, however the land is used, damage to the environment is kept within prescribed limits." . . . The CWA is not a land-use code; it is a paradigm of environmental regulation. Such regulation is an accepted exercise of federal power. . . .

Because I would affirm the judgment of the Court of Appeals, I respectfully dissent.

In 2006 the Supreme Court handed down its most recent decision concerning the scope of "navigable waters" in two consolidated cases, Rapanos v. United States and Carabell v. U.S. Army Corps of Engineers.

RAPANOS v. UNITED STATES
126 S. Ct. 2208 (2006)

JUSTICE SCALIA announced the judgment of the Court, and delivered an opinion, in which THE CHIEF JUSTICE, JUSTICE THOMAS, and JUSTICE ALITO join. . . .

---

13. The majority appears to believe that its position is consistent with *Riverside Bayview* because of that case's reservation of the question whether the Corps' jurisdiction extends to "certain wetlands not necessarily adjacent to other waters," 474 U.S., at 124, n.2. But it is clear from the context that the question reserved by *Riverside Bayview* did not concern "isolated" waters, such as those at issue in this case, but rather "isolated" wetlands. See id., at 131-132, n.8 ("We are not called upon to address the question of the authority of the Corps to regulate discharges of fill material into wetlands that are not adjacent to bodies of open water . . ."). . . . If, as I believe, actually navigable waters lie at the very heart of Congress' commerce power and "isolated," nonnavigable waters lie closer to (but well within) the margin, "isolated wetlands," which are themselves only marginally "waters," are the most marginal category of "waters of the United States" potentially covered by the statute. It was the question of the extension of federal jurisdiction to that category of "waters" that the *Riverside Bayview* Court reserved. That question is not presented in this case.

I

The Corps' current regulations interpret "the waters of the United States" to include, in addition to traditional interstate navigable waters, 33 CFR §328.3(a)(1) (2004), "[a]ll interstate waters including interstate wetlands," §328.3(a)(2); "[a]ll other waters such as intrastate lakes, rivers, streams (including intermittent streams), mudflats, sandflats, wetlands, sloughs, prairie potholes, wet meadows, playa lakes, or natural ponds, the use, degradation, or destruction of which could affect interstate or foreign commerce," §328.3(a)(3); "[t]ributaries of [such] waters," §328.3(a)(5); and "[w]etlands adjacent to [such] waters [and tributaries] (other than waters that are themselves wetlands)," §328.3(a)(7). The regulation defines "adjacent" wetlands as those "bordering, contiguous [to], or neighboring" waters of the United States. §328.3(c). It specifically provides that "[w]etlands separated from other waters of the United States by man-made dikes or barriers, natural river berms, beach dunes, and the like are 'adjacent wetlands.'"

II

In these consolidated cases, we consider whether four Michigan wetlands, which lie near ditches or man-made drains that eventually empty into traditional navigable waters, constitute "waters of the United States" within the meaning of the Act. Petitioners in No. 04-1034, the Rapanos and their affiliated businesses, deposited fill material without a permit into wetlands on three sites near Midland, Michigan: the "Salzburg site," the "Hines Road site," and the "Pine River site." The wetlands at the Salzburg site are connected to a man-made drain, which drains into Hoppler Creek, which flows into the Kawkawlin River, which empties into Saginaw Bay and Lake Huron. The wetlands at the Hines Road site are connected to something called the "Rose Drain," which has a surface connection to the Tittabawassee River. And the wetlands at the Pine River site have a surface connection to the Pine River, which flows into Lake Huron. It is not clear whether the connections between these wetlands and the nearby drains and ditches are continuous or intermittent, or whether the nearby drains and ditches contain continuous or merely occasional flows of water.

   The United States brought civil enforcement proceedings against the Rapanos petitioners. The District Court found that the three described wetlands were "within federal jurisdiction" because they were "adjacent to other waters of the United States. . . ." On appeal, the United States Court of Appeals for the Sixth Circuit affirmed, holding that there was federal jurisdiction over the wetlands at all three sites because "there were hydrological connections between all three sites and corresponding adjacent tributaries of navigable waters."

   Petitioners in No. 04-1384, the Carabells, were denied a permit to deposit fill material in a wetland located on a triangular parcel of land about one mile from Lake St. Clair. A man-made drainage ditch runs along one side of the wetland, separated from it by a 4-foot-wide man-made berm. The berm is largely or entirely impermeable to water and blocks drainage from the wetland, though it may permit occasional overflow to the ditch. The ditch empties into another ditch or a drain, which connects to Auvase Creek, which empties into Lake St. Clair.

   . . . The District Court ruled that there was federal jurisdiction because the wetland "is adjacent to neighboring tributaries of navigable waters and has a significant nexus to 'waters of the United States.'" Again the Sixth Circuit affirmed, holding that the Carabell wetland was "adjacent" to navigable waters.

We granted certiorari and consolidated the cases to decide whether these wetlands constitute "waters of the United States" under the Act, and if so, whether the Act is constitutional.

III

... We have twice stated that the meaning of "navigable waters" in the Act is broader than the traditional understanding of that term, SWANCC, *Riverside Bayview*. We have also emphasized, however, that the qualifier "navigable" is not devoid of significance. SWANCC.

We need not decide the precise extent to which the qualifiers "navigable" and "of the United States" restrict the coverage of the Act. Whatever the scope of these qualifiers, the CWA authorizes federal jurisdiction only over "waters." The only natural definition of the term "waters," our prior and subsequent judicial constructions of it, clear evidence from other provisions of the statute, and this Court's canons of construction all confirm that "the waters of the United States" in §1362(7) cannot bear the expansive meaning that the Corps would give it.

The Corps' expansive approach might be arguable if the [CWA] defined "navigable waters" as "water of the United States." But "the waters of the United States" is something else. The use of the definite article ("the") and the plural number ("waters") show plainly that §1362(7) does not refer to water in general. In this form, "the waters" refers more narrowly to water "[a]s found in streams and bodies forming geographical features such as oceans, rivers, [and] lakes," or "the flowing or moving masses, as of waves or floods, making up such streams or bodies." WEBSTER'S NEW INTERNATIONAL DICTIONARY 2882 (2d ed. 1954) (hereinafter WEBSTER'S SECOND). On this definition, "the waters of the United States" include only relatively permanent, standing or flowing bodies of water. . . . All of these terms connote continuously present, fixed bodies of water, as opposed to ordinarily dry channels through which water occasionally or intermittently flows. . . . None of these terms encompasses transitory puddles or ephemeral flows of water.

The restriction of "the waters of the United States" to exclude channels containing merely intermittent or ephemeral flow also accords with the commonsense understanding of the term. In applying the definition to "ephemeral streams," "wet meadows," storm sewers and culverts, "directional sheet flow during storm events," drain tiles, man-made drainage ditches, and dry arroyos in the middle of the desert, the Corps has stretched the term "waters of the United States" beyond parody. The plain language of the statute simply does not authorize this "Land Is Waters" approach to federal jurisdiction. . . .

... [T]he CWA itself categorizes the channels and conduits that typically carry intermittent flows of water separately from "navigable waters," by including them in the definition of "'point source.'" The Act defines "'point source'" as "any discernible, confined and discrete conveyance, including but not limited to any . . . ditch, channel, tunnel, [or] conduit . . . from which pollutants are or may be discharged." It also defines "'discharge of a pollutant'" as "any addition of any pollutant *to* navigable waters *from* any point source." The definitions thus conceive of "point sources" and "navigable waters" as separate and distinct categories. The definition of "discharge" would make little sense if the two categories were significantly overlapping. The separate classification of "ditch[es], channel[s], and conduit[s]"—which are terms ordinarily used to describe the watercourses through which *intermittent* waters typically flow—shows that these are, by and large, *not* "waters of the United States."

Moreover, only the foregoing definition of "waters" is consistent with the CWA's stated "policy of Congress to recognize, preserve, and protect the primary responsibilities and rights of the States to prevent, reduce, and eliminate pollution, [and] to plan the development and use (including restoration, preservation, and enhancement) of land and water resources. . . ." §1251(b). . . .

[T]he Government's expansive interpretation would "result in a significant impingement of the States' traditional and primary power over land and water use." Regulation of land use, as through the issuance of the development permits sought by petitioners in both of these cases, is a quintessential state and local power. The extensive federal jurisdiction urged by the Government would authorize the Corps to function as a *de facto* regulator of immense stretches of intrastate land—an authority the agency has shown its willingness to exercise with the scope of discretion that would befit a local zoning board. See 33 CFR §320.4(a)(1) (2004). We ordinarily expect a "clear and manifest" statement from Congress to authorize an unprecedented intrusion into traditional state authority. The phrase "the waters of the United States" hardly qualifies.

Likewise, . . . the Corps' interpretation stretches the outer limits of Congress's commerce power and raises difficult questions about the ultimate scope of that power. Even if the term "the waters of the United States" were ambiguous as applied to channels that sometimes host ephemeral flows of water (which it is not), we would expect a clearer statement from Congress to authorize an agency theory of jurisdiction that presses the envelope of constitutional validity.

In sum, on its only plausible interpretation, the phrase "the waters of the United States" includes only those relatively permanent, standing or continuously flowing bodies of water "forming geographic features" that are described in ordinary parlance as "streams[,] . . . oceans, rivers, [and] lakes." The phrase does not include channels through which water flows intermittently or ephemerally, or channels that periodically provide drainage for rainfall. The Corps' expansive interpretation of the "the waters of the United States" is thus not "based on a permissible construction of the statute." Chevron U.S.A., Inc. v. Natural Resources Defense Council, Inc., 467 U.S. 837, 843 (1984).

IV

In *Carabell*, the Sixth Circuit held that the nearby ditch constituted a "tributary" and thus a "water of the United States" under 33 CFR §328.3(a)(5) (2004). Likewise in *Rapanos*, the Sixth Circuit held that the nearby ditches were "tributaries" under §328(a)(5). But *Rapanos II* also stated that, even if the ditches were not "waters of the United States," the wetlands were "adjacent" to *remote* traditional navigable waters in virtue of the wetlands' "hydrological connection" to them. This statement reflects the practice of the Corps' district offices, which may "assert jurisdiction over a wetland without regulating the ditch connecting it to a water of the United States." We therefore address in this Part whether a wetland may be considered "adjacent to" remote "waters of the United States," because of a mere hydrologic connection to them. . . .

... [O]*nly* those wetlands with a continuous surface connection to bodies that are "waters of the United States" in their own right, so that there is no clear demarcation between "waters" and wetlands, are "adjacent to" such waters and covered by the Act. Wetlands with only an intermittent, physically remote hydrologic connection to "waters of the United States" do not implicate the boundary-drawing problem of *Riverside Bayview*, and thus lack the necessary connection to covered waters that we described as a "significant nexus" in SWANCC. Thus, establishing that wetlands such as those at the Rapanos and Carabell sites are covered by the Act requires two findings: First, that the adjacent channel contains a "wate[r] of the United States," (i.e., a relatively permanent body of water connected to traditional interstate navigable waters); and second, that the wetland has a continuous surface connection with that water, making it difficult to determine where the "water" ends and the "wetland" begins. ...

VIII

Because the Sixth Circuit applied the wrong standard to determine if these wetlands are covered "waters of the United States," and because of the paucity of the record in both of these cases, the lower courts should determine, in the first instance, whether the ditches or drains near each wetland are "waters" in the ordinary sense of containing a relatively permanent flow; and (if they are) whether the wetlands in question are "adjacent" to these "waters" in the sense of possessing a continuous surface connection that creates the boundary-drawing problem we addressed in *Riverside Bayview*.

We vacate the judgments of the Sixth Circuit in both No. 04-1034 and No. 04-1384, and remand both cases for further proceedings.

CHIEF JUSTICE ROBERTS, concurring.

Five years ago, this Court rejected the position of the Army Corps of Engineers on the scope of its authority to regulate wetlands under the Clean Water Act. [SWANCC]. The Corps had taken the view that its authority was essentially limitless; this Court explained that such a boundless view was inconsistent with the limiting terms Congress had used in the Act. ...

Agencies delegated rulemaking authority under a statute such as the Clean Water Act are afforded generous leeway by the courts in interpreting the statute they are entrusted to administer. Given the broad, somewhat ambiguous, but nonetheless clearly limiting terms Congress employed in the CWA, the Corps and the EPA would have enjoyed plenty of room to operate in developing *some* notion of an outer bound to the reach of their authority.

[While the Corps and EPA initiated a rulemaking to consider "issues associated with the scope of waters that are subject to the [CWA], in light of the U.S. Supreme Court decision in [SWANCC]," "the proposed rulemaking went nowhere. Instead, the Corps chose to adhere to its essentially boundless view of the scope of its power. The upshot today is another defeat for the agency."]

It is unfortunate that no opinion commands a majority of the Court on precisely how to read Congress' limits on the reach of the Clean Water Act. Lower courts and regulated entities will now have to feel their way on a case-by-case basis. This situation is certainly not unprecedented. What is unusual in this instance, perhaps, is how readily the situation could have been avoided.

JUSTICE KENNEDY, concurring in the judgment.

These consolidated cases require the Court to decide whether the term "navigable waters" in the Clean Water Act extends to wetlands that do not contain and are not adjacent to waters that are navigable in fact. In [SWANCC], the Court held, under the circumstances presented there, that to constitute " 'navigable waters' " under the Act, a water or wetland must possess a "significant nexus" to waters that are or were navigable in fact or that could reasonably be so made. In the instant cases neither the plurality opinion nor the dissent by JUSTICE STEVENS chooses to apply this test; and though the Court of Appeals recognized the test's applicability, it did not consider all the factors necessary to determine whether the lands in question had, or did not have, the requisite nexus. In my view the cases ought to be remanded to the Court of Appeals for proper consideration of the nexus requirement.

I . . .

A . . .

The statutory term to be interpreted and applied in the two instant cases is the term "navigable waters." The outcome turns on whether that phrase reasonably describes certain Michigan wetlands the Corps seeks to regulate. Under the Act "[t]he term 'navigable waters' means the waters of the United States, including the territorial seas." §1362(7). In a regulation the Corps has construed the term "waters of the United States" to include not only waters susceptible to use in interstate commerce—the traditional understanding of the term "navigable waters of the United States[]"—but also tributaries of those waters and, of particular relevance here, wetlands adjacent to those waters or their tributaries. 33 CFR §§328.3(a)(1), (5), (7) (2005). The Corps views tributaries as within its jurisdiction if they carry a perceptible "ordinary high water mark." §328.4(c); 65 Fed. Reg. 12,823 (2000). An ordinary high-water mark is a "line on the shore established by the fluctuations of water and indicated by physical characteristics such as clear, natural line impressed on the bank, shelving, changes in the character of soil, destruction of terrestrial vegetation, the presence of litter and debris, or other appropriate means that consider the characteristics of the surrounding areas." 33 CFR §328.3(e).

. . . Under the Corps' regulations, wetlands are adjacent to tributaries, and thus covered by the Act, even if they are "separated from other waters of the United States by man-made dikes or barriers, natural river berms, beach dunes and the like." §328.3(c). . . .

II

Twice before the Court has construed the term "navigable waters" in the Clean Water Act. In *United States v. Riverside Bayview Homes, Inc.,* the Court upheld the Corps' jurisdiction over wetlands adjacent to navigable-in-fact waterways. The property in *Riverside Bayview,* like the wetlands in the *Carabell* case now before the Court, was located roughly one mile from Lake St. Clair, though in that case, unlike *Carabell,* the lands at issue formed part of a wetland that directly abutted a navigable-in-fact creek. In regulatory provisions that remain in effect, the Corps had concluded that wetlands perform important functions such as filtering and purifying water draining into adjacent water bodies, slowing the flow of runoff into lakes, rivers, and streams so as to prevent flooding and erosion, and providing critical habitat for aquatic animal species. Recognizing that "[a]n agency's construction of a statute it is charged with enforcing is entitled to deference if it is reasonable and not in conflict with the expressed intent of Congress," the Court held that "the Corps' ecological judgment about the relationship between waters and their adjacent wetlands provides an adequate basis for a legal judgment that adjacent wetlands may be defined as waters under the Act." The Court reserved, however, the question of the Corps' authority to regulate wetlands other than those adjacent to open waters.

In *SWANCC*, the Court considered the validity of the Corps' jurisdiction over ponds and mudflats that were isolated in the sense of being unconnected to other waters covered by the Act. The property at issue was an abandoned sand and gravel pit mining operation where "remnant excavation trenches" had "evolv[ed] into a scattering of permanent and seasonal ponds." Asserting jurisdiction pursuant to a regulation called the "Migratory Bird Rule," the Corps argued that these isolated ponds were "waters of the United States" (and thus "navigable waters" under the Act) because they were used as habitat by migratory birds. The Court rejected this theory. "It was the significant nexus between wetlands and 'navigable waters,'" the Court held, "that informed our reading of the [Act] in *Riverside Bayview Homes*." Because such a nexus was lacking with respect to isolated ponds, the Court held that the plain text of the statute did not permit the Corps' action.

Riverside Bayview and *SWANCC* establish the framework for the inquiry in the cases now before the Court: Do the Corps' regulations, as applied to the wetlands in *Carabell* and the three wetlands parcels in *Rapanos*, constitute a reasonable interpretation of "navigable waters" as in *Riverside Bayview* or an invalid construction as in *SWANCC*? Taken together these cases establish that in some instances, as exemplified by *Riverside Bayview*, the connection between a nonnavigable water or wetland and a navigable water may be so close, or potentially so close, that the Corps may deem the water or wetland a "navigable water" under the Act. In other instances, as exemplified by *SWANCC*, there may be little or no connection. Absent a significant nexus, jurisdiction under the Act is lacking. Because neither the plurality nor the dissent addresses the nexus requirement, this separate opinion, in my respectful view, is necessary.

A

The plurality's opinion begins from a correct premise. As the plurality points out, and as *Riverside Bayview* holds, in enacting the Clean Water Act Congress intended to regulate at least some waters that are not navigable in the traditional sense. *Riverside Bayview, SWANCC.* This conclusion is supported by "the evident breadth of congressional concern for protection of water quality and aquatic ecosystems." It is further compelled by statutory text, for the text is explicit in extending the coverage of the Act to some nonnavigable waters. . . . [33 U.S.C. §1344(g)(1).] . . .

From this reasonable beginning the plurality proceeds to impose two limitations on the Act; but these limitations, it is here submitted, are without support in the language and purposes of the Act or in our cases interpreting it. First, . . . the plurality would conclude that the phrase "navigable waters" permits Corps and EPA jurisdiction only over "relatively permanent, standing or flowing bodies of water"—a category that in the plurality's view includes "seasonal" rivers, that is, rivers that carry water continuously except during "dry months," but not intermittent or ephemeral streams. Second, the plurality asserts that wetlands fall within the Act only if they bear "a continuous surface connection to bodies that are 'waters of the United States' in their own right"—waters, that is, that satisfy the plurality's requirement of permanent standing water or continuous flow. . . .

As a fallback the plurality suggests that avoidance canons would compel its reading even if the text were unclear. In SWANCC, as one reason for rejecting the Corps' assertion of jurisdiction over the isolated ponds at issue there, the Court observed that this "application of [the Corps'] regulations" would raise significant questions of Commerce Clause authority and encroach on traditional state land-use regulation. As SWANCC observed, and as the plurality points out here, the Act states that "[i]t is the policy of the Congress to recognize, preserve, and protect the primary responsibilities and rights of States to prevent, reduce, and eliminate pollution, [and] to plan the development and use . . . of land and water resources." The Court in SWANCC cited this provision as evidence that a clear statement supporting jurisdiction in applications raising constitutional and federalism difficulties was lacking.

The concerns addressed in SWANCC do not support the plurality's interpretation of the Act. In SWANCC, by interpreting the Act to require a significant nexus with navigable waters, the Court avoided applications—those involving waters without a significant nexus—that appeared likely, as a category, to raise constitutional difficulties and federalism concerns. Here, in contrast, the plurality's interpretation does not fit the avoidance concerns it raises. On the one hand, when a surface-water connection is lacking, the plurality forecloses jurisdiction over wetlands that abut navigable-in-fact waters—even though such navigable waters were traditionally subject to federal authority. On the other hand, by saying the Act covers wetlands (however remote) possessing a surface-water connection with a continuously flowing stream (however small), the plurality's reading would permit applications of the statute as far from traditional federal authority as are the waters it deems beyond the statute's reach. Even assuming, then, that federal regulation of remote wetlands and nonnavigable waterways would raise a difficult Commerce Clause issue notwithstanding those waters' aggregate effects on national water quality, the plurality's reading is not responsive to this concern. As for States' "responsibilities and rights," §1251(b), it is noteworthy that 33 States plus the District of Columbia have filed an *amici* brief in this litigation asserting that the Clean Water Act is important to their own water policies. These *amici* note, among other things, that the Act protects downstream States from out-of-state pollution that they cannot themselves regulate. . . .

Finally, it should go without saying that because the plurality presents its interpretation of the Act as the only permissible reading of the plain text, the Corps would lack discretion, under the plurality's theory, to adopt contrary regulations. THE CHIEF JUSTICE suggests that if the Corps and EPA had issued new regulations after SWANCC they would have "enjoyed plenty of room to operate in developing *some* notion of an outer bound to the reach of their authority" and thus could have avoided litigation of the issues we address today. That would not necessarily be true under the opinion THE CHIEF JUSTICE has joined. New rulemaking could have averted the disagreement here only if the Corps had anticipated the unprecedented reading of the Act that the plurality advances.

B

While the plurality reads nonexistent requirements into the Act, the dissent reads a central requirement out—namely, the requirement that the word "navigable" in "navigable waters" be given some importance. Although the Court has held that the statute's language invokes Congress' traditional authority over waters navigable in fact or susceptible of being made so, the dissent would permit federal regulation whenever wetlands lie alongside a ditch or drain, however remote and insubstantial, that eventually may flow into traditional navigable waters. The deference owed to the Corps' interpretation of the statute does not extend so far. . . .

Consistent with SWANCC and *Riverside Bayview* and with the need to give the term "navigable" some meaning, the Corps' jurisdiction over wetlands depends upon the existence of a significant nexus between the wetlands in question and navigable waters in the traditional sense. The required nexus must be assessed in terms of the statute's goals and purposes. Congress enacted the law to "restore and maintain the chemical, physical, and biological integrity of the Nation's waters," and it pursued that objective by restricting dumping and filling in "navigable waters." With respect to wetlands, the rationale for Clean Water Act regulation is, as the Corps has recognized, that wetlands can perform critical functions related to the integrity of other waters— functions such as pollutant trapping, flood control, and runoff storage. Accordingly, wetlands possess the requisite nexus, and thus come within the statutory phrase "navigable waters," if the wetlands, either alone or in combination with similarly situated lands in the region, significantly affect the chemical, physical, and biological integrity of other covered waters more readily understood as "navigable." When, in contrast, wetlands' effects on water quality are speculative or insubstantial, they fall outside the zone fairly encompassed by the statutory term "navigable waters."

Although the dissent acknowledges that wetlands' ecological functions vis-à-vis other covered waters are the basis for the Corps' regulation of them, it concludes that the ambiguity in the phrase "navigable waters" allows the Corps to construe the statute as reaching all "non-isolated wetlands," just as it construed the Act to reach the wetlands adjacent to navigable-in-fact waters in *Riverside Bayview*. This, though, seems incorrect. The Corps' theory of jurisdiction in these consolidated cases—adjacency to tributaries, however remote and insubstantial—raises concerns that go beyond the holding of *Riverside Bayview*; and so the Corps' assertion of jurisdiction cannot rest on that case.

As applied to wetlands adjacent to navigable-in-fact waters, the Corps' conclusive standard for jurisdiction rests upon a reasonable inference of ecologic interconnection, and the assertion of jurisdiction for those wetlands is sustainable under the Act by showing adjacency alone. That is the holding of *Riverside Bayview*. Furthermore, although the *Riverside Bayview* Court reserved the question of the Corps' authority over "wetlands that are not adjacent to bodies of open water," and in any event addressed no factual situation other than wetlands adjacent to navigable-in-fact waters, it may well be the case that *Riverside Bayview*'s reasoning—supporting jurisdiction without any inquiry beyond adjacency—could apply equally to wetlands adjacent to certain major tributaries. Through regulations or adjudication, the Corps may choose to identify categories of tributaries that, due to their volume of flow (either annually or on average), their proximity to navigable waters, or other relevant considerations, are significant enough that wetlands adjacent to them are likely, in the majority of cases, to perform important functions for an aquatic system incorporating navigable waters.

The Corps' existing standard for tributaries, however, provides no such assurance. As noted earlier, the Corps deems a water a tributary if it feeds into a traditional navigable water (or a tributary thereof) and possesses an ordinary high-water mark, defined as a "line on the shore established by the fluctuations of water and indicated by [certain] physical characteristics." This standard presumably provides a rough measure of the volume and regularity of flow. Assuming it is subject to reasonably consistent application, it may well provide a reasonable measure of whether specific minor tributaries bear a sufficient nexus with other regulated waters to constitute "navigable waters" under the Act. Yet the breadth of this standard—which seems to leave wide room for regulation of drains, ditches, and streams remote from any navigable-in-fact water and carrying only minor water-volumes towards it— precludes its adoption as the determinative measure of whether adjacent wetlands are likely to play an important role in the integrity of an aquatic system comprising navigable waters as traditionally understood. Indeed, in many cases wetlands adjacent to tributaries covered by this standard might appear little more related to navigable-in-fact waters than were the isolated ponds held to fall beyond the Act's scope in SWANCC.

When the Corps seeks to regulate wetlands adjacent to navigable-in-fact waters, it may rely on adjacency to establish its jurisdiction. Absent more specific regulations, however, the Corps must establish a significant nexus on a case-by-case basis when it seeks to regulate wetlands based on adjacency to nonnavigable tributaries. Given the potential overbreadth of the Corps' regulations, this showing is necessary to avoid unreasonable applications of the statute. Where an adequate nexus is established for a particular wetland, it may be permissible, as a matter of administrative convenience or necessity, to presume covered status for other comparable wetlands in the region. That issue, however, is neither raised by these facts nor addressed by any agency regulation that accommodates the nexus requirement outlined here.

This interpretation of the Act does not raise federalism or Commerce Clause concerns sufficient to support a presumption against its adoption. To be sure, the significant-nexus requirement may not align perfectly with the traditional extent of federal authority. Yet in most cases regulation of wetlands that are adjacent to tributaries and possess a significant nexus with navigable waters will raise no serious constitutional or federalism difficulty. As explained earlier, moreover, and as exemplified by SWANCC, the significant-nexus test itself prevents problematic applications of the statute. . . .

III

In both the consolidated cases before the Court the record contains evidence suggesting the possible existence of a significant nexus according to the principles outlined above. Thus the end result in these cases and many others to be considered by the Corps may be the same as that suggested by the dissent, namely, that the Corps' assertion of jurisdiction is valid. Given, however, that neither the agency nor the reviewing courts properly considered the issue, a remand is appropriate, in my view, for application of the controlling legal standard. . . .

JUSTICE STEVENS, with whom JUSTICE SOUTER, JUSTICE GINSBURG, and JUSTICE BREYER join, dissenting. . . .

In my view, the proper analysis is straightforward. The Army Corps has determined that wetlands adjacent to tributaries of traditionally navigable waters preserve the quality of our Nation's waters by, among other things, providing habitat for aquatic animals, keeping excessive sediment and toxic pollutants out of adjacent waters, and reducing downstream flooding by absorbing water at times of high flow. The Corps' resulting decision to treat these wetlands as encompassed within the term "waters of the United States" is a quintessential example of the Executive's reasonable interpretation of a statutory provision. See Chevron U.S.A., Inc. v. Natural Resources Defense Council, Inc. . . .

I . . .

Prior to their destruction, the wetlands at all three sites had surface connections to tributaries of traditionally navigable waters. The Salzburg wetlands connected to a drain that flows into a creek that flows into the navigable Kawkawlin River. The Hines Road wetlands connected to a drain that flows into the navigable Tittabawassee River. And the Pine River wetlands connected with the Pine River, which flows into Lake Huron.

At trial, the Government['s] . . . wetland expert . . . testified that the wetlands at these three sites provided ecological functions in terms of "habitat, sediment trapping, nutrient recycling, and flood peak diminution." He explained:

> [G]enerally for all of the . . . sites we have a situation in which the flood water attenuation in that water is held on the site in the wetland . . . such that it does not add to flood peak. By the same token it would have some additional water flowing into the rivers during the drier periods, thus, increasing low water flow.
>
> . . . . .
>
> By the same token on all of the sites to the extent that they slow the flow of water of the site they will also accumulate sediment and thus trap sediment and hold nutrients for use in those wetland systems later in the season as well. . . .

II

Our unanimous opinion in *Riverside Bayview* squarely controls these cases. There, we evaluated the validity of the very same regulations at issue today. These regulations interpret "waters of the United States" to cover all traditionally navigable waters; tributaries of these waters; and wetlands adjacent to traditionally navigable waters or their tributaries. Although the particular wetland at issue in *Riverside Bayview* abutted a navigable creek, we framed the question presented as whether the Clean Water Act "authorizes the Corps to require landowners to obtain permits from the Corps before discharging fill material into wetlands adjacent to navigable bodies of water *and their tributaries*."

We held that . . . the Corps' decision to interpret "waters of the United States" as encompassing such wetlands was permissible. We recognized the practical difficulties in drawing clean lines between land and water, and deferred to the Corps' judgment that treating adjacent wetlands as "waters" would advance the "congressional concern for protection of water quality and aquatic ecosystems."

Contrary to the plurality's revisionist reading today, *Riverside Bayview* nowhere implied that our approval of "adjacent" wetlands was contingent upon an understanding that "adjacent" means having a "continuous surface connection" between the wetland and its neighboring creek. Instead, we acknowledged that the Corps defined "adjacent" as including wetlands "'that form the border of or are in reasonable proximity to other waters'" and found that the Corps reasonably concluded that adjacent wetlands are part of the waters of the United States. Indeed, we explicitly acknowledged that the Corps' jurisdictional determination was reasonable even though

> "not every adjacent wetland is of great importance to the environment of adjoining bodies of water. . . . If it is reasonable for the Corps to conclude that in the majority of cases, adjacent wetlands have significant effects on water quality and the ecosystem, its definition can stand. That the definition may include some wetlands that are not significantly intertwined with the ecosystem of adjacent waterways is of little moment, for where it appears that a wetland covered by the Corps' definition is in fact lacking in importance to the aquatic environment . . . the Corps may always allow development of the wetland for other uses simply by issuing a permit."

In closing, we emphasized that the scope of the Corps' asserted jurisdiction over wetlands had been specifically brought to Congress' attention in 1977, that Congress had rejected an amendment that would have narrowed that jurisdiction, and that even proponents of the amendment would not have removed wetlands altogether from the definition of "waters of the United States."

Disregarding the importance of *Riverside Bayview*, the plurality relies heavily on the Court's subsequent opinion in [SWANCC]. In stark contrast to *Riverside Bayview*, however, SWANCC had nothing to say about wetlands, let alone about wetlands adjacent to traditionally navigable waters or their tributaries. Instead, SWANCC dealt with a question specifically reserved by *Riverside Bayview*, namely, the Corps' jurisdiction over isolated waters—"'waters that are *not* part of a tributary system to interstate waters or to navigable waters of the United States, the degradation or destruction of which could affect interstate commerce.'" At issue in SWANCC was "an abandoned sand and gravel pit . . . which provide[d] habitat for migratory birds" and contained a few pools of "nonnavigable, isolated, intrastate waters." The Corps had asserted jurisdiction over the gravel pit under its 1986 Migratory Bird Rule, which treated isolated waters as within its jurisdiction if migratory birds depended upon these waters. The Court rejected this jurisdictional basis since these isolated pools, unlike the wetlands at issue in *Riverside Bayview*, had no "significant nexus" to traditionally navigable waters. In the process, the Court distinguished *Riverside Bayview*'s reliance on Congress' decision to leave the Corps' regulations alone when it amended the Act in 1977, since "'[i]n both Chambers, debate on the proposals to narrow the definition of navigable waters centered largely on the issue of wetlands preservation'" rather than on the Corps' jurisdiction over truly isolated waters.

Unlike SWANCC and like *Riverside Bayview*, the cases before us today concern wetlands that are adjacent to "navigable bodies of water [or] their tributaries." Specifically, these wetlands abut tributaries of traditionally navigable waters. As we recognized in *Riverside Bayview*, the Corps has concluded that such wetlands play important roles in maintaining the quality of their adjacent waters, and consequently in the waters downstream. Among other things, wetlands can offer "nesting, spawning, rearing and resting sites for aquatic or land species"; "serve as valuable storage areas for storm and flood waters"; and provide "significant water purification functions." These values are hardly "*independent*" ecological considerations as the plurality would have it—instead, they are integral to the "chemical, physical, and biological integrity of the Nation's waters." Given that wetlands serve these important water quality roles and given the ambiguity inherent in the phrase "waters of the United States," the Corps has reasonably interpreted its jurisdiction to cover non-isolated wetlands. . . .

The Corps' exercise of jurisdiction is reasonable even though not every wetland adjacent to a traditionally navigable water or its tributary will perform all (or perhaps any) of the water quality functions generally associated with wetlands. *Riverside Bayview* made clear that jurisdiction does not depend on a wetland-by-wetland inquiry. Instead, it is enough that wetlands adjacent to tributaries generally have a significant nexus to the watershed's water quality. If a particular wetland is "not significantly intertwined with the ecosystem of adjacent waterways," then the Corps may allow its development "simply by issuing a permit." . . .

IV

While I generally agree with Parts I and II-A of JUSTICE KENNEDY's opinion, I do not share his view that we should replace regulatory standards that have been in place for over 30 years with a judicially crafted rule distilled from the term "significant nexus" as used in SWANCC. To the extent that our passing use of this term has become a statutory requirement, it is categorically satisfied as to wetlands adjacent to navigable waters or their tributaries. *Riverside Bayview* and SWANCC together make this clear. SWANCC's only use of the term comes in the sentence: "It was the significant nexus between the wetlands and 'navigable waters' that informed our reading of the [Clean Water Act] in *Riverside Bayview*." Because *Riverside Bayview* was written to encompass "wetlands adjacent to navigable waters and their tributaries," and reserved only the question of isolated waters, its determination of the Corps' jurisdiction applies to the wetlands at issue in these cases.

Even setting aside the apparent applicability of *Riverside Bayview*, I think it clear that wetlands adjacent to tributaries of navigable waters generally have a "significant nexus" with the traditionally navigable waters downstream. Unlike the "nonnavigable, isolated, intrastate waters" in SWANCC, these wetlands can obviously have a cumulative effect on downstream water flow by releasing waters at times of low flow or by keeping waters back at times of high flow. This logical connection alone gives the wetlands the "limited" connection to traditionally navigable waters that is all the statute requires—and disproves JUSTICE KENNEDY's claim that my approach gives no meaning to the word "'navigable[.]'" Similarly, these wetlands can preserve downstream water quality by trapping sediment, filtering toxic pollutants, protecting fish-spawning grounds, and so forth. While there may exist categories of wetlands adjacent to tributaries of traditionally navigable waters that, taken cumulatively, have no plausibly discernible relationship to any aspect of downstream water quality, I am skeptical. And even given JUSTICE KENNEDY's "significant nexus" test, in the absence of compelling evidence that many such categories do exist I see no reason to conclude that the Corps' longstanding regulations are overbroad.

JUSTICE KENNEDY's "significant nexus" test will probably not do much to diminish the number of wetlands covered by the Act in the long run. JUSTICE KENNEDY himself recognizes that the records in both cases contain evidence that "should permit the establishment of a significant nexus," and it seems likely that evidence would support similar findings as to most (if not all) wetlands adjacent to tributaries of navigable waters. But JUSTICE KENNEDY's approach will have the effect of creating additional work for all concerned parties. Developers wishing to fill wetlands adjacent to ephemeral or intermittent tributaries of traditionally navigable waters will have no certain way of knowing whether they need to get §404 permits or not. And the Corps will have to make case-by-case (or category-by-category) jurisdictional determinations, which will inevitably increase the time and resources spent processing permit applications. These problems are precisely the ones that *Riverside Bayview*'s deferential approach avoided. Unlike JUSTICE KENNEDY, I see no reason to change *Riverside Bayview*'s approach—and every reason to continue to defer to the Executive's sensible, bright-line rule.

V . . .

I would affirm the judgments in both cases, and respectfully dissent from the decision of five Members of this Court to vacate and remand. I close, however, by noting an unusual feature of the Court's judgments in these cases. It has been our practice in a case coming to us from a lower federal court to enter a judgment commanding that court to conduct any further proceedings pursuant to a specific mandate. That prior practice has, on occasion, made it necessary for Justices to join a judgment that did not conform to their own views. In these cases, however, while both the plurality and JUSTICE KENNEDY agree that there must be a remand for further proceedings, their respective opinions define different tests to be applied on remand. Given that all four Justices who have joined this opinion would uphold the Corps' jurisdiction in both of these cases—and in all other cases in which either the plurality's or JUSTICE KENNEDY's test is satisfied—on remand each of the judgments should be reinstated if *either* of those tests is met.

NOTES AND QUESTIONS ON THE NPDES PERMIT PROGRAM'S JURISDICTIONAL BOUNDARIES

1. *Point to the Point Source.* Determining the appropriate line between point and nonpoint source pollution has not been easy. Which of the following might be a point source? Trash from a riverfront industrial building and rainwater that leaks into the building and enters the river as runoff? Compare Hudson Riverkeeper Fund, Inc. v. Harbor at Hastings Assoc., 917 F. Supp. 251 (S.D.N.Y. 1996) with Hudson River Fishermen's Ass'n v. Arcuri, 862 F. Supp. 73 (S.D.N.Y. 1994). A trap-shooting facility on the edge of a navigable body of water? See Stone v. Naperville Park Dist., 38 F. Supp. 2d 651 (N.D. Ill. 1999); Connecticut Coastal Fishermen's Ass'n v. Remington Arms Co., 989 F.2d 1305 (2d Cir. 1993).

2. *"Navigable Waters": Where to Draw the Line?* The *Rapanos* opinions raise a series of issues, among them: (1) Which opinion or opinions control? (2) What rule(s) of law does the controlling opinion (or do the controlling opinions) announce? (3) What is the holding of the Court in *Riverside Bayview*, and what is the impact of *Rapanos*, if any, on this decision? (4) Similarly, what is the Court's holding in

SWANCC and what impact, if any, does *Rapanos* have on that decision? (5) Is *Rapanos* likely to have an effect on the scope of CWA jurisdiction over wetlands, and, if so, in what ways? (6) What options do the opinions leave regulators to try to bring greater clarity to, or to revise, the definition of navigable waters? (7) What role is *Chevron* deference likely to play in the validity of any actions regulators take? (8) What are Congress's options in light of *Rapanos*? (9) What role do possible constitutional issues play in the various opinions?

Because *Rapanos* was decided in June 2006, as this chapter was being developed, it is too early to know how it will be interpreted. The Army Corps of Engineers has indicated that it plans to issue guidance that will help facilitate interpretation of *Rapanos*.

A few courts have already applied *Rapanos*. Three decisions are summarized below. Consider whether you agree with the courts' opinions. In United States v. Gerke, 464 F.3d 723 (7th Cir. 2006), the Seventh Circuit concluded the Kennedy opinion is controlling. The court gave the following instructions for the District Court to follow on remand:

> The test [Justice Kennedy] proposed is that "wetlands possess the requisite nexus, and thus come within the statutory phrase 'navigable waters,' if the wetlands, either alone or in combination with similarly situated lands in the region, significantly affect the chemical, physical, and biological integrity of other covered waters more readily understood as 'navigable.' When, in contrast, wetlands' effects on water quality are speculative or insubstantial, they fall outside the zone fairly encompassed by the statutory term 'navigable waters.'" This test is narrower (so far as reining in federal authority is concerned) than the plurality's in most cases, though not in all because Justice Kennedy also said that "by saying the Act covers wetlands (however remote) possessing a surface-water connection with a continuously flowing stream (however small), the plurality's reading would permit applications of the statute as far from traditional federal authority as are the waters it deems beyond the statute's reach."
>
> Thus, any conclusion that Justice Kennedy reaches in favor of federal authority over wetlands in a future case will command the support of five Justices (himself plus the four dissenters), and in *most* cases in which he concludes that there is no federal authority he will command five votes (himself plus the four Justices in the *Rapanos* plurality), the exception being a case in which he would vote against federal authority only to be outvoted 8-to-1 (the four dissenting Justices plus the members of the *Rapanos* plurality) because there was a slight surface hydrological connection. The plurality's insistence that the issue of federal authority be governed by strict rules will on occasion align the Justices in the plurality with the *Rapanos* dissenters when the balancing approach of Justice Kennedy favors the landowner. But that will be a rare case, so as a practical matter the Kennedy concurrence is the least common denominator (always, when his view favors federal authority).

In Northern California River Watch v. City of Healdsburg, 457 F.3d 1023 (9th Cir. 2006), the Ninth Circuit similarly held that Justice Kennedy's *Rapanos* concurrence is controlling. The court held that CWA jurisdiction existed over a wetland by finding a significant nexus between the wetland involved and the adjacent traditionally navigable water, after stating that the Kennedy test makes adjacency of wetlands to a navigable water insufficient to establish CWA jurisdiction; instead, it is now necessary to establish a significant nexus between wetlands and such adjacent navigable waters. Is this how you read *Rapanos*? If not, has it caused you to change your view? If so, why? If not, why not?

For a third interpretation of *Rapanos*, see United States v. Chevron Pipe Line Co., 437 F. Supp. 2d 605 (N.D. Tex. 2006). In that case the court noted that the Supreme Court "failed to reach a consensus of a majority as to the jurisdictional boundary of the CWA." It characterized Justice Kennedy's concurring opinion as advancing an "ambiguous test—whether a 'significant nexus' exists to waters that are/were/might be navigable." The court continued that "[t]his test leaves no guidance on how to implement its vague, subjective centerpiece. That is, exactly what is 'significant' and how is a 'nexus' determined?" The court indicated that it would "feel its way on a case-by-case basis," as Chief Justice Roberts had surmised would happen in his concurrence in *Rapanos*. In ruling on a motion for summary judgment, the court held that "this Court must look to see if there is a genuine issue of material fact as to whether the farthest traverse of the spill [a Chevron pipe had failed, resulting in an oil spill] is a navigable-in-fact water or adjacent to an open body of navigable water." The court granted Chevron's motion, holding that the United States had failed to show that any oil from the spill reached an "actual navigable water." The court held that an unnamed channel/tributary, and Ennis Creek, did not qualify as navigable waters and therefore the fact that oil may have reached those areas was not sufficient to establish CWA jurisdiction.

3. *The "Addition" Element for NPDES Jurisdiction.* In addition to needing a point source and a navigable water to trigger NPDES jurisdiction, a third element is the "addition" of a pollutant. The "addition" element has been analyzed in the context of dams, among others. Dams can have substantial adverse environmental impacts on the stream system that they impound and modify, including impeding fish runs, altering stream temperatures and the chemical balance of streams, and modifying flood cycles. In National Wildlife Fed'n v. Gorsuch, 693 F.2d 156 (D.C. Cir. 1982), Judge Wald, writing for a unanimous panel, held that dams do not "add" pollutants. The Court also concluded that "Congress did not want to interfere any more than necessary with state water management, of which dams are an important component. . . ." The issue of NPDES coverage of water transfers has continued to be contentious. In South Florida Water Mgmt. Dist. v. Miccosukee Tribe, 541 U.S. 95 (2004), the Court vacated an Eleventh Circuit decision that an NPDES permit is required for transferring water from one navigable water into another. The Court remanded the case for factfinding as to whether the two waters involved in that case were "meaningfully distinct." The Court indicated that if two volumes of water are "simply two parts of the same water body, pumping water from one into the other cannot constitute an 'addition' of pollutants." EPA issued a memorandum in August 2005* in which it concluded that an NPDES permit generally is not required for water transfers from one body of water to another. The agency also has proposed a rule that will exempt certain transfers of water between water bodies. National Pollutant Discharge Elimination System (NPDES) Water Transfers, 71 Fed. Reg. 32,887 (2006; to be codified at 40 C.F.R. pt. 122). In Catskill Mountains Chapter of Trout Unlimited, Inc. v. New York City Dep't of Envtl. Prot., 451 F.3d 77 (2d Cir. 2006), the Second Circuit appears to have been less than fully persuaded by EPA's interpretation, holding that a water transfer from one body of water to another constitutes a discharge that requires an NPDES permit.

---

*Agency Interpretation on Applicability of Section 402 of the Clean Water Act to Water Transfers (by Ann R. Klee, General Counsel, and Benjamin H. Grumbles, Assistant Administrator for Water), http://www.epa.gov/ogc/documents/water_transfers.pdf.

4. *What Is a "Pollutant"?* The final element required to trigger NPDES permitting requirements is that the material discharged be a "pollutant." Courts have tended to interpret the definition of "pollutant," contained in CWA §502(6) and 40 C.F.R. §122.2, broadly. In Sierra Club Lone Star Chapter v. Cedar Point Oil Co., 73 F.3d 546, 564-568 (5th Cir. 1996), the Fifth Circuit ruled that the list of substances in the definition of "pollutant" in CWA §502(6) is not exclusive: "it seems clear that, while the listing of a specific substance in the definition of pollutant may be significant, the fact that a substance is not specifically included does not remove it from the coverage of the statute." The court further held that courts are empowered to make independent determinations that a particular substance is (or is not) a pollutant. Romero-Barcelo v. Brown, 478 F. Supp. 646, 665 (D.P.R. 1979), *vacated and remanded on other grounds,* 643 F.3d 835 (1st Cir. 1981), *rev'd sub nom.* Weinberger v. Romero-Barcelo, 456 U.S. 305, 309 (1982), defined the term to include unexploded bombs that the military fired into the ocean during training exercises. On the other hand, the Ninth Circuit held that mussel shells and their by-products were not "pollutants" on the ground that they are the "natural biological processes of the mussels, not the waste product of a transforming human process." Association to Protect Hammersley, Eld & Totten Inlets v. Taylor Res., Inc., 299 F.3d 1007, 1017 (9th Cir. 2002). The Ninth Circuit held in Fairhurst v. Hagener, 422 F.3d 1146 (9th Cir. 2005), that Montana wildlife officials did not need a NPDES permit to use a federally registered pesticide to rid a river of non-native trout, on the ground that the pesticides that were intentionally applied to water for a beneficial purpose and in compliance with the Federal Insecticide, Fungicide, and Rodenticide Act (FIFRA) and "that produce no residue and unintended effects are not chemical wastes" are not "pollutants" under the CWA. In No Spray Coalition, Inc. v. City of New York, 351 F.3d 602 (2d Cir. 2003), the Second Circuit remanded to the district court a citizen suit alleging that pesticide spraying that reached navigable waters violated the CWA. The Second Circuit held that each statute (CWA and FIFRA) stands on its own. It raised but did not address the question of whether spraying that is consistent with FIFRA must be deemed also to comply with the CWA. In November 2006, EPA promulgated a rule in which it excludes from NPDES permit requirements applications of pesticides to navigable waters in two circumstances. 71 Fed. Reg. 68,483 (Nov. 27, 2006).

5. *Groundwater.* Groundwater is not explicitly dealt with in the CWA. The federal court precedents are split on whether discharges into aquifers that are hydrologically connected to jurisdictional surface streams require NPDES permits. Two cases that provide fairly thorough discussions of this issue came out on opposite sides. Umatilla Water Quality Protective Ass'n v. Smith Frozen Foods, 962 F. Supp. 1312 (D. Or. 1997), held that the CWA does not apply to discharges into groundwater hydrologically connected to surface water because (1) the Act is ambiguous, (2) EPA had never offered a formal or consistent interpretation of the Act that would subject groundwater discharges to the NPDES program, and (3) Oregon administered a separate permit program for surface and groundwater discharges without objection from EPA for 25 years. In light of the lack of clear congressional or agency guidance, it was reasonable to protect the reliance interest of Oregon groundwater permittees, especially since the difficulty of determining when a hydrologic connection exists "would expose potentially hundreds of . . . permittees to current or future litigation and legal liability if they or DEQ . . . happened to make the 'wrong' choice about which kind of permit discharges to groundwater require." Id. at 1320. Idaho Rural Council v. Bosma, 143 F. Supp. 2d 1169,

1178-1181 (D. Idaho 2001), held that the CWA does apply to groundwater that is hydrologically connected to surface water.

6. *The Relationship between the NPDES Permit Scheme and the Jurisdictional Reach of Other Environmental Laws.* Under some circumstances, the existence of NPDES jurisdiction potentially exempts a discharger from obligations that it otherwise might face under other environmental laws. For example, Resource Conservation and Recovery Act (RCRA) §1004(27) exempts some discharges regulated under the CWA from its definition of solid waste (see Chapter 8), and Comprehensive Environmental Response, Compensation, and Liability Act (CERCLA) §107(j) limits liability for federally permitted releases (see Chapter 9). In Defenders of Wildlife v. EPA, 420 F.3d 946 (9th Cir. 2005), the Ninth Circuit vacated EPA's approval of Arizona's application to administer the NPDES permit program, holding that, *inter alia*, (1) ESA §7(a)(2) obligates EPA to protect listed species when EPA decides to approve a transfer of permitting authority and (2) EPA failed adequately to consider the effect on listed species as part of its transfer decision. Arizona had argued that the CWA's list of factors that applications for authorization must meet should be read to mean that ESA §7(a)(2) does not apply to such decisions, but the court rejected this view. See id. at 967. In reaching its decision, the court noted that there is a split in the circuits. *Defenders of Wildlife* is reproduced as a principal case in section B of Chapter 5.

Problem 7-1

EPA has authorized the State of Nirvana regulatory agency to implement the NPDES program in the state. Assume that you are a staff attorney with the Nirvana regulatory agency and that your main responsibility involves working with technical staff in the Department to interpret and apply the CWA. A new inspector has joined your unit. The new person approaches you one day and states:

> I was driving across the bridge at the St. Marks Wildlife Refuge last weekend. The bridge is currently undergoing some maintenance work. It's being painted, and there's also some reinforcement work being done. There were a few workers out there over the weekend, and I noticed that some liquid material from the containers the workers were using was spilling occasionally into the marsh below the bridge. The marsh serves as habitat for migratory birds and is hydrologically connected to the Gulf of Mexico.

Analyze whether this maintenance operation is subject to CWA permitting authority.

D.   ESTABLISHMENT OF TECHNOLOGY-BASED EFFLUENT LIMITATIONS

The heart of the CWA is subchapter III, which allows the federal government to impose technology-based effluent limitations on point source discharges. EPA develops effluent limitations on a national basis for different industries, and sometimes regulates more precisely by industrial subcategory. CWA §§304(b), (m), 306.

Chemical Mfrs. Ass'n v. NRDC, 470 U.S. 116, 120 (1985), makes it clear that the agency has considerable discretion to establish such subcategories—subcategories are necessarily "rough hewn." The agency develops standards by looking at the existing state of the art in an industry and potential advances in waste treatment technology. The process of establishing national standards for a particular industry is often expensive and time-consuming. The permitting agency uses "best professional judgment" (BPJ) to establish permit limits for facilities not covered by a national rule. CWA §402(a); 40 C.F.R. §122.44(a). The permit writer, in determining BPJ, considers the same factors as EPA considers in establishing nationwide effluent limits. 40 C.F.R. §125.3(d).

Technology-based regulation requires point sources to use the best available technology to treat their wastes, rather than requiring levels of treatment based on water quality goals. This has led to charges that the standards impede economic efficiency because they discourage or prohibit the adoption of the least costly treatment alternative. See Note, Technology-Based Emission and Effluent Standards and the Achievement of Ambient Environmental Standards, 91 Yale L.J. 792 (1982). Critics have charged that this approach of establishing national technology-based categorical standards for various industries is inefficient because it employs a "one size fits all" approach to regulation. This issue comes up in Weyerhaeuser Co. v. Costle, 590 F.2d 1011 (D.C. Cir. 1978), discussed below at page 634, in which regulated parties that challenged EPA regulations argued, among other things, that the agency is obligated to take into account the actual environmental impact on receiving waters in setting permit limits for particular dischargers. One commentator's succinct summary and criticism of this centerpiece of the CWA regulatory scheme is that the technology-based approach

> is not finely tuned to the condition of the specific waterbody nor does it vary based on the relationship between the discharge and water quality. Rather, a technology based approach imposes similar limitations on similar dischargers irrespective of the effect of the discharge on water quality or the specific waterbody. Consequently, although "end of pipe" controls frequently improve stream conditions, the technology-based approach may under or over regulate the affected discharger.

Warren, Total Maximum Daily Loads: A Watershed Approach to Improved Water Quality, ALI-ABA Course of Study Clean Water Act: Law and Regulations 115 (Oct. 23-25, 2002).

The NPDES permit program's reliance on national, technology-based pollution control limits includes two crucial distinctions. First, sources are divided, as they are in the Clean Air Act, between existing and new ones. Second, pollutants are divided into four categories for purposes of standard setting and compliance deadlines: (1) conventional pollutants, generally those that are biodegradable; (2) toxic pollutants, those that are not biodegradable and create a risk of substantial human health impairment; (3) nonconventional, nontoxic pollutants; and (4) heat, which is treated as a separate category because its adverse impacts are more site-specific than those of the first three categories. It also includes a series of variance provisions that create a degree of flexibility in this national program.

The 1972 CWA required all dischargers, by 1977, to meet effluent limitations based on application of BPT (best practicable technology currently available). The Act imposed a more stringent standard, BAT (best available technology economically achievable), for 1983. New sources were subject to BADT (best available demonstrated control technology) and were required to meet new source performance standards (NSPS). Congress anticipated that BADT limits would be the most stringent of the technology-based controls, since new sources could reduce discharges more cost-effectively than could existing plants. See, e.g., CPC Int'l, Inc. v. Train, 540 F.2d 1329 (8th Cir. 1976). Congress later extended its deadlines for achieving certain standards. In 1977, Congress amended the CWA to require dischargers of "conventional" pollutants to meet BCT (best conventional technology) limits rather than the more stringent BAT, thus creating an intermediate level of technology-based controls between BPT and BAT.

Once EPA establishes technology-based regulations for an industrial category, they constitute floors—not ceilings—that must be incorporated into all NPDES permits (subject to limited variances in the Act). Effluent limitations may specify, among other things, (1) numerical limits on the discharge from individual units of production, (2) maximum daily and 30-day average permissible concentrations in unit waste streams of listed pollutants, and (3) specific treatment and process modification designs that must be employed. R. Zener, Guide to Federal Environmental Law 96 (1981). Permits issued to individual sources also may require monitoring and reporting for pollutants for which numerical limits are not set.

1.   A National, Industry-Wide Approach

An early issue in the implementation of the CWA concerned whether EPA could issue uniform industry-wide limitations that would bind all permittees. The Supreme Court resolved this issue in the following case.

E. I. DU PONT DE NEMOURS & CO. v. TRAIN
430 U.S. 112 (1977)

MR. JUSTICE STEVENS delivered the opinion of the Court.

Inorganic chemical manufacturing plants operated by the eight petitioners . . . discharge various pollutants into the Nation's waters and therefore are "point sources" within the meaning of the Federal Water Pollution Control Act (Act), as added and amended by §2 of the Federal Water Pollution Control Act Amendments of 1972. The Environmental Protection Agency has promulgated industrywide regulations imposing three sets of precise limitations on petitioners' discharges. The first two impose progressively higher levels of pollution control on existing point sources after July 1, 1977, and after July 1, 1983, respectively. The third set imposes limits on "new sources" that may be constructed in the future.

These cases present three important questions of statutory construction: (1) whether EPA has the authority under §301 of the Act to issue industrywide regulations limiting discharges by existing plants; (2) whether the Court of Appeals, which admittedly is authorized to review the standards for new sources, also has jurisdiction under §509 to review the regulations concerning existing plants; and (3) whether the new-source standards issued under §306 must allow variances for individual plants. . . .

The Statute

The statute, enacted on October 18, 1972, authorized a series of steps to be taken to achieve the goal of eliminating all discharges of pollutants into the Nation's waters by 1985, §101(a)(1).

The first steps required by the Act are described in §304, which directs the Administrator to develop and publish various kinds of technical data to provide guidance in carrying out responsibilities imposed by other sections of the Act. Section 304(b) goes into great detail concerning the contents of these regulations. They must identify the degree of effluent reduction attainable through use of the best practicable or best available technology for a class of plants. The guidelines must also "specify factors to be taken into account" in determining the control measures applicable to point sources within these classes. A list of factors to be considered then follows. The Administrator was also directed to develop and publish, within one year, elaborate criteria for water quality accurately reflecting the most current scientific knowledge, and also technical information on factors necessary to restore and maintain water quality. §304(a). . . .

Section 306 directs the Administrator to publish within 90 days a list of categories of sources discharging pollutants and, within one year thereafter, to publish regulations establishing national standards of performance for new sources within each category. Section 306 contains no provision for exceptions from the standards for individual plants; on the contrary, subsection (e) expressly makes it unlawful to operate a new source in violation of the applicable standard of performance after its effective date. The statute provides that the new-source standards shall reflect the greatest degree of effluent reduction achievable through application of the best available demonstrated control technology.

Section 301(b) defines the effluent limitations that shall be achieved by existing point sources in two stages. By July 1, 1977, the effluent limitations shall require the application of the best practicable control technology currently available; by July 1, 1983, the limitations shall require application of the best available technology economically achievable. The statute expressly provides that the limitations which are to become effective in 1983 are applicable to "categories and classes of point sources"; this phrase is omitted from the description of the 1977 limitations. While §301 states that these limitations "shall be achieved," it fails to state who will establish the limitations.

Section 301(c) authorizes the Administrator to grant variances from the 1983 limitations. Section 301(e) states that effluent limitations established pursuant to §301 shall be applied to all point sources. . . .

The Regulations

The various deadlines imposed on the Administrator were too ambitious for him to meet. For that reason, the procedure which he followed in adopting the regulations applicable to the inorganic chemical industry and to other classes of point sources is somewhat different from that apparently contemplated by the statute. Specifically, as will appear, he did not adopt guidelines pursuant to §304 before defining the effluent limitations for existing sources described in §301(b) or the national standards for new sources described in §306. This case illustrates the approach the Administrator followed in implementing the Act.

EPA began by engaging a private contractor to prepare a Development Document. This document provided a detailed technical study of pollution control in the industry. The study first divided the industry into categories. For each category, present levels of pollution were measured and plants with exemplary pollution control were investigated. Based on this information, other technical data, and economic studies, a determination was made of the degree of pollution control which could be achieved by the various levels of technology mandated by the statute. The study was made available to the public and circulated to interested persons. It formed the basis of "effluent limitation guideline" regulations issued by EPA after receiving public comment on proposed regulations. These regulations divide the industry into 22 subcategories. Within each subcategory, precise numerical limits are set for various pollutants. The regulations for each subcategory contain a variance clause, applicable only to the 1977 limitations. . . .

The Issues

The broad outlines of the parties' respective theories may be stated briefly. EPA contends that §301(b) authorizes it to issue regulations establishing effluent limitations for classes of plants. The permits granted under §402, in EPA's view, simply incorporate these across-the-board limitations, except for the limited variances allowed by the regulations themselves and by §301(c). The §304(b) guidelines, according to EPA, were intended to guide it in later establishing §301 effluent-limitation regulations. Because the process proved more time-consuming than Congress assumed when it established this two-stage process, EPA condensed the two stages into a single regulation.

In contrast, petitioners contend that §301 is not an independent source of authority for setting effluent limitations by regulation. Instead, §301 is seen as merely a description of the effluent limitations which are set for each plant on an individual basis during the permit-issuance process. Under the industry view, the §304 guidelines serve the function of guiding the permit issuer in setting the effluent limitations. . . .

   I

We think §301 itself is the key to the problem. The statutory language concerning the 1983 limitation, in particular, leaves no doubt that these limitations are to be set by regulation. Subsection (b)(2)(A) of §301 states that by 1983 "effluent limitations *for categories and classes* of point sources" are to be achieved which will require "application of the best available technology economically achievable for such *category or class.*" (Emphasis added.) These effluent limitations are to require elimination of all discharges if "such elimination is technologically and economically achievable for a *category or class* of point sources." (Emphasis added.) This is "language difficult to reconcile with the view that individual effluent limitations are to be set when each permit is issued." American Meat Institute v. EPA, 526 F.2d 442, 450 (C.A. 7 1975). The statute thus focuses expressly on the characteristics of the "category or class" rather than the characteristics of individual point sources. Normally, such classwide determinations would be made by regulation, not in the course of issuing a permit to one member of the class.

Thus, we find that §301 unambiguously provides for the use of regulations to establish the 1983 effluent limitations. Different language is used in §301 with respect to the 1977 limitations. Here, the statute speaks of "effluent limitations for point sources," rather than "effluent limitations for categories and classes of point sources." Nothing elsewhere in the Act, however, suggests any radical difference in the mechanism used to impose limitations for the 1977 and 1983 deadlines. For instance, there is no indication in either §301 or §304 that the §304 guidelines play a different role in setting 1977 limitations. Moreover, it would be highly anomalous if the 1983 regulations and the new-source standards were directly reviewable in the Court of Appeals, while the 1977 regulations based on the same administrative record were reviewable only in the District Court. The magnitude and highly technical character of the administrative record involved with these regulations makes it almost inconceivable that Congress would have required duplicate review in the first instance by different courts. We conclude that the statute authorizes the 1977 limitations as well as the 1983 limitations to be set by regulation, so long as some allowance is made for variations in individual plants, as EPA has done by including a variance clause in its 1977 limitations.

The question of the form of §301 limitations is tied to the question whether the Act requires the Administrator or the permit issuer to establish the limitations. Section 301 does not itself answer this question, for it speaks only in the passive voice of the achievement and establishment of the limitations. But other parts of the statute leave little doubt on this score. Section 304(b) states that "[f]or the purpose of adopting or revising effluent limitations . . . the Administrator shall" issue guideline regulations; while the judicial-review section, §509(b)(1), speaks of "the Administrator's action . . . in approving or promulgating any effluent limitation or other limitation under section 301. . . ." And §101(d) requires us to resolve any ambiguity on this score in favor of the *Administrator*. It provides that "(e)xcept as otherwise expressly provided in this Act, the *Administrator* of the Environmental Protection Agency . . . shall administer this Act." (Emphasis added.) In sum, the language of the statute supports the view that §301 limitations are to be adopted by the Administrator, that they are to be based primarily on classes and categories, and that they are to take the form of regulations. . . .

What, then, is the function of the §304(b) guidelines? As we noted earlier, §304(b) requires EPA to identify the amount of effluent reduction attainable through use of the best practicable or available technology and to "specify factors to be taken into account" in determining the pollution control methods "to be applicable to point sources . . . within such categories or classes." These guidelines are to be issued "[f]or the purpose of adopting or revising effluent limitations under this Act." As we read it, §304 requires that the guidelines survey the practicable or available pollution-control technology for an industry and assess its effectiveness. The guidelines are then to describe the methodology EPA intends to use in the §301 regulations to determine the effluent limitations for particular plants. . . .

III

The remaining issue in this case concerns new plants. Under §306, EPA is to promulgate "regulations establishing Federal standards of performance for new sources. . . ." §306(b)(1)(B). A "standard of performance" is a "standard for the control of the discharge of pollutants which reflects the greatest degree of effluent reduction which the Administrator determines to be achievable through application of the best available demonstrated control technology, . . . including, where practicable, a standard permitting no discharge of pollutants." §306(a)(1). In setting the standard, "[t]he Administrator may distinguish among classes, types, and sizes within categories of new sources . . . and shall consider the type of process employed (including whether batch or continuous)." §306(b)(2). As the House Report states, the standard must reflect the best technology for "that category of sources, and for classes, types, and sizes within categories." H.R. Rep. No. 92-911, p. 111 (1972), Leg. Hist. 798.

The Court of Appeals held:

> Neither the Act nor the regulations contain any variance provision for new sources. The rule of presumptive applicability applies to new sources as well as existing sources. On remand EPA should come forward with some limited escape mechanism for new sources." *Du Pont II*, 541 F.2d, at 1028.

The court's rationale was that "[p]rovisions for variances, modifications, and exceptions are appropriate to the regulatory process." Ibid.

The question, however, is not what a court thinks is generally appropriate to the regulatory process; it is what Congress intended for *these* regulations. It is clear that Congress intended these regulations to be absolute prohibitions. The use of the word "standards" implies as much. So does the description of the preferred standard as one "permitting *no* discharge of pollutants." (Emphasis added.) It is "unlawful for *any* owner or operator of *any* new source to operate such source in violation of any standard of performance applicable to such source." §306(e) (emphasis added). In striking contrast to §301(c), there is no statutory provision for variances, and a variance provision would be inappropriate in a standard that was intended to insure national uniformity and "maximum feasible control of new sources."

2. Relevant Factors in Setting National Standards

With the Supreme Court having established that EPA may issue industry-wide technology-based standards, numerous questions arose concerning interpretation and application of the legal framework for establishing such standards. As might be expected, EPA regulations establishing such national standards were challenged on a wide variety of grounds. Prominent issues included the role that cost should play in EPA's analysis, and the role of "receiving water capacity"—that is, the extent to which "dilution could be the solution to pollution." The following case addresses these questions.

WEYERHAEUSER CO. v. COSTLE
590 F.2d 1011 (D.C. Cir. 1978)

McGowan, Circuit Judge: . . .

[The pulp and paper mill industry challenged EPA's BPT standards. The court's description of the pulp and paper waste disposal process and its disposition of the industry's two major challenges to the regulations follow.]

B.

To make paper from trees is an old art; to do it without water pollution is a new science. In papermaking, logs or wooden chips must be ground up or "cooked" in one of several processes until only cellulose pulp is left. The pulp is bleached and made into various types and grades of paper. The cooking solutions and wash water that are left contain a variety of chemicals produced during "cooking" and other processes, including acids and large quantities of dissolved cellulose-breakdown products. Indeed, in some pulping processes, more of the wood is discarded in the waste water than is used to make paper. EPA has selected three parameters for measuring the pollutant content of the industry's effluent, all of which have been used extensively in this and other industries' measurements: total suspended solids (TSS), biochemical oxygen demand (BOD), and pH. TSS reflects the total amount of solids in solution, while BOD reflects the amount of biodegradable material in solution, and pH measures the acidity of the solution.[6]

EPA has divided this segment of the industry into 16 subcategories, and further subdivided it into 66 subdivisions, for the purposes of its rulemaking effort. As noted, some of petitioners' challenges concern all of the regulations for the whole industry, while other challenges are directed to regulations for particular industry subcategories. Actually, of the 16 subcategories in the whole industry, only the three that use some form of the "sulfite process" have evoked particularized challenges. The reaction of sulfite mill operators stems from the limitations' greater economic impact on them. That impact in turn results from the fact that the sulfite process creates one of the highest pollution loads of any industrial process, and certainly the highest within the pulping industry. In fact, the Act's legislative history focused in particular on injury to shellfish in rivers and bays caused by sulfite wastes. A Legislative History of the Water Pollution Control Act Amendments of 1972 718-21 (1973) [hereinafter referred to as Legislative History]. . . .

V.   *The Agency's Interpretation of the Statute* . . .

1.

Some of the paper mills that must meet the effluent limitations under review discharge their effluents into the Pacific Ocean. Petitioners contend that the ocean can dilute or naturally treat effluent, and that EPA must take this capacity of the ocean ("receiving water capacity") into account in a variety of ways. They urge what they term "common sense," i.e., that because the amounts of pollutant involved are small

---

6. As the Second Circuit recently noted, "Biochemical Oxygen Demand is not strictly speaking a pollutant at all." C & H Sugar Co. v. EPA, 553 F.2d 280, 282 n.7 (2d Cir. 1977). BOD is a measure of how much oxygen is used by organisms in water that break down biodegradable pollutants. As such, it indicates how much dissolved oxygen in the water will be used in fermenting the wastes. It is important because that fermentation process is capable of depleting so much of the water's oxygen supply that fish and other life in the water asphyxiate. The BOD level is also important because it correlates with the level of harmful organic chemicals. Accordingly, effluent with high BOD can cause damage even when dumped into waters that have more than ample amounts of dissolved oxygen. The same is true of pH: effluent high in toxic acids may cause damage even when dumped into sea water, whose salts buffer its pH level. It is well recognized that EPA can use pollution parameters that are not harmful in themselves, but act as indicators of harm. See American Paper Inst. v. Train, 543 F.2d 328, 349 (1976) (color can be used as a pollution parameter).

in comparison to bodies of water as vast as Puget Sound or the Pacific Ocean, they should not have to spend heavily on treatment equipment, or to increase their energy requirements and sludge levels, in order to treat wastes that the ocean could dilute or absorb.[41]

EPA's secondary response to this claim was that pollution is far from harmless, even when disposed of in the largest bodies of water. As congressional testimony indicated, the Great Lakes, Puget Sound, and even areas of the Atlantic Ocean have been seriously injured by water pollution. Even if the ocean can handle ordinary wastes, ocean life may be vulnerable to toxic compounds that typically accompany those wastes. In the main, however, EPA simply asserted that the issue of receiving water capacity could not be raised in setting effluent limitations because Congress had ruled it out. We have examined the previous legislation in this area, and the 1972 Act's wording, legislative history, and policies, as underscored by its 1977 amendments. These sources, which were thoroughly analyzed in a recent opinion of the administrator of the Agency, fully support EPA's construction of the Act. They make clear that based on long experience, and aware of the limits of technological knowledge and administrative flexibility, Congress made the deliberate decision to rule out arguments based on receiving water capacity. . . .

Moreover, by eliminating the issue of the capacity of particular bodies of receiving water, Congress made nationwide uniformity in effluent regulation possible. Congress considered uniformity vital to free the states from the temptation of relaxing local limitations in order to woo or keep industrial facilities.[46] In addition, national uniformity made pollution clean-up possible without engaging in the divisive task of favoring some regions of the country over others.

More fundamentally, the new approach implemented changing views as to the relative rights of the public and of industrial polluters. Hitherto, the right of the polluter was pre-eminent, unless the damage caused by pollution could be proven. Henceforth, the right of the public to a clean environment would be pre-eminent, unless pollution treatment was impractical or unachievable. The Senate Committee declared that "[t]he use of any river, lake, stream or ocean as a waste treatment system is unacceptable" regardless of the measurable impact of the waste on the body of water in question. Legislative History at 1425 (Senate Report). The Conference Report stated that the Act "specifically bans pollution dilution as an alternative to waste treatment." Id. at 284. This new view of relative rights was based in part on the hard-nosed assessment of our scientific ignorance: "we know so little about the

41. Apart from this simple "common sense" version of the argument, there is a more sophisticated economic version called the "optimal pollution" theory. This economic theory contends that there is a level or type of pollution that, while technologically capable of being controlled, is uneconomic to treat because the benefit from treatment is small and the cost of treatment is large. See generally W. Baxter, People or Penguins: The Case for Optimal Pollution (1974); B. Ackerman, S. Rose-Ackerman, J. Sawyer & D. Henderson, The Uncertain Search for Environmental Quality (1974). These economic theories are premised on a view that we have both adequate information about the effects of pollution to set an optimal test, and adequate political and administrative flexibility to keep polluters at that level once we allow any pollution to go untreated. As discussed in this section, it appears that Congress doubted these premises.

46. "[T]he greatest political barrier to effective pollution control is the threat by industrial polluters to move their factories out of any State that seriously tries to protect its environment." Legislative History, at 577 (remarks of Rep. Reuss). "Varying local revenue capabilities, economic pressures, and citizen interest have often stagnated community and State initiative." Id. at 156 (remarks of EPA Administrator Ruckelshaus). See American Frozen Food Inst. v. Train, 539 F.2d 107, 129 (1976).

ultimate consequences of injection of new matter into water that (the Act requires) a presumption of pollution. . . ." Id. at 1332 (remarks of Sen. Buckley). It also was based on the widely shared conviction that the nation's quality of life depended on its natural bounty, and that it was worth incurring heavy cost to preserve that bounty for future generations. . . .

The Act was passed with an expectation of "mid-course corrections," Legislative History, at 175 (statement of Sen. Muskie), and in 1977 Congress amended the Act, although generally holding to the same tack set five years earlier. Pub. L. No. 95-217, 91 Stat. 1584. Notably, during those five years, representatives of the paper industry had appeared before Congress and urged it to *change* the Act and to incorporate receiving water capacity as a consideration. Nonetheless, Congress was satisfied with this element of the statutory scheme. . . .

2.

Petitioners also challenge EPA's manner of assessing two factors that all parties agree must be considered: cost and non–water quality environmental impacts. They contend that the Agency should have more carefully balanced costs versus the effluent reduction benefits of the regulations, and that it should have also balanced those benefits against the non–water quality environmental impacts to arrive at a "net" environmental benefit conclusion. Petitioners base their arguments on certain comments made by the Conferees for the Act, and on the fact that the Act lists non–water quality environmental impacts as a factor the Agency must "take into account."

In order to discuss petitioners' challenges, we must first identify the relevant statutory standard. Section 304(b)(1)(B) of the Act identifies the factors bearing on BPCTCA in two groups. First, the factors shall

> include consideration of the total cost of application of technology in relation to the effluent reduction benefits to be achieved from such application,

and second, they

> shall also take into account the age of equipment and facilities involved, the process employed, the engineering aspects of the application of various types of control techniques, process changes, non–water quality environmental impact (including energy requirements), and such other factors as the Administrator deems appropriate[.]

The first group consists of two factors that EPA must compare: total cost versus effluent reduction benefits. We shall call these the "comparison factors." The other group is a list of many factors that EPA must "take into account": age, process, engineering aspects, process changes, environmental impacts (including energy), and any others EPA deems appropriate. We shall call these the "consideration factors." Notably, section 304(b)(2)(B) of the Act, which delineates the factors relevant to setting 1983 BATEA limitations, tracks the 1977 BPCTCA provision before us except in one regard: in the 1983 section, *all* factors, including costs and benefits, are consideration factors, and no factors are separated out for comparison.

Based on our examination of the statutory language and the legislative history, we conclude that Congress mandated a particular structure and weight for the 1977 comparison factors, that is to say, a "limited" balancing test.[52] In contrast, Congress did not mandate any particular structure or weight for the many consideration factors. Rather, it left EPA with discretion to decide how to account for the consideration factors, and how much weight to give each factor. In response to these divergent congressional approaches, we conclude that, on the one hand, we should examine EPA's treatment of cost and benefit under the 1977 standard to assure that the Agency complied with Congress' "limited" balancing directive. On the other hand, our scrutiny of the Agency's treatment of the several consideration factors seeks to assure that the Agency informed itself as to their magnitude, and reached its own express and considered conclusion about their bearing. More particularly, we do not believe that EPA is required to use any specific structure such as a balancing test in assessing the consideration factors, nor do we believe that EPA is required to give each consideration factor any specific weight.

Our conclusions are based initially on the section's wording and apparent logic. By singling out two factors (the comparison factors) for separate treatment, and by requiring that they be considered "in relation to" each other, Congress elevated them to a level of greater attention and rigor. Moreover, the comparison factors are a closed set of two, making it possible to have a definite structure and weight in considering them and preventing extraneous factors from intruding on the balance.

By contrast, the statute directs the Agency only to "take into account" the consideration factors, without prescribing any structure for EPA's deliberations. As to this latter group of factors, the section cannot logically be interpreted to impose on EPA a specific structure of consideration or set of weights because it gave EPA authority to "upset" any such structure by exercising its discretion to add new factors to the mix. Instead, the listing of factors seems aimed at noting all of the matters that Congress considered worthy of study before making limitation decisions, without preventing EPA from identifying other factors that it considers worthy of study. So long as EPA pays some attention to the congressionally specified factors, the section on its face lets EPA relate the various factors as it deems necessary.

The legislative history reveals that clear congressional policies support the section's facial structure. The original House and Senate versions of the section differed significantly. A major point of contention between the two versions involved the House's stronger concern over the economic effects of imposing stringent effluent limitations. Ultimately a compromise was reached at Conference and accepted by both houses. It provided, first, that the Agency must use "limited" cost-benefit balancing in deriving 1977 standards, but not in arriving at the 1983 standards. Legislative History, at 170 (statement of Sen. Muskie). A "mid-course" evaluation was then to

---

52. Senator Muskie described the "limited" balancing test:

The modification of subsection 304(b)(1) is intended to clarify what is meant by the term "practicable." The *balancing test between total cost and effluent reduction benefits* is intended to limit the application of technology only where the additional degree of effluent reduction is *wholly out of proportion to the costs* of achieving such marginal level of reduction for any class or category of sources.

The Conferees agreed upon this limited cost-benefit analysis in order to maintain uniformity within a class and category of point sources subject to effluent limitations, and to avoid imposing on the Administrator any requirement to consider the location of sources within a category or to ascertain water quality impact of effluent controls, or to determine the economic impact of controls on any individual plant in a single community.

Legislative History, at 170 (emphasis added).

occur in the mid- to late-1970's, after the Act had been in effect for several years but before full implementation of the 1983 standards. Id. at 175. The latter step was designed to allow Congress to rewrite the 1983 standards in order to continue the cost-benefit balancing during that period as well, if Congress found after early experience that such a course was necessary. Section 315 of the Act (establishing a National Study Commission to consider mid-course changes).

Thus the fact that Congress indicated its greater concern for cost-benefit calculation in the short run by making cost and benefit "comparison factors" for 1977, but only "consideration factors" for 1983, demonstrates the more relaxed view it took of EPA's treatment of consideration factors relevant to both the 1977 and 1983 standards. Indeed, after studying the need for mid-course correction, Congress decided to retain the 1972 arrangement, which, except for limited modifications not germane here, gives the Agency more complete discretion in considering the relevant factors in the future.[53]

Judicial decisions have carefully observed that the cost and benefit factors require more rigorous EPA consideration of cost versus benefit in the 1977 standards than in the 1983 standards. *American Paper Inst., supra,* 543 F.2d at 338 (cost-benefit balancing in 1977, not in 1983). Since the consideration factors specified in the 1977 provision track the language of all of the factors including cost and benefit in the 1983 provision, these cases support a lower level of administrative rigor and judicial review with respect to the 1977 consideration factors than with respect to the costs and benefit factors relevant to that year's limitations. We are fortified in this view by its coincidence with the Agency's interpretation. As the Supreme Court held last year, the EPA's construction of this Act is entitled to some deference. *Du Pont, supra,* 430 U.S. at 134-35.

Consequently, we must review the comparison factors to determine if EPA weighed them through the "limited" balancing test as intended by Congress. On the other hand, we may review the consideration factors only to determine if EPA was fully aware of them and reached its own express conclusions about them. Since the two types of factors are separate, we divide our discussion accordingly.

A.

Petitioners do not challenge the cost-benefit analysis for the whole industry. They do, however, challenge the analysis for the sulfite sector, contending that EPA used an "overall" instead of an "incremental" method of balancing, and that its figures on the cost of BPCTCA for the dissolving sulfite subcategory were underestimates. We uphold EPA's determination against both contentions.

EPA's approach was similar to the one we upheld in *American Paper Inst., supra,* 543 F.2d at 338-39. The Agency assessed the costs of internal and external effluent treatment measures, not only for the industry, but also for each subcategory.

---

53. When the mid-course study by the National Study Commission was completed and congressional hearings were held, Congress concluded that "little contained in the study of the Commission could be construed as justifying major change in the direction established in 1972. . . . With respect to the industrial program (which includes the regulations at issue in this case), the committee recognizes and applauds the significant success that most of the Nation's major industries have attained." S. Rep. No. 370, 95th Cong., 1st Sess. 1. reprinted in (1977) U.S. Code Cong. & Admin. News pp. 4326, 4327. Accordingly, the 1977 amendments did not change the factors involved in §304(b)(2).

This included a separate cost assessment for the sulfite subcategories. An economic analysis was prepared to determine the impact of the costs on the industry. It found that the industry as a whole would readily absorb the cost of compliance with the 1977 standards, estimated at $1.6 billion. Out of 270 mills employing 120,000 people, eight mills would likely be closed and 1800 people laid off. The Agency noted that the impact on the three heavily polluting sulfite subcategories would be the greatest. Of less than 30 sulfite mills, three would probably close, resulting in 550 people being laid off.

Against these costs, EPA balanced the main effluent reduction benefit: overall 5,000 fewer tons per day of BOD discharged into the nation's waters. EPA refined this balance by calculating the cost per pound of BOD removed for each subcategory. Although sulfite mills must make large investments in waste treatment facilities, the cost-benefit balance is favorable for the limitations on these mills, because of the large volume of waste they produce and thus the greater treatment efficiency.

Petitioners' first contention is that EPA not only should have calculated the overall cost-benefit balance, but also should have made an "incremental" calculation of that balance. More precisely, they contend that EPA must undertake to measure the costs and benefits of each additional increment of waste treatment control, from bare minimum up to complete pollution removal. In support of this contention, they point to Senator Muskie's description of cost-benefit balancing, which suggests a focus on the "additional degree" or "marginal" amount of effluent reduction. See note 52 *supra*. Petitioners concede that we accepted EPA's calculation of the overall cost-benefit balance, without any further marginal or incremental analysis, in *American Paper Inst., supra*, 543 F.2d at 338. Nonetheless, they suggest that the present case can be distinguished, because in these proceedings, unlike in *American Paper Inst.*, industry representatives submitted an incremental breakdown of costs and benefits to the Agency.

The failure of *American Paper Inst.* to require EPA to perform its own incremental analysis is justified for a number of reasons beyond some oversight on the part of paper industry petitioners in that case. While EPA has no discretion to avoid cost-benefit balancing for its 1977 standards, it does have some discretion to decide how it will perform the cost-benefit balancing task. "[E]ven with th[e] 1977 standard, the cost of compliance was not a factor to be given primary importance," *American Iron & Steel Inst., supra*, 526 F.2d at 1051, and, as such, cost need not be balanced against benefits with pinpoint precision. A requirement that EPA perform the elaborate task of calculating incremental balances would bog the Agency down in burdensome proceedings on a relatively subsidiary task. Hence, the Agency need not on its own undertake more than a net cost-benefit balancing to fulfill its obligation under section 304.

However, when an incremental analysis has been performed by industry and submitted to EPA, it is worthy of scrutiny by the Agency, for it may "avoid the risk of hidden imbalances between cost and benefit." Id. at 1076 n.19 (Adams, J., concurring). If such a "hidden imbalance" were revealed here, and if the Agency had ignored it, we might remand for further consideration. But in this case the incremental analysis proffered by industry showed that the last and most expensive increment of BOD treated in sulfite mills cost less than $.15 per pound of BOD removed, which is below the average cost of treatment in most of the industry's subcategories. We would be reluctant to find that EPA had ignored a "hidden imbalance" when the most unfavorable incremental cost-benefit balance that is challenged falls well within the range of averages for the industry as a whole. . . .

_____

While *Weyerhaeuser* focused on the application of a technology-based approach in setting BPT-based limits, the following case applies this approach with respect to BAT-based limits.

ASSOCIATION OF PACIFIC FISHERIES v. EPA
615 F.2d 794 (9th Cir. 1980)

KENNEDY, Circuit Judge:

In 1972 Congress, intending "to restore and maintain the chemical, physical, and biological integrity of the Nation's waters," amended the Federal Water Pollution Control Act (Act), 33 U.S.C. §1251 *et seq.* Congress established national pollution goals to be achieved by specific dates. By July 1, 1977, industries discharging pollutants into the nation's waters were to have achieved "the best practicable control technology currently available (BPT)." Section 301(b)(1)(A). By 1983, industry is to achieve "the best available technology economically achievable (BEA)." Section 301(b)(2)(A). The Environmental Protection Agency (EPA or Agency) was entrusted with the responsibility of defining and policing the efficient and prompt achievement of these goals. Section 304.

This case involves a challenge to regulations promulgated by the Agency establishing effluent guidelines for the Canned and Preserved Seafood Processing Point Source Category. 40 C.F.R. §§408.10 *et seq.* Petitioner Association of Pacific Fisheries is a trade association representing canners and fresh and frozen fish processors in affected subcategories. The remaining petitioners process seafood in all the subcategories at issue on this appeal.

The EPA's regulations governing the fish processing industry were promulgated in two phases. . . . [P]etitioners challenge several of the regulations promulgated during phase II of the Agency's proceedings. These phase II regulations covered nineteen separate subcategories. The subcategories were determined by the species of fish being processed; whether there was mechanization in the processing technique; for Alaska processors, the location of the plant, i.e., whether the plant was located in a "population or processing center"; and in some cases, the production capacity of the plant. At issue are the regulations which apply to Alaskan hand-butchered salmon (Subpart P), Alaskan mechanized salmon (Subpart Q), west coast hand-butchered salmon (Subpart R), west coast mechanized salmon (Subpart S), Alaskan bottomfish (Subpart T), west coast bottomfish (Subparts U and V), Alaskan scallops (Subpart AC), and herring fillets (Subparts AE and AF). See 40 C.F.R. §§408.160-408.226, 408.290-408.296, 408.310-408.326.

The effluent which is the subject of the regulations consists of unused fish residuals. This discharge includes heads, tails, and internal residuals of the processed fish. Substantial quantities of water are used at various stages of the plant operations. This water comes into contact with the fish residuals and contains pollutants when discharged. The regulations prescribe limitations on discharge, and utilize three measures of pollution: five-day biochemical oxygen demand (BOD_5); total suspended solids (TSS); and oil and grease (O & G).[2] The regulations establish daily maximum levels and monthly average levels for each subcategory, and are measured in terms of the amount of pollutant per thousand pounds of fish processed. . . .

By 1983 the fisheries must comply with more rigorous technology requirements and effluent limitations. For nonremote facilities, the Agency directed that a dissolved air flotation unit be installed at each location and that the end-of-pipe effluent be channeled through this system before it is discharged into the receiving water. These regulations apply to all nonremote subcategories except Subpart V, Conventional Bottomfish. There, the Administrator has prescribed aerated lagoons. . . . Remote Alaska fish processors will be required by the 1983 regulations to screen the effluent before discharging it into the receiving waters. . . .

1983 Regulations

The regulations promulgated by the Administrator for 1983 are to reflect the "best available technology economically achievable." Section 301(b)(2)(A). For the regulations to be affirmed, the Agency must demonstrate that the technology required is "available" and the effluent limitations are "economically achievable."

A.   DISSOLVED AIR FLOTATION UNIT.

A dissolved air flotation unit is the prescribed technology for the following subcategories: west coast hand-butchered salmon (Subpart R), west coast mechanized salmon (Subpart S), non-Alaskan mechanized bottomfish (Subpart V), and non-Alaskan herring fillet (Subpart AF).

The system operates as follows: Effluent passes into a holding tank. Air enters the effluent under pressure and attaches to solid particles. Buoyed by the air, the particles rise to the surface and are skimmed off. The particles can be used as animal feed or fertilizer. The clarified water is withdrawn from the bottom of the tank. Before entering the receiving waters, this effluent remainder must be within certain maximum limitations. The regulations set forth limitations for BOD_5, TSS, O & G, and acidity for each category.

The numerical limitations were based on the assumption that a DAF unit will reduce BOD_5 by 75%, TSS by 90%, and O & G by 90%. Petitioners claim these figures were the result of a single study conducted by the British Columbia seafood industry in conjunction with the Canadian Fisheries Research Board. The study measured the amount of reduced pollutants in the effluent from a salmon processing plant. The DAF unit reduced the BOD_5 by 80%, the TSS by 90%, and the oil and grease by 95%. Petitioners argue that the Agency was arbitrary and capricious in basing its 1983 technology regulations on a single study.

2. BOD_5, five-day biochemical oxygen demand, is a measure of the oxygen-consuming potentialities of organic matter in the effluent. The BOD_5 test measures the extent to which the biological degradation of organic waste matter over a five-day period removes oxygen from the water. This test does not identify what kind of organic material is present in the effluent, but merely indicates the presence of biodegradable matter.

TSS describes the quantity of undissolved solid matter suspended in the effluent. As with BOD, the TSS measure does not identify the nature or the physical and chemical characteristics of the matter present in the effluent.

Oil and grease describes the volume of naturally-occurring fish oil in the effluent.

The legislative history of the 1983 regulations indicates that regulations establishing BEA can be based on statistics from a single plant. The House Report states:

> It will be sufficient for the purposes of setting the level of control under available technology, that there be one operating facility which demonstrates that the level can be achieved or that there is sufficient information and data from a relevant pilot plant or semi-works plant to provide the needed economic and technical justification for such new source. [L.H. at 798.]

Although only one salmon study was in the record, the Administrator also considered numerous other DAF studies involving herring, groundfish, stickwater, sardines, shrimp, tuna, mackerel, scabbard, yellow croaker, and menhaden bailwater. Each of these studies revealed a substantial reduction in pollution levels. Although the pollution reduction in some studies was not as dramatic as others, the EPA is not charged with burden of showing that all DAF units could meet the limitations, but rather that the best existing DAF units can meet the limitations. Further, to the extent that some of these studies are best viewed as implicating "transfer technology," the Agency did not misuse its discretion in finding the technology to be transferable to the subcategories at issue. The EPA's data base was sufficient to show that the technology required to meet the 1983 limitations is "available." . . .

The next question is whether the Agency properly evaluated the costs of meeting the 1983 guidelines. In describing the role of costs in promulgating BEA, the Conference Report stated:

> While cost should be a factor in the Administrator's judgment, no balancing test will be required. The Administrator will be bound by a test of reasonableness. In this case, the reasonableness of what is "economically achievable" should reflect an evaluation of what needs to be done to move toward the elimination of the discharge of pollutants and what is achievable through the application of available technology without regard to cost.

L.H. at 170. Although the wording of the statute clearly states that the 1983 limitations must be "economically achievable," there is some disagreement among the circuits as to whether the costs of compliance should be considered in a review of the 1983 limitations. We hold, in agreement with the court in *Weyerhaeuser, supra,* 590 F.2d at 1044-45, that the EPA must consider the economic consequences of the 1983 regulations, along with the other factors mentioned in section 304(b)(2)(B).

Petitioners maintain that the Agency must balance the ecological benefits against the associated costs in determining whether the technology is economically achievable. They cite in support of this proposition *Appalachian Power Co. v. Train, supra.* In remanding the 1983 regulations affecting electrical power companies, the court there stated:

> [I]n choosing among alternative strategies, EPA must not only set forth the cost of achieving a particular level of heat reduction but must also state the expected environmental benefits, that is to say the effect on the environment, which will take place as a result of reduction, for it is only after EPA has fully explicated its course of conduct in this manner that a reviewing court can determine whether the agency has, in light of the goal to be achieved, acted arbitrarily or capriciously in adopting a particular effluent reduction level.

Id. at 1364-65. According to petitioners, the Agency did not consider the incremental benefit to the environment to be achieved by the dissolved air flotation units, and the regulations must be set aside. We cannot agree. As noted by the court in *Weyerhaeuser, supra*, 590 F.2d at 1045-46, the language of the statute indicates that the EPA's consideration of costs in determining BPT and BEA was to be different. In prescribing the appropriate 1977 technology, the Agency was to "include consideration of the total cost of application of *technology in relation to the effluent reduction benefits to be achieved from such application.*" Section 304(b)(1)(B) (emphasis added). In determining the 1983 control technology, however, the EPA must "take into account . . . the cost of achieving such effluent reduction," along with various other factors. Section 304(b)(2)(B). The conspicuous absence of the comparative language contained in section 304(b)(1)(B) leads us to the conclusion that Congress did not intend the Agency or this court to engage in marginal cost-benefit comparisons.

The intent of Congress is stated in 33 U.S.C. §1251(a)(1): "(I)t is the national goal that the discharge of pollutants into the navigable waters be eliminated by 1985. . . ." The regulations that will be applied in 1983 are intended to result "in reasonable further progress toward the national goal of eliminating the discharge of all pollutants. . . ." 33 U.S.C. §1311(b)(2)(A). These express declarations of congressional intent cannot be ignored in determining the reasonableness of the 1983 regulations. So long as the required technology reduces the discharge of pollutants, our inquiry will be limited to whether the Agency considered the cost of technology, along with the other statutory factors, and whether its conclusion is reasonable. Of course, at some point extremely costly more refined treatment will have a de minimis effect on the receiving waters. But that point has not been reached in these BEA regulations.

The record discloses that the Agency studied the cost of complying with the 1983 regulations. It set forth the cost of compliance for plants that produced various amounts of effluent per minute, both in terms of capital costs and operation and maintenance costs. The projections include estimates of the costs of construction, labor, power, chemicals and fuel. Although land acquisition costs were not considered, the amount of land necessary for the air flotation unit is minimal. In contrast to our conclusion regarding aerated lagoons, the Agency was not arbitrary in concluding that the DAF unit could be installed on existing plant locations without necessitating additional land acquisitions.

Finally, it does not appear that the cost of complying with the 1983 regulations is unreasonable. The cost of compliance for the Northwest Canned Salmon subcategory, for example, is estimated to be $157,000 for initial investment and $32,000 of annual expenditures for the average size plants. According to the EPA's economic analysis, the total annual costs of pollution abatement averaged between one and two percent of the total sales figures of each subcategory. Depreciation is available for the capital outlays and tax deductions are available for business expenses. The Agency concluded that the benefits justified the costs, and petitioners have not shown that conclusion to be arbitrary or capricious.

Although the number of plants estimated to close as a result of the 1983 regulations was not stated clearly to us, it appears to be a lesser proportion of affected plants than that which we approved for the 1977 regulations. Since Congress contemplated the closure of some marginal plants, we do not consider the regulations to be arbitrary and capricious.

For these reasons, we conclude that the 1983 regulations requiring dissolved air flotation units for West Coast fish processors should be upheld.

B. AERATED LAGOONS

The aerated lagoon is the required technology for the non-Alaskan conventional bottomfish subcategory. 40 C.F.R. §408.213. Aerated lagoons are still ponds in which waste water is treated biologically. They are usually three to four feet deep. With oxidation taking place in the upper eighteen inches, the water will remain in the lagoon from three to fifty days. Mechanically aerated lagoons are between six and twenty feet deep and receive oxygen from a floating aerator. Because of the length of detention time, the lagoons must be large in relation to the square footage of a processing plant to handle peak wasteload production.

Petitioners contend that the data are insufficient to determine if the limitations are achievable. The Agency relied on one study conducted with perch and smelt wastewater. Although the record also makes a vague reference to a shrimp processing lagoon in Florida, the record contains no information about its similarities to or differences from the technology at issue. The record does not disclose the analytic approach utilized, the transferability of the technology, or even the person or persons who conducted the study. Therefore, we limit our discussion to the smelt and perch wastewater study.

Although the 1983 regulations can be based on information from a single model plant, the study must demonstrate the effectiveness of the required technology. The smelt perch study does not reach this standard. The study measured the BOD_5 and TSS contained in the wastewater before entry to the lagoon (BOD_5 4.5, TSS 2.3), but the record reveals only the reduction in BOD_5 in the effluent leaving the lagoon. Although the BOD_5 level would comply with the 1983 limitations, there is no indication as to whether the TSS and O & G levels would be sufficiently reduced.

The Agency is charged with the duty of articulating the reasons for its determination. Since there are no data upon which to determine that the TSS and O & G levels will be reduced sufficiently to comply with the 1983 limitations, we remand these regulations to the Agency for further findings.

The final question presented is whether the Agency gave adequate consideration to costs in the determination that aerated lagoons are achievable technology. The major disadvantage of aerated lagoons is that they require large amounts of readily accessible land. The Agency did not consider the cost of acquiring land in determining the economic impact of the regulations. The reason given for this omission is that the costs of acquiring land are "site-specific" and vary depending upon the location and surrounding area. Although this may be true, it does not follow that the cost of acquiring land should be completely ignored in determining whether the technology is achievable. Where a significant amount of land proximate to a plant is an inherent requirement of a control technology, the Agency must attempt to determine the economic impact of acquiring the land. The Agency may set forth the amount of land necessary for various size plants, the average cost of land in the vicinity of identified processing plants, and, finally, whether it is reasonable to conclude that land will be available for the aerated lagoons.

We recognize this holding may be at odds with American Iron and Steel Inst. v. EPA, 526 F.2d 1027, 1053 (3d Cir. 1976). The court there determined that the cost of land acquisition should not be considered because it is "inherently site-specific" and that petitioners have the burden of showing "the magnitude of these excluded costs factors." Id. at 1053. We respectfully disagree on both counts.

The Agency has successfully projected other average costs that might be termed "site-specific" such as the cost of in-plant process changes, the cost of barging and screening, and the cost of other control technology. Each of these costs is subject to variability, depending on plant design and location. Similarly, when a significant amount of land is required for implementation of the regulation, we think the Agency must take land availability or land cost into account in some manner before it can make a reasoned determination that the regulations are economically achievable, especially when actual plant sites can be studied for this purpose. Failure to do so results in an incomplete consideration of the economic impact of the regulations. This is especially true where, as here, it appears many plant sites are located on waterfront areas where proximate land is not available or is in all probability expensive. That the cost or practicality of acquiring land is difficult to discern does not excuse the Agency from making some estimate of those factors. The amount of land necessary for this control technology is quite significant, and we think it is essential that the Agency give express consideration to that aspect of the 1983 regulations. . . .

The agency must show that the regulations are achievable. These regulations, based on data that fail to consider land acquisition cost or availability, are not the result of reasoned decisionmaking.

We therefore remand the regulation requiring aerated lagoons to the Agency in order that it may promulgate new 1983 regulations for the non-Alaskan conventional bottomfish subcategory. The remaining regulations are sustained upon the reasoning set forth above.

AFFIRMED in part and REMANDED in part.

3. *Variances*

As we discussed above, one of the criticisms of the national categorical standards framework is that its "one size fits all" approach is inefficient and unfair. The CWA contains a number of "variance" provisions that are intended to provide some relief from this framework. The Supreme Court's decision in the following case addresses the issue of "variances."

EPA v. NATIONAL CRUSHED STONE ASSOCIATION
449 U.S. 64 (1980)

JUSTICE WHITE delivered the opinion of the Court.

In April and July 1977, the Environmental Protection Agency (EPA), acting under the Federal Water Pollution Control Act (Act), as amended, 86 Stat. 816, 33 U.S.C. §1251 et seq., promulgated pollution discharge limitations for the coal mining industry and for that portion of the mineral mining and processing industry comprising the crushed-stone, construction-sand, and gravel categories. Although the Act does not expressly authorize or require variances from the 1977 limitation, each set of regulations contained a variance provision. . . .

To obtain a variance from the 1977 uniform discharge limitations a discharger must demonstrate that the "factors relating to the equipment or facilities involved, the process applied, or other such factors relating to such discharger are fundamentally different from the factors considered in the establishment of the guidelines." Although a greater than normal cost of implementation will be considered in acting on a request for a variance, economic ability to meet the costs will not be considered.[5] A variance, therefore, will not be granted on the basis of the applicant's economic inability to meet the costs of implementing the uniform standard. . . .

We granted certiorari to resolve the conflict between the decisions below and Weyerhaeuser Co. v. Costle, 590 F.2d 1011 (D.C. Cir. 1978), in which the variance provision was upheld.

I . . .

Section 301(c) of the Act explicitly provides for modifying the 1987 (BAT) effluent limitations with respect to individual point sources. A variance under §301(c) may be obtained upon a showing "that such modified requirements (1) will represent the maximum use of technology within the economic capability of the owner or operator; and (2) will result in reasonable further progress toward the elimination of the discharge of pollutants." Thus, the economic ability of the individual operator to meet the costs of effluent reductions may in some circumstances justify granting a variance from the 1987 limitations.

No such explicit variance provision exists with respect to BPT standards, but in E. I. du Pont de Nemours & Co. v. Train, 430 U.S. 112 (1977), we indicated that a variance provision was a necessary aspect of BPT limitations applicable by regulations to classes and categories of point sources. Id., at 128. The issue in this case is whether the BPT variance provision must allow consideration of the economic capability of an individual discharger to afford the costs of the BPT limitation. For the reasons that follow, our answer is in the negative.

II

The plain language of the statute does not support the position taken by the Court of Appeals. Section 301(c) is limited on its face to modifications of the 1987 BAT limitations. It says nothing about relief from the 1977 BPT requirements. Nor does the language of the Act support the position that although §301(c) is not itself applicable to BPT standards, it requires that the affordability of the prescribed 1977 technology be considered in BPT variance decisions. This would be a logical reading of the statute only if the factors listed in §301(c) bore a substantial relationship to the considerations underlying the 1977 limitations as they do to those controlling the 1987 regulations. This is not the case.

The two factors listed in §301(c)—"maximum use of technology within the economic capability of the owner or operator" and "reasonable further progress toward

5. EPA has explained its position as follows:

> Thus a plant may be able to secure a BPT variance by showing that the plant's own compliance costs with the national guideline limitation would be x times greater than the compliance costs of the plants EPA considered in setting the national BPT limitation. A plant may not, however, secure a BPT variance by alleging that the plant's own financial status is such that it cannot afford to comply with the national BPT limitation. [43 Fed. Reg. 50,042 (1978).]

the elimination of the discharge of pollutants"—parallel the general definition of BAT standards as limitations that "require application of the best available technology economically achievable for such category or class, which will result in reasonable further progress toward . . . eliminating the discharge of all pollutants. . . ." §301(b)(2). A §301(c) variance, thus, creates for a particular point source a BAT standard that represents for it the same sort of economic and technological commitment as the general BAT standard creates for the class. As with the general BAT standard, the variance assumes that the 1977 BPT standard has been met by the point source and that the modification represents a commitment of the maximum resources economically possible to the ultimate goal of eliminating all polluting discharges. No one who can afford the best available technology can secure a variance.

There is no similar connection between §301(c) and the considerations underlying the establishment of the 1977 BPT limitations. First, §301(c)'s requirement of "reasonable further progress" must have reference to some prior standard. BPT serves as the prior standard with respect to BAT. There is, however, no comparable, prior standard with respect to BPT limitations. Second, BPT limitations do not require an industrial category to commit the maximum economic resources possible to pollution control, even if affordable. Those point sources already using a satisfactory pollution control technology need take no additional steps at all. The §301(c) variance factor, the "maximum use of technology within the economic capability of the owner or operator," would therefore be inapposite in the BPT context. It would not have the same effect there that it has with respect to BAT's, i.e., it would not apply the general requirements to an individual point source.

More importantly, to allow a variance based on the maximum technology affordable by the point source, even if that technology fails to meet BPT effluent limitations, would undercut the purpose and function of BPT limitations. Rather than the 1987 requirement of the best measures economically and technologically feasible, the statutory provisions for 1977 contemplate regulations prohibiting discharges from any point source in excess of the effluent produced by the best practicable technology currently available in the industry. . . .

NOTES AND QUESTIONS ON TECHNOLOGY-BASED STANDARDS

1. *Challenges to EPA's Technology-Based Standards. Du Pont* upholds EPA's discretion to promulgate uniform national effluent standards, *Weyerhaeuser* and *API* explore some of the issues associated with establishing such standards, and *National Crushed Stone* discusses the notion of variances under the CWA's national categorical standards approach. Within the parameters of this framework, the establishment of effluent limitations has been extremely difficult and involves considerable judgment by the agency. First, the agency must rely on the regulated community for much of its data on available technologies, reduction rates, and the costs of achieving possible discharge levels. Industry has naturally had incentives to withhold data, inflate costs, and challenge EPA's methodologies for making each of these judgments. Second, the agency must constantly balance what is technically feasible with cost considerations and deal with the problem of being unable to quantify the environmental benefits of the mandated effluent limitations. Third, these limitations are established through informal notice and comment rulemaking. Regulations frequently are challenged on procedural grounds, as *ultra vires*, or as arbitrary because they failed to adequately

consider relevant data or statutory factors. Some of the issues covered in these challenges are summarized in the notes below.

2. *Good, Better, Best.* In setting BPT and BAT regulations, can EPA base the regulations solely on the performance of the best plants, or must all plants within an industrial subcategory be considered in setting an effluent limitation? Hooker Chem. & Plastics Corp. v. Train, 537 F.2d 620 (2d Cir. 1976), holds that the agency correctly limited the range of plants to the more technologically advanced ones because the legislative history supported the use of "the average of the best existing performance." *National Crushed Stone* affirms this holding. Chemical Mfrs. Ass'n v. EPA, 870 F.2d 177, 207-211 (5th Cir.), *clarified on rehearing*, 885 F.2d 253 (5th Cir. 1989), followed these cases to hold that EPA could base BPT for the organic chemical, plastics, and synthetic fiber industry on its use by 99 out of 304 plants and further could use the practice of 71 plants as the "average of the best" and need not distinguish between cold- and warm-weather plants. Cold-weather-area plants could apply biological treatment, but warm-weather ones needed design and operations changes. Kennecott v. EPA, 780 F.2d 445 (4th Cir. 1985), summarized and applied the law of inter-industry technology transfers, concluding that "Congress contemplated that EPA might use technology from other industries to establish the Best Available Technology."

The issue of the availability of foreign and hypothetical technologies arose early in the administration of the CWA. Is a technology that is not in actual use in any plant within the United States "available" for the purpose of establishing BAT? See Kennecott v. EPA, 780 F.2d 445 (4th Cir. 1985); American Frozen Food Inst. v. Train, 539 F.2d 107 (D.C. Cir. 1976). A technology is not per se unavailable just because it is not in use in any plant, but the agency's burden of justification increases. In Hooker Chem. & Plastics Corp. v. Train, 537 F.2d 620 (2d Cir. 1976), the court found that the agency's record was inadequate on the issue of feasibility because EPA had failed to specify adequately the facts underlying its conclusion that technologies would become commercially feasible and thus available. It is difficult for industry to show that the technology is not technically available if a model plant meets the EPA standard. See CPC Int'l, Inc. v. Train, 540 F.2d 1329 (8th Cir. 1976), in which the wet corn milling industry was faced with a plant that met BOD standards and was thus reduced to the unsuccessful argument that the capital and operating costs were excessive.

A zero-discharge BAT effluent limitations guideline for water and sand discharges from the coastal oil and gas industry, with the exception of Cook Inlet, Alaska, was upheld in Texas Oil & Gas Ass'n v. EPA, 161 F.3d 923 (5th Cir. 1998). The court noted that the industry petitions

> face an especially difficult challenge . . . given the proportion of dischargers already practicing zero at the time of the rulemaking. The EPA found that 100 percent of coastal oil and gas facilities outside of Cook Inlet, Louisiana and Texas, and at least 62 percent of facilities in Louisiana and Texas, were practicing zero discharge in 1992.

What does this decision tell us about the technology-forcing nature of BAT in at least some cases? For a case in which the court approved EPA's decision to choose a BAT that allows various requirements to be implemented on a case-by-case basis because of variability in topography, climate, and other factors and that similarly approved EPA's rejection of a treatment option that would be "economically prohibitive" and not likely to result in significant environmental benefits, see Waterkeeper Alliance, Inc. v. EPA, 399 F.3d 486 (2nd Cir. 2005).

3. *Variances from Technology-Based Standards.* As noted above, Congress has established a limited number of variances from technology-based standards. See, e.g., CWA §301(c), (*l*), and (n); 40 C.F.R. §125. Variances are intended to provide flexibility in what otherwise was thought to be a rigid scheme of national regulation, as the *Train* decision, *supra*, reflects. The availability of variances depends to some extent on the type of pollutant involved. Section 301(*l*), added in 1977, provided: "The Administrator may not modify any requirement of this section as it applies to any specific pollutant which is on the toxic pollutant list under section 307(a)(1) of this title." Chemical Mfrs. Ass'n v. NRDC, 470 U.S. 116 (1985), however, held that EPA's decision to grant variances on the ground that the discharger's situation was fundamentally different from its industrial class was within its discretion:

> Section 301(*l*) states that EPA may not "modify" any requirement of §301 insofar as toxic materials are concerned. EPA insists that §301(*l*) prohibits only those modifications expressly permitted by other provisions of §301, namely, those that §301(c) and §301(g) would allow on economic or water-quality grounds. Section 301(*l*), it is urged, does not address the very different issue of FDF variances. This view of the agency charged with administering the statute is entitled to considerable deference; and to sustain it, we need not find that it is the only permissible construction that EPA might have adopted but only that EPA's understanding of this very "complex statute" is a sufficiently rational one to preclude a court from substituting its judgment for that of EPA. Train v. NRDC, 421 U.S. 60, 75, 87, (1975). . . .

In 1987 Congress ratified *Chemical Mfrs. Ass'n.* See CWA §301(*l*), (n).

4. *Permit Shields.* A discharge in excess of the amount specified in an NPDES permit is a violation of the Act and potentially makes the discharger vulnerable to the enforcement sections discussed in Chapter 10. The converse is also true. Atlantic States Legal Found. v. Eastman Kodak Co., 12 F.3d 353 (2d Cir. 1994), held that an NPDES permit operates as a shield from citizen suits for discharges that comply with the terms of the permit. "Once within the NPDES or SPDES [State Pollutant Discharge Elimination System] scheme, . . . polluters may discharge pollutants not specifically listed in their permits so long as they comply with the appropriate reporting requirements and abide by any new limitations imposed on such pollutants." EPA interprets *Kodak* to apply to pollutants for which no limits exist in the permit but that were identified during the permit process. Piney Run Pres. Ass'n v. County Comm'rs of Carroll County, 268 F.3d 255 (4th Cir. 2001), upheld EPA's interpretation of §402(k)'s permit shield provision, notably the position that a discharger is not liable for the discharge of pollutants not listed in the permit but disclosed to the permitting authorities.

5. *Bubbles and Effluent Credit Trading.* In January 2003, EPA issued its Water Quality Trading Policy Statement, 68 Fed. Reg. 1608 (2003). The agency characterized water quality trading as a "voluntary, incentive-based approach that can offer greater efficiency in restoring or protecting water bodies." EPA established several ground rules for trading schemes, including (1) demarcating areas in which trades may take place ("within a watershed or a defined area for which a TMDL has been approved"); (2) identifying the types of pollutants that may be traded (generally, nutrients or sediment loads, though EPA indicated that it may support trades of other pollutants as well under certain circumstances); (3) highlighting the need to establish baselines for trading; and (4) reviewing the circumstances in which trading

may occur (e.g., to maintain water quality where WQSs are attained, and intra-plant trading). Id. at 1610-1611.

EPA's Assistant Administrator for Water, Benjamin Grumbles, announced in June 2006 that 93 NPDES permits providing for water quality trading have been issued for 233 facilities in seven states. He indicated that EPA planned to issue a water quality trading toolkit for permit writers, and that EPA's goal is for one-third of all NPDES permits issued in FY 2007 to incorporate water quality trading. EPA Touts Water Quality Trading as Effective for Gulf, Chesapeake Bay, 37 Env't Rep. (BNA) 1161 (2006).

Some NGOs have signaled their desire that any trading scheme protect against localized "hot spots," among other issues. Further, trades between point and non-point sources are likely to be particularly challenging for a variety of reasons. Issues to watch include the extent to which trading schemes create enforceable obligations under the CWA for nonpoint sources, and the degree to which these schemes make point sources accountable for reductions by nonpoint sources. Stephenson et al., Toward an Effective Watershed-Based Effluent Allowance Trading System: Identifying the Statutory and Regulatory Barriers to Implementation, 5 Envtl. Law. 775 (1999), argue that the CWA limits watershed-based effluent allowance trading and suggest amendments to remove barriers to an effective trading scheme. For an example of a water trading initiative at the state level, Pennsylvania has authorized and begun to implement a new trading program intended to generate nutrient reduction credits as part of the state's effort to reduce nitrogen, phosphorus, and sediment pollution in the Chesapeake Bay watershed. First Sale of Nutrient Credits Executed under Pennsylvania Trading Program, Daily Env't Rep. (BNA) (November 13, 2006), at A-10.

Problem 7-2

EPA has developed BAT effluent limitations for the dry-cleaning industry. This industry's effluent consists primarily of two pollutants, PERC and TCE. EPA's national survey identified one plant that could achieve the PERC limit EPA set, and another plant that could achieve the TCE limit EPA set. No plant that EPA studied could achieve both limitations. The industry has challenged EPA's effluent limitations. Who would you expect to prevail in this challenge?

E.   WATER QUALITY STANDARDS

The [CWA] §303(d) focus on ambient water quality standards has returned the nation to a water quality program that was not considered implementable 35 years ago when there was a paucity of data and analytical tools for determining causes of impairment and assigning responsibility to various sources. . . . Having returned the focus to ambient water quality conditions, are we better positioned than we were years ago? Do we have more and better data and analytical methods? Do we have a better understanding of watershed events and processes responsible for water quality violations? These are the science questions facing the nation as we implement Section 303(d) of the Clean Water Act. [National Research Council, Assessing the TMDL Approach to Water Quality Management 16 (2001).]

1. *Theory and Current Function*

Water quality standards were the heart of the pre-1972 federal regulatory program, as discussed in the introduction to this chapter. A Senate report on the predecessor of the 1972 Federal Water Pollution Control Act Amendments, the proposed Federal Water Pollution Control Act Amendments of 1971, explained the theory behind the 1965 Act:

> The standards are intended to function in two ways:
>
> 1. As a measure of performance, the standards are expected to establish the maximum level of pollution allowable in interstate waters.
> 2. The standards are also intended to provide an avenue of legal action against polluters. If the wastes discharged by polluters reduce water quality below the standards, actions may be begun against the polluters. [S. Rep. No. 92-414, at 4 (1971), reprinted in 1972 U.S.C.C.A.N. 3668.]

The theory did not pan out. States dragged their feet in submitting standards, and enforcement was nil. By 1971, despite considerable efforts by the states to control pollution through water quality standards, Congress concluded that this approach was hopelessly flawed and that a switch to technology-based effluent limitations was necessary. The Senate report went on to pinpoint the major flaw in a receiving water quality approach: "Water quality standards, in addition to their deficiencies in relying on the assimilative capacity of receiving water, often cannot be translated into effluent limitations defendable by court tests because of the imprecision of models for water quality and the effects of effluents in most waters." Id. at 18.

Many members of the Senate wanted to drop the water quality standards approach entirely, but in the end the Senate accepted a House amendment to continue and expand the program. Thus, the technology-based effluent limitations imposed by §301(b), and discussed in section D of this chapter, were superimposed on the water quality-based approach. Under today's CWA, permittees must meet technology-based requirements; but under CWA §301(b)(1)(C), they also must comply with "any more stringent limitation, including those necessary to meet water quality standards. . . ." Thus, if implementation of technology-based requirements will not suffice to protect a particular body of water adequately, in theory the permitting agency is obligated to include in the dischargers' permits more stringent controls that will suffice. Water quality standards, in short, are intended to serve as a "safety net" or "supplementary basis" for the protection of our nation's waters. EPA v. California ex rel. State Water Res. Control Bd., 426 U.S. 200, 205 n.12 (1976).

In recent years the role of water quality standards has increased significantly. Even greater reliance on such standards and the strategies to achieve them likely is in store for the future. This is because of the substantial improvements still needed in the quality of our waters, and the likelihood that the application of technology-based controls will not be enough to protect our waters for the uses for which we would like them to be available (swimming, fishing, drinking, etc.). Thus, effective implementation of the "safety net" embodied by the water quality standards approach is needed if we are to achieve our clean water goals. As EPA put it in its 1998 Water Quality Criteria and Standards Plan—Priorities for the Future 2 (June 1998):

> [N]ot all of the Nation's waters have achieved the Clean Water Act goal of "fishable and swimmable," and significant water pollution problems still exist. Approximately 40 percent of the Nation's assessed waters still do not meet water quality goals and about half of the Nation's 2000 major watersheds have water quality problems.
>
>   Given these facts, there is a critical need for improved water quality standards and a set of tools to implement those standards.

Setting and Reviewing WQS: Required Elements and Distribution of Responsibility. It is up to the states in the first instance to establish water quality or ambient standards for waters in their jurisdiction. CWA §303. All of the states have assumed this responsibility. EPA Office of Inspector General, Water: Proactive Approach Would Improve EPA's Water Quality Standards Program i (Sept. 29, 2000). EPA must approve state water quality standards, and the federal agency is obligated to promulgate its own standards under some circumstances if it determines that the state standards are deficient. See, e.g., CWA §303(b).

The first step a state must take in developing water quality standards is to designate uses for its water bodies. CWA §303(c)(2)(A) directs states to consider a series of possible uses, including "public water supplies, propagation of fish and wildlife, recreational purposes, and agricultural, industrial, and other purposes, and also taking into consideration their use and value for navigation." EPA's regulations currently provide some boundaries for the states' designation of uses. Among them, a state may (1) designate several uses for a water body, and (2) establish a "higher quality use" than is currently in place. The CWA limits a state's ability to alter use designations to make them less demanding. 40 C.F.R. §131.10(g), (h). Further, the "fishable-swimmable" standard in CWA §101(a)(2) was to have been achieved by 1983; states that propose not to achieve such uses must explain why. 40 C.F.R. §131.10(j). Finally, states are supposed to set their water quality standards so that waters leaving a state do not undermine the ability of downstream states to meet their own water quality standards. Id. §131.10(b). The Supreme Court offered its gloss on this last obligation in its 1991 decision in Arkansas v. Oklahoma, excerpted below.

EPA has traditionally allowed states substantial discretion in designating the uses for different water bodies. In June 2002, EPA convened a national symposium to identify and discuss the issues relating to designation of uses. The proceedings from the symposium suggest that a consensus exists that "better refined use designations" are needed, while there is disagreement about issues such as the definition of existing uses and how national policy goals concerning uses should be reconciled with the views of local residents. Proceedings Summary Report, National Symposium, Designating Attainable Uses for the Nation's Waters, June 3-4, 2002, at 16 (prepared for EPA's Office of Science and Technology by Great Lakes Environmental Center).

In addition to designating uses for a water body, a state must establish "water quality criteria" that are sufficient to protect the designated uses. 40 C.F.R. §131.11(a)(1). Criteria are "elements of State water quality standards, expressed as constituent concentrations, levels or narrative statements, representing a quality of water that supports a particular use." 40 C.F.R. §131.3(b). CWA §304(a)(1) requires EPA to develop its own water quality criteria to help states determine appropriate water quality standards for particular designated uses. The agency has done so periodically.* These criteria are based on the "latest scientific knowledge" concerning the relationships between "pollutant concentrations and environmental and human health effects." Id. When EPA recommends criteria, states often rely on them in setting their own, but do not always do so.

Based on the designated uses each state has established and its water quality criteria, which must protect the designated uses, each state establishes water quality standards for the water bodies in its jurisdiction. States submit proposed water quality standards to EPA for review; EPA either approves the state standards or rejects them on the ground that they are inconsistent with the CWA, in which case EPA may promulgate its own standards. CWA §303(b), (c)(4)(A); 40 C.F.R. §131.22(b). The CWA requires states to engage in a triennial review of their water quality standards and directs them to refine the standards as appropriate. CWA §303(c); 40 C.F.R. §131.20.

The final significant aspect of the legal framework governing the establishment of water quality standards involves a concept known as "antidegradation." EPA's antidegradation policy "ensures that existing water quality is maintained and protected." EPA, Water Quality Criteria and Standards Plan—Priorities for the Future 5 (June 1998); 40 C.F.R. §131.12(a)(1). The policy protects existing uses of water bodies. The policy also seeks to maintain and protect waters that exceed fishable/swimmable levels by providing that such waters may be degraded to the point where they merely support existing uses only if doing so is necessary to "accommodate important economic or social development in the area." Even in such cases, however, the state must adequately protect existing uses, and it must "assure . . . the highest regulatory requirements for point sources, and all cost effective and reasonable best management practices for non-point sources." Id. §131.12(a)(2). Water quality must be maintained for "outstanding natural resource" waters. Id. §131.12(a)(3). Some commentators have suggested that antidegradation holds special promise as a proactive tool to prevent waters from becoming "unusable" in the first place, comparing it to the reactive approach of the TMDL program (discussed in the following section) of cleaning up water bodies after they are no longer available for designated uses. See, e.g., Dernbach, Why Lawyers Should Care, 19 Envtl. F. 30, 46 (July/August 2002).

To sum up, water quality standards have become increasingly important, particularly as EPA and the states struggle with controlling discharges into impaired waters. One of the key questions involves the respective roles of these federalism partners in determining the appropriate content of such standards—what the water quality standards (WQS) should be for a particular water body. In Mississippi Comm'n on Natural Res. v. Costle, 625 F.2d 1269 (5th Cir. 1980), the Fifth Circuit upheld EPA's refusal to approve Missisippi's water quality standard for dissolved oxygen, which is necessary for the protection and propagation of fish and aquatic life, and the agency's imposition of its own, more stringent standards instead. The court explained the legal framework as follows:

> For EPA to promulgate a water quality standard, it must determine that the state's standard "is not consistent with the applicable requirements of (the Act)" or that "a revised or new standard is necessary to meet the requirements of (the Act)." 33 U.S.C. §1313(c)(3), (c)(4)(B) (1976). Review is therefore centered around two

*In January 2003, for example, EPA announced nine "ecoregional nutrient criteria." 68 Fed. Reg. 557 (2003). In 1973 EPA issued its "Blue Book," in 1976 it issued the "Red Book," and in 1999 it published a compilation of nationally recommended water quality criteria for 157 pollutants. EPA, National Recommended Water Quality Criteria—Correction 1 (April 1999).

issues: first, whether EPA's disapproval of Mississippi's DO standard was proper; and second, whether EPA properly promulgated the substitute standard. . . .

Congress did place primary authority for establishing water quality standards with the states [citing §101(b)]. . . . [T]he legislative history reflects congressional concern that the Act not place in the hands of a federal administrator absolute power over zoning watershed areas. The varied topographies and climates in the country call for varied water quality solutions.

Despite this primary allocation of power, the states are not given unreviewable discretion to set water quality standards. All water quality standards must be submitted to the federal Administrator. 33 U.S.C. §1313(c)(2) (1976). The state must review its standards at least once every three years and make the results of the review available to the Administrator. Id. §1313(c)(1). EPA is given the final voice on the standard's adequacy [under §303(c)(3)]. . . . In addition, EPA can override state water quality standards by changing the effluent limits in NPDES permits whenever a source interferes with water quality. Id. §1312.

EPA's role also is more dominant when water quality criteria are in question. Although the designation of uses and the setting of criteria are interrelating chores, the specification of a waterway as one for fishing, swimming, or public water supply is closely tied to the zoning power Congress wanted left with the states. The criteria set for a specific use are more amenable to uniformity. Congress recognized this distinction by placing with EPA the duty to develop and publish water quality criteria reflecting the latest scientific knowledge shortly after the amendment's passage and periodically thereafter. Id. §1314(a)(1). EPA correctly points out that by leaving intact the Mississippi use designations it has acted in the manner least intrusive of state prerogatives. . . .

We conclude that EPA did not exceed its statutory authority in disapproving the state water quality standard. [Id. at 1275-1277.]

For a more recent consideration of the CWA's allocation of responsibility between EPA and the states concerning water quality standards, see Defenders of Wildlife v. EPA, 415 F.3d 1121 (10th Cir. 2005).

NOTES AND QUESTIONS

1. *EPA's Responsibilities as Part of the Triennial Review of State Water Quality Standards.* The D.C. Circuit considered EPA's role in National Wildlife Fed'n v. Browner, 127 F.3d 1126, 1130 (D.C. Cir. 1997), holding that while states must submit existing water quality standards to EPA upon completion of their triennial review,

> EPA, however, is not automatically required under the Act to review and approve those standards. Instead, EPA observes, the agency is granted discretionary authority under §303(c)(4)(B) of the Act to force a state to accept "a revised or new standard . . . [if] necessary to meet the requirements of" the Act. 33 U.S.C. §1313(c)(4)(B) (1988). This discretionary power is reflected as well in the agency's regulations. Therefore, under §131.20 of the regulations states are only required to submit existing water quality standards to EPA to enable it to make an informed decision about whether to exercise its discretion to supplant the state standards. . . .

2. *Challenges Remain in Implementing Water Quality–Based Approaches.* As this section reflects, EPA and the states have struggled in their efforts to implement the water quality standards–based approach to water protection contained in the

CWA. See, e.g., EPA, Strategy for Water Quality Standards and Criteria: Strengthening the Foundation of Programs to Protect and Restore the Nation's Waters (EPA-823-R-03-010, August 2003). In a June 2003 report, the GAO recommended that EPA simplify the changing of designated uses and enhance uniformity in the process. U.S. GAO, Water Quality: The EPA Should Improve Guidance and Support to Help States Develop Standards that Better Target Cleanup Efforts (2003).

2. Spillover Effects and Treatment of New Dischargers to Impaired Waters

Two important questions that have been raised concerning water quality standards–based approaches involve (1) how to treat "spillover" effects (i.e., the impacts of pollution spilling over from one state to another) and (2) the circumstances in which a new discharge is allowable into a water body that exceeds water quality standards. The following Supreme Court case discusses both issues.

ARKANSAS v. OKLAHOMA
503 U.S. 91 (1991)

JUSTICE STEVENS delivered the opinion of the Court.

Pursuant to the Clean Water Act, the Environmental Protection Agency (EPA or agency) issued a discharge permit to a new point source in Arkansas, about 39 miles upstream from the Oklahoma state line. The question presented in this litigation is whether the EPA's finding that discharges from the new source would not cause a detectable violation of Oklahoma's water quality standards satisfied the EPA's duty to protect the interests of the downstream State. Disagreeing with the Court of Appeals, we hold that the Agency's action was authorized by the statute.

I

In 1985, the city of Fayetteville, Arkansas, applied to the EPA, seeking a permit for the city's new sewage treatment plant under the National Pollution Discharge Elimination System (NPDES). After the appropriate procedures, the EPA, pursuant to §402(a)(1) of the Act, 33 U.S.C. §1342(a)(1), issued a permit authorizing the plant to discharge up to half of its effluent (to a limit of 6.1 million gallons per day) into an unnamed stream in northwestern Arkansas. That flow passes through a series of three creeks for about 17 miles, and then enters the Illinois River at a point 22 miles upstream from the Arkansas-Oklahoma border.

The permit imposed specific limitations on the quantity, content, and character of the discharge and also included a number of special conditions, including a provision that if a study then underway indicated that more stringent limitations were necessary to ensure compliance with Oklahoma's water quality standards, the permit would be modified to incorporate those limits.

Respondents challenged this permit before the EPA, alleging, inter alia, that the discharge violated the Oklahoma water quality standards. Those standards provide that "no degradation [of water quality] shall be allowed" in the upper Illinois River, including the portion of the river immediately downstream from the state line.

Following a hearing, the Administrative Law Judge (ALJ) concluded that the Oklahoma standards would not be implicated unless the contested discharge had "something more than a mere *de minimis* impact" on the State's waters. He found that the discharge would not have an "undue impact" on Oklahoma's waters and, accordingly, affirmed the issuance of the permit.

On a petition for review, the EPA's Chief Judicial Officer first ruled that §301(b)(1)(C) of the Clean Water Act "requires an NPDES permit to impose any effluent limitations necessary to comply with applicable state water quality standards." He then held that the Act and EPA regulations offered greater protection for the downstream State than the ALJ's "undue impact" standard suggested. He explained the proper standard as follows:

> [A] mere theoretical impairment of Oklahoma's water quality standards—i.e., an infinitesimal impairment predicted through modeling but not expected to be actually detectable or measurable—should not by itself block the issuance of the permit. In this case, the permit should be upheld if the record shows by a preponderance of the evidence that the authorized discharges would not cause an actual detectable violation of Oklahoma's water quality standards.

On remand, the ALJ made detailed findings of fact and concluded that the city had satisfied the standard set forth by the Chief Judicial Officer. Specifically, the ALJ found that there would be no detectable violation of any of the components of Oklahoma's water quality standards. The Chief Judicial Officer sustained the issuance of the permit.

Both the petitioners (collectively Arkansas) and the respondents in this litigation sought judicial review. Arkansas argued that the Clean Water Act did not require an Arkansas point source to comply with Oklahoma's water quality standards. Oklahoma challenged the EPA's determination that the Fayetteville discharge would not produce a detectable violation of the Oklahoma standards.

The Court of Appeals did not accept either of these arguments. The court agreed with the EPA that the statute required compliance with Oklahoma's water quality standards, and did not disagree with the Agency's determination that the discharges from the Fayetteville plant would not produce a detectable violation of those standards. Nevertheless, relying on a theory that neither party had advanced, the Court of Appeals reversed the Agency's issuance of the Fayetteville permit. The court first ruled that the statute requires that "where a proposed source would discharge effluents that would contribute to conditions currently constituting a violation of applicable water quality standards, such [a] proposed source may not be permitted." Then the court found that the Illinois River in Oklahoma was "already degraded," that the Fayetteville effluent would reach the Illinois River in Oklahoma, and that effluent could "be expected to contribute to the ongoing deterioration of the scenic [Illinois R]iver" in Oklahoma even though it would not detectably affect the river's water quality. . . .

II

Interstate waters have been a font of controversy since the founding of the Nation. E.g., Gibbons v. Ogden, 9 Wheat. 1 (1824). This Court has frequently resolved disputes between States that are separated by a common river, e.g., that border the same body of water, or that are fed by the same river basin, see, e.g., New Jersey v. New York, 283 U.S. 336 (1931).

Among these cases are controversies between a State that introduces pollutants to a waterway and a downstream State that objects. See, e.g., Missouri v. Illinois, 200 U.S. 496. In such cases, this Court has applied principles of common law tempered by a respect for the sovereignty of the States. Compare id., at 521, with Georgia v. Tennessee Copper Co., 206 U.S. 230, 237 (1907). In forging what "may not improperly be called interstate common law," Illinois v. Milwaukee, 406 U.S. 91, 105-106 (1972) (*Milwaukee I*), however, we remained aware "that new federal laws and new federal regulations may in time pre-empt the field of federal common law of nuisance." Id., at 107.

In Milwaukee v. Illinois, 451 U.S. 304 (1981) (*Milwaukee II*), we held that the Federal Water Pollution Control Act Amendments of 1972 did just that. In addressing Illinois' claim that Milwaukee's discharges into Lake Michigan constituted a nuisance, we held that the comprehensive regulatory regime created by the 1972 amendments pre-empted Illinois' federal common law remedy. We observed that Congress had addressed many of the problems we had identified in *Milwaukee I* by providing a downstream State with an opportunity for a hearing before the source State's permitting agency, by requiring the latter to explain its failure to accept any recommendations offered by the downstream State, and by authorizing the EPA, in its discretion, to veto a source State's issuance of any permit if the waters of another State may be affected. *Milwaukee II*, 451 U.S., at 325-326.

In *Milwaukee II*, the Court did not address whether the 1972 amendments had supplanted state common law remedies as well as the federal common law remedy. See id., at 310, n.4. On remand, Illinois argued that §510 of the Clean Water Act, 33 U.S.C. §1370, expressly preserved the State's right to adopt and enforce rules that are more stringent than federal standards. The Court of Appeals accepted Illinois' reading of §510, but held that section did "no more than to save the right and jurisdiction of a state to regulate activity occurring within the confines of its boundary waters." Illinois v. Milwaukee, 731 F.2d 403, 413 (CA7 1984).

This Court subsequently endorsed that analysis in International Paper Co. v. Ouellette, 479 U.S. 481 (1987), in which Vermont property owners claimed that the pollution discharged into Lake Champlain by a paper company located in New York constituted a nuisance under Vermont law. The Court held the Clean Water Act taken "as a whole, its purposes and its history" pre-empted an action based on the law of the affected State and that the only state law applicable to an interstate discharge is "the law of the State in which the point source is located." Id., at 493, 487. Moreover, in reviewing §402(b) of the Act, the Court pointed out that when a new permit is being issued by the source State's permit-granting agency, the downstream State

> "does not have the authority to block the issuance of the permit if it is dissatisfied with the proposed standards. An affected State's only recourse is to apply to the EPA Administrator, who then has the discretion to disapprove the permit if he concludes that the discharges will have an undue impact on interstate waters. §1342(d)(2). . . . Thus the Act makes it clear that affected States occupy a subordinate position to source States in the federal regulatory program. Id., at 490-491."

Unlike the foregoing cases, this litigation involves not a state-issued permit, but a federally issued permit. To explain the significance of this distinction, we comment further on the statutory scheme before addressing the specific issues raised by the parties.

III

The Clean Water Act anticipates a partnership between the States and the Federal Government, animated by a shared objective: "to restore and maintain the chemical, physical, and biological integrity of the Nation's waters." 33 U.S.C. §1251(a). Toward this end, the Act provides for two sets of water quality measures [effluent limitations and water quality standards]. . . .

IV

The parties have argued three analytically distinct questions concerning the interpretation of the Clean Water Act. First, does the Act require the EPA, in crafting and issuing a permit to a point source in one State, to apply the water quality standards of downstream States? Second, even if the Act does not require as much, does the Agency have the statutory authority to mandate such compliance? Third, does the Act provide, as the Court of Appeals held, that once a body of water fails to meet water quality standards no discharge that yields effluent that reach the degraded waters will be permitted?

In these cases, it is neither necessary nor prudent for us to resolve the first of these questions. In issuing the Fayetteville permit, the EPA assumed it was obligated by both the Act and its own regulations to ensure that the Fayetteville discharge would not violate Oklahoma's standards. As we discuss below, this assumption was permissible and reasonable and therefore there is no need for us to address whether the Act requires as much. . . .

Our decision not to determine at this time the scope of the Agency's statutory obligations does not affect our resolution of the second question, which concerns the Agency's statutory authority. Even if the Clean Water Act itself does not require the Fayetteville discharge to comply with Oklahoma's water quality standards, the statute clearly does not limit the EPA's authority to mandate such compliance.

Since 1973, EPA regulations have provided that an NPDES permit shall not be issued "[w]hen the imposition of conditions cannot ensure compliance with the applicable water quality requirements of all affected States." 40 CFR §122.4(d)(1991). Those regulations—relied upon by the EPA in the issuance of the Fayetteville permit—constitute a reasonable exercise of the Agency's statutory authority.

Congress has vested in the Administrator broad discretion to establish conditions for NPDES permits. Section 402(a)(2) provides that for EPA-issued permits "[t]he Administrator shall prescribe conditions . . . to assure compliance with the requirements of [§402(a)(1)] and *such other requirements as he deems appropriate.*" 33 U.S.C. §1342(a)(2) (emphasis added). Similarly, Congress preserved for the Administrator broad authority to oversee state permit programs: "No permit shall issue . . . if the Administrator . . . objects in writing to the issuance of such permit as being outside the guidelines and requirements of this chapter." 33 U.S.C. §1342(d)(2).

The regulations relied on by the EPA were a perfectly reasonable exercise of the Agency's statutory discretion. The application of state water quality standards in the interstate context is wholly consistent with the Act's broad purpose "to restore and maintain the chemical, physical, and biological integrity of the Nation's waters." 33 U.S.C. §1251(a). Moreover, as noted above, §301(b)(1)(C) expressly identifies the achievement of state water quality standards as one of the Act's central objectives. The Agency's regulations conditioning NPDES permits are a well-tailored means of achieving this goal.

Notwithstanding this apparent reasonableness, Arkansas argues that our description in *Ouellette* of the role of affected States in the permit process and our characterization of the affected States' position as "subordinate," see 479 U.S., at 490-491, indicates that the EPA's application of the Oklahoma standards was error. We disagree. Our statement in *Ouellette* concerned only an affected State's input into the permit process; that input is clearly limited by the plain language of §402(b). Limits on an affected State's direct participation in permitting decisions, however, do not in any way constrain the EPA's authority to require a point source to comply with downstream water quality standards. . . .

Similarly, we agree with Arkansas that in the Clean Water Act Congress struck a careful balance among competing policies and interests, but do not find the EPA regulations concerning the application of downstream water quality standards at all incompatible with that balance. Congress, in crafting the Act, protected certain sovereign interests of the States; for example, §510 allows States to adopt more demanding pollution-control standards than those established under the Act. Arkansas emphasizes that §510 preserves such state authority only as it is applied to the waters of the regulating State. Even assuming Arkansas' construction of §510 is correct, that section only concerns state authority and does not constrain the EPA's authority to promulgate reasonable regulations requiring point sources in one State to comply with water quality standards in downstream States.

For these reasons, we find the EPA's requirement that the Fayetteville discharge comply with Oklahoma's water quality standards to be a reasonable exercise of the Agency's substantial statutory discretion.

V

The Court of Appeals construed the Clean Water Act to prohibit any discharge of effluent that would reach waters already in violation of existing water quality standards. We find nothing in the Act to support this reading. . . .

Although the Act contains several provisions directing compliance with state water quality standards, see, e.g., §1311(b)(1)(C), the parties have pointed to nothing that mandates a complete ban on discharges into a waterway that is in violation of those standards. The statute does, however, contain provisions designed to remedy existing water quality violations and to allocate the burden of reducing undesirable discharges between existing sources and new sources. See, e.g., §1313(d). Thus, rather than establishing the categorical ban announced by the Court of Appeals—which might frustrate the construction of new plants that would improve existing conditions—the Clean Water Act vests in the EPA and the States broad authority to develop long-range, area-wide programs to alleviate and eliminate existing pollution. See, e.g., §1288(b)(2).

To the extent that the Court of Appeals relied on its interpretation of the Act to reverse the EPA's permitting decision, that reliance was misplaced.

VI

The Court of Appeals also concluded that the EPA's issuance of the Fayetteville permit was arbitrary and capricious because the Agency misinterpreted Oklahoma's water quality standards. The primary difference between the court's and the Agency's interpretation of the standards derives from the court's construction of the Act. Contrary to the EPA's interpretation of the Oklahoma standards, the Court of Appeals read those standards as containing the same categorical ban on new discharges that the court had found in the Clean Water Act itself. Although we do not believe the text of the Oklahoma standards supports the court's reading (indeed, we note that Oklahoma itself had not advanced that interpretation in its briefs in the Court of Appeals), we reject it for a more fundamental reason—namely, that the Court of Appeals exceeded the legitimate scope of judicial review of an agency adjudication. . . .

As discussed above, an EPA regulation requires an NPDES permit to comply "with the applicable water quality requirements of all affected States." 40 CFR §122.4(d) (1991). This regulation effectively incorporates into federal law those state-law standards the Agency reasonably determines to be "applicable." In such a situation, then, state water quality standards—promulgated by the States with substantial guidance from the EPA and approved by the Agency—are part of the federal law of water pollution control.

Two features of the body of law governing water pollution support this conclusion. First, as discussed more thoroughly above, we have long recognized that interstate water pollution is controlled by federal law. Recognizing that the system of federally approved state standards as applied in the interstate context constitutes federal law is wholly consistent with this principle. Second, treating state standards in interstate controversies as federal law accords with the Act's purpose of authorizing the EPA to create and manage a uniform system of interstate water pollution regulation.

Because we recognize that, at least insofar as they affect the issuance of a permit in another State, the Oklahoma standards have a federal character, the EPA's reasonable, consistently held interpretation of those standards is entitled to substantial deference. In these cases, the Chief Judicial Officer ruled that the Oklahoma standards—which require that there be "no degradation" of the upper Illinois River—would only be violated if the discharge effected an "actually detectable or measurable" change in water quality.

This interpretation of the Oklahoma standards is certainly reasonable and consistent with the purposes and principles of the Clean Water Act. As the Chief Judicial Officer noted, "unless there is some method for measuring compliance, there is no way to ensure compliance." Moreover, this interpretation of the Oklahoma standards makes eminent sense in the interstate context: If every discharge that had some theoretical impact on a downstream State were interpreted as "degrading" the downstream waters, downstream States might wield an effective veto over upstream discharges. . . .

In its review of the EPA's interpretation and application of the Oklahoma standards, the Court of Appeals committed three mutually compounding errors.

First, the court failed to give due regard to the EPA's interpretation of its own regulations, as those regulations incorporate the Oklahoma standards. Instead the court voiced its own interpretation of the governing law and concluded that "where a proposed source would discharge effluents that would contribute to conditions currently constituting a violation of applicable water quality standards, such [a] proposed source may not be permitted." 908 F.2d, at 620. As we have already pointed out, that reading of the law is not supported by the statute or by any EPA regulation. The Court of Appeals sat in review of an agency action and should have afforded the EPA's interpretation of the governing law an appropriate level of deference.

Second, the court disregarded well-established standards for reviewing the factual findings of agencies and instead made its own factual findings. The troubling nature of the court's analysis appears on the face of the opinion itself: At least four times, the court concluded that "there was substantial evidence before the ALJ to support" particular findings which the court thought appropriate, but which were contrary to those actually made by the ALJ. Although we have long recognized the "substantial evidence" standard in administrative law, the court below turned that analysis on its head. A court reviewing an agency's adjudicative action should accept the agency's factual findings if those findings are supported by substantial evidence on the record as a whole. The court should not supplant the agency's findings merely by identifying alternative findings that could be supported by substantial evidence.

Third, the court incorrectly concluded that the EPA's decision was arbitrary and capricious. This error is derivative of the court's first two errors. Having substituted its reading of the governing law for the Agency's, and having made its own factual findings, the Court of Appeals concluded that the EPA erred in not considering an important and relevant fact—namely, that the upper Illinois River was (by the court's assessment) already degraded. . . .

In sum, the Court of Appeals made a policy choice that it was not authorized to make. Arguably, as that court suggested, it might be wise to prohibit any discharge into the Illinois River, even if that discharge would have no adverse impact on water quality. But it was surely not arbitrary for the EPA to conclude—given the benefits to the river from the increased flow of relatively clean water and the benefits achieved in Arkansas by allowing the new plant to operate as designed—that allowing the discharge would be even wiser. It is not our role, or that of the Court of Appeals, to decide which policy choice is the better one, for it is clear that Congress has entrusted such decisions to the Environmental Protection Agency.

Accordingly, the judgment of the Court of Appeals is REVERSED.

NOTES AND QUESTIONS

1. *Dirty Hands.* Is *Oklahoma* a classic case of lack of clean hands or, alternatively, a *de minimis* injury case? Suppose a state adopts a nondegradation standard for its portion of an interstate watercourse and enforces it against its own dischargers. A discharge in an adjoining state threatens to migrate across state lines and violate the host state's antidegradation standard. Does EPA have a mandatory duty to deny or condition the NPDES permit? See Lininger, Narrowing the Preemptive Scope of the Clean Water Act as a Means of Enhancing Environmental Protection, 20 Harv. Envtl. L. Rev. 165, 178-179 (1996). Professor Merrill argues the federal common law and international law should be that a state can protect its resources from extraterritorial pollution only if the pollution would violate rules that it has adopted and enforced against its own citizens. Golden Rules for Transboundary Pollution, 46 Duke L.J. 931 (1997). How does this differ from the standard for EPA denial of upstream NPDES permits adopted in *Oklahoma*?

2. *Did Downstream States Win or Lose?* Professor Glicksman argues that the apparent opportunity that the Court's decision in Arkansas v. Oklahoma provides downstream states to preserve the quality of water resources shared with other states may be illusory for several reasons. First, the Court refused to decide whether the statute requires rather than merely permits EPA to apply affected-state water quality standards to source-state point sources. He contends that the plain language of the statute (particularly §§301(b)(1)(C) and 401(a)(2)), its principal purposes, and the "quasi-sovereign" interest of each state in protecting the integrity of its environment all support an affirmative answer to the question. Second, political factors may make EPA reluctant to impose significant constraints on source-state industries for the benefit of downstream users. Third, the threshold showing that a downstream state must make to force an upstream discharger to comply with its water quality standards is likely to be insurmountable due to the difficulty of tracing adverse effects on the state's water quality to one out of a number of upstream dischargers. He urges the adoption of a series of statutory amendments to buttress the rights of downstream states to protect themselves against out-of-state discharges, including a provision entitling a downstream state to relief upon proof that an upstream point source or group of point sources is causing or contributing to water quality violations in the affected state. Watching the River Flow: The Prospects for Improved Interstate Water Pollution Control, 43 Wash. U. J. Urb. & Contemp. L. 119, 144-145, 166-174 (1993).

3. The Role of TMDLs in Achieving Water Quality Standards

a. Overview

As we have learned, states are required to establish water quality standards that will protect the designated uses of waters within their jurisdictions, with EPA providing oversight and, in some cases, taking on the job itself if a state's performance is inadequate. As we also have learned, the CWA quite clearly (in §301(b)(1)(C)) requires that NPDES permits specify limits that will meet these standards. Yet the reality is that, despite the regulatory and other efforts undertaken over the past 30 years, close to one-half of the nation's assessed waters do not meet water quality goals.

Total maximum daily loads (TMDLs) represent, in one commentator's view, the "new frontier" in accomplishing the CWA's goal of restoring and protecting our nation's waters. Warren, Total Maximum Daily Loads: A Watershed Approach to Improved Water Quality, ALI-ABA Course of Study Clean Water Act: Law and Regulations 115 (Oct. 23-25, 2002). The characterization of TMDLs as a "new frontier" might seem surprising given the inclusion of the TMDL provisions in the 1972 version of the CWA and the fact that the TMDL program's focus on ambient conditions harks back to pre-1972 water pollution initiatives. Professor Houck's apt phrase is that "[t]he TMDL process represents, in the short life of environmental law, an ancient approach to pollution control. . . . From the very first hint of federal involvement in water pollution control 50 years ago, states and pollution dischargers have fought a running battle to defend and, where lost, return to the local primacy and utilitarianism of regulation by water quality standards." O. Houck, The Clean Water Act TMDL Program: Law, Policy, and Implementation 12 (2d ed. 2002). The explanation lies in the limited progress made in implementing TMDLs for the first couple of decades of implementation of the CWA, and in the importance many attach to TMDLs, despite the track record of water quality–based approaches, as a potentially useful mechanism for advancing the CWA's goals.

The TMDL program is fairly straightforward at a broad conceptual level. It contains three key components. First, CWA §303(d) obligates states to identify and develop a priority ranking of waters where effluent limitations are not stringent enough to achieve an applicable water quality standard. The priority ranking is to be based on the "severity of the pollution and the uses to be made of such waters." §303(d)(1)(A). This list of impaired waters is sometimes referred to as the "CWA 303(d) list." Next, the government must set total TMDLs for specified pollutants for these waters—the maximum pollutant loading that the water body can handle without violating water quality standards. The TMDL is to take into account seasonal variations and incorporate a margin of safety that takes into account "any lack of knowledge concerning the relationship between effluent limitations and water quality." §303(d)(1)(C). Third, the government authorities must allocate this total loading among the various sources. Congress added §304(l) in 1987 to establish a time frame for implementing control strategies for point sources that discharge toxic pollutants. The details, as might be expected, have proven quite complex and raised numerous issues, discussed below.

The theory behind §303(d) was explained in House debates, where the theory originated and was incorporated into the final bill in conference:

> Section 303 contains provisions for the identification of waters where the technological standards are not stringent enough to implement applicable water quality standards. For these waterways, the States are required to establish load limits which are to be approved by the Administrator. These load limits would indicate, for those pollutants which are suitable for such calculations, the maximum quantity which can be discharged into the water and still not result in a violation of the water quality standards. It is believed that this information is needed for planning and enforcement and the managers expect that the States and the Administrator will be diligent and will make these studies in a timely fashion. [1972 Legislative History, at 246.]

b. Progress to Date in Implementing the TMDL program

Progress in implementing the water quality–based TMDL program was slow during the first 20-plus years of the CWA. Oliver Houck offers the following summary of the theory and reality of TMDL development, and the slow early pace of implementation:

> Section 303(d) provided a structure for water quality–based regulation. States would identify waters that remained polluted after the application of technology standards, they would determine the . . . TMDLs of pollutants that would bring these waters up to grade, and they would then allocate these loads among discharge sources in discharge permits and state water quality plans. If the states did not do it, EPA would.
>
> Only the states did none of it, and neither did EPA—until a series of federal court cases in the late 1980s and early 1990s began to crack the defenses, catching EPA and the states by surprise. A wave of litigation followed, state by state, compelling listings of impaired waters and schedules for first-ever TMDLs. [Houck, *supra*, at 5.]

The pace of TMDL development has picked up considerably over the past decade, in part because of citizen suits, although adoption and implementation of

TMDLs remains very much a work in progress. As of August 2006, EPA's website indicates that states have listed more than 35,000 waters as impaired (compared with the list of 22,000 such waters in December 2002, when the previous edition of this text was developed). http://oaspub.epa.gov/waters/national_rept.control. As of August 2006, EPA had approved more than 19,000 TMDLs, a significant increase over the 6,853 TMDLs the agency had approved as of December 2002. http://oaspub.epa.gov/waters/national_rept.control.

c. A More In-Depth Look at the TMDL Program

As noted above, each phase of the TMDL process has proven controversial. The first step in the §303 process is listing (although we divide the TMDL process into three basic steps, the grouping is artificial to some extent and there is overlap among the categories). There has been considerable inconsistency among the states in their approach to exercising this responsibility. For example, some states fail to include waters that do not meet water quality standards because of atmospheric deposition or temperature problems.* A 2001 National Research Council report indicates that some states have included waters on §303(d) lists without the data needed to show impairment or in spite of the fact that effluent limitations may address the problem. The NRC suggests a more in-depth process for listing to address these threshold issues. National Research Council, Assessing the TMDL Approach to Water Quality Management 52 (2001). There also has been litigation over the listing process. The Ninth Circuit, for example, has upheld EPA's view that a state's §303(d) list should include all impaired waters, including waters impaired by nonpoint sources. Pronsolino v. Nastri, 291 F.3d 1123 (9th Cir. 2002). Indiana's experience with its listing process reflects the dynamic and imprecise nature of the lists. Based on its five-year assessment of its water bodies, in 2002 Indiana's Department of Environmental Management more than doubled its number of impaired waters, from 209 to 428; in doing so, it made clear that the increase "does not necessarily mean the state's waterways have become more polluted but is merely a reflection of the assessment process being completed. . . ." The State indicated that the increase in the number of impaired waters is due to the collection of additional data. The State's ultimate conclusion based on this assessment was that "nearly all of the state's water bodies are polluted enough to limit their use for fishing, swimming, or drinking." State to Develop Remediation Plans as Number of Impaired Waterways Grows, 33 Env't Rep. (BNA) 2658 (2002).

Determining the TMDLs and allocating the total allowable loading among point sources and nonpoint sources have proven enormously difficult as well. Assessing the assimilative capacity of a water body can be extremely challenging technically, requiring consideration of flow and a wide variety of other factors. A TMDL is composed of waste load allocations (WLAs, or point source contributions), load allocations (LAs, or nonpoint source contributions), natural background, and a margin of safety. 40 C.F.R. §130.32. Each of these may be enormously complex. The National Research Council, for example, found that determination of the required "margin of safety" has proved contentious. National Research Council, *supra*, at 76. More

---

*National Clarifying Guidance for 1998 State and Territory Clean Water Act Section 303(d) Listing Decisions, http://www.epa.gov/OWOW/tmdl/lisgid.html.

generally, even the regulations seem to acknowledge the likelihood of significant variability in implementation, providing that load allocations are "best estimates . . . which may range from reasonably accurate estimates to gross allotments, depending on the availability of data and appropriate techniques for predicting the loading." 40 C.F.R. §130.2(g). TMDLs for water bodies for which narrative (rather than numeric) water quality standards have been established raise an additional set of challenges.

The Ninth Circuit's 2002 *Pronsolino* decision, which follows, addresses the threshold question of the types of waters a state must include in its §303(d) list and, in particular, whether §303(d) covers waters impaired solely by nonpoint sources.

PRONSOLINO v. NASTRI
291 F.3d 1123 (9th Cir. 2002)

BERZON, Circuit Judge: . . .

II. *Factual and Procedural Background*

A. THE GARCIA RIVER TMDL

In 1992, California submitted to the EPA a list of waters pursuant to §303(d)(1)(A). Pursuant to §303(d)(2), the EPA disapproved California's 1992 list because it omitted seventeen water segments that did not meet the water quality standards set by California for those segments. Sixteen of the seventeen water segments, including the Garcia River, were impaired only by nonpoint sources of pollution. After California rejected an opportunity to amend its §303(d)(1) list to include the seventeen sub-standard segments, the EPA, again acting pursuant to §303(d)(2), established a new §303(d)(1) list for California, including those segments on it. California retained the seventeen segments on its 1994, 1996, and 1998 §303(d)(1) lists.

California did not, however, establish TMDLs for the segments added by the EPA. Environmental and fishermen's groups sued the EPA in 1995 to require the EPA to establish TMDLs for the seventeen segments, and in a March 1997 consent decree the EPA agreed to do so. According to the terms of the consent decree, the EPA set March 18, 1998, as the deadline for the establishment of a TMDL for the Garcia River. When California missed the deadline despite having initiated public comment on a draft TMDL and having prepared a draft implementation plan, the EPA established a TMDL for the Garcia River. The EPA's TMDL differed only slightly from the state's draft TMDL.

The Garcia River TMDL for sediment is 552 tons per square mile per year, a sixty percent reduction from historical loadings. The TMDL allocates portions of the total yearly load among the following categories of nonpoint source pollution: a) "mass wasting" associated with roads; b) "mass wasting" associated with timber-harvesting; c) erosion related to road surfaces; and d) erosion related to road and skid trail crossings.

B. THE APPELLANTS

In 1960, appellants Betty and Guido Pronsolino purchased approximately 800 acres of heavily logged timber land in the Garcia River watershed. In 1998, after re-growth of the forest, the Pronsolinos applied for a harvesting permit from the California Department of Forestry ("Forestry").

In order to comply with the Garcia River TMDL, Forestry and/or the state's Regional Water Quality Control Board required, among other things, that the Pronsolinos' harvesting provide for mitigation of 90% of controllable road-related sediment run-off and contain prohibitions on removing certain trees and on harvesting from mid-October until May 1. The Pronsolinos' forester estimates that a large tree restriction will cost the Pronsolinos $750,000.

Larry Mailliard, a member of the Mendocino County Farm Bureau, submitted a draft harvesting permit on February 4, 1998, for a portion of his property in the Garcia River watershed. Forestry granted a final version of the permit after incorporation of a 60.3% reduction of sediment loading, a requirement included to comply with the Garcia River TMDL. Mr. Mailliard's forester estimates that the additional restrictions imposed to comply with the Garcia River TMDL will cost Mr. Mailliard $10,602,000. . . .

C. Proceedings Below

. . . [T]he Pronsolinos challenged the EPA's authority to impose TMDLs on rivers polluted only by nonpoint sources of pollution and sought a determination of whether the Act authorized the Garcia River TMDL. . . .

On August 6, 2000, the district court entered final judgment in favor of the EPA. The Pronsolinos timely filed this appeal. . . .

III. Analysis

A. Deference to the EPA . . .

The EPA regulations pertinent to §303(d)(1) lists and TMDLs focus on the attainment of water quality standards, whatever the source of any pollution. For instance, the EPA's regulations define TMDLs as the "sum of the individual WLAs [wasteload allocations] for point sources and LAs [load allocations] for nonpoint sources and natural background." 40 C.F.R. §130.2(i). Section 130.2 also defines a "wasteload allocation" as the "portion of a receiving water's loading capacity that is allocated to one of its existing or future point sources of pollution," §130.2(h), and a "load allocation" as the "portion of a receiving water's loading capacity that is attributed either to one of its existing or future nonpoint sources of pollution or to natural background sources," §130.2(g). The load allocation regulation also advises that, if possible, "natural and nonpoint source loads should be distinguished." Id. No reason appears why, under this TMDL definition, the amount of either point source loads or nonpoint source loads cannot be zero. If the wasteload allocation is zero, then the TMDL would cover only the nonpoint sources and natural background sources. So read, the regulation provides that a TMDL can apply where there is no wasteload allocation for point source pollution. . . .

Section 130.7 evinces the same understanding. That regulation directs states to identify those waters listed pursuant to §303(d)(1) that still require the establishment of TMDLs if:

> (i) Technology-based effluent limitations required by sections 301(b), 306, 307, or other sections of the Act; (ii) More stringent effluent limitations (including prohibitions)

required . . . ; and (iii) Other pollution control requirements (e.g., best management practices) required by local, State, or Federal authority are not stringent enough to implement any water quality standards . . . applicable to such waters.

§130.7(b)(1). "Best management practices" pertain to nonpoint sources of pollution. So, again, section 130.7 does not distinguish between sources of pollution for purposes of applying the TMDL requirement. Instead, control requirements applicable to either type of pollution receive equal treatment in the quest to achieve water quality standards.

Also consistent with application of the §303(d)(1) listing and TMDL requirements to waters impaired only by nonpoint sources is the regulation addressing water quality standards. Section 130.3 explains that "such standards serve the dual purposes of establishing the water quality goals for a specific water body and serving as the regulatory basis for establishment of water quality–based treatment controls and strategies beyond the technology-based level of treatment required. . . ." 40 C.F.R. §130.3. One purpose of water quality standards therefore—and not surprisingly—is to provide federally approved goals to be achieved *both* by state controls and by federal strategies *other* than point-source technology-based limitations. This purpose pertains to waters impaired by both point and nonpoint source pollution. The regulations addressing states' water quality management plans, intended to attain the promulgated water quality standards, confirm this understanding. Such plans must include, among other things, TMDLs, effluent limitations, and "*nonpoint* source management and control." 40 C.F.R. §130.6 (emphasis added).

In short, the EPA's regulations concerning §303(d)(1) lists and TMDLs apply whether a water body receives pollution from point sources only, nonpoint sources only, or a combination of the two. The EPA has issued directives concerning the states' CWA §303(d) requirements in conformity with this understanding of its regulations. See, e.g., Memorandum from Geoffrey Grubbs, Director, EPA Assessment and Watershed Protection Division, to Water Quality Branch Chiefs and TMDL Coordinators (Aug. 13, 1992) (Section 303(d)(1)(A) "applies equally to segments affected by point sources only, a combination of point and nonpoint sources, and nonpoint sources only."); EPA, National Clarifying Guidance for 1998 State and Territory Clean Water Act Section 303(d) Listing Decisions 6 (1997) ("Consistent with longstanding EPA policy, regulations, and practice, States should include waterbodies impaired by nonpoint sources alone on 1998 section 303(d)(1)(A) lists. . . .").

[After reviewing EPA's position, the court decided that this position warranted judicial deference.]

B. PLAIN MEANING AND STRUCTURAL ISSUES

1. THE COMPETING INTERPRETATIONS

Section 303(d)(1)(A) requires listing and calculation of TMDLs for "those waters within [the state's] boundaries for which the effluent limitations required by section [301(b)(1)(A)] and section [301(b)(1)(B)] of this title *are not stringent enough to implement any water quality standard* applicable to such waters." §303(d) (emphasis added). The precise statutory question before us is whether, as the Pronsolinos maintain, the term "not stringent enough to implement . . . water quality standards" as used in §303(d)(1)(A) must be interpreted to mean *both* that application of effluent limitations will not achieve water quality standards *and* that the waters at issue are subject to effluent limitations. As only waters with point source pollution are subject to effluent limitations, such an interpretation would exclude from the §303(d) listing and TMDL requirements waters impaired only by nonpoint sources of pollution.

The EPA, as noted, interprets "not stringent enough to implement . . . water quality standards" to mean "not adequate" or "not sufficient . . . to implement any water quality standard," and does not read the statute as implicitly containing a limitation to waters initially covered by effluent limitations. According to the EPA, if the use of effluent limitations will not implement applicable water quality standards, the water falls within §303(d)(1)(A) regardless of whether it is point or nonpoint sources, or a combination of the two, that continue to pollute the water.

2. THE LANGUAGE AND STRUCTURE OF §303(D)

Whether or not the appellants' suggested interpretation is entirely implausible, it is at least considerably weaker than the EPA's competing construction. The Pronsolinos' version necessarily relies upon: (1) understanding "stringent enough" to mean "strict enough" rather than "thoroughgoing enough" or "adequate" or "sufficient";[14] (2) reading the phrase "not stringent enough" in isolation, rather than with reference to the stated goal of implementing "any water quality standard applicable to such waters." Where the answer to the question "not stringent enough for what?" is "to implement any [applicable] water quality standard," the meaning of "stringent" should be determined by looking forward to the broad goal to be attained, not backwards at the inadequate effluent limitations. One might comment, for example, about a teacher that her standards requiring good spelling were not stringent enough to assure good writing, as her students still used bad grammar and poor logic. Based on the language of the contested phrase alone, then, the more sensible conclusion is that the §303(d)(1) list must contain any waters for which the particular effluent limitations will not be adequate to attain the statute's water quality goals.

Placing the phrase in its statutory context supports this conclusion. Section 303(d) begins with the requirement that each state identify those waters within its boundaries. . . . §303(d)(1)(A). So the statute's starting point for the listing project is a compilation of each and every navigable water within the state. Then, only those waters that will attain water quality standards after application of the new point source technology are excluded from the §303(d)(1) list, leaving all those waters for which that technology will not "implement any water quality standard applicable to such waters." §303(d)(1)(A); see American Wildlands v. Browner, 260 F.3d 1192, 1194 (10th Cir. 2001) ("Each state is required to identify all of the waters within its borders not meeting water quality standards and establish [TMDLs] for those waters.") (citing §303(d)); *Pronsolino*, 91 F. Supp. 2d at 1347. The alternative construction, in contrast,

14. Stringent means "rigorous, strict, thoroughgoing; rigorously binding or coercive." Oxford English Dictionary Online (2001). Defining "stringent" as "rigorous" or "strict" would lend support to the Pronsolinos' interpretation. If "stringent" means "thoroughgoing," however, §303(d)(1)(A) would encompass the EPA's broader reading of the statute. Also, "stringent enough" may have a slightly different meaning from "stringent" standing alone, such as "adequate" or "sufficient." See 1 Legislative History of the Water Pollution Control Act Amendments of 1972 at 792 (1973) (Legislative History) (H.R. Rep. 92-911 to accompany H.R. 11896 (March 11, 1972)) (using the term "are inadequate" in place of "not stringent enough").

would begin with a subset of all the state's waterways, those that have point sources subject to effluent limitations, and would result in a list containing only a subset of that subset—those waters as to which the applicable effluent limitations are not adequate to attain water quality standards.

The Pronsolinos' contention to the contrary notwithstanding, no such odd reading of the statute is necessary in order to give meaning to the phrase "for which the effluent limitations required by section [301(b)(1)(A)] and section [301(b)(1)(B)] . . . are not stringent enough." The EPA interprets §303(d)(1)(A) to require the identification of any waters not meeting water quality standards only if specified effluent limitations would not achieve those standards. 40 C.F.R. §130.2(j). If the pertinent effluent limitations would, if implemented, achieve the water quality standards but are not in place yet, there need be no listing and no TMDL calculation. Id.

So construed, the meaning of the statute is different than it would be were the language recast to state only that "[e]ach State shall identify those waters within its boundaries . . . [not meeting] any water quality standard applicable to such waters." Under the EPA's construction, the reference to effluent limitations reflects Congress' intent that the EPA focus initially on implementing effluent limitations and only later avert its attention to water quality standards. . . .

Given all these language considerations, it is not surprising that the only time this court addressed the reach of §303(d)(1)(A), it rejected a reading of §303(d)(1)(A) similar to the one the Pronsolinos now proffer. In *Dioxin*, 57 F.3d at 1526-27, the plaintiffs argued that the phrase "not stringent enough" prohibited the EPA from listing under §303(d)(1)(A) and establishing TMDLs for toxic pollutants, until after the implementation and proven failure of §301(b)(1)(A) "best practicable technology" effluent limitations. Toxic pollutants, however, are not subject to "best practical technology" controls, but to more demanding "best available technology," precisely because of their toxicity. Id.

The court in *Dioxin* held that the EPA acted within its statutory authority in setting TMDLs for toxic pollutants, even though the effluent limitations referenced by §303(d)(1)(A) did not apply to those pollutants. 57 F.3d at 1528. The court explained that, since best practical technology effluent limitations do not apply to toxic pollutants, those limitations are, as a matter of law, "not stringent enough" to achieve water quality standards. Id. In other words, *Dioxin* read §303(d)(1)(A) as applying to all waters in the state, not only to the subset covered by certain kinds of effluent controls, and it understood "not stringent enough" to mean "not adequate for" or "inapplicable to."

Nothing in §303(d)(1)(A) distinguishes the treatment of point sources and non-point sources as such; the only reference is to the "effluent limitations required by" §301(b)(1). So if the effluent limitations required by §301(b)(1) are "as a matter of law" "not stringent enough" to achieve the applicable water quality standards for waters impaired by point sources not subject to those requirements, then they are also "not stringent enough" to achieve applicable water quality standards for other waters not subject to those requirements, in this instance because they are impacted only by nonpoint sources. Additionally, the *Dioxin* court, applying *Chevron* deference, upheld the EPA's interpretation of §303(d) "as requiring TMDLs where existing pollution controls will not lead to attainment of water standards," 57 F.3d at 1527; see also 40 C.F.R. §130.7(b), a holding that directly encompasses waters polluted by nonpoint sources.

3. THE STATUTORY SCHEME AS A WHOLE

The Pronsolinos' objection to this view of §303(d), and of *Dioxin*, is, in essence, that the CWA as a whole distinguishes between the regulatory schemes applicable to point and nonpoint sources, so we must assume such a distinction in applying §§303(d)(1)(A) and (C). We would hesitate in any case to read into a discrete statutory provision something that is not there because it is contained elsewhere in the statute. But here, the premise is wrong: There is no such general division throughout the CWA.

Point sources are treated differently from nonpoint sources for many purposes under the statute, but not all. In particular, there is no such distinction with regard to the basic purpose for which the §303(d) list and TMDLs are compiled, the eventual attainment of state-defined water quality standards. Water quality standards reflect a state's designated *uses* for a water body and do not depend in any way upon the source of pollution. See §303(a)-(c). . . .

Additionally, §303(d) follows the subsections setting forth the requirements for water quality standards, §303(a)-(c)—which, as noted above, apply without regard to the source of pollution—and precedes the "continuing planning process" subsection, §303(e), which applies broadly as well. Thus, §303(d) is structurally part of a set of provisions governing an interrelated goal-setting, information-gathering, and planning process that, unlike many other aspects of the CWA, applies without regard to the source of pollution.

True, there are, as the Pronsolinos point out, two sections of the statute as amended, §208 and §319, that set requirements exclusively for nonpoint sources of pollution. But the structural inference we are asked to draw from those specialized sections—that no *other* provisions of the Act set requirements for waters polluted by nonpoint sources—simply does not follow. Absent some irreconcilable contradiction between the requirements contained in §§208 and 319, on the one hand, and the listing and TMDL requirements of §303(d), on the other, both apply.

There is no such contradiction. Section 208 provides for federal grants to encourage the development of state areawide waste treatment management plans for areas with substantial water quality problems, §208(a), (f), and requires that those plans include a process for identifying and controlling nonpoint source pollution "to the extent feasible." §208(b)(2)(F). Section 319, added to the CWA in 1987, directs states to adopt "nonpoint source management programs;" provides grants for nonpoint source pollution reduction; and requires states to submit a report to the EPA that "identifies those navigable waters within the State which, without additional action to control nonpoint sources of pollution, cannot reasonably be expected to attain or maintain applicable water quality standards or the goals and requirements of this chapter." §319(a)(1)(A). This report must also describe state programs for reducing nonpoint source pollution and the process "to reduce, to the maximum extent practicable, the level of pollution" resulting from particular categories of nonpoint source pollution. §319(a)(1)(C), (D).

The CWA is replete with multiple listing and planning requirements applicable to the same waterways (quite confusingly so, indeed), so no inference can be drawn from the overlap alone. See, e.g., §208(b); §303(d)(1)(A), (d)(1)(B), (d)(3), (e); CWA §304(*l*); §319(a). Nor are we willing to draw the more discrete inference that the §303(d) listing and TMDL requirements cannot apply to nonpoint source pollutants because the planning requirements imposed by §208 and §319 are qualified ones—

"to the extent feasible" and "to the maximum extent practicable"—while the §303(d) requirements are unbending. For one thing, the water quality standards set under §303 are functional and may permit more pollution than it is "feasible" or "practicable" to eliminate, depending upon the intended use of a particular waterway. For another, with or without TMDLs, the §303(e) plans for attaining water quality standards must, without qualification, account for elimination of nonpoint source pollution to the extent necessary to meet those standards. §303(e)(3)(F). . . .

Essentially, §319 encourages the states to institute an approach to the elimination of nonpoint source pollution similar to the federally mandated effluent controls contained in the CWA, while §303 encompasses a water quality based approach applicable to all sources of water pollution. As various sections of the Act encourage different, and complementary, state schemes for cleaning up nonpoint source pollution in the nation's waterways, there is no basis for reading any of those sections—including §303(d)—out of the statute.

There is one final aspect of the Act's structure that bears consideration because it supports the EPA's interpretation of §303(d): The list required by §303(d)(1)(A) requires that waters be listed if they are impaired by a combination of point sources and nonpoint sources; the language admits of no other reading. Section 303(d)(1)(C), in turn, directs that TMDLs shall be established at a level necessary *to implement* the applicable water quality standards. . . . Id. (emphasis added). So, at least in blended waters, TMDLs must be calculated with regard to nonpoint sources of pollution; otherwise, it would be impossible "to implement the applicable water quality standards," which do not differentiate sources of pollution. This court has so recognized. *Browner*, 20 F.3d at 985 ("Congress and the EPA have already determined that establishing TMDLs is an effective tool for achieving water quality standards in waters impacted by non-point source pollution.").

Nothing in the statutory structure—or purpose—suggests that Congress meant to distinguish, as to §303(d)(1) lists and TMDLs, between waters with one insignificant point source and substantial nonpoint source pollution and waters with only nonpoint source pollution. Such a distinction would, for no apparent reason, require the states or the EPA to monitor waters to determine whether a point source had been added or removed, and to adjust the §303(d)(1) list and establish TMDLs accordingly. There is no statutory basis for concluding that Congress intended such an irrational regime.

Looking at the statute as a whole, we conclude that the EPA's interpretation of §303(d) is not only entirely reasonable but considerably more convincing than the one offered by the plaintiffs in this case.

C.   FEDERALISM CONCERNS

The Pronsolinos finally contend that, by establishing TMDLs for waters impaired only by nonpoint source pollution, the EPA has upset the balance of federal-state control established in the CWA by intruding into the state's traditional control over land use. That is not the case.

The Garcia River TMDL identifies the maximum load of pollutants that can enter the Garcia River from certain broad categories of nonpoint sources if the river is to attain water quality standards. It does not specify the load of pollutants that may be received from particular parcels of land or describe what measures the state should take to implement the TMDL. Instead, the TMDL expressly recognizes that "implementation and monitoring" "are state responsibilities" and notes that, for this reason, the EPA did not include implementation or monitoring plans within the TMDL.

Moreover, §303(e) requires—separately from the §303(d)(1) listing and TMDL requirements—that each state include in its continuing planning process "adequate implementation, including schedules of compliance, for revised or new water quality standards" "for all navigable waters within such State." §303(e)(3). The Garcia River TMDL thus serves as an informational tool for the creation of the state's implementation plan, independently—and explicitly—required by Congress.

California chose both *if* and *how* it would implement the Garcia River TMDL. States must implement TMDLs only to the extent that they seek to avoid losing federal grant money; there is no pertinent statutory provision otherwise requiring implementation of §303 plans or providing for their enforcement. *See* CWA §309; CWA §505.[19]

Finally, it is worth noting that the arguments that the Pronsolinos raise here would apply equally to nonpoint source pollution controls for blended waters. Yet, as discussed above, Congress definitely required that the states or the EPA establish TMDLs for all pollutants in waters on §303(d)(1) lists, including blended waters.

We conclude that the Pronsolinos' federalism basis for reading §303 against its own words and structure is unfounded.

IV.   Conclusion

For all the reasons we have surveyed, the CWA is best read to include in the §303(d) listing and TMDLs requirements waters impaired only by nonpoint sources of pollution. . . . We therefore hold that the EPA did not exceed its statutory authority in identifying the Garcia River pursuant to §303(d)(1)(A) and establishing the Garcia River TMDL, even though the river is polluted only by nonpoint sources of pollution.

The decision of the district court is AFFIRMED.

NOTES AND QUESTIONS

1. *Additional Issues Relating to Listing.* Numerous issues have arisen concerning the nature of states' listing authority and responsibility and EPA's oversight obligations. For example, under what circumstances may a state decline to list a water body on the basis that the data supporting listing are problematic? When do listing decisions trigger ESA consultation requirements? See American Littoral Soc'y v. EPA, 199 F. Supp. 2d 217 (D.N.J. 2002); Sierra Club v. EPA, 162 F. Supp. 2d 406 (D. Md. 2001).

19. See also Professor Houck's summary:

> Within the statutory scheme §319 is the carrot, funding state programs for nonpoint source abatement statewide, for all waters whether they are currently above standard or below. In keeping with its broad sweep, §319's provisions are voluntary. States may choose to participate or not. . . . Section 303(d), on the other hand, addresses a narrower and more nasty job: the chronically polluted waters of the United States. For this problem zone, enter a stick: quantified pollution load allocations. The nature of the allocations and of the implementing controls remains up to the states, but states do have to come up with them. [The Clean Water Act TMDL Program 62.]

2. *More on the Content of TMDLs*. In NRDC v. Muszynski, 268 F.3d 91 (2d Cir. 2001), the Second Circuit, in a challenge to EPA's approval of a phosphorus TMDL for 19 New York City reservoirs, held that EPA could establish an annual TMDL as a measure of mass per time "where such an alternative measure best serves the purpose of effective regulation of pollutant levels in waterbodies." The challengers alleged that TMDLs have to be expressed in daily loads. In Friends of the Earth, Inc. v. EPA, 446 F.3d 140 (D.C. Cir. 2006), the D.C. Circuit vacated non-daily loads incorporated into a TMDL on the ground that TMDLs must be daily loads. The D.C. Circuit rejected the reasoning of the *Muszynski* Second Circuit decision that reading "daily" to mean daily would be "absurd," noting that "agencies seeking to demonstrate absurdity have an exceptionally high burden" and that EPA had failed to meet that burden. Id. at 146. EPA issued a Memorandum clarifying its position on the issues involved in November 2006. Memo Clarifying EPA's Position on the Use of Daily Time Increment When Establishing Total Maximum Daily Loads for Pollutants, Daily Env't Rep. (BNA) (Nov. 15, 2006), at E-1.

3. *Federalism Issues: EPA's Responsibility in Setting TMDLs*. One of the most frequently litigated issues has concerned when EPA must step in to set TMDLs. Several courts, including the Ninth and Tenth Circuits, rejected challenges under numerous theories to lack of progress in setting TMDLs. See, e.g., San Francisco Baykeeper v. Whitman, 297 F.3d 877 (9th Cir. 2002); Hayes v. Whitman, 264 F.3d 1017 (10th Cir. 2001). An attorney for environmental groups in several TMDL cases characterizes the state of the case law as follows:

> [R]egardless of legal theory (constructive submission, mandatory duty, arbitrary and capricious, abuse of discretion, unreasonable delay, etc.), [several circuit and district courts] declined to order EPA to step in to set TMDLs. The standard for ordering EPA to comply is nearly insurmountable, requiring both (1) an explicit refusal by a state to take *any* TMDL action, and (2) unreasonable EPA delay in declaring such refusal a "constructive submission" of no TMDLs. Not surprisingly, no state is so bold as to declare the intent to refuse to participate in the TMDL program, and EPA has many reasons for delay. Thus, despite the hype, the constructive submission doctrine and related theories appear moribund. [May, Recent Developments in TMDL Litigation 1999-2002 135 (ALI-ABA Course on Clean Water Act Course of Study Materials, Oct. 23-25, 2002).]

4. *The Role of Consent Decrees*. EPA has negotiated consent decrees in numerous states to resolve TMDL-related litigation. These cases typically establish schedules for the involved state to complete its responsibilities, but may involve a host of substantive and other issues as well. EPA maintains information concerning these decrees and other developments in TMDL litigation on its website. http://www.epa.gov/owow/tmdl/lawsuit1.html.

5. *State Courts Have a Role in TMDL Litigation*. The Minnesota Court of Appeals held in In re Annandale and Maple Lake NPDES/SPS Permit, 702 N.W.2d 768 (Minn. Ct. App. 2005), that the state could not issue an NPDES permit to a proposed wastewater treatment plant because the facility would contribute to the impairment of §303(d) waters. It also held that a TMDL does not need to be in place before a discharge to an impaired water may be approved, so long as the new discharge "does not cause or contribute to the violation of water quality standards." A Virginia appellate court reached the same conclusion on the latter point. Crutchfield v. State Water Control Bd., 612 S.E.2d 249, 255 (Va. App. 2005). On the other hand, a Texas

court ruled that a TMDL-type allocation must be in place before new discharges can be authorized into impaired waters. City of Waco v. Texas Natural Res. Conservation Comm'n, Cause No. GV1-03893, et seq., (May 6, 2004).

6. *Outstanding Issues.* In theory, TMDLs are to be allocated in part to point sources, and the permits of these sources are to be modified to reflect the load allocated to them. It remains to be seen how effective this mechanism will be, but the mechanism is fairly well established. EPA has stated that "[w]hen a TMDL is developed for waters impaired by point sources only, the issuance of a . . . (NPDES) permit(s) provides the reasonable assurance that the wasteload allocations contained in the TMDL will be achieved." EPA, Guidelines for Reviewing TMDLs under Existing Regulations Issued in 1992 (May 20, 2002). The waters are murkier when it comes to the application of TMDLs in the nonpoint source context. The TMDL program is intended to identify nonpoint pollution as a source of impairment. See, e.g., *Pronsolino, supra.* EPA contemplates that states, in developing and allocating a TMDL, may allocate a portion of the total load to nonpoint sources. 40 C.F.R. §130.32(b)(7). How much of a burden is the government likely to impose on nonpoint sources? Will this burden be sufficient to achieve the TMDL program's goals of achieving WQSs? Are the government's current tools adequate for it to ensure that nonpoint source discharges conform to the amounts allocated to them in the TMDL process (the "load allocations")? EPA explains how the approach is supposed to work, and that the end result is supposed to be that the TMDL will achieve water quality standards, as follows:

> When a TMDL is developed for waters impaired by both point and nonpoint sources, and the WLA is based on an assumption that nonpoint source load reductions will occur, EPA's 1991 TMDL Guidance states that the TMDL should provide reasonable assurances that nonpoint source control measures will achieve expected load reductions in order for the TMDL to be approvable. This information is necessary for EPA to determine that the TMDL, including the load and wasteload allocations, has been established at a level necessary to implement water quality standards. [EPA, Guidelines for Reviewing TMDLs under Existing Regulations Issued in 1992 (May 20, 2002).]

The devil is likely to be in the details, in short. A state is required to provide assurances persuading EPA that the state's nonpoint source control measures will achieve the expected load reductions. Absent such assurances, EPA is not supposed to provide the required approval. Key implementation questions, therefore, will include (a) the types of assurances states are providing; (b) the level of EPA scrutiny of such assurances; (c) EPA action in cases where the assurances do not pass muster; and (d) monitoring and follow-up on the implementation end to determine whether the allocated reductions are actually occurring and, if not, the adequacy of steps taken to put the program on the intended track.

7. *Updated EPA Guidance on TMDLs.* In an August 2, 2006, memorandum EPA clarifies its 1991 Guidance for Water Quality-Based Decisions: The TMDL Process. The agency's memorandum reinforces that all TMDLs "must be established at a level necessary to meet water quality standards," and identifies a series of situations in which different approaches to TMDL development and implementation (including "staged implementation," adaptive approaches, and the like) are used. Benita Best-Wong, Clarification Regarding "Phased" Total Maximum Daily Loads (Aug. 2, 2006).

4. Section 401 Certifications

Section 401 of the CWA gives states another tool to advance water protection goals. Certain types of projects that may discharge pollutants into waters, such as power plants, are subject to federal permitting. Section 401 gives states a special "seat at the table" in such proceedings. In S.D. Warren Co. v. Maine Bd. of Envtl. Prot., 126 S. Ct. 1843 (2006), the Court unanimously held that state regulators have authority under §401 to require water flowing through dams to meet their water quality standards. The Court held that water passing through a dam constitutes a "discharge" that triggers the §401 certification requirement. The Court distinguished §401 "discharges" from §402 "discharges of a pollutant," holding that the latter but not the former require "addition" of a "pollutant." At least one commentator has concluded that, as a result, the *Warren* case is "not likely to have significant implications for the scope of state NPDES permit authority." Glick, State Authority & Hydropower, Water Rep. No. 28 (June 15, 2006). The following case explores the parameters of this mechanism.

PUD NO. 1 OF JEFFERSON COUNTY v. WASHINGTON DEPARTMENT OF ECOLOGY
511 U.S. 700 (1994)

JUSTICE O'CONNOR delivered the opinion of the Court.

Petitioners, a city and a local utility district, want to build a hydroelectric project on the Dosewallips River in Washington State. We must decide whether respondent state environmental agency (hereinafter respondent) properly conditioned a permit for the project on the maintenance of specific minimum stream flows to protect salmon and steelhead runs. . . .

I

The State of Washington has adopted comprehensive water quality standards intended to regulate all of the State's navigable waters. The State created an inventory of all the State's waters, and divided the waters into five classes. Each individual fresh surface water of the State is placed into one of these classes. The Dosewallips River is classified AA, extraordinary. . . .

In addition to these specific standards applicable to Class AA waters, the State has adopted a statewide antidegradation policy. That policy provides:

(a) Existing beneficial uses shall be maintained and protected and no further degradation which would interfere with or become injurious to existing beneficial uses will be allowed.

(b) No degradation will be allowed of waters lying in national parks, national recreation areas, national wildlife refuges, national scenic rivers, and other areas of national ecological importance. . . .

(f) In no case, will any degradation of water quality be allowed if this degradation interferes with or becomes injurious to existing water uses and causes long-term and irreparable harm to the environment. [WAC 173-201-035(8).]

As required by the Act, EPA reviewed and approved the State's water quality standards. See 33 U.S.C. §1313(c)(3). Upon approval by EPA, the state standard became "the water quality standard for the applicable waters of that State." 33 U.S.C. §1313(c)(3).

States are responsible for enforcing water quality standards on intrastate waters. §1319(a). In addition to these primary enforcement responsibilities, §401 of the Act requires States to provide a water quality certification before a federal license or permit can be issued for activities that may result in any discharge into intrastate navigable waters. 33 U.S.C. §1341. Specifically, §401 requires an applicant for a federal license or permit to conduct any activity "which may result in any discharge into the navigable waters" to obtain from the State a certification "that any such discharge will comply with the applicable provisions of sections [1311, 1312, 1313, 1316, and 1317 of this title]." 33 U.S.C. §1341(a). Section 401(d) further provides that "[a]ny certification . . . shall set forth any effluent limitations and other limitations, and monitoring requirements necessary to assure that any applicant . . . will comply with any applicable effluent limitations and other limitations, under section [1311 or 1312 of this title] . . . and with any other appropriate requirement of State law set forth in such certification." 33 U.S.C. §1341(d). The limitations included in the certification become a condition on any federal license. Ibid.

II

Petitioners propose to build the Elkhorn Hydroelectric Project on the Dosewallips River. If constructed as presently planned, the facility would be located just outside the Olympic National Park on federally owned land within the Olympic National Forest. The project would divert water from a 1.2-mile reach of the river (the bypass reach), run the water through turbines to generate electricity and then return the water to the river below the bypass reach. Under the Federal Power Act, 16 U.S.C. §791a et seq., the Federal Energy Regulatory Commission (FERC) has authority to license new hydroelectric facilities. As a result, petitioners must get a FERC license to build or operate the Elkhorn Project. Because a federal license is required, and because the project may result in discharges into the Dosewallips River, petitioners are also required to obtain state certification of the project pursuant to §401 of the Clean Water Act, 33 U.S.C. §1341.

[The river supports coho and chinook salmon and steelhead trout. The Washington State Department of Ecology imposed a minimum stream flow requirement of 100 to 200 cubic feet per second. A state administrative appeals board rejected the condition because it was imposed to enhance, not maintain, the fishery and thus was outside the scope of §401. The state Supreme Court upheld the minimum flow requirements, and the Supreme Court accepted certiorari to resolve a conflict among state supreme courts about the scope of §401.]

III

The principal dispute in this case concerns whether the minimum stream flow requirement that the State imposed on the Elkhorn Project is a permissible condition of a §401 certification under the Clean Water Act. To resolve this dispute we must first determine the scope of the State's authority under §401. We must then determine whether the limitation at issue here, the requirement that petitioners maintain minimum stream flows, falls within the scope of that authority.

A

There is no dispute that petitioners were required to obtain a certification from the State pursuant to §401. Petitioners concede that, at a minimum, the project will result in two possible discharges—the release of dredged and fill material during the construction of the project, and the discharge of water at the end of the tailrace after the water has been used to generate electricity. Petitioners contend, however, that the minimum stream flow requirement imposed by the State was unrelated to these specific discharges, and that as a consequence, the State lacked the authority under §401 to condition its certification on maintenance of stream flows sufficient to protect the Dosewallips fishery.

If §401 consisted solely of subsection (a), which refers to a state certification that a "discharge" will comply with certain provisions of the Act, petitioners' assessment of the scope of the State's certification authority would have considerable force. Section 401, however, also contains subsection (d), which expands the State's authority to impose conditions on the certification of a project. Section 401(d) provides that any certification shall set forth "any effluent limitations and other limitations . . . necessary to assure that *any applicant*" will comply with various provisions of the Act and appropriate state law requirements. 33 U.S.C. §1341(d) (emphasis added). The language of this subsection contradicts petitioners' claim that the State may only impose water quality limitations specifically tied to a "discharge." The text refers to the compliance of the applicant, not the discharge. Section 401(d) thus allows the State to impose "other limitations" on the project in general to assure compliance with various provisions of the Clean Water Act and with "any other appropriate requirement of State law." Although the dissent asserts that this interpretation of §401(d) renders §401(a)(1) superfluous, we see no such anomaly. Section 401(a)(1) identifies the category of activities subject to certification—namely, those with discharges. And §401(d) is most reasonably read as authorizing additional conditions and limitations on the activity as a whole once the threshold condition, the existence of a discharge, is satisfied. . . .

We agree with the State that ensuring compliance with §303 is a proper function of the §401 certification. Although §303 is not one of the statutory provisions listed in §401(d), the statute allows States to impose limitations to ensure compliance with §301 of the Act, 33 U.S.C. §1311. Section 301 in turn incorporates §303 by reference. See 33 U.S.C. §1311(b)(1)(C); see also H.R. Conf. Rep. No. 95-830, p. 96 (1977), U.S. Code Cong. & Admin. News 1977, pp. 4326, 4471 ("Section 303 is always included by reference where section 301 is listed"). As a consequence, state water quality standards adopted pursuant to §303 are among the "other limitations" with which a State may ensure compliance through the §401 certification process. This interpretation is consistent with EPA's view of the statute. . . . [3]

3. The dissent asserts that §301 is concerned solely with discharges, not broader water quality standards. Although §301 does make certain discharges unlawful, see 33 U.S.C. §1311(a), it also contains a broad enabling provision which requires States to take certain actions, to wit: "In order to carry out the objective of this chapter [viz. the chemical, physical, and biological integrity of the Nation's water] there shall be achieved . . . not later than July 1, 1977, any more stringent limitation, including those necessary to meet water quality standards, . . . established pursuant to any State law or regulations. . . ." 33 U.S.C. §1311(b)(1)(C). This provision of §301 expressly refers to state water quality standards, and is not limited to discharges.

B

Having concluded that, pursuant to §401, States may condition certification upon any limitations necessary to ensure compliance with state water quality standards or any other "appropriate requirement of State law," we consider whether the minimum flow condition is such a limitation. Under §303, state water quality standards must "consist of the designated uses of the navigable waters involved and the water quality criteria for such waters based upon such uses." 33 U.S.C. §1313(c)(2)(A). In imposing the minimum stream flow requirement, the State determined that construction and operation of the project as planned would be inconsistent with one of the designated uses of Class AA water, namely "[s]almonid [and other fish] migration, rearing, spawning, and harvesting." App. to Pet. for Cert. 83a-84a. The designated use of the river as a fish habitat directly reflects the Clean Water Act's goal of maintaining the "chemical, physical, and biological integrity of the Nation's waters." 33 U.S.C. §1251(a). Indeed, the Act defines pollution as "the man-made or man induced alteration of the chemical, physical, biological, and radiological integrity of water." §1362(19). Moreover, the Act expressly requires that, in adopting water quality standards, the State must take into consideration the use of waters for "propagation of fish and wildlife." §1313(c)(2)(A).

Petitioners assert, however, that §303 requires the State to protect designated uses solely through implementation of specific "criteria." According to petitioners, the State may not require them to operate their dam in a manner consistent with a designated "use"; instead, say petitioners, under §303 the State may only require that the project comply with specific numerical "criteria."

We disagree with petitioners' interpretation of the language of §303(c)(2)(A). Under the statute, a water quality standard must "consist of the designated uses of the navigable waters involved *and* the water quality criteria for such waters based upon such uses." 33 U.S.C. §1313(c)(2)(A) (emphasis added). The text makes it plain that water quality standards contain two components. We think the language of §303 is most naturally read to require that a project be consistent with both components, namely, the designated use and the water quality criteria. Accordingly, under the literal terms of the statute, a project that does not comply with a designated use of the water does not comply with the applicable water quality standards.

Consequently, pursuant to §401(d) the State may require that a permit applicant comply with both the designated uses and the water quality criteria of the state standards. In granting certification pursuant to §401(d), the State "shall set forth any . . . limitations . . . necessary to assure that [the applicant] will comply with any . . . limitations under [§303] . . . and with any other appropriate requirement of State law." A certification requirement that an applicant operate the project consistently with state water quality standards—i.e., consistently with the designated uses of the water body and the water quality criteria—is both a "limitation" to assure "compl[iance] with . . . limitations" imposed under §303, and an "appropriate" requirement of state law. . . .

The State also justified its minimum stream flow as necessary to implement the "antidegradation policy" of §303, 33 U.S.C. §1313(d)(4)(B). When the Clean Water Act was enacted in 1972, the water quality standards of all 50 States had antidegradation provisions. These provisions were required by federal law. By providing in 1972 that existing state water quality standards would remain in force until revised, the

Clean Water Act ensured that the States would continue their antidegradation programs. See 33 U.S.C. §1313(a). EPA has consistently required that revised state standards incorporate an antidegradation policy. And, in 1987, Congress explicitly
recognized the existence of an "antidegradation policy established under [§303]."
§1313(d)(4)(B).

EPA has promulgated regulations implementing §303's antidegradation
policy. . . . These regulations require States to "develop and adopt a statewide antidegradation policy and identify the methods for implementing such policy." 40 CFR
§131.12 (1993). These "implementation methods shall, at a minimum, be consistent
with the . . . [e]xisting instream water uses and the level of water quality necessary to
protect the existing uses shall be maintained and protected." Ibid. EPA has explained
that under its antidegradation regulation, "no activity is allowable . . . which could
partially or completely eliminate any existing use." EPA, Questions and Answers on
Antidegradation 3 (Aug. 1985). Thus, States must implement their antidegradation
policy in a manner "consistent" with existing uses of the stream. The State of Washington's antidegradation policy in turn provides that "[e]xisting beneficial uses shall be
maintained and protected and no further degradation which would interfere with or
become injurious to existing beneficial uses will be allowed." WAC 173-201-
035(8)(a)(1986). The State concluded that the reduced stream flows would have
just the effect prohibited by this policy. The Solicitor General, representing EPA,
asserts, and we agree, that the State's minimum stream flow condition is a proper
application of the state and federal antidegradation regulations, as it ensures that an
"existing in-stream water us[e]" will be "maintained and protected." 40 CFR
§131.12(a)(1)(1993).

Petitioners also assert more generally that the Clean Water Act is only concerned
with water "quality," and does not allow the regulation of water "quantity." This is an
artificial distinction. In many cases, water quantity is closely related to water quality; a
sufficient lowering of the water quantity in a body of water could destroy all of its
designated uses, be it for drinking water, recreation, navigation or, as here, as a fishery.
In any event, there is recognition in the Clean Water Act itself that reduced stream
flow, i.e., diminishment of water quantity, can constitute water pollution. First, the
Act's definition of pollution as "the man-made or man induced alteration of the
chemical, physical, biological, and radiological integrity of water" encompasses
the effects of reduced water quantity. 33 U.S.C. §1362(19). This broad conception
of pollution—one which expressly evinces Congress' concern with the physical and
biological integrity of water—refutes petitioners' assertion that the Act draws a
sharp distinction between the regulation of water "quantity" and water "quality."
Moreover, §304 of the Act expressly recognizes that water "pollution" may result
from "changes in the movement, flow, or circulation of any navigable waters . . . ,
including changes caused by the construction of dams." 33 U.S.C. §1314(f). This
concern with the flowage effects of dams and other diversions is also embodied in the
EPA regulations, which expressly require existing dams to be operated to attain
designated uses.

Petitioners assert that two other provisions of the Clean Water Act, §§101(g) and
510(2), 33 U.S.C. §§1251(g) and 1370(2), exclude the regulation of water quantity
from the coverage of the Act. Section 101(g) provides "that the authority of each State
to allocate quantities of water within its jurisdiction shall not be superseded, abrogated
or otherwise impaired by this chapter." 33 U.S.C. §1251(g). Similarly, §510(2) provides that nothing in the Act shall "be construed as impairing or in any manner

affecting any right or jurisdiction of the States with respect to the waters . . . of such States." 33 U.S.C. §1370. In petitioners' view, these provisions exclude "water quantity issues from direct regulation under the federally controlled water quality standards authorized in §303."

This language gives the States authority to allocate water rights; we therefore find it peculiar that petitioners argue that it prevents the State from regulating stream flow. In any event, we read these provisions more narrowly than petitioners. Sections 101(g) and 510(2) preserve the authority of each State to allocate water quantity as between users; they do not limit the scope of water pollution controls that may be imposed on users who have obtained, pursuant to state law, a water allocation. In California v. FERC, 495 U.S. 490, 498 (1990), construing an analogous provision of the Federal Power Act, we explained that "minimum stream flow requirements neither reflect nor establish 'proprietary rights' " to water. Moreover, the certification itself does not purport to determine petitioners' proprietary right to the water of the Dosewallips. . . .

IV

Petitioners contend that we should limit the State's authority to impose minimum flow requirements because FERC has comprehensive authority to license hydro-electric projects pursuant to the FPA, 16 U.S.C. §791a et seq. In petitioners' view, the minimum flow requirement imposed here interferes with FERC's authority under the FPA. . . .

No such conflict with any FERC licensing activity is presented here. FERC has not yet acted on petitioners' license application, and it is possible that FERC will eventually deny petitioners' application altogether. Alternatively, it is quite possible, given that FERC is required to give equal consideration to the protection of fish habitat when deciding whether to issue a license, that any FERC license would contain the same conditions as the state §401 certification. Indeed, at oral argument the Deputy Solicitor General stated that both EPA and FERC were represented in this proceeding, and that the Government has no objection to the stream flow condition contained in the §401 certification. . . .

In summary, we hold that the State may include minimum stream flow requirements in a certification issued pursuant to §401 of the Clean Water Act insofar as necessary to enforce a designated use contained in a state water quality standard. The judgment of the Supreme Court of Washington, accordingly, is AFFIRMED.

While the Court held that a state may set minimum flow standards in exercising its §401 certification requirements, must it do so? See, e.g., Great Basin Mine Watch v. Hankins, 456 F.3d 955 (9th Cir. 2006). Though the Supreme Court in the preceding case appeared to give a broad reading to a state's authority under §401 to protect its waters, in the following case the Ninth Circuit identified limits in this authority, notably that it does not empower the states to address nonpoint source releases.

OREGON NATURAL DESERT ASSOCIATION v. DOMBECK
172 F.3d 1092 (9th Cir. 1998)

SCHROEDER, Circuit Judge:

The United States Forest Service appeals the district court's ruling that pollution from cattle grazing is subject to the certification requirement of §401 of the Clean Water Act, 33 U.S.C. §1341. This appeal requires us to consider whether the term "discharge" in §1341 includes releases from nonpoint sources as well as releases from point sources. We conclude from the language and structure of the Act that the certification requirement of §1341 was meant to apply only to point source releases. Accordingly, we reverse.

The background of this case can be briefly described. In 1993 the Forest Service issued a permit allowing Robert and Diana Burril to graze 50 head of cattle in Oregon's Malheur National Forest. The cattle graze several months a year in and around Camp Creek and the Middle Fork of the John Day River, polluting these waterways with their waste, increased sedimentation, and increased temperature. In 1994 Oregon Natural Desert Association (ONDA) filed an action under the citizen suit provision of the Clean Water Act, 33 U.S.C. §1365, as well as the Administrative Procedures Act, 5 U.S.C. §702. ONDA alleged that the Forest Service had violated 33 U.S.C. §1341 by issuing the grazing permit without first obtaining the State of Oregon's certification that the grazing would not violate the state's water quality standards. The Burrils, Grant County, and the Eastern Oregon Public Lands Coalition intervened as defendants and the Confederated Tribes of the Warm Springs Reservation intervened as plaintiffs. The district court granted the plaintiffs' summary judgment motion, concluding that the Forest Service must obtain certification for activities that will potentially cause nonpoint source pollution. . . .

The crux of this case is whether the Burrils' Forest Service grazing permit requires certification from the State of Oregon. The resolution of this question hinges on the interpretation of the term "discharge" as used in §1341. . . .

The appellees argued before us and the district court that "discharge" in §1341 refers to pollution from both point sources and nonpoint sources. In accepting this argument below, the district court relied exclusively on §502[(12), (16)] of the Act. . . . The district court reasoned that because the unqualified term "discharge" is defined as including, but not limited to, point source releases, it must include releases from nonpoint sources as well. The court therefore concluded that the term "discharge" encompassed nonpoint source pollution like runoff from grazing. It rejected the government's position that the unqualified term "discharge" is limited to point sources but includes both polluting and nonpolluting releases. . . .

The Clean Water Act, when examined as a whole, cannot support the conclusion that §1341 applies to nonpoint sources. . . .

The Clean Water Act . . . overhauled the regulation of water quality. Direct federal regulation now focuses on reducing the level of effluent that flows from point sources. This is accomplished through the issuance of permits under the National Pollutant Discharge Elimination System (NPDES). See 33 U.S.C. §1342. The Act prohibits the release of pollutants from point sources except in compliance with an NPDES permit. 33 U.S.C. §1311. . . .

We must reach the same conclusion with regard to the scope of the term "discharge" in §1341. Prior to 1972, the provision required the state to certify that a licensed activity would "not violate applicable water quality standards." Pub. L.

92-224, §21(b)(1), 84 Stat. 91 (1970). Now, the statute requires certification that any discharge from the licensed activity "will comply with the applicable provisions of sections 1311, 1312, 1313, 1316, and 1317" of Title 33. 33 U.S.C. §1341(a)(1). The statute was thus amended "to assure consistency with the bill's changed emphasis from water quality standards to effluent limitations based on the elimination of any discharge of pollutants." S. Rep. No. 414, at 69 (1971), reprinted in 1972 U.S.C.C.A.N. at 3764, 3735. The term "discharge" in §1341 is limited to discharges from point sources.

All of the sections cross-referenced in §1341 relate to the regulation of point sources. Appellees contend section 1313, requiring states to establish water quality standards, relates to nonpoint source pollution because it addresses water quality standards and implementation plans. The section does not itself regulate nonpoint source pollution. Water quality standards are established in part to regulate point source pollution. They provide "a supplementary basis . . . so that numerous point sources, despite individual compliance with effluent limitations, may be further regulated to prevent water quality from falling below acceptable levels." EPA v. California ex. rel. State Water Resources Control Bd., 426 U.S. 200, 205 n.12 (1976). In Oregon Natural Resources Council [v. United States Forest Service, 834 F.2d 842, 850 (9th Cir. 1987)], we held that the reference to water quality standards in §1311(b)(1)(C) did not sweep nonpoint sources into the scope of §1311. For similar reasons, §1313 does not sweep nonpoint sources into the scope of §1341.

Appellees' reliance on the Supreme Court's decision in PUD No. 1 v. Washington Dep't of Ecology, 511 U.S. 700 (1994), is similarly misplaced. In that case, the State of Washington issued a §1341 certification for a dam, conditioned on minimum stream flows in order to protect fisheries. The Court held that such a condition was permissible under §1341 even though it did not relate to an effluent discharge from the dam. Thus, a state is free to impose such water-quality limitations "once the threshold condition, the existence of a discharge, is satisfied." Id. at 712. The Supreme Court in PUD No. 1 did not broaden the meaning of the term "discharge" under §1341. . . .

The terminology employed throughout the Clean Water Act cuts against ONDA's argument that the term "discharge" includes nonpoint source pollution like runoff from grazing. Neither the phrase "nonpoint source discharge" nor the phrase "discharge from a nonpoint source" appears in the Act. Rather, the word "discharge" is used consistently to refer to the release of effluent from a point source. By contrast, the term "runoff" describes pollution flowing from nonpoint sources. The term "runoff" is used throughout 33 U.S.C. §1288, describing urban wastewater plans, and 33 U.S.C. §1314(f), providing guidelines for identification of nonpoint sources of pollution. Section 1341 contains no reference to runoff.

Had Congress intended to require certification for runoff as well as discharges, it could easily have written §1341 to mirror the language of §1323, which directs federal agencies "engaged in any activity which may result in the discharge or runoff of pollutants" to comply with applicable water quality standards. 33 U.S.C. §1323(a). Section 1323 plainly applies to nonpoint sources of pollution on federal land. ONDA does not seek relief under this provision, however, because absent the issuance of an NPDES permit under §1342, a citizen suit under the Clean Water Act may not be based on a violation of 33 U.S.C. §1323. See 33 U.S.C. §1365(f).

We have recognized the distinction between the terms "discharge" and "runoff":

> Nonpoint source pollution is not specifically defined in the Act, but is pollution
> that does not result from the "discharge" or "addition" of pollutants from a point source.
> Examples of nonpoint source pollution include runoff from irrigated agriculture and
> silvicultural activities.

We have further noted that "Congress had classified nonpoint source pollution as
runoff caused primarily by rainfall around activities that employ or create pollutants.
Such runoff could not be traced to any identifiable point of discharge."

F.   ISSUES RELATED TO MUNICIPAL
TREATMENT OPERATIONS

[The materials in this section are located at the casebook's website.]

G.   ISSUES RELATED TO AGRICULTURAL POLLUTION,
INCLUDING CAFOS

[The materials in this section are located at the casebook's website.]

H.   ISSUES RELATED TO NONPOINT
SOURCE POLLUTION

In part because of the progress made in addressing point source pollution, nonpoint
source pollution "causes the majority of water body impairment throughout the
country." Adler, Controlling Nonpoint Source Water Pollution: Is Help on the
Way (from the Courts or EPA)?, 31 Envtl. L. Rep. (ELI) 10270 (2001). The CWA
does not provide a general definition of "nonpoint source pollution," although it
specifically exempts certain discharges from the definition of point sources.
§502(14). There is consensus that, essentially, nonpoint source pollution results
when "water, such as precipitation, runs over land surfaces and into bodies of
water." U.S. GAO, Water Quality: Better Data and Evaluation of Urban Runoff
Programs Needed to Assess Effectiveness 6 (June 2001). EPA's description puts it
nicely:

> NPS pollution is caused by rainfall or snowmelt moving over and through the ground. As
> the runoff moves, it picks up and carries away natural and human-made pollutants,
> finally depositing them into lakes, rivers, wetlands, coastal waters, and even our under-
> ground sources of drinking water. [What Is Nonpoint Source (NPS) Pollution?

Questions and Answers, www.epa.gov/owow/nps/qa.html (taken from EPA's Polluted brochure, EPA-841-F-94-005, 1994).]

Nonpoint source pollution comes from numerous diffuse sources. Significant nonpoint sources of pollution include paved urban areas, agricultural practices, forestry, and mining. EPA offers the following list:

- Agricultural areas (fertilizers, herbicides, and insecticides, salt from irrigation practices, sediment, and bacteria and nutrients from livestock)
- Urban runoff (oil, grease, and toxic chemicals)
- Construction sites (sediment)
- Forest lands (sediment)
- Abandoned mines (acid drainage)
- Residential areas (fertilizers, herbicides and insecticides, pet wastes, and faulty septic systems
- Atmospheric deposition [Id.]

While the legal divide between point and nonpoint source pollution is not always clear (as discussed earlier in this chapter), the legal consequences of falling on one side or the other can be dramatic. In marked contrast to the permit-driven approach taken to regulate point sources, in some cases requiring reductions that force some members of the regulated party community out of business, Congress and EPA have taken a much less aggressive approach with respect to nonpoint sources. One observer paints a gloomy picture of efforts over the years to address nonpoint sources:

> Despite periodic statutory amendments designed to turn this situation [the fact that nonpoint source pollution causes the majority of water body impairment] around, the numbers never seem to change very much. Polluted runoff from row crop agriculture, logging, grazing, development, and other sources, along with other activities such as dams, water diversions, and the like that significantly alter aquatic and riparian habitat, continue to impair both human and ecological uses of our rivers, lakes, and coastal waters. While significant amounts of money have been spent and substantial programs have been developed to address the problem, the nature and magnitude of the problem does not seem to have changed significantly. [Adler, *supra*, at 10,270.]

Professor Ruhl's characterization is at least equally skeptical of the efficacy of past and ongoing efforts: "Efforts to address nonpoint source water pollution in the CWA . . . have been feeble, unfocused, and underfunded." Ruhl, Farms, Their Environmental Harms, and Environmental Law, 27 Ecology L.Q. 265, 298 (2000).

Congress's initial approach in the 1972 CWA for controlling nonpoint sources of pollution, set forth in CWA §208, contemplated that states would develop and submit to EPA areawide waste treatment management plans that included a process for identifying nonpoint sources and for establishing procedures and methods to control the pollution from such sources to the extent feasible. Federal funds and technical assistance would be available to help states with the planning process. This program became moribund in the early 1980s. Oliver Houck summarizes the experience with the §208 program:

> A 1972 program to address [nonpoint source] pollution through state and watershed planning under §208 of the CWA produced volumes of studies and no

measurable improvement. In its 1984 Water Quality Inventory, EPA listed several reasons for this lack of progress, among them the diffuse nature of nonpoint sources, difficulties in tracing pollution to sources, and the lack of baseline data on stream conditions. Not mentioned, perhaps out of tact, was the more fundamental political difficulty of dealing with agriculture, silviculture, and municipalities. [O. Houck, The Clean Water Act TMDL Program: Law, Policy, and Implementation 30 (2d ed. 2002).]

Congress tried again in 1987. The rhetoric was impressive, or at least ambitious. Congress's goal was to control nonpoint sources of pollution "in an expeditious manner so as to enable the goals of this Act to be met through the control of both point and nonpoint sources of pollution." Water Quality Act of 1987, Pub. L. No. 100-4, §319. Section 319 served as the statutory home for this goal of invigorating the effort to control nonpoint sources. Section 319 is an example of a voluntary approach to devolution, presumably to be accompanied by fiscal support that would provide incentives to the states to implement the scheme set forth in the section. It was supposed to offer attractive (primarily financial) carrots to induce state engagement but did not carry much of a stick.

Section 319 required each state to prepare and submit to EPA an "assessment report" that (1) identifies navigable waters that, "without additional action to control nonpoint sources of pollution, cannot reasonably be expected" to attain WQSs; (2) identifies categories of nonpoint sources and particular nonpoint sources that are significant contributors to these impaired waters; (3) describes the process that the state would use to identify best management practices (BMPs) to reduce, "to the maximum extent practicable, the level of pollution" resulting from these sources; and (4) identifies and describes the state programs for controlling nonpoint source pollution. §319(a). Section 319 also required each state to prepare and submit to EPA a "management program" for controlling nonpoint source pollution. This program was supposed to detail, among other things, the best management practices the state was going to use to address nonpoint source pollution, identify how the state would implement its BMP approach, and provide a timetable for implementing the program. §319(b). These reports were due no later than the fall of 1988 (18 months after February 1987), and Congress gave EPA 180 days after receipt to review and approve or disapprove them. §319(c), (d). Congress offered the prospect of financial and technical assistance as an incentive for states to undertake these reporting and management program development activities, and by 1991, all 50 states and the territories had received EPA approval (by 1995 seven tribes had done so as well). EPA, Nonpoint Source Management Program, Pointer No. 4, EPA841-F-96-004D.

Several commentators have suggested that the §319 initiative, like its predecessor, has produced limited environmental results. Oliver Houck, for example, concludes that the §319 program "was the epitome of a voluntary program, and it produced about the same results as its predecessor had in 1972: a volume of studies, a number of voluntary programs, and little noticeable cleanup of nonpoint source pollution." Houck, *supra*, at 31. Professor Ruhl cites several critiques of this sort. Ruhl, *supra*, at 299 n.211. EPA, on the other hand, reports that as of 1995 the agency had awarded states, territories, and tribes $370 million under §319 to implement NPS pollution controls, and it has catalogued several projects in which various efforts to reduce pollution from nonpoint sources have paid environmental dividends.* At the

---

*EPA, Nonpoint Source Management Program, Pointer No. 4, EPA841-F-96-004D; U.S. EPA, Section 319 Success Stories, EPA 841-S-94-004 (Nov. 1994), available at http://www.epa. gov/owow/nps/Success319.

end of 2005, EPA issued a guidance document intended to encourage and help states, local governments, and others manage urban runoff from parking lots, buildings, and homes in particular.*

One of the interesting issues to watch concerns the extent to which the trading schemes that EPA is encouraging will create enforceable obligations under the CWA for nonpoint sources, or perhaps make point sources accountable for reductions by nonpoint sources. EPA issued its Watershed Trading Policy in January 2003. 68 Fed. Reg. 1608. EPA has also issued The Water Quality Trading Assessment Handbook to facilitate trading in watersheds. http://www.epa.gov/owow/watershed/trading.htm. EPA officials have expressed their hope that such trading schemes will stimulate reductions in nonpoint source pollution. Some states have used trading to facilitate nonpoint source controls as well. Klahn, TMDLs: Another New Regulation?, TRENDS, July/August 2003, at 12.

Despite some successes, there is little dispute that nonpoint source pollution remains a significant contributor to water quality problems throughout the United States, as we have demonstrated above, and that the cost of addressing these sources is significant. The GAO reports that total federal annual spending for nonpoint-related programs is about $3 billion, but also notes EPA's estimate that roughly $9 billion is needed annually to tackle the issues effectively. U.S. GAO, Water Quality, Federal Role in Addressing — and Contributing to — Nonpoint Source Pollution 4, 5 (Feb. 1999). According to the GAO, even this substantial annual funding requirement understates the actual amounts of money needed, since it does not include some potentially significant sources of NPS pollution; nor does it include the operation and maintenance costs associated with the best management practices EPA believes are needed. Id. at 4, 7.

Beyond the CWA, several other initiatives have the potential to address nonpoint source pollution. In 1990 Congress amended the Coastal Zone Management Act to require that any state with a federally approved coastal zone management plan develop a "coastal nonpoint pollution program subject to federal review and approval." 16 U.S.C. §1455b. Other federal agencies have contributed substantial amounts to addressing nonpoint source pollution and have undertaken a wide variety of programs to address such pollution. USDA, for example, contributed about 80 percent of federal funding to address NPS pollution in FY 1998; and the Department of the Interior contributed about $1.4 billion from FY 1994 to FY 1998. U.S. GAO, Water Quality, *supra*, at 6. EPA reports that a joint initiative to reduce the threat to drinking water from leaking storage tanks has been quite effective. EPA, Protecting the Nation's Drinking Water from Leaking Underground Storage Tanks (2005).

I.   THE §404 PROGRAM

1.   *The Problem: From Hazard to Ecosystem*

Throughout most of our history, marshes and swamps have been considered health menaces, and much effort, supported by national and state land grant laws, has

---

*National Management Measures to Control Nonpoint Source Pollution from Urban Areas, available at http://www.epa.gov/owow/nps/urbanmm/index.html.

been devoted to draining and filling these lands. At the national level, the nation's chief construction agency, the U.S. Army Corps of Engineers, acquired jurisdiction over many wetlands in the late nineteenth century for the purpose of navigation protection. The Corps historically exercised this jurisdiction by allowing all dredging and filling that did not impair the navigable capacity of rivers and harbors. One-half of the 215 million acres of wetlands that existed at the time of European settlement were drained and filled. The U.S. Fish & Wildlife Service estimates that there now are about 100 million acres of wetlands. U.S. Fish & Wildlife Service, Report to Congress on the Status and Trends of Wetlands in the Coterminous United States 1986 to 1997, at 9 (2000).

Over the past few decades the environmental movement increasingly has focused on the ecological value of wetlands. In 1987, the Conservation Foundation convened a National Wetlands Policy Forum, which issued a report that proposed the adoption of a "no net loss" goal for wetlands conversion. Both the Clinton adminis-tration and the first Bush administration adopted "no net loss" as the guiding wetlands policy. Conservation Foundation, Protecting America's Wetlands: An Action Agenda—The Final Report of the National Wetlands Policy Forum (1988). In December 2002 the second Bush administration issued an "Interagency National Wetlands Mitigation Action Plan" and a "Regulatory Guidance Letter" in which it "affirm[ed] its commitment to the goal of no net loss of the nation's wetlands." Bush Administration's Interagency National Wetlands Mitigation Action Plan, 34 Env't Rep. (BNA) 55 (2003). The CEQ's Conserving America's Wetlands 2006: Two Years of Progress Implementing the President's Goal (April 2006) indicates that on Earth Day 2004, President Bush announced a goal of moving beyond "no net loss" of wetlands and achieving an "overall increase in the amount and quality of wetlands in America." The "no net loss (or better)" concept has helped to focus a spotlight on a wide array of questions relating to wetlands, such as how they should be delineated, the appropriate parameters for mitigation when natural wetlands are converted under §404, and the restoration of degraded wetlands.

2. *The Allocation of Regulatory Jurisdiction*

EPA and the Corps of Engineers share responsibility under §404 of the CWA for regulating activities that may adversely impact wetlands. The Corps of Engineers continues to exercise its historical jurisdiction to issue dredge and fill permits. EPA, however, has a significant role in the process as well. Among other things, it has established guidelines that the Corps must follow in considering projects (see the discussion of §404(b) below). EPA also has the authority to veto any permit that would have an unreasonable adverse effect on water supplies, fish, wildlife, or recreation areas. §404(c). EPA has used its authority sparingly. Through 1994, EPA had used its veto authority 11 times. Liebesman, Clean Water Act's Section 404 Program—Overview 97, 115-116 (ALI-ABA Course of Study Materials, Wetlands Law and Regulation, May 31-June 2, 2000). Congress authorized the Corps to issue general permits, in lieu of specific ones, in some situations for relatively minor activities. CWA §404(e). Two commentators estimate that the "mean individual permit application costs over $271,596 to prepare (ignoring the cost of mitigation, design changes, costs of carrying capital and other costs), while the cost of preparing a nationwide permit appli-cation averages $28,915." Sunding & Zilberman, Non-Federal and Non-Regulatory

Approaches to Wetlands Conservation: A Post-SWANCC Exploration of Conservation Alternatives 7 (2003).

3. Activities Regulated under CWA §404

The "discharge of dredged or fill material into . . . navigable waters . . ." triggers a permit scheme contained in §404 of the CWA. This is a different permitting mechanism from the NPDES permit scheme established by §402 of the Act. A project that falls within the scope of the §404 process may also trigger NEPA. Utahns for Better Transp. v. United States Dep't of Transp., 305 F.3d 1152 (10th Cir. 2002). Defining the jurisdictional boundaries of the §404 program has proved contentious over the years. The three key elements are (1) the discharge (2) of dredged or fill material (3) into navigable waters.

Section C.2, above, discusses the third element, the definition of "navigable waters." It contains excerpts of three of the key Supreme Court cases, the 1985 *Riverside Bayview*, 2001 *SWANCC*, and 2006 *Rapanos* decisions. As that discussion reflects, the debate over the appropriate scope of navigable waters continues.

The second element required to create §404 jurisdiction, the definition of "discharge," has received considerable attention in recent years as well. In the early 1990s the Corps adopted the "Tulloch" rule (named after the case that precipitated its development, North Carolina Wildlife Fed'n v. Tulloch, No. C90-713-CIV-5-B0 (E.D.N.C. 1992) (the case was dismissed after settlement), which included various incidental discharges or redeposits of dredged material as discharges subject to §404 jurisdiction. 33 C.F.R. §323.2(d)(1)(iii). In 1998, however, the D.C. Circuit invalidated the Tulloch rule, holding that activities that involve "incidental fallback" are not discharges because they do not involve "addition" of a pollutant. American Mining Cong. v. United States Army Corps of Eng'rs, 145 F.3d 1399 (D.C. Cir. 1998). The court stated that "the straightforward statutory term 'addition' cannot reasonably be said to encompass the situation in which material is removed from the waters of the United States and a small portion of it happens to fall back. Because incidental fallback represents a net withdrawal, not an addition, of material, it cannot be a discharge." Judge Williams did observe that since §404 "sets out no bright line between incidental fallback . . . and regulable redeposits . . . a reasoned attempt by the agencies to draw such a line would be entitled to considerable deference."

EPA and the Corps responded to *American Mining Cong.* by issuing a rule providing that redeposits will be evaluated on a case-by-case basis. 40 Fed. Reg. 25,120 (1999). In 2001 the Corps and EPA revised their definition of "incidental fallback." They included a 26-page preamble in which they explained that they intended to construe the phrase narrowly. 66 Fed. Reg. 4550 (2001). For a decision finding that activities qualify as discharges triggering §404 jurisdiction, see United States v. Deaton, 209 F.3d 331 (4th Cir. 2000) (holding that a landowner who dug a ditch across a wetland on his property and sidecast dirt excavated from the ditch into a wetland violated the CWA). Similarly, Borden Ranch P'ship v. United States Army Corps of Eng'rs, 261 F.3d 810 (9th Cir. 2001), held that a process known as "deep ripping" requires a §404 permit. The "deep ripping" involved dragging four- to seven-foot-long prongs through soil in wetland areas, among others, in order to convert a ranch to a vineyard and orchard, and resulted in the excavation and redeposition of wetland soils. The court held that the destruction of wetlands resulting from this practice qualified as a discharge and triggered §404 jurisdiction. The Supreme Court affirmed, in a one-sentence, 4-4 decision (Justice Kennedy not participating). Borden Ranch P'ship v. United States Army Corp of Eng'rs, 537 U.S. 99 (2002). In Save Our Cmty. v. EPA, 971 F.2d 1155 (5th Cir. 1992), the Fifth Circuit held that *draining* a wetland does not require a permit because it does not involve the discharge of material.

The definitions of dredge and fill material have triggered considerable litigation and controversy as well. In May 2002, EPA and the Corps announced that the Corps was adopting EPA's definition of "fill material." 67 Fed. Reg. 31,129 (2002). Resource Inv., Inc. v. United States Army Corps of Eng'rs, 151 F.3d 1162 (9th Cir. 1998), held that construction of a landfill in wetlands is not subject to Corps jurisdiction because it deposits solid waste, not material excavated or dredged from waters of the United States. In Kentuckians for the Commonwealth, Inc. v. Rivenburgh, 317 F.3d 425 (4th Cir. 2003), the court considered and affirmed the agencies' judgment that §404, rather than §402, applies to the deposition of overburden from mountain coal mining into navigable streams.

4. *Substantive Criteria*

For projects that are subject to §404 jurisdiction, the scope of the Corps' discretion to determine whether a permit is in the "public interest" (33 C.F.R. Part 320) is considerable. See Water Works & Sewer Bd. v. United States Army Corps of Eng'rs, 983 F. Supp. 1052, 1067 (N.D. Ala. 1997) (scope of §404 "public interest review is essentially the same as the extent of review permitted under NEPA analysis"). 33 C.F.R. §320.4(a)(1) directs the Corps to consider 12 general policies:

> All factors which may be relevant to the proposal must be considered including the cumulative effects thereof: among those are conservation, economics, aesthetics, general environmental concerns, wetlands, historic properties, fish and wildlife values, flood hazards, floodplain values, land use, navigation, shore erosion and accretion, recreation, water supply and conservation, water quality, energy needs, safety, food and fiber production, mineral needs, considerations of property ownership and, in general, the needs and welfare of the people.

33 C.F.R. §320.4(a) and (b) highlight the value of wetlands and, consistent with CWA §404(b)(1), require the Corps, in exercising its §404 authority for projects involving wetlands, to adhere to regulations that EPA has developed in which EPA provides several environmental guidelines concerning when a §404 permit should be issued. EPA's regulations, set forth in 40 C.F.R. §230.12(a)(3)(i)-(iv), limit the permitting agency's flexibility by providing that a proposed discharge site falls short when:

> (i)   There is a practicable alternative to the proposed discharge that would have less adverse effect on the aquatic ecosystem, so long as such alternative does not have other significant adverse environmental consequences; or
>
> (ii) The proposed discharge will result in significant degradation of the aquatic ecosystem under Sec. 230.10(b) or (c); or
>
> (iii) The proposed discharge does not include all appropriate and practicable measures to minimize potential harm to the aquatic ecosystem; or
>
> (iv) There does not exist sufficient information to make a reasonable judgment as to whether the proposed discharge will comply with these Guidelines.

Probably the most important substantive criterion is the Corps' water dependency standard. Before the Corps can approve a non-water-dependent activity, it must determine whether a practicable alternative site is available that would cause less damage to wetlands. 40 C.F.R. §230.10(a). The regulations define "practicable" as "available and capable of being done after taking into consideration cost, existing technology, and logistics in light of overall project purposes." 40 C.F.R. §230.3(q). For non-water-dependent projects, it is "presumed" that a practicable alternative exists. This presumption does not rise to the level of an automatic bar to issuance of a permit, but the applicant has the burden of demonstrating otherwise. Utahns for Better Transp. v. United States Dep't of Transp., 305 F.3d 1152, 1162, 1186-1190 (10th Cir. 2002), held that an applicant must make a "persuasive showing concerning the lack of alternatives" if it is to overcome the CWA's presumption for non-water-dependent projects that there is a practicable alternative to dredging or filling wetlands. Houck, Hard Choices: The Analysis of Alternatives under Section 404 of the Clean Water Act and Similar Environmental Laws, 60 U. Colo. L. Rev. 773 (1989), critically examines the consideration of alternatives and recommends that the water dependency test be "dispositive." William Want's wetlands treatise, Law of Wetlands Regulation §§6:17-6:21 (2006), reviews the judicial and agency decisions applying this criterion.

A second important issue that has arisen in the permitting context involves the circumstances in which it is appropriate to allow mitigation—that is, replacement of wetlands lost or damaged by a project.

> In the context of existing wetland regulation, mitigation generally refers to avoidance, minimization, and compensation. These steps are frequently applied in a sequential manner. First, a party seeking a permit for a project that affects wetlands must demonstrate that the least environmentally damaging alternative will be used. Second, the permit applicant must develop a plan to minimize the environmental harm from any unavoidable impacts. For example, the applicant might minimize the impact of a project by scheduling construction in a manner that would reduce interference with spawning or nesting seasons. Finally, the applicant must compensate for or offset any harm done to wetland functions and values which is not avoided or minimized. The applicant satisfies the compensation requirement by enhancing, restoring, creating, or preserving other wetlands that may be located on or off the project site. [Gardner, Banking on Entrepreneurs: Wetlands, Mitigation Banking, and Takings, 81 Iowa L. Rev. 527, 535-536 (1996).]

EPA and the Corps have taken several actions over the years to promote mitigation, including recognizing the idea of "mitigation banking." In 2002, in response to complaints about the effectiveness of mitigation efforts, EPA, the Corps, and the Departments of Agriculture, Commerce, Interior, and Transportation released the National Wetlands Mitigation Action Plan. http://www.mitigationactionplan.gov/index.html.

The track record of mitigation efforts is mixed. The National Research Council (NRC), in its 2001 report Compensating for Wetland Losses under the Clean Water Act (June 2001), indicates that annually from 1993 to 2000, 24,000 acres of wetlands were permitted to be filled, and 42,000 acres were required as compensatory mitigation (1.8 acres mitigated or gained for every acre permitted or lost). It notes that if the mitigation conditions in permits were observed, the result would be a net gain in jurisdictional wetland area and function. But the NRC committee was not convinced that commitments on paper are being translated into reality because, among other things, "the literature on compensatory mitigation suggests that required mitigation projects often are not undertaken or fail to meet permit conditions." It said that "the magnitude of the shortfall [compared with the goal of no net loss] is not precisely known and cannot be determined from current data." Id. at 3.

EPA and the Corps proposed a rule in March 2006 that proposes standards to mitigate the loss of wetlands. Compensatory Mitigation for Losses of Aquatic Resources, 71 Fed. Reg. 15,520 (2006). In August 2006, the Army Corps of Engineers issued a guidance for monitoring compensatory mitigation projects that is intended to improve the quality of such monitoring. The guidance specifies that, among other things, project managers should conduct final field visits to assess on-site conditions, and that all Department of the Army permits that require compensatory mitigation must include the following condition:

> Your responsibility to complete the required compensatory mitigation as set forth in Special Condition X will not be considered fulfilled until you have demonstrated mitigation success and have received written verification from the U.S. Army Corps of Engineers. [U.S. Army Corps of Engineers, Regulatory Guidance Letter No. 06-03 5 (Aug. 3, 2006).]

NOTES AND QUESTIONS

1. *The ESA Operates as a Limit on the Corps' §404 Authority.* As noted in Chapter 5, 16 U.S.C. §1536(a)(2) requires that all federal agencies ensure that their actions will not jeopardize the continued existence of species listed as threatened or endangered. Once a federal action is found to jeopardize a listed species, the agency has an absolute mandate to prevent the destruction of the listed species, TVA v. Hill, 437 U.S. 153 (1978), unless a cabinet-level committee exempts the species from the Act. 16 U.S.C. §1536(e)-(h). See Riverside Irrigation Dist. v. Andrews, 568 F. Supp. 583 (D. Colo. 1983), aff'd, 758 F.2d 508 (10th Cir. 1985) (dam developer may not discharge sand and gravel pursuant to a permit during the construction of a dam because the operation of the dam and the altered water flow might have an adverse impact on a whooping crane habitat 250 to 300 miles downstream). The agencies' duties to protect species are well outlined in Roosevelt Campobello Park Comm'n v. EPA, 684 F.2d 1041 (1st Cir. 1982). See generally Tarlock, The Endangered Species Act & Western Water Rights, 20 Land & Water L. Rev. 1 (1985). Section 9 of the ESA prohibits private parties from taking a species. Water diversions may be a §9 taking, United States v. Glenn-Colusa Irrigation Dist., 788 F. Supp. 1126 (E.D. Cal. 1992), and the Supreme Court has upheld EPA regulations that define habitat destruction as a taking under some circumstances. Babbitt v. Sweet Home Chapter of Communities for a Great Oregon, 515 U.S. 687 (1995). See section B of Chapter 5.

2. *Bush Administration Initiatives Regarding Wetlands.* In addition to its endorsement of a "no net loss +" goal, discussed above at page 688, the Bush administration has announced some successes in conserving and restoring wetlands. The CEQ's Conserving America's Wetlands 2006: Two Years of Progress Implementing the President's Goal (April 2006) reports that since President Bush announced in 2004 the goal of achieving an increase in wetland quantity and quality, "we have restored, created, protected, or improved 1,797,000 acres of wetlands." The U.S. Fish & Wildlife Service issued a report, U.S. Fish & Wildlife Service Status and Trends of Wetlands in the Coterminous United States 1998-2004, which shows a

net gain in wetlands. Some groups have challenged this assertion, claiming that the Service figures show a net loss of wetlands during the same time period. New Report Shows "Net Gain" in Acreage; Critic Says Figures Actually Show Net Loss, 37 Env't Rep. (BNA) 751 (2006).

3. *Nonregulatory and State Strategies for Managing and Protecting Wetlands.* Sunding & Zilberman, *supra,* reviews three alternative strategies for managing and protecting wetlands that might not fall within the scope of the §404 program. It considers "non-regulatory federal programs embedded principally in the nation's farm policy," such as the Conservation Reserve Program (CRP), the Wetlands Reserve Program (WRP), and Swampbuster. The 2002 Farm Act provides financial incentives to farmers under the CRP to retire environmentally sensitive cropland from production for 10 to 15 years, with an enrollment limit of 39 million acres. Under the WRP, the 2002 Farm Act allows property owners voluntarily to limit future use of their land and yet retain ownership for up to 2.275 million acres; it also compensates landowners for permanent and 30-year conservation easements and for agreeing to restore and protect wetlands. For a 2006 update on the CRP and WRP, see Claassen, Emphasis Shifts in U.S. Conservation Policy, Amber Waves (July 2006). EPA and the Corps of Engineers have identified a number of federal and state alternatives to the CWA for protecting wetlands. 68 Fed. Reg. 1991, 1995 (2003).

4. In National Ass'n of Home Builders v. U.S. Army Corps of Eng'rs, 440 F.3d 459 (D.C. Cir. 2006), the D.C. Circuit held that a challenge to the "Tulloch II" rule, involving the definition of discharges of dredged material, is ripe for review and remanded the case to the district court.

J. WATERSHED OR "PLACE-BASED" APPROACHES TO WATER PROTECTION

The preceding sections of this chapter make three fundamental points: (1) in addition to expressing a commitment to clean up our nation's waters by reducing discharges of pollutants into them, the CWA (as well as other statutes) provides a series of tools for accomplishing this goal; (2) use of these tools over the past 30 years has produced substantial reductions in discharges of various types of pollutants, which in turn has yielded many significant improvements in water quality; (3) but considerably more needs to be done if we are to come close to the goal of cleaning up our waters so that they can be available for such seemingly basic uses as fishing, swimming, drinking, and various forms of recreation. Watershed or "place-based" approaches continue to gain popularity as a possible framework for taking on some of the remaining challenges.

This section briefly reviews three features of watershed-based approaches to water protection. It begins with a definition of the concept. It then offers examples of the substantial support that seems to have emerged for such approaches. Third, the section summarizes some of the insights gleaned to date from experimentation with watershed-based approaches.

EPA defines a watershed-based approach as one that "focuses multi-stakeholder efforts within hydrologically defined boundaries to protect and restore our aquatic resources and ecosystems." Memorandum from G. Tracy Mehan, III, EPA Assistant

Administrator, Office of Water, Committing EPA's Water Program to Advancing the Watershed Approach (Dec. 3, 2002). The agency also has described a watershed as a "geographic area in which all the falling water drains to a common water body, i.e., river, lake or stream." It notes that watersheds may be "as small as a few acres or larger than several states." And it suggests that, based on U.S. Geological Survey data, the country can be "divided into 2,149 medium-sized watersheds, averaging about 1,700 square miles in each area." EPA, Watershed Success Stories: Applying the Principles and Spirit of the Clean Water Action Plan 3, 4 (Sept. 2000). The agency has elaborated on this definition in the context of state watershed approaches by characterizing such approaches as having five key components:

> (1) the delineation of a state into natural geographic (e.g., watershed/basin) management areas; (2) a series of management steps or phases to guide regulatory and non-regulatory actions within geographic areas (i.e., monitoring, assessment, planning, implementation); (3) the integration of CWA and other water resource programs through the coordinated implementation of management steps and the formation of partnerships; (4) a process for involving stakeholders; and (5) a focus on environmental results. [EPA, A Review of Statewide Watershed Management Approaches, Final Report 1 (April 2002).]

EPA has placed considerable hope in watershed-based approaches as a tool for improving water quality. This was evident during the Clinton administration, as reflected in its 1998 Clean Water Action Plan and the 2000 *Success Stories* report cited above, and Bush administration EPA officials hold the same view. Tracy Mehan, head of EPA's Office of Water from 2001 to 2003, stated,

> I firmly believe that [a watershed-based] approach . . . offers the most cost-effective opportunity to tackle today's challenges. Administrator Whitman shares my belief. She feels strongly that a watershed or "place-based" approach is one of the most important environmental guiding principles for her as well as for this Administration. By working together with a diverse array of partners, I believe we can identify and implement successful strategies to maintain and restore the chemical, physical and biological integrity of our waters. No doubt, many of these strategies will be tailored to specific problems in specific communities. Hence, the importance of the watershed as a social and hydrological reality. Here is where communities, neighbor to neighbor, can engage, educate and persuade one another in a mutual quest for shared goals. [Mehan, *supra*.]

One concrete example of the Bush administration's apparent commitment to watershed-based approaches is its 2002 initiative directing the Corps of Engineers to "use watershed and ecosystem approaches when determining compensatory mitigation requirements, consider the resource needs of the watersheds where impacts will occur, and also consider the resource needs of neighboring watersheds." Wetlands Regulatory Guidance Action Plan Issued to Address Wetlands Mitigation Measures, Daily Env't Rep. (BNA), at A-3 (Dec. 31, 2002) (quoting the guidance letter).

Many state officials appear to share EPA's enthusiasm for watershed approaches. A Wisconsin official, for example, lauds such approaches for a long list of reasons, including the following:

> States should concede to a watershed-based approach because it focuses stakeholders on what a particular lake, river, wetland or aquifer needs and what they can do collectively to meet that need. This focus helps better integrate and coordinate the myriad of state,

federal and local programs and efforts by groups and citizens. It helps leverage financial and other resources to stretch protection and restoration efforts farther. It decreases duplication, and it allows projects to draw on the different strengths, authorities and ideas that different governmental units and partners possess. . . .

[I]t provides ownership to those people most affected by the resource—and most responsible for its conditions. Such ownership of problems and solutions will ultimately determine success in protecting or restoring the watershed. . . . [Sylvester, The Watershed Approach: The Path to Further Progress, ECOStates 10, 11 (Spring 2000).]

EPA reports that more than 20 states have adopted statewide watershed management approaches. EPA, A Review of Statewide Watershed Management Approaches, *supra*. Based on case studies of 8 such states (Kentucky, Massachusetts, New Jersey, North Carolina, Ohio, Oregon, Texas, and Washington), EPA offered the following five conclusions:

- State managers and staff are overwhelmingly supportive of the statewide watershed management approach despite a number of programmatic and institutional barriers.
- The key to a successful statewide watershed program[] appears to be one that recognizes the important value of inter-agency and state-local partnerships and is supported by an adequate coordination infrastructure.
- The rotating basin approach to statewide watershed management should be viewed as a framework for focusing resources and coordinating activities and not an end in itself. [EPA explains that the "most common form of statewide watershed management" is the "5-year, 5-step rotating basin approach."]
- EPA needs to focus more resources and attention on improving federal-state oversight and building state watershed management capacity as part of its strategy to support the watershed approach.
- EPA and states need to begin documenting the resource and environmental gains attributed to the statewide watershed management approach. [Id. at 41-45.]

EPA's study identified numerous barriers to the success of state watershed strategies. These include, at a programmatic level, (1) "state-level program management barriers" (e.g., the reality that state managers have specific responsibilities for implementing the NPDES program or other features of the CWA that may compete with watershed-related activities for priority attention); (2) "EPA program management barriers" (EPA's fragmented and output-oriented approach to oversight undermines efforts to operate in an integrated and environmental results-driven fashion); (3) difficulties in coordinating across programs and among agencies (a barrier that will resonate with anyone who has sought to design and implement a joint initiative); and (4) challenges in engaging the public and coordinating with local governments. Id. at 15-27.

At a practical level, what effect does "watershed" management have on a state's use of the specific tools and strategies embodied in the state monitoring and permitting programs discussed in this chapter, and vice versa? EPA offered some interesting insights about this relationship. It found that "statewide watershed management has resulted in dramatic improvements in both the quantity and quality of data," although it identified numerous deficiencies in basin-wide monitoring. In contrast, the agency found little overlap between watershed management approaches and states' obligations to develop water quality standards because of a number of factors, including the different cycles involved (triennial review for WQSs and five-year basin cycles used for watershed management). EPA found that "TMDL development and statewide watershed approaches can provide mutual benefits." For example, key elements of watershed management, such as interagency collaboration, stakeholder involvement, and intensive monitoring, can "provide benefits and set the stage for more effective TMDL programs." States appear to have had mixed experiences in their efforts to integrate or coordinate NPDES permitting efforts with watershed management. Some states apparently found that basin-wide NPDES permitting was a net positive because it proved more strategic and efficient, while many states experienced significant difficulties in pursuing such permitting (because of uneven permitting workloads across basins, special EPA initiatives that divert attention from basin-oriented approaches, etc.). Finally, EPA found that states have not fully integrated their nonpoint source programs into their watershed management approaches. Again, the reasons vary, but in part the lack of integration stems from the multitude of actors involved (e.g., state officials may be focusing on one aspect of the pollution while local officials are focused on another). Id. at 4-6.

In conclusion, some strides have been made in the design and implementation of watershed-based approaches at the federal and state levels. Yet the jury is very much still out as to the extent to which watershed management is likely to change significantly the regulatory and nonregulatory landscape for reducing water pollution. The opportunity to consider the possibilities for integrating such approaches with the types of tools outlined in the rest of this chapter, in a way that advances the goals of water protection and minimizes some of the obstacles identified above, is part of what makes environmental law such an interesting field to study.

NOTES AND QUESTIONS

1. Case studies of other watershed-based efforts have been developed. See, e.g., EPA, Watershed Success Stories, *supra* (reviewing experiences with respect to 30 watersheds throughout the United States); ECOStates 10, 12, 13 (Spring 2000) (brief case studies of such efforts in Florida, Louisiana, and Wisconsin). The NRC issued a report in which it recommended a "watershed"-type approach to handle water-related issues in southwestern Pennsylvania. Natural Research Council, Regional Cooperation for Water Quality Improvement in Southwestern Pennsylvania (2005).* In a July 2006 report to the Washington governor, the Puget Sound Partnership recommended a comprehensive approach to protect and restore the Puget Sound ecosystem. http://www.pugetsoundpartnership.org.

2. Watershed approaches inherently contemplate place-based, place-tailored strategies to reduce pollution. We referred above to criticisms that the CWA is overly rigid. To what extent do the CWA and other laws provide the tools needed to implement such strategies? How good, in short, is the match between current statutory authority and the design and implementation of watershed strategies? What types of changes need to be made to the environmental laws to facilitate the implementation of such strategies? See, e.g., Stephenson et al., Toward an Effective Watershed-Based Effluent Allowance Trading System: Identifying the Statutory and Regulatory Barriers to Implementation, 5 The Envtl. Law. 775 (1999).

*For a December 2005 report on concerns with the Great Lakes ecosystem, see Prescription for Great Lakes Ecosystem Protection and Restoration, http://www.restorethelakes.org/PrescriptionforGreatLakes.pdf (commissioned by the Healing Our Waters-Great Lakes Coalition).

VIII

CONTROLLING TOXIC SUBSTANCES AND HAZARDOUS WASTES

Chapters 6 and 7 examined the two basic media protection programs, the Clean Air and Clean Water Acts. The next logical medium would be soil or the Earth's crust. Soil, however, has never been identified as a specific environmental medium for regulatory purposes. The reasons may be both legal and physical. Many of the major air and water pollution sources can be identified, characterized, and subjected to a technology-based regulatory regime. The sources of soil contamination are much more diffuse. In addition, airsheds are true commons and watercourses are quasi-commons because all entitlements are correlative. In contrast, the Earth is divided into discrete ownership units and thus regulation raises more substantial constitutional questions. Finally, discharges into air and water can migrate long distances, whereas soil contamination is localized. Thus, it is not surprising that the protection of soil takes place indirectly through the regulation of toxic pollutants. The focus has been on the unsafe discharge of specific pollutants into the workplace, the ground, aquifers and streams, and, to a lesser extent, the air. Several agencies regulate, under a host of statutes and often with potentially overlapping jurisdiction, the release of toxic materials into all environmental media and into foods.

Congress enacted the Clean Air and Clean Water Acts in 1970 and 1972. The assumption regarding the core of the pollution problem was that a fairly small number of environmental pollutants that were present in large quantities were causing a limited amount of harm to large numbers of people (e.g., SO_2 was a respiratory irritant and waterborne bacteria caused infectious diseases). In a few situations, however, a few persons were apparently threatened with severe harm from being exposed to small quantities of a few pollutants (e.g., a heavy metal in the air or water might cause cancer; SO_2 could cause emphysema in sensitive population groups). Brief statutory provisions were added, almost as an afterthought, to handle pollutants that could not be adequately regulated under the principal ambient and technology-based Clean Air and Clean Water Act provisions. By the mid-1970s, policymakers began to realize that their perspective on the pollution problem might be wrong—that in fact hundreds or thousands of environmental contaminants might cause severe harm to large numbers of persons if exposure even to trace quantities occurred over long periods of time, no matter what the pathway.

These observations raise the problem, which will be addressed throughout this chapter and the next, of how a "hazardous" or "toxic" pollutant is any different from the pollutants that were the focus of most of the regulatory programs encountered in Chapters 6 and 7. A pollutant may irritate the skin or mucous membranes; depress the functions of the nervous system; damage blood, liver, kidney, or brain cells; interfere with important enzyme systems; or cause damage to the reproductive system. Most effects of this type are reversible; generally, when the exposure stops the individual gradually returns to normal. To take a simple example, alcohol-induced central nervous system depression disappears a few hours after a person stops drinking. The effects of many conventional pollutants are reversible under most conditions of exposure. But essentially nonreversible effects also may occur, sometimes after prolonged exposure at low levels. Examples include severe tissue damage from acid or alkali burns, mutations that are passed on to succeeding generations, teratogens that deform the developing fetus—and cancer.

In the public mind, cancer is the most important harm produced by the discharge of toxic substances. The prevention of increased cancer risk has been the driving force behind toxic or hazardous substances regulation since the start of the environmental movement. The basic "environmentalist" thesis is that the majority of human cancers are caused by human exposure to specific substances and that these cancers are potentially preventable by eliminating or reducing exposure levels. See Proctor, Cancer Wars: How Politics Shapes What We Know and Don't Know about Cancer 35-53 (1995). In this chapter, we will examine the theories of cancer causation that lie behind toxic substances regulation as well as inquire whether recent developments in cancer theory suggest a need to reexamine basic regulatory assumptions.

Recent concern related to exposure to toxic substances is due in part to the expansion of the chemical industry after World War II. The industry produced thousands of new chemicals, most of which are organic (carbon-containing) compounds. Because life itself is based in part on carbon compounds, interference by newly invented compounds with evolutionary ones may play havoc with human life processes if exposure occurs. See Colburn et al., Our Stolen Future (1996) (discussing the effects of endocrine-disrupting chemicals).

The key questions for environmental policymakers are: What compounds are dangerous to humans in the quantities in which they are likely to be encountered? What regulatory responses are appropriate? In particular, how are prolonged low-level, low-risk exposures to chemicals to be addressed? Although many hazardous compounds are capable of inducing disease or causing death, the effects of everyday low-level exposures on human health are extremely difficult to determine. The Surgeon General stated long ago, "We believe that toxic chemicals are adding to the disease burden of the United States in a significant, although as yet not precisely defined, way. In addition, we believe that this problem will become more important in the years ahead." Senate Comm. on Env't and Pub. Works, 96th Cong., 2d Sess., Health Effects of Toxic Pollution: A Report from the Surgeon General iii (Comm. Print 1980). The uncertainty that caused the Surgeon General to describe the problem as not "precisely defined" represents the major issue awaiting you in this chapter.

A. DEFINING THE PROBLEM: RISK AND UNCERTAINTY

1. *The Nature of Environmental Risk*

PAGE, A GENERIC VIEW OF TOXIC CHEMICALS AND SIMILAR RISKS
7 Ecology L.Q. 207, 207-223 (1978)

A new type of environmental problem is emerging which differs in nature from the more familiar pollution and resource depletion problems. This type of problem, which may be called *environmental risk*,[1] has rapidly increased in importance over the last few decades and may indeed become the dominant type of environmental problem. Environmental risk problems are exemplified by: the risk of leakage and contamination in the disposal of nuclear wastes [and] the production of synthetic chemicals which may be toxic, carcinogenic, mutagenic, or teratogenic. . . . [Environmental risk possesses nine characteristics, discussed below. The first four emphasize scientific uncertainty and often are the focus of cost-benefit analysis. The remaining five concern regulatory management of risk.]

Ignorance of mechanism is the first characteristic of environmental risk problems. The present state of knowledge of the mechanisms by which a risk is effected is both limited and limiting. Ignorance of mechanism may be present at any number of levels of risk creation, from the generation of the hazard (e.g., the release of radiation from the nuclear fuel cycle) or transmission of the hazard's effect (e.g., dispersion of radiation in the ambient environment or food chain) to an organism's response to exposure, particularly health-related responses (e.g., sensitivity to "hot particles" and other forms of radiation). The mechanisms of generation, transmission, and response are understood so poorly that any management of these problems is truly decision making under pervasive uncertainty. . . .

The *potential for catastrophic costs* is the second common characteristic of environmental risk. What little is known about mechanism in each case establishes that each is a gamble with high stakes. But what is known about mechanism precludes specification of just how catastrophic and likely the costs might be. Ignorance of mechanism colors the next two characteristics as well.

The third characteristic is a *relatively modest benefit* associated with environmental risk gamble. . . . [T]here appears to be at some level a strong asymmetry between potential costs and benefits . . . for most . . . environmental risks. . . . The situation with spray cans and ozone depletion is . . . clear cut. The benefit of fluorocarbons can be directly measured in markets in terms of a cheaper and finer spray compared with the alternatives, which include pump spray. These benefits accrue regardless of the potential effects of the fluorocarbons on the ozone layer. They appear modest indeed compared with the potentially catastrophic costs which might result from ozone depletion. Correspondingly, for the potentially toxic chemical Red Dye No. 40, the benefit is the cosmetic effect the color provides in foods. Again this benefit is modest compared with the potential of the chemical as a carcinogen. This

---

1. "Environmental risk" will be defined specifically in terms of nine characteristics discussed *infra*. "Risk" has several distinct meanings depending on its usage. In "environmental risk," the term draws attention to the potential adverse consequences, for which the underlying probability may be highly uncertain. . . .

asymmetry in the orders of magnitude of potential costs and benefits has important implications for environmental decision making in terms of the degree of proof necessary to warrant precautionary action.

An environmental risk gamble may be thought of as a seesaw with the potential costs on one side of the pivot and the potential benefits on the other. The distances from the pivot represent the relative magnitudes of benefits and costs. Figure 8-1 illustrates the freon propellant example. The distance from zero to B represents the benefit of the convenience of using propellants. Forgoing this convenience is the cost of opting out of the gamble. The distance from zero to C–B represents the net cost of taking the gamble and losing. The net cost is the potential, relatively large "catastrophic" cost reduced by the comparatively small benefit of using propellants that will accrue even if propellants do deplete the ozone.

In Figure 8-1 the potential costs, due to their magnitude, are considerably farther from the pivot than the modest benefits. If both hypotheses were of equal weight the seesaw would tip toward the potentially great loss. Common sense then suggests that the gamble is too risky to undertake.

However, there is a dilemma. There often are reasons to believe that the probabilities of the safe and catastrophic hypotheses are not equal and that the catastrophic outcome is considerably less likely than the favorable outcome. For many potentially toxic chemicals, . . . what little is known about mechanism suggests that the probability of the catastrophic outcome is low, much lower than the probability of the favorable outcome. Just how low is impossible to say with confidence, because of the incomplete knowledge of mechanism. Due to the fragmentary knowledge of mechanism, the likelihood of the catastrophic hypotheses cannot be determined objectively, but must be assessed subjectively, based upon whatever knowledge is available.

Low subjective probability of the catastrophic outcome is the fourth characteristic of environmental risk. Common sense suggests that the low subjective probability of the catastrophic costs should be taken into account in balancing costs and benefits. In terms of the seesaw illustration, the probabilities of the benign and catastrophic hypotheses can be thought of as weight placed upon the seesaw at distances from the pivot equal to the magnitude of the respective potential costs and benefits. A heavy weight close to the pivot can more than balance a light weight farther from the pivot. With a low subjective probability of the catastrophic outcome and a high subjective probability of the favorable outcome, it is no longer clear which way the seesaw will tip. The fourth characteristic, low subjective probability of the potential catastrophe, introduces a second asymmetry which tends to counterbalance the asymmetry of potential high costs and modest benefits.

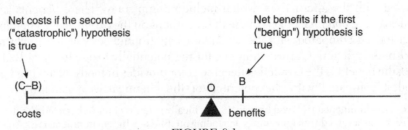

FIGURE 8-1
Net Costs and Benefits Associated with Two Hypotheses

Whether the greater likelihood of the favorable outcome compensates for its smaller relative size is a fundamental question of environmental risk management. In the extreme case, the problem is called a "zero-infinity dilemma": a virtually zero probability of a virtually infinite catastrophe.

In the seesaw illustration, common sense may suggest that an environmental risk is worth taking as long as the seesaw, with the probability of weights added, tips in the direction of benign hypothesis. This interpretation is formally equivalent to the expected value criterion, which says that a gamble is worth taking only if the product of the benefits and their likelihood is greater than the product of the adverse outcome and its likelihood. The analogy to the seesaw is used to suggest that the expected value criterion has some natural appeal as a way of balancing potential costs and benefits and their probabilities.

There are obvious limitations to the expected value criterion. It focuses on outcomes rather than processes; because of the uncertainties involved it may be difficult or even impossible to estimate the magnitudes of the outcomes or their probabilities. The various uncertainties surrounding the quantification of costs, benefits, and probabilities are illustrated in Figure 8-2. The range of uncertainty associated with benefits, represented by a, is the uncertainty of *efficacy*. . . . The corresponding range of uncertainty associated with *costs*, represented by b, is typically much larger than the uncertainty of efficacy. In addition, there is uncertainty as to the *likelihood* of each hypothesis (c and d).

The uncertainties surrounding the potential costs, benefits, and probabilities often are so strong that the decision maker avoids numerical quantification altogether. Even so, the magnitudes of the costs, benefits, and probabilities are essential considerations in environmental risk decision making, and informal estimations of costs, benefits, and probabilities cannot be avoided. Moreover, a decision to forgo a final verdict on a chemical's use and to allow, or prevent, its use pending the collection of more information, is still a decision made under uncertainty. . . .

The five remaining characteristics common to environmental risk problems bear more directly on the institutional problems encountered in their management. The first of these is the *internal transfer of benefits* associated with these risks. In the case of the freon propellants, the benefits—added convenience and possibly lower manufacturing costs—are transferred through markets and reflected in product prices. The economic term for costs and benefits thus transferred is "internal."

In contrast to an internal transfer, the adverse effects of environmental risk gambles usually are transferred directly through the environment rather than through the market. A direct, non-market transfer of an effect is called an economic externality. The *external transfer of costs* is the sixth characteristic of environmental risk.

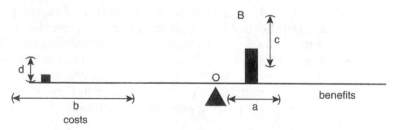

FIGURE 8-2
Costs and Benefits Weighted by Probability

The failure of markets to internalize these potentially catastrophic costs is the primary reason for regulation of environmental risk problems. . . .

The seventh characteristic of environmental risk, *collective risk*, is also related to the environmental transfer of effect. A risk is collective when it is borne by many people simultaneously. Since environmental transfer often means a diffusion of effect, major environmental risk problems have the potential to affect millions of people at the same time. The effectiveness of insurance, liability law, and other traditional compensatory mechanisms in protecting against loss resulting from risk is limited in the case of collective risk. The larger the potential loss and the more widespread its effects, the more difficult it is to insure. Society is more [averse] to collective risks than to individual risks, which often are managed through insurance markets.

The eighth characteristic of environmental risk is *latency*, the extended delay between the initiation of hazard, or exposure to it, and the manifestation of its effect. For many carcinogens, the latency is 20 to 30 years. Indeed, the mutagenic effect of a chemical may not show up for several generations. As a result of latency, those bearing environmental risks may not be the ones enjoying the benefits of the decision. Moreover, in most cases, latency is sufficiently long and the risk sufficiently diffuse so that the risk is borne involuntarily, if not unknowingly. Since an acute, or short-term, effect usually is much easier to discover and trace than a chronic, or long-term effect, long latencies increase the likelihood that the potential effects of environmental risks will be masked by other factors.

The ninth characteristic of environmental risk is *irreversibility*. Even when an effect is theoretically reversible, as a practical matter there are important elements of irreversibility when reversal of the effect inescapably requires a long time, especially when reversal entails a high cost in addition to a long time. Irreversibility can be essentially absolute, as is the case with plutonium's half-life of 24,000 years. It can also be measured on a scale of tens of generations, as is the case with mutagens. In the freon propellant example, the stratospheric effects of ozone depletion might last a hundred years after fluorocarbon emissions are stopped. Within this essentially irreversible period of stratospheric change, however, the resulting climate modification could produce further irreversible effects, such as species extinction.

The last two characteristics, latency and irreversibility of effect, have profound ethical and institutional implications. They raise questions concerning fair distributions of risk over time and how institutions can be designed to anticipate adverse effects, rather than merely to react to existing, known effects. . . .

NOTES AND QUESTIONS

1. Page asserts that the risks posed to those exposed to toxic substances possess a series of common characteristics that tend to set them apart from other kinds of risks. Do any of the air or water pollution problems analyzed in the preceding two chapters exemplify these common characteristics? Why is ignorance of mechanism arguably the predominant such characteristic? What are the implications of ignorance of mechanism for application of the expected value criterion described by Page? Which of the common characteristics arguably justify governmental intervention to assist in risk reduction efforts?

2. Assuming that those responsible for setting public policy on environmental matters determine that government intervention to reduce the risks created by

exposure to toxic substances is appropriate, the next logical question is what form that intervention should take. The issue of whether a risk is serious enough to warrant action (be it public or private) is often called the risk assessment question. The issue of how to manage the risk, once it is decided that it crosses some threshold level of significance that has been established to trigger risk-reducing action, is often referred to as the risk management question. The first excerpt below describes the risk assessment process as it applies to toxic substances. The second excerpt describes EPA's current approach to assessing the risk of exposure to potentially carcinogenic substances.

2. Risk Assessment, Risk Management, Cancer, and the Environment

ADLER, AGAINST "INDIVIDUAL RISK": A SYMPATHETIC CRITIQUE OF RISK ASSESSMENT
153 U. Pa. L. Rev. 1121, 1133-1139, 1161-1162 (2005)

Risk assessment, generically, is a set of techniques for quantifying the fatalities or fatality risks resulting from various hazards. These techniques can also be used to quantify nonfatal illness or injury, or the risk of nonfatal illness or injury. However, because death is the central and paradigmatic harm addressed by health and safety regulators, my presentation will focus there. The best-developed variant of risk assessment, in current regulatory practice, is *toxic* risk assessment: a quantitative description of the fatalities and fatality risks caused by toxic chemicals. But risk assessment with respect to a much wider array of death's causes is also possible and, to some extent, practiced.

Let's start with the toxins. Toxic risk assessment is, in effect, quantitative toxicology and dates from the nineteenth century. Toxic risk assessment by U.S. governmental entities is more recent than that, but still has a substantial history. Toxic risk assessment at the federal level was pioneered by [the federal Food and Drug Administration (FDA)]. This agency is charged with implementing a statute that generally precludes foods containing "poisonous or deleterious" substances and that imposes even stricter standards on "food additives": such additives must be "safe," and carcinogenic food additives are flatly prohibited by the (in)famous "Delaney Clause." . . . As for the threat of cancer: there are various escape routes around the absolutism of the Delaney Clause—for example, FDA takes the position that the Clause does not apply to the nonfunctional carcinogenic constituents of additives—and in the 1970s FDA commenced a practice of quantifying the potency of certain food carcinogens. The 1 in 1 million cutoff for individual cancer risk derives from FDA practice during this period.

The widespread use of toxic risk assessment at other federal agencies began in the 1980s. This development had multiple triggers, including three apparent ones: (1) the *Industrial Union* case [excerpted at page 000 below], which forced OSHA to follow FDA's lead and, more generally, made clear that the courts would not permit federal agencies engaged in health and safety regulation to impose large costs on the regulated entities without some effort to justify such costs through a quantification of benefits, even in cases (as with OSHA) where the underlying statute was quite pro-safety; (2) the 1983 appointment, as EPA administrator, of William Ruckelshaus, who made risk assessment his top priority and actually succeeded in infusing such techniques into administrative routines throughout the large EPA bureaucracy; and (3) the publication, also in 1983, of a seminal study by the National Research Council, Risk Assessment in the Federal Government: Managing the Process (the so-called Red Book), which further popularized the practice of risk assessment and, perhaps more importantly, did much to standardize it. By the 1990s, risk assessment had become such a familiar feature of the regulatory landscape that OMB, in its guidance to federal agencies regarding Executive Order 12,866, instructed that the regulatory impact analysis required by this Executive Order prior to the issuance of major rules should include a "risk assessment":

> Estimating the benefits and costs of risk-reducing regulations [requires, inter alia] . . . a risk assessment that . . . characterizes the probabilities of occurrence of outcomes of interest. . . .
>
> . . . The risk assessment should generate a credible, objective, realistic, and scientifically balanced analysis; present information on hazard, dose-response, and exposure (or analogous material for non-health assessments); and explain the confidence in each assessment. . . .

So risk assessment is now standard practice for federal agencies that regulate toxins, as well as other health and safety agencies, at the major rulemaking stage. But the practice of toxic risk assessment is really much broader than that. For example, the overwhelming majority of EPA risk assessments do not involve major rules, but other categories of administrative decision, such as clean-up decisions with respect to individual Superfund sites.

The Red Book framework for toxic risk assessment has been the canonical framework since its publication and runs as follows. There are four parts to toxic risk assessment: hazard identification, dose-response assessment, exposure assessment, and risk characterization. Hazard identification is a preliminary step: the risk analyst verifies that the allegedly toxic substance is indeed a toxin, that there is sufficient evidence of a causal link to disease and death. If so, the analysis moves on to the two central parts of the risk-assessment inquiry, namely dose-response assessment and exposure assessment. Dose-response assessment means quantifying the link between different doses of the toxin and premature death. This inquiry is, in effect, *physiological*: it seeks to determine how frequently the ingestion, inhalation, or dermal uptake of the toxin, into humans' bodies, leads to cancer or other fatal illnesses. This physiological inquiry is almost always grounded in two types of data—rodent bioassays, in which the differing rates of fatal illness in groups of rodents fed different doses of the toxin are measured, and human epidemiological data—and eventuates in a dose-response curve. The X-axis of the curve represents human doses of the toxin; the Y-axis, the risk to a person exposed to that dose of dying prematurely as a result.

Exactly how to draw this curve, based on the animal or epidemiological evidence, is a technical (but important!) issue in risk assessment [See Figure 8-3]. While dose-response assessment is physiological, exposure assessment is *topographical* and *demographic*. The aim here is to characterize the pattern of exposures to the toxin that will occur under various contingencies (for regulatory purposes, as a result of different regulatory options, including the status quo option of inaction). This assessment depends on where the toxin is located; on how much toxin currently exists, and would be produced under various contingencies, at the source; on the toxin's so-called "fate and transport," i.e., how the toxin migrates through the air, the water, and other

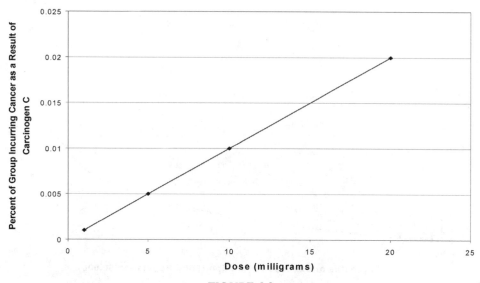

FIGURE 8-3
Dose-Response Curve for Carcinogen C

environmental pathways; and on how the human population is distributed at varying distances from the source of the toxin. What "source" means depends, of course, on the toxin and the regulatory program. It might be a single waste dump, a group of smokestacks (for example all smokestacks in factories in a given industrial category), a food type (in which case the relevant pathway is direct ingestion by food consumers), containers of hazardous workplace chemicals (in which case the relevant pathway is air transport to workers or direct worker contact with the containers), and so on. A relatively complete exposure assessment will predict the dose of the toxin that each member of the population will receive as a result of the evaluated source. Typically, members of the population will not be identified by name, but rather by their doses. That is: a relatively complete exposure assessment will produce a predicted distribution, by numbers and percentiles, of lifetime doses resulting from the analyzed source, for the status quo option of regulatory inaction and, ideally, for each regulatory contingency being assessed. [See Figure 8-4.]

To be sure, the toxic exposure assessments produced by regulatory agencies or their contractors are often not this detailed. If the agency's program focuses on risk to the maximally exposed individual, then the full pattern of dosages that will occur in the status quo, or as a result of various regulatory interventions, is irrelevant. The analyst might estimate the dosage received by the maximally exposed individual by generating a full distribution of doses across the population, then using a very high percentile as maximum exposure; or she might do so more directly by maximizing the parameters underlying her exposure model and determining what dosage results. Concretely, this might mean estimating the maximum exposure to a toxic air pollutant emitted from a factory by looking at the exposure incurred by the person living closest to the factory, on the conservative assumptions that he lives there for his entire lifetime and that his inhalation rate is at the high end of the population distribution of such rates.

The final stage of risk assessment [is] risk characterization. . . . "Risk characterization" means combining the dose-response assessment (which correlates doses and

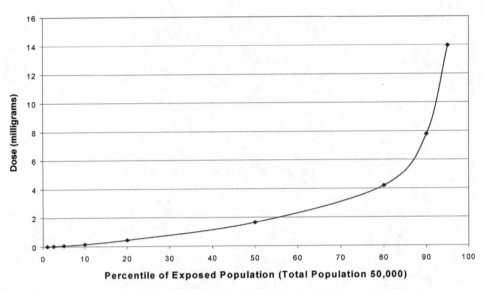

FIGURE 8-4

Exposure Assessment for Carcinogen C in Source S

fatality risks) and the exposure assessment (which predicts doses, across the population or at least for some segment) so as to generate a prediction of the fatalities and fatality risks resulting from the toxin under various contingencies. The risk assessment jargon for total fatalities, as I have already noted, is "population risk"; the jargon for the risk of death incurred by one or another individual is "individual risk." Using the dose-response assessment and exposure assessment to predict "population risk" is somewhat laborious. In general, to do that, the analyst needs a full population distribution of doses, and even then the analyst cannot simply "read" an estimate of total deaths off the dose-response curve, but instead must use probability theory to generate a probability distribution of total deaths and then a point estimate of "population risk" equaling the mean number of total deaths.

Generating a prediction of "individual risk" is more straightforward. For example, if the analyst possesses a full or truncated exposure assessment showing the dosage of the toxin to the "maximally exposed" individual, then the "individual risk" to that person is simply the risk corresponding to that dosage given by the dose-response curve. And if the analyst possesses a full or truncated exposure assessment showing the exposure to the "representative" individual—the person at the median or mean of the dosage distribution—then the "individual risk" incurred by this "ordinary Joe" is the risk for his dosage predicted by our physiological graph, the dose-response curve. . . .

Traditionally, non-cancer and cancer risk assessments have been performed somewhat differently. Toxic effects other than cancer have been seen to have a physiological threshold. The difference, crudely, stems from the special causal mechanism for cancer—DNA damage to some cells, followed by proliferation of those cells—such that a dose so small as to be genotoxic to but a single cell might, in unfortunate circumstances, lead to fatal cancer for the organism.

Dose-response evaluation is therefore performed differently for non-cancer toxicity than for cancers. Experiments and epidemiological studies are still used to produce dose-response data points pairing doses of the toxin with incremental risks (frequencies) of death or some other adverse effect, relative to background. But instead of fitting a linear function to these data points, or some other function without a threshold, the analyst instead identifies the so-called NOAEL ("no observed adverse effect level"): the "highest tested dose at which no statistically significant elevation over background in the incidence of the adverse effect was observed." So-called safety factors are then applied to the NOAEL dose to produce a conservative estimate of the physiologically safe level. Typically, this means dividing the NOAEL dose by a factor of 10, 100, or 1000. The resultant dose, termed the "reference dose" (RfD) by EPA, is the physiologically safe dose, to a high degree of certainty: that dose, and lower doses, do not (it can be said with great confidence) produce an incremental risk of death.

This difference between the procedure for estimating non-cancer and cancer risk leads to a difference in how "individual risks" for noncarcinogens are expressed. The "individual risk" incurred by a particular person, given her exposure to a non-carcinogen, is expressed as a ratio of the dose to the RfD — not as a probability number. For example, if the RfD for the toxin is a lifetime dose of 100 grams, and the exposure assessment predicts that the maximally exposed individual will receive a lifetime dose of 25 grams, she will be ascribed an "individual risk" index of 1/4. If the exposure assessment instead predicts a maximal exposure of 200 grams, the "individual risk" index to the maximally exposed person is 2. These nonprobabilistic indices of "individual risk" are less meaningful than the probabilistic indices employed for carcinogens. All that a nonprobabilistic index number less than 1 means is this: to a high degree of certainty, the incremental fatality risk incurred by that person is zero. All that a nonprobabilistic index number greater than 1 means is the negation, namely it cannot be stated with a high degree of confidence that the individual incurs a zero incremental fatality risk. . . .

NOTES AND QUESTIONS

1. Risk assessment is the process of deciding how dangerous a substance is. It draws on a variety of disciplines, including toxicology, biostatistics, epidemiology, economics, and demography. Its objective is to ascertain the nature of the adverse effects of exposure and to produce quantitative estimates of the probability that an individual will experience those effects as a result of a specified exposure, the consequences of exposure to an entire population (i.e., the number of cases of disease or death), or both. Carnegie Commission on Science, Technology, and Government, Risk and the Environment: Improving Regulatory Decision Making, June 1993, at 76. See also Shere, The Myth of Meaningful Environmental Risk Assessment, 19 Harv. Envtl. L. Rev. 409, 412 (1995). Risk assessment serves a screening function by helping to guide regulators in making decisions on which substances and activities merit regulation. Risk management is the process of deciding what to do about an assessed risk or group of risks. Unlike risk assessment, it "explicitly involves consideration of a wide range of legal, economic, political, and sociological factors." Carnegie Commission, *supra*, at 32. "The 'conventional wisdom' (which some believe needs rethinking) stresses that risk management must not influence the processes and assumptions made in risk assessment, so the two functions must be kept conceptually and administratively separate." Id. at 76.

2. What is the relationship among risk assessment, risk management, and regulation? In Flue-Cured Tobacco Coop. Stabilization Corp. v. EPA, 4 F. Supp. 2d 435 (M.D.N.C. 1998), representatives of the tobacco industry sued to invalidate a report in which EPA concluded that secondhand or environmental tobacco smoke (ETS) causes lung cancer in humans. The plaintiffs argued that issuance of the report violated the Radon Gas and Indoor Air Quality Research Act of 1986, Pub. L. No. 99-499, 100 Stat. 1758-1760 (1986), which authorizes EPA to develop a research program on indoor air pollutants, but not "to carry out any regulatory program or any activity other than research, development, and related reporting, information dissemination, and coordination activities specified in [the Act]." According to the plaintiffs, the risk assessment reflected in the report amounted to regulatory, not research, activity because under EPA's own Guidelines for Carcinogen Risk Assessment, 51 Fed. Reg. 33,992 (1986), regulatory decisionmaking involves two components—risk assessment and risk management—and because EPA had issued regulations for every other substance it had classified as a Group A human carcinogen.

The court refused to equate risk assessment with regulation. The Radon Act authorized EPA to engage in research on the effects of indoor air pollution, and "researching health effects is indistinguishable from assessing risk to health. Congress' directives to research the effects of indoor air pollution on human health and disseminate the findings encompass risk assessment." 4 F. Supp. 2d at 441-442. Although "[r]isk assessment is a component of regulation[,] . . . Congress' prohibition of regulation is not a prohibition against the components comprising regulation." Id. at 443. The Fourth Circuit later vacated the judgment, concluding that the district

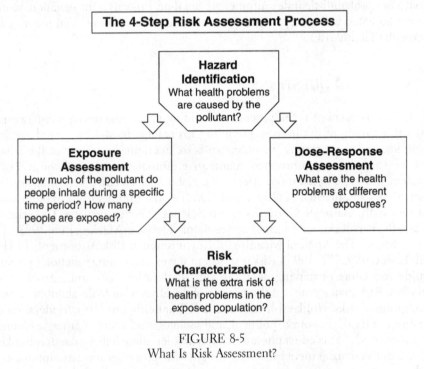

FIGURE 8-5
What Is Risk Assessment?

Source: Risk Assessment for Toxic Air Pollutants: A Citizen's Guide—EPA 450/3-90-024 (Mar. 1991).
http://www.epa.gov/oar/oaqps/air_risc/3_90_024.html

court lacked subject matter jurisdiction because the report was not a judicially review-able final agency action. 313 F.3d 852 (4th Cir. 2002). In the meantime, a subcommittee of the National Toxicology Program's Board of Scientific Counselors had voted unanimously to endorse the conclusion that ETS is carcinogenic.

3. In 2006, EPA and the National Academy of Sciences contracted to update the Red Book discussed in the Adler excerpt to reflect new scientific developments in areas such as genomics, nanotechnology, and biomonitoring. Previously, EPA had already revised its own risk assessment guidelines for exposure to carcinogens:

ENVIRONMENTAL PROTECTION AGENCY, NOTICE OF AVAILABILITY; DOCUMENTS ENTITLED GUIDELINES FOR CARCINOGEN RISK ASSESSMENT AND SUPPLEMENTAL GUIDANCE FOR ASSESSING SUSCEPTIBILITY FROM EARLY-LIFE EXPOSURE TO CARCINOGENS
70 Fed. Reg. 17,766 (2005)

In the 1983 Risk Assessment in the Federal Government: Managing the Process, the National Academy of Sciences recommended that Federal regulatory agencies establish "inference guidelines" to promote consistency and technical quality in risk assessment, and to ensure that the risk assessment process is maintained as a scientific effort separate from risk management. A task force within EPA accepted that recommendation and requested that EPA scientists begin to develop such guidelines. [These guidelines replace those published by EPA in 1986.]

Features of the Guidelines

Use of default options—Default options are approaches that EPA can apply in risk assessments when scientific information about the effects of an agent on human health is unavailable, limited, or of insufficient quality. Under the final Guidelines, EPA's approach begins with a critical analysis of available information, and then invokes defaults if needed to address uncertainty or the absence of critical information.

Consideration of mode of action—Cancer refers to a group of diseases involving abnormal, malignant tissue growth. Research has revealed that the development of cancer involves a complex series of steps and that carcinogens may operate in a number of different ways. The final Guidelines emphasize the value of understanding the biological changes and how these changes might lead to the development of cancer. They also discuss ways to evaluate and use such information, including information about an agent's postulated mode of action [MOA], or the series of steps and processes that lead to cancer formation. Mode-of-action data, when available and of sufficient quality, may be used to draw conclusions about the potency of a chemical, its potential effects at low doses, whether findings in animals are relevant to humans, and which populations or lifestages may be particularly susceptible.

Fuller characterization of carcinogenic potential—In the final Guidelines, an agent's human carcinogenic potential is described in a weight-of-evidence narrative. The narrative summarizes the full range of available evidence and describes any conditions associated with conclusions about an agent's hazard potential. For example, the narrative may explain that a chemical appears to be carcinogenic by some routes of exposure but not by others (e.g., by inhalation but not ingestion). Similarly, a hazard may be attributed to exposures during sensitive life-stages of development but not at other times. The narrative also summarizes uncertainties and key default options that have been invoked. . . .

Consideration of differences in susceptibility—The Guidelines explicitly recognize that variation may exist among people in their susceptibility to carcinogens. Some subpopulations may experience increased susceptibility to carcinogens throughout their life, such as people who have inherited predisposition to certain cancer types or reduced capacity to repair genetic damage. Also, during certain lifestages the entire population may experience heightened susceptibility to carcinogens. In particular, EPA notes that childhood may be a lifestage of greater susceptibility for a number of reasons: rapid growth and development that occurs prenatally and after birth, differences related to an immature metabolic system, and differences in diet and behavior patterns that may increase exposure. . . .

Risk Assessment Guidelines at EPA . . .

1.3.   KEY FEATURES OF THE CANCER GUIDELINES

1.3.1.   CRITICAL ANALYSIS OF AVAILABLE INFORMATION AS THE STARTING POINT FOR EVALUATION

As an increasing understanding of carcinogenesis is becoming available, these cancer guidelines adopt a view of default options that is consistent with EPA's mission to protect human health while adhering to the tenets of sound science. Rather than viewing default options as the starting point from which departures may be justified by new scientific information, these cancer guidelines view a critical analysis of all of the available information that is relevant to assessing the carcinogenic risk as the starting point from which a default option may be invoked if needed to address uncertainty or the absence of critical information. . . . The primary goal of EPA actions is protection of human health; accordingly, as an Agency policy, risk assessment procedures, including default options that are used in the absence of scientific data to the contrary, should be health protective.

Use of health-protective risk assessment procedures as described in these cancer guidelines means that estimates, while uncertain, are more likely to overstate than understate hazard and/or risk. [The National Research Council (NRC)] reaffirmed the use of default options as "a reasonable way to cope with uncertainty about the choice of appropriate models or theory." . . .

Encouraging risk assessors to be receptive to new scientific information, NRC discussed the need for departures from default options when a "sufficient showing" is made. . . . NRC envisioned that principles for choosing and departing from default options would balance several objectives, including "protecting the public health, ensuring scientific validity, minimizing serious errors in estimating risks, maximizing incentives for research, creating an orderly and predictable process, and fostering openness and trustworthiness." . . .

The basis for invoking a default option depends on the circumstances. Generally, if a gap in basic understanding exists or if agent-specific information is missing, a default option may be used. If agent-specific information is present but critical analysis reveals inadequacies, a default option may also be used. . . .

In the absence of sufficient data or understanding to develop . . . a robust, biologically based model, an appropriate policy choice is to have a single preferred curve-fitting model for each type of data set. Many different curve-fitting models have been developed, and those that fit the observed data reasonably well may lead to several-fold differences in estimated risk at the lower end of the observed range. In addition, goodness-of-fit to the experimental observations is not by itself an effective means of discriminating among models that adequately fit the data. To provide some measure of consistency across different carcinogen assessments, EPA uses a standard curve-fitting procedure for tumor incidence data. Assessments that include a different approach should provide an adequate justification and compare their results with those from the standard procedure. Application of models to data should be conducted in an open and transparent manner.

1.3.2. MODE OF ACTION

The use of mode of action[3] in the assessment of potential carcinogens is a main focus of these cancer guidelines. This area of emphasis arose because of the significant scientific advances that have developed concerning the causes of cancer induction. . . . Significant information should be developed to ensure that a scientifically justifiable mode of action underlies the process leading to cancer at a given site. In the absence of sufficiently, scientifically justifiable mode of action information, EPA generally takes public health–protective, default positions regarding the interpretation of toxicologic and epidemiologic data: Animal tumor findings are judged to be relevant to humans, and cancer risks are assumed to conform with low dose linearity.

Understanding of mode of action can be a key to identifying processes that may cause chemical exposures to differentially affect a particular population segment or lifestage. Some modes of action are anticipated to be mutagenic and are assessed with a linear approach. This is the mode of action of radiation and several other agents that are known carcinogens. Other modes of action may be modeled with either linear or nonlinear[4] approaches after a rigorous analysis of available data under the guidance provided in the framework for mode of action analysis.

3. The term "mode of action" is defined as a sequence of key events and processes, starting with interaction of an agent with a cell, proceeding through operational and anatomical changes, and resulting in cancer formation. A "key event" is an empirically observable precursor step that is itself a necessary element of the mode of action or is a biologically based marker for such an element. Mode of action is contrasted with "mechanism of action," which implies a more detailed understanding and description of events, often at the molecular level, than is meant by mode of action. . . . There are many examples of possible modes of carcinogenic action, such as mutagenicity, mitogenesis, inhibition of cell death, cytotoxicity with reparative cell proliferation, and immune suppression.

4. The term "nonlinear" is used here in a narrower sense than its usual meaning in the field of mathematical modeling. In these cancer guidelines, the term "nonlinear" refers to threshold models (which show no response over a range of low doses that include zero) and some nonthreshold models (e.g., a quadractic model, which shows some response at all doses above zero). In these cancer guidelines, a nonlinear model is one whose slope is zero at (and perhaps above) a dose of zero. A low-dose-linear model is one whose slope is greater than zero at a dose of zero. A low-dose-linear model approximates a straight line only at very low doses; at higher doses near the observed data, a low-dose-linear model can display curvature. The term "low-dose-linear" is often abbreviated "linear," although a low-dose-linear model is not linear at all doses. Use of nonlinear approaches does not imply a biological threshold dose below which the response is zero. Estimating thresholds can be problematic; for example, a response that is not statistically significant can be consistent with a small risk that falls below an experiment's power of detection.

1.3.3.   WEIGHT OF EVIDENCE NARRATIVE

The cancer guidelines emphasize the importance of weighing all of the evidence in reaching conclusions about the human carcinogenic potential of agents. This is accomplished in a single integrative step after assessing all of the individual lines of evidence, which is in contrast to the step-wise approach in the 1986 cancer guidelines. Evidence considered includes tumor findings, or lack thereof, in humans and laboratory animals; an agent's chemical and physical properties; its structure-activity relationships (SARs) as compared with other carcinogenic agents; and studies addressing potential carcinogenic processes and mode(s) of action, either *in vivo* or *in vitro*. Data from epidemiologic studies are generally preferred for characterizing human cancer hazard and risk. However, all of the information discussed above could provide valuable insights into the possible mode(s) of action and likelihood of human cancer hazard and risk. The cancer guidelines recognize the growing sophistication of research methods, particularly in their ability to reveal the modes of action of carcinogenic agents at cellular and subcellular levels as well as toxicokinetic processes. . . .

The weight of evidence narrative to characterize hazard summarizes the results of the hazard assessment and provides a conclusion with regard to human carcinogenic potential. The narrative explains the kinds of evidence available and how they fit together in drawing conclusions, and it points out significant issues/strengths/limitations of the data and conclusions. Because the narrative also summarizes the mode of action information, it sets the stage for the discussion of the rationale underlying a recommended approach to dose-response assessment.

In order to provide some measure of clarity and consistency in an otherwise free-form, narrative characterization, standard descriptors are used as part of the hazard narrative to express the conclusion regarding the weight of evidence for carcinogenic hazard potential. There are five recommended standard hazard descriptors: *"Carcinogenic to Humans," "Likely to Be Carcinogenic to Humans," "Suggestive Evidence of Carcinogenic Potential," "Inadequate Information to Assess Carcinogenic Potential,"* and *"Not Likely to Be Carcinogenic to Humans."* . . .

1.3.5.   SUSCEPTIBLE POPULATIONS AND LIFESTAGES

An important use of mode of action information is to identify susceptible populations and lifestages. It is rare to have epidemiologic studies or animal bioassays conducted in susceptible individuals. This information need can be filled by identifying the key events of the mode of action and then identifying risk factors, such as differences due to genetic polymorphisms, disease, altered organ function, lifestyle, and lifestage, that can augment these key events. . . .

2.   *Hazard Assessment*

2.1.   OVERVIEW OF HAZARD ASSESSMENT AND CHARACTERIZATION

2.1.1.   ANALYSES OF DATA

The purpose of hazard assessment is to review and evaluate data pertinent to two questions: (1) Whether an agent may pose a carcinogenic hazard to human beings, and (2) under what circumstances an identified hazard may be expressed. Hazard assessment involves analyses of a variety of data that may range from observations of tumor responses to analysis of structure-activity relationships (SARs). . . .

2.2. ANALYSIS OF TUMOR DATA

Evidence of carcinogenicity comes from finding tumor increases in humans or laboratory animals exposed to a given agent or from finding tumors following exposure to structural analogues to the compound under review. The significance of observed or anticipated tumor effects is evaluated in reference to all the other key data on the agent. . . .

2.2.1. HUMAN DATA

Human data may come from epidemiologic studies or case reports. . . . The most common sources of human data for cancer risk assessment are epidemiologic investigations. Epidemiology is the study of the distribution of disease in human populations and the factors that may influence that distribution. The goals of cancer epidemiology are to identify distribution of cancer risk and determine the extent to which the risk can be attributed causally to specific exposures to exogenous or endogenous factors. Epidemiologic data are extremely valuable in risk assessment because they provide direct evidence on whether a substance is likely to produce cancer in humans, thereby avoiding issues such as: species-to-species inference, extrapolation to exposures relevant to people, effects of concomitant exposures due to lifestyles. Thus, epidemiologic studies typically evaluate agents under more relevant conditions. When human data of high quality and adequate statistical power are available, they are generally preferable over animal data and should be given greater weight in hazard characterization and dose-response assessment, although both can be used.

Null results from epidemiologic studies alone generally do not prove the absence of carcinogenic effects because such results can arise either from an agent being truly not carcinogenic or from other factors such as: inadequate statistical power, inadequate study design, imprecise estimates, or confounding factors. . . . [But] data from a well designed and well conducted epidemiologic study that does not show positive results, in conjunction with compelling mechanistic information, can lend support to a conclusion that animal responses may not be predictive of a human cancer hazard.

2.2.2. ANIMAL DATA

Various whole-animal test systems are currently used or are under development for evaluating potential carcinogenicity. Cancer studies involving chronic exposure for most of the lifespan of an animal are generally accepted for evaluation of tumor effects (. . . but see Ames and Gold, 1990). . . . Other studies of special design are useful for observing formation of preneoplastic lesions or tumors or investigating specific modes of action. Their applicability is determined on a case-by-case basis.

2.2.2.1. Long-Term Carcinogenicity Studies

The objective of long-term carcinogenesis bioassays is to determine the potential carcinogenic hazard and dose-response relationships of the test agent. Carcinogenicity rodent studies are designed to examine the production of tumors as well as preneoplastic lesions and other indications of chronic toxicity. . . . Current standardized carcinogenicity studies in rodents test at least 50 animals per sex per dose group in each of three treatment groups and in a concurrent control group, usually for 18 to 24 months, depending on the rodent species tested. The high dose in long-term studies is generally selected to provide the maximum ability to detect treatment-related carcinogenic effects while not compromising the outcome of the study through excessive toxicity or inducing inappropriate toxicokinetics (e.g., overwhelming absorption or detoxification mechanisms). The purpose of two or more lower doses is to provide some information on the shape of the dose-response curve. . . .

2.2.2.1.1.   Dosing Issues

With regard to the appropriateness of the high dose, an adequate high dose would generally be one that produces some toxic effects without unduly affecting mortality from effects other than cancer or producing significant adverse effects on the nutrition and health of the test animals. . . .

2.2.3.   STRUCTURAL ANALOGUE DATA

For some chemical classes, there is significant available information, largely from rodent bioassays, on the carcinogenicity of analogues. Analogue effects are instructive in investigating carcinogenic potential of an agent as well as in identifying potential target organs, exposures associated with effects, and potential functional class effects or modes of action. . . . Confidence in conclusions is a function of how similar the analogues are to the agent under review in structure, metabolism, and biological activity. It is important to consider this confidence to ensure a balanced position. . . .

2.3.5.   EVENTS RELEVANT TO MODE OF CARCINOGENIC ACTION

Knowledge of the biochemical and biological changes that precede tumor development (which include, but are not limited to, mutagenesis, increased cell proliferation, inhibition of programmed cell death, and receptor activation) may provide important insight for determining whether a cancer hazard exists and may help inform appropriate consideration of the dose-response relationship below the range of observable tumor response. Because cancer can result from a series of genetic alterations in the genes that control cell growth, division, and differentiation, the ability of an agent to affect genotype (and hence gene products) or gene expression is of obvious importance in evaluating its influence on the carcinogenic process. . . .

Furthermore, carcinogenesis involves a complex series and interplay of events that alter the signals a cell receives from its extracellular environment, thereby promoting uncontrolled growth. Many, but not all, mutagens are carcinogens, and some, but not all, agents that induce cell proliferation lead to tumor development. Thus, understanding the range of key steps in the carcinogenic process upon which an agent might act is essential for evaluating its mode of action. . . .

2.4.   MODE OF ACTION—GENERAL CONSIDERATIONS AND FRAMEWORK FOR ANALYSIS

2.4.1.   GENERAL CONSIDERATIONS

The interaction between the biology of the organism and the chemical properties of the agent determine whether there is an adverse effect. Thus, mode of action analysis is based on physical, chemical, and biological information that helps to explain key events in an agent's influence on development of tumors. . . .

Information for mode of action analysis generally includes tumor data in humans and animals and among structural analogues, as well as the other key data. The more complete the data package and the generic knowledge about a given mode of action, the more confidence one has and the more one can rely on assessment of available data rather than reverting to default options to address the absence of information on mode of action. . . . Many times there will be conflicting data and gaps in the information base; it is important to carefully evaluate these uncertainties before reaching any conclusion. . . .

3.3.1. CHOOSING AN EXTRAPOLATION APPROACH

The approach for extrapolation below the observed data considers the understanding of the agent's mode of action at each tumor site. Mode of action information can suggest the likely shape of the dose-response curve at lower doses. The extent of inter-individual variation is also considered, with greater variation spreading the response over a wider range of doses.

Linear extrapolation should be used when there are MOA data to indicate that the dose-response curve is expected to have a linear component below the [point of departure (POD)]. Agents that are generally considered to be linear in this region include:

- Agents that are DNA-reactive and have direct mutagenic activity, or
- Agents for which human exposures or body burdens are high and near doses associated with key precursor events in the carcinogenic process, so that background exposures to this and other agents operating through a common mode of action are in the increasing, approximately linear, portion of the dose-response curve.

When the weight of evidence evaluation of all available data are insufficient to establish the mode of action for a tumor site and when scientifically plausible based on the available data, linear extrapolation is used as a default approach, because linear extrapolation generally is considered to be a health-protective approach. Nonlinear approaches generally should not be used in cases where the mode of action has not been ascertained. Where alternative approaches with significant biological support are available for the same tumor response and no scientific consensus favors a single approach, an assessment may present results based on more than one approach.

A *nonlinear approach* should be selected when there are sufficient data to ascertain the mode of action and conclude that it is not linear at low doses and the agent does not demonstrate mutagenic or other activity consistent with linearity at low doses. . . .

Both linear and nonlinear approaches may be used when there are multiple modes of action. . . .

3.3.2. EXTRAPOLATION USING A LOW-DOSE, LINEAR MODEL

Linear extrapolation should be used in two distinct circumstances: (1) when there are data to indicate that the dose-response curve has a linear component below the POD, or (2) as a default for a tumor site where the mode of action is not established. For linear extrapolation, a line should be drawn from the POD to the origin, corrected for background. This implies a proportional (linear) relationship between risk and dose at low doses. (Note that the dose-response curve generally is not linear at higher doses.) . . .

3.3.3. NONLINEAR EXTRAPOLATION TO LOWER DOSES

A nonlinear extrapolation method can be used for cases with sufficient data to ascertain the mode of action and to conclude that it is not linear at low doses but with not enough data to support a toxicodynamic model that may be either nonlinear or linear at low doses. Nonlinear extrapolation having a significant biological support may be presented in addition to a linear approach when the available data and a weight of evidence evaluation support a nonlinear approach, but the data are not strong enough to ascertain the mode of action applying the Agency's mode of action framework. If the mode of action and other information can support chemical-specific modeling at low doses, it is preferable to default procedures. . . .

3.4.   EXTRAPOLATION TO DIFFERENT HUMAN EXPOSURE SCENARIOS

. . . [S]pecial problems arise when the human exposure situation of concern suggests exposure regimens, e.g., route and dosing schedule, that are substantially different from those used in the relevant animal studies. Unless there is evidence to the contrary in a particular case, the cumulative dose received over a lifetime, expressed as average daily exposure prorated over a lifetime, is recommended as an appropriate measure of exposure to a carcinogen. That is, the assumption is made that a high dose of a carcinogen received over a short period of time is equivalent to a corresponding low dose spread over a lifetime. This approach becomes more problematical as the exposures in question become more intense but less frequent, especially when there is evidence that the agent has shown dose-rate effects. . . .

NOTES AND QUESTIONS

1. *Competing Theories of Cancer Causation.* Beginning in the 1950s, the United States began an all-out effort to find *the* cause of cancer and *a* cure. At the time, viruses were suspected by many scientists to be that cause. By the 1970s much of the blame had shifted to environmental exposure to industrial chemicals, but in the early 1980s some scientists concluded that lifestyle and diet were the major determinants of cancer incidence. Some scientists believe that 90 percent of human cancer may have "environmental" origins, that is, nonhereditary origins such as diet, lifestyle, and type of work. See, e.g., Table 8-1. Other scientists question this conclusion based on the enormous difficulty of demonstrating a precise connection between various cancers and their nonhereditary causes. According to some scientists, environmental exposure is responsible for at most 2 percent of annual cancer deaths. Trichopoulos et al., What Causes Cancer?, Sci. Am. (Sept. 1996), at 80. Trying to link cancer to a cause illustrates Talbot Page's conclusion that uncertainty makes environmental risk regulatory decisions a high-stakes gamble involving the health of millions of individuals.

TABLE 8-1
Cancer Deaths in the United States

Attribution	Percent
Diet	35
Tobacco	30
Infection (speculative)	10
Sexual/reproductive behavior	7
Occupational	4
Alcohol	3
Geophysical (sunlight, radiation)	3
Pollution	2
Other and unknown	6

Source: Based on Doll & Peto, The Causes of Cancer: Quantitative Estimates of Avoidable Risks of Cancer in the United States Today, 66 J. Nat'l Cancer Inst. (1981) (Table 20).

Cancer theory is again changing. Scientists are exploring the idea of a more complex relationship between genetic predisposition and environmental factors ranging from diet and lifestyle to exposure to carcinogenic toxins discharged into air and water and onto soil. See S. Steingraber, Living Downstream: An Ecologist Looks at Cancer and the Environment 256-259 (1997). To many in the environmental community, genetic susceptibility may be the basis for more stringent regulation intended to protect target populations—if they can be scientifically and ethically identified—because "heritable genes that predispose their hosts to cancer by creating special susceptibilities to the effects of carcinogens have undoubtedly been with us for a long time." Id. at 260. Others argue that genetic susceptibility, especially combined with lifestyle evidence, reinforces the argument that current methods for regulating toxic and other chemicals is neither scientifically nor economically justified. Genes that normally prompt cell division can cause uncontrollable cell multiplication, resulting in cancer, when they mutate. These defective growth genes are called oncogenes. Mutations in DNA also can inactivate tumor suppressor cells, allowing other mutations to proliferate. Katzenstein, Unraveling Cancer's Riddles, 13 Am. Health (Nov. 1994), at 76. Defective genes may be inherited or healthy genes may be subject to damage by external forces, such as exposure to sunlight or chemicals, which tends to accumulate over time. To make matters even more complicated, researchers once again believe that certain cancers of the liver, cervix, and prostate are linked to viruses. Altman, Virus Link to Rare Form of Prostate Cancer Revives Suspicion of Medical Detectives, N.Y. Times, Feb. 25, 2006, at A8.

Throughout this progression through the pathogenic, environmental behavioral, and genetic hypotheses of cancer causation, researchers maintained that reducing or eliminating cancer would require understanding its cause on the molecular level. Scientists assert that they have begun to better understand the disease's mechanisms of action. In Tozzi v. U.S. Dep't of Health and Human Serv., 271 F.3d 301 (D.C. Cir. 2001), the court rejected the claim that the Department of Health and Human Services and the National Institute of Environmental Health Sciences erroneously relied on mechanistic evidence (evidence of the actual biochemical processes by which a substance causes cancer) in upgrading dioxin from a chemical that is reasonably anticipated to be a human carcinogen to one that is known to be a human carcinogen under the National Toxicology Program's biennial Report on Carcinogens, published under the Public Health Service Act.

Professor Tarlock has described the impact of modern genetic theory as follows:

> Environmental law is still premised on the one-hit theory of cancer that posits that there are no safe exposure thresholds. As cancer researchers increasingly focus on genetic explanations of cancer, these theories are being replaced by theories that examine how environmental factors may act in conjunction with genetic and acquired suscepti-bility. The scientific validity of the one-hit theory has now been questioned by one of the originators of the theory, and modern genetic theory suggests that cancer is in part caused by the genetic susceptibility of individuals. In short, cancer is more likely to be the result of multiple hits rather than a single hit as previously assumed. But, the one-hit hypothesis may still be valid in some circumstances. [Tarlock, Is There a There There in Environ-mental Law?, 19 J. Land Use & Envtl. L. 213, 247-248 (2004).]

2. *The Role of Smoking.* Smoking is by far the single most important preventable cause of death in the United States and the leading cause of death by cancer in both sexes. Tobacco smoke contains numerous chemical carcinogens. Researchers asserted in 1996 that they found a direct link between one of these, benzo[a]pyrene, and human cancer mutations. Denissenko et al., Preferential Formation of Benzo(a)pyrene Adducts at Lung Cancer Mutational Hotspots, 274 Science 430 (1996). According to the Centers for Disease Control and Prevention (CDC), lung cancer is the leading cause of cancer death; smoking causes about 90 percent of lung cancer deaths in men and almost 80 percent in women. In 2003 an estimated 171,900 new cases of lung cancer occurred and approximately 157,200 people died from lung cancer. The surgeon general has con-cluded that smoking also causes cancers of the oral cavity, pharynx, larynx, esophagus, and bladder.* In 2000, tobacco use caused 18.1 percent of all deaths in the United States, more than ten times as much as motor vehicle crashes. Mokdad et al., Actual Causes of Death in the United States, 2000, 291 J. Am. Med. Ass'n 1238 (2006).**

Exposed nonsmokers are also at risk. In a 1992 report, Respiratory Health Effects of Passive Smoking: Lung Cancer and Other Disorders, EPA/600/6-90/006F (Dec. 1992), EPA classified secondhand, or environmental, tobacco smoke (ETS) as a human carcinogen and attributed to it about 3,000 annual lung cancer deaths and respiratory impairment in hundreds of thousands of children. In 2006, the California Air Resources Board identified ETS as a Toxic Air Contaminant that may cause or contribute to death or serious illness. The study upon which the agency's decision was based also "found links between ETS exposure and increased incidences of breast cancer in non-smoking, pre-menopausal women. ETS had already been linked to adult incidences of lung and nasal sinus cancer, heart disease, eye and nasal irritation, and asthma."***

---

*See http://www.cdc.gov/TOBACCO/sgr/sgr_2004/Factsheets/2.htm. "[T]obacco kills more people every year than alcohol, illicit drugs, automobile accidents, violent crime, and AIDS com-bined." Hanson & Logue, The Costs of Cigarettes: The Economic Case for Ex Post Incentive-Based Regulation, 107 Yale L.J. 1163, 1167 (1998).

**If current trends continue, tobacco use will kill a billion people worldwide during the twenty-first century, ten times more than in the twentieth century. Tobacco use kills more than 1.4 million people each year. N.Y. Times, July 11, 2006, at A17.

***California EPA News Release, California Identifies Second-Hand Smoke as a "Toxic Air Contaminant" (Jan. 26, 2006), available at http://www.arb.ca.gov/newsrel/nr012606.htm.

The Surgeon General of the United States in a 2006 report called exposure to secondhand smoke "an alarming public health hazard" and found that it causes premature death and disease in children and adults who do not smoke. In particular, exposure "has immediate adverse effects on the cardiovascular system and causes coronary heart disease and lung cancer." Nonsmokers exposed to secondhand smoke at work or at home increase their risk of developing heart disease by 25-30 percent and lung cancer by 20-30 percent. In addition, the report concluded that "[t]he scientific evidence indicates that there is no risk-free level of exposure to secondhand smoke." Finally, the report concluded that segregation of smokers and nonsmokers does not eliminate the risk; only complete elimination of indoor smoking fully protects nonsmokers.*

3. A *Cancer "Epidemic"*? The stringency of toxic substances regulation is often justified in part as an attempt to prevent a cancer epidemic. If the cancer risk has been unduly exaggerated, support for the costly regulatory programs that are the focus of this chapter and the next may be undercut. No one questions that cancer now accounts for a greater percentage of deaths than it once did. But is increased environmental exposure to blame?

One possibility is that people who would have died at a young age of infectious diseases before the discovery of antibiotics and other drugs now live long enough to die of cancer. But in 1980 researchers at the National Cancer Institute (NCI) detected, after adjusting their data for increased longevity, what they believed to be a 9 percent increase in cancer in white males and a 14 percent increase in white females over the period 1969 to 1976—a possible 10,000 new cancer cases a year in the United States. Pollack & Horm, Trends in Cancer Incidence and Mortality in the United States: 1969-76, 64 J. Nat'l Cancer Inst. 1091 (1980). A NRC study concluded that all forms of cancer mortality except lung and stomach were increasing in persons over age 54. The Director of Science Policy at NCI concluded that less than half of the increased incidence of cancer could be explained by smoking, and that occupationally related cancers were increasing significantly. Culliton, Government Says Cancer Rate Is Increasing, 209 Science 998 (1980). On the basis of this kind of information, some observers predicted the outbreak of a cancer epidemic after high-risk chemicals had ample time to reach humans through the environment and after the lapse of the long latency periods between exposure and the onset of disease. Large quantities of high-risk chemicals were not manufactured until the 1960s. Davis & Magee, Cancer and Industrial Chemical Production, 206 Science 1356 (1980).

This prognosis was not universally embraced. Two prominent British epidemiologists concluded that the data "do not . . . suggest that the United States is beginning to experience an epidemic of cancer due to new factors." Doll & Peto, The Causes of Cancer: Quantitative Estimates of Avoidable Risks of Cancer in the United States Today, 66 J. Nat'l Cancer Inst. 1191 (1981). Some scientists have attributed part of the increase in cancer incidence to better detection methods for certain kinds of cancers. Further, studies indicated that, for the first time since the 1930s, the incidence of new cancers fell (by 0.7 percent) between 1990 and 1995 (compared with an increase of 1.2 percent between 1973 and 1990). See Kolata, Environment and Cancer: The Links Are Elusive, N.Y. Times, Dec. 13, 2005, at D1, D6 (reporting Oxford University epidemiologist's findings that rates of cancer have been steadily dropping for 50 years,

*See Department of Health and Human Services, The Health Consequences of Involuntary Exposure to Tobacco Smoke (2006), available at www.surgeongeneral.gov/library/secondhandsmoke/.

if tobacco-related cancers are excluded). Opinions differ on whether the decline rebuts the thesis that cancer is largely attributable to environmental factors or reflects the effectiveness of efforts to reduce environmental exposures. A reduction in cigarette smoking among American men was responsible for some of the dip, but researchers credited part to reduced occupational exposure to industrial carcinogens as well as improved treatments. Brody, Decline Is Seen in Death Rates from Broad Range of Cancers, N.Y. Times, Nov. 14, 1996, at A15.

According to the American Cancer Society's annual statistical report,* cancer surpassed heart disease in 2002 for the first time as the top killer of Americans younger than 85, in part, at least, because of greater improvements in treating heart disease than cancer. The number of deaths from either cause fell compared with previous years, primarily due to a reduction in the number of people who smoke. Between 1965 and 2000, the proportion of American adult smokers fell from 42 to 22 percent. Cancer deaths have declined about 1 percent each year since 1999 as a result of earlier detection, prevention efforts, and better treatment. The report indicates that one-third of all cancers are related to smoking and another third to obesity, poor diet, and lack of exercise.

Too great a focus on the national cancer rate may mask increases in the cancer rate among small groups of people exposed to carcinogens. The evidence correlating occupational and environmental exposures to particular chemicals with site-specific cancers improves steadily and does reveal, if not epidemics, outbreaks of cancer. Many occupational correlations exist—for example, mesothelioma (cancer of the lung lining) with asbestos, angiosarcoma (liver cancer) with polyvinylchloride, and leukemia with benzene. What position did EPA take in its 2005 guidelines on the different risks facing sensitive subpopulations and the general population?**

4. *The Role of Diet.* What do Table 8-1 and the American Cancer Society's 2005 report suggest should be the prevailing strategy for reducing cancer mortality in the United States? Perhaps the industrial contribution to the problem of cancer is too tiny, nature's role too large, and personal choice too determinative to justify much environmental and occupational safety regulatory activity. Should the focus of regulation therefore shift to dietary and other lifestyle choices? How effective would this shift be?

Some scientists contend that the human body is awash in naturally occurring carcinogens and mutagens.*** Foods that contain natural carcinogens include animal fat, coffee, peanut butter, pepper, browned foods, and some vegetables.**** The synergistic effects of eating the wrong foods and exposure to other cancer risk factors exacerbate the difficulties of the cancer risk assessment process. The risk of liver cancer, for example, is 70 times greater for a person who eats peanut butter containing

---

*Cancer Facts and Figures: 2005, available at http://www.cancer.org/downloads/STT/CAFF2005PWSecured4.pdf.

**See also EPA, Supplemental Guidance for Assessing Susceptibility from Early-Life Exposure to Carcinogens (2005), available at http://cfpub.epa.gov/ncea/cfm/recordisplay.cfm?deid=116283 (calling for consideration of possible sensitive subpopulations and life stages in cancer risk assessments).

***See Ames, Dietary Carcinogens and Anticarcinogens, 221 Science 1256, 1258 (1983); Feinberg, A Cookbook for a Consistent Food Safety Standard for Carcinogenic Foods: Looking for the Ingredients of a Food Rather than Its Recipe, 5 J. Pharmacy & Law 67, 70 (1996) (referring to "the significant amount of new evidence showing that the risk of cancer from natural foods dwarfs the risks from non-natural foods").

****See also Clark & Snedeker, 9 J. Toxicology & Envtl. Health (Part B) 265 (2006) (discussing effects of naturally occurring mycotoxin that contaminates a variety of foods and beverages).

aflatoxin and who also is infected with hepatitis B than for a person who does not have hepatitis B. Hepatitis B by itself increases cancer risks by only 7 percent. Kolata, Environment and Cancer: The Links Are Elusive, N.Y. Times, Dec. 13, 2005, at D1, D6.

Foods may be relevant as positive as well as negative risk factors. Cancer is thwarted by natural cell repair mechanisms and cancer-inhibiting chemicals in common foods that contain vitamin E, carotene, selenium, and ascorbic and uric acids. Ames, *supra*, at 1259. Certain foods can increase the activity of enzymes that convert chemicals to carcinogens, while other foods inactivate enzymes that detoxify chemicals. A single food, such as broccoli, can affect both kinds of enzymes. Some researchers therefore advocate increased consumption of fruits, vegetables, antioxidants, and fiber and decreased consumption of fat (along with not smoking) as the best way to reduce cancer risks.*

What implications does this information have for the one-hit theory of cancer (one molecule of carcinogen can initiate cancer by striking a single body cell)? Do the data suggest that regulators should reexamine their assumption that no threshold dose exists for regulated carcinogens? Is it possible to conduct meaningful cancer risk assessments in light of the data? For one view, see generally Calabrese & Blain, A Single Exposure to Many Carcinogens Can Cause Cancer, 28 Envtl. L. Rep. (ELI) 10254 (1998).

Richard Merrill, former General Counsel of the FDA, suggested shifting the emphasis from the regulation of dietary carcinogens to requiring labels on foods that cannot practically be eliminated from the diet, as Congress did for saccharin. Merrill, Reducing Diet-Induced Cancer through Federal Regulation: Opportunities and Obstacles, 38 Vand. L. Rev. 513 (1985). Are there any legal obstacles to regulation requiring information disclosure? See Philip Morris, Inc. v. Reilly, 312 F.3d 24 (1st Cir. 2002) (analyzing whether state statute requiring tobacco product manufacturers to report for potential public disclosure the constituents of each brand effected an unconstitutional taking).

5. *The Role of Exercise.* The degree of exercise that an individual engages in also may affect his or her cancer risk. The tissues of physically active people tend to be very sensitive to the effects of insulin. In sedentary people, the muscles and liver are less sensitive to insulin, causing reduced glucose uptake by muscle and continued production of insulin by the liver, even when the body does not need it. "Insulin-resistant" individuals tend to have relatively high blood sugar. The reason that insulin levels may affect cancer risk is that insulin is a growth hormone. If it is oversecreted, it may lead to the kind of uncontrolled proliferation of cells that is characteristic of cancer. As a result, "[s]everal types of cancer whose incidence is dramatically reduced in people who exercise seem to have a connection to insulin sensitivity and glucose metabolism." Brisk walking three or four times a week may reduce the risk of colorectal cancer, for example, by as much as 40 percent. Shaw, The Deadliest Sin, Harv. Mag., March-April 2004, at 36, 42.

---

*Ames & Gold, Too Many Rodent Carcinogens: Mitogenesis Increases Mutagenesis, 249 Science 970 (1990). Compare Kolata, Which of These Foods Will Stop Cancer? (Not So Fast), N.Y. Times, Sept. 27, 2005, at D1 (stating that "scientists say they really do not know whether dietary changes will make a difference" and that "[i]t is turning out to be much more difficult than anyone expected to discover if diet affects cancer risk. Hypotheses abound, but convincing evidence remains elusive.").

6. *Animal Tests.* The insufficiency of data (particularly epidemiological data) concerning the risks of exposure to carcinogens at commonly experienced low levels, coupled with insufficient understanding of the etiology of carcinogenesis, creates the need for the controversial leaps of faith involved in risk assessment default assumptions. Federal regulation relies overwhelmingly on rodent bioassay data. See generally Pastoor & Stevens, Historical Perspective of the Cancer Bioassay, 31 Scandinavian J. Work, Env't & Health 1129 (Supp. 1 2005). To demonstrate low-level cancer risk, regulators have to somehow extrapolate from the high-dose region of the dose-response curve of an actual animal experiment, where tumor rates run 5 to 50 percent, to the low-dose region of a hypothetical human dose-response curve, where there is a projected incidence of one cancer per 100 thousand to 100 million people. This process is probably the "most contentious judgment in carcinogen risk assessment." Rosenthal et al., Legislating Acceptable Cancer Risk from Exposure to Toxic Chemicals, 19 Ecology L.Q. 269, 287 (1992). To show incontrovertibly (with 95 percent confidence) that a low dose of one substance causes fewer than one cancer in a million subjects would require 6 million test animals. Because of the assumptions that must be made in order to rely on smaller experiments (still involving hundreds or thousands of test animals), the major models, all of which may fit the experimental data and have some plausible scientific basis, can differ by a factor of 100,000 in terms of the dose size that creates a risk of one cancer per million subjects. See Figure 8-6. The impact of conservative assumptions may therefore be quite large.

Some scientists are not willing to accept the chain of inferences upon which a conclusion that a substance is carcinogenic to humans depends—animal evidence, large-dose experiments, the one-hit no-threshold theory, and so on.[*] Other scientists question the premises reflected in the linear, no-threshold model that some risk is present at all levels of exposure above zero, and that the risk estimates at low levels should be calculated by linear extrapolation from observed data at higher doses. See, e.g., Goldman, Cancer Risk of Low-Level Exposure (Chemical and Radiation Exposure), 271 Science 1821 (1996). Such criticisms can prove troublesome to regulators. In Chlorine Chemistry Council v. EPA, 206 F.3d 1285 (D.C. Cir. 2000), excerpted in section E.3 below, industry petitioners challenged EPA's decision to set a zero-level maximum contaminant level goal under the Safe Drinking Water Act for chloroform, even though the agency conceded that recent evidence supported the conclusions that there is a safe threshold level of exposure to that chemical and that the chloroform dose-response curve should be considered nonlinear. The court vacated EPA's action on the ground that it was inconsistent with its obligation to act on the basis of the best available evidence.

[*]For example, some scientists question the legitimacy of using rodent bioassays to assess cancer risks to humans. Bender, Societal Risk Reduction: Promise and Pitfalls, 3 N.Y.U. Envtl. L.J. 255, 290 n.158 (1995). The Ninth National Toxicology Report on Carcinogens, issued by the National Institute for Environmental Health Sciences in 2000, removed saccharin from the list of suspected carcinogens on the ground that tests showing that it caused bladder tumors in rats did not apply to humans because of differences in mechanisms in the two species. U.S. Report Adds to List of Carcinogens, N.Y. Times, May 16, 2000, at D4. See also Baxter Healthcare Corp. v. Denton, 15 Cal. Rptr. 3d 430 (Cal. Ct. App. 2004) (upholding trial court's judgment declaring that chemical plasticizer contained in medical devices posed no significant risk of causing cancer in humans, even though it was undisputed that the substance causes liver cancer in rats and mice, because a preponderance of the evidence demonstrated that the biological mechanism by which the substance causes liver cancer in laboratory animals does not function in humans).

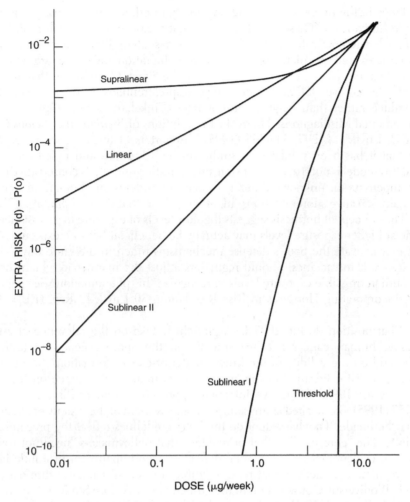

FIGURE 8-6
Results of Alternative Extrapolation Models for the Same Experimental Data

Critics of extrapolation from animal test data also charge that high-dose testing is flawed. They argue that exposure of test animals to massive or maximum tolerated doses (MTDs) may cause cell proliferation, which itself increases the risk of cell mutation and cancer, and of toxic side effects that predispose animals to cancers that would not occur at lower doses. It is therefore not clear whether cancer incidence in test animals is attributable to the inherent carcinogenicity of the substance tested or to the use of MTDs. Ames & Gold, *supra*.

Most scientists, however, support the continued use of animal bioassays because, in the absence of epidemiological data, they are the best available method of assessing carcinogenic potential, their results are representative of the results of workplace exposures, and their usefulness has been verified: all chemicals known to induce cancer in humans that have been studied under adequate experimental protocols also have induced cancer in laboratory animals. See, e.g., Baxter Healthcare Corp. v. Denton, 15 Cal. Rptr. 3d 430, 435 (Cal. Ct. App. 2004) ("There is a 'broad scientific acceptance of the inference that carcinogenicity in other animals means carcinoge-nicity in humans.'"). These scientists claim that measurements of cell proliferation have failed to demonstrate any correlation between such proliferation and either doses or tumor rates, and speculate that, even if cell proliferation and cancer are associated, the proliferation may be the cause rather than the effect. Carcinogens that also have toxic effects may even kill rapidly dividing cells preferentially. If so, the use of MTDs may reduce rather than heighten tumor rates. Finkel, A Second Opinion on an Environmental Misdiagnosis: The Risky Prescriptions of *Breaking the Vicious Circle*, 3 N.Y.U. Envtl. L.J. 295, 343-345 (1995). Supporters of linearity, including EPA, assert that it has been validated in studies of both humans and rodents and that, even if this model is not strictly defensible on scientific grounds, its conservative nature can compensate for unknown differences between rodents and humans and protect potentially sensitive subpopulations. Id. at 342; Rosenthal et al., *supra*, at 287-289.

The concept of hormesis suggests that low levels of exposure to a substance that is toxic at higher exposure levels may actually be beneficial because exposure at low levels may activate the body's defense mechanisms much in the same way that the body responds to vaccines. Should regulators adjust the manner in which they set maximum permissible exposure levels to recognize this phenomenon? See generally Cross, Incorporating Hormesis in Risk Regulation, 30 Envtl. L. Rep. (ELI) 10778 (2000).

What position do the 2005 EPA guidelines take on the relevance of animal studies to human cancer risk assessments, on the appropriateness of testing at MTDs, and on the validity of the linear model of cancer formation? According to one account, EPA began "moving away from its traditional reliance on high-dose studies" in the 1990s. Stone, A Molecular Approach to Cancer Risk, 268 Science 356, 357 (1995). Stone cited as an example a reassessment of the toxicity of atrazine, a popular herbicide. To what extent do the 2005 guidelines reflect the precautionary principle? The "core idea" of that principle is that policymakers "need not wait for conclusive evidence of environmental damage or the impairment of public health before regulating an activity that poses credible risks of substantial future damage." Tarlock, Biodiversity Conservation in the United States: A Case Study in Incomplete-ness and Indirection, 32 Envtl. L. Rep. (ELI) 10529 (2002). EPA's own economists claimed that the 2005 guidelines would make it harder for the agency to demonstrate the benefits of regulating carcinogenic chemicals because accepted methods do not exist for quantifying benefits when nonlinear extrapolation models are used. See Inside EPA Weekly, April 29, 2005, at 4.

7. *Good Science, Bad Science, and Ignorance of Mechanism*. The critics of pre-vailing methodologies have claimed that government officials misuse science to bolster predetermined positions and that the public overreacts to environmental health threats because the government rarely explains them properly. Junk Science: Federal Government's Misuse of Science, Nat'l Rev., Oct. 24, 1994, at 22. One of these authors has suggested that the limits of scientific verification be recognized:

> The hope was that good science would provide objective criteria to make regulatory decisions about issues such as toxic risks.
>   This model began to break down in the environmental area when scientists were asked to opine on issues with high ranges of uncertainty. There was no consensus about cutting edge scientific issues to report. We now realize that there are two problems with the good-versus-bad science model. First, good science is a political construct that has too

often been used to deflect hard questions about the social costs of technology. However, there is a second and more profound problem, which is less a function of abused or sloppy science than of the internal protocols of science. Good science, defined as elegant hypothesis construction and testing, is often inadequate to provide the necessary information and thus, the rational guidance for scientifically sound decision making. The research may be scientifically valid, but it may lack the cross-disciplinary integration and informed speculation needed to be useful to a policy maker.

In short, the whole good-versus-bad science debate is becoming irrelevant. Science is increasingly criticized not because it is bad, but because it provides inadequate guidance to answer questions posed by legislatures and administrators. There are two fundamental reasons for the difficulties of applying science to the issues brought to a board for resolution. The first reason is that the questions are framed as scientific questions when they are actually scientifically informed value judgments. Scientists are pushed to give answers to questions that are framed as positive or verifiable, but the questions are normative because a decision must be made before acceptable verification procedures can be followed. [Tarlock, The Non-equilibrium Paradigm in Ecology and the Partial Unraveling of Environmental Law, 27 Loy. L.A. L. Rev. 1121, 1133-1134 (1994).]

8. *Treatment Breakthroughs*. Many scientists now believe that, although a person may inherit a genetic predisposition to cancer, it may take decades for the genetic mutations to occur that are a prerequisite to development of the disease. The genetic changes that lead to even a cancer of a particular kind often differ from person to person. Yet scientists have hypothesized that the crucial changes that produce a tumor involve a limited number of pathways. The cell mutations that may lead to cancer include those that accelerate cell growth, eliminate the genes that normally slow growth, allow cells to keep dividing indefinitely, allow cancerous cells to recruit normal tissue to nourish them, block the immune system from destroying cancerous cells, and activate genes normally used in embryo development and in healing wounds to assist in spreading the cancer. Genetic predisposition to a particular kind of cancer starts out with a gene mutation that puts a person's cells on one of these pathways. Scientists have developed the capability to identify every gene that is active in a cancer cell and determine which portions of the genes have been changed. They are also able to "turn off" any gene in a cancerous cell and see what happens to it. If they can develop medications or other treatments that prevent the kinds of mutations described above from occurring, they may be able to prevent the development or spread of cancerous cells, or at least render them quiescent. Kolata, Slowly, Cancer Genes Tender Their Secrets, N.Y. Times, Dec. 27, 2005, at D1, D6.

9. *Framing the Issues*. You should consider the following questions as you move through this chapter and the next: To what extent will economic markets and common law liability provide sufficient incentives to keep hazardous substances in check? Would changes in the common law have to be made (e.g., in allocation of the burden of proof, statutes of limitations, the standard of liability, and causation requirements) to render common law actions a sufficient mechanism for controlling exposure to toxic substances? Should regulatory decisions depend on whether risks, injuries, and other costs exceed the benefits of further use of the toxic substance in question? Should the burden rest on the agency to prove risk, or should an agency be able to require that a suspect substance be strictly contained or removed from commerce pending a demonstration that satisfies the agency that the substance is safe?

NOTE ON REGULATION OF THE TOBACCO INDUSTRY

[The materials in this Note are located at the casebook's website.]

B.   RISK AND THE COMMON LAW

The common law offers many forms of relief to a plaintiff who can prove that the defendant has caused or is causing actual harm: damages, injunctions, and other equitable relief. But what about the plaintiff who is merely endangered and cannot yet show any actual harm? This section addresses the relief the common law offers to persons who are threatened but not yet injured by the low-probability, delayed, but potentially serious harms that hazardous substances may cause.

VILLAGE OF WILSONVILLE v. SCA SERVICES, INC.
86 Ill. 2d 1, 426 N.E.2d 824 (1981)

CLARK, Justice . . .

[SCA hauled away chemical wastes generated by its customers and delivered them to its chemical waste disposal site, which it had operated since 1977 within and adjacent to the village. These wastes included substances that can cause pulmonary diseases, cancer, brain damage, and birth defects to exposed individuals. After testing waste samples, SCA deposited the waste in 15-foot-deep, 50-foot-wide, and 250- to 350-foot-long trenches. SCA buried most of the materials in 55-gallon steel drums, and the rest in double-wall paper bags. It then placed uncompacted clay between groups of containers and between the top drum and the top clay level of the trench.

The landfill was bordered on three sides by farmland and on the fourth by the village. The mine site, the village, and much of the surrounding area was located above an abandoned coal mine. About 50 percent of the coal was left in pillars to support the earth above the mine. Testimony at trial established that pillar failure might occur in any mine where there was a readjustment of stress. The 73 water wells in the village were used mostly to water gardens and wash cars, but one was used for drinking water. The trenches were built in an area with a surface layer of about 10 feet of wind-blown silt and clay material. Beneath that material was 40-65 feet of dense and relatively impermeable glacial till composed of a thin sand layer that contained groundwater.

The village sued to enjoin operation of the waste disposal site on the ground that it presented a public nuisance. The trial court ordered the defendant to close the site, remove the wastes and the contaminated soil, and restore the site to its former condition. After examining the testimony presented during the 104-day trial, the Supreme Court upheld the trial court's findings that chemical wastes had spilled from the metal drums and paper bags in which they were transported to the site, that explosions and fires might result from chemical interactions, that chemicals might overflow the trenches or migrate down to groundwater through the soil, and that waste migration and infiltration into groundwater could be hastened by subsidence in the abandoned mine beneath the site. The defendant relied on the testimony of Raymond Harbison, a pharmacology professor at Vanderbilt University and consultant to EPA (referred to by the court as USEPA), who offered the opinion that the site was the most advanced scientific landfill in the country and that the "absolute confinement" of the materials to the site rendered the interaction of the chemicals an impossibility. The trial court had discounted Harbison's testimony in the light of the other evidence presented.]

The trial court herein concluded that defendant's chemical-waste-disposal site constitutes both a private and a public nuisance. Professor Prosser has defined a private nuisance as "a civil wrong, based on a disturbance of rights in land" (Prosser, Torts sec. 86, at 572 (4th ed. 1971)). . . . [A] public nuisance is ". . . the doing of or the failure to do something that injuriously affects the safety, health or morals of the public, or works some substantial annoyance, inconvenience or injury to the public." (Id. sec. 88, at 583 n.29.) It is generally conceded that a nuisance is remediable by injunction or a suit for damages. . . .

[The court then found that Illinois law required that before the trial court may find that a prospective nuisance exists, it must balance the social utility of the defendant's activity against the plaintiff's right to use its property without deleterious effects. The trial court conducted such a balancing process, contrary to the defendant's assertions. The defendant did not dispute a trial court's authority to enjoin a prospective nuisance, but it argued that the trial court erred by failing "to require a showing of a substantial risk of certain and extreme future harm before enjoining operation of the defendant's site."] The defendant argues that the proper standard to be used is that an injunction is proper only if there is a "dangerous probability" that the threatened or potential injury will occur. The defendant further argues that the appellate court looked only at the potential consequences of not enjoining the operation of the site as a nuisance and not at the likelihood of whether harm would occur. . . .

We agree with the defendant's statement of the law, but not with its urged application to the facts of this case. Again, Professor Prosser has offered a concise commentary. He has stated that

> [o]ne distinguishing feature of equitable relief is that it may be granted upon the threat of harm which has not yet occurred. The defendant may be restrained from entering upon an activity where it is highly probable that it will lead to a nuisance, although if the possibility is merely uncertain or contingent he may be left to his remedy after the nuisance has occurred.

(Prosser, Torts sec. 90, at 603 (4th ed. 1971).) This view is in accord with Illinois law. In [Fink v. Board of Trustees, 218 N.E.2d 240 (1966)], . . . [t]he court stated:

> While, as a general proposition, an injunction will be granted only to restrain an actual, existing nuisance, a court of equity may enjoin a threatened or anticipated nuisance, where it clearly appears that a nuisance will necessarily result from the contemplated act or thing which it is sought to enjoin. This is particularly true where the proof shows that the apprehension of material injury is well grounded upon a state of facts from which it appears that the danger is real and immediate. While care should be used in granting injunctions to avoid prospective injuries, there is no requirement that the court must wait until the injury occurs before granting relief.

(71 Ill. App. 2d 226, 281-82.) We agree.

In this case there can be no doubt but that it is highly probable that the chemical-waste-disposal site will bring about a substantial injury. . . . [W]e think it is sufficiently clear that it is highly probable that the instant site will constitute a public nuisance if, through either an explosive interaction, migration, subsidence, or the "bathtub effect," the highly toxic chemical wastes deposited at the site escape and contaminate the air, water, or ground around the site. That such an event will occur was positively attested to by several expert witnesses. A court does not have to wait for it to happen before it can enjoin such a result. Additionally, the fact is that the condition of a nuisance is already present at the site due to the location of the site and the manner in which it has been operated. Thus, it is only the damage which is prospective. Under these circumstances, if a court can prevent any damage from occurring, it should do so.

The defendant next asserts that error occurred in the courts below when they failed to defer to the [Illinois Environmental Protection Agency (IEPA)] and the USEPA, as well as when they failed to give weight to the permits issued by the IEPA. This assertion has no merit, however, because the data relied upon by the IEPA in deciding to issue a permit to the defendant were data collected by the defendant, data which have been proved at trial to be inaccurate. In particular, defendant's experts concluded that any subsidence at the site would be negligible. The IEPA (as well as the USEPA) adopted this inaccurate conclusion in deciding to issue a permit to the defendant. . . .

The next issue we consider is whether the trial court erroneously granted a permanent injunction. The defendant argues . . . that the courts below did not balance the equities in deciding to enjoin the defendant from continuing to operate the waste-disposal site. Defendant cites Harrison v. Indiana Auto Shredders Co. (7th Cir. 1975), 528 F.2d 1107, for the proposition that the court must balance the relative harm and benefit to the plaintiff and defendant before a court may enjoin a nuisance. . . .

In *Harrison*, . . . [t]he court stated:

> Reasonableness is the standard by which the court should fashion its relief in ordinary nuisance cases, . . . and reasonableness is also the appropriate standard for relief from environmental nuisance. Ordinarily a permanent injunction will not lie unless (1) either the polluter seriously and imminently threatens the public health or (2) he causes non-health injuries that are substantial and the business cannot be operated to avoid the injuries apprehended. . . .

(Id. at 1123.) The court concluded in *Harrison* that since the defendant was not in violation of any relevant zoning standards, and since the [activity] did not pose an imminent hazard to the public health, the defendant should not be prevented from continuing to operate. The court then ordered that the defendant be permitted a reasonable time to "launder its objectionable features." (528 F.2d 1107, 1125.)

This case is readily distinguishable for the reason that the gist of this case is that the defendant is engaged in an extremely hazardous undertaking at an unsuitable location, which seriously and imminently poses a threat to the public health. We are acutely aware that the service provided by the defendant is a valuable and necessary one. We also know that it is preferable to have chemical-waste-disposal sites than to have illegal dumping in rivers, streams, and deserted areas. But a site such as defendant's, if it is to do the job it is intended to do, must be located in a secure place, where it will pose no threat to health or life, now, or in the future. This site was intended to be a permanent disposal site for the deposit of extremely hazardous chemical-waste materials. Yet this site is located above an abandoned tunneled mine where subsidence is occurring several years ahead of when it was anticipated. Also, the permeability-coefficient samples taken by defendant's experts, though not conclusive alone, indicate the soil is more permeable at the site than expected. Moreover, the spillage, odors, and dust caused by the presence of the disposal site indicate why it was inadvisable to locate the site so near the plaintiff village.

Therefore, we conclude that in fashioning relief in this case the trial court did balance relative hardship to be caused to the plaintiffs and defendant, and did fashion reasonable relief when it ordered the exhumation of all material from the site and the reclamation of the surrounding area. The instant site is akin to Mr. Justice Sutherland's observation that "Nuisance may be merely a right thing in a wrong place—like a pig in the parlor instead of the barnyard." Village of Euclid v. Ambler Realty Co. (1926), 272 U.S. 365, 388.

We are also cognizant of amicus USEPA's suggestion in its brief and affidavits filed with the appellate court which urge that we remand to the circuit court so that alternatives to closure of the site and exhumation of the waste materials may be considered. The USEPA states:

> Heavy equipment may damage drums, releasing wastes and possibly causing gaseous emissions, fires, and explosions. Repackaging and transporting damaged drums also risks releasing wastes. Workers performing the exhumation face dangers from contact with or inhalation of wastes; these risks cannot be completely eliminated with protective clothing and breathing apparatus. Nearby residents may also be endangered.

It is ironic that the host of horribles mentioned by the USEPA in support of keeping the site open includes some of the same hazards which the plaintiffs have raised as reasons in favor of closing the site.

The USEPA continues that while it is not suggesting a specific alternative remedy to closure, possible alternative remedies exist:

> A proper cap of low permeability can ensure that little or no rain water can infiltrate the site, and thus that little leachate will be formed. Leachate-collection sumps can also be installed to remove whatever leachate is formed. Ground water monitoring can generally detect any migration of waste constituents, and counterpumping of contaminated ground water (or other measures) can protect against further migration.

We note, however, that the USEPA does not suggest how the location of the disposal site above an abandoned tunneled mine and the effects of subsidence can be overcome. . . .

Affirmed and remanded.

RYAN, Justice, concurring. . . .

I am concerned that the holding of *Fink,* quoted by the majority, may be an unnecessarily narrow view of the test for enjoining prospective tortious conduct in general. . . .

I believe that there are situations where the harm that is potential is so devastating that equity should afford relief even though the possibility of the harmful result occurring is uncertain or contingent. The Restatement's position applicable to preventative injunctive relief in general is that "[t]he more serious the impending harm, the less justification there is for taking the chances that are involved in pronouncing the harm too remote." (Restatement (Second) of Torts sec. 933, at 561, comment b

(1979).) If the harm that may result is severe, a lesser possibility of it occurring should be required to support injunctive relief. Conversely, if the potential harm is less severe, a greater possibility that it will happen should be required. Also, in the balancing of competing interests, a court may find a situation where the potential harm is such that a plaintiff will be left to his remedy at law if the possibility of it occurring is slight. This balancing test allows the court to consider a wider range of factors and avoids the anomalous result possible under a more restrictive alternative where a person engaged in an ultrahazardous activity with potentially catastrophic results would be allowed to continue until he has driven an entire community to the brink of certain disaster. A court of equity need not wait so long to provide relief.

Although the "dangerous probability" test has certainly been met in this case, I would be willing to enjoin the activity on a showing of probability of occurrence substantially less than that which the facts presented to this court reveal, due to the extremely hazardous nature of the chemicals being dumped and the potentially catastrophic results.

NOTES AND QUESTIONS

1. *Imminence.* Traditionally, injunctive relief is appropriate only if a damage remedy would not be adequate. According to one source, a damage remedy is inadequate if the plaintiff will suffer imminent, substantial, and irreparable injury in the absence of an injunction. Irreparable harm includes damage for which adequate compensation cannot be provided. Injury is "imminent," according to the majority view, if there is "a threat that harm will occur in the immediate future" and "the anticipated harm is 'practically certain' to result from the act which [the plaintiff] seeks to enjoin." Hellerich, Note, Imminent Irreparable Injury: A Need for Reform, 45 S. Cal. L. Rev. 1025, 1031-1032 (1972). Did the *Wilsonville* court apply this version of the blackletter law? Which is the sounder test of the power to issue injunctions to enjoin risky hazardous waste disposal practices—the rule that Judge Clark applied or the approach of Judge Ryan's concurring opinion? Does Talbot Page's risk "seesaw" (see section A.1 above) offer a better standard for injunctions than the *Wilsonville* majority or concurrence did? Which of the following situations would be enjoinable under each of the three approaches: (1) an ax poised to fall on your wrist, (2) exposure to smallpox, (3) exposure to asbestos dust?

As you will see in this chapter, Congress has authorized the federal district courts to enjoin activities that pose imminent threats to the public health or the environment. Under §7002(a)(1)(B) of the Resource Conservation and Recovery Act, for example, private citizens may sue to enjoin any person who has contributed or is contributing to waste management activities "which may present an imminent and substantial endangerment to health or the environment." In Interfaith Cmty. Org. v. Honeywell Int'l, Inc., 399 F.3d 248 (3d Cir. 2005), the court upheld the district court's injunction requiring the defendant to excavate and remove 1.5 million tons of solid waste that had been deposited at a tidal wetlands site. The appellate court found no credible evidence that either a containment cap or shallow groundwater treatment, the remedies favored by the defendant, would be effective. It also found that the district court properly considered the cost-benefit analysis evidence presented by the parties, and decided upon a "reasonable and narrow" injunction that was only what was necessary to abate the endangerment and was consistent with the public interest.

2. *Public Nuisance and Equitable Relief.* Historically, courts of equity, sitting without a jury, ordered abatement of a public nuisance only under unusual circumstances. When evidence of injury to the public was conflicting or doubtful, equity would not intervene but would leave the issue of fact to trial by jury. Should courts show a similar reluctance today? See Mugler v. Kansas, 123 U.S. 623, 673 (1887).

Courts in public nuisance actions have long allowed individuals to sue as representatives of the public, but only if they can demonstrate a "special injury," which some courts define as an injury different in kind from that suffered by other members of the public. The problem with that test is that "the broader the injury to the community and the more the plaintiff's injury resembles an injury also suffered by other members of the public, the *less* likely that the plaintiff can bring a *public* nuisance lawsuit." Antolini, Modernizing Public Nuisance: Solving the Paradox of the Special Injury Rule, 28 Ecology L.Q. 755, 761 (2001).

3. *Resolving Uncertainty and Proving Causation.* One of the editors of this casebook has asserted that the *Wilsonville* court's "summary of the evidence and the law leaves little doubt that courts now have more discretion to resolve the uncertainty issue in the public's favor when hazardous wastes are involved." Tarlock, Anywhere but Here: An Introduction to State Control of Hazardous Waste Facility Location, 2 UCLA J. Envtl. L. & Pol'y 1, 21 (1981). Subsequent cases, however, demonstrate that the courts have not always exercised that discretion in favor of plaintiffs complaining of harm attributable to hazardous waste management. In Adkins v. Thomas Solvent Co., 487 N.W.2d 715 (Mich. 1992), for example, the plaintiffs claimed that toxic chemicals released at the defendant's property had contaminated groundwater in the area. Although the chemicals had not polluted the plaintiffs' property, the plaintiffs alleged that the releases had caused a diminution in value of their land because of public concern about contaminants in the general area. The court refused to "relax" the boundaries of traditional nuisance doctrine to permit recovery by the plaintiffs. It concluded that the plaintiffs did not demonstrate a risk of illness or a threat to safety, that property depreciation alone is an insufficient basis to impose liability, and that negative publicity resulting in unfounded fears did not constitute a significant interference with the use and enjoyment of land. A damage award might result in "a reordering of a polluter's resources for the benefit of persons who have suffered no cognizable harm at the expense of those claimants who have been subjected to a substantial and unreasonable interference." Id. at 727.*

Other courts have been more accommodating to the plaintiffs in toxics cases. In Walker Drug Co. v. La Sal Oil Co., 972 P.2d 1238 (Utah 1998), the court ruled that a nuisance suit would not lie for unsubstantiated fears of third persons concerning contamination of adjacent property, but that stigma damages are recoverable when a plaintiff demonstrates that defendants caused temporary physical injury to plaintiff's land, and repair of that injury would not return the value of the property to its prior

---

*See also Adams v. Star Enter., 51 F.3d 417 (4th Cir. 1995) (refusing to impose liability on oil distribution facility for underground oil plume because the claim that the oil spill resulted in the attachment of a stigma to the community and caused a decline in property values was too speculative); Duff v. Morgantown Energy Ass'n, 421 S.E.2d 253 (W. Va. 1992) (refusing to enjoin construction and operation of proposed cogeneration facility because neighboring landowners failed to prove that the facility would result in "devastating harm or is certain to result in serious damages or irreparable injury"). The court in In re Tutu Wells Contamination Litig., 909 F. Supp. 991, 998 (D.V.I. 1995), criticized the approach in *Adams* as likely to lead to "underdeterrence of environmental contamination which may or may not otherwise be the subject of government laws and regulations."

level "because of a lingering negative public perception." Cf. Bradley v. Armstrong Rubber Co., 130 F.3d 168 (5th Cir. 1997) (recognizing the propriety of awarding stigma damages for permanent physical injury to the land to promote policy of redressing economic loss). Is a property owner entitled to a decrease in real estate tax valuation based on the stigma caused by contamination on the assessed property itself or on adjacent property? See Dealers Mfg. Co. v. County of Anoka, 615 N.W.2d 76 (Minn. 2000).

The difficulty of proving causation often stymies common law tort actions filed by plaintiffs exposed to toxic substances. See, e.g., Anglado v. Leaf River Forest Prod., Inc., 716 So. 2d 543 (Miss. 1998), where the court granted summary judgment to a pulp mill operator on trespass and nuisance claims filed by downstream riparian owners because the plaintiffs failed to prove that the dioxin and other chemicals to which they were exposed came from the defendant's pulp mill. The dissenting justice complained that the plaintiffs' burden of proof should not require such "fingerprinting" of the defendant's waste.

4. *Regulatory Compliance.* The Wilsonville site had been heralded as one of the most modern, safest chemical waste disposal facilities in the country, a site to which unsafely disposed-of wastes that had been exhumed elsewhere should be sent. The fully permitted site had been under constant federal and state surveillance since its inception. Is it significant that the site in *Wilsonville* was fully authorized under state and federal law? Compare Green v. Castle Concrete Co., 509 P.2d 588 (Colo. 1973) with Armory Park Neighborhood Ass'n v. Episcopal Cmty. Serv., 712 P.2d 914, 921-922 (Ariz. 1985). Does it make a difference whether the plaintiff files a private or a public nuisance claim? See Desruisseau v. Isley, 553 P.2d 1242, 1245-1246 (Ariz. App. 1976). Cf. City of Sunland Park v. Harris News, Inc., 124 P.3d 566, 578 (N.M. Ct. App. 2005) (stating that, while violation of a municipal ordinance is not sufficient to prove either a nuisance in fact or a nuisance per se in a public nuisance action, violation of a state statute declaring certain conduct to be a public nuisance will be considered a nuisance per se). What is the effect of proof of a regulatory violation on a negligence cause of action? See Regional Airport Auth. v. LFG, LLC, 255 F. Supp. 2d 688 (W.D. Ky. 2003).

Some state statutes foreclose the courts from enjoining the construction or operation of a hazardous waste disposal facility that conforms to the state's hazardous waste facility siting statute. Landowners are instead limited to seeking (1) compensation in an inverse condemnation action for loss of property value or use at the time a facility is constructed, and (2) the incremental damages caused by a subsequent "modification" in the approved design or operation of the facility. Utah Code Ann. §19-6-206. It is unclear whether the statute allows recovery of damages for personal injury. If not, does the statute unconstitutionally foreclose potential plaintiffs' right to bring an action at common law? See Duke Power Co. v. Carolina Envtl. Study Group, Inc., 438 U.S. 59 (1978); Bormann v. Board of Supervisors, 584 N.W.2d 309 (Iowa 1998).* But see Moon v. North Idaho Farmers Ass'n, 96 P.3d 637 (Idaho 2004) (holding that statute immunizing crop residue burning from nuisance or trespass liability was not a taking of property of grower's neighbors under federal or state law because plaintiff's land was not appropriated, they did not lose access or complete

---

*Cf. Glicksman, Federal Preemption and Private Legal Remedies for Pollution, 134 U. Pa. L. Rev. 121, 179-182 (1985) (arguing that federal statutory preemption of all state common law remedies for harms caused by pollution would raise due process concerns).

use of the property, and the right to maintain a nuisance is not an easement under Idaho law).

5. *Class Actions and Environmental Torts*. Under what circumstances is it appropriate for a court to allow those allegedly injured by pollution to bring a class action? See Mejdrech v. Met-Coil Sys. Corp., 319 F.3d 910 (7th Cir. 2003).

A subcategory of environmental tort cases—toxic tort cases—has raised a series of difficult questions concerning the kinds of interests that the legal system should protect against harm resulting from the conduct of others. Consider the following analysis.

LIN, THE UNIFYING ROLE OF HARM IN ENVIRONMENTAL LAW
2006 Wis. L. Rev. 897, 922-930, 945-946, 955-968, 984

. . . Harm is the most widely accepted justification for the exercise of police power and it is the rationale most applicable to environmental regulation.

At first glance, harm may appear to be a simple and objective concept, capable of ready definition. But . . . the concept is surprisingly elusive. One possible conception, for example, would define harm with respect to utilitarian goals of maximizing happiness, pleasure, or the fulfillment of subjective preferences. In this framework, harm would be synonymous with pain or the frustration of one's preferences. Such an account of harm, however, is simply too subjective to provide a workable basis for defining the permissible scope of government power. A harm principle* based on this conceptualization of harm would be boundless because "[a]ny sort of conduct to which some people object will inflict pain of various sorts and will interfere with the satisfaction of some people's preferences."

[John Stuart Mill] suggested that harm involves "encroachment" on others' rights, or the injuring of "certain interests" of another, "which, either by express legal provision or by tacit understanding, ought to be considered as rights." . . . As commentators have pointed out, Mill's distinctions rely heavily on unstated moral and social assumptions that may not be universally shared. . . .

[Others have suggested that the concept of harm entails a wrongful violation of another's rights.] Intuitive notions of harm, however, do not necessarily incorporate wrongfulness. For example, . . . harm in environmental law—whether in nuisance, regulatory law, or otherwise—does not always require wrongdoing. Consider the operation of a brickyard in a residential area. If the brickyard's presence long predates construction of the neighboring residences, and if the brickyard complies with applicable regulations, its operations could hardly be termed wrongful. Yet the noise and dust it generates surely harm its neighbors, and the brickyard's operations would almost certainly qualify as a nuisance. Likewise, the release of pollutants by a power plant during normal operations may harm nearby residents, even if such releases are lawful under the plant's permit and subject to the most advanced emission control devices available.

---

*Professor Lin defines the harm principle as "jurisdictional in nature" in that "it is a touchstone for identifying one class of conduct that society has the power to regulate. . . . [I]t is the means of delineating the scope of legal authority."—EDS.

Including wrongfulness in the concept of harm thus seems contingent on the criminal law context of [the] inquiry. The primary purpose of criminal law is to punish and to deter wrongful conduct that has resulted in or is likely to result in harm if allowed to proceed. Civil law, however, has a broader reach: tort law seeks to compensate for harm and to foster corrective justice as well as to deter; and public law seeks to accomplish these aims and others as well. The differences between criminal and civil law suggest that . . . [in the context of environmental harm], the element of wrongfulness [should be] set aside. Consistent with this approach, and perhaps reflecting the origins of environmental law, the Restatement (Second) of Torts defines harm as a "loss or detriment in fact of any kind to a person resulting from any cause." . . .

If harm is a setback to one's interests, the obvious question is as follows: what sort of interests can give rise to harm? . . .

The definition of harm found in the Restatement (Second) of Torts hints at the wide range of interests that might be implicated:

> [H]arm . . . is the detriment or loss to a person which occurs by virtue of, or as a result of, some alteration or change in his person, or in physical things, and also the detriment resulting to him from acts or conditions which impair his physical, emotional, or aesthetic well-being, his pecuniary advantage, his intangible rights, his reputation, or his other legally recognized interests.

With respect to environmental harm in particular, one commentator has suggested various classes of harm: immediate and future physical injury to people, emotional distress from fear of future injury, social and economic disruption, remediation costs, property damage, ecological damage, and regulatory harms.

The variety of interests just mentioned raises a number of issues. First, the absence of an obvious unifying theme suggests that the task of determining what interests matter is a subjective one—perhaps hopelessly so. As a commentator has noted, "what constitutes harm . . . will be governed by one's view of the good." Even physical injuries . . . qualify as harms "not because harm is a matter of unadorned fact," but because most reasonable normative accounts of harm would encompass such injuries. The Restatement's definition, which limits the interests that can be harmed to "legally recognized interests," underscores the normative nature of harm and begs the question of what interests are to be legally recognized.

Second, if a setback to any interest qualified as a harm, the harm principle might become useless as a limit on societal jurisdiction. And if indirect harms—that is, setbacks to interests that flow from long chains of causation—are considered regardless of their magnitude, virtually any activity could be said to be "harmful." "Almost every act in a complex, crowded, industrial society involves externalities, but we would not expect [the] government to institute rules for all of them." Thus, implicit in the harm principle may be limits as to the types and the insignificance of interests that the principle will protect. Absent such limits, harm may lose its force and utility as a critical principle for determining the legitimacy of government action, regulation, or judicial intervention. . . .

[Professor Lin argues that the law of takings, discussed in Chapter 5 above, and the rules governing standing to sue, discussed in Chapter 3 above, demonstrate that "[h]arm is not purely subjective; it depends on social norms, not on mere personal judgments or preferences." He asserts that physical injury, emotional injury, and damage to property represent "easy, core cases of harm." His primary interest is several contexts "that present more difficult questions of harm." In each context, "society has not conclusively determined that harm is present, and there is debate over if and how society should respond." According to Lin, "[u]nderstanding how these cutting-edge issues of harm might be resolved will help shape future environmental law."]

. . . [F]ear, anxiety, and other emotional injuries constitute serious setbacks to welfare interests. In the environmental context, the fear that may accompany toxic exposure can debilitate individuals and communities. The term "dread" is often used to describe this kind of fear, which is a serious and substantial setback to the affected individuals' welfare interests. The latent hazards characteristic of environmental problems are dreaded not only because of their involuntary nature, catastrophic potential, and fatal consequences, but also because they often have no clearly defined end. People exposed to invisible contaminants, unlike victims of natural disasters such as floods or hurricanes, may be left without closure for years or decades. As case studies of Love Canal, Times Beach, and other communities exposed to toxics have found, the emotional impacts may ultimately include loss of trust in society's institutions and fracturing of the affected community.

Various trends likely will draw more attention to psychological injury in the future. First, rapidly developing technologies will give rise to new fears. New technologies with the potential for significant, unprecedented, and wide-ranging impacts include nanotechnology, biotechnology, and cloning. Potentially catastrophic environmental risks posed by the use or misuse of these technologies are already beginning to arouse widespread concern. . . .

Despite the potentially devastating impacts and growing importance of psychological injury, Congress and the Environmental Protection Agency (EPA) generally have not recognized fear as a harm in environmental statutes. Environmental law, in contrast to areas of law such as that governing hostile work environments, gives relatively little weight to emotional impacts. Nuisance actions against environmental pollution, for example, cannot rely on emotional injuries alone. . . . For most environmental statutes, Congress did not expressly consider fear as a harm. Rather, the more direct, tangible, and easily quantified health effects have driven the regulatory process. The question is not whether reasonable fear is a harm, but why environmental law generally has failed to treat reasonable fear as harm. Absent adequate justification for differential treatment, environmental law should address fear in a manner consistent with other areas of law. . . .

Exposure to toxics can give rise not only to fear, of course, but also to various physical changes in the body. Technological advances have enhanced scientists' ability to detect subcellular changes—such as chromosomal aberrations—and other potential precursors of toxic illness. These advances pose the question of whether the existence of such precursors, in the absence of a clinical diagnosis of illness, constitutes harm.

Existing safety and environmental regulations may limit the level and duration of exposure to toxic substances, but they do not eliminate all exposure or risk. Thus, an exposed individual may appear healthy, having no physical injuries or symptoms of illness, yet face a heightened level of risk. Because no physical harm is manifest—at least not yet—some might say there is no harm at all. Although courts increasingly allow plaintiffs in cases of toxic exposure to recover medical monitoring costs, such people are otherwise uncompensated for their heightened risk.

Technological advances in the detection and measurement of biomarkers will force reconsideration of such cases and of the nature of harm. Biomarkers are chemical substances or events in the human body that provide concrete evidence of exposure to a chemical, the effects of such exposure, and a person's susceptibility to disease. Of particular interest to this discussion are biomarkers of effect. These cellular responses to toxic exposure may signal or even increase the risk of adverse health consequences. As scientists develop more sophisticated analyses of biomarkers of effect, they will be able to measure bodily changes that are quantitatively or qualitatively predictive of health impairment resulting from toxic exposure. . . .

The question posed by such developments is whether the exposed individual has suffered harm. In contrast to the cancer victim, a person having high levels of [chromosomal aberrations (CAs)] has not yet suffered an obvious setback to welfare interests. Nevertheless, our growing knowledge about CAs may soon give rise to the ability to diagnose disease in such people before any symptoms appear. This development will blur the line between good health and disease, and that blurring will have implications for the law. For instance, tort law generally requires that a potential plaintiff be harmed before bringing suit. Whether high CA levels constitute harm may determine who can bring an action, as well as when an action can or must be brought. . . .

Illness is harm because it is a setback to physical well-being. Subcellular damage per se, however, does not constitute illness. Rather, it is a physical effect that may be a precursor or predictor of illness. Cancer, for instance, develops in a multistage process in which four to six critical genes must mutate before a malignant tumor appears. Such mutations may result from exposure to a mutagen, but they also may arise spontaneously in the process of cell division. Cancer results when a "sufficient number of mutations" have occurred in the "genes that control a cell's replication and repair functions so that the cell reproduces endlessly." As the process of cancer development illustrates, the presence of subcellular damage hardly guarantees that an individual will become ill.

There is thus a very significant qualitative difference between a person who has subcellular damage and a person who has cancer, as the judicial skepticism of subcellular injury claims reflects. Subcellular damage is extremely common, and it does not have the same impacts as a cancer diagnosis on daily life or on one's more ultimate interests. Moreover, it is the relative frequency of chromosomal aberrations, and not simply their presence or absence, that has predictive force. Because even single low-level exposures to carcinogens may cause damage to DNA, and because people who will never develop cancer nonetheless have cells containing damaged DNA, a view that any subcellular damage qualifies as harm means that virtually any activity—such as living in a house with ordinary background levels of radiation or breathing in cigarette smoke while visiting a casino—could be deemed harmful.

Even so, the difficulty of drawing a line between good health and disease cautions against an outright rejection of subcellular damage as harm. . . .

[I]n deciding whether subcellular damage constitutes harm, it is more important to focus on what the physical phenomena represent, rather than on the phenomena themselves. The ultimate question, in other words, is whether particular levels of subcellular damage make a difference to the welfare of the exposed individual. The answer to that question depends on whether any risk associated with subcellular damage is a harm. . . .

The question of whether risk constitutes harm is particularly important to toxic tort claims. Tort law has traditionally demanded physical, emotional, or economic injury as a prerequisite to recovery. Negligent behavior that imposes risk on another person, but causes no such injury, does not give rise to a cause of action. This is in contrast to preventative environmental regulation, which inherently regulates the risk of harm. Risk of harm is the inevitable object of regulation because regulation generally seeks to prevent harm before it occurs. Such regulation is consistent with the harm principle because reducing or eliminating the risk of physical harm protects one's fundamental welfare interest in not being physically injured. Tort law, however, requires proof of harm that has actually occurred. The question is whether risk alone can satisfy that requirement. [Lin explains that he is referring to "risk" as an objective conception—"that is, risk that has some objective existence in the physical world."]

... [W]e begin with a relatively simple case: if a sufficiently large population is exposed to a toxic substance, we might predict that a certain number of illnesses and deaths will result. In such a case, where risk is spread across a population, the harm is certain, although the victims are indeterminate. This is a clear instance of harm, because physical harm almost certainly will occur.

Such harm is distinct from "risk harm," which presents the more difficult question of whether there is harm when an individual is exposed to a one in one-hundred risk of cancer, but ultimately does not develop the disease. Here, the answer is less obvious because one cannot rely on the indisputably harmful nature of physical injuries. On the one hand, everyday activities are filled with numerous unrealized risks—risks that result in no physical harm and provide no recognized basis for a tort action. We simply accept such risks as part of daily life. ... The adage "no harm, no foul" would seem to suggest that risk harm is no harm at all.

On the other hand, even when the risked physical harm does not come to pass, being subjected to risk by others is an unsettling matter, particularly when the risk exposure occurs without one's knowledge or consent. ... [A] person who only after the fact becomes aware of high-level radiation exposure might still claim harm, even if no radiation-induced illness ever develops. [Professor Claire] Finkelstein contends that people subjected to such risks have been harmed because they have suffered an objective setback to their interests; the person exposed to radiation is now in a class of people with a higher risk of developing cancer, and thus is doing substantially less well in life. ...

... As with the concept of harm generally, whether risk constitutes harm is ultimately a question of social norms. ...

Ultimately, whether a risk constitutes harm depends on factors in addition to the probability and magnitude of harm. Because harm is a normative concept, society may reach very different judgments about the harmfulness of quantitatively similar risks. Indeed, gaps between public perceptions of risk and probabilistic notions of risk have widened over the last few decades. ... Studies of expressed preferences have found that public perceptions of risk depend on factors such as controllability, voluntariness, and equity, not just on raw probabilities. ...

The risks to the individual exposed to toxic substances ... are very different from the risks involved in skydiving. Risks from exposure to environmental toxins are not voluntary, readily observable, well understood, or equally distributed among the population. Even if it is theoretically possible to avoid such risks, it is often prohibitively difficult or costly to do so. These factors point toward a low social tolerance for such risks, and hence a judgment that such risks qualify as harm. Indeed, the involuntary nature of such risks may explain why they constitute harm: the imposition of involuntary risks infringes on individual autonomy, which is the core value that the harm principle seeks to promote.

The conclusion that involuntary risk is a harm does not necessarily dictate the recognition of a tort action. The use of substances that generate health or environmental risks, such as preservatives or pesticides, may reduce other risks. And government regulation may be a more appropriate response to risk than an enforceable "right" against risk, particularly for broadly distributed, low-level risks. . . . Notwithstanding the variety of possible responses to harm, the point remains: the imposition of significant involuntary risk is a serious setback to one's welfare because it interferes with one's autonomy. . . .

Harm is indeed the pivotal concern of much of environmental law. The aims of toxic tort, nuisance, and statutory environmental law are to prevent, deter, mitigate, and compensate for harm. Harm, however, is not an objective concept possessing a fixed meaning. Rather, harm is a normative concept dependent on social judgments about the interests that matter, bound up in social visions of the good and the bad.

Some commentators within and outside of environmental law have bemoaned the expansion of the concept of harm. The main complaint is that the harm principle, originally set forth by Mill as a limit on government power, is often employed to justify the regulation of morals under the guise of preventing harm. If harm is too broadly understood, jurisdiction to legislate might extend to almost any behavior. The expansion of the traditional concept of harm in environmental law beyond physical injury, however, does not—for the most part—pose such a danger. Rather, it reflects a more sophisticated understanding of the relationship between humans and the environment. . . .

[The realization that "many of our activities can, and do, cause harm to others"] does not dictate government involvement wherever harm is present; case-by-case policy decisions are still necessary. In such decisions, the nature and extent of harm at issue should be a critical consideration—as should interests in autonomy and other factors. . . . [T]he harm principle is not without limits even in our more informed and interconnected world. Most of modern environmental law is not really about deontological harm to the environment; it is about setbacks to fundamental human interests. These setbacks lie firmly within the harm principle. . . .

NOTE ON THE COMMON LAW APPROACH TO RISK AS INJURY

As the materials in this chapter demonstrate, one of the major innovations of environmental law has been to use the concept of risk as a proxy for injury for the common law's insistence that injury be established by proof that an action in fact caused demonstrable harm. This is a radical and thus controversial departure from the common law baseline reflected in Restatement of Torts (Second) §433B, which requires that a plaintiff prove that defendant's conduct is a substantial factor in bringing about harm. Although the test replaces the older "but for" standard of cause in fact, it still imposes a substantial burden on plaintiffs. To recover for a "toxic tort," a plaintiff must generally prove (1) exposure in an amount and over a period of time sufficient to cause the disease complained of, (2) the occurrence of the disease, (3) the elapse of an appropriate time interval between exposure and the disease, (4) a scientifically recognized relationship between the chemicals and the disease, and (5) the absence of alternative, equally probable explanations. See In re Paoli R.R. Yard PCB Litig., 916 F.2d 829 (3d Cir. 1990).

In particular, the required demonstration of causation has been more rigorous in the tort context, including toxic tort cases, than in regulatory contexts. In In re "Agent Orange" Product Liab. Litig., 597 F. Supp. 740, 781 (E.D.N.Y. 1984), aff'd, 818 F.2d 145 (2d Cir. 1987), Judge Weinstein stated that in a tort action as opposed to an action to review a risk-based regulation, "a far higher probability (greater than 50%) is required since the law believes it unfair to require an individual to pay for another's tragedy unless it is shown that it is more likely than not that he caused it." The moral basis of the necessity to prove cause in fact is expressed most clearly in criminal law, which adopts a "beyond a reasonable doubt" standard and a presumption of innocence to reduce the risk of factual error and preserve the moral force of the criminal law by preserving individual freedom. In re Winship, 397 U.S. 358, 363 (1970).

Nevertheless, the courts have developed novel theories of liability and causes of action, and litigants have sought to establish others that would facilitate the ability of plaintiffs to seek relief in toxic tort cases.

Market Share Liability. When regulators began to implement the modern environmental statutes, they had to confront what scientists have long known: most environmental decisions must be made under conditions of extreme uncertainty (Page's "ignorance of mechanism"). The regulated community seized on the pervasive uncertainty to argue that decisions should wait until "good science" provided conclusive evidence of harm. Beginning with EPA's decision to cancel DDT's pesticide registration based on the chemical's human health risks, however, the agency increasingly accepted risk as a sufficient basis to justify regulation, rather than insisting upon proof of past harm. Probabilistic cause has a limited basis in the common law. The leading case is Sindell v. Abbott Lab., 607 P.2d 924 (Cal. 1980). Plaintiff alleged that she developed a malignant bladder tumor and other precancerous growths from DES, an anti-miscarriage drug. Because she could not identify the manufacturer of the drug that she ingested, the plaintiff sued the entire industry. To allow the plaintiff to recover, the California Supreme Court applied the rule of Summers v. Tice, 199 P.2d 1 (Cal. 1948), to create a new rule of market share liability. In *Summers*, one of two hunters shot the plaintiff, and the court shifted the burden to the two defendants to absolve themselves. The court's approach is sometimes referred to as the alternative liability approach. Under the Restatement (Second) of Torts §433B(3), "[w]here the conduct of two or more actors is tortious, and it is proved that harm has been caused to the plaintiff by only one of them, but there is uncertainty as to which one has caused it, the burden is upon each such actor to prove that he has not caused the harm." The *Sindell* court applied the alternative liability theory:

> . . . [W]e hold it to be reasonable in the present context to measure the likelihood that any of the defendants supplied the product which allegedly injured plaintiff by the percentage which the DES sold by each of them for the purpose of preventing miscarriage bears to the entire production of the drug sold by all for that purpose. . . .
>
> If plaintiff joins in the action the manufacturers of a substantial share of the DES which her mother might have taken, the injustice of shifting the burden of proof to defendants to demonstrate that they could not have made the substance which injured plaintiff is significantly diminished. . . .
>
> The presence in the action of a substantial share of the appropriate market also provides a ready means to apportion damages among the defendants. Each defendant will be held liable for the proportion of the judgment represented by its share of that

market unless it demonstrates that it could not have made the product which caused plaintiff's injuries. . . . Once plaintiff has met her burden of joining the required defendants, they in turn may cross-complaint against other DES manufacturers, not joined in the action, which they can allege might have supplied the injury-causing product. [607 P.2d at 937.]

Sindell has been adopted in several other states, but other courts have rejected it. For example, Smith v. Eli Lilly & Co., 560 N.E.2d 324 (Ill. 1990), rejected market share liability because it is difficult to make allocations, there is a high risk that they will be arbitrary, and the rule provides a disincentive to disclose and recall products on the market. Multiple causal agent cases are different from the usual toxic tort case where the consequence of exposure is uncertain. Does this explain the New Jersey Supreme Court's rejection of a collective liability approach in favor of one that requires toxic tort plaintiffs to establish factual proof of frequent, regular, and proximate exposure to a product and medical and/or scientific proof of a nexus between exposure and plaintiff's condition? James v. Bessemer Processing Co., 714 A.2d 898 (N.J. 1998). Compare Conde v. Velsicol Chem. Corp., 24 F.3d 809 (6th Cir. 1994) (expert testimony that exposure to chlordane was "consistent with" the plaintiffs' health problems did not demonstrate that the exposure caused their injuries).

Commingled Product Theory. A tort action brought by a group of local governments and public and private water suppliers against companies engaged in the design, manufacture, or distribution of gasoline containing methyl tertiary butyl ether (MTBE) provided the occasion for the modification of the market share liability theory as an additional means of addressing scientific uncertainty relating to causation of injuries traceable to exposure to toxic substances. In re Methyl Tertiary Butyl Ether ("MTBE") Products Liab. Litig., 379 F. Supp. 2d 348 (S.D.N.Y. 2005). The plaintiffs sought relief for the defendants' alleged contamination or threatened contamination of groundwater with MTBE. The defendants moved to dismiss the complaints (which had been filed in 15 states) because the plaintiffs failed to identify which defendants' MTBE-containing gasoline proximately caused their harm. The plaintiffs conceded that they could not identify the offending product due to its fungible nature and the commingling of many suppliers' petroleum products during transportation and distribution. The issue was whether plaintiffs could proceed on their tort claims based on the theory of collective liability.

After explaining and distinguishing among the theories of concert of action, alternative, enterprise, or market share liability, the court described the latter as "uniquely suited to fungible product cases because such products (1) create the problem of non-identification in the first place, and (2) pose equal risks of harm to those exposed to the product." Id. at 376. The court found that MTBE presented as compelling a circumstance for the application of market share liability as DES, the drug at issue in *Sindell*. It also explained that courts on occasion have fashioned new approaches to tort liability to permit plaintiffs to pursue recovery when the circumstances raise unforeseen barriers to relief. The MTBE cases "suggest the need for one more theory, which can be viewed as a modification of market share liability, incorporating elements of concurrent wrongdoing." Id. The court described its new theory of "commingled product" market share liability as follows:

> When a plaintiff can prove that certain gaseous or liquid products (e.g., gasoline, liquid propane, alcohol) of many suppliers were present in a completely commingled or

blended state at the time and place that the risk of harm occurred, and the commingled product caused a single indivisible injury, then each of the products should be deemed to have caused the harm. [Id. at 377-378.]

Accordingly, if a defendant's indistinct product was present in the area of contamination and was commingled with the products of other suppliers, all of the suppliers can be held severally liable for any harm arising from an incident of contamination. Damages would be apportioned by reference to a defendant's share of the market at the time a risk of harm was created to a class of potential victims. A defendant may exculpate itself by proving that its product was not present at the relevant time and place and therefore could not have been part of the new commingled or blended product. Plaintiffs invoking this theory must identify those defendants believed to have contributed to the commingled product that caused the injury, after conducting "some investigation so that they can make a good faith identification of the defendants whom they believe caused their injury." Id. at 378. The court explained that its modification of market share liability was distinguishable from previous applications of market share liability because the product of each supplier is known to be present and it is also known that the commingled product caused the harm. "What is *not known* is what percentage of each supplier's goods is present in the blended product that caused the harm." Id. at 378-379. In addition, the theory applies even though the harm caused by the commingled product does not necessarily have a long latency period before the discovery of the harm because this fact has no effect on the victim's ability to identify the actual tortfeasor. The court then predicted how each of the 15 states involved in the suit would react to the new liability theory. See also In re MTBE Products Liab. Litig., 415 F. Supp. 2d 261 (S.D.N.Y. 2005).

As the Lin article indicates, persons claiming exposure to toxic chemicals have sought recovery for a variety of alleged harms, including the increased risk of future injury stemming from the exposure, immune system impairment, the costs of medical monitoring, the fear of contracting cancer, and post-traumatic stress disorder. Endorsement of these novel causes of action is another route to recognition of probabilistic cause. According to Lin, what is the unifying thread that provides the basis for deciding whether or not these should be recognized as legitimate causes of action? Which of the causes of action does his analysis support? Judicial receptivity has been mixed.

Fear of Illness. In Sterling v. Velsicol Chem. Corp., 855 F.2d 1188 (6th Cir. 1988), plaintiffs established defendant's liability for personal injuries sustained as a result of drinking and using well water contaminated by organic chemical toxicants from defendant's negligent operation of a nearby hazardous waste disposal site. Unlike the plaintiff in *Wilsonville*, the plaintiffs in *Sterling* had already sustained a variety of physical injuries. The court nevertheless required the plaintiffs to show to "a reasonable medical certainty" that the contaminated water caused bodily harm. Damages may not be "speculative or conjectural" and may not be based on a mere "probability" or "likelihood," especially for diseases that may result from a variety of causes that "inflict society at random, often with no known specific origin." Id. at 1200. How does this test compare to the test in *Wilsonville*?

Applying the reasonable medical certainty test, the court in *Sterling* held that fear of increased risk of cancer was "clearly" a present injury and compensable, but only for "reasonable" fear. The mere risk of cancer and kidney and liver diseases was noncompensable because the risk was 25-30 percent, not the required 50-plus percent (i.e., "more probable than not"). The court denied damages for immune system impairment and learning disorders entirely because no generally accepted scientific theory of causation exists for these injuries. It also denied damage awards for post-traumatic stress disorder, holding that drinking the contaminated water was not sufficiently stressful and that no recurring fear existed. Compare In re Berg Litig., 293 F.3d 1127 (9th Cir. 2002) (Price Anderson Act does not allow claims for emotional distress or medical monitoring absent present physical injury). Even if a court refuses to recognize a separate cause of action for fear of illness or other injury, it may allow a plaintiff who prevails on a more traditional cause of action (such as trespass, nuisance, or negligence) to recover for emotional distress as an element of damages for that claim. See, e.g., Nnadili v. Chevron U.S.A. Inc., 435 F. Supp. 2d 93 (D.D.C. 2006).

Medical Monitoring. The leading case of Ayers v. Township of Jackson, 525 A.2d 287 (N.J. 1987), rejected the creation of a new tort of "cancerphobia," in part because the damages were too speculative and it would be difficult to adjudicate damage claims. The court did recognize a right to recover damages for the medical expenses necessary to monitor the enhanced risk caused by exposure. Theer v. Philip Carey Co., 628 A.2d 724 (N.J. 1993), however, limits *Ayers* to cases of direct exposure where the plaintiff suffered some injury. In Bower v. Westinghouse Elec. Corp., 522 S.E.2d 424 (W. Va. 1999), the court endorsed a cause of action for medical monitoring costs as "a well-grounded extension of traditional common-law tort principles" in the sense that a claim for medical monitoring is essentially a claim for future damages. The court did not insist that the plaintiff seeking such costs demonstrate the existence of any present physical harm or even the probable likelihood that a serious disease will result from the exposure. It remarked that "significant economic damage may be inflicted on those exposed to toxic substances, notwithstanding the fact that the physical harm resulting from such exposure is often latent." Thus, the exposure itself and the concomitant need for testing constitute the injury. The West Virginia Supreme Court refused to extend *Bower* to recognize a separate cause of action for the recovery of the costs of future inspection and monitoring of real property located next to a chemical dump, where the plaintiffs had not yet demonstrated that their properties had been exposed to a hazardous substance. Carter v. Monsanto Co., 575 S.E.2d 342 (W. Va. 2002).

The Supreme Court of Alabama reached a result diametrically opposed to that in *Bower* in Hinton v. Monsanto Co., 813 So. 2d 827 (Ala. 2001). It held that a complaint that does not allege any past or present personal injury to the plaintiff does not state a cause of action for medical monitoring and study when the plaintiff alleges that he has been exposed to hazardous contamination by the defendant's conduct. Alabama law has long required a manifest, present injury before a plaintiff may recover in tort. The court found insufficient justification to abandon that principle. Recognition of a cause of action for medical monitoring "based upon nothing more than an increased risk that an injury or an illness might one day occur" would require the courts to decide cases "based upon nothing more than speculation and conjecture." Id. at 830. The court noted the possible "ill effects" of this kind of "drastic departure" from traditional tort law rules and asserted that, even though there were important competing considerations, a cost-benefit analysis counseled against recognition of the cause of action in these circumstances.

The Michigan Supreme Court reached the same result in Henry v. Dow Chem. Co., 701 N.W.2d 784 (Mich. 2005). The plaintiffs brought a class action against Dow, alleging that it negligently released dioxin into the floodplain where the plaintiffs lived and worked, creating the risk of future disease. The plaintiffs sought to require Dow to pay to monitor the class for possible future manifestations of dioxin-related disease. The court declined to provide the remedy sought, holding that the plaintiffs did not present a viable negligence claim because they did not allege a present injury. It interpreted Michigan negligence law as requiring proof of present physical injuries and economic losses that result from those injuries. According to the court, recognition of a cause of action for medical monitoring in the absence of present physical injuries would create a potentially limitless pool of plaintiffs. Litigation of pre-injury claims could drain resources needed to compensate those with manifest physical injuries and a more immediate need for medical care. "Simply put," the court stated, "recognition of a medical monitoring cause of action may do more harm than good—not only for Michigan's economy but also for 'other potential plaintiffs who are not before the court and who depend on a tort system that can distinguish between reliable and serious claims on the one hand, and unreliable and relatively trivial claims on the other.'" Id. at 696. Although the court was unsure what the consequences of granting the relief requested might be, it feared that they "may well be disastrous," including "wreak[ing] enormous harm on Michigan's citizens and its economy." Finally, the court invoked the principle of separation of powers, referring to the judiciary's obligation to exercise caution and defer to the legislature when called upon to make "potentially societally dislocating change to the common law." Id. at 697. One judge dissented, asserting that the court's result "inexcusably" rendered the plaintiffs' physical health secondary to defendant's economic health. The dissent warned that the rejection of the medical monitoring cause of action would induce corporations to continue to operate in ways that harm nearby residents. "And it is the people of our state who will pay the costs—with their money and with their lives—of allowing defendant to contaminate our environment with no repercussions. Sadly, this Court has resorted to a cost-benefit analysis to determine and, consequently, degrade the value of human life, and this is an analysis I cannot support." Id. at 715.

Increased Risk. Potter v. Firestone Tire & Rubber Co., 863 P.2d 795 (Cal. 1993), recognizes a limited tort of enhanced risk exposure. Firestone maintained a toxic landfill that contaminated plaintiffs' wells. Plaintiffs manifested no immediate injuries but sued for fear of an increased risk of cancer. The court held that there is a tort of increased risk of cancer that does not require a showing of physical injury. But it adopted a very high objective standard to prevent medical research into products like prescription drugs from being chilled, to prevent liability insurance for toxic liability risks from becoming unavailable or unaffordable, and to ensure that compensation remains available for those individuals who actually develop cancer or other physical harms. Plaintiff must prove that it is more likely than not that cancer will develop, except in cases of fraud, oppression, or malice. This exception applied to Firestone because it ignored warnings about the dangers of careless waste disposal practices.*

Lin, Beyond Tort: Compensating Victims of Environmental Toxic Injury, 78 S. Cal. L. Rev. 1439 (2005), proposes a "risk-based" administrative system of liability and compensation for exposure to toxic pollutants. Under Professor Lin's proposed system, levies would be assessed against polluters based on the amounts discharged, the degree of likely human exposure, the risk of harm from exposure, and the expected costs of

---

*Compare Bonnette v. Conoco, Inc., 837 So. 2d 1219 (La. 2003) (declining to allow damage recovery for a "slightly" increased risk of developing cancer as a result of exposure to soil containing asbestos particles).

harm to victims. The levies would be used to compensate individuals according to the health risk they bear as a result of toxic exposures.*

DAUBERT v. MERRELL DOW PHARMACEUTICALS, INC.
509 U.S. 579 (1993)

JUSTICE BLACKMUN delivered the opinion of the Court.

In this case we are called upon to determine the standard for admitting expert scientific testimony in a federal trial.

[Petitioners, minor children born with serious birth defects, and their parents sued Merrell Dow (Merrell or respondent), alleging that the birth defects had been caused by the mothers' ingestion of Bendectin, a prescription antinausea drug marketed by Merrell. Merrell moved for summary judgment, contending that Bendectin does not cause birth defects in humans and that petitioners would not be able to come forward with any admissible evidence that it does. Merrell relied on an affidavit of a well-credentialed physician and epidemiologist, Dr. Lamm, with expertise on the risks from exposure to various chemical substances. In his review of the literature on Bendectin and human birth defects, Dr. Lamm located no study finding Bendectin to be a human teratogen (i.e., a substance capable of causing malformations in fetuses). Dr. Lamm concluded that maternal use of Bendectin during the first trimester of pregnancy had not been shown to be a risk factor for human birth defects.

Instead of contesting this characterization of the published record, petitioners submitted the testimony of eight more well-credentialed experts, all of whom concluded that Bendectin can cause birth defects. Petitioners' experts relied on "in vitro" (test tube) and "in vivo" (live) animal studies; "pharmacological studies of the chemical structure of Bendectin that purported to show similarities between the structure of the drug and that of other substances known to cause birth defects; and the 'reanalysis' of previously published epidemiological (human statistical) studies."

The district court awarded summary judgment to Merrell, stating that scientific evidence is admissible only if the principle upon which it is based is "sufficiently established to have general acceptance in the field to which it belongs." Petitioners' evidence did not meet this standard.] Given the vast body of epidemiological data concerning Bendectin, the court held, expert opinion which is not based on epidemiological evidence is not admissible to establish causation. Thus, the animal-cell studies, live-animal studies, and chemical-structure analyses on which petitioners had relied could not raise by themselves a reasonably disputable jury issue regarding causation. Petitioners' epidemiological analyses, based as they were on recalculations of data in previously published studies that had found no causal link between the drug and birth defects, were ruled to be inadmissible because they had not been published or subjected to peer review.

[The Ninth Circuit affirmed. Citing Frye v. United States, 293 F. 1013 (D.C. Cir. 1923), it] stated that expert opinion based on a scientific technique is inadmissible

---

*For more on these novel toxic exposure–based causes of action, see Martin & Martin, Tort Actions for Medical Monitoring: Warranted or Wasteful?, 20 Colum. J. Envtl. L. 121 (1995); Wells, The Grin without the Cat: Claims for Damages from Toxic Exposure without Present Injury, 18 Wm. & Mary J. Envtl. L. 285 (1994); Donath, Comment, Curing Cancerphobia Phobia: Reasonableness Redefined, 62 U. Chi. L. Rev. 1113 (1995). A collection of articles titled Toxic Torts and the Environmental Lawyer can be found at 17 Nat. Resources & Env't (Spring 2003).

unless the technique is "generally accepted" as reliable in the relevant scientific community. The court declared that expert opinion based on a methodology that diverges "significantly from the procedures accepted by recognized authorities in the field . . . cannot be shown to be 'generally accepted as a reliable technique.'" . . .

II

A

In the 70 years since its formulation in the *Frye* case, the "general acceptance" test has been the dominant standard for determining the admissibility of novel scientific evidence at trial. Although under increasing attack of late, the rule continues to be followed by a majority of courts, including the Ninth Circuit.

The *Frye* test has its origin in a short and citation-free 1923 decision concerning the admissibility of evidence derived from a systolic blood pressure deception test, a crude precursor to the polygraph machine. In what has become a famous (perhaps infamous) passage, the then Court of Appeals for the District of Columbia described the device and its operation and declared:

> Just when a scientific principle or discovery crosses the line between the experimental and demonstrable stages is difficult to define. Somewhere in this twilight zone the evidential force of the principle must be recognized, and while courts will go a long way in admitting expert testimony deduced from a well-recognized scientific principle or discovery, *the thing from which the deduction is made must be sufficiently established to have gained general acceptance in the particular field in which it belongs.* 293 F., at 1014 (emphasis added). . . .

[Petitioners contended that the *Frye* test was superseded by the Federal Rules of Evidence.] Here there is a specific Rule that speaks to the contested issue. Rule 702, governing expert testimony, provides:

> If scientific, technical, or other specialized knowledge will assist the trier of fact to understand the evidence or to determine a fact in issue, a witness qualified as an expert by knowledge, skill, experience, training, or education, may testify thereto in the form of an opinion or otherwise.

Nothing in the text of this Rule establishes "general acceptance" as an absolute prerequisite to admissibility. Nor does respondent present any clear indication that Rule 702 or the Rules as a whole were intended to incorporate a "general acceptance" standard. The drafting history makes no mention of *Frye*, and a rigid "general acceptance" requirement would be at odds with the "liberal thrust" of the Federal Rules and their "general approach of relaxing the traditional barriers to 'opinion' testimony." Beech Aircraft Corp. v. Rainey, 488 U.S., at 169 (citing Rules 701 to 705). See also Weinstein, Rule 702 of the Federal Rules of Evidence Is Sound; It Should Not Be Amended, 138 F.R.D. 631 (1991) ("The Rules were designed to depend primarily upon lawyer-adversaries and sensible triers of fact to evaluate conflicts"). Given the Rules' permissive backdrop and their inclusion of a specific rule on expert testimony that does not mention "general acceptance," the assertion that the Rules somehow assimilated *Frye* is unconvincing. *Frye* made "general acceptance" the exclusive test for admitting expert scientific testimony. That austere standard, absent from, and incompatible with, the Federal Rules of Evidence, should not be applied in federal trials.

B

That the *Frye* test was displaced by the Rules of Evidence does not mean, however, that the Rules themselves place no limits on the admissibility of purportedly scientific evidence. Nor is the trial judge disabled from screening such evidence. To the contrary, under the Rules the trial judge must ensure that any and all scientific testimony or evidence admitted is not only relevant, but reliable.

The primary locus of this obligation is Rule 702, which clearly contemplates some degree of regulation of the subjects and theories about which an expert may testify. "*If scientific*, technical, or other specialized *knowledge will assist the trier of fact* to understand the evidence or to determine a fact in issue" an expert "may testify *thereto*." (Emphasis added.) The subject of an expert's testimony must be "scientific . . . knowledge." The adjective "scientific" implies a grounding in the methods and procedures of science. Similarly, the word "knowledge" connotes more than subjective belief or unsupported speculation. The term "applies to any body of known facts or to any body of ideas inferred from such facts or accepted as truths on good grounds." Webster's Third New International Dictionary 1252 (1986). Of course, it would be unreasonable to conclude that the subject of scientific testimony must be "known" to a certainty; arguably, there are no certainties in science. See, e.g., Brief for American Association for the Advancement of Science et al. as Amici Curiae 7-8 ("Science is not an encyclopedic body of knowledge about the universe. Instead, it represents a *process* for proposing and refining theoretical explanations about the world that are subject to further testing and refinement"). But, in order to qualify as "scientific knowledge," an inference or assertion must be derived by the scientific method. Proposed testimony must be supported by appropriate validation—i.e., "good grounds," based on what is known. In short, the requirement that an expert's testimony pertain to "scientific knowledge" establishes a standard of evidentiary reliability. . . .

C

Faced with a proffer of expert scientific testimony, then, the trial judge must determine at the outset, pursuant to Rule 104(a), whether the expert is proposing to testify to (1) scientific knowledge that (2) will assist the trier of fact to understand or determine a fact in issue. This entails a preliminary assessment of whether the reasoning or methodology underlying the testimony is scientifically valid and of whether that reasoning or methodology properly can be applied to the facts in issue. We are confident that federal judges possess the capacity to undertake this review. Many factors will bear on the inquiry, and we do not presume to set out a definitive checklist or test. But some general observations are appropriate.

Ordinarily, a key question to be answered in determining whether a theory or technique is scientific knowledge that will assist the trier of fact will be whether it can be (and has been) tested. "Scientific methodology today is based on generating hypotheses and testing them to see if they can be falsified; indeed, this methodology is what distinguishes science from other fields of human inquiry." Green 645. See also K. Popper, Conjectures and Refutations: The Growth of Scientific Knowledge 37 (5th ed. 1989) ("[T]he criterion of the scientific status of a theory is its falsifiability, or refutability, or testability").

Another pertinent consideration is whether the theory or technique has been subjected to peer review and publication. Publication (which is but one element of peer review) is not a *sine qua non* of admissibility; it does not necessarily correlate with reliability, and in some instances well-grounded but innovative theories will not have been published. Some propositions, moreover, are too particular, too new, or of too limited interest to be published. But submission to the scrutiny of the scientific community is a component of "good science," in part because it increases the likelihood that substantive flaws in methodology will be detected. The fact of publication (or lack thereof) in a peer reviewed journal thus will be a relevant, though not dispositive, consideration in assessing the scientific validity of a particular technique or methodology on which an opinion is premised.

Additionally, in the case of a particular scientific technique, the court ordinarily should consider the known or potential rate of error, and the existence and maintenance of standards controlling the technique's operation.

Finally, "general acceptance" can yet have a bearing on the inquiry. A "reliability assessment does not require, although it does permit, explicit identification of a relevant scientific community and an express determination of a particular degree of acceptance within that community." United States v. Downing, 753 F.2d, at 1238. Widespread acceptance can be an important factor in ruling particular evidence admissible, and "a known technique which has been able to attract only minimal support within the community," id. at 1238, may properly be viewed with skepticism.

The inquiry envisioned by Rule 702 is, we emphasize, a flexible one. Its overarching subject is the scientific validity—and thus the evidentiary relevance and reliability—of the principles that underlie a proposed submission. The focus, of course, must be solely on principles and methodology, not on the conclusions that they generate. . . .

III

. . . Respondent expresses apprehension that abandonment of "general acceptance" as the exclusive requirement for admission will result in a "free-for-all" in which befuddled juries are confounded by absurd and irrational pseudoscientific assertions. In this regard respondent seems to us to be overly pessimistic about the capabilities of the jury and of the adversary system generally. Vigorous cross-examination, presentation of contrary evidence, and careful instruction on the burden of proof are the traditional and appropriate means of attacking shaky but admissible evidence. Additionally, in the event the trial court concludes that the scintilla of evidence presented supporting a position is insufficient to allow a reasonable juror to conclude that the position more likely than not is true, the court remains free to direct a judgment, Fed. Rule Civ. Proc. 50(a), and likewise to grant summary judgment, Fed. Rule Civ. Proc. 56. . . . These conventional devices, rather than wholesale exclusion under an uncompromising "general acceptance" test, are the appropriate safeguards where the basis of scientific testimony meets the standards of Rule 702.

Petitioners and, to a greater extent, their amici exhibit a different concern. They suggest that recognition of a screening role for the judge that allows for the exclusion of "invalid" evidence will sanction a stifling and repressive scientific orthodoxy and will be inimical to the search for truth. It is true that open debate is an essential part of both legal and scientific analyses. Yet there are important differences between the quest for truth in the courtroom and the quest for truth in the laboratory. Scientific conclusions are subject to perpetual revision. Law, on the other hand, must resolve disputes finally and quickly. The scientific project is advanced by broad and wide-ranging consideration of a multitude of hypotheses, for those that are incorrect will eventually be shown to be so, and that in itself is an advance. Conjectures that are probably wrong are of little use, however, in the project of reaching a quick, final, and binding legal judgment—often of great consequence—about a particular set of events in the past. We recognize that, in practice, a gatekeeping role for the judge, no matter how flexible, inevitably on occasion will prevent the jury from learning of authentic insights and innovations. That, nevertheless, is the balance that is struck by Rules of Evidence designed not for the exhaustive search for cosmic understanding but for the particularized resolution of legal disputes. . . .

NOTES AND QUESTIONS

1. *The Scope of the* Daubert *Ruling.* Does *Daubert* require a higher standard for reviewing the trial judge's admissibility rulings on expert testimony than the standard that applies to other evidentiary rulings? General Elec. Co. v. Joiner, 522 U.S. 136 (1997), holds that *Daubert* does not modify the prior abuse-of-discretion standard. In Weisgram v. Marley Co., 528 U.S. 440 (2000), the Court held that if the court of appeals decides that the district court should have excluded the plaintiff's expert testimony and that the remaining evidence is insufficient to justify a jury verdict for the plaintiff, the appellate court may instruct the district court to enter judgment against the plaintiff. *Weisgram* describes the standards for the admissibility of expert testimony set forth in *Daubert* and its progeny as "exacting standards of reliability." Id. at 455. In Kumho Tire Co. v. Carmichael, 526 U.S. 1377 (1999), the Court extended *Daubert* to the testimony of engineers and other experts who are not scientists. The trial judge's "gatekeeping" obligation therefore applies not only to testimony based on scientific knowledge, but also to testimony based on technical and other specialized knowledge. Because *Daubert*'s test of reliability is flexible, the list of specific factors set forth there "neither necessarily nor exclusively applies to all experts or in every case."

In 2000, Rule 702 was amended by the addition of the following language at the end of the previous version of the rule: "if (1) the testimony is based upon sufficient facts or data, (2) the testimony is the product of reliable principles and methods, and (3) the witness has applied the principles and methods reliably to the facts of the case." The Advisory Committee notes indicate that the amendment "affirms the trial court's role as gatekeeper and provides some general standards that the trial court must use to assess the reliability and helpfulness of proffered expert testimony." Although no attempt was made to "codify" the specific factors set forth in *Daubert* for assessing the reliability of expert testimony, the "standards set forth in the amendment are broad enough to require consideration of any or all of the specific *Daubert* factors where appropriate." Additional factors also may be relevant.

A trial court ruling on the admissibility of expert scientific testimony need not take into account all of the factors the Court mentioned in *Daubert* as being relevant to the question of whether the testimony represents scientific knowledge. In Ellis v. Gallatin Steel Co., 390 F.3d 461 (6th Cir. 2004), the court concluded that the failure to consider the absence of peer review or scholarly writing did not preclude admission of testimony relating to an assessment of a local real estate market.

The test for admissibility of scientific expert testimony in state courts is not necessarily the same as for federal court. In Goeb v. Tharaldson, 615 N.W.2d 800 (Minn. 2000), the court refused to abandon the *Frye* general acceptance test, as modified by previous Minnesota Supreme Court decisions to require an additional showing that the particular evidence derived from a novel scientific test has a foundation that is scientifically reliable, in favor of the *Daubert* approach. The court reached that result even though the applicable Minnesota rule of evidence was identical to Rule 702 of the Federal Rules of Evidence. The court reasoned that the *Daubert* approach confers upon "judges uneducated in science the authority to determine what is scientific," whereas *Frye* "ensures that the persons most qualified to assess scientific validity of a technique have the determinative voice." Id. at 813. See also Donalson v. Central Ill. Pub. Serv. Co., 767 N.E.2d 314, 323 (2002) ("Illinois law is unequivocal: the exclusive test for the admission of expert testimony is governed by the standard first expressed in [*Frye*]").

2. *Independence and Peer Review.* On remand in *Daubert,* the plaintiffs' proffered evidence was found inadmissible. The Ninth Circuit indicated that one significant factor in determining reliability is

> whether the experts are proposing to testify about matters growing naturally and directly out of research they have conducted independent of the litigation, or whether they have developed their opinions expressly for purposes of testifying. . . .
>
> That an expert testifies based on research he has conducted independent of the litigation provides important, objective proof that the research comports with the dictates of good science. For one thing, experts whose findings flow from existing research are less likely to have been biased toward a particular conclusion by the promise of remuneration; when an expert prepares reports and findings before being hired as a witness, that record will limit the degree to which he can tailor his testimony to serve a party's interests. Then, too, independent research carries its own indicia of reliability, as it is conducted, so to speak, in the usual course of business and must normally satisfy a variety of standards to attract funding and institutional support. Finally, there is usually a limited number of scientists actively conducting research on the very subject that is germane to a particular case, which provides a natural constraint on parties' ability to shop for experts who will come to the desired conclusion. . . . [Daubert v. Merrell Dow Pharmaceuticals, Inc., 43 F.3d 1311, 1317 (9th Cir. 1995).]

None of the plaintiffs' experts based their testimony concerning Bendectin's effect on limb reduction defects on research conducted before they were hired to testify in *Daubert* or related cases. Because the plaintiffs' proffered expert testimony was not based on independent research, they had to produce other evidence that was objective and verifiable, such as scrutiny through peer review and publication. But none of the plaintiffs' experts had published their work on Bendectin in scientific journals, and no other scientists had verified, refuted, or commented on that work. "It's as if there were a tacit understanding within the scientific community that what's going on here is not science at all, but litigation." Id. at 1318.*

---

*For other post-*Daubert* cases in which expert testimony was excluded, see Marmo v. Tyson Fresh Meats, Inc., 457 F.3d 748 (8th Cir. 2006) (upholding trial court's decision to exclude testimony of toxicologist concerning extent of injuries caused by exposure to air pollution because she had never examined the plaintiff); Dodge v. Cotter Corp., 328 F.3d 1212 (10th Cir. 2003) (trial court should have excluded testimony of geologist, toxicologist, and oncologist due to absence of sufficient findings on the reliability of their expert testimony); Nelson v. Tennessee Gas Pipeline Co., 243 F.3d 244 (6th Cir.

3. *Science and Risk Regulation. Daubert* excludes the kind of evidence that is routinely used to set toxic exposure standards, extrapolations from animal studies. See In re Paoli R.R. Yard PCB Litig., 35 F.3d 717, 743 (3d Cir. 1994). Does *Daubert* foreclose risk-based regulation and reliance on new fields of applied science because it makes it easier to attack science-based regulation? Should the standard of proof of causation be less for public health-based regulation than for tort liability?

Regulatory science, the science demanded by regulators to support public health and biodiversity regulations, is often done in response to a specific regulatory program. Regulatory science is driven by policy questions raised by public officials rather than by research agendas set by individual scientists. Often, environmental regulations require scientists to answer questions that they consider nonscientific, or at least to answer questions that arise in a form different from the way they arise within traditional scientific research. Thus, prior research data and research designs are generally not adequate to answer the question posed by legislation. In short, scientists are asked to answer questions that are not classically "scientific." The answer often involves moral judgments about resource worth. Would a *Daubert* approach reject such judgments as unscientific, and therefore insufficient to justify regulatory action? Is regulatory science likely to be able to meet the *Daubert* criteria, such as falsifiability? Must all environmental standards designed to limit external costs be grounded in the scientific method as applied in *Daubert*? Does the last part of Justice Blackmun's opinion adequately address these concerns?* See generally Kelly, The Dangers of *Daubert* Creep in the Regulatory Realm, 14 J.L. & Pol'y 165 (2006) (addressing the "danger that *Daubert* can undermine administrative law by fostering an attitude of skepticism of agency action based upon science and creating a rhetorical weapon with which to attack agency policy-making").

C.　EARLY STATUTORY EXAMPLES OF PRECAUTIONARY REGULATION OF RISK

Environmental legislation often goes beyond the common law in authorizing the abatement of dangers posed by hazardous substances. Professor Applegate has summarized one rationale for shifting the focus of concern from harm to risk as a means of

---

2001) (upholding exclusion of expert testimony that sought to establish that personal injuries were caused by exposure to PCBs due to lack of peer review and failure to show temporal relationship between exposure and symptoms); Kalamazoo River Study Group v. Rockwell Int'l Corp., 171 F.3d 1065 (6th Cir. 1999) (affirming district court's issuance of summary judgment for PRP in CERCLA cost recovery action due to unreliability of testimony by plaintiff's expert witness on causation of contamination); Seneca Meadows, Inc. v. ECI Liquidating, Inc., 427 F. Supp. 2d 279 (W.D.N.Y. 2006) (relying on absence of peer review and general acceptance in relevant scientific community to exclude testimony in CERCLA case). Cf. New Mexico v. General Elec. Co., 335 F. Supp. 2d 1266 (D.N.M. 2004) (admitting expert testimony on the impact of groundwater contamination). A study by the RAND Institute for Civil Justice found that the proportion of expert evidence that district courts have excluded increased after *Daubert*. L. Dixon & B. Gill, Changes in the Standards for Admitting Expert Evidence in Federal Civil Cases Since the Daubert Decision (2001), available at http://www.rand.org/publications/MR/MR1439/MR1439.pdf.

*For further reading, see Capra, The *Daubert* Puzzle, 32 Ga. L. Rev. 699 (1998); Symposium, Scientific Evidence after the Death of *Frye*, 15 Cardozo L. Rev. 1745 (1994); Gagen, What Is an Environmental Expert? The Impact of *Daubert*, *Joiner*, and *Kumho Tire* on the Admissibility of Scientific Expert Evidence, 19 UCLA J. Envtl. L. & Pol'y 401 (2001/2002).

redressing the deficiencies in common law standards in controlling risks to health and the environment.

> [R]egulation of risk instead of harm . . . contrasts with, and is a reaction to, the traditional tort law rule that damages can be recovered only for actual harm or for the definite likelihood of future harm to the individual plaintiff. Toxic effects are extremely difficult to prove under the preponderance of the evidence standard of civil litigation because of the great uncertainty caused by the passage of time (latency), the relative unlikelihood of causation (rarity of effect), and the possibility of other causes (nonsignature diseases) present in most toxic substances cases. As a result, tort law fails to internalize these costs and serves as a poor deterrent to toxic risk creation.
>
> An important impetus for governmental regulation was the desire to overcome this obstacle to successful recovery for toxic injury. . . . Risk is an expression of uncertainty; it is easier to prove than actual harm. Regulation based on risk permits regulatory action based on *ex ante* collective danger rather than *ex post* individual injury, and also operates preventively to avert injury to the public as a whole. [Applegate, The Perils of Unreasonable Risk: Information, Regulatory Policy, and Toxic Substances Control, 91 Colum. L. Rev. 261, 271-273 (1991).]

The question of whether Congress intended to depart from common law standards was raised in two landmark cases. In each case, brief federal statutes authorized the abatement of conditions that "endangered" the public health. In each, the strict common law approach denying abatement of risks was first embraced by the majority of a three-judge panel and then rejected on fuller consideration en banc. The second of the two cases, *Ethyl Corp.*, is excerpted below. The first case, Reserve Mining Co. v. EPA, 514 F.2d 492 (8th Cir. 1975), is discussed in the notes following *Ethyl Corp.*

ETHYL CORP. v. EPA
541 F.2d 1 (D.C. Cir. 1976)

[Section 211(c)(1)(A) of the Clean Air Act authorized the Administrator of EPA to regulate gasoline additives if their emissions products "will endanger the public health or welfare." After rulemaking proceedings in which EPA reviewed a number of inconclusive scientific studies indicating that lead emissions harmed the health of urban populations, particularly children, the Administrator determined that leaded gasoline emissions presented "a significant risk of harm," thereby endangering the public health within the meaning of the statute. The Administrator therefore set standards requiring an annual reduction in the lead content of gasoline.

In upholding those standards, the court, in an opinion by Judge Skelly Wright, made the following observations about the meaning of the critical statutory language and the scope of the agency's decisionmaking authority:]

. . . Case law and dictionary definition agree that endanger means something less than actual harm. When one is endangered, harm is *threatened*; no actual injury need ever occur. Thus, for example, a town may be "endangered" by a threatening plague or hurricane and yet emerge from the danger completely unscathed. A statute allowing for regulation in the face of danger is, necessarily, a precautionary statute. Regulatory action may be taken before the threatened harm occurs; indeed, the very existence of such precautionary legislation would seem to *demand* that regulatory action precede, and, optimally, prevent, the perceived threat. As should be apparent, the "will endanger" language of Section 211(c)(1)(A) makes it such a precautionary statute.

The Administrator read it as such, interpreting "will endanger" to mean "presents a significant risk of harm." We agree with the Administrator's interpretation. . . .

. . . While the dictionary admittedly settles on "probable" as its measure of danger, we believe a more sophisticated case-by-case analysis is appropriate. Danger, the Administrator recognized, is not set by a fixed probability of harm, but rather is composed of reciprocal elements of risk and harm, of probability and severity. Cf. Reserve Mining Co. v. EPA, [514 F.2d 492, 519-520 (8th Cir. 1975)]. That is to say, the public health may properly be found endangered both by a lesser risk of a greater harm and by a greater risk of a lesser harm.[32] Danger depends upon the relation between the risk and harm presented by each case, and cannot legitimately be pegged to "probable" harm, regardless of whether that harm be great or small. . . .

. . . Where a statute is precautionary in nature, the evidence difficult to come by, uncertain, or conflicting because it is on the frontiers of scientific knowledge, the regulations designed to protect the public health, and the decision that of an expert administrator, we will not demand rigorous step-by-step proof of cause and effect. Such proof may be impossible to obtain if the precautionary purpose of the statute is to be served. Of course, we are not suggesting that the Administrator has the power to act on hunches or wild guesses. . . . The Administrator may apply his expertise to draw conclusions from suspected, but not completely substantiated, relationships between facts, from trends among facts, from theoretical projections from imperfect data, from probative preliminary data not yet certifiable as "fact," and the like. We believe that a conclusion so drawn—a risk assessment—may, if rational, form the basis for health-related regulations under the "will endanger" language of Section 211.[58]

32. This proposition must be confined to reasonable limits, however. In Carolina Environmental Study Group v. United States, 510 F.2d 796 (1975), a division of this court found the possibility of a Class 9 nuclear reactor disaster, a disaster of ultimate severity and horrible consequences, to be so low that the Atomic Energy Commission's minimal consideration of the effects of such a disaster in an environmental impact statement prepared for a new reactor was sufficient. Likewise, even the absolute certainty of de minimis harm might not justify government action. Under §211 the threatened harm must be sufficiently significant to justify health-based regulation of national impact. . . .

58. . . . Petitioners argue that the Administrator must decide that lead emissions "will endanger" the public health solely on "facts," or, in the words of the division majority, by a "chain of scientific facts or reasoning leading [the Administrator] ineluctably to this conclusion. . . ." Petitioners demand sole reliance on *scientific* facts, on evidence that reputable scientific techniques certify as certain. Typically, a scientist will not certify evidence unless the probability of error, by standard statistical measurement, is less than 5%. That is, scientific fact is at least 95% certain.

Such certainty has never characterized the judicial or the administrative process. It may be that the "beyond a reasonable doubt" standard of criminal law demands 95% certainty. But the standard of ordinary civil litigation, a preponderance of the evidence, demands only 51% certainty. A jury may weigh conflicting evidence and certify as adjudicative (although not scientific) fact that which it believes is more likely than not. . . . Inherently, such a standard is flexible; inherently, it allows the fact-finder to assess risks, to measure probabilities, to make subjective judgments. Nonetheless, the ultimate finding will be treated, at law, as fact and will be affirmed if based on substantial evidence, or, if made by a judge, not clearly erroneous.

The standard before administrative agencies is no less flexible. Agencies are not limited to scientific fact, to 95% certainties. Rather, they have at least the same fact-finding powers as a jury, particularly when, as here, they are engaged in rule-making. "Looking to the future, and commanded by Congress to make policy, a rule-making agency necessarily deals less with 'evidentiary' disputes than with normative conflicts, projections from imperfect data, experiments and simulations,

All this is not to say that Congress left the Administrator free to set policy on his own terms. To the contrary, the policy guidelines are largely set, both in the statutory term "will endanger" and in the relationship of that term to other sections of the Clean Air Act. These prescriptions direct the Administrator's actions. Operating within the prescribed guidelines, he must consider all of the information available to him. Some of the information will be factual, but much more of it will be speculative—scientific estimates and "guesstimates" of probable harm, hypotheses based on still-developing data, etc. Ultimately, he must act, in part on "factual issues," but largely "on choices of policy, on an assessment of risks, [and] on predictions dealing with matters on the frontiers of scientific knowledge. . . ." Amoco Oil Co. v. EPA, [501 F.2d 722, 741 (D.C. Cir. 1974)]. A standard of danger—fear of uncertain or unknown harm— contemplates no more.

[After reviewing the evidence in the administrative record, Judge Wright concluded that EPA complied with all statutory requirements and that its reasons provided a rational basis for its actions. Judge Wilkey dissented, contending that "the paucity of scientific evidence pointing to any firm conclusion, [and] the gaps in logic supporting the Administrator's analysis" rendered the regulations arbitrary and capricious. He argued that, by dispensing with any requirement that EPA rely on proof of actual harm which has already occurred, that is, by countenancing risk assessment, the majority had "grant[ed] the plainest license for the wildest speculation."]

NOTES AND QUESTIONS

1. *The Terminology of Risk Assessment.* Footnote 58 of *Ethyl* is an excellent statement of the jurisprudence of risk assessment. Judge Wright referred to both risk and uncertainty. According to Professor Hornstein, risk exists when one can calculate an outcome's "expected value" with reasonable confidence by multiplying its magnitude by its probability. Uncertainty exists when one's understanding of the underlying probabilities is "so shaky that expected values (losses) cannot be calculated with much confidence at all." Hornstein, Reclaiming Environmental Law: A Normative Critique of Comparative Risk Analysis, 92 Colum. L. Rev. 562, 571 (1992). See also Sunstein, Irreversible and Catastrophic, 91 Cornell L. Rev. 841, 848 (2006). Footnote 58 also distinguishes between legal and scientific "facts." Is a 51 to 94 percent certainty sufficient to support either kind of "fact"?

2. Reserve Mining. The *Reserve Mining* litigation involved an attempt to halt the company's discharge of mine tailings (the crushed rock residue discarded in the mining process) resembling asbestos fibers into Lake Superior. Concern that discharge of the fibers into the air and water created a cancer risk for those exposed to them prompted the United States, the states of Michigan, Wisconsin, and Minnesota,

---

educated predictions, differing assessments of possible risks, and the like." Amoco Oil Co. v. EPA, 501 F.2d at 735. An agency's finding of fact differs from that of a jury or trial judge primarily in that it is accorded more deference by a reviewing court. Thus, as a matter of administrative law, the Administrator found *as fact* that lead emissions "will endanger" the public health. That in so doing he did not have to rely solely on proved scientific fact is inherent in the requirements of legal fact-finding. Petitioners' assertions of the need to rely on "fact" confuse the two terminologies. We must deal with the terminology of law, not science. At law, unless the administrative or judicial task is peculiarly factual in nature, or Congress expressly commands a more rigorous finding, assessment of risks as herein described typifies both the administrative and the judicial fact-finding function, and is not the novel or unprecedented theory that petitioners contend.

and several environmental groups to bring suit in federal district court to enjoin further discharges into either medium. The effort to halt discharges into the water was based in part on a provision of the pre-1972 Federal Water Pollution Control Act (FWPCA) authorizing the United States to secure abatement of discharges into interstate waters that, among other things, "endanger[ed] . . . the health or welfare of persons." 33 U.S.C. §1160(g)(1).

The district court ordered Reserve's facility to shut down, holding that its operation violated the FWPCA and state air pollution regulations, and that both the air and water discharges constituted common law nuisances. After a panel of the Eighth Circuit stayed the decision, the entire court, sitting en banc, modified the order and remanded. Focusing on the discharges into Lake Superior, the court remarked that

> [i]n assessing probabilities in this case, it cannot be said that the probability of harm is more likely than not. Moreover, the level of probability does not readily convert into a prediction of consequences. On this record it cannot be forecast that the rates of cancer will increase from drinking Lake Superior water or breathing Silver Bay air. The best that can be said is that the existence of this asbestos contaminant in air and water gives rise to a reasonable medical concern for the public health. The public's exposure to asbestos fibers in air and water creates some health risk. Such a contaminant should be removed. [514 F.2d at 520.]

The issue under §1160(g)(1) was whether the discharges "endangered" the public health or welfare. The court found that Congress used the term "in a precautionary or preventive sense, and, therefore, evidence of potential harm as well as actual harm comes within the purview of that term." Id. at 528. The appellate court confirmed the district court's finding that, due to "an acceptable but unproved theory" that the tailings might be carcinogenic, the discharges constituted an endangerment subject to abatement. Id. at 529.

Nevertheless, the court refused to order an immediate shutdown of the plant, basing its decision on the need to "strike a proper balance between the benefits conferred and the hazards created" by the facility. Id. at 535. The benefits of the plant included a $350 million capital investment, construction of two company towns, jobs for more than 3,000 employees, and payment of substantial state and local taxes. The mine was responsible for 12 percent of total U.S. production of taconite. On the other hand, the probability of harm from exposure to tailings discharged into the water was low because, even though "[s]erious consequences could result" if the risk materialized, the probability did "not rest on a history of past health harm attributable to ingestion but on a medical theory implicating the ingestion of asbestos fibers as a causative factor in increasing the rates of gastrointestinal cancer among asbestos workers." Id. at 536. In addition, the court credited the intervening union's claim that ill health effects resulting from prolonged unemployment should the plant shut down might be more certain than the harm attributable to exposure to the tailings. Ultimately, the court concluded:

> Some pollution and ensuing environmental damage are, unfortunately, an inevitable concomitant of a heavily industrialized economy. In the absence of proof of a reasonable risk of imminent or actual harm, a legal standard requiring immediate cessation of industrial operations will cause unnecessary economic loss, including unemployment,

and, in a case such as this, jeopardize a continuing domestic source of critical metals without conferring adequate countervailing benefits.

We believe that on this record the district court abused its discretion by immediately closing this major industrial plant. In this case, the risk of harm to the public is potential, not imminent or certain, and Reserve says it earnestly seeks a practical way to abate the pollution. A remedy should be fashioned which will serve the ultimate public weal by insuring clean air, clean water, and continued jobs in an industry vital to the nation's welfare. . . . [Id. at 537.]

The court therefore afforded Reserve "a reasonable time to stop discharging its wastes into Lake Superior," during which the company would take steps to arrange for land disposal of its waste. Id.

3. Village of Wilsonville, Ethyl Corp., *and* Reserve Mining *Compared.* What standards did the courts use in *Village of Wilsonville* and *Reserve Mining* to decide whether to enjoin the alleged risk-creating activities? Would the danger factually documented in *Reserve Mining* have justified injunctive relief under the standard applied by the majority in the *Wilsonville* case? Under the standard adopted by the concurrence in *Wilsonville*? Which of the three approaches is closest to that suggested by the Page excerpt at the beginning of this chapter?

Ethyl Corp. arose in a different procedural context in that the court of appeals was reviewing a decision rendered by an administrative agency to assess its reasonableness in light of the evidence, rather than making a de novo determination as to the scope of the danger presented by lead emissions from automobiles. Nevertheless, the statutory standards at issue in *Ethyl* and *Reserve Mining* are quite similar. What differences, if any, do you detect in the two courts' interpretation and application of the "endangerment" standard? The result of considering both the *probability* that actual harm will eventually occur and the *magnitude* or severity of that harm if it does occur sometimes is called "risk," but it is also sometimes called "danger." As Judge Wright indicates, "danger . . . is not set by a fixed probability of harm, but rather is composed of reciprocal elements of . . . probability and severity." *Ethyl*, 541 F.2d at 18.

If danger or risk depends on two interdependent factors, probability and magnitude of harm, and neither factor can be considered in isolation, then what was the court in *Reserve Mining* doing when, in addressing the remedies to be applied, it reassessed the "probabilities of harm" and then refused to sustain the trial court's injunction? Was it incorrectly applying its own analytic framework by permitting the timing of relief to hinge on probability alone? See Henderson & Pearson, Implementing Federal Environmental Policies: The Limits of Aspirational Commands, 78 Colum. L. Rev. 1429, 1453-1456 (1978).

To justify delaying relief rather than granting an immediate injunction, the *Reserve Mining* court repeatedly contrasted the "potential" threat to the public health it found to exist with an "imminent" danger to public health. The implication is that only an "imminent" hazard merits immediate relief, and Reserve's discharges did not present one. Yet is it correct to say that the danger in *Reserve* was not imminent? Had it been many years earlier and had Reserve Mining been almost ready to open the mine and dump the first load of tailings into the lake, the danger could have been imminent. But at the time of the decision the danger existed, and the statute said nothing about showing imminent *harm* before relief could be granted.

4. *The Role of Public Input.* What should be the role of those who live near and those who work in a plant engaged in activities alleged to create risks similar to those

involved in *Reserve Mining* in deciding the fate of those activities? One view is that "it is more important in a democracy that the public have the decision it wants, rationally or irrationally, right or wrong, than that the 'correct' decision be made." Green, Limitations on the Implementation of Technology Assessment, 14 Atomic Energy L.J. 59, 82 (1972). In 1983, EPA held a series of public workshops in Tacoma, Washington, in which it informed the public that a copper smelter's emissions of arsenic, a known carcinogen, created a cancer risk for workers and nearby residents. The plant's employees responded that unemployment and the emotional and economic stress resulting from it created worse health risks than those posed by the plant's operation. 16 Env't Rep. (BNA) 648 (1985). While some residents and editorialists argued that the issue was too sophisticated for public input, EPA Administrator William Ruckelshaus concluded that the community reached some sort of consensus and that the agency was informed by the public's nontechnical concerns. Pildes & Sunstein, Reinventing the Regulatory State, 62 U. Chi. L. Rev. 1, 89-90 (1995). The plant was closed, but the overcapacity of the copper industry may have played at least as great a role as environmental factors. Sunstein, On the Divergent American Reactions to Terrorism and Climate Change, AEI-Brookings Joint Center for Regulatory Studies, Working Paper 06-13 (May 2006), available at http://ssrn.com/abstract=901217, contends that the divergence between the belief of many Americans that aggressive action to reduce the risks of terrorist events are worth taking, but that aggressive actions to reduce the risk of global climate change are not, is based on "intuitive cost-benefit analysis, affected by bounded rationality."

    5. *The Impact of* Ethyl *and* Reserve Mining. In 1970, before the adoption of a spate of environmental legislation, Professor James Krier wrote that "burden of proof rules at present have an inevitable bias against protection of the environment. . . ." Krier, Environmental Litigation and the Burden of Proof, in Law and the Environment 105, 107 (M. Baldwin & J. Page eds., 1970). *Ethyl* and *Reserve Mining* have decisively influenced judicial interpretation of practically all subsequently adopted regulatory statutes that attempt to protect health and the environment before actual harm occurs. Indeed, the rationale that they provide stretches across the breadth of pollution control legislation, from the provisions contained in all the major pollution control statutes for direct abatement by court action when the federal government can show that "imminent and substantial endangerment" to health and the environment exists, to the threshold showing of danger necessary to trigger regulation under conventional ambient and emissions standards provisions. Interestingly, the statutory provisions at issue in both cases have since been amended. Look at §211(c)(1) of the Clean Air Act and §504(a) of the Clean Water Act. Do they endorse or refute the courts' decisions in *Ethyl* and *Reserve Mining*, respectively? See also H.R. Rep. No. 95-294 (1977) (explaining the amendments to §211(c)(1)).

    6. *False Positives and False Negatives.* Debate over the advisability of precautionary regulation often revolves around the distinction between false positives and false negatives. A false positive arises when a regulation to address an environmental risk turns out, after the accumulation of more information, to have been unnecessary. A false negative occurs when information reveals that a decision not to regulate was premised on the erroneous conclusion that the risk presented either did not exist or was acceptably low. Overregulation based on a false positive imposes costs on the regulated community and on the consumers of the products and services they produce. Underregulation based on a false negative imposes costs on those who incur

risk as a result of exposure to the unregulated substance or activity. Cranor, Regulating Toxic Substances: A Philosophy of Science and the Law 8 (1993). One argument in favor of precautionary regulation is that the costs imposed by a false positive tend to be less (or less serious) than the often irreversible costs emanating from a false negative. What are some examples that support this view? See Guruswamy, Global Warming: Integrating United States and International Law, 32 Ariz. L. Rev. 221 (1990). The opposing view is that false positives may pose greater threats to public health than false negatives because regulation may induce conduct or the use of alternative substances that pose even greater risks than those being regulated. Banning a pesticide may allow the proliferation of molds that create health risks. A crackdown on nuclear power plant operating practices may require more frequent shutdowns and start-ups, even though these activities are the stages of operation that pose the greatest risk of an accident. See Cross, The Public Role in Risk Control, 24 Envtl. L. 887 (1994).

7. A *Postscript on* Ethyl. After the decision in *Ethyl*, studies revealed that combustion of lead-containing fuels was the principal source of lead in the environment, that the blood lead level of urban children directly correlated with the lead content of gasoline, and that high blood lead levels caused psychological and behavioral problems in those children. In 1982 and 1985, EPA approved stricter phase-down regulations. In the 1990 Clean Air Act amendments, Congress banned the sale of leaded gasoline for use as fuel in any motor vehicle effective January 1, 1996. 42 U.S.C. §7545(n).

D. DEALING WITH RISK THROUGH COMPARATIVE RISK ASSESSMENT AND COST-BENEFIT ANALYSIS

Much of the rest of this chapter concerns federal regulatory statutes that go quite far in shifting the burden of proving safety to risk-generating enterprises. Although the details differ from statute to statute, a common analytical framework for assessing regulation of risk applies in a variety of contexts. For each statute, Congress had to answer two basic questions. The first is the risk assessment question: what criteria should the agency vested with responsibility to implement the statute apply in deciding whether to regulate a particular activity or substance, or, putting it slightly differently, what is the threshold showing of risk that will suffice to trigger the agency's authority to regulate? The second major question is the risk management question: once the agency has decided to regulate a particular risk, what standards should it employ in choosing the appropriate method and extent of regulation?

Subsequent sections of this chapter and the next address the details of how Congress and regulatory agencies such as EPA have answered these questions. This section provides an overview of some of the issues raised by the use of the two fundamental concepts traced in section A.2 of this chapter—risk assessment (particularly the comparative and quantitative varieties) and risk management—in regulation that is designed to address the health and environmental risks posed by the generation, use, and management of toxic materials.

1. The Rationale for Comparative Risk Assessment

The Diagnosis. Federal environmental regulation began in earnest in 1970, with the passage of NEPA and the Clean Air Act. Collectively, the many environmental statutes adopted by Congress during the next two decades applied to activities that used toxic substances in otherwise useful endeavors and that generated hazardous waste in every environmental medium—air, water, and land.

By the 1990s, however, it was clear to many that more regulation did not always mean better regulation. In particular, critics of this accretion of risk-regulating commands charged that federal environmental regulation had resulted in a serious misallocation of expenditures both by regulators and the regulated community. See generally Glicksman & Chapman, Regulatory Reform and (Breach of) the Contract with America: Improving Environmental Policy or Destroying Environmental Protection?, 5 Kan. J.L. & Pub. Pol'y (Winter 1996), at 9, 13-15. According to the Carnegie Commission on Science, Technology, and Government, Risk and the Environment: Improving Regulatory Decision Making 73 (1993), "[t]he fundamental problem in regulatory decisionmaking at the agency level, as at the presidential and interagency level, is how to set priorities. It is a great challenge for science-based regulatory agencies to compare and rank individual risks and families of risks within the universe they regulate." Although the Commission praised the tendency of regulators to be responsive to the public in prioritizing their regulatory agendas, it also warned that "setting priorities on a 'chemical of the month' basis may result in over-regulation of some hazards, underregulation of others, and reduction of agency credibility.

One of the most forceful of the critics was then–Circuit Judge Stephen Breyer, whose book Breaking the Vicious Circle: Toward Effective Risk Regulation (1993) proffered the thesis that federal regulation often focused on the wrong risks. One result of such regulation is that even though cancer is "the engine that drives much of health risk regulation," id. at 6, current regulation would prevent only a small portion of annual cancer deaths in the United States. Breyer described three particular problems that plague federal risk regulation. First, regulation often reflects too much of a good thing. By seeking to eliminate the last 10 percent of the risk, regulators impose enormous costs without achieving significant incremental risk reductions. In addition, agencies rarely select the least-cost means of regulation. Second, agencies such as EPA lack a rational agenda selection mechanism. Breyer's charge echoed a 1987 EPA report, Unfinished Business: A Comparative Assessment of Environmental Problems, in which the agency concluded that its regulatory efforts tended to be more responsive to public perceptions of which risks were the most serious than to the views of its own scientific experts. The report described a mismatch between the agency's focus on medium to low risks, such as groundwater pollution, and the inadequacy of its efforts to address serious risks such as indoor air pollution and global warming.* Third, different agencies use different methods for assessing risks and too often ignore the effect of regulation of one environmental medium upon another.

Breyer attributed these problems to irrational public perceptions of risk, overly prescriptive and compartmentalized legislation, and the use by regulators of excessively conservative assumptions to deal with uncertainty. That conservative posture

---

*See also EPA, Science Advisory Board, Reducing Risk: Setting Priorities and Strategies for Environmental Protection (1990) (confirming this analysis and urging a reordering of agency priorities to redress the existing misallocation of resources).

exacerbates public concern, which contributes to continuing irrationality in the perception of risk and inappropriate responses by legislators and regulators alike.

The Prescription. The analytical technique that emerged as the most promising candidate for reallocating risk reduction efforts was comparative risk assessment (CRA), the process by which scientists determine which environmental risks are the most serious. The goal of this ranking process is to assign priorities to environmental problems so that the limited (and often shrinking) risk reduction resources available are directed at the most serious risks first. Better allocation of these resources will spread them further and generate a higher rate of return on the regulatory investment. Ideally, CRA would take the form of "societal risk reduction" analysis, a comparison of *all* health and safety risks, so that, for example, risk reduction investments could be rechanneled from environmental regulation to expanded childhood vaccinations and crime prevention measures, if those initiatives would prove more productive in terms of risk reduction payoffs. See generally Bender, Societal Risk Reduction: Promise and Pitfalls, 3 N.Y.U. Envtl. L.J. 255 (1995). Breyer urged the creation of a centralized, multidisciplinary team of experts to fulfill the utilitarian promise of CRA. Risk reduction decisions based on the scientific underpinnings of CRA could prevent capture of regulators by the supporters of an irrational risk reduction agenda. See Cross, The Risk of Reliance on Perceived Risks, 3 Risk: Issues in Health and Safety 59 (1992).

"Risk-Risk" Analysis. Some proponents of CRA have argued that regulation can cause as well as avert harm and that, before deciding to regulate, agencies should compare the harms attributable to and avoided by regulation to ensure that the former does not exceed the latter and that regulation is not counterproductive. According to this theory, sometimes referred to as "risk-risk" or "richer is safer" analysis,

> [i]ndividuals with more disposable income are less likely to die, to become ill, or to suffer accidental injuries. Thus, a regulation that reduces disposable income might have an incidental effect of increasing death, illness, and injury. Consequently, a regulation that imposes significant costs could produce a negative health effect that more than counteracts the positive health effect from reduced exposure to harmful substances. [Cross, When Environmental Regulations Kill: The Role of Health/Health Analysis, 22 Ecology L.Q. 729, 731 (1995).]*

By one estimate, each $7.25 million spent on regulation will cause one death. Keeney, Mortality Risks Induced by Economic Expenditures, 10 Risk Analysis 147 (1990).

In a concurring opinion in International Union, UAW v. OSHA, 938 F.2d 1310 (D.C. Cir. 1991), Judge Stephen Williams relied on both the theory and Keeney's figures to support his contention that less stringent regulations under the Occupational Safety and Health (OSH) Act would not necessarily have adverse effects on worker health and safety. In American Dental Ass'n v. Martin, 984 F.2d 823 (7th Cir. 1993), the court turned aside an attack on regulations under the OSH Act designed to prevent workplace exposure to bloodborne pathogens based on OSHA's failure to use risk-risk

---

*See also Wildavsky, Richer Is Safer, 60 Pub. Interest 23 (1980); Calandrillo, Responsible Regulation: A Sensible Cost-Benefit, Risk versus Risk Approach to Federal Health and Safety Regulation, 81 B.U. L. Rev. 957, 964 (2001) (risk-risk analysis "simply means that the risks unintentionally created by the imposition of a new regulation should never outweigh the risks reduced or alleviated by that regulation"); Goode, For Good Health, It Helps to Be Rich and Important, N.Y. Times, June 1, 1999, at D1 (summarizing "an explosion of research" demonstrating that social class is one of the most powerful predictors of health).

analysis. Although the court accepted the theoretical basis for risk-risk analysis, it concluded that the challengers failed to quantify such "indirect" costs of regulation as increased costs of medical care, and therefore that the agency's decision to ignore those costs was not arbitrary. The intervening union in *Reserve Mining* also relied on a rudimentary version of risk-risk analysis in arguing against plant closure. What was the union's argument? See also NRDC v. EPA, 902 F.2d 962, 972-973 (D.C. Cir. 1990) (rejecting argument that the national ambient air quality standards for lead issued under the Clean Air Act were flawed because EPA failed to consider the adverse health consequences of unemployment that would result from issuance of the standards); United States v. Vertac Chem. Corp., 33 F. Supp. 2d 769, 779-780 (E.D. Ark. 1998) (rejecting challenge to hazardous substance cleanup based on EPA's failure to consider risks of injuries and fatalities to workers involved in the cleanup), *vacated on other grounds*, 247 F.3d 706 (8th Cir. 2001). In Union Elec. Co. v. EPA, 427 U.S. 246 (1976), reproduced in Chapter 6, Justice Powell concurred with the majority's holding that EPA lacked the authority to reject a state implementation plan under the Clean Air Act on the ground that it was infeasible. He added, however, that the adverse effects on public health that would result from shutting down an electric utility might outweigh the adverse health effects attributable to continued air pollution, and that "Congress, if fully aware of this Draconian possibility, would strike a different balance." Id. at 271. For a statutory analogue of risk-risk analysis, see 42 U.S.C. §7412(f)(1)(C).

2.   *Quantitative Risk Assessment*

CARNEGIE COMMISSION ON SCIENCE, TECHNOLOGY, AND GOVERNMENT, RISK AND THE ENVIRONMENT: IMPROVING REGULATORY DECISION MAKING
76 (1993)

Numerical estimates derived from risk assessment serve as inputs to several very different kinds of decisions, including (1) "acceptable risk" determinations (wherein action is taken if the risk exceeds some "bright line," which can be zero); (2) "cost-benefit" determinations, where the risks reduced by a proposed action are translated into benefits (e.g., lives saved, life-years extended), expressed in dollar amounts, and compared to the estimated costs of implementing the action and some rule of thumb regarding how much cost it is wise to incur to achieve a given level of benefit (e.g., $10 million to save one additional life); and (3) "cost-effectiveness" determinations, where the action that maximizes the amount of risk reduction (not necessarily expressed in dollar terms) per unit of cost is favored.

INDUSTRIAL UNION DEPARTMENT, AFL-CIO v. AMERICAN PETROLEUM INSTITUTE
448 U.S. 607 (1980)

Mr. JUSTICE STEVENS announced the judgment of the Court and delivered an opinion, in which THE CHIEF JUSTICE and Mr. JUSTICE STEWART joined and in [parts] of which Mr. JUSTICE POWELL joined.

... This litigation concerns a standard promulgated by the Secretary of Labor [under the Occupational Safety and Health Act of 1970] to regulate occupational exposure to benzene, a substance which has been shown to cause cancer at high exposure levels. The principal question is whether such a showing is a sufficient basis for a standard that places the most stringent limitation on exposure to benzene that is technologically and economically possible.

The Act delegates broad authority to the Secretary to promulgate different kinds of standards. The basic definition of an "occupational safety and health standard" is found in §3(8), which provides: "The term 'occupational safety and health standard' means a standard which requires conditions, or the adoption or use of one or more practices, means, methods, operations, or processes, reasonably necessary or appropriate to provide safe or healthful employment and places of employment." 29 U.S.C. §652(8). ... Where toxic materials or harmful physical agents are concerned, a standard must also comply with §6(b)(5), which provides [that] "[t]he Secretary, in promulgating standards dealing with [such materials], shall set the standard which most adequately assures, to the extent feasible, on the basis of the best available evidence, that no employee will suffer material impairment of functional capacity even if such employee has regular exposure for the period of his working life." 29 U.S.C. §655(b)(5). ...

[After finding a causal connection between benzene and leukemia (a cancer of the white blood cells), the Secretary set an exposure limit on airborne concentrations of benzene of one part benzene per million parts of air (1 ppm). The Court of Appeals for the Fifth Circuit held that the regulation was invalid because the Occupational Safety and Health Administration (OSHA) failed to show that the exposure limit was "reasonably necessary or appropriate to provide safe or healthful employment" as required by §3(8), and because §6(b)(5) does "not give OSHA the unbridled discretion to adopt standards designed to create absolutely risk-free workplaces regardless of costs." The court read the two provisions as requiring the agency to assess whether the benefits expected from the standard bore a reasonable relationship to the costs it imposed. Although OSHA estimated the costs of compliance, it did not demonstrate substantial evidence of any discernible benefits.]

We agree with the Fifth Circuit's holding that §3(8) requires the Secretary to find, as a threshold matter, that the toxic substance in question poses a significant health risk in the workplace and that a new, lower standard is therefore "reasonably necessary or appropriate to provide safe or healthful employment and places of employment." ...

I

[Benzene, a colorless liquid that evaporates rapidly under ordinary atmospheric conditions, was produced in large quantities in the United States by the petroleum, petrochemical, and steel industries. It was used to manufacture products that included motor fuels, solvents, detergents, and other organic chemicals. "The entire population of the United States is exposed to small quantities of benzene, ranging from a few parts per billion to 0.5 ppm, in the ambient air. Over one million workers are subject to additional low-level exposures as a consequence of their employment." Most of those workers were employed in a limited number of occupations, including gasoline service stations, benzene production operations, chemical processing, and rubber manufacturing.]

Benzene is a toxic substance. . . . [T]he principal risk of harm comes from inhalation of benzene vapors. When these vapors are inhaled, the benzene diffuses through the lungs and is quickly absorbed into the blood. Exposure to high concentrations produces an almost immediate effect on the central nervous system. Inhalation of concentrations of 20,000 ppm can be fatal within minutes; exposures in the range of 250 to 500 ppm can cause vertigo, nausea, and other symptoms of mild poisoning. Persistent exposures at levels above 25-40 ppm may lead to blood deficiencies and diseases of the blood-forming organs, including aplastic anemia, which is generally fatal.

. . . As early as 1928, some health experts theorized that there might . . . be a connection between benzene in the workplace and leukemia. In the late 1960's and early 1970's a number of epidemiological studies were published indicating that workers exposed to high concentrations of benzene were subject to significantly increased risk of leukemia. In a 1974 report . . . , the National Institute for Occupational Safety and Health (NIOSH), OSHA's research arm, noted that these studies raised the "distinct possibility" that benzene caused leukemia. . . .

[Additional studies published between 1974 and 1976 tended to confirm the view that benzene can cause leukemia at high exposure levels. NIOSH interpreted these studies as providing "conclusive" proof of a causal connection between benzene and leukemia. Acknowledging that the dose-response data it had found lacking earlier were still not available, NIOSH nevertheless recommended that the exposure limit be set low as possible. OSHA responded in 1977 by issuing a permanent standard that reduced the benzene exposure limit from 10 to 1 ppm. OSHA explained that benzene had been shown to cause leukemia at exposures below 25 ppm and that a 1 ppm exposure limit was feasible.]

In its published statement giving notice of the proposed permanent standard, OSHA did not ask for comments as to whether or not benzene presented a significant health risk at exposures of 10 ppm or less. Rather, it asked for comments as to whether 1 ppm was the minimum feasible exposure limit. [T]his formulation of the issue . . . was consistent with OSHA's general policy with respect to carcinogens. Whenever a carcinogen is involved, OSHA will presume that no safe level of exposure exists in the absence of clear proof establishing such a level and will accordingly set the exposure limit at the lowest level feasible. . . . Given OSHA's cancer policy, it was in fact irrelevant whether there was any evidence at all of a leukemia risk at 10 ppm. The important point was that there was no evidence that there was not some risk, however small, at that level. . . .

. . . [T]he benzene standard is an expensive way of providing some additional protection for a relatively small number of employees. . . . [O]nly 35,000 employees would gain any benefit from the regulation in terms of a reduction in their exposure to benzene. [The record indicated that compliance costs would be $1,390 per employee in the rubber industry and $82,000 per employee in the petroleum refining industry.]

. . . [I]t appears from the economic impact study done at OSHA's direction that [the benefits of regulation] may be relatively small. . . . [T]he actual exposures outlined in that study are often considerably lower [than the current 10 ppm standard]. For example, for the period 1970-1975 the petrochemical industry reported that, out of a total of 496 employees exposed to benzene, only 53 were exposed to levels between 1 and 5 ppm and only 7 (all at the same plant) were exposed to between 5 and 10 ppm.

II

... The written explanation of the standard ... demonstrates that there is ample justification for regulating occupational exposure to benzene and that the prior limit of 10 ppm, with a ceiling of 25 ppm (or a peak of 50 ppm) was reasonable. It does not, however, provide direct support for the Agency's conclusion that the limit should be reduced from 10 ppm to 1 ppm.

The evidence in the administrative record of adverse effects of benzene exposure at 10 ppm is sketchy at best. OSHA noted that there was "no dispute" that certain nonmalignant blood disorders ... could result from exposures of 25-40 ppm. It then stated that several studies had indicated that relatively slight changes in normal blood values could result from exposures below 25 ppm and perhaps below 10 ppm. OSHA did not attempt to make any estimate based on these studies of how significant the risk of nonmalignant disease would be at exposures of 10 ppm or less. Rather, it stated that because of the lack of data concerning the linkage between low-level exposures and blood abnormalities, it was impossible to construct a dose-response curve at this time.[33] OSHA did conclude, however, that the studies demonstrated that the current 10 ppm exposure limit was inadequate to ensure that no single worker would suffer a nonmalignant blood disorder as a result of benzene exposure. Noting that it is "customary" to set a permissible exposure limit by applying a safety factor of 10-100 to the lowest level at which adverse effects had been observed, the Agency stated that the evidence supported the conclusion that the limit should be set at a point "substantially less than 10 ppm" even if benzene's leukemic effects were not considered. OSHA did not state, however, that the nonmalignant effects of benzene exposure justified a reduction in the permissible exposure limit to 1 ppm.

[The plurality described the evidence of an increased cancer risk due to benzene exposure as "even sketchier." The agency cited no empirical evidence to support the conclusion that exposure to benzene at or below 10 ppm "had ever in fact caused leukemia."] In the end OSHA's rationale for lowering the permissible exposure limit to 1 ppm was based, not on any finding that leukemia has ever been caused by exposure to 10 ppm of benzene and that it will not be caused by exposure to 1 ppm, but rather on a series of assumptions indicating that some leukemias might result from exposure to 10 ppm and that the number of cases might be reduced by reducing the exposure level to 1 ppm. In reaching that result, the Agency first unequivocally concluded that benzene is a human carcinogen. Second, it concluded that industry had failed to prove that there is a safe threshold level of exposure to benzene below which no excess leukemia cases would occur. ...

Third, the Agency applied its standard policy with respect to carcinogens, concluding that, in the absence of definitive proof of a safe level, it must be assumed that any level above zero presents some increased risk of cancer. ... [T]here are a number of scientists and public health specialists who subscribe to this view, theorizing that a

---

33. "A dose-response curve shows the relationship between different exposure levels and the risk of cancer [or any other disease] associated with those exposure levels. Generally, exposure to higher levels carries with it a higher risk, and exposure to lower levels is accompanied by a reduced risk." 581 F.2d, at 504, n.24. OSHA's comments with respect to the insufficiency of the data were addressed primarily to the lack of data at low exposure levels. OSHA did not discuss whether it was possible to make a rough estimate, based on the more complete epidemiological and animal studies done at higher exposure levels, of the significance of the risks attributable to those levels, nor did it discuss whether it was possible to extrapolate from such estimates to derive a risk estimate for low-level exposures.

susceptible person may contract cancer from the absorption of even one molecule of a carcinogen like benzene.[41]

Fourth, the Agency reiterated its view of the Act, stating that it was required by §6(b)(5) to set the standard either at the level that has been demonstrated to be safe or at the lowest level feasible, whichever is higher. If no safe level is established, as in this case, the Secretary's interpretation of the statute automatically leads to the selection of an exposure limit that is the lowest feasible. . . . [T]he Agency selected 1 ppm as a workable exposure level, and then determined that compliance with that level was technologically feasible and that "the economic impact of . . . [compliance] will not be such as to threaten the financial welfare of the affected firms or the general economy." 43 Fed. Reg. 5939 (1978). It therefore held that 1 ppm was the minimum feasible exposure level within the meaning of §6(b)(5) of the Act.

Finally, [OSHA] . . . concluded that some benefits were likely to result from reducing the exposure limit from 10 ppm to 1 ppm. This conclusion was based, again, not on evidence, but rather on the assumption that the risk of leukemia will decrease as exposure levels decrease. Although the Agency had found it impossible to construct a dose-response curve that would predict with any accuracy the number of leukemias that could be expected to result from exposures at 10 ppm, at 1 ppm, or at any intermediate level, it nevertheless "determined that the benefits of the proposed standard are likely to be appreciable." 43 Fed. Reg. 5941 (1978). . . .

It is noteworthy that at no point in its lengthy explanation did the Agency quote or even cite §3(8) of the Act. It made no finding that any of the provisions of the new standard were "reasonably necessary or appropriate to provide safe or healthful employment and places of employment." Nor did it allude to the possibility that any such finding might have been appropriate.

III

Our resolution of the issues in these cases turns, to a large extent, on the meaning of and the relationship between §3(8) . . . and §6(b)(5). . . .

In the Government's view, §3(8)'s definition of the term "standard" has no legal significance or at best merely requires that a standard not be totally irrational. It takes the position that §6(b)(5) is controlling and that it requires OSHA to promulgate a standard that either gives an absolute assurance of safety for each and every worker or reduces exposures to the lowest level feasible. The Government interprets "feasible" as meaning technologically achievable at a cost that would not impair the viability of the industries subject to the regulation. The respondent industry representatives, on the other hand, argue that the Court of Appeals was correct in holding that the "reasonably

41. The so-called "one hit" theory is based on laboratory studies indicating that one molecule of a carcinogen may react in the test tube with one molecule of DNA to produce a mutation. The theory is that, if this occurred in the human body, the mutated molecule could replicate over a period of years and eventually develop into a cancerous tumor. . . .

In light of the improbability of a person's contracting cancer as a result of a single hit, a number of the scientists testifying on both sides of the issue agreed that every individual probably does have a threshold exposure limit below which he or she will not contract cancer. The problem, however, is that individual susceptibility appears to vary greatly and there is no present way to calculate each and every person's threshold. Thus, even industry witnesses agreed that if the standard must ensure with absolute certainty that every single worker is protected from any risk of leukemia, only a zero exposure limit would suffice.

necessary and appropriate" language of §3(8), along with the feasibility requirement of §6(b)(5), requires the Agency to quantify both the costs and the benefits of a proposed rule and to conclude that they are roughly commensurate.

... [W]e think ... that §3(8) ... requires the Secretary, before issuing any standard, to determine that it is reasonably necessary and appropriate to remedy a significant risk of material health impairment. Only after the Secretary has made the threshold determination that such a risk exists with respect to a toxic substance, would it be necessary to decide whether §6(b)(5) requires him to select the most protective standard he can consistent with economic and technological feasibility, or whether, as respondents argue, the benefits of the regulation must be commensurate with the costs of its implementation. Because the Secretary did not make the required threshold finding in these cases, we have no occasion to determine whether costs must be weighed against benefits in an appropriate case. ...

... [W]e think it is clear that the statute was not designed to require employers to provide absolutely risk-free workplaces whenever it is technologically feasible to do so, so long as the cost is not great enough to destroy an entire industry. Rather, both the language and structure of the Act, as well as its legislative history, indicate that it was intended to require the elimination, as far as feasible, of significant risks of harm. ...

By empowering the Secretary to promulgate standards that are "reasonably necessary or appropriate to provide safe or healthful employment and places of employment," the Act implies that, before promulgating any standard, the Secretary must make a finding that the workplaces in question are not safe. But "safe" is not the equivalent of "risk-free." There are many activities that we engage in every day—such as driving a car or even breathing city air—that entail some risk of accident or material health impairment; nevertheless, few people would consider these activities "unsafe." Similarly, a workplace can hardly be considered "unsafe" unless it threatens the workers with a significant risk of harm.

Therefore, before he can promulgate any permanent health or safety standard, the Secretary is required to make a threshold finding that a place of employment is unsafe—in the sense that significant risks are present and can be eliminated or lessened by a change in practices. This requirement applies to permanent standards promulgated pursuant to §6(b)(5) ... [f]or there is no reason why §3(8)'s definition of a standard should not be deemed incorporated by reference into §6(b)(5). ...

In the absence of a clear mandate in the Act, it is unreasonable to assume that Congress intended to give the Secretary the unprecedented power over American industry that would result from the Government's view of §§3(8) and 6(b)(5), coupled with OSHA's cancer policy. ... In light of the fact that there are literally thousands of substances used in the workplace that have been identified as carcinogens or suspect carcinogens, the Government's theory would give OSHA power to impose enormous costs that might produce little, if any, discernible benefit.

If the Government was correct in arguing that neither §3(8) nor §6(b)(5) requires that the risk from a toxic substance be quantified sufficiently to enable the Secretary to characterize it as significant in an understandable way, the statute would make such a "sweeping delegation of legislative power" that it might be unconstitutional under the Court's reasoning in A.L.A. Schechter Poultry Corp. v. United States, 295 U.S. 495, 539, and Panama Refining Co. v. Ryan, 293 U.S. 388. A construction of the statute that avoids this kind of open-ended grant should certainly be favored. ...

Given the conclusion that the Act empowers the Secretary to promulgate health and safety standards only where a significant risk of harm exists, the critical issue becomes how to define and allocate the burden of proving the significance of the risk in a case such as this, where scientific knowledge is imperfect and the precise quantification of risks is therefore impossible. The Agency's position is that there is substantial evidence in the record to support its conclusion that there is no absolutely safe level for a carcinogen and that, therefore, the burden is properly on industry to prove, apparently beyond a shadow of a doubt, that there is a safe level for benzene exposure. The Agency argues that, because of the uncertainties in this area, any other approach would render it helpless, forcing it to wait for the leukemia deaths that it believes are likely to occur before taking any regulatory action.

We disagree. As we read the statute, the burden was on the Agency to show, on the basis of substantial evidence, that it is at least more likely than not that long-term exposure to 10 ppm of benzene presents a significant risk of material health impairment. Ordinarily, it is the proponent of a rule or order who has the burden of proof in administrative proceedings. See 5 U.S.C. §556(d). In some cases involving toxic substances, Congress has shifted the burden of proving that a particular substance is safe onto the party opposing the proposed rule. The fact that Congress did not follow this course in enacting the [OSH] Act indicates that it intended the Agency to bear the normal burden of establishing the need for a proposed standard. [The Court concluded that OSHA failed to carry its burden of proof.] . . .

Contrary to the Government's contentions, imposing a burden on the Agency of demonstrating a significant risk of harm will not strip it of its ability to regulate carcinogens, nor will it require the Agency to wait for deaths to occur before taking any action. First, the requirement that a "significant" risk be identified is not a mathematical straitjacket. It is the Agency's responsibility to determine, in the first instance, what it considers to be a "significant" risk. Some risks are plainly acceptable and others are plainly unacceptable. If, for example, the odds are one in a billion that a person will die from cancer by taking a drink of chlorinated water, the risk clearly could not be considered significant. On the other hand, if the odds are one in a thousand that regular inhalation of gasoline vapors that are 2% benzene will be fatal, a reasonable person might well consider the risk significant and take appropriate steps to decrease or eliminate it. Although the Agency has no duty to calculate the exact probability of harm, it does have an obligation to find that a significant risk is present before it can characterize a place of employment as "unsafe."[62]

Second, OSHA is not required to support its finding that a significant risk exists with anything approaching scientific certainty. Although the Agency's findings must be supported by substantial evidence, 29 U.S.C. §655(f), §6(b)(5) specifically allows the Secretary to regulate on the basis of the "best available evidence." . . . [T]his provision requires a reviewing court to give OSHA some leeway where its findings must be made on the frontiers of scientific knowledge. Thus, so long as they are supported by a body of reputable scientific thought, the Agency is free to use conservative assumptions in interpreting the data with respect to carcinogens, risking error on the side of overprotection rather than underprotection. . . .

. . . We express no opinion on what . . . factual determinations would warrant a conclusion that significant risks are present which make promulgation of a new standard reasonably necessary or appropriate. . . .

62. . . . [W]hile the Agency must support its finding that a certain level of risk exists by substantial evidence, we recognize that its determination that a particular level of risk is "significant" will be based largely on policy considerations. At this point we have no need to reach the issue of what level of scrutiny a reviewing court should apply to the latter type of determination.

In this case the record makes it perfectly clear that the Secretary relied squarely on a special policy for carcinogens that imposed the burden on industry of proving the existence of a safe level of exposure, thereby avoiding the Secretary's threshold responsibility of establishing the need for more stringent standards. . . .

The judgment of the Court of Appeals remanding the petition for review to the Secretary for further proceedings is affirmed. . . .

[JUSTICE POWELL joined all portions of the plurality opinion quoted above except that dealing with allocation of the burden of proof. He took the position that, even if OSHA had met its threshold burden, the regulations would have been invalid because OSHA failed to determine that the economic impact of the benzene standard bore a reasonable relationship to the expected benefits. The standard "is neither 'reasonably necessary' nor 'feasible,' as required by statute, if it calls for expenditures wholly disproportionate to the expected health and safety benefits."

JUSTICE REHNQUIST concurred in the judgment, expanding on the plurality's concern about the scope of OSHA's authority. He concluded that the "standardless delegation" contained in §6(b)(5) violated the nondelegation doctrine by failing to provide OSHA with any guidance on the appropriate level of control for hazardous substances for which a "safe" level is either unknown or impractical.]

Mr. JUSTICE MARSHALL, with whom Mr. JUSTICE BRENNAN, Mr. JUSTICE WHITE, and Mr. JUSTICE BLACKMUN join, dissenting. . . .

. . . The critical problem in cases like the ones at bar is scientific uncertainty. While science has determined that exposure to benzene at levels above 1 ppm creates a definite risk of health impairment, the magnitude of the risk cannot be quantified at the present time. . . . [T]he existing evidence may frequently be inadequate to enable the Secretary to make the threshold finding of "significance" that the Court requires today. . . .

. . . [T]he Secretary concluded that benefits will result, that those benefits "may" be appreciable, but that the dose-response relationship of low levels of benzene exposure and leukemia, nonmalignant blood disorders, and chromosomal damage was impossible to determine. The question presented is whether, in these circumstances, the Act permits the Secretary to take regulatory action, or whether he must allow continued exposure until more definitive information becomes available.

. . . Nothing in the Act purports to prevent the Secretary from acting when definitive information as to the quantity of a standard's benefits is unavailable. Where, as here, the deficiency in knowledge relates to the extent of the benefits rather than their existence, I see no reason to hold that the Secretary has exceeded his statutory authority. . . .

. . . The plurality does not show how [the significant risk] requirement can be plausibly derived from the "reasonably necessary or appropriate" clause. . . . In short, the plurality's standard is a fabrication bearing no connection with the acts or intentions of Congress. . . .

. . . [I]t seems clear that the Secretary found a risk that is "significant" in the sense that the word is normally used. There was some direct evidence of chromosomal damage, nonmalignant blood disorders, and leukemia at exposures at or near 10 ppm and below. In addition, expert after expert testified that the recorded effects of benzene exposure at higher levels justified an inference that an exposure level above 1 ppm was dangerous. The plurality's extraordinarily searching scrutiny of this factual record reveals no basis for a conclusion that quantification is, on the basis of "the best available evidence," possible at the present time. . . .

Under these circumstances, the plurality's requirement of identification of a "significant" risk will have one of two consequences. If the plurality means to require the Secretary realistically to "quantify" the risk in order to satisfy a court that it is "significant," the record shows that the plurality means to require him to do the impossible. But the regulatory inaction has very significant costs of its own. The adoption of such a test would subject American workers to a continuing risk of cancer and other serious diseases; it would disable the Secretary from regulating a wide variety of carcinogens for which quantification simply cannot be undertaken at the present time. . . .

. . . [T]he record amply demonstrates that in light of existing scientific knowledge, no purpose would be served by requiring the Secretary to take steps to quantify the risk of exposure to benzene at low levels. Any such quantification would be based not on scientific "knowledge" as that term is normally understood, but on considerations of policy. For carcinogens like benzene, the assumptions on which a dose-response curve must be based are necessarily arbitrary. To require a quantitative showing of a "significant" risk, therefore, would either paralyze the Secretary into inaction or force him to deceive the public by acting on the basis of assumptions that must be considered too speculative to support any realistic assessment of the relevant risk. . . .

NOTES AND QUESTIONS

1. *Nondelegation and Precautionary Regulation.* In his concurrence in *Benzene*, Justice Rehnquist contended that §6(b)(5) of the OSH Act constituted an impermissible delegation of legislative authority to OSHA. The same issue arose in American Trucking Ass'ns, Inc. v. EPA, 175 F.3d 1027 (D.C. Cir. 1999), where the court invalidated national ambient air quality standards issued by EPA under the Clean Air Act on nondelegation grounds. On rehearing, the court had this to say about the role of the nondelegation doctrine in the *Benzene* plurality opinion:

> To be sure, the plurality in the *Benzene* case ostensibly relied on the doctrine to support its interpretation of the [OSH] Act. But a careful reading of the plurality opinion (not, of course, an opinion of the Court, which would bind us) reveals that the doctrine was only a makeweight, tossed into the analysis, in light of Justice Rehnquist's concurrence, to help justify the result. The plurality, disturbed at the seemingly draconian impact of the Secretary of Labor's standard as applied to several industries, analytically conflated the scope of the Secretary's discretion—the legitimate concern of the nondelegation doctrine—with the regulatory consequences of his interpretation of the statute. The latter concern is not really germane to the doctrine; indeed, the Secretary was actually claiming he had less discretion than the plurality thought he had. Accordingly, the *Benzene* plurality opinion gives only lip service to the nondelegation doctrine; the boundaries limiting the scope of congressional delegation to the executive branch remain only dimly perceivable. [American Trucking Ass'ns, Inc. v. EPA, 195 F.3d 4, 14 (D.C. Cir. 1999).]

The Supreme Court reversed the D.C. Circuit in Whitman v. American Trucking Ass'ns, Inc., 531 U.S. 457 (2001), reproduced in Chapter 6, section D.1.b. The Court held that §109(b)(1) of the Clean Air Act fits "well within the outer limits of our nondelegation precedents" and that it is not necessary for Congress to provide a "determinate criterion" for saying how much of a regulated harm is too much.

2. *The Functions of Risk Assessment.* The Carnegie Commission excerpt indicates that a risk assessment can perform three functions. To begin with, it can assist a regulator in determining whether a risk is acceptable or should be reduced through regulation of the activities that create it. After accumulating voluminous evidence, OSHA concluded that workers were being exposed to excessive amounts of benzene and reduced the existing PEL by a factor of 10. On what grounds did the Fifth Circuit and the plurality opinion conclude that OSHA's risk assessment did not support issuance of the benzene standard? According to the Carnegie Commission, risk assessment also serves to inform the agency whether the costs of regulation justify the benefits and whether the regulatory method being considered is cost-effective. Did OSHA quantify the cost of compliance or the benefits that would result from reducing the risks presented by workplace exposure to benzene? Did it compare the costs and benefits of reducing PELs from 10 to 1 ppm? Did the statute require that it do so? Why did OSHA establish a PEL of 1 ppm rather than, say, 5 or 3 ppm?

3. According to OSHA, what is the relationship between §§3(8) and 6(b)(5) of the OSH Act? How did the industry petitioners view these two provisions? According to the plurality, what standards did Congress provide for OSHA's application of risk assessment and risk management inquiries?

4. According to the plurality, how did Congress intend to allocate the burden of proof in situations involving uncertainty concerning the level of risk presented by workplace exposure to toxic substances such as benzene? Which statutory provisions were determinative? How did Justice Marshall's interpretation of congressional intent differ? Do the two interpretations correspond to the approaches reflected in the Page excerpt, *Wilsonville, Reserve Mining,* or *Ethyl?* Does the plurality opinion induce OSHA to quantify the results of future risk assessments? Given the scientific uncertainties attendant on determining the effects of low-level exposures to carcinogens, how can the agency justify such quantitative efforts?

One observer has concluded that "OSHA learned its lesson" after *Benzene* and began to use mathematical models to quantify the risks posed by exposure to low concentrations of toxic materials such as ethylene oxide. Shere, The Myth of Meaningful Environmental Risk Assessment, 19 Harv. Envtl. L. Rev. 409, 425 (1995). These models relied on a series of conservative assumptions to extrapolate the data observed in animal experiments to the low-dose regions of the dose-response curve relevant to human exposure. The ethylene oxide PEL was upheld in Public Citizen Health Research Group v. Tyson, 796 F.2d 1479 (D.C. Cir. 1986). See also Graham, The Risk Not Reduced, 3 N.Y.U. Envtl. L.J. 382, 386 (1995) (*Benzene* was "[t]he turning point for quantitative risk assessment"). Professor Adler, whose description of the risk assessment process was excerpted earlier in this chapter, postulates that the *Benzene* case left OSHA with room to maneuver:

> *Industrial Union's* linkage between significant risk and "individual risk" might have been rejected as dictum. An agency more self-confident than OSHA might have read the case as mandating a de minimis threshold but permitting that to be specified in "population risk" terms—as some number of premature deaths that would be caused by the workplace toxin absent OSHA intervention. Instead, OSHA's practice in regulating workplace carcinogens has been to follow the letter of *Industrial Union*: the agency determines whether the existing concentration of a workplace carcinogen is a "significant risk," warranting OSHA intervention, by determining whether a worker exposed to that concentration for his entire working lifetime (forty-five years of exposure, five days a week, eight hours a day) would incur an "individual risk" of premature death that

exceeds, or at least is not too far below, 1 in 1000. Interestingly, OSHA's approach is more eclectic once it has determined that the status quo level of a workplace carcinogen poses a "significant risk." Considerations of "population risk," "individual risk," and economic and technical "feasibility" all seem to bear on the agency's decision as to what the permissible level of the carcinogen should be. [Adler, Against "Individual Risk": A Sympathetic Critique of Risk Assessment, 153 U. Pa. L. Rev. 1121, 1170-1171 (2005).]

5. The agency learned its lesson with respect to benzene as well. The Supreme Court's invalidation of the benzene standard restored the old 10 ppm standard. In 1987, OSHA amended the benzene standard by reducing the permissible exposure limit to an eight-hour time-weighted average of 1 ppm. 52 Fed. Reg. 34,460. The basis for the amended standard was a finding that employees exposed to benzene face a significant health risk (in the form of aplastic anemia, leukemia, and other blood disorders) and that the standard would substantially reduce that risk. The current standard, which is still 1 ppm, is at 29 C.F.R. §1910.1028(c)(1). About 70 percent of benzene emissions into the ambient air today come from road and nonroad vehicles. See EPA Air Toxics Study May Prompt Focus on New Mobile Source Controls, Inside EPA Weekly, Jan. 6, 2006, at 1, 8.

6. The *Benzene* decision can be read to require OSHA to determine acceptable risk levels solely on the basis of health concerns, before considering factors such as cost and technological feasibility. "[I]t is difficult to imagine how one could go about rationally making a choice between acceptable risks without relying on nonhealth factors like cost and technology. . . . [W]e accept risk precisely on account of non-health factors." Applegate, The Perils of Unreasonable Risk: Information, Regulatory Policy, and Toxic Substances Control, 91 Colum. L. Rev. 261, 275-276 (1991). Is there some other basis upon which an agency could premise a decision that an unregulated risk is acceptable? Does quantitative risk assessment perform an allocative function?

NOTE ON FEDERAL GENERIC CANCER POLICIES FOR REGULATING CARCINOGENS

The primary motivation behind "generic" agency cancer policies like the one employed by OSHA in the *Benzene* case is to create a uniform, systematic agency approach to risk assessment. Before the adoption of generic approaches, federal regulatory resources were stretched thin from the effort to reestablish in separate administrative proceedings that a scientific basis existed for the various methodological shortcuts for inferring a human cancer risk (e.g., use of animal data). Months or years could pass while an agency laboriously went through the same defense of its methodology, as manufacturers made the same attacks on agency methodology that they had made in prior proceedings on other substances. The generic approach would enable an agency to provide its answers to disputed fundamental questions in advance of proceedings on specific substances as guidance to its own decisionmakers, regulated entities, and public participants. The development of EPA's cancer policy is explored in §A.2 above. OSHA developed its own cancer policy through rulemaking. 45 Fed. Reg. 5002 (1980). In 1981, OSHA deleted those portions of the policy that it deemed inconsistent with the *Benzene* decision. 46 Fed. Reg. 4889.

A student of these agency policies has discerned three types: presumption-rebuttal, weight-of-the-evidence, and leave-it-to-the-scientists. M. E. Rushefsky, Making Cancer Policy (1986). The OSHA policy represents the presumption-rebuttal approach. The regulatory process establishes presumptions and sets stringent conditions on when and how these presumptions may be rebutted. EPA's 2005 carcinogen risk assessment guidelines take a weight-of-the-evidence approach, in which all relevant data are used. A weight-of-the-evidence approach is more flexible, and, when implemented by the agencies, is more open to considering negative data on carcinogenicity. The OSHA policy restricted the circumstances in which negative data could be considered. In the third approach, leave-it-to-the-scientists, a separate body conducts risk assessments; this constitutes the clearest separation of risk assessment from risk management. Industry groups typically endorse the weight-of-the-evidence approach. Labor, public interest, and environmental organizations want regulatory agencies to act on limited positive evidence.

Some administrative law specialists maintain that generic rulemaking increases agency consistency, public understanding, and efficiency in resolving individual cases; saves money; avoids relitigation of issues; provides an accessible procedure for diverse interests to make their views known; clarifies agency policy; and enhances the predictability of agency decisions. E.g., McGarity, Substantive and Procedural Discretion in Administrative Resolution of Science Policy Questions: Regulating Carcinogens in EPA and OSHA, 67 Geo. L.J. 729 (1979). Potential disadvantages include oversimplification, inappropriate mixing of scientific knowledge with risk assessment policy, overallocation of agency resources to guideline development, and the freezing of science.

3. Criticisms of Comparative and Quantitative Risk Assessment

Instrumental Criticisms. Despite its appeal as a screening mechanism for determining which risks merit regulation and as an allocative mechanism for ordering regulatory priorities, risk assessment, especially in its comparative and quantitative forms, has come under heavy attack from a variety of perspectives. The uncertainties that surround the use of comparative risk assessment are well known. "Risk comparisons assume that a great deal is known about the relationship between risk factors and human disease, and that risk assessment methods have a high degree of quantitative validity and predictability. Unfortunately, neither assumption is well established." Silbergeld, The Risks of Comparing Risks, 3 N.Y.U. Envtl. L.J. 405, 408 (1995). Information is often lacking, for example, about the physical processes that give rise to toxic risks. Campbell-Mohn & Applegate, Learning from NEPA: Guidelines for Responsible Risk Legislation, 23 Harv. Envtl. L. Rev. 93, 94 (1999). Few would contest the notion that, as a result of these uncertainties, cancer risk assessors possess considerable discretion in the choice of extrapolation models and exposure assumptions and the interpretation of data. Because of the many controversial assumptions and extrapolation models built into the risk assessment process, "each of which may skew the analysis by a factor of ten or more, . . . [t]he hard fact is that quantitative risk assessment generates numbers that are meaningless." Shere, The Myth of Meaningful Environmental Risk Assessment, 19 Harv. Envtl. L. Rev. 409, 413-414 (1995). The consequences of the exercise of that discretion, however, are a matter of some debate.

On the one hand, critics of prevailing risk assessment methodologies charge that the use of overly conservative assumptions in risk assessment models generates over-regulation and unwarranted public concern. E.g., Viscusi, Equivalent Frames of Reference for Judging Risk Regulation Policies, 3 N.Y.U. Envtl. L.J. 431 (1995). On the other hand, supporters of regulation based on current practices have responded that the biases reflected in risk assessments are not uniformly pro-regulatory in nature. Carcinogenesis tends to be the primary if not exclusive focus of many risk assessments. See Heinzerling, Reductionist Regulatory Reform, 8 Fordham Envtl. L.J. 459, 489 (1997). Because carcinogenesis may not be the most sensitive endpoint, this focus may fail to take into account the risk of other adverse health effects, such as neurotoxic and teratogenic effects. Further, substance-by-substance risk assessments may fail to factor synergistic effects into the analysis. Hornstein, Reclaiming Environmental Law: A Normative Critique of Comparative Risk Analysis, 92 Colum. L. Rev. 562, 572 (1992). Because risk assessments have tended to assume that all people are equally susceptible to the risk of adverse effects, and "have generally failed to examine susceptibility as a function of race, ethnicity, and income," they have produced regulations that fail to protect particularly sensitive subgroups. Israel, An Environmental Justice Critique of Risk Assessment, 3 N.Y.U. Envtl. L.J. 469, 503 (1995).

Environmentalists and other supporters of regulation have attacked other justifications for increased reliance on CRA as well. They claim that the evidence does not support the contention that the regulatory budget has been misallocated. They question the assertion that regulation has been directed at trivial risks, both because the number of cancer deaths attributed by Justice Breyer and others to certain activities may be understated and because society has expressed concern over smaller numbers of fatalities caused by other activities, such as the use of handguns. They claim that the costs of regulatory compliance tend to be overstated because cost estimates typically do not take into account economies of scale as demand for control technology increases, cost savings attributable to technological innovation, or the productive economic uses (such as substitute products) that regulatory expenditures generate. Finkel, A Second Opinion on an Environmental Misdiagnosis: The Risky Prescriptions of *Breaking the Vicious Circle*, 3 N.Y.U. Envtl. L.J. 295, 307, 369, 372 (1995).

Critics of CRA charge that the need to generate sufficient reliable data to enable decisionmakers to compare the costs and benefits of a series of risk reduction alternatives would impose a crushing analytical burden that would paralyze regulatory agencies such as EPA. Applegate, Worst Things First: Risk, Information, and Regulatory Structure in Toxic Substances Control, 9 Yale J. on Reg. 277, 325 (1992). "The fact that much of the information is within the control of the regulated industry, which has every incentive to delay new regulations, only exacerbates the potential for delay." McGarity, A Cost-Benefit State, 50 Admin. L. Rev. 1, 26 (1998). The critics also argue that legislation prescribing the methodology of CRA may limit analytical flexibility and hinder the development of more accurate risk assessment techniques.

Proposals to increase reliance on risk-risk analysis and societal risk reduction have proven to be particularly controversial. Risk-risk analysis has been characterized as everything from "a provocative thesis worthy of further research [that] is currently far too speculative to serve as a firm foundation" for regulatory policy decisions, Bender, Societal Risk Reduction: Promise and Pitfalls, 3 N.Y.U. Envtl. L.J. 255, 283 (1995), to "close to analysis gone haywire." Finkel, *supra*, at 324. For a particularly jaundiced view of risk-risk analysis, see Watkins, Pollution Can Save Your Life, N.Y. Times, June 19, 1997, at A15. The General Accounting Office criticized the Office of

Information and Regulatory Affairs within the OMB, which endorsed the use of risk-risk analysis in the early 1990s, for failing to recognize that a correlation between wealth and health may not be causal in nature. GAO, Risk-Risk Analysis: OMB's Review of a Proposed OSHA Rule, GAO/PEMD-92-93 (1992). In other words, "wealthy people might be wealthy partly because they are healthy, rather than the other way around." Heinzerling, *supra*, at 479. In addition, risk-risk analysis improperly assumes that money spent on regulation yields no economic gains such as new jobs. Heinzerling & Ackerman, The Humbugs of the Anti-Regulatory Movement, 87 Cornell L. Rev. 650, 669 (2002). Even those who support risk-risk analysis as a theoretical matter have characterized as implausible the $7.25 million figure often used as the amount of regulatory expenditure that corresponds to each death attributable to lost income: "either the implicit value of life estimate is too high or the amount of expenditure that will lead to the loss of a statistical life is too low." Viscusi, *supra*, at 458. Societal risk reduction is a flawed analytical technique, according to its critics, because its use would free up relatively little money for more efficient risk reduction, given that environmental regulatory expenditures are much smaller than the resources (e.g., defense expenditures) devoted to other risk-producing activities. Finkel, *supra*, at 373-374. In addition, the overwhelming bulk of resources saved through a reallocation of risk reduction efforts away from environmental regulation would be private compliance costs rather than government expenditures. As a result, absent new taxes on risk-creating activities, much of the money saved might not wind up being committed to alternative risk reduction projects. Bender, *supra*, at 275-276.

Normative Criticisms. The attacks on CRA have extended beyond qualms over data availability and quarrels over the validity of current analytical methodology to broader policy-based critiques. EPA's 1987 Unfinished Business report noted the discrepancy between public and expert perceptions of risk. Justice Breyer advocated the creation of a centralized administrative group whose function would be the rationalization of the process by which environmental risks are targeted. Breyer, Breaking the Vicious Circle: Toward Effective Risk Regulation 60-63 (1993). Critics of CRA, however, contend that reliance on public perceptions of risk to set the regulatory agenda is far from irrational. The differences between public and expert perceptions of risk may be due to differences in perspective rather than to ignorance or irrationality. The experts tend to view risk in terms of the total number of fatalities expected to result from the activities under consideration. The public tends to consider a wider range of factors, such as whether the risk is voluntarily or involuntarily incurred, familiar or unfamiliar, concentrated or disbursed, natural or man-made, preventable or unpreventable, reversible or irreversible, and chronic or catastrophic. See Sandman, A Formula for Effective Risk Communication (1991); Freeman & Godsil, The Question of Risk: Incorporating Community Perceptions into Environmental Risk Assessments, 21 Fordham Urb. L.J. 547 (1994). Cognitive error theory postulates, for example, that because people tend to weigh the probability of an event by the ease with which relevant information comes to mind, they may overestimate low risks of catastrophic events but underestimate higher risks of more diffuse, chronic harms. Similarly, critics of CRA contest its tendency to ignore equitable considerations by focusing on aggregate effects and downplaying society's distaste for risks that affect the poor, the elderly, children, racial minorities, and future generations disproportionately. Hornstein, *supra*, at 600-601.

What are the consequences of these differing perceptions for the development of a mechanism for ranking risks according to their severity? At the very least, the public's perceptions arguably ought not to be excluded from the debate through exclusive reliance on the risk rankings of a technocratic body of experts. Because the debate involves "competing rationalities,"

> it unarguably follows that the choice of approach is an ethical and political one that technical experts have neither the knowledge nor the authority to dictate, because the issue transcends technocratic expertise. Were we to defer to agencies simply on the basis of their technical proficiency, the ethical-political question would be begged entirely. Agencies could be expected to resort to methods the use of which denies the very values at stake . . . [and] methodological proclivities would bias agency risk processing in the direction of too much public risk—as viewed from the public's perspective. [Gillette & Krier, Risk, Courts, and Agencies, 138 U. Pa. L. Rev. 1027, 1085 (1990).]

In short, the trade-offs involved "are not resolvable as technocratic exercises" and the delegation to an expert body of authority to determine which risks are "reasonable" "both avoids and obscures the real policy decision being made. These decisions are fundamentally political and must be based on broader sets of values, many of which are not quantifiable." Applegate, *supra*, at 300.

Why not simply increase public participation in the risk assessment process? Although the use of comparative risk assessment does not necessarily preclude public input that reflects values other than utilitarianism, the technical nature of the process may discourage such input, and the experts responsible for ranking risks, because of their inclination to deride the public's irrationality toward risk, may subordinate these values to the more concrete considerations reflected in aggregate risk reduction figures. A process that fails to incorporate public concerns in this manner is likely to be perceived as illegitimate and undemocratic. See Finkel, *supra*, at 357. Moreover, the kind of centralized body of experts envisioned by Justice Breyer may insulate itself from everyone except representatives of special interest groups. The information-intensive nature of risk-based decisionmaking tends to favor such resource-rich groups in producing the information relied on by the experts in making their decisions. The decisionmaking process also tends to be more accessible to these groups because of its length and complexity. As a result, "risk-based decisionmaking can itself become a device by which politically powerful groups can effectuate their interests—now clothed as merely the objective determinations of 'science'—at the expense of less powerful groups." Hornstein, Lessons from Federal Pesticide Regulation on the Paradigms and Politics of Environmental Law Reform, 10 Yale J. on Reg. 369, 416 (1993).

Finally, the skeptics contend that CRA tends to pose "false choices" in the sense that it encourages decisionmakers to trade off one environmental risk against another instead of developing alternative, creative solutions that involve efforts to reduce all of those risks.

> Comparative risk analysis tends to undermine [the] forward-looking enterprise [of current environmental law]. . . . By tending to compare environmental risks with each other, rather than to alternative possibilities, comparative risk analysis emphasizes the wrong risk baseline, one that fails to capture the law's moral direction (as well as its abhorrence of market externalities). The result is an ideological scheme, based on an inward-looking set of comparisons, that is decidedly biased toward the status quo. . . . By exacerbating uncertainty in the current standing of a given risk, comparative risk analysis can dramatically complicate the willingness or ability of entrepreneurs to capitalize

improvements such as pollution-control processes or environmentally benign products. [Hornstein, Reclaiming Environmental Law, *supra*, at 616-617.]

Reform Proposals. A variety of proposals to incorporate comparative and quantitative risk assessment into agency decisionmaking have surfaced, some of which take into account the foregoing criticisms. For example, Professor Applegate has proposed shifting the focus of legislative control of agency action back from the standard-setting phase to the priority-setting stage of the regulatory process by requiring that EPA develop a multi-year plan of action, based on statutory criteria such as achievement of the greatest overall risk reduction possible with available budgetary resources. EPA would be bound to conform its actions to the plan, except in emergencies or in the event that new data become available. Congressional control of the priority-setting process would force public debate on how to allocate risk reduction expenditures and improve both the effectiveness and efficiency of regulation.

Further Reading. For a collection of further criticisms of risk assessment as a mechanism for improving environmental policy, see Risk Symposium, 63 U. Cin. L. Rev. 1533 (1995). For further evaluation of the usefulness of comparative risk assessment, see generally Symposium, Risk in the Republic: Comparative Risk Analysis and Public Policy, 8 Duke Envtl. L. & Pol'y F. 1-180 (1997). Campbell-Mohn & Applegate, *supra*, suggest a series of guidelines for risk assessment legislation.

4. Comparing the Costs and Benefits of Hazardous Substance Control

Quantification of regulatory benefits may be relevant at the risk management as well as at the risk assessment stage. Once the agency decides it is authorized to regulate, it must decide how to trade off health benefits against the added economic costs of hazardous substances control. Quantification places a numerical value on risk that can be compared with regulatory costs, allowing the agency to choose the regulatory option that produces the greatest net benefit. The following case addresses the question that the Supreme Court left open in the *Benzene* decision: whether the Occupational Safety and Health Act requires that OSHA engage in cost-benefit analysis when promulgating health standards for toxic materials.

AMERICAN TEXTILE MANUFACTURERS INSTITUTE, INC. v. DONOVAN
452 U.S. 490 (1981)

Justice Brennan delivered the opinion of the Court.

[In 1978, OSHA issued a standard limiting occupational exposure to cotton dust, an airborne particle by-product of the preparation and manufacture of cotton products, exposure to which may cause a respiratory illness known as byssinosis, or "brown lung" disease. OSHA determined that exposure to cotton dust represents a significant health hazard to employees, and that the standard, which the agency deemed both technologically and economically feasible, would lead to a significant reduction in the prevalence of byssinosis.[25] Representatives of the cotton industry challenged the validity of the standard.]

II

The principal question presented in these cases is whether the Occupational Safety and Health Act requires the Secretary, in promulgating a standard pursuant to §6(b)(5) of the Act, 29 U.S.C. §655(b)(5), to determine that the costs of the standard bear a reasonable relationship to its benefits. Relying on §§6(b)(5) and 3(8) of the Act, 29 U.S.C. §§655(b)(5) and 652(8), petitioners urge not only that OSHA must show that a standard addresses a significant risk of material health impairment, see Industrial Union Dept. v. American Petroleum Institute, 448 U.S., at 639 (plurality opinion), but also that OSHA must demonstrate that the reduction in risk of material health impairment is significant in light of the costs of attaining that reduction. Respondents on the other hand contend that the Act requires OSHA to promulgate standards that eliminate or reduce such risks "to the extent such protection is technologically and economically feasible." . . .

A

. . . Although their interpretations differ, all parties agree that the phrase "to the extent feasible" contains the critical language in §6(b)(5) for purposes of these cases.

The plain meaning of the word "feasible" supports respondents' interpretation of the statute. According to Webster's Third New international Dictionary of the English Language 831 (1976), "feasible" means "capable of being done, executed, or effected." Thus, §6(b)(5) directs the Secretary to issue the standard that "most adequately assures . . . that no employee will suffer material impairment of health," limited only by the extent to which this is "capable of being done." In effect ʌ en, . . . Congress itself defined the basic relationship between costs and benefits, by placing the "benefit" of worker health above all other considerations save those making attainment of this "benefit" unachievable. Any standard based on a balancing of costs and benefits by the Secretary that strikes a different balance than that struck by Congress would be inconsistent with the command set forth in §6(b)(5). Thus, cost-benefit analysis by OSHA is not required by the statute because feasibility analysis is.[29]

---

25. . . . In distinct contrast with its Cancer Policy, OSHA expressly found that "exposure to cotton dust presents a significant health hazard to employees," and that "cotton dust produced significant health effects at low levels of exposure." . . . OSHA relied on dose-response curve data (the Merchant Study) showing that 25% of employees suffered at least Grade ½ byssinosis at a 500 µg/m³ PEL standard. Examining the Merchant Study in light of other studies in the record, the agency found that "the Merchant study provides a reliable assessment of health risk to cotton textile workers from cotton dust." OSHA concluded that the "prevalence of byssinosis should be significantly reduced" by the 200 µg/m³ PEL. It is difficult to imagine what else the agency could do to comply with this Court's decision in [Benzene].

29. In these cases we are faced with the issue whether the Act requires OSHA to balance costs and benefits in promulgating a single toxic material and harmful physical agent standard under §6(b)(5). Petitioners argue that without cost-benefit balancing, the issuance of a single standard might result in a "serious misallocatio[n] of the finite resources that are available for the protection of worker safety and health," given the other health hazards in the workplace. This argument is more properly addressed to other provisions of the Act which may authorize OSHA to explore costs and benefits for deciding between issuance of several standards regulating different varieties of health and

When Congress has intended that an agency engage in cost-benefit analysis, it has clearly indicated such intent on the face of the statute. [A] recent example is the Outer Continental Shelf Lands Act Amendments of 1978, 43 U.S.C. §1347(b), providing that offshore drilling operations shall use "the best available and safest technologies which the Secretary determines to be economically feasible, wherever failure of equipment would have significant effect on safety, health, or the environment, except where the Secretary determines that the incremental benefits are clearly insufficient to justify the incremental costs of using such technologies." . . . Congress uses specific language when intending that an agency engage in cost-benefit analysis. See Industrial Union Dept. v. American Petroleum Institute, 448 U.S. at 710, n.27 (MARSHALL, J., dissenting). Certainly in light of its ordinary meaning, the word "feasible" cannot be construed to articulate such congressional intent. We therefore reject the argument that Congress required cost-benefit analysis in §6(b)(5).

B

Even though the plain language of §6(b)(5) supports this construction, we must still decide whether §3(8), the general definition of an occupational safety and health standard, either alone or in tandem with §6(b)(5), incorporates a cost-benefit requirement for standards dealing with toxic materials or harmful physical agents. Section 3(8) of the Act, 29 U.S.C. §652(8) (emphasis added), provides:

> The term "occupational safety and health standard" means a standard which requires conditions, or the adoption or use of one or more practices, means, methods, operations, or processes, *reasonably necessary or appropriate* to provide safe or healthful employment and places of employment.

Taken alone, the phrase "reasonably necessary or appropriate" might be construed to contemplate some balancing of the costs and benefits of a standard. Petitioners urge that, so construed, §3(8) engrafts a cost-benefit analysis requirement on the issuance of §6(b)(5) standards, even if §6(b)(5) itself does not authorize such analysis. We need not decide whether §3(8), standing alone, would contemplate some form of cost-benefit analysis. For even if it does, Congress specifically chose in §6(b)(5) to impose separate and additional requirements for issuance of a subcategory of occupational safety and health standards dealing with toxic materials and harmful physical agents: it required that those standards be issued to prevent material impairment of health to the extent feasible. Congress could reasonably have concluded that health standards should be subject to different criteria than safety standards because of the special problems presented in regulating them.

Agreement with petitioners' argument that §3(8) imposes an additional and overriding requirement of cost-benefit analysis on the issuance of §6(b)(5) standards would eviscerate the "to the extent feasible" requirement. Standards would inevitably be set at the level indicated by cost-benefit analysis, and not at the level specified by §6(b)(5). For example, if cost-benefit analysis indicated a protective standard of 1,000 μg/m³ PEL, while feasibility analysis indicated a 500 μg/m³ PEL, the agency would be forced by the cost-benefit requirement to choose the less stringent point. We cannot

---

safety hazards, e.g., §6(g) of the Act, 29 U.S.C. §655(g); or for promulgating other types of standards not issued under §6(b)(5). We express no view on these questions.

believe that Congress intended the general terms of §3(8) to countermand the specific feasibility requirement of §6(b)(5). Adoption of petitioners' interpretation would effectively write §6(b)(5) out of the Act. We decline to render Congress' decision to include a feasibility requirement nugatory, thereby offending the well-settled rule that all parts of a statute, if possible, are to be given effect. . . . [32]

[The Court concluded that the record contained substantial evidence to support the conclusion that the cotton dust standard was feasible because, even though some marginal employers might shut down rather than comply, the standard would not threaten the industry as a whole.]

NOTES AND QUESTIONS

1. The Court relied on the plain meaning of the word "feasible" in §6(b)(5) of the OSH Act to support its resolution of the issue of whether OSHA must engage in cost-benefit analysis when it promulgates occupational safety and health standards for toxic materials. Did the Court rely on the plain meaning of the word "safe" in the *Benzene* case? Was the Court's interpretation of the relationship between §§6(b)(5) and 3(8) in the *Cotton Dust* case consistent with its interpretation of the same relationship in *Benzene*? Why might cost-benefit analysis be required when OSHA issues occupational safety and health standards that do not deal with toxic materials? See International Union, UAW v. OSHA, 37 F.3d 665 (D.C. Cir. 1994); International Union, UAW v. OSHA, 938 F.2d 1310 (D.C. Cir. 1991).

2. The cotton industry argued that, absent a requirement that OSHA engage in cost-benefit analysis, agency standards might result in a misallocation of worker protection resources. Why? What was the Court's response to this argument? Does §6(g) of the OSH Act provide a model for requiring comparative risk assessment? Cf. American Iron and Steel Inst. v. OSHA, 182 F.3d 1261 (11th Cir. 1999) (judicial review of OSHA's priority setting in determining the appropriate subjects of regulation is deferential).

3. *Different Approaches to Risk Management.* We have now examined a number of attempts by courts, legislatures, and regulatory agencies to respond to the economic impact of efforts to reduce risks. In *Wilsonville* the court took the costs and benefits of closing the hazardous waste disposal site into account in enjoining the further operation of the facility. In *Reserve Mining* and *Ethyl*, the statutes applied in those cases merely required abatement if public health was "endangered," without explicitly requiring the high costs involved to be taken into account in any particular manner, if at all. But in *Reserve Mining* the court explicitly took the economic costs of enjoining Reserve's taconite discharges into Lake Superior into account in fashioning delayed

---

32. This is not to say that §3(8) might not require the balancing of costs and benefits for standards promulgated under provisions other than §6(b)(5) of the Act. . . . Furthermore, the mere fact that a §6(b)(5) standard is "feasible" does not mean that §3(8)'s "reasonably necessary or appropriate" language might not impose additional restraints on OSHA. For example, all §6(b)(5) standards must be addressed to "significant risks" of material health impairment. In addition, if the use of one respirator would achieve the same reduction in health risk as the use of five, the use of five respirators was "technologically and economically feasible," and OSHA thus insisted on the use of five, then the "reasonably necessary or appropriate" limitation might come into play as an additional restriction on OSHA to choose the one-respirator standard. In this case we need not decide all the applications that §3(8) might have, either alone or together with §6(b)(5).

injunctive relief, and in *Ethyl* EPA took costs into account in scheduling the phase-in of its gasoline lead content standards.

Do these cases and other federal environmental statutory provisions reveal a consistent pattern in the treatment of the costs and benefits of risk reduction? A former general counsel of the Food and Drug Administration (FDA) discerns three categories of legislation for preventing human exposure to carcinogenic substances. First, some statutes reflect a "no risk" policy, which requires the implementing agency to prevent any human exposure. Second, some laws restrict the agency to the regulation of significant risks. Third, some statutes require that other criteria, such as the techno-logical capabilities of regulated industries, moderate agency efforts to protect human health. The differences in these approaches are attributable to a mix of considerations, including the fact that most of the statutes are directed at the reduction of other health hazards in addition to cancer. R. Merrill, Federal Regulation of Cancer-Causing Chemicals, Report to the Administrative Conference of the United States 22-32 (1982). Where in Professor Merrill's taxonomy do the statutory provisions discussed in *Reserve Mining, Ethyl, Benzene,* and *Cotton Dust* belong? Professor Rodgers posits a different categorization scheme: the cost-oblivious, cost-effective, cost-sensitive, and strict cost-benefit models. Rodgers, Benefits, Costs, and Risks: Oversight of Health and Environmental Decision Making, 4 Harv. Envtl. L. Rev. 191 (1980). Cost-benefit analysis is not the same as cost-effectiveness analysis, which serves the allied but more limited purpose of ensuring that the agency selects the least costly method for attaining a predetermined goal. More cost-effective solutions produce better cost-benefit ratios. For another attempt to discern patterns in the role Congress has assigned to cost considerations in the health and safety protection statutes, see S. Shapiro & R. Glicksman, Risk Regulation at Risk: Restoring a Pragmatic Approach ch. 3 (2003) (concluding that Congress typically requires that agencies consider costs in some fashion, but not by engaging in cost-benefit analysis).

4. What is the rationale for cost-benefit analysis in the environmental regulatory context, and what are its advantages and disadvantages from practical and normative points of view? See the Note on Cost-Benefit Analysis in Chapter 3, section C.

E.   PREVENTING THE ENTRY OF TOXIC SUBSTANCES INTO THE STREAM OF COMMERCE

Over the years, agencies and programs have been established to deal with hazardous substances, with recent focus on deleterious long-term effects, such as cancer, of these substances. A detailed analysis of the legislative acts enacted by Congress concerning toxic substances [Table 8-2] reveals an evolution of thought in that each reflects the scientific views that existed at the time of enactment. Consequently, these acts are not uniform in their view of the disease, the role chemical substances might play in its incidence, and what ought to be done about potential toxic substances and potential carcinogens. [Office of Science and Technology Policy, Chemical Carcinogens; Review of the Science and Its Associated Principles, 50 Fed. Reg. 10,372, 10,373 (1985).]

More can be done to control hazardous substances than merely bringing common law actions to enjoin a nuisance or setting emissions and effluent standards, using the classic approach of the Clean Air and Clean Water Acts. Commerce in all

TABLE 8-2
Federal Laws Related to Exposures to Toxic Substances*

Legislation	Agency	Area of Concern
Food, Drug, and Cosmetic Act	FDA	Food, drugs, food additives, color additives, new drugs, animal and feed additives, and medical devices
Federal Insecticide, Fungicide, and Rodenticide Act	EPA	Pesticides
Dangerous Cargo Act	DOT, USCG	Water shipment of toxic materials
Atomic Energy Act	NRC	Radioactive substances
Federal Hazardous Substances Act	CPSC	Toxic household products
Federal Meat Inspection Act	USDA	Food, feed, color additives, and pesticide residues
Poultry Products Inspection Act		
Egg Products Inspection Act		
Occupational Safety and Health Act	OSHA, NIOSH	Workplace toxic chemicals
Poison Prevention Packaging Act	CPSC	Packaging of hazardous household products
Clean Air Act	EPA	Air pollutants
Hazardous Materials Transportation Uniform Safety Act	DOT	Transport of hazardous materials
Clean Water Act	EPA	Water pollutants
Marine Protection, Research, and Sanctuaries Act	EPA	Ocean dumping
Consumer Product Safety Act	CPSC	Hazardous consumer products
Lead-Based Paint Poison Prevention Act	CPSC, HEW (HHS), HUD	Use of lead paint in federally assisted housing
Safe Drinking Water Act	EPA	Drinking water contaminants
Resource Conservation and Recovery Act	EPA	Solid waste, including hazardous wastes
Toxic Substances Control Act	EPA	Hazardous chemicals not covered by other laws, including pre-market review
Federal Mine Safety and Health Act	DOL, NIOSH	Toxic substances in coal and other mines
Comprehensive Environmental Response, Compensation, and Liability Act	EPA	Hazardous substances, pollutants, and contaminants

*Dates of enactment and amendment omitted.

substances that pre-market screening shows to be likely to subject the public to unacceptable hazards may be restricted or banned entirely. The Toxic Substances Control Act (TSCA) of 1976, which purports to screen all existing and new toxic substances, authorizes EPA to regulate the manufacture and use of toxic substances in this manner. Another strategy allows a product to be marketed until its hazards become known and then restricts its marketing or use only so far as necessary to protect the public. Federal regulation of pesticides under the Federal Insecticide, Fungicide, and Rodenticide Act (FIFRA) exemplifies this approach. Bhagwat, Modes of Regulatory Enforcement and the Problem of Administrative Discretion, 50 Hastings L.J. 1275 (1999), explores the justification for and consequences of ex ante review of regulated conduct. Although Bhagwat concludes that granting an agency the power to engage in ex ante review of private behavior may be desirable for practical reasons, he also concludes that such authorizations provide agencies with enormous substantive discretion and a great deal of power to coerce regulated entities.

As the OST excerpt at the beginning of this section indicates, Congress has delegated to several different federal agencies the power to restrict the manufacture of toxic chemicals and their incorporation into otherwise useful products. These statutory delegations reflect diverse approaches to risk assessment and risk management. Some of the statutory schemes listed in Table 8-2, such as the Clean Air and Clean Water Acts and the Occupational Safety and Health Act, are covered in earlier portions of this book. Others, those that regulate and impose liability for hazardous waste management, are treated in section F of this chapter and in Chapter 9. This section focuses on a few representative examples of the regulation of the manufacture and use of toxic chemicals authorized by federal law. As you study these materials, consider what approaches to risk assessment and risk management Congress has chosen, why it may have chosen them, and whether the choices are appropriate.

1.   Regulation of Chemical Manufacturing and Use

a.   The Toxic Substances Control Act

(1)   Introduction

In 1976, Congress passed the Toxic Substances Control Act (TSCA), 15 U.S.C. §§2601-2629, which empowers EPA to regulate the manufacture of most of the chemical substances not already regulated, based on the risks they pose to health or the environment. Rather than focusing on the use of products or the disposal of wastes (although it reaches that far), TSCA's emphasis falls high in the stream of commerce, at the premanufacture phase. EPA is supposed to review each new chemical marketed annually, as well as the approximately 62,000 chemicals in commerce shortly after TSCA was enacted, to determine if they "may present an unreasonable risk of injury to health or the environment." §4(a)(1)(A)(i). By the end of 2005, EPA's Office of Pollution Prevention and Toxics was tracking more than 80,000 chemicals available for sale and use in the United States. Physicians Comm. for Responsible Medicine v. Johnson, 436 F.3d 326, 328 (2d Cir. 2006). TSCA exempts some materials because they are regulated under other statutes and others because political lobbies were powerful enough to secure their exclusion. §3(2)(B).

Despite these exemptions, TSCA represents the closest thing to a comprehensive chemical substance control statute that Congress has ever enacted. Yet TSCA has disappointed its proponents, who do not believe that its testing and premanufacture review provisions have improved chemical product safety. Indeed, the most important issues that this discussion addresses are whether TSCA succeeds as a legal device for shifting the burden of proof of safety to chemical manufacturers, and whether the test of "unreasonable risk," which appears repeatedly in TSCA, can be applied with a balanced emphasis on health protection and economic productivity.*

(2)   A Summary of TSCA

The TSCA scheme is not difficult to summarize. See Figure 8-7. Subject to some important exemptions, TSCA requires that manufacturers or others engaging in commerce in a new chemical substance, or making a significant new use of an existing chemical substance, give EPA premanufacturing notice (PMN) of data and test results regarding the substance. EPA then determines if the new chemical presents an unreasonable risk or if testing must be done to enable that determination to be made. §5. EPA must compile an inventory of chemicals already in commerce and determine if the chemicals on the inventory present unreasonable risks. Manufacturers or others responsible for putting chemicals in commerce must perform tests on both new and existing chemical substances and mixtures if EPA determines that they present unreasonable risks or that existing information is insufficient to allow an informed preliminary assessment to be made. §4. EPA may limit or forbid the manufacture of new or existing chemicals that studies have shown present an unreasonable risk to health or the environment. §6. These provisions were intended to put the burden of proof on the manufacturer whenever EPA raises the issue of a chemical's safety. In theory, this burden may be very difficult to discharge. In practice, however, critics feel that EPA still assumes, or has been forced to assume, most of the burden of showing that a chemical presents an unreasonable risk.

(3)   Premanufacturing Notice for New Chemicals

No one may manufacture a new chemical substance (i.e., one not on the inventory of existing chemicals) or manufacture or process an existing chemical substance for a "significant new use" without providing at least 90 days prior notice to EPA. §5(a)(1). This premanufacture notification of intent to manufacture or make a significant new use may have to be accompanied by existing data and, in theory at least, new information. For specific requirements, see §§8(a)(2); 5(b)(1), (2); 5(d)(1). The statute affords trade secrets protection to those who submit these PMNs. See §14; section E.2 below. If the data submitted to EPA are insufficient to permit a reasoned conclusion about the health and environmental risks posed by the substance, and allowing commerce in the chemical may present an unreasonable risk, the Administrator may issue an administrative order or seek a court injunction to limit or prohibit its use. §5(e). Manufacturers sometimes withdraw PMNs to avoid the issuance of §5(e) orders or interim regulations under §5(f) to protect against unreasonable risks.

---

*For more extensive coverage of the practical aspects of TSCA's applications, see generally Hathaway et al., A Practitioner's Guide to the Toxic Substances Control Act: Parts I, II, and III, 24 Envtl. L. Rep. (ELI) 10,207 (May 1994); id. at 10,285 (June 1994); id. at 10,357 (July 1994).

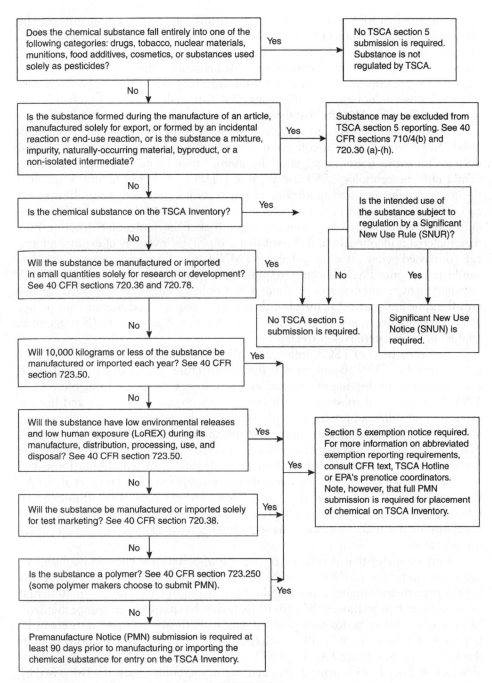

FIGURE 8-7
Steps for Determining Whether a Premanufacture Submission Is Required for a
Chemical Substance

Source: http://www.epa.gov/opptintr/newchems/whofiles.htm#pmnchrt

Suppose that EPA considers living, genetically modified microorganisms to be chemical substances subject to TSCA. These would include microorganisms used for bioremediation at CERCLA sites, enhanced oil recovery, metal extraction, and specialty chemical production. The unpredictable behaviors of these organisms, according to EPA, presents uncertainties about the risks they pose. EPA wants to require PMN submissions for new microorganisms that contain deliberately modified hereditary traits. Does TSCA authorize the agency to do so?

Suppose that EPA is considering requiring PMN for newly developed nanomaterial. Nanotechnology is "a collection of technologies for building materials and devices 'from the bottom up,' atom by atom." Van Lente, Note, Building the World of Nanotechnology, 38 Case W. Res. J. Int'l L. 173, 174 (2006). It involves the design, production, and application of structures and devices by controlling shape and size at the nanoscale (a nanonmeter encompasses about 8-10 atoms).[*] Representatives of the nanotechnology industry argue that if the molecular structure of a nanomaterial is identical to that of a substance on EPA's inventory of existing chemicals (discussed below), it is not subject to PMN. Under this view, carbon nanotubes would not require PMN because graphite is an existing chemical on the TSCA inventory. Environmental groups respond that unless a chemical substance has not only the same molecular structure, but also the same physical and chemical properties as a listed substance, it is subject to PMN. Which conception of the PMN program as applied to nanomaterials is correct?

Section 5(h)(4) of TSCA authorizes EPA to exempt manufacturers of new chemicals from the PMN requirement if the manufacture, processing, distribution in commerce, use, or disposal of a substance will not present an unreasonable risk. In 1995, EPA exempted substances with very low environmental releases and human exposures, regardless of production volume, unless the substance may cause serious acute or chronic human health effects or significant environmental effects. 40 C.F.R. §723.50. The change was part of an effort by EPA to streamline the PMN process so that it could concentrate its limited resources on identifying and controlling those new chemical substances most likely to present unreasonable risks. See Hinds et al., EPA's Premanufacture Notification Revisions: New Twists, New Opportunities, 19 Chemical Reg. Rep. (BNA) 58 (1995). Has EPA demonstrated a sensitivity to resource misallocation that makes statutorily mandated comparative risk assessment procedures unnecessary?

EPA estimates that it reviews an average of 2,300 new chemical substances each year under the PMN process. Nevertheless, critics have not been impressed with its performance in implementing the PMN requirements. The information that must be submitted by those subject to PMN review has hardly been comprehensive. Many PMNs contain no toxicological test data at all. By one estimate, only about 15 percent of PMNs include health or safety test data. Woolf, Why Modernization of the U.S. Toxic Substance Law Is Good for Public Health and Business, 6 Sustainable Dev. & Pol'y L. #3 (Spring 2006), at 6. Agency scientists assess the risk posed by substances for which there are no toxicological data based on their structural similarity to known toxic chemicals (known as a structure-activity relationship). Is this practice justifiable on the basis of a desire to allocate scarce investigative resources

---

[*]See also Lemley, Patenting Nanotechnology, 58 Stan. L. Rev. 601, 602 (2005) ("Nanotechnology is the study and use of the unique characteristics of materials at the nanometer scale, between the classical large-molecule level to which traditional physics and chemistry apply and the atomic level in which the bizarre rules of quantum mechanics take effect.").

efficiently? See EDF v. EPA, 598 F.2d 62 (D.C. Cir. 1978) (EPA justified regulation of less-chlorinated PCBs under §307(a) of the Clean Water Act on the basis of available information concerning more-chlorinated PCBs). About 90 percent of chemicals for which PMNs are submitted wind up not being restricted under TSCA. Through 1988, for example, EPA had received about 11,600 PMNs and subjected only 190 of them to §5(e) orders. Almost 90 percent of those orders simply required the use of protective clothing by those working with the substance. Hanan, Pushing the Environmental Regulatory Focus a Step Back: Controlling the Intro-duction of New Chemicals under the Toxic Substances Control Act, 18 Am. J.L. & Med. 395 (1992).

(4)   Screening Existing Chemicals

The original TSCA inventory contained about 55,000 chemicals and chemical groups. 45 Fed. Reg. 49,974 (1980). EPA must supplement the inventory to include all new chemicals for which PMN notices are filed. §8(b). Although TSCA does not specifically state that EPA must systematically study this backlog to determine which chemicals may pose an unreasonable risk, the inventory requirement would be pointless without such a review. Nevertheless, as of 2002, EPA had "no toxicity infor-mation on 43 percent of the nearly 3,000 organic chemicals produced or imported in amounts above one million pounds annually, and a full set of basic toxicity informa-tion [was] available for only 7 percent." Greer & Steinzor, Bad Science, 19 Envtl. F. 28, 34 (Jan./Feb. 2002).

Section 8(d) of TSCA requires EPA to issue rules requiring any person who manufactures, processes, or distributes in commerce any chemical substance, or who proposes to engage in one of those activities, to submit to EPA copies and lists of unpublished health and safety studies conducted by, known to, or reasonably ascer-tainable by that person, on the listed chemicals manufactured, imported, or processed. The list is at 40 C.F.R. §716.120. See, e.g., 53 Fed. Reg. 22,300 (1988) (requiring testing of 33 chemicals for human health effects and chemical fate to benefit the agency's RCRA program).

EPA's existing chemicals program screens chemicals currently in production or use to determine whether they present potential health or environmental risks. EPA may decide that a chemical requires additional testing or that it presents significant risks that warrant regulatory action. To establish the order in which chemicals will be reviewed, EPA assigns them a priority based on factors such as whether the chemical is associated with other regulatory activity, whether it has been referred to EPA by another agency, and whether data or assessments already exist. Of the inventoried chemicals that have been screened, relatively few have received more than cursory attention.

(5)   The Issuance of Test Rules

The most intensive testing requirements for potentially injurious chemicals—new and existing—are provided in §4 of TSCA. EPA may mandate a series of particular tests if it believes they are necessary to determine the safety of a chemical substance. Once a test is completed, EPA may carry out its PMN duties under §5 or make a determination of unreasonable risk under §6 and promulgate rules limiting or banning the chemical's use. The tests required under §4 are referred to collectively as the chemical's "test rule" because TSCA specifies notice-and-comment rulemaking procedures.

Each test rule must include standards for the development of test data for the substance or mixture being tested. §4(b)(1)(B). The Act specifies a not-surprising list of effects (e.g., carcinogenesis, mutagenesis), characteristics (e.g., acute and chronic toxicity), and methodologies that may be used in formulating standards. §4(b)(2)(A). To help EPA set priorities, §4(e) created an Interagency Testing Committee (ITC), which lists chemicals for priority testing. After listing, EPA has one year either to propose a test rule or to publish reasons for not doing so. EPA may also list a chemical after rulemaking. §5(b)(4). EPA has added chemicals included on the ITC list to its own lists of substances for which manufacturers must file Preliminary Assessment forms in accordance with §8(a) and unpublished health and safety studies under §8(d). See, e.g., 69 Fed. Reg. 24,517 (2004) (§8(d) rule requiring manufacturers of 15 chemicals on the ITC's §4(e) Priority Testing List to submit unpublished health and safety data to EPA).

By the end of 2002, the ITC had recommended information reporting or testing for about 4,200 chemicals and deferred information reporting or testing for another 38,000. Bergeson et al., TSCA—Chemical Testing Issues, 35 Envtl. L. Rep. (ELI) 10085, 10086 (2005). But by 2005, EPA had issued test rules for only 185 of the approximately 82,000 chemicals on the TSCA inventory. Woolf, *supra*, at 6.

What must EPA demonstrate to justify issuance of a test rule? Section 4 authorizes testing requirements in two situations. First, EPA may issue a test rule if it finds that (1) the manufacture, distribution in commerce, processing, use, or disposal of a chemical substance may present an unreasonable risk of injury to health or the environment, (2) there are insufficient data to reasonably assess the effects of those activities on health or the environment, and (3) testing is necessary to develop the data. §4(a)(1)(A). In Chemical Mfrs. Ass'n v. EPA, 859 F.2d 977 (D.C. Cir. 1988), CMA challenged a test rule for 2-ethylhexanoic acid (EHA). The court upheld EPA's view that TSCA authorizes issuance of a test rule where EPA finds that there is "a more-than-theoretical basis for concluding that the substance is sufficiently toxic, and human exposure to it is sufficient in amount, to generate" an unreasonable risk. EPA can establish the existence and extent of human exposure based on inferences drawn from the circumstances of the substance's manufacture and use. It must rebut industry-supplied evidence attacking those inferences only if that evidence renders the probability of exposure in the amount found by EPA "no more than theoretical or speculative. The probability of infrequent or even one-time exposure to individuals can warrant a test rule, so long as there is a more-than-theoretical basis for determining that exposure in such doses presents an 'unreasonable risk of injury to health.' " Id. at 979.

Because the standard of judicial review of test rules is the substantial evidence test, §19(c)(1)(B)(i), Professor Applegate has described §4(a)(1)(A) test rules as predicated on

> a third order probability: EPA must promulgate a test rule when it finds a probability (substantial evidence) of a probability (may present) of a probability (risk). Moreover, each probability is a very different type of calculation: risk is a statement of frequency of effect; "may present" is a statement of the confidence in the induction from known data to frequency; and substantial evidence is a statement of the overall certainty with which the foregoing statements are made. Risk and "may present" take an *ex ante* perspective;

substantial evidence is an *ex post* evaluation. [Applegate, The Perils of Unreasonable Risk: Information, Regulatory Policy, and Toxic Substances Control, 91 Colum. L. Rev. 261, 322 (1991).]

Second, EPA may issue a test rule if a chemical substance is or will be produced in substantial quantities and "(I) it enters or may reasonably be anticipated to enter the environment in substantial quantities or (II) there is or may be significant or substantial exposure to such substance or mixture," provided again that insufficient data exist to assess the risk, and testing is necessary to supply the data. §4(a)(1)(B). Chemical Mfrs. Ass'n v. EPA, 899 F.2d 344 (5th Cir. 1990), involved the scope of EPA's authority under this provision. The chemical industry challenged a regulation requiring manufacturers of the chemical cumene to engage in toxicological testing. EPA based its rule on the following finding:

> Under [§4(a)(1)(B)], EPA finds that cumene is produced in substantial quantities and that there is substantial environmental release with the potential for substantial human exposure from manufacturing, processing, use, and disposal. . . . Workers potentially exposed to cumene range between 700 to 800. During manufacturing, processing, and use an estimated 3 million pounds of cumene are lost to the atmosphere per year in fugitive emissions. Although this amount is only approximately one fifth the estimated atmospheric release of cumene from land transportation vehicles, the industrial releases are localized and may result in more significant exposures to the general population living near these facilities than the more ubiquitous vehicle emissions. Over half of the cumene manufacturing and processing plants are located in two major metropolitan areas, thus increasing the potential human exposure to 15 to 16 million people. [Id. at 348-349.]

CMA argued (1) that a finding of "substantiality" under either clause (I) or (II) of §4(a)(1)(B)(i) requires a showing that the quantity or level of exposure is such that if the chemical were "highly toxic" it could "realistically be expected" to cause health or environmental harm; (2) that in order to make a proper finding under §4(a)(1)(B)(i)(I) of entry into the environment in substantial quantities, EPA must determine not only that the substance will enter the environment in such quantities, but also that it will persist there; and (3) that whether "human exposure" is "substantial" depends on more than simply the number of persons exposed, no matter how brief the exposure or how small its quantity or what the circumstances are in which the exposure occurs.

The court rejected all three assertions, but remanded the regulations to EPA on the basis of CMA's fourth argument. CMA contended that EPA did not articulate any understandable basis — either in the form of a general definition of or a set of criteria respecting the statutory term "substantial," or in its analysis of the specific evidence respecting cumene — for its ultimate determinations that the quantities of cumene that entered the environment from the facilities in question were "substantial" and that the potentially resulting human exposure to cumene was "substantial." The court ordered the agency to explain the basis on which its §4(a)(1)(B)(i)(I) and (II) "substantiality" findings were made. The court added:

> Under the statutory wording, it is clear that mere entry into the environment of some quantities of the chemical does not suffice for clause (I), rather the quantities entering must be "substantial"; likewise, for clause (II), just any human exposure to the chemical does not suffice, for that human exposure must be "substantial" (or "significant," but here

there is no "significant" finding). A focus on quantity, without more, is hence of little help in understanding what is meant by "substantial."

We recognize that "substantial" is an inherently imprecise word. We are also aware that in this context no definition or group of criteria can be established which will function like a mathematical formula, so that for every given set of facts a specific, predictable answer will always be forthcoming. Room must be left for the exercise of judgment. [899 F.2d at 359.]

Had you been an attorney for the agency, how would you have advised it to respond to the court's remand order? On remand, EPA adopted a 1 million–pound threshold for "substantial production" under §4(a)(1)(B)(i), and a threshold value for "substantial releases" of 1 million pounds per year or the release of 10 percent or more of total production volume, whichever is lower. The agency also determined that "substantial exposure" means exposure to large numbers of people, which it described as 1,000 workers, 10,000 consumers, and/or 100,000 persons in the general population. Finally, it concluded that it lacked sufficient experience to define generic criteria for making a finding of "significant" human exposure. Instead, a finding of "significant" exposure would generally be made on a case-by-case basis, taking into consideration, among other factors, the manner of use, substance-specific physical properties, concentration levels, and the duration and frequency of the exposure to the substance. Exposure might be "significant" where the potential exposed population is not large but the conditions of exposure are unique and create unusually great concern about the substance's potential for adverse effects. 58 Fed. Reg. 28,736 (1993). Under what circumstances may EPA order chemical testing under §4(a)(1)(B) in which it would not be able to order testing under §4(a)(1)(A)? Even in the absence of formal findings invoking the authority to issue test rules, EPA may have made de facto findings sufficient to trigger a mandatory duty under TSCA to issue a test rule. See Physicians Comm. for Responsible Medicine v. Johnson, 436 F.3d 326 (2d Cir. 2006) (holding, however, that EPA had not made such de facto findings with respect to high-volume-production chemicals).

One congressional staffer has argued that §4(a)(1)

> creates a classic "Catch-22" situation. The Agency must already have sufficient data to demonstrate that a chemical poses an unreasonable risk of injury to human health or the environment before it can start a data collection rulemaking. Based on the circular logic of this provision, EPA must already have the data needed to evaluate a chemical's risk in order to compel companies to submit the missing data.

Woolf, *supra*, at 6. Is this an accurate characterization of EPA's authority under §4(a)(1)?

(6)   Regulation of Chemical Substances under TSCA

If the results of testing, PMN review, or screening of the inventory of existing chemicals indicate that there is a "reasonable basis to conclude" that commerce in a chemical "presents or will present" an unreasonable risk to health or the environment, the Administrator may impose a variety of restraints on the marketing of a chemical, including absolute bans, production quotas, bans or limitations on particular uses or at certain concentrations, and labeling requirements. §6(a). See also §6(b).

If time is of the essence, a §6 rule may be made effective almost immediately. §§5(f)(2), 6(d)(2)(B). If even faster action seems necessary, the Administrator may file a civil action for immediate seizure of "an imminently hazardous chemical substance or mixture" or for other temporary or permanent relief necessary to "protect health or the environment from the unreasonable risk associated with" the substance or mixture. §7(a)(1), (b). What is an "imminently hazardous chemical substance or mixture"? See §7(f).

TSCA specifically regulates the production, use, and disposal of polychlorinated biphenyls (PCBs), the only chemicals singled out by name for special attention in the Act. PCBs have long been used for their chemical stability, fire resistance, and electrical resistance properties. They are frequently used in electrical transformers and capacitors. PCBs are extremely toxic to humans and wildlife.* The statute prohibits the manufacture, processing, and sale of PCBs, subject to limited exemptions when unreasonable risk would not result and when good faith efforts to find PCB substitutes were ongoing. With certain exceptions, §6(e) permits PCBs to be used only in conditions of total enclosure. EPA may authorize unenclosed PCB uses that "present no unreasonable risk of injury to health or the environment." What factors must EPA consider in determining whether a risk is unreasonable? See EDF v. EPA, 636 F.2d 1267 (D.C. Cir. 1980), where the court upheld EPA's use of §6(c)(1) criteria, including adverse economic impacts, in determining unreasonable risk of injury under §6(e)(2)(B).

The following case deals with the scope of EPA's authority under §6(a) to regulate other chemical substances not banned by the statute itself, but that present unreasonable risks.

CORROSION PROOF FITTINGS v. EPA
947 F.2d 1201 (5th Cir. 1991)

Jerry E. Smith, Circuit Judge.

[EPA issued a final rule under §6 of TSCA that prohibited the manufacture, importation, processing, and distribution of asbestos in almost all products. Petitioners claimed that the rulemaking procedures were flawed and that the rule was not promulgated on the basis of substantial evidence. The court agreed and remanded to EPA.]

I

Asbestos is a naturally occurring fibrous material that resists fire and most solvents. Its major uses include heat-resistant insulators, cements, building materials, fireproof gloves and clothing, and motor vehicle brake linings. Asbestos is a toxic material, and occupational exposure to asbestos dust can result in mesothelioma, asbestosis, and lung cancer. . . .

*Head, PCBs—The Rise and Fall of an Industrial Miracle, 19 Nat. Resources & Env't No. 4 (Spring 2005), at 14, argues, however, that while animal studies indicate that PCBs can cause cancer and other diseases in animals, "more studies are needed on chronic, low-level exposure risks, particularly involving PCBs in the food chain, . . . to determine if there is reason for continued concern regarding exposure at low levels from various environmental sources."

[Based on its review of over one hundred studies of asbestos, EPA concluded that asbestos is a potential carcinogen at all levels of exposure, regardless of the type of asbestos or the size of the fiber. It issued a rule prohibiting the manufacture, importation, processing, and distribution in commerce of most asbestos-containing products. Based on its finding that asbestos constituted an unreasonable risk to health and the environment, it also promulgated a staged ban of most commercial uses of asbestos. The ban was to go into effect in three stages, depending upon how toxic each substance was and how soon adequate substitutes would be available. EPA estimated that the rule would save either 202 or 148 lives, depending upon whether the benefits were discounted, at a cost of approximately $450-800 million, depending upon the price of substitutes.]

III.   Rulemaking Defects

[The petitioners alleged that the rulemaking procedure was flawed because EPA did not allow cross-examination of all of its witnesses and because it did not notify anyone until after the hearings were over that it intended to use "analogous exposure" estimates and a substitute pricing assumption to support its rule. The court concluded that, considering the importance TSCA accords to cross-examination, EPA should have afforded interested parties full cross-examination on all of its major witnesses. "Precluding cross-examination of EPA witnesses — even a minority of them — is not the proper way to expedite the finish of a lengthy rulemaking procedure." The court also criticized the agency's failure to provide prior public notice that it intended to use "analogous exposure" data to calculate the expected benefits of certain product bans. "EPA should not hold critical analysis in reserve and then use it to justify its regulation despite the lack of public comment on the validity of its basis. Failure to seek public comment on such an important part of the EPA's analysis deprived its rule of the substantial evidence required to survive judicial scrutiny."]

IV.   The Language of TSCA

A.   STANDARD OF REVIEW

Our inquiry into the legitimacy of the EPA rulemaking begins with a discussion of the standard of review governing this case. EPA's phase-out ban of most commercial uses of asbestos is a TSCA §6(a) rulemaking. TSCA provides that a reviewing court "shall hold unlawful and set aside" a final rule promulgated under §6(a) "if the court finds that the rule is not supported by substantial evidence in the rulemaking record . . . taken as a whole." 15 U.S.C. §2618(c)(1)(B)(i). . . .

Contrary to the EPA's assertions, the arbitrary and capricious standard found in the APA and the substantial evidence standard found in TSCA are different standards, even in the context of an informal rulemaking. . . . "The substantial evidence standard mandated by [TSCA] is generally considered to be more rigorous than the arbitrary and capricious standard normally applied to informal rulemaking," Environmental Def. Fund v. EPA, 636 F.2d 1267, 1277 (D.C. Cir. 1980), and "affords a considerably more generous judicial review" than the arbitrary and capricious test. Abbot Laboratories v. Gardener, 387 U.S. 136 (1967). The test "imposes a considerable burden on the agency and limits its discretion in arriving at a factual predicate." Mobil Oil Corp. v. FPC, 483 F.2d 1238, 1258 (D.C. Cir. 1973). . . .

B. The EPA's Burden under TSCA

... We conclude that the EPA has presented insufficient evidence to justify its asbestos ban. We base this conclusion upon two grounds: the failure of the EPA to consider all necessary evidence and its failure to give adequate weight to statutory language requiring it to promulgate the least burdensome, reasonable regulation required to protect the environment adequately. ...

1. Least Burdensome and Reasonable

TSCA requires that the EPA use the least burdensome regulation to achieve its goal of minimum reasonable risk. This statutory requirement can create problems in evaluating just what is a "reasonable risk." Congress' rejection of a no-risk policy, however, also means that in certain cases, the least burdensome yet still adequate solution may entail somewhat more risk than would other, known regulations that are far more burdensome on the industry and the economy. The very language of TSCA requires that the EPA, once it has determined what an acceptable level of non-zero risk is, choose the least burdensome method of reaching that level.

In this case, the EPA banned, for all practical purposes, all present and future uses of asbestos—a position the petitioners characterize as the "death penalty alternative," as this is the most burdensome of all possible alternatives listed as open to the EPA under TSCA. TSCA not only provides the EPA with a list of alternative actions, but also provides those alternatives in order of how burdensome they are. The regulations thus provide for EPA regulation ranging from labeling the least toxic chemicals to limiting the total amount of chemicals an industry may use. Total bans head the list as the most burdensome regulatory option.

By choosing the harshest remedy given to it under TSCA, the EPA assigned to itself the toughest burden in satisfying TSCA's requirement that its alternative be the least burdensome of all those offered to it. Since, both by definition and by the terms of TSCA, the complete ban of manufacturing is the most burdensome alternative—for even stringent regulation at least allows a manufacturer the chance to invest and meet the new, higher standard—the EPA's regulation cannot stand if there is any other regulation that would achieve an acceptable level of risk as mandated by TSCA. ...

The EPA considered, and rejected, such options as labeling asbestos products, thereby warning users and workers involved in the manufacture of asbestos-containing products of the chemical's dangers, and stricter workplace rules. EPA also rejected controlled use of asbestos in the workplace and deferral to other government agencies charged with worker and consumer exposure to industrial and product hazards, such as OSHA, the [Consumer Product Safety Commission], and the [Mine Safety and Health Administration]. The EPA determined that deferral to these other agencies was inappropriate because no one other authority could address all the risk posed "throughout the life cycle" by asbestos, and any action by one or more of the other agencies still would leave an unacceptable residual risk.[16]

---

16. EPA argues that OSHA can only deal with workplace exposures to asbestos and that the CPSC and MSHA cannot take up the slack, as the CPSC can impose safety standards for asbestos products based only upon the risk to consumers, and MSHA can protect against exposure only in the mining and milling process. These agencies leave unaddressed dangers posed by asbestos exposure through product repair, installation, wear and tear, and the like.

Much of the EPA's analysis is correct, and the EPA's basic decision to use TSCA as a comprehensive statute designed to fight a multi-industry problem was a proper one that we uphold today on review. What concerns us, however, is the manner in which the EPA conducted some of its analysis. TSCA requires the EPA to consider, along with the effects of toxic substances on human health and the environment, "the benefits of such substance[s] or mixture[s] for various uses and the availability of substitutes for such uses," as well as "the reasonably ascertainable economic consequences of the rule, after consideration of the effect on the national economy, small business, technological innovation, the environment, and public health." Id. §2605(c)(1)(C)-(D).

The EPA presented two comparisons in the record: a world with no further regulation under TSCA, and a world in which no manufacture of asbestos takes place. The EPA rejected calculating how many lives a less burdensome regulation would save, and at what cost. Furthermore the EPA, when calculating the benefits of its ban, explicitly refused to compare it to an improved workplace in which currently available control technology is utilized. This decision artificially inflated the purported benefits of the rule by using a baseline comparison substantially lower than what currently available technology could yield.

Under TSCA, the EPA was required to evaluate, rather than ignore, less burdensome regulatory alternatives. TSCA imposes a least-to-most-burdensome hierarchy. In order to impose a regulation at the top of the hierarchy—a total ban of asbestos—the EPA must show not only that its proposed action reduces the risk of the product to an adequate level, but also that the actions Congress identified as less burdensome also would not do the job. The failure of the EPA to do this constitutes a failure to meet its burden of showing that its actions not only reduce the risk but do so in the Congressionally mandated *least burdensome* fashion. . . .

This comparison of two static worlds is insufficient to satisfy the dictates of TSCA. While the EPA may have shown that a world with a complete ban of asbestos might be preferable to one in which there is only the current amount of regulation, the EPA has failed to show that there is not some intermediate state of regulation that would be superior to both the currently regulated and the completely banned world. Without showing that asbestos regulation would be ineffective, the EPA cannot discharge its TSCA burden of showing that its regulation is the least burdensome available to it.

Upon an initial showing of product danger, the proper course for the EPA to follow is to consider each regulatory option, beginning with the least burdensome, and the costs and benefits of regulation under each option. The EPA cannot simply skip several rungs, as it did in this case, for in doing so, it may skip a less-burdensome alternative mandated by TSCA. Here, although the EPA mentions the problems posed by intermediate levels of regulation, it takes no steps to calculate the costs and benefits of these intermediate levels. Without doing this it is impossible, both for the EPA and for this court on review, to know that none of these alternatives was less burdensome than the ban in fact chosen by the agency. . . .

2.   THE EPA'S CALCULATIONS

[The court expressed its concern over EPA's failure to compute the costs and benefits of its ban past the year 2000.] In performing its calculus, the EPA only included the number of lives saved over the next thirteen years, and counted any additional lives saved as simply "unquantified benefits." The EPA and intervenors now seek to use these unquantified lives saved to justify calculations as to which the benefits seem far outweighed by the astronomical costs. For example, the EPA plans to save about three lives with its ban of asbestos pipe, at a cost of $128-227 million (i.e., approximately $43-76 million per life saved). Although the EPA admits that the price tag is high, it claims that the lives saved past the year 2000 justify the price.

Such calculations not only lessen the value of the EPA's cost analysis, but also make any meaningful judicial review impossible. While TSCA contemplates a useful place for unquantified benefits beyond the EPA's calculation, unquantified benefits never were intended as a trump card allowing the EPA to justify any cost calculus, no matter how high.

The concept of unquantified benefits, rather, is intended to allow the EPA to provide a rightful place for any remaining benefits that are impossible to quantify after the EPA's best attempt, but which still are of some concern. But the allowance for unquantified costs is not intended to allow the EPA to perform its calculations over an arbitrarily short period so as to preserve a large unquantified portion.

Unquantified benefits can, at times, permissibly tip the balance in close cases. They cannot, however, be used to effect a wholesale shift on the balance beam. Such a use makes a mockery of the requirements of TSCA that the EPA weigh the costs of its actions before it chooses the least burdensome alternative. . . .

3. REASONABLE BASIS

In addition to showing that its regulation is the least burdensome one necessary to protect the environment adequately, the EPA also must show that it has a reasonable basis for the regulation. 15 U.S.C. §2605(a). . . .

Most problematical to us is the EPA's ban of products for which no substitutes presently are available. In these cases, the EPA bears a tough burden indeed to show that under TSCA a ban is the least burdensome alternative, as TSCA explicitly instructs the EPA to consider "the benefits of such substance or mixture for various uses and the availability of substitutes for such uses." Id. §2605(c)(1)(C). These words are particularly appropriate where the EPA actually has decided to ban a product, rather than simply restrict its use, for it is in these cases that the lack of an adequate substitute is most troubling under TSCA.

As a general matter, we agree with the EPA that a product ban can lead to great innovation, and it is true that an agency under TSCA, as under other regulatory statutes, "is empowered to issue safety standards which require improvements in existing technology or which require the development of new technology." Chrysler Corp. v. Department of Transp., 472 F.2d 659, 673 (6th Cir. 1972). As even the EPA acknowledges, however, when no adequate substitutes currently exist, the EPA cannot fail to consider this lack when formulating its own guidelines. Under TSCA, therefore, the EPA must present a stronger case to justify the ban, as opposed to regulation, of products with no substitutes.

We note that the EPA does provide a waiver provision for industries where the hoped-for substitutes fail to materialize in time. Under this provision, if no adequate substitutes develop, the EPA temporarily may extend the planned phase-out.

The EPA uses this provision to argue that it can ban any product, regardless of whether it has an adequate substitute, because inventive companies soon will develop good substitutes. The EPA contends that if they do not, the waiver provision will allow the continued use of asbestos in these areas, just as if the ban had not occurred at all.

The EPA errs, however, in asserting that the waiver provision will allow a continuation of the status quo in those cases in which no substitutes materialize. By its own terms, the exemption shifts the burden onto the waiver proponent to convince the EPA that the waiver is justified. As even the EPA acknowledges, the waiver only "may be granted by [the] EPA in very limited circumstances." 54 Fed. Reg. at 29,460. . . .

We also are concerned with the EPA's evaluation of substitutes even in those instances in which the record shows that they are available. The EPA explicitly rejects considering the harm that may flow from the increased use of products designed to substitute for asbestos, even where the probable substitutes themselves are known carcinogens. The EPA justifies this by stating that it has "more concern about the continued use and exposure to asbestos than it has for the future replacement of asbestos in the products subject to this rule with other fibrous substitutes." Id. at 29,481. The agency thus concludes that any "[r]egulatory decisions about asbestos which poses well-recognized, serious risks should not be delayed until the risk of all replacement materials are fully quantified." Id. at 29,483. . . .

[T]he EPA cannot say with any assurance that its regulation will increase workplace safety when it refuses to evaluate the harm that will result from the increased use of substitute products. While the EPA may be correct in its conclusion that the alternate materials pose less risk than asbestos, we cannot say with any more assurance than that flowing from an educated guess that this conclusion is true.

Considering that many of the substitutes that the EPA itself concedes will be used in the place of asbestos have known carcinogenic effects, the EPA not only cannot assure this court that it has taken the least burdensome alternative, but cannot even prove that its regulations will increase workplace safety. Eager to douse the dangers of asbestos, the agency inadvertently actually may increase the risk of injury Americans face. The EPA's explicit failure to consider the toxicity of likely substitutes thus deprives its order of a reasonable basis. [The court went on to construe TSCA to require that, whenever interested parties introduce credible studies and evidence showing the toxicity of substitutes, EPA consider whether its regulations would represent a net increase in safety or whether the increased risk resulting from dangerous substitutes renders regulation unreasonable.]

4.   UNREASONABLE RISK OF INJURY

The final requirement the EPA must satisfy before engaging in any TSCA rulemaking is that it only take steps designed to prevent "unreasonable" risks. In evaluating what is "unreasonable," the EPA is required to consider the costs of any proposed actions and to "carry out this chapter in a reasonable and prudent manner [after considering] the environmental, economic, and social impact of any action." 15 U.S.C. §2601(c). . . .

That the EPA must balance the costs of its regulations against their benefits further is reinforced by the requirement that it seek the least burdensome regulation. While Congress did not dictate that the EPA engage in an exhaustive, full-scale cost-benefit analysis, it did require the EPA to consider both sides of the regulatory equation, and it rejected the notion that the EPA should pursue the reduction of workplace risk at any cost. See American Textile Mfrs. Inst., 452 U.S. at 510 n.30 ("unreasonable risk" statutes require "a generalized balancing of costs and benefits["]). Thus,

"Congress also plainly intended the EPA to consider the economic impact of any actions taken by it under . . . TSCA." *Chemical Mfrs. Ass'n*, 899 F.2d at 348.

Even taking all of the EPA's figures as true, and evaluating them in the light most favorable to the agency's decision (non-discounted benefits, discounted costs, analogous exposure estimates included), the agency's analysis results in figures as high as $74 million per life saved. . . .

While we do not sit as a regulatory agency that must make the difficult decision as to what an appropriate expenditure is to prevent someone from incurring the risk of an asbestos-related death, we do note that the EPA, in its zeal to ban any and all asbestos products, basically ignored the cost side of the TSCA equation. The EPA would have this court believe that Congress, when it enacted its requirement that the EPA consider the economic impacts of its regulations, thought that spending $200-300 million to save approximately seven lives (approximately $30-40 million per life) over thirteen years is reasonable. . . .

The EPA's willingness to argue that spending $23.7 million to save less than one-third of a life reveals that its economic review of its regulations, as required by TSCA, was meaningless. As the petitioners' brief and our review of EPA case law reveals, such high costs are rarely, if ever, used to support a safety regulation. If we were to allow such cavalier treatment of the EPA's duty to consider the economic effects of its decisions, we would have to excise entire sections and phrases from the language of TSCA. Because we are judges, not surgeons, we decline to do so.[23] . . .

NOTES AND QUESTIONS

1. Did EPA make a finding that asbestos posed an unreasonable risk? What factors did the agency consider in reaching that conclusion? Did EPA consider the availability of substitutes for the products it banned? Did it provide a mechanism for relief from product bans in the event that substitutes were not available? What, then, were the flaws in the agency's reasoning process? For a much more sympathetic and deferential review of the agency's consideration of regulatory alternatives in a Clean Air Act rulemaking, compare Allied Local and Regional Mfrs. Caucus v. EPA, 215 F.3d 61, 74 (D.C. Cir. 2000) (characterizing industry's argument that the regulation of VOC emissions from commercial products might have counterproductive consequences as "a series of theoretical possibilities" rather than "fact-based predictions"). What role do unquantified benefits play in determinations of the reasonableness of risk under TSCA? How much money would be a reasonable amount to spend to save a life? How did the court in *Corrosion Proof Fittings* interpret the relationship between the seven subsections of §6(a)? What is the significance of that relationship? What must EPA do on remand to abide by the court's interpretation of §6(a)?

On what basis did the court in *Corrosion Proof Fittings* conclude not only that EPA failed to prove that its regulation would increase workplace safety, but also that the asbestos ban rule might inadvertently increase the risk of injury? Is this portion of

23. . . . As the petitioners point out, the EPA regularly rejects, as unjustified, regulations that would save more lives at less cost. For example, over the next 13 years, we can expect more than a dozen deaths from ingested toothpicks—a death toll more than twice what the EPA predicts will flow from the quarter-billion dollar bans of asbestos pipe, shingles, and roof coatings. See L. Budnick, Toothpick-Related Injuries in the United States, 1979 through 1982, 252 J. Am. Med. Ass'n, Aug. 10, 1984, at 796 (study showing that toothpick-related deaths average approximately one per year).

the court's opinion an example of the risk-risk analysis described at pages 759-760, *supra*? Relying on an article written by Justice Scalia before he became a judge, two observers suggest that judicial review of the substantive validity of risk regulation ought to revolve around the basic precept that agency action is justifiable only if it "does more good than harm." See Warren & Marchant, "More Good than Harm": A First Principle for Environmental Agencies and Reviewing Courts, 20 Ecology L.Q. 379 (1993).

2. *The Meaning of "Unreasonable Risk."* TSCA repeatedly instructs EPA to apply the standard of "unreasonable risk of injury to health or the environment" in making decisions. If "unreasonable risk" is suspected or determined to be present, EPA may, among other things, issue a test rule (§4(a), (b)), place a chemical on a list for priority attention (§4(e)), require PMN of new chemicals (§5(b)(2)(B)), regulate chemicals under §6, and regulate imminent hazards (§7). See Table 8-3.

Other sections apply slightly different standards to agency determinations under TSCA. Under §4(f), EPA has a nondiscretionary duty to take action within six months under other TSCA provisions if available data indicate that "there may be a reasonable basis to conclude that a chemical substance or mixture presents a significant risk of serious or widespread harm to human beings from cancer, gene mutations, or birth defects." What is the difference between the "unreasonable risk" and "significant risk" standards? EPA at times has taken the position that the "significant risk" standard is stricter than the "unreasonable risk" standard. Can you devise an argument that, while economic considerations are relevant to determinations of unreasonable risk, they have no bearing on determinations of significant risk under §4(f)?

3. *TSCA and the Burden of Proof.* Before TSCA, the production of a new but potentially dangerous chemical could be enjoined only if the government or some other plaintiff could prove that a legal wrong—e.g., a tort such as negligence or a crime such as public nuisance—had occurred and that the manufacturer's action threatened to cause imminent, substantial, and irreparable harm. In civil trials, the burden of persuading the trier of fact that the plaintiff's interpretation of the facts was more probably true than not true rested on the plaintiff. TSCA arguably shifted the burden of persuasion to the manufacturer, which must prove to EPA's satisfaction that it is more probably true than not true that its chemical does not present an unreasonable risk of injury to health and to the environment. Moreover, in assessing whether a chemical presents an unreasonable risk, EPA does not have to determine that a scientifically acceptable, proven chain of causation links the chemical with its effects. The logic of federal risk regulation, established in *Reserve Mining, Ethyl,* and their judicial and legislative progeny, pointedly rejects this view.

Other risk regulation statutes also may be examined in terms of evidentiary burdens. Latin, The "Significance" of Toxic Health Risks: An Essay on Legal Decisionmaking under Uncertainty, 10 Ecology L.Q. 339 (1982), for example, argues that the Supreme Court's "reductionist" approach in the *Benzene* decision to allocation of the burden of proof in the face of scientific uncertainty seriously misinterpreted the OSH Act. Latin supports allocating the burden of proof in risk regulation statutes in a manner that fulfills Congress's desire to resolve uncertainty on the side of precautionary action, using *Reserve Mining* as a model.

4. *The Impact of* Corrosion Proof Fittings. More than 15 years after the Fifth Circuit's decision, no other case involving TSCA had cited *Corrosion Proof Fittings* (other than for a discussion of the relationship between the "substantial evidence" and "arbitrary and capricious" tests for judicial review or for a discussion of standing

TABLE 8-3
Summary of EPA's Authority under TSCA

Source of EPA's Authority	Nature of EPA's Authority	Conditions for Exercise of EPA's Authority
§4(a)	Require testing on health and environmental effects of chemical substances	Chemical substance may present an unreasonable risk of injury to health or the environment, or chemical substance is or will be produced in substantial quantities with substantial human or environmental exposure
§4(f)	Take action under §§5, 6, or 7 of TSCA to prevent or reduce risk or publish a finding that a risk is not unreasonable	Reasonable basis to conclude that chemical substance presents or will present a significant risk of serious or widespread harm to human beings from cancer, gene mutations, or birth defects
§5(e)	Issue orders prohibiting or limiting manufacture, use, etc. of chemical substances pending development of further information	Finding that chemical substance is manufactured or produced in the United States
§5(f)	Issue orders or regulations or apply to federal court for injunction prohibiting or limiting manufacture, use, etc. of chemical substance	Finding of reasonable basis to conclude that manufacture, use, etc. of chemical substance subject to premanufacture notification under §5 presents or will present an unreasonable risk of injury to health or the environment before EPA can regulate under §6
§6(a)	Regulate chemical substances, including a prohibition on manufacture, use, etc. to the extent necessary to protect adequately against the risk using the least burdensome requirements	Finding of reasonable basis to conclude that manufacture, use, etc. of chemical substance presents or will present an unreasonable risk of injury to health or the environment
§7(a)	Commence civil action in federal court for seizure of imminently hazardous chemical substance or for other relief	Finding that chemical substance presents an imminent and unreasonable risk of serious or widespread injury to health or the environment
§8(b)	Compile inventory of substances subject to premanufacture notification requirements of §5(a)	Finding that chemical substance is manufactured or processed in the United States

issues), and no other case involving any other federal pollution statute had relied on its principal holding.* Nevertheless, the damage may already have been done. During the first 30 years after TSCA's adoption, EPA issued regulations to prohibit or restrict the use of only five chemicals, none after 1989. Woolf, *supra*, at 6-7.

Did the *Corrosion Proof Fittings* court misconstrue how Congress intended to allocate the burden of proof in connection with the issuance of regulations under §6 of TSCA? The decision created shock waves at EPA. "[T]here is a strong view within EPA that if the asbestos rule cannot withstand judicial scrutiny despite an enormous commitment of resources by EPA, then the §6 standard for regulating existing chemicals may simply be too high a standard for the Agency to meet." Hathaway et al., A Practitioner's Guide to the Toxic Substances Control Act: Part III, 24 Envtl. L. Rep. (ELI) 10,357 (1994). See also Woolf, *supra*, at 7 (claiming that "many TSCA practitioners believ[e] that EPA could never meet the statutory standard as interpreted by the court").

Has *Corrosion Proof Fittings* imposed an unrealistic burden on EPA to quantify risk in order to justify regulation under §6(a)? In the wake of *Corrosion Proof Fittings*, the GAO made the following pessimistic assessment:

> In current state-of-the-art risk assessments, some uncertainty and some basis for a legal challenge almost always exist. Furthermore, the costs to the economy of regulating a chemical are usually much more easily documented than the risks of the chemical or the benefits associated with controlling it, according to EPA officials. . . .
>
> The court's decision [in *Corrosion Proof Fittings*] is especially revealing about section 6 because EPA spent 10 years preparing the rule. In addition, asbestos is generally regarded as one of the substances for which EPA has the most scientific evidence or documentation of substantial adverse health effects. . . . Officials of EPA's Office of Pollution Prevention and Toxics told us that with the court decision in the asbestos case, EPA most likely will not attempt to issue regulations under section 6 for comprehensive bans or restrictions on chemicals. [GAO, Toxic Substances Control Act— Legislative Changes Could Make the Act More Effective, GAO/RCED 94-103, 1994 WL 840961 (1994).]

See also the scathing attack on *Corrosion Proof Fittings* in McGarity, The Courts and the Ossification of Rulemaking: A Response to Professor Seidenfeld, 75 Tex. L. Rev. 525, 541-548 (1997) (arguing that the court "sent EPA on a potentially endless analytical crusade in search of the holy grail of *the* least burdensome alternative that still protected adequately against unreasonable risk," that the court afforded "not one whit" of deference to EPA's interpretation of the statute, and that the opinion left EPA with the choice of adopting regulations "that were sufficiently inoffensive to the regulated industry to avoid legal challenge or . . . giving up the quest altogether").

Following the Fifth Circuit's decision, EPA turned primarily to market-based mechanisms to control the use of asbestos. For discussion of the history of regulation of asbestos in the United States, see Garlow, Asbestos—The Long-Lived Mineral, 19 Nat. Resources & Env't No. 4 (Spring 2005), at 36.

5. Corrosion Proof Fittings *and the Standard of Judicial Review under TSCA.* Do the hybrid rulemaking procedures, the substantial evidence standard of judicial review, and the unreasonable risk standard, as interpreted by the court in *Corrosion*

---

*The case was cited, however, to support the conclusion that not all asbestos-containing products are inherently dangerous for purposes of toxic tort litigation. Cimino v. Raymark Indus., Inc., 151 F.3d 297, 331 (5th Cir. 1998).

Proof Fittings, make regulation under §6 impossible to sustain? If so, can EPA resort to its authority under §5 to address risks that it would rather pursue under §6? Consider the following:

> The court's analysis shows the basic flaw in evaluating regulations based on complex scientific analysis under the substantial evidence standard of review. In many instances, qualitative indicators of risk may suggest regulation. However, these qualitative indicators of risk may prove, as the EPA noted in its final asbestos rule, "unquantifiable." The unquantifiable nature of these risks exists because of technological limitations or limited agency resources. It is entirely possible that, at one level of practical scientific investigation, a reasonable conclusion could be drawn that a risk exists and is potentially large. To go to the next level of scientific investigation and actually calculate these risks with precision, however, may be completely impractical. . . . In the final analysis, the substantial evidence standard of review removes judicial deference to agency expertise when EPA deems it impractical and unsafe to waive regulation in order to make further scientific findings. Rather, it is in these situations that deference to agency expertise is warranted. [Hanan, Pushing the Environmental Regulatory Focus a Step Back: Controlling the Introduction of New Chemicals under the Toxic Substances Control Act, 18 Am. J.L. & Med. 395, 415-416 (1992).]

In Central and South West Serv., Inc. v. EPA, 220 F.3d 683 (5th Cir. 2000), the court interpreted §6(e) of TSCA as creating a rebuttable presumption that all uses of PCBs present an unreasonable risk of injury to health and the environment. This interpretation dictated the conclusion that the substantial evidence standard of review provided by §19(c)(1)(B)(i) applies only when a petitioner challenges EPA's decision to depart from the outright ban and to permit or expand the use of PCBs. A petitioner challenging an EPA rule restricting or prohibiting the use of PCBs is subject to the "arbitrary and capricious" standard of review. Does this result make sense as a matter of policy? Is it consistent with the language of §19(c)(1)(B)(i) of TSCA?

NOTE ON INTEGRATION OF TSCA WITH OTHER REGULATORY SCHEMES

Section 9 of TSCA is intended to prevent regulatory activity under that law from overlapping with or duplicating regulation under other federal statutes. If EPA has a reasonable basis to conclude that certain activities involving chemical substances or mixtures present an unreasonable risk, and it determines that the risk may be prevented or reduced to a sufficient extent under another law not within EPA jurisdiction, EPA must submit to the agency administering that law a report describing the risk and the activities presenting it. If the agency receiving the report either declares that the activities do not present an unreasonable risk or decides to regulate those activities, EPA is barred by §9(a) from acting under §§6 or 7 of TSCA. Section 9(b) requires EPA to coordinate actions taken under TSCA with actions taken under other EPA-administered statutes. If EPA determines that a risk to health or the environment could be addressed sufficiently under such other statutes, regulation must proceed under those laws unless, in the Administrator's discretion, TSCA regulation would be in the public interest. See also §6(c)(1). Section 9(c) provides that the exercise of EPA's authority under TSCA will not be regarded as the issuance or enforcement of occupational health and safety standards under the OSH Act. In issuing its asbestos ban regulations, did EPA make the findings required by §9? Did the court in *Corrosion Proof Fittings* second-guess EPA's determinations?

Ruggerio, Referral of Toxic Chemical Regulation under the Toxic Substances Control Act: EPA's Administrative Dumping Ground, 17 B.C. Envtl. Aff. L. Rev. 75, 77 (1989), contends that §9 has "become an escape hatch for the EPA to avoid regulatory responsibility that it should legitimately exercise." Writing before the *Corrosion Proof Fittings* decision, the author pointed in particular to EPA's referral of regulatory responsibility for all toxic substances in any way associated with the workplace to OSHA. She claimed that the result has been an increased risk of adverse health consequences because the OSH Act is weaker than TSCA. See also U.S. General Accounting Office, *supra* (laws such as the Clean Air Act or the OSH Act lack TSCA's flexibility to ban or restrict a chemical's production, use, or disposal).

Problem 8-1

In 2002, EPA began receiving complaints that people working in buildings with new carpets were experiencing headaches, nausea, skin rashes, and other symptoms. In 2005, X-Pose-A, Inc., a private laboratory in Massachusetts, issued a report on a recently completed animal bioassay in which the lab had exposed mice to emissions from several brands of new carpets. The report indicated that neurotoxicity, pulmonary irritation, and death had occurred in a small but statistically significant percentage of the exposed animals. EPA scientists received permission to repeat the carpet emissions tests on the X-Pose-A premises. The results were similar to the ones produced in the tests conducted by X-Pose-A scientists. EPA scientists were unable to replicate the findings in subsequent tests in EPA's own labs, however. Those tests did not even indicate mild toxicity: no deaths, no severe or moderate sensory irritation, and no clear evidence of neurotoxicity arose. In 2006, EPA sent the three sets of test results to a panel of scientists unaffiliated with either EPA or any carpet manufacturers for peer review. The panel recently concluded that the findings were irreconcilable. The panel also indicated that it was unable to detect methodological flaws in any of the tests.

EPA is considering whether to take action to control the risks to the public health posed by exposure to carpet emissions in the workplace. Does it have sufficient information to make that decision? If not, how may it solicit more information? If so, should it regulate or refer the matter to another agency? If it decides to regulate, should it regulate under TSCA or another statute? If it decides to regulate under TSCA, what is the threshold showing necessary to justify regulation?

NOTE ON FEDERAL REGULATION OF ASBESTOS AND LEAD

[The materials in this note are located at the casebook's website.]

b.   Regulation of Pesticide Use: The Federal Insecticide, Fungicide, and Rodenticide Act

[The materials in this section are located at the casebook's website.]

NOTE ON ALTERNATIVE PEST CONTROL MECHANISMS

[The materials in this note are located at the casebook's website.]

c. Regulation of Drinking Water Supplies: The Safe Drinking Water Act

The Nature of the Problem. The distribution of drinking water may contribute to the dissemination of harmful substances. Ingestion of water contaminated by pathogens such as cryptosporidium, giardia, and *E. coli* can cause severe diarrhea, abdominal cramps, vomiting, and fever. The Centers for Disease Control estimated that 900,000 people experience illness and 900 people die each year in the United States as the result of pathogenic organisms in drinking water. S. Rep. No. 104-169, at 6 (1995). Chemical pollution is also a concern. According to a Senate committee, "[a]bout 10 percent of ground water wells supplying drinking water systems are contaminated with man-made chemicals—an estimated 3 percent at levels above EPA health standards." Id. at 7. Almost all surface waters are contaminated with these substances, usually at much lower levels. A scientific study published in 2006 concluded that an increased risk of bladder cancer was associated with the intake of tap water in the United States, Canada, Finland, France, and Italy, and suggested the presence of carcinogenic chemicals as the reason. Villanueva et al., Total and Specific Fluid Consumption as Determinants of Bladder Cancer Risk, 118 Int'l J. Cancer 2040 (2006).

Drinking Water Regulations. The Safe Drinking Water Act (SDWA) of 1974, 42 U.S.C. §§300j-26, established a federal regulatory system to ensure the safety of public drinking water systems. The Act authorizes EPA to issue maximum contaminant level goals (MCLGs) and subject most public water systems to national primary drinking water regulations (NPDWRs). These regulations identify contaminants with potential adverse effects on public health and specify maximum contaminant levels (MCLs) or treatment techniques. §§300g, 300f(1). A "contaminant" is broadly defined to include "any physical, chemical, biological, or radiological substance or matter in water." §300f(6). A public water system is "a system for the provision to the public of piped water for human consumption . . . if such system has at least fifteen service connections or regularly serves at least twenty-five individuals." §300f(4)(A). "Human consumption" includes bathing, showering, cooking, dishwashing, and maintaining oral hygiene. United States v. Midway Heights County Water Dist., 695 F. Supp. 1072 (E.D. Cal. 1988).

In 1986 Congress amended the statute in an effort to force more aggressive EPA regulation of drinking water contaminants. The amendments required EPA to publish MCLGs and promulgate NPDWRs for 83 listed contaminants by June 1989 and to publish a priority list every three years of contaminants "known or anticipated to occur in public water systems" that require NPDWRs. By the end of 1995, EPA had issued or proposed NPDWRs for 88 contaminants and identified an additional 25 substances for regulation. S. Rep. No. 104-169, *supra*, at 9-10. But the provision requiring EPA to regulate a specified number of contaminants provoked widespread criticism.

This single provision of the Safe Drinking Water Act has provoked more critical comment than virtually any other element of environmental law. Some of the 83 contaminants for which standards are required occur so infrequently in public water systems that the costs of monitoring (for a substance not present) far outweigh any health benefit that could be realized at the few systems that may detect the contaminant. In other cases, the available science is so uncertain that standards incorporate extravagant margins of safety (30,000-fold for one contaminant), making it impossible to assert that expenditures to implement the regulation are a public health necessity. Finally, the mandate that EPA set standards for an additional 25 contaminants every 3 years regardless of the threat posed by these contaminants in drinking water is for many the quintessential example of an arbitrary Federal law imposing burdens on consumers and the taxpayers of other governments with no rational relationship to the public benefits that might be realized. [Id. at 12-13.]

In short, the statute "unintentionally discourages EPA from concentrating its resources on regulating contaminants that pose the highest health risks," requiring instead that the agency "regulate a long list of contaminants, regardless of the seriousness of the threat they pose to public health and regardless [of] the frequency with which they occur in drinking water." Id. at 1.

Congress set out to "give EPA flexibility to set drinking water standards based on peer-reviewed science and the benefits and risks associated with contaminants," and to minimize the impact of the statute on local drinking water systems struggling to keep up with the growing burdens imposed by the Act's regulatory requirements. Id. at 2. In the Safe Drinking Water Act Amendments of 1996, Pub. L. No. 104-182, 110 Stat. 1613, Congress required that EPA issue MCLGs and NPDWRs for each contaminant that may have an adverse effect on health and that is known or is substantially likely to occur in public water systems "with a frequency and at levels of public health concern," provided that, in the sole judgment of the Administrator, regulation "presents a meaningful opportunity for health risk reduction for persons served by public water systems." 42 U.S.C. §300g-1(b)(1)(A). EPA must periodically publish a list of contaminants not subject to NPDWRs that are known or are anticipated to occur in public water systems and that may require regulation. These substances must include those regulated under CERCLA and pesticides registered under FIFRA. EPA's decision to list or not list a particular contaminant is exempt from judicial review. §300g-1(b)(1)(B)(i). As for unregulated contaminants, EPA must select for consideration those that present the greatest public health concern, taking into consideration the effects of the contaminants on subgroups that are at greater risk of adverse health effects than the general population. §300g-1(b)(1)(C).

What is the relationship between the MCLGs and the NPDWRs? See Figure 8-8. The MCLGs must be set "at the level at which no known or anticipated adverse effects on the health of persons occur and which allows an adequate margin of safety." §300g-1(b)(4)(A). Is the margin of safety concept well suited to the regulation of carcinogenic drinking water contaminants? In International Fabricare Inst. v. EPA, 972 F.2d 384 (D.C. Cir. 1992), chemical companies and an association of dry cleaning businesses challenged the establishment of MCLGs and MCLs for 38 organic and inorganic chemicals. The petitioners attacked the MCLGs on the ground, among others, that EPA's decision to set zero-level MCLGs for known or probable carcinogens failed to take into account new scientific evidence concerning the possibility that there are threshold levels of exposure to the substances regulated. The court rejected the attack, concluding that the petitioners' "evidence" amounted to nothing more than the opinions of a few scientists who were out of the mainstream. The court was also not persuaded that EPA placed undue reliance on animal studies. Compare that result with the following case.

CHLORINE CHEMISTRY COUNCIL v. EPA
206 F.3d 1286 (D.C. Cir. 2000)

STEPHEN F. WILLIAMS, Circuit Judge:

[Chloroform is a nonflammable, colorless liquid that is one of four compounds classified as total trihalomethanes (TTHMs), which are by-products of chlorination, the most widely used technique for ensuring the safety of drinking water. Although chlorination plays a significant role in the control of microbial pathogens, EPA concluded on the basis of rodent tumor data that chloroform, a by-product of this process, is a probable human carcinogen. In particular, EPA concluded in 1998 that chloroform exhibits a "nonlinear mode of carcinogenic action."] In other words, exposures to chloroform below some threshold level pose no risk of cancer. But in promulgating the MCLG [under the SDWA] it retained the existing standard of zero, which was based on the previously held assumption that there was no safe threshold. EPA justified its action on a variety of grounds, including an alleged need

Applicability (§300g-1(b)(1)(A)).
   (i) the contaminant may have an adverse effect on the health of persons;
   (ii) the contaminant is known to occur or there is a substantial likelihood that it will occur in public water systems with a frequency and at levels of public health concern; and
   (iii) in the sole judgment of EPA regulation presents a meaningful opportunity for public health risk reduction

Regulatory Goal (§300g-1(b)(4)(A)). EPA must set maximum contaminant level goal (MCLG) at the level at which no known or anticipated adverse effects on the health of persons occur and which allows an adequate margin of safety.

Regulatory Standard (§300g-1(b)(4)(B)). EPA must set maximum contaminant level (MCL) as close to the MCLG as is feasible (as defined in §300g-1(b)(4)(D)), with exceptions specified in §300g-1(b)(5)-(6).

FIGURE 8-8
National Primary Drinking Water Regulations under the SDWA

to consult the report of its Science Advisory Board ("SAB"), which would not be available until after the statutory deadline for rulemaking had expired. Petitioners, including the Chlorine Chemistry Council, a trade association comprised of chlorine and chlorine product manufacturers, petitioned this court for review, arguing that EPA violated its statutory mandate to use the "best available" evidence when implementing the provisions of the Safe Drinking Water Act. 42 U.S.C. §300g-1(b)(3)(A). We agree. . . .

On July 29, 1994, EPA issued a proposed rule on disinfectants and disinfection byproducts in water. This included a zero MCLG for chloroform, based on EPA's finding of an *absence* of data to suggest a threshold level below which there would be no potential carcinogenic effects. The Agency's default method of inferring risk at exposure levels for which it has no adequate data is linear extrapolation from cancer incidence inferred at exposures for which it does have data. See EPA's Proposed Guidelines for Carcinogen Risk Assessment, 61 Fed. Reg. 17,960, 17,968 (1996). Thus, either if the evidence supports linearity, *or* if there is "insufficient" evidence of nonlinearity, EPA assumes that if a substance causes cancer at *any* exposure it will do so at *every* nonzero exposure (though with cancer incidence declining with exposure). But EPA acknowledges its authority "to establish nonzero MCLGs for carcinogens if the scientific evidence" indicates that a "safe threshold" exists. And petitioners here assume the validity of the linear default assumption.

[The 1996 amendments to the SDWA included a timetable for EPA's issuance of rules relating to disinfectants and disinfection by-products associated with water treatment. 42 U.S.C. §300g-1(b)(2)(C). The deadline for regulating chloroform was November 1998. Based on the findings and recommendations of an advisory group formed by EPA in 1997 to collect and analyze new information, EPA published two Notices of Data Availability specific to chloroform. The Notices discussed the findings of the experts, which had been subjected to peer review, that although chloroform was "a likely carcinogen to humans above a certain dose range, [it was] unlikely to be carcinogenic below a certain dose range." The experts recommended "the nonlinear or margin of exposure approach [as] the preferred approach to quantifying the cancer risk associated with chloroform exposure."]

EPA agreed. It said that "[a]lthough the precise mechanism of chloroform carcinogenicity is not established," nevertheless "the chloroform dose-response should be considered nonlinear." Rather than operating through effects on DNA, which is consistent with linearity, chloroform evidently works through "cytotoxicity" (i.e., damage to the cells) followed by regenerative cell proliferation. Employing the threshold approach that it found was entailed by chloroform's mode of action, EPA then calculated an MCLG of 600 parts per billion ("ppb"), based solely on carcinogenicity. This level built in a 1000-fold margin of error in relation to the maximum safe dosage implied from the animal studies used by EPA. But because even lower chlorine doses cause liver toxicity (a non-cancer effect), EPA proposed an MCLG of 300 ppb.

When EPA came to promulgate its final rule in December 1998, however, its MCLG was again zero. It stuck with 1994's zero level despite its explicit statement that it now "believe[d] that the underlying science for using a nonlinear extrapolation approach to evaluate the carcinogenic risk from chloroform is well founded." It justified the action on the basis that "additional deliberations with the Agency's SAB on the analytical approach used" and on the underlying scientific evidence were needed "prior to departing from a long-held EPA policy." It could not complete such additional deliberations by the November 1998 statutory deadline, and, moreover, the rulemaking would not affect the enforceable MCL for TTHMs. . . .

On February 11, 2000, the day of oral argument, EPA released a draft report by the SAB on chloroform. The report concluded that chloroform exhibits a "cytotoxic" mode of action. Such a mode of action (unlike a "genotoxic" mechanism, which acts directly on a cell's DNA) involves no carcinogenic effects at low doses; thus a non-linear approach is "scientifically reasonable." . . .

. . . [P]etitioners argue that EPA's decision to adopt a zero MCLG in the face of scientific evidence establishing that chloroform is a threshold carcinogen was inconsistent with the Safe Drinking Water Act. Section 300g-1(b)(3)(A) of the Act states unequivocally that "to the degree that an Agency action is based on science, the Administrator shall use . . . the best available, peer-reviewed science and supporting studies conducted in accordance with sound and objective scientific practices." In promulgating a zero MCLG for chloroform EPA openly overrode the "best available" scientific evidence, which suggested that chloroform is a threshold carcinogen.

EPA provides several arguments in defense of its action. First, it argues that to establish a nonzero MCLG would be a "precedential step," that represents "a major change in the substance of regulatory decisions related to chloroform." We do not doubt that adopting a nonzero MCLG is a significant step, one which departs from previous practice. But this is a change in result, not in policy. The change in outcome occurs simply as a result of steadfast application of the relevant rules: first, the statutory mandate to set MCLGs at "the level at which no known or anticipated adverse effect on the health of persons occur," 42 U.S.C. §300g-1(b)(4)(A), as determined on the basis of the "best available" evidence; and second, EPA's Carcinogen Risk Assessment guidelines, stating that when "adequate data on mode of action show that linearity is not the most reasonable working judgment and provide sufficient evidence to support a nonlinear mode of action," the default assumption of linearity drops out. The fact that EPA has arrived at a novel, even politically charged, outcome is of no significance either for its statutory obligation or for fulfillment of its adopted policy.

Second, and similarly, EPA supports its action on the basis that "it could not complete the deliberations with the SAB" before the November 1998 deadline. But however desirable it may be for EPA to consult an SAB and even to revise its conclusion in the future, that is no reason for acting against its own science findings in the meantime. The statute requires the agency to take into account the "best *available*" evidence. 42 U.S.C. §300g-1(b)(3)(A) (emphasis added). EPA cannot reject the "best available" evidence simply because of the possibility of contradiction in the future by evidence unavailable at the time of action—a possibility that will *always* be present. . . .

Finally, EPA argues that its statements in the 1998 Notice of Data Availability do not represent its "ultimate conclusions" with respect to chloroform, and thus in adopting a zero MCLG it did not reject what it considered to be the "best available" evidence. In fact, the zero MCLG merely represented an "interim risk management decision" pending the final SAB report. We find these semantic somersaults pointless. First, whether EPA has adopted its 1998 NODA as its "ultimate conclusion" is irrelevant to whether it represented the "best available" evidence. All scientific conclusions are subject to some doubt; future, hypothetical findings always have the potential to resolve the doubt (the new resolution itself being subject, of course, to falsification by later findings). What is significant is Congress's requirement that the action be taken on the basis of the best available evidence *at the time* of the rulemaking. The word "available" would be senseless if construed to mean "expected to be available at some future date." Second, EPA cannot avoid this result by dubbing its action "interim." The statute applies broadly to any "[a]gency action"; whether the action is interim is irrelevant. . . .

NOTES AND QUESTIONS

1. Under EPA's 1996 proposed cancer risk guidelines, how did EPA ascertain the level of risk at exposure levels for which it lacked adequate data? Under what circumstances did EPA apply the linear, no-threshold approach to ascertaining the risk of exposure to a carcinogenic substance? On what basis did the Chlorine Chemistry Council contend that issuance of a zero-level MCLG for chloroform was inappropriate? How did EPA attempt to defend its decision to set a zero-level MCLG in this case? What provision of the statute did the court find that EPA violated? Compare City of Waukesha v. EPA, 320 F.3d 228 (D.C. Cir. 2003) (rejecting assertion that EPA failed to use the best available scientific evidence in issuing national primary drinking water standards for radionuclides). What is EPA's approach to choosing an extrapolation approach under the 2005 carcinogen risk assessment guidance excerpted in section A.2 of this chapter?

2. The MCLG for a drinking water contaminant is not binding on public water systems. It is the MCL that establishes the maximum concentration of the relevant contaminant in drinking water that may be distributed. Why, then, did the Chlorine Chemistry Council have standing to challenge EPA's issuance of a zero-level MCLG for chloroform; how was it injured by EPA's action? In a portion of the opinion omitted from the casebook, the court held that the Council had standing because EPA sometimes uses MCLGs to set remediation levels for cleanups under the Comprehensive Environmental Response, Compensation, and Liability Act. The Council's members alleged that they faced liability for the cleanup of chloroform at Superfund sites across the country, and thus faced higher cleanup costs under a zero-level than under a higher MCLG.

Before the 1996 amendments, the NPDWRs* had to specify a MCL "which is as close to the [MCLG] as is feasible." This provision generated three principal criticisms. First, small drinking water systems might not be able to afford compliance with MCLs arrived at using this methodology, even if larger systems could. Second, compliance costs might outweigh the resulting benefits for some contaminants, particularly low-potency carcinogens. "The only identifiable benefit that can be stated for

---

*EPA also has the authority to issue secondary drinking water regulations to protect against contaminants that may adversely affect the odor or appearance of drinking water or otherwise adversely affect the public welfare. §§300g-1(c), 300f(2).

some standards is to prevent a handful of cancer cases nationwide, in some cases at costs that exceed tens of millions of dollars per cancer case avoided." S. Rep. No. 104-169, *supra*, at 14. Third, treatment technologies needed to achieve the MCLs might increase the risks posed by other contaminants. For example, chlorine, which is used to kill pathogenic organisms, might increase the cancer risk from disinfection by-products. "Read literally, the statute requires EPA to 'over control' some contaminants to a degree that overall public health risks from drinking water would be greater using the best available technology that is feasible than risks would be if the standard were set at a less stringent level."* Id.

In response to these concerns, the 1996 amendments altered the manner in which EPA sets MCLs. Section 300g-1(b)(3)(C)(i) now requires that, in promulgating MCLs, EPA analyze the quantifiable and nonquantifiable health risk reduction benefits and costs likely to occur as a result of regulation, as well as the incremental costs and benefits associated with each alternative contaminant level considered. Based on this analysis, EPA must determine when it proposes a NPDWR whether the benefits of an MCL that represents the maximum feasible level of control justify the costs. §300g-1(b)(4)(C). What does "feasible" mean in this context? See §300g-1(b)(4)(D). If EPA decides that they do not, it may establish an MCL that "maximizes health risk reduction benefits at a cost that is justified by the benefits." §300g-1(b)(6)(A). EPA also may set an MCL at a level other than the feasible level if the technology, treatment techniques, and other means used to determine the feasible level would result in an increase in the health risk from drinking water by increasing the concentration of other contaminants in drinking water or interfering with the efficacy of drinking water treatment techniques used to comply with other NPDWRs. §300g-1(b)(5)(A). In this situation, EPA must choose a level for the MCL that minimizes the overall risk posed by exposure to the contaminant being regulated and the other affected contaminants. §300g-1(b)(5)(B). Is this provision an example of "risk-risk" analysis?

Even before the 1996 amendments, EPA could issue NPDWRs that require the use of treatment techniques in lieu of establishing an MCL if it is not economically or technologically feasible to ascertain the level of the contaminant. §§300g-1(b)(7)(A), 300f(1)(C)(ii). This authority remains intact. American Water Works Ass'n v. EPA, 40 F.3d 1266 (D.C. Cir. 1994), involved challenges to EPA's pre-1996 NPDWRs for lead. NRDC challenged EPA's decisions to establish a treatment technique instead of an MCL. It argued that because it was economically and technologically feasible to ascertain the level of lead in water, EPA was obliged to set an MCL for lead. According to NRDC, "feasible" means "physically capable of being done at reasonable cost." EPA, however, argued that "feasible" means "capable of being accomplished in a manner consistent with the SDWA," and that subjecting public water systems to an MCL for lead would frustrate the statute's goals. If public water systems were required to comply with an MCL for lead, they would have to undertake corrosion control techniques that would increase the levels of other contaminants at the same time that

---

*EPA addressed this problem in its Disinfectants and Disinfection By products Rule, 63 Fed. Reg. 69,390 (1998). The chloroform MCLG vacated in the *Chlorine Chemistry Council* decision excerpted above was part of the Disinfection By products Rule. EPA regulations require drinking water utilities serving more than 100,000 people to submit cryptosporidium monitoring plans and to control the by-products formed during disinfection. 71 Fed. Reg. 69 (2006).

they were reducing the amount of lead leached from customers' plumbing. The court deferred to EPA's interpretation:

> The Congress clearly contemplated that an MCL would be a standard by which both the quality of the drinking water and the public water system's efforts to reduce the contaminant could be measured. See 42 U.S.C. §300g-1(b)(5). Because lead generally enters drinking water from corrosion in pipes owned by customers of the water system, an MCL for lead would be neither; ascertaining the level of lead in water at the meter (i.e., where it enters the customer's premises) would measure the public water system's success in controlling the contaminant but not the quality of the public's drinking water (because lead may still leach into the water from the customer's plumbing), while ascertaining the level of lead in water at the tap would accurately reflect water quality but effectively hold the public water system responsible for lead leached from plumbing owned by its customers.
>   . . . A single national standard (i.e., an MCL) for lead is not suitable for every public water system because the condition of plumbing materials, which are the major source of lead in drinking water, varies across systems and the systems generally do not have control over the sources of lead in their water. In this circumstance the EPA suggests that requiring public water systems to design and implement custom corrosion control plans for lead will result in optimal treatment of drinking water overall, i.e., treatment that deals adequately with lead without causing public water systems to violate drinking water regulations for other contaminants.
>   Viewing the Act as a whole, we cannot say that the statute demonstrates a clear congressional intent to require that the EPA set an MCL for a contaminant merely because it can be measured at a reasonable cost. In light of the purpose of the Act to promote safe drinking water generally, we conclude that the EPA's interpretation of the term "feasible" so as to require a treatment technique instead of an MCL for lead is reasonable. [40 F.3d at 1271.]

Enforcement. EPA delegates primary enforcement responsibility to the states, provided they comply with EPA drinking water standards. 40 C.F.R. §142.10. EPA may assume enforcement if the state fails to commence appropriate enforcement action. §300g-3(a)(1)(A). The SDWA also authorizes EPA to bring a civil action in federal district court to require compliance with the statute. The court may provide such relief "as protection of the public health may require." §300g-3(b). In United States v. Massachusetts Water Resources Auth., 256 F.3d 36 (1st Cir. 2001), the court affirmed the district court's refusal to require the Authority to build a filtration plant to treat water drawn from a reservoir to supply the metropolitan Boston area. The district court had agreed with the Authority that a less expensive system of ozonation and chloramination would adequately protect against the risk of disease from waterborne pathogens, and that the expenditure of $180 million for a plant that would achieve less than a 1 percent improvement in treatment capacity was unwarranted. The First Circuit concluded that, as long as a court issues a judgment ensuring that the public system provides water that is safe according to EPA standards, it retains flexibility to tailor the specifics of an equitable remedy that will accomplish that goal. The court found no evidence that the narrow goal of filtration (as opposed to the broader aim of safe drinking water) was an overarching congressional priority. United States v. Alisal Water Corp., 431 F.3d 643 (9th Cir. 2005), upheld as an appropriate exercise of judicial discretion under §300g-3(b) the district court's order requiring the owners of various private water systems to divest themselves of some of their systems based on their numerous violations of SDWA regulations.

The SDWA authorizes EPA to take whatever actions it deems necessary to protect the public health if it finds that a contaminant that is present in or is likely to enter a public water system or underground source of drinking water may present an imminent and substantial endangerment to the health of persons. §300i. In United States v. Midway Heights County Water Dist., 695 F. Supp. 1072 (E.D. Cal. 1988), the court approved an EPA order that the district bring its water up to the quality demanded by the NPDWRs. The court rejected the district's claim that, to prove that the water system "may present" such an endangerment, the government had to show that the failure to comply with MCLs had already caused illness among the district's customers. The Act "authorizes preventative actions. . . . The widespread contamination of the system with organisms which are accepted indicators of the potential for the spread of serious disease in an untreated water system presents the imminent and substantial endangerment. This court need not wait to exercise its authority until water district customers have actually fallen ill from drinking Midway Heights water." Id. at 1076.

Similarly, Trinity Am. Corp. v. EPA, 150 F.3d 389 (4th Cir. 1998), upheld an emergency order requiring a polyurethane foam plant located above a groundwater aquifer to sample groundwater near its property and provide bottled water to anyone with access to groundwater not meeting the standards. It made no difference that there was no evidence that anyone was actually drinking contaminated water. As long as the risk of harm was imminent, the harm itself need not be. "EPA must demonstrate the 'imminent likelihood' that the public may consume contaminated water unless prompt action is taken to 'prevent' a 'potential hazard from occurring.'" Id. at 399. Compare W.R. Grace & Co. v. EPA, 261 F.3d 330 (3d Cir. 2001), where the court vacated and remanded a §300i emergency order that required Grace to conduct a long-term cleanup of an aquifer contaminated by ammonia. The court found that EPA failed to provide a rational basis for its determination that cleanup to the specified level was necessary to protect the health of those who might use a public drinking water system that derived its water from the aquifer or that the remedial approach chosen (the removal of excess ammonia) was necessary.

Constitutionality. In Nebraska v. EPA, 331 F.3d 995 (D.C. Cir. 2003), the court rejected a facial attack on the SDWA as beyond the scope of Congress's authority under the Commerce Clause and as a violation of the Tenth Amendment.

Problem 8-2

Section 300g-1(b)(1)(B)(i)(I) of the SDWA requires that EPA compile a list once every five years of contaminants not already covered by NPDWRs "which are known or anticipated to occur in public water systems, and which may require regulation" under the SDWA. EPA must then decide whether or not to regulate each of the listed contaminants. EPA recently published one such list, including on it 20 contaminants. EPA explained that it had excluded 10 other contaminants (contaminants A-J) not already subject to regulation but known to occur in public water systems because it concluded that the financial burdens imposed on local governments operating public water systems were already onerous and that requiring local governments to monitor and regulate those 10 contaminants would not be financially feasible. EPA indicated that it would consider including the 10 excluded substances on the next five-year list.

Several months later, EPA decided to issue NPDWRs for 4 of the contaminants included on the previous list. The agency indicated that it had decided not to issue NPDWRs for 9 of the listed contaminants (contaminants K-S) on the ground that requiring public water systems to comply with MCLs for them would impose economic costs on those systems that would exceed the environmental benefits attributable to regulation. EPA chose not to regulate 5 other contaminants on the list (contaminants T-X) on the ground that no evidence had been presented to EPA that exposure to the contaminants would cause adverse health effects. Finally, it chose not to regulate 2 other contaminants (contaminants Y and Z) because, although exposure to those contaminants might create adverse effects, EPA determined that local governments operating public water systems could achieve higher levels of public health protection by devoting the resources that would be required to comply with NPDWRs for contaminants Y and Z to providing better facilities for the disposal of solid waste in landfills located near public drinking water supplies.

EPA has just issued final NPDWRs for the first of the remaining 4 listed contaminants, hexaflurgapilon-1,2,3. EPA conceded that this substance is a suspected human carcinogen. It nevertheless established a maximum contaminant level goal (MCLG) above zero for that contaminant because it was unable to determine that there is no safe threshold level of exposure to hexaflurgapilon-1,2,3. Further, EPA established the MCL for hexaflurgapilon-1,2,3 at 10 percent above the MCLG, even though it would have been feasible for public water systems to reduce concentrations of hexaflurgapilon-1,2,3 further to 5 percent above the MCLG. EPA justified that decision on the ground that the 10 percent level produced a better cost-benefit ratio than the 5 percent level.

An environmental public interest group, Better Water's Our Only Game (BWOOG), has properly filed petitions for review of each of these EPA decisions. BWOOG has attacked the validity of the following decisions: (1) EPA's decision to exclude contaminants A-J from the five-year list of unregulated contaminants; (2) EPA's decisions not to issue NPDWRs for contaminants K-S, T-X, and Y-Z; and (3) EPA's decisions to set an MCLG for hexaflurgapilon-1,2,3 at an above-zero level and to set an MCL for hexaflurgapilon-1,2,3 at 10 percent instead of 5 percent above the MCLG. How should the court resolve BWOOG's challenges?

d. Regulation of Chemicals in Food: The Federal Food, Drug, and Cosmetic Act

LES v. REILLY
968 F.2d 985 (9th Cir. 1992)

SCHROEDER, Circuit Judge:

[EPA denied an administrative petition requesting that it revoke a final order permitting the use of four pesticides as food additives although they had been found to induce cancer. The petitioners challenged the order on the ground that it violated the Delaney clause, 21 U.S.C. §348(c)(3), which prohibits the use of any food additive that is found to induce cancer.]

The Federal Food, Drug, and Cosmetic Act (FFDCA), 21 U.S.C. §§301-394, is designed to ensure the safety of the food we eat by prohibiting the sale of food that is "adulterated." 21 U.S.C. §331(a). Adulterated food is in turn defined as food containing any unsafe food "additive." 21 U.S.C. §342(a)(2)(C). A food "additive" is defined broadly as "any substance the intended use of which results or may reasonably be expected to result . . . in its becoming a component . . . of any food." 21 U.S.C. §321(s). A food additive is considered unsafe unless there is a specific exemption for the substance or a regulation prescribing the conditions under which it may be used safely. 21 U.S.C. §348(a).

Before 1988, the four pesticide chemicals with which we are here concerned—benomyl, mancozeb, phosmet and trifluralin—were all the subject of regulations issued by the EPA permitting their use. In October 1988, however, the EPA published a list of substances, including the pesticides at issue here, that had been found to induce cancer. Regulation of Pesticides in Food: Addressing the Delaney Paradox Policy Statement, 53 Fed. Reg. 41,104, 41,119 (1988). As known carcinogens, the four pesticides ran afoul of a special provision of the FFDCA known as the Delaney clause, which prescribes that additives found to induce cancer can never be deemed "safe" for purposes of the FFDCA. The Delaney clause is found in FFDCA section 409, 21 U.S.C. §348. That section limits the conditions under which the Secretary may issue regulations allowing a substance to be used as a food additive:

> No such regulation shall issue if a fair evaluation of the data before the Secretary—(A) fails to establish that the proposed use of the food additive, under the conditions of use to be specified in the regulation, will be safe: Provided, That no additive shall be deemed to be safe if it is found to induce cancer when ingested by man or animal, or if it is found, after tests which are appropriate for the evaluation of the safety of food additives, to induce cancer in man or animal. . . . [21 U.S.C. §348(c)(3).]

The FFDCA also contains special provisions which regulate the occurrence of pesticide residues on raw agricultural commodities. Section 402 of the FFDCA, 21 U.S.C. §342(a)(2)(B), provides that a raw food containing a pesticide residue is deemed adulterated unless the residue is authorized under section 408 of the FFDCA, 21 U.S.C. §346a, which allows tolerance regulations setting maximum permissible levels and also provides for exemption from tolerances under certain circumstances. When a tolerance or an exemption has been established for use of a pesticide on a raw agricultural commodity, then the FFDCA allows for the "flow-through" of such pesticide residue to processed foods, even when the pesticide may be a carcinogen. This flow-through is allowed, however, only to the extent that the concentration of the pesticide in the processed food does not exceed the concentration allowed in the raw food. The flow-through provisions are contained in section 402 which provides:

> That where a pesticide chemical has been used in or on a raw agricultural commodity in conformity with an exemption granted or a tolerance prescribed under section 346a of this title [FFDCA section 408] and such raw agricultural commodity has been subjected to processing such as canning, cooking, freezing, dehydrating, or milling, the residue of such pesticide chemical remaining in or on such processed food shall, notwithstanding the provisions of sections 346 and 348 of this title [FFDCA sections 406 and 409], not be deemed unsafe if such residue in or on the raw agricultural commodity has been removed to the extent possible in good manufacturing practice and the concentration of such residue in the processed food when ready to eat is not greater than the tolerance prescribed for the raw agricultural commodity.

21 U.S.C. §342(a)(2)(C). It is undisputed that the EPA regulations at issue in this case allow for the concentration of cancer-causing pesticides during processing to levels in excess of those permitted in the raw foods.

[I]n October 1988 . . . EPA announced a new interpretation of the Delaney clause: the EPA proposed to permit concentrations of cancer-causing pesticide residues greater than that tolerated for raw foods so long as the particular substances posed only a "de minimis" risk of actually causing cancer. Finding that benomyl, mancozeb, phosmet and trifluralin (among others) posed only such a de minimis risk, the Agency announced that it would not immediately revoke its previous regulations authorizing use of these substances as food additives.

The issue before us is whether the EPA has violated section 409 of the FFDCA, the Delaney clause, by permitting the use of carcinogenic food additives which it finds to present only a de minimis or negligible risk of causing cancer. The Agency acknowledges that its interpretation of the law is a new and changed one. From the initial enactment of the Delaney clause in 1958 to the time of the rulings here in issue, the statute had been strictly and literally enforced. . . .

The language is clear and mandatory. The Delaney clause provides that no additive shall be deemed safe if it induces cancer. 21 U.S.C. §348(c)(3). The EPA states in its final order that appropriate tests have established that the pesticides at issue here induce cancer in humans or animals. The statute provides that once the finding of carcinogenicity is made, the EPA has no discretion. As a leading work on food and drug regulation notes:

> [T]he Delaney Clause leaves the FDA room for scientific judgment in deciding whether its conditions are met by a food additive. But the clause affords no flexibility once FDA scientists determine that these conditions are satisfied. A food additive that has been found in an appropriate test to induce cancer in laboratory animals may not be approved for use in food for any purpose, at any level, regardless of any "benefits" that it might provide. [R. Merrill & P. Hutt, Food and Drug Law 78 (1980).] . . .

The Agency asks us to look behind the language of the Delaney clause to the overall statutory scheme governing pesticides, which permits the use of carcinogenic pesticides on raw food without regard to the Delaney clause. Yet section 402 of the FFDCA, 21 U.S.C. §342(a)(2)(C), expressly harmonizes that scheme with the Delaney clause by providing that residues on processed foods may not exceed the tolerance level established for the raw food. The statute unambiguously provides that pesticides which concentrate in processed food are to be treated as food additives, and these are governed by the Delaney food additive provision contained in section 409. If pesticides which concentrate in processed foods induce cancer in humans or animals, they render the food adulterated and must be prohibited.

The legislative history, too, reflects that Congress intended the very rigidity that the language it chose commands. The food additive Delaney clause was enacted in response to increasing public concern about cancer. It was initially part of a bill, introduced in the House of Representatives in 1958 by Congressman Delaney, to amend the FFDCA. The bill, intended to ensure that no carcinogens, no matter how small the amount, would be introduced into food, was at least in part a response to a decision by the FDA to allow a known carcinogen, the pesticide Aramite, as an approved food additive. Of the FDA's approval for sale of foods containing small quantities of Aramite, Congressman Delaney stated:

> The part that chemical additives play in the cancer picture may not yet be completely understood, but enough is known to put us on our guard. The safety of the public health demands that chemical additives should be specifically pretested for carcinogenicity, and this should be spelled out in the law. The precedent established by the Aramite decision has opened the door, even if only a little, to the use of carcinogens in our foods. That door should be slammed shut and locked. That is the purpose of my anticarcinogen provision.

The scientific witnesses who testified before Congress stressed that because current scientific techniques could not determine a safe level for carcinogens, all carcinogens should be prohibited. . . . Thus, the legislative history supports the conclusion that Congress intended to ban all carcinogenic food additives, regardless of amount or significance of risk, as the only safe alternative.

Throughout its 30-year history, the Delaney clause has been interpreted as an absolute bar to all carcinogenic food additives. . . . Further, Congress has repeatedly ratified a strict interpretation of the Delaney clause by reenacting all three FFDCA provisions which contain Delaney clauses without changing the Agency's interpretation. See 21 U.S.C. [§§348, 360b, 376].

The EPA contends that the legislative history shows that Congress never intended to regulate pesticides, as opposed to other additives, with extraordinary rigidity under the food additives provision. The Agency is indeed correct that the legislative history of the food additive provision does not focus on pesticides, and that pesticides are regulated more comprehensively under the Federal Insecticide, Fungicide, and Rodenticide Act (FIFRA). Nevertheless, the EPA's contention that Congress never intended the food additive provision to encompass pesticide residues is belied by the events prompting passage of the provision into law: FDA approval of Aramite was the principal impetus for the food additive Delaney clause and Aramite was itself a regulated pesticide. Thus, Congress intended to regulate pesticides as food additives under section 409 of the FFDCA, at least to the extent that pesticide residues concentrate in processed foods and exceed the tolerances for raw foods.

Finally, the EPA argues that a de minimis exception to the Delaney clause is necessary in order to bring about a more sensible application of the regulatory scheme. It relies particularly on a recent study suggesting that the criterion of concentration level in processed foods may bear little or no relation to actual risk of cancer, and that some pesticides might be barred by rigid enforcement of the Delaney clause while others, with greater cancer-causing risk, may be permitted through the flow-through provisions because they do not concentrate in processed foods. See National Academy of Sciences, Regulating Pesticides in Food: The Delaney Paradox (1987). . . . Revising the existing statutory scheme, however, is neither our function nor the function of the EPA. . . . If there is to be a change, it is for Congress to direct.

The EPA's refusal to revoke regulations permitting the use of benomyl, mancozeb, phosmet and trifluralin as food additives on the ground the cancer risk they pose is de minimis is contrary to the provisions of the Delaney clause prohibiting food additives that induce cancer. . . .

NOTES AND QUESTIONS

1. *Tolerances for Pesticide Residues.* At the time of the *Les* decision, §408 of the Federal Food, Drug, and Cosmetic Act (FFDCA), 21 U.S.C. §346a, authorized EPA to issue tolerances for residues on raw agricultural commodities of pesticides not generally recognized as safe, taking into account the necessity for the production of an adequate and economical food supply and the ways in which consumers might be affected by those pesticides or by related deleterious substances. EPA granted tolerances for residues of pesticides that induced tumors in laboratory animals when it perceived the risks to humans as relatively small (generally, less than one in a million). Hornstein, Lessons from Federal Pesticide Regulation on the Paradigms and Politics of Environmental Law Reform, 10 Yale J. on Reg. 369, 389-390 (1993). The Food and Drug Administration (FDA) is responsible for enforcing these tolerances. EPA's discretion in approving pesticide residues on processed foods was narrower. Section 402(a)(2)(C) of the FFDCA, 21 U.S.C. §342(a)(2)(C), allowed for the flow-through of such residues, notwithstanding §409 (which contains the food additive Delaney clause), 21 U.S.C. §348, but only in amounts not exceeding the tolerance prescribed for the raw agricultural commodity. How did EPA explain its October 1988 decision to approve concentrations of pesticide residues in processed foods that exceeded those amounts?

2. *The Delaney Clause and Comparative Risk Assessment.* EPA's concern that the literal application of the food additive Delaney clause might prevent the use of less risky products helps to explain its reliance on the *de minimis* doctrine in *Les*:

> Because pesticides approved in earlier decades were not adequately tested to identify their carcinogenic potential and were grandfathered in under earlier standards, EPA is concerned that strict application of the Delaney Clause to new pesticides prevents the replacement of more dangerous older chemicals with safer new ones. Because EPA does not have the administrative flexibility to approve new pesticides that are carcinogenic, older high risk pesticides are retained on the market while less toxic alternatives are discouraged because the smaller risk they pose might still trigger a registration rejection. [Rosenthal et al., Legislating Acceptable Cancer Risk from Exposure to Toxic Chemicals, 19 Ecology L.Q. 269, 299 (1992).]

What is the "paradox" referred to in the 1987 NAS study cited by the court in *Les*? See 139 Cong. Rec. S12139 (daily ed. Sept. 21, 1993) (statement of Senator Nickles). Compare Turner, Delaney Lives! Reports of Delaney's Death Are Greatly Exaggerated, 28 Envtl. L. Rep. (ELI) 10003, 10006 (1998) (characterizing the paradox as "a nonexistent legal inconsistency").

3. *EPA's Coordination Policy.* Were the FFDCA provisions governing the marketing of foods containing carcinogenic pesticide residues consistent with the treatment of carcinogenic pesticides under FIFRA? What risk management approach did each statute employ?

> The consequences of [the] "flow through" provision [of 21 U.S.C. §342(a)(2)(C)] are in fact more severe than what is statutorily mandated. When the pesticide registrant seeks a section 408 tolerance for a specific crop, it must address the need for a section 409 food additive tolerance by showing whether the residues concentrate during specific processes such as drying, milling, or juicing. The EPA coordinates its regulatory decisions under sections 408 and 409 of the FFDCA by revoking a section 408 tolerance where

section 409 regulations are needed but cannot be established. The EPA also coordinates its regulatory actions under FIFRA and the FFDCA by not permitting under FIFRA a pesticide use that would result in adulterated food. Therefore, when a section 409 tolerance is revoked, EPA revokes both the section 408 tolerance and the FIFRA registration for that use. This is referred to as EPA's "coordination policy." [Curme, Regulation of Pesticide Residues in Foods: Proposed Solutions to Current Inadequacies under FFDCA and FIFRA, 49 Food & Drug L.J. 609, 614-615 (1994).]

Does the coordination policy "unlawfully incorporate[] the Delaney clause into the standard for raw product tolerances"? See Ely, An Obscure EPA Policy Is to Blame, EPA J., Jan./Feb./Mar. 1993, at 44. How did the *Les* court respond to EPA's use of FIFRA to justify its 1988 regulations?

Shortly after the decision in *Les*, various associations of food processors and fresh fruit and vegetable growers filed a petition with EPA challenging its policies in linking its regulatory activities under the various pesticide provisions of FIFRA and the FFDCA. The petition charged that the coordination policy was both unnecessary and unlawful, in that it required that the agency ignore the risk/benefit standards of FIFRA and FFDCA §408. The petitioners requested repeal of the coordination policy so that §408 tolerances could remain in effect (or be established) for pesticide uses even when, under the *Les* decision, the associated §409 tolerances had to be revoked (or could not be established).

The agency largely denied the petition in 1996. It retained most aspects of the coordination policy intact because, although the Delaney clause does not directly govern §408 tolerances or FIFRA registrations, EPA has a responsibility to avoid inconsistent action under FIFRA and the FFDCA. "Legally used pesticides should not result in illegal food." The Pesticide Coordination Policy; Response to Petitions, 61 Fed. Reg. 2378, 2379. EPA noted its willingness, however, to consider an exception to the coordination approach to avert severe economic disruption:

> EPA believes [that coordination] is best accomplished by treating the Delaney clause as indicating that Congress had a heightened concern for carcinogenic pesticide residues in processed food where those residues exceed the section 408 tolerance. Thus, EPA, in making the risk/benefit balancing determination called for under FIFRA and section 408 for a carcinogenic pesticide, takes into account the likelihood that residues of the pesticide will exceed the section 408 tolerance in processed food and the added weight such overtolerance residues are due in light of the Delaney clause.
>
> Additionally, in evaluating the benefits provided by use of a pesticide in the FIFRA and section 408 risk/benefit decision, EPA must consider the extent to which use of a pesticide could result in adulterated food. Adulterated food resulting from use of a pesticide would decrease any benefits the pesticide provided to society. Thus, the Delaney clause's effect of denying a [tolerance] for carcinogenic pesticides affects benefits determinations as well as risk evaluations under FIFRA and section 408. . . .
>
> . . . EPA cannot rule out the possibility that in a given situation the balance of factors supporting a coordination policy may shift away from a pre-market clearance procedure and toward the more costly and inefficient process of after-the-fact enforcement. For example, application of the coordination policy may result in the cancellation of a use or group of uses that is so central to the production of a certain crop that the revocation of that use or uses would severely disrupt domestic production of that commodity with attendant consequences to the price and availability of food to the consumer. In these circumstances, EPA believes it may be appropriate to allow an exception to the coordination policy. [Id. at 2380-2381.]

4. *Scientific Advances and Zero Tolerance.* Have scientific advances in methodologies for measuring trace amounts of chemicals in foods made the Delaney clause obsolete? Senator Edward Kennedy thought so when he remarked in 1995 that

> there has been a revolution in food science and biochemistry since 1958, when the Delaney class was enacted. We now have the technology to identify cancer-causing chemicals in foods, in far smaller trace amounts than possible 40 years ago. We also understand that animals may develop tumors from certain chemicals through pathways of animal biology that humans do not have. Zero tolerance, therefore, means something different today than it did in 1958. . . . In 1958, testing equipment might have considered zero risk to be a 1 in 100,000 chance of causing cancer. Today, we have scientific instruments that can detect risk levels as low as 1 in 1 billion. Clearly a modern standard of risk is warranted. [141 Cong. Rec. S10267 (daily ed. July 19, 1995).]

The *Les* decision put dozens of tolerances and pesticide registrations at risk of revocation. See Hornstein, *supra*, at 445.

5. *The 1996 FFDCA Amendments.* Concerns over the economic impact of a literal application of the food additive Delaney clause and over its questionable scientific underpinnings culminated in adoption of the Food Quality Protection Act of 1996, Pub. L. No. 104-170, 110 Stat. 1489, which amended the FFDCA. Section 408 of the FFDCA now provides that a pesticide chemical residue is unsafe, and subject to the prohibition on adulterated food in §402(a)(2)(B), unless it is in compliance with a tolerance or covered by an exemption issued by EPA. For purposes of the amended §408, "food" means either a raw agricultural commodity or processed food. What effect does this definition have on the dual standard for tolerances previously in effect under §§408 and 409? For a good description of the relationship between FIFRA and the FFDCA after the 1996 amendments, see NRDC v. Johnson, 461 F.3d 164 (2d Cir. 2006). EPA may issue a tolerance only if it regards exposure to food with pesticide residues that comply with the tolerance as safe. To reach that conclusion, EPA must determine "that there is a reasonable certainty that no harm will result from aggregate exposure" to the residue. If EPA is unable to determine a level of exposure at which a residue will not cause or contribute to a known or anticipated harm to human health, it may leave a tolerance in effect only if it finds either that use of the pesticide that produces the residue protects consumers from adverse health effects that would pose a greater risk than the dietary risk from the residue, or that use of the pesticide is necessary to avoid a significant disruption in domestic production of an adequate, wholesome, and economical food supply.

The 1996 amendments also responded to a study finding that physiological differences between adults and children make children more sensitive to pesticide exposure. National Academy of Sciences, Board on Agriculture, Pesticides in the Diets of Infants and Children (1993). Under amended §408(b)(2)(C), when EPA issues or modifies a tolerance, it must assess the risks of the pesticide residue on infants and children, given their "special susceptibility," and ensure that there is a reasonable certainty that no harm will result to them from aggregate exposure to the residue. EPA must build into a tolerance an additional tenfold margin of safety for infants and children to account for pre- and postnatal toxicity. Suppose the agency adopts a presumption that the extra tenfold margin of safety is needed to protect infants and children, but allows the presumption to be rebutted on a case-by-case basis if test and exposure data indicate that an additional uncertainty factor is unnecessary. Does the statute permit such an approach?

What effect does the amended FFDCA have on the food additive Delaney clause of §409(c)(3)(A)? Weinstein et al., in The Food Quality Protection Act: A

New Way of Looking at Pesticides, 28 Envtl. L. Rep. (ELI) 10555, 10556 (1998), explain that the amended Act exempts pesticide residues from §409 and the Delaney clause by removing them from the definition of food additives, but that the prohibition against establishing tolerances for carcinogenic food additives otherwise remains in place. Although the 1996 Act did not amend §409 of the FFDCA, it provides that regulations establishing tolerances for pesticide residues on processed food issued under §409 before adoption of the 1996 amendments will be treated as §408 regulations and subject to modification under that section. 21 U.S.C. §346a(j)(2). Does the amended FFDCA afford EPA more flexibility in its regulation of food additives? Too much flexibility? Is the "reasonable certainty of no harm" standard too vague? Does it make sense to impose a uniform level of risk, regardless of the benefits afforded by pesticide use? Or does the new standard for tolerances take account of the degree of benefits provided by a pesticide?

   Section 408(a)(2) now provides that if a tolerance is in effect for a pesticide residue on a raw agricultural commodity, a residue present on processed food because the food is made from that commodity will not be regarded as unsafe within the meaning of §402(a)(2)(B), even if EPA has not established a tolerance for the processed food, if the pesticide has been used on the raw commodity in conformity with a §408 tolerance, the residue has been removed to the extent possible in good manufacturing practice, and the concentration of the pesticide in the processed food is not greater than the tolerance for the residue in the raw commodity. What is the relationship between this provision and the pre-1996 version of §402(a)(2)(C), which was repealed by the 1996 amendments? Do the provisions of the 1996 law affect the coordination policy? Amended §408(l)(1) provides that, to the extent practicable, when EPA suspends or revokes a tolerance for a pesticide residue on food, it must coordinate that action with "any related necessary action" under FIFRA. Under §408(l)(2)-(3), if EPA cancels or suspends a pesticide registration under FIFRA due to dietary risks to humans posed by the presence of residues on food, it must revoke any tolerance that allows the presence in food of the pesticide or any residue that results from its use. Do the 1996 amendments protect consumers against the cumulative risks of ingesting the residues of many different pesticides in raw and processed foods? See Weinstein et al., *supra*, at 10557-10558 (the statute requires consideration of aggregate exposure from dietary and nondietary sources).

2.   *Proprietary Rights to Information versus the Public's Right to Know*

a.   Market Failure and the Availability of Information on Toxic Substances

WAGNER, COMMONS IGNORANCE: THE FAILURE OF ENVIRONMENTAL LAW TO PRODUCE NEEDED INFORMATION ON HEALTH AND THE ENVIRONMENT
53 Duke L.J. 1619, 1622, 1631-1634, 1639-1641, 1650-1651, 1653-1654, 1656-1657, 1663-1664, 1670, 1677-1679, 1699 (2004)

Rational choice theory and the large body of laws premised on it understand that those who inflict invisible and costly harms on others are disinclined to document the problems, much less take responsibility for them. Indeed, rational choice theory predicts that if wrongdoers are going to invest in research at all, they will dedicate resources to concealing and contesting incriminating information and producing exculpatory excuses and alibis. The criminal justice system is certainly familiar with this natural reaction to culpability. Yet, for some reason, environmental law has largely failed to come to grips with this inescapable feature of human nature. Instead, environmental law innocently assumes that information linking actors to resulting invisible harms will arise serendipitously, and, even more surprising, that the actors will either volunteer or accept this incriminating information without fuss or fanfare. . . .

[Professor Wagner turns her attention to the reasons for the "pervasive ignorance" that exists in the United States concerning how hazardous substances affect human health and the environment.] So, what accounts for this pervasive commons ignorance in the United States? The complexity of the systems is an important impediment to producing better information. But this is not the whole explanation. Research in other fields is also complex, and yet discoveries in health care and technology greatly outpace the minimal advancements in assessing man's impact on health and the environment.

Much of the blame belongs to industry's rational and vigorous resistance to producing information about the damage that it may cause to the commons. In other areas of scientific inquiry, private actors contribute substantially to advancements in public knowledge because the research promises to provide simultaneous private gains. No equivalent benefit attaches to research on the adverse effects of human activities on health or the environment. Rather than presenting the opportunity for private profit, these questions pose the opposite equation for private actors generating externalities. These actors vastly prefer ignorance over research because most documentation of externalities will ultimately affect them negatively. Thus, rather than contribute to enlightenment, actors seem more willing to contribute to, and even invest in, the perpetuation of ignorance.

Although it is rarely noticed, ignorance regarding the harm that private actors are causing health and the environment is just another external cost of their activities that they are able to pass on to society. The common law courts have sometimes appreciated this, requiring actors to disprove that they caused harm when they are best situated to know how their activities might affect others. Similarly, externality theory supports requiring actors to internalize the costs of researching an externality, because these costs are imposed on society by the actor's conduct. As long as there are predictable, nonobvious harms that flow from an activity, it is the actors' duty to investigate and disclose these harms before taking action. Otherwise, the externality and the ignorance surrounding it will be self-perpetuating. . . .

In Professor Mary Lyndon's classic article about the lack of safety research on toxic products,* she details the ways in which the market discourages manufacturers from conducting research on the long-term safety of potentially toxic products. Professor Lyndon's analysis reveals that the market penalizes, rather than rewards, actors who document the negative effects of their products when the effects are neither obvious nor visible and immediate. Although Professor Lyndon focuses on the disincentives for manufacturers to research long-term product safety, her analysis applies

---

*Lyndon, Information Economics and Chemical Toxicity: Designing Laws to Produce and Use Data, 87 Mich. L. Rev. 1795 (1989).

even more forcefully to actors who discharge pollution, whose responsibility for down-stream effects is even more difficult to discern.

According to Professor Lyndon, there are at least three reasons that actors will not find it in their interest to document the potential harm from their products or polluting activities. First, the out-of-pocket (direct) costs associated with conducting safety research are not only expensive but also may not produce definitive results. Indeed, even after protracted testing, the results generally cannot completely exonerate a product or activity, nor do they enable the manufacturer to quantify risks in a definitive way. Given the lack of inexpensive screening tests, actors will rarely be able to obtain information about the harms created by their product or activity at low cost. Thus, financial realities and lack of research efficacy combine to explain why long-term safety testing is generally not an attractive investment for actors.

Second, virtually no market benefits accrue to actors who produce research on the long-term safety of products or activities. Professor Lyndon demonstrates that when safety representations cannot be easily validated or compared, consumers are unlikely to make purchasing or investment decisions based upon a manufacturer's self-serving statements about safety. Moreover, given that the results are rarely determinative, even thorough safety research will seldom provide a clear market signal of "safety." Even if research results were definitive and comparable between different products and activities, advertising that a product or activity did not cause cancer in animals might not impress consumers or be received positively in the marketplace.

Third, for toxicity and safety testing, there are few guarantees about what the testing will reveal. Any possible good news, moreover, is always tempered by looming uncertainties. Most screening tests produce false positives by design. Yet even when "no effect" is observed in a toxicity study, the testing cannot ensure that the product is safe—only that it did not cause a few types of adverse effects (e.g., cancer) in one exposure setting (e.g., ingestion by rats). On the other hand, a bad result is almost always definitive in the following sense: When a substance does cause cancer in laboratory animals, uncertainty about how those results could or should be extrapolated to humans does not materially diminish the impact of the adverse result. The best that can be said is that bad news encourages more testing to refine and improve the outlook for the product or activity.

Beyond the lack of market incentives for developing information on externalities, actors also have legitimate concerns about increased tort liability that could result from producing incriminating information about the harms caused by their products or activities. Common law tort liability is generally imposed only after injured parties prove that the defendant's activity caused their harm. Producing and publicizing internal research on such harms is, therefore, a risky proposition. Once plaintiffs' attorneys seize on a firm's internal research suggesting that harm may result from the firm's products or activities, catastrophic liability may follow. Under such information-triggered common law regimes, actors benefit from knowing nothing, in part because it deprives plaintiffs of the evidence that they need to bring their case.

That remaining ignorant about the impact of their products and activities is an effective strategy is evident in practice. Industries do not volunteer information on the long-term safety of their products and activities, and they lobby against laws requiring them to share even basic internal information. . . . [I]gnorance is not merely a byproduct of a market system that fails to offer incentives to provide this information; ignorance actually represents a willful, strategic choice. . . . Remaining ignorant about the potential harms caused by one's products and activities increases the likelihood that the actor can avoid tort suits and stay out of the range of plaintiffs' attorneys' radar. . . .

. . . In addition, whatever positive incentives may exist are mitigated because the information—once produced and publicized—becomes a public good. Thus actors producing useful information, unless it pertains exclusively to them, will be unable to capture its full benefit. Any good news that safety testing may yield is of little value to a manufacturer unless it is publicized. But once publicized, competitors can capitalize on the information without bearing any of the costs of producing it. Although theoretically actors will produce information on the harm resulting from their activities if the benefits outweigh the costs, when the information is also useful to competitors, the resulting reduction in benefit will be added to the tally in determining whether the information is worth the investment. For example, investments in research on improving screening methods for detecting neurological harms from exposure to toxic products not only helps the investing actor assess the harm caused by its activities, but can be used by others. Thus, if private actors develop enhanced capabilities for detecting these harms, they help produce a public good for which they will not be compensated adequately. . . .

If actors believe that information about their activities has a negative value, they might not only resist producing this information, but also may make it more difficult for third parties to produce it. . . . Actors will invest as much in obstructing research as they expect to lose if the information is made publicly available. Moreover, to the extent that actors enjoy superior access to or control over information essential to assess externalities, they may be able to increase the costs of third-party research simply by preventing access to key information. If actors believe that they have much to lose from public enlightenment about externalities—particularly, for example, if there is a potential for mass liability—they might even take affirmative steps to discredit or counter the claims made by third parties. Even if these efforts ultimately fail, the actors benefit by postponing the ultimate "day of reckoning"— sometimes indefinitely. . . .

[In addition, a]ctors have developed a number of imaginative approaches to obscure or discredit potentially troublesome third-party research suggesting that their activities cause harm. The easiest approach is for an actor simply to publicize only the positive information about a product or activity, while keeping potentially damaging information private. Because actors control access to key information, this tactic allows them to present a misleadingly positive account of the externalities associated with their products and activities that helps to offset damaging research produced by outsiders. . . .

More aggressive efforts to manufacture uncertainty take on a variety of forms, but they generally involve either blatant, underhanded attacks on third-party research or investments in "counter-research" carefully designed to produce results more favorable to an actor's interests. Although in many areas there is no scientific consensus about certain issues and presenting another side of an issue is legitimate, the manufactured critiques and studies discussed here involve a strategic, ends-oriented effort to undermine credible research and obscure scientific consensus. Many actors have launched a frontal assault on academic or public research that documents how their products or activities harm the public health or the environment. In some cases, because of the inherent complexity of the studies, even high-quality technical research can be at least temporarily discredited by making groundless challenges about the methods used, the reliability of the data collected, the qualifications of the researcher conducting the study, or by suggesting that the review processes are flawed. These "hired gun" attacks on third-party research are common in high-stakes cases when acceptance of the results could lead to shattering liability and publicity. . . .

In addition to attacking the credibility of the research and in some cases the researcher, affected actors have also financed counter-research designed to refute third-party research, either by producing different results or by suggesting that the results of the independent research cannot be reproduced—a devastating critique within the scientific community. By hiring scientists willing to "collaborate" closely with the sponsoring industry (under contracts that require sponsor control of the research), sponsors historically have been able to exert dramatic control over the outcome of research, to the point of designing studies, framing research questions, and even editing and ghostwriting articles. . . .

Most environmental laws do aspire to ensure that needed information on environmental harms is developed and, in some cases, the laws even demand that actors bear full responsibility for producing this information. Every major environmental statute includes among its opening goals a declaration that externalities be identified and regulated so that the public and the environment will be fully protected, or at least protected to the extent reasonable or feasible. . . .

Despite these noble statutory intentions, however, the regulation- and litigation-driven implementation of these laws nevertheless allows actors to escape much of the responsibility for producing vital information on the externalities that they create. . . .

[With certain exceptions], actors are generally off the hook when it comes to identifying and analyzing the harms created by their products and activities. . . . Typically actors are only required to provide information about the nature of the activity and not information about its possible adverse effects. Indeed, . . . existing laws allow most private actors to avoid responsibility for providing any information about the harms created by their products and activities. It is instead left to the public, particularly government agencies, to collect and assess this information. . . .

It is bad enough that environmental laws—contrary to their promise—fail to require actors to produce information needed to assess their externalities. But some environmental laws lead to a still worse state of affairs: the laws sometimes reward actors for their ignorance, penalize them for producing useful knowledge, and provide mechanisms for them to attack damaging public science that suggests they are causing harm. . . .

Under the current regulatory system, volunteering adverse information on the effects or even the existence of harms associated with one's product or activity is equivalent to shooting oneself in the foot. Regulation and enforcement increase in lockstep with the availability of public information on adverse effects. Whereas no information means no regulation, a solid body of uncontested, adverse information will almost certainly lead to intrusive regulation, enforcement activity, and sometimes even a ban on the activity or product. . . . [A]s long as information is neither required nor rewarded but instead is used punitively by the regulatory system, the decision about whether to voluntarily conduct and report research on one's product's or activity's externalities is an easy one. Ignorance is bliss. . . .

With such strong reasons to resist producing information, it is no surprise that actors not only avoid learning about the adverse harms created by their products or activities but, once such news is discovered, actively seek legal protections to limit the disclosure of the incriminating information. By claiming broad protections, actors can raise the costs to others of accessing this information or, in some cases, can even bar access completely. [Professor Wagner goes on to describe "several discrete legal protections" that allow actors to claim confidentiality privileges for privately held, damaging information and that bar most public access to the information, often even by EPA. These include protection for trade secrets or confidential business information, privacy protections, litigation settlements, nondisclosure contracts, state privilege laws, and national security legislation. She also points out that several laws, such as the Information Quality Act (which is discussed in the notes below) "actually facilitate the ability of actors to disparage credible research" by providing "opportunities for private actors to contest the quality of research and taint the integrity of researchers, even when the actors' charges are without scientific merit."]

NOTES

1. *Information Sources.* Other observers agree that neither workers nor consumers are likely to generate significant amounts of information concerning toxic risks because of the high cost and low individual benefit involved. The tort system is an inadequate means of remedying the resulting data deficiency due to the absence of information, the inability to generate data, and the institutional incompetence of the judiciary. That leaves government regulation as the best source of the data necessary for effective regulation of the manufacture and use of toxic substances. Shifting the cost of generating the data to those who manufacture and use toxic chemicals in their products is both efficient (because internalization of the cost of detecting externalities will result in prices that more accurately reflect the true cost of their production) and equitable (because the primary beneficiaries of the chemicals ought to pay for the cost of ascertaining the extent of the risks they impose). See Applegate, The Perils of Unreasonable Risk: Information, Regulatory Policy, and Toxic Substances Control, 91 Colum. L. Rev. 261 (1991).

2. Among the corrective mechanisms that Professor Wagner recommends to the problems she has identified in the excerpt is legislation that would make it illegal to invoke trade secret and other protections to classify information about the adverse effects of products and activities that threaten public health and the environment, and the adoption of a requirement, backed by civil and criminal sanctions, that all health-related information be reported to the government. She also supports imposing sanctions on those who abuse litigation and administrative mechanisms to delay regulation and "harass and discredit public scientists." Wagner, *supra*, at 1734. She recommends the creation of incentives to produce information by basing environmental regulatory standards on worst-case predictions and reducing regulation when credible information suggests that harms have been overestimated. Finally, she asserts that most basic research used for regulation should be performed by disinterested government or federally funded academic scientists not influenced by sponsors or financial incentives.

3. *The Information Quality Act.* The Information Quality Act, referred to by Professor Wagner, requires OMB to issue guidelines to federal agencies "for ensuring and maximizing the quality, objectivity, utility, and integrity of information (including statistical information) disseminated by Federal agencies." Pub. L. No. 106-554, §515, 114 Stat. 2763, 2763A-153 (2000) (codified at 44 U.S.C. §3516 note). Each agency to which the guidelines apply must issue its own, similar guidelines and establish administrative mechanisms allowing affected persons to seek and obtain

correction of information that does not comply with the guidelines. Written in large part by industry lobbyists, the statute provides interest groups with the means to force environmental agencies to withdraw from public dissemination reports or other documents containing information that does not meet the OMB tests for "quality, objectivity, utility, and integrity." In one case, for example, a trade association of companies that produce salt for food and other uses alleged that the Department of Health and Human Services violated the IQA by reporting on its website, in medical journals, and in at least one report the results of studies showing that decreased use of salt by all Americans could lower blood pressure and by recommending that people limit salt intake. In Salt Inst. v. Thompson, 440 F.3d 156 (4th Cir. 2006), the court held that the plaintiffs lacked standing to bring a suit under the IQA to challenge HHS's dissemination of the information. For further discussion of the IQA, see page 213.

b. Trade Secrets and Information Property

The federal statutory provisions requiring chemical manufacturers and users to disclose information about those substances to the government give rise to a potential conflict between the desire to protect industry investments in proprietary information and the need for the dissemination of sufficient information to the government and the public. The government needs information about toxic substances to make rational decisions about whether and how to reduce risk-generating activities. The public needs the information to make informed choices about matters such as whether to live near a risk-producing activity and whether to consume a product containing a potentially toxic substance.

The stakes can be very high on both sides. It may cost as much as $15 million annually to develop a potential commercial pesticide, for example, and the development process may take 20 years. Further, "f[o]r every manufacturing-use pesticide the average company finally markets, it will have screened and tested 20,000 others." Ruckelshaus v. Monsanto Co., 467 U.S. 986, 998 (1984). The information generated by a pesticide manufacturer and submitted to EPA in support of its application for registration is typically valuable to the manufacturer "beyond its instrumentality in gaining that particular application. Monsanto uses this information to develop additional end-use products and to expand the uses of its registered products. The information would also be valuable to Monsanto's competitors. For that reason, Monsanto has instituted stringent security measures to ensure the secrecy of the data." Id.* What is at stake for members of the public is the ability to participate meaningfully in the regulatory process and to make informed choices about the degree of exposure risk they are willing to incur.

Both TSCA and FIFRA require the submission of enormous quantities of technical data. Both also provide significant protection to proprietary information that constitutes trade secrets, confidential business information, or privileged information under the Trade Secrets Act, 18 U.S.C. §1905; the Freedom of Information Act, 5 U.S.C. §552; or state statutes or common law. TSCA removes this protection from data that EPA determines must be disclosed to protect health or the environment against an unreasonable risk of injury, and from certain health and safety studies

---

*See generally McGarity & Shapiro, The Trade Secret Status of Health and Safety Testing Information: Reforming Agency Disclosure Policies, 93 Harv. L. Rev. 837 (1980).

submitted for regulatory purposes. TSCA §14(a)(3), (b). Section 14(b) bars EPA from disclosing processes used in the manufacture or processing of a chemical substance or mixture. From 1977 to 1990, more than 90 percent of all PMNs for new chemicals were deemed confidential business information by EPA. Bass & MacLean, Enhancing the Public's Right-to-Know About Environmental Issues, 4 Vill. Envtl. L.J. 287, 310 (1993).

Under FIFRA a pesticide registrant must mark and separately submit required trade secrets and commercial or financial information. FIFRA §136h(a). EPA may not disclose such information. Information concerning test results on registered pesticides or the effects of pesticides on the environment is available to the public, except for information that discloses manufacturing or quality control processes, the details of testing methods, or the identity or percentages of inert ingredients. Even that information, however, may be disclosed if in EPA's judgment it is necessary to protect against unreasonable risks. §136h(d)(1). Both TSCA and FIFRA provide stiff penalties for the willful disclosure of protected information by agency personnel.

Both statutes permit subsequent reliance on data submitted in connection with earlier health and safety studies, but with protections accorded the company that first generated the information. Under TSCA, for a five-year period after its submission of data, a manufacturer may obtain EPA-adjudicated "fair and equitable" reimbursement from companies that rely upon its test results in their own submissions to EPA. TSCA §4(c)(3). Under FIFRA, the operation of a more complex exclusive use and compensation scheme turns on how long the information has existed—for 10 years post-1978, no use; for the next 15 years, compensated use. FIFRA §136a(c)(1)(F).

The Supreme Court addressed the constitutionality of FIFRA's data use provisions in *Ruckelshaus, supra*. It held that Monsanto's health and environmental data regarding potential commercial pesticides were property susceptible to taking under the Fifth Amendment, although they were intangible trade secrets. It also held that EPA's use of data submitted to it by Monsanto after the effective date of 1978 amendments to FIFRA to assist the agency's consideration of another's request for registration was not a taking. Monsanto had no reasonable, investment-backed expectation that EPA would regard the information as confidential beyond the limits prescribed in the amended statute. The requirement that a registration applicant give up its property interest in the data did not amount to an unconstitutional condition on the right to a valuable government benefit (registration). In Sygenta Crop Prot., Inc. v. EPA, 444 F. Supp. 2d 435 (M.D.N.C. 2006), EPA issued pesticide registrations to the competitors of the plaintiff pesticide manufacturer, based on data submitted by the plaintiff when it initially registered a similar pesticide, after the agency issued a registration for the plaintiff's new pesticide that was conditioned on its agreement to withdraw registration for the original pesticide. Both EPA and the plaintiff agreed that the new pesticide was safer. The court rejected the plaintiff's claims that EPA's actions resulted in a violation of procedural or substantive due process or the equal protection clause.

c. Public Disclosure Requirements and Right-to-Know Acts

OSHA's Hazard Communication Standard. OSHA's Hazard Communication Standard, 29 C.F.R. §1910.1200, dating back to 1974, is one of the first examples of federally mandated disclosure of the risks of exposure to toxic substances. The purpose of the Standard is to ensure evaluation of the hazards of produced or imported chemicals and transmission to employers and employees of information concerning known chemical hazards. Employers need not perform tests on the health effects of exposure to chemicals, but they must develop and implement at each workplace a written hazard communication program that includes a list of the hazardous chemicals known to be present, the methods the employer will use to inform employees of the hazards, the labeling of containers of hazardous substances leaving the workplace, and the preparation of material safety data sheets (MSDSs) that contain information about chemical substances in the workplace.

The Emergency Planning and Community Right-to-Know Act. Perhaps the most important federal disclosure program today is the 1986 Emergency Planning and Community Right-to-Know Act (EPCRA), 42 U.S.C. §§11001-11050. The Act was passed in response to the 1984 disaster at Union Carbide's plant in Bhopal, India, where thousands of people were killed or injured as a result of the accidental release of methyl isocyanide into the air. It requires local and federal governments and industry to prepare emergency response plans and to disclose the manufacture or use of hazardous chemicals. The following excerpt analyzes the potential benefits of EPCRA's reporting and disclosure requirements.

KARKKAINEN, INFORMATION AS ENVIRONMENTAL REGULATION: TRI AND PERFORMANCE BENCHMARKING, PRECURSOR TO A NEW PARADIGM?
89 Geo. L.J. 257, 260-263, 270, 277, 284, 294-295 (2001)

... Conventional environmental reporting typically demands only the minimum information necessary to gauge compliance with a fixed regulatory standard. Like the regulations they are designed to support, reported data are fragmentary and narrowly tailored to program requirements that vary by medium, industry, pollutant, and source. Consequently, data are difficult to aggregate, compare, rank, or track over time. In contrast, [the Toxic Release Inventory (TRI)] establishes a broadly accessible, objective, open-ended, cross-media metric of facility-level environmental performance that is not tied to any particular regulatory standard. Because TRI data are reported in standard units, they can be aggregated to produce profiles and performance comparisons at the level of the facility, firm, industrial sector, community, metropolitan region, state, watershed or other critical ecosystem, and the nation as a whole. ...

By creating this performance metric, TRI both compels and enables facilities and firms to monitor their own environmental performance. It also encourages them to compare, rank, and track performance among production processes, facilities, operating units, and peer or competitor firms. By enabling an unprecedented degree of self-monitoring, aggregation, disaggregation, comparison, ranking, and tracking of environmental performance, TRI produces information that is far more valuable to reporting entities than that produced by conventional forms of environmental reporting. It enables managers to engage in both internal and comparative benchmarking to establish performance baselines, set improvement targets, track progress toward those targets, and hold operational units within the firm accountable for meeting them. In this way, TRI empowers managers to translate the firm's general environmental goals into specific performance objectives, and to incorporate environmental management almost seamlessly into their overall business strategy and ongoing operations. This is a radical departure from externally imposed, fixed regulatory standards that, in effect, demand a series of discrete and costly side adjustments to achieve compliance. Moreover, in contrast to fixed regulatory standards that effectively become performance ceilings as well as floors, TRI-induced benchmarking creates an implicit open-ended performance standard that demands continuous improvement in relation to one's peers and to one's own past performance. . . .

The ready availability of TRI data also enhances transparency and accountability to external parties. It subjects the environmental performance of facilities and firms to an unprecedented degree of scrutiny by their peers, competitors, investors, employees, consumers, community residents, environmental organizations, activists, elected officials, regulators, and the public in general. Just like facility and firm managers, these external parties use TRI data to monitor performance over time, compare facilities and firms against their peers, and track their progress toward explicit or implicit improvement goals. These external monitors often have powerful tools at their disposal, including political, market, community, and regulatory pressures, which they use to discipline poor performers and reward superior performance outcomes as measured by TRI. TRI-generated transparency thus unleashes, strengthens, and exploits multiple pressures, all tending to push in the direction of continuous improvement as facilities and firms endeavor to leapfrog over their peers to receive credit for larger improvements or superior performance. . . .

Conventional approaches to environmental regulation are nearing a dead end, limited by the capacity of regulators to acquire the information necessary to set regulatory standards and keep pace with rapid changes in knowledge, technology, and environmental conditions. A pervasive information bottleneck constrains the extent, effectiveness, efficiency, and responsiveness of the regulatory system.

. . . Many leading advocates of market-based reforms explicitly recognize that the problems of conventional command regulation stem largely from the inability of the regulator to acquire sufficient information. But upon closer examination, market-based substitutes turn out to suffer from similar information problems, limiting their usefulness as a corrective. . . .

Neither conventional regulation nor tradeable permits are inherently well-suited to institutional learning and adaptation to new information. Both approaches presume that, by amassing sufficient scientific and technical information prior to setting the regulatory standard, the regulator can get the right standard the first time, essentially making a permanent judgment as to the appropriate level of pollution. If conventional regulations are based on erroneous judgments or produce unintended consequences, they can be suspended or modified, tightened or relaxed, either as a formal matter or de facto, by adjusting the pace and stringency of the enforcement effort. But these adjustments are slow, painful, cumbersome, and costly to both regulators and regulated entities, and they occur infrequently. This places a heavy burden on the regulator to "get it right" the first time so as to avoid having to make costly corrections, further raising the information bar to regulation in the first instance, and slowing the pace of regulatory change. . . .

How can simple information disclosure like that required under TRI drive improvements in pollution performance? After all, the skeptic might regard TRI as the quintessential "paperwork" requirement—the only formal demand it makes of the regulated entity is the production and disclosure of information. Although firms have flexibility to choose their own improvement targets, why should they bother to do so at all? How, in other words, can TRI spur firms to reduce pollution?

. . . TRI works by establishing an objective, quantifiable, standardized (and therefore comparable), and broadly accessible metric that transforms the firm's understanding of its own environmental performance, while facilitating unprecedented levels of transparency and accountability. Firms and facilities are compelled to self-monitor and, therefore, to "confront disagreeable realities" concerning their environmental performance "in detail and early on," even prior to the onset of market, community, or regulatory reactions to the information they are required to make public. Simultaneously, they are subjected to the scrutiny of a variety of external parties, including investors, community residents, and regulators, any of whom may desire improved environmental performance and exert powerful pressures on poor performers to up-grade their performance as measured by the TRI yardstick.

NOTES AND QUESTIONS

1. According to Professor Karkkainen, how does the TRI represent an improvement over conventional statutory reporting requirements in terms of the kinds of information it will generate? How will the reporting requirements of EPCRA yield improved environmental performance rather than just increased information to the government and the public?

2. *The Toxic Release Inventory.* The most widely publicized reporting program under the EPCRA is the §313 annual toxic chemical release reporting requirement. Each facility subject to §313 must submit to EPA annual reports describing each toxic chemical on a list published by EPA that was manufactured, processed, or otherwise used at the facility during the preceding calendar year in quantities exceeding the threshold quantities designated pursuant to §313(f). The first annual Toxic Release Inventory (TRI) compiled by EPA covered reports filed by 18,500 companies on releases of 329 chemicals to the environment in 1987. These companies released 10.4 billion pounds of toxic substances—2.7 billion pounds were emitted into the air, 3.9 billion pounds to landfills and pits, and 3.3 billion pounds to treatment and disposal facilities. In 2004, by comparison, the total amount of toxic chemicals released into the environment in the United States by the 23,600 facilities in the TRI database was about 4.2 billion pounds. The largest contributor was the metal mining sector (1.1 billion pounds). Hazardous waste and solvent recovery facilities reported releases of 195 million pounds, while electric utilities were responsible for 16 million pounds. 37 Env't Rep. (BNA) 803 (2006).

Section 313(d) of the EPCRA authorizes EPA to add chemicals to or delete chemicals from the TRI list. In Troy Corp. v. Browner, 120 F.3d 277 (D.C. Cir.), *rehearing denied*, 129 F.3d 1200 (D.C. Cir. 1997), the court upheld in large part the addition of 286 chemicals to the TRI under §313(d)(2)(B). It rejected the contention that the statute requires EPA to consider the likelihood of human exposure to listed chemicals that pose risks of chronic adverse effects. Why might EPA choose not to consider exposure? Would the result be the same if EPA were considering listing a substance under §313(d)(2)(A)? See also Fertilizer Inst. v. Browner, 163 F.3d 774 (3d Cir. 1998) (upholding listing of nitrate compounds based on long-term consequences of exposure rather than long-term exposure). In Dayton Power & Light Co., 44 F. Supp. 2d 356 (D.D.C. 1999), the court upheld an EPA regulation that requires TRI reporting by electricity-generating facilities that combust coal or oil to generate power. It did not matter that the companies did not manufacture or otherwise use toxic chemicals to manufacture products. The release of TRI chemicals found in the coal and oil during the production of electricity was sufficient to justify listing.

In American Chemistry Council v. Johnson, 406 F.3d 738 (D.C. Cir. 2005), a chemical industry association challenged EPA's denial of its petition to remove methyl ethyl ketone (MEK) from the TRI list. Exposure to MEK itself (which is a volatile organic compound) does not cause adverse health effects. Rather, MEK is a precursor to the formation of tropospheric ozone, which is known to cause adverse health effects. The court agreed with the association that EPA should delete MEK from the TRI list. It characterized the issue as whether a chemical may meet the "chronic health effects" requirement of §313(d)(2)(B) or the "significant adverse effect on the environment" requirement of §313(d)(2)(C) on the basis of its contribution to the formation of tropospheric ozone. The court held that the answer is no; a chemical may not be listed solely on the basis of its contribution to the creation of a toxic chemical. At a minimum, a chemical must cause harm via exposure to be toxic to qualify for listing.

TRI release forms are available publicly (except for protected trade secrets), §§313(h)-(j), 322(a)(1), (2)(A), (b), and environmental groups have seen that the press is fully informed. Does the decline in annual releases since 1987 indicate that public dissemination of information on releases has induced reporting companies to reduce the volumes of their releases, perhaps out of fear of adverse publicity? Should statutory disclosure requirements substitute for some or all of the regulations designed to control the manufacture and use of toxic substances discussed in the preceding sections of this chapter?

3. *Other Reporting Requirements under the EPCRA.* Under §302 of the EPCRA, EPA must publish a list of extremely hazardous substances. If a release of one of those substances in an amount above reportable quantities under CERCLA occurs at a facility at which the chemical is produced, used, or stored, the facility must notify the local emergency planning committee in the affected area. §304(a)(1), (b). In Huls Am., Inc. v. Browner, 83 F.3d 445 (D.C. Cir. 1996), the petitioner argued that EPA improperly denied its petition under §302(a)(4) to remove isophorone diisocyanate (IPDI) from the list of extremely hazardous substances. Huls argued that by focusing primarily upon one factor, toxicity, in deciding that IPDI should remain on the emergency hazardous substances list, EPA improperly ignored the other factors set forth in the statute, which include reactivity, volatility, dispersibility, combustibility, and flammability. The court upheld the reasonableness of EPA's view that it need not consider all of the factors in every case. What single word in §302(a)(4) supports that holding? Huls also argued that EPA acted arbitrarily by relying on toxicity data derived from animal tests conducted by the National Institute of Occupational Safety and Health (NIOSH) because it extrapolated the NIOSH data from animal studies conducted under extreme conditions that were unlikely to occur in reality and bore no relationship to the accidental releases addressed by §304. The court characterized the validity of extrapolation of the results of toxicity tests conducted at high concentrations as the type of technical question that merits deference.

4. *State Disclosure Laws.* States such as California and New Jersey have imposed additional disclosure requirements on businesses and landowners involved with toxic materials. California's Safe Drinking Water and Toxic Enforcement Act of 1986 (Proposition 65), Cal. Health and Safety Code §§25180.7,

25249.5-25249.13, forbids any business from knowingly and intentionally exposing any individual to a chemical known to the state to cause cancer or reproductive toxicity without first giving a clear and reasonable warning. §25249.6. Businesses may satisfy their obligations by labeling consumer products and posting or publishing notices, provided that the warnings are clear and reasonable. §25249.11(f). In Ingredient Commc'n Council, Inc. v. Lungren, 4 Cal. Rptr. 2d 216 (Cal. App. 1992), the court held that a court determining the adequacy of a warning method may review its effectiveness in operation.

Proposition 65 exempts from the warning requirements any exposure that "poses no significant risk assuming lifetime exposure at the level in question for substances known to the state to cause cancer . . . based on evidence and standards of comparable scientific validity to the evidence which form the scientific basis for the listing of such chemical. . . ." Cal. Health and Safety Code §25249.10(c). In Baxter Healthcare Corp. v. Denton, 15 Cal. Rptr. 3d 430 (Cal. Ct. App. 2004), the court upheld a trial court's finding that a chemical plasticizer used in medical devices qualified for the exemption because a preponderance of the evidence demonstrated that, even though it was undisputed that the plasticizer causes liver cancer in rats and mice, the biological mechanism by which it causes liver cancer in laboratory animals does not function in humans.

Rechtschaffen, The Warning Game: Evaluating Warnings under California's Proposition 65, 23 Ecology L.Q. 303 (1996), contends that Proposition 65 "has had mixed success in realizing its underlying statutory goals of providing individuals with sufficient information to make meaningful choices and reducing exposure to toxic chemicals." Id. at 306-307. He argues that the program has not succeeded in promoting informed choice, in part because inadequate implementing regulations have allowed businesses to provide vague and uninformative warnings that consumers are likely to ignore. But the statute has encouraged product reformulation through the use of substitute chemicals, and concerns over negative publicity have helped to reduce toxic air emissions and other environmental exposures. In sum, Proposition 65 "is an excellent illustration of the important contribution that information disclosure laws can make to protect the environment," although the author makes eight specific recommendations for enhancing the statute's utility.[*]

Do the EPCRA and California's Proposition 65 reflect the same approach? Consider the following:

> What drives Proposition 65 is a background liability rule that leads polluting firms to welcome fixed regulatory standards as a relatively more palatable alternative and, consequently, to produce the risk assessment information upon which the regulatory standard-setting enterprise depends. While Proposition 65 may induce close self-monitoring on the part of polluting firms to ensure that their activities do not exceed thresholds that might expose them to Proposition 65 liability, it does not produce a TRI-like stream of generally available and comparable performance data. Consequently, it does not promote the kinds of performance monitoring, bench marking, and transparency that are so central to TRI's operative success. It is the latter, TRI-inspired approach

[*]See also Rechtschaffen, How to Reduce Lead Exposures with One Simple Statute: The Experience of Proposition 65, 29 Envtl. L. Rep. (ELI) 10581 (1999) (contending that information disclosure has been more effective than traditional federal regulatory programs at inducing reformulation of products to include less lead) ; Rechtschaffen & Williams, The Continued Success of Proposition 65 in Reducing Toxic Exposures, 35 Envtl. L. Rep. (ELI) 10850 (2005) (examining product reformulations caused by enforcement of Proposition 65's warning requirements).

that appears from this vantage point to hold the greater potential to change the face of environmental regulation. [Karkkainen, *supra*, at 347.]

5. *Mandatory Disclosure and National Security Concerns.* The public dissemination of information about industrial chemical use creates a risk that information about the whereabouts and content of dangerous chemicals could become available to potential terrorists. In the Chemical Safety Information, Site Security and Fuels Regulatory Relief Act, Pub. L. No. 106-40, 113 Stat. 207 (1999), Congress required that EPA assess the increased risk of terrorist and other criminal activity associated with the posting on the Internet or the compilation in government electronic databases of information contained in risk management plans filed under §112(r) of the Clean Air Act relating to an evaluation of worst-case release scenarios. Based on that assessment, EPA must issue regulations concerning the management of that information so as to minimize the risk of terrorist and criminal activity by restricting access to the information. Following the terrorist attacks of September 11, 2001, some federal agencies, including EPA, removed information from their websites due to fear that its continuing availability could pose national security risks.

The debate that surrounded the establishment of a new federal homeland security agency highlighted the potential clash between promoting the public's right to know about the location and extent of the risks of exposure to toxic materials and the desire to diminish access to that kind of potentially sensitive information to prevent its improper use. In the Homeland Security Act of 2002, Pub. L. No. 107-296, 116 Stat. 2135, Congress addressed the balance by creating a new exception to the Freedom of Information Act. Section 214(a) of the 2002 statute provides that, notwithstanding any other provision of law, "critical infrastructure information" that is voluntarily submitted to the Department of Homeland Security for use by that agency regarding the security of critical infrastructure is exempt from disclosure under the FOIA. In addition, such information may not, without the written consent of the submitter, be used by the Department, by any other federal, state, or local agency, or by any third party in any civil action arising under federal or state law if the information is submitted in good faith. The Act defines "critical infrastructure information" in part to mean "information not customarily in the public domain and related to the security of critical infrastructure," but it does not define critical infrastructure. A submission is "voluntary" if it occurs in the absence of the Department of Homeland Security's exercise of legal authority to compel access to or submission of that information. Environmental groups feared that the 2002 Act could provide incentives for some regulated entities to voluntarily submit information concerning violations of environmental laws in order to preclude the use of that information to support government or private enforcement action. The 2002 Act does not purport to limit the ability of state or federal agencies or third parties to obtain critical infrastructure information lawfully and properly disclosed to the public and to use that information in any manner permitted by law.

6. *Assessment of EPCRA.* For an assessment of the EPCRA asserting that it has failed to inform low-income communities of color about local environmental risks, see Durham-Hammer, Left to Wonder: Reevaluating, Reforming, and Implementing the Emergency Planning and Community Right-to-Know Act of 1986, 29 Colum. J. Envtl. L. 323 (2004).

F.   PREVENTING HARM FROM HAZARDOUS WASTE

Human and environmental exposure to chemical wastes creates the same kinds of risks as those considered in previous sections of this chapter. Chemical wastes may explode, ignite, or bring instant death from inhalation of their fumes during generation, treatment, storage, transportation, or disposal processes. More often, they work incrementally, like other toxic substances, revealing their effects over longer periods. Human exposure occurs via direct contact with the skin, inhalation, or ingestion of contaminated drinking water and food. Potential adverse health impacts range from acute and chronic damage to the respiratory, nervous, alimentary, and urological systems to cancer, birth defects, and permanent genetic impairment. Environmental disruption can range from the instant death of exposed plant and animal life to long-term disruption of ecological systems.

Chemical waste dumps probably account for a large degree of the popular consciousness of the risks created by improper hazardous waste management. These dumps result from the accumulation, often over a period of years or decades, of large quantities of dangerous residues on generators' premises or at sites to which the wastes have been transported. Although the wastes result largely from industrial processes, they also may include infectious organic materials from hospitals and scientific laboratories. As time passes, storage containers, ponds, and burial grounds are adversely affected by corrosion, breakage, natural processes, and acts of vandalism, so that the waste material disperses in ground and surface waters, soil, and the air.

The Love Canal dump site near Niagara Falls, New York, illustrates the problem. Until the early 1940s, the Hooker Chemical Company used a mile-long, abandoned hydroelectric canal about 40 feet deep and 20 yards wide as a dump for wastes from its operations. The wastes included benzene, PCBs, and pesticides. After Hooker abandoned and bulldozed the site, it sold it in 1953 to the Niagara Falls Board of Education for one dollar. The Board promptly built a school and playground in the middle of the site, and over one hundred residences were built near the school. Health problems eventually began to plague residents of the area, even though dumping had ceased decades earlier. The afflictions included cancer; spontaneous abortion; malformed fetal organ systems; and skin, neurological, kidney, and liver disorders. In 1977, chemicals that had "floated up" on water from heavy rains and snows that had accumulated for several years in the clay-lined canal appeared in residents' basements. See M. Brown, Laying Waste (1980). The resulting publicity was a crucial impetus for the adoption of CERCLA, discussed in the next chapter.

Although the federal Clean Air Act and Clean Water Act are discussed in detail in Chapters 6 and 7, the special provisions for hazardous emissions and effluents considered there also place them conceptually among the legislative measures that Congress has adopted for regulating hazardous wastes. The bulk of this section plows new ground; it is devoted to a study of the regulation of the management of hazardous waste under the Resource Conservation and Recovery Act (RCRA).

1. Regulation of Hazardous Air Pollutants under the Clean Air Act

[See Chapter 6, section I.1.]

2. Regulation of Toxic Water Pollutants under the Clean Water Act

[See Chapter 7, section D.]

3. Regulation of Hazardous Waste Management under the Resource Conservation and Recovery Act

a. Introduction to the Management of Hazardous Waste

Each year millions of tons of hazardous waste are generated in the United States by large industrial facilities such as chemical manufacturers, electroplating companies, petroleum refineries, and by smaller businesses such as dry cleaners, auto repair shops, hospitals, exterminators, and photo-processing centers. The hazardous waste disposal problem is largely a groundwater protection problem. Groundwater trapped in underground aquifers supplies one-quarter of all fresh water used in the United States. The "most pernicious" consequence of land disposal is that improperly maintained waste sites have caused many drinking water wells to be closed. H.R. Rep. No. 94-1491, at 89 (1976). Careless waste disposal has caused the loss of millions of dollars' worth of usable groundwater.

NOTE ON POLLUTION PREVENTION

There are three basic strategies for minimizing the risks created by hazardous wastes: (1) treatment, storage, or disposal; (2) process changes, to reduce waste stream volume; and (3) resource recovery (e.g., recycling). To date, Congress has relied mostly on the first strategy. It has assumed that little can be done to reduce the volume of waste generated if we want to preserve the benefits of the chemical era. Further, Congress has chosen to avoid mandating the adoption of the specific technologies used in resource recovery. Many policymakers now agree that the second and third strategies represent the best long-term options.

Despite their focus on waste management, both Congress and EPA have recognized the force of the argument that it is better to prevent the generation of waste in the first place than to control how waste is managed. In 1990, Congress enacted the Pollution Prevention Act (PPA), 42 U.S.C. §§13101-13109. The Act declares it to be the national policy to prevent or reduce pollution at the source whenever feasible, to recycle in an environmentally sound manner pollution that cannot be prevented, and to dispose of or release pollution into the environment only as a last resort. §13101(b). The PPA requires that EPA establish a pollution prevention office, authorizes it to make matching grants to states to promote the use of source reduction techniques by businesses, and expands its authority to collect data to better track source reduction activities. §§13103-13107.

EPA published its Pollution Prevention Strategy in 1991. 56 Fed. Reg. 7849. The agency cited studies showing that pollution prevention can be the most effective way to reduce risks, as well as the most cost-efficient; pollution prevention therefore harmonizes environmental protection and economic efficiency. EPA announced its intention to work with industry to achieve reasonable prevention goals (such as a 50 percent reduction in environmental releases) by assisting in the identification of opportunities to profit from prevention. It also stated that a strong regulatory and enforcement program under existing statutory authorities is necessary to provide further incentives to prevent pollution. EPA therefore would build pollution prevention principles into its regulatory programs. EPA deemed pollution prevention to be critical to overcoming some of the limitations in traditional approaches to pollution control, such as the use of treatment technologies that solve one pollution problem while creating a new one in a different medium.

> Air pollution control devices or industrial wastewater treatment plants prevent wastes from going into the air or water, but the toxic ash and sludge that these systems produce can become hazardous waste problems themselves. Wastes disposed of on the land or in deep wells may contaminate ground water, and evaporation from ponds and lagoons can convert solid or liquid wastes into air pollution problems. . . . While cross-media connections are complex and difficult to manage, part of the solution should be to reduce or even eliminate pollution at the source. Prevention reduces emissions, discharges or wastes released to all parts of the ecosystem, thereby eliminating a potential cross-media "shell-game." [Id. at 7853.]

Pollution prevention also could help to address the problems caused by dispersed sources such as nonpoint sources of water pollution for which treatment technologies may not be practical or economical.

Neither the Act nor EPA's pollution prevention strategy have yet generated any significant litigation, but the courts have cited the statute and the strategy in interpreting other statutes. In Monsanto Co. v. EPA, 19 F.3d 1201 (7th Cir. 1994), the company petitioned for review of EPA's denial of its request for additional time to comply with national emission standards for hazardous air pollutants issued under §112 of the Clean Air Act. EPA granted Monsanto a two-year extension under §112(c)(1)(B)(ii) to allow the company to install water-scrubbing equipment designed to satisfy the standard. When the equipment did not work as well as anticipated, Monsanto requested an additional extension so that it could install a secondary filtration system to catch harmful emissions not captured by the primary system. EPA denied this second request, but the court found the denial to be contrary to the PPA and EPA's own pollution prevention strategy because it would induce companies to adopt a "quick fix" solution that would change the form of the problem (by removing the environmental hazard from the air but creating a hazardous waste disposal problem) rather than eliminate it. If a company like Monsanto has a choice between two control strategies, EPA may grant a waiver for a pollution prevention strategy even if that strategy would take slightly longer to implement than the less desirable strategy.

Although RCRA, to which we turn next, focuses primarily on traditional techniques for regulating hazardous waste management, it also reflects the application of pollution prevention principles. RCRA requires that all generators of hazardous waste certify in the manifest that must accompany shipments of hazardous waste that they have established a program to reduce the volume or toxicity of their waste to the extent economically practicable. §3002(b)(1). In addition, if a generator wishes to receive a permit for the treatment, storage, or disposal of hazardous waste on the premises where the waste is generated, it must provide an annual certification that such a program is in place. §3005(h)(1).*

b.   A Summary of RCRA

Local, state, and federal law have controlled hazardous wastes piecemeal for decades. The techniques included public nuisance laws and emergency health measures, although a few states have adopted more comprehensive legislation. Tort suits also acted as a deterrent to negligent hazardous waste management. In the 1970s, however, the inadequacy of these predominantly local or stopgap strategies prompted Congress to adopt the Solid Waste Disposal Act, better known as the Resource Conservation and Recovery Act (RCRA), 42 U.S.C. §§6901-6991i, which is the focus of the remainder of this section.

RCRA distinguishes between nonhazardous solid waste and hazardous waste, each of which is subject to a separate regulatory program. Subtitle D authorizes EPA to establish guidelines for regulation of nonhazardous solid waste disposal facilities by the states. As it was initially adopted, Subtitle D envisioned federal financial and technical assistance to the states, with a minimal federal regulatory presence. Subtitle C, on the other hand, which addresses hazardous waste, represents perhaps the furthest developed application of the regulatory paradigm for pollution control. EPA has promulgated several thousand pages of regulations under Subtitle C. As a result, environmental practitioners in this field must immerse themselves in a regulatory exegesis. Frankly, the experience is not for everyone.

Touted as a comprehensive, "cradle to grave" system, RCRA provides for the listing of certain specific wastes as hazardous and the identification of characteristics that subject nonlisted wastes to the regulatory scheme of Subtitle C. Hazardous waste generators must comply with recordkeeping, reporting, and container labeling requirements, as well as assist federal and state regulators in tracking the movement of hazardous waste through the preparation of written manifests to accompany waste shipments. Waste transporters must abide by regulatory standards issued under the Hazardous Materials Transportation Uniform Safety Act as well as RCRA. The most extensive controls apply to entities engaged in the treatment, storage, or disposal of hazardous waste (TSD facilities). These entities may not operate without a permit, which requires compliance with performance standards for location, design, construction, operation, closure, and post-closure care. RCRA bars or severely restricts the extent to which certain untreated hazardous wastes may be disposed of on land. Anyone violating these requirements is subject to the usual array of civil and criminal sanctions. As it has in other environmental statutes, Congress has authorized the states to run their own hazardous waste regulatory programs, so long as they satisfy or exceed minimum EPA requirements. The states may adopt more stringent requirements than those contained in RCRA or EPA implementing regulations. See, e.g., Secured Envtl. Mgmt., Inc. v. Texas Natural Res. Conservation Comm'n, 97 S.W.3d 246

---

*See generally Guidance to Hazardous Waste Generators on the Elements of a Waste Minimization Program, 58 Fed. Reg. 31,114 (1993); Ochsner, Pollution Prevention: An Overview of Regulatory Incentives and Barriers, 6 N.Y.U. Envtl. L.J. 586 (1998); Strasser, Cleaner Technology, Pollution Prevention and Environmental Regulation, 9 Fordham Envtl. L.J. 1 (1997) (urging adoption of multimedia approach to regulation to encourage pollution prevention).

TABLE 8-4
Summary of EPA's Regulatory Authority under Subtitle C of RCRA

Source of Regulatory Authority	Nature of Regulatory Authority
§3001	Identify and list hazardous wastes
§3002	Promulgate standards applicable to hazardous waste generators "as may be necessary to protect human health and the environment"
§3003	Promulgate standards applicable to hazardous waste transporters "as may be necessary to protect human health and the environment"
§3004	Promulgate performance standards applicable to facilities that treat, store, or dispose of hazardous waste (TSD facilities) "as may be necessary to protect human health and the environment" Implement land disposal restrictions (LDRs) on particular hazardous wastes Issue treatment standards for hazardous wastes subject to LDRs Require corrective action for releases of hazardous wastes or their constituents
§3005	Require permits for TSD facilities Issue TSD facility permits
§3006	Authorize states to issue TSD facility permits
§3007	Inspect and obtain samples from sources that generate, transport, treat, store, or dispose of hazardous waste
§3008	Pursue civil or criminal enforcement of Subtitle C

(Tex. App. 2002) (prohibiting disposal of hazardous waste in salt dome formations). Table 8-4 provides a summary of EPA's authority to implement Subtitle C of RCRA.

As the statute's name suggests, RCRA is designed to encourage the recovery of useful materials through process substitution and properly conducted recycling and reuse, thereby minimizing the amount of waste generated, as well as to ensure the proper management of hazardous waste. §1003(a)(4), (6). The Act declares a national policy of reducing or eliminating the generation of hazardous waste as expeditiously as possible, "wherever feasible," and of managing waste that is nevertheless generated in a manner that minimizes threats to health and the environment. §1003(b). Although these objectives seem complementary in theory, in practice there is considerable tension between them.

c. Distinguishing Waste from Useful Materials: Legitimate versus Sham Recycling

The potential for activities that increase reuse to thwart the statute's safe management objective has manifested itself in EPA's efforts to define what constitutes a waste. Neither Subtitle C nor Subtitle D applies to materials unless they qualify as solid wastes. (Hazardous wastes are a subset of solid wastes. See §1004(5)). Whether a material is or is not a waste is probably the single most perplexing question raised by RCRA. Resolution of that question is the crucial determinant of the statute's scope. The statute defines solid waste in §1004(27). EPA's definition, located at 40 C.F.R. §261.2, is considerably more complex, if not convoluted. The following case reviews some of the history of EPA's interpretation of the parameters of the term "solid waste."

OWEN ELECTRIC STEEL CO. OF SOUTH CAROLINA, INC. v. BROWNER
37 F.3d 146 (4th Cir. 1994)

RUSSELL, Circuit Judge:

The sole issue in this case is whether the "slag" produced by petitioner Owen Electric Steel Company ("Owen") at its Cayce, South Carolina, facility as a byproduct of steel production is "discarded," and therefore constitutes a "solid waste" under 42 U.S.C. §6903(27). . . .

. . . Owen is engaged in the production of steel. The steel is produced in an electric arc furnace. In the course of production, crushed limestone (calcium carbonate) is added to the furnace to remove certain non-ferrous constituents from the molten metal. In this process, the non-ferrous constituents bind with the limestone, creating "slag," which is essentially limestone and dolomite (magnesium carbonate) with trace amounts of metallic oxides. The slag then floats to the surface of the molten metal and is removed.

The slag is continuously processed at the Owen's plant. . . . Following processing, the slag is placed in holding bays, where the slag lies on bare soil for tempering and weathering. During this process, known as "curing," the slag is hydrated and undergoes phase changes where its bulk increases volumetrically. This curing process generally takes six months. After this time, the slag becomes dimensionally stable and, as a result, amenable for use as a construction aggregate. The slag generated at Owen's Cayce facility is sold to the construction industry for use as a road base material or for other commercial purposes. . . .

[RCRA requires that an operator of a facility that treats, stores, or disposes of hazardous wastes (a TSD facility, or TSDF) obtain a permit from EPA or an authorized state. Owen applied for and received a TSDF permit for its Cayce facility. The permit identified the slag processing area (SPA) as a solid waste management unit (SWMU). Owen protested that classification and petitioned for review when EPA adhered to its original determination.]

We must determine whether the EPA properly classified the SPA as an SWMU. . . . The legislative history . . . unequivocally states: "[T]he term 'solid waste management unit' [in amended RCRA §3004] is used to reaffirm the Administrator's responsibility to examine all units at [a TSDF] from which hazardous constituents might migrate, irrespective of whether the units were intended for the management of solid and/or hazardous waste." H.R. Rep. No. 98-198, pt. 1, at 60 (1983). Accordingly, in order to conclude that the SPA is an SWMU, the EPA need only find that Owen's slag is a "solid waste" [under §1004(27)].

. . . At issue is whether Owen's slag constitutes "other discarded material." Owen argues that its slag is not a "discarded material" because it is ultimately recycled and used in roadbeds. EPA counters that, because the slag lies dormant, exposed, on the ground for six months before such use, it is discarded even if it is later "picked up" and used in another capacity. . . .

A series of cases have addressed the meaning of "discarded material." In American Mining Cong. v. EPA, 824 F.2d 1177 (D.C. Cir. 1987) ("*AMC I*"), the District of Columbia Circuit was faced with the question of

> whether, in light of [Congress's] expressly stated objectives and the underlying problems that motivated it to enact RCRA in the first instance, Congress was using the term "discarded" in its ordinary sense—"disposed of" or "abandoned"—or whether Congress was using it in a much more open-ended way, so as to encompass materials no longer useful in their original capacity though destined for immediate reuse in another phase of the industry's ongoing production process.

Id. at 1185. The court of appeals settled upon the former option, emphasizing that it found the statutory language unambiguous. The court observed that the legislative history and policies underlying RCRA supported its conclusion. In the court's opinion, only materials that are "disposed of" or "abandoned" "become part of the waste disposal problem," id. at 1186, with which RCRA is concerned.

Were *AMC I* the final case offering interpretation of the phrase "discarded material," Owen might be victorious here: because Owen's slag is eventually recycled, it cannot be said to have been discarded. Subsequent cases, however, have read *AMC I* narrowly. First, in American Petroleum Inst. v. EPA, 906 F.2d 729 (D.C. Cir. 1990), the EPA asserted that the District of Columbia Circuit's holding in *AMC I* precluded it from regulating as waste hazardous slag that was delivered to a plant for metal reclamation. The court of appeals held otherwise, explaining:

> The issue in AMC [I] was whether the EPA could, under the RCRA, treat as "solid wastes" "materials that are recycled and reused in an *ongoing* manufacturing or industrial process." [AMC I, 824 F.2d at 1186.] We held that it could not because
>
> > [t]hese materials have not yet become part of the waste disposal problem; rather, *they are destined for beneficial reuse or recycling in a continuous process by the generating industry itself.*
>
> Id. Materials subject to such a process were not "discarded" because they were never "disposed of, abandoned, or thrown away."
>
> AMC [I] is by no means dispositive of EPA's authority to regulate K061 slag. Unlike the materials in question in AMC [I], K061 is indisputably "discarded" *before* being subject to metals reclamation. Consequently, it *has* "become part of the waste disposal problem."

American Petroleum Inst., 906 F.2d at 741 (emphasis provided by the *American Petroleum Inst.* court).

Next, in American Mining Cong. v. EPA, 907 F.2d 1179 (D.C. Cir. 1990) ("*AMC II*"), petitioners, relying on *AMC I*, claimed that three hazardous wastes were not solid wastes on the basis that "sludges [containing the wastes] from wastewater that are stored in surface impoundments and that *may* at some time in the future be reclaimed are not 'discarded'." AMC II, 907 F.2d at 1186 (emphasis in original). The court of appeals rejected petitioners' reading of *AMC I*, stating:

> Petitioners read AMC [I] too broadly. AMC [I]'s holding concerned only materials that are "destined for *immediate reuse* in another phase of the industry's ongoing production process," and that "have not yet become part of the waste disposal problem." Nothing in

AMC [I] prevents the agency from treating as "discarded" the wastes at issue in this case, which are managed in land disposal units that *are* part of wastewater treatment systems, which have therefore become "part of the waste disposal problem," and which are not part of the ongoing industrial processes.

Finally, in United States v. ILCO, Inc., 996 F.2d 1126 (11th Cir. 1993), ILCO, Inc. ("ILCO") purchased spent batteries from various sources and then recycled them. ILCO contended that, because it recycled the spent batteries, they had not been discarded and, therefore, were not solid waste. The Eleventh Circuit rejected this argument, stating:

> ILCO argues that it has never "discarded" the plates and groups [of the batteries] and, therefore, the material it recycles is not "solid waste" as defined in §6903(27). The lead plates and groups are, no doubt, valuable feedstock for a smelting process. Nevertheless, EPA, with congressional authority, promulgated regulations that classify these materials as "discarded solid waste." *Somebody* has discarded the battery in which these components are found. This fact does not change just because a reclaimer has purchased or finds value in the components.[4]

From these cases, we glean that the fundamental inquiry in determining whether a byproduct has been "discarded" is whether the byproduct is *immediately* recycled for use in the same industry; if not, then the byproduct is justifiably seen as "part of the waste disposal problem," AMC I, 824 F.2d at 1186, and therefore as a "solid waste." We think it reasonable and permissible . . . for the EPA to adhere to this inquiry in determining whether a material is "discarded."

Moreover, we find no abuse of discretion in EPA's conclusion that, under this interpretation, Owen's slag constitutes "discarded material" and therefore "solid waste." The slag is not immediately used in Owen's production process; rather, the slag must sit, untouched, for some six months before it is sold to other entities. The EPA is justified in finding that, where a byproduct sits untouched for six months, it cannot be said that the material was *"never* 'disposed of, abandoned, or thrown away.'" *American Petroleum Inst.*, 906 F.2d at 741 (emphasis added) (quoting AMC I, 824 F.2d at 1193). The EPA is also justified to conclude that, because the slag is sold to others for use in roadbed construction, it is not "destined for beneficial reuse or recycling in a continuous process by the generating industry itself," AMC I, 824 F.2d at 1186. In short, the EPA did not abuse its discretion in concluding that Owen's slag is "part of the waste disposal problem." . . .

We conclude that Owen's slag is "solid waste" and that, therefore, the SPA was appropriately determined to be an SWMU. Owen's petition for relief is therefore denied.

---

4. . . . The crucial element of the Eleventh Circuit's reasoning is that the batteries became, in the words of *AMC I*, "part of the waste disposal problem," as soon as the various owners of the batteries discarded them. That ILCO, a third party, then agreed to recycle the batteries, thereby, at least in some sense, ameliorating the waste disposal problem, is irrelevant in the sense that that subsequent act does not divest the EPA of jurisdiction over the waste. In other words, once the batteries were discarded they became classified as solid waste; subsequent treatment is irrelevant.

NOTES AND QUESTIONS

1. What is the "ordinary sense" of the terms "disposed of" and "abandoned"? How did the *AMC I* court appear to interpret those terms? How long after generation may the agency properly regard a material as a waste under that approach? When does a material generated by a production process become "part of the waste disposal problem"? How did the decisions in *American Petroleum Inst.* and *AMC II* alter the inquiry? Had Owen used its slag in one of its own production processes, would the result in the principal case have been different?

2. *The Regulatory Definition of a Solid Waste.* EPA's RCRA regulations define a "solid waste" as follows:

§261.2   *Definition of Solid Waste*

(a)(1) A *solid waste* is any discarded material that is not excluded by §261.4(a).[a] . . .

(2) A *discarded material* is any material which is:

(i) *Abandoned*, as explained in paragraph (b) of this section; or

(ii) *Recycled*,[b] as explained in paragraph (c) of this section; or

(iii) Considered *inherently waste-like*, as explained in paragraph (d) of this section; . . .

(b) Materials are solid waste if they are *abandoned* by being:

(1) Disposed of; or

(2) Burned or incinerated; or

(3) Accumulated, stored, or treated (but not recycled) before or in lieu of being abandoned by being disposed of, burned, or incinerated.

(c) Materials are solid wastes if they are *recycled*—or accumulated, stored, or treated before recycling—as specified in paragraphs (c)(1) through (c)(4) of this section.

(1) *Used in a manner constituting disposal.*[c]

(2) *Burning for energy recovery.*

(3) *Reclaimed.*[d]

(4) *Accumulated speculatively.* . . .

(d) *Inherently waste-like materials.* The following are solid wastes when they are recycled in any manner [which are listed as such in the regulations].

a. Section 261.4 provides that certain materials "are not solid wastes" for purposes of Subtitle C, including domestic sewage, industrial wastewater discharges that are point source discharges subject to regulation under the Clean Water Act's NPDES permit program, irrigation return flows, certain nuclear material regulated under the Atomic Energy Act, and materials subjected to in-situ mining techniques which are not removed from the ground as part of the extraction process. Finally, §261.4(a)(8) excludes from the definition of a solid waste certain "secondary materials that are reclaimed and returned to the original process or processes in which they were generated where they are reused in the production process."

b. Section 261.1(c)(7) provides that "[a] material is 'recycled' if it is used, reused, or reclaimed."

c. This includes materials that are "[a]pplied to or placed on the land in a manner that constitutes disposal" or "[u]sed to produce products that are applied to or placed on the land or are otherwise contained in products that are applied to or placed on the land (in which cases the product itself remains a solid waste)." §261.2(c)(1)(i).

d. Section 261.1(c)(4) provides that "[a] material is 'reclaimed' if it is processed to recover a usable product, or if it is regenerated. Examples are recovery of lead values from spent batteries and regeneration of spent solvents."

(e) *Materials that are not solid waste when recycled.*
    (1) Materials are not solid wastes when they can be shown to be recycled by being:
        (i) Used or reused[e] as ingredients in an industrial process to make a product, provided the materials are not being reclaimed; or
        (ii) Used or reused as effective substitutes for commercial products; or
        (iii) Returned to the original process from which they are generated, without first being reclaimed or land disposed. The material must be returned as a substitute for feedstock materials. In cases where the original process to which the material is returned is a secondary process, the materials must be managed such that there is no placement on the land. . . .
    (2) The following materials are solid wastes, even if the recycling involves use, reuse, or return to the original process (described in paragraphs (e)(1)(i)-(iii) of this section):
        (i) Materials used in a manner constituting disposal, or used to produce products that are applied to the land; or
        (ii) Materials burned for energy recovery, used to produce a fuel, or contained in fuels; or
        (iii) Materials accumulated speculatively;[f] or
        (iv) Materials listed in paragraphs (d)(1) and (d)(2) of this section.

Should the materials involved in *Owen Elec.* or any of the cases cited in that opinion have qualified for exclusion from regulation under §261.4(a)(8)? Why do you think EPA defined solid waste in §261.2(c) to include some recycled materials? Doesn't RCRA seek to encourage the processing of material that would otherwise be waste to recover usable products? What effect will designation of such materials as solid wastes have on companies contemplating such recovery efforts? What is the function of §261.2(e)(1) and (2)? Do these provisions seem circular to you? Is there any escape from this regulatory morass?

AMERICAN PETROLEUM INSTITUTE v. EPA (*API II*)
216 F.3d 50 (D.C. Cir. 2000)

Before: WILLIAMS, SENTELLE and ROGERS, Circuit Judges . . .
PER CURIAM:

[Petroleum refiners, including the American Petroleum Institute (API), and petrochemical manufacturers, including the Chemical Manufacturers Association (CMA), challenged EPA's decision to regulate under Subtitle C of RCRA certain materials generated by the petroleum refining industry.]
    In petroleum refining, impurities are removed and usable hydrocarbon fractions are isolated from crude oil feedstock. Large quantities of water are used, and the resulting wastewaters contain a small percentage of residual oil. These "oil-bearing

___

e. Section 261.1(c)(5) provides that "[a] material is 'used or reused' if it is either: (i) Employed as an ingredient (including use as an intermediate) in an industrial process to make a product (for example, distillation bottoms from one process used as feedstock in another process). However, a material will not satisfy this condition if distinct components of the material are recovered as separate end products (as when metals are recovered from metal-containing secondary materials); or (ii) Employed in a particular function or application as an effective substitute for a commercial product (for example, spent pickle liquor used as phosphorous precipitant and sludge conditioner in wastewater treatment)."
    f. For an example of activities that amount to speculative accumulation, see Parker v. Scrap Metal Processors, Inc., 386 F.3d 993, 1011-1012 (11th Cir. 2004).

wastewaters" are destined for ultimate discharge, but only after a three-step treatment process is first applied. The first phase of treatment, known as "primary treatment," removes certain materials including the oil. This phase has at least two beneficial consequences: (1) it meets a Clean Water Act requirement that refineries remove oil from their wastewater, and (2) it allows refineries to recover a not insignificant quantity of oil (up to 1,000 barrels a day across the industry) which is cycled back into the refinery production process.

Industry petitioners and EPA disagree over when these wastewaters become discarded for purposes of the solid waste definition. While no one disputes that discard has certainly occurred by the time the wastewaters move into the later phases of treatment, the question is whether discard happens before primary treatment, allowing regulation of wastewater as solid waste at that point, or not until primary treatment is complete and oil has been recovered for further processing.

EPA's initial proposal excluded oil-bearing wastewaters. However, it changed its mind in 1994 and concluded that even before the oil is recovered in primary treatment, "the wastewaters are discarded materials and hence solid wastes subject to regulation under RCRA." EPA stated: "Primary wastewater treatment operations exist to treat plant wastewaters." It noted that the percentage of oil in the wastewater is very small and "not significant in the context of a refinery's overall production activities," and that the Clean Water Act mandates such treatment. For these stated reasons, EPA concluded that "[c]learly, wastewater treatment is the main purpose of the systems in question, and any oil recovery is of secondary import." . . .

Industry petitioners . . . contend that . . . oil-bearing wastewaters cannot be regulated because they are (as claimed in API's *AMC I* brief) unquestionably in-process materials not yet discarded. Alternately, . . . [p]etitioners emphasize that primary treatment yields valuable oil that is reinserted into the refining processes in a continuous operation. They also claim that oil recovery operations began long before Clean Water Act regulations required it. In sum, they contend that oil recovery in primary treatment is a part of in-process oil production.

At bottom, the parties disagree over the proper characterization of primary treatment. Is it simply a step in the act of discarding? Or is it the last step in a production process before discard? Our prior cases have not had to draw a line for deciding when discard has occurred. . . .

It may be permissible for EPA to determine that the predominant purpose of primary treatment is discard. Legal abandonment of property is premised on determining the intent to abandon, which requires an inquiry into facts and circumstances. Where an industrial by-product may be characterized as discarded or "in process" material, EPA's choice of characterization is entitled to deference. See *AMC II*, 907 F.2d at 1186. However, the record must reflect that EPA engaged in reasoned decisionmaking to decide which characterization is appropriate. The record in this case is deficient in that regard. EPA has noted two purposes of primary treatment and concludes, "[c]learly, wastewater treatment is the main purpose." As English teachers have long taught, a conclusion is not "clear" or "obvious" merely because one says so.

EPA points out that primary treatment only recovers a small amount of oil relative to the entire output of a typical refining facility. However, the oil is still valuable and usable, so that reason alone cannot show discard. The rock of a diamond mine may only contain a tiny portion of precious carbon, but that is enough to keep miners busy. In the refining industry, the net amount of oil recovered may reach 1,000 barrels a day. It is plausible to claim, as industry petitioners do, that refiners engage in primary treatment first and foremost to recover this usable resource. At the very least, EPA cannot merely rely on the small relative amount of oil recovered from primary treatment without further explanation.

EPA also notes that the Clean Water Act requires primary treatment before discharge. If refiners got nothing from primary treatment, this might be a compelling rationale because it would be hard to explain why, other than to discard, refiners would engage in a costly treatment activity with no economic benefits. However, petitioners claim they would engage in primary treatment regardless of the treatment standards in order to recover the desired oil. EPA does not explain why this possibly valid motivation is not compelling. EPA makes no attempt to balance the costs and benefits of primary treatment, or otherwise to explain why the Clean Water Act requirements are the real motivation behind primary treatment. Indeed, without further explanation, it is not inherently certain why a substance is definitively "discarded" if its possessor is continuing to process it, even though the possessor's decision to continue processing may have been influenced, or even predominantly motivated, by some external factor. Otherwise put, it is not so obvious as EPA would have us hold that if the industry petitioners conceded that their overriding motivation in further processing the wastewaters was compliance with Clean Water Act regulations that they would then conclusively be discarding the material in question even while further processing it. If the non–Clean Water Act benefits of the initial treatment are enough to justify firms' incurring the costs (petitioners point to material in the record that may support such a proposition), the EPA would have to reconcile that fact with any conclusion that the Clean Water Act purpose was primary.

In short, EPA has not set forth why it has concluded that the compliance motivation predominates over the reclamation motivation. Perhaps equally importantly it has not explained why that conclusion, even if validly reached, compels the further conclusion that the wastewater has been discarded. Therefore, because the agency has failed to provide a rational explanation for its decision, we hold the decision to be arbitrary and capricious. We therefore vacate the portion of EPA's decision declining to exclude oil-bearing wastewaters from the statutory definition of solid waste, and remand for further proceedings. We do not suggest any particular result on remand, only a reasoned one demonstrating when discard occurs if EPA wishes to assert jurisdiction.

NOTES AND QUESTIONS

1. Why didn't *AMC I* or *AMC II* control the result in this case? How did the purpose of the activities of the petroleum refining industry bear on the proper characterization of the wastewaters that contained residual oil? What defects did the court identify in EPA's justification for subjecting the oil-bearing wastewaters to RCRA regulation?

2. *More on Recycling and Solid Waste.* Suppose that secondary materials generated by one industry are destined for recycling in another industry. Are those materials necessarily "discarded" and therefore solid wastes under §1003(27) of RCRA and §261.2 of EPA's regulations? In Safe Food and Fertilizer v. EPA, 350 F.3d 1263 (D.C. Cir. 2003), *remanded on rehearing*, 365 F.3d 46 (D.C. Cir. 2004), the issue was whether secondary materials recycled to make zinc fertilizer, as well as the zinc fertilizer itself, were solid wastes under RCRA. The court accepted EPA's argument

that they were not, based on two factors. First, market participants treated the recycled feedstocks more like valuable products than like negatively valued wastes, managing them in ways inconsistent with treatment of discarded materials. Second, the fertilizers derived from the recycled feedstocks were chemically indistinguishable from analogous commercial products made from virgin materials (the court referred to this as the "identity principle"). Under EPA's regulations, feedstocks were exempt from Subtitle C regulation if they were not speculatively accumulated and met certain storage, recordkeeping, and notice requirements consistent with the use of feedstocks as valued commodities rather than wastes. The zinc fertilizers produced from the recycled materials were exempt if they complied with maximum concentration levels for six contaminants (including several heavy metals and dioxins).

3. *Legitimate versus Sham Recycling.* EPA has sought to determine which recycled materials are subject to regulation as Subtitle C solid wastes by distinguishing between legitimate and sham recycling. Section 261.6(a)(2) of EPA's regulations provides that "[r]ecyclable materials used in a manner constituting disposal" are subject to a special set of provisions, §266.20, called the Product Rule. Under the Product Rule, items produced for the general public's use "that are used in a manner that constitutes disposal and that contain recyclable materials" are exempt from some hazardous waste regulations "if the recyclable materials have undergone a chemical reaction in the course of producing the products so as to become inseparable by physical means" and the products meet EPA's treatment standards (which are discussed later in this chapter) for each recyclable material that they contain. §266.20(b). In United States v. Marine Shale Processors, 81 F.3d 1361 (5th Cir. 1996), the issue was whether soil contaminated with toxic wastes generated at a wood treatment facility (SWP) qualified as "recyclable materials," given that SWP sent them to a hazardous waste recycler. The recycler burned the soil in a rotary kiln as part of its manufacturing process, producing air particles that contained carcinogenic metals. The court analyzed the issue as follows:

The United States points out that EPA has consistently interpreted the Product Rule to include a requirement that the substance at issue be produced from a process of legitimate, as opposed to sham, recycling. According to these documents, sham recycling, as opposed to legitimate recycling, occurs when the hazardous waste purportedly recycled contributes in no significant way to the production of the product allegedly resulting from the recycling. . . . In other words, the sham versus legitimate recycling inquiry focuses on the purpose or function the hazardous waste allegedly serves in the production process. If the waste does not in fact serve its alleged function in the process, then sham recycling is occurring.

Although the text of 40 C.F.R. §266.20(b) itself does not mention sham or legitimate recycling, the distinction is inherent in the language "[e]mployed as an ingredient . . . in an industrial process to make a product" in 40 C.F.R. §261.1(c)(5)(i). A hazardous waste is not "employed as an ingredient" if it contributes in no legitimate way to the product's production. EPA's interpretation of its own regulation as including a distinction between sham and legitimate recycling is entitled to deference. . . . A substance cannot be an ingredient in making something if it is merely along for the ride. . . .

[The court provided two examples of processes that would not qualify as "legitimate" recycling.] Hypothetical Facility A generates a large amount of liquid organic waste. In order to rid itself of the waste, Facility A heats the liquid to very high temperatures in the presence of oxygen, causing the carbon and hydrogen in the organic waste to burn away. The temperatures in the heating device are so high as to make irrelevant any heat contribution from the burning of the organic waste.[5] Facility A has incinerated, not recycled, its organic waste. To the extent that Facility A has made a product, it has done so without using its hazardous waste.

Hypothetical Facility B also generates a large amount of liquid organic waste. In order to rid itself of the waste, the facility dumps it into soil. Facility B then digs up the soil containing the waste and heats it to very high temperatures in the presence of oxygen, causing the carbon and hydrogen in the organic waste to burn. The temperatures in the heating device are so high as to make irrelevant any heat contribution from the burning of the organic waste. The soil, however, conglomerates together and forms something that Facility B calls "aggregate." Under such circumstances, Facility B has not recycled its hazardous waste. The only difference between Facilities A and B is that Facility B dumped its waste in soil first. If the organic waste provides neither energy nor materials, then the organic material contributes nothing to the production of the "aggregate." Facility B could have manufactured the exact same "aggregate" by dumping virgin soil into its heating device.

SWP argues that producing a product is recycling. This contention ignores the fact that the hazardous waste in [the recycler's] "feedstocks" may simply be along for the ride. At bottom, SWP's argument depends on the idea that soil contaminated with organic waste is a fundamentally distinct substance from the organic waste itself. We do not agree. . . . Incineration does not cease to be incineration when one dumps the waste to be incinerated into a temporary medium like soil.

Id. at 1365-1366. The court remanded so that the district court could consider whether SWP's organic waste was a legitimate ingredient in the production of any product by the recycler.

In another portion of the principal case, the court addressed EPA's decision to regulate as hazardous waste under RCRA certain residual oil, known as "petrochemical recovered oil," that results from the use of refined petroleum products and other feedstocks to produce petrochemical products such as organic chemicals. This residual oil can be inserted back into the petroleum refining process. EPA was concerned that if additional unneeded materials present in petrochemical recovered oil were excluded from regulation, it would allow for sham recycling. If extra materials were added to petrochemical recovered oil that provide no benefit to the industrial process, petrochemical producers would be engaged in an act of discard under the guise of recycling. EPA raised this concern because some of the residual oil samples it tested were contaminated with chlorinated or other halogenated materials that were unexpected. Industry argued that EPA lacks the authority to regulate any petrochemical recovered oil under any circumstances because such materials are not "discarded." The court disagreed and upheld EPA's approach, concluding that EPA can regulate material "discarded" through sham recycling even though it cannot regulate under RCRA materials that are not discarded.

4. *Another Timing Question: When Is Immediate Not Imminent?* The AMC I court required that recycled materials be "destined for immediate reuse" in an ongoing production process to avoid characterization as discarded material. Both the AMC II and Owen Elec. cases emphasized that aspect of AMC I. But exactly what does "immediate reuse" mean? In Association of Battery Recyclers, Inc. v. EPA, 208 F.3d 1047 (D.C. Cir. 2000), the National Mining Association and the American Iron and

---

5. An easier case is presented if the organic compound is a low energy hazardous waste, thus making it an inappropriate fuel. In a third possibility, the facility does not use the lion's share of the heat produced from the burning of its organic waste.

Steel Institute challenged an EPA regulation that regarded as solid waste secondary materials destined for recycling by the mineral processing industry in its production processes if they exhibit a characteristic of hazardous waste and are stored by means other than tanks, containers, buildings, or properly maintained pads. Such materials stored in any other way were considered solid wastes regardless of the length of their storage before recycling. The petitioners relied on *AMC I*, but EPA argued that subsequent cases had sharply limited the scope of that case. EPA claimed it was prohibited from treating secondary materials as discarded only if "reclamation is continuous in the sense that there is no interdiction in time" in that materials move from one step of a recovery process to another without a break in the process for storage.

The court invalidated the regulation. First, it concluded that the materials destined for recycling were neither thrown away nor abandoned. Thus, *AMC I* precluded EPA from characterizing them as discarded. Remarkably, the court added that "[l]ater cases in this court do not limit *AMC I*, as EPA supposes." Id. at 1054. *AMC II*, for example, stands only for the proposition that EPA may regulate as solid waste materials that "may at some time in the future be reclaimed." The secondary materials at issue in this case *would* be reclaimed. Second, the court contested EPA's assumption that "immediate," as the court in *AMC I* used that word, means "at once." Instead, the court concluded that it means "direct," as in "the immediate cause of the accident." In this case, EPA improperly regulated materials that were not a by-product of solid waste, but rather a direct by-product of industrial processes that were destined for reuse as part of a continuous industrial process. EPA thus exceeded the scope of its authority by subjecting to Subtitle C regulation these in-process secondary materials.

5. *Proposed Regulatory Revisions*. In response to *Association of Battery Recyclers*, EPA proposed revisions to the definition of solid waste to identify certain recyclable materials that are not subject to regulation under Subtitle C. 68 Fed. Reg. 61,558 (2003). The proposal also would establish criteria for determining whether or not hazardous secondary materials are recycled legitimately. EPA proposed that any material that is generated and reclaimed in a continuous process within the same industry is not "discarded" for purposes of Subtitle C, provided that the recycling process is legitimate. Thus, when generation and reclamation occur on a continuous basis within a single industry, secondary materials would not be regulated as solid wastes. The proposal would require that reclamation of excluded materials within the generating industry produce a product or ingredient that can be used or reused without any further reclamation. Generation and reclamation of materials would take place in a "continuous process" only if the materials are handled exclusively by facilities or entities (except for transporters) that are within the generating industry, and the materials are not "speculatively accumulated." A generator could not ship excluded materials to a broker or other middleman before they are received at a reclamation facility. EPA concluded that the potential for environmental harm from deregulating the type of recycling covered in the proposal is likely to be small compared with other types of recycling practices.

The agency's proposed criteria for distinguishing between legitimate and sham recycling would apply not only to materials excluded from regulation under the proposal, but more broadly to recycling of hazardous waste, as well as recycling of hazardous secondary materials that are not considered wastes when they are recycled. The proposed criteria for materials that are legitimately recycled are as follows: (1) The secondary material to be recycled is managed as a valuable commodity.

(2) The secondary material provides a useful contribution to the recycling process or to a product of the recycling process. Evaluation of this criterion should include consideration of the economics of the recycling transaction. (3) The recycling process yields a valuable product or intermediate that is (i) sold to a third party or (ii) used by the recycler or the generator as an effective substitute for a commercial product or as a useful ingredient in an industrial process. (4) The product of the recycling process (i) does not contain significant amounts of hazardous constituents that are not found in analogous products, (ii) does not contain significantly elevated levels of any hazardous constituents that are found in analogous products, and (iii) does not exhibit a hazardous characteristic that analogous products do not exhibit.

EPA solicited comments on a regulatory option that would provide a broader regulatory conditional exclusion from RCRA regulation for essentially all materials that are legitimately recycled by reclamation, whether the recycling is done within the generating industry or between industries. But this exclusion would apply only to hazardous secondary materials that are legitimately recycled by reclamation.

6. *A State Approach to Defining Waste.* In Waste Mgmt. of the Desert, Inc. v. Palm Springs Recycling Ctr., Inc., 869 P.2d 440 (Cal. 1994), the California Supreme Court considered whether recyclable materials qualified as "wastes" within the meaning of a state statute authorizing cities to grant exclusive franchises for solid waste handling services and barring commercial generators of recyclable materials from selling them to someone other than the exclusive franchisee. The court held that they did not. The analysis revolved around whether the recyclable materials were discarded and whether they had economic value. The court concluded that the statute's repeated references to "solid waste" indicates that "the Legislature was concerned with just what it said—waste—and not with materials of economic value to their owner."

> The commonly understood meaning of "waste" is something discarded "as worthless or useless." (Amer. Heritage Dict. (1985) p. 1365, col. 1.) If the owner sells his property—that is, receives value for it—the property cannot be said to be worthless or useless in an economic sense and is thus not waste from the owner's perspective. Conversely, if the owner voluntarily disposes of the property without receiving compensation or other consideration in exchange—that is, throws it away—the obvious conclusion is that the property has no economic value to the owner. The concept of value is in this sense related to the manner in which the property is disposed. . . .
>
> [The statute defined the term "solid waste" as including several enumerated types of materials and "other discarded solid and semisolid wastes." Thus, the court reasoned, "an item is not waste until it is discarded."] This returns us to the concept of value. Property that is sold for value—for example, a recyclable—is not "discarded" under any traditional understanding of the term. "Discard" means "to throw away." (Amer. Heritage Dict. (2d college ed. 1982) p. 402, col. 1.) It is not synonymous with the broader term "dispose," which means "To transfer or part with, as by giving or selling." (Id., at p. 407, col. 2.) A homeowner, for example, can dispose of used furniture, clothing, or automobiles by discarding them or by selling them, but either method of disposition necessarily precludes the other. If he sells the property, he cannot discard it; and if he discards it, he cannot sell it. That "discard" connotes throwing away or abandoning has been well recognized in cases dealing with waste and related issues. [AMC 1] (D.C. Cir. 1987) 824 F.2d 1177, 1184. . . .
>
> The proper rule is this: If the owner of property disposes of it for compensation—in common parlance, sells it—it is not waste because it has not been discarded. The owner is not required under the Act to transfer this property to the exclusive franchisee.

But, consistent with the purpose of the Act, an owner cannot discard property as he sees fit. Discarding the property renders the property waste and subjects it to the Act. [869 P.2d at 442-445.]

If the court in *Owen Elec.* had used the American Heritage Dictionary, would it have reached a different result? Would the recyclable materials in *Waste Mgmt. of the Desert* be "solid waste" under RCRA? If RCRA's definition of solid waste were governed by the economic value and valuable materials concepts relied upon by the *Waste Mgmt. of the Desert* court, would the decisions in *Owen Elec.*, in the *API II* case, or in the other cases cited in the notes following the last two principal cases have been different? Should Congress amend RCRA §1003(27) to define solid waste as material that has no economic value and that has been discarded as opposed to being disposed of for compensation? What would be the benefits of adopting such a definition? Compare Safe Air for Everyone v. Meyer, 373 F.3d 1035, 1043 n.8 (9th Cir. 2004) (stating that "the issue of monetary value does not affect the analysis of whether materials are 'solid waste' under RCRA").

7. *Nonindustrial Solid Wastes.* RCRA solid wastes can turn up in some rather unlikely places. In Connecticut Coastal Fishermen's Ass'n v. Remington Arms Co., 989 F.2d 1305 (2d Cir. 1993), the court concluded that debris in Long Island Sound from lead shot and clay targets discharged by patrons of a gun club was solid waste under RCRA. Without deciding how long materials must accumulate after they have served their original, intended purpose but before they are discarded, the court held that the lead shot and clay targets had accumulated long enough to qualify as solid waste. Compare Potomac Riverkeeper, Inc. v. National Capital Skeet and Trap Club, Inc., 388 F. Supp. 2d 582 (D. Md. 2005) (refusing to grant summary judgment to defendant in RCRA citizen suit; the plaintiff alleged that the buildup of lead in soil at site of skeet and trap range at which operations had ceased amounted to open dumping in violation of RCRA and constituted an imminent and substantial endangerment). In Military Toxics Project v. EPA, 146 F.3d 948 (D.C. Cir. 1998), however, the court deferred to EPA's decision to exempt from the definition of a solid waste military munitions that, after being fired, hit the ground and remain there. According to EPA, such munitions are not discarded because they are used for their intended purpose. See also Otay Land Co. v. U.E. Ltd., L.P., 440 F. Supp. 2d 1152 (S.D. Cal. 2006); WaterKeeper Alliance v. United States Dep't of Defense, 152 F. Supp. 2d 163 (D.P.R. 2001) (rejecting contention that ordnance becomes discarded material as soon as it hits land; munitions cannot be considered discarded until some time after they have served their intended purpose).

If a city decides to undertake an insecticide spraying program to control mosquito-borne diseases, would implementation of the program involve disposal of solid waste subject to Subtitle C of RCRA (assuming the pesticides qualify as hazardous)? See No Spray Coalition, Inc. v. City of New York, 252 F.3d 148 (2d Cir. 2001).

Suppose that some Idaho farmers are in the business of growing bluegrass. To harvest bluegrass seed, the farmers cut the crop close to the ground, after which it dries out and ripens. They then use a combine to separate the seed from the straw, leaving the straw on the field. They prepare the seed for commercial distribution, but leave the straw and stubble (the part of the crop not cut from the ground) on the field. The farmers then burn the straw and stubble in a practice called "open burning." An environmental group has sued a group of bluegrass farmers under the citizen suit provision of RCRA, §7002(a)(1)(B), to force them to stop open burning. They allege that the straw and stubble are solid wastes and that open burning amounts to the handling, treatment, and disposal of solid waste that may present an imminent and substantial endangerment to health because the smoke from open burning creates severe respiratory problems for nearby residents. The group alleges that it is necessary for bluegrass farmers to remove the post-harvest straw and stubble in order to maintain high bluegrass seed yields when they plant another crop; thus, they claim, the primary purpose of open burning is to remove the straw and stubble from the fields. The growers respond that open burning benefits them because (1) it extends the productive life of their fields; (2) it restores beneficial minerals and fertilizers to the fields (allowing them to purchase less of these materials than they would otherwise have to do to produce a bountiful crop); (3) it reduces or eliminates insects, reducing the need for pesticide use; and (4) it blackens the soil, which maximizes sunlight absorption and increases future crop yields. Accordingly, the growers contend, the straw and stubble are not solid wastes, and §7002(a)(1)(B) provides no authority for the court to enjoin open burning. If both sides move for summary judgment, which side should prevail? See Safe Air for Everyone v. Meyer, 373 F.3d 1035 (9th Cir. 2004).

Problem 8-3

For years the cement industry has lined its kilns with refractory bricks containing chromium. The bricks sometimes leach chromium in amounts sufficient to render the material hazardous under EPA's toxicity characteristic leaching procedure (described in the next section). When a kiln reached the end of its useful life (due to cracking of the bricks, for example), kiln owners often would crush the bricks from the inactive kiln and use the pulverized bricks as a raw material in the manufacture of cement. The manufacturing process involved burning the raw materials in industrial furnaces. Initially, EPA took the position that spent bricks are not solid wastes when they are reused as ingredients in an industrial process. When the agency adopted land disposal restrictions for hazardous debris under §3004 of RCRA, however, it defined hazardous debris to include chromium-containing spent bricks from cement kilns. The regulations also precluded thermal destruction as an acceptable treatment method for spent bricks, and defined thermal destruction to include the use of industrial furnaces at cement plants.

ABC Cement Company no longer manufactures kilns with chromium-containing refractory bricks. It has a considerable inventory of these bricks, however. Some of them are in active kilns that will one day be taken out of service, some are in inactive kilns that have not yet been dismantled, and some have never been used and are stored in the company's warehouse. The company is considering challenging EPA's regulations barring the use of pulverized refractory brick as raw materials in cement manufacturing through treatment in industrial furnaces. The company would claim that the bricks do not constitute solid waste, are therefore not hazardous waste, and are therefore not subject to regulation under §3004. Is ABC likely to prevail in such a challenge?

d. Identification and Listing of Hazardous Wastes

Overview of the Hazardous Waste Designation Process. The trigger for regulatory action under Subtitle C of RCRA is formal designation of a solid waste as hazardous.

The statute defines a hazardous waste as a solid waste that, because of its quantity, concentration, or characteristics, may cause or significantly contribute to an increase in mortality or serious illness or pose a substantial hazard to human health or the environment when improperly managed. §1004(5). EPA is required to issue criteria for identifying the characteristics of hazardous waste and for listing particular hazardous wastes, taking into account factors such as toxicity, persistence, degradability in nature, potential for accumulation in tissue, flammability, and corrosiveness. §3001(a). It must then issue regulations that actually identify the characteristics of hazardous waste and list particular wastes that are hazardous and therefore subject to regulation under Subtitle C. §3001(b)(1).

EPA's regulations establish several mechanisms by which a solid waste may qualify as hazardous.* First, a solid waste is hazardous if it is specifically listed as such by EPA. 40 C.F.R. §261.3(a)(2)(ii). This method, which is reflected in the statutes of some states and European countries,** simply requires a generator to consult the lists published by EPA to see if a substance is regulated under Subtitle C. See id. §262.11(b). Second, a waste is hazardous if it meets any of the characteristics of a hazardous waste: ignitability, corrosivity, reactivity, or toxicity. Id. §§261.3(a)(2)(i), 261.20. A generator of a solid waste that is not listed as hazardous must determine whether the waste is nevertheless regulated under Subtitle C on the basis of its characteristics by testing the waste using EPA-approved methods, or by "[a]pplying knowledge of the waste in light of the materials or the processes used." Id. §262.11(c)(2). Third, a mixture of a listed hazardous waste and another solid waste is hazardous unless EPA has specifically excluded it. Id. §261.3(a)(2)(iv). Fourth, a mixture of a waste that is hazardous because of its characteristics and a nonhazardous solid waste is hazardous if the resulting mixture exhibits any of the characteristics of a hazardous waste. Id. §261.3(a)(2)(iii). Fifth, the "derived from" rule provides that, with certain exceptions, any solid waste generated from the treatment, storage, or disposal of a hazardous waste is hazardous. Id. §261.3(c)(2)(i). The "derived from" rule was meant to prevent hazardous waste generators and owners of treatment, storage, and disposal facilities from evading regulation by "minimally processing or managing a hazardous waste and claiming that resulting residue was no longer the listed waste, despite the continued hazards that could be posed by the residue even though it does not exhibit a [hazardous waste] characteristic." 60 Fed. Reg. 66,344, 66,346 (1995).

Listing and Delisting of Hazardous Wastes. EPA relies on listing as the predominant strategy for bringing wastes into the RCRA scheme because testing by generators for characteristics such as carcinogenicity, mutagenicity, and teratogenicity is generally impractical. This difficulty explains at least in part why EPA has not expanded the list of characteristics that render a waste hazardous beyond the four that appear in the regulations. Instead, EPA listed the constituents of hazardous waste streams that have been shown in reputable scientific studies to have toxic, carcinogenic, mutagenic, or teratogenic effects on human or other forms of life and generally required that these waste streams be managed under Subtitle C. 40 C.F.R. Part 261, Appendices VII-VIII.

---

*Certain solid wastes, such as household waste, waste generated by the growing or harvesting of crops or the raising of animals, mining overburden returned to the mine site, and wastes associated with the exploration or production of crude oil, natural gas, or geothermal energy, are excluded from the definition of hazardous waste. 40 C.F.R. §261.4(b). See also RCRA §§3001(b)(2)-(3), 8002.

**State law definitions of hazardous waste may be more expansive than RCRA definitions. See 42 U.S.C. §6929.

Because industrial wastes tend to be generated in complex mixtures of many separate substances, EPA has listed scores of hazardous waste streams, typical waste sources, and hazardous waste–generating processes, as well as hundreds of specific hazardous substances. See id. §§261.31-261.33, 261.35. In Dithiocarbamate Task Force v. EPA, 98 F.3d 1394 (D.C. Cir. 1996), the court invalidated a series of waste listings because EPA failed to consider all of the regulatory factors for determining whether a waste containing toxic constituents is capable of posing a substantial threat to health or the environment when improperly managed. But in Environmental Def. Fund v. EPA, 210 F.3d 396 (D.C. Cir. 2000), the court upheld EPA's decision not to list 14 solvent wastes as hazardous, rejecting the claim that EPA violated its own regulations by examining only the toxicity of the spent solvents and not the toxicity of other constituents that might mix with the solvents to form a larger waste stream.

Section 261.11(a)(3) of EPA's regulations requires that EPA list a waste as hazardous if it contains any of the toxic constituents listed in an appendix to the regulations and if, based on a consideration of designated factors, it is capable of posing a substantial present or potential hazard to human health or the environment when improperly managed. In American Petroleum Inst. v. EPA, 216 F.3d 51 (D.C. Cir. 2000), API challenged EPA's listing of refinery residuals on the ground that the wastes do not pose a substantial hazard. The court upheld the listings. It concluded that EPA appropriately took the position that it would regulate a waste posing a substantial risk to highly exposed individuals, even if the substance poses a relatively small risk to the population at large.

RCRA authorizes waste generators to petition the agency to delist their wastes. §3001(f). To succeed, the petitioner must demonstrate that a specific waste generated by an individual facility is not hazardous because of plant-specific variations in raw materials, processes, or other factors.

Characteristic Hazardous Wastes. Of the four characteristics, toxicity has proven the most difficult to apply. Cf. United States v. Elias, 269 F.3d 1003 (9th Cir. 2001) (rejecting the claim that the regulatory definition of reactive waste was so vague as to render criminal convictions for its violation unconstitutional). Initially, EPA established an extraction procedure (EP) leach test for measuring toxicity. Under the EP test, the toxicity of a waste was determined by measuring the potential for its toxic constituents to leach out and contaminate groundwater at levels that would create health or environmental concerns under conditions of improper management. See 45 Fed. Reg. 33,110 (1980). In 1990, the agency replaced that test with the Toxicity Characteristic Leaching Procedure (TCLP) test. The purpose of the TCLP test remains the determination of whether a waste poses a threat to health or the environment if it is mismanaged, but this test requires the use of a limited number of leaching fluids and eliminates an exception to the requirement that large solid pieces of waste be reduced to particles before testing. Edison Elec. Inst. v. EPA, 2 F.3d 438, 442 (D.C. Cir. 1993). EPA also added 25 organic chemicals to the list of toxic constituents of concern. For a more extensive description of how the TCLP test is conducted, see Association of Battery Recyclers, Inc. v. EPA, 208 F.3d 1047 (D.C. Cir. 2000).

The Mixture and "Derived From" Rules. As indicated above, the mixture rule subjects to Subtitle C regulation any solid waste that is mixed with a listed hazardous waste. The "derived from" rule provides that a waste derived from the treatment, storage, or disposal of a listed waste is also hazardous. In Shell Oil Co. v. EPA, 950 F.2d 741 (D.C. Cir. 1991), the court stunned EPA by vacating both rules on procedural grounds more than a dozen years after their adoption. EPA reissued the mixture and "derived from" rules in 2001. 66 Fed. Reg. 27,266. It asserted that the rules continue to be necessary to protect health and the environment from unacceptable risk. EPA nevertheless excluded from Subtitle C regulation derivatives of wastes listed solely for the characteristics of ignitability, reactivity, and/or corrosivity when they no longer exhibit any characteristic of hazardous waste. Mixtures of wastes listed solely for these characteristics that no longer exhibit any hazardous waste characteristic were already excluded from regulation. Wastes that exhibit a hazardous waste characteristic at the point of generation and then are subsequently decharacterized remain subject to land disposal restriction requirements.

In American Chemistry Council v. EPA, 337 F.3d 1060 (D.C. Cir. 2003), the court upheld the 2001 version of the mixture and "derived from" rules. It was reasonable for EPA to assume that all mixtures of and derivatives from hazardous wastes are themselves hazardous until it can be shown otherwise. Placing the burden on the regulated entity to show the lack of a hazardous characteristic in a mixture or derivative avoids placing on EPA the nearly impossible burden of anticipating the hazardousness or non-hazardousness of every conceivable mixture or derivative that a generator might create. In addition, Congress wanted EPA to err on the side of caution, and the rules were a reasonable exercise of such caution.

NOTE ON MUNICIPAL WASTE COMBUSTION ASH

Many local governments burn their solid wastes. Some do so to recover energy. EPA described the waste produced by waste-to-energy (WTE) facilities as follows:

> Approximately 25 percent (dry weight) of the waste that is combusted remains as ash, amounting to around eight million tons of municipal waste combustor (MWC) ash generated annually. While the ash may be collected at a number of locations within a WTE facility, it typically is characterized as either "bottom ash" or "fly ash." Bottom ash collects at the bottom of the combustion unit and comprises approximately 75-80% of the total ash by weight. Fly ash collects in the air pollution control devices that "clean" the gases produced during the combustion of the waste and comprises around 20-25% of the total by weight. The fly ash from a WTE facility's different air pollution control devices typically is consolidated and then combined with the bottom ash via enclosed conveyors at the bottom of the MWC where it is cooled and conveyed to a storage area. EPA estimates that nearly 80% of WTE facilities routinely combine their ash. [60 Fed. Reg. 6666-6667 (1995).]

The issue facing EPA in 1980 was whether to treat MWC ash generated by a WTE facility as a hazardous waste subject to Subtitle C regulation or as a nonhazardous solid waste that could be disposed of in state-regulated, Subtitle D landfills. Why would EPA even consider treating the ash that results from the burning of nonhazardous, municipal solid waste as hazardous waste? The Seventh Circuit provided the following answer:

> To borrow a phrase from computer programmers, resource recovery quite literally is "garbage in, garbage out," but the garbage that emerges from the incineration process—ash—is fundamentally different in its chemical composition from the plastic, paper, and other rubbish that goes in. It does not follow that the generation of hundreds of tons of a whole new substance with the characteristic of a hazardous waste should be exempt from

regulation just because Congress wanted to spare individual households and municipalities from a complicated scheme if they inadvertently handled hazardous waste. [EDF v. City of Chicago, 948 F.2d 345, 351 (7th Cir. 1991).]

EPA's 1980 regulations excluded "household waste." Although most waste generated by households is nonhazardous in nature, a small portion—such as cleaning fluids and batteries—would have qualified as hazardous under RCRA absent the exclusion. The regulations provided that residues remaining after treatment of household wastes, including incineration, also would be exempt from Subtitle C. As a result, a WTE facility burning only household waste could dispose of the resulting MWC ash in a Subtitle D landfill. If a facility burned nonhazardous industrial waste along with household waste, however, any incinerator ash it produced was deemed hazardous, even though the raw material input was not.

In 1984, Congress enacted §3001(i) of RCRA, titled "Clarification of Household Waste Exclusion." Four years later, an environmental group sued Chicago in a RCRA citizen suit, claiming that it was illegally disposing of more than 100,000 tons of MWC ash annually at Subtitle D landfills. The issue in City of Chicago v. EDF, 511 U.S. 328 (1994), was whether EPA correctly interpreted §3001(i) as continuing to exempt MWC ash from the definition of hazardous waste. If not, the city would have to dispose of its MWC ash in Subtitle C landfills.

Relying on the plain meaning rule, the Court chose not to defer to EPA's interpretation. "[S]o long as a facility recovers energy by incineration of the appropriate wastes, it (the facility) is not subject to Subtitle C regulation as a facility that treats, stores, disposes of, or manages hazardous waste. The provision quite clearly does not contain any exclusion for the ash itself." Id. at 334. Citing §1003(b)(1), the Court refused to "interpret the statute to permit MWC ash sufficiently toxic to qualify as hazardous to be disposed of in ordinary landfills." Id. at 335. In short, "while a resource recovery facility's management activities are excluded from Subtitle C regulation, its generation of toxic ash is not." Id. at 337. Justice Stevens dissented, arguing that under §3001(i), both the input and the output of a WTE facility are nonhazardous.

The City of Chicago decision did not indicate the exact point at which the ash generated by a WTE facility becomes a hazardous waste. EPA subsequently announced that it interpreted §3001(i) to first subject the ash to Subtitle C when it exits the combustion building following the combustion and air pollution control processes. It is at this point that the facility owner or operator must determine whether the ash generated at the facility exhibits the toxicity characteristic. EPA asserted that this result promotes Congress's intent to remove impediments to the operation of commercially viable resource recovery facilities. If regulation applied to ash inside the building, the facility might need to sample and analyze ash at multiple points. The cost of installing multiple handling and storage systems to convey separate ash streams—bottom ash and fly ash—to different conditioning systems and of analyzing the two different ash streams would likely be twice the cost of operating the facility without these changes. See 60 Fed. Reg. 6666 (1995).

Puder, Trash, Ash, and the Phoenix: A Fifth Anniversary Review of the Supreme Court's City of Chicago Waste-to-Energy Combustion Ash Decision, 26 B.C. Envtl. Aff. L. Rev. 473 (1999), concludes that City of Chicago has not threatened the viability of the WTE industry, largely because combined WTE combustion ash continues to pass the TCLP test. Chicago, however, decided to close its municipal garbage incinerators rather than retrofit them with environmental controls.

NOTES AND QUESTIONS

1. *Dueling Objectives.* The desire to both encourage legitimate recycling and prevent activities that pose threats to health and the environment is part of the reason that EPA has had such difficulty ascertaining the appropriate scope of the term "solid waste" under RCRA. Both the majority and dissenting opinions in *City of Chicago* recognized that the same tension affected EPA's implementation of the household waste exclusion. How did EPA's interpretation resolve that tension? What was the argument behind the claim that EPA's approach conflicted with RCRA's primary objective?

Is the text of §3001(i) as clear as the majority asserted? Justice Stevens contended that it was not. What arguments were available to the city to make its case that its activities were exempt from regulation under Subtitle C? Do RCRA's definitions shed light on the persuasiveness of these arguments? What was the majority's response?

2. *Contingent Management.* Some critics of RCRA have urged the adoption of a "contingent management" approach based on the theory that the risk posed by a waste depends on not only its chemical composition, but also the manner in which it is managed. A waste stream otherwise subject to Subtitle C (because it satisfies one of the four characteristics of hazardous waste) would be exempt if it were managed in a manner that mitigates the health and environmental risks it poses. Acceptable management might take the form of a requirement that the risk of exposure posed by disposal of the waste in a Subtitle D facility be less than some quantitative level (such as an excess cancer risk of one in a million).

EPA endorsed a form of "contingent management" when it relied on §3004(y) of RCRA to exempt from Subtitle C nonchemical military munitions transported or stored in compliance with waste management regulations issued by the Departments of Defense and Transportation. In Military Toxics Project v. EPA, 146 F.3d 948 (D.C. Cir. 1998), the court upheld the exemption as reasonable. Narrowly construed, the decision does not extend to conditional exemption for wastes managed by the generating industry without oversight by another agency. But the court's rationale may support such an extension. The court interpreted §§3001(a), 3002(a), 3003(a), and 3004(a) as vesting in EPA the power to decide whether a waste should be regulated under Subtitle C based on whether regulation is necessary to protect health and the environment. Gaba, Regulation by Bootstrap: Contingent Management of Hazardous Wastes under the Resource Conservation and Recovery Act, 18 Yale J. on Reg. 85 (2001), argues that the legality of contingent management is far from clear.

e.   Regulation of Hazardous Waste Generation and Transportation

Regulation of Hazardous Waste Generation under RCRA. Each generator of solid waste is responsible for determining whether its wastes qualify as hazardous. 40 C.F.R. §262.11. If a generator contracts to have its hazardous waste moved off-site for treatment or disposal, it must originate for each waste shipment a detailed paper manifest, select responsible transporters, specify a fully permitted TSD facility to which delivery is to be made, and report irregularities if receipt is not confirmed. It also must comply with packaging, labeling, and placarding requirements. Generally, hazardous waste generators may not accumulate waste on-site for more than 90 days without engaging in storage requiring a TSD facility permit. §3002; 40 C.F.R. Part 262. Certain small-quantity generators are subject to less onerous requirements. EPA standardized the content and appearance of the manifest form in 2005. 70 Fed. Reg. 10,776.

Regulation of Hazardous Waste Exports. Section 3017 of RCRA prohibits the export of hazardous wastes unless the government of the receiving country has agreed to accept them or the shipment complies with the terms of an agreement between the United States and that country regarding the export of hazardous waste. See 40 C.F.R. §262.52. The Basel Convention on the Control of Transboundary Movements of Hazardous Wastes and Their Disposal, 28 I.L.M. 657 (1989), amended in 1995, restricts the international movement of wastes. The Convention prohibits transfers of hazardous wastes between parties and nonparties unless they are consistent with environmentally sound management. Transfers between parties may proceed only if the exporting state cannot dispose of the wastes adequately, the exported wastes are required as raw materials in recycling or recovery, or the transfer otherwise conforms to criteria developed by the parties. The Convention bars all transboundary movements of hazardous waste between Organization for Economic Development and Cooperation and European Union states. The United States is a signatory to the Convention but has not ratified it due to the absence of implementing legislation. It has continued to export hazardous wastes under the "environmentally sound management" exception.* Guruswamy, International Environmental Law 309-310 (2d ed. 2003).

Regulation of Hazardous Waste Transportation under RCRA and HMTUSA. Tank car explosions or derailments typify the kinds of accidents that can result during the transportation of hazardous waste. The Subtitle C requirements applicable to hazardous waste transporters are designed to ensure that wastes remain within the regulated waste handling system. Section 3003, which is aimed at "midnight dumping" by "gypsy haulers," requires compliance with recordkeeping and labeling regulations as well as participation in the manifest system. The implementation of §3003 must be consistent with the requirements of the Hazardous Materials Transportation Uniform Safety Act (HMTUSA), as amended by the Safe Accountable, Flexible, Efficient Transportation Equity Act: A Legacy for Users, Pub. L. No. 109-59, 119 Stat. 1144 (2005) (codified as amended at 49 U.S.C. §§5101-5127). The purpose of HMTUSA is "to provide adequate protection against the risks to life and property inherent in the transportation of hazardous material in commerce." §5101. The statute grants to the Secretary of Transportation the authority to designate materials as hazardous if their transportation may pose an unreasonable risk to health and safety or property, §5103(a), and to prescribe regulations for the safe transportation of those materials. The Director of the Transportation Security Administration must develop and implement a process for carrying out background checks for drivers hauling hazardous materials. §5103a(g). Motor carriers may transport hazardous materials in commerce only if they have a safety permit, which requires compliance with motor carrier safety rules and financial responsibility requirements. §5109(a). The Secretary must issue standards for states to implement highway routing requirements

---

*The convention defines environmentally sound management as "taking all practicable steps to ensure that hazardous wastes or other wastes are managed in a manner which will protect human health and the environment against the adverse effects which may result from such wastes." Art. 2(8). See generally Portas, The Basel Convention, Back to the Future, 6 Sustainable Dev. L. & Pol'y 38 (Spring 2006).

designed to enhance public safety. §5112(b). The DOT regulations for the transportation of hazardous materials are at 49 C.F.R. Parts 172-173, 178-179.

HMTUSA preempts state and local requirements if compliance with both them and federal requirements is impossible or if compliance with the state or local provision is an obstacle to the implementation of HMTUSA. §5125(a). Some state or local laws (such as those dealing with designation or packaging of hazardous material and container design and manufacture) are preempted if they are "not substantively the same" as ones promulgated under HMTUSA. §5125(b)(1). States may not establish designations for highway routes over which hazardous materials may be transported except in accordance with HMTUSA. §5125(c). The Secretary may waive the preemptive effect of HMTUSA if the state or local requirement is at least as protective as HMTUSA and does not unreasonably burden interstate commerce. §5125(e).*

f. Regulation of Hazardous Waste Treatment, Storage, and Disposal

(1)   TSD Facility Permits and Performance Standards

The most complicated provisions of RCRA are those that establish a permit system for on- or off-site treatment, storage, and disposal (TSD) of hazardous waste and require compliance by TSD facilities with an extensive array of regulatory requirements. As of late 2003, there were 367 commercial hazardous waste facilities operating in North America, most of which were waste and wastewater recycling operations. 34 Env't Rep. (BNA) 2441 (2003). Section 3005(a) of RCRA prohibits the treatment, storage, or disposal of hazardous waste, or the construction of a new TSD facility, except in accordance with a permit. EPA (or a state authorized by EPA to administer the TSD facility permit program under §3006) may issue a permit only if the applicant demonstrates compliance with §§3004 and 3005 (§3005(c)(1)), and it may revoke a permit upon finding that the permit holder is not complying with the permit or the requirements of §3004. §3005(d). EPA has authorized most states to implement at least some aspects of the TSD facility permit program. The regulations issued by EPA under §3004 are those that the agency deems "necessary to protect human health and the environment." §3004(a).

EPA's regulations prescribe location, design, and construction standards aimed at preventing waste releases during the life of the facility and thereafter. In addition, they establish performance standards for groundwater protection implemented through monitoring and, if necessary, corrective action (i.e., remediation of a contaminated TSD facility). Some of the regulatory requirements apply to all kinds of TSD facilities (e.g., 40 C.F.R. Part 264, Subparts A-I), while others apply to specific kinds of facilities, such as surface impoundments, waste piles, landfills, and incinerators (id., Subparts J-O). The TSD facility regulations are meant to prevent landfill

---

*Compare Chlorine Inst. v. California Highway Patrol, 29 F.3d 495 (9th Cir. 1994) (HMTUSA preempted state requirement that hazardous shipments on California highways be accompanied by escort vehicles) with Massachusetts v. United States Dep't of Transp., 93 F.3d 890 (D.C. Cir. 1996) (state requirement that hazardous waste carriers post a bond before picking up or dropping off hazardous waste within the state not preempted). In Skull Valley Band of Goshute Indians v. Nielson, 376 F.3d 1223 (10th Cir. 2004), the court held that the Nuclear Waste Policy Act preempted Utah statutes that regulated the storage and transportation of spent nuclear fuel.

leachate from leading to another Love Canal, discussed in the introduction to section F of this chapter. The regulations require that permit holders comply with detailed requirements for chemical treatment, restrictions on the disposal of liquids, site location (away from wetlands and other critical areas), and final site closure. Liner systems must be designed to prevent migration of wastes into adjacent soils or groundwater or surface water during facility life and during a post-closure period, generally 30 years. Certain facilities must have a monitoring program to determine the facility's impact on groundwater. §3004(p).

For a facility to be closed, landfills must be covered, storage and treatment facilities must be decontaminated, and the hazardous wastes must be removed from the facility. The post-closure plan must include an extended period of groundwater monitoring and maintenance activities to ensure the integrity of the final ground cover or containment structures. Deed restrictions required by the regulations in effect create an easement or restrictive covenant that runs with land containing a closed hazardous waste facility. The restrictions must inform subsequent purchasers that the facility is under post-closure RCRA status. The post-closure restriction may be released only if all wastes, waste residues, and contaminated soils are removed from the facility. See 40 C.F.R. §264.119.

The owner or operator of a TSD facility that is in existence on the effective date of statutory or regulatory changes that first subject it to Subtitle C regulation, that notifies EPA of its operations, and that applies for a permit is treated as if it had a permit until EPA or an authorized state rules on the permit application. §3005(e)(1). These "interim status" facilities must comply with standards that are analogous to but in many respects less stringent than those applicable to finally permitted facilities. 40 C.F.R. Part 264.

In 2005 EPA authorized the issuance of "standardized permits" for TSD facilities that generate and store or non-thermally treat hazardous waste on-site. Those permits also are available to facilities that receive hazardous waste generated off-site by a generator under the same ownership as the receiving facility, and that store or non-thermally treat the hazardous waste. EPA estimated that the facilities eligible for the standardized permit represent 50 percent of the 11 major types of hazardous waste management units. The standardized permit is intended to streamline the permitting process by allowing TSD facilities to obtain and modify permits more easily without lessening the degree of environmental protection achieved. The standardized permit consists of two parts: a uniform portion, required in all cases, and a supplemental portion that is required at the discretion of EPA or an authorized state. 70 Fed. Reg. 53,420 (2005).

NOTE ON FINANCIAL RESPONSIBILITY AND INSURANCE ISSUES

[The materials in this note are located at the casebook's website.]

(2)   Land Disposal Restrictions and Treatment Requirements

Dissatisfied with EPA's progress in promulgating RCRA regulations, Congress adopted the Hazardous and Solid Waste Amendments of 1984 (HSWA). The motivating force behind these amendments to RCRA was a desire to restrict the disposal of hazardous wastes on land. Congress declared that

certain classes of land disposal facilities are not capable of assuring long-term containment of certain hazardous wastes, and to avoid substantial risk to human health and the
environment, reliance on land disposal should be minimized or eliminated, and land
disposal, particularly landfill and surface impoundment, should be the least favored
method for managing hazardous waste.

§1002(b)(7). Congress also found that the extent of improper hazardous waste management would likely require expensive, complex, and time-consuming corrective
action. §1002(b)(6). The objectives of RCRA therefore were expanded to include
ensuring that hazardous waste management practices are conducted in a manner
that protects health and the environment, requiring proper waste management to
reduce the need for corrective action, and minimizing hazardous waste generation
and land disposal of hazardous waste through treatment and other means.
§1003(a)(4)-(6).

The RCRA provisions designed to achieve those goals reflect the same technology-
forcing approach reflected in the Clean Air and Clean Water Acts. HSWA requires,
for example, that permits issued after its adoption compel the use by certain kinds of
land disposal facilities of liners (described in incredible detail in §3004(o)(5)(B)) and
leachate collection systems. §3004(o)(1). The centerpiece of the 1984 amendments,
however, is a series of provisions (known collectively as the land disposal restrictions,
or LDRs) that limit the land disposal of hazardous wastes. HSWA bans the placement
of non-containerized or bulk liquid hazardous wastes in salt dome formations, salt bed
formations, underground mines, and caves until EPA finds that those activities are
protective of health and the environment and issues performance and permitting
standards. §3004(b)(1). It also prohibits the placement of these wastes in landfills.
§3004(c)(1).

HSWA also prohibits the land disposal of certain dioxin-containing wastes and
halogenated and nonhalogenated solvents. Land disposal includes placement of hazardous waste in facilities such as landfills, surface impoundments, and injection wells.
§3004(k). EPA may lift the ban by issuing a finding that the prohibition of one or more
methods of land disposal of these wastes "is not required in order to protect human
health and the environment for as long as the waste remains hazardous," taking into
account the long-term uncertainties associated with land disposal; the goal of managing hazardous waste in an appropriate manner in the first instance; and the persistence, toxicity, mobility, and bioaccumulation propensity of the wastes and their
hazardous constituents. The statute precludes such a finding for an untreated hazardous waste unless EPA determines, "to a reasonable degree of certainty, that there will
be no migration of hazardous constituents for as long as the waste remains hazardous."
§3004(e)(1). A similar set of restrictions applies to the land disposal of liquid hazardous wastes containing free cyanides, metals above specified concentrations, PCBs, and
halogenated organic compounds. §3004(d)(1).

HSWA required that EPA review all of the hazardous wastes subject to the
restrictions of §3004(d)-(e) that are disposed of by underground injection into deep
injection wells. The agency was then to issue regulations by 1988 prohibiting such
disposal if "it may reasonably be determined" that it may not be protective of health
and the environment, taking into account the same factors that apply to land disposal
of the wastes listed in §3004(d)-(e). If EPA failed to make a timely determination for a
particular waste, the statute automatically barred its disposal into a deep injection well.
§3004(f)(3). The 1984 amendments also compelled EPA to issue LDRs for all other

hazardous wastes listed under §3001 in accordance with a statutory schedule. If EPA failed to issue timely restrictions or determine that restrictions are unnecessary, the statute itself, in a series of so-called hammer provisions, either restricted or banned land disposal. §3004(g)(6).

The scope of the LDRs was at issue in NRDC v. EPA, 907 F.2d 1146 (D.C. Cir. 1990). The chemical industry claimed that EPA could not ban the disposal of hazardous waste by deep injection under §3004(f)-(g) and require site-specific deep injection permits because it had failed to make the determination, required by §§3004(f)(2) and 3004(g)(5), that absent a site-specific permitting process, deep injection of hazardous waste might not be protective of human health and the environment for as long as the wastes remain hazardous. But the court found that EPA may ban any method of land disposal of wastes governed by §3004(g) without first determining that the method is not protective of human health and the environment. Indeed, RCRA commands EPA to impose LDRs unless it has made an affirmative determination of safety. Industry also challenged EPA's application of the no-migration standard to the prohibition on disposal by deep injection on the ground that §3004(f) does not contain a no-migration standard similar to the ones set forth in §3004(d)(1), (e)(1), and (g)(5). The court rejected the attack, holding that it was within EPA's discretion to decide that a disposal method would not be sufficiently protective of health and the environment for purposes of §3004(f)(2) unless it satisfied the no-migration standard.

The issue raised by NRDC in the same case was whether the no-migration standard would be violated if hazardous constituents seeped out of a storage area at a time when some of the stored wastes were still hazardous, but not those actually escaping from the area. "Hazardous *constituents*," which are chemical compounds listed in 40 C.F.R. Part 261, Appendix VIII, are defined by molecular formulae without reference to their concentrations. A *waste* is hazardous only if various factors, including the concentration of its hazardous constituents, actually make it hazardous to human health or the environment. NRDC supported a literal reading of the no-migration standard: the migration of even a single molecule would preclude a finding that a land disposal method is protective of health and the environment, even if migrating waste was itself not hazardous. But the court found the phrase "as long as the wastes remain hazardous" to be ambiguous. Because the consistency of wastes may vary throughout an injection zone or disposal unit, wastes near the perimeter may no longer be hazardous even though wastes in another part still are. It was not clear whether hazardous constituents in those nonhazardous wastes could migrate without violating the no-migration standard or whether migration of hazardous constituents was barred until all wastes throughout the injection zone were no longer hazardous. EPA interpreted "the wastes" to refer to the wastes containing the hazardous constituents that are leaving the injection zone. The court deferred to EPA's position that hazardous constituents may migrate so long as they do not do so in high enough concentrations to be hazardous wastes. Does the statutory language support this result?

Section 3004(j) prohibits the storage of hazardous waste subject to the LDRs, unless it is solely for the purpose of accumulating quantities of the waste necessary to facilitate proper recovery, treatment, or disposal. EPA took the position that the storage of hazardous waste pending development of treatment capacity is not exempt from that prohibition. In Edison Elec. Inst. v. EPA, 996 F.2d 326 (D.C. Cir. 1993), the petitioners argued that when treatment capacity is not available, the only way to "facilitate proper recovery, treatment, or disposal" is to accumulate and store the waste until sufficient capacity does become available. The court agreed with EPA that §3004(j) does not authorize the indefinite storage of wastes pending development of treatment methods or disposal capacity. Which HSWA policy does this result arguably promote?

The LDRs are not as absolute as the description above would seem to indicate. First, RCRA authorizes EPA to defer the effective date of the LDRs of §3004(d)-(g) under certain circumstances. §3004(h). Second, and more important, the statute requires EPA to issue treatment standards simultaneously with the issuance of regulations to implement the LDRs. These standards must specify "those levels or methods of treatment, if any, which substantially diminish the toxicity of the waste or substantially reduce the likelihood of migration of hazardous constituents from the waste so that short-term and long-term threats to human health and the environment are minimized." §3004(m)(1). A hazardous waste that has been treated to the level or by a method specified in these treatment regulations is no longer subject to the LDRs. §3004(m)(2). Thus, HSWA in effect imposes a ban on the land disposal of *untreated* hazardous waste.

COLUMBIA FALLS ALUMINUM CO. v. EPA
139 F.3d 914 (D.C. Cir. 1998)

RANDOLPH, Circuit Judge:
[Small manufacturers of aluminum challenged regulations adopted by EPA under §3004 of RCRA that established a treatment standard for "spent potliner"—a by-product of primary aluminum reduction—and prohibited the land disposal of untreated spent potliner. Aluminum is produced by dissolving aluminum oxide in a molten cryolite bath and introducing a direct electric current to produce aluminum metal. The process occurs in electrolytic steel cells, or pots, lined with brick and carbon. The lining serves as the cathode for the electrolysis process. Over the useful life of the pots, the carbon lining absorbs the cryolite solution and degrades. When the liner cracks, the pot is removed and the steel shell is stripped away, leaving the spent potliner.

At the time EPA issued its regulations, only Reynolds Metals Company was engaged in full-scale treatment of spent potliner. Reynolds' treatment process involved crushing spent potliner to particle size and adding limestone, which reacted with the fluoride in spent potliner to transform it into relatively insoluble calcium fluoride. The mixture was fed into a rotary kiln and heated, after which it was cooled and deposited in an on-site monofill. EPA's treatment standard did not specify a particular technology, but EPA understood that Reynolds provided virtually all capacity for treating spent potliner. EPA expressed the treatment standard in terms of numerical concentration limits for constituents in the waste, including cyanide, toxic metals such as arsenic, polycyclic aromatic hydrocarbons (PAHs), and fluoride. The standards for cyanide and the PAHs were based on a "total composition concentration analysis." For fluoride and the metals, treatment standards were expressed in terms of the TCLP.]

 . . . The TCLP is designed to simulate the mobility or leachability of toxic constituents into groundwater following disposal of a hazardous waste in a municipal solid waste landfill. In 1990 EPA adopted the TCLP as the required test for measuring the mobility of toxic metals in all solid wastes.

For solid wastes, the TCLP involves reducing a sample of the waste to particle size and mixing it with an extraction fluid. One of two extraction fluids is used depending on the alkalinity of the waste being tested. Any solid is then discarded and the remaining liquid, called the TCLP extract, is analyzed for toxic contaminants. A solid waste exhibits the characteristic of toxicity if it contains any one of a number of contaminants specified by EPA at a concentration equal to or greater than the regulatory level. . . .

[EPA postponed the effective date of the treatment standard and the prohibition on land disposal of untreated spent potliner. According to the agency, even though the wastes as tested using the TCLP would have complied with the treatment standards for one of the wastes, actual sampling data showed potentially high concentrations of hazardous constituents in the leachate from Reynolds' landfill. Eventually, though, EPA concluded that Reynolds' treatment represented an improvement over the disposal of untreated spent potliner, and it allowed the prohibition on land disposal of untreated potliner to go into effect. The aluminum manufacturers claimed that it was arbitrary and capricious for EPA to continue using the TCLP to measure compliance with the treatment standard once it knew that the test did not accurately predict the mobility of toxic constituents in the actual leachate.]

As discussed above, the concentration limits for fluoride and the toxic metals in spent potliner are expressed in terms of the TCLP. Thus the TCLP cannot be divorced from the standard itself. Because these constituents cannot be destroyed, the goal of treatment is to minimize their mobility. The treatment standard is in fact a model intended to predict the degree to which these constituents will leach following disposal. The problem, as EPA has admitted, is that the model does not work. The leachate "generated from actual disposal of the treatment residues is more hazardous than initially anticipated." 62 Fed. Reg. at 37,695. When tested by the TCLP, the treated spent potliner exhibited numbers that were lower than the regulatory levels for toxic constituents, but tests of the actual leachate revealed numbers above the concentration limits. . . . In its proposal to revoke the delisting of Reynolds' treated spent potliner, EPA described the "residue leachate concentrations" as "orders of magnitude higher than the average predicted TCLP leachate values." 62 Fed. Reg. 41,005, 41,008-09 (1997).

EPA attributes the failure of the TCLP to several factors. It acknowledged . . . that the "extreme alkaline pH conditions that exist in [Reynolds'] monofill were not anticipated by the Agency and are not analogous to" conditions simulated by the TCLP. 62 Fed. Reg. at 1994. The TCLP is premised on a "generic mismanagement scenario" in which hazardous waste is deposited in a municipal solid waste landfill, where other wastes would act as buffer agents. Reynolds disposes of treated spent potliner in a monofill—a landfill receiving only spent potliner—where the high pH level remains undiluted. . . . EPA stated:

> In hindsight, it is now apparent that spent potliners are themselves highly alkaline and contain cyanide, arsenic, and fluoride—constituents which are most soluble under alkaline pH. . . . EPA had failed to take into account the effect of alkaline disposal conditions on potliners and potliner treatment residues when promulgating . . . the treatment standard for [the wastes involved]. . . .

62 Fed. Reg. at 37,695. Despite these flaws, the Agency concluded: "Although it is now apparent that the TCLP is not a good model for disposal conditions to which [the

wastes] would be subject, the treatment standard still requires use of the TCLP and any results so obtained that do not exceed the treatment standard are in compliance." 62 Fed. Reg. at 37,696 n.12.

We cannot make sense of EPA's conclusion. Why should the treatment standard for spent potliner be maintained when that standard has no correlation to the actual fate of toxic constituents upon disposal? Petitioners ask this question; EPA gives no good answer. An agency's use of a model is arbitrary if that model "bears no rational relationship to the reality it purports to represent." American Iron & Steel Inst. v. EPA, 115 F.3d 979, 1005 (D.C. Cir. 1997). Models need not fit every application perfectly, nor need an agency "justify the model on an ad hoc basis for every chemical to which the model is applied." Chemical Mfrs. Ass'n v. EPA, 28 F.3d 1259, 1265 (D.C. Cir. 1994). If, however, "the model is challenged, the agency must provide a full analytical defense." Eagle-Picher Indus., Inc. v. EPA, 759 F.2d 905, 921 (D.C. Cir. 1985). Furthermore, EPA "retains a duty to examine key assumptions as part of its affirmative burden of promulgating and explaining a non-arbitrary, noncapricious rule." Small Refiner Lead Phase-Down Task Force v. EPA, 705 F.2d 506, 534 (D.C. Cir. 1983). Here EPA knows that "key assumptions" underlying the TCLP are wrong and yet has offered no defense of its continued reliance on it. . . .

In this case, there is not only no evidence that treated spent potliner is exposed to the disposal conditions that the TCLP simulates, but all available evidence indicates that the treated residue is disposed of in quite different circumstances. It is impossible to say at this point whether the TCLP would be an inaccurate predictor for spent potliner's leachability following all forms of treatment. Certain aspects of the Reynolds treatment process — disposal in a dedicated monofill and the additives it uses — increase alkalinity. The TCLP may or may not work well for other spent potliner treatment technologies. . . .

We therefore conclude that EPA's use of the TCLP is arbitrary and capricious. As a result, we must vacate the treatment standard itself because the concentration limits for fluoride and the metals, including arsenic, are expressed only in terms of the TCLP. . . . Vacating the treatment standard for spent potliner also requires us to vacate the prohibition on land disposal. Contrary to EPA's arguments on appeal, we believe Congress intended treatment standards and land disposal restrictions to operate in tandem. The statutory language indicates as much. RCRA §3004(m) requires that "simultaneously" with the promulgation of prohibitions on land disposal, the Administrator of the EPA shall "promulgate regulations specifying" treatment standards. 42 U.S.C. §6924(m)(1). These regulations are to "become effective on the same date" as any land disposal prohibition. Id. §6924(m)(2).

Pragmatic considerations also strongly suggest that the treatment standard and land disposal restriction are intended to work together. Banning land disposal is a relatively simple task, one that could be accomplished by administrative fiat, but promulgating treatment standards is more complicated. To ensure that EPA would act promptly, Congress enacted an absolute deadline of May 8, 1990 — the so-called "hard hammer" — for all hazardous wastes listed or identified as of the time of the 1984 Amendments. This was a powerful incentive for regulatory action because a ban on land disposal without a means of treatment would threaten the closure of entire industries. Under RCRA §3004(j), generators of a waste prohibited from land disposal are also barred from storing it. If we were to vacate the treatment standard for spent potliner without vacating the prohibition on land disposal, aluminum manufacturers might be forced to cease production. . . .

... The spent potliner treatment standard and the prohibition on land disposal are vacated and remanded.

Our decision leaves EPA without a regulation governing spent potliner. If EPA wishes to promulgate an interim treatment standard, the Agency may file a motion in this court to delay issuance of this mandate in order to allow it a reasonable time to develop such a standard.

NOTES AND QUESTIONS

1. What was the flaw in EPA's treatment standard for spent potliner? Does the *Columbia Falls* decision threaten the viability of other treatment standards issued under §3004(m)? What relief did the court grant? Should it have left the LDRs in effect despite invalidation of the spent potliner treatment standard? EPA reissued numerical treatment standards on remand "to assure that spent potliners remain prohibited from land disposal." 63 Fed. Reg. 51,254, 51,256 (1998). For another case involving alleged misapplication of the TCLP, see Association of Battery Recyclers, Inc. v. EPA, 208 F.3d 1047 (D.C. Cir. 2000).

2. *Risk-Based versus Technology-Based Treatment Standards.* The courts have been called on in several other instances to review the legality of §3004(m) treatment standards and the LDRs with which they are associated. In Hazardous Waste Treatment Council v. EPA, 886 F.2d 355 (D.C. Cir. 1989), the legality of EPA regulations governing land disposal of solvents and dioxins under §3004(e) was at issue. The court concluded that §3004(m) authorizes EPA to base treatment standards on either risk-based screening levels or best demonstrated available technology, as long as the effect is to minimize short-term and long-term threats to health and the environment. What provisions in §3004(m) might the court have relied on to support that reading of the statute? The court remanded the treatment regulations because EPA did not adequately explain why it chose technology-based rather than risk-based screening levels. In particular, EPA impermissibly relied on criticism by members of Congress of the agency's proposal to use risk-based screening levels. Why is it inappropriate for an agency finalizing proposed regulations to respond to the comments of members of the legislature whose votes contributed to enactment of a statute? On remand, EPA expressed a preference for risk-based treatment levels. Why would risk-based levels arguably be preferable as a matter of policy to technology-based treatment standards? Despite this preference, EPA justified the adoption of technology-based standards for solvents and dioxins because it was not yet able, due to the scientific uncertainties involved, to identify constituent concentration levels at which wastes no longer pose risks. See 55 Fed. Reg. 6640 (1990). EPA later announced that, in light of new and more reliable health-based and ecological data, it might soon be able to establish risk-based levels for some chemicals to minimize threats to health and the environment. 64 Fed. Reg. 63,381, 63,444 (1999).

3. *Land Treatment.* In American Petroleum Inst. v. EPA, 906 F.2d 729 (D.C. Cir. 1990), the court held that RCRA bars EPA from authorizing land treatment of petroleum refining hazardous wastes under §3004(m). Land treatment involves placing hazardous waste on the ground with the expectation that the hazardous constituents will become less hazardous over time. Citing §3004(k), EPA concluded that it is a type of land disposal. In a land treatment facility, the treatment of hazardous waste occurs only after the waste has been land disposed. But RCRA requires that hazardous

wastes be treated *before* land disposal. What language of §3004(m) supports this analysis?

In Louisiana Envtl. Action Network v. EPA, 172 F.3d 65 (D.C. Cir. 1999), the court upheld an EPA regulation allowing variances under §3004(m) from treatment standards if treatment would likely discourage aggressive remediation. The agency was concerned that the application of overly stringent treatment requirements to waste already in a landfill could discourage excavation and thus prevent any treatment at all. The court interpreted the *API* case, discussed in the previous paragraph, as holding that, because land disposal pursuant to §3004(m)(2) is dependent on compliance with §3004(m)(1) treatment requirements, land disposal itself cannot constitute the "treatment" required by §3004(m)(1). *API* "says nothing," however, about whether EPA, in measuring whether treatment will substantially diminish toxicity or substantially reduce the likelihood of migration, may look beyond the predisposal context.

4. *Treatment of Characteristic Hazardous Wastes.* Both industry and environmental groups challenged the treatment standards for certain characteristic hazardous wastes in Chemical Waste Mgmt. v. EPA, 976 F.2d 2 (D.C. Cir. 1992). Industry argued that EPA lacks the authority to mandate treatment of these wastes beyond the point at which they cease to display hazardous characteristics, claiming that, once a waste ceases to meet the regulatory definition of a hazardous waste, it ceases to be subject to Subtitle C. The court, siding with the agency, held that EPA may bar land disposal of certain wastes unless they have been treated to reduce risks beyond those presented by the characteristics themselves. Environmental petitioners challenged EPA's endorsement of dilution as an acceptable method of treatment. They argued that RCRA requires the use of technological treatment because dilution does not minimize threats to health and the environment or substantially reduce waste toxicity. The court concluded that RCRA does not require the use of best demonstrated available technology in all situations and that, in principle, dilution can constitute an acceptable form of treatment for ignitable, corrosive, or reactive characteristic hazardous wastes. But it also held that dilution is appropriate only if it removes the characteristic and reduces hazardous constituents that are present in sufficient concentrations to pose a threat to human health or the environment. EPA's justification for the use of dilution sufficed only for corrosive wastes, and, even for those wastes, only to the extent that the wastes do not contain hazardous constituents that, following dilution, would themselves present a continuing danger to health or the environment.

Congress amended RCRA in 1996 to allow solid waste identified as hazardous solely on the basis of its characteristics to escape RCRA treatment requirements if it is disposed of at facilities regulated under the Clean Water Act or the Safe Drinking Water Act, provided the waste no longer exhibits a hazardous characteristic at the time of disposal. EPA retains the authority to impose treatment standards or additional requirements on these wastes if necessary to protect health and the environment. §3004(g)(7)-(11).

NOTE ON SITING TSD FACILITIES AND ENVIRONMENTAL JUSTICE

Until the 1970s, location of TSD facilities was regulated, if at all, by local communities through the exercise of the zoning power. Many communities welcomed such facilities because they added jobs and increased tax revenues. After Love Canal, the perception of the value of these facilities changed and TSD facilities became paradigm examples of the NIMBY ("not in my backyard") syndrome. See Resolving Locational Conflict (R. Lake ed., 1987). TSD facilities are widely regarded as LULUs (locally undesirable land uses). A LULU is a broad term used to identify land uses that pose a higher level of market failure than that usually associated with an alien land use entering a neighborhood. Fear of the risks that TSD and nuclear waste facilities may pose has sparked intense opposition that cuts across geographical, political, and social class lines. The federal government's approach has been to rely on state siting powers subject to minimal EPA oversight. However, §3004(o)(7) of RCRA requires that EPA promulgate criteria for acceptable TSD location "necessary to protect human health and the environment," and §104(c)(3) of CERCLA required that by 1989 each state provide the agency with assurances that it has adequate TSD capacity to handle all hazardous wastes expected to be generated in the state for the next 20 years.

Within a very short period of time after the LULU problem was identified, an "expert" consensus emerged that local opposition would prevent the introduction and expansion of TSD facilities, thus creating a national or regional capacity problem. Proponents of facility siting contended that local opposition should be overridden. Some states responded by adopting laws, patterned on earlier laws relating to power plants, that preempt local authority over TSD facility siting decisions. Some laws provide for expansion of public participation and more intense site review; others seek to "bribe" host communities through negotiated siting agreements that offer direct and indirect compensation for accepting a new risk. One review of attempts to site facilities concluded that "[f]ew laws have failed so completely as the federal and state statutes designed to create new facilities for the disposal of hazardous and radioactive wastes." M. Gerrard, Whose Backyard, Whose Risk: Fear and Fairness in Toxic and Nuclear Waste Siting 1 (1994).*

Much of the concern over the siting of TSD facilities has concentrated on their location in poor and minority neighborhoods. In 1987, the United Church of Christ Commission on Racial Justice issued a report that found race to be the most significant variable in the location of hazardous waste facilities and that these facilities were concentrated in areas with high minority populations. Toxic Wastes and Race in the United States: A National Report on the Racial and Socio-Economic Characteristics of Communities with Hazardous Waste Sites (1987). This conclusion forms the basis of the environmental justice or environmental racism movement, see R. Bullard, Dumping in Dixie: Race, Class, and Environmental Quality (1990), but the link between racial discrimination and the location of new and expanded facilities is disputed. The initial environmental justice suits, which alleged intentional discrimination, did not succeed. See Lazarus, Pursuing "Environmental Justice": The Distributional Effects of Environmental Protection, 87 Nw. U. L. Rev. 787, 834 (1993). A second generation of lawsuits was commenced under Title VI of the Civil Rights Act of 1964, which prohibits discrimination in the distribution of federal or federally financed benefits, including regulatory decisions. President Clinton's 1994 Executive Order 12898, 3 C.F.R. 859 (1995), and EPA's Interim Guidance for Investigating

---

*For analysis of the political and sociological theory of facility siting, see B. Davy, Essential Injustice: When Legal Institutions Cannot Resolve Environmental and Land Use Disputes (1997); Tarlock, Benjamin Davy's Essential Injustice: A Comparative and Philosophical Analysis of the LULU Siting Mess, 22 Harv. Envtl. L. Rev. 607 (1998).

Title VI Administrative Complaints Challenging Permits (Feb. 5, 1998) allow plaintiffs to infer a disparate impact from permits that result in a net increase in pollution. Is the presence of disparate impact arising from the location of a TSD or other facility that generates adverse environmental impacts sufficient to maintain a private right of action for a violation of the Civil Rights Act?

SOUTH CAMDEN CITIZENS IN ACTION v. NEW JERSEY DEPARTMENT OF ENVIRONMENTAL PROTECTION
274 F.3d 771 (3d Cir. 2001)

GREENBERG, Circuit Judge . . .

This matter comes on before this court on appeals by defendant-appellant New Jersey Department of Environmental Protection ("NJDEP") and intervenor-appellant St. Lawrence Cement Co., L.L.C. ("St. Lawrence") from the district court's order granting preliminary injunctive relief to plaintiffs, South Camden Citizens in Action and ten residents of the Waterfront South neighborhood of Camden, New Jersey. Plaintiffs brought this action pursuant to 42 U.S.C. §1983 . . . claiming NJDEP discriminated against them by issuing an air permit to St. Lawrence to operate a facility that would have an adverse disparate racial impact upon them in violation of Title VI of the Civil Rights Act of 1964, 42 U.S.C. §§2000d to 2000d-7.

Our opinion focuses on whether, following the Supreme Court's recent decision in Alexander v. Sandoval, 532 U.S. 275 (2000), plaintiffs can maintain this action under section 1983 for disparate impact discrimination in violation of Title VI and its implementing regulations. For the reasons we set forth, we hold that an administrative regulation cannot create an interest enforceable under section 1983 unless the interest already is implicit in the statute authorizing the regulation, and that inasmuch as Title VI proscribes only intentional discrimination, the plaintiffs do not have a right enforceable through a 1983 action under the EPA's disparate impact discrimination regulations. Because the district court predicated its order granting injunctive relief on section 1983, we will reverse. . . .

[T]he residents of Waterfront South are predominantly minorities and the neighborhood is disadvantaged environmentally. Waterfront South contains two Superfund sites, several contaminated and abandoned industrial sites, and many currently operating facilities, including chemical companies, waste facilities, food processing companies, automotive shops, and a petroleum coke transfer station. Moreover, NJDEP has granted permits for operation of a regional sewage treatment plant, a trash-to-steam incinerator and a co-generation power plant in the neighborhood. As a result, Waterfront South, though only one of 23 Camden neighborhoods, hosts 20% of the city's contaminated sites and, on average, has more than twice the number of facilities with permits to emit air pollution than exist in the area encompassed within a typical New Jersey zip code.

[St. Lawrence supplied cement materials to the ready-mix concrete industry. It processed ground granulated blast furnace slag (GBFS), a sand-like by-product of the steel-making industry, used in portland cement. In 1998, St. Lawrence wanted to open a GBFS grinding facility on a site in Camden it leased from the South Jersey Port Corporation (the Port). When St. Lawrence applied to NJDEP for construction and operation permits, community members voiced their opposition based on environmental justice and air quality concerns. Plaintiffs filed an administrative complaint with EPA and a request for a grievance hearing with NJDEP, alleging that NJDEP's permit review procedures violated Title VI of the Civil Rights Act of 1964 because those procedures did not include an analysis of the allegedly racially disparate adverse impact of the facility. NJDEP did not respond to the grievance hearing request. Instead, it issued St. Lawrence's final air permit.

Plaintiffs then filed a complaint against NJDEP, alleging that it violated Title VI by intentionally discriminating against them in violation of §601, 42 U.S.C. §2000d, by issuing the air quality permit. They asserted that the facility's operation under the air permit would have an adverse disparate impact on them in violation of §602, 42 U.S.C. §§2000d-1. St. Lawrence intervened. The district court, on April 19, 2001, granted plaintiffs' request for a preliminary injunction (*South Camden I*). It found that §602 and its implementing regulations contained an implied private right of action and remanded to NJDEP for a Title VI analysis.]

South Camden I, however, had a short shelf life. On April 24, 2001, the Supreme Court issued its decision in *Sandoval*, holding that "[n]either as originally enacted nor as later amended does Title VI display an intent to create a freestanding private right of action to enforce regulations promulgated under §602. We therefore hold that no such right of action exists." 121 S. Ct. at 1523. [Instead of dissolving the injunction, the district court allowed plaintiffs to amend their complaint to add a claim to enforce §602 through §1983.] On May 10, 2001, the court issued a supplemental opinion and order continuing the preliminary injunction based on plaintiffs' section 1983 claim and again remanding the matter to NJDEP for a Title VI analysis (*South Camden II*). [The court relied on Powell v. Ridge, 189 F.3d 387 (3d Cir. 1999), in which the court had held that there was a private right of action to enforce a regulation implementing Title VI and that a disparate impact discrimination claim could be maintained under §1983 for a violation of a regulation promulgated pursuant to §602.]

. . . Naturally, in view of *Sandoval*, the overarching legal issue on this appeal is whether plaintiffs can advance a cause of action to enforce section 602 of Title VI and its implementing regulations through section 1983. If they cannot, then the only basis on which they can obtain relief is to demonstrate that the NJDEP engaged in intentional discrimination, a possibility that we do not address on this appeal.

We start our legal analysis with a consideration of *Sandoval*, in which the Court held that a private right of action is not available to enforce disparate impact regulations promulgated under Title VI, thus overruling *Powell* at least to the extent that it held to the contrary. In *Sandoval*, . . . [t]he Court . . . found that section 602's text and structure did not evince an intent to create a private right of action and that the regulations alone were insufficient to create [one]. Therefore, the Court held that a private right of action was not available to enforce regulations promulgated under section 602. However, inasmuch as the plaintiffs in *Sandoval* did not advance a cause of action under section 1983 to enforce Title VI and its implementing regulations, the majority did not consider whether such an action is available.

Resolution of this issue, therefore, requires us to examine whether disparate impact regulations promulgated pursuant to section 602 may, and if so do, create a right that may be enforced through a section 1983 action.

Section 1983 provides, in relevant part:

Every person who, under color of any statute, ordinance, regulation, custom, or usage, of any State or Territory or the District of Columbia, subjects, or causes to be subjected, any

citizen of the United States or other person within the jurisdiction thereof to the deprivation of any rights, privileges, or immunities secured by the Constitution and laws,
shall be liable to the party injured in any action at law, suit in equity, or other proper
proceeding for redress.

Therefore, section 1983 provides a remedy for deprivation under color of state law of
"any rights . . . secured by the Constitution and laws." In Maine v. Thiboutot, 448 U.S.
1, 6-8 (1980), the Supreme Court . . . held that causes of action under section 1983 are
not limited to claims based on constitutional or equal rights violations. Rather, certain
rights created under federal statutes are enforceable through section 1983 as well. This
rule, however, is limited by two well-recognized exceptions. First, a section 1983 remedy
is not available "where Congress has foreclosed such enforcement of the statute in the
enactment itself." Wright v. City of Roanoke Redev. & Hous. Auth., 479 U.S. 418, 423
(1987). Second, the remedy is not available "where the statute did not create enforceable
rights, privileges, or immunities within the meaning of §1983." Id.

The Supreme Court has established a three-part test to determine whether a
federal statute creates an individual right enforceable through a section 1983 action:

> First, Congress must have intended that the provision in question benefit the plaintiff.
> Second, the plaintiff must demonstrate that the right assertedly protected by the statute is
> not so "vague and amorphous" that its enforcement would strain judicial competence.
> Third, the statute must unambiguously impose a binding obligation on the States. In
> other words, the provision giving rise to the asserted right must be couched in mandatory,
> rather than precatory, terms.

Blessing v. Freestone, 520 U.S. 329, 340-41 (1997). If a plaintiff satisfies each of these
elements, and therefore establishes and identifies a federal right that allegedly has
been violated, a rebuttable presumption that the right is enforceable through section
1983 arises. We have found two circumstances, which in harmony with *Wright*, are
sufficient to rebut this presumption: where "Congress specifically foreclosed a remedy
under §1983, [either] expressly, by forbidding recourse to §1983 in the statute itself, or
impliedly, by creating a comprehensive enforcement scheme that is incompatible
with individual enforcement under §1983." *Powell*, 189 F.3d at 401. In the former
case, the plaintiff's claim must fail. In the latter case, however, the burden shifts to the
defendant to "make the difficult showing that allowing a §1983 action to go forward in
these circumstances 'would be inconsistent with Congress' carefully tailored
scheme.'" Id.

Here, plaintiffs seek to enforce a prohibition on disparate impact discrimination
that does not appear explicitly in Title VI, but rather is set forth in EPA regulations.
They contend that the regulations are a valid interpretation of Title VI.[6] Section 601 of
Title VI provides:

> No person in the United States shall, on the ground of race, color, or national origin, be
> excluded from participation in, be denied the benefits of, or be subjected to discrimi-
> nation under any program or activity receiving Federal financial assistance.

---

6. We assume without deciding that the regulations are valid, as neither NJDEP nor
St. Lawrence timely challenged them in the district court and our analysis does not turn on their
validity. That being said, like the Court stated in *Sandoval*, we observe that there does seem to be
considerable tension between the section 602 regulations proscribing activities that have a disparate
impact and section 601's limitation to interdiction only of intentionally discriminatory activities.

42 U.S.C. §2000d. Section 602 provides, in relevant part:

> Each Federal department and agency which is empowered to extend Federal financial assistance to any program or activity, by way of grant, loan, or contract other than a contract of insurance or guaranty, is authorized and directed to effectuate the provisions of section 2000d [Section 601] of this title with respect to such program or activity by issuing rules, regulations, or orders of general applicability which shall be consistent with achievement of the objectives of the statute authorizing financial assistance in connection with which the action is taken.

Id. §2000d-1. Finally, the EPA regulations at issue provide:

> No person shall be excluded from participation in, be denied the benefits of, or be subjected to discrimination under any program or activity receiving EPA assistance on the basis of race, color, [or] national origin. . . .
>
> A recipient shall not use criteria or methods of administering its program which have the effect of subjecting individuals to discrimination because of their race, color, national origin, or sex, or have the effect of defeating or substantially impairing accomplishment of the objectives of the program with respect to individuals of a particular race, color, national origin, or sex.

40 C.F.R. §§7.30 & 7.35(b). According to plaintiffs, these statutory provisions and their complementary regulations prohibiting discriminatory impacts in administering programs create a federal right enforceable through section 1983.

This contention raises the question of whether a regulation can create a right enforceable through section 1983 where the alleged right does not appear explicitly in the statute, but only appears in the regulation. . . .

In considering whether a regulation in itself can establish a right enforceable under section 1983, we initially point out that a majority of the Supreme Court never has stated expressly that a valid regulation can create such a right. . . . [The courts of appeals had split on the question of whether a regulation alone may create a right enforceable under §1983.]

. . . To start with, we reiterate that in *Sandoval* the Court made the critical point that "[l]anguage in a regulation may invoke a private right of action that Congress through statutory text created, but it may not create a right that Congress has not." 121 S. Ct. at 1522. Furthermore, . . . the Court's focus in *Wright* was on tying Congress' intent to create federal rights through the statute to the particular federal right claimed. It was of paramount importance that Congress intended to create such a right in the statute, with the regulation then defining the right that Congress already conferred through the statute.

Moreover, it is apparent that in the Court's section 1983 jurisprudence after *Wright* dealing with whether a plaintiff is advancing an enforceable right, the primary consideration has been to determine if Congress intended to create the particular federal right sought to be enforced. . . .

Therefore, we follow *Wright*, in accordance with its actual holding, [and] the teaching of *Sandoval*, . . . and hold that the EPA's disparate impact regulations cannot create a federal right enforceable through section 1983. To the extent, if any, that *Powell* might be thought on a superficial reading to suggest otherwise, in the light of *Sandoval* we cannot regard it as stating controlling law.

Since the time of the Supreme Court's decision in *Sandoval*, it hardly can be argued reasonably that the right alleged to exist in the EPA's regulations, namely to be free of disparate impact discrimination in the administration of programs or activities receiving EPA assistance, can be located in either section 601 or section 602 of Title VI.

In reaching our result, we emphasize the following. *Sandoval* made it clear that section 601 proscribes intentional discrimination only. In discussing whether section 602 and its implementing regulations created an implied right of action, the Court first considered whether Congress intended to create a federal right in favor of the plaintiffs. . . . [T]he Court found that there was no evidence of congressional intent to create new rights under section 602. Rather, "§602 limits agencies to 'effectuat[ing]' rights already created by §601." [121 S. Ct. at 1521.]

Inasmuch as the Court found previously that the only right conferred by section 601 was to be free of intentional discrimination, it does not follow that the right to be free from disparate impact discrimination can be located in section 602. In fact, it cannot. . . . [T]he regulations do more than define or flesh out the content of a specific right conferred upon the plaintiffs by Title VI. Instead, the regulations implement Title VI to give the statute a scope beyond that Congress contemplated, as Title VI does not establish a right to be free of disparate impact discrimination. Thus, the regulations are "too far removed from Congressional intent to constitute a 'federal right' enforceable under §1983." Harris v. James, 127 F.3d 993, 1009 (11th Cir. 1997).

Accordingly, if there is to be a private enforceable right under Title VI to be free from disparate impact discrimination, Congress, and not an administrative agency or a court, must create this right. In this regard, we point out what should be obvious: the scope of conduct subject to being interdicted by limitations on actions having a disparate impact is far broader than limitations on intentional discrimination. . . .

We emphasize that the implications of this case are enormous. . . . It is plain that in view of the pervasiveness of state and local licensing provisions and the likely applicability of Title VI to the agencies involved, the district court's opinion has the potential, if followed elsewhere, to subject vast aspects of commercial activities to disparate impact analyses by the relevant agencies. Indeed, we noted in *Powell* that "[a]t least 40 federal agencies have adopted regulations that prohibit disparate-impact discrimination pursuant to [§602]." *Powell*, 189 F.3d at 393. While we do not express an opinion on whether that would be desirable, we do suggest that if it is to happen, then Congress and not a court should say so as a court's authority is to interpret rather than to make the law. . . .

McKEE, Circuit Judge, dissenting: . . .

The issue here, simply stated, is whether §1983 provides an independent avenue to enforce disparate impact regulations promulgated under §602 of Title VI. That is the same question that was posed in *Powell*. We answered it in the affirmative in *Powell*, and the answer was not overturned by the subsequent *holding* in *Sandoval*. . . .

The majority reasons that inasmuch as the *Sandoval* majority did not find the requisite Congressional intent for a private cause of action in the statute there can be no enforceable right under §1983. . . .

However,

[An enforceable right under §1983] is a different inquiry than that involved in determining whether a private right of action can be implied in a particular statute. In right of action cases we employ the four-factor test [from Cort v. Ash, 422 U.S. 66 (1975)] to determine whether Congress intended to create the private remedy asserted for the violation of statutory rights. The test reflects a concern, grounded in separation of powers, that Congress rather than the courts controls the availability of remedies for violations of statutes. *Because §1983 provides an alternative source of express congressional authorization of private suits, these separation-of-powers concerns are not present in a §1983 case.* Consistent with this view, we recognize an exception to the general rule that §1983 provides a remedy for violation of federal statutory rights only when Congress has affirmatively withdrawn the remedy. [Wilder v. Virginia Hosp. Assoc., 496 U.S. 498, 508 n.9 (1990) (emphasis added).] . . .

NOTES AND QUESTIONS

1. What procedural opportunities to seek redress for alleged discrimination in plant siting did the Supreme Court's decision in *Sandoval* preclude? Why didn't EPA's Title VI regulations provide a basis for the plaintiffs' suit to enjoin NJDEP's permitting of the St. Lawrence facility? See also Save Our Valley v. Sound Transit, 335 F.3d 932 (9th Cir. 2003) (holding that a Department of Transportation regulation prohibiting the recipients of federal funds from taking actions that have the effect of discriminating on the basis of race did not create an individual right that can be enforced under §1983).

What opportunities does Title VI continue to provide for halting the siting of TSD and other pollution-generating facilities after the principal case? Mank, *South Camden Citizens in Action v. New Jersey Department of Environmental Protection*: Will Section 1983 Save Title VI Disparate Impact Suits?, 32 Envtl. L. Rep. (ELI) 10454 (2002), states that environmental justice advocates can continue to file Title VI administrative complaints with EPA. Accordingly, "EPA still needs to consider how to address environmental justice challenges similar to the South Camden situation." Id. at 10477. Professor Mank asserts that the district court "correctly interpreted EPA's §602 disparate impact regulations to impose an independent duty on [federal funds] recipients to go beyond compliance with existing regulations to examine whether a permit decision will have significantly unjustified disparate impacts on a minority group protected by the statute." Id.

A subsequent effort by the plaintiffs in the principal case to prove a violation of §601 of Title VI due to intentional discrimination by the NJDEP, and to demonstrate an actionable nuisance against St. Lawrence, failed. South Camden Citizens in Action v. New Jersey Dep't. of Envtl. Prot., 62 Env't Rep. Cas. (BNA) 1175 (D.N.J. 2006).

2. *Environmental Injustice.* Researchers have determined that black Americans are 79 percent more likely than white Americans to live in neighborhoods that present the greatest risk of exposure to pollution injurious to human health. In some states (including Kansas, Kentucky, Minnesota, Oregon, and Washington), more than 40 percent of blacks live in high-risk neighborhoods. In addition, there are 12 states in which Hispanics are more than twice as likely as non-Hispanics to live in the most polluted areas.*

---

*Among the counties with the highest potential health risk from air pollution in 2000 were Washington County, OH; Wood County, WV; Muscatine County, IA; Leflore County, MS; Cowlitz

3. *The Dormant Commerce Clause and TSD Facility Siting.* Are there other laws that either facilitate or restrict the siting of TSD facilities? The courts have created important limitations on state power to exclude TSD facilities through aggressive use of the dormant Commerce Clause to limit state attempts to impose limitations on all forms of waste imports. See section G below. Section 3009 of RCRA allows state and local government to adopt regulations more stringent than EPA's, but courts have held that RCRA preempts state and local siting policies that in effect amount to a total facility ban. Blue Circle Cement, Inc. v. Board of County Comm'rs, 27 F.3d 1499 (10th Cir. 1994). The court did suggest that a county could justify a total ban under §3009 "if the county consisted only of densely populated residential areas and the hazardous waste activity in fact posed a significant threat to health or safety."

4. *The Basel Convention and TSD Facility Siting.* The Basel Convention on the Control of Transboundary Movements of Hazardous Wastes and Their Disposal, 28 I.L.M. 657 (1989), discussed above, does not conflict with any U.S. TSD siting approach, but it may increase the demand for domestic TSD capacity. The Convention does not formally require that each nation treat its own wastes, but it does so indirectly by restricting the export of hazardous wastes to poor host countries. The Basel Convention differs from RCRA in several respects. First, host countries can ban all imports. For example, the Bamako Convention seeks to make Africa free of non-African wastes.* Second, the Basel Convention recognizes that different countries have different "capacities" to control hazardous wastes. Article 4(2)(a) requires that host states take appropriate measures but recognizes a sliding-scale concept. But Article 4(2)(e) forbids an export state from allowing an export if the disposal level in the host state is not environmentally sound. The host state must prevent the import if it reaches the same conclusion.

(3)   Corrective Action Requirements

[The materials in this section are located at the casebook's website.]

NOTE ON PROTECTION OF GROUNDWATER UNDER THE SAFE DRINKING WATER ACT

[The materials in this note are located at the casebook's website.]

(4)   Underground Storage Tanks

[The materials in this section are located at the casebook's website.]

County, WA; Henry County, IN; Tooele County, UT; Scott County, IA; Gila County, AZ; and Whiteside County, IL. Pace, More Blacks Live with Pollution, AP, Dec. 13, 2005. For access to recent information about environmental justice issues, see ABA, The Law of Environmental Justice: Update Service, http://www.abanet.org/environ/committees/envtab/ejupdates.html.

*Kaminsky, Assessment of the Bamako Convention on the Ban of Imports into Africa and the Control of Transboundary Movement and Management of Hazardous Wastes within Africa, 5 Geo. Envtl. L. Rev. 77 (1992).

g.   Regulation of Nonhazardous Solid Waste

Although the portion of the Solid Waste Disposal Act (SWDA) of 1976 that is better known as RCRA has received the lion's share of the attention of EPA, the state agencies, the regulated community, and academic commentators, the SWDA also addresses the environmental risks posed by the management of nonhazardous municipal solid waste. The SWDA finds that land disposal of solid as well as hazardous waste without proper planning and management can threaten health and the environment, that open dumping is particularly harmful to all environmental media as well as to the public health, and that alternative methods of land disposal are needed to prevent cities from running out of suitable solid waste disposal capacity. §1002(b). The objectives of the SWDA therefore include providing technical and financial assistance to state and local governments to develop solid waste management plans, prohibiting future open dumping and requiring the upgrading of existing open dumps, providing guidelines for solid waste management practices, and establishing a cooperative effort among all levels of government and private enterprise to recover valuable materials and energy from solid waste. §1003(a).

These objectives have a far less prescriptive feel about them than do the statutory objectives that deal with the management of hazardous waste. Congress envisioned state and local governments retaining most of the authority to regulate solid waste management practices; the federal government's role would revolve around the provision of information and financial resources. Subtitle D reflects that allocation of authority. The SWDA requires EPA to adopt suggested guidelines for solid waste management that describe attainable levels of performance and provide minimum criteria for use by the states in defining the practices that constitute the open dumping of solid waste. §1008(a). See also §4004(a) (EPA must issue regulations that distinguish between open dumps and sanitary landfills). EPA also must publish guidelines to assist the states in developing and implementing solid waste management plans. §4002(b). See 40 C.F.R. Part 256.

States must submit their plans for EPA approval. At a minimum, each state plan is required to prohibit the establishment of new open dumps and require that all solid wastes be either used for resource recovery or disposed of in sanitary landfills. §4003(a)(2). See also §4005(a) (after the promulgation of EPA's §1008(a) criteria, the open dumping of solid or hazardous waste is prohibited). An open dump is a solid waste disposal facility that is neither a sanitary landfill nor a hazardous waste TSD facility. §1004(14). A sanitary landfill is a facility that complies with the design and performance criteria issued by EPA under §4004. §1004(26). The prohibition on open dumping is not enforceable by EPA, but citizen suits may be brought to enjoin prohibited open dumping. §4005(a). The court in Parker v. Scrap Metal Processors, Inc., 386 F.3d 993, 1012-1013 (11th Cir. 2004), found a violation of the prohibition on open dumping. State plans also must provide for the closing or upgrading of open dumps and, more generally, for whatever combination of resource conservation or recovery and solid waste disposal practices is necessary for sound waste management. §4003(a)(3), (6). EPA must approve a state plan if it satisfies the requirements of §4003 and provides for plan revisions after notice and public hearing. §4007(a). States with approved plans are eligible for federal financial assistance. §4007(b).

Efforts to reduce nonhazardous solid waste through recycling have not gone smoothly. The Container Recycling Institute reported that 131 billion beverage containers were discarded in 2004 (up from 127 billion in 2003, and 121 billion in 2002), that the amount of can and bottle waste was rising, and that recycling rates for these materials were holding steady or declining. In 1992, when recycling rates were highest, about 67 billion containers were discarded and about 72 billion were recycled. In 2004, only about one-third of containers were recycled. 36 Env't Rep. (BNA) 12 (2005).

h. Liability for Imminent Hazards

MEGHRIG v. KFC WESTERN, INC.
516 U.S. 479 (1996)

Justice O'Connor delivered the opinion of the Court.

We consider whether §7002 of [RCRA], 42 U.S.C. §6972, authorizes a private cause of action to recover the prior cost of cleaning up toxic waste that does not, at the time of suit, continue to pose an endangerment to health or the environment. We conclude that it does not.

[In 1988, KFC discovered during the course of a construction project on one of its "Kentucky Fried Chicken" restaurants in Los Angeles that the property was contaminated with petroleum. KFC spent $211,000 removing and disposing of the contaminated soil to comply with a county health department order. In 1991, it brought a citizen suit under §7002(a) of RCRA to recover its cleanup costs from the previous owners of the property, the Meghrigs. KFC claimed that the contaminated soil had previously posed an "imminent and substantial endangerment" for purposes of §7002(a)(1)(B), and that the Meghrigs were responsible for "equitable restitution" of KFC's cleanup costs because, as prior owners, they had contributed to the waste's "past or present handling, storage, treatment, transportation, or disposal." The district court dismissed KFC's complaint, holding that §7002(a) does not authorize either recovery of past cleanup costs or a cause of action for remediation of waste no longer posing an "imminent and substantial endangerment" at the time suit is filed. The Ninth Circuit reversed on both grounds, and the Meghrigs appealed.]

. . . Unlike the Comprehensive Environmental Response, Compensation and Liability Act of 1980 (CERCLA), RCRA is not principally designed to effectuate the cleanup of toxic waste sites or to compensate those who have attended to the remediation of environmental hazards. . . . RCRA's primary purpose, rather, is to reduce the generation of hazardous waste and to ensure the proper treatment, storage, and disposal of that waste which is nonetheless generated, "so as to minimize the present and future threat to human health and the environment." 42 U.S.C. §6902(b).

Chief responsibility for the implementation and enforcement of RCRA rests with [EPA], see §§6928, 6973, but like other environmental laws, RCRA contains a citizen suit provision, §6972, which permits private citizens to enforce its provisions in some circumstances.

Two requirements of §6972(a) defeat KFC's suit against the Meghrigs. The first concerns the necessary timing of a citizen suit brought under §6972(a)(1)(B): That section permits a private party to bring suit against certain responsible persons, including former owners, "who ha[ve] contributed or who [are] contributing to the past or present handling, storage, treatment, transportation, or disposal of any solid or hazardous waste which *may present* an *imminent* and substantial endangerment to health or the environment." (Emphasis added.) The second defines the remedies a district court can award in a suit brought under §6972(a)(1)(B): Section 6972(a) authorizes district courts "*to restrain* any person who has contributed or who is contributing to the past or present handling, storage, treatment, transportation, or disposal of any solid or hazardous waste . . . , *to order such person to take such other action as may be necessary, or both.*" (Emphasis added.)

It is apparent from the two remedies described in §6972(a) that RCRA's citizen suit provision is not directed at providing compensation for past cleanup efforts. Under a plain reading of this remedial scheme, a private citizen suing under §6972(a)(1)(B) could seek a mandatory injunction, i.e., one that orders a responsible party to "take action" by attending to the cleanup and proper disposal of toxic waste, or a prohibitory injunction, i.e., one that "restrains" a responsible party from further violating RCRA. Neither remedy, however, is susceptible of the interpretation adopted by the Ninth Circuit, as neither contemplates the award of past cleanup costs, whether these are denominated "damages" or "equitable restitution."

In this regard, a comparison between the relief available under RCRA's citizen suit provision and that which Congress has provided in the analogous, but not parallel, provisions of CERCLA is telling. CERCLA was passed several years after RCRA went into effect, and it is designed to address many of the same toxic waste problems that inspired the passage of RCRA. Compare 42 U.S.C. §6903(5) (RCRA definition of "hazardous waste") and §6903(27) (RCRA definition of "solid waste") with §9601(14) (CERCLA provision incorporating certain "hazardous substance[s]," but not the hazardous and solid wastes defined in RCRA, and specifically not petroleum). CERCLA differs markedly from RCRA, however, in the remedies it provides. CERCLA's citizen suit provision mimics §6972(a) in providing district courts with the authority "to order such action as may be necessary to correct the violation" of any CERCLA standard or regulation. 42 U.S.C. §9659(c). But CERCLA expressly permits the Government to recover "all costs of removal or remedial action," §9607(a)(4)(A), and it expressly permits the recovery of any "necessary costs of response, incurred by any . . . person consistent with the national contingency plan," §9607(a)(4)(B). . . . See [also] §9613(f)(1). Congress thus demonstrated in CERCLA that it knew how to provide for the recovery of cleanup costs, and that the language used to define the remedies under RCRA does not provide that remedy.

That RCRA's citizen suit provision was not intended to provide a remedy for past cleanup costs is further apparent from the harm at which it is directed. Section 6972(a)(1)(B) permits a private party to bring suit only upon a showing that the solid or hazardous waste at issue "may present an imminent and substantial endangerment to health or the environment." The meaning of this timing restriction is plain: An endangerment can only be "imminent" if it "threaten[s] to occur immediately," Webster's New International Dictionary of English Language 1245 (2d ed. 1934), and the reference to waste which "may present" imminent harm quite clearly excludes waste that no longer presents such a danger. As the Ninth Circuit itself intimated in Price v. United States Navy, 39 F.3d 1011, 1019 (1994), this language "implies that there must be a threat which is present now, although the impact of the threat may not be felt until later." It follows that §6972(a) was designed to provide a remedy that ameliorates present or obviates the risk of future "imminent" harms, not a remedy that compensates for past cleanup efforts. . . .

Other aspects of RCRA's enforcement scheme strongly support this conclusion. Unlike CERCLA, RCRA contains no statute of limitations, compare §9613(g)(2) . . . , and it does not require a showing that the response costs being sought are reasonable, compare §§9607(a)(4)(A) and (B) (costs recovered under CERCLA must be "consistent with the national contingency plan"). If Congress had intended §6972(a) to function as a cost-recovery mechanism, the absence of these provisions would be striking. Moreover, with one limited exception, . . . a private party may not bring suit under §6972(a)(1)(B) without first giving 90 days' notice to the Administrator of the EPA, to "the State in which the alleged endangerment may occur," and to potential defendants, see §§6972(b)(2)(A)(i)-(iii). And no citizen suit can proceed if either the EPA or the State has commenced, and is diligently prosecuting, a separate enforcement action, see §§6972(b)(2)(B) and (C). Therefore, if RCRA were designed to compensate private parties for their past cleanup efforts, it would be a wholly irrational mechanism for doing so. Those parties with insubstantial problems, problems that neither the State nor the Federal Government feel compelled to address, could recover their response costs, whereas those parties whose waste problems were sufficiently severe as to attract the attention of Government officials would be left without a recovery.

      . . . [EPA] (as amicus) . . . joins KFC in arguing that §6972(a) does not in all circumstances preclude an award of past cleanup costs. The Government posits a situation in which suit is properly brought while the waste at issue continues to pose an imminent endangerment, and suggests that the plaintiff in such a case could seek equitable restitution of money previously spent on cleanup efforts. Echoing a similar argument made by KFC, the Government does not rely on the remedies expressly provided in §6972(a), but rather cites a line of cases holding that district courts retain inherent authority to award any equitable remedy that is not expressly taken away from them by Congress. See, e.g., Hecht Co. v. Bowles, 321 U.S. 321 (1944).

      RCRA does not prevent a private party from recovering its cleanup costs under other federal or state laws, see §6972(f) . . . , but the limited remedies described in §6972(a), along with the stark differences between the language of that section and the cost recovery provisions of CERCLA, amply demonstrate that Congress did not intend for a private citizen to be able to undertake a cleanup and then proceed to recover its costs under RCRA. As we explained in Middlesex County Sewerage Auth. v. National Sea Clammers Ass'n, 453 U.S. 1, 14 (1981), where Congress has provided "elaborate enforcement provisions" for remedying the violation of a federal statute, as Congress has done with RCRA and CERCLA, "it cannot be assumed that Congress intended to authorize by implication additional judicial remedies for private citizens suing under" the statute. . . .

      Without considering whether a private party could seek to obtain an injunction requiring another party to pay cleanup costs which arise after a RCRA citizen suit has been properly commenced, cf. United States v. Price, 688 F.2d 204, 211-213 (C.A.3 1982) (requiring funding of a diagnostic study is an appropriate form of relief in a suit brought by the Administrator under §6973), or otherwise recover cleanup costs paid out after the invocation of RCRA's statutory process, we agree with the Meghrigs that a private party cannot recover the cost of a past cleanup effort under RCRA, and that KFC's complaint is defective for the reasons stated by the District Court. Section 6972(a) does not contemplate the award of past cleanup costs, and §6972(a)(1)(B) permits a private party to bring suit only upon an allegation that the contaminated site presently poses an "imminent and substantial endangerment to health or the environment," and not upon an allegation that it posed such an endangerment at some time in the past. The judgment of the Ninth Circuit is reversed.

NOTES AND QUESTIONS

1. Did Justice O'Connor understand the relationship between RCRA and CERCLA? What do you make of her assertion that CERCLA's definition of "hazardous substances" does not include hazardous or solid wastes under RCRA? If a cost recovery suit is available under CERCLA, why does it make any difference if reimbursement may not be sought under RCRA?

2. *Cost Reimbursement and Cleanup Incentives.* What meaning, if any, did Justice O'Connor attribute to the provision in §7002(a)(1) authorizing the district courts to order the defendant to "take such other action as may be necessary"? Under her reading of the statute, was it necessary to interpret that phrase? What if, after *Meghrig*, a property owner begins cleaning up hazardous waste on its property and, while the cleanup is ongoing, commences a citizen suit against a person who allegedly disposed of the waste on the property; could the plaintiff recover cleanup costs incurred to date? If so, what would be the source of the district court's authority to require cost reimbursement—RCRA, other federal statutes, state law, or some other source of law? What if the plaintiff commences suit under §7002(a)(1)(B) before it spends any money responding to the contamination; would the court have the authority to order the defendant to finance the cleanup? See United States v. Domestic Indus., Inc., 32 F. Supp. 2d 855, 870-872 (E.D. Va. 1999) (private party defendant in action by United States alleging violations of RCRA may not recover through contribution or indemnity action against third-party defendants for civil penalties or cleanup costs for land not yet cleaned up); Express Car Wash Corp. v. Irinaga Bros., Inc., 967 F. Supp. 1188 (D. Or. 1997).

What incentives does *Meghrig*'s reading of RCRA's citizen suit provision create for a property owner who discovers the presence of hazardous waste attributable to the actions of a past generator, transporter, or TSD facility owner? In Avondale Fed. Sav. Bank v. Amoco Oil Co., 170 F.3d 692 (7th Cir. 1999), the court ruled that RCRA's citizen suit provision does not allow a court to award restitution for cleanup costs incurred by the current site owner after the filing of the citizen suit and that an injunction against the defendant (a former site owner) to prevent off-site contamination was premature because no harm was imminent. Judge Wood penned a strong dissent, arguing that the majority's result on the restitution issue creates perverse disincentives for current site owners to mitigate damage by cleaning up contaminated sites pending resolution of a pending citizen suit. It also creates incentives for defendants to stall, because "the longer the lawsuit runs, the more likely it is that another party will as a practical matter be forced to take it upon itself to clean up the defendants' messes." Id. at 697. What is the likely impact of *Avondale* on brownfields development? See also Albany Bank & Trust Co. v. Exxon Mobil Corp., 310 F.3d 969 (7th Cir. 2002) (investigation costs not recoverable in RCRA citizen suit).

3. *Equitable Discretion and Environmental Remedies.* The courts do not always read narrowly the scope of the federal courts' remedial powers in enforcing federal legislation. In United States v. Lane Labs–USA Inc., 427 F.3d 219 (3d Cir. 2005), the court distinguished *Meghrig* in holding that the federal district courts have the power to order a defendant found to be in violation of the FFDCA to pay restitution to consumers, pursuant to a provision vesting in those courts the authority "to restrain violations" of the Act. The government in that case charged the defendant with inappropriately advertising and promoting its products as effective in the prevention, treatment, and cure of cancer. Characterizing the issue as a "close call," the court

stated that, even "[t]hough the [FFDCA] does not specifically authorize restitution, such specificity is not required where the government properly invokes a court's equitable jurisdiction under this statute." Id. at 223. The court found that the statute and its legislative history indicated that Congress intended to protect the financial interests of consumers as well as their health. It emphasized that restitution serves a deterrent function and concluded that it was appropriate for the courts to award restitution to prevent further violations. The case was different from *Meghrig* because the latter was a citizen suit, not an enforcement action initiated by the government. The equitable powers of the federal courts are broader when the public interest is involved, as opposed to a mere private controversy. See also United States v. Rx Depot, Inc., 438 F.3d 1052 (10th Cir. 2006) (holding that an order of disgorgement is permitted under the FFDCA if it furthers statutory purposes).

4. *Imminent Hazards.* Section 7003 of RCRA authorizes EPA to bring suit in federal district court to enjoin activities that may present an imminent and substantial endangerment to health or the environment. EPA also may issue administrative orders "as may be necessary to protect public health and the environment." How does the scope of relief available to EPA under §7003 compare with the relief available in a §7002 citizen suit to abate an imminent and substantial endangerment? The court in United States v. Bliss, 667 F. Supp. 1298 (E.D. Mo. 1987), explained that liability under §7003 is strict and may be imposed on any person, including waste generators and transporters, whose past conduct contributed to the current endangerment.

In Interfaith Cmty. Org. v. Honeywell Int'l, Inc., 399 F.3d 248 (3d Cir. 2005), the court provided an extended discussion of the test for the issuance of injunctive relief under §7002(a)(1)(B). It indicated that Congress intended that the courts err on the side of protecting the public health and the environment in responding to citizen suits brought under §7002(a)(1)(B). It concluded that the plaintiff in such a suit need not demonstrate that there is a potential population at risk, quantify the risk posed by the defendant's activities, or show that contaminants are present at levels above those considered acceptable by the state in which the defendant's operations occur. "Proof of contamination in excess of state standards may support a finding of liability, and may alone suffice for liability in some cases, but its required use is without justification in the statute." Id. at 261.* Cf. Parker v. Scrap Metal Processors, Inc., 386 F.3d 993, 1015 (11th Cir. 2004) (stating that a plaintiff suing under §7002(a)(1)(B) must show that "there is a potential for an imminent threat of a serious harm"). A plaintiff suing under §7002(a)(1)(B) must prove that a particular defendant's waste was of a type that could contribute to an imminent and substantial endangerment that may exist. See Prisco v. A&D Carting Corp., 168 F.3d 593 (2d Cir. 1999).

Problem 8-4

EPA and the state of Iowa spent $10 million dollars cleaning up a pesticide formulation facility operated by Dead Bugs, Inc. (DBI) from 1974 through 1981, when DBI was adjudged to be bankrupt. EPA sought to recover its response costs under §7003 of RCRA from eight pesticide manufacturers who did business with DBI by hiring DBI to formulate their technical-grade pesticides into commercial-

---

*See also California Dep't of Toxic Substance Control v. Interstate Non-Ferrous Corp., 298 F. Supp. 2d 930, 980-981 (E.D. Cal. 2003) (stating that endangerment does not require proof of actual harm and that plaintiff need not quantify the endangerment to show that it is substantial).

grade pesticides. According to EPA, it was a common practice in the pesticide industry for manufacturers of active pesticide ingredients to contract with formulators such as DBI to produce a commercial-grade product that could then be sold to farmers and other consumers. Formulators such as DBI mix the manufacturer's active ingredients with inert materials using the specifications provided by the manufacturer. The resulting commercial-grade product is then packaged by the formulator and either shipped back to the manufacturer or shipped directly to customers of the manufacturer. The complaint alleged that although DBI performed the actual mixing or formulation process, the defendants owned the technical-grade pesticide, the work in process, and the commercial-grade pesticide while the pesticide was in DBI's possession. The complaint also alleged that the generation of pesticide-containing wastes through spills, cleaning of equipment, mixing and grinding operations, and production of batches that do not meet specifications is an "inherent" part of the formulation process. EPA alleged that the defendants were liable under §7003 for the cleanup costs incurred at the DBI site because, by virtue of their relationships with DBI, they "contributed to" the handling, storage, treatment, or disposal of hazardous wastes.

Does §7003 authorize the government to seek reimbursement for cleanup costs it has incurred in responding to an imminent and substantial endangerment? Is there any reason to treat the government differently from a private party in this regard? Cf. 28 U.S.C. §2415 (establishing a statute of limitations for civil actions by the United States based on express or implied contract or sounding in tort). Assuming that the United States may seek cost reimbursement under §7003, must the endangerment continue to exist at the time suit is commenced?

G.   THE INTERSTATE WASTE WARS

SDDS, INC. v. SOUTH DAKOTA
47 F.3d 263 (8th Cir. 1995)

MAGILL, Circuit Judge.

. . . At issue in this §1983 suit is whether the referendum of a measure permitting [South Dakota Disposal Systems, Inc. (SDDS)] to operate a large-scale municipal solid waste disposal (MSWD) facility in South Dakota violates the dormant commerce clause. . . . Because we find that the referendum was the latest in a series of protectionist roadblocks erected by South Dakota, we hold that the referendum violates the dormant commerce clause. . . .

I.   Background

[In November 1988, SDDS filed with the South Dakota Department of Water and Natural Resources (DWNR) an application for a permit to site, construct and operate a MSWD facility (the Lonetree facility). The Board of Minerals and the Environment (BME), a branch of the DWNR, found the Lonetree facility to be environmentally safe and in the public interest and issued a one-year permit in

September 1989. It issued a five-year renewal permit in 1990 based on similar findings. The South Dakota Supreme Court concluded, however, that the BME's factual findings in support of the original one-year permit did not permit the court to determine whether the facility was in the public interest. The same court held later that the renewal permit was also void from its inception.]

[An initiative on the November 1990 ballot] required legislative approval of any large-scale SWD facility in addition to the administrative approval required of all SWD facilities regardless of size. Legislative approval was conditioned upon a finding that the facility was environmentally safe and in the public interest. Under South Dakota law, the Secretary of State is required to publish a pamphlet containing an Attorney General's explanation of and public comment on each initiated or referred measure. [This pamphlet becomes part of the legislative history of the measure.] The Attorney General's explanation of the November 1990 initiative stated that it would apply retroactively to existing facilities (i.e., the Lonetree facility), and that only one facility (i.e., the Lonetree facility) would be affected. The initiative was passed in the November 1990 election.

[After the legislature passed a statute approving the Lonetree facility, the Attorney General certified a referendum on that approval and prepared an explanation of the approval and published arguments pro and con.] The Attorney General's explanation states that the legislature found the facility to be environmentally safe and in the public interest and that the DWNR permits were "declared invalid in a court decision." The three-sentence "pro" statement mentions public support for the facility in the Edgemont area, the issuance of permits by the DWNR and the legislature, and the economic impact of the facility.

The "con" statement is the most significant part of the explanatory pamphlet in terms of length and impact. Because of the importance of this statement, we set it out at length:

> Referred Law is a direct public vote on the Lonetree mega-garbage dump near Edgemont. South Dakota Disposal Systems, Inc. (SDDS), Lonetree's owner, has stated 95% of the waste will come from out-of-state. [BME] and the legislature gave SDDS approval to bring in 65 railroad cars of garbage per day, seven days per week.
>
> ACTion for the Environment has referred that approval to a vote because South Dakota is not the nation's dumping grounds. A "NO" vote will prevent Lonetree from operating, and keep its imported garbage out of South Dakota.
>
> [EPA] stated that all landfills eventually deteriorate, and new technologies only delay leaks further into the future (Federal Register, August 30, 1988). NIMBY (not in my backyard) exists because people do not want their soil, air and water contaminated. . . .
>
> . . . Lonetree is not an option for South Dakota communities. It is an out-of-state dump.
>
> To the extent we become the nation's dumping grounds, we undermine successful recycling efforts elsewhere. Vote "NO" on Lonetree.

[In November 1992, the referendum was defeated, effectively vetoing the Lonetree facility and nullifying the legislature's approval of the facility. SDDS challenged the initiative that required dual legislative and administrative approval. In *SDDS III*, a state court judge upheld the initiative, rejecting dormant Commerce Clause claims like those at issue in this case. SDDS did not appeal. The South Dakota Supreme Court later held that the decision in *SDDS III* did not collaterally estop SDDS from attacking the legality of the referendum. On remand, the district court upheld the referendum against a Commerce Clause challenge. SDDS appealed.]

A.   THE GENERAL FRAMEWORK: VARYING LEVELS OF SCRUTINY

The Supreme Court has established a two-step approach to the dormant commerce clause. The first step requires us to determine whether a challenged state measure discriminates against out-of-state articles (i.e., is a protectionist measure). Discrimination may take one of three forms. . . . First, a measure may facially discriminate against out-of-state articles. See, e.g., Philadelphia v. New Jersey, 437 U.S. 617 (1978) (facial discrimination where state statute prohibited importation of waste "which originated or was collected outside the territorial limits of the State"). No one contends that the referendum is facially discriminatory. However, facial discrimination is merely one of the ways in which a state may "artlessly disclose an avowed purpose to discriminate." Dean Milk Co. v. City of Madison, 340 U.S. 349, 354 (1951).

The other two forms of discrimination are more subtle and require us to examine the overall effect of the challenged measures.[7] A second way in which a challenged measure may discriminate is that a facially neutral measure may have a discriminatory purpose. . . . Third, a facially neutral measure may have a discriminatory effect. See, e.g., Maine v. Taylor, 477 U.S. 131, 148 n.19 (1986) (discriminatory effect may be found where state "respond[s] to legitimate local concerns by discriminating arbitrarily against interstate trade").

At the second step of the analysis, we apply the appropriate level of scrutiny. The Supreme Court has established two levels of scrutiny. The determinative factor is the presence or absence of discrimination against interstate commerce. If the state measure is discriminatory, it is subjected to the "strictest scrutiny," Oregon Waste Sys., Inc. v. Department of Envtl. Quality, 511 U.S. 93, 101 (1994), and a "virtually per se rule of invalidity" applies. Id. at 100.[8] If "other legislative objectives are credibly advanced and there is no patent discrimination against interstate trade," the measure is subjected to a more flexible balancing test. Pike v. Bruce Church, 397 U.S. 137, 142 (1970). . . .

B.   WHAT LEVEL OF SCRUTINY: IS THERE DISCRIMINATION?

Although the referendum is not facially discriminatory, we find that . . . the referred measure was defeated for a discriminatory purpose. We also find that the referendum has a discriminatory effect against interstate commerce. We therefore apply the "strictest scrutiny" to the referendum.

1.   DOES THE REFERENDUM HAVE A DISCRIMINATORY PURPOSE?

The presence of a discriminatory purpose is one of three ways to trigger strict scrutiny. The record is replete with direct and indirect evidence of an avowed discriminatory purpose behind the referendum.

The record contains two pieces of direct evidence of a discriminatory purpose. First, in SDDS III, [the judge] noted that the initiative "was purposely drafted to insure

7. "[T]he evil of protectionism can reside in legislative means as well as legislative ends." Philadelphia, 437 U.S. at 626. Facial discrimination generally involves a discriminatory purpose and a discriminatory effect, while the other two forms of discrimination involve one or the other.

8. . . . The only way that discriminatory state action can withstand this level of scrutiny is if the state demonstrates that the out-of-state articles are more dangerous than are in-state articles. Neither party to this appeal makes any such claim.

that, except for Lonetree, the Initiated Measure would not apply to existing or fore-seeable future landfills that dispose of South Dakota waste." The dual administrative and legislative approval required by the initiative was specifically designed and intended to hinder the importation of out-of-state waste into South Dakota. The purpose of the first and only referendum under the initiative cannot be divorced from the purpose of the initiative itself. The initiative was drafted to defeat a specific "out-of-state dump" by requiring an additional approval, and the referendum concerns that very approval for the same "out-of-state dump." We believe that the discriminatory purpose behind the initiative infected the referendum as well. Second, the legislative history of the referred measure is brimming with protectionist rhetoric. The state-sponsored pamphlet that accompanied the referendum contained a "con" statement that exhorted voters to vote against the "out-of-state dump" because "South Dakota is not the nation's dumping grounds," and "[a] 'NO' vote will prevent Lonetree from operating, and keep its imported garbage out of South Dakota." This is ample evidence of a discriminatory purpose to trigger strict scrutiny.

. . . [T]here is [also] substantial indirect evidence that the referendum was moti-vated by a discriminatory purpose. In [Hunt v. Washington State Apple Advertising Comm'n, 432 U.S. 333, 352 (1977)], the Supreme Court found "it somewhat suspect" that the means used to achieve the state's "ostensible . . . purpose" were relatively inef-fective. Likewise, South Dakota has employed a highly ineffective means to pursue its ostensible purpose of environmental protection. After the initiative passed, a large-scale MSWD facility in South Dakota was required to obtain two things: an administrative permit and legislative authorization. South Dakota argues that large MSWD facilities generally pose a greater risk to the environment than do smaller facilities. We will assume for the sake of our decision that this is true. However, although the general difference in risk between larger and smaller facilities justifies a general requirement of legislative approval for large MSWD facilities, a general difference in risk, without more, is insufficient to support a particular denial of legislative approval. South Dakota must demonstrate not only that there are legitimate interests justifying the general requirement of dual approval, but it must also show that this particular review furthered those goals. . . . South Dakota has completely failed to demonstrate that the referen-dum that denied legislative approval for the Lonetree facility in any way furthered the state's legitimate concerns with safety and environmental protection.

South Dakota's most significant environmental protection device is the admin-istrative permitting process for SWD facilities. . . . SDDS sought a permit for the Lonetree facility from the DWNR, and when the permit was contested, the BME held hearings to determine whether the Lonetree facility was environmentally safe and in the public interest. The permit was granted, appealed, remanded, reissued, reap-pealed, renewed, and ultimately voided. The fact that SDDS's permit for the Lonetree facility was so carefully scrutinized indicates that the administrative permitting process is a relatively effective means of environmental protection. In fact, South Dakota admits that the Lonetree facility is safe and in the public interest if operated in accordance with the DWNR permit conditions. . . . Thus, the dual process provides an incremental benefit over the administrative process alone to the extent that the legislature is able to detect unsafe facilities that are not detected by the DWNR.

Because the benefit of legislative review is that it screens out unsafe large facil-ities that survived the administrative review process, the benefit of each legislative review is directly proportional to the amount of scrutiny of the environmental effects of the proposed facility that occurs in that review.[9] The challenged referendum cannot be said to have provided any benefits because the body that disapproved the Lonetree facility (i.e., the South Dakota electorate) was provided with: (1) no standards or information to use to evaluate the benefits and risks of the Lonetree facility; and (2) information that leads to an unreliable result. . . . The voters simply voted yes or no without any criteria and with severely limited information to guide them in evaluating the effects of the Lonetree facility. Thus, because the voters were not provided with any meaningful criteria, the defeat of the referred measure cannot be seen as improving environmental protection.

[The court next noted that "voters were bombarded with protectionist propaganda that renders the result of the referendum unreliable as an environmental review." No connection was made in the "con" statement between "vague and general statements" such as the eventual degeneration of all landfills and the specific Lonetree facility. The few specific environmental concerns mentioned were "sandwiched between . . . pleas to reject 'imported garbage' and the 'out-of-state dump.' This protectionist concern clearly emerges as the dominant reason to reject the referred measure. . . . Such propaganda does nothing to enhance any meaningful review of the environmental impact; it merely allows protectionism to run rampant."]

2.   DOES THE REFERENDUM HAVE A DISCRIMINATORY EFFECT?

Alternatively, even if South Dakota had not openly declared a discriminatory purpose, the referendum is discriminatory in its effect, and this type of discrimination will also trigger strict scrutiny. . . . The structure of the "garbage market" in South Dakota is such that the referendum has a discriminatory effect. South Dakota generates 600,000 to 700,000 tons of MSW each year. In addition to this in-state waste, three facilities accept out-of-state waste (they accepted 60,000 tons in 1992). As a result of the low rate of domestic waste generation and the costs of regulation, the existing disposal facilities in South Dakota are fairly small; the largest facility disposes of 125,000 tons per year. New facilities must be large scale in order to recover the costs imposed by environmental regulations. The Lonetree facility was designed to accept 1.5 million tons of MSW per year. According to the literature accompanying the referendum, 95% of this waste would originate outside South Dakota.

. . . Here South Dakota is attempting to exclude out-of-state trash that has a "negative" value, thus forcing other states to bear the cost of disposing of the trash when the market would otherwise dispose of the trash in South Dakota. . . . Thus, because the garbage market of South Dakota is such that the referendum so predominantly affects only out-of-staters, we believe that the referendum of S.B. 169 is discriminatory in effect, and must receive strict scrutiny.

C.   APPLICATION OF STRICT SCRUTINY

Once strict scrutiny is triggered, "the burden falls on the State to justify [the measure] both in terms of the local benefits flowing from the statute and the

---

9. Viewing the benefit in this manner distinguishes the dual permitting measure from the absolute bans on large landfills that have been approved in dicta. There is a legitimate state interest in environmental protection, and the absolute ban is the best, or at least a permissible way to achieve this goal. South Dakota's legislative review process, by contrast, although supported by the same state interest in the abstract, simply does nothing to further this purported goal. Thus, the fact that legislative review is less restrictive than an absolute ban, rather than being an asset, proves fatal.

unavailability of a nondiscriminatory alternative adequate to preserve the local interests at stake." *Hunt*, 432 U.S. at 353. We find that the referendum fails both prongs of this test because the record demonstrates that (1) the denial of legislative approval by the referendum does not further the legitimate goal of environmental safety, and therefore provides no local benefits; and (2) a nondiscriminatory alternative is available because legislative review of the Lonetree facility may be obtained without a referendum in which the predominant argument is the imported nature of the garbage at Lonetree.

In order to survive strict scrutiny under the commerce clause, South Dakota first must demonstrate that the referendum on the Lonetree facility provided some local benefits. . . . Although the goal of environmental protection is [such] a permissible [benefit], . . . the referendum . . . simply does nothing to advance this goal. Because there is already one procedure in place to protect the environment, and this second review provides only an incremental amount of additional protection, this referendum in which voters were distracted by distinctly non-environmental concerns provided no local benefit. South Dakota has not carried its burden to prove that this referendum resulted in increased environmental protection.

To survive strict scrutiny, South Dakota must also demonstrate the lack of a nondiscriminatory alternative to this referendum under the dual permitting scheme. . . . The most obvious alternative is a legislative discussion in which interstate trade issues are not the dominant issues discussed. This alternative may be easily achieved through a fuller discussion of the environmental issues. . . . The alternative would more fully achieve the desired effect of protecting the environment by forcing consideration of the environmental issues without the distortions of reasoning that result from the emphasis on protectionist propaganda.

Thus, . . . we conclude that the referendum fails the required strict scrutiny. We therefore hold that South Dakota's referendum of S.B. 169 violates the dormant aspects of the commerce clause of the United States Constitution. . . .

NOTES AND QUESTIONS

1. *The Dormant Commerce Clause and Economic Protectionism. SDDS* applies the Supreme Court's dormant Commerce Clause "waste" jurisprudence. State public health quarantines have long been an exception to the general rule that a state cannot discriminate against interstate commerce. Bowman v. Chicago & N.W. Ry. Co., 12 U.S. 465 (1888). Although efforts to prohibit or make more costly the disposal of out-of-state wastes could be characterized as quarantines, the Supreme Court has consistently invalidated as protectionist waste import bans or laws that subject out-of-state wastes to differential costs or otherwise distort interstate markets. Philadelphia v. New Jersey, 437 U.S. 617 (1978), invalidated a New Jersey law that prohibited the import of out-of-state waste for disposal in New Jersey landfills. The law was not a quarantine because the danger arose after disposal, thus negating any difference between in- and out-of-state wastes. The statute was facially discriminatory and thus subject to the Court's "virtually per se rule of invalidity." No state law that treats out-of-state wastes differently has survived the Court's strict scrutiny analysis to ferret out protectionist legislation.

For an interesting example of the interstate enmities that may result from waste export efforts, see Trade Trash for Culture? Not Virginia, N.Y. Times, Jan. 18, 1999, at A1. Virginia's efforts to halt the export of solid waste from states like New York were challenged in Waste Mgmt. Holdings, Inc. v. Gilmore, 252 F.3d 316 (4th Cir. 2001). The court granted summary judgment to the plaintiffs in their dormant Commerce Clause challenges to statutory provisions that capped the amount of municipal solid waste that may be accepted by Virginia landfills, restricted the use of barges and trucks to transport such waste in the state, and required a state agency to condition the carrying of municipal solid waste on Virginia roads on the provision by truck owners of financial assurances not applicable to truckers carrying other cargo. Using the strict scrutiny test applicable to measures adopted for a discriminatory purpose, the court invalidated these provisions because the state failed to show that it adopted the least discriminatory alternative that addressed the state's concerns over health and safety risks. Similarly, in Harper v. Public Serv. Comm'n, 427 F. Supp. 2d 707 (S.D. W. Va. 2006), the court concluded that a state statute prohibiting solid waste haulers from operating within the state without first receiving a certificate of convenience and necessity violated the dormant Commerce Clause. It found that the certification requirement imposed a substantial barrier to entry into the trash collection and disposal market. Applying the *Pike* balancing test discussed in *SDDS*, the court reasoned that the resulting significant burdens on interstate commerce outweighed the purported local benefits of universal service at reasonable rates and environmental protection.

One justification for *Philadelphia* and subsequent cases is that waste is an article of commerce and must be allocated exclusively by national markets that increase efficiency and promote a national union. The counter-theory is that waste import bans and similar laws reflect not economic protectionism but environmental externality prevention. The externality theory has not impressed the Court. Oregon Waste Sys., Inc. v. Department of Envtl. Quality, 511 U.S. 93 (1994); Chemical Waste Mgmt. v. Hunt, 504 U.S. 334 (1992). In each case the Court invalidated waste disposal laws that imposed differential fees on the disposal or treatment of out-of-state wastes. Alabama attempted in *Hunt* to justify its additional fee on out-of-state waste as a health and safety measure, but the Court found "absolutely no evidence" that out-of-state wastes are more dangerous than in-state wastes. Oregon tried to rely on an exception suggested in *Hunt*, but Justice Thomas was unimpressed:

> Respondent's principal defense of the higher surcharge on out-of-state waste is that it is a "compensatory tax" necessary to make shippers of such waste pay their "fair share" of the costs imposed on Oregon by the disposal of their waste in the State. In [*Hunt*] we noted the possibility that such an argument might justify a discriminatory surcharge or tax on out-of-state waste. . . . To justify a charge on interstate commerce as a compensatory tax, a State must, as a threshold matter, identif[y] the [intrastate tax] burden for which the State is attempting to compensate. . . . Once the burden has been identified, the tax on interstate commerce must be shown to roughly approximate—but not to exceed—the amount of the tax on interstate commerce. . . . [W]e have little difficulty concluding that the Oregon surcharge is not [a compensatory] tax. Oregon does not impose a specific charge of at least $2.25 per ton on shippers of waste generated in Oregon, for which the out-of-state surcharge might be considered compensatory. In fact, the only analogous charge on the disposal of waste is $0.85 per ton, approximately one-third of the amount imposed on waste from other States. . . . Respondent's failure to identify a specific charge . . . is fatal. [511 U.S. at 102-104.]

Justice Rehnquist dissented in both cases because the results presented states with a Hobson's choice: either ban all landfills or accept all wastes, thus increasing risks to the public.

Despite predictions that the nation will soon run short of waste disposal capacity, the combined dump capacity of the nation's three largest waste haulers increased from 5,342 million tons in 2000 to 6,620 million tons in 2004. The increase was due to expansion of existing dumps and more efficient compacting methods. See Bailey, Waste Yes, Want Not: Rumors of Dump Space Were Greatly Exaggerated, N.Y. Times, Aug. 12, 2005, at C1, C3.

2. *Resource versus Economic Protectionism.* The Court's antiprotectionist jurisprudence applies to *intrastate* discrimination, too. Fort Gratiot Sanitary Landfill, Inc. v. Michigan Dep't of Natural Res., 504 U.S. 353 (1992), applied *Philadelphia* to a state statute that barred counties from accepting out-of-county wastes unless their mandatory solid waste plan explicitly authorized it. While the statute allowed counties to accept out-of-state wastes, one county denied an application to accept out-of-state waste because the plan did not authorize out-of-county waste. Michigan argued, relying on Pike v. Bruce Church, that the statute regulated evenhandedly to achieve local interests and that any burden it imposed on interstate commerce was not clearly excessive in relation to those benefits; the Court, however, found the statute as protectionist as New Jersey's import ban. The fact that some Michigan counties accept out-of-state waste did not adequately distinguish the case from *Philadelphia.* The Court did suggest that a state could determine a safe capacity level and limit the amount of wastes that landfill operators accept per year based on this projection. But in *Oregon Waste Sys., supra,* the Court rejected Oregon's argument that conserving scarce landfill space for home-generated waste was resource, not economic, protectionism; a state may not give its own citizens preferred access to its natural resources over out-of-state consumers.

Eastern Ky. Res. v. Fiscal Court of Magoffin County, 127 F.3d 532 (6th Cir. 1997), upheld a state requirement that area solid waste plans identify "any additional capacity authorized for out-of-area municipal and solid waste." The statute was neither facially discriminatory nor invalid under the *Pike* balancing test, and there was no evidence that the state tried to prevent the acceptance of out-of-state waste. A similar result was reached in United Waste Sys., Inc. v. Wilson, 189 F.3d 762 (8th Cir. 1999). The court upheld an Iowa statute that required each city and county in the state to designate a solid waste facility in a mandated plan, but permitted the local government to send its waste elsewhere in the state or out of state. The purposes included state tracking of the destination of the state's waste and the collection of tipping fees to finance recycling. The court found that this was an evenhanded, nonprotectionist regulatory scheme with "only an attenuated effect on interstate commerce." But cf. Waste Management of Pa., Inc. v. Shinn, 938 F. Supp. 1243 (D.N.J. 1996). In 1991, New Jersey exported 2.7 of the 7.1 million tons of solid waste that it generated each year. In 1994, it adopted a statewide solid waste management plan with the goal of state self-sufficiency by 2000, but a district court held that the goal "discriminates against out-of-state waste disposal facilities in favor of in-state economic interests without serving any legitimate local interest which could not be addressed by less restrictive means." Id. at 1256. If New Jersey actually develops sufficient disposal and recycling capacity for all solid waste generated in the state, would this be unconstitutional? Could a state have different capacity quotas for in- and out-of-state waste? See Environmental Tech. Council v. Sierra Club, 98 F.3d 774 (4th Cir. 1996).

If a court determines that a local measure has extraterritorial effect, it is likely to strike it down as violative of the dormant Commerce Clause. See, e.g., National Solid Wastes Mgmt. Ass'n v. Meyer, 165 F.3d 1151 (7th Cir. 1999) (striking down as an improper "clog on interstate commerce" a Wisconsin statute allowing out-of-state waste to be disposed of in Wisconsin only if the community where the waste originates adopts an ordinance incorporating the mandatory components of Wisconsin's recycling program); National Solid Wastes Mgmt. Ass'n v. Charter County, 303 F. Supp. 2d 835 (E.D. Mich. 2004) (invalidating county regulation making it unlawful for a landfill to accept solid waste that is not regulated by a beverage container deposit law that has bottle return rates comparable to those reported by Michigan agency). Compare National Solid Wastes Mgmt. Ass'n v. Granholm, 344 F. Supp. 2d 559 (E.D. Mich. 2004) (requirements that out-of-state jurisdictions impose limits on solid waste disposal in landfills comparable to those in Michigan to be eligible for disposal in Michigan, and that out-of-state solid waste be inspected before being deposited in Michigan landfill, did not discriminate against out-of-state waste).

3. *Flow Control.* In the 1980s, there was great interest in building new recycling centers to limit the need for new landfill capacity. Because the centers require a constant supply of waste to be operated efficiently, towns adopted flow control ordinances requiring all nonhazardous waste to be deposited at the facility. In C & A Carbone, Inc. v. Town of Clarkstown, 511 U.S. 383 (1994), the Court held that an ordinance requiring that all of the town's wastes be deposited at a transfer station, and charged a tipping fee before being recycled or landfilled, unlawfully discriminated against interstate commerce. Clarkstown argued that its ordinance did not discriminate because it did not differentiate waste on the basis of its geographic origin; *all* solid waste had to be processed at the designated transfer station before it left the town. Thus, the town claimed, instead of erecting a barrier to the import or export of solid waste, the ordinance required only that the waste be channeled through the designated facility. The Supreme Court characterized the service of processing and disposing of waste, not the waste itself, as the article of commerce. The ordinance discriminated against interstate commerce by allowing only the favored operator to process waste within the town. Its "essential vice" was that it barred the import of the processing service, thereby hoarding solid waste, and the demand to get rid of it, for the benefit of the preferred processing facility and squelching competition in the waste-processing service from outside providers. That kind of discrimination in favor of local business or investment is per se invalid, unless the municipality can demonstrate that it has no other means to advance its legitimate local interest. The Court distinguished Maine v. Taylor, 477 U.S. 131 (1986), which upheld a ban on the import of baitfish because Maine had no other way to prevent the spread of parasites and the adulteration of native fish species. The Court found that Clarkstown had nondiscriminatory alternatives, such as the adoption of safety regulations to ensure that competitors like Carbone do not underprice the market by cutting corners on safety. Clarkstown could not justify the flow control ordinance as a way to steer solid waste away from out-of-town disposal sites that it might deem harmful to the environment because such an effort would amount to an improper extraterritorial application of the town's police power. Although a central purpose of the flow control ordinance was to ensure the profitability of the town-sponsored facility, revenue generation alone cannot justify discrimination against interstate commerce.

How far does *Carbone* extend? Houlton Citizens' Coalition v. Town of Houlton, 175 F.3d 178 (1st Cir. 1999), upheld a local waste management scheme requiring all generators of residential rubbish within the town either to use the town's chosen contractor or to haul their own trash to a designated repository, and granting the exclusive right to collect third-party residential waste to the town's contractor. The court did not interpret *Carbone* as banning every flow control ordinance coupled with

an exclusive contractual arrangement in favor of an in-state operator. If the scheme allows out-of-state as well as in-state haulers to compete fairly for the waste hauling contract, as this one did, the scheme is not facially discriminatory. Applying the *Pike* balancing test, the court found no Commerce Clause violation because the strong local interest in efficient and effective waste management outweighed the "virtually invisible burden that the Town's scheme places on interstate commerce." Id. at 189.*
But in National Waste Mgmt. Ass'n v. Daviess County, 434 F.3d 898 (6th Cir. 2005), *rehearing denied*, 446 F.3d 647 (6th Cir. 2006), the court struck down an ordinance specifying that the county would provide universal municipal solid waste collection within its jurisdiction through the grant of nonexclusive franchises, that all franchise agreements would require the party providing waste collection service to dispose of the waste it collects at the county's landfill or transfer station, and that no waste hauler would be allowed to collect municipal solid waste in the county unless granted a franchise by the county. The ordinance prevented waste haulers from using in-state facilities other than the county's and from using out-of-state facilities, making it facially discriminatory against out-of-state interests. The absence of discrimination against out-of-state waste collectors made no difference because the ordinance discriminated against out-of-state waste disposal facilities.

Does it make any difference whether a flow control ordinance requires that waste be delivered to a privately or publicly owned facility? See United Haulers Ass'n, Inc. v. Oneida-Herkimer Solid Waste Mgmt. Auth., 438 F.3d 150 (2d Cir. 2006); United Haulers Ass'n, Inc. v. Oneida-Herkimer Solid Waste Mgmt. Auth., 261 F.3d 245 (2d Cir. 2001). Suppose that a county adopts an ordinance that prohibits the disposal of waste generated within the county at any landfill whose operator refuses to sign a designation agreement obligating it to collect and remit to the county a per-ton contract fee designed to meet the "financial need" of the county in implementing its solid waste management plan. If no out-of-state county agrees to sign a designation agreement, thus precluding out-of-state disposal, does the ordinance violate the dormant Commerce Clause? See Maharg, Inc. v. Van Wert Solid Waste Mgmt. Dist., 249 F.3d 549 (6th Cir. 2001).

4. *Economic Protectionism versus Environmental Justice.* One rationale for the Court's dormant Commerce Clause jurisprudence is that facially discriminatory legislation is a good indicator that out-of-state interests have been excluded from the political process. E.g., Eule, Laying the Dormant Commerce Clause to Rest, 91 Yale L.J. 425 (1982). But environmentalists have been critical of cases such as *SDDS* because no weight is given to the states' interest in allocating landfill and treatment capacity. Engel, Reconsidering the National Market in Solid Waste: Trade-offs in Equity, Efficiency, Environmental Protection and State Autonomy, 73 N.C. L. Rev. 1481 (1995). Professor Engel found that waste exports move from richer,

_____

*See also IESI AR Corp. v. Northwest Arkansas Solid Waste Mgmt. Dist., 433 F.3d 600 (8th Cir. 2005) (upholding under *Pike* balancing test a flow control ordinance requiring that solid waste be disposed of either in the district in which the ordinance was enacted or in out-of-state landfills because, among other things, the ordinance favored some out-of-state interests over in-state interests by exempting solid waste bound for landfills outside the state); National Solid Waste Mgmt. Ass'n v. Pine Belt Regional Solid Waste Mgmt. Auth., 389 F.3d 491 (5th Cir. 2004) (holding that flow control ordinance did not violate the *Pike* test because regional waste management authority had legitimate local purpose of ensuring economic viability of its landfill and the ordinance did not have a disparate impact on interstate commerce; the burdens imposed on the interstate contracts of companies that collected, processed, and disposed of solid waste were no greater than the burdens imposed on intrastate contracts).

generally eastern states to poorer, southern and midwestern ones. Is there an environmental justice case for abandoning the *Philadelphia* per se rule? See Verchick, The Commerce Clause, Environmental Justice and the Interstate Garbage Wars, 70 So. Cal. L. Rev. 1239 (1997).

5. *Market Participation.* The market participation doctrine exempts direct state participation in the market from dormant Commerce Clause scrutiny. The state, however, cannot impose conditions on the sale of state-owned natural resources. South-Central Timber Dev., Inc. v. Wunnicke, 467 U.S. 82 (1984), held that an Alaskan statute requiring that all timber purchased from the state be processed in-state violated the Commerce Clause.

National Solid Waste Mgmt. Ass'n v. Williams, 146 F.3d 595 (8th Cir. 1998), upheld under the market participation doctrine a state solid waste plan that required all public agencies to use local facilities if a state-approved county plan was in place. See also BFI Waste Sys. of N. Am., Inc. v. Broward County, 265 F. Supp. 2d 1332 (2003) (finding that contract between county and solid waste hauler requiring hauler to deliver waste it collected to designated facilities was exempt from Commerce Clause scrutiny because the county was acting as a market participant in both the solid waste collection and disposal markets). But Huish Detergents, Inc. v. Warren County, 214 F.3d 707 (6th Cir. 2000), held that the doctrine did not justify an agreement between a local government and its exclusive franchisee that required the franchisee to process all waste at a single transfer station owned by the city. The county was not acting in a proprietary capacity in forcing all municipal waste to flow through the city's transfer station, and it was not purchasing processing services with public funds or selling its own processing services. Similarly, the county did not act as a market participant in prohibiting out-of-state disposal of municipal waste because it neither bought nor sold disposal services with municipal funds. The court struck down both the requirement that the franchisee process waste at the county's transfer station and the prohibition on out-of-state disposal as per se discriminatory.

6. *Funding Hazardous Waste Remediation.* State schemes for financing the cleanup of hazardous waste sites also may run afoul of the dormant Commerce Clause. See, e.g., CWM Chem. Serv., L.L.C. v. Roth, 787 N.Y.S.2d 780 (N.Y. App. Div. 2004), *aff'd as modified*, 846 N.E.2d 448 (N.Y. 2006). Cf. American Trucking Ass'ns, Inc. v. New Jersey, 852 A.2d 142 (N.J. 2004) (holding that hazardous waste transporter registration fee discriminated against interstate commerce by charging a flat fee unrelated to the transporter's level of activity in the state).

7. *New Jersey versus Pennsylvania.* The Congressional Research Service reported in 2004 that interstate shipments of municipal solid waste increased 170 percent over the preceding decade, to a total of more than 39 million tons in 2003. The five largest exporting states were New York, New Jersey, Missouri, Illinois, and Maryland. Pennsylvania was the largest importer, with most of its imports coming from New York and New Jersey. 35 Env't Rep. (BNA) 2055 (2004).

IX

LIABILITY FOR AND REMEDIATION OF HAZARDOUS SUBSTANCE CONTAMINATION

The regulatory programs for the management of toxic substances and hazardous waste discussed in the preceding chapter are primarily prospective in orientation. Even if statutes such as RCRA succeed in preventing harm from the operation of active waste treatment, storage, and disposal facilities, many inactive or abandoned dump sites will continue to threaten health and natural systems. Sites no longer receiving wastes often are difficult to clean up for several reasons. Some sites are true "orphan" sites: no one knows who operated or used them. Others are the work of "midnight dumpers" or "gypsy haulers," who significantly lowered their overhead costs by treating unoccupied land as a waste commons and then disappeared. Some businesses that generated the substances sent to the site, transported those substances to the site, or owned the site at the time of disposal may have gone out of business or into bankruptcy. These factors often make it difficult to identify parties that are capable of financing remediation. Even if it is possible to locate those parties, attempts to allocate responsibility among them may be frustrating. The nature or quantity of wastes present at a site, and the amounts sent or managed by the various identified contributors, may be impossible to establish because records have been lost or destroyed, if any existed at all. It may seem unfair to assign responsibility to a solvent entity whose contribution to the site appears to have been minimal, while assets of more culpable businesses or individuals do not exist or cannot be reached.

Finally, even if entities with the resources to finance site remediation are available, and a reasonable allocation of cleanup costs among them can be made, selecting the appropriate remedy is typically an arduous task. Remediation may be physically impossible, such as where groundwater has been contaminated with dense, non-aqueous-phase liquids (those with a specific gravity greater than that of water). Where it is not, questions concerning the appropriate extent of remediation abound. Should efforts be made to restore contaminated resources to their precontamination state? What role should cost play in the selection of a remedy? If a multi-million-dollar cleanup technology is capable of reducing the risk of disease attributable to exposure by 99 percent, but simply capping the site can reduce the risk by 95 percent at a fraction of the cost, which remedy should be chosen?

The price tag of cleaning up sites at which hazardous substances have been released into the environment runs well into the billions of dollars. EPA reported in 2004 that it will cost up to $253 billion over the next 30 years to clean up about

350,000 contaminated sites. EPA, Cleaning up the Nation's Waste Sites: Markets and Technology Trends (2004). The principal weapon available to the federal government in its efforts to finance and implement the remediation of these sites is the Comprehensive Environmental Response, Compensation, and Liability Act (CERCLA), 42 U.S.C. §§9601-9675. CERCLA authorizes EPA to issue orders requiring responsible parties to engage directly in remediation efforts. It also authorizes the government to clean up contaminated sites and to seek reimbursement of its cleanup costs from responsible parties. Although CERCLA fails to enunciate clearly the standard of liability it imposes, the courts uniformly interpreted it early in the statute's history as creating a strict liability scheme. Perhaps because of the problems in identifying solvent responsible parties described earlier, the government as well as private plaintiffs began seeking cost recovery from entities that seemed to have increasingly peripheral connections with contaminated sites. These efforts prompted concerns about the fairness of imposing substantial liabilities on parties whose responsibility for site contamination seemed questionable. As materials later in this chapter will indicate, the courts have responded by incorporating into CERCLA's liability scheme principles of causation and fault that have moved the statutory liability scheme closer to the traditional tort law model and Congress has adopted a host of liability exemptions.

The first two sections of this chapter provide some background information on CERCLA. Section A discusses the history of CERCLA's adoption and amendment, while section B summarizes the statutory scheme and provides an assessment of its impact. Sections C-E analyze the statutory provisions relating to liability for response costs, imminent and substantial endangerments, and natural resource damages, respectively. The regulatory component of CERCLA is the subject of section F, which focuses on the process of determining how clean a site must be after cleanup. The final section of this chapter addresses the effect of the discovery of hazardous substances on real estate transactions, both under CERCLA and under state law, although that topic is implicated in much of the earlier material in this chapter as well.

A.   THE HISTORY AND PURPOSES OF CERCLA

SUPERFUND AMENDMENTS AND REAUTHORIZATION ACT OF 1986

House Report No. 99-253, pt. 1, at 1-2 (1985), reprinted in 1986 U.S.C.C.A.N. 3124-3125

Hazardous waste contamination of the Nation's ground and surface water resources has become perhaps the most significant and troublesome water quality problem facing the country for the remainder of this century. With the ability to render vast quantities of water unfit for use without treatment, toxins that leach and flow [from] thousands of active and abandoned waste sites all across the Nation pose costly and often controversial cleanup and public health problems for government officials at all levels.

During the late 1970s, Federal laws then in existence were found to be inadequate for dealing with the problem of abandoned toxic waste sites such as "Love

Canal" in Niagara Falls, New York and the "Valley of the Drums" in Brooks, Kentucky. Special funds in other statutes were simply inadequate for meeting the large costs of cleaning up the thousands of often buried and corroding drums of toxic wastes found at these sites, and so were the laws that would have allowed regulators to hold those responsible for these toxic dumps—the generators, transporters and waste site operators—for the costs of cleaning them up.

On December 11, 1980, the Congress responded to these inadequacies in the Federal laws by enacting the "Comprehensive Environmental Response, Compensation, and Liability Act of 1980" (P.L. 96-510), commonly referred to as the "Superfund" law.

The Origins of CERCLA. CERCLA represents Congress's effort to rectify decades of careless waste disposal practices. The basic idea behind CERCLA is simple: it places responsibility for cleaning up sites on the responsible parties but provides seed money for federal cleanups and site study. The implementation of these concepts, however, has proved anything but simple. Part of the problem stems from the genesis of the Act. CERCLA was patched together during the last days of the Carter administration. At the last minute, the Senate bypassed the conference procedures and presented the House with a quickly worked out compromise between the versions being considered by the two legislative bodies. As a result, there is little conventional legislative history. A court commented acerbically that CERCLA is "so badly drafted as to be virtually incomprehensible," that it has achieved a "quirky notoriety," and that it resembles King Minos's labyrinth in ancient Crete. See In re Acushnet River & New Bedford Harbor Proceedings Re Alleged PCB Pollution, 675 F. Supp. 22, 26 n.2 (D. Mass. 1987).*

Implementation Problems. The new statutory program quickly ran into difficulty. Congress originally anticipated that only a few hundred facilities needed cleanup and that the task could be accomplished relatively expeditiously by "removing containers or scraping a few inches of soil off the ground." H.R. Rep. No. 99-253, pt. 1, at 54 (1985), reprinted in 1986 U.S.C.C.A.N. 2836. It established a fund of $1.6 billion, originally called the Hazardous Substance Response Trust Fund but more commonly known as the Superfund. The fund was financed by taxes on chemical feedstocks, on certain imported substances from chemical feedstocks, and on domestic and imported petroleum and by a corporate environmental tax equal to a small percentage of an alternative minimum taxable income in excess of $2 million annually. In addition, the statute authorized the federal government to replenish the fund when it was reimbursed for its cleanup costs in litigation against responsible parties initiated under §107 or in litigation settlements. The initial $1.6 billion fund, however, turned out to be woefully inadequate, even taking into account the government's ability to replenish it with

---

*See also Commander Oil Corp. v. Barlo Equipment Corp., 215 F.3d 321, 326 (2d Cir. 2000) (denigrating "CERCLA's miasmatic provisions"); Dedham Water Co. v. Cumberland Farms Dairy, Inc., 805 F.2d 1074, 1081 (1st Cir. 1986) (CERCLA's legislative history is shrouded in mystery); Cadlerock Properties Joint Venture, L.P. v. Schilberg, 35 Envtl. L. Rep. 20,150 (D. Conn. 2005) ("wading through CERCLA's morass of statutory provisions can often seem as daunting as cleaning up one of the sites the statute is designed to cover"). See generally Nagle, CERCLA's Mistakes, 38 Wm. & Mary L. Rev. 1405 (1997) (discussing various theories of statutory interpretation that might be used to resolve interpretational questions attributable to CERCLA's poor drafting).

recoveries from responsible parties in litigation. The number of sites in need of remediation far outstripped what Congress initially anticipated. Instead of the quick and
simple cleanups Congress had envisioned, CERCLA remediation often involved the
pumping and treatment of contaminated groundwater aquifers that lasted for years.

The 1986 and Subsequent Amendments. When Congress reauthorized CERCLA
in 1986, it provided EPA with more money to finance cleanups, but it also curtailed
some of the agency's discretion in response to perceived mismanagement by EPA. The
Superfund Amendments and Reauthorization Act (SARA) increased the trust fund,
now formally renamed the Superfund, to $8.6 billion to be spent over five years. Con-
gress added another $5.1 billion in 1990. SARA imposed deadlines on EPA to initiate
and implement various phases of remediation at sites on the agency's National Priorities
List. It established more detailed criteria for the selection of remedies and provided
enhanced opportunities for public participation in the remedy selection process. These
developments helped to transform CERCLA, perhaps inadvertently, into a quasi-
regulatory statute. Congress has amended CERCLA several times since 1986 in an
effort to mitigate the alleged unfairness of the statute's liability scheme. As indicated
below, these amendments clarified the scope of preexisting liability exemptions (such
as the lender liability or "innocent landowner" exemptions) or created new ones.

Superfund Financing and the Pace of Cleanup. Congress allowed the special
taxes that used to finance the Superfund to expire in 1995 and has since refused to
reauthorize them. By the end of fiscal year 2003, the Superfund had no tax revenue
left. Since then, cleanups have been financed by general revenue that Congress
appropriates to the program, by interest earned on amounts in the fund, and by
litigation recoveries. Annual congressional funding for the Superfund declined by
35 percent between fiscal year 1993 and fiscal year 2003, adjusting for inflation.
GAO, Superfund Program: Breakdown of Appropriations Data, GAO-04-475R
(May 14, 2004). To make matters worse, cost recoveries in litigation brought by the
government declined too. Cost recovery awards peaked in 2001 at about $562 million,
falling to about $110 million in 2004. Schiffer, How Litigation Shaped Superfund, 22
Envtl. F. No. 4 (July/August 2005), at 17, 24.*

These developments had two consequences. First, a greater share of the cleanup
costs incurred by EPA must now be derived from general revenues, thus shifting a
significant share of the responsibility for paying for the cleanup of Superfund sites
from industry to the public at large. Second, the pace of cleanups has slowed. Between
1992 and 2000, an average of 77 site cleanups were completed each year. Between
2001 and 2005, that number fell to 42.** Some EPA officials indicated that the
decline was due to the increased complexity and cost of remediating the remaining
sites. Others claim, however, that cleanup projects ready for initiation were delayed
due to lack of money.*** Support for the latter view came in 2004, when EPA's own

---

*But see Bourdeau & Jawetz, 25 Years of Superfund Liability: Progress Made, Progress
Needed, 37 Env't Rep. (BNA) 97, 99 (2006) (reporting that, despite the expiration of the special
tax sources of the Superfund in 1995, responsible parties spent more than $2.6 billion on cleanup
work between 1995 and 1998, 17 percent of all such expenditures at sites on the National Priorities
List since 1980).

**See Steinzor & Clune, The Toll of Superfund Neglect: Toxic Waste Dumps and Commu-
nities at Risk (2006), available at http://www.progressivereform.org/articles/Superfund_061506.pdf.

***See Seelye, Bush Proposing to Shift Burden of Toxic Cleanups to Taxpayers, N.Y. Times,
Feb. 24, 2002, at A1; Hernandez, Political Battle Looming over Superfund Plan, N.Y. Times,
Apr. 15, 2002, at A22.

inspector general reported that the agency delayed or scaled back cleanups at some sites due to a funding shortfall of $174.9 million in fiscal year 2003. In particular, EPA could not provide any funding for new projects at 10 sites for which Superfund financing was requested.[*]

B. AN OVERVIEW OF CERCLA

The Cleanup Process. CERCLA authorizes the president (who has delegated his authority to EPA) to respond to hazardous substance releases and recover cleanup costs from parties responsible for creating the problems. Section 104(a)(1) of the Act authorizes EPA to take any response measure consistent with the National Contingency Plan (NCP) that is necessary to protect the public health or welfare or the environment in two situations: (1) whenever a hazardous substance is released or there is a substantial threat of a release into the environment; or (2) whenever there is a release or substantial threat of a release of a pollutant or contaminant that may present an imminent and substantial danger to the public health or welfare. The statute designates certain substances as hazardous by reference to other federal laws. §101(14). EPA may add others to the list if they present substantial danger to the public health or welfare or the environment when released. §102(a).

Response actions may take one of two forms: short-term responses to emergencies such as a spill or leak, called removal actions; and long-term, permanent cleanups, called remedial actions. See §101(23)-(24). EPA may not undertake remedial action unless the state in which the release of hazardous substance occurs has entered into a contract or cooperative agreement with EPA that provides assurances that the state will maintain all future removal and remedial actions. The state also must agree to pay a minimum of 10 percent of the cost of a cleanup. §104(c)(3). A hazardous waste management facility may not receive wastes from a Superfund site unless the facility is in compliance with RCRA. §121(d)(3).

The National Contingency Plan and the National Priorities List. CERCLA requires that EPA issue a national hazardous substance response plan to establish procedures and standards for responding to hazardous substance releases. §105(a). This NCP, published at 40 C.F.R. Part 300, acts as a kind of blueprint for CERCLA cleanups. The NCP must include methods for discovering and investigating facilities at which hazardous substances are located, for evaluating and remedying releases or threats thereof, for determining the appropriate extent of remediation, and for ensuring that remedial actions are cost-effective. Persons in charge of a facility who have knowledge of a release in excess of EPA-designated reportable quantities must notify the government or risk criminal penalties. §103(a)-(b). The 1986 amendments added a series of rules, discussed in section F.2, for remedy selection, §121, which have been incorporated into the NCP.

The NCP also must include criteria for determining priorities for responding to releases or threatened releases throughout the United States, based on relative risk to public health or welfare or the environment. EPA must use these criteria to compile a

[*]35 Env't Rep. (BNA) 118 (2004). At the end of fiscal year 2005, EPA reported that its funding needs for fiscal year 2005 cleanups exceeded appropriated funding levels. See EPA, Fiscal Year 2004 Annual Report, available at http://www.epa.gov/superfund/action/process.

National Priorities List (NPL) of response targets, including, to the extent practicable, one facility designated by each state as the one presenting the greatest threat.* §105(a)(8). EPA has included in the NCP a Hazard Ranking System (HRS) for determining which sites merit inclusion on the NPL; sites that receive a sufficiently high HRS score are placed on the NPL. As of mid-2006, the NPL contained about 1,245 sites that awaited cleanup. A site's inclusion on the NPL does not commit EPA to remediation there, nor does it impose liability on anyone for the costs of any response taken at the site. Rather, the NPL's purpose is to "identify, quickly and inexpensively, sites that may warrant further action under CERCLA." Eagle-Picher Indus., Inc. v. EPA, 759 F.2d 905, 911 (D.C. Cir. 1985). But, under EPA regulations, only sites on the NPL are eligible to receive money from the Superfund for remediation. 40 C.F.R. §300.425(b)(1). Between 1980 and 2004, nearly 17,000 response actions were conducted under CERCLA. Remedial actions at sites on the NPL accounted for less than 10 percent of these.**

The Superfund. Money from the Superfund may be used to pay costs incurred by the federal government in responding to releases or threatened releases, reimburse private parties for expenditures approved by EPA and incurred in a manner consistent with the NCP, pay for the costs of assessing natural resource damages attributable to hazardous substance releases, and reimburse local governments for carrying out temporary emergency measures. A person who presents a claim to the owner or operator of a facility from which a release occurred and to other responsible parties that is not satisfied within 60 days may seek reimbursement from the Superfund. §112(a). If the United States pays a claim out of the fund, it is subrogated to the claimant's right to recover from responsible parties. §112(c)(1).

Abatement Orders. As an alternative to cleaning up the site by itself or through contractors, the federal government may bring suit in federal district court to require responsible parties to abate an imminent and substantial endangerment due to an actual or threatened release of hazardous substances. The district courts are authorized to grant whatever relief "the public interest and the equities of the case may require." EPA may issue administrative orders to accomplish the same result. §106(a). A person who willfully violates such an order without sufficient cause is subject to fines of up to $25,000 per day of noncompliance. A person who complies with a §106 order is eligible for reimbursement from the Superfund if it can demonstrate that it was not responsible for the release. §106(b).

Cost Recovery and Natural Resource Damage Actions. If EPA expends fund monies for a removal or remedial action instead of using §106 to force responsible parties to perform the cleanup, it may recover its costs from four classes of "potentially responsible parties" (PRPs): (1) current owners or operators of vessels or facilities that contain hazardous substances, (2) owners or operators at the time of disposal, (3) persons who arranged for disposal, and (4) certain persons who transported hazardous substances to the facility at which the release occurred. §107(a). The courts have tended to interpret these categories of PRPs broadly. The statute affords limited defenses to liability that have expanded over the years. The ground rules for the imposition of §107 liability appear to depart significantly from the standards of liability that apply in more traditional civil litigation such as common law tort actions. Liability is retroactive (i.e., the statute applies to activities that took place before CERCLA's

*The NPL is at 40 C.F.R. Part 300, Appendix B.

**E² Inc., Superfund Benefits Analysis (Jan. 28, 2005) (draft report prepared by contractor for EPA), available at http://www.epa.gov/superfund/news/benefits.pdf.

adoption), strict, and in many cases joint and several. The causal link that a CERCLA plaintiff must demonstrate between a PRP's activities and the release that caused the incurrence of response costs is sometimes tenuous. CERCLA also authorizes federal and state agencies to seek recovery for injury to, destruction of, or loss of natural resources attributable to hazardous substance releases. See section E.

In certain circumstances, private parties may bring cost recovery actions against PRPs, but they normally may not sue for injuries to public natural resources, and the statute provides no cause of action for personal injuries or property damage. CERCLA includes a citizen suit provision that authorizes litigation against persons alleged to be in violation of statutory or regulatory provisions and against EPA for failure to perform nondiscretionary duties. §310.

Responding to assertions that CERCLA's liability net unfairly and unwisely sweeps too broadly, Congress has whittled away at the scope of response cost and natural resource damage liability. In the Superfund Recycling Equity Act of 1999, Congress created exemptions from arranger liability for the disposal of hazardous substances for certain entities engaged in recycling transactions. 42 U.S.C. §9627. In the Small Business Liability Relief and Brownfields Revitalization Act of 2002, Congress exempted from arranger liability entities that sent small volumes of materials to facilities listed on the NPL and certain persons who sent municipal solid waste to such facilities. It also exempted from owner-operator liability contiguous property owners and bona fide prospective purchasers. See CERCLA §107(o)-(r). The 2002 amendments created a program designed to facilitate the cleanup of brownfields sites and the conversion of such sites to productive use. §107(k). In addition, §113(f)(1), added in 1986, provides another mechanism for mitigating potential unfairness by authorizing PRPs held jointly and severally liable to file contribution actions against other PRPs.

Assessments of CERCLA. CERCLA's track record is a mixed one. On the one hand, according to Senator Baucus of Montana, Superfund's underlying principle that the "polluter pays" "changed our country for the better" by "deterr[ing] pollution[,] . . . encourag[ing] environmental audits and investments in technology that prevent pollution[, and making] . . . everyone realize pollution does carry a price and that polluters must be held accountable."* By one account,

> EPA has achieved a high level of success [under CERCLA]. After starting out with little or no practical knowledge of the problems to be addressed, the Agency has, over time, developed institutional capability and expertise, solved problems, improved relationships, and ultimately established a program that operates effectively and performs a critical function in society. Tens of thousands of contaminated sites have been evaluated, short-term removal actions have been taken at several thousand of those sites, and longer term remedial actions are slowly being completed at the most severely contaminated sites. A topic of intense public concern—once dominated by controversy and emotion—has been brought under control, buttressed by sound technical understanding and a general public recognition that actions that should be taken are being taken. [Quarles & Steinberg, The Superfund Program at Its 25th Anniversary, 36 Envtl. L. Rep. (ELI) 10364, 10365-66 (2006).]

---

*Superfund Reform Act of 1994: Hearings on S. 1834 before the Subcomm. on Superfund, Recycling, and Solid Waste Management, of the Sen. Comm. on Env't and Pub. Works, 103d Cong., pt. 2, at 1 (1994).

On the other hand, Senator Baucus conceded that "Superfund has not lived up to its goal of quickly and economically cleaning up toxic dumps" and that it is perhaps "best known for expensive cleanups, excessive delays, and for being a cash cow for lawyers." By one account, "[n]o other environmental statute has been the source of so much controversy—or so much litigation." Quarles & Steinberg, *supra*, at 10364. The statute's liability system has repeatedly been criticized as both unfair and inefficient.* Critics have charged that too much money has been allocated not to cleanup but to "transaction costs," including legal costs incurred by PRPs seeking contribution from other PRPs:

> At a purely practical level, the allocation system is encumbered by the huge evidentiary challenges of determining whose waste went to which site, especially with respect to activities that occurred two, three, four, or five decades earlier, even sometimes dating back to the 19th century. This funding mechanism has raised vast amounts of money to pay for many costly cleanups, but the investigation, negotiation, and litigation it has spawned are notorious. It is not a system one wants to lean on except under absolute necessity. [Id. at 10366.]

Still others complain that the cleanup mechanism is "inherently highly inefficient," id., and that too few sites have been cleaned up to justify the billions of dollars thrown at the problem. They have attacked the remedies chosen by EPA as too expensive, inefficient, and inconsistent from site to site. See, e.g., Hamilton & Viscusi, Calculating Risks: The Spatial and Political Dimensions of Hazardous Waste Policy (1999) (criticizing the CERCLA remediation process for failure to consider explicit trade-offs that balance benefits and costs and supporting more flexible remedy decisions based on comparative risk assessment). The friction between federal and state governments generated by the statute's allocation of responsibility also has caused concern. Finally, according to some observers, CERCLA helped to depress the market value of older industrial facilities and divert investments from inner city industrial areas characterized by chronically high levels of unemployment to undeveloped "greenfield" sites.**

Given these conflicting assessments, what does the ultimate balance sheet of CERCLA look like? In 2005, EPA's Science Advisory Board issued a draft report, Superfund Benefits Analysis, in which it concluded that the benefits of CERCLA substantially outweigh its costs. The benefits it cited include improving human health, improving contaminated sites, improving natural resources, reducing the risks associated with commercial and industrial properties, increasing the willingness of the financial community to use those properties, deterring the use of hazardous substances, avoiding the uncontrolled release of such substances, increasing emergency preparedness, and increasing scientific knowledge and research. The benefits of remedial actions were estimated to be about $63 billion.***

---

*See, e.g., Bourdeau & Jawetz, *supra*, at 101 (claiming that "[e]ven at typical [S]uperfund sites, no one disputes the basic proposition that the CERCLA liability scheme is unfair." See also Menell, The Limitations of Legal Institutions for Addressing Environmental Risks, 5 J. Econ. Persp. 93 (1991).

**See generally H.R. Rep. No. 103-582, pt. 1, at 76-77 (1994); S. Rep. No. 103-349, at 4-5 (1994).

***E^2 Inc., Superfund Benefits Report (Jan. 28, 2005), available at http://www.epa.gov/superfund/news/benefits.pdf. For access to several reports on the effectiveness of CERCLA, see http://www.rff.org/Superfund.cfm#completed.

The controversy over CERCLA is likely to continue. EPA continues to add an average of 20 to 30 new sites to the NPL each year, and response actions continue to occur at more than 300 newly discovered releases annually. See Bourdeau & Jawetz, *supra*, at 100. Moreover, as EPA has acknowledged, one in four Americans still live within three miles of a Superfund site, and about 3 to 4 million children live within one mile of such sites.*

The rest of this chapter supplies the meat to this barebones description of CERCLA and provides an opportunity for you to make your own assessment of CERCLA. It may be useful to return to this section as you proceed through the chapter to refresh your recollection as to how the various components of CERCLA fit together.

C. LIABILITY FOR REMEDIATION OF HAZARDOUS SUBSTANCES

1. Proving a Prima Facie Case for CERCLA Liability

The forerunner of modern statutory environmental law was the common law tort action. The causes of action available to a plaintiff whose person or property was injured as a result of the polluting activities of another traditionally have been negligence, trespass, nuisance, and strict liability for abnormally dangerous activities. Chapter 8, section B addresses some aspects of the application of tort law to environmental risk. For present purposes, what is relevant is the need for plaintiffs in each of these traditional causes of action to demonstrate a central core of elements that includes some demonstration of culpability on the defendant's part. A plaintiff suing in negligence, for example, must demonstrate that the defendant was under a duty to the plaintiff and that it breached that duty. The duty to refrain from negligent conduct is meant to protect one person from the risk that a legally protected interest will be invaded by harm resulting from hazards created by another. Restatement (Second) of Torts §281, cmt. e. Although trespass to land began as a strict liability cause of action, more recently the courts have tended to regard it as an intentional tort. See, e.g., United Proteins, Inc. v. Farmland Indus., Inc., 915 P.2d 80 (Kan. 1996). To succeed in a private nuisance action, the plaintiff has to prove that any damage suffered was the result of an intentional and unreasonable invasion or an unintentional invasion that is actionable under the rules governing negligence or strict liability actions. Restatement (Second) of Torts §822. Even in an action seeking to impose strict liability for abnormally dangerous activity, a court following the Restatement's approach will "weigh the probability and severity of foreseeable harm, whether the activity is unusual or is in an inappropriate location, and other factors. Thus, fault plays a role in [this] assessment." Farber, Toxic Causation, 71 Minn. L. Rev. 1219, 1223 (1987).

Similarly, the common law required proof of a causal connection between the defendant's acts or omissions and the harm suffered by the plaintiff. A defendant is liable in a negligence action only if its negligence was a "legal" or proximate cause of

---

*See EPA, Superfund's 25th Anniversary: Capturing the Past, Charting the Future, available at http://www.epa.gov/superfund/25anniversary/.

the plaintiff's harm. Restatement (Second) of Torts §430. Negligent conduct is a legal cause of another's harm if the conduct was a substantial factor in bringing about the harm (a cause in fact) and the relationship between the defendant's conduct and the plaintiff's harm is not sufficiently remote as to render the harm unforeseeable. Id. §431. This requirement could pose substantial problems for the plaintiff whose property was damaged by a leaking hazardous waste disposal site. It is not unusual for many companies to dispose of wastes at the same site. If the wastes from these various sources mixed together before the site began leaking, the plaintiff may find it impossible to prove that any particular company's conduct caused all or even an identifiable portion of the contamination.

Situations in which multiple defendants contributed to the plaintiff's harm also raise questions concerning the appropriate allocation of liability. Traditionally, the plaintiff was entitled to recover nothing unless he or she could prove that a particular member of a group of multiple defendants caused the damage and identify the extent of that damage. The Restatement provides that if two or more persons, acting independently, tortiously cause distinct harms or a single harm that can reasonably be apportioned according to the contribution of each, then each defendant is liable only for the portion of the total harm it caused. Restatement (Second) of Torts §881. It is only if multiple defendants tortiously contributed to a single and indivisible harm that each party is jointly and severally liable for the entire harm. Id. §875. Normally, the burden of proving that tortious conduct caused the plaintiff's harm is on the plaintiff. Id. §433B(1). When, however, the conduct of two or more persons combined to bring about harm and one of them seeks to limit its liability on the ground that the harm is apportionable, the burden of proving apportionment is on that defendant. Id. §433B(2).

One of the recurring questions posed in this chapter is how CERCLA's liability system departs from these traditional principles. The starting point, of course, is the statute. Under §107(a)-(b), what must a plaintiff seeking reimbursement for response costs or compensation for damaged natural resources show in order to prevail? Is proof of culpability necessary? See §101(32); 33 U.S.C. §1321; Town of Munster v. Sherwin-Williams Co., 27 F.3d 1268, 1272 (7th Cir. 1994). Must the plaintiff prove a causal link between acts or omissions on the defendant's part and the release that triggered the incurrence of response costs? Cf. Bob's Beverage, Inc. v. Acme, Inc., 264 F.3d 692 (6th Cir. 2001) (facility owner not liable in contribution action, because any release that occurred during its ownership did not cause any increase in incurrence of response costs). What role, if any, does foreseeability on the defendant's part play? Is liability joint and several?

Amoco Oil Co. v. Borden, Inc., 889 F.2d 664, 668 (5th Cir. 1989), summarized the plaintiff's burden of proof in a CERCLA §107 action as follows:

> To establish a prima facie case of liability in a CERCLA cost recovery action, a plaintiff must prove: (1) that the site in question is a "facility" . . . ; (2) that the defendant is a responsible person under §[107(a)]; (3) that a release or a threatened release of a hazardous substance has occurred; and (4) that the release or threatened release has caused the plaintiff to incur response costs. If the plaintiff establishes each of these elements and the defendant is unable to establish the applicability of one of the defenses listed in §[107(b)], the plaintiff is entitled to summary judgment on the liability issue.

Other courts also require proof that response costs were necessary and have been incurred in a manner consistent with the NCP. See, e.g., Regional Airport Auth. v.

LFG, LLC, 460 F.3d 697, 703 (6th Cir. 2006) (stating that "whether the costs were 'necessary' is a threshold issue for recovery under §107(a)," and holding that costs were not necessary, because lead concentration levels were below levels EPA deemed acceptable before cleanup began). In Young v. United States, 394 F.3d 858 (10th Cir. 2005), the court held that the plaintiff failed to demonstrate that its costs of investigating the extent of contamination on its property were necessary or consistent with the NCP, because the costs were not tied to the actual cleanup of hazardous substance releases. No nexus existed between the costs the plaintiff spent and any effort to clean up the contamination that had spread to his property from neighboring land. The plaintiff's land continued to be contaminated, and the plaintiff testified that he did not intend to spend any money on cleanup activities. See also Minnesota v. Kalman W. Abrams Metals, Inc., 155 F.3d 1019, 1025 (8th Cir. 1998) (disallowing cost recovery claim because state agency "obstinately insisted on employing an untried, high-risk, high-cost remedy" and failed to study the nature and extent of the contamination problem).

Proof that a remedial action was inconsistent with the NCP is not necessarily a complete defense to a §107 cost recovery action, however.* To avoid or reduce liability, a PRP must also show that the failure to comply with NCP procedures resulted in the incurrence of avoidable response costs. See United States v. Burlington N. R.R. Co., 200 F.3d 679 (10th Cir. 1999).

Sections C.3-4 address the second and fourth elements of a prima facie case identified by the *Amoco Oil* court. The rest of section C.1 relates to the first and third elements.

a. Release or Threatened Release

FERTILIZER INSTITUTE v. EPA
935 F.2d 1303 (D.C. Cir. 1991)

HENDERSON, Circuit Judge:
. . . CERCLA requires parties to notify the EPA whenever a reportable quantity (RQ) of a hazardous substance is released into the environment. 42 U.S.C. §9603. Additionally CERCLA vests the EPA with authority to determine what constitutes the RQ of any given hazardous substance and thereby enables the EPA to determine what releases must be reported. 42 U.S.C. §9602(a). . . .

[EPA issued final regulations which set RQs for radionuclides.[1] In the preamble to the rule, EPA provided its interpretation of what constitutes a "release" of hazardous substances into the environment, thereby triggering the notification requirement. Numerous businesses and trade associations petitioned for review of the regulations.]

---

*The requirements for cost recovery differ depending on who the plaintiff is. If the United States, a state, or an Indian tribe establishes a prima facie case for response costs in an action under §107(a), the burden shifts to the PRP to prove that the agency's response was inconsistent with the NCP. United States v. W.R. Grace & Co., 429 F.3d 1224, 1232 n.13 (9th Cir. 2005). If any other person brings a cost recovery action, the plaintiff must show as part of its prima facie case that the response costs were incurred in a manner "consistent with" the NCP.

1. Radionuclides are chemical elements with unstable nuclei and they release charged particles (ions). In other words, radionuclides are radioactive elements.

The preamble to the EPA's final rule states in part:

> The Agency considers the stockpiling of an RQ of a hazardous substance to be a release because any activity that involves the placement of a hazardous substance into any unenclosed containment structure wherein the hazardous substance is exposed to the environment is considered a release. An unenclosed containment structure may allow the hazardous substance to emit, escape, or leach into the air, water, or soil. Thus, the placement of an RQ of a hazardous substance in an unenclosed structure would constitute a "release" regardless of whether an RQ of the substance actually volatilizes into the air or migrates into surrounding water or soil. The same rule applies to the placement of material containing radionuclides in tanks or other containment structures outside a building. If the tank or containment structure is not totally sealed off from the environment, the placement into the containment structure of an amount of a hazardous substance that equals or exceeds an RQ constitutes a reportable release. [54 Fed. Reg. at 22,526 (footnote omitted).] . . .

In the preamble, [EPA also] interprets CERCLA to require notification whenever a hazardous substance is placed into an "unenclosed containment structure." The EPA defines an unenclosed containment structure as "any surface impoundment, lagoon, tank, or other holding device that has an open side with the contained materials directly exposed to the ambient environment." According to this interpretation, therefore, "the placement of an RQ of a hazardous substance in an unenclosed structure would constitute a 'release' regardless of whether an RQ of the substance actually volatilizes into the air or migrates into surrounding water or soil." Id.

The EPA's interpretation of CERCLA's reporting requirement cannot be reconciled with CERCLA's express terms. Rather than defining a release as the movement of a substance from a facility into the environment (as does CERCLA), the EPA defines a release as the placement of a substance into a facility that is exposed to the environment. For the EPA's interpretation to come within CERCLA's meaning, the exposure of a substance to the environment must be equivalent to the release of that substance into the environment. But this is not so. A simple example exposes the flaw in the EPA's analysis: a company could place a non-volatile substance into an open-air storage container and the consequences of the open-air storage would be no different from those that would occur if the company had placed the substance [in] a closed container. Nonetheless, under the EPA's interpretation, the company would have to report the transfer of the substance to the container notwithstanding the non-volatile substance's inability to escape into the air.

Even in the final rule, the EPA cannot escape the inconsistency caused by equating the mere exposure of a substance to the environment to the release of that substance into the environment. At one point the EPA asserts:

> An unenclosed containment structure may allow the hazardous substance to emit, escape, or leach into the air, water, or soil. Thus, the placement of an RQ of a hazardous substance in an unenclosed structure would constitute a "release" regardless of whether an RQ of the substance actually volatilizes into the air or migrates into surrounding water or soil.

54 Fed. Reg. at 22,526. Implicit in this passage is the recognition that the mere exposure of a substance to the environment does not always result in the release of that substance into the environment. The EPA attempts to gloss over this incongruity by arguing that the placement of a substance into an unenclosed containment

structure creates such a great threat of a release that the EPA is justified in treating it as an actual release. This argument, however, is precisely foreclosed by CERCLA. CER-CLA provides that the EPA must be notified when a hazardous substance is actually released into the environment. 42 U.S.C. §9603(a). Nowhere in the statute is there any language requiring that the EPA be notified when there is a threatened release. This omission is especially significant given the sections of CERCLA that expressly distinguish between threats of releases and actual releases. See, e.g., 42 U.S.C. §§9604, 9606. These sections give the EPA the authority to act with reference both to releases and to threatened releases. Under these circumstances, we must presume that Congress's failure to subject threatened releases to the reporting requirement was intentional. Accordingly we reject the EPA's claim that the threat of a release from an unenclosed containment structure is sufficient to allow the EPA to require reporting when a reportable quantity of a hazardous material is put in the structure. Under CERCLA's provisions, nothing less than the actual release of a hazardous material into the environment triggers its reporting requirement. . . .

NOTES AND QUESTIONS

1. For purposes of EPA's reporting regulations, what is an unenclosed containment structure? What was EPA's rationale for defining a release to include placement of hazardous substances into such a structure? According to the court, what was the flaw in that reasoning? If EPA reissued its reporting regulations to include within the definition of a release the placement of a volatile substance into an unenclosed structure, would the regulations be valid? What bearing does your answer to that question have on the persuasiveness of the court's "simple example"? Part of the definition of a "release" in §101(22) of CERCLA is "the abandonment or discarding of barrels, containers, and other closed receptacles containing any hazardous substance or pollutant or contaminant. . . ." The court omitted this language when it quoted the definition of a "release." Is this language relevant? If so, which way does it cut?

To prove a violation of CERCLA's reporting requirements, must a defendant know that a reportable quantity of a hazardous substance has been released, or merely that a hazardous substance has been released? Must that knowledge be actual or may it be constructive? See §103(a); Sierra Club v. Tyson Foods, Inc., 299 F. Supp. 2d 693, 707 (W.D. Ky. 2003).

2. *Releases and Cost Recovery Actions.* Other cases have addressed the scope of the term release in the context of §107 cost recovery actions. See, e.g., Westfarm Assoc. Ltd. P'ship v. Washington Suburban Sanitary Comm'n, 66 F.3d 669 (4th Cir. 1995). The court held that the movement of perchloroethylene (PCE) through cracks in a public sewer system onto neighboring property was a release, even though the PCE migrated from another person's land after having been previously released there. Suppose that the government discovers that a metal smelting facility shipped drums of ore contaminated by lead, a hazardous substance under CERCLA, to Mexico to avoid the costs of disposal in the United States. The government orders the facility to recover the drums by a certain date and dispose of their contents in a permitted RCRA TSD facility. The facility fails to pick up the drums by the agency's deadline. What arguments can the government make that a release has occurred? Is the government likely to prevail? See A & W Smelter & Refiners, Inc. v. Clinton, 146

F.3d 1107 (9th Cir. 1998). Compare Pakootas v. Teck Cominco Metals, Ltd., 452 F.3d 1066, 1074-1075 (9th Cir. 2006) (holding that release occurred when hazardous substances leached from heavy metals slag into facility consisting of a portion of the Columbia River, not previously, when lead-zinc smelter discharged slag into the river, or when the slag "escaped" into the United States where the Columbia River crossed the border between the United States and Canada).

Suppose that an employee is exposed to a hazardous substance in the course of his employment inside a chemical plant. The employee returns home each night with traces of the substance on his clothes. As a result, the employee's family members are exposed to the substance. Has a release into the environment occurred? See Greco v. United Tech. Corp., 890 A.2d 1269, 1281-1286 (Ct. 2006); Ruffing v. Union Carbide Corp., 746 N.Y.S.2d 798 (N.Y. Sup. 2002), aff'd on other grounds, 766 N.Y.S.2d 439 (A.D. 2003).

NOTE ON THE EXTRATERRITORIAL APPLICATION OF CERCLA

Does CERCLA apply to a release in another country that has adverse effects within the United States? In Pakootas v. Teck Cominco Metals, Ltd., 59 Env't Rep. Cas. (BNA) 1870 (E.D. Wash. 2004), the defendant, a Canadian corporation, moved to dismiss an action to enforce a unilateral administrative order (UAO) issued by EPA. Teck argued, among other things, that the court lacked subject matter jurisdiction because CERCLA does not apply to a Canadian corporation for actions taken by that corporation which occur within Canada. The court denied the motion to dismiss. It regarded the order not as an attempt to regulate Teck's Canadian smelter, but instead as an effort to deal with the adverse effects in the United States of the smelter's operation. The court noted that the presumption against extraterritorial application of U.S. statutes does not apply where failure to extend the scope of the statute to a foreign setting will result in adverse effects within the United States. Although the remedy sought might have the incidental effect of altering Teck's future disposal practices, what the order sought to do was remedy an existing condition at a facility wholly within the United States (in Washington state). On appeal, Teck argued that, in the absence of a clear statement by Congress that it intended CERCLA to apply extraterritorially, the presumption against extraterritorial application of U.S. law prohibited the application of CERCLA to Teck in Canada. The court responded that the UAO

> defines the facility as being entirely within the United States, and Teck does not argue that the Site is not a CERCLA facility. Because the CERCLA facility is within the United States, this case does not involve an extraterritorial application of CERCLA to a facility abroad. The theory of Pakootas's complaint, seeking to enforce the terms of the [UAO] to a "facility" within the United States, does not invoke extraterritorial application of United States law precisely because this case involves a domestic facility.

Pakootas v. Teck Cominco Metals, Ltd., 452 F.3d 1066, 1074 (9th Cir. 2006). Accordingly, the court did not have to decide whether the presumption against extraterritorial application of domestic law applied. International transboundary pollution disputes in general, and Teck Cominco in particular, are discussed further in Chapter 11, section A.

b. Hazardous Substance

Section 101(14)'s definition of a hazardous substance incorporates by reference materials regulated under the Clean Air and Clean Water Acts, RCRA, and TSCA. EPA may designate as hazardous additional substances which, when released into the environment, may present substantial danger to the public health or welfare or the environment. §102(a). Cost recovery actions rarely turn on disputes over whether hazardous substances are present at the site. PRPs typically concede that they are and fight over whether they are responsible for putting them there.

Occasionally, however, this element of a prima facie case presents difficulties. See, e.g., Massachusetts v. Blackstone Valley Elec. Co., 67 F.3d 981 (1st Cir. 1995) (addressing whether ferric ferrocyanide (FFC) was a hazardous substance, even though it was not specifically named in any of the lists incorporated into §101(14) and EPA had never designated it under §102, because the NCP listed cyanides as a hazardous substance, and EPA alleged that FFC qualified as a cyanide). See also Narragansett Elec. Co. v. EPA, 407 F.3d 1 (1st Cir. 2005) (describing EPA's answer).

Must a substance be present in certain minimal concentrations to be regarded as hazardous? In United States v. Alcan Aluminum Corp., 964 F.2d 252 (3d Cir. 1992) (*Alcan Butler*), Alcan tried to convince the court to read a threshold concentration requirement into the definition of hazardous substances. It argued that it should not be held liable for response costs incurred by the government in cleaning up the Susquehanna River, because the level of hazardous substances in its emulsion was below that which naturally occurred in the river. The government responded that §101(14) contains no quantitative requirement, and the court agreed. Alcan argued in the alternative that the government must prove that its emulsion caused or contributed to the release. The court again disagreed, holding that CERCLA requires the plaintiff to prove that the release caused the incurrence of response costs and that the defendant is a generator of hazardous substances at the facility, but not that the generator's substances themselves caused the release. See also Johnson v. James Langley Operating Co., 226 F.3d 957 (8th Cir. 2000).

The last sentence of §101(14) excludes from the definition of a hazardous substance certain petroleum products. In *Alcan Butler*, the Second Circuit held that Alcan's emulsion, which contained used oil to which substances listed as hazardous under CERCLA had been added, was not covered by the petroleum exclusion. See also Tosco Corp. v. Koch Indus., Inc., 216 F.3d 886 (10th Cir. 2000) (holding that the petroleum exclusion did not apply, because hazardous substances had commingled with petroleum products in the soil and groundwater). In Wilshire Westwood Assoc. v. Atlantic Richfield Corp., 881 F.2d 801 (9th Cir. 1989), on the other hand, the exclusion applied to unrefined and refined gasoline, even though some of its indigenous components and refining additives had themselves been designated as hazardous under CERCLA.

c. Facility

A CERCLA "facility" includes more than the usual image of a leaking dump site. It includes "virtually any place at which hazardous wastes have been dumped, or otherwise disposed of," such as roadsides where hazardous waste was dumped. United States v. Northeastern Pharmaceutical & Chem. Co., 810 F.2d 726, 743 (8th Cir.

1986). Facilities also include shipping containers holding barrels of arsenic trioxide on board a vessel, United States v. M/V Santa Clara I, 887 F. Supp. 825 (D.S.C. 1995), and a drenching operation for cleaning harvested fruit, during which hazardous pesticide residue was rinsed off and disposed of. Burlington N. R.R. v. Woods Indus., Inc., 815 F. Supp. 1384 (E.D. Wash. 1993). But cf. Miami-Dade County v. United States, 345 F. Supp. 2d 1319, 1340 (S.D. Fla. 2004) (airplane engines, parts, and containers were not facilities). Is a publicly owned treatment works a facility? What is the argument that it is not? See Westfarm Assoc. Ltd. P'ship v. Washington Suburban Sanitary Comm'n, 66 F.3d 669 (4th Cir. 1995). Suppose wind blew lead-based paint off a building onto adjacent property. If lead is a hazardous substance, has a "release" occurred from a "facility"? In Castaic Lake Water Agency v. Whittaker Corp., 272 F. Supp. 2d 1053, 1076 (C.D. Cal. 2003), the court rejected the argument that groundwater in a valley constituted a facility. But in Pakootas v. Teck Cominco Metals, Ltd., 452 F.3d 1066, 1074 (9th Cir. 2006), the court held that an area in and along the Columbia River contaminated by heavy metals slag was a facility, because contaminated substances had "come to be located" there.

CERCLA excludes from the definition of a facility "any consumer product in consumer use." §101(9). Several courts have concluded that a house containing asbestos is exempt from the definition of a facility under this provision. See, e.g., Kane v. United States, 15 F.3d 87 (8th Cir. 1994); Dayton Indep. School Dist. v. United States Mineral Prod. Co., 906 F.2d 1059, 1065 & n.4 (5th Cir. 1990). Not all courts agree. In California v. Blech, 976 F.2d 525 (9th Cir. 1992), the court concluded that structures containing asbestos building material as distinguished, for example, from containers of such materials for consumer use, satisfied the broad definition of a facility. How should a court following the view of the Eighth and Fifth Circuits regard an abandoned house containing asbestos? See Dayton Indep. School Dist., supra. Do asbestos bricks that are no longer part of a building but that are lying around a site in damaged and friable condition constitute a facility? See Bancamerica Commercial Corp. v. Trinity Indus., Inc., 900 F. Supp. 1427 (D. Kan. 1995), aff'd in part, rev'd in part, and remanded, 100 F.3d 792 (10th Cir. 1996). What about support pillars and the undersides of the buildings erected over railroad tracks that were coated with asbestos-containing materials? See National R.R. Passenger Corp. v. New York City Housing Auth., 819 F. Supp. 1271 (S.D.N.Y. 1993). Is a public trap and skeet shooting range where lead shot falls back to the ground a facility, or is it covered by the "consumer product in consumer use" exception? Must the range itself qualify as a consumer product to trigger the exception, or is it enough that the ammunition and targets were consumer products in consumer use? See Otay Land Co. v. U.E. Ltd., L.P., 440 F. Supp. 2d 1152 (S.D. Cal. 2006).

Exactly what does a facility include? In United States v. Township of Brighton, 153 F.3d 307, 313 (6th Cir. 1998), the court held that the "facility" included the entire property operated as a dump, not just the contaminated portion. While "the bounds of a facility should be defined at least in part by the bounds of the contamination, . . . an area that cannot be reasonably or naturally divided into multiple parts or functional units should be defined as a single 'facility,' even if it contains parts that are noncontaminated." In Sierra Club v. Seaboard Farms, 387 F.3d 1167 (10th Cir. 2004), the court held that a pig-farming operation that consisted of two farms on contiguous sections of land, each with eight buildings, was a single "facility" for purposes of determining whether the facility's emissions exceeded the reportable quantities under §103. The farm was a "site or area where a hazardous substance has . . . come to be located" under §101(9)(B), was managed as one facility, and had a single purpose—producing swine products.* Compare New Jersey Tpk. Auth. v. PPG Indus., Inc., 197 F.3d 96, 105 (3d Cir. Nov. 1999) (rejecting argument that entire eastern spur of the New Jersey Turnpike was a single facility); Niagara Mohawk Power Corp. v. Consolidated Rail Corp., 291 F. Supp. 2d 105, 124-125 (N.D.N.Y. 2003) (railway property was not part of same facility as nearby manufactured gas plant, because the former was naturally divisible from the latter and had no connection with property upon which gas plant was operated).

Problem 9-1

A tanker truck parked at a trucking terminal ruptured, resulting in the release of hazardous industrial chemicals into the environment. The chemicals would have been delivered to a manufacturer for use in its production process had the rupture not occurred. One of the companies whose chemicals escaped from the ruptured tanker cleaned up the spill and then sued the other shippers and the owner of the truck for reimbursement in a CERCLA contribution action. The defendants claim, first, that CERCLA does not apply because it is limited to disposals of hazardous substances at inactive or abandoned waste sites, and, second, that even if the statute is not confined to waste disposal sites, the release here did not occur at a facility because that term excludes consumer products in consumer use. How should the court rule?

2. Recoverable Response Costs

Section 107(a) authorizes plaintiffs in actions for reimbursement of cleanup costs to recover "all costs of removal or remedial action incurred by the United States Government or a State or an Indian tribe not inconsistent with the [NCP]." The terms removal and remedial actions are defined at §101(23)-(24). The distinction is significant, because the procedural and substantive requirements set forth in the NCP are more detailed and onerous for remedial than for removal actions. Morrison Enter. v. McShares, Inc., 302 F.3d 1127, 1136 (10th Cir. 2002). Compare 40 C.F.R. §§300.65, 300.68.

Given the significance of the distinction, how does one distinguish between a removal and a remedial action? According to one court, the two statutory definitions overlap: "[a]ttempting to untie the Gordian knot of these definitions solely based on their plain meanings is thus unavailing." United States v. W.R. Grace & Co., 429 F.3d 1224, 1239 (9th Cir. 2005). The court deferred to EPA's position in that case that

---

*See also United States v. 150 Acres of Land, 204 F.3d 698, 709 (6th Cir. 2000) (merely formal division in land records does not amount to a "reasonable or natural division" where the contaminated and noncontaminated parcels were transferred under one deed); Axel Johnson, Inc. v. Carroll Carolina Oil Co., 191 F.3d 409 (4th Cir. 1999) (refusing to allow former facility owner to limit liability by designating as separate facilities areas it helped contaminate and those it did not contaminate); Sierra Club v. Tyson Foods, Inc., 299 F. Supp. 2d 693, 708-711 (W.D. Ky. 2003) (holding that entire chicken farm site was a single facility, and rejecting claim that each poultry house was a separate facility for purposes of §103 reporting requirements).

the removal/remedial distinction boils down to whether the exigencies of the situation were such that the EPA did not have time to undertake the procedural steps required for a remedial action, and, in responding to such a time-sensitive threat, the EPA sought to minimize and stabilize imminent harms to human health and the environment.

Id. at 1241. See also id. at 1245 ("removal actions encompass interim, partial time-sensitive responses taken to counter serious threats to public health"). Applying the distinction, the court upheld EPA's decision that the cleanup of a massive, closed asbestos mining site was a removal action. The court relied heavily on evidence that, "absent immediate attention, the airborne toxic particles [at the site] would continue to pose a substantial threat to public health. To combat this widespread, looming threat, the EPA had no choice but to undertake an aggressive removal action of an expansive scope." Id. at 1247. Another court opined that "[t]he one consistent thread in the decisions dealing with whether an action is 'remedial' or 'removal' in nature is that 'removal actions generally are immediate or interim responses, and remedial actions generally are permanent responses.'" City of Moses Lake v. United States, 416 F. Supp. 2d 1015, 1022-1023 (E.D. Wash. 2005). How many removal and remedial actions may there be at a single facility? See Colorado v. Sunoco, Inc., 337 F.3d 1233, 1241 (10th Cir. 2003).

Exactly what kinds of costs qualify as recoverable response costs?

Overhead and Oversight Costs. When EPA undertakes removal or remedial action under §104(a) of CERCLA, it may recover from those responsible for contaminating the affected facility not only the costs incurred directly by private contractors hired by the government to perform the remediation, but also the agency's costs of supervising the contractor's performance. It also may recover in a §107(a) cost recovery action the indirect overhead costs of administering the Superfund program allocated by the agency to a site remediated by the government or its contractors. See, e.g., W.R. Grace & Co., supra, at 1249-1250 (upholding EPA methodology that allocated indirect costs based on total site-specific expenditures incurred for a particular site).

EPA sometimes authorizes PRPs to perform cleanups. CERCLA conditions delegation of the task of conducting a remedial investigation and feasibility study on the agreement by such parties to reimburse the government for its costs of overseeing those investigatory activities. See §104(a)(1). May the government also recover its costs of overseeing a cleanup paid for and conducted by private parties? Does it make any difference whether the response action is a removal or a remedial action? See §§101(23), (24), 111(c)(8). The Third Circuit initially said no to the first question in United States v. Rohm and Haas Co., 2 F.3d 1265 (3d Cir. 1993). But the court overruled that decision in United States v. E.I. Dupont de Nemours & Co., 432 F.3d 161 (3d Cir. 2005), holding that EPA may recover its costs of supervising either a removal action or a remedial action conducted by a PRP pursuant to a unilateral administrative order issued under §106. The court found that the definitions of both removal action in §101(24) and remedial action in §101(25) cover oversight costs. It reasoned that oversight actions qualify as monitoring and enforcement activities and are also covered by the catch-all phrase in §101(24) that authorizes EPA to take any other action "necessary to prevent, minimize, or mitigate damage to the public health or welfare or to the environment" resulting from a release or threatened release. Finally, the court concluded that recovery of EPA's oversight costs is consistent with CERCLA's "functional objectives" because EPA's technical and supervisory expertise is often a key element of a successful CERCLA cleanup. See also Atlantic Richfield Co. v. American Airlines, Inc., 98 F.3d 564 (10th Cir. 1996).

What incentives did *Rohm and Haas* arguably create for EPA in deciding whether to conduct remediations itself under §104(a) or to issue §106 orders requiring private parties to take responsibility for cleanups? What effects might the decision have had on the availability of the Superfund to finance future cleanups?* Did the decision create incentives for private party cleanups? If so, what effect might those incentives have had on the Superfund?**

Medical Monitoring Costs. Disputes over the kinds of costs recoverable under §107(a) also have arisen in private cost recovery actions brought under §107(a)(1)-(4)(B). Most courts have determined that medical monitoring costs are not recoverable. The plaintiffs in Daigle v. Shell Oil Co., 972 F.2d 1527 (10th Cir. 1992), sought to establish a fund to finance long-term "medical monitoring" or "medical surveillance" designed to detect, prevent, or treat any latent disease that may have been caused by exposure to toxic fumes emanating from an NPL site. What language in §101(23)-(24) arguably supports private plaintiffs' right to reimbursement for such costs? Is there a counter-argument? The *Daigle* court concluded that long-term health monitoring of the sort requested by the plaintiffs had nothing to do with preventing contact between a "release or threatened release" and the public, because the release had already occurred. But in Williams v. Allied Automotive, Autolite Div., 704 F. Supp. 782 (N.D. Ohio 1988), the court allowed recovery of private medical monitoring costs. It found that the definition of "removal" clearly contemplates actions necessary to determine whether physical removal of contaminants is necessary in a given case.

Property Losses and Relocation Costs. The ability of private individuals to recover under CERCLA for property losses resulting from contamination is limited. In Wehner v. Syntex Corp., 681 F. Supp. 651 (N.D. Cal. 1987), the court refused to permit private plaintiffs, who filed a §107(a) action after they sold their property to the federal government at less than market value, to recover for loss of property destroyed or diminished in value as a result of dioxin contamination. The plaintiffs argued that the cost of permanent relocation under §101(24) includes the lost value on the homes they sold to the government, but the court held that loss of value to a home, like loss of capacity of contaminated water wells, is a nonrecoverable economic loss.***

Recovery of damages not covered by CERCLA must be pursued in state court. Suppose that a property owner recovers damages in a state common law tort action for diminution in the value of its property caused by the defendant's conduct in negligently removing an underground storage tank on the property. May the property owner also recover from the same defendant response costs incurred in cleaning up the contamination? Compare Minyard Enter., Inc. v. Southeastern Chem. & Solvent Co., 184 F.3d 373, 375 (4th Cir. 1999) with Braswell Shipyards, Inc. v. Beazer East, Inc., 2 F.3d 1331 (4th Cir. 1993).

---

*See Jacob, Note, Government Reimbursement of Costs to Oversee Private Party Clean up Actions: An Analysis of United States v. Rohm & Haas Co., 57 Alb. L. Rev. 1255, 1259-1260 (1994).

**See Schmidt, Rohm and Haas Was Right: Recovery of Government Oversight Costs in Private Party Response Actions, 19 Wm. & Mary Envtl. L. & Pol'y Rev. 253, 284 (1995).

***On recoverability of relocation costs, see Colorado v. Idarado Mining Co., 916 F.2d 1486, 1499 (10th Cir. 1990); Tanglewood East Homeowners v. Charles-Thomas, Inc., 849 F.2d 1568, 1575 (5th Cir. 1988); Romeo v. General Chem. Corp., 922 F. Supp. 287, 290 (N.D. Cal. 1994).

Attorneys' Fees. The issue in Key Tronic Corp. v. United States, 511 U.S. 809 (1994), was whether a private plaintiff could recover its attorneys' fees under §107(a). The answer turned on whether the "enforcement activities" referred to in §101(25)'s definition of "response" included a private party's attorneys' fees associated with bringing a cost recovery action. The starting point for analysis was Alyeska Pipeline Serv. Co. v. Wilderness Soc'y, 421 U.S. 240 (1975), which recognized the general practice of not awarding attorneys' fees to private litigants absent explicit statutory authorization. The Court found no such authorization in §107(a), pointing out that elsewhere in the statute (e.g., §310(f), the citizen suit provision), Congress had authorized the recovery of attorneys' fees. The reference in §101(25) to "enforcement activity" is not sufficiently explicit to embody private cost recovery under §107. The Court added, however, that an attorney's work, such as identifying PRPs, that is "closely tied to the actual cleanup" may constitute a necessary cost of response, since that kind of work might be performed by nonlawyers such as engineers or private investigators. *Alyeska* does not apply, because those costs are not incurred in pursuing litigation. In Village of Milford v. K-H Holding Corp., 390 F.3d 926, 936 (6th Cir. 2004), the court clarified the Sixth Circuit's "ambiguous" precedents on the recovery of attorneys' fees as follows:

> A CERCLA plaintiff may recover attorney's fees if the activities for which the fees are incurred could have been performed by a non-attorney, are closely tied to an actual cleanup, are not related to litigation, and are otherwise necessary. Such activities may include, but are not limited to, identification of PRPs.*

Do the same limitations on the recovery of attorneys' fees apply in the context of a cost recovery action brought by the United States? See United States v. Dico, 266 F.3d 864 (8th Cir. 2001) (upholding fee award); United States v. Chapman, 146 F.3d 1166 (9th Cir. 1998) (same); B.F. Goodrich v. Betkoski, 99 F.3d 505, 528 (2d Cir. 1996).

The increased difficulty of recovering attorneys' fees (along with other factors, such as a weakening of the joint and several liability standard discussed below, and the limitations imposed on the ability of PRPs to bring contribution actions against other PRPs that resulted from cases like *Aviall*, at page 946) contributed to a reduction of voluntary cleanup activity. Site owners may be willing to initiate cleanup if they are confident of their ability to bring private cost recovery or contribution actions against other PRPs and to recover their legal and litigation costs in doing so, in addition to the cleanup costs themselves. If attorneys' fees and court costs are not recoverable, these owners have less incentive to do anything other than wait until the government, through administrative or judicial action, forces them to begin cleanup.

Other Costs. Syms v. Olin Corp., 408 F.3d 95 (2d Cir. 2005), held that costs incurred to repair damage caused by cleanup crews are not usually recoverable as response costs under CERCLA, because a response cost is necessary only when it addresses a threat to health or the environment posed by a hazardous substance. Caldwell Trucking PRP v. Rexon Tech. Corp., 421 F.3d 234 (3d Cir. 2005), held that prejudgment interest may be awarded in a §113 contribution action, but that it is not mandatory.

---

*See also Syms v. Olin Corp., 408 F.3d 95 (2d Cir. 2005) (expenses incurred in negotiating site access were not recoverable response costs because they were not directly related to litigation and primarily protected the interests of the landowning plaintiff, but summary judgment was inappropriate with respect to the landowners' time spent admitting contractors to the site).

3. *Standard of Liability*

a. Strict, Retroactive, and Joint and Several Liability

CERCLA is virtually silent on the standard of liability that applies to cost recovery actions under §107(a), but the courts have interpreted the statute as a sharp departure from the requirements of common law tort litigation. First, "[t]he traditional elements of tort culpability . . . simply are absent from the statute." United States v. Monsanto Co., 858 F.2d 160, 168 (4th Cir. 1988). Section 101(32) defines liability to mean the standard of liability applicable to the oil spill liability provisions of the Clean Water Act, 33 U.S.C. §1321, and the courts have uniformly agreed that this reference reveals Congress's intention to impose strict liability. E.g., United States v. Northeastern Pharmaceutical & Chem. Co., Inc., 579 F. Supp. 823, 844 (W.D. Mo. 1984), *aff'd in part, rev'd in part, and remanded*, 810 F.2d 726 (8th Cir. 1986).

Second, the plaintiff in a §107(a) cost recovery action need not demonstrate the same kind of causal link between the defendant's activities and the plaintiff's harm traditionally required in tort litigation.

> CERCLA does not require the plaintiff to prove that the defendant caused actual harm to the environment at the liability stage. Harm to the environment is material only when allocating responsibility. . . . Instead, CERCLA focuses on whether the defendant's release or threatened release caused harm to the plaintiff in the form of response costs. If so, and if the other elements [of a prima facie case] are established, the defendant is liable under CERCLA.

Control Data Corp. v. SCSC Corp., 53 F.3d 930, 935 (8th Cir. 1995). As another court put it, "The argument that the government must prove a direct causal link between the incurrence of response costs and an actual release caused by a particular defendant has been rejected by 'virtually every court' that has directly considered the issue." United States v. Hercules, Inc., 247 F.3d 706, 716 n.8 (8th Cir. 2001).

Monsanto held that the government need not prove a nexus between the waste that particular PRPs sent to the site and the resulting environmental harm. Given the synergistic and migratory capacities of leaking chemical waste and the technological infeasibility of tracing waste to its source, all of which Congress understood, requiring a CERCLA plaintiff to "fingerprint" wastes would frustrate the statutory goal of facilitating prompt remediation. A requirement of proof of a causal link also would render the affirmative defenses of §107(b), discussed below, superfluous. All that is necessary for a cost recovery plaintiff to prevail against generator PRPs is evidence that those PRPs sent hazardous substances to the site and that substances like those contained in their wastes were found at the site. A CERCLA plaintiff must nevertheless show "some connection" between the actions of the defendant and the contamination. Accordingly, the plaintiff will not prevail if it cannot show that hazardous substances generated by the defendant ever made their way to the site of the release. New Jersey Tpk. Auth. v. PPG Indus., Inc., 197 F.3d 96, 105 (3d Cir. 1999).

Under *Monsanto*'s test for causation, could the owner of a jar of copper pennies found at a leaking landfill be held liable if free copper, a CERCLA hazardous substance, is found in the landfill? See §107(o)-(p). What if a PRP can show that its wastes were removed from the site before any release occurred? The *Monsanto* court implied that such a PRP would not be liable. In Artesian Water Co. v. Government of New Castle County, 659 F. Supp. 1269 (D. Del. 1987), *aff'd*, 851 F.2d 643 (3d Cir. 1988), the court declined to apply the strict traditional "but for" rule of causation ("but for" the presence of defendant's waste, the release would not have occurred) and instead imposed a federal common law requirement that the defendant's conduct, along with other contributing causes, was "a material element and substantial factor" in causing the release. Can a generator escape liability by showing that the containers it sent to the site were never breached? Intact drums contribute little if any risk; effectively, there is no "release" from such drums. Percolation of escaped liquid wastes into soil and synergistic interactions of leaked chemicals cause most problems. In B.F. Goodrich v. Betkoski, 99 F.3d 505, 516-517 (2d Cir. 1996), the court rejected the district court's conclusion that a hazardous substance generator is not liable if the substances it sent to the facility would only be released by an intervening force.

Third, CERCLA liability is retroactive in the sense that it applies to activities that took place before the statute's adoption in 1980. Thus, PRPs may be liable for response costs and natural resource damages even if those activities were lawful at the time they occurred. See, e.g., State ex rel. Brown v. Georgeoff, 562 F. Supp. 1300 (N.D. Ohio 1983). Efforts to convince the courts that CERCLA's retroactive liability scheme amounts to a bill of attainder, an ex post facto law, or a violation of the due process rights of PRPs have failed. In *Monsanto*, for example, the court held that retroactive liability did not violate due process. See, e.g., United States v. Vertac Chem. Corp., 453 F.3d 1031, 1047-1048 (8th Cir. 2006).

Liability under CERCLA may be joint and several. While CERCLA does not mandate joint and several liability, it permits it where harm is indivisible, based on "traditional and evolving principles of federal common law." *Monsanto*, 858 F.2d at 171. The following case is particularly instructive in its review of how the courts have elaborated on these principles.

IN THE MATTER OF BELL PETROLEUM SERVICES, INC.
3 F.3d 889 (5th Cir. 1993)

E. Grady Jolly, Circuit Judge:

[EPA sought to recover its response costs stemming from a discharge of chromium waste that contaminated a local water supply. Responding to complaints about discolored drinking water, a state agency determined that the contamination originated from rinsing operations conducted at a chrome-plating shop that was operated successively from 1971 through 1977 by John Leigh, Bell, and a division of Chromalloy American Corporation (which later merged with Sequa Corporation).

In December 1988, EPA filed an action against Bell, Sequa, and Leigh to recover the costs it incurred in studying, designing, and constructing an alternate water supply system for the community. The district court decided to resolve the case in three phases: liability, recoverability of EPA's response costs, and "responsibility." It determined that the relative culpability of the parties and the "divisibility of liability" issues would be decided during Phase III. Although the district court ruled that CERCLA did not require EPA to prove causation, it ruled that "Leigh, Bell and

Sequa caused the contamination."[4] At the end of the Phase II proceeding, the district court held that the defendants were liable for EPA's response costs.

The district court subsequently approved, over Sequa's objection, a proposed consent decree in which EPA settled its claims against Bell for past and future costs for $1 million. It concluded that there was no nonspeculative method of dividing the liability among the defendants because, among other things, important records had been lost. In the alternative, it concluded that equitable factors supported allocation of 35 percent of the responsibility to Bell, 35 percent to Sequa, and 30 percent to Leigh. The court also approved a second consent decree in which Leigh agreed to pay $100,000 of EPA's past and future costs. The court then held Sequa jointly and severally liable for $1.8 million, including the costs of the alternate water supply system as well as for all future costs incurred by EPA in designing and implementing a permanent remedy. Sequa appealed the imposition of joint and several liability.]

Joint and Several Liability . . .

A. COMMON LAW: THE RESTATEMENT OF TORTS

Although joint and several liability is commonly imposed in CERCLA cases,[7] it is not mandatory in all such cases. Instead, Congress intended that the federal courts determine the scope of liability in CERCLA cases under traditional and evolving common law principles, guided by the Restatement (Second) of Torts.

Section 433 of the Restatement provides that

(1) Damages for harm are to be apportioned among two or more causes where (a) there are distinct harms, or (b) there is a reasonable basis for determining the contribution of each cause to a single harm.

4. Approximately a month after the district court entered its findings of fact and conclusions of law on causation, our court decided Amoco Oil Co. v. Borden, Inc., 889 F.2d 664 (5th Cir. 1989). In *Amoco*, we noted that, "in cases involving multiple sources of contamination, a plaintiff need not prove a specific causal link between costs incurred and an individual generator's waste." Id. at 670 n.8. Other courts have likewise concluded that proof of causation is not required in CERCLA cases. E.g., United States v. Alcan Aluminum Corp. (*Alcan-PAS*), 990 F.2d 711, 721 (2d Cir. 1993) (the government is not required to "show that a specific defendant's waste caused incurrence of clean-up costs"); United States v. Alcan Aluminum Corp. (*Alcan-Butler*), 964 F.2d 252, 266 (3d Cir. 1992) ("the Government must simply prove that the defendant's hazardous substances were deposited at the site from which there was a release and that the release caused the incurrence of response costs"); United States v. Monsanto Co., 858 F.2d 160, 170 (4th Cir. 1988) (. . . "Congress has, therefore, allocated the burden of disproving causation to the defendant who profited from the generation and inexpensive disposal of hazardous waste.").

7. Many of the cases in which joint and several liability has been imposed involve hazardous waste sites at which numerous substances have been commingled. In such cases, determining the contribution of each cause to a single harm will often require a very complex assessment of the relative toxicity, migratory potential, and synergistic capacity of the hazardous wastes at issue. Under such circumstances, it is hardly surprising that defendants have had difficulty in meeting their burden of proving that apportionment is feasible. See O'Neil v. Picillo, 883 F.2d 176, 178-79 (1st Cir. 1989) ("The practical effect of placing the burden on defendants has been that responsible parties rarely escape joint and several liability, courts regularly finding that where wastes of varying (and unknown) degrees of toxicity and migratory potential commingle, it simply is impossible to determine the amount of environmental harm caused by each party.").

(2) Damages for any other harm cannot be apportioned among two or more causes. [Restatement (Second) of Torts, §433A.]

The nature of the harm is the key factor in determining whether apportionment is appropriate. Distinct harms—e.g., where two defendants independently shoot the plaintiff at the same time, one wounding him in the arm and the other wounding him in the leg—are regarded as separate injuries. Although some of the elements of damages . . . may be difficult to apportion, "it is still possible, as a logical, reasonable, and practical matter, . . . to make a rough estimate which will fairly apportion such subsidiary elements of damages." Id., comment b on subsection (1).

The Restatement also discusses "successive" harms, such as when "two defendants, independently operating the same plant, pollute a stream over successive periods of time." Id., comment c on subsection (1). Apportionment is appropriate, because "it is clear that each has caused a separate amount of harm, limited in time, and that neither has any responsibility for the harm caused by the other." Id.

The final situation discussed by the Restatement in which apportionment is available involves a single harm that is "divisible"—perhaps the most difficult type of harm to conceptualize. . . . [One] example involves pollution of a stream by two or more factories. There, "the interference with the plaintiff's use of the water may be treated as divisible in terms of degree, and may be apportioned among the owners of the factories, on the basis of evidence of the respective quantities of pollution discharged into the stream." Id.

Apportionment is inappropriate for other kinds of harm, which, "by their very nature, are normally incapable of any logical, reasonable, or practical division." Id., comment on subsection (2). . . . "Where two or more causes combine to produce such a single result, incapable of division on any logical or reasonable basis, and each is a substantial factor in bringing about the harm, the courts have refused to make an arbitrary apportionment for its own sake, and each of the causes is charged with responsibility for the entire harm." Id.

Apportionment is also inappropriate in . . . "exceptional" cases, "in which injustice to the plaintiff may result." Id., comment h on subsection (1). For example, "one of two tortfeasors [may be] so hopelessly insolvent that the plaintiff will never be able to collect from him the share of the damages allocated to him." Id. Where the court deems it unjust to require the innocent plaintiff to bear the risk of one of the tortfeasors' insolvency, it may refuse to apportion damages in such a case. Id. . . .

Section [433B(2)] of the Restatement sets forth the burdens of proof . . . as follows:

Where the tortious conduct of two or more actors has combined to bring about harm to the plaintiff, and one or more of the actors seeks to limit his liability on the ground that the harm is capable of apportionment among them, the burden of proof as to the apportionment is upon each such actor.

[This rule] will not permit a defendant to escape liability altogether, but only to limit its liability, if it can meet its burden of proving the amount of the harm that it caused. If it is unable to do so, it is liable for the full amount of the harm. According to the Restatement, the typical case to which this rule applies "is the pollution of a stream by a number of factories which discharge impurities into it." Id., comment c on subsection (2). . . .

B. THE JURISPRUDENCE

The first published case to address the scope of liability under CERCLA is United States v. Chem-Dyne Corp., 572 F. Supp. 802 (S.D. Ohio 1983). . . . [In that case,] the court concluded that provisions for joint and several liability were deleted from CERCLA "in order to avoid its universal application to inappropriate circumstances." Id. at 810. It relied on the Restatement for guidance in applying federal common law. . . .

[In] United States v. Ottati & Goss, Inc., 630 F. Supp. 1361 (D.N.H. 1988), . . . the court . . . imposed joint and several liability [on multiple generators,] because "the exact amount or quantity of deleterious chemicals or other noxious matter [could not] be pinpointed as to each defendant[, and] [t]he resulting proportionate harm to surface and groundwater [could not] be proportioned with any degree of accuracy as to each individual defendant." Id. at 1396. . . .

On the other hand, [the *Alcan-Butler* case] involved the Butler Tunnel Site, a network of approximately five square miles of underground mines, tunnels, caverns, pools, and waterways, drained by the Butler Tunnel into the Susquehanna River in Pennsylvania. During the 1970s, millions of gallons of liquid wastes containing hazardous substances were disposed of through a borehole that led directly into the mine workings. In 1985, 100,000 gallons of contaminated water were released from the site into the river.

The government filed a cost-recovery action against 20 defendants; all but Alcan settled. [The Third Circuit remanded the district court's imposition of joint and several liability to give Alcan the opportunity to limit or avoid liability by proving its personal contribution to the harm]. Thus, under the Third Circuit's approach, Alcan could escape liability altogether if it could prove that its "emulsion did not or could not, when mixed with other hazardous wastes, contribute to the release and the resultant response costs." Id. at 270. . . .

[The Second Circuit "essentially adopted" the Third Circuit's approach to joint and several liability in *Alcan-PAS*, concluding that Alcan should have the opportunity to show that the harm caused at a waste disposal and treatment center operated by PAS was capable of reasonable apportionment.] The court stated that Alcan could escape liability if it could prove that its oil emulsion, when mixed with other hazardous wastes, did not contribute to the release and resulting clean-up costs. It acknowledged that "causation is being brought back into the case—through the backdoor, after being denied entry at the frontdoor—at the apportionment stage." [990 F.2d at 722]. However, it pointed out that causation was "reintroduced only to permit a defendant to escape payment where its pollutants did not contribute more than background contamination and also cannot concentrate." Id. . . .

A "moderate" approach to joint and several liability was adopted in United States v. A & F Materials Co., Inc., 578 F. Supp. 1249 (S.D. Ill. 1984). . . . The court concluded that a rigid application of the Restatement approach to joint and several liability was inappropriate [because] Congress was "concerned about the issue of fairness, and joint and several liability is extremely harsh and unfair if it is imposed on a defendant who contributed only a small amount of waste to a site." Id. at 1256.

The court concluded that six factors delineated in an unsuccessful amendment to CERCLA proposed by Representative (now Vice President) Gore could be used to "soften" the modern common law approach to joint and several liability in appropriate circumstances. Under this "moderate" approach, a court has the power to impose joint and several liability upon a defendant who cannot prove its contribution to an injury, but it also has the discretion to apportion damages in such a situation according to the "Gore factors":

> (i) the ability of the parties to demonstrate that their contribution to a discharge[,] release or disposal of a hazardous waste can be distinguished; (ii) the amount of the hazardous waste involved; (iii) the degree of toxicity of the hazardous waste involved; (iv) the degree of involvement by the parties in the generation, transportation, treatment, storage, or disposal of the hazardous waste; (v) the degree of care exercised by the parties with respect to the hazardous waste concerned, taking into account the characteristics of such hazardous waste; and (vi) the degree of cooperation by the parties with Federal, State, or local officials to prevent any harm to the public health or the environment.

Id. at 1256. The court stated that its moderate approach would promote fairness by allowing courts . . . to make rational distinctions based on such factors as the amount and toxicity of a particular defendant's contribution to a waste site. . . .

To summarize, our review of the jurisprudence leads us to conclude that there are three distinct, although closely-related, approaches to the issue of joint and several liability. The first is the "*Chem-Dyne* approach," which relies almost exclusively on the principles of the Restatement (Second) of Torts. Under that approach, a defendant who seeks to avoid the imposition of joint and several liability is required to prove the amount of harm it caused.

The second approach, the "*Alcan* approach," . . . recognizes that, under the unique statutory liability scheme of CERCLA, the plaintiff's common law burden of proving causation has been eliminated. . . . [But] the *Alcan* approach suggests that a defendant may escape liability altogether if it can prove that its waste, even when mixed with other wastes at the site, did not cause the incurrence of response costs.

The third approach is the "moderate" approach taken in *A & F*[, which] . . . applies the principles of the Restatement in determining whether there is a reasonable basis for apportionment. If there is not, the court may impose joint and several liability; the court, however, retains the discretion to refuse to impose joint and several liability where such a result would be inequitable.

. . . The major differences among the cases concern the timing of the resolution of the divisibility question, whether equitable factors should be considered, and whether a defendant can avoid liability for all, or only some portion, of the damages. . . .

. . . We also agree with the majority view that equitable factors, such as those listed in the Gore amendment, are more appropriately considered in actions for contribution among jointly and severally liable parties, than in making the initial determination of whether to impose joint and several liability. We therefore conclude that the *Chem-Dyne* approach is an appropriate framework for resolving issues of joint and several liability in CERCLA cases. . . . [W]e nevertheless recognize that the Restatement principles must be adapted, where necessary, to implement congressional intent with respect to liability. . . . [14]

C.   Application of Joint & Several Liability . . .

. . . In the district court, the EPA contended that there was no reasonable basis for apportionment, because the harm to the Trinity Aquifer was a single harm, and [that a] single harm is the equivalent of an indivisible harm, thus mandating the imposition of joint and several liability. Apparently now recognizing the lack of support for that position, the EPA on appeal acknowledges that apportionment is available, at least theoretically, when there is a reasonable basis for determining the contribution of each cause to a single harm. It asserts, however, that Sequa failed to meet its burden of proof on that issue. . . .

Essentially, the question whether there is a reasonable basis for apportionment depends on whether there is sufficient evidence from which the court can determine the amount of harm caused by each defendant. If [so], joint and several liability should not be imposed in the absence of exceptional circumstances. . . .

Our review of the record convinces us that Sequa met its burden of proving that, as a matter of law, there is a reasonable basis for apportionment. . . .

. . . [M]ost CERCLA cost-recovery actions involve numerous, commingled hazardous substances with synergistic effects and unknown toxicity. In contrast, this case involves only one hazardous substance — chromium — and no synergistic effects. The chromium entered the groundwater as the result of similar operations by three parties who operated at mutually exclusive times. Here, it is reasonable to assume that the respective harm done by each of the defendants is proportionate to the volume of chromium-contaminated water each discharged into the environment. [The court accordingly concluded that "there is sufficient evidence from which a reasonable . . . approximation of each defendant's individual contribution to the contamination can be made."]

During the Phase III hearing, [Sequa's] expert, Henderson, calculated the total amount of chromium that had been introduced into the environment by Leigh, Bell, and Sequa, collectively and individually. The second expert, Mooney, calculated the

---

14. The dissent's proposal for an "equitable divisibility" phase is indeed creative. Notwithstanding our respect for so fertile a mind, we do not believe that the plain language of CERCLA will support the application of such equitable factors in determining liability. Under CERCLA, a defendant has contribution rights only against other defendants who have not resolved their liability in an administrative or judicially approved settlement. CERCLA §113(f). No provision of CERCLA grants a defendant a right to hold the EPA liable for eliminating its contribution rights by entering into consent decrees with other jointly and severally liable defendants. In sum, CERCLA simply does not contemplate a proceeding in which a jointly and severally liable, non-settling defendant can force the EPA to bear the costs resulting from settlements that, although judicially approved, are later thought, for equitable reasons, to be unfair or otherwise inadequate. Because the EPA settled with Bell and Leigh (pursuant to judicially-approved consent decrees which are not before us on appeal), there can be no action for contribution. We cannot agree that the EPA "bargained" for the risk that its consent decrees with Bell and Leigh would be undermined in such a manner.

amount of chromium that would have been introduced into the environment by each operator on the basis of electrical usage records. . . . [19] . . .

PARKER, District Judge, concurring in part and dissenting in part:

[Judge Parker took the position that, while the harm suffered by the Trinity Aquifer was "theoretically capable of apportionment," Sequa failed to meet its factual burden of proving apportionability by a preponderance of the evidence. Sequa introduced evidence concerning the relative times of facility ownership by each of the defendants, but its attempts to show the actual level or quantity of plating activity conducted during those periods of time proved futile. Judge Parker also concluded that the majority's adoption of the *Chem-Dyne* approach precluded the district court's alternative ruling based on "equitable apportionment." Nevertheless, those equitable apportionment findings were relevant to what Judge Parker would have regarded as a contribution claim by Sequa. In resolving that claim, the district court should have considered "the impact of the consent decrees on the defendants' statutory equitable cost allocation rights."]

. . . I would hold that when, in a case such as this one, the EPA finds it advantageous to enter into a settlement with jointly and severally liable defendants, thereby shielding the settling defendants from contribution *liability* (by operation of CERCLA's §9613(f)(2)), the EPA must bear the risk of its bargain being proved less than satisfying upon district court resolution of a non-settling defendant's, consent decree-attacking, §9613(f)(1) equitable cost allocation claim. Under the facts of this case, the EPA cannot have it both ways. It cannot enjoy the benefits of joint and several liability and at the same time enter into consent decrees with the otherwise jointly and severally liable defendants to destroy a non-settling defendant's statutory right to an equitable allocation of costs under 42 U.S.C. §9613(f)(1). . . .

Under the facts of this case, Sequa's equitable cost allocation rights are not limited to 42 U.S.C. §9613(f)(2), which provision focuses on providing for *offset* contribution. In short, because Sequa raised its claims for an equitable, proportionate cost allocation ruling in what amounts to a contribution claims proceeding—before the district court embraced the consent decrees shielding Bell and Leigh, under 42 U.S.C. §9613(f)(2), from contribution liability—Sequa is entitled to invoke the broader equitable response cost allocation remedy contained in 42 U.S.C. §9613(f)(1). . . .

NOTES AND QUESTIONS

1. Consider carefully each of the three approaches to joint and several liability that the court in *Bell Petroleum* discerned in previous CERCLA cases. What role, if any, does proof of causation play under each approach?

19. The dissent's assertion that we are advocating a standard of proof of less than a preponderance of the evidence is incorrect. Sequa is, of course, required to prove its contribution to the harm by a preponderance of the evidence. Our point is that such proof need not rise to the level of certainty; evidence sufficient to permit a rough approximation is all that is required under the Restatement. Although the dissent acknowledges that certainty is not required, the evidence it would require Sequa to adduce in order to escape joint and several liability rises far above the level necessary to satisfy the preponderance of the evidence standard. We seriously doubt that any CERCLA defendant would ever be able to satisfy the dissent's rigorous proof requirements—which would be the equivalent of a mandate of joint and several liability in all CERCLA cases. . . .

2. *Whose Common Law?* According to the court, Congress intended that the imposition of joint and several liability in CERCLA litigation be governed by common law principles. Whose common law? CERCLA is a federal statute; the Restatement of Torts, which is to provide guidance, is a compendium of state common law rules. How does the result in *Bell Petroleum* differ from the results in the two *Alcan* cases? Which of the cases is likely to be most helpful to PRPs seeking to avoid the imposition of joint and several liability? How often will a case whose facts are analogous to those in *Bell Petroleum* arise? See, e.g., United States v. Vertac Chem. Corp., 453 F.3d 1031 (8th Cir. 2006) (upholding district court decision that distinguished *Bell Petroleum* and concluding that PRP failed to demonstrate divisibility). Note that EPA's argument on joint and several liability before the Court of Appeals differed from the argument it made before the district court. What would have been the effect of accepting the argument that the agency made at the district court level?

United States v. Hercules, Inc., 247 F.3d 706 (8th Cir. 2001), described various scenarios in which a PRP may be able to avoid joint and several liability based on the divisibility of the harm. The court noted that divisibility generally limits the scope of, but does not eliminate CERCLA liability, because it is essentially a defense to joint and several liability. It also observed that the divisibility doctrine is "conceptually distinct" from contribution or allocation of damages. The divisibility inquiry is guided not by equitable considerations (as is the case with contribution) but by principles of causation alone. A defendant seeking to establish divisibility need not prove that its waste could not have contributed to any harm at the contaminated site. Instead, it may prove divisibility of harm based on volumetric, chronological, or other types of evidence.*

3. *Joint and Several Liability and Contribution.* Both the majority and the dissenting judge in *Bell Petroleum* appeared to be bothered by the unfairness of making Sequa jointly and severally liable for more than $1.8 million in past costs and an unknown quantity of costs yet to be incurred. How did their approaches for dealing with the potential inequities of joint and several liability differ? Why was it so important for Sequa to avoid joint and several liability? Why wouldn't it have been able to seek contribution from its original co-defendants, Bell and Leigh, if the Fifth Circuit had upheld the district court's decision to impose joint and several liability? Under the respective approaches of the majority and the dissent, who bears the risk that a settlement between EPA and less than all PRPs at a site will, in retrospect, appear to be unfair to nonsettling PRPs?

Suppose that a site has two areas of contamination, a pond and a plant. The government settles a cost recovery action against a PRP (BIC) in which BIC agrees to pay for the costs of remediating the plant contamination. BIC was solely responsible for that contamination. The government then pursues a cost recovery action against a second PRP (BN) for the costs of remediating the pond contamination, and the court finds that BIC and BN are jointly and severally liable for that contamination. The court also rules that the pond and plant contamination are divisible. How much credit should BN be given for the costs of the plant contamination that BIC agreed to pay? See United States v. Burlington N. R.R. Co., 200 F.3d 679 (10th Cir. 1999).

*For an unsuccessful attempt to establish geographic divisibility, see Chem-Nuclear Sys., Inc. v. Bush, 139 F. Supp. 2d 30 (D.D.C. 2001), *aff'd*, 292 F.3d 254 (D.C. Cir. 2002). City of Wichita v. Trustees of the APCO Oil Corp. Liquidating Trust, 306 F. Supp. 2d 1040, 1106 (D. Kan. 2003), found that the relative size of a party's contaminant plume is a fair and equitable measure of that party's response costs for all costs except facility-specific source control measures.

4. Alcan was ultimately unable to avoid joint and several liability in either the *Butler* or *PAS* cases. In *Butler*, Alcan reiterated its position that, as a matter of law, it could not be liable for any of the government's response costs because its waste was present in the emulsion at the site at concentrations below the naturally occurring levels, and therefore could not have caused any environmental harm. It did not introduce any evidence on the relative toxicity, migratory potential, or synergistic characteristics of the various wastes dumped into the borehole or address whether its emulsion could have reacted with other wastes. The district court granted summary judgment to the government for the full amount of its unreimbursed response costs. United States v. Alcan Aluminum Corp., 892 F. Supp. 648 (M.D. Pa. 1995), *aff'd*, 96 F.3d 1434 (3d Cir. 1996) (Table).

Alcan suffered the same fate in *PAS*. The district court found that Alcan's emulsion was contaminated with PCBs, which are not naturally occurring substances and therefore have no background levels. Accordingly, Alcan failed to escape liability. The next question was whether Alcan could nevertheless limit its liability by showing that there was a reasonable basis for apportionment. The district court and Second Circuit on appeal agreed that Alcan failed to demonstrate divisibility. Alcan failed to show that its emulsion was distinct or to provide any reasonable basis for dividing the harm at the site. It also failed to account for the emulsion's chemical interaction with other hazardous substances already at the site. United States v. Alcan Aluminum Corp., 315 F.3d 179 (2d Cir. 2003).

The PRPs in Acushnet Co. v. Mohasco Corp., 191 F.3d 69 (1st Cir. 1999), had more success. The court affirmed the district court's dismissal of a series of contribution claims on the ground that the defendants demonstrated that their share of the hazardous substances deposited at the site constituted no more than background amounts of those substances in the environment and could not contribute to produce higher amounts. This path to avoiding liability was a logical derivative of §113(f)'s authorization to take equitable factors into account when determining a contribution defendant's fair share of response costs. Observers predicted that the decision would make it more difficult for PRPs that contributed large amounts to a site to foist off a significant share of liability onto *de minimis* PRPs. Attorneys for large PRPs responded that it would discourage settlements with the government.

Problem 9-2

For years, Acme Company sent wastes containing heavy metals to the Sparkling Dump Site (SDS). Bilt-More, Inc. and Carson Company sent wastes containing volatile organic compounds (VOCs) for disposal at the site. The wastes were disposed of in shallow lagoons. Releases from the lagoons have resulted in contamination of soil at and adjacent to the SDS with both heavy metals and VOCs. The groundwater in the vicinity of the SDS has been contaminated only with VOCs, because heavy metals are often relatively immobile in soil and have not migrated to the groundwater underneath or adjacent to the site. The remedy chosen by EPA was removal of the contaminated soil and extraction of the groundwater, followed by removal of the VOCs through air stripping, and reinjection of the groundwater into the aquifer. EPA spent $100,000 removing the contaminated soil and $1 million cleaning up the groundwater. EPA sued Acme, Bilt-More, and Carson in a §107(a) cost recovery action, and moved for summary judgment to establish that each defendant is jointly and severally liable for the agency's response costs. Before the district court ruled on the motion, EPA entered a consent decree with Carson in which Carson agreed to pay $100,000 to the agency in return for EPA's dismissal of its §107(a) action against the company. Assuming that Acme and Bilt-More are appropriate PRPs under §107(a)(3), what arguments can each company make to try to limit its liability for EPA's response costs? As counsel for one of the remaining PRPs, what kinds of evidence would you want to develop to support your opposition to EPA's motion?

b. Affirmative Defenses to Liability

CERCLA imposes strict liability and seems to create attenuated causation requirements in §107(a) cost recovery actions. Section 107(b) provides a few affirmative defenses to liability, and some courts have recognized additional equitable defenses. According to one court, this liability framework discourages PRPs from "carelessly allowing their wastes to run into one large, unidentifiable morass at the waste site, confident in the knowledge that the government must identify the wastes and prove causation." Violet v. Picillo, 648 F. Supp. 1283, 1293 (D.R.I. 1986), *overruled on other grounds by* United States v. Davis, 794 F. Supp. 67 (D.R.I. 1992). The joint and several liability scheme provides the same incentives. Does this reasoning suggest that a strict liability scheme removes incentives to act with due care?

The "Act of God" Defense. United States v. Alcan Aluminum Corp., 892 F. Supp. 648 (M.D. Pa. 1995), *aff'd*, 96 F.3d 1434 (3d Cir. 1996) (Table), illustrates the limited availability of §107 defenses in general and the "act of God" defense in particular. The court found that no reasonable factfinder could have concluded that a hurricane was the sole cause of the release and resulting response costs, that the effects of the hurricane could have been prevented or avoided "by the exercise of due care or foresight," §101(1), and that heavy rainfall was not an "exceptional" natural phenomenon. See also United States v. W.R. Grace & Co.-Conn., 280 F. Supp. 2d 1149, 1174 (D. Mont. 2003) (presence of asbestos was not an act of God).

The "Act of War" Defense. In United States v. Shell Oil Co., 281 F.3d 812 (9th Cir. 2002), PRPs unsuccessfully argued that the federal government's requisitioning and regulation of the production of aviation fuel during World War II constituted an act of war under §107(b)(2):

> [T]wo treatises that discuss the issue suggest that "act of war" has a narrow meaning. One suggests the "act of war" defense requires "massive violence." The other suggests that it requires "natural or man-made catastrophes beyond the control of any responsible party." Case law in other contexts also suggests a narrow definition of "act of war." [Id. at 827.]

The "Third Party" Defense. Of much greater practical significance than either of the two preceding defenses is the "third party" defense of §107(b)(3). The exclusion for persons in a contractual relationship generally precludes lessors, employees, and independent contractors such as transporters from invoking the third party defense. But see New York v. Fried, 430 F. Supp. 2d 151 (S.D.N.Y. 2006) (refusing to find "third party" defense unavailable to landlord who did not cause tenant's release). Suppose that a PRP acquired the contaminated property through a tax deed after the delinquency of the party whose activities contaminated the site. Is there a contractual relationship between the two parties for purposes of §107(b)(3)?

See Continental Tile Co. v. The Peoples Gas Light and Coke Co., 30 Envtl. L. Rep. (ELI) 20,192, 1999 WL 753933 (N.D. Ill. 1999). Acts or omissions of a third party that occurred after dissolution of a contractual relationship do not disqualify a PRP from invoking the "third party" defense, Shapiro v. Alexanderson, 743 F. Supp. 268, 271 (S.D.N.Y. 1990), and there must be a connection between the contractual relationship and the act or omission that resulted in the contamination to defeat the defense. New York v. Lashins Arcade Co., 91 F.3d 353, 360 (2d Cir. 1996) (where a purchaser of contaminated property successfully invoked the defense).*

In Lincoln Properties, Ltd. v. Higgins, 823 F. Supp. 1528, 1542 (E.D. Cal. 1992), the court held that the requirement that the release be "caused solely by" the unrelated third party

> incorporates the concept of proximate or legal cause. If the defendant's release was not foreseeable, and if its conduct — including acts as well as omissions — was "so indirect and insubstantial" in the chain of events leading to the release, then the defendant's conduct was not the proximate cause of the release and the third party defense may be available.

Under this standard, a county was not responsible for the release into soil and groundwater of PCE introduced into the county's leaking sewer lines by dry cleaners.**

Suppose that PCBs are released upstream from the property of a riparian landowner. Does the riparian owner's failure to take affirmative action to prevent the spread of the PCBs preclude it from invoking the "third party" defense? See Kalamazoo River Study Group v. Rockwell Int'l, 3 F. Supp. 2d 799 (W.D. Mich. 1998).

The "Innocent Landowner" Defense. The 1986 amendments to CERCLA added a new defense for innocent landowners in §101(35). How does this defense relate to the "third party" defense of §107(b)(3)?

> [Section 101(35)] is intended to clarify and confirm that under limited circumstances landowners who acquire property without knowing of any contamination at the site and without reason to know of any contamination . . . may have a defense to liability under section 107 and therefore should not be held liable for cleaning up the site if such persons satisfy the remaining requirements of section 107(b)(3). A person who acquires property through a land contract or deed or other instrument transferring title or possession that meets the requirements of this definition may assert that an act or omission of a third party should not be considered to have occurred in connection with a contractual relationship as identified in section 107(b) and therefore is not a bar to the defense. [H.R. Rep. No. 99-962, at 186-187 (1986), reprinted in 1986 U.S.C.C.A.N. 2835, 3279-3280.]

What limits does §101(35)(C) place on the availability of the defense? What effect does sale of property by an "innocent landowner" have on its ability to use the

---

*But cf. State ex rel. Howes v. W.R. Peele, Sr. Trust, 876 F. Supp. 733, 745 (E.D.N.C. 1995) (the contractual relationship between the defendant and the third party need not relate to the handling of the hazardous substance or allow the defendant some control over the third party's activities to defeat the defense).

**But see Westfarm Assoc. Ltd. P'ship v. Washington Suburban Sanitary Comm'n, 66 F.3d 669 (4th Cir. 1995) (sewer commission was liable because "it had the power to abate the foreseeable release of PCE, yet failed to exercise that power"). United States v. Chrysler Corp., 157 F. Supp. 2d 849 (N.D. Ohio 2001), also discusses the incorporation of proximate causation principles into the "third party" defense.

defense? See Westwood Pharmaceuticals, Inc. v. National Fuel Gas Distrib. Corp., 964 F.2d 85, 90-91 (9th Cir. 1992). What is the function of §101(35)(D)?

To prevail in asserting the "innocent landowner" defense, a PRP must show, among other things, that at the time it acquired the facility, it did not know and had no reason to know that any hazardous substance which is the subject of the release or threatened release was disposed of at the facility. §101(35)(A)(i). Congress provided guidance on the meaning of "reason to know" when it adopted the Small Business Liability Relief and Brownfields Revitalization Act, Pub. L. No. 107-118, 115 Stat. 2356 (2002), which amended §101(35)(B). What conditions does the statute place upon a PRP seeking to qualify for the "innocent landowner" defense? In City of Wichita v. Trustees of the APCO Oil Corp. Liquidating Trust, 306 F. Supp. 2d 1040, 1050-1051 (D. Kan. 2003), the court interpreted §101(35)(B) as requiring that an innocent landowner make all appropriate inquiries prior to purchasing a piece of property and lack actual knowledge of the pollution at the time of purchase. When the landowner subsequently discovers contamination, it must take reasonable steps to control the problem.

What incentives does the defense create for prospective purchasers? EPA issued rules setting standards for conducting all appropriate inquiry into previous ownership, uses, and environmental conditions for purposes of §101(35)(B)(ii) and (iii). 70 Fed. Reg. 66,070 (2005). Prospective landowners who do not conduct all appropriate inquiries before or on the date of obtaining ownership of the property may lose their ability to claim protection from CERCLA liability as an innocent landowner, bona fide prospective purchaser, or contiguous property owner (referred to below). For a description of what an owner must demonstrate to qualify for each of these defenses, see id. at 66,073-66,074.*

What if the purchaser can demonstrate that lack of diligence was routine for buyers at that time and place? See In re Hemingway Transport, Inc., 174 B.R. 148, 169 (Bankr. D. Mass. 1994). Those who inherit property may be entitled to more lenient treatment than those who purchase it. United States v. Pacific Hide & Fur Depot, Inc., 716 F. Supp. 1341 (D. Idaho 1989).

Other Statutory Defenses. The 2002 Brownfields Revitalization Act added a couple of other new affirmative defenses to owner and operator liability. These defenses are discussed below in connection with the materials on owner-operator liability. See also §107(q)-(r).

Equitable Defenses. At one time, the courts disagreed on whether additional equitable defenses are available to PRPs. Courts allowing these defenses tended to reason that, "because the government in a cost recovery case seeks the equitable remedy of restitution defendants should not be barred from raising equitable defenses." United States v. Iron Mountain Mines, Inc., 812 F. Supp. 1528, 1546, (E.D. Cal. 1992). Other courts concluded that, because equitable concerns are relevant in other CERCLA contexts (such as in a §113(f) contribution action), they are not relevant in a §107(a) action. Recent cases almost uniformly bar the assertion of

---

*See generally Freeman & Giler, AAI Rule Will Have Significant Impact on Parties Seeking Liability Protections, 35 Env't Rep. (BNA) 2127 (2004) (discussing proposed versions of the rules). Do the provisions of the Brownfields Amendments apply to conduct that occurred before the adoption of the statute? See United States v. Domenic Lombardi Realty, Inc., 290 F. Supp. 2d 198, 210 (D.R.I. 2003) (applying preexisting version of the "innocent landowner" defense).

equitable defenses.* California v. Neville Chem. Co., 358 F.3d 661, 672 (9th Cir. 2004); California Dep't of Toxic Substances Control, 217 F. Supp. 2d 1028, 1038-1040 (C.D. Cal. 2002).

Problem 9-3

Allen operated a junkyard on land surrounded by residential property. Among the materials disposed of at the junkyard were used electrical transformers that contained PCBs, a toxic chemical. Allen placed those transformers, along with the other junk he received, in an open pit in the ground. When Allen ceased junkyard operations on the site, he covered up the pit with dirt and placed sod over the pit. Several years later, Allen hired a real estate agent, Walsh, to sell the property. Walsh showed the property to Leonard, who planned to use it for residential purposes after constructing a new house. At that time, Walsh informed Leonard that the land had at some point in the past been used as a junkyard and that local officials had objected to the junkyard operations on several occasions on aesthetic grounds. Leonard did not investigate past uses of the site further.

After Leonard purchased the property, but before he began constructing the house, he noticed that pools of colored liquid formed on a portion of the land whenever it rained heavily. Leonard called Walsh to inquire whether the latter knew what the cause of the pooling might be. Walsh said that he did not, but suggested that Leonard hire a chemist from a nearby environmental engineering firm to sample the pools to identify the nature of the pooled liquids. Leonard did so, and found out that the pools contained a combination of water and PCBs. Leonard decided to hire a construction company to excavate the land underneath the pools. The construction company dug up 50 tons of PCB-contaminated soil. Leonard directed the company to place the soil on large sheets of plastic and to cover the soil piles with more plastic until Leonard could figure out the proper way to dispose of the contaminated soil. Two weeks later, during a heavy rainstorm, the plastic covers blew off the piles and portions of the soil washed onto a neighbor's property. When the neighbor informed the local health department, the health department requested that EPA investigate the situation. EPA tested the soil, determined that it was contaminated with PCBs, and traced the source of the contaminated soil to Leonard's property. EPA spent $5 million removing the dispersed 50 tons of contaminated soil, excavating other portions of Leonard's property, and removing an additional 50 tons of PCB-contaminated soil that it discovered as a result of the excavation process.

EPA brought a cost recovery action in federal district court against Leonard, seeking reimbursement of the $5 million in cleanup costs. Leonard asserted two defenses, the "third party" defense and the "innocent landowner" defense. EPA has moved for summary judgment and a determination that Leonard is liable for the agency's response costs. Should the court grant summary judgment to EPA? If not, what issues of fact would be relevant at trial?

---

*CERCLA may bar efforts by plaintiffs to pursue equitable claims as well. See, e.g., Regional Airport Auth. v. LFG, LLC, 460 F.3d 697, 710-712 (6th Cir. 2006) (refusing to allow claim for equitable indemnification because CERCLA provides an adequate remedy at law).

NOTE ON STRATEGIC BANKRUPTCY

[The materials in this note are located at the casebook's website.]

4. Potentially Responsible Parties

a. Owners and Operators

LONG BEACH UNIFIED SCHOOL DISTRICT v. DOROTHY B. GODWIN CALIFORNIA LIVING TRUST
32 F.3d 1364 (9th Cir. 1994)

KOZINSKI, Circuit Judge.

We must decide whether the holder of an easement burdening land which contains a hazardous waste facility is, by virtue of that interest alone, liable for cleanup costs as an "owner" or "operator" under [CERCLA].

[The school district bought land from two private trusts. Before the sale, the land was occupied by a tenant, which maintained a waste pit on it. The district knew about the pit before the transaction, because the trusts' site assessment had revealed the contamination, estimating cleanup costs at $249,000. As a condition of the sale, the district required the trusts to put $250,000 in escrow for cleanup. When that amount turned out to be inadequate to pay for the cleanup, the district "responded, as people with toxic waste-ridden property are wont to, by bringing a CERCLA action in federal district court." The seller and the tenant that polluted the land settled, agreeing to pay the district a substantial share of the anticipated cleanup costs. The case continued against M & P, which held an easement to run a pipeline across the property. The district claimed that M & P were liable as "owners" or "operators" under §107.]

Obviously "owner" and "operator" are distinct concepts, else Congress wouldn't have used two words. Like other courts, we read these categories in the disjunctive. In other words, a party may be liable either as an owner or as an operator (or both, of course). We therefore consider whether M & P fall into either of these categories.

A. The holder of an easement can clearly be an operator under CERCLA. For example, CERCLA expressly includes pipelines in its definition of "facility." 42 U.S.C. §9601(9). As a result, when a party uses the easement to operate a pipeline that releases hazardous materials,[3] it is liable as an operator provided the other statutory elements are satisfied. . . .

But the district doesn't allege that M & P's pipelines are leaking toxic waste, nor is there anything on the record to suggest this is the case. Rather, the district merely points to the fact that defendants' pipelines crossed [the tenant's] waste pit and claims this put defendants "in a position to prevent" the contamination.

This allegation is not sufficient to render the defendants operators under the statute. To be an operator of a hazardous waste facility, a party must do more than

___

3. We do not reach the closer question of an easement holder's liability when he leases his right to use land to someone else, who then operates such a pipeline. As discussed below, operator liability generally turns on the defendant's control over the facility. The easement holder's liability, therefore, should hinge on his degree of participation in operating the facility.

stand by and fail to prevent the contamination. It must play an active role in running the facility, typically involving hands-on, day-to-day participation in the facility's management. Exercising the right to pass a pipeline over someone's property is as far removed from active management of the property as one could get, short of having no connection to the property at all. This is much less than the active control we require before someone will be held liable as an "operator" under CERCLA.

B. In the alternative, the district argues that, as holders of easements across the facility, M & P are the property's "owners." We suspect the district would be less eager to call someone else an owner of its property if there were gold there, rather than a toxic waste pit. It's human nature, we suppose, to be more generous with one's misfortunes.

CERCLA gives no definition of "owner" and therefore does not tell us whether parties owning an interest that is much less than a fee—such as an easement—are to be deemed owners for purposes of CERCLA liability. Rather, 42 U.S.C. §9601(20)(A) defines "owner or operator" as "any person owning or operating" a toxic waste facility, which is a bit like defining "green" as "green." [The court deemed it appropriate to "read the statute as incorporating the common law definitions of its terms."]

The common law does not regard an easement holder as the owner of the property burdened by it. Rather, an easement is merely the right to use someone's land for a specified purpose, such as a driveway, a drainage ditch or even a pipeline. . . .

Common law courts have consistently distinguished between ownership of an easement and ownership of the burdened land. . . . Given this well established distinction, we see no basis for holding that easement holders are owners for purposes of CERCLA liability.

Sound public policy supports this reading of the statute. Vast numbers of easements encumber land title records throughout the United States, establishing such diverse rights as the running of utility poles, cables and railroad track, irrigation, overflight, passage on foot, even use of a swimming pool—not to mention "scenic" easements, which preserve the "scenic and historical attractiveness" of the dominant estate. Subjecting holders of these interests to CERCLA liability would not only disserve the statute's purposes—which is to make polluters pay for the damage they cause—but it would vastly and unjustifiably increase the potential number of CERCLA defendants. Among these would surely be legitimate, non-polluting actors such as telephone and electric companies which, in running pipelines and cables, have no greater responsibility for the nation's toxic waste problem than the public at large. Nor is it clear what these entities have to offer beyond a deep pocket[6]—no doubt a wonderful thing to find in a defendant, but not a sufficient basis for the imposition of liability. Without a much clearer expression from Congress that the term owner is meant to encompass holders of easements, we see no basis for construing the statute as plaintiff suggests. . . .

6. One commentator, in advocating ownership liability for easement holders, suggests these entities could provide useful monitoring of waste disposal. But it's not only unfair to impose this burden on these entities, and inefficient to pay for cleanup by increasing the price of activities, such as phone service, that do not themselves generate toxic waste. It's also not clear this monitoring would add much to what subsequent purchasers are already required to do. After all, detecting toxic waste can be a complex and costly matter, and the experts hired by a prospective buyer are presumably more likely to find such waste than, say, a telephone repairman. Finally, because easement holders exercise no control over the owner of the servient estate beyond preventing him from interfering with the easement, it's not clear how easement holders could stop the pollution if they did discover it.

NOTES AND QUESTIONS

1. *Liability of Easement Holders.* Does Judge Kozinski's opinion move the law of CERCLA liability closer to common law norms with respect to culpability and causation? If empirical evidence indicated that it would be efficient for easement holders to monitor waste disposal, would it be appropriate to make them liable as owners or operators? Should public easement holders, such as public utilities, be treated differently than private entities?* Compare Louisiana v. Braselman Corp., 78 F. Supp. 2d 543 (E.D. La. 1999) (owner of railroad tracks qualified as a past owner at the time of disposal under §107(a)(2) because tracks themselves were a facility contaminated with creosote).

Suppose that EPA constructed a remedy at a site on the NPL that included underground pipes to carry contaminated groundwater to an on-site treatment unit. A utility company installing cable access facilities in an adjacent public right-of-way accidentally ruptured one of the pipes, causing a release of the contaminated groundwater. Is the utility liable as an operator of the contaminated site? See United States v. Qwest Corp., 353 F. Supp. 2d 1048 (D. Minn. 2005).

2. *Passive Disposal.* Suppose that A dumps hazardous substances in a pit on property she owns. Before A sells the property to B, she covers the pit with soil and grass. After the sale, B does not engage in any activities relating to the management of hazardous substances and does not disturb the land surrounding the pit dug by A. Nevertheless, hazardous substances leak out of the pit into soil and groundwater beneath the pit. Then B sells the property to C. When EPA discovers that groundwater in the vicinity of the property is contaminated, it determines that the pit on C's land is the source of the contamination. EPA brings a cost recovery action against A, B, and C. Clearly, absent successful invocation of the "innocent landowner" defense of §101(35), C is liable under §107(a)(1) as the current owner of the property. Just as clearly, A is liable under §107(a)(2) as the owner at the time of disposal. But what about B? Is B also liable as a past owner under §107(a)(2)? The answer may turn on the meaning of "disposal" in §107(a)(2). See §101(29). What argument can EPA make that B is indeed liable as an owner at the time of disposal?

The courts have reached conflicting conclusions in cases involving this kind of "passive disposal." In holding a past owner liable on the basis of passive disposal, the court in Nurad, Inc. v. William E. Hooper & Sons Co., 966 F.2d 837 (4th Cir. 1992), relied on a literal interpretation of §101(29), which does not require active human participation. Does this result create desirable incentives for owners such as B? See id. at 845-846. Or does it merely make available to §107 cost recovery plaintiffs another category of entities with potentially deep pockets? United States v. Petersen Sand & Gravel, Inc., 806 F. Supp. 1346 (N.D. Ill. 1992), came out the other way. It did so, in part, based on a comparison of a "release" under CERCLA and a "disposal" under RCRA:

> [I]t is the contextual relationship in the statute between "release" and "disposal" that convinces this court that "disposal" does not contemplate passive migration. A "release" or a threatened "release" is a precondition to the authority to act under CERCLA, and it is undisputed that a "release" includes the kind of passive migration at issue here. . . .

*For arguments that *Long Beach* was incorrectly decided, see Whitener, Comment, Cleaning Up the Confusion: *Long Beach, Grand Trunk*, and the Scope of Easement Holder Liability Under CERCLA, 45 Emory L.J. 805 (1996).

A "release" includes a "disposal," but a "disposal" does not include a "release." In some way, therefore, "release" must be more inclusive than "disposal." Congress could have made operator liability depend on a "release"; instead, Congress designed the entire CERCLA response scheme to activate whenever a "release" occurred, but limited the liability for operators to those who were operators during a "disposal." Some distinction must have been intended, and the so-called innocent owner defense shows that the distinction must have been between active and passive events.* [Id. at 1351.]

Does this view account for the inclusion of spilling and leaking in the definition of disposal? Is it relevant that the definition of a release includes the word "leaching" but the definition of disposal does not? See United States v. CDMG Realty Co., 96 F.3d 706, 715 (3d Cir. 1996).

As the last sentence of the quote from *Petersen Sand & Gravel* indicates, the court also concluded that the innocent landowner defense in §101(35) revealed Congress's intention that owners during passive disposal not be liable. Can you re-create the court's argument? Does the *Petersen Sand & Gravel* approach improperly import concepts of culpability and causation into §107? Does it discourage private cleanups? The court in *Petersen Sand & Gravel* indicated that "state common law that protects land purchasers from the intentional failure to disclose hidden defects would also prevent a malevolent owner from carrying out an environmentally irresponsible scheme." 806 F. Supp. at 1353. United States v. 150 Acres of Land, 204 F.3d 698, 705 (6th Cir. 2000), characterized the *Petersen Sand & Gravel* approach as "the better view."

Carson Harbor Village, Ltd. v. Unocal Corp., 270 F.3d 863 (9th Cir. 2001), contains a thorough review of the cases addressing the passive migration issue. The majority suggested that the cases fall into a continuum, ranging from the "active only approach" to cases, including *Nurad*, that conclude that disposal includes passive migration. The majority perched itself on a middle ground. Based on CERCLA's plain meaning, purposes, structure, and legislative history, the court held that the gradual passive migration of contamination through soil was not a disposal that rendered a past owner liable. The court acknowledged, however, that disposal may include passive migration under other circumstances.

3. Suppose that *P*, a prospective purchaser of property, undertakes a soil investigation to determine whether the property is contaminated. *P* acquires title, but later resells the land to *Q*. After the sale by *P* to *Q*, *Q* learns that *P*'s investigation stirred up hazardous substances in a buried waste pit, causing them to leach into the surrounding soil. Is *P* liable as an owner at the time of disposal? What bearing, if any, does §101(35)(B) have on this question? See *CDMG Realty Co., supra*, at 721.

4. May an individual corporate employee be liable as an operator? In United States v. Gurley, 43 F.3d 1188 (8th Cir. 1994), the court held that such an individual may be liable, if he or she (1) had authority to determine whether hazardous wastes would be disposed of and to determine the method of disposal and (2) actually exercised that authority, either by personally performing the tasks necessary to dispose of the hazardous wastes or by directing others to perform those tasks. The court in

---

*Cf. Coeur d'Alene Tribe v. Asarco Inc., 280 F. Supp. 2d 1094, 1113-1114 (D. Idaho 2003) (holding that passive water migration was a release for purposes of the statute of limitations on natural resource damages, 42 U.S.C. §9607(f)(1)); Castaic Lake Water Agency v. Whittaker Corp., 272 F. Supp. 2d 1053, 1076-1077 (C.D. Cal. 2003) (holding that the passive migration of contaminants from a source into groundwater wells constituted leaching, and therefore a release).

Redwing Carriers, Inc. v. Saraland Apartments, 94 F.3d 1489 (11th Cir. 1996), reached a similar conclusion regarding limited partners. For more on various aspects of corporate liability, see section C.4.f.

5. *Liability of Lessees as Owners and Operators.* Courts interpreting the scope of owner liability under §107(a)(1) and (2) have concluded that, in certain circumstances, a person can qualify as an owner even if he or she does not hold a fee simple in the contaminated facility. May a lessee qualify as an owner for purposes of §107(a)? See Commander Oil Corp. v. Barlo Equipment Corp., 215 F.3d 321 (2d Cir. 2000).

6. *Contiguous Property Owners and Bona Fide Prospective Purchasers.* The Small Business Liability Relief and Brownfields Revitalization Act created an exception from owner and operator liability for certain innocent owners of properties adjacent to contaminated facilities.* See §107(q). A person that fails to qualify for the contiguous property owner defense because that person knew or had reason to know that the property was or could be contaminated may nevertheless qualify as a bona fide prospective purchaser. Who qualifies as such a purchaser? See §101(40). A bona fide prospective purchaser whose potential liability is based solely on the purchaser's being considered an owner or operator of the facility will not be liable as long as that person does not impede the performance of a response action. §107(r)(1). If there are unrecovered response costs incurred by the United States at a facility owned by a person who is not liable as a bona fide prospective purchaser, the United States will have a lien on the facility for the unrecovered response costs if the response action increases the fair market value of the facility above the fair market value that existed before initiation of the response action. §107(r)(2)-(3).

For discussion of the differences between the innocent landowner and bona fide prospective purchaser defenses, see City of Wichita v. Trustees of the APCO Oil Corp. Liquidating Trust, 306 F. Supp. 2d 1040, 1051-1052 (D. Kan. 2003). The court noted, for example, that the latter permits persons with actual knowledge to purchase a contaminated facility without incurring liability, but that the former is confined to purchases that occurred after the adoption of the 2002 amendments.

b.   Arrangers

As the material in section C.3.a indicates, those who send hazardous substances to a facility at which a release later occurs may be liable under §107(a)(3) as persons who "by contract, agreement, or otherwise arranged for disposal or treatment, or arranged with a transporter for transport for disposal or treatment," of those hazardous substances. Moreover, as United States v. Monsanto Co., 858 F.2d 160 (4th Cir. 1988), reveals, the government need not prove a causal nexus between the waste sent to the site by the generator and the resulting environmental harm to render it liable. It is enough if hazardous substances of the same kind as those sent by the generator are present at the facility at the time of the release. What single word in §107(a) supports that result? A question that has engendered more difficulty than the requisite link between the generator and the release is exactly what it means to "arrange for disposal or treatment" of hazardous substances.

---

*For criticism of the 2002 amendments, see Kettles, Bad Policy: CERCLA's Amended Liability for New Purchasers, 21 UCLA J. Envtl. L. & Pol'y 1 (2002/2003).

SOUTH FLORIDA WATER MANAGEMENT DISTRICT v. MONTALVO
84 F.3d 402 (11th Cir. 1996)

BLACK, Circuit Judge:

In this appeal, we are asked to define the limits of "arranged for" liability under §107(a)(3) of [CERCLA].

[Chemspray and Chemairspray, both of which were allegedly controlled by Juan Montalvo, provided pesticide formulating and aerial spraying services in south Florida. Their businesses were located on the "Chemairspray Site" (or "the Site"), which consisted of two pieces of land. Chemairspray, the company providing spraying services, leased a 10-acre parcel on which it maintained an airstrip. Chemspray owned the adjacent 14-acre plot on which it formulated pesticides from chemicals supplied by chemical manufacturers. Chemairspray contracted with farmers and ranchers throughout south Florida to spray their lands with aerial pesticides and herbicides. Its operations contaminated the Chemairspray Site with pesticide wastes as a result of spills of pesticides on the airstrip and surrounding land during the mixing and loading of pesticides into the applicating tanks of planes. Further contamination resulted from the release of pesticide wastes during the rinsing out of the applicating tanks after spraying runs.

In 1985, the Florida environmental agency sued New Farm, Inc., which had purchased the property leased by Chemairspray, to compel cleanup of the Site. By then, contamination had spread to adjacent lands owned by the South Florida Water Management District (SFWMD). In 1988, New Farm and SFWMD sued Chemairspray, Chemspray, and Montalvo (collectively, "the Sprayers") for response costs under CERCLA. After the Sprayers admitted their liability, the district court found them jointly and severally liable for 75 percent[1] of the costs incurred in cleaning up the Site. The Sprayers filed a third-party complaint seeking contribution from farmers and ranchers ("the Landowners"), alleging that the Landowners had "arranged for" the disposal of hazardous substances within the meaning of §107(a)(3).]

... Since the Sprayers have not alleged the Landowners expressly agreed to dispose of hazardous substances at the Site, the question becomes whether the Landowners, by virtue of their contracting with the Sprayers for aerial spraying services, are parties who "otherwise arranged for" the disposal of hazardous substances.

... CERCLA does not define the phrase "arranged for." Congress has left this task to the courts, and the courts have at times struggled with the contours of "arranger" liability under §107(a)(3). When analyzing whether a particular transaction amounted to an arrangement to dispose, courts have focused on various factors. For example, where the transaction involved a sale, courts have asked whether there was a transfer of a "useful" or "waste" product. In several cases, courts have considered whether the defendant intended to dispose of a substance at the time of a transaction. Courts have also looked to whether a defendant made the "crucial decision" to place hazardous substances in the hands of a particular facility. See United States v. A & F Materials Co., 582 F. Supp. 842, 845 (S.D. Ill. 1984). ...

... The Sprayers assert the following supports finding the Landowners "arranged for" the disposal of pesticide wastes at the Chemairspray Site: (1) the Landowners

---

1. As the current owner of the property, New Farm was found to be a "covered person" under §107(a)(1) of CERCLA and held liable for 25 percent of the clean-up costs.

contracted with the Sprayers to have pesticides applied to their property; (2) the Landowners owned the pesticides throughout the application process; (3) the generation of hazardous wastes was a necessary incident to the application process; and (4) the Sprayers acted as the Landowners' agents and/or independent contractors in applying the pesticides and handling the pesticide wastes.[8]

The only link alleged between the Landowners and the Sprayers is the Landowners' contracting with the Sprayers for aerial spraying services. The Sprayers contend this is sufficient to establish liability. . . . We disagree. The Landowners contracted to have pesticides applied to their property. They did not agree to have pesticides and contaminated rinse water spilled onto the Chemairspray Site.

For the Landowners to have "arranged for" the disposal of the pesticide wastes, they must have done more than simply contracted for aerial spraying services. The Sprayers must demonstrate the Landowners took some affirmative act to dispose of the wastes. The allegations in the Sprayers' complaint do not disclose the Landowners took such an act. The Landowners did not assist the Sprayers in loading the planes or rinsing out the applicating tanks. Indeed, the Sprayers have not even alleged the Landowners knew about the spills at the Site. Nor have the Sprayers alleged the Landowners had either the duty or authority to monitor or control the Sprayers' activities. In other words, there are no allegations from which we can infer the Landowners implicitly agreed to the disposal of these wastes.

The Sprayers analogize this case to the Eighth Circuit's decision in *Aceto* to demonstrate the Landowners effectively controlled the disposal of wastes at the Site. In *Aceto*, the United States and the State of Iowa sued a group of chemical manufacturers under CERCLA to recover costs incurred in cleaning up the site of a pesticide formulation business. The plaintiffs alleged the manufacturers sent raw chemicals to the formulator for mixing and conversion into commercial pesticides. "Inherent" in the formulating process was the generation of hazardous wastes through "spills, cleaning of equipment, mixing and grinding operations, production of batches which [did] not meet specifications, and other means." According to the complaint, the manufacturers specified what pesticides they wanted produced, and retained ownership of the chemicals throughout the formulating process. Once the pesticides had been formulated, they were either shipped back to the manufacturers or forwarded to their customers. Under these circumstances, the Eighth Circuit concluded the plaintiffs in *Aceto* had stated a claim for "arranged for" liability under CERCLA, and upheld the denial of the manufacturers' motion to dismiss.

The service contracted for in *Aceto* bears little resemblance to the service the Landowners purchased in this case. The chemical manufacturers in *Aceto* contracted for formulating services requiring the mixing of active and inactive chemicals according to the manufacturers' specifications. Since the manufacturers provided the chemicals to the formulator, specified what pesticides the formulator was to mix, and retained ownership of the chemicals and pesticides throughout the formulating

---

8. This last allegation . . . adds nothing to the Sprayers' claim. The Sprayers have not alleged any basis for an agency relationship beyond the Landowners having contracted for spraying services. Characterizing this act as creating an agency between the parties does not lead to the conclusion the Landowners "arranged for" the disposal of hazardous wastes. While common law principles of agency are relevant in determining CERCLA liability in some instances, see [United States v. Aceto Agric. Chems. Corp., 872 F.2d 1373, 1382 (8th Cir. 1989)], they add nothing to the analysis here. The Sprayers must establish the Landowners "arranged for" the disposal of the pesticide wastes. Whether or not the Landowners' conduct also created an agency/independent contractor relationship is irrelevant.

process, it was possible to infer the manufacturers exercised some control over the formulator's mixing process.

In contrast, the Landowners contracted with the Sprayers to have formulated pesticides sprayed on their property. That the Landowners owned the pesticides during the application process does not, by itself, imply the kind of control over the Sprayers' application procedures that the chemical manufacturers had over the formulator's process in *Aceto*.

In *Aceto*, the mixing and packaging of pesticides "inherently" involved the creation of hazardous wastes such that the manufacturers should have expected the formulator would have to dispose of these wastes as part of the service they were purchasing. The service the Sprayers contracted for—aerial pesticide spraying—does not obviously involve the creation and disposal of hazardous wastes. Granted, the Sprayers have alleged the generation of pesticide wastes was a "necessary incident" to the application process. This may be so, but the Sprayers have not alleged the Landowners knew about this incidental by-product of the service they were purchasing. Whereas it was possible to infer the chemical manufacturers in *Aceto* knew about the creation of hazardous wastes given the service they were being provided, we cannot infer the Landowners had similar knowledge that spraying their crop and pasture lands with pesticides entailed the spilling of pesticides and draining of contaminated rinse water. Without this knowledge, the Landowners cannot be said to have acquiesced to the Sprayers' disposal of the wastes.

. . . CERCLA liability . . . is not boundless. The Sprayers cannot escape the fact they were the parties who spilled the hazardous substances that contaminated the Chemairspray Site. . . . Essentially, the Sprayers seek to hold the Landowners liable merely because the Landowners contracted for a service that involved the application of hazardous substances. We think this stretches the meaning of "arranged for" too far.

At the same time, we decline the Landowners' invitation to broadly exclude from CERCLA's reach cases where a plaintiff seeks to hold a defendant liable because the defendant contracted for a service involving the use and disposal of hazardous substances. We emphasize that whether or not a party has "arranged for" the disposal of a hazardous substance depends on the particular facts of each case. . . . [W]e conclude the Sprayers have simply not alleged the Landowners had sufficient knowledge of or control over the Sprayers' disposal practices to be held liable under this provision. . . .

NOTES AND QUESTIONS

1. What factors induced the court to conclude that the Landowners had not "arranged for" disposal under §107(a)(3)? Must a PRP have engaged in affirmative acts of disposal to be liable as an arranger? See Redwing Carriers, Inc. v. Saraland Apartments, 94 F.3d 1489, 1506 (11th Cir. 1996). Must it have been physically involved in those acts? Must the defendant have been actively involved in arranging to dispose of the waste to be liable as an arranger?* Must it have had knowledge of the disposal?

*See GenCorp., Inc. v. Olin Corp., 390 F.3d 433, 446-447 (6th Cir. 2004) (stating that, although active involvement in arranging to dispose of waste at a particular location and in a particular manner is not a prerequisite to arranger liability, a PRP "may not become an arranger through inadvertence"; the alleged arranger must have had "some intent to make preparations for the disposal of hazardous waste," even if the evidence of that intent may be inferred from the circumstances).

Must it have had a duty to control the activities that led to the disposal? If so, is arranger liability simply a codification of negligence law? Is such an interpretation consistent with Congress's intention to impose strict liability?

Arrangers are liable under §107(a)(3) based on arrangements to dispose of hazardous substances that they "owned or possessed." In United States v. Vertac Chem. Corp., 46 F.3d 803 (8th Cir. 1995), the court stated that proof of authority to control the handling and disposal of hazardous substances might be sufficient to impose liability, even absent proof of actual ownership or possession. Similarly, in American Cyanamid Co. v. Capuano, 381 F.3d 6, 25 (1st Cir. 2004), the court concluded that a broker that arranges for the disposal of hazardous waste by exercising control over the waste may be deemed to be in "constructive possession" of the waste for purposes of the arranger liability provisions. GenCorp., Inc. v. Olin Corp., 390 F.3d 433 (6th Cir. 2004), reached the same result. The court stated that when Congress enacted CERCLA, "it did so against a statutory and common-law backdrop that had long dignified constructive ownership as a legitimate means by which to establish criminal and other forms of liability for individuals and entities that did not have title to or physically possess certain items." As a result, "courts quite appropriately infer that Congress meant the phrase 'ownership or possession' to include constructive ownership or possession." Id. at 448. In that case, the court found constructive possession because, even if the alleged arranger never held title to the plant at which the hazardous substances had been generated, it had an active interest in the plant through its option to buy the plant. It also had representation on the committee that oversaw the construction, operation, and management of the plant and that approved the design plans, capital appropriations requests, and budgets of the plant (all of which contemplated off-site waste disposal).

Can a party that disposes of its own waste qualify as an arranger? See Pakootas v. Teck Cominco Metals, Ltd., 452 F.3d 1066, 1079-1082 (9th Cir. 2006) (stating that §107(a)(3) "does not make literal or grammatical sense as written").

2. How did the court in *Montalvo* distinguish the *Aceto* case? Why was it appropriate to infer that the chemical manufacturers in *Aceto* knew about the creation of hazardous wastes but not appropriate to draw a similar inference with respect to the Landowners in *Montalvo*? If, as the court pointed out, the Sprayers "were the parties who spilled the hazardous substances," wasn't it also the case that the pesticide formulators spilled the wastes in *Aceto*? The pesticide manufacturers in *Aceto* argued that they hired Aidex, the company that formulated their technical-grade pesticides into commercial-grade products, "to formulate, not to dispose," and that they could be held liable as arrangers only if they intended to dispose of a waste. But the Eighth Circuit refused to be bound by the PRPs' characterization of their relationship with the formulator. Further, the court found it significant that Aidex performed a process on products owned by the manufacturers for the manufacturers' benefit and at their direction. Compare United States v. Hercules, Inc., 247 F.3d 706 (8th Cir. 2001), where the court found Uniroyal, a party to a toll conversion agreement, liable as an arranger even though it lacked control over the process by which Vertac manufactured dioxin for it, using an ingredient supplied by Uniroyal.

Was the pesticide exemption in §107(i) relevant to the analysis in *Montalvo*? Would the pesticide exemption apply to the application of a pesticide to grain stored in a grain elevator if the pesticide leaked out of the elevator and contaminated a nearby water supply? See Cameron v. Navarre Farmers Union Coop. Ass'n, 76 F. Supp. 2d 1178 (D. Kan. 1999).

3. *Useful Products or Hazardous Substance?* The court in *Montalvo* referred to cases in which PRPs sought to avoid liability by claiming that they were transferring a useful product rather than disposing of a hazardous substance. The argument has had mixed success. The *Aceto* court rejected it. So did the court in United States v. Pesses, 794 F. Supp. 151 (W.D. Pa. 1992). The PRPs argued that they sold valuable scrap metal which the contaminated site operator used as raw material in its manufacturing processes or for resale, and that therefore they did not arrange for treatment or disposal of hazardous substances. The court reasoned that if a transaction involves the "sale of a new, useful product containing a hazardous substance, as opposed to the sale of a substance merely to 'get rid of it,' CERCLA liability may not attach." Id. at 156. Here, however, the PRPs were liable as arrangers even though they did not retain ownership of the materials they sent to the site operator and had no control over how it handled the materials because they decided to place the materials into the operator's hands. Similarly, in California v. Summer del Caribe, Inc., 821 F. Supp. 574 (N.D. Cal. 1993), C & C sold solder dross to a metal reclamation facility, which reclaimed and resold the usable portion of the dross and stored the unusable remainder in drums at the site. The drums leaked. C & C argued that it sold a useful product, but the court interpreted the useful product rule to apply only to the sale of a new product, manufactured specifically for the purpose of sale or of a product that remains useful for its normal purpose in its existing state. Here, the solder dross was manufactured as a by-product of C & C's can manufacturing process. According to the court, C & C was liable, because it sold the dross "to get rid of or treat the by-product of its manufacturing process." Id. at 581. Compare United States v. Mallinckrodt, 343 F. Supp. 2d 809 (E.D. Mo. 2004) (petroleum company that sent drums containing lead-based paint to drum reconditioning facility not eligible for the "useful products" defense).

The Ninth Circuit rejected the "useful products" defense in Cadillac Fairview/ California, Inc. v. Dow Chem. Co., 41 F.3d 562 (9th Cir. 1994). Unlike in *Aceto*, the PRPs there sold the materials containing hazardous substances to the owner of the facility at which the release occurred. Dow sold fresh styrene to rubber companies for the manufacture of synthetic rubber. The rubber companies shipped contaminated styrene back to Dow for the removal of contaminants. Dow returned fresh styrene to the rubber companies for further production of synthetic rubber. The court noted that "[r]emoval and release of the hazardous substances was not only the inevitable consequence, but the very purpose of the return of the contaminated styrene to Dow." Id. at 566. It made no difference that contaminated styrene had value on the market and that Dow credited the accounts of the rubber companies for each pound they sent to Dow for treatment. A trier of fact could reasonably conclude that the transfer of contaminated styrene to Dow by the rubber companies was not a sale of a useful product but an arrangement for treatment of a hazardous waste.

In other cases, the courts accepted the "useful products" characterization. In Florida Power & Light Co. v. Allis Chalmers Corp., 893 F.2d 1313 (11th Cir. 1990), the manufacturers of transformers containing PCBs were not liable as arrangers. The manufacturers sold the transformers to a utility, which used them for 40 years before reselling them as scrap. The release occurred at the site of the metal reclamation facility. The court found no evidence that the manufacturers intended to dispose of hazardous waste when they sold the transformers. In Edward Hines Lumber Co. v. Vulcan Materials Co., 685 F. Supp. 651 (N.D. Ill.), *aff'd*, 861 F.2d 155 (7th Cir. 1988), manufacturers who sold chemicals to a wood treatment facility were not liable as arrangers for a threatened release from a holding pond containing those chemicals. The "crucial inquiry" was the reason for the transaction in the hazardous substance, and the chemical manufacturers did not decide how the hazardous substance would be disposed of after its use in the wood treatment process.

Other courts also have focused on the intention of the party supplying the allegedly useful product. In Amcast Industrial Corp. v. Detrex Corp., 2 F.3d 746 (7th Cir. 1993), for example, the court held that Detrex, which delivered TCE to Amcast, a manufacturer of copper fittings, was not liable as an arranger for the cost of cleaning up TCE accidentally spilled during the filling of Amcast's storage tanks. The court reasoned that the words "arranged for" imply intentional action. "But when the shipper is not trying to arrange for the disposal of hazardous wastes, but is arranging for the delivery of a useful product," it is not liable as an arranger if a mishap occurs en route. Id. at 751. Is examination of a PRP's state of mind consistent with the strict liability nature of CERCLA?

The Seventh Circuit also accepted the "useful product" characterization in G.J. Leasing Co. v. Union Elec. Co., 54 F.3d 379 (7th Cir. 1995). Union Electric sold a decommissioned power plant to Sarnelli Brothers, a salvage contractor. Sarnelli resold it to G.J., retaining the right to salvage valuable metals from the equipment. Both Sarnelli and G.J. knew that there was asbestos in the equipment and parts of the building. Sarnelli "went through the power plant like a tornado and left the building a shambles. Some of the asbestos insulation was torn or smashed." Id. at 383. Further damage occurred when G.J.'s contractor, Schwartz, converted the property into a transportation facility. The court held that Union Electric was not liable to G.J. for the cost of asbestos removal under §107(a)(3). "[T]he sale of a product [the building] which contains a hazardous substance cannot be equated to the disposal of the substance itself or even the making of arrangements for its subsequent disposal." Id. at 384. The release of the asbestos fibers "was due to the ham-handed methods employed by Sarnelli Brothers and by Schwartz. . . . It seems very odd, even in Superfund Cloud-cuckooland, to attribute the negligent, unforeseeable conduct of the buyer's agent to the seller." Id. at 385.

Another case absolving an alleged arranger of liability based on the "useful product" defense was United States v. Gordon Stafford, Inc., 810 F. Supp. 182 (N.D. W. Va. 1993). ARCO sold surplus electrical transformers at public auction. The purchaser sold them to Stafford, who, after discovering that the transformers contained high concentrations of PCBs, arranged for their disposal. ARCO escaped liability as an arranger. The transformers were not at the end of their useful life when ARCO sold them, and "[a] sale without additional evidence that the transaction includes an arrangement for disposal of a hazardous substance does not create CERCLA liability." Id. at 185. See also United States v. Petersen Sand & Gravel, Inc., 806 F. Supp. 1346 (N.D. Ill. 1992) (utility that sold fly ash, a by-product of coal combustion, for use in making road base was not liable as an arranger because it did not arrange for disposal at the particular site at which the release occurred after one of the road base manufacturers sent the ash to the disposal site instead of using it as a component of road base).

What factors make it more or less likely that the "useful product" argument will prevail? In Morton Int'l, Inc. v. A.E. Staley Mfg. Co., 343 F.3d 669, 677 (3d Cir. 2003), the court concluded that analysis of arranger liability "should focus on these principal factors: (1) ownership or possession of a material by the defendant; and (2) the defendant's knowledge that the processing of that material can or will result in the release of hazardous waste; or (3) the defendant's control over the production process." What if a useful product is mixed with a hazardous waste; is the resulting mixture a useful product or a hazardous waste? Does the answer depend on the quantity of waste added to the mixture? See A & W Smelter and Refiners, Inc. v. Clinton, 146 F.3d 1107 (9th Cir. 1998).

Suppose Acme recommends that Cleaners, Inc. use PCE, a hazardous substance, in its dry-cleaning equipment, designs the layout of that equipment, and sells the equipment to Cleaners and installs it at Cleaners' facilities. Once Cleaners begins operations, the equipment facilitates leakage of PCE into the city sewer system. If EPA sues to recover its response costs from Cleaners, can Cleaners seek contribution from Acme as an arranger, or should Acme prevail based on the "useful product" defense? See Berg v. Popham, 412 F.3d 1122 (9th Cir. 2005); Berg v. Popham, 113 P.3d 604 (Alaska 2005); California Dep't of Toxic Substances Control v. Payless Cleaners, 368 F. Supp. 2d 1069, 1075-1080 (E.D. Cal. 2005); R.R. Street & Co., Inc. v. Pilgrim Enter., Inc., 166 S.W.2d 232 (Tex. 2005).

4. *De Micromis and Municipal Solid Waste Exemptions.* The 2002 Brownfields Revitalization Act discussed above created new exemptions for persons who otherwise might have been liable as arrangers or transporters of hazardous substances. Specifically, it provides an exemption for those who, before April 1, 2001, arranged for the disposal of minimal quantities of materials containing hazardous substances. Under what circumstances is the exemption unavailable? See §107(o). What is the rationale for the exemption? The Act also exempts from response cost liability certain persons who sent municipal solid waste to an NPL site. Which persons are eligible for the defense, and under what circumstances? What is municipal solid waste for these purposes? See §107(p).

Problem 9-4

Zeus owns property contaminated by lead that leached into the soil and groundwater from crushed battery casings dumped there over several years. EPA discovered elevated levels of lead in the soil and groundwater underneath and adjacent to the property and incurred response costs in excess of $6 million. Many of the crushed battery casings that contaminated the property were transported to the Zeus site by a battery cracking plant operated by Crackling Batteries Co. (CBC). The CBC plant reclaimed lead from dead lead acid batteries, most of which were from cars. CBC obtained dead batteries from gas stations and auto parts facilities such as the Retail Auto Parts Stores (RAPS). The dead batteries purchased from RAPS were depleted and no longer capable of providing electrical power to cars. CBC purchased the batteries solely for the lead they contained, and the prices CBC paid fluctuated directly with the price of lead.

The batteries CBC purchased required processing before the lead within them could be reused. CBC melted or "guillotined" the top off a battery to remove the lead plates from within it, and then smelted the recovered lead for a variety of new uses, including the manufacture of lead solder, pipe, and shot; sheet and plumber's caulking lead; and ingot lead for battery manufacturers. After CBC removed the lead, it washed and crushed the casings and loaded them into a truck for transportation to the Zeus dump site. Tons of pieces of crushed battery casings were found at the Zeus site. When CBC purchased batteries, it assumed complete ownership and control of them.

RAPS relinquished all ownership interest in and control over the batteries and was not directly involved in CBC's transportation, processing, recycling, or disposal activity.

In 1998 the United States sued Zeus, CBC, and RAPS to recover its response costs. Zeus and CBC settled, but RAPS denied liability. The government's theory is that RAPS is liable as an arranger for disposal. Both parties have filed summary judgment motions on the issue of liability. How should the court rule? Suppose instead that the suit were filed in 2003. Would the result be different? See §127(e)-(f), added to CERCLA by the Superfund Recycling Equity Act, Pub. L. No. 106-113, 113 Stat. 1501, 1537 (1999).*

c. Transporters

[The materials in this section are located at the casebook's website.]

d. Lenders and Trustees

The issue of whether a party may become liable under CERCLA even if it is not directly involved in the activities resulting in hazardous substance contamination has arisen in a series of CERCLA contexts. One issue involves the extent to which those who lend money to facilities requiring remediation are liable under §107(a). CERCLA includes a "secured creditor exemption" in §101(20)(A), which provides that the term "owner or operator" "does not include a person who, without participating in the management of a vessel or facility, holds indicia of ownership primarily to protect his security interest in the vessel or facility."

The courts disagreed on the scope of the exemption. United States v. Fleet Factors Corp., 901 F.2d 1550 (11th Cir. 1990), took the position that a secured creditor could become liable as an operator under §107(a)(2)

> by participating in the financial management of a facility to a degree indicating a capacity to influence the corporation's treatment of hazardous wastes. It is not necessary for the secured creditor actually to involve itself in the day-to-day operations of the facility in order to be liable—although such conduct will certainly lead to the loss of the protection of the statutory exemption. Nor is it necessary for the secured creditor to participate in management decisions relating to hazardous waste. Rather, a secured creditor will be liable if its involvement with the management of the facility is sufficiently broad to support the inference that it could affect hazardous waste disposal decisions if it so chose. [Id. at 1557-1558.]

The Ninth Circuit, however, ruled that the mere capacity or unexercised right to control facility operations does not take a lender outside the scope of the secured creditor exemption. It held that "there must be some actual management of the facility before a secured creditor will fall outside the exception." In re Bergsoe Metal Corp., 910 F.2d 668, 672 (9th Cir. 1990).

In 1996, Congress enacted the Asset Conservation, Lender Liability, and Deposit Insurance Protection Act, Pub. L. No. 104-208, which added new subsections

---

*See also United States v. Malinckrodt, 343 F. Supp. 2d 809 (E.D. Mo. 2004); California Dep't of Toxic Substance Control v. Interstate Non-Ferrous Corp., 298 F. Supp. 2d 930 (E.D. Cal. 2003).

(E)-(G) to §101(20) of CERCLA. What approach to the lender liability issue do the 1996 amendments reflect? Does the statute codify *Fleet Factors* or *Bergsoe Metal Corp.*? See Policy on Interpreting CERCLA Provisions Addressing Lenders and Involuntary Acquisitions by Government Entities, 62 Fed. Reg. 36,424 (1997). Under what circumstances will a foreclosing lender incur liability as an owner or operator?

The 1996 Act also addressed fiduciary liability by adding §107(n) to CERCLA. Under what circumstances and to what extent may fiduciaries incur response cost liability? See Canadyne-Georgia Corp. v. NationsBank, N.A. (South), 183 F.3d 1269 (11th Cir. 1999).

Problem 9-5

In 2000, Blanchard purchased a steel manufacturing plant previously owned by Clevenger. To finance the purchase, Blanchard arranged a loan from Downing Savings & Loan. Under the terms of the loan, Downing provided sufficient capital to Blanchard to purchase the site and business and authorized Blanchard to seek additional advances of up to $5 million in working capital. In return, Downing took a security interest in the plant and its assets. Over the next two years, Blanchard applied for and received from Downing $5 million in working capital advances. In January 2003, Blanchard defaulted on its loan payments for the initial loan and the subsequent advances, and Downing foreclosed on its security interest in the plant and its assets.

In February 2003, Downing leased the plant site to Howard for one year. At the same time, Downing sold to Howard all of the plant equipment, inventory, and other assets previously owned by Blanchard. Under the terms of the lease, Howard was responsible for paying all taxes, insurance, mortgage costs, and other maintenance expenses on the plant site. The lease agreement gave Howard a right of first refusal if Downing decided to sell the plant at the expiration of the lease. In February 2004, after Downing's management informed Howard that it intended to sell the property, Howard purchased the plant site from Downing. To facilitate the transaction, Downing financed the mortgage Howard took out on the real property, in exchange for which Downing took a security interest in the land.

The security interest agreement between Downing and Howard gave Downing the right to demand monthly reports from Howard on inventory status and monthly expenditures and receipts. Downing had the right to prohibit Howard from procuring financing from other lenders or executing liens on any of the plant's equipment, the right to approve all major expenses incurred by Howard, including payroll expenditures, the right to approve all contracts entered into by Howard, and the right to inspect the plant facilities on a monthly basis. Downing also retained the right to attend all meetings held by Howard's board of directors and to provide advice to Howard's management on any matters discussed at those meetings.

Between February 2003 and September 2006, Downing's senior loan officer, Reniff, visited the plant site to review Howard's accounts receivables and analyze its inventory and raw materials. During the first year, Reniff made monthly visits to the plant. After that, he visited the plant on a bimonthly basis. Each of the visits took less than a day, during which Reniff toured the plant facilities and spent a few hours in the office reviewing financial records. Reniff attended four meetings of Howard's board of directors during this period. At one of those meetings Stafford, Howard's president, discussed with other members of the board the plant's waste management practices.

Shortly after that meeting Howard entered into a contract with Gonder pursuant to which Gonder picked up and removed from the site every six months barrels of liquid waste collected at the plant's loading dock. Reniff reviewed the contract before it was executed but did not communicate with anyone at Howard about it before Stafford signed the contract on behalf of Howard.

In September 2006, during a routine plant inspection, state environmental officials discovered that a variety of hazardous substances had contaminated the plant site. Some of those substances resulted from operations at the plant during Clevenger's and Blanchard's ownership, and some resulted from operations conducted by Howard since February 2003. In particular, the state agency determined that hazardous substances leaked out of the barrels near the loading dock before they were picked up by Gonder.

After being notified of the situation by the state agency, EPA conducted a cleanup at the site. EPA subsequently filed a cost recovery action under §107 against Blanchard, Clevenger, Howard, and Stafford. Clevenger filed an action for contribution against Downing. Downing has filed a motion for summary judgment, claiming that it is protected from liability under the secured creditor exemption. How should the court rule on that motion?

Direct Action against Insurers. Section 108(c)(2) of CERCLA allows a §107 cost recovery action to be asserted directly against a guarantor that has provided evidence of financial responsibility pursuant to §108(b) if the insured PRP is in bankruptcy or is likely to be insolvent at the time of judgment. RCRA has a similar provision. Under §3004(t)(2) of RCRA, in any case where the owner or operator of a TSD facility is in bankruptcy or reorganization, any claim arising from conduct for which evidence of financial responsibility must be provided under §3004(t) may be asserted directly against the guarantor providing such evidence of financial responsibility. See *South Carolina Dep't of Health and Envtl. Control v. Commerce & Indus. Ins. Corp.*, 372 F.3d 245 (4th Cir. 2004).

e. Local Governments

[The materials in this section are located at the casebook's website.]

f. Corporate Liability

UNITED STATES v. BESTFOODS
524 U.S. 51 (1998)

JUSTICE SOUTER delivered the opinion of the Court.

... The issue before us, under [CERCLA], is whether a parent corporation that actively participated in, and exercised control over, the operations of a subsidiary may, without more, be held liable as an operator of a polluting facility owned or operated by the subsidiary. We answer no, unless the corporate veil may be pierced. But a corporate parent that actively participated in, and exercised control over, the operations of the facility itself may be held directly liable in its own right as an operator of the facility. . . .

[While manufacturing chemicals at a plant in Michigan, Ott Chemical Co. (Ott I) dumped hazardous substances, significantly polluting the site. In 1965, CPC International Inc. (which later changed its name to Bestfoods) incorporated a wholly owned subsidiary, Ott Chemical Co. (Ott II), to buy Ott I's assets in exchange for CPC stock. Ott II continued to pollute its surroundings. The managers of Ott I became officers of Ott II. Some Ott II officers and directors performed duties for both Ott II and CPC. In 1972, CPC sold Ott II to Story, which operated the plant until its bankruptcy in 1977. A state agency subsequently discovered massive chemical contamination of the soil and water at the site. Cordova/California, a wholly owned subsidiary of Aerojet-General Corp., purchased the site from the bankruptcy trustee in 1977. Cordova/California created its own wholly owned subsidiary, Cordova/Michigan, which manufactured chemicals at the site until 1986.

After EPA developed a remedial plan for the site, the United States filed a §107 cost recovery action against CPC, Aerojet, Cordova/California, and Cordova/Michigan, but not Ott I and Ott II, which were defunct. The issue was whether CPC and Aerojet, the parent corporations of Ott II and the Cordova companies, were liable under §107(a)(2). The district court concluded that a parent corporation may incur operator liability both directly, when it operates the facility, and indirectly, when the corporate veil can be pierced under state law. It ruled that a parent is directly liable as an operator under §107(a)(2) if it "actively participat[ed] in and exercis[ed] control over the subsidiary's business during a period of waste disposal," but not on the basis of "mere oversight" of the subsidiary's business in a manner consistent with the investment relationship between parent and subsidiary. Under this test, CPC and Aerojet were liable as operators, based on CPC's selection of Ott II's board of directors, the presence of CPC officials among Ott II's executives, and the significant role in shaping Ott II's environmental compliance policy played by a CPC official, G.R.D. Williams.

In a split decision, the Sixth Circuit reversed in part. The majority acknowledged that a parent company might be directly liable as an operator of a facility owned by its subsidiary: "At least conceivably, a parent might independently operate the facility in the stead of its subsidiary; or, as a sort of joint venturer, actually operate the facility alongside its subsidiary." But it rejected the district court's analysis, concluding that a parent corporation will be liable as an operator based on its control of a subsidiary which owns the facility only when the requirements necessary to pierce the corporate veil under state law are met. According to the court, the liability of the parent as an operator depends on whether its controls over the subsidiary and the extent and manner of its involvement with the facility amount to a sufficient abuse of the corporate form to warrant such piercing. Applying Michigan law, the court held that neither CPC nor Aerojet was liable as an operator, because the parent and subsidiary corporations maintained separate personalities, and the parents did not use the subsidiary corporate form to perpetrate fraud or subvert justice.

The Supreme Court granted *certiorari* "to resolve a conflict among the Circuits over the extent to which parent corporations may be held liable under CERCLA for operating facilities ostensibly under the control of their subsidiaries."*]

---

*Some courts had held that a parent may be held liable for controlling affairs of its subsidiary only when the corporate veil can be pierced, but others had concluded that a parent actively involved in the affairs of its subsidiary may be held directly liable as an operator of the facility, regardless of whether the corporate veil can be pierced.

III

It is a general principle of corporate law deeply "ingrained in our economic and legal systems" that a parent corporation (so-called because of control through ownership of another corporation's stock) is not liable for the acts of its subsidiaries. Douglas & Shanks, Insulation from Liability Through Subsidiary Corporations, 39 Yale L.J. 193 (1929) (hereinafter Douglas). Thus it is hornbook law that "the exercise of the 'control' which stock ownership gives to the stockholders . . . will not create liability beyond the assets of the subsidiary. That 'control' includes the election of directors, the making of by-laws . . . and the doing of all other acts incident to the legal status of stockholders. Nor will a duplication of some or all of the directors or executive officers be fatal." Id. at 196. Although this respect for corporate distinctions when the subsidiary is a polluter has been severely criticized in the literature, nothing in CERCLA purports to reject this bedrock principle, and against this venerable common-law backdrop, the congressional silence is audible. The Government has indeed made no claim that a corporate parent is liable as an owner or an operator under §107 simply because its subsidiary is subject to liability for owning or operating a polluting facility.

But there is an equally fundamental principle of corporate law, applicable to the parent-subsidiary relationship as well as generally, that the corporate veil may be pierced and the shareholder held liable for the corporation's conduct when, *inter alia*, the corporate form would otherwise be misused to accomplish certain wrongful purposes, most notably fraud, on the shareholder's behalf. Nothing in CERCLA purports to rewrite this well-settled rule, either. . . . [T]he failure of the statute to speak to a matter as fundamental as the liability implications of corporate ownership demands application of the rule that "[i]n order to abrogate a common-law principle, the statute must speak directly to the question addressed by the common law," United States v. Texas, 507 U.S. 529, 534 (1993). The Court of Appeals was accordingly correct in holding that when (but only when) the corporate veil may be pierced,[9] may a parent corporation be charged with derivative CERCLA liability for its subsidiary's actions.[10]

IV

A

If the Act rested liability entirely on ownership of a polluting facility, this opinion might end here; but CERCLA liability may turn on operation as well as ownership,

9. There is significant disagreement among courts and commentators over whether, in enforcing CERCLA's indirect liability, courts should borrow state law, or instead apply a federal common law of veil piercing. Since none of the parties challenges the Sixth Circuit's holding that CPC and Aerojet incurred no derivative liability, the question is not presented in this case, and we do not address it further.

10. Some courts and commentators have suggested that this indirect, veil-piercing approach can subject a parent corporation to liability only as an owner, and not as an operator. See, e.g., Lansford-Coaldale Joint Water Auth. v. Tonolli Corp., [4 F.3d 1209, 1220 (3d Cir. 1993)]; Oswald, Bifurcation of the Owner and Operator Analysis under CERCLA, 72 Wash. U. L.Q. 223, 281-282 (1994) (hereinafter Oswald). We think it is otherwise, however. If a subsidiary that operates, but does not own, a facility is so pervasively controlled by its parent for a sufficiently improper purpose to warrant veil piercing, the parent may be held derivatively liable for the subsidiary's acts as an operator.

and nothing in the statute's terms bars a parent corporation from direct liability for its own actions in operating a facility owned by its subsidiary. As Justice (then-Professor) Douglas noted almost 70 years ago, derivative liability cases are to be distinguished from those in which "the alleged wrong can seemingly be traced to the parent through the conduit of its own personnel and management" and "the parent is directly a participant in the wrong complained of." Douglas, at 207, 208. In such instances, the parent is directly liable for its own actions. The fact that a corporate subsidiary happens to own a polluting facility operated by its parent does nothing, then, to displace the rule that the parent "corporation is [itself] responsible for the wrongs committed by its agents in the course of its business," Mine Workers v. Coronado Coal Co., 259 U.S. 344, 395 (1922), and whereas the rules of veil-piercing limit derivative liability for the actions of another corporation, CERCLA's "operator" provision is concerned primarily with direct liability for one's own actions. It is this direct liability that is properly seen as being at issue here.

Under the plain language of the statute, any person who operates a polluting facility is directly liable for the costs of cleaning up the pollution. See 42 U.S.C. §9607(a)(2). This is so regardless of whether that person is the facility's owner, the owner's parent corporation or business partner, or even a saboteur who sneaks into the facility at night to discharge its poisons out of malice. If any such act of operating a corporate subsidiary's facility is done on behalf of a parent corporation, the existence of the parent-subsidiary relationship under state corporate law is simply irrelevant to the issue of direct liability.

This much is easy to say; the difficulty comes in defining actions sufficient to constitute direct parental "operation." . . . In a mechanical sense, to "operate" ordinarily means "[t]o control the functioning of; run: operate a sewing machine." American Heritage Dictionary 1268 (3d ed. 1992). And in the organizational sense more obviously intended by CERCLA, the word ordinarily means "[t]o conduct the affairs of; manage: operate a business." Id. So, under CERCLA, an operator is simply someone who directs the workings of, manages, or conducts the affairs of a facility. To sharpen the definition for purposes of CERCLA's concern with environmental contamination, an operator must manage, direct, or conduct operations specifically related to pollution, that is, operations having to do with the leakage or disposal of hazardous waste, or decisions about compliance with environmental regulations.

B

With this understanding, we are satisfied that the Court of Appeals correctly rejected the District Court's analysis of direct liability. But we also think that the appeals court erred in limiting direct liability under the statute to a parent's sole or joint venture operation, so as to eliminate any possible finding that CPC is liable as an operator on the facts of this case. . . .

By emphasizing that "CPC is directly liable under section 107(a)(2) as an operator because CPC actively participated in and exerted significant control over Ott II's business and decision-making," the District Court applied the "actual control" test of whether the parent "actually operated the business of its subsidiary," as several Circuits have employed it, see, e.g., Jacksonville Elec. Auth. v. Bernuth Corp., 996 F.2d 1107, 1110 (11th Cir. 1993) (parent is liable if it "actually exercised control over, or was otherwise intimately involved in the operations of, the [subsidiary] corporation immediately responsible for the operation of the facility").

The well-taken objection to the actual control test, however, is its fusion of direct and indirect liability; the test is administered by asking a question about the relationship between the two corporations (an issue going to indirect liability) instead of a question about the parent's interaction with the subsidiary's facility (the source of any direct liability). If, however, direct liability for the parent's operation of the facility is to be kept distinct from derivative liability for the subsidiary's own operation, the focus of the enquiry must necessarily be different under the two tests. "The question is not whether the parent operates the subsidiary, but rather whether it operates the facility, and that operation is evidenced by participation in the activities of the facility, not the subsidiary. Control of the subsidiary, if extensive enough, gives rise to indirect liability under piercing doctrine, not direct liability under the statutory language." Oswald, at 269. The District Court was therefore mistaken to rest its analysis on CPC's relationship with Ott II, premising liability on little more than "CPC's 100-percent ownership of Ott II" and "CPC's active participation in, and at times majority control over, Ott II's board of directors." The analysis should instead have rested on the relationship between CPC and the Muskegon facility itself.

In addition to (and perhaps as a reflection of) the erroneous focus on the relationship between CPC and Ott II, . . . [t]he District Court emphasized the facts that CPC placed its own high-level officials on Ott II's board of directors and in key management positions at Ott II, and that those individuals made major policy decisions and conducted day-to-day operations at the facility. . . .

In imposing direct liability on these grounds, the District Court failed to recognize that "it is entirely appropriate for directors of a parent corporation to serve as directors of its subsidiary, and that fact alone may not serve to expose the parent corporation to liability for its subsidiary's acts." American Protein Corp. v. AB Volvo, 844 F.2d 56, 57 (2d Cir. 1988).

. . . [I]t cannot be enough to establish liability here that dual officers and directors made policy decisions and supervised activities at the facility. The Government would have to show that, despite the general presumption to the contrary, the officers and directors were acting in their capacities as CPC officers and directors, and not as Ott II officers and directors, when they committed those acts. The District Court made no such enquiry here. . . .

In sum, the District Court's focus on the relationship between parent and subsidiary (rather than parent and facility), combined with its automatic attribution of the actions of dual officers and directors to the corporate parent, erroneously, even if unintentionally, treated CERCLA as though it displaced or fundamentally altered common law standards of limited liability. . . . [Such an approach would essentially create] a relaxed, CERCLA-specific rule of derivative liability that would banish traditional standards and expectations from the law of CERCLA liability. But, as we have said, such a rule does not arise from congressional silence, and CERCLA's silence is dispositive. . . .

We accordingly agree with the Court of Appeals that a participation-and-control test looking to the parent's supervision over the subsidiary, especially one that assumes that dual officers always act on behalf of the parent, cannot be used to identify operation of a facility resulting in direct parental liability. Nonetheless, a return to the ordinary meaning of the word "operate" in the organizational sense will indicate why we think that the Sixth Circuit stopped short when it confined its examples of direct parental operation to exclusive or joint ventures, and declined to find at least the possibility of direct operation by CPC in this case.

In our enquiry into the meaning Congress presumably had in mind when it used the verb "to operate," we recognized that the statute obviously meant something more than mere mechanical activation of pumps and valves, and must be read to contemplate "operation" as including the exercise of direction over the facility's activities. The Court of Appeals recognized this by indicating that a parent can be held directly liable when the parent operates the facility in the stead of its subsidiary or alongside the subsidiary in some sort of a joint venture. [But] a dual officer or director might depart so far from the norms of parental influence exercised through dual officeholding as to serve the parent, even when ostensibly acting on behalf of the subsidiary in operating the facility. Yet another possibility, suggested by the facts of this case, is that an agent of the parent with no hat to wear but the parent's hat might manage or direct activities at the facility.

Identifying such an occurrence calls for line drawing yet again, since the acts of direct operation that give rise to parental liability must necessarily be distinguished from the interference that stems from the normal relationship between parent and subsidiary. . . . The critical question is whether, in degree and detail, actions directed to the facility by an agent of the parent alone are eccentric under accepted norms of parental oversight of a subsidiary's facility.

There is, in fact, some evidence that CPC engaged in just this type and degree of activity at the Muskegon plant. The District Court's opinion speaks of an agent of CPC alone who played a conspicuous part in dealing with the toxic risks emanating from the operation of the plant. G.R.D. Williams worked only for CPC; he was not an employee, officer, or director of Ott II, and thus, his actions were of necessity taken only on behalf of CPC. The District Court found that "CPC became directly involved in environmental and regulatory matters through the work of . . . Williams, CPC's governmental and environmental affairs director. Williams . . . became heavily involved in environmental issues at Ott II." . . .

We think that these findings are enough to raise an issue of CPC's operation of the facility through Williams's actions, though we would draw no ultimate conclusion from these findings at this point. . . . [The Court remanded, "on the theory of direct operation set out here, for reevaluation of Williams's role, and of the role of any other CPC agent who might be said to have had a part in operating the Muskegon facility."]

NOTES AND QUESTIONS

1. *Parent and Subsidiary Corporations, and Piercing the Corporate Veil.* It is important to distinguish between liability imposed on a parent corporation as a result of its own activities and liability that stems solely from the parent's ownership of another corporation. The Supreme Court in *Bestfoods* described the distinction as one between direct and indirect (or derivative) liability. What is the difference between the two? On remand in *Bestfoods*, the district court found that CPC was not directly liable as an operator. The government failed to prove that G.R.D. Williams, or any other CPC officer or director, engaged in activities that were sufficiently "eccentric" to impose operator liability. The court also rejected the contention that CPC was derivatively liable as a successor to Ott I, because Ott I's acquisition constituted a de facto merger with CPC. Bestfoods v. Aerojet-General Corp., 173 F. Supp. 2d 729 (W.D. Mich. 2001).

In assessing a parent corporation's indirect liability either as an owner or operator, when is it appropriate to pierce the corporate veil? Suppose a company forms a subsidiary to purchase the assets of a corporation with potential CERCLA liability for the purpose of avoiding that liability. The formation of a wholly owned, undercapitalized subsidiary whose day-to-day operations are controlled by the parent is an easy case for imposing liability on the parent. For example, in Idaho v. Bunker Hill Co., 635 F. Supp. 665 (D. Idaho 1986), a parent that capitalized a subsidiary at $1100 and received $27 million in dividends was deemed an owner or operator. But in Browning-Ferris Indus. of Illinois, Inc. v. Ter Maat, 195 F.3d 953, 960-961 (7th Cir. 1999), the court determined that piercing on the basis of undercapitalization that nevertheless complied with minimum capitalization requirements under state law was inappropriate. The factors traditionally considered by the state courts in determining whether to pierce the corporate veil include: (1) inadequate capitalization in light of the purposes for which the corporation was organized, (2) extensive control by the parent shareholders, (3) intermingling of subsidiary and parent accounts and property, (4) failure to observe the formalities of separateness, such as separate records, (5) diversion of funds from the subsidiary to the parent, and (6) existence of nonfunctioning officers or directors.*

Direct liability, as the Court points out in *Bestfoods*, is premised on the relationship between the parent and the contaminated site. In Lansford-Coaldale Joint Water Auth. v. Tonolli Corp., 4 F.3d 1209 (3d Cir. 1993), the court described a split of opinion among the circuits in assessing whether a parent corporation may be directly liable as an operator under CERCLA:

> Courts have fashioned two competing standards for the imposition of operator liability: what we term the "actual control" test and the "authority-to-control" test. Under the actual control standard, a corporation will only be held liable for the environmental violations of another corporation when there is evidence of substantial control exercised by one corporation over the activities of the other. In contrast, under the authority-to-control test, operator liability is imposed as long as one corporation had the capability to control, even if it was never utilized. [Id. at 1221.]

Does the opinion in *Bestfoods* take a position on this issue? After *Bestfoods*, under what circumstances will a parent corporation be directly liable as an operator for response costs under CERCLA? In United States v. Kayser-Roth Corp., 272 F.3d 89 (1st Cir. 2001), the court affirmed a lower court finding that a parent was directly liable on the basis of its pervasive control over the subsidiary's environmental affairs.**

Should the tests for determining whether a parent corporation is liable as an operator also apply in the context of arranger or transporter liability? See United States v. TIC Inv. Corp., 68 F.3d 1082, 1091-1092 (8th Cir. 1995) (concluding that "in order for a parent corporation to incur direct arranger liability for a subsidiary's off-site disposal practices, there must be some causal connection or nexus between the parent

---

*For a case in which the court pierced the corporate veil based on the control exercised by the parent over the subsidiary, see United States v. Union Corp., 259 F. Supp. 2d 356, 389 (E.D. Pa. 2003). For a case in which the court refused to pierce the corporate veil, see Pfohl Bros. Landfill Site Steering Comm. v. Allied Waste Sys., Inc., 255 F. Supp. 2d 134, 178-183 (W.D.N.Y. 2003).

**Compare Atlanta Gas Light Co. v. UGI Util, Inc., 463 F.3d 1201 (11th Cir. 2006) (parent not liable as operator); BP Amoco Chem. Co. v. Sun Oil Co., 316 F. Supp. 2d 166 (D. Del. 2004) (parent not liable because there was no evidence that parent employee's activities at subsidiary's facility were eccentric under accepted norms of parental oversight of a subsidiary's facility).

corporation's conduct and the subsidiary's arrangement for disposal, or the off-site disposal itself"). What should the test for transporter liability of a parent corporation be?

2. *Successor and Dissolved Corporations.* The courts have imposed operator liability on successor as well as parent corporations. United States v. General Battery Corp., 423 F.3d 294 (3d Cir. 2005), involved both choice of law and substantive questions concerning successor liability. The court concluded that successor liability is governed by federal common law, as derived from the general doctrine of successor liability in operation in most states. It recognized that successor environmental liability rests at the intersection of tort and corporate law, both of which are largely governed by state law. But state approaches vary, and the unpredictability of relying on divergent state approaches supports the application of uniform federal common law. A uniform and predictable approach is likely to better promote CERCLA's objectives by encouraging settlements and facilitating a more liquid market in brownfield assets. Not all courts agree. Atchison, Topeka & Santa Fe Ry. v. Brown & Bryant, Inc., 159 F.3d 358 (9th Cir. 1997), ruled that the parameters of successor liability under CERCLA are governed by state corporation law, not federal common law. Did the Supreme Court in *Bestfoods* shed any light on which approach to the choice of law question is correct?[*]

On the substantive question of when to impose successor liability, the court in *General Battery* found that the general rule of corporate successor liability followed in most states (sometimes referred to as the "mere continuation" test) is that the successor is not liable for the activities of an acquired corporation unless (1) the successor assumes liability, (2) the transaction amounts to a consolidation or merger, (3) the transaction is fraudulent and intended to provide an escape from liability, or (4) the purchasing corporation is a mere continuation of the selling company. The *General Battery* case turned on whether there had been a de facto merger. The successor is liable as a result of a de facto merger if (1) there has been a continuation of the enterprise of the seller corporation, (2) there is a continuity of shareholders, (3) the seller corporation ceases its ordinary business operations and liquidates and dissolves as soon as possible, and (4) the purchasing corporation assumes the obligations of the seller ordinarily necessary for the uninterrupted continuation of the seller's normal business operations. The court held that the successor was liable under that standard.[**] Finally, the court held that, after the *Bestfoods* decision, the "substantial continuity" doctrine, which is a more expansive successor liability rule than that accepted in most states, is untenable as a basis for successor liability under CERCLA. In New York v. National Serv. Indus., Inc., 460 F.3d 201 (2d Cir. 2006), the court declined to decide whether CERCLA incorporates or displaces state law for purposes of determining successor liability; under either federal or state law, the successor was not liable following a de facto merger in the absence of continuity of ownership. Must the successor have knowledge of the predecessor's potential CERCLA liability at the

---

[*]See generally Aronovsky, Federalism and CERCLA: Rethinking the Role of Federal Law in Private Cleanup Cost Disputes, 33 Ecology L.Q. 1 (2006) (favoring the application of uniform federal common law).

[**]See also North Shore Gas Co. v. Salomon Inc., 152 F.3d 642 (7th Cir. 1998) (holding that, assuming predecessor was liable, asset purchaser was too, despite the general rule that an asset purchaser does not acquire the liabilities of the seller, because the transaction amounted to a de facto merger, and the purchaser was a mere continuation of the seller).

time of an asset purchase to become liable under the substantial continuity test? See Gould, Inc. v. A & M Battery & Tire Serv., 950 F. Supp. 653 (M.D. Pa. 1997).

May a corporation or partnership that has been dissolved in accordance with state law and whose assets have been distributed incur liability under CERCLA as an owner or operator at the time of disposal? Canadyne-Georgia Corp. v. Cleveland, 72 F. Supp. 2d 1373 (M.D. Ga. 1999), reviews the cases and holds that, to the extent that state dissolution laws might affect the capacity of a PRP to be sued under CERCLA, those laws are preempted.

3. *Corporate Officers and Shareholders.* The courts seem to be more wary of interpreting CERCLA's liability provisions expansively when individuals rather than organizations are named as PRPs. Corporate officers apparently will not be held liable, either as operators or arrangers, merely on the basis of their position in the corporate hierarchy. Officers who actively participate in or actually exercise substantial control over hazardous substance management, however, may be liable. See, e.g., United States v. TIC Inv. Corp., 68 F.3d 1082 (8th Cir. 1995) (arranger liability); Sidney S. Arst Co. v. Pipefitters Welfare Educ. Fund, 25 F.3d 417 (7th Cir. 1994) (operator liability). Should corporate officers who control day-to-day corporate activities but not liability-creating conduct be liable? See United States v. USX Corp., 68 F.3d 811 (3d Cir. 1995) (only officers who actively participate in the process of accepting hazardous wastes for transport and have a substantial role in the selection of a disposal facility may be liable as transporters under §107(a)(4), although actual knowledge of and acquiescence in a subordinate's decisions may be enough). Likewise, Jacksonville Elec. Auth. v. Bernuth Corp., 996 F.2d 1107 (11th Cir. 1993), established that individual shareholders are liable as operators only when they actually participated in facility operations or in the activities which resulted in disposal, or actually exercised control over, or were otherwise intimately involved in the operations of, the corporation immediately responsible for the operation of the facility.*

Problem 9-6

Blackhawk operated a trucking terminal on the Maggyland site from 1961 to 1971, when it sold the site to Apartments, Inc. In 1973, Apartments, Inc. sold the site to Maggyland Limited, which contracted with Constructor Co. to build an apartment complex. In 1984, Al Adams and Adams, Inc. became general partners in Maggyland Limited, holding a 1 percent interest. Adams was president and majority shareholder of Adams, Inc. At the same time, Lynch Properties, Inc. became a limited partner in Maggyland Limited, holding the other 99 percent. Beginning in 1984, the partners in Maggyland Limited vested day-to-day responsibility for managing the apartment complex in Management Co. The general and limited partners remained responsible for approving rent increases and capital improvements in the apartment complex, which

---

*See also Raytheon Constructors, Inc. v. ASARCO, Inc., 368 F.3d 1214 (10th Cir. 2003) (holding that, under *Bestfoods*, a minority shareholder was not liable either as an operator or an arranger). But see Carter-Jones Lumber Co. v. LTV Steel Co., 237 F.3d 745 (6th Cir. 2001) (individual shareholder's control of corporation justified piercing of corporate veil and imposing joint and several liability). For further reading, see Oswald, Strict Liability of Individuals under CERCLA: A Normative Analysis, 20 B.C. Envtl. Aff. L. Rev. 579 (1993).

included repaving the parking lot and maintaining natural gas lines on the property. Both of these projects involved movement and dispersal of contaminated soil, although none of the partners knew at the time about the contamination.

While Blackhawk operated its trucking terminal, its trucks routinely carried substances that included asphalt. Its employees dumped unused asphalt into a pit on the site and hazardous substances which Blackhawk employees disposed of at the site mixed with the asphalt, creating a black, tar-like substance that oozed from the pit into surrounding soil and groundwater. Some of the hazardous substances at the site resulted from the washing of Blackhawk's trucks. To contain these substances, Blackhawk built levees, using heavy equipment to move earth. The result was the movement of hazardous substances near the levees and mixture of those substances with surrounding soil. Although Blackhawk did not inform Apartments, Inc. of the history of hazardous substance disposal and release when Blackhawk sold the site to Apartments, Inc., the presence of hazardous substances in the area was common knowledge.

In 1988, the state environmental agency responded to complaints from Maggyland Apartment residents that tar-like substances were seeping to the surface at the site. The state agency notified EPA, which discovered tar, asphalt, pesticides, chlorinated benzenes, and polynuclear hydrocarbons in the soil and groundwater at the Maggyland site. The pesticides chlordane and dieldrin were initially sprayed at the site at the direction of Management Co., which was responsible for lawn care at the apartment complex. EPA had registered the two pesticides under FIFRA before the spraying, but it revoked the registrations before 1984. EPA incurred nearly $2 million in response costs over the next ten years removing or containing these contaminants.

EPA has brought an action for reimbursement of its response costs under §107(a) of CERCLA against Blackhawk; Apartments, Inc.; Maggyland Limited; Constructor Co.; Al Adams; Adams, Inc.; Lynch Properties, Inc.; and Management Co. Which of the defendants, if any, should the court hold liable?

5. Contribution and Private Cost Recovery Actions

Section 113(f)(1) of CERCLA entitles any person to seek contribution from any other person who is liable or potentially liable under §106 or §107. May a person who is not the subject of a prior or pending CERCLA enforcement action bring such a contribution action?

COOPER INDUSTRIES, INC. v. AVIALL SERVICES, INC.
543 U.S. 147 (2004)

JUSTICE THOMAS delivered the opinion of the Court.

Section 113(f)(1) of [CERCLA] allows persons who have undertaken efforts to clean up properties contaminated by hazardous substances to seek contribution from other parties liable under CERCLA. . . . The issue we must decide is whether a private party who has not been sued under §106 or §107(a) may nevertheless obtain contribution under §113(f)(1) from other liable parties. We hold that it may not.

I ...

After CERCLA's enactment in 1980, litigation arose over whether §107, in addition to allowing the Government and certain private parties to recover costs from PRPs, also allowed a PRP that had incurred response costs to recover costs from other PRPs. More specifically, the question was whether a private party that had incurred response costs, but that had done so voluntarily and was not itself subject to suit, had a cause of action for cost recovery against other PRPs. Various courts held that §107(a)(4)(B) and its predecessors authorized such a cause of action.

After CERCLA's passage, litigation also ensued over the separate question whether a private entity that had been sued in a cost recovery action (by the Government or by another PRP) could obtain contribution from other PRPs. As originally enacted in 1980, CERCLA contained no provision expressly providing for a right of action for contribution. A number of District Courts nonetheless held that, although CERCLA did not mention the word "contribution," such a right arose either impliedly from provisions of the statute, or as a matter of federal common law. That conclusion was debatable in light of two decisions of this Court that refused to recognize implied or common-law rights to contribution in other federal statutes.

Congress subsequently amended CERCLA in [SARA, enacted in 1986] to provide an express cause of action for contribution, codified as CERCLA §113(f)(1). . . .

SARA also created a separate express right of contribution, §113(f)(3)(B), for "[a] person who has resolved its liability to the United States or a State for some or all of a response action or for some or all of the costs of such action in an administrative or judicially approved settlement." In short, after SARA, CERCLA provided for a right to cost recovery in certain circumstances, §107(a), and separate rights to contribution in other circumstances, §§113(f)(1), 113(f)(3)(B).

II

[Cooper owned and operated four contaminated aircraft engine maintenance sites in Texas until 1981, when it sold them to Aviall. Aviall later discovered that both it and Cooper had contaminated the facilities through leaks and spills of hazardous substances onto the ground and into the groundwater. Aviall notified the Texas Natural Resource Conservation Commission (Commission), which informed Aviall that it was violating state environmental laws, directed Aviall to clean up the site, and threatened to pursue an enforcement action if Aviall failed to do so. Neither the Commission nor EPA took any judicial or administrative measures to compel cleanup by Aviall.

Under the state's supervision, Aviall cleaned up the properties and then sold them to a third party, remaining contractually responsible for the cleanup. After Aviall incurred approximately $5 million in cleanup costs, it sued Cooper in federal district court in Texas, seeking to recover contribution under §113(f)(1). The district court granted Cooper's motion for summary judgment, holding that §113(f)(1) relief was unavailable to Aviall because it had not been sued under CERCLA §106 or §107. A divided panel of the Fifth Circuit affirmed, but on rehearing en banc, that court reversed by a divided vote. The majority held that §113(f)(1) allows a PRP to obtain contribution from other PRPs regardless of whether the PRP has been sued under §106 or §107. Three members of the en banc court dissented for essentially the reasons given by the district court and the panel majority.]

III

A

Section 113(f)(1) does not authorize Aviall's suit. The first sentence, the enabling clause that establishes the right of contribution, provides: "Any person *may* seek contribution . . . *during or following* any civil action under section 9606 of this title or under section 9607(a) of this title" (emphasis added). The natural meaning of this sentence is that contribution may only be sought subject to the specified conditions, namely, "during or following" a specified civil action.

Aviall answers that "may" should be read permissively, such that "during or following" a civil action is one, but not the exclusive, instance in which a person may seek contribution. We disagree. First, as just noted, the natural meaning of "may" in the context of the enabling clause is that it authorizes certain contribution actions— ones that satisfy the subsequent specified condition—and no others.

Second, and relatedly, if §113(f)(1) were read to authorize contribution actions at any time, regardless of the existence of a §106 or §107(a) civil action, then Congress need not have included the explicit "during or following" condition. In other words, Aviall's reading would render part of the statute entirely superfluous, something we are loath to do. Likewise, if §113(f)(1) authorizes contribution actions at any time, §113(f)(3)(B), which permits contribution actions after settlement, is equally superfluous. There is no reason why Congress would bother to specify conditions under which a person may bring a contribution claim, and at the same time allow contribution actions absent those conditions.

The last sentence of §113(f)(1), the saving clause, does not change our conclusion. That sentence provides: "Nothing in this subsection shall diminish the right of any person to bring an action for contribution in the absence of a civil action under section 9606 of this title or section 9607 of this title." The sole function of the sentence is to clarify that §113(f)(1) does nothing to "diminish" any cause(s) of action for contribution that may exist independently of §113(f)(1). In other words, the sentence rebuts any presumption that the express right of contribution provided by the enabling clause is the exclusive cause of action for contribution available to a PRP. The sentence, however, does not itself establish a cause of action; nor does it expand §113(f)(1) to authorize contribution actions not brought "during or following" a §106 or §107(a) civil action; nor does it specify what causes of action for contribution, if any, exist outside §113(f)(1). Reading the saving clause to authorize §113(f)(1) contribution actions not just "during or following" a civil action, but also before such an action, would again violate the settled rule that we must, if possible, construe a statute to give every word some operative effect.

Our conclusion follows not simply from §113(f)(1) itself, but also from the whole of §113. As noted above, §113 provides two express avenues for contribution: §113(f)(1) ("during or following" specified civil actions) and §113(f)(3)(B) (after an administrative or judicially approved settlement that resolves liability to the United States or a State). Section 113(g)(3) then provides two corresponding 3-year limitations periods for contribution actions, one beginning at the date of judgment, §113(g)(3)(A), and one beginning at the date of settlement, §113(g)(3)(B). Notably absent from §113(g)(3) is any provision for starting the limitations period if a judgment or settlement never occurs, as is the case with a purely voluntary cleanup. The lack of such a provision supports the conclusion that, to assert a contribution claim under §113(f), a party must satisfy the conditions of either §113(f)(1) or §113(f)(3)(B).

Each side insists that the purpose of CERCLA bolsters its reading of §113(f)(1). Given the clear meaning of the text, there is no need to resolve this dispute or to consult the purpose of CERCLA at all. As we have said: "[I]t is ultimately the provisions of our laws rather than the principal concerns of our legislators by which we are governed." Oncale v. Sundowner Offshore Serv., Inc., 523 U.S. 75, 79 (1998). Section 113(f)(1) authorizes contribution claims only "during or following" a civil action under §106 or §107(a), and it is undisputed that Aviall has never been subject to such an action.[5] Aviall therefore has no §113(f)(1) claim.

B

Aviall and amicus Lockheed Martin contend that, in the alternative to an action for contribution under §113(f)(1), Aviall may recover costs under §107(a)(4)(B) even though it is a PRP. [The majority refused to address this issue, because it had not been properly raised below.]

C

In addition to leaving open whether Aviall may seek cost recovery under §107, we decline to decide whether Aviall has an implied right to contribution under §107. Portions of the Fifth Circuit's opinion below might be taken to endorse the latter cause of action; others appear to reserve the question whether such a cause of action exists. To the extent that Aviall chooses to frame its §107 claim on remand as an implied right of contribution (as opposed to a right of cost recovery), we note that this Court has visited the subject of implied rights of contribution before. We also note that, in enacting §113(f)(1), Congress explicitly recognized a particular set (claims "during or following" the specified civil actions) of the contribution rights previously implied by courts from provisions of CERCLA and the common law. Nonetheless, we need not and do not decide today whether any judicially implied right of contribution survived the passage of SARA. . . .

JUSTICE GINSBURG, with whom JUSTICE STEVENS joins, dissenting.

[The dissenters favored a ruling on the issue of whether Aviall had a right of contribution under §107.] Federal courts, prior to the enactment of §113(f)(1), had correctly held that PRPs could "recover [under §107] a proportionate share of their costs in actions for contribution against other PRPs"; nothing in §113 retracts that right. Accordingly, I would not defer a definitive ruling by this Court on the question whether Aviall may pursue a §107 claim for relief against Cooper.

NOTES AND QUESTIONS

1. What was the key language in §113(f)(1) that the majority relied on to support its holding? The Fifth Circuit en banc majority had relied on a combination of the first and last sentences of §113(f)(1) to support its conclusion that a PRP may sue for contribution even if it has not already been the subject of an enforcement action

---

5. Neither has Aviall been subject to an administrative order under §106; thus, we need not decide whether such an order would qualify as a "civil action under section 9606 . . . or under section 9607(a)" of CERCLA. 42 U.S.C. §9613(f)(1).

under §106 or §107. Can you re-create what that court's argument might have been? How did the Supreme Court majority interpret the last sentence of §113(f)(1)? Justice Thomas noted that both sides argued that the purpose of CERCLA bolstered their readings of the statutory text, but that the clarity of the text precluded the need to consider statutory purposes.[*]

2. *The Consequences of* Aviall. What do you suppose the effect of the Court's holding in the principal case will be on the conduct of the owners of contaminated sites that have not yet been sued by the government? Is that result consistent or inconsistent with the purposes of CERCLA? According to some estimates, voluntary cleanups comprise as much as 90 percent of all cleanups of sites contaminated by hazardous substances. See Hill Fix Eyed after Supreme Court Ruling Limits Voluntary Cleanups, Inside E.P.A. Weekly, at 1, 9 (Dec. 17, 2004).

3. Is an administrative order a "civil action" for purposes of §113(f)(1)? See footnote 5 of the principal case; Pharmacia Corp. v. Clayton Chem. Acquisition, LLC, 382 F. Supp. 2d 1079 (S.D. Ill. 2005) (no).

4. May a court in a §113 contribution action issue a declaratory judgment determining liability for response costs to be incurred in the future? See §113(g)(2); Gussack Realty Corp. v. Xerox Corp., 224 F.3d 85 (2d Cir. 2000); Boeing Co. v. Cascade Corp., 207 F.3d 1177, 1191-1192 (9th Cir. 2000). Declaratory relief facilitates voluntary cleanups by eliminating uncertainty as to a PRP's share of cleanup costs yet to be incurred. See United States v. Davis, 261 F.3d 1, 46-47 (1st Cir. 2001).

NOTES AND QUESTIONS ON CONTRIBUTION AND PRIVATE COST RECOVERY

PRP Options after Aviall. After *Aviall*, what options are available to PRPs who wish to pay for a cleanup and then seek at least partial reimbursement from other PRPs? One option is to wait until the PRP is the subject to a suit under §106 or §107 of CERCLA and then bring a §113(f)(1) contribution action against other PRPs. A second possibility is to enter an administrative settlement with EPA or a state. See §113(f)(3)(B); Atlanta Gas Light Co. v. UGI Util, Inc., 463 F.3d 1201 (11th Cir. 2006); Boarhead Farm Agreement Group v. Advanced Envtl. Tech. Corp., 381 F. Supp. 2d 427 (E.D. Pa. 2005) (not allowing party who entered consent decree with EPA to remediate a site to bring a contribution action against other PRPs, even in the absence of a §106 or §107 action, "would torture the meaning of the statute and discourage PRPs not sued from cooperating and settling with PRPs who were sued without the costs and delay of litigation"). An administrative consent order between a PRP and a state that settles exclusively state law claims, however, does not trigger a right to contribution under §113(f)(3)(B). See Consolidated Edison Co. of New York, Inc. v. UGI Util., Inc., 423 F.3d 90 (2d Cir. 2005). Some courts after *Aviall* held that an administrative order by consent (AOC) issued by EPA under §106 does not qualify as a "settlement" for purposes of §113(f)(3)(B). See, e.g., Pharmacia Corp. v. Clayton Chem. Acquisition, LLC, 382 F. Supp. 2d 1079 (S.D. Ill. 2005). In response, EPA and

---

[*]For thorough analysis of the arguments the parties made in their briefs before the Court and the Court's likely analysis, see Hyson, The *Aviall* Case: Will the Supreme Court Deny Recovery under CERCLA to PRPs Who Voluntarily Incur Response Costs?, 34 Envtl. L. Rep. (ELI) 10,824 (2004). Professor Hyson, whose article was written before the Supreme Court's decision, argues that the Fifth Circuit's decision was correct.

the Justice Department issued a document in 2005, Interim Revisions to CERCLA Removal, RI/FS and RD AOC Models to Clarify Contribution Rights and Protection under Section 113(f). The document seeks to establish that an AOC is a settlement agreement with the federal government that resolves the settling party's liability and protects its right to seek contribution from non-settling PRPs. Among other things, the agencies changed their model language for AOCs by henceforth calling them administrative settlement agreements and orders on consent. See Rosen, Agency Revises Language in Consent Orders to Ease Concerns about Contribution Rights, 36 Env't Rep. (BNA) 1768 (2005).

A third option for PRPs is to bring a private cost recovery action under §107(a)(4)(B). That option is clearly available to an innocent landowner who incurs response costs and wants to seek reimbursement from PRPs. Before the *Aviall* decision, courts uniformly held that a PRP may not bring such a cost recovery action against another PRP. The question is what effect, if any, *Aviall* has on those precedents. The Supreme Court in *Aviall* refused to address the issue of whether a PRP can bring a §107(a) cost recovery against other PRPs.

Some courts have concluded that the pre-*Aviall* precedents on this issue are no longer valid.* In Vine Street LLC v. Keeling, 362 F. Supp. 2d 754 (E.D. Tex. 2005), the court held that when a PRP is unable to bring a §113(f) contribution claim (because, for example, it is a volunteer), it may bring a cost recovery action under §107(a). "Quite simply, a [PRP] that voluntarily works with a government agency to remedy environmentally contaminated property should not have to wait to be sued to recover cleanup costs since Section 113(f)(1) is not meant to be the only way to recover cleanup costs." Id. at 763. Another district court concluded that CERCLA's purposes support allowing PRPs barred from pursuing §113(f) contribution claims to bring §107 claims:

> If the section 107 sluiceway is closed, CERCLA would ensure contribution for responsible parties who are forced to incur remediation costs beyond their pro rata share (via section 113(f)). In contrast, responsible parties who voluntarily incur remediation costs in excess of their pro rata share would have no CERCLA remedy. The Court sees no basis for treating responsible parties so differently based solely on what prompted them to incur remediation costs. Moreover, given the broad categories of entities that are considered responsible parties under CERCLA, it is hard to imagine many cases in which purely "innocent parties" would ever be motivated to initiate an action under section 107. . . .
>
> Ultimately, interpreting section 107 to forbid current owners and other responsible parties from seeking reimbursement for voluntary cleanups would encourage these parties to wait for a governmental entity or an innocent party to take decisive action before initiating any investigation or remediation. . . . [T]his effect is contrary to CERCLA's clear goals of encouraging voluntary remediations. [City of Bangor v. Citizens Commc'n Co., 437 F. Supp. 2d 180, 222-223 (D. Me. 2006).]

The court in Consolidated Edison Co. of New York, Inc. v. UGI Util., Inc., 423 F.3d 90 (2d Cir. 2005), adopted a similar position. It concluded that a contrary ruling would impermissibly discourage voluntary cleanups and undercut CERCLA's purposes. The court noted that a party that has expended funds for cleanup solely due to the imposition of liability through a state administrative order might not have incurred

---

*Other courts have admitted to utter confusion as to the impact of *Aviall* on previous circuit court rulings on various cost recovery and contribution questions. See, e.g., Adobe Lumber, Inc. v. Hellman, 415 F. Supp. 2d 1070 (E.D. Cal. 2006).

"necessary costs of response," and therefore might not be eligible to bring a §107(a) action, but declined to resolve the question. Finally, without committing itself, the court indicated that a person sued under §107(a) may be able to bring a counterclaim under §113(f)(1) for offsetting contribution against the §107(a) volunteer plaintiff. The Second Circuit extended the ruling in *Consolidated Edison* in Schaefer v. Town of Victor, 457 F.3d 188 (2d Cir. 2006), concluding that a person who eventually enters into a consent agreement with EPA or a state may sue under §107(a), even if it began a voluntary cleanup before entering the agreement.*

Other courts of appeals have followed suit. In Atlantic Research Corp. v. United States, 459 F.3d 827 (8th Cir. 2006), the court held that a private party that voluntarily undertakes cleanup for which it may be held liable and that is therefore ineligible under *Aviall* to bring a §113(f)(1) contribution action may pursue an action for direct recovery or contribution under §107 against another liable party.** In the process, it overruled pre-*Aviall* case law from the Eighth Circuit. The court reasoned that it no longer makes sense to view §113 as a liable party's exclusive remedy, given its unavailability to those who voluntarily incur cleanup costs. It added, however, that §107 plaintiffs may not recover their full response costs.

Some courts have reached a different set of conclusions. In Elementis Chem. Inc. v. T H Agric. and Nutrition, L.L.C., 373 F. Supp. 2d 257 (S.D.N.Y. 2005), the court ruled that a PRP that had conducted a voluntary cleanup could not bring a private cost recovery action under §107(a). Prohibiting volunteers from filing cost recovery actions might encourage them to concede liability and enter settlement agreements with the government, thereby enabling them to bring contribution actions under §113(f)(3)(B). Encouraging settlements is consistent with congressional intent.*** E.I. DuPont De Nemours and Co. v. United States, 460 F.3d 515 (3d Cir. 2006), used similar reasoning. It rejected the notion that CERCLA's broad remedial purpose demands recognition of a PRP's express right to bring a §107 cost recovery action. The court found it less than clear that Congress wanted to encourage voluntary cleanups by allowing those conducting them to sue other PRPs for cost recovery. While Congress sought to encourage settlements when it adopted SARA, a cleanup conducted as a result of a settlement with the federal government (unlike a voluntary cleanup) is subject to EPA oversight. EPA itself expressed serious doubts about *sua sponte* voluntary cleanups before the enactment of SARA. The provisions of CERCLA that encourage settlement, allow contribution by PRPs that settle, and establish minimal cleanup standards for government cleanups to ensure safe, effective, and reliable cleanups are consistent with that wariness and with the pre-*Aviall* case law barring PRP volunteers from suing under §107.

*See also Seneca Meadows, Inc. v. ECI Liquidating, Inc., 427 F. Supp. 2d 279, 289 (W.D.N.Y. 2006) (noting that an effort by a PRP previously held partially liable in a §113(f)(1) contribution action to pursue a §107 action does not seek to undercut that allocation of responsibility by seeking recovery from other PRPs of a portion of its share of response costs, as opposed to all of its response costs).
**The court in *Atlantic Research* declined to use the term "PRP," preferring the term "liable party." It stated that *Aviall* had weakened the term "PRP," which may be read to confer on a party that has not been held liable a legal status that it should not bear. *Atlantic Research*, 457 F.3d at 831 n.6.
***See also Aviall Serv., Inc. v. Cooper Indus. LLC, 63 Env't Rep. Cas. (BNA) 1622 (N.D. Tex 2006) (deciding, on remand from the Supreme Court's decision in *Aviall*, that PRPs may not bring a private cost recovery action under §107 and that there is no implied right of contribution under either §107 or federal common law); City of Waukesha v. Viacom Int'l Inc., 362 F. Supp. 2d 1025 (E.D. Wis. Mar. 2005).

Still another option for a PRP unable to pursue a contribution action under §113(f)(1) is to sue on the basis of an implied federal common law right to contribution for PRPs. This strategy has met with some success. In *Atlantic Research, supra,* the court, in an alternative holding, recognized an implied right to contribution under §107 itself.* See also Raytheon Aircraft Co. v. United States, 435 F. Supp. 2d 1136, 1149-1151 (D. Kan. 2006). But in Niagara Mohawk Power Corp. v. Consolidated Rail Corp., 436 F. Supp. 2d 398 (N.D.N.Y. 2006), the court refused to allow a PRP that had incurred and was incurring expenditures under two consent orders with the state environmental agency to bring an implied cause of action for contribution under §107. See also *DuPont,* discussed earlier. The Supreme Court granted *certiorari* in *Atlantic Research* in January 2007, presumably to clear up some of the confusion engendered by its decision in *Aviall.*

Resolving Contribution Claims. Section 113(f)(1) provides that, in resolving contribution claims, a federal court "may allocate response costs among liable parties using such equitable factors as the court determines are appropriate." One court likened the process to "trying to figure out what makes Coke taste the way it does." Browning-Ferris Indus. of Ill., Inc. v. Ter Maat, 13 F. Supp. 2d 756, 777 (N.D. Ill. 1998), *aff'd in part, rev'd in part on other grounds,* 195 F.3d 953 (7th Cir. 1999). Most courts agree that liability in a §113(f)(1) contribution action is several, rather than joint and several. Elementis Chromium, L.P. v. Coastal States Petroleum Co., 450 F.3d 607, 612-613 (5th Cir. 2006). But see Browning-Ferris Indus. of Illinois, Inc. v. Ter Maat, 195 F.3d 953, 956 (7th Cir. 1999) (CERCLA does not preclude the imposition of joint and several liability in a contribution action based on equitable considerations).

The factors that courts most frequently use to allocate responsibility in CERCLA contribution actions are the so-called Gore factors, discussed in the *Bell Petroleum Services* case in section C.3.a. Essentially, "[t]hose parties who can show that their contribution to the harm is relatively small in terms of amount of waste, toxicity of the waste, involvement with the waste, and care, stand in a better position to be allocated a smaller portion of response costs." Control Data Corp. v. SCSC Corp., 53 F.3d 930, 935 (8th Cir. 1995). In Boeing Co. v. Cascade Corp., 207 F.3d 1177 (9th Cir. 2000), the court noted that courts may consider factors other than the Gore factors, such as volume, as the basis for cost allocation. But in Beazer East, Inc. v. Mead Corp., 412 F.3d 429 (3d Cir. 2005), the court ruled that CERCLA does not allow a court to prioritize the parties' relative contributions of waste, based on the "polluter pays" principle, over their contractual intent to allocate environmental liability among themselves.

What is the role of causation in CERCLA contribution litigation? In *Browning-Ferris, supra,* the court concluded that liability may be imposed on a contribution defendant on the basis of either "but for" causation or proof that the defendant's activities were a "sufficient condition" of cleanup cost incurrence. "The resulting

---

*The court stated that a contrary ruling in that case, in which the plaintiff had brought a §107 action against the United States, based on a contract to retrofit rocket motors for the federal government, would be absurd and unjust. If a person who voluntarily incurs cleanup costs is barred from bringing a §107 cost recovery action against the federal government, "the government could insulate itself from responsibility for its own pollution by simply declining to bring a CERCLA action or refusing a liable party's offer to settle. This bizarre outcome would eviscerate CERCLA whenever the government, itself, was partially responsible for a site's contamination." *Atlantic Research,* 457 F.3d at 837.

inquiry thus focuses not only on causation, but also on fault—a negligence concept foreign to the initial determination of responsibility under CERCLA." Nagle, CERCLA, Causation, and Responsibility, 78 Minn. L. Rev. 1493, 1523 (1994). Is it true that, as §107 has been interpreted, the concept of negligence is always foreign to the initial determination of responsibility under CERCLA?

Is it appropriate for a court to determine that a PRP is liable in the liability phase of a bifurcated CERCLA §107(a) action, but then to refuse to allocate any response costs to it? See Kalamazoo River Study Group v. Rockwell Int'l Corp., 274 F.3d 1043 (6th Cir. 2001). See also Kalamazoo River Study Group v. Rockwell Int'l Corp., 355 F.3d 574, 591-592 (6th Cir. 2003) (upholding district court's decision in contribution action allocating only 10 percent of investigation costs and none of future remediation costs to PRP it had previously deemed liable).

Contribution Protection. Section 113(f)(2) provides that "[a] person who has resolved its liability to the United States or a State in an administrative or judicially approved settlement shall not be liable for claims for contribution regarding matters addressed in the settlement." Courts determine the scope of the "matters addressed" in a settlement by referring to the location, time frame, hazardous substances, and cleanup costs covered by the agreement, and whatever other factors bear upon the reasonable expectations of the parties to the settlement and an equitable apportionment of response costs. Akzo Coatings, Inc. v. Aigner Corp., 30 F.3d 761, 766 (7th Cir. 1994). See also American Cyanamid Co. v. Capuano, 381 F.3d 6, 17-18 (1st Cir. 2004) (consent decree requiring that PRP contribute to soil remediation costs did not provide contribution protection for costs of groundwater remediation); United States v. Alexander, 981 F.2d 250 (5th Cir. 1993) (distinguishing between off-site and on-site remediation costs). What is the effect of a settlement between two private PRPs on a subsequent contribution action? See Boeing Co. v. Cascade Corp., 207 F.3d 1177, 1189-1190 (9th Cir. 2000).

When a joint tortfeasor enters a settlement that does not fully satisfy the plaintiff's claim, one approach to determining the effect of the settlement on the liability of nonsettlors, called the "pro tanto" approach, is to reduce the nonsettlors' share of liability by the dollar amount of the settlement. This approach is endorsed by the Uniform Contribution Among Tortfeasors Act (UCATA). A second approach, reflected in the Uniform Comparative Fault Act (UCFA), is to reduce that share by the settling party's proportionate share. *American Cyanamid, supra,* refused to choose between the UCATA and UCFA approaches because CERCLA provides district courts with the discretion to allocate response costs among PRPs, and determining how a settlement affects the liability of non-settling PRPs is within that discretion. Would a complete bar on contribution actions against settling PRPs raise constitutional concerns? See Waste Management of Pa., Inc., v. City of York, 910 F. Supp. 1035, 1042-1043 (M.D. Pa. 1995). Can the contribution protection provisions of CERCLA work a compensable taking of the property of a PRP denied the ability to seek contribution against another settling PRP? See United States v. Davis, 261 F.3d 1, 28 (1st Cir. 2001).

Private Cost Recovery. Section 107(a)(1)-(4)(B) imposes liability on PRPs for any necessary costs of response incurred by any party other than federal, state, or Indian tribe plaintiffs consistent with the NCP. Assuming that a completely innocent plaintiff or a PRP allowed to file a §107(a) cost recovery action brings such a claim, when are response costs "necessary"? Suppose that the private cost recovery plaintiff has an independent business reason for cleaning up site contamination (such as a desire to convert the property to a new use). Is it precluded from recovery under §107(a)(1)-(4)(B)? See Carson Harbor Village, Ltd. v. Unocal Corp., 270 F.3d 863, 871-872 (9th Cir. 2001).

Suppose that X Corp. is the owner of a facility at which a release of hazardous substances occurs. EPA files a cost recovery action against X Corp. and a number of companies that sent hazardous substances to the site (the generators). X Corp. brings cross-claims against the generators. Ins. Co., X's insurer, then files a §107(a) cost recovery action against the generators, seeking to impose joint and several liability against them. Should the court rule on the merits of Ins. Co.'s suit? See California Dep't of Toxic Substances Control v. City of Chico, 297 F. Supp. 2d 1227 (E.D. Cal. 2004); §112(c)(2). Suppose that a release of hazardous substances occurred that contaminated soil near a town's underground drinking water supply. The town's water supply currently meets all Safe Drinking Water Act standards. If the town spends money monitoring the soil on its property, then sues the owner of the facility that releases the hazardous substances under §107(a), can the PRP defend itself by arguing that the response costs were not "necessary" because the drinking water supply was not compromised? See Village of Milford v. K-H Holding Corp., 390 F.3d 926 (6th Cir. 2004).*

Proof of consistency with the NCP is part of the private plaintiff's prima facie case. But see Village of Milford v. K-H Holding Corp., 390 F.3d 926 (6th Cir. 2004) (consistency with the NCP is not required for monitoring and investigation costs). Is that also true for cost recovery actions brought by the United States or a state? For private contribution actions under §113(f)? See Morrison Enter. v. McShares, Inc., 302 F.3d 1127 (10th Cir. 2002) (analyzing the effect of compliance with a state-issued, EPA-approved consent decree). Proof of substantial compliance is sufficient. A private plaintiff's failure to solicit public comment and provide opportunities for public participation may itself demonstrate inconsistency with the NCP. Comprehensive input from a state environmental agency may satisfy the public participation requirement. Bedford Affiliates v. Sills, 156 F.3d 416, 428 (2d Cir. 1998).**

May an environmental group, acting as "private attorneys-general," bring a citizen suit to compel PRPs to clean up sites themselves? See Cadillac Fairview/Calif., Inc. v. Dow Chem. Co., 840 F.2d 691, 697 (9th Cir. 1988) (no). Should the result be different if a state is the plaintiff? See §121(e)(2); Colorado v. Idarado Mining Co., 916 F.2d 1486 (10th Cir. 1990). What kinds of relief may private persons seek under CERCLA's citizen suit provision, §310?

---

*See also City of Wichita v. Trustees of the APCO Oil Corp. Liquidating Trust, 306 F. Supp. 2d 1040, 1090-1096 (D. Kan. 2003) (concluding that payments to environmental consulting firm that performed cleanup, payments to state environmental agency for oversight and participation in cleanup, payments to vendors, payments to attorneys for PRP identification, and motor pool expenses were "necessary," but that payroll costs for city were not).

**Compare Carson Harbor Village, Ltd. v. County of Los Angeles, 433 F.3d 1260 (9th Cir. 2006), where the court held that state agency involvement did not suffice, because instead of overseeing the cleanup, as in *Bedford Affiliates*, the agency merely inspected the property after the cleanup to verify compliance with the remedial action plan. The court also held that the private cost recovery plaintiff violated the NCP by failing to assess viable alternatives at the feasibility study stage. See also Regional Airport Auth. v. LFG, LLC, 460 F.3d 697, 707-709 (6th Cir. 2006) (state failed to present preferred alternative to the public for comment).

D.   LIABILITY FOR IMMINENT AND SUBSTANTIAL ENDANGERMENTS

EPA's Options. To avoid spending money from the Superfund responding to a hazardous substance release, EPA may turn to §106 of CERCLA, which authorizes the United States to bring a civil action in federal district court to abate an imminent and substantial endangerment resulting from an actual or threatened release. EPA also may issue administrative orders "as may be necessary to protect public health and welfare and the environment." The government has four different ways to require a PRP to conduct remediation: a settlement approved in a judicial consent decree, a court order after litigation in a §106 action, a settlement reflected in an administrative consent order, and a unilateral §106 administrative order (UAO).* The fourth option is attractive, because EPA can schedule more cleanups if PRPs instead of the Superfund finance them under a unilateral order. Further, an administrative order permits EPA to mandate the federal remedy of choice by specifying the precise behavior it expects, as if the PRPs were subject to a regulatory regime.

Civil Abatement Actions. The government's authority under §106(a) both to bring lawsuits and to issue UAOs depends upon whether a site presents an "imminent and substantial endangerment to the public health or welfare or the environment." What does this term mean? Is it broad enough to authorize a cleanup at every site on the NPL? See United States v. Reilly Tar & Chem. Corp., 546 F. Supp. 1100 (D. Minn. 1982). What is the significance of the words "imminent" and "endangerment"? Recall the *Reserve Mining* and *Ethyl* cases in Chapter 8. Does the "imminent and substantial endangerment" standard merely adopt unchanged the old common law standard for injunctive relief from a prospective nuisance? *Reserve Mining* noted that the common law required "an immediate threat of harm" before a nuisance could be abated. 514 F.2d at 529 n.71. The *Ethyl* court agreed. 541 F.2d at 20 n.36.

The court summarized existing case law relating to the scope of the government's authority to issue a UAO under §106 in United States v. E.I. du Pont de Nemours & Co., 341 F. Supp. 2d 215, 246-248 (W.D.N.Y. 2004). EPA need not show that people may be endangered to support a §106 order; possible endangerment to the public welfare or the environment alone may suffice. It also indicated that an endangerment need not be immediate to be imminent. Imminence refers to the nature of the threat rather than identification of the time when the endangerment liability arose. The cases also have concluded that the government need not provide quantitative proof of actual harm and that an endangerment is considered substantial if there is reasonable cause for concern that someone or something may be exposed to a risk of harm by a release or threatened release of hazardous substances if remedial action is not taken.

Section 106 Administrative Orders. A PRP that complies with a UAO may sue for reimbursement from the Superfund if it can show that it is not liable for response costs or that EPA abused its discretion in selecting its preferred remedy. §106(b)(2). But if a PRP refuses to carry out a UAO, EPA may seek enforcement in federal district court, fines of up to $25,000 per day of violation, and punitive damages equal to three times the costs incurred by the federal fund as a result of the refusal to carry out the order.

---

*See Mugdan, The Use of CERCLA Section 106 Administrative Orders to Secure Remedial Action, C98 ALI-ABA 113 (Oct. 27, 1994).

§§106(b)(1), 107(c)(3). May punitive damages be assessed in addition to actual response costs? See United States v. Parsons, 936 F.2d 526 (11th Cir. 1991). United States v. Parsons, 723 F. Supp. 757, 764 (N.D. Ga. 1989), held that financial inability to pay is not a good defense to a §107(c)(3) punitive damage penalty.

Suppose that EPA issues a §106 UAO to a PRP. The PRP completes the portion of the cleanup for which it accepts responsibility, refusing to undertake the rest of the cleanup deemed necessary by EPA to protect public health and the environment. May the PRP seek reimbursement from the Superfund for the portion of the cleanup it completed under §106(b)(2)(A)? Does efficiency support a negative answer? If EPA denies the claim on the ground that the cleanup is not complete, what forum is available for the PRP to seek review of that determination? See §106(b)(2)(B). What if the PRP fails to complete the cleanup because it becomes insolvent? May it seek reimbursement under §106(b)(2)(A)? See Employers Ins. of Wausau v. Browner, 52 F.3d 656 (7th Cir. 1995).

Do the limits on judicial review in §106(b) present constitutional problems? In General Elec. Co. v. Johnson, 362 F. Supp. 2d 327 (D.D.C. 2005), the court rejected GE's contentions that the mere issuance of a UAO under §106 triggers a deprivation of property without due process due to the absence of a pre-deprivation hearing, that CERCLA fails to provide a meaningful judicial hearing at any time because a UAO under §106 may only be challenged under the APA's "arbitrary and capricious" standard without allowing the PRP to present evidence, and that the fines and penalties under §§106 and 107 are so coercive that the PRP is effectively forced to forgo judicial review of the UAO. The court refused to dismiss GE's claim that EPA has a pattern and practice of administering §106 (in conjunction with §§107 and 113) in a manner that denies PRPs due process.

Suppose that the United States enters a judicially approved settlement that fully reimburses the government for all past and future cleanup costs at a contaminated site. May the government issue a UAO under §106 to another party that had refused to settle, requiring it to undertake cleanup at the same site? What bearing do §§113(f)(3)(A) and 122(c)(2) have on the question? What are the policy implications of not allowing the government to proceed against the nonsettlor under §106? See United States v. Occidental Chem. Corp., 200 F.3d 143 (3d Cir. 1999).

E.   LIABILITY FOR DAMAGE TO NATURAL RESOURCES

Interior's Initial Natural Resource Damage Regulations. CERCLA authorizes the recovery of damages for injuries to natural resources in §107(a)(1)-(4)(C). Section 301(c)(1) required the president to issue natural resource damage assessment regulations by the end of 1982. In Ohio v. United States Dep't of the Interior, 880 F.2d 432 (D.C. Cir. 1989), the court struck down several important provisions of the regulations issued by the Interior Department pursuant to §301(c)(1). The primary issue in the case was whether the agency's "lesser of" rule was valid. That rule stated that damages to natural resources would be measured by the *lesser of* (1) restoration or replacement costs or (2) diminution of use values. The state and environmental petitioners claimed that the statute requires damages to be sufficient in every case to restore, replace, or acquire the equivalent of the damaged resources. Interior responded that CERCLA does not establish any floor for damages, instead leaving it up to the agency to decide what the proper measure of damages should be. Although under §107(f)(1) all damages recovered must be spent restoring or replacing the injured resources, Interior argued that the amount recovered from PRPs need not be sufficient to complete the job.

The court explained the significance of this difference of opinion by way of example:

> [I]magine a hazardous substance spill that kills a rookery of fur seals and destroys a habitat for seabirds at a sealife reserve. The lost use value of the seals and seabird habitat would be measured by the market value of the fur seals' pelts (which would be approximately $15 each) plus the selling price per acre of land comparable in value to that on which the spoiled bird habitat was located. Even if, as likely, that use value turns out to be far less than the cost of restoring the rookery and seabird habitat, it would nonetheless be the only measure of damages eligible for the presumption of recoverability under the Interior rule. [Id. at 442.]

The court invalidated the "lesser of" rule. Section 107(f)(1) requires sums recovered by the United States as trustee to be used to restore or replace the injured resources. This mandate, the court concluded, reflects the "paramount restorative purpose" of the natural resource damage provisions. If the Interior Department were correct that Congress authorized the agency to measure damages by the lesser of restoration costs or diminution in use values, and if the latter would be significantly less than the former in many cases, then Congress would have established a damage assessment and recovery scheme that would be insufficient in most cases to achieve this paramount purpose. The court also relied on the fifth sentence of §107(f)(1), which indicates that restoration costs will not serve as a ceiling on damage recoveries.[*]

Interior tried to justify the "lesser of" rule as economically efficient. It argued that requiring the payment of restoration costs would be a waste of money whenever restoration cost exceeds the use value of the resource. The court characterized Interior's position as "nothing more or less than cost-benefit analysis." It did not dispute that Congress intended the natural resource damage provisions to operate efficiently, requiring, for example, that restoration of injured resources take place as cost-effectively as possible. But it found that Interior's argument was based on an assumption that natural resources are fungible goods just like any others, and that the value to society generated by a particular resource can be accurately measured in every case. Congress rejected precisely that assumption because it was skeptical of society's ability to measure the true "value" of natural resources.

The court also overturned the regulations' hierarchy of methods for determining use values, which limited damages to the price commanded by the injured resource on the open market, unless the trustee finds that the market for that resource is not reasonably competitive. The court agreed with the environmental petitioners that Congress did not intend to limit use values to market prices and directed the agency on remand to consider allowing trustees to derive use values by summing up all

---

[*]See also Manus, Natural Resource Damages from Rachel Carson's Perspective: A Rite of Spring in American Environmentalism, 37 Wm. & Mary L. Rev. 381, 430 (1996) (stating that "[o]n a theoretical level, using market value to assess the damages for injury to natural resources would have gutted [natural resource damage] law of any element of [the] principled belief that humans instinctively value nature for far more than its service to us").

reliably calculated use values. The court took issue with Interior's decision to limit the role of nonconsumptive values, such as option and existence values, in the calculation of use values.

Industry litigants also attacked the portion of the assessment regulations that governed the measurement of the use value of a damaged resource. The regulations equated lost use value with diminution of the market price when the injured resource is traded in a market. If the damaged resource is not itself traded in a market, but a similar resource is, an appraisal technique could be used to determine lost use value. When neither of these two situations applies, nonmarketed resource methodologies, including contingent valuation (CV), could be used. Industry charged that CV is too speculative and amounts to little more than ordinary public opinion polling, but the court held that Interior's decision to endorse CV was reasonable.

The Regulations on Remand. In 1994, the Interior Department reissued the regulations on remand from *Ohio.* Those regulations allowed trustees to recover the costs of restoration, rehabilitation, replacement, or acquisition of equivalent resources (RRRA) in all cases. Trustees could add to that basic measure of damages the value of the resource services lost to the public from the date of the release to the date RRRA activities are completed. Option and existence values could be used to value damaged resources only if trustees could not calculate use values. Interior authorized the use of CV to assess lost use values, but sought comments on whether to impose additional limitations on its use. Do these changes respond adequately to the *Ohio* court's decision? See Robinson, Note, The Role of Nonuse Values in Natural Resource Damages: Past, Present, and Future, 75 Tex. L. Rev. 189, 205-207 (1996) (no).

In Kennecott Utah Copper Corp. v. United States Dep't of the Interior, 88 F.3d 1191 (D.C. Cir. 1996), the court invalidated the provisions that appeared to permit trustees to recover both the cost of restoring the injured resources and the cost of restoring the services provided by those resources. The effect of the decision was to reinstate the pre-1994 approach, which measured the level of restoration of injured resources as the level of services provided by the resources before they were damaged. The court also ruled that CERCLA does not require trustees to choose the most cost-effective restoration option as the measure of damages and that the agency did not err when it failed to adopt a standard to prevent trustees from selecting restoration options whose costs are grossly disproportionate to the value of the injured resource.

The Debate over CV. Those who support the use of CV methodology for assessing natural resource damages contend that it is the only methodology capable of quantifying the inherently subjective nonuse values. Further, research suggests that the values obtained through CV reasonably reflect actual resource costs. The critics of CV claim that it is "an economic and social science aberration, lacking reliability, trustworthiness, and a theoretically defensible foundation, which is good for little more than creating inflated damage claims intended for leveraging disproportionate settlements." Binger et al., Contingent Valuation Methodology in the Natural Resource Damage Regulatory Process: Choice Theory and the Embedding Phenomenon, 35 Nat. Resources J. 443, 444 (1995) (referred to below as "Choice Theory"). CV's critics charge that the underlying surveys are entirely hypothetical and that respondents typically lack sufficient information about resource value to make meaningful bids. See Binger et al., The Use of Contingent Valuation Methodology in Natural Resource Damage Assessments: Legal Fact and Economic Fiction, 89 Nw. U. L. Rev. 1029 (1995). At best, CV "is still largely in an embryonic state of development" and should not be used until it can be reliably ascertained whether CV "is actually linked to the real values that citizens place on environmental goods." Choice Theory, *supra*, at 458-459. Heyde, Comment, Is Contingent Valuation Worth the Trouble?, 62 U. Chi. L. Rev. 331, 333 (1995), argues that CV should be abandoned, "not because it gives bad estimates, but because it would not be worth the cost of developing and litigating" CV studies even if they were completely accurate. Further, any attempt to devise a " 'perfect' damages figure tends to commod-ify our understanding of natural resources, thereby undermining the proper relation-ship that society should have with these resources." Id.

Natural Resource Damage Litigation. Relatively few natural resource damage cases have been litigated. The uncertainties involved in predicting judicial receptivity to natural resource damage claims and the complexity of the Interior Department's regulations (which even government lawyers have characterized as a "cookbook for litigation") may be partially responsible. Bourdeau & Jawetz, 25 Years of Superfund Litigation: Progress Made, Progress Needed, 37 Env't Rep. (BNA) 97, 99 (2006). In Idaho v. Southern Refrigerated Transport, Inc., 1991 WL 22479 (D. Idaho Jan. 24, 1991), the court concluded that damages for injuries to fish killed by a release should be based on a combination of commercial, existence, and recreational values. It derived the commercial component from guidelines based on average prices set by commercial fish hatcheries and the recreational component from a study of the recreational value of steelhead salmon conducted by several federal land management agencies. The court refused to add a component based on existence value because the studies relied on by the state were unpersuasive. The end result was a figure of $7,672 recreational value and $31,702 commercial value for 137 dead adult steelhead.

F.   THE CERCLA CLEANUP PROCESS

1.   An Overview of the Cleanup Process

The courts frequently describe CERCLA's dual goals as adequate remediation of hazardous substance releases that pose threats to public health and the environment (see Figure 9-1) and imposition of liability for the costs of remediation on those responsible for the release. See, e.g., Key Tronic Corp. v. United States, 511 U.S. 809, 815 (1994). When Congress adopted SARA in 1986, it sought to provide more guidance to EPA in its selection of remedies and to increase consistency of cleanups from site to site. Section 121 governs the question of how clean a site must be at the end of remediation. This provision, and EPA's implementing regulations and guid-ance documents, have added meat to CERCLA's initial regulatory skeleton. It is generally agreed, however, that §121 has failed to ensure expeditious or efficient cleanups that conform to consistently applied standards.

Section 104(a)(1) of CERCLA authorizes EPA to respond to a release or threatened release of a hazardous substance into the environment or of any pollutant or contaminant that may present an imminent and substantial danger to the public health or welfare. Remedial actions must conform to the cleanup standards adopted pursuant to §121, see §104(c)(4), as well as to the procedural and substantive dictates of the NCP. The contents of the NCP are sketched out in §105(a). Section 105(a)(8)

Before

Source: U.S. EPA

The East Ditch, located at the south end of Bowers Landfill, contained discarded tires and debris.

During

Source: U.S. EPA

1993: After excavating soil, the west field was graded and seeded to support wetlands.

After

Source: U.S. EPA

1997: Wetlands that were created during the cleanup flourish with a variety of plants and wildlife.

FIGURE 9-1
A Superfund Success Story: Bowers Landfill, Pickaway County, Ohio, Before, During, and After Remediation

Source: http://www.epa.gov/superfund/action/process/bowphoto.htm.

requires that EPA devise criteria for determining which releases or threatened releases most urgently demand remedial action, taking into account relative risk to public health or welfare or the environment. Based on these criteria, EPA must include in the NCP a list of sites, known as the national priorities list (NPL), representing the "top priorit[ies] among known response targets." §105(a)(8)(B).

For every NPL site, EPA's contractors or PRPs prepare an elaborate study of site conditions and cleanup options called the Remedial Investigation and Feasibility Study (RI/FS) in conformity with agency specifications. The process usually takes at least two years and is expensive ($1 million for a study is not uncommon). Once the RI/FS is prepared, EPA documents its preferred remedy in a record of decision (ROD). EPA affords PRPs an opportunity to negotiate a consent decree under which they can carry out the cleanup dictated by the ROD.

2. The National Priorities List

CARUS CHEMICAL COMPANY v. EPA
395 F.3d 434 (D.C. Cir. 2005)

GINSBURG, Chief Judge.

[Carus Chemical Company operated a manufacturing plant on a parcel of land that was part of a larger property known as the Matthiessen & Hegeler Zinc Company Site. The Zinc Company operated a smelter and a rolling mill on the property for more than 100 years. During that time, two large slag piles accumulated at the site, one of which was located adjacent to (and partly in) the Little Vermilion River and partly on Carus's property. EPA placed the entire Matthiessen & Hegeler site on the NPL, based on its belief that the substances in the slag piles posed a threat to human health and the environment. Carus challenged that decision as arbitrary and capricious.]

In order to identify candidates for the NPL, the EPA promulgated the Hazard Ranking System (HRS), a comprehensive methodology and mathematical model the agency uses to "evaluate[] the observed or potential release of hazardous substances" and to "quantif[y] the environmental risks a site poses." Tex Tin Corp. v. EPA, 992 F.2d 353, 353 (D.C. Cir.1993).

In order to evaluate a waste site using the HRS, the EPA first identifies the "sources" of contamination, the "[h]azardous substances associated with these sources," and the "[p]athways potentially threatened by these hazardous substances." HRS §2.2. The HRS lists four possible pathways: soil exposure, air migration, ground water migration, and the one relevant to this case, surface water migration. For each pathway deemed potentially affected in light of conditions at the site, the agency calculates a score based upon particular "threats." The surface water migration pathway is scored based upon threats to drinking water, to the human food chain, and to the environment. With respect to each pathway and threat to be scored, the HRS calls for the EPA to measure three so-called factor categories: "likelihood of release (or likelihood of exposure)"; "waste characteristics"; and "targets," which may include an individual, a human population, resources, and sensitive environments. The agency's measurements of the first two categories are relevant to this case.

The "[l]ikelihood of release is a measure of the likelihood that a waste has been or will be released to the environment." Id. §2.3. When, as in this case, the EPA determines there has already been a release, it assigns a fixed number for this component of the overall score of the pathway, regardless of the level of that release.

With respect to waste characteristics, the HRS first requires the EPA to "select the hazardous substance potentially posing the greatest hazard for the pathway." Id. §2.4.1. The agency is then to evaluate persistence, bioaccumulation, and toxicity factors pertaining to that substance (only the last of which features in this case).

For each substance being scored, the agency uses a toxicity factor value between 0 and 10,000, reflecting the potential of that substance to cause adverse health effects. For a single substance there may be multiple toxicity factor values, each corresponding to a route of exposure (e.g., inhalation, ingestion) through which that substance may come into contact with humans. If there are, and if the agency has "usable toxicity data" for more than one such exposure route, then it should "consider all exposure routes and use the highest assigned value, regardless of exposure route, as the toxicity factor value." Id. §2.4.1.1. [EPA places any site with a score greater than 28.50 on a scale of 0 to 100 on the NPL.]

... EPA determined that hazardous substances were being released into the Little Vermilion River. Because the observed release was into a river, the agency scored the surface water migration pathway, and because Illinois classified that river as a fishery, the agency scored that pathway for the threat it posed to the human food chain.

Following the method set forth in the HRS, the EPA then assessed the "waste characteristics" of the hazardous substances found at the site, namely, cadmium, copper, lead, nickel, and zinc. Carus's principal dispute is over the EPA's choice, purportedly in compliance with HRS §2.4.1.1, to use the toxicity factor value for cadmium corresponding to the inhalation route of exposure. Plugging this value into the model, the EPA calculated a score of 100 for the pathway and a total score of 50 for the Matthiessen & Hegeler site. [EPA placed the site on the NPL, over Carus's objections.] ...

Carus raises two separate challenges to the EPA's decision to place the Matthiessen & Hegeler site on the NPL. First, Carus argues the agency wrongly interpreted HRS §2.4.1.1 as requiring it to use a toxicity factor value for cadmium corresponding to a route of exposure (inhalation) unlikely to occur in light of the conditions at the site. Had the agency instead applied the toxicity factor value corresponding to the ingestion route of exposure, Carus maintains, the HRS score for the site would have been below 28.50. Second, Carus contends the sampling data and the documents it submitted during the comment period rendered unreasonable the EPA's reliance solely upon data collected earlier by the Illinois EPA.

A. THE EPA'S INTERPRETATION OF HRS §2.4.1.1

As the EPA understands HRS §2.4.1.1, and as it applied that regulation in the rulemaking under review, the agency was required to use the toxicity factor value for the inhalation of cadmium even though it was scoring the surface water migration pathway. Carus takes exception to that interpretation, arguing it is nonsensical to read the rule as mandating the use of a toxicity factor value corresponding to an exposure route (inhalation) unlikely to present a threat considering the pathway being scored.

... The EPA has consistently interpreted §2.4.1.1 as requiring it to use the highest toxicity factor value for a substance regardless of the most likely route of exposure. Indeed, the protest Carus now advances—that there is no scientific justification for using the toxicity factor value for a route of exposure that is improbable in light of the pathway being scored—was made and rejected when the EPA first issued the regulation. At that time, the agency defended its interpretation of the rule as follows:

> EPA recognizes that toxicity values for substances are route-specific. However, the three pathways . . . receiving a toxicity factor value are substance migration pathways, not human exposure routes. Multiple human exposure routes are possible for each substance migration pathway (e.g., volatile substances in ground water or surface water used for drinking can be inhaled during showering), and, therefore, use of a single route-specific toxicity value is not necessarily appropriate. . . . For this reason, and to avoid the added complexity of route-specific toxicity evaluations, EPA decided to base the toxicity factor on the highest route-specific value (if more than one is available). . . . [T]his may, in a few site situations, overstate toxicity. . . .

. . . [W]e must uphold the EPA's interpretation because it accords both with the text of the regulation and with what we know of the agency's understanding of the rule when it was issued.

As for the former, the regulation reads in relevant part as follows:

> *Toxicity Factor.* Evaluate toxicity for those hazardous substances at the site that are available to the pathway being scored. For all pathways and threats, except the surface water environmental threat, evaluate human toxicity as specified below. . . .
>
>   For hazardous substances having usable toxicity data for multiple exposure routes (for example, inhalation and ingestion), consider all exposure routes and use the highest assigned value, regardless of exposure route, as the toxicity factor value.

HRS §2.4.1.1. The EPA's interpretation clearly hews close to the text. The rule first directs the agency to "[e]valuate [the] toxicity" of each hazardous substance "available to the pathway being scored," and then unequivocally requires that, when the substance being scored has "usable toxicity data for multiple exposure routes"—as does cadmium—the EPA "consider all exposure routes and use the highest assigned value, regardless of exposure route."

. . . [Carus claimed that the rule, if read properly,] allows the use of only those toxicity factor values corresponding to routes of exposure the EPA finds are a threat at the site. In support of this interpretation, Carus points to the reference, in the opening sentence of the rule, to the "pathway being scored." According to Carus, this phrase modifies not just the preceding clause of the same sentence but the entire rule, thus requiring the EPA to decide whether exposure via a particular route is likely, considering the pathway being scored, before it uses a toxicity factor value corresponding to that exposure route.

. . . Even if we owed no deference to the agency, however, we would not be persuaded by Carus's alternative reading of the rule. First, the phrase "available to the pathway" plainly limits only the universe of hazardous substances the EPA may use in scoring a pathway; the phrase cannot reasonably be read to limit, as Carus suggests, the universe of toxicity factor values upon which the agency may draw. Second, Carus would read out of the regulation the direction to use the highest toxicity factor value "regardless of exposure route," in contravention of the principle that every word of a legal text should be given effect. . . .

B.   CARUS'S SUBMISSIONS TO THE EPA

Carus also claims the EPA relied upon insufficient and out-dated sampling data obtained by its Illinois counterpart in 1991 and 1993. Carus apparently believes more recent data from samples collected by GeoSyntec Consulting shows the EPA erred in listing the Matthiessen & Hegeler site on the NPL. Before considering this argument we must address two anterior matters.

. . . Carus asserts the documents it submitted to the EPA "establish[ed] risk-based clean-up levels"—whatever that may mean—and "evaluate[d] possible remedial alternatives," both of which contributions the agency apparently failed to consider. Perhaps so, but Carus did and still does nothing to explain how either consideration could have affected the HRS score for the Matthiessen & Hegeler site. Nor does Carus refute the EPA's response that it had no obligation to consider such matters because they are irrelevant to the decision to list a site on the NPL.

In the EPA's response to public comments it explained that the data compiled by GeoSyntec, far from contradicting the data upon which the agency relied, "confirmed the presence of . . . cadmium and lead in soil samples" taken from around the slag piles. The EPA also responded to Carus's claim the GeoSyntec data showed the levels of hazardous substances present in the Little Vermilion River were below applicable limits; the agency explained that an "observed release" of a hazardous substance may be established "[e]ven though levels may be lower than regulatory limits . . . if the measured levels are significantly higher than background levels." In sum, the EPA concluded Carus did not present "any specific comments [showing] that the data used in the HRS scoring [were] incorrect or why [Geosyntec's] data would suggest that the site score is incorrect." Just so. . . .

NOTES AND QUESTIONS

1. Why did EPA place the Mathhiessen & Hegeler site on the NPL? Does it make any sense for EPA to gauge the risk presented by the site, based on a pathway of exposure that was unlikely to occur? How did EPA justify its reliance on the inhalation route of exposure? Why did the court endorse that decision?

2. *Placing Sites on the NPL.* EPA explained the function of the NPL in the preamble to the 1984 version of the NCP:

> The purpose of the NPL . . . is primarily to serve as an informational tool for use by EPA in identifying sites that appear to present a significant risk to public health or the environment. The initial identification of a site in the NPL is intended primarily to guide EPA in determining which sites warrant further investigation designed to assess the nature and extent of the public health and environmental risks associated with the site and to determine what response action, if any, may be appropriate. Inclusion of a site on the NPL does not establish that EPA necessarily will undertake response actions. Moreover, listing does not require any action of any private party, nor does it determine the liability of any party for the cost of cleanup at the site.
>
> In addition, although the HRS scores used to place sites on the NPL may be helpful to the Agency in determining priorities for cleanup and other response activities among sites on the NPL, EPA does not rely on the scores as the sole means of determining such priorities. . . . The information collected to develop HRS scores to choose sites for the NPL is not sufficient in itself to determine the appropriate remedy for a

particular site. After a site has been included on the NPL, EPA generally will rely on further, more detailed studies conducted at the site to determine what response, if any, is appropriate. . . . After conducting these additional studies EPA may conclude that it is not feasible to conduct response action at some sites on the NPL because of more pressing needs at other sites. Given the limited resources available in the [Superfund], the Agency must carefully balance the relative needs for response at the numerous sites it has studied. It is also possible that EPA will conclude after further analysis that no action is needed at the site because the site does not present a significant threat to public health, welfare or the environment. [49 Fed. Reg. 37,070, 37,071 (1984).]

Nevertheless, NPL listing has real-world consequences: "listing a site virtually assures costly clean-up of the site, and . . . this probability in turn has significant immediate consequences for both surrounding property values and the liability of [PRPs]." Board of Regents v. EPA, 86 F.3d 1214, 1217 (D.C. Cir. 1996). See also Mead Corp. v. Browner, 100 F.3d 152, 155 (D.C. Cir. 1996) ("listing drastically increases the chances of costly activity").

Owners of NPL sites have challenged not only the application of the HRS, but the HRS itself. In Eagle-Picher Indus., Inc. v. EPA, 759 F.2d 905 (D.C. Cir. 1985), the court held that the HRS represented a reasonable effort by EPA to reconcile the need for certainty before acting with the need for inexpensive and expeditious procedures for identifying potentially hazardous sites. The court also deferred to EPA's application to the petitioners' sites of the predictive model upon which the HRS was based. EPA conceded that the model was imperfect, but the court refused to second-guess the agency's conclusion that efforts to refine it would not be worth the cost and time involved.

3. *Additional Challenges to Placement on the NPL.* EPA has had mixed success in defending its decisions to place facilities on the NPL. In National Gypsum Co. v. EPA, 968 F.2d 40 (D.C. Cir. 1992), the court vacated and remanded an NPL listing

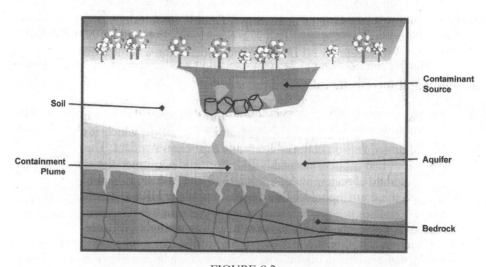

FIGURE 9-2
Contaminated Groundwater

Source: http://www.epa.gov/superfund/tools/gw/brochure.htm.

because EPA acted arbitrarily in assessing both the site's toxicity and persistence scores.* But in Bradley Mining Co. v. EPA, 972 F.2d 1356 (D.C. Cir. 1992), the D.C. Circuit refused to vacate an NPL listing and rejected the assertion that EPA failed to demonstrate that mercury found in an adjacent lake was caused by mining operations or that it incorrectly calculated the risk that the mercury would contaminate usable groundwater.** See Figure 9-2 for a representation of groundwater contamination and its sources.

May EPA aggregate noncontiguous areas into a single NPL site on the basis of factors such as whether the areas were part of the same operation and whether the PRPs are the same? See 48 Fed. Reg. 40,658 (1983); 42 U.S.C. §§9604(d)(4), 9605(a)(8)(B); *Mead Corp., supra.*

4. *Deferral to Voluntary State Cleanups.* At the request of a state, EPA is generally required to defer final listing on the NPL of a site that qualifies as a brownfield site as defined by §101(39) of CERCLA if EPA determines that the state, or another party under an agreement with the state, is conducting a response action at the site that will provide long-term protection of human health and the environment. Alternatively, EPA must defer the listing if the state is actively pursuing an agreement to perform such a response action with a person that the state believes capable of conducting it. If EPA later determines that the state or other party is not making reasonable progress toward completing a response action at the site, EPA may list it on the NPL. §105(h).

5. *The Fate of Love Canal.* EPA removed the Love Canal landfill site whose discovery was instrumental in the passage of CERCLA from the NPL in 2004. 69 Fed. Reg. 58,322. The site was covered with a 70-acre cap and equipped with a permanent leachate collection and treatment system. EPA indicated that it would continue to engage in annual monitoring and review of institutional controls.

3.   The National Contingency Plan and Cleanup Standards

Once EPA decides that a site, whether it is placed on the NPL or not, merits remediation, the agency must determine what kind of cleanup is appropriate. The process of selecting a remedy — the so-called how clean is clean problem — is one that entails consideration of the technical feasibility of alternative remedial possibilities, how costly each of those possibilities will be to implement, whether each of the alternatives adequately addresses the health and environmental risks posed by the site in its existing, contaminated state, and whether any additional risk reduction benefits likely to accrue from one alternative compared to another are worth the resulting cost increases. In short, the issues that arise in selecting a remedy under

---

*See also Tex Tin Corp. v. EPA, 992 F.2d 353 (D.C. Cir. 1993) (invalidating NPL listing due to EPA's failure to justify its conclusion that arsenic contained in slag piles was capable of becoming airborne); Kent County v. EPA, 963 F.2d 391 (D.C. Cir. 1992) (EPA's reliance on a single unfiltered groundwater sample in scoring a landfill was arbitrary and capricious).

**See also Honeywell Int'l, Inc. v. EPA, 372 F.3d 441 (D.C. Cir. 2004) (rejecting claim that NPL listing was improper because EPA failed to indicate that contemplated remedial action posed serious environmental risks and finding that EPA adequately supported its conclusion that a fishery existed within the boundaries of the observed release).

CERCLA are precisely the same risk management issues addressed in depth in Chapter 8, which covered an array of approaches to management of the risks presented by exposure to toxic substances.

CERCLA did not originally contain cleanup standards. Instead, it contained only a vague mandate to

> select appropriate remedial actions determined to be necessary . . . which are to the extent practicable in accordance with the national contingency plan and which provide for that cost-effective response which provides a balance between the need for protection of public health and welfare and the environment . . . and the availability of amounts from the [Superfund]. [§104(c)(4).]

Frustrated with the inconsistency of cleanup standards from site to site, Congress adopted §121 of CERCLA in the 1986 SARA legislation to curtail EPA's discretion. In response to intense lobbying by environmental and industry groups, Congress sought to strike a balance among (1) technology forcing, (2) the implementation of health-based standards, and (3) cost-effectiveness considerations. As you read the following case and the notes that follow it, consider these questions: Which of these interests does the balance favor? Which provisions of §121 reflect these priorities? Do the 1986 amendments represent an improvement over the approach reflected in §104(c)(4) as it existed before the amendments?

OHIO v. EPA
997 F.2d 1520 (D.C. Cir. 1993)

Before MIKVA, Chief Judge, EDWARDS and RANDOLPH, Circuit Judges.

PER CURIAM: . . .

[According to the court, the NCP is "the means by which EPA implements CERCLA." It "provide[s] the organizational structure and procedures" for responding to releases and threats thereof under §104(a)(1) of CERCLA. 40 C.F.R.§300.1.]

Petitioners, whom we shall call "the States," include both states and private parties contending that EPA's changes to the NCP in 1985 and 1990 are inconsistent with the requirements of CERCLA. The petitions for review challenge two general categories of NCP provisions. One category involves claims that the NCP unlawfully diminishes the level of environmental protectiveness in the remedy selection process and cleanup provisions of CERCLA. (These claims are resolved in Parts [II and III] of the opinion.) The second category involves claims that the NCP improperly limits the States' participation in the cleanup process while increasing their financial burden. (These claims are resolved in Part V of the opinion.) . . .

II

The States first challenge several elements of the NCP definition of legally "applicable" or "relevant and appropriate" environmental standards, known as "ARARs." CERCLA does not define ARARs, but the statute does require that remedial actions at Superfund sites result in a level of cleanup or standard of control that at least meets the legally applicable or otherwise relevant and appropriate federal (or stricter state) requirements. 42 U.S.C. §9621(d)(2)(A). The NCP defines "applicable requirements" as follows:

> Applicable requirements means those cleanup standards, standards of control, and other substantive requirements, criteria, or limitations promulgated under federal environmental or state environmental or facility siting laws that specifically address a hazardous substance, pollutant, contaminant, remedial action, location, or other circumstance found at a CERCLA site.

Only those state standards that are identified by a state in a timely manner and that are more stringent than federal requirements may be applicable. 40 C.F.R. §300.5. "Relevant and appropriate requirements" are those substantive requirements that, while not "applicable," nonetheless "address problems or situations sufficiently similar to those encountered at the CERCLA site that their use is well suited to the particular site." Id. . . .

D. Does the NCP Improperly Fail to Apply Zero-Level Maximum Contaminant Level Goals ("MCLGs") as ARARs?

The States challenge EPA's decision that Maximum Contaminant Level Goals ("MCLGs") established under the Safe Drinking Water Act ("SDWA") do not have to be attained for contaminants whose MCLG has been set at a level of zero. . . .

The SDWA is specifically referenced in section 121(d)(2)(A) of CERCLA as one of the federal laws containing ARARs for Superfund cleanups. The SDWA identifies two standards for exposure to contaminants. The first, Maximum Contaminant Level Goals ("MCLGs"), are generally unenforceable goals that reflect the level for a given contaminant at which "no known or anticipated adverse effects on the health of persons occur and which allows an adequate margin of safety." 42 U.S.C. §300g-1(b)(4). Many MCLGs for carcinogens are set at zero. The second type of standards, Maximum Contaminant Levels ("MCLs")—the actual maximum permissible concentration levels under the SDWA—must be set as close as "feasible" to their corresponding MCLGs, taking into account available technology and cost. 42 U.S.C. §300g-1(b)(4)-(5).

While MCLGs are unenforceable under the SDWA, section [121(d)(2)(A)] of CERCLA converts them into enforceable goals. . . . Consistent with this requirement, the NCP generally requires the attainment of MCLGs. When the MCLG for a contaminant has been set at a level of zero, however, the NCP requires only that the MCL be attained. In essence, EPA has made a categorical determination that MCLGs set at a level of zero are never "relevant and appropriate under the circumstances" of a release.

This determination was based on EPA's conclusion "that it is impossible to detect whether 'true' zero has actually been attained." 55 Fed. Reg. 8752 (1990). . . .

The States contend that EPA's decision concerning zero-level MCLGs is inconsistent with CERCLA's mandate that all remedial actions attain MCLGs. This argument ignores the full language of the section, which imposes the requirement "where such goals . . . are relevant and appropriate under the circumstances of the release or threatened release." 42 U.S.C. §9621(d)(2)(A). This language leaves EPA with discretion to determine when MCLGs are relevant and appropriate. . . .

[The court also rejected the states' claim that EPA abused its discretion by concluding that zero-level MCLGs are never relevant and appropriate.] As we understand EPA's scientific analysis, one can never prove a true zero level. If the measuring device indicates zero, this shows only that the device is not sufficiently sensitive to detect the presence of any contaminants. It does not show the total absence of the contaminants. In other words, if one asserts that zero contaminants are present, this can be *falsified* by showing the presence of some detectable level, but it can never be shown to be *true*. EPA chose to set MCLGs for carcinogens at zero under the SDWA because they "are goals which may or may not be practically achievable and the practicality of these goals should be factored into the MCLs," not the MCLGs. 50 Fed. Reg. 46,896 (1985). In contrast, EPA concluded that "ARARs must be measurable and attainable since their purpose is to set a standard that an actual remedy will attain." 55 Fed. Reg. 8752 (1990).

[The states also argued that EPA could and should have selected a method of measurement approximating zero by setting "a goal of achieving the analytical detection limits for specific carcinogens."] That EPA could do this, however, does not mean it is required to do so. Section 121 requires the selection of MCLs where MCLGs are unattainable. That is what the NCP does. That conclusion is reasonable given EPA's discretion to determine when ARARs are relevant and appropriate.

III . . .

A. DOES THE NCP ESTABLISH AN IMPROPER COST-BENEFIT ANALYSIS IN THE REMEDY SELECTION PROCESS?

[Section 121(d)(1) requires the selection of remedial actions "at a minimum which assures protection of human health and the environment," while §121(b)(1) requires the selection of remedial actions that are cost-effective. Both EPA and the States agreed that §121(d)(1) prohibits EPA from considering cost when it determines the level of protectiveness to be achieved by a remedial action.] The States contend, however, that two provisions in the NCP implicitly authorize the use of cost-benefit analysis, thereby permitting cost to be considered in determining the level of protectiveness to be achieved by a remedial action. In making this argument, the States distort the language of the NCP, which is carefully structured so "that protection of human health and the environment will not be compromised by other selection factors, such as cost." [55 Fed. Reg. 8726.]

The States first point to a provision in the NCP authorizing EPA to balance nine different criteria, including both protection of human health and cost, in selecting a remedy. But while the NCP identifies nine criteria to be used in selecting a remedy, all of the criteria are not given equal weight. Instead, they are divided into three classifications: threshold criteria, primary balancing criteria, and modifying criteria. Under this structure, "[o]verall protection of human health and the environment and compliance with ARARs (unless a specific ARAR is waived) are threshold requirements that each alternative must meet in order to be eligible for selection." 40 C.F.R. §300.430(f)(1)(i)(A). EPA explained in the preamble to the NCP that remedial alternatives "must be demonstrated to be protective . . . in order to be eligible for consideration in the balancing process by which the remedy is selected." 55 Fed. Reg. 8726 (1990). The identification of threshold criteria therefore undermines the States' claim that by listing nine criteria, the NCP permits the level of protectiveness to be affected by cost.

The States also point us to the NCP's definition of "cost-effectiveness," which states that "[a] remedy shall be cost-effective if its costs are proportional to its overall effectiveness." 40 C.F.R. §300.430(f)(1)(ii)(D). The States contend that this language actually authorizes the use of cost-benefit analysis. In making this argument, though, the States ignore the first sentence of the same section of the NCP that they are challenging. It states: "Each remedial action shall be cost-effective, provided that it first satisfies the threshold criteria set forth in §300.430(f)(1)(ii)(A) and (B)." Id. Thus, . . . the NCP explicitly prohibits consideration of costs in the manner complained of by the States.

B.   DOES THE NCP IMPROPERLY FAIL TO REQUIRE THE SELECTION OF PERMANENT REMEDIES TO THE MAXIMUM EXTENT PRACTICABLE?

The States next argue that the NCP is inconsistent with section 121(b)(1)'s requirement that the President select remedial actions "that utilize[] permanent solutions . . . to the maximum extent practicable." The NCP classifies permanence as one of the five primary balancing criteria, along with reduction of toxicity, mobility, or volume; short-term effectiveness; implementability; and cost. 40 C.F.R. §300.430(f)(1)(i)(B). The States reason that because the selection of permanent remedies "is one of the overarching statutory principles of remedy selection under CERCLA," the other balancing criteria, particularly cost, should play no role in EPA's determination whether a permanent remedy is to be selected. In essence, the States would like permanence to be treated as an additional threshold criterion that must be evaluated independently of cost.

The flaw in the States' argument is in the premise that permanence is an overarching statutory principle. This premise is not supported by the statutory language. Section 121(b)(1) . . . places as much emphasis on the selection of cost-effective remedies as it does on the selection of permanent remedies. . . . [T]here is nothing in section 121 to suggest that selecting permanent remedies is more important than selecting cost-effective remedies. . . .

. . . Given the statutory requirement to achieve a number of competing goals, EPA's decision concerning how much emphasis to place on the selection of permanent remedies is a reasonable one.

C.   DOES THE NCP CANCER RISK RANGE IMPROPERLY FAIL TO PROTECT HUMAN HEALTH AND THE ENVIRONMENT WITHOUT REGARD TO COST?

The States next challenge EPA's use of a cancer risk range between 10^{-6} and 10^{-4} in the NCP, arguing that an exposure level greater than 10^{-6} is never appropriate. A 10^{-4} risk subjects the surrounding population to an increased lifetime cancer risk of 1 in 10,000. A 10^{-6} risk subjects the surrounding population to an increased lifetime cancer risk of 1 in 1,000,000. When EPA develops objectives for a remedial action at a site, it selects a remediation goal that "establish[es] acceptable exposure levels that are protective of human health." 40 C.F.R. §300.430(e)(2)(i). EPA attempts to use health-based ARARs to set the goal, but if ARARs are nonexistent or unsuitable for use, EPA establishes the goal based on criteria in the NCP. "For known or suspected carcinogens, acceptable exposure levels are generally concentration levels that represent an excess upper bound lifetime cancer risk to an individual of between 10^{-6} and 10^{-4}. . . ." 40 C.F.R. §300.430(e)(2)(i)(A)(2). The NCP expresses a preference for remedial actions that achieve a level of 10^{-6}[;] however, the ultimate decision depends on a balancing of nine criteria, including cost.

The States contend that by permitting cost to play a role in determining the level of exposure, the cancer risk range fails to meet the requirement in [§121] that remedial actions be "protective of human health." The States' argument necessarily depends, though, on the notion that an exposure level greater than 10^{-6} is not protective of human health. CERCLA requires the selection of remedial actions "that are protective of human health," not as protective as conceivably possible. A "risk range of 10^{-4} to 10^{-6} represents EPA's opinion on what are generally acceptable levels." 55 Fed. Reg. 8716 (1990). Although cost cannot be used to justify the selection of a remedy that is not protective of human health and the environment, it can be considered in selecting from options that are adequately protective. [The court also pointed out that many ARARs, which Congress specifically intended be used as cleanup standards under CERCLA, are set at risk levels less stringent than 10^{-6}.] . . .

V . . .

A.   Does the NCP Improperly Limit the States' Ability to Take Actions Authorized by CERCLA?

The States . . . argue that Subpart F of the NCP impermissibly precludes state officials from applying for cleanup and related enforcement authority pursuant to section 104 of CERCLA, and from exercising authority that is properly assignable to them under the statute.

. . . Under [§104(d)(1)(A)], states may apply for enforcement authority and the President "shall make a determination" regarding any such application within ninety days. If a state is determined to be capable of carrying out the policies of the statute, section 104 allows the President to delegate all of the responsibilities authorized in section 104 as well as the authority to take "related enforcement actions." Moreover, a delegation under this section authorizes states to carry out these actions on behalf of federal authorities, not merely in conjunction with them. See id. §§9604(d)(3) (states may act "on behalf of the President"), 9611(f) (President may delegate to states authority to obligate federal funds and settle claims against Superfund). . . .

The NCP regulations pertaining to state participation in CERCLA response actions [implicate two types of state-led response actions.] The first involves a state acting as the lead agency in a federally financed cleanup ("state-led, fund-financed"); in such a situation, the NCP limits state participation to preparing proposed remedial plans and the final record of decision ("ROD") setting forth the selected remedy. Specifically, states must first enter into a cooperative agreement with EPA in order to receive Superfund financing. The state may then perform initial site assessment activities, conduct the remedial investigation ("RI"), do the feasibility study ("FS"), draft and recommend a proposed remedial action plan, and prepare the final ROD. However, in state-led, fund-financed actions, the state may not publish a remedial plan that has not been approved by EPA, or proceed with the response action unless EPA has concurred in, and adopted, the ROD. Thus, all final authority is reserved to EPA.

The second type of state-led response action . . . involves a state acting as the lead agency in potentially responsible party ("PRP") or state funded cleanups. In these actions ("state-led, non-fund-financed"), states need not get EPA concurrence to publish and implement a remedy, but, under the NCP, the states are barred from invoking CERCLA authority. In other words, a state may not even apply for such authority pursuant to section 104. Thus, if a state elects to proceed on its own authority, there is a risk that EPA will take later actions or select different remedies under CERCLA that could potentially expose the state or the PRP to additional liabilities. The States contend that, without the ability to invoke CERCLA authority as the lead agency, state officials are severely handicapped in their ability to enforce and settle cleanup obligations. [The states contested the NCP's blanket prohibition on state selection of the remedy in fund-financed cleanups and on state use of CERCLA authority in non-fund-financed cleanups.]

The first question . . . is whether CERCLA requires the grant of authority to a state under section 104 whenever it is sought. The answer to this question is obvious: under the statute, EPA's determination (on behalf of the President) to delegate section 104 responsibilities to state officers is clearly discretionary. The statute directs that states "*may* apply to the President to carry out actions authorized in this section. . . . [T]he President *may* enter into a contract . . . with the State . . . to carry out such actions." 42 U.S.C. §9604(d)(1)(A) (emphasis added). Naturally, terms such as "may" are indicative of discretionary authority. Furthermore, cooperative contracts are "subject to such terms and conditions as the President may prescribe." 42 U.S.C. §9604(d)(1)(B). . . . Thus, the statute manifestly does not *require* EPA to delegate full CERCLA authority in either state-led, fund-financed, or state-led, non-fund-financed responses.

. . . [T]he States have raised a second question challenging EPA's determination to preclude all states from even applying for enforcement authority that is otherwise permissible under section 104. . . . [The NCP] categorically precludes states from taking CERCLA actions that are not included in the NCP codification of delegable duties, irrespective of the state's capabilities. For instance, [it] does not allow delegation of the authority to select the final remedy, despite the fact that such authority is one of those enumerated in CERCLA section 104. . . . In effect, EPA has determined in a rulemaking that no state may qualify to exercise *all* of the potentially delegable authority of section 104.

To the extent that the NCP merely defines the terms of arrangements governing "cooperative agreements" under 42 U.S.C. §9604(d)(1)(A) we can see no problem with the regulations. CERCLA expressly provides that such cooperative agreements are to be governed by the terms and conditions of EPA's choosing. Id. §9604(d)(1)(B). Thus, in one sense, the NCP provisions . . . merely provide for a uniform set of conditions to which states entering into cooperative agreements must adhere. Viewed as such, the provisions are a valid exercise of the Agency's rulemaking authority.

Moreover, the conditions EPA has placed on state participation under the cooperative agreements are far from arbitrary. Since EPA bears ultimate responsibility under the statute to ensure appropriate remedial responses at release sites, it is not surprising that the Agency also intends to control final remedial selection. Similarly, at least with regard to fund-financed cleanups, EPA must also protect scarce federal resources. Subpart F of the NCP is one means of accomplishing these two legitimate ends.

The problem with EPA's blanket prohibition in the latest version of the NCP is that it reflects an inexplicable change in policy. . . . In neither [the 1982 nor the 1985 versions of the NCP] was an entire category of powers excluded. Thus, the provisions of the current NCP that expressly exclude states from exercising enforcement and remedy selection authority represent a departure from EPA's previous policy of making individualized determinations based on state capability.

[EPA must supply a "reasoned explanation" to justify its "significant change in policy."] In the present case, EPA offered only the most general and cursory explanation for the new blanket exclusion—the necessity of retaining federal control over remedy selection to ensure consistency. Yet, the Agency never explained the relationship between remedial consistency and statutory objectives, nor did it substantiate its assumption that state remedy selection would lead to less consistency than the present system in which remedies are selected by diverse EPA field offices. Given that EPA may condition any cooperative agreement as it deems necessary, we see no reason to assume that greater remedial inconsistency would follow from state remedy selection. . . .

NOTES AND QUESTIONS

1. How did the court respond to the states' challenges to the NCP provisions dealing with cost and permanence? CERCLA remedies must be "protective of human health and the environment." §121(b)(1). On what basis did the states contend that the cancer risk range chosen by EPA conflicted with this mandate? Why did the court disagree? Given the language of §121(d)(2)(A), how did EPA justify not establishing MCLGs under the SDWA as ARARs at sites with carcinogenic hazardous substances in the principal case? For a case in which EPA's choice of a cancer risk level of 10^{-5} rather than 10^{-4} was upheld, see United States v. Burlington N. R.R. Co., 200 F.3d 679 (10th Cir. 1999).

2. ARARs. SARA's cleanup standard for remedial actions is tied to "legally applicable" standards adopted under other federal and state environmental laws. The statute, however, does not define which standards or other federal and state laws are "legally applicable." The legislative history indicates that a statutory standard is legally applicable if the statute "subjects to regulation" a hazardous substance, even though the statute does not "apply directly to the situation involved at the hazardous waste site." H.R. Rep. No. 99-253, pt. 5, at 53 (1985). In addition, the cleanup must attain other standards that are "relevant and appropriate" under the circumstances of the release or threatened release. "[W]hat is a 'Relevant and Appropriate' provision of a federal or state environmental statute constitutes a judgmental determination that it would be desirable to comply with such provisions when carrying out the Superfund cleanup but that such provisions do not, as a matter of law, apply to the Superfund site." Whitney, Superfund Reform: Clarification of Cleanup Standards to Rationalize the Remedy Selection Process, 20 Colum. J. Envtl. L. 183, 192 (1995). ARARs are thus not themselves standards but a source of standards. Because neither CERCLA nor the NCP provides across-the-board standards for remedy selection, ARARs must be identified on a site-by-site basis. May an ARAR include a state or local requirement not adopted until after EPA's selection of the final remedy? See Missouri v. Indep. Petrochem. Corp., 104 F.3d 159 (8th Cir. 1997).

There are three different kinds of ARARs: ambient or chemical-specific, performance or action-specific, and location-specific requirements. The first category includes standards that can be expressed as maximum permissible concentrations of particular substances or similar numerical limits. Action-specific requirements are often technology-based requirements derived from statutes such as RCRA with respect to certain kinds of activities at the site of the cleanup. The third category entails restrictions derived from the presence of hazardous substances in sensitive environments, such as wetlands or floodplains. See Whitney, *supra*, at 229.

Does the mere presence of a particular substance at an NPL site mandate the application of a chemical-specific ARAR, such as a MCLG, promulgated by EPA under another statute for that substance? According to one CERCLA practitioner, "the mere presence of chemicals at a site is not sufficient to trigger chemical-specific ARARs" and "EPA must evaluate additional information to determine what remedies would protect human health and the environment and devise an acceptable risk range. . . . [T]he agency cannot determine whether a chemical at the site indeed presents a 'problem' unless it ascertains whether the chemical presents an actual risk of groundwater contamination or other exposure." Thus, "EPA is obliged to consider the extent to which site-specific factors may eliminate or control the risk" and "if protection can be provided by controlling exposure to contaminants through engineering controls or institutional controls, treatment may be unnecessary."*

3. *Institutional Controls.* The NCP allows the use of institutional controls that prevent access to contaminated areas as part of a final remedy "where necessary." 40 C.F.R. §300.430(a)(1)(iii)(D). They may not, however, substitute for active response measures as the sole remedy unless active measures are not practicable. In Superfund-financed remedial actions, institutional controls, such as deed and water use restrictions, well drilling prohibitions, and building permits, must be reliable and remain in place after initiation of state maintenance. Id. §300.510(c)(1). May the purchase of contaminated property adjacent to the source of a release qualify as an appropriate institutional control?**

The Uniform Environmental Covenants Act, which was adopted by the National Conference of Commissioners on Uniform State Laws in 2003, "creates a legal infrastructure for creating, modifying, terminating, and enforcing institutional controls." Edwards, National Conference Adopts Uniform Environmental Covenants Act, 35 Trends No. 3, at 12, 13 (Jan./Feb. 2004).***

4. *Natural Attenuation.* Are there any circumstances in which the dilution, dispersion, and biodegradation of contaminants without human intervention should be permitted to suffice as a remedy under §121? Would natural attenuation qualify as "remedial action"? What would the likely reaction of local residents be to the selection of natural attenuation? The National Research Council concluded that natural attenuation is an appropriate and cost-effective remedy for a few types of groundwater contaminants, but not for most common classes of contaminants. See Council Says

---

*Rodburg, Understanding the Role of ARARs in Determining Site Specific Cleanup Goals for Contaminated Soils and Waste Areas, C948 ALI-ABA 93, 95-97, 99, 109-110 (1994).

**The Government Accountability Office concluded that relying on institutional controls as a major component of a site's remedy without first considering whether they can be implemented in a reliable and enforceable manner could jeopardize the effectiveness of the remedy. See Improved Effectiveness of Controls at Sites Could Better Protect the Public, GAO-05-163 (January 2005), available at http://www.gao.gov/docsearch/pastweek.html. See generally Borinsky, The Use of Institutional Controls in Superfund and Similar State Laws, 7 Fordham Envtl. L.J. 1 (1995); Opper, CERCLA Institutional Controls and the Role of Local Government, 35 Env't Rep. (BNA) 2602 (2004).

***At least ten states have adopted some version of the Act, which makes institutional controls on contaminated or formerly contaminated property enforceable, even after foreclosure or other transfer of ownership. 36 Env't Rep. (BNA) 1665-1666 (2005). The Act can be found at http://www.environmentalcovenants.org/ueca/DesktopDefault.aspx?tabindex=1&tabid=86.

Natural Attenuation Works; Extensive Data, Public Involvement Needed, 31 Env't Rep. (BNA) 382 (2000).

   5. *The State Role in Remedy Selection.* Because ARARs incorporate state as well as federal laws, the states have a significant role in determining the extent of cleanup under CERCLA. What constraints on state participation in CERCLA cleanups did the states protest in the principal case? Why did the court remand to EPA? The states have grappled with PRPs and EPA over the appropriate remedies at particular sites as well. In Colorado v. Idarado Mining Co., 916 F.2d 1486 (10th Cir. 1990), the state sought an injunction requiring PRP compliance with a state-devised cleanup plan that differed from the remedy chosen by EPA, relying on §121(e)(2). The court ruled that CERCLA envisions only state enforcement of federally selected remedies and that the state's proper role was involvement in the federal remedy selection under §121(f). Orders issued by EPA under §106 may preempt conflicting state and local laws. United States v. City & County of Denver, 100 F.3d 1509 (10th Cir. 1996). But United States v. Colorado, 990 F.2d 1565 (10th Cir. 1993), concluded that §121 did not bar Colorado from enforcing its state RCRA program against a federally owned and operated facility. The United States argued unsuccessfully that the state's role when a CERCLA response action is underway is confined to the ARARs process.

   6. *RCRA Corrective Action.* Contamination may occur not only at inactive dump sites and industrial facilities, but also at active TSD facilities. RCRA authorizes EPA to require corrective action at TSD facilities seeking RCRA permits. See 42 U.S.C. §6924(u)-(v); Florida Power & Light Co. v. EPA, 145 F.3d 1414, 1416 (D.C. Cir. 1998). EPA faces similar questions in determining the appropriate extent of corrective action as it faces in the CERCLA remedy selection process.

G.   THE EFFECT OF THE DISCOVERY OF HAZARDOUS SUBSTANCES ON REAL ESTATE TRANSACTIONS

How has CERCLA affected real estate transactions? Coupled with the expanded common law duty to disclose material facts in connection with the sale of property, CERCLA has prompted sellers of property to disclose the existence of hazardous wastes.* Brokers who misrepresent the condition of the property also may be liable to buyers. Sheehy v. Lipton Indus., Inc., 507 N.E.2d 781 (Mass. App. Ct. 1987). These CERCLA-mandated disclosures may have discouraged the development of some brownfield properties. Is the presence of environmental contamination an encumbrance on title that renders title unmarketable? See In re Country World Casinos, 181 F.3d 1146 (10th Cir. 1999).

   Due Diligence Investigations. As indicated in section C.3.b, CERCLA includes defenses for innocent landowners and bona fide prospective purchasers. §§101(35), (40), 107(b)(3), (r). Site investigation may help prospective purchasers and lenders avoid purchasing contaminated properties. It also may help them avoid liability under

---

*See T & E Indus., Inc. v. Safety Light Corp., 587 A.2d 1249 (N.J. 1991) (strict liability for abnormally dangerous activities); Russell-Stanley Corp. v. Plant Indus., Inc., 595 A.2d 534 (N.J. Super. 1991) (landlord's liability to tenant for activities of previous tenant). But see Hydro-Mfg., Inc. v. Kayser-Roth Corp., 640 A.2d 950 (R.I. 1994) (previous owners of contaminated property not liable to remote purchasers on tort or failure to disclose theories).

CERCLA and similar state laws if contamination is later found, by enhancing the chances that these defenses will be available. These "due diligence" investigations combine legal and technical assessment of the status of a site's contamination and regulatory compliance.* They are routinely performed on sites at which manufacturing has occurred or where substances such as asbestos, lead paint, or urea formaldehyde may have been used. Site assessments must be conducted in a manner consistent with good commercial and customary practices to provide the basis for invocation of the innocent landowner defense. A Phase I environmental site assessment (ESA), which is performed to identify environmental conditions likely to give rise to liability under CERCLA or similar state laws, is composed of four phases: records review, site reconnaissance, interviews with owners and occupants and local government officials, and an evaluation and report stating whether the assessment has revealed evidence of contamination.** If the Phase I ESA reveals actual or potential contamination, a further Phase II ESA, composed of site sampling, lab analysis, and recommendations for remediation, may be conducted to assess the nature and extent of contamination.

   State Disclosure Laws. The consequences of the presence of hazardous substances on real estate transactions may extend beyond the creation of CERCLA liability for the purchaser who does not qualify for the "innocent landowner" defense. Some states intervene in transactions involving potentially contaminated land. New Jersey's Environmental Cleanup Responsibility Act (ECRA), N.J. Stat. Ann. §§13:1K-6 to K-14, adopted in 1983, "was the first statute to link real estate and business transactions to environmental audits and cleanups. . . . [It] sought to decrease the growing number of waste sites by requiring businesses to perform environmental audits." D'Alonzo et al., Comment, ECRA to ISRA: Is It More Than Just a Name Change?, 7 Vill. Envtl. L.J. 51, 52-53 (1996). One court described ECRA as follows:

> ECRA's unique approach to solving the hazardous waste problem implements "market forces to bring about the reversal of environmental pollution." Dixon Venture v. Joseph Dixon Crucible Co., 122 N.J. 228, 236-37 (1991). ECRA makes the transfer or the closure of an "industrial establishment" contingent upon compliance with the Act and thereby, internalizes the cost of clean-up within those transactions. [Grand Street Artists v. General Elec. Co., 19 F. Supp. 2d 242, 249 (D.N.J. 1998).]***

ECRA required the owners and operators of industrial facilities to investigate the environmental condition of their property before closing or transferring operations. State regulations required notification of planned closings or transfers and the

---

   *See generally Forte, Environmental Due Diligence: A Guide to Liability Risk Management in Commercial Real Estate Transactions, 5 Fordham Envtl. L.J. 349 (1994).
   **See Conrad, Sliding Scale or Slippery Slope? The New ASTM's Standard Practices for Environmental Site Assessments, 23 Envtl. L. Rep. (ELI) 10181 (1993); Carlisle & Johnson, The Impact of CERCLA on Real Estate Transactions, 4 S.C. Envtl. L.J. 129, 135 (1995).
   ***See also Gergen, Note, The Failed Promise of the "Polluter Pays" Principle: An Economic Analysis of Landowner Liability for Hazardous Waste, 69 N.Y.U. L. Rev. 624, 655 (1994) ("the New Jersey legislature hoped that [ECRA] would provide a means by which the state could motivate the privately financed cleanup of hazardous waste sites without having to discover waste sites itself, incur cleanup costs on its own, or seek reimbursement in a subsequent recovery action as is required under the [state's] Spill Act and CERCLA").

preparation of either a negative declaration (specifying that there has been no discharge of hazardous substances at the site or that any such discharge has been cleaned up) or a cleanup plan for remediation of contamination. Cleanup plans had to be accompanied by a surety bond or its equivalent to cover the anticipated cost of the cleanup and had to address both on-site and off-site contamination attributable to site operations. In re Adoption of N.J.A.C. 7:26B, 608 A.2d 288 (N.J. 1992). Current site owners were responsible for remediating contamination, even if it was caused by previous owners. See Superior Air Prod. Co. v. N.L. Indus., Inc., 522 A.2d 1025 (N.J. Super. App. Div. 1987).

The transferee of property transferred in violation of ECRA could sue a noncomplying transferor to recover the cost of ECRA compliance. New West Urban Renewal Co. v. Westinghouse Elec. Corp., 909 F. Supp. 219, 225 (D.N.J. 1995). A noncomplying owner or operator was strictly liable for all remediation costs. N.J. Stat. Ann. §13:1K-13. Transactions subject to but not in compliance with ECRA could be voided by the buyer, N.J. Stat. Ann. §13:1K-13(a), but a buyer need not void the transaction in order to sue for damages. May a purchaser of contaminated property sue in a negligence action a consultant whose ECRA report failed to disclose the contamination, even if the report was prepared for purposes of site closure rather than sale, based on a breach of a duty stemming from ECRA? The court in Grand Street Artists, supra, said yes, at least where there was some indication that the consultant knew that the premises would be sold once the ECRA closure process was completed.

Critics charged that ECRA delayed the process and increased the cost of transferring commercial and industrial property, causing some industry to leave the state. Responding to these criticisms, the state legislature adopted the Industrial Site Recovery Act (ISRA), N.J. Pub. L. 1993, c. 139, which amended and renamed ECRA. ISRA sought to promote certainty and efficiency in the regulatory process and privatization of the cleanup process without incurring unnecessary health and environmental risks. See Motiuk et al., New Jersey's Hazardous Site Remediation Program: The Year of Reform, 832 PLI/Corp 585 (Dec.-Jan. 1993) (ISRA is designed "to minimize governmental involvement in certain business transactions"). ISRA still requires the owner or operator of an industrial establishment planning to close or transfer ownership of operations to notify the state Department of Environmental Protection (DEP) and submit either a negative declaration or a proposed remedial action work plan that complies with state remediation standards for soil, groundwater, and surface water. The DEP must approve the transfer and may rescind approval of a negative declaration if material information is withheld. But ISRA expanded the exemptions from notification and remediation requirements and established an expedited review process. It also sought to ease the financial burdens of compliance by authorizing insurance and self-guarantees as funding sources. D'Alonzo et al., supra, at 76. ISRA requires the seller to disclose information to the other parties to the transaction, by, for example, attaching a copy of any approved negative declaration or approved remedial action work plan to a sale or transfer agreement. Inderbitzin, Taking the Burden off the Buyer: A Survey of Hazardous Waste Disclosure Statutes, 1 Envtl. Law. 513 (1995), citing N.J. Stat. Ann. §13:1K-9(b)(2).

How effective has ECRA/ISRA been at achieving its goals? To what extent has it generated unintended adverse consequences for New Jersey's economy? On the one hand, ISRA prompted hundreds of site cleanups. On the other hand, it may not have induced industrial landowners to engage in more rapid cleanups with fewer litigation-related transaction costs.

> In addition, critics of ISRA charge that it has discouraged corporate transactions and slowed needed urban redevelopment in New Jersey by subjecting sellers to potentially great environmental liability. Moreover, some have argued that ISRA discourages the cleanup of older industrial sites by deterring not only potential sellers but also potential buyers of industrial sites from taking part in land transfers because of concerns over regulatory delays. . . .
>   . . . ISRA may have some role in motivating cleanups, but it appears to be unable to encourage the discovery and reporting of larger polluted sites. [Gergen, *supra*, at 663-664, 667.]

Gergen recommends as alternatives to both CERCLA and ISRA the adoption of a set of rules placing more emphasis on motivating the discovery and reporting of hazardous waste contamination by landowners.

Brownfields Revitalization. Critics of CERCLA have long complained that the statute's liability scheme creates disincentives to economic development of contaminated property. Former EPA Administrator Carol Browner testified before Congress that many old industrial sites lay abandoned because the threat of CERCLA liability discouraged developers from buying contaminated property, cleaning it up, and developing it. The result was that developers had incentives to use undeveloped or "greenfield" sites to avoid liability, "thereby contributing to suburban sprawl and exacerbating the woes of the inner city, the unemployment, etc."[*] Similarly, CERCLA may encourage protracted litigation rather than expeditious cleanups; a refusal by lenders to foreclose on contaminated properties, often followed by abandonment of the sites; and a reluctance by purchasers of properties previously devoted to commercial or industrial use to investigate possible contamination due to fear that the information revealed might trigger liability. Kibel, The Urban Nexus: Open Space, Brownfields, and Justice, 25 B.C. Envtl. Aff. L. Rev. 589, 600-601 (1998). CERCLA therefore "helped to deepen the post-industrial economic decline in many city neighborhoods. From an investment and business standpoint, these abandoned properties, or brownfields, became untouchables."[**] Id. at 601.

Chang & Sigman, The Effect of Joint and Several Liability under Superfund on Brownfields, University of Pennsylvania Law School, Institute for Law and Economics, Research Paper No. 05-21 (Sept. 5, 2005),[***] identify four different reasons why joint and several liability under CERCLA may discourage the purchase of contaminated property, despite the tendency for land prices to reflect the expected transfer of liability: (1) A sale may increase the share of liability that a seller and a buyer may expect to pay as a group. (2) A sale may increase the amount of damages that the government can expect to recover from the defendants at trial. (3) A sale may increase the total litigation costs that a buyer and seller may face as a group. (4) Game theory

---

[*]Superfund Reform Act of 1994: Hearings on S. 1834 Before the Subcomm. on Superfund, Recycling, and Solid Waste Management of the Senate Comm. on Env't and Public Works, 103d Cong., 2d Sess. 12 (Feb. 10, 1994) (testimony of Carol Browner).

[**]The term "brownfields" developed to describe "former industrial properties that were now unused due to uncertainty over environmental remediation liability." Kibel, *supra*, at 603. For a primer on the brownfields problem, see Jacobs, Basic Brownfields, 12 J. Nat. Resources & Envtl. L. 265 (1996-1997).

[***]This paper is available at http://ssrn.com/abstract_id=804464.

suggests that a sale may increase the amount that the government can expect to extract from defendants in a settlement.

The Small Business Liability Relief and Brownfields Revitalization Act, Pub. L. No. 107-118, 115 Stat. 2356 (2002), ordered EPA to establish a program to provide grants to inventory, characterize, assess, and conduct planning related to brownfield sites and perform targeted assessments at those sites. CERCLA §107(k)(2)(A). Brownfield sites comprise real property whose expansion, redevelopment, or reuse may be complicated by the presence or potential release of hazardous substances. Exclusions are listed at §101(39)(B). In particular, EPA may make grants to "eligible entities" (local governments, state agencies, or Indian tribes) to engage in these activities at brownfield sites. The statute also directs the president to establish a program to provide grants to eligible entities to provide assistance for the remediation of brownfield sites. §107(k)(3). In determining whether a site characterization and assessment or a remediation grant is appropriate, the president or an eligible entity must consider a series of factors. These include the extent to which a grant will facilitate the creation of, preservation of, or addition to a park, greenway, undeveloped property, recreational property, or other property used for nonprofit purposes; the extent to which a grant will meet the needs of a community that is unable to draw on other sources of funding for environmental remediation and subsequent redevelopment; and the extent to which a grant will facilitate the use or reuse of existing infrastructure. §107(k)(3)(C).

EPA must publish guidance to assist eligible entities in applying for grants and award grants to eligible entities that have the highest rankings under criteria set forth in the statute. These include the potential of the proposed project to stimulate economic development and the extent to which a grant would address or facilitate identification and reduction of threats to human health and the environment, particularly to minority and sensitive populations. §107(k)(5)(C). Each grant must be subject to an agreement that requires the recipient to comply with applicable federal and state laws and ensures that the cleanup protects health and the environment. §107(k)(9). The Brownfields Revitalization Act also authorized EPA to make grants to states or Indian tribes to conduct response actions.

The 2002 amendments bar the federal government from taking enforcement action under §106(a) or §107(a) of CERCLA with respect to eligible response sites at which there is a release or threatened release of hazardous substances, and a person is conducting or has completed a response action that complies with the state program. §128(b). An eligible response site is one that meets CERCLA's definition of a brownfield site (excluding facilities for which EPA is conducting or has conducted a preliminary assessment or site inspection and for which EPA has determined that the site qualifies for possible listing on the NPL). §101(41). Under certain circumstances, federal enforcement is appropriate even for an eligible response site. See §128(b)(1)(B).

CERCLA and Federal Facilities. When a federal agency enters a contract for the sale of real property on which hazardous waste was stored, disposed of, or known to have been released, §120(h)(3)(B) of CERCLA requires that it notify the prospective purchaser and include in the deed a covenant warranting that it will take all necessary remedial action. Hercules, Inc. v. EPA, 938 F.2d 276 (D.C. Cir. 1991), held that notification is required even if the contamination occurred before government ownership. The Community Environmental Response Facilitation Act, Pub. L. No. 102-426, 106 Stat. 2174 (1992), sought to encourage the redevelopment of closed military bases. It requires the federal government to investigate property on which it plans to terminate military operations to determine the likelihood of a release or threatened release of hazardous substances or petroleum products. Deeds for properties covered by the Act must include a covenant warranting that the United States will take any necessary corrective action. §120(h)(4). A 1996 appropriations bill exempts property leased rather than sold by the federal government from the obligation to supply this covenant. Pub. L. No. 104-106, §2834, 110 Stat. 186, 559 (1996).

X

ENFORCEMENT OF
ENVIRONMENTAL LAW

Enforcement is the set of actions that governments or others take to achieve compliance within the regulated community.

EPA, Principles of Environmental Enforcement,
1-4 (July 15, 1992).

A strong and vital enforcement program is critical to the success of EPA's environmental programs.

EPA, Environmental Protection Agency 1999 Annual Plan
Request to Congress, A Credible Deterrent to Pollution
and Greater Compliance with the Law, Objective #1 Overview (1999).

A. INTRODUCTION

EPA has long considered promoting and producing compliance with environmental regulatory requirements to be a critical aspect of environmental governance. Goal 9 of EPA's 2000 Strategic Plan is to maintain a "credible deterrent to pollution and [produce] greater compliance with the law." EPA Strategic Plan 2000, at 55. In this Plan EPA notes that "[p]rotecting the public and the environment from risks posed by violations of environmental requirements is, and always has been, basic to EPA's mission." Id. In its current Strategic Plan, the Agency states that "[e]nviron-mental laws and regulations are designed to protect human health and safeguard the environment. But they can achieve their purpose only when companies and facilities comply with requirements." EPA Strategic Plan 2003, p. 111.

In recent years EPA has put a premium on exercising its traditional authority to identify violations and pursue alleged significant violators through civil and/or criminal enforcement actions, while also expanding its "toolbox" of strategies for promoting compliance. The agency explains its goal of blending traditional enforce-ment with "compliance assistance" and "compliance incentive" strategies as follows: "While maintaining a strong regulatory enforcement program, EPA and its state and local partners are also expanding the use of innovative tools for ensuring compliance by providing assistance and incentives to the regulated community." EPA Strategic

Plan 2000, at 55. The agency's strategy of using a combination of tools has been characterized as an integrated approach to compliance assurance. Stoughton et al., Toward Integrated Approaches to Compliance Assurance, 31 Envtl. L. Rep. (ELI) 11266 (2001).

This chapter provides an introduction to three key elements of contemporary environmental enforcement. First, it reviews the key actors who engage in the actual work of promoting compliance. Second, it covers the key legal authorities that are available for government officials, as well as citizens, to enforce the law. Finally, the chapter explores some of the recent strategies that EPA and its state partners have developed in their "policy toolboxes" to achieve the goal of compliance.

B. THE ACTORS

There are four major categories of actors in the environmental enforcement arena: federal officials, state personnel, citizens (environmental nongovernmental organizations, or ENGOs), and regulated parties. We review the roles of each, including some of the areas of overlap and tension.

1. Federal Officials

This chapter focuses on the role of the Environmental Protection Agency (EPA) in its capacity as the federal entity primarily responsible for promoting compliance with the major pollution control laws, such as the Clean Water and Clean Air Acts, and RCRA (other agencies, such as the Department of the Interior (DOI), also have enforcement responsibilities under various environmental laws, such as the Endangered Species Act, as other chapters reflect). EPA staff (1) develop enforcement priorities and the policies to carry them out; (2) conduct enforcement work—inspections, negotiations with regulated parties, administrative enforcement actions, and referral of civil and criminal enforcement cases to the Department of Justice for further action; and (3) authorize and oversee the performance of the states in the increasing number of jurisdictions in which states have taken over primary responsibility for implementation of federal environmental programs.

EPA's headquarters enforcement office is known as the Office of Enforcement and Compliance Assurance (OECA). Figure 10-1 shows OECA's organizational chart. Other EPA headquarters offices play a role in enforcement and promoting compliance, including the "program offices," such as the Office of Water, the Office of Air and Radiation, and the Office of Solid Waste and Emergency Response (OSWER).

EPA's ten regional offices also play an integral role in enforcement. Perhaps surprisingly, there is no uniform structure for how the regions are organized to perform their enforcement and compliance functions; the regional offices have evolved their own structures over the years. John B. Stephenson, Director of Natural Resources and Environment for the Government Accountability (formerly General Accounting) Office (GAO), testified before Congress in 2006 that EPA's regions "vary substantially in the actions they take to enforce environmental requirements" and that there are

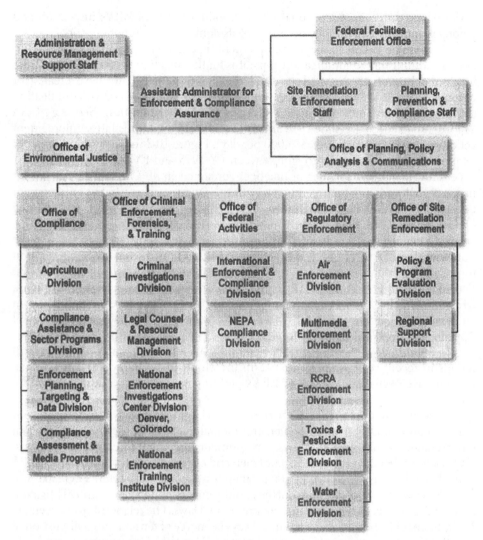

FIGURE 10-1

Office of Enforcement and Compliance Assurance Organization Chart

Source: http://www.epa.gov/compliance/about/us.html.

"philosophical" differences among the regions in their views about enforcement.[*]
Regardless of their structures and philosophical predispositions, the regional offices
play several critical roles in enforcement and compliance work. They serve as the
primary interlocutors between headquarters (where much of environmental policy,
including policy in the enforcement arena, is set) and the states (where, as discussed
below, much of the actual implementation work is performed), and they oversee state

---

[*]Statement of John B. Stephenson, U.S. GAO, Environmental Compliance and Enforcement: EPA's Efforts to Improve and Make More Consistent Its Compliance and Enforcement
Activities 2, 3 (June 2006), available at http://www.gao.gov/new.items/d06840t.pdf.

performance. Further, the regional offices conduct much of EPA's inspection and enforcement activity, and they do much of its compliance promotion work.

In addition to developing and implementing enforcement policies, EPA maintains an administrative adjudication apparatus for the litigation that is brought administratively. Recent iterations of many of the environmental laws have created or expanded EPA's authority to pursue violators through administrative adjudication (in addition to strengthening its judicial enforcement authorities). See, e.g., CAA §113(d) (enacted as part of the 1990 amendments to allow administrative enforcement actions, with penalties of up to $25,000 per day). Figure 10-2 indicates the number of administrative actions EPA brought between FY 1975 and FY 2005.

EPA's consolidated rules of practice, contained in 40 C.F.R. Part 22, govern much of EPA's administrative enforcement work. Agency administrative enforcement cases initially are heard, and decided, by a Presiding Officer. Appeals of Presiding Officer decisions are made to the agency's Environmental Appeals Board (EAB), an entity created within EPA in 1992 for this purpose. The Board generally serves as the final agency decision maker, although it has the discretion to refer any case or motion to the EPA Administrator. EAB decisions are subject to judicial review. See, e.g., Pepperell Assoc. v. EPA, 246 F.3d 15 (1st Cir. 2001); City of San Diego v. Whitman, 242 F.3d 1097, 1101 (9th Cir. 2001); 5 U.S.C. §704. For an article on the EAB from an insider, see Firestone, The Environmental Protection Agency's Environmental Appeals Board, 1 Envtl. Law. 1 (1994).

EPA's Office of the Inspector General (OIG) has issued a significant number of reports in recent years on performance in the enforcement and compliance arena. Several have been quite critical of EPA's performance and the performance of the states.*

The other major federal agency actor is the U.S. Department of Justice. The four major sections of DOJ that work on environmental matters are its civil environmental enforcement, environmental crimes, environmental defense, and appellate sections. DOJ's lawyers handle much of the court civil and criminal litigation on behalf of EPA and other federal agencies. In addition to "main Justice" in Washington, D.C., many of the U.S. Attorneys' offices throughout the country play a significant role in civil litigation and criminal prosecutions under the environmental laws. The relationship between the Department of Justice and EPA has not always been free of tension. For a discussion of the allocation of enforcement authority between EPA and the Department of Justice, see Devins & Herz, The Battle That Never Was: Congress, the White House, and Agency Litigation Authority, 61 Law & Contemp. Probs. 205 (Winter 1998).

Parts of the executive branch, including the Office of Information and Regulatory Affairs (OIRA), which is located within the Office of Management and Budget and reviews EPA regulations, have the potential to become involved in environmental enforcement policy as well. EPA also uses OMB's Program Assessment Rating Tool (PART) to evaluate its performance, including in the enforcement arena.

Congress (including its committees and one of its research arms, the Government Accountability Office) has the capacity to play an important role in enforcement matters on several fronts. For a recent GAO statement that is critical of EPA

---

*See, e.g., EPA Performance Measures Do Not Effectively Track Compliance Outcomes, Report No. 2006-P-00006 (Dec. 15, 2005), www.epa.gov/oig/reports/2006/20051215-2006-P-00006.pdf; and Limited Knowledge of the Universe of Regulated Entities Impedes EPA's Ability to Demonstrate Changes in Regulatory Compliance, Report No. 2005-P-00024 (Sept. 19, 2005), www.epa.gov/oig/reports/2005/20050919-2005-P-00024.pdf.

	CAA	CWA/SDWA	RCRA	TOTALS
FY75	0	738	0	738
FY76	210	915	0	1,125
FY77	297	1,128	0	1,425
FY78	129	730	0	859
FY79	404	506	0	910
FY80	86	569	0	655
FY81	112	562	159	833
FY82	21	329	237	587
FY83	41	781	436	1,258
FY84	141	1,644	554	2,339
FY85	122	1,031	327	1,480
FY86	143	990	235	1,368
FY87	191	1,214	243	1,648
FY88	224	1,345	309	1,878
FY89	336	2,146	453	2,935
FY90	249	1,780	366	2,395
FY91	214	2,177	364	2,755
FY92	354	1,977	291	2,622
FY93	279	2,216	282	2,777
FY94	435	1,841	115	2,391
FY95	232	1,774	92	2,098
FY96	242	998	238	1,478
FY97	391	1,642	423	2,456
FY98	499	1,590	398	2,487
FY99	542	1,390	558	2,490
FY00	379	1,271	3,416	4,049
FY01	341	1,557	306	2,204
FY02	300	1,452	292	2,044
FY03	359	1,806	320	2,485
FY04	461	2,043	387	2,891
FY05	635	2,327	398	3,360

Sources: EPA, Annual Report on Enforcement and Compliance Assurance Accomplishments in 1999, Ex. B-5; and EPA, National Enforcement Trends—FY 2005, http://cfpub.epa.gov/compliance/resources/reports/nets/index.cfm.

FIGURE 10-2
EPA Administrative Actions by Statute, FY 1975 to FY 2005*

*Includes administrative compliance orders issued, administrative penalty order complaints, field citations, and HQCAA mobile-source NOVs with penalties.

enforcement, see Statement of John B. Stephenson, *supra*, at 8, 13 (finding significant disparities in regional approaches to enforcement and substantial problems with enforcement data, and concluding that EPA actions have "thus far achieved only limited success and illustrate both the importance and the difficulty of addressing the long-standing problems in ensuring the consistent application of enforcement requirements").

Finally, the federal courts are involved at virtually every step of the enforcement process—from determining the validity of the norms or standards allegedly violated, to deciding whether violations for which liability should attach occurred, to fashioning appropriate relief when actionable violations are found.

2.   *State Officials*

The other major government actors in the environmental enforcement arena are, of course, the state officials. As explained in Chapter 1, section C.4, beginning in the 1970s Congress has adopted a series of laws that have "federalized" environmental law to a significant degree. To a large extent, these laws, the regulations promulgated to implement them, and the cases that have interpreted them, represent the corpus of this textbook.

As explained in Chapter 2, in many of these laws (e.g., the Clean Air Act, Clean Water Act, and RCRA), Congress adopted a "cooperative federalism" structure. Under this structure, EPA, while retaining overall responsibility for administering these laws and achieving their purposes, authorizes interested and qualified states to implement them within their respective jurisdictions. In the Clean Water Act, for example, Congress indicates that its intent is to "recognize, preserve, and protect the primary responsibilities and right of States to prevent, reduce, and eliminate pollution." CWA §101(b). Under some laws, EPA is obligated to "delegate" programs to a state to administer once EPA has determined that the state is capable of performing this role. Under most statutes, states achieve delegation by adopting their own versions of federal laws, which the states then administer, rather than by implementing the federal law itself.

EPA has authorized states to administer a significant number of environmental programs in recent years. The result is that states have become increasingly important players in the implementation of federal environmental laws. According to R. Steven Brown, now the Executive Director of the Environmental Council of the States (ECOS), the Washington, D.C.–based association of state environmental agencies, "A remarkable, and largely unnoticed, change in environmental protection has occurred over the past five to 10 years. The States have become the primary environmental protection agencies across the nation." Brown, The States Protect the Environment, ECOStates (Summer 1999).

A 2001 ECOS Report to Congress reports that states administer more than 75 percent of the major federal delegable environmental programs, up from less than 40 percent in 1993.* According to one accounting, states now are responsible for as much as 80 percent of all enforcement under the federal pollution laws. 31 Env't Rep. (BNA) 113 (2000). Figure 10-3 presents data on state administrative enforcement

---

*Environmental Council of the States, Report to Congress, State Environmental Agency Contributions to Enforcement and Compliance n.1 (April 2001), available at http://www.ecos.org/files/687_file_ECOS_20RTC_20f.pdf.

Administrative Actions:

Statute	FY89	FY90	FY91	FY92	FY93	FY94	FY95	FY96	FY97	FY98	FY99
SDWA/CWA	3,100	3,298	3,180	2,748	3,960	4,063	4,231	4,598	7,051	6,960	3,602
CAA	1,139	1,312	1,687	1,411	2,005	2,050	1,833	1,534	1,919	2,410	2,036
RCRA	1,189	1,350	1,495	1,389	1,744	1,609	1,235	841	444	727	1,278
Totals	5,428	6,590	6,362	5,548	7,709	7,722	7,299	6,973	9,414	10,097	6,916

Judicial Referrals:

Statute	FY89	FY90	FY91	FY92	FY93	FY94	FY95	FY96	FY97	FY98	FY99
SDWA/CWA	489	429	297	204	383	162	169	169	151	146	223
CAA	96	156	190	258	174	325	124	198	164	146	158
RCRA	129	64	57	112	133	91	104	66	64	60	126
Totals	714	649	544	574	690	578	397	433	379	352	507

Source: EPA, Annual Report on Enforcement and Compliance Assurance Accomplishments in 1999, Ex. B-7.

FIGURE 10-3
State Environmental Agencies' Formal Administrative Actions and Judicial
Referrals, FY 1989 to FY 1999

actions and judicial referrals. In a 1999 Executive Order on federalism, President Clinton supported shifting authority to states, instructing federal agencies to "grant the States the maximum administrative discretion possible" in administering federal programs. Exec. Order No. 13,132, 64 Fed. Reg. 43,255 (1999). The Bush administration has favored devolution as well.

State capacity and investment in the environmental enforcement and compliance arena increased significantly during much of the 1980s and 1990s. Brown reports that from 1986 to 1996, for example, state environmental staffs expanded in size by about 60 percent. Significant variations continue to exist between and among the states. Further, there have been periodic ebbs and flows in state resources. For example, in the early 2000s, budget shortfalls in many states caused some retrenchment. Brown, Coping with the Budget Crunch: When the Axe Falls—How State Environmental Agencies Deal with Budget Cuts, ECOStates (Winter 2002).

States that EPA authorizes to administer environmental programs remain subject to federal oversight. EPA's 1986 Revised Policy Framework for State/EPA Enforcement Agreements, revised several times since then, creates a general framework that governs the relationship between EPA and the states. Among other things, this framework establishes criteria that EPA and the states use to assess government performance, and it identifies the circumstances in which EPA may take its own enforcement action in authorized states. In 1995, EPA and the states decided to "reinvent" their relationship by establishing the National Environmental Performance Partnership System (NEPPS), which the Environmental Law Institute (ELI) has described as "the most substantial nation-wide reform in the EPA-state relationship since those relationships were first established over twenty-five years ago. ELI, An Independent Review of the State-Federal Environmental Partnership Agreements 11 (1996). More recently, EPA has been working with the states to implement an approach they have called the State Review Framework, or SRF. OECA describes the origins and purposes of the SRF as follows:

> OECA has worked closely with EPA regions, the . . . [ECOS], state media associations and other state representatives to jointly develop a framework and process for conducting reviews of core enforcement programs in the CWA-NPDES, RCRA Subtitle C and the CAA Stationary Sources programs. The goals of the reviews are to promote consistent levels of activity in state and regional enforcement programs, consistent oversight of state and regional enforcement programs, and consistent levels of environmental protection across the country. In July of 2005, full implementation of SRF was initiated with the goal of completing reviews of all states and territories by the end of FY 2007. [EPA, Final FY07 Update to . . . [OECA] National Program Managers' Guidance 21 (April 2006).]

Congress's decision to give EPA overall responsibility for achieving the goals of the federal environmental laws, while requiring or authorizing EPA to delegate primary implementation authority to qualified states and then oversee state performance, has been the source of considerable tension. EPA's head of enforcement during the Clinton presidency indicated that "forging an effective, cooperative relationship with the states on enforcement" was the "most significant" challenge he faced. Mason, Snapshot Interview: Steven A. Herman, 12 Nat. Resources & Env't 286 (1998).

Views differ about the effectiveness of this uneasy partnership. Professor Richard Stewart, in an important early article, suggested that "[t]he success of federal programs has been gravely compromised by . . . dependence upon state and local governments" because of the lack of state buy-in to federal strategies. Stewart, Pyramids of Sacrifice? Problems of Federalism in Mandating State Implementation of National Environmental Policy, 86 Yale L.J. 1196 (1977). A multitude of audits and evaluations in recent years similarly have raised questions about state and federal performance in their respective roles in the enforcement arena.* On the other hand, Professor Evan Ringquist is one of several political scientists who have highlighted improvements in state capacity and performance: "[M]any states have tossed away their recalcitrant stance toward strong environmental programs, and in many instances state governments, not the 'feds,' are at the forefront in efforts to protect the environment." Ringquist, Environmental Protection at the State Level: Politics and Progress in Controlling Pollution xiii (1993). Rechtschaffen & Markell, Reinventing Environmental Enforcement & the State/Federal Relationship (2003), examine the effectiveness of the state-federal partnership in the enforcement arena and identify several strategies for strengthening the relationship and improving its performance.

---

*See, e.g., Statement of John B. Stephenson, *supra*, at 2; EPA Office of Inspector General, Water Enforcement: State Enforcement of Clean Water Act Dischargers Can Be More Effective (Aug. 2001), available at http://www.epa.gov/oig/reports/2001/finalenfor.pdf.

3.   *Environmental Nongovernmental Organizations (ENGOs) and Regulated Parties*

Two other groups of actors play significant roles in the enforcement and compliance arena. First, there are private citizens and nongovernmental organizations that have an interest in such matters. They play a variety of roles in seeking to promote compliance with the environmental laws. Of greatest significance in this chapter, they act as "private attorneys general" under many of the federal environmental laws. As we discuss in more detail below, most of the major federal environmental laws empower citizens to bring enforcement actions against regulated parties that allegedly are violating environmental requirements. Professor Jeffery Miller has noted that "citizen suits have become more than an occasionally used safety valve. Under the Clean Water Act they are now a frequently used federal judicial enforcement mechanism." Miller, Citizen Suits: Private Enforcement of Federal Pollution Control Laws 15 (1987). Common law causes of action, such as private nuisance, also discussed below, are another mechanism available to citizens to address violations, at least in some instances. Citizens also have become increasingly active in monitoring the performance of individual facilities in various ways, including by serving on "good neighbor committees."*

Finally, citizen groups such as NRDC, US PIRG, and the Environment Working Group have reviewed government and regulated-party performance more systematically. See, e.g., U.S. PIRG Education Fund, Troubled Waters: An Analysis of Clean Water Act Compliance, July 2003-December 2004 (March 2006) (concluding that there is significant noncompliance with the Clean Water Act); Environmental Working Group, Prime Suspects: The Law Breaking Polluters America Fails to Inspect (July 2000).

Last, but certainly not least, there are the regulated parties themselves, and their consultants and other representatives. A significant aspect of the debate in the enforcement and compliance arena these days, in the United States as well as worldwide, involves determining how best to encourage regulated parties to be proactive in managing their operations in a way that minimizes noncompliance, facilitates timely identification of problems when they arise, and promotes timely remediation and other responses. There is a burgeoning interest, for example, in having regulated parties conduct audits and, more generally, develop and implement environmental management systems (EMSs). As we discuss in more detail in the final section of this chapter, EPA has committed to encouraging adoption of EMSs and similar proactive approaches that "improve compliance, prevent pollution, and integrate other means of improving environmental performance." EPA, Position Statement on Environmental Management Systems (EMSs), 71 Fed. Reg. 5664 (2006).

Thus, while government is clearly part of the solution to the issue of noncompliance, it is widely accepted that the public at large, including environmental and community NGOs, and the regulated community, occupy important parts of this landscape as well, although details concerning their appropriate roles remain in issue.

Having summarized the roles of some of the major actors in the world of environmental enforcement, we close this section on enforcement actors by returning to

---

*Lewis & Henkel, Good Neighbor Agreements: A Tool for Environmental and Social Justice, 23 Soc. Just. 134 (Winter 1996), available at http://www.cpn.org/topics/environment/goodneighbor.html.

the state-federal relationship for a closer look at some of the legal issues that have surfaced. A significant issue in this relationship is when EPA legally may file a lawsuit against a regulated party for alleged violations of environmental requirements if a state agency has already filed a lawsuit or otherwise initiated legal action against the regulated party. A 1999 Eighth Circuit decision, Harmon Indus., Inc. v. Browner, caused considerable consternation among federal officials and some scholars by holding that EPA legally may not file a lawsuit against a regulated party under RCRA if the delegated state agency already has pursued a legal action against that party. An excerpt of that case follows.

HARMON INDUSTRIES, INC. v. BROWNER
191 F.3d 894 (8th Cir. 1999)

HANSEN, Circuit J.

Harmon Industries, Inc. (Harmon) filed this action pursuant to the Administrative Procedure Act, 5 U.S.C. §706 (1994), seeking judicial review of a final decision of the United States Environmental Protection Agency (EPA). The district court granted summary judgment in favor of Harmon and reversed the decision of the EPA. The EPA appeals. We affirm.

I. Facts and Procedural Background

Harmon Industries operates a plant in Grain Valley, Missouri, which it utilizes to assemble circuit boards for railroad control and safety equipment. In November 1987, Harmon's personnel manager discovered that maintenance workers at Harmon routinely discarded volatile solvent residue behind Harmon's Grain Valley plant. This practice apparently began in 1973 and continued until November 1987. Harmon's management was unaware of its employees' practices until the personnel manager filed his report in November 1987. Following the report, Harmon ceased its disposal activities and voluntarily contacted the Missouri Department of Natural Resources (MDNR). The MDNR investigated and concluded that Harmon's past disposal practices did not pose a threat to either human health or the environment. The MDNR and Harmon created a plan whereby Harmon would clean up the disposal area. Harmon implemented the clean up plan. While Harmon was cooperating with the MDNR, the EPA initiated an administrative enforcement action against Harmon in which the federal agency sought $2,343,706 in penalties. Meanwhile, Harmon and the MDNR continued to establish a voluntary compliance plan. In harmonizing the details of the plan, Harmon asked the MDNR not to impose civil penalties. Harmon based its request in part on the fact that it voluntarily self-reported the environmental violations and cooperated fully with the MDNR.

On March 5, 1993, while the EPA's administrative enforcement action was pending, a Missouri state court judge approved a consent decree entered into by the MDNR and Harmon. In the decree, MDNR acknowledged full accord and satisfaction and released Harmon from any claim for monetary penalties. MDNR based its decision to release Harmon on the fact that the company promptly self-reported its violation and cooperated in all aspects of the investigation. After the filing of the consent decree, Harmon litigated the EPA claim before an administrative law judge (ALJ). The ALJ found that a civil penalty against Harmon was appropriate in this case. The ALJ rejected the EPA's request for a penalty in excess of $2 million but the ALJ did impose a civil fine of $586,716 against Harmon. A three-person Environmental Appeals Board panel affirmed the ALJ's monetary penalty. Harmon filed a complaint challenging the EPA's decision in federal district court on June 6, 1997. In its August 25, 1998, summary judgment order, the district court found that the EPA's decision to impose civil penalties violated the Resource Conservation and Recovery Act and contravened principles of res judicata. The EPA appeals to this court.

II. Discussion

A. THE PERMISSIBILITY OF OVERFILING

When reviewing a federal agency's interpretation of a federal statute, a federal court must defer to the agency's interpretation only if it finds that the agency's interpretation is consistent with the plain language of the statute or represents a reasonable interpretation of an ambiguous statute. We review de novo a district court's findings and conclusions regarding the correctness of an agency's statutory interpretations.

The Resource Conservation and Recovery Act (RCRA) permits states to apply to the EPA for authorization to administer and enforce a hazardous waste program. See 42 U.S.C. §6926(b). If authorization is granted, the state's program then operates "in lieu of" the federal government's hazardous waste program. The EPA authorization also allows states to issue and enforce permits for the treatment, storage, and disposal of hazardous wastes. "Any action taken by a State under a hazardous waste program authorized under [the RCRA] [has] the same force and effect as action taken by the [EPA] under this subchapter." 42 U.S.C. §6926(d). Once authorization is granted by the EPA, it cannot be rescinded unless the EPA finds that (1) the state program is not equivalent to the federal program, (2) the state program is not consistent with federal or state programs in other states, or (3) the state program is failing to provide adequate enforcement of compliance in accordance with the requirements of federal law. See 42 U.S.C. §6926(b). Before withdrawing a state's authorization to administer a hazardous waste program, the EPA must hold a public hearing and allow the state a reasonable period of time to correct the perceived deficiency. See 42 U.S.C. §6926(e).

Missouri, like many other states, is authorized to administer and enforce a hazardous waste program pursuant to the RCRA. Despite having authorized a state to act, the EPA frequently files its own enforcement actions against suspected environmental violators even after the commencement of a state-initiated enforcement action. See Bryan S. Miller, Harmonizing RCRA's Enforcement Provisions: RCRA Overfiling in Light of Harmon Industries v. Browner, 5 Environmental Law. 585 (1999). The EPA's process of duplicating enforcement actions is known as overfiling. The permissibility of overfiling apparently is a question of first impression in the federal circuit courts. After examining this apparent issue of first impression, the district court concluded that the plain language of section 6926(b) dictates that the state program operate "in lieu" of the federal program and with the "same force and effect" as EPA action. Accordingly, the district court found that, in this case, the RCRA precludes the EPA from assessing its own penalty against Harmon.

The EPA contends that the district court's interpretation runs contrary to the plain language of the RCRA. Specifically, the EPA cites section 6928 of the RCRA, which states that:

(1) Except as provided in paragraph (2), whenever on the basis of any information the [EPA] determines that any person has violated or is in violation of any requirement of this subchapter, the [EPA] may issue an order assessing a civil penalty for any past or current violation, requiring compliance immediately or within a specified time period, or both, or the [EPA] may commence a civil action in the United States district court in the district in which the violation occurred for appropriate relief, including a temporary or permanent injunction.

(2) In the case of a violation of any requirement of [the RCRA] where such violation occurs in a State which is authorized to carry out a hazardous waste program under section 6926 of this title, the [EPA] shall give notice to the State in which such violation has occurred prior to issuing an order or commencing a civil action under this section. [42 U.S.C. §6928(a)(1) and (2).]

The EPA argues that the plain language of section 6928 allows the federal agency to initiate an enforcement action against an environmental violator even in states that have received authorization pursuant to the RCRA. The EPA contends that Harmon and the district court misinterpreted the phrases "in lieu of" and "same force and effect" as contained in the RCRA. According to the EPA, the phrase "in lieu of" refers to which regulations are to be enforced in an authorized state rather than who is responsible for enforcing the regulations. The EPA argues that the phrase "same force and effect" refers only to the effect of state issued permits. The EPA contends that the RCRA, taken as a whole, authorizes either the state or the EPA to enforce the state's regulations, which are in compliance with the regulations of the EPA. The only requirement, according to the EPA, is that the EPA notify the state in writing if it intends to initiate an enforcement action against an alleged violator.

Both parties argue that the plain language of the RCRA supports their interpretation of the statute. We also are ever mindful of the long-established plain language rule of statutory interpretation as we inquire into the scope of the EPA's enforcement powers under the RCRA. Such an inquiry requires examining the text of the statute as a whole by considering its context, "object, and policy." Pelofsky v. Wallace, 102 F.3d 350, 353 (8th Cir. 1996).

An examination of the statute as a whole supports the district court's interpretation. The RCRA specifically allows states that have received authorization from the federal government to administer and enforce a program that operates "in lieu of" the EPA's regulatory program. 42 U.S.C. §6926(b). While the EPA is correct that the "in lieu of" language refers to the program itself, the administration and enforcement of the program are inexorably intertwined.

The RCRA gives authority to the states to create and implement their own hazardous waste program. The plain "in lieu of" language contained in the RCRA reveals a congressional intent for an authorized state program to supplant the federal hazardous waste program in all respects including enforcement. Congressional intent is evinced within the authorization language of section 6926(b) of the RCRA. Specifically, the statute permits the EPA to repeal a state's authorization if the state's program "does not provide adequate enforcement of compliance with the requirements of" the RCRA. Id. This language indicates that Congress intended to grant states the primary role of enforcing their own hazardous waste program. Such an indication is not undermined, as the EPA suggests, by the language of section 6928. Again, section 6928(a)(1) allows the EPA to initiate enforcement actions against suspected environmental violators, except as provided in section 6928(a)(2). Section 6928(a)(2) permits the EPA to enforce the hazardous waste laws contained in the RCRA if the agency gives written notice to the state. Section 6928(a)(1) and (2), however, must be interpreted within the context of the entire Act. Harmonizing the section 6928(a)(1) and (2) language that allows the EPA to bring an enforcement action in certain circumstances with section 6926(b)'s provision that the EPA has the right to withdraw state authorization if the state's enforcement is inadequate manifests a congressional intent to give the EPA a secondary enforcement right in those cases where a state has been authorized to act that is triggered only after state authorization is rescinded or if the state fails to initiate an enforcement action. Rather than serving as an affirmative grant of federal enforcement power as the EPA suggests, we conclude that the notice requirement of section 6928(a)(2) reinforces the primacy of a state's enforcement rights under RCRA. Taken in the context of the statute as a whole, the notice requirement operates as a means to allow a state the first chance opportunity to initiate the statutorily permitted enforcement action. If the state fails to initiate any action, then the EPA may institute its own action. Thus, the notice requirement is an indicator of the fact that Congress intended to give states, that are authorized to act, the lead role in enforcement under RCRA.

The "same force and effect" language of section 6926(d) provides additional support for the primacy of states' enforcement rights under the RCRA when the EPA has authorized a state to act in lieu of it. The EPA argues that the "same force and effect" language is limited to state permits because the words appear under a heading that reads: "Effect of State Permit." The EPA contends that the "same force and effect" language indicates only that state-issued permits will have the same force and effect as permits issued by the federal government. The EPA claims that the district court was incorrect when it applied the "same force and effect" language to encompass the statute's enforcement mechanism. We disagree.

Regardless of the title or heading, the plain language of section 6926(d) states that "[a]ny action taken by a State under a hazardous waste program authorized under this section shall have the same force and effect as action taken by the [EPA] under this subchapter." 42 U.S.C. §6926(d). In this context, the meaning of the text is plain and obvious. "Any action" under this provision broadly applies to any action authorized by the subchapter, and this language is not limited to the issuance of permits. The state authorization provision substitutes state action (not excluding enforcement action) for federal action. It would be incongruous to conclude that the RCRA authorizes states to implement and administer a hazardous waste program "in lieu of" the federal program where only the issuance of permits is accorded the same force and effect as an action taken by the federal government. Contrary to the EPA's assertions, the statute specifically provides that a "[s]tate is authorized to carry out [its hazardous waste program] in lieu of the Federal program . . . and to issue and enforce permits." 42 U.S.C. §6926(b). Issuance and enforcement are two of the functions authorized as part of the state's hazardous waste enforcement program under the RCRA. Nothing in the statute suggests that the "same force and effect" language is limited to the issuance of permits but not their enforcement. We believe that if Congress had intended such a peculiar result, it would have stated its preference in a clear and unambiguous manner. Absent such an unambiguous directive, we will apply a common sense meaning to the text of the statute and interpret its provisions in a manner logically consistent with the Act as whole.

Utilizing a sort of reverse plain language argument, the EPA contends that its approach is logically consistent with the framework of the RCRA. The EPA cites the statute's citizen suit provision for the proposition that limitations on a part[y]'s right to act are expressly stated within the statute itself. See 42 U.S.C. §6972(b)(1)(B). Section 6972(b)(1)(B), provides that "if the [EPA] or State has commenced and is diligently prosecuting a civil or criminal action in a court of the United States or a State," then a private citizen suit is not permitted. Id. The EPA argues that if Congress had intended to limit the EPA's right to file an enforcement action, it would have expressly stated its intention as it did in the citizen suit context. We find the EPA's argument unpersuasive. Section 6972(b)(1)(B) of the RCRA provides the parameters for private litigation. In the course of providing such parameters, Congress apparently found it necessary to delineate exactly when and how a private citizen may initiate a civil action against an alleged environmental violator. In contrast, section 6926 of the RCRA addresses the interplay between federal and state authorization. Section 6926 also contains express language that establishes the primacy of states' enforcement rights once the EPA has granted a state authorization. The mere fact that Congress did not choose to employ the exact same language as contained in an unrelated part of the act does not detract from the plain language used in the state authorization section. Again, Congress provided that the state's program should operate in lieu of the federal program and that the state action should operate with the same force and effect as action taken by the EPA. See 42 U.S.C. §6926(b) and (d). We find the language contained in the state authorization section of the Act to be as unambiguous as the citizen suit provision. In fact, we find it revealing that, under the citizen suit provision, Congress chose to forbid a private citizen from acting if the EPA or a state was diligently pursuing a civil action. See 42 U.S.C. §6972(b)(1)(B). Utilizing the same reverse plain language argument, one can assume that if Congress intended to allow the federal government and the states to initiate competing enforcement actions, it would have chosen the words "and/or" rather than simply "or." The word "or" indicates that Congress did not contemplate competing enforcement actions between the federal government and the states. Thus, when the EPA has authorized a state program, the plain language of the text indicates that primary enforcement powers are vested in the states. See 42 U.S.C. §6926.

Even assuming some ambiguity exists in the statutory language, the primacy of the states' enforcement rights, once the EPA has authorized a state to act, is illustrated further through the RCRA's legislative history. The United States House of Representatives stated after its hearings that, through the RCRA, it intended to vest primary enforcement authority in the states. See H.R. Rep. 1491, 94th Cong., 2nd Sess. 24, reprinted in 1976 U.S.C.C.A.N. 6262 ("It is the Committee's intention that the States are to have primary enforcement authority and if at any time a State wishes to take over the hazardous waste program it is permitted to do so, provided that the State laws meet the Federal minimum requirements for both administering and enforcing the law"). The House Report states that although the "legislation permits the states to take the lead in the enforcement of the hazardous wastes [sic] laws[,] . . . the Administrator [of the EPA] is not prohibited from acting in those cases where the state fails to act, or from withdrawing approval of the state hazardous waste plan and implementing the federal hazardous waste program pursuant to . . . this act." 1976 U.S.C.C.A.N. 6269. The House Report also states that the EPA, "after giving the appropriate notice to a state that is authorized to implement the state hazardous waste program, that violations of this Act are occurring and the state [is] failing to take action against such violations, is authorized to take appropriate action against those persons in such state not in compliance with the hazardous waste title." Id. at 6270. The House Report thus supports our interpretation of the statute—that the federal government's right to pursue an enforcement action under the RCRA attaches only when a state's authorization is revoked or when a state fails to initiate any enforcement action.

There is no support either in the text of the statute or the legislative history for the proposition that the EPA is allowed to duplicate a state's enforcement authority with its own enforcement action. The EPA argues that the statute and legislative history support its contention that it may initiate an enforcement action if it deems the state's enforcement action inadequate. The EPA's argument misses the point. Without question, the EPA can initiate an enforcement action if it deems the state's enforcement action inadequate. Before initiating such an action, however, the EPA must allow the state an opportunity to correct its deficiency and the EPA must withdraw its authorization. See 42 U.S.C. §6926(b) and (e). Consistent with the text of the statute and its legislative history, the EPA also may initiate an enforcement action after providing written notice to the state when the authorized state fails to initiate any enforcement action. See 42 U.S.C. §6928(a)(2). The EPA may not, however, simply fill the perceived gaps it sees in a state's enforcement action by initiating a second enforcement action without allowing the state an opportunity to correct the deficiency and then withdrawing the state's authorization.

A contrary interpretation would result in two separate enforcement actions. Such an interpretation, as explained above, would derogate the RCRA's plain language and legislative history. Companies that reach an agreement through negotiations with a state authorized by the EPA to act in its place may find the agreement undermined by a later separate enforcement action by the EPA. While, generally speaking, two separate sovereigns can institute two separate enforcement actions, those actions can cause vastly different and potentially contradictory results. Such a potential schism runs afoul of the principles of comity and federalism so clearly embedded in the text and history of the RCRA. When enacting the RCRA, Congress intended to delegate the primary enforcement of EPA-approved hazardous waste programs to the states. In fact, as we have noted above, the states' enforcement action has the "same force and effect as an action taken by" the EPA. See 42 U.S.C. §6926(d). In EPA authorized states, the EPA's action is an alternative method of enforcement that is permitted to operate only when certain conditions are satisfied. See 42 U.S.C. §6926(b) and (e); 42 U.S.C. §6928(b). The EPA's interpretation simply is not consistent with the plain language of the statute, its legislative history, or its declared purpose. Hence, it is also an unreasonable interpretation to which we accord no deference. Therefore, we find that the EPA's practice of overfiling, in those states where it has authorized the state to act, oversteps the federal agency's authority under the RCRA.

B. RES JUDICATA

As an alternative basis to support its grant of summary judgment, the district court concluded that principles of res judicata also bar the EPA's enforcement action by reason of the Missouri state court consent decree. The EPA argues that the state court judgment has no effect on its enforcement action against Harmon because the two actions lack the elements essential for a finding of res judicata. We review de novo a district court's summary judgment determinations.

Principles of res judicata embodied in the Full Faith and Credit Act, 28 U.S.C. §1738 (1982), see also U.S. Const. art. 4, §1, require federal courts to give preclusive effect to the judgments of state courts whenever the state court from which the judgment emerged would give such an effect. See Hickman v. Electronic Keyboarding, Inc., 741 F.3d 230, 232 (8th Cir. 1984). In this case, we must determine whether Missouri law would give res judicata effect to the consent decree entered between Harmon and the MDNR in Missouri state court.

In Missouri, res judicata requires "(1) [i]dentity of the thing sued for; (2) identity of the cause of action; (3) identity of the persons and parties to the action; and (4) identity of the quality of the person for or against whom the claim is made." Prentzler v. Schneider, 411 S.W.2d 135, 138 (Mo. 1966) (en banc).

In this case, the four Missouri law res judicata requirements are satisfied. In both the state court action and the EPA administrative enforcement action, the parties sought to enforce a hazardous waste program pursuant to the RCRA. In both the state action and the agency action, the complaints named Harmon as the defendant. In addition, both actions involved the enforcement of regulations based upon identical facts and legal principles. The only dispute is whether the parties are identical.

A party is identical when it is the same party that litigated a prior suit or when a new party is in privity with a party that litigated a prior suit. See United States v. Gurley, 43 F.3d 1188, 1197 (8th Cir. 1994). Privity exists when two parties to two separate suits have "a close relationship bordering on near identity." Id. As the United States and the State of Missouri are not the same party, we must resolve whether their relationship in the enforcement action is nearly identical.

The statutory language of the RCRA provides the framework for the party identity analysis. Pursuant to 42 U.S.C. §6926(b), the federal program operates "in lieu of" the state program. Section 6926(d) of the same statute mandates that "[a]ny action taken by a State under a hazardous waste program authorized under this section shall have the same force and effect as action taken by the [EPA] under this subchapter." 42 U.S.C. §6926(d). As we determined in Part II(A) of this opinion, the plain language of the RCRA permits the State of Missouri to act in lieu of the EPA. When such a situation occurs, Missouri's action has the same force and effect as an action initiated by the EPA. Accordingly, the two parties stand in the same relationship to one another. The EPA argues that it has enforcement interests sufficiently distinct from the interests of the State of Missouri. We explained in *Hickman*, however, that privity under Missouri law is satisfied when the two parties represent the same legal right. As the district court correctly indicated, privity is not dependent upon the subjective interests of the individual parties. In this case, the State of Missouri advanced the exact same legal right under the statute as the EPA did in its administrative action. Accordingly, the identity of the parties requirement is satisfied.

The EPA contends that even if principles of res judicata are satisfied under Missouri law, the doctrine of sovereign immunity precludes applying res judicata to the United States unless the United States was the actual party in the prior lawsuit. Before addressing the merits of the EPA's claim, we note that the EPA did not raise the sovereign immunity defense before the district court. Harmon argues that in failing to raise the issue at the district court level, the EPA has waived its right to assert sovereign immunity on appeal. Sovereign immunity, however, is a jurisdictional threshold matter and it is well-established that questions of subject matter jurisdiction can be raised for the first time on appeal. See DeWitt Bank & Trust Co. v. United States, 878 F.2d 246 (8th Cir. 1989).

Turning to the merits of the EPA's sovereign immunity defense, we conclude that the defense is forestalled by the United States Supreme Court's decision in Montana v. United States, Id. 147 (1979). In *Montana*, the Supreme Court held that "one who prosecutes or defends a suit in the name of another to establish and protect his own right is as much bound as he would be if he had been a party to the record." 440 U.S. at 154). The Court found in *Montana* that although the United States was not a party to a prior suit, it "had a sufficient laboring oar in the conduct of the state-court litigation to actuate principles of estoppel." Id. at 155. The EPA argues that it had no laboring oar in the State of Missouri's enforcement action. Such an argument ignores the RCRA. Unlike the present case, *Montana* did not involve a statute that authorized the state to proceed "in lieu of" the federal government and "with the same force and effect" as the federal government. In *Montana*, the United States controlled the details of the prior suit directly. In RCRA cases, however, the federal government authorizes the state to act in its place. It cedes its authority to the state pursuant to the authorization plan contained in the statute. See 42 U.S.C. §6926(b). The "laboring oar" is pulled on much earlier in the process. It occurs at the authorization stage when the EPA grants the state permission to enforce the EPA's interests through the state's own hazardous waste program. After authorization, the state "prosecutes" enforcement actions "in lieu of" the federal government and operates as if it were the EPA. See 42 U.S.C. §6926(b) and (d). Hence, pursuant to *Montana*, the United States must be bound by prior judgments involving state action as authorized by the RCRA. See also United States v. County of Cook, Illinois, 167 F.3d 381, 389 (7th Cir. 1999) (questioning when sovereign immunity to claim preclusion exists); United States v. ITT Rayonier, Inc., 627 F.2d 996, 1002 (9th Cir. 1980) (applying res judicata against the EPA). Accordingly, we find that principles of res judicata as defined by Missouri law foreclose the EPA's enforcement action against Harmon. . . .

III. Conclusion

For the reasons stated herein, we affirm the judgment of the district court.

NOTES AND QUESTIONS ABOUT THE ACTORS IN ENVIRONMENTAL ENFORCEMENT AND COMPLIANCE

1. *Some Courts Have Disagreed with* Harmon's *Interpretation of RCRA.* In United States v. Power Eng'g Co., 303 F.3d 1232 (10th Cir. 2002), the United States filed a civil enforcement action against a metal refinishing/chrome electroplating business after Colorado had issued an administrative compliance order and an administrative civil penalty order for the same RCRA violations. The Tenth Circuit held that RCRA did not preclude the federal enforcement action, disagreeing with the Eighth Circuit in its reading of several key RCRA provisions. The court, finding the statute to be ambiguous, deferred to EPA's view that EPA's authorization of a state permit program does not deprive the federal agency of its enforcement powers. The court also held that the federal enforcement action was not barred by res judicata because the federal and state governments were separate parties and therefore not in privity for res judicata purposes. Similarly, in United States v. Murphy Oil USA, Inc., 143 F. Supp. 2d 1054 (W.D. Wis. 2001), the court declined to adopt *Harmon*'s conclusion

that giving the states authority to implement and enforce RCRA's hazardous waste program affords the states the sole right to enforce the statute unless EPA withdraws a state's authorization or the state fails to take any enforcement action. The court found that *Harmon* "rested on a flawed interpretation" of §3006(b) and that the structure of RCRA suggests that the administration and enforcement of state regulations are not "inextricably intertwined." Id. at 1116. The court held that RCRA authorizes the federal government to bring enforcement action in states authorized to implement and enforce the hazardous waste program, "provided only that notice is given to the state." Id. at 1117.

2. *Do Different Environmental Statutes Treat "Overfiling" Differently?* Other courts have distinguished *Harmon* and declined to follow it in addressing overfiling under other statutes, such as the Clean Air and Clean Water Acts, on the ground that the statutory language is different. See United States v. Murphy Oil USA, Inc., 143 F. Supp. 2d 1054, 1090-1092 (W.D. Wis. 2001); United States v. LTV Steel Co., 118 F. Supp. 2d 827 (N.D. Ohio 2000); United States v. City of Youngstown, 109 F. Supp. 2d 739 (N.D. Ohio 2000). What is the key language in RCRA §3006 governing the permissibility of "overfiling" by EPA? What is the key language of §3008? What is the key language in the Clean Air and Clean Water Acts? Does this difference in statutory language provide a basis for limiting *Harmon*'s holding concerning the validity of federal overfilings to RCRA?

3. *State Overfiling?* While rare as far as we know, there also is the possibility of a state engaging in its own version of overfiling activity—that is, filing suit after EPA has done so. Suppose, for example, that EPA recovers a penalty under a CWA civil enforcement action from a defendant that violated the terms of a permit issued by a state that EPA has authorized to administer the NPDES permit program. May the state, having declined to participate in the federal enforcement action, pursue its own enforcement action for the same violations? See State Water Control Bd. v. Smithfield Foods, Inc., 542 S.E.2d 766 (Va. 2001) (finding privity between the State Board and EPA under the facts of that case and stating that privity does not require that the parties have a shared subjective intent).

4. What strategies should federal and state enforcement authorities use to foster coordination in the enforcement arena? For a 2003 government initiative, see U.S. DOJ and National Association of Attorneys General, Guidelines for Joint State/Federal Civil Environmental Enforcement Litigation (March 2003).

5. *The Role of Citizen Suits.* Because the major environmental laws allow citizens to file citizen suits as "private attorneys general," numerous questions have arisen concerning the role of such suits vis-à-vis state and/or federal enforcement actions involving the same alleged violator. The Supreme Court in *Gwaltney* (excerpted in section C below) characterized the role of citizen suits as "to supplement rather than to supplant governmental action." Why is supplementation of government enforcement desirable? Professor Plater has argued that the pressures placed on enforcement officials are too substantial to justify exclusive reliance on them as "watchdogs [to] protect us all from marketplace excesses. The backstop enforcement [under the citizen suit provisions] has been a vital credibility factor that drives the bureaucracy's implementation of the law." Plater, The Embattled Social Utilities of the Endangered Species Act—A Noah Presumption and Caution against Putting Gasmasks on the Canaries in the Coalmine, 27 Envtl. L. 845, 871-872 (1997). The Senate Report cited by the Court in *Gwaltney* stated that citizen suits "perform[] a public service." S. Rep. No. 92-414, *supra*, 1972 U.S.C.C.A.N. at 3747. But the benefits of citizen

enforcement sometimes come with a price. In Hallstrom v. Tillamook County, 493 U.S. 20, 29 (1989), the Court acknowledged the tension between Congress's desire to "encourag[e] citizen enforcement of environmental regulations and [its desire to avoid] burdening the federal courts with excessive numbers of citizen suits." Further, as the Court suggested in *Gwaltney*, citizen suits may undermine government discretion in addressing violations and thereby undercut government's ability to use its entire arsenal of tools to produce results it believes will best promote compliance and desired environmental results. Section C below reviews the issues that have emerged as this tension has played out in the courts.

6. Because the shape of our cooperative federalism approach has changed dramatically in recent years, so that states now perform a very substantial majority of environmental work, the performance of the states in conducting such enforcement, and of EPA in overseeing it, is quite important in evaluating the effectiveness of the nation's environmental enforcement efforts. The state-federal relationship in enforcement has received considerable attention over the years, much of it critical. In addition to several EPA Office of Inspector General reports, the GAO has issued a series of evaluations of the relationship and of enforcement-related performance. It concluded in 1995 that, due in large part to lack of funding, states have had difficulty performing key enforcement functions. The GAO has noted that the relationship is tense and has identified several contributing factors, including states' concerns that EPA acts inconsistently in its oversight across regions, sometimes micromanages state programs, fails to provide sufficient technical support, and often does not adequately consult states before making key decisions affecting them.*

7. Not all environmental statutes use a "cooperative federalism" approach. Fischman & Hall-Rivera, A Lesson for Conservation from Pollution Control Law: Cooperative Federalism for Recovery under the Endangered Species Act, 27 Colum. J. Envtl. L. 45 (2002), assess whether the ESA should move in this direction.

8. There has been a substantial amount of debate in recent years about the theoretical underpinnings of the decision to "federalize" environmental law. Professor Richard Revesz has authored a series of articles that have played an important role in raising such questions, including: Revesz, Rehabilitating Interstate Competition: Rethinking the "Race-to-the-Bottom" Rationale for Federal Environmental Regulation, 67 N.Y.U. L. Rev. 1210 (1992); Revesz, Federalism and Interstate Environmental Externalities, 144 U. Pa. L. Rev. 2341 (1996); and Revesz, Federalism and Environmental Regulation: A Public Choice Analysis, 115 Harv. L. Rev. 553 (2001). Rechtschaffen & Markell, *supra*, review the scholarship pro and con on these issues, as well as some of the constitutional doctrines that have the potential to influence the shape of our cooperative federalism approach. We cover these issues in more detail in Chapter 2.

*U.S. GAO, EPA and the States—Environmental Challenges Require a Better Working Relationship, GAO/RCED 95-64 (Apr. 3, 1995), available at http://archive.gao.gov/t2pbatl/154202.pdf. For further discussion of the relationship between state and federal enforcement, see generally Hodas, Enforcement of Environmental Law in a Triangular Federal System: Can There Not Be a Crowd When Enforcement Authority Is Shared by the United States, the States, and Their Citizens?, 54 Md. L. Rev. 1552 (1995); Rechtschaffen & Markell, Reinventing Environmental Enforcement & the State/Federal Relationship, (2003); Markell, The Role of Deterrence-Based Enforcement in a "Reinvented" State/Federal Relationship: The Divide between Theory and Reality, 24 Harv. Envtl. L. Rev. 1 (2000).

C. THE LEGAL AUTHORITIES

What legal authorities influence how the actors approach their responsibilities or opportunities in the enforcement and compliance arena? Our focus here is primarily on the authorities in the major environmental laws. Each of these laws contains one or more enforcement provisions—provisions that, perhaps most significantly: (1) empower government officials to monitor compliance with environmental requirements (via inspections, self-reporting, etc.), and (2) authorize the government to pursue administrative, civil, and/or criminal enforcement in appropriate instances. Many of these laws also contain provisions that authorize citizens to bring legal action in some circumstances. Following our coverage of statutory authorities, we cover the common law doctrines of public and private nuisance briefly.

1. The Government's Information-Gathering Authority

The capacity to monitor compliance is a critical element of our nation's environmental regulatory scheme. EPA's enabling statutes give the agency several tools for performing this responsibility, including the authority to require regulated parties to monitor their own performance and the power to review compliance itself, as Figure 10-4 reflects.

The government may demand that regulated entities keep records, install and use specified monitoring equipment, take samples, and submit reports. The best-known of the self-reporting approaches are the CWA's discharge monitoring reports (DMRs). These reports track a party's permitted limits and its actual performance in light of those limits. In many cases, the DMRs on their face reveal whether a regulated party is operating in compliance with its obligations under a permit. Regulated parties must submit these reports to the government. DMRs also are accessible to citizens, and citizens have used them in many cases as the basis for filing citizen suits under the Clean Water Act against the submitters. The *Gwaltney* case, excerpted below, is an example. Congress's 1990 Amendments to the Clean Air Act contain a similar self-reporting requirement that is modeled after the Clean Water Act DMRs. See Van Cleve & Holman, Promise and Reality in the Enforcement of the Amended Clean Air Act, Part I: EPA's "Any Credible Evidence" and "Compliance Assurance Monitoring" Rules, 27 Envtl. L. Rep. (ELI) 10097 (1997). Congress, also in the 1990 Clean Air Act Amendments, mandates that certain sources of air pollution install continuous emissions monitoring (CEM) systems or their equivalent. CAA §412(a); Reitze & Schell, Self-Monitoring and Self-Reporting of Routine Air Pollution Releases, 24 Colum. J. Envtl. L. 63, 107 (1999).

Congress has been fairly creative with some of the tools it has created to encourage identification of violations. It has adopted both bounty provisions (that reward individuals who provide information) and whistleblower provisions (that are intended to protect individuals who do so from retribution from the regulated party). See, e.g., CAA §113(f) and CWA §507, respectively; Knox v. United States Dep't of Labor, 434 F.3d 721 (4th Cir. 2006).

EPA's enabling legislation typically empowers EPA to enter regulated premises, copy records, inspect monitoring equipment, and take samples of its own, in addition to requiring regulated parties to track their own performance, as Figure 10-4 indicates.

CWA	CAA	CERCLA	RCRA
§308(a)(A). Empowers EPA to require the operator of a point source to sample, file reports, and maintain records. §308(a)(B). Authorizes EPA inspections.	§114. Recordkeeping, Inspections, Monitoring and Entry: Requires owners/operators of emission sources to monitor emissions, keep records, and provide reports. Gives the Administrator a right of entry to these facilities for inspection purposes.	§104(e). Information Gathering and Access: Authorizes the president and his employees to access information and investigate facilities where hazardous substances may be stored, released, or threatened to be released.	§3007. Inspections: Authorizes EPA inspection of facilities where hazardous wastes are or have been generated, stored, treated, disposed of, or transported from. §3013. Monitoring, Analysis, and Testing: Authorizes the Administrator to investigate if hazardous waste is discovered that may present a substantial threat to public safety.

FIGURE 10-4
Selected Information-Gathering Authorities

Inspections have been characterized as the "backbone" of EPA's compliance monitoring efforts. Reitze & Holmes, Inspections Under the Clean Air Act, 1 The Envtl. Law. 29, 36 (1994). Professor Reitze summarizes EPA's goals for its inspections efforts as follows:

(1) Assess compliance status and verify proper self-monitoring and reporting;
(2) Detect and document violations and obtain evidence to support enforcement actions;
(3) Identify environmental problems and provide information on compliance patterns in the regulated community;
(4) Perform an oversight function when done by EPA and/or the state reviewing the effectiveness of programs delegated to a state;
(5) Provide data on the adequacy of programs and the need for additional control;
(6) Promote compliance through information and technology transfer communicated by inspectors;
(7) Provide data to support the issuance of permits;
(8) Provide government agency employees experience and familiarity with industrial processes and facilities;
(9) Make the source aware of any problems;
(10) Deter violations; and
(11) Determine whether compliance orders have been obeyed.

The size of the regulated community far outstrips governments' ability to engage in meaningful monitoring of a significant percentage of regulated parties. Former

	FY99	FY00	FY01	FY02	FY03	FY04	FY05
CAA Stationary	1,406	1,284	1,046	440*	491*	409*	1,745
CAA CFCs	1,227	579	122	265	255	255	195
CAA Mobile Source	39	34	8	6	3	801	266
Asbestos D & R	437	151	325	98	270	276	209
NPDES Minors	965	1,141	876	1044	1221	1348	1386
NPDES Majors	949	640	758	871	565	645	512
Pretreatment IUS	0	277	273	94	164	158	NR
Pretreatment POTWs	0	115	134	115	90	135	140
CWA 311	1,424	1,549	1,269	786	1141	969	1159
CWA 404	1,079	964	699	643	558	471	453
EPCRA 313	513	472	321	267	262	298	244
EPCRA non-313	521	1,366	613	466	725	672	661
FIFRA	259	799	858	810	338	472	215
RCRA-HW	2,214	1,746	1,521	1,400	1,643	1,627	1,552
RCRA-UST	1,482	1,185	1,259	1,080	1,327	1,415	1,216
SDWA-PWSS	449	488	362	327	228	358	355
SDWA-UIC	6,880	6,227	5,663	6,218	7,190	8,143	8,416
TSCA	2,003	1,400	1,453	2,738	2,376	1,792	1,611
TOTAL	21,847	20,417	17,560	17,668	18,877	20,244	20,335

Source: EPA, National Enforcement Trends—FY 2005, http://cfpub.epa.gov/compliance/resources/reports/nets/index.cfm.

FIGURE 10-5
EPA Regional Inspections*

*EPA notes that "the drop in CAA EPA inspection count is due, at least in part, to implementation in that year of a new CAA Compliance Monitoring Strategy (CMS), which changed the definition of a CAA inspection."

EPA enforcement official Eric Schaeffer noted in 1996 that "[b]y one estimate, at least 700,000 facilities are subject to one or more federal environmental laws, while the federal government and states together conduct fewer than 100,000 inspections per year."** EPA itself conducts roughly 20,000 annual inspections, as Figure 10-5 reflects (the states conduct the vast majority of government inspections).

The resulting reliance on regulated-party self-monitoring has raised concerns about the credibility and reliability of the data produced through such efforts. See, e.g., U.S. GAO, Environmental Enforcement: EPA Cannot Ensure the Accuracy of Self-Reported Compliance Data (1993).

Government inspection efforts have not fared especially well under scrutiny either. In addition to concerns that not enough inspections are being done, the GAO and OIG have concluded that in some cases the quality of inspections performed is not adequate to evaluate compliance effectively. They also have found

**Schaeffer, Encouraging Voluntary Compliance without Compromising Enforcement: EPA's 1995 Auditing Policy, in Conference Proceedings, Fourth International Conference on Environmental Compliance and Enforcement 451, 453 (1996).

that, for numerous reasons, data from inspections are not being reported accurately or in a timely way.* In 1999, EPA established its Office of Environmental Information as a way to improve the management of data. See http://www.epa.gov.oei. In 2002, EPA published its Guidelines for Ensuring and Maximizing the Quality, Objectivity, Utility, and Integrity of Information Disseminated by the Environmental Protection Agency (Oct. 2002), available at http://www.epa.gov/quality/informationguidelines/documents/EPA_InfoQualityGuidelines.pdf. Data-related issues have been a long-standing challenge, and it remains to be seen how effective OEI and others will be in addressing some of the critical deficiencies that exist in EPA's management of data.

Credible data about levels of compliance, numbers of inspections, and the like are obviously critical to the effort to promote compliance with the law and to understand the effect of such efforts. Because of the institutional challenges described above, however, the gap between goal and reality in this area means that our understanding of the state of compliance with environmental requirements is less than complete, at best. As one longtime EPA attorney put it, "there is . . . an obvious need for completely accurate and timely compliance data—something which EPA and the states cannot currently assure." Mugdan, Federal Environmental Enforcement in EPA Region 2, 10 Envtl. L. N.Y. 49, 63 (1999). A December 2005 EPA Office of Inspector General Report concludes that, because of data and other issues, EPA "does not know if compliance is actually going up or down."**

NOTES AND QUESTIONS ABOUT EPA'S INFORMATION-GATHERING AUTHORITIES

1. *The Fourth Amendment.* In many situations EPA needs a warrant before it may legally conduct an inspection without a regulated party's consent, but the Supreme Court noted in Marshall v. Barlow's, Inc., 436 U.S. 307, 320-321 (1978), that "[p]robable cause in the criminal sense is not required" for an administrative warrant. Instead, the government must show either that reasonable suspicion of a violation exists or that it desires to enter the premises as part of a neutral inspection scheme. Warrants are not needed under certain circumstances, including if the regulated party consents, if an emergency exists, or if the "open field" doctrine applies. In Dow Chem. Co. v. United States, 476 U.S. 227 (1986), EPA made an in-plant inspection of Dow's 2,080-acre Michigan plant to check for air quality violations. The agency decided that a second inspection was necessary and informed Dow that it intended to take aerial photographs of the facility; Dow objected. Rather than obtain a civil search warrant, EPA contracted with a private concern to take sophisticated photographs of the facility. Dow sued, claiming that EPA lacked the authority under §114 of the CAA to engage in site inspections by aerial photography and that, even if it had that authority, the flight and the photographs constituted an unreasonable search of its property in violation of the Fourth Amendment. The Supreme Court held that EPA's statutory "right of entry to,

*See, e.g., U.S. GAO, Improved Inspections and Enforcement Would Ensure Safer Underground Storage Tanks (May 8, 2002); EPA OIG, Water Enforcement: State Enforcement of Clean Water Act Dischargers Can Be More Effective, Report No. 2001-P-00013, 23-24, 27 (Aug. 2001); EPA OIG Audit Report, Enforcement: Compliance with Enforcement Instruments, Report No. 2001-P-00006 (Mar. 29, 2001).

**EPA, OIG, EPA Performance Measures Do Not Effectively Track Compliance Outcomes, Report No. 2006-P-00006 11 (Dec. 15, 2005), available at www.epa.gov/oig/reports/2006/20051215-2006-P-00006.pdf.

upon, or through any premises" was broad enough to encompass the use of aerial photography. The Court also held that, although Dow had a legitimate expectation of privacy within the interior of its covered buildings, the open areas of the plant did not qualify as a "curtilage" area entitled to protection as a place where the occupants have such an expectation. Instead, the complex was more like an open field, the owner of which is not entitled to an expectation of privacy for activities engaged in there. See generally Tillitt, Note, The Open Fields Doctrine: New Limitations on Environmental Surveillance, 17 Va. Envtl. L.J. 245 (1998).

2. *The Fifth Amendment.* The obligation to maintain and disclose records has been upheld in the context of challenges under the Fourth and Fifth Amendments. Courts have required regulated parties to disclose information even in situations where such records may prove to be self-incriminating. Marchetti v. United States, 390 U.S. 39, 55-57 (1968); United States v. Ward, 448 U.S. 242, 255 (1980).

3. *Takings.* The Takings Clause has been invoked in connection with government efforts to enter onto property. In Hendler v. United States, 175 F.3d 1374 (Fed. Cir. 1999), EPA installed and operated groundwater monitoring wells on private property in an attempt to mitigate the adverse effects of groundwater pollution originating on an adjacent hazardous waste site. The Federal Circuit concluded that the property owners were entitled to no damages, holding that the decline in value suffered by the property owners on the portion of their land that suffered a partial physical taking was more than offset by special benefits conferred by the government's cleanup actions, in the form of the elimination of a need for the property owners to engage in a Phase Two investigation of the extent of contamination on its property. The court also affirmed the trial court's conclusion that the retained property suffered no severe damage. Compare Scogin v. United States, 33 Fed. Cl. 568 (1995), where the court held that the government's intermittent use of plaintiff's mooring facility for several weeks to load and unload cleanup equipment was not a taking, that a lease allowing a government contractor to use plaintiff's land in a more substantial manner for remedial purposes after a federal district court ordered him to allow government access was without the plaintiff's consent and therefore did not preclude a taking, and that further proceedings were necessary to determine whether the rental received constituted just compensation. See also Boise Cascade Corp. v. United States, 296 F.3d 1339 (Fed. Cir. 2002) (involving alleged taking under the Endangered Species Act); McKay v. United States, 199 F.3d 1376 (Fed. Cir. 1999).

4. *FOIA as an Information-Gathering Tool.* Much of the information obtained by the government is available to the public, though there are exceptions to public access contained in FOIA and some of the environmental enabling legislation. See, e.g., Gersh & Danielson v. EPA, 871 F. Supp. 407 (D. Colo. 1994); cf. Doe v. Browner, 902 F. Supp. 1240 (D. Nev. 1995), *aff'd in part, dismissed in part sub nom.* Kasza v. Browner, 133 F.3d 1159 (9th Cir. 1998).

5. For a case involving a claim that the government violated the CAA whistle-blower provision, 42 U.S.C. §7622, by retaliating against an employee who raised concerns about asbestos in the workplace, see Knox v. United States Dep't of Labor, 434 F.3d 721 (4th Cir. 2006).

6. EPA's use of its inspection authorities under CERCLA has been the subject of considerable litigation. The stakes can be high. The Sixth Circuit upheld a $1.9 million civil penalty against a party for failing to respond adequately to an EPA information request under CERCLA §104(e). United States v. Gurley, 384 F.3d 316 (6th Cir. 2004). Suppose that EPA assumes primary responsibility for a removal

action under CERCLA. The agency requests that the owner of the contaminated site provide unconditional access to the agency and its employees for purposes of conducting the cleanup. The site owner responds that EPA may enter the site to undertake the cleanup, but that the owner reserves the right to object on constitutional grounds to the use of any evidence EPA gathers in subsequent criminal proceedings against the owner. The site owner fears that EPA may initiate criminal proceedings under the CAA on the basis of evidence that may become available to it if EPA enters the site. EPA enters the site and completes the cleanup, and then sues the site owner, which it alleges is liable for civil penalties for violating CERCLA's access provisions, §104(e), by refusing to grant unconditional access. Is the site owner liable? See United States v. Omega Chem. Corp., 156 F.3d 994 (9th Cir. 1998). In United States v. Tarkowski, 248 F.3d 596 (7th Cir. 2001), the court affirmed the district court's denial of EPA's request for an order requiring a property owner to allow EPA to enter his property under §104(e) of CERCLA to engage in testing and implement response actions. The district court had found EPA's request for access to be arbitrary and capricious because it was far more extensive than necessary to address the identified threat of contamination, which was minimal. Compare United States v. W.R. Grace & Co., 134 F. Supp. 2d 1182 (D. Mont. 2001) (issuing order allowing EPA immediate access to former vermiculite mining site under §104(e)); United States v. Martin, 30 Envtl. L. Rep. (ELI) 20,756 (N.D. Ill. 2000) (ordering former site owner to respond to EPA request for information under §104(e) because the agency satisfied the "low threshold" of showing a reasonable basis to believe there may be a release or threat of a release at the site under investigation, and imposing a penalty of $75 a day for past noncompliance).

7. Two commentators have examined quite thoroughly many of the issues associated with obtaining information from regulated parties under the CAA, dividing the issues into nine categories: (1) the identity of the inspectors, (2) types of inspections, (3) how inspections are planned, (4) consensual searches, (5) warrants, (6) pre-entry activity, (7) post-entry activities (chain of custody, inspection of records, etc.), (8) liability of government inspectors, and (9) possible responses to an inspection. Reitze & Holmes, Inspections under the Clean Air Act, 1 Envtl. Law. 29 (1994).

8. EPA and the states have undertaken a number of steps to encourage regulated parties to be more proactive in uncovering violations, notifying the government, and correcting them. We discuss EPA's self-audit policy and other such initiatives in section D.

2. The Government's Civil Litigation Authorities

Successful implementation of regulatory controls on activities with the potential to damage the environment ultimately depends on compliance with regulatory requirements. Cohen, Empirical Research on the Deterrent Effect of Environmental Monitoring and Enforcement, 30 Envtl. L. Rep. (ELI) 10245 (2000), reviews the literature on the relationship between enforcement and corporate compliance. The deterrence-based theory underlying EPA's traditional approach to enforcement is that regulated entities lack strong incentives to comply with costly controls in the absence of a credible threat of enforcement. See Hodas, Enforcement of Environmental Law in a Triangular Federal System: Can Three Not Be a Crowd When Enforcement Authority Is Shared by the United States, the States, and Their Citizens?, 54 Md. L. Rev. 1552, 1553-1554 (1995). Compliance is often aided by the knowledge that permit

or standard violations will be subject to enforcement actions. The federal environmental laws contain an array of enforcement choices, including civil and criminal
enforcement options, as Figure 10-6 shows.

Each year EPA provides its penalty recoveries and other key information relating
to its enforcement performance. Figure 10-7 shows the dollar values for EPA enforcement actions in FY 2005.

What enforcement options are available to the federal government? Some statutes contemplate four possible avenues for pursuing alleged violators: (1) the issuance
of administrative compliance orders that set timetables for correcting violations; (2) the
imposition of administrative civil penalties; (3) the initiation of civil litigation in which
the government can request injunctive relief, civil penalty assessments, or both; and
(4) criminal prosecution (which is discussed in the next section). This list can be
misleading, however, because agencies generally view judicial or formal administrative
enforcement proceedings as a last resort. An early empirical study of water pollution
enforcement, W. Irwin et al., The Water Pollution Control Act of 1972, Institutional
Assessment, Enforcement (1975) (2 vols.), found that states prefer graduated enforcement processes that stress cooperation with dischargers and negotiation over technical
and economic feasibility issues, but that EPA took a harder enforcement line.

Administrative Compliance Orders. The CAA's civil enforcement provisions typify the options available to EPA under the pollution control laws, though its provisions
are unusually elaborate. Assuming that EPA has complied with applicable state notification and waiting requirements, it may issue an order requiring compliance with
applicable statutory, regulatory, permit, or SIP provisions. CAA §113(a)(1)(A). Compliance orders must "state with reasonable specificity the nature of the violation and
specify a time for compliance which the Administrator determines is reasonable,
taking into account the seriousness of the violation and any good faith efforts to comply
with applicable requirements." Id. §113(a)(4). Based on concerns that EPA had
abused the discretion this provision afforded it to fashion schedules of compliance,
Congress amended the statute in 1990 to require that compliance with an administrative order be achieved "as expeditiously as practicable, but in no event longer than
one year after the date the order was issued." Id. Administrative compliance orders are
nonrenewable. Id. Figure 10-8 illustrates the number of administrative compliance
orders issued from 1996 to 2005.

Administrative Civil Penalties. Congress added the power to impose civil penalties without judicial intervention to EPA's arsenal relatively late in the game. Under
some of the statutes, such as the CWA and CAA, Congress has started incrementally in
the sense that it has created lower penalty ceilings for administrative enforcement than
it has established for judicial enforcement. Under the CAA, for example, EPA may
issue administrative orders assessing civil penalties of up to $32,500 per day of viola-
tion, provided the total penalty does not exceed $270,000 (with limited exceptions),
while the statute does not create a similar ceiling for penalties obtained through civil
judicial litigation. CAA §113(d)(1).* The Clean Water Act similarly establishes ceilings on penalty amounts recoverable through administrative enforcement that it does
not impose for civil litigation. Compare CWA §1319(g) with CWA §1319(d). RCRA
does not draw such a distinction; EPA may assess administrative or judicial civil
penalties under RCRA of up to $32,500 per day of noncompliance. RCRA

---

*While Congress initially set these limits at $25,000 and $200,000, respectively, the Federal
Civil Penalties Adjustment Act of 1990 requires periodic adjustments to account for inflation. For
the most recent adjustments, see Penalty Adjustment and Table, 40 CFR §19.4 (2005).

	CWA	CAA	RCRA
	§309(a). Compliance orders: Authorizes EPA to issue compliance orders requiring compliance. §309(b) and (d). Civil actions: Authorizes the Administrator to file civil actions for injunctive relief and/or payment of penalties of up to $25,000/day. §309(c). Criminal penalties: Authorizes criminal prosecutions. §309(g). Administrative penalties: Authorizes Class I and Class II administrative enforcement penalties for violations, with ceilings on the total penalty that may be imposed.	§113(b). Civil actions: Authorizes civil enforcement actions, for permanent or temporary injunctive relief, as well as civil penalties up to $25,000/ day. §113(c). Criminal penalties: Authorizes criminal prosecutions. §113(d). Administrative assessment of civil penalties: Authorizes Administrator to issue civil penalties of up to $25,000/day, generally with a ceiling on the total penalty that may be imposed.	§3008(a) and (g). Compliance orders: Authorizes administrator to issue orders assessing civil penalties of up to $25,000 per day of violation and requiring compliance. §3008(d). Criminal penalties: Authorizes criminal prosecutions. §3013. Monitoring, analysis, and testing: Authorizes orders that mandate owners or operators of facilities where hazardous waste is found or released that may cause a substantial threat to public welfare to monitor, test, analyze, and report to ascertain the extent of the hazard. §7003. Imminent hazard: Authorizes actions in situations that may present an imminent and substantial endangerment.

FIGURE 10-6
Selected Enforcement Authorities

	Criminal Penalties Assessed	Civil Judicial Penalties Assessed	Administrative Penalties Assessed	$ Value of Judicial Injunctive Relief	$ Value of Administrative Injunctive Relief
CAA	NR*	$26,908,150	$7,044,700	$2,151,461,500	$17,816,581
CWA	NR	$16,471,404	$7,025,481	$6,449,999,571	$178,231,967
RCRA	NR	$81,937,064	$4,472,345	$2,150,500	$19,905,938
TOTALS	**$100M**	**$125,316,618**	**$18,542,526**	**$8,603,611,571**	**$215,954,486**

*NR = Not Reported

Source: EPA, National Enforcement Trends—FY 2005, http://cfpub.epa.gov/compliance/resources/reports/nets/index.cfm..

FIGURE 10-7
Dollar Value of FY 2005 EPA Enforcement Actions by Statute

	FY96	FY97	FY98	FY99	FY00	FY01	FY02	FY03	FY04	FY05
CAA	154	209	277	298	219	192	144	197	198	187
CWA	504	815	849	621	727	452	546	655	775	843
RCRA	35	44	49	50	42	35	34	31	28	28
TOTAL	693	1,068	1,175	969	988	679	724	883	1,001	1,058

Source: EPA, Annual Report on Enforcement and Compliance Assurance Accomplishments in 1999, p. B-3; EPA, Annual Report on Enforcement and Compliance Assurance Accomplishments in 2001, p. 68; and EPA, National Enforcement Trends—FY 2005, http://cfpub.epa.gov/compliance/resources/reports/nets/index.cfm.

FIGURE 10-8
EPA Administrative Compliance Orders Issued

§3008(a)(3). Figure 10-9 details EPA's use of authority to issue administrative penalty order complaints over the past decade.

Administrative civil penalties generally may be assessed only after EPA conducts formal adjudicatory proceedings in accordance with §§554 and 556 of the APA, though there are exceptions. See, e.g., CAA §113(d)(2), (3). Under the CWA, more rigorous procedures are required for Class II penalties (which may not exceed $157,500) than for Class I penalties (which may not exceed $32,500). CWA §309(g)(2); Penalty Adjustment and Table, 40 C.F.R. §19.4 (2005).

Aside from establishing maximum amounts, the statutes afford EPA considerable discretion in determining the size of the penalty. Under the CAA, EPA must take into account factors that include the size of the business, the economic impact of the penalty on the business, the violator's compliance history and good faith efforts to comply, the duration of the violation, the economic benefit of noncompliance, and the seriousness of the violation. CAA §113(e)(1). See also CWA §309(g)(3); RCRA §3008(a)(3). EPA has developed guidance documents under many of its statutes that elaborate on the approach EPA should take in determining appropriate penalty amounts. See, e.g., EPA, Hazardous Waste Civil Enforcement Response

	FY96	FY97	FY98	FY99	FY00	FY01	FY02	FY03	FY04	FY05
CAA	88	126	156	193	160	170	156	162	263	448
CWA	153	329	389	436	544	442	518	580	699	779
RCRA	88	139	155	197	212	154	258	289	359	370
TOTAL	329	594	700	826	916	766	932	1,031	1,321	1,597

Source: EPA Annual Report on Enforcement and Compliance Assurance Accomplishments in 1999, p. B-3; EPA Annual Report on Enforcement and Compliance Assurance Accomplishments in 2001, p. 69; and EPA, National Enforcement Trends—FY 2005, http://cfpub.epa.gov/compliance/resources/reports/nets/index.cfm.

FIGURE 10-9
EPA Administrative Penalty Order Complaints

Policy (Dec. 2003). Civil liability under the federal environmental statutes is typically strict liability, and EPA is authorized under statutes such as the CWA to impose civil penalties even in the absence of evidence that a violation caused actual harm to the environment. See, e.g., Kelly v. EPA, 203 F.3d 519 (7th Cir. 2000) (noting, in the course of upholding a civil penalty imposed by EPA for filling in a wetland without a CWA §404 permit, that driving a car without a license is not necessarily dangerous but is nevertheless illegal).

The 1990 CAA amendments authorized EPA inspectors to issue field citations for minor violations. These citations, which have been analogized to traffic tickets, may impose fines of up to $5,000 per day. Congress exempted field citations from APA formal adjudication procedures in an effort to streamline the enforcement process. See CAA §113(d)(3); Miskiewicz & Rudd, Civil and Criminal Enforcement of the Clean Air Act After the 1990 Amendments, 9 Pace Envtl. L. Rev. 281, 314-316 (1992).

Judicial Civil Litigation. As an alternative to administrative enforcement, EPA may pursue alleged violators in federal court. The federal district courts have the authority to issue injunctive relief, temporary or permanent, and impose civil penalties based on factors similar to those EPA must consider in calculating administrative civil penalties. See CAA §113(b), (e); CWA §309(b), (d); RCRA §3008(a)(3). One rationale for the imposition of civil penalties is that they can act as a deterrent. In one case, the court explained that it chose to impose a penalty of nearly $5 million for RCRA violations to provide a deterrent to both the defendant "and others who might choose the path of wealth and greed over human decency. Perhaps [the defendant] and others like him will not cho[o]se the errant path in the future." United States v. Hill, 98 F. Supp. 2d 280, 283 (N.D.N.Y. 2000). The district courts have broad discretion in determining the appropriate penalty amount. The following decision by the Fourth Circuit reviews some of the issues associated with the calculation of penalties.

UNITED STATES v. SMITHFIELD FOODS
191 F.3d 516 (4th Cir. 1999)

ERVIN, Circuit J.

Smithfield Foods, Inc. ("Smithfield"') appeals a grant of summary judgment in favor of the United States finding Smithfield liable for multiple Clean Water Act violations. Smithfield also challenges the court's imposition of a corresponding $12.6 million civil penalty. . . .

On the penalty issue, Smithfield contends that the district court erred in calculating the penalty, especially with respect to its determination of economic benefit and the denial of "good-faith" credit to Smithfield for its compliance efforts.

For the reasons that follow, we affirm the district court's grant of summary judgment on liability. We remand the penalty determination to the district court with instructions to recalculate the civil penalty as directed by this opinion.

I.

The facts of this case are undisputed and are comprehensively set out in the district court's published opinion, United States v. Smithfield Foods, Inc., 965 F. Supp. 769, 772-781 (E.D. Va. 1997). To properly analyze this case, however, the major events bear repeating. Smithfield owns and operates two swine slaughtering and processing plants, Smithfield Packing Co. and Gwaltney of Smithfield, Ltd. Both plants are located on the Pagan River, a tributary of the James River, in Isle of Wight County, Virginia. The wastewater discharged from these plants is treated in two of Smithfield's facilities, Outfall 001 and Outfall 002. From at least August 1991 to August 1997, treated wastewater was discharged from Outfall 001 into the Pagan River. From at least August 1991 until June 1996, treated wastewater was discharged from Outfall 002 into the Pagan River. Smithfield stopped discharging wastewater into the Pagan River when it successfully connected its plants to the Hampton Roads Sanitation District ("HRSD") system.

A.

Smithfield's wastewater discharges contained numerous pollutants that were regulated under the CWA and thus, could not be discharged into the waters of the United States unless specifically authorized by permit. Permits are governed by the National Pollutant Discharge Elimination System ("NPDES"), under which polluters obtain an NPDES permit to discharge lawfully certain pollutants in specific amounts. See 33 U.S.C.A. §1342 (West 1986 & Supp. 1999). Regulation of NPDES permits is overseen by the Environmental Protection Agency ("EPA"), see 33 U.S.C.A. §1342(a), but locally administered by the Commonwealth of Virginia through its agent, the Virginia State Water Control Board ("the Board"). See 33 U.S.C.A. §§1251(b), 1342(b) (West 1986 & Supp. 1999). The Board is authorized to enforce the CWA subject to the guidance and approval of the EPA. See 33 U.S.C.A. §1319.

Smithfield's discharges were authorized by an NPDES permit ("the Permit") issued in 1986, modified in 1990, and reissued in 1992. The Permit placed restrictions on the amount and concentration of certain pollutants allowed in wastewater released to the Pagan River and required Smithfield to monitor, sample, analyze, and issue reports concerning its discharges. The results of Smithfield's wastewater sampling program were periodically compiled into Discharge Monitoring Reports ("DMRs") and submitted to the Board. . . .

B.

The government filed suit in the United States District Court for the Eastern District of Virginia on December 16, 1996, seeking injunctive relief and penalties for a range of effluent limit violations, submission of false DMRs, submission of late reports, and destruction of records. . . .

The district court held a bench trial . . . in July 1997. The court reviewed evidence and heard from both sides' experts who opined on the proper calculations for each of the factors to be considered under the CWA's penalty statute. In the end, the district court found Smithfield liable for 6,982 days of violations and, after weighing the mitigating and aggravating circumstances, assessed a penalty of $12.6 million. . . .

III.

Smithfield's second major challenge is to the district court's assessment of a $12.6 million penalty. We review the factual findings that formed the basis of the district court's penalty calculation for clear error, but the highly discretionary calculations necessary to award civil penalties are reviewed for abuse of discretion.

The CWA sets out six factors intended to assist courts in determining the appropriate civil penalty. *See* CWA §309(d), 33 U.S.C.A. §1319(d) (Supp. 1999). Section 309(d) provides that "the court shall consider the seriousness of the violation or violations, the economic benefit (if any) resulting from the violation, any history of such violations, any good-faith efforts to comply with the applicable requirements, the economic impact of the penalty on the violator, and such other matters as justice may require." Id.

These factors are designed to give district courts direction in fashioning penalties for CWA violations, but once applied in a specific case, we have given and will continue to give the district court's final penalty calculation wide discretion. Because of the difficulty of determining an appropriate penalty in a complex case such as this one, we give deference to the "highly discretionary calculations that take into account multiple factors [that] are necessary in order to set civil penalties under the Clean Water Act." Tull v. United States, 481 U.S. 412, 427 (1987).

Although Smithfield contests several of the district court's discretionary decisions, such as the method used to count each violation and the alleged trebling of the penalty, Smithfield's major allegations of error relate to the court's economic benefit calculation and its refusal to grant Smithfield good-faith credit for its compliance efforts. We consider each of these arguments in turn. . . .

B.

Smithfield next argues that the district court erred as a matter of law by allegedly calculating the penalty by trebling the amount of economic benefit calculated. Pointing to the text of the Act, Smithfield contends that, unlike other federal statutes, the CWA does not provide for trebling and therefore the court committed reversible error by assessing a penalty equal to exactly three times the amount of economic benefit calculated. We see no indication that the district court "simply trebled the amount of economic benefit." On the contrary, we find that the district court correctly applied the CWA in assessing Smithfield's penalty.

In calculating the penalty, the district court properly began by determining that the statutory maximum based on Smithfield's violations was $174.55 million. *See Smithfield*, 972 F. Supp. at 353. Thereafter, the court evaluated two different methods used to assess penalties—the top-down method and the bottom-up method—and to Smithfield's advantage, chose the bottom-up method.[7] Under the bottom-up method, the court begins with the violator's estimated economic benefit from noncompliance, which here was $4.2 million, and then adjusts up or down based on the court's evaluation of the six factors set out in §309(d). After evaluating and discussing the effect of each of the factors, the court found a $12.6 million penalty appropriate.

---

7. As noted by the district court, the CWA does not require the use of either method, however, courts have applied both. See, e.g., *Tyson Foods*, 897 F.2d at 1142 (using top-down method in which a court begins with the statutory maximum and adjusts downward based on evaluation of §309(d) factors); Hawaii's Thousand Friends v. City & County of Honolulu, 821 F. Supp. 1368, 1395 (D. Haw. 1993) (same). But see United States v. Municipal Auth. of Union Twp., 150 F.3d 259, 265 (3d Cir. 1998) (applying the bottom-up method) (known as *"Dean Dairy"*); *Monsanto*, 1998 WL 156691, at *16 (same).

When calculating Smithfield's penalty, the district court took into account all six of the statutorily mandated factors and sufficiently detailed its findings as to whether the evidence in each area had a mitigating or aggravating impact on the total penalty. The court properly exercised its discretion in weighing the evidence and determining the credibility of key witnesses and, in doing so, made several decisions that were highly favorable to Smithfield. In the end, however, the court found that Smithfield's thousands of CWA violations warranted a penalty far in excess of the economic benefit calculation.

We find that the court's analysis was complete and in line with what is required under the statute. It is clear from its opinion that the court's exhaustive examination of the facts formed the basis of its final penalty calculation, rather than simply multiplying the economic benefit by three as Smithfield contends.

But even if the court had simply trebled the economic benefit to determine the appropriate penalty, that was within its discretion, as long as it was below the statutory maximum of $174.55 million. As mentioned, the Supreme Court has emphasized that under the CWA, the highly discretionary calculations necessary to assess civil penalties are particularly within the purview of trial judges, see *Tull*, 481 U.S. at 426-427, and we have continually given these determinations wide deference, reviewing them only for abuse of discretion. The government asked for a $20 million penalty, but based on its analysis of the relevant factors, the district court determined that $12.6 million was more appropriate, which is approximately 7.2% of the maximum penalty that could have been assessed. Finding that the court did not abuse its discretion in calculating the penalty, we reject Smithfield's contention that the district court erred as a matter of law in determining the penalty.

C.

Smithfield also argues that the district court erred as a matter of law by failing to give Smithfield credit for certain capital costs incurred and user fees paid when calculating economic benefit.

As one of the six factors the court must use to calculate CWA penalties, economic benefit is assessed to keep violators from gaining an unfair competitive advantage by violating the law. This is accomplished by including as part of the penalty an approximation of the amount of money the violator has saved by failing to comply with its permit. The rationale for including this measure as part of the violators' fine is "to remove or neutralize the economic incentive to violate environmental regulations." As noted in the Senate Report accompanying the 1987 amendment adding the economic benefit factor to §309(d), and as recognized by courts, the precise economic benefit a polluter has gained by violating its effluent limits may be difficult to prove, so "[r]easonable approximations of economic benefit will suffice" (referring to S. Rep. No. 50, 99th Cong., 1st Sess. 25 (1985)).

The statute does not define economic benefit and courts have applied different methods to determine the appropriate amount.[10] The district court used the common "cost-avoided" method here whereby economic benefit is measured by determining

---

10. In *Dean Dairy*, the Third Circuit calculated a violator's economic benefit by determining that the company would have lost $417,000 per year in revenues from a customer it would have had to drop in order to reduce production enough to comply with its permit. 150 F.3d at 262-267. In most cases, however, the court applies the cost-avoided method applied by the district court in the instant case.

"the avoided and/or delayed cost of compliance, TTT [using] the weighted average cost of capital (WACC) as a discount/interest rate." The rationale behind this method is that "[w]hen a company delays or avoids certain costs of capital and operations and maintenance necessary for compliance, the company is able to use those funds for other income-producing activities, such as investing that money in their own company." Id. The cost-avoided method has been utilized elsewhere, and was chosen by the district court in its discretion in part based on the court's evaluation of the credibility of the government's expert witness. The cost-avoided method is not in conflict with the CWA or basic economic principles. On the contrary, it represents a logical method by which a violator in Smithfield's position can be disgorged of any profits it attained through its non-compliance. Finding no fault with the district court's choice to apply the cost-avoided method in this case, we reject Smithfield's claim that its application was in error.

Smithfield further alleges that even under the cost-avoided method, the district court should have given Smithfield credit for (1) capital expenses incurred to build a pretreatment facility and to modify a sludge lagoon in preparation for connecting to HRSD, and (2) future user fees paid that Smithfield claims allowed HRSD to construct the necessary facilities for Smithfield's connection. In support of this argument, Smithfield repeatedly asserts that these are expenses it would have gotten credit for had it built its own direct discharge treatment system.

Smithfield decided to connect to HRSD in 1991 and, from that time until HRSD became available in 1996 and 1997, Smithfield was responsible for complying with its 1992 Permit requirements. Its decision to ignore these requirements in the interim certainly benefited Smithfield financially because, by failing to comply with the 1992 Permit limits, Smithfield avoided the costs of pollution control its competitors were simultaneously incurring by complying with the law. It is these costs that constitute Smithfield's economic benefit.

These capital expenses and user fees can reduce the economic benefit that Smithfield experienced from 1991 to 1996 or 1997 only in so far as they are duplicative of costs Smithfield should have incurred for interim compliance. The building of its pretreatment facility and the paying of user fees for future HRSD use were not costs Smithfield incurred to aid in compliance from 1991 to 1996 or 1997 and, therefore, should not have been credited to Smithfield during the district court's economic benefit calculation. . . .

D.

Finally, Smithfield alleges that the district court erred when it failed to give Smithfield credit for its good-faith efforts to comply by connecting to HRSD. Specifically, Smithfield argues that it should have received credit for its efforts to connect to HRSD because, even if it was mistaken, Smithfield believed that connecting to HRSD was the only applicable requirement in the interim.

Section 309(d) of the CWA requires a district court to consider "any good-faith efforts to comply with the applicable requirements" as a mitigating factor in the penalty calculation. 33 U.S.C.A. §1319(d). In practice, a court evaluates the evidence to determine whether the permittee took any actions to reduce the number of violations or attempted to lessen the impact of their discharges on the environment.

In its opinion, the district court began by acknowledging that Smithfield should receive credit for its decision to connect to HRSD when available, a decision that would eventually reduce its discharges to zero. The court went on, however, to focus

its inquiry on whether there were any good-faith efforts to comply with the requirements set out in Smithfield's Permits during the relevant period—from 1991 until
1996 or 1997 when Smithfield connected to HRSD. In evaluating the facts presented
at trial, the court found little evidence that the defendants made any good-faith efforts
to comply because Smithfield did not facilitate its connection to HRSD or mitigate its
discharges by treating its wastewater or decreasing its releases of pollutants in the
interim.

The court looked beyond these obvious facts, however, for other signs that
Smithfield might have tried to mitigate its violations by evaluating Smithfield's
other business practices. In doing so, the court found that during the relevant period
Smithfield cut back on the number of times it curtailed production to achieve compliance, ignored the advice of its own consultants who pointed out serious deficiencies
in the operation and maintenance of Smithfield's existing wastewater treatment plant,
and dismissed evidence that its treatment plant employees were inadequately trained.
Other than agreeing to connect to HRSD, the court found that Smithfield "apparently
believed they could discharge as much and as frequently as they wanted into the Pagan
River. . . ."

The district court's finding of liability, with which we agree, was based on the
notion that Smithfield impermissibly ignored its explicit obligations under its 1992
Permit by failing to comply with effluent limitations for the entire period between its
decision to connect to HRSD and the time the connection was made. It is only
reasonable, therefore, that Smithfield's efforts towards connecting to HRSD would
not suffice as good-faith efforts to comply with its applicable permit requirements
since, during this entire interim period, Smithfield made no effort to heed the specific
limits established by its 1992 Permit.

Furthermore, the evidence supports the district court's ruling. The testimony
presented at trial and the documentary evidence on which the court relied in making
these factual findings illustrate that Smithfield did not make efforts to decrease its
violations and, instead, relied on the unreasonable notion that as long as it connected
to HRSD within three months of availability, it was unnecessary to comply with the
specific effluent limitations listed in its 1992 Permit during the five year interim.
Finding that the district court's factual determinations regarding Smithfield's lack
of good-faith efforts to comply with applicable requirements were not clearly
erroneous, we affirm its findings on this issue.

IV.

For the foregoing reasons, we affirm the district court's grant of summary judgment on
liability. We reverse and remand the penalty determination to the district court with
instructions to recalculate the civil penalty to the extent required by this opinion.

AFFIRMED IN PART, REVERSED IN PART, AND REMANDED . . .

NOTES AND QUESTIONS CONCERNING THE
GOVERNMENT'S CIVIL LITIGATION AUTHORITIES

1. Many of the statutes contemplate that one of the main factors to be taken into
account in determining an appropriate penalty amount is the "economic benefit" the

violator gained because of its violations. The notion is that a penalty should be high enough to disgorge the violator's economic benefit, so that the penalty puts the violator in no better shape than its competitors that complied with their legal obligations. The other major factor is the "gravity" of the violation. Typically this may be used to increase the amount of a penalty (to ensure that the violator is put in worse shape through the enforcement action than it would be in if it had complied with its obligations).

2. As the principal case reflects, courts have varied in their approaches to determining appropriate penalties. The Third Circuit, for example has approved either the "top down" or "bottom up" approach. United States v. Allegheny Ludlum Corp., 366 F.3d 164, 178 n.6 (3rd Cir. 2004).

3. Determination of economic benefit in particular cases is not always straightforward, but EPA has developed the BEN computer model to assist in this effort. EPA OECA, BEN User's Manual (Sept. 1999). In particular, the model is intended to "calculate the economic benefit a violator derives from delaying and/or avoiding compliance with environmental statutes." Id. at 1-1. EPA has continued to tweak its BEN model over the years. EPA announced revisions to its approach to calculating economic benefit in August 2005. Calculation of the Economic Benefit of Noncompliance in EPA's Civil Penalty Enforcement Cases. 70 Fed. Reg. 50,326 (2005). An EPA SAB Illegal Competitive Advantage Economic Benefit Advisory Panel, established to review the role of illegal competitive advantage (ICA) in penalty calculation (i.e., the role of increased revenues from profits resulting from the illegal activity), issued its Advisory on September 7, 2005. In its February 2006 response to the SAB report, EPA notes that "[o]nly about ten published EPA decisions have involved benefit recapture based upon increased revenues." The agency notes that because of the infrequency of these cases it is not going to modify the BEN model to address them.

EPA summarizes its methodology for calculating economic benefits as follows:

> BEN calculates the economic benefits gained from delaying and avoiding required environmental expenditures. Such expenditures can include: (1) Capital investments (e.g., pollution control equipment), (2) One-time nondepreciable expenditures (e.g., setting a reporting system, or acquiring land), (3) Annually recurring costs (e.g., operating and maintenance costs). Each of these expenditures can be either delayed or avoided. BEN's baseline assumption is that capital investments and one-time nondepreciable expenditures are merely delayed over the period of noncompliance, whereas annual costs are avoided entirely over this period. BEN does allow you, however, to analyze any combination of delayed and avoided expenditures.
>
> The economic benefit calculation must incorporate the economic concepts of the "time value of money." Stated simply, a dollar today is worth more than a dollar tomorrow, because you can invest today's dollar to start earning a return immediately. Thus, the further in the future the dollar is, the less it is worth in "present-value" terms. Similarly, the greater the time value of money (i.e., the greater the "discount" or "compound" rate used to derive the present value), the lower the present value of future costs. . . .
>
> A violator may gain illegal competitive advantages in addition to the usual benefits of noncompliance. These may be substantial benefits, but they are beyond the capability of BEN or any computer program to assess. Instead BEN asks you a series of questions about possible illegal competitive advantages so that you may identify cases where they are relevant. EPA is in the process of developing guidance protocols for such situations. You can obtain a copy of these protocols from EPA's enforcement economics toll-free

helpline at 888-ECON-SPT. Meanwhile, if illegal competitive advantage is an issue you should consult an expert or the helpline. [BEN User's Manual, at 1-2, 1-3.]

EPA also has developed a computer model known as ABEL to help it to evaluate ability to pay.

4. All of the statutes authorize the imposition of penalties for each day of violation. Suppose that an abandoned fish cannery violated its regulatory obligation to notify EPA of its intention to remove asbestos. Three years later, EPA sought civil penalties in federal district court under the CAA. The court regarded the failure to notify as a "continuing violation" and held the company separately liable for each day from the date it should reasonably have given notice to the date state officials learned of the removal. On appeal, the cannery argues that the failure to notify occurred on a single day and it is therefore subject to penalties under CAA §113(b) only for that date. Should the district court's decision be reversed? See United States v. Trident Seafoods Corp., 60 F.3d 556 (9th Cir. 1995). Suppose that a point source violates an effluent limitation that contains a monthly average limitation on discharges. Has it engaged in a violation for one day or 30 days? United States v. Allegheny Ludlum Corp., 366 F.3d 164 (3d Cir. 2004).

5. EPA may impose a variety of sanctions in addition to penalties. For example, the agency may seek to revoke the violator's authority to operate. RCRA §3008(a)(3). In addition, EPA may prohibit violators from contracting with the government under some circumstances. See, e.g., CWA §508. For an example of a state decision to revoke a company's incinerator operating permit on the ground that the company's past performance warranted this result, see the January 6, 2006, letter from Michigan's Department of Environmental Quality to the President of Michigan Waste Services, LLC; Michigan Denies Permit for Disposal Unit after Revoking Firm's Incinerator License, State Env't Daily (BNA) (Jan. 12, 2006).

6. *Possible Defenses to Enforcement.* The target of a government enforcement action has any number of potential defenses available. In addition to the "I did not do it" defense, another defense that occasionally is available is the statute of limitations. How long may the government wait before seeking to enforce the provisions of the environmental laws? The general federal statute of limitations that applies to enforcement actions in the absence of more specific statutory provisions requires commencement of an "action, suit or proceeding for the enforcement of any civil fine, penalty, or forfeiture" within five years from the date when the claim first accrued. 28 U.S.C. §2462. 3M Co. (Minnesota Mining & Mfg.) v. Browner, 17 F.3d 1453 (D.C. Cir. 1994), held that §2462 applies to civil penalty cases brought before agencies (in this case under TSCA) on the basis that an administrative complaint qualifies as "an action, suit or proceeding" and it is one "for the enforcement of" a civil penalty. The distinction between a one-time and a continuing violation, which arises in the context of civil penalty calculations, is also relevant to the application of the statute of limitations. The relief sought may matter as well. In United States v. Telluride Co., 146 F.3d 1241 (10th Cir. 1998), the Tenth Circuit concluded that §2462 did not apply to the government's request for an injunction requiring the developer to restore the affected wetlands because it did not seek compensation for injury beyond that caused by the defendant, and therefore was not a "penalty" for purposes of §2462. See also United States v. Banks, 115 F.3d 916, 918-919 (11th Cir. 1997) (§2462 applies only to civil penalties, not to claims for equitable relief).

Due process also may provide a defense in some cases. General Elec. Co. v. EPA, 53 F.3d 1324 (D.C. Cir. 1995), refused to fine GE for improper processing of

PCBs under TSCA on the ground that GE lacked fair notice of the regulatory interpretation upon which EPA relied in citing the company because the agency's interpretation "is so far from a reasonable person's understanding of the regulation that [the agency] could not fairly have informed GE of [its] perspective." Id. at 1330. The lack of clarity of the regulations was highlighted by the disagreement about their meaning among different divisions of EPA and by EPA's failure to adhere to a consistent interpretation over time. Professor Lazarus suggests that the court in the GE case "created, in effect, a good faith defense based on due process." Lazarus, Meeting the Demands of Integration in the Evolution of Environmental Law: Reforming Environmental Criminal Law, 83 Geo. L.J. 2407, 2528 (1995).

7. Problem 10-1,on page 1038, raises several issues concerning the overfiling issue discussed in *Harmon* and the following notes, and government enforcement, as well as two topics discussed below, citizen suit enforcement (section C.4) and EPA's Self-Audit and Supplemental Environmental Projects (SEPs) policies (section D).

3. *Criminal Liability*

The History of Environmental Criminal Prosecution in a Nutshell. The pursuit of criminal sanctions under the environmental statutes has waxed and waned over time. Most of the environmental statutes adopted in the 1970s authorized the imposition of criminal penalties. See Lazarus, Meeting the Demands of Integration in the Evolution of Environmental Law: Reforming Environmental Criminal Law, 83 Geo. L.J. 2407, 2446 (1995). This authority was rarely used during that "environmental decade," and when it was it tended to be in egregious cases involving intentional activity that resulted in serious environmental harm. The initial push for more widespread criminal enforcement came in 1982, when EPA's General Counsel, responding to charges that the Reagan administration EPA was too soft on corporate polluters, announced that criminal prosecution would play a more important role in the government's enforcement efforts. See Brickey, Environmental Crime at the Crossroads: The Intersection of Environmental and Criminal Law Theory, 71 Tul. L. Rev. 487, 493 (1997). The Justice Department created its Environmental Crimes Unit (later elevated to a Department Section) at about the same time, and it obtained almost 700 guilty pleas and convictions during the next ten years. Id. at 495-496; Brickey, The Rhetoric of Environmental Crime: Culpability, Discretion, and Structural Reform, 84 Iowa L. Rev. 115 (1998). The adoption of the Pollution Prosecution Act of 1990, Pub. L. No. 101-593, 104 Stat. 2954, enhanced EPA's investigatory authority and increased the number of EPA criminal investigators.

Controversy emerged again during the 1992 presidential campaign amidst charges that the George H. W. Bush administration's Justice Department declined to prosecute environmental criminal violations or settled for inappropriately lenient sanctions for political reasons. These allegations prompted a series of congressional inquiries into improper political influence as well as an internal review by the Clinton administration's Justice Department. The resulting reports largely exonerated the Department's practices as appropriate exercises of prosecutorial discretion. Lazarus, *supra*, at 2410-2411; Brickey, Crossroads, *supra*, at 496-497. Figure 10-10 details EPA's criminal enforcement activity from 1995 to 2005.

Criminal Culpability and Environmental Crimes. The increased resort to criminal prosecution raised a series of legal and policy questions, not the least of

	FY95	FY96	FY97	FY98	FY99	FY00	FY01	FY02	FY03	FY04	FY05
Cases initiated	562	548	551	636	471	477	482	484	471	425	372
Referrals	256	262	278	266	241	236	256	250	228	168	NR*
Defendants	245	221	322	350	324	360	372	325	247	293	320
Years of sentence	74	93	195.9	172.9	208.3	146.2	212	215	146	77	186
Fines ($ millions)	23.2	76.7	169.3	92.8	61.6	122		94.7	62	71	47	100

*In FY 2005 EPA terminated the count of criminal referrals as an internal criminal enforcement program measure, Id., note 2.

Source: EPA, Annual Report on Enforcement and Compliance Assurance Accomplishments in 2001, p. 64; EPA, FY 1998-FY 2005 Criminal Enforcement Program Activities.

FIGURE 10-10
Criminal Program Statistics

which is the one at issue in the principal case that follows this introductory material: what degree of culpability must the government prove to convict an individual or corporation of a criminal offense under the environmental statutes?** A few provisions of the environmental statutes impose criminal liability for negligent conduct, e.g., CWA §309(c)(1) and CAA §113(c)(4). In United States v. Hanousek, 176 F.3d 1116 (9th Cir. 1999), the court held that criminal liability under the CWA for discharging harmful quantities of oil into navigable waters turns on proof that the defendant acted negligently. The government need not demonstrate that the defendant's actions constituted "criminal negligence," an elevated standard requiring a *gross* deviation from the standard of care that a reasonable person would observe in the situation. Instead, the court held that proof of *ordinary* negligence as defined in tort law was sufficient because it is well established that a public welfare statute (like the CWA) may impose criminal liability upon that lesser standard without violating the Due Process Clause. See also United States v. Hong, 242 F.3d 528 (4th Cir. 2001) (affirming corporate officer's conviction for negligent violation of CWA's pretreatment requirements). The Tenth Circuit (citing the *Hanousek* decision discussed above) held in United States v. Ortiz, 427 F.3d 1278, 1279 (10th Cir. 2005), that the CWA "criminalizes any act of ordinary negligence that leads to the discharge of a pollutant into the navigable waters of the United States."

The so-called knowing endangerment provisions provide for culpability under a recklessness standard, imposing severe criminal penalties on persons who place other persons at imminent risk of death or serious bodily injury. E.g., RCRA 3008(f)(1)(C). For an example of a successful prosecution for violation of RCRA's imminent endangerment provision, see United States v. Hansen, 262 F.3d 1217 (11th Cir. 2001). Many of the federal environmental criminal statutes, however, require proof that the defendant acted knowingly. E.g., CWA §309(c)(2); RCRA §3008(d); CAA §113(c)(1).

**See generally Solow & Sarachan, Criminal Negligence Prosecutions under the Federal Clean Water Act: A Statistical Analysis and an Evaluation of the Impact of *Hanousek* and *Hong*, 32 Envtl. L. Rep. (ELI) 11153 (2002); Buente & Thomson, The Changing Face of Federal Environmental Criminal Law: Trends and Developments—1999-2001, 31 Envtl. L. Rep. (ELI) 11340 (2001); Lazarus, *supra*. Section 2.02(2) of the Model Penal Code describes four different criminal states of mind: purposeful, knowing, reckless, and negligent.

The determination of the required standard of culpability is often demanding even in the best of circumstances. "Few areas of criminal law pose more difficulty than the proper definition of the *mens rea* required for any particular crime." United States v. Bailey, 444 U.S. 394, 403 (1980). What makes application of these provisions particularly difficult in the environmental context is that "Congress avoided addressing at all what it meant by the mens rea requirements it enacted." Lazarus, *supra*, at 2454. Thus, "ambiguity abounds in [the] federal [environmental] statutes, especially with respect to the appropriate mens rea in criminal provisions." Id. at 2466. The Conference Committee report on the 1980 amendments to RCRA, for example, states that the Committee did not seek to define "knowing," but left the process of fleshing out the meaning of that term "to the courts under general principles." H.R. Rep. No. 96-1444, at 39 (1980). Two commentators assert that "[e]nvironmental cases decided since late 1998 signal the continuing erosion of the *mens rea*, or scienter, requirements under federal environmental laws." See Buente & Thomson, *supra*, at 11345.

The principal case which follows considers the application of the "knowing" mens rea requirement in the context of a prosecution under the Clean Water Act.

UNITED STATES v. AHMAD
101 F.3d 386 (5th Cir. 1996)

JERRY E. SMITH, Circuit Judge: . . .

[In 1992, Attique Ahmad purchased the "Spin-N-Market No. 12," a convenience store and gas station located in Conroe, Texas. The gas station had two pumps, each of which was fed by an 8,000-gallon underground gasoline tank. Ahmad discovered that one of the tanks, which held high-octane gasoline, was leaking. The leak allowed water to enter into the tank and contaminate the gas, preventing Ahmad from selling it. In October 1993, Ahmad hired CTT Environmental Services (CTT), a tank testing company, to examine the tank. A CTT employee told Ahmad that the leak could not be repaired until it was completely emptied, which CTT offered to do. When Ahmad inquired whether he could empty the tank himself, the CTT employee replied that it would be dangerous and illegal to do so. She testified at trial that Ahmad responded, "Well, if I don't get caught, what then?"

In January 1994, Ahmad rented a hand-held motorized water pump from a hardware store, telling an employee that he was planning to use it to remove water from his backyard. Two witnesses testified that they subsequently saw Ahmad pumping gasoline into the street and discharging it into a manhole. Another witness testified that he asked Ahmad what he was doing; Ahmad replied that he was removing the water from the tank. Ahmad dumped about 4,700 gallons of gasoline into the street and the manhole in front of the Spin-N-Market. The gasoline discharged by Ahmad into the street entered a storm drain. The gas flowed through a pipe that empties into Possum Creek, which feeds into the San Jacinto River and eventually into Lake Houston. Several vacuum trucks were required to decontaminate the creek. The gasoline that Ahmad discharged into the manhole flowed through the sanitary sewer system and into the city's sewage treatment plant. When plant employees discovered a 1,000-gallon pool of gasoline in one of the intake ponds, they diverted it into an emergency lagoon. The plant supervisor ordered evacuation of nonessential personnel and called firefighters and a hazardous materials crew to the scene. The fire department determined that the gasoline created a risk of explosion and ordered the evacuation of two nearby schools. No one was injured, but fire officials testified at trial that the discharge created a "tremendous explosion hazard" that could have led to "hundreds, if not thousands, of deaths and injuries" and millions of dollars of property damage.]

Ahmad was indicted for [violating] the [Clean Water Act (CWA) by] knowingly discharging a pollutant from a point source into a navigable water of the United States without a permit, in violation of 33 U.S.C. §§1311(a) and 1319(c)(2)(A) (count one); [and] knowingly operating a source in violation of a pretreatment standard, in violation of 33 U.S.C. §§1317(d) and 1319(c)(2)(A) (count two). . . . At trial, Ahmad did not dispute that he had discharged gasoline from the tank or that eventually it had found its way to Possum Creek and the sewage treatment plant. Instead, he contended that his discharge of the gasoline was not "knowing," because he had believed he was discharging water. . . .

II.

Ahmad argues that the district court improperly instructed the jury on the *mens rea* required for counts one and two. The instruction on count one stated in relevant part:

> For you to find Mr. Ahmad guilty of this crime, you must be convinced that the government has proved each of the following beyond a reasonable doubt:
>
> (1) That on or about the date set forth in the indictment,
> (2) the defendant knowingly discharged
> (3) a pollutant
> (4) from a point source
> (5) without a permit to do so.

On count two, the court instructed the jury:

> In order to prove the defendant guilty of the offense charged in Count 2 of the indictment, the government must prove beyond a reasonable doubt each of the following elements:
>
> (1) That on or about the date set forth in the indictment
> (2) the defendant,
> (3) who was the owner or operator of a source,
> (4) knowingly operated that source by discharging into a public sewer system or publicly owned treatment works
> (5) a pollutant that created a fire or explosion hazard in that public sewer system or publicly owned treatment works.

Ahmad contends that the jury should have been instructed that the statutory *mens rea*—knowledge—was required as to each element of the offenses, rather than only with regard to discharge or the operation of a source. . . .

The language of the CWA is less than pellucid. Title 33 U.S.C. §1319(c)(2)(A) says that "any person who knowingly violates" any of a number of other sections of the

CWA commits a felony. One of the provisions that §1319(c)(2)(A) makes it unlawful to violate is §1311(a), which, when read together with a series of definitions in §1362, prohibits the addition of any pollutant to navigable waters from a "point source." That was the crime charged in count one. Section 1319(c)(2)(A) also criminalizes violations of §1317(d), which prohibits the operation of any "source" in a way that contravenes any effluent standard, prohibition, or pretreatment standard. That was the crime charged in count two.

The principal issue is to which elements of the offense the modifier "knowingly" applies. The matter is complicated somewhat by the fact that the phrase "knowingly violates" appears in a different section of the CWA from the language defining the elements of the offenses. Ahmad argues that within this context, "knowingly violates" should be read to require him knowingly to have acted with regard to each element of the offenses. The government, in contrast, contends that "knowingly violates" requires it to prove only that Ahmad knew the nature of his acts and that he performed them intentionally. Particularly at issue is whether "knowingly" applies to the element of the discharge's being a pollutant, for Ahmad's main theory at trial was that he thought he was discharging water, not gasoline.

The Supreme Court has spoken to this issue in broad terms. In United States v. X-Citement Video, Inc., 513 U.S. 64 (1994), the Court . . . reaffirmed the long-held view that "the presumption in favor of a scienter requirement should apply to each of the statutory elements which criminalize otherwise innocent conduct."

Although X-Citement Video is the Court's most recent pronouncement on this subject, it is not the first. In Staples v. United States, 511 U.S. 600, 619-20 (1994), the Court found that the statutes criminalizing knowing possession of a machinegun require that defendants know not only that they possess a firearm but that it actually is a machinegun. Thus, an awareness of the features of the gun—specifically, the features that make it an automatic weapon—is a necessary element of the offense. More generally, the Court also made plain that statutory crimes carrying severe penalties are presumed to require that a defendant know the facts that make his conduct illegal.

Our own precedents are in the same vein. In United States v. Baytank (Houston), Inc., 934 F.2d 599, 613 (5th Cir. 1991), we concluded that a conviction for knowing and improper storage of hazardous wastes under 42 U.S.C. §6928(d)(2)(A) requires "that the defendant know factually what he is doing—storing, what is being stored, and that what is being stored factually has the potential for harm to others or the environment, and that he has no permit. . . ." This is directly analogous to the interpretation of the CWA that Ahmad urges upon us. Indeed, we find it eminently sensible that the phrase "knowingly violates" in §1319(c)(2)(A), when referring to other provisions that define the elements of the offenses §1319 creates, should uniformly require knowledge as to each of those elements rather than only one or two. To hold otherwise would require an explanation as to why some elements should be treated differently from others, which neither the parties nor the case law seems able to provide.

In support of its interpretation of the CWA, the government cites cases from other circuits. We find these decisions both inapposite and unpersuasive on the point for which they are cited. In United States v. Hopkins, 53 F.3d 533, 537-41 (2d Cir. 1995), the court held that the government need not demonstrate that a §1319(c)(2)(A) defendant knew his acts were illegal. The illegality of the defendant's actions is not an element of the offense, however. In United States v. Weitzenhoff, 35 F.3d 1275 (9th Cir. 1994), the court similarly was concerned almost exclusively with whether the language of the CWA creates a mistake-of-law defense. Both cases are easily distinguishable, for neither directly addresses mistake of fact or the statutory construction issues raised by Ahmad.

The government also protests that CWA violations fall into the judicially created exception for "public welfare offenses," under which some regulatory crimes have been held not to require a showing of *mens rea*. On its face, the CWA certainly does appear to implicate public welfare.

As recent cases have emphasized, however, the public welfare offense exception is narrow. The *Staples* Court, for example, held that the statute prohibiting the possession of machineguns fell outside the exception, notwithstanding the fact that "[t]ypically, our cases recognizing such offenses involve statutes that regulate potentially harmful or injurious items." *Staples*, 511 U.S. at 607.

Though gasoline is a "potentially harmful or injurious item," it is certainly no more so than are machineguns. Rather, *Staples* held, the key to the public welfare offense analysis is whether "dispensing with *mens rea* would require the defendant to have knowledge only of traditionally lawful conduct." Id. at 618. The CWA offenses of which Ahmad was convicted have precisely this characteristic, for if knowledge is not required as to the nature of the substance discharged, one who honestly and reasonably believes he is discharging water may find himself guilty of a felony if the substance turns out to be something else.

The fact that violations of §1319(c)(2)(A) are felonies punishable by years in federal prison confirms our view that they do not fall within the public welfare offense exception. As the *Staples* Court noted, public welfare offenses have virtually always been crimes punishable by relatively light penalties such as fines or short jail sentences, rather than substantial terms of imprisonment. Serious felonies, in contrast, should not fall within the exception "absent a clear statement from Congress that *mens rea* is not required." Id. at 618. Following *Staples*, we hold that the offenses charged in counts one and two are not public welfare offenses and that the usual presumption of a *mens rea* requirement applies. With the exception of purely jurisdictional elements, the *mens rea* of knowledge applies to each element of the crimes.

Finally, the government argues that the instructions, considered as a whole, adequately conveyed to the jury the message that Ahmad had to have known that what he was discharging was gasoline in order for the jury to find him guilty. We disagree.

At best, the jury charge made it uncertain to which elements "knowingly" applied. At worst, and considerably more likely, it indicated that only the element of discharge need be knowing. The instructions listed each element on a separate line, with the word "knowingly" present only in the line corresponding to the element that something was discharged. . . .

The obvious inference for the jury was that knowledge was required only as to the fact that something was discharged, and not as to any other fact. In effect, with regard to the other elements of the crimes, the instructions implied that the requisite *mens rea* was strict liability rather than knowledge. . . .

Because the charge effectively withdrew from the jury's consideration facts that it should have been permitted to find or not find, this error requires reversal. . . .

NOTES AND QUESTIONS ABOUT CRIMINAL ENFORCEMENT

1. *"How Far Does 'Knowingly' Travel?"* What was the government's position in *Ahmad*? What stance did the defendant, and ultimately the court, take? What if

Ahmad had argued, not that he thought the substance he dumped into the sewer was water, but that he didn't know that dumping gasoline into the sewer was prohibited by the CWA; would that argument have provided the basis for a good defense? See the *Hopkins* and *Weitzenhoff* cases, cited in *Ahmad*. In United States v. Weintraub, 273 F.3d 139 (2d Cir. 2001), the defendant was charged, pursuant to CAA §113(c)(1), with knowingly violating an asbestos work practice standard promulgated under §113 of the CAA. The court held that the government had to prove knowledge of facts and circumstances that comprise a violation of the statute, but not specific knowledge that the defendant's conduct was illegal. That meant proof of knowledge of enough facts to distinguish conduct that is likely culpable from conduct that is entirely innocent. In that case, the government had to show that the defendant knew the substance involved was asbestos, but it did not have to show that the defendant knew the friability of the asbestos or the minimum quantities required to trigger the work practice standard. Of what relevance is the distinction between a mistake of law and mistake of fact referred to by the court in *Ahmad*? See United States v. Kelley Tech. Coatings, Inc., 157 F.3d 432, 438 (6th Cir. 1998); United States v. Wilson, 133 F.3d 251, 260-262 (4th Cir. 1997); Uiselt, What a Criminal Needs to Know Under Section 309(c)(2) of the Clean Water Act: How Far Does "Knowingly" Travel?, 8 The Envtl. Law. 303 (2002).

The rule of lenity dictates that statutory ambiguities be resolved in a criminal defendant's favor to avoid penalizing conduct the defendant could not fairly have known was proscribed. The courts have reversed criminal convictions under the environmental statutes on the basis of this doctrine. See, e.g., United States v. Plaza Health Lab., Inc., 3 F.3d 643 (2d Cir. 1993) (holding that a human being was not a point source for purposes of §301(a) of the CWA).

2. *Liability of Responsible Corporate Officers.* The environmental statutes not only subject corporate entities to criminal liability; they also impose liability on responsible corporate officers. E.g., CWA §309(c)(6); CAA §113(c)(6). The Supreme Court endorsed the "responsible corporate officer" doctrine in United States v. Dotterweich, 320 U.S. 277 (1943), upholding the imposition of criminal sanctions under the food and drug laws on a corporate officer on the basis of his position in the corporate hierarchy, even though he had no personal knowledge of the criminal conduct engaged in by other corporate employees. Is the authority to control the illegal activity enough to invoke the doctrine, or must the officer have actually exercised control? See United States v. Iverson, 162 F.3d 1015 (9th Cir. 1998). May an individual be held criminally liable for violating a CWA permit to which he is not a party? See United States v. Cooper, 173 F.3d 1192, 1201 (9th Cir. 1999).

3. *The Public Welfare Doctrine.* How broad is the public welfare doctrine? The court in *Ahmad* rejected the government's plea to rely on the public welfare doctrine to find the requisite criminal culpability on Ahmad's part. The Supreme Court has concluded that when criminal liability provisions are intended to protect the public welfare by regulating dangerous activities that create a risk of widely distributed harm, and the statute contains no mens rea requirement or is otherwise unclear as to what that requirement should be, the courts should assume that the legislature intended to lighten the government's burden of proof on the mens rea element of the crime. United States v. Dotterweich, 320 U.S. 277 (1943).

4. *Civil versus Criminal Enforcement.* The Department of Justice has developed policy concerning the integration of civil and criminal investigations. See U.S. DOJ, Integrated Enforcement Policy, Directive 99-21 (April 20, 1999); U.S. DOJ, Global

Settlement Policy, Directive 99-20 (April 20, 1999). For a review of parallel proceedings, see Meisner & Bornstein, Judicial Decision Will Significantly Impact Coordination of Investigations by the SEC and DOJ, BNA Corp. Accountability Report (Feb. 10, 2006). When *should* the government initiate criminal as opposed to civil enforcement proceedings? Should environmental violations be regarded as "white collar" crimes for which civil penalties are typically the most appropriate enforcement mechanism? EPA stated in its RCRA Compliance/Enforcement Guidance Manual (Oct. 1984) that, due to the "profound consequences" of criminal prosecution for the defendant, it would confine criminal referrals "to situations that—when measured by the nature of the conduct, the compliance history of the subject(s), or the gravity of the environmental consequences—reflect the most serious cases of environmental misconduct." Id. at 9-1. The extent of the environmental contamination or the human health hazard attributable to the prohibited conduct is of "primary importance." Id. at 9-2. Similarly, federal prosecutors have noted that evidence of deceit, degree of economic gain, and nature of harm to the environment are all important factors in deciding whether to pursue civil or criminal penalties. See 26 Env't Rep. (BNA) 527 (1995). Some private practitioners suggest that the federal government has "over-criminalized" environmental law in recent years. See, e.g., Buente & Thomson, The Changing Face of Federal Environmental Criminal Law: Trends and Developments—1999-2001, 31 Envtl. L. Rep. (ELI) 11340 (2001). Others have suggested that the growing criminalization of environmental law, and the lack of predictability about when the government will proceed with a criminal prosecution, have the potential to undermine compliance rather than promote it:

> The disturbing trend toward criminalization of environmental violations continues. EPA criminal investigators are likely to appear in any enforcement effort by EPA. It has reached the point where it is impossible to counsel clients on what kinds of violations will not be treated criminally. While EPA may revel in this lack of predictability, it is becoming more and more difficult for companies, plant managers, and environmental professionals to operate from day to day without fear of being indicted. . . . This atmosphere of fear and unpredictability undermines industry's ability to make intelligent decisions regarding the operation of its facilities and to attract and retain highly competent individuals to run them. In the long run, this will undermine environmental compliance and cause relations between EPA and industry to become increasingly hostile, instead of cooperative, to the detriment of the environment. [Gaynor & Lippard, Environmental Enforcement: Industry Should Not Be Complacent, 32 Envtl. L. Rep. (ELI) 10488, 10489 (2002).]

5. *False Statements*. The environmental statutes have separate provisions criminalizing the knowing omission of material information or submission of false material statements or certifications in applications, records, reports, or other documents and the knowing falsification of or tampering with monitoring devices. E.g., CWA §309(c)(4); RCRA §3008(d)(3); CAA §113(c)(2). The government continues to prosecute false statements, tampering, and related offenses. See, e.g., United States v. White, 270 F.3d 356 (6th Cir. 2001); United States v. Fern, 155 F.3d 1318 (11th Cir. 1998). See also Brickey, Rhetoric, *supra*, at 115 (false statement and monitoring charges often accompany alleged substantive violations because defendants file false statements and lie to cover up regulatory noncompliance).

6. For a survey of recent developments in criminal enforcement of the environmental laws, see Solow, The State of Environmental Crime Enforcement: An Annual

Survey, 37 Env't Rep. (BNA) 465 (2006). See also Buente & Thomson, *supra*. For recent developments in the sentencing arena, see United States v. Booker, 543 U.S. 220 (2005) (holding that the U.S. sentencing guidelines are advisory, not mandatory); United States v. Hillyer, 457 F.3d 357 (4th Cir. 2006); United States v. Barken, 412 F.3d 1131 (9th Cir. 2005) (applying *Booker*). For a discussion of EPA's joint prosecution effort with OSHA to address worker endangerment, see Pasfield, Worker Endangerment Initiative Survives First Test in Environmental Crimes Trial, 37 Env't Rep. (BNA) 1596 (2006).

4. *Private Enforcement of Statutory Violations: Citizen Suits*

The federal environmental laws typically allow citizens to bring suit against violators. See, e.g., CWA §505; CAA §304; RCRA §7002. We make two points concerning citizen suits in the first section of this chapter that are worth repeating here. First, citizen suits are intended to "supplement," not displace, government enforcement actions, as the Supreme Court reinforces in its *Gwaltney* decision, excerpted below. Second, despite this "supplemental" role, citizens have been quite active under several statutes in filing suits against violators, especially under the Clean Water Act for violations that violators disclose in their publicly accessible DMRs. The question of when citizens may bring suit has raised numerous issues and triggered considerable litigation. *Gwaltney* is one of the seminal decisions.

GWALTNEY OF SMITHFIELD, LTD. v. CHESAPEAKE BAY FOUNDATION, INC.
484 U.S. 49 (1987)

JUSTICE MARSHALL delivered the opinion of the Court.

In this case, we must decide whether §505(a) of the Clean Water Act [CWA], also known as the Federal Water Pollution Control Act, 33 U.S.C. §1365(a), confers federal jurisdiction over citizen suits for wholly past violations.

I.

The holder of a federal NPDES permit [issued under the Act] is subject to enforcement action by the Administrator [of EPA] for failure to comply with the conditions of the permit. . . . The holder of a state NPDES permit is subject to both federal and state enforcement action for failure to comply. §§1319, 1342(b)(7). In the absence of federal or state enforcement, private citizens may commence civil actions against any person "alleged to be in violation of" the conditions of either a federal or state NPDES permit. §1365(a)(1). If the citizen prevails in such an action, the court may order injunctive relief and/or impose civil penalties payable to the United States Treasury. §1365(a).

[In 1974, Virginia issued a CWA permit to a predecessor of Gwaltney authorizing the discharge of seven pollutants from the company's meat-packing plant into the Pagan River in Smithfield, Virginia. The permit established effluent limitations, monitoring requirements, and other conditions of discharge. Between 1981 and 1984, Gwaltney repeatedly violated the permit by exceeding applicable effluent limitations for five of the covered pollutants. The last reported violation occurred in May 1984, after Gwaltney installed upgraded waste treatment technology.

Chesapeake Bay Foundation and NRDC notified Gwaltney, EPA, and the Virginia State Water Control Board in February 1984 that they intended to commence a citizen suit under the CWA based on Gwaltney's permit violations. The two nonprofit organizations filed suit in June 1984, alleging that Gwaltney "has violated . . . [and] will continue to violate its NPDES permit." They sought declaratory and injunctive relief, civil penalties, and an award of attorneys' fees and costs. The district court granted partial summary judgment for the plaintiffs, finding Gwaltney "to have violated and to be in violation" of the Act. Before the district court reached a decision on the appropriate remedy, Gwaltney moved to dismiss the action for lack of subject matter jurisdiction. It argued that §505(a) requires that a defendant be violating the Act at the time of suit; Gwaltney's last recorded violation occurred several weeks before plaintiffs filed their complaint. The district court denied the motion, concluding that §505 authorizes citizens to bring enforcement actions on the basis of wholly past violations. It held in the alternative that it had jurisdiction under §505 because the complaint alleged in good faith that Gwaltney was continuing to violate its permit at the time suit was filed. The Court of Appeals affirmed.]

II.

A.

It is well settled that "the starting point for interpreting a statute is the language of the statute itself." The Court of Appeals concluded that the "to be in violation" language of §505 is ambiguous, whereas petitioner asserts that it plainly precludes the construction adopted below. We must agree with the Court of Appeals that §505 is not a provision in which Congress' limpid prose puts an end to all dispute. But to acknowledge ambiguity is not to conclude that all interpretations are equally plausible. The most natural reading of "to be in violation" is a requirement that citizen-plaintiffs allege a state of either continuous or intermittent violation—that is, a reasonable likelihood that a past polluter will continue to pollute in the future. Congress could have phrased its requirement in language that looked to the past ("to have violated"), but it did not choose this readily available option.

Respondents urge that the choice of the phrase "to be in violation," rather than phrasing more clearly directed to the past, is a "careless accident," the result of a "debatable lapse of syntactical precision." But the prospective orientation of that phrase could not have escaped Congress' attention. Congress used identical language in the citizen suit provisions of several other environmental statutes that authorize only prospective relief. See, e.g., [CAA §304; RCRA §7002; TSCA §20]. Moreover, Congress has demonstrated in yet other statutory provisions that it knows how to avoid this prospective implication by using language that explicitly targets wholly past violations.[2]

2. For example, the Solid Waste Disposal Act was amended in 1984 to authorize citizen suits against any "past or present" generator, transporter, owner, or operator of a treatment, storage, or disposal facility "who has contributed or who is contributing" to the "past or present" handling, storage, treatment, transportation, or disposal of certain hazardous wastes. 42 U.S.C. §6972(a)(1)(B).

Respondents seek to counter this reasoning by observing that Congress also used the phrase "is in violation" in §309(a) of the Act, which authorizes the Administrator of EPA to issue compliance orders. That language is incorporated by reference in §309(b), which authorizes the Administrator to bring civil enforcement actions. Because it is little questioned that the Administrator may bring enforcement actions to recover civil penalties for wholly past violations, respondents contend, the parallel language of §309(a) and §505(a) must mean that citizens, too, may maintain such actions.

Although this argument has some initial plausibility, it cannot withstand close scrutiny and comparison of the two statutory provisions. The Administrator's ability to seek civil penalties is not discussed in either §309(a) or §309(b); civil penalties are not mentioned until §309(d), which does not contain the "is in violation" language. This Court recently has recognized that §309(d) constitutes a separate grant of enforcement authority: "Section 1319 [§309] does not intertwine equitable relief with the imposition of civil penalties. Instead each kind of relief is separately authorized in a separate and distinct statutory provision. Subsection (b), providing injunctive relief, is independent of subsection (d), which provides only for civil penalties." Tull v. United States, 481 U.S. 412, 425 (1987).

In contrast, §505 of the Act does not authorize civil penalties separately from injunctive relief; rather, the two forms of relief are referred to in the same subsection, even in the same sentence. 33 U.S.C. §1365(a). The citizen suit provision suggests a connection between injunctive relief and civil penalties that is noticeably absent from the provision authorizing agency enforcement. A comparison of §309 and §505 thus supports rather than refutes our conclusion that citizens, unlike the Administrator, may seek civil penalties only in a suit brought to enjoin or otherwise abate an ongoing violation. . . .

B.

Our reading of the "to be in violation" language of §505(a) is bolstered by the language and structure of the rest of the citizen suit provisions in §505 of the Act. These provisions together make plain that the interest of the citizen-plaintiff is primarily forward-looking.

One of the most striking indicia of the prospective orientation of the citizen suit is the pervasive use of the present tense throughout §505. A citizen suit may be brought only for violation of a permit limitation "which is in effect" under the Act. 33 U.S.C. §1365(f). Citizen-plaintiffs must give notice to the alleged violator, the Administrator of EPA, and the State in which the alleged violation "occurs." §1365(b)(1)(A). A Governor of a State may sue as a citizen when the Administrator fails to enforce an effluent limitation "the violation of which is occurring in another State and is causing an adverse effect on the public health or welfare in his State." §1365(h). The most telling use of the present tense is in the definition of "citizen" as "a person . . . having an interest which is or may be adversely affected" by the defendant's

---

Prior to 1984, the Solid Waste Disposal Act contained language identical to that of §505(a) of the Clean Water Act, authorizing citizen suits against any person "alleged to be in violation" of waste disposal permits or standards. 42 U.S.C. §6972(a)(1). Even more on point, the most recent Clean Water Act amendments permit EPA to assess administrative penalties without judicial process on any person who "has violated" the provisions of the Act. Water Quality Act of 1987, §314, Pub. L. 100-4, 101 Stat. 46.

violations of the Act. §1365(g). This definition makes plain what the undeviating use of the present tense strongly suggests: the harm sought to be addressed by the citizen suit lies in the present or the future, not in the past.

Any other conclusion would render incomprehensible §505's notice provision, which requires citizens to give 60 days' notice of their intent to sue to the alleged violator as well as to the Administrator and the State. §1365(b)(1)(A). If the Administrator or the State commences enforcement action within that 60-day period, the citizen suit is barred, presumably because governmental action has rendered it unnecessary. §1365(b)(1)(B). It follows logically that the purpose of notice to the alleged violator is to give it an opportunity to bring itself into complete compliance with the Act and thus likewise render unnecessary a citizen suit. If we assume, as respondents urge, that citizen suits may target wholly past violations, the requirement of notice to the alleged violator becomes gratuitous. Indeed, respondents, in propounding their interpretation of the Act, can think of no reason for Congress to require such notice other than that "it seemed right" to inform an alleged violator that it was about to be sued.

Adopting respondents' interpretation of §505's jurisdictional grant would create a second and even more disturbing anomaly. The bar on citizen suits when governmental enforcement action is under way suggests that the citizen suit is meant to supplement rather than to supplant governmental action. The legislative history of the Act reinforces this view of the role of the citizen suit. The Senate Report noted that "[t]he Committee intends the great volume of enforcement actions [to] be brought by the State," and that citizen suits are proper only "if the Federal, State, and local agencies fail to exercise their enforcement responsibility." S. Rep. No. 92-414, p. 64 (1971). Permitting citizen suits for wholly past violations of the Act could undermine the supplementary role envisioned for the citizen suit. This danger is best illustrated by an example. Suppose that the Administrator identified a violator of the Act and issued a compliance order under §309(a). Suppose further that the Administrator agreed not to assess or otherwise seek civil penalties on the condition that the violator take some extreme corrective action, such as to install particularly effective but expensive machinery, that it otherwise would not be obliged to take. If citizens could file suit, months or years later, in order to seek the civil penalties that the Administrator chose to forgo, then the Administrator's discretion to enforce the Act in the public interest would be curtailed considerably. The same might be said of the discretion of state enforcement authorities. Respondents' interpretation of the scope of the citizen suit would change the nature of the citizens' role from interstitial to potentially intrusive. We cannot agree that Congress intended such a result. . . .

III.

Our conclusion that §505 does not permit citizen suits for wholly past violations does not necessarily dispose of this lawsuit, as both lower courts recognized. The District Court found persuasive the fact that "[respondents'] allegation in the complaint, that Gwaltney was continuing to violate its NPDES permit when plaintiffs filed suit[,] appears to have been made fully in good faith." On this basis, the District Court explicitly held, albeit in a footnote, that "even if Gwaltney were correct that a district court has no jurisdiction over citizen suits based entirely on unlawful conduct that occurred entirely in the past, the Court would still have jurisdiction here." The Court of Appeals acknowledged, also in a footnote, that "[a] very sound argument can be made that [respondents'] allegations of continuing violations were made in good faith," but expressly declined to rule on this alternative holding. Because we agree that §505 confers jurisdiction over citizen suits when the citizen-plaintiffs make a good-faith allegation of continuous or intermittent violation, we remand the case to the Court of Appeals for further consideration.

Petitioner argues that citizen-plaintiffs must prove their allegations of ongoing noncompliance before jurisdiction attaches under §505. We cannot agree. The statute does not require that a defendant "be in violation" of the Act at the commencement of suit; rather, the statute requires that a defendant be "alleged to be in violation." Petitioner's construction of the Act reads the word "alleged" out of §505. As petitioner itself is quick to note in other contexts, there is no reason to believe that Congress' drafting of §505 was sloppy or haphazard. We agree with the Solicitor General that "Congress's use of the phrase 'alleged to be in violation' reflects a conscious sensitivity to the practical difficulties of detecting and proving chronic episodic violations of environmental standards." Brief for United States as Amicus Curiae 18. Our acknowledgment that Congress intended a good-faith allegation to suffice for jurisdictional purposes, however, does not give litigants license to flood the courts with suits premised on baseless allegations. Rule 11 of the Federal Rules of Civil Procedure, which requires pleadings to be based on a good-faith belief, formed after reasonable inquiry, that are "well grounded in fact," adequately protects defendants from frivolous allegations.

Petitioner contends that failure to require proof of allegations under §505 would permit plaintiffs whose allegations of ongoing violation are reasonable but untrue to maintain suit in federal court even though they lack constitutional standing. Petitioner reasons that if a defendant is in complete compliance with the Act at the time of suit, plaintiffs have suffered no injury remediable by the citizen suit provisions of the Act. Petitioner, however, fails to recognize that our standing cases uniformly recognize that allegations of injury are sufficient to invoke the jurisdiction of a court. . . .

Petitioner also worries that our construction of §505 would permit citizen-plaintiffs, if their allegations of ongoing noncompliance become false at some later point in the litigation because the defendant begins to comply with the Act, to continue nonetheless to press their suit to conclusion. According to petitioner, such a result would contravene both the prospective purpose of the citizen suit provisions and the "case or controversy" requirement of Article III. Longstanding principles of mootness, however, prevent the maintenance of suit when "'there is no reasonable expectation that the wrong will be repeated.'" United States v. W.T. Grant Co., 345 U.S. 629, 633 (1953). In seeking to have a case dismissed as moot, however, the defendant's burden "is a heavy one." [Id.] The defendant must demonstrate that it is *absolutely clear* that the allegedly wrongful behavior could not reasonably be expected to recur." United States v. Phosphate Export Ass'n, Inc., 393 U.S. 199, 203 (1968) (emphasis added). Mootness doctrine thus protects defendants from the maintenance of suit under the Clean Water Act based solely on violations wholly unconnected to any present or future wrongdoing, while it also protects plaintiffs from defendants who seek to evade sanction by predictable "protestations of repentance and reform." United States v. Oregon State Medical Society, 343 U.S. 326, 333 (1952).[6]

6. Under the Act, plaintiffs are also protected from the suddenly repentant defendant by the authority of the district courts to award litigation costs "whenever the court determines such an award is appropriate." 33 U.S.C. §1365(d). The legislative history of this provision states explicitly that the

Because the court below erroneously concluded that respondents could maintain an action based on wholly past violations of the Act, it declined to decide whether respondents' complaint contained a good-faith allegation of ongoing violation by petitioner. We therefore remand the case for consideration of this question. . . .

NOTES AND QUESTIONS ABOUT CITIZEN SUITS

1. *Continuous and Intermittent Violations and Mootness.* On what basis did the Court in *Gwaltney* conclude that EPA may seek to recover civil penalties for past violations but that private citizens may not? Given that Gwaltney's violations ceased before the filing of the complaint against it, what was the purpose of the Court's remand order? After *Gwaltney*, why can't a permit holder consistently defeat citizen suits by ceasing violations as soon as it receives notice that someone intends to file a citizen suit and repeating the process if violations recur and it receives another notice of an intended suit?

On remand in *Gwaltney*, the Fourth Circuit held that the plaintiff may prevail "either (1) by proving violations that continue on or after the date the complaint is filed, or (2) by adducing continuing evidence from which a reasonable trier of fact could find a likelihood of a recurrence in intermittent or sporadic violations." Chesapeake Bay Found., Inc. v. Gwaltney of Smithfield, Ltd., 844 F.2d 170, 171-172 (4th Cir. 1988). The same court subsequently upheld the district court's finding of ongoing violations because, at the time the original suit was filed, there was a reasonable likelihood of intermittent or sporadic violations, even though, as it turned out, such violations did not recur. Chesapeake Bay Found., Inc. v. Gwaltney of Smithfield, Ltd., 890 F.2d 690, 693-694 (4th Cir. 1989). The court also refused to dismiss the case as moot. For an example of a more recent review of mootness, in which the Sixth Circuit panel expressed different views about whether the mootness test had been met, see Ailor v. City of Maynardville, 368 F.3d 587 (6th Cir. 2004). What is a sporadic violation? See Sierra Club v. Shell Oil Co., 817 F.2d 1169 (5th Cir. 1987) (given that CWA effluent limitations assume 95-99 percent compliance, permit compliance rates above 95 percent do not put a company in violation of an NPDES permit).

In a separate concurrence in *Gwaltney*, Justice Scalia suggested that the adoption of remedial measures "that clearly eliminate the cause of the violation" preclude a finding of a continuous violation. In Carr v. Alta Verde Indus., Inc., 931 F.2d 1055, 1065 (5th Cir. 1991), the court refused to dismiss a CWA citizen suit as moot because improvements to the defendant's wastewater disposal system did not make it "absolutely clear" that the violations could not reasonably be expected to recur. In Atlantic States Legal Found., Inc. v. Tyson Foods, Inc., 897 F.2d 1128 (11th Cir. 1990), the court concluded that even if post-filing improvements moot a request for injunctive relief, they do not necessarily moot a request for civil penalties.

2. *The Notice Requirement.* What is the effect of failing to provide the requisite prior notice? In Hallstrom v. Tillamook County, 493 U.S. 20 (1989), the Court held that the 60-day notice requirement of RCRA's citizen suit provision, §7002(b), is a jurisdictional prerequisite. Accordingly, when a plaintiff fails to comply with it, the

---

award of costs "should extend to plaintiffs in actions which result in successful abatement but do not reach a verdict. For instance, if as a result of a citizen proceeding and before a verdict is issued, a defendant abated a violation, the court may award litigation expenses borne by the plaintiffs in prosecuting such actions." S. Rep. No. 92-414, p. 81 (1972), 2 Leg. Hist. 1499.

suit must be dismissed. In dissent, Justice Marshall argued that dismissal was not the only possible sanction for noncompliance. The purposes of the notice requirement would be equally well served by staying the proceedings for 60 days. Moreover, that sanction would be more consistent than dismissal would be with Congress's objective of encouraging citizen suits. Issues concerning the adequacy of notice have been raised as well. E.g., Hawksbill Sea Turtle v. Federal Emergency Mgmt. Agency, 126 F.3d 461, 471 (3d Cir. 1997) (ESA); Washington Trout v. McCain Foods, Inc., 45 F.3d 1351, 1354-1355 (9th Cir. 1995) (CWA).

3. *The Role of Citizen Suits Revisited: The Issue of Multiple Enforcement Actions.* As noted above, citizen suits play an important role in environmental enforcement but they are considered to be supplementary to state and federal enforcement. In its *Gwaltney* decision, the Supreme Court described citizens' "interstitial" role in enforcement as follows:

> The bar on citizen suits when governmental enforcement action is under way suggests that the citizen suit is meant to supplement rather than to supplant governmental action. The legislative history of the [Clean Water] Act reinforces this view of the role of the citizen suit. The Senate Report noted that "[t]he Committee intends the great volume of enforcement actions [to] be brought by the State," and that citizen suits are proper only "if the Federal, State, and local agencies fail to exercise their enforcement responsibility." S. Rep. No. 92-414, p. 64 (1971), reprinted in 2 A Legislative History of the Water Pollution Control Act Amendments of 1972, p. 1482 (1973). [Gwaltney of Smithfield v. Chesapeake Bay Found., 484 U.S. 49, 60 (1987).]

Some environmental statutes preclude citizen suits if federal or state authorities have commenced and are "diligently prosecuting" their own civil or criminal enforcement action against the alleged violator. See, e.g., CWA §505(b)(1)(B); CAA §304(b)(1)(B). The question of what constitutes "diligent prosecution" for purposes of determining whether a court action precludes a citizen suit has arisen in a variety of contexts. Is a citizen suit barred if a state entered into a consent decree with the defendant before the filing of the citizen suit? See Knee Deep Cattle Co. v. Bindana Inv. Co., 94 F.3d 514 (9th Cir. 1996). Is the amount of civil penalties sought by a state relevant to whether prosecution was diligent? See Friends of the Earth, Inc. v. Laidlaw Envtl. Serv. (TOC), Inc., 528 U.S. 167 (2000). For further discussion of what constitutes diligent prosecution, see Arkansas Wildlife Fed'n v. ICI Americas, Inc., 29 F.3d 376, 382-383 (8th Cir. 1994).

The CWA was amended in 1987 so that it now bars citizen suits seeking civil penalties if EPA has filed an *administrative* enforcement action or a state "has commenced and is diligently prosecuting an action under a State law comparable to [§1319(g), EPA's administrative enforcement authority]." §309(g)(6)(A). Several of the circuit courts have had occasion to apply §309 to determine whether it bars citizen suits in the context of a variety of administrative enforcement actions. In Paper, Allied-Indus., Chem. and Energy Workers Int'l Union v. Continental Carbon Co., 428 F.3d 1285, 1288 (10th Cir. 2005), the court summarized several of the other appellate courts' decisions, and adopted the Eleventh Circuit's "rough comparability" approach, rather than what it characterized as the "more forgiving" "overall comparability" standard that it indicates the First and Eighth Circuits have adopted. The court held that "three categories of state-law provisions—penalty-assessment, public participation, and judicial review—must be roughly comparable to the corresponding categories of federal provisions." The Eighth Circuit addressed the "comparability" element of §309(g)(6)(A) in *Arkansas Wildlife Fed'n, supra*, at 381, in holding that a state administrative enforcement action barred a citizen suit. The court reached two conclusions concerning the definition of "comparability." The first:

> We agree with the reasoning in *Scituate* [North & South Rivers Watershed Ass'n v. Town of Scituate, 949 F.2d 552 (1st Cir. 1991)], that the comparability requirement may be satisfied so long as the state law contains comparable penalty provisions which the state is authorized to enforce, has the same overall enforcement goals as the federal CWA, provides interested citizens a meaningful opportunity to participate at significant stages of the decision-making process, and adequately safeguards their legitimate substantive interests.

The court added, however, that a state statute that seemingly is comparable for the reasons discussed in the preceding quoted language is only "presumptively" so; the plaintiffs have an opportunity to demonstrate that, on the facts of the case, the state did not provide a "meaningful opportunity to participate in the administrative enforcement case." Id. at 382. For a decision holding that a state law is not comparable to EPA's and, therefore, action under the state law did not bar a citizen suit, see McAbee v. Fort Payne, 318 F.3d 1248 (11th Cir. 2003) (applying the "rough comparability" test).

One of the nuances in §309(g)(6)(A) is that when a violation is being pursued by a state in an administrative enforcement action, the violation may not be the subject of a "civil penalty action" brought under CWA §505. A number of courts have wrestled with the question of whether §309(g)(6)(A) bars not only citizen suits seeking civil penalties, but also such suits seeking injunctive relief. The Eighth Circuit, in the *Arkansas Wildlife Fed'n* decision, and the First Circuit in the *Scituate* case, each held that the §309(g)(6)(A) bar should be read broadly to bar injunctive and penalty-based claims. The Southern District of New York has come out the other way on the ground that the statutory language is "clear and unambiguous" that the bar to citizen suits applies only to civil penalty actions. Coalition for a Livable West Side v. New York City Dep't of Envtl. Prot., 830 F. Supp. 194, 196-197 (S.D.N.Y. 1993). The Tenth Circuit came out on the same side as the Southern District in Paper, Allied-Indus., Chem. and Energy Workers Int'l Union v. Continental Carbon Co., 428 F.3d 1285, 1289 (10th Cir. 2005).

The CAA does not contain comparable language concerning the preclusive effect of state administrative enforcement actions, and the Fifth Circuit has held that, as a result, state administrative enforcement actions under that Act do not have preclusive effect. Texans United for a Safe Economy Educ. Fund v. Crown Central Petroleum Corp., 207 F.3d 789 (5th Cir. 2000). The Third Circuit, in Baughman v. Bradford Coal Co., 592 F.2d 215 (3d Cir. 1979), suggested that in some cases an administrative action could be preclusive under the CAA, delineating several factors for determining whether agency action was tantamount to "a civil action in a court of the United States or a State" for purposes of §304(b)(1)(B) of the CAA. These factors include whether the administrative tribunal has "the power to accord relief which is the substantial equivalent to that available to the EPA in federal court," especially the power to enjoin and to assess meaningful penalties, and whether the agency's procedures are comparable to the procedures applicable to federal court suits brought by the EPA. 592 F.2d at 219. See also Student PIRG v. Fritzsche, Dodge & Olcott, Inc., 759 F.2d 1131, 1138-1139 (3d Cir. 1985) (concluding, after applying the same analytical framework, that an agency proceeding was not the equivalent of a civil action in court).

In some statutes, Congress has clearly indicated that certain types of pending administrative proceedings bar citizen suits. E.g., TSCA §20(b)(1)(B); 33 U.S.C. §1415(g)(2)(C) (Marine Protection, Research, and Sanctuaries Act of 1972). On the other hand, the First Circuit held in Esso Standard Oil Co. (Puerto Rico) v. Rodriguez-Perez, 455 F.3d 1 (1st Cir. 2006), that while a government judicial RCRA (§6972(b)(1)(B)) enforcement action bars citizen suits, a government administrative RCRA enforcement action does not.

Another issue in this arena is: what are the consequences for a citizen suit if a government enters into a settlement with an alleged violator after the citizen files suit? The Second Circuit, in Atlantic States Legal Found. v. Eastman Kodak Co., 933 F.2d 124 (2d Cir. 1991), held that a citizen suit could not continue after the state entered into a settlement with the defendant, so long as the state settlement "reasonably assures that the violations alleged in the complaint have ceased and will not recur." The court held that the state case precluded the citizen suit even though the state did not initiate its enforcement proceeding during the 60-day statutory notice period. The court allowed the citizens to seek recovery of their attorneys' fees on the ground that their action may have helped trigger the state settlement. A year later, the same circuit held that another citizen suit by the same plaintiff was not moot, in a situation in which a local government agency entered into a settlement after the citizen had filed suit and the settlement reasonably assured that the violations would not recur. The court distinguished the two cases on several grounds, including the size of the penalties involved (in the first case, the total penalty was $2 million, while in the latter it was under $10,000) and the identity of the government actors (in the first case it was the state, while in the second it was a local government environmental agency). Atlantic States Legal Found. v. Pan Am. Tanning Corp., 993 F.2d 1017 (2d Cir. 1993).

4. *The Scope of the Citizen Suit Provisions.* What kinds of alleged violations may form the basis for citizen suits? May a citizen suit be brought under the CWA for alleged violations of state water quality standards? In Northwest Envtl. Advocates v. City of Portland, 56 F.3d 979 (9th Cir. 1995), *reh'g denied,* 74 F.3d 945 (9th Cir. 1996), the court ruled that such a suit was proper, provided the defendant's permit includes an explicit condition that its discharges would not cause violations of water quality standards. Compare Oregon Natural Res. Council v. United States Forest Serv., 834 F.2d 842 (9th Cir. 1987) (citizen suit could not be brought to enjoin alleged violation of state water quality standard by a nonpoint source).

May a suit be brought to enforce state standards that exceed federal minimum requirements? The Second Circuit said no in Atlantic States Legal Found. v. Kodak, 12 F.3d 353, 358-360 (2d Cir. 1993). The Ninth Circuit has considered this issue as well. Community Ass'n for Restoration of the Env't v. Henry Bosma Dairy, 305 F.3d 943 (9th Cir. 2002); Ashoff v. Ukiah, 130 F.3d 409 (9th Cir. 1997). For discussion of the broad scope of citizen suits under RCRA, see Interfaith Cmty. Org. v. Honeywell Int'l, 399 F.3d 248 (3d Cir. 2005); Note, Interfaith Community Organization v. Honeywell International: The Third Circuit Affirms the Citizen Suit Use of the [RCRA] and Orders the $400 Million Cleanup of a Polluted Site, 19 Tul. Envtl. L.J. 121 (2006); Maine People's Alliance v. Mallinckrodt, Inc., 471 F.3d 277 (1st Cir. 2006).

5. *Citizen Suits against the Government.* Citizens may sue environmental agencies to force them to perform nondiscretionary duties. See, e.g., ESA §11(g)(1)(C); CAA §304(a)(2); CWA §505(a)(2); RCRA §7002(a)(2). In an early case, NRDC v. Train, 545 F.2d 320 (2d Cir. 1976), the court ordered EPA in a citizen suit under the

CAA to list lead as a criteria pollutant. Compare NRDC v. Thomas, 885 F.2d 1067 (2d Cir. 1989). Citizen suits against the government often seek to force it to comply with statutory deadlines. See, e.g., NRDC v. Train, 510 F.2d 692 (D.C. Cir. 1974) (suit to compel issuance of effluent limitation guidelines under the CWA). Is it possible that successful citizen suits ultimately will undermine EPA's implementation of the federal pollution control laws by forcing it to allocate resources based on the preferences of interest groups and individual judges rather than its own expertise? What effect may the presence of a statutory deadline have on a court's discretion to deny injunctive relief? See Forest Guardians v. Babbitt, 174 F.3d 1178 (10th Cir. 1998). In the absence of a statutory deadline, could disgruntled litigants allege unreasonable delay under §706(1) of the APA rather than pursue a citizen suit under the relevant environmental law? See, e.g., National Wildlife Fed'n v. Adamkus, 936 F. Supp. 435, 442-443 (W.D. Mich. 1996). For an analysis of this issue, see Glicksman, The Value of Agency-Forcing Citizen Suits to Enforce Nondiscretionary Duties, 10 Widener L. Rev. 353 (2004).

6. *Citizen Suits to Force Enforcement.* Is a citizen suit to compel EPA to enforce a pollution control requirement against an alleged violator appropriate? See Heckler v. Chaney, 470 U.S. 821 (1985), which holds that agency decisions not to take enforcement action are presumptively immune from judicial review. Sierra Club v. Whitman, 268 F.3d 898 (9th Cir. 2001), concluded that the decisions concerning whether to issue a finding of violation under §309(a)(3) of the CWA, and whether to enforce once such a finding has been issued, are both discretionary and therefore not the appropriate subject of a citizen suit to force EPA to pursue enforcement action. Dubois v. Thomas, 820 F.2d 943, 948 (8th Cir. 1987), stated: "Only if the Administrator has discretion to allocate its own resources can a rational enforcement approach be achieved. We hold that any duties imposed by §309(a)(3) to investigate or make findings are discretionary." Andreen, Beyond Words of Exhortation: The Congressional Prescription for Vigorous Federal Enforcement of the Clean Water Act, 55 Geo. Wash. L. Rev. 202, 250 (1987), argues that "[t]he legislative history of the [CWA] clearly demonstrates that Congress never meant to create a loophole through which the EPA could defeat a citizen suit seeking compulsory administrative enforcement by simply refusing to issue a finding of violation." Compare Blomquist, Rethinking the Citizen as Prosecutor Model of Environmental Enforcement under the Clean Water Act: Some Overlooked Problems of Outcome Independent Values, 22 Ga. L. Rev. 337 (1988) (criticizing prosecutorial discretion delegated to private citizens by the CWA).

May a private citizen sue to compel EPA to assume enforcement of a delegated state program, such as the NPDES permit program under the CWA, or to revoke the state's program on the ground that the state is improperly implementing the program? See CWA §402(c)(3); Save the Valley, Inc. v. EPA, 99 F. Supp. 2d 981 (S.D. Ind. 2000), *summary judgment granted in part, denied in part,* 223 F. Supp. 2d 997 (2002).

7. *The Constitutionality of Citizen Suits.* Abell, Note, Ignoring the Trees for the Forests: How the Citizen Suit Provision of the Clean Water Act Violates the Constitution's Separation of Powers Principle, 81 Va. L. Rev. 1957 (1995), argues that citizen suit provisions conflict with norms of separation of powers by transferring the power of prosecutorial discretion to private citizens, thereby undermining the executive branch's prosecutorial function and seizing significant executive power for Congress. In his concurrence in Friends of the Earth, Inc. v. Laidlaw, 528 U.S. 167 (2000), Justice Kennedy stated that "[d]ifficult and fundamental questions are raised when we ask whether exactions of public fines by private litigants, and the

delegation of Executive power which might be inferable from the authorization, are permissible in view of the responsibilities committed to the Executive by Article II of the Constitution." Id. at 197. In his dissent in the same case, Justice Scalia suggested that citizen suits are "constitutionally bizarre." Id. at 210. As this section reflects, a majority of the Court have not yet adopted these views. Craig, Will Separation of Powers Challenges "Take Care" of Environmental Citizen Suits? Article II, Injury-in-Fact, Private "Enforcers," and Lessons from *Qui Tam* Litigation, 72 U. Colo. L. Rev. 93 (2001), supports the constitutionality of citizen suits.

8. *Attorneys' Fees*. The ability of public interest groups to recover their attorneys' fees and court costs can be an important inducement to initiate citizen suits. The citizen suit provisions authorize an award of attorneys' and expert witnesses' fees. Some of the statutes explicitly restrict fee awards to prevailing or substantially prevailing parties. E.g., CWA §505(d); CERCLA §310(f); RCRA §7002(e). The Tenth Circuit construed the RCRA attorneys' fee provision, 42 U.S.C. §6972(e), in Browder v. City of Moab, 427 F.3d 717, 723 (10th Cir. 2005), holding that the plaintiff was a prevailing party because it prevailed on at least one claim, even though it lost on others, and noting that the district court "retains discretion to adjust the award commensurate with the degree of success obtained."

In its 2001 decision in Buckhannon Bd. & Care Home, Inc. v. West Virginia Dep't of Health & Human Res., 532 U.S. 598, 600 (2001), the Court, analyzing the attorneys' fees provision of the Fair Housing Amendments Act of 1988 (FHAA), rejected the theory that a party that has "achieved the desired result because the lawsuit brought about a voluntary change in the defendant's conduct," even though the party failed to obtain a judgment on the merits or a court-ordered consent decree, is a "catalyst" and therefore eligible to recover attorneys' fees as a "prevailing party." Is the language in different environmental statutes authorizing recovery of attorneys' fees likely to produce the same result as *Buckhannon*? See Amigo Bravos v. EPA, 324 F.3d 1166 (10th Cir. 2003) (CWA); Sierra Club v. EPA, 322 F.3d 718 (D.C. Cir. 2003) (CAA); Loggerhead Turtle v. The County Council of Volusia County, Florida, 307 F.3d 1318 (11th Cir. 2002) (ESA).

The amount as well as the availability of fee awards is often at issue. In Pennsylvania v. Delaware Valley Citizens' Council for Clean Air, 483 U.S. 711 (1987), a plurality of the Court ruled that the CAA citizen suit provision does not permit enhancement of a reasonable "lodestar" fee to compensate for the attorney's risk of not being paid. City of Burlington v. Dague, 505 U.S. 557 (1992), established that courts may not enhance fee awards in RCRA or CWA citizen suits above the lodestar amount to reflect the fact that the plaintiff's attorneys were retained on a contingent-fee basis and thus assumed the risk of receiving no payment at all. Axline, Decreasing Incentives to Enforce Environmental Laws: City of Burlington v. Dague, 43 Wash. U. J. Urb. & Contemp. L. 257, 273 (1993), argues that "*Dague* decreases the incentives for attorneys to represent citizen groups in statutorily authorized enforcement actions," making it less likely that statutory objectives will be realized.

9. *Post*-Gwaltney *Case Law*. Steel Co. v. Citizens for a Better Env't, 523 U.S. 83 (1998), held that plaintiffs lacked standing to sue for wholly past reporting violations under EPCRA because the complaint "fails the third test of standing, redressability." Among other things, the Court held that requiring the company to pay EPCRA civil penalties to the Treasury and to reimburse the citizens group's litigation expenses did not satisfy this prong of the standing test. Has the majority's decision significantly impaired the usefulness of citizen suits as a supplement to government enforcement

against regulated private entities? Is the decision unique to EPCRA, or does its reasoning apply to other citizen suit provisions as well? See generally *Steel Company Colloquium*, 12 Tul. Envtl. L.J. 1-86 (1998).

In his dissenting opinion in *Steel Company*, Justice Stevens took issue with the majority's treatment of the redressability question by noting that the Court had acknowledged that the environmental group would have had standing if Congress had authorized some payment to it for successful pursuit of an EPCRA filing violation. The majority failed to make clear why payment to the Treasury did not also suffice. The issue of a private individual's standing to sue under a statute that does provide for a bounty was raised in Vermont Agency of Natural Res. v. Stevens, 529 U.S. 765 (2000). The False Claims Act (FCA), 31 U.S.C. §3730(b)(1), authorizes a private person to bring a *qui tam* action (an action pursued by the private plaintiff on behalf of the sovereign as well as on his or her own behalf) against a person who has knowingly filed with the United States a false or fraudulent claim for payment. A successful FCA plaintiff recovers from the defendant a bounty equal to 15-30 percent of the ultimate damage award; the rest goes to the government. Stevens brought a FCA claim against the Vermont agency, alleging that it had submitted false claims to EPA by overstating the amount of time spent by its employees on federally funded projects. The Court held that Stevens met Article III standing requirements. The bounty Stevens would receive if he prevailed provided him with an "interest" in the outcome of the suit, but it was not an interest in obtaining compensation for or preventing the violation of a "legally protected right." Stevens nevertheless demonstrated sufficient injury in fact to satisfy Article III because he was a partial assignee of the government's damage claim, and an assignee has standing to assert the injury in fact suffered by the assignor. Stevens lost on the merits, however, because the Court held that the FCA does not authorize *qui tam* actions against a state.

Two years after its decision in *Steel Company*, and 13 years after its decision in *Gwaltney*, the Court issued Friends of the Earth, Inc. v. Laidlaw Envtl. Serv. (TOC), Inc., 528 U.S. 167 (2000). An excerpt from this case, and questions concerning key elements of standing following the decision, appears in Chapter 3, section A.1 of the text, and we refer the reader there.

For a recent D.C. Circuit decision that addresses standing, involving a challenge to an EPA rule, see NRDC v. EPA, 464 F.3d 1 (D.C. Cir. 2006) (holding that NRDC had standing to challenge EPA's rule because "increases in risk can at times be 'injuries in fact' sufficient to confer standing," and the plaintiffs met the "injury in fact" prong by showing a "substantial probability" of injury).

10. A threshold question for citizen suits is whether the relevant statute provides for a private right of action. Most of the major environmental regulatory statutes contain specific citizen suit provisions that allow citizens to sue under particular circumstances, but not all environmental laws do so. See, e.g., George v. New York City Dep't of City Planning, 436 F.3d 102 (2d Cir. 2006).

Problem 10-1

Chemicals, Inc. (CI), located in a state that EPA has authorized to administer the CWA NPDES program (covered in Chapter 7), has had an NPDES permit since 1998. It never had a violation until 2007. On January 3, 2007, an CI engineer discovered that CI's treatment system is not working properly. The reason for the malfunction is that beginning on January 2, 2007, CI increased its production in order to meet new orders and it therefore began generating more waste. The plant engineer thought that the existing biological treatment system was adequate to treat this expanded volume of waste, but the malfunctioning of the system shows that the engineer was wrong.

On January 10, 2007, CI informed the State environmental agency (the DEP) by letter of the violation and advised the DEP that the company would take steps immediately to fix the treatment system. The company followed up with a letter on March 1 in which it informed the DEP that while the company thought the problem was an anomaly and would take care of itself, to be safe it would install an upgraded biological treatment unit. The company expressed its commitment to full compliance with the environmental laws and its willingness to work with the DEP to be a model company.

The upgraded biological treatment unit that the company has ordered will cost $100,000, and it will cost an additional $1,000 per month to operate (to buy new biological organisms, etc.). It will take the company until January 1, 2008, to install the equipment and make it operational. The company will pay the $100,000 cost of the equipment on January 1, 2008, when it becomes operational. The company typically gets a 10 percent return on its money.

The penalty for violating the CWA is a maximum of $32,500 for each day a violation continues.

Assume the following facts:

1. In determining an appropriate penalty, the State DEP typically begins by calculating the statutory maximum.
2. The DEP also typically determines the economic benefit of noncompliance. In doing so, it uses EPA's BEN model. The basic methodology is described in the EPA's 1999 BEN User's Manual (this is a paraphrased version of the methodology):

   BEN calculates the economic benefits gained from delaying and avoiding required environmental expenditures. Such expenditures can include (1) capital investments (e.g., pollution control equipment), (2) one-time nondepreciable expenditures (e.g., setting a reporting system, or acquiring land), (3) annually recurring costs (e.g., operating and maintenance costs). Each of these expenditures can be either delayed or avoided. BEN's baseline assumption is that capital investments and one-time nondepreciable expenditures are merely delayed over the period of noncompliance, whereas annual costs are avoided entirely over this period. BEN does allow you, however, to analyze any combination of delayed and avoided expenditures.

   The economic benefit calculation must incorporate the economic concepts of the "time value of money." Stated simply, a dollar today is worth more than a dollar tomorrow, because you can invest today's dollar to start earning a return immediately. Thus, the further in the future the dollar is, the less it is worth in "present-value" terms. Similarly, the greater the time value of money (i.e., the greater the "discount" or "compound" rate used to derive the present value), the lower the present value of future costs.

3. In addition, the DEP generally calculates what it refers to as the "gravity" component of the penalty, based on the seriousness of the violations, good faith efforts to comply, and so forth. Assume that DEP staff have already taken this step and determined that the gravity component of the penalty should be $50,000.

4. The DEP has adopted EPA's 2000 Self-Audit Policy, 65 Fed. Reg. 9618 (2000) and the federal agency's 1998 Supplemental Environmental Projects (SEPs) Policy, 63 Fed. Reg. 24,796 (1998). CI is interested in using one or both of these policies to persuade the DEP to minimize the penalty. Ideally, CI would like to avoid paying any penalty at all.

5. Attorneys for the DEP, CI, and a local citizens group that is concerned about CI's dischargers, Save America's Environment (SAE), are meeting next week to discuss the violations and possible ways to address them. The SAE attorney has notified both the DEP and CI attorneys that it believes a significant penalty is warranted, and that SAE also endorses requiring CI to improve the environmental management of its facility, including changing its production process to reduce its generation of hazardous materials that require treatment. The SAE attorney also has informed the DEP and CI attorneys that SAE is considering filing a citizen suit against CI for its violations.

6. An EPA attorney is planning to attend the meeting as well. EPA has informed the DEP that EPA thinks the violations warrant a penalty, and that EPA may initiate its own judicial enforcement action if the DEP does not resolve the case satisfactorily soon.

Each lawyer should prepare for the meeting by considering the following issues: (1) the maximum potential penalty for CI, (2) the amount of economic benefit that CI has gained through its noncompliance, (3) the extent to which the Self-Audit policy and/or the SEPs policy (the former is excerpted below and both are discussed later in this chapter) should be used to shape the outcome, (4) the issues associated with any lawsuit SAE might bring, (5) the issues associated with any lawsuit EPA might bring, and (6) the strategy each party should pursue during the meeting and thereafter.

5.   *Common Law versus Statutory Causes of Action*

In addition to statutory causes of action, either the government or a person may have a cause of action against an entity causing environmental harm, based on common law doctrines such as public and private nuisance. The *Boomer* case, set forth immediately below, is a landmark case in which the court in a common law nuisance action refused to order the closing of a plant responsible for generating air pollution that adversely affected neighboring property. The notes following *Boomer* consider not only alternative approaches to the damages versus injunction question, but also the issue of whether judicial receptivity to requests for injunctive relief should differ depending upon whether the substantive source of law is common law or statutory or depending upon the identity of the plaintiff.

BOOMER v. ATLANTIC CEMENT CO.
26 N.Y.2d 219, 257 N.E.2d 870, 309 N.Y.S.2d 312 (1970)

BERGAN, Judge.

Defendant operates a large cement plant near Albany. These are actions for injunction and damages by neighboring land owners alleging injury to property from dirt, smoke and vibration emanating from the plant. A nuisance has been found after trial, temporary damages have been allowed; but an injunction has been denied.

The public concern with air pollution arising from many sources in industry and in transportation is currently accorded ever wider recognition accompanied by a growing sense of responsibility in State and Federal Governments to control it. Cement plants are obvious sources of air pollution in the neighborhoods where they operate.

But there is now before the court private litigation in which individual property owners have sought specific relief from a single plant operation. The threshold question raised by the division of view on this appeal is whether the court should resolve the litigation between the parties now before it as equitably as seems possible; or whether, seeking promotion of the general public welfare, it should channel private litigation into broad public objectives.

A court performs its essential function when it decides the rights of parties before it. Its decision of private controversies may sometimes greatly affect public issues. Large questions of law are often resolved by the manner in which private litigation is decided. But this is normally an incident to the court's main function to settle controversy. It is a rare exercise of judicial power to use a decision in private litigation as a purposeful mechanism to achieve direct public objectives greatly beyond the rights and interests before the court.

Effective control of air pollution is a problem presently far from solution even with the full public and financial powers of government. In large measure adequate technical procedures are yet to be developed and some that appear possible may be economically impracticable.

It seems apparent that the amelioration of air pollution will depend on technical research in great depth; on a carefully balanced consideration of the economic impact of close regulation; and of the actual effect on public health. It is likely to require massive public expenditure and to demand more than any local community can accomplish and to depend on regional and interstate controls.

A court should not try to do this on its own as a by-product of private litigation and it seems manifest that the judicial establishment is neither equipped in the limited nature of any judgment it can pronounce nor prepared to lay down and implement an effective policy for the elimination of air pollution. This is an area beyond the circumference of one private lawsuit. It is a direct responsibility for government and should not thus be undertaken as an incident to solving a dispute between property owners and a single cement plant—one of many—in the Hudson River valley. . . .

The ground for the denial of injunction, notwithstanding the finding both that there is a nuisance and that plaintiffs have been damaged substantially, is the large disparity in economic consequences of the nuisance and of the injunction. This theory cannot, however, be sustained without overruling a doctrine which has been consistently reaffirmed in several leading cases in this court and which has never been disavowed here, namely that where a nuisance has been found and where there has been any substantial damage shown by the party complaining an injunction will be granted.

The rule in New York has been that such a nuisance will be enjoined although marked disparity be shown in economic consequence between the effect of the injunction and the effect of the nuisance.

The problem of disparity in economic consequence was sharply in focus in Whalen v. Union Bag & Paper Co., 208 N.Y. 1, 101 N.E. 805. A pulp mill entailing an investment of more than a million dollars polluted a stream in which plaintiff, who owned a farm, was "a lower riparian owner." The economic loss to plaintiff from this pollution was small. This court, reversing the Appellate Division, reinstated the injunction granted by the Special Term against the argument of the mill owner that in view of "the slight advantage to plaintiff and the great loss that will be inflicted on defendant" an injunction should not be granted. "Such a balancing of injuries cannot be justified by the circumstances of this case," Judge Werner noted. He continued: "Although the damage to the plaintiff may be slight as compared with the defendant's expense of abating the condition, that is not a good reason for refusing an injunction."

Thus the unconditional injunction granted at Special Term was reinstated. The rule laid down in that case, then, is that whenever the damage resulting from a nuisance is found not "unsubstantial," viz., $100 a year, injunction would follow. . . .

Although the court at Special Term and the Appellate Division held that injunction should be denied, it was found that plaintiffs had been damaged in various specific amounts up to the time of the trial and damages to the respective plaintiffs were awarded for those amounts. The effect of this was, injunction having been denied, plaintiffs could maintain successive actions at law for damages thereafter as further damage was incurred.

The court at Special Term also found the amount of permanent damage attributable to each plaintiff, for the guidance of the parties in the event both sides stipulated to the payment and acceptance of such permanent damage as a settlement of all the controversies among the parties. The total of permanent damages to all plaintiffs thus found was $185,000. . . .

This result at Special Term and at the Appellate Division is a departure from a rule that has become settled; but to follow the rule literally in these cases would be to close down the plant at once. This court is fully agreed to avoid that immediately drastic remedy; the difference in view is how best to avoid it.*

One alternative is to grant the injunction but postpone its effect to a specified future date to give opportunity for technical advances to permit defendant to eliminate the nuisance; another is to grant the injunction conditioned on the payment of permanent damages to plaintiffs which would compensate them for the total economic loss to their property present and future caused by defendant's operations. For reasons which will be developed the court chooses the latter alternative.

If the injunction were to be granted unless within a short period—e.g., 18 months—the nuisance be abated by improved methods, there would be no assurance that any significant technical improvement would occur.

The parties could settle this private litigation at any time if defendant paid enough money and the imminent threat of closing the plant would build up the pressure on defendant. If there were no improved techniques found, there would inevitably be applications to the court at Special Term for extensions of time to perform on showing of good faith efforts to find such techniques.

Moreover, techniques to eliminate dust and other annoying by-products of cement making are unlikely to be developed by any research the defendant can undertake within any short period, but will depend on the total resources of the

*Respondent's investment in the plant is in excess of $45,000,000. There are over 300 people employed there.

cement industry nationwide and throughout the world. The problem is universal wherever cement is made.

For obvious reasons the rate of the research is beyond control of defendant. If at the end of 18 months the whole industry has not found a technical solution a court would be hard put to close down this one cement plant if due regard be given to equitable principles.

On the other hand, to grant the injunction unless defendant pays plaintiffs such permanent damages as may be fixed by the court seems to do justice between the contending parties. All of the attributions of economic loss to the properties on which plaintiffs' complaints are based will have been redressed.

The nuisance complained of by these plaintiffs may have other public or private consequences, but these particular parties are the only ones who have sought remedies and the judgment proposed will fully redress them. The limitation of relief granted is a limitation only within the four corners of these actions and does not foreclose public health or other public agencies from seeking proper relief in a proper court.

It seems reasonable to think that the risk of being required to pay permanent damages to injured property owners by cement plant owners would itself be a reasonable effective spur to research for improved techniques to minimize nuisance. . . .

Thus it seems fair to both sides to grant permanent damages to plaintiffs which will terminate this private litigation. The theory of damage is the "servitude on land" of plaintiffs imposed by defendant's nuisance. (See United States v. Causby, 328 U.S. 256, 261, 262, 267, where the term "servitude" addressed to the land was used by Justice Douglas relating to the effect of airplane noise on property near an airport.) . . .

JASEN, Judge (dissenting). . . .

I see grave dangers in overruling our long-established rule of granting an injunction where a nuisance results in substantial continuing damage. In permitting the injunction to become inoperative upon the payment of permanent damages, the majority is, in effect, licensing a continuing wrong. It is the same as saying to the cement company, you may continue to do harm to your neighbors so long as you pay a fee for it. Furthermore, once such permanent damages are assessed and paid, the incentive to alleviate the wrong would be eliminated, thereby continuing air pollution of an area without abatement. . . .

This kind of inverse condemnation may not be invoked by a private person or corporation for private gain or advantage. Inverse condemnation should only be permitted when the public is primarily served in the taking or impairment of property. The promotion of the interests of the polluting cement company has, in my opinion, no public use or benefit.

Nor is it constitutionally permissible to impose servitude on land, without consent of the owner, by payment of permanent damages where the continuing impairment of the land is for a private use. This is made clear by the State Constitution (art. I, §7, subd. (a)) which provides that "[p]rivate property shall not be taken for *Public use* without just compensation" (emphasis added). It is, of course, significant that the section makes no mention of taking for a *private* use. . . .

I would enjoin the defendant cement company from continuing the discharge of dust particles upon its neighbors' properties unless, within 18 months, the cement company abated this nuisance. . . .

*NOTES AND QUESTIONS ABOUT COMMON LAW VERSUS
STATUTORY CAUSES OF ACTION*

1. Did *Boomer* consider all relevant costs in balancing the equities? Is harm to persons other than the plaintiffs relevant? See Juergensmeyer, Control of Air Pollution through the Assertion of Private Rights, 1967 Duke L.J. 1126.

2. *Common Law versus Statutory Standards for Injunctive Relief.* Should the relief provided for proven statutory violations be the same as for common law nuisances? The Court in the *Snail Darter* case, TVA v. Hill, 437 U.S. 153 (1978), excerpted in Chapter 5, held that the ESA foreclosed the exercise of traditional judicial equitable discretion and required an injunction preventing completion of the Tellico Dam to save the darter. In Weinberger v. Romero-Barcelo, 456 U.S. 305 (1982), on the other hand, the Supreme Court upheld the district court's refusal to enjoin the Navy from continuing to drop bombs off the coast of Puerto Rico while it applied for a permit under the CWA, even though the activity clearly violated §301(a) of the Act. Distinguishing the *Snail Darter* case, the Court reasoned that issuance of the requested injunction was not the only means of vindicating the statute's purposes. The district court acted well within its traditional equitable discretion, which Congress intended to preserve, by ordering the Navy to apply for a permit but not shutting down training activities in the interim. The reasoning in *Romero-Barcelo* is also evident in Amoco Prod. Co. v. Village of Gambell, 480 U.S. 531 (1987), where the Court refused to enjoin an offshore oil and gas lease as a violation of the Alaska National Interest Lands Conservation Act (ANILCA), 16 U.S.C. §3120(a)(3)(C). The Court determined that an injunction was not warranted because the Act did not prohibit all federal resource development. Instead, ANILCA established a process for the consideration of the effects of federal land use on subsistence resources. Because the district court found that oil and gas exploration would not significantly restrict subsistence uses, the statutory policy of protecting such uses was not undermined by denial of injunctive relief. Further, the Court concluded that a presumption that a violation of the Act caused irreparable damage, which the appellate court had engaged in, was contrary to traditional equitable principles. Although "the balance of harms will usually favor the issuance of an injunction to protect the environment," 480 U.S. at 545, injury to subsistence resources from oil exploration was not at all probable in that case.

3. *Does the Identity of the Plaintiff Matter?* Would it have made any difference if the plaintiff in *Romero-Barcelo* had been the federal government instead of the governor of Puerto Rico and EPA had supported the issuance of an injunction? See footnote 12 of Justice White's opinion in *Romero-Barcelo*. In United States v. Bethlehem Steel Corp., 38 F.3d 862 (7th Cir. 1994), the court stated that the law of injunctions differs when the plaintiff is the government or a "private attorney general" as opposed to a private individual. In the former case, at least where the activity sought to be enjoined may endanger the public health, "injunctive relief is proper, without resort to balancing." Id. at 868. "In cases of public health legislation, the emphasis shifts from irreparable injury to concern for the general public interest." Id. (quoting EDF, Inc. v. Lamphier, 714 F.2d 331, 337-338 (4th Cir. 1983)). The court upheld an injunction against continued noncompliance with RCRA and the SDWA issued without regard to a balancing of the equities or a finding of irreparable harm.

Does *Bethlehem Steel* support the proposition that the government is automatically entitled to an injunction each time it proves a statutory violation? In United States v. Marine Shale Processors, 81 F.3d 1329 (5th Cir. 1996), the court stated that "when the United States or a sovereign state sues in its capacity as protector of the public interest, a court may rest an injunction entirely upon a determination that the activity at issue constitutes a risk of danger to the public." Id. at 1359. It added that, "[t]o be sure, a court of equity must exercise its discretion with an eye to the congressional policy as expressed in the relevant statute, but some of *Bethlehem Steel*'s language may tread too closely to the view, rejected in [*Romero-Barcelo*], that a court is 'mechanically obligated to grant an injunction for every violation of law' when the United States is the plaintiff." Id. at 1360. United States v. Massachusetts Water Res. Auth., 256 F.3d 36 (1st Cir. 2001), stated that "[t]he role a court plays in deciding whether to grant a statutory injunction is different than the one it plays when it weighs the equitable claims of two private parties in a suit seeking injunctive relief. . . . [I]n the context of statutory injunctions, the court's freedom to make an independent assessment of the equities and the public interest is circumscribed to the extent that Congress has already made such assessments with respect to the type of case before the court." Id. at 47. The court nevertheless concluded that Congress intended that courts considering alleged violations of the SDWA retain their traditional equitable discretion and that the district court did not exceed its authority by refusing to issue an injunction requiring that a public water system install filtration technology.

4. *The Scope of Judicial Discretion in Fashioning Particular Forms of Injunctive Relief.* In *Boomer*, the court refused to grant an injunction that required the installation of equipment to correct the problem. Should the common law be technology forcing? What should be the standard of required technology? 1 W. Rodgers, Environmental Law: Air and Water §2.7 (1986). One of the purported goals of tort law is to force those who cause harm to internalize the resulting costs. It is has been suggested that it is fairer to force internalization on those who are in a good position to spread widely the costs of the harm. Does injunctive relief further this goal? See Calabresi, Some Thoughts on Risk Distribution and the Law of Torts, 70 Yale L.J. 499, 534-536 (1961).

More generally, how much discretion does or should a federal district court have in a citizen suit to determine the nature of the relief granted? Suppose that the court finds that the plaintiff has proven that a citizen suit defendant has violated a permit under the Clean Water Act. Is the court limited to ordering compliance or may it mandate the manner of compliance? See NRDC v. Southwest Marine, Inc., 236 F.3d 985, 1000-1002 (9th Cir. 2000).

D.   EMERGING ISSUES IN ENVIRONMENTAL ENFORCEMENT AND THE EXPANSION OF THE ENFORCEMENT POLICY TOOLBOX

Much of this chapter focuses on what might be considered "traditional enforcement tools," notably monitoring compliance and bringing, and defending against, alleged violations. One of the primary purposes of such traditional enforcement is "deterrence," which EPA defines as causing "people [to] change their behavior to avoid a sanction." EPA, Office of Enforcement, Principles of Environmental Enforcement 2-3 (Feb. 1992). The agency has long believed that deterrence must be an important part of an enforcement program. In his book on EPA's environmental enforcement efforts,

Professor Mintz describes EPA's traditional emphasis on deterrence-based enforcement as follows:

> With the brief exception of the Gorsuch era of the early 1980s, both the EPA's written enforcement policies and its actual practices have consistently emphasized the initiation of formal enforcement actions against violators of federal environmental standards. . . . The formal, legalistic nature of EPA's enforcement efforts is reflected in the agency's system for measuring and publicizing enforcement success. It is also evident in the EPA's sizeable legal staff, the high volume of cases it regularly refers to the Justice Department for civil action or criminal prosecution, the monetary value of the civil and administrative penalties it has assessed against violators, and the large body of enforcement policies, guidance documents, and studies it has issued that require or urge the use of formal enforcement methods. [Mintz, Enforcement at the EPA: High Stakes and Hard Choices 102 (1995).]

While deterrence-based enforcement has continued to be an important part of EPA's enforcement toolbox, there has been increasing debate about "what works best" in promoting compliance with environmental requirements. In recent years some members of the regulated community, and many state officials, among others, have increasingly sounded the theme that an approach based on cooperation is more likely to produce compliance in many cases than an approach based on deterrence. Rechtschaffen & Markell, Reinventing Environmental Enforcement & the State/Federal Relationship (2003). EPA itself has given increasing emphasis in recent years to cooperative approaches. EPA's FY 2007 update to its national enforcement guidance, for example, identifies compliance assistance and compliance incentives (each of which is described below in more detail), as well as traditional enforcement, as tools needed to address environmental risks and noncompliance patterns. EPA, Final FY07 Update to . . . [OECA] National Program Managers' Guidance 11 (April 2006).

The growing enthusiasm for "cooperative approaches" is not necessarily matched by empirical support that they work. With respect to the idea that self-policing approaches almost surely will yield improved environmental performance, for example, Shelley Metzenbaum has noted that "[s]urprisingly, we are far from a clear answer [concerning] whether EMSs [environmental management systems] predictably improve environmental performance." Metzenbaum, Information-Driven, 17 Envtl. F. 26, 33 (Mar./Apr. 2000). On the other hand, it also seems clear that exclusive reliance on deterrence-based enforcement is unlikely to be of maximum effectiveness for numerous reasons, including the fact that there simply aren't enough government officials to monitor the compliance of the regulated community or to take enforcement action when violations occur. Schaeffer, Encouraging Voluntary Compliance without Compromising Enforcement: EPA's 1995 Auditing Policy, in Conference Proceedings, Fourth International Conference on Environmental Compliance and Enforcement 451, 453 (1996). What is indisputable at this point is that much remains to be learned before definitive statements are possible as to the relative effectiveness of different approaches in different settings. See Silberman, Does Environmental Deterrence Work? Evidence and Experience Say Yes, but We Need to Understand How and Why, 30 Envtl. L. Rep. (ELI) 10523 (2000).

A second overarching issue that has swept the enforcement world involves the debate about what we should be measuring in gauging the effectiveness of enforcement and other compliance promotion efforts. Traditionally, EPA and the states have focused primarily on what some have characterized as "enforcement beans"—the level of government activities, such as the number of inspections conducted, the number of enforcement actions brought, and the amount of penalty dollars sought and collected. Most observers agree that this information has some value, for the reasons that EPA's Michael Stahl has identified:

> These outputs have some virtues as performance measures. They provide a sense of enforcement "presence" and the extent to which deterrence is being used to bring about compliance. They are simple, clear, easily understood, and depict what has been produced for a given level of resources invested. [M. Stahl, Beyond the Bean Count: Measuring Performance of Regulatory Compliance Programs, The Public Manager (Fall 1999), at 31.]

These measures, however, also have significant shortcomings, particularly when used as the exclusive benchmarks for performance, as Stahl also explains:

> [O]utput measures reveal very little about the state of compliance. Is an increase in enforcement outputs good news (i.e., the government was able to identify and correct a higher percentage of noncompliance) or bad news (i.e., noncompliance is increasing)? . . . [O]utput measures do not describe the changes in behavior or other improvements that resulted from government action to ensure compliance. Knowing that [EPA] . . . issued over 2,000 enforcement cases in a year does not give any indication about how many tons of pollutants were removed from the environment from those cases. . . . [O]utput measures say nothing about the extent to which important social objectives or problems are being addressed. Knowing that [OSHA] . . . conducted thousands of inspections in a year does not indicate whether work place injury rates are declining. [Id. at 32.]

Concern that traditional measures of enforcement performance did not provide good pictures of the effects of enforcement activity has led EPA and the states to explore expanding the measures used in order to better capture these effects. See, e.g., EPA Performance Measures Do Not Effectively Track Compliance Outcomes, Report No. 2006-P-00006 3 (Dec. 15, 2005), www.epa.gov/oig/reports/2006/20051215-2006-P-00006.pdf, discussing EPA's use of "intermediate outcome" measures (e.g., compliance rates and changes in compliance) and "end outcome" measures (e.g., improved environmental conditions resulting from particular activities) as well as output and input measures. See generally Metzenbaum, Making Measurement Matter: The Challenge and Promise of Building a Performance-Focused Environmental Protection System (Brookings Inst. 1998).

While progress in increasing the range of compliance strategies, and refining measures of performance has been mixed,* these two phenomena have contributed to the emergence of a fairly broad-based desire to expand the toolbox for promoting compliance and to expand the measures used to evaluate performance. These phenomena have made the process of environmental enforcement quite dynamic in recent years. EPA and the states have experimented with a wide variety of compliance promotion strategies that fall along a continuum with deterrence-based approaches on one end and cooperation-based approaches on the other. We divide these initiatives

*Performance Measures, *supra*; U.S. GAO, Environmental Protection: EPA's and States' Efforts to Focus State Enforcement Programs on Results, GAO/RCED-98-113 (May 1998).

into four categories: (1) compliance assistance, (2) compliance incentives, (3) "spotlighting," and (4) performance tracking. The lines between the categories are by no means clear in all cases. Instead, there is considerable overlap in some areas. Brief summaries of some of these initiatives are provided below.

1. Compliance Assistance

In recent years EPA has made a significant commitment to upgrading its capacity to provide "compliance assistance," which the agency defines as "providing information and technical assistance to the regulated community to help it meet the requirements of environmental law." EPA Office of Enforcement and Compliance Assurance, Guide for Measuring Compliance Assistance Outcomes 4 (June 2002). EPA characterizes as compliance assistance "attempts to ensure that the regulated community understands its obligations by providing clear and consistent descriptions of regulatory requirements" and helping the regulated community "find cost-effective ways to comply and to go 'beyond compliance' in improving their environmental performance through the use of pollution prevention and other innovative technologies." Id.

EPA groups compliance assistance activities into the following categories: telephone assistance, workshops, presentations, compliance assistance tools, and on-site visits. One of its significant initiatives in this area is the creation of Internet-based Compliance Assistance Centers (www.assistancecenters.net). The primary focus of these centers is to provide compliance assistance to small and medium-sized businesses, local governments, and federal facilities. In 2006, EPA "celebrated ten years of helping regulated facilities" and others through the centers. EPA reports that in FY 2005 these centers were visited more than 1.4 million times. EPA, FY 2005 Compliance & Enforcement Annual Results, at 17.

A second major EPA compliance assistance initiative was its launching of the National Assistance Clearinghouse (http://cfpub.epa.gov/clearinghouse) in 2001. The Clearinghouse website provides "quick access to compliance assistance tools, contacts, and planned activities from US EPA, its partners, and other compliance assistance providers. . . . " Id.

In its June 2002 Guide for Measuring Compliance Assistance Outcomes and in a more focused report, The National Nitrate Compliance Initiative Report, EPA OECA, EPA 300-R-02-003 (Apr. 2002), EPA summarizes one of its recent compliance assistance initiatives, known as the National Nitrate Compliance Initiative, which involved educating the metal finishing sector about EPCRA §313 requirements (discussed in Chapter 8, section E.2.c) and EPA's audit policy. In late 1999, EPA determined that up to 1,000 facilities (or roughly 40 percent of the covered regulated community) were failing to comply with their reporting obligations under the TRI program for nitrate compounds. EPA considered this widespread reporting failure to be significant because of the inherent risks that nitrates pose (EPA terms them "toxic chemicals that can pose serious risks to human health and the environment") and because, among other things, there had been recent "[c]atastrophic releases" that caused adverse health effects; for example, an incident in Pennsylvania led EPA Region III to issue an emergency order under the Safe Drinking Water Act in June 2000 to provide bottled water to more than 4,000 people because a facility had contaminated local drinking water and more than 21 miles of Connoquenessing Creek with dangerous levels of nitrates.

EPA adopted a "nationally consistent enforcement response" (the National Nitrate Compliance Initiative) to address this widespread noncompliance. EPA first sought to raise awareness about the reporting obligations and the extent of non-compliance by issuing an Enforcement Alert that urged regulated parties to disclose violations under EPA's Self-Audit and Small Business policies (both of which are discussed below). EPA reports that many facilities did so. For the parties that did not pursue voluntary disclosure under these policies following distribution of the Enforcement Alert, EPA followed up by issuing Notice of Opportunity to Show Cause letters that invited these parties either to show EPA that they were not in violation of their reporting obligations or to accept a settlement that included a modest fine and a commitment to report properly in the future. The agency subsequently issued an alternative settlement that included an even more modest penalty and a commitment by the party to undertake a compliance audit of all of its obligations under EPCRA §313.

EPA reports that, through this initiative, nearly 600 companies agreed to audit more than 1,000 facilities for EPCRA §313 regulatory obligations (including nitrate reporting). The agency also reports that the initiative increased reporting of nitrate releases from 60 percent to 90 percent. Further, through a follow-up phone survey, EPA determined that 78 percent of the respondents reported that they changed their behavior as a result of the mailing. EPA lists the following examples of the types of changes made:

- Conducted an audit
- Made a process, operating, or material change
- Developed an internal monitoring/reporting system
- Researched alternatives and substitutions
- Obtained further technical assistance [June 2002 Guide, at 6.]

This initiative has features that come within the rubric of "compliance assistance," such as its effort to educate regulated parties about their reporting obligations. It also contains elements, such as promised reductions in penalty amounts for voluntarily reporting and for conducting self-audits, which are in the nature of "compliance incentives." The latter category of EPA strategies to encourage compliance is discussed next.

2.   Compliance Incentives

To complement its development of a variety of compliance assistance strategies, in recent years EPA has launched a number of initiatives referred to as "compliance incentive"–based approaches. EPA has defined compliance incentives as approaches that "encourage regulated entities to voluntarily discover, disclose and correct violations or clean up contaminated sites before they are identified by the government for enforcement investigation or response." EPA, Operating Principles for an Integrated Enforcement and Compliance Assurance Program 8 (Interim Final Nov. 18, 1996).

EPA's "Self-Audit" Policy, Incentives for Self-Policing: Discovery, Disclosure, Correction and Prevention of Violations, 65 Fed. Reg. 19618 (2000), is perhaps its best-known compliance incentive policy. The policy is intended to provide incentives for regulated parties to detect, promptly disclose, and expeditiously correct violations. The incentives take four shapes. Regulated entities that commit violations but meet the nine conditions in the policy qualify for 100 percent mitigation of the gravity-based component of a civil penalty. Regulated parties that meet all of the conditions except the first (systematic discovery of violations) qualify for a 75 percent mitigation of any gravity-based civil penalty. Further, EPA will not recommend criminal prosecution for regulated parties that disclose violations of criminal law under certain conditions outlined in the policy. Finally, EPA will not routinely request audit reports.

Figure 10-11 contains EPA's statistics concerning regulated parties' use of the Self-Audit policy.

An excerpt from the Self-Audit policy follows.

ENVIRONMENTAL PROTECTION AGENCY, INCENTIVES FOR SELF-POLICING: DISCOVERY, DISCLOSURE, CORRECTION AND PREVENTION OF VIOLATIONS
65 Fed. Reg. 19,618-19,624 (2000)

[Parts I.A and I.B review the history of the Self-Audit policy, which is a revision of EPA's 1995 policy.]

PURPOSE . . .

EPA's enforcement program provides a strong incentive for compliance by imposing stiff sanctions for noncompliance. Enforcement has contributed to the dramatic expansion of environmental auditing as measured in numerous recent surveys. For example, in a 1995 survey by Price Waterhouse LLP, more than 90% of corporate respondents who conduct audits identified one of the reasons for doing so as the desire to find and correct violations before government inspectors discover them. . . .

At the same time, because government resources are limited, universal compliance cannot be achieved without active efforts by the regulated community to police themselves. More than half of the respondents to the same 1995 Price Waterhouse survey said that they would expand environmental auditing in exchange for reduced penalties for violations discovered and corrected. While many companies already

	1999	2000	2001	2002	2003	2004	2005
Number of audit policy disclosures for facilities	990	2190	1095	957	614	1223	1487
Number of audit policy disclosures for companies	260	429	397	500	379	491	627

Source: EPA, National Enforcement Trends—FY 2005, http://cfpub.epa.gov/compliance/resources/reports/nets/index.cfm.

FIGURE 10-11
Self-Audit Policy Statistics

audit or have compliance management programs in place, EPA believes that the incentives offered in this Policy will improve the frequency and quality of these self-policing efforts.

D. Incentives for Self-Policing

1. ELIMINATING GRAVITY-BASED PENALTIES

In general, civil penalties that EPA assesses are comprised of two elements: the economic benefit component and the gravity-based component. The economic benefit component reflects the economic gain derived from a violator's illegal competitive advantage. Gravity-based penalties are that portion of the penalty over and above the economic benefit. They reflect the egregiousness of the violator's behavior and constitute the punitive portion of the penalty. . . .

Under the Audit Policy, EPA will not seek gravity-based penalties for disclosing entities that meet all nine Policy conditions, including systematic discovery. ("Systematic discovery" means the detection of a potential violation through an environmental audit or a compliance management system that reflects the entity's due diligence in preventing, detecting and correcting violations.) EPA has elected to waive gravity-based penalties for violations discovered systematically, recognizing that environmental auditing and compliance management systems play a critical role in protecting human health and the environment by identifying, correcting and ultimately preventing violations.

However, EPA reserves the right to collect any economic benefit that may have been realized as a result of noncompliance, even where the entity meets all other Policy conditions. Where the Agency determines that the economic benefit is insignificant, the Agency also may waive this component of the penalty.

EPA's decision to retain its discretion to recover economic benefit is based on two reasons. First, facing the risk that the Agency will recoup economic benefit provides an incentive for regulated entities to comply on time. Taxpayers whose payments are late expect to pay interest or a penalty; the same principle should apply to corporations and other regulated entities that have delayed their investment in compliance. Second, collecting economic benefit is fair because it protects law-abiding companies from being undercut by their noncomplying competitors, thereby preserving a level playing field.

2. 75% REDUCTION OF GRAVITY-BASED PENALTIES

Gravity-based penalties will be reduced by 75% where the disclosing entity does not detect the violation through systematic discovery but otherwise meets all other Policy conditions. The Policy appropriately limits the complete waiver of gravity-based civil penalties to companies that conduct environmental auditing or have in place a compliance management system. However, to encourage disclosure and correction of violations even in the absence of systematic discovery, EPA will reduce gravity-based penalties by 75% for entities that meet conditions D(2) through D(9) of the Policy. EPA expects that a disclosure under this provision will encourage the entity to work with the Agency to resolve environmental problems and begin to develop an effective auditing program or compliance management system.

3.   No Recommendations for Criminal Prosecution

In accordance with EPA's Investigative Discretion Memo dated January 12, 1994, EPA generally does not focus its criminal enforcement resources on entities that voluntarily discover, promptly disclose and expeditiously correct violations, unless there is potentially culpable behavior that merits criminal investigation. When a disclosure that meets the terms and conditions of this Policy results in a criminal investigation, EPA will generally not recommend criminal prosecution for the disclosing entity, although the Agency may recommend prosecution for culpable individuals and other entities. . . .

Important limitations to the incentive apply. It will not be available, for example, where corporate officials are consciously involved in or willfully blind to violations, or conceal or condone noncompliance. Since the regulated entity must satisfy conditions D(2) through D(9) of the Policy, violations that cause serious harm or which may pose imminent and substantial endangerment to human health or the environment are not eligible. Finally, EPA reserves the right to recommend prosecution for the criminal conduct of any culpable individual or subsidiary organization.

While EPA may decide not to recommend criminal prosecution for disclosing entities, ultimate prosecutorial discretion resides with the U.S. Department of Justice, which will be guided by its own policy on voluntary disclosures. . . . In addition, where a disclosing entity has met the conditions for avoiding a recommendation for criminal prosecution under this Policy, it will also be eligible for either 75% or 100% mitigation of gravity-based civil penalties, depending on whether the systematic discovery condition was met.

4.   No Routine Requests for Audit Reports

EPA reaffirms its Policy . . . to refrain from routine requests for audit reports. That is, EPA has not and will not routinely request copies of audit reports to trigger enforcement investigations. Implementation of the 1995 Policy has produced no evidence that the Agency has deviated, or should deviate, from this Policy. In general, an audit that results in expeditious correction will reduce liability, not expand it. However, if the Agency has independent evidence of a violation, it may seek the information it needs to establish the extent and nature of the violation and the degree of culpability.

For discussion of the circumstances in which EPA might request an audit report to determine Policy eligibility, see the explanatory text on cooperation, section I.E.9.

E.   Conditions

Section D describes the nine conditions that a regulated entity must meet in order for the Agency to decline to seek (or to reduce) gravity-based penalties under the Policy. . . .

1.   Systematic Discovery of the Violation through an Environmental Audit or a Compliance Management System

Under Section D(1), the violation must have been discovered through either (a) an environmental audit, or (b) a compliance management system that reflects due diligence in preventing, detecting and correcting violations. Both "environmental audit" and "compliance management system" are defined in Section B of the Policy.

The revised Policy uses the term "compliance management system" instead of "due diligence," which was used in the 1995 Policy. This change in nomenclature is intended solely to conform the Policy language to terminology more commonly in use by industry and by regulators to refer to a systematic management plan or systematic efforts to achieve and maintain compliance. No substantive difference is intended by substituting the term "compliance management system" for "due diligence," as the Policy clearly indicates that the compliance management system must reflect the regulated entity's due diligence in preventing, detecting and correcting violations.

Compliance management programs that train and motivate employees to prevent, detect and correct violations on a daily basis are a valuable complement to periodic auditing. Where the violation is discovered through a compliance management system and not through an audit, the disclosing entity should be prepared to document how its program reflects the due diligence criteria defined in Section B of the Policy statement. These criteria, which are adapted from existing codes of practice—such as Chapter Eight of the U.S. Sentencing Guidelines for organizational defendants, effective since 1991—are flexible enough to accommodate different types and sizes of businesses and other regulated entities. The Agency recognizes that a variety of compliance management programs are feasible, and it will determine whether basic due diligence criteria have been met in deciding whether to grant Audit Policy credit.

As a condition of penalty mitigation, EPA may require that a description of the regulated entity's compliance management system be made publicly available. The Agency believes that the availability of such information will allow the public to judge the adequacy of compliance management systems, lead to enhanced compliance, and foster greater public trust in the integrity of compliance management systems.

2.   VOLUNTARY DISCOVERY

Under Section D(2), the violation must have been identified voluntarily, and not through a monitoring, sampling, or auditing procedure that is required by statute, regulation, permit, judicial or administrative order, or consent agreement. The Policy provides three specific examples of discovery that would not be voluntary, and therefore would not be eligible for penalty mitigation: emissions violations detected through a required continuous emissions monitor, violations of NPDES discharge limits found through prescribed monitoring, and violations discovered through a compliance audit required to be performed by the terms of a consent order or settlement agreement. The exclusion does not apply to violations that are discovered pursuant to audits that are conducted as part of a comprehensive environmental management system (EMS) required under a settlement agreement. In general, EPA supports the implementation of EMSs that promote compliance, prevent pollution and improve overall environmental performance. Precluding the availability of the Audit Policy for discoveries made through a comprehensive EMS that has been implemented pursuant to a settlement agreement might discourage entities from agreeing to implement such a system. . . .

The voluntary requirement applies to discovery only, not reporting. That is, any violation that is voluntarily discovered is generally eligible for Audit Policy credit, regardless of whether reporting of the violation was required after it was found.

3.   PROMPT DISCLOSURE

Section D(3) requires that the entity disclose the violation in writing to EPA within 21 calendar days after discovery. . . . If a statute or regulation requires the entity to report the violation in fewer than 21 days, disclosure must be made within the time limit established by law. . . .

The 21-day disclosure period begins when the entity discovers that a violation has, or may have, occurred. The trigger for discovery is when any officer, director, employee or agent of the facility has an objectively reasonable basis for believing that a violation has, or may have, occurred. The "objectively reasonable basis" standard is measured against what a prudent person, having the same information as was available to the individual in question, would have believed. It is not measured against what the individual in question thought was reasonable at the time the situation was encountered. If an entity has some doubt as to the existence of a violation, the recommended course is for the entity to proceed with the disclosure and allow the regulatory authorities to make a definitive determination. Contract personnel who provide on-site services at the facility may be treated as employees or agents for purposes of the Policy. . . .

In the multi-facility context, EPA will ordinarily extend the 21-day period to allow reasonable time for completion and review of multi-facility audits where: (a) EPA and the entity agree on the timing and scope of the audits prior to their commencement; and (b) the facilities to be audited are identified in advance. In the acquisitions context, EPA will consider extending the prompt disclosure period on a case-by-case basis. The 21-day disclosure period will begin on the date of discovery by the acquiring entity, but in no case will the period begin earlier than the date of acquisition.

In summary, Section D(3) recognizes that it is critical for EPA to receive timely reporting of violations in order to have clear notice of the violations and the opportunity to respond if necessary. Prompt disclosure is also evidence of the regulated entity's good faith in wanting to achieve or return to compliance as soon as possible. The integrity of Federal environmental law depends upon timely and accurate reporting. The public relies on timely and accurate reports from the regulated community, not only to measure compliance but to evaluate health or environmental risk and gauge progress in reducing pollutant loadings. EPA expects the Policy to encourage the kind of vigorous self-policing that will serve these objectives and does not intend that it justify delayed reporting. When violations of reporting requirements are voluntarily discovered, they must be promptly reported. When a failure to report results in imminent and substantial endangerment or serious harm to the environment, Audit Policy credit is precluded under condition D(8).

4.   DISCOVERY AND DISCLOSURE INDEPENDENT OF GOVERNMENT OR THIRD PARTY PLAINTIFF

Under Section D(4), the entity must discover the violation independently. That is, the violation must be discovered and identified before EPA or another government agency likely would have identified the problem either through its own investigative work or from information received through a third party. This condition requires regulated entities to take the initiative to find violations on their own and disclose them promptly instead of waiting for an indication of a pending enforcement action or third-party complaint.

Section D(4)(a) lists the circumstances under which discovery and disclosure will not be considered independent. For example, a disclosure will not be independent where EPA is already investigating the facility in question. However, under subsection (a), where the entity does not know that EPA has commenced a civil investigation and proceeds in good faith to make a disclosure under the Audit Policy, EPA may, in its discretion, provide penalty mitigation under the Audit Policy. The subsection (a) exception applies only to civil investigations; it does not apply in the criminal context. Other examples of situations in which a discovery is not considered independent are where a citizens' group has provided notice of its intent to sue, where a third party has already filed a complaint, where a whistleblower has reported the potential violation to government authorities, or where discovery of the violation by the government was imminent. Condition D(4)(c)—the filing of a complaint by a third party—covers formal judicial and administrative complaints as well as informal complaints, such as a letter from a citizens' group alerting EPA to a potential environmental violation.

Regulated entities that own or operate multiple facilities are subject to section D(4)(b) in addition to D(4)(a). EPA encourages multi-facility auditing and does not intend for the "independent discovery" condition to preclude availability of the Audit Policy when multiple facilities are involved. Thus, if a regulated entity owns or operates multiple facilities, the fact that one of its facilities is the subject of an investigation, inspection, information request or third-party complaint does not automatically preclude the Agency from granting Audit Policy credit for disclosures of violations self-discovered at the other facilities, assuming all other Audit Policy conditions are met. However, just as in the single-facility context, where a facility is already the subject of a government inspection, investigation or information request (including a broad information request that covers multiple facilities), it will generally not be eligible for Audit Policy credit. The Audit Policy is designed to encourage regulated entities to disclose violations before any of their facilities are under investigation, not after EPA discovers violations at one facility. Nevertheless, the Agency retains its full discretion under the Audit Policy to grant penalty waivers or reductions for good-faith disclosures made in the multi-facility context. EPA has worked closely with a number of entities that have received Audit Policy credit for multi-facility disclosures, and entities contemplating multi-facility auditing are encouraged to contact the Agency with any questions concerning Audit Policy availability.

5. CORRECTION AND REMEDIATION

Under Section D(5), the entity must remedy any harm caused by the violation and expeditiously certify in writing to appropriate Federal, State, and local authorities that it has corrected the violation. Correction and remediation in this context include responding to spills and carrying out any removal or remedial actions required by law. The certification requirement enables EPA to ensure that the regulated entity will be publicly accountable for its commitments through binding written agreements, orders or consent decrees where necessary.

Under the Policy, the entity must correct the violation within 60 calendar days from the date of discovery, or as expeditiously as possible. EPA recognizes that some violations can and should be corrected immediately, while others may take longer than 60 days to correct. For example, more time may be required if capital expenditures are involved or if technological issues are a factor. If more than 60 days will be required, the disclosing entity must so notify the Agency in writing prior to the conclusion of the 60-day period. In all cases, the regulated entity will be expected to do its utmost to achieve or return to compliance as expeditiously as possible. . . .

6.   PREVENT RECURRENCE

Under Section D(6), the regulated entity must agree to take steps to prevent a recurrence of the violation after it has been disclosed. Preventive steps may include, but are not limited to, improvements to the entity's environmental auditing efforts or compliance management system.

7.   NO REPEAT VIOLATIONS

Condition D(7) bars repeat offenders from receiving Audit Policy credit. Under the repeat violations exclusion, the same or a closely related violation must not have occurred at the same facility within the past 3 years. The 3 year period begins to run when the government or a third party has given the violator notice of a specific violation, without regard to when the original violation cited in the notice actually occurred. Examples of notice include a complaint, consent order, notice of violation, receipt of an inspection report, citizen suit, or receipt of penalty mitigation through a compliance assistance or incentive project.

When the facility is part of a multi-facility organization, Audit Policy relief is not available if the same or a closely related violation occurred as part of a pattern of violations at one or more of these facilities within the past 5 years. If a facility has been newly acquired, the existence of a violation prior to acquisition does not trigger the repeat violations exclusion.

The term "violation" includes any violation subject to a Federal, State or local civil judicial or administrative order, consent agreement, conviction or plea agreement. Recognizing that minor violations sometimes are settled without a formal action in court, the term also covers any act or omission for which the regulated entity has received a penalty reduction in the past. This condition covers situations in which the regulated entity has had clear notice of its noncompliance and an opportunity to correct the problem. . . .

8.   OTHER VIOLATIONS EXCLUDED

Section D(8) provides that Policy benefits are not available for certain types of violations. Subsection D(8)(a) excludes violations that result in serious actual harm to the environment or which may have presented an imminent and substantial endangerment to public health or the environment. When events of such a consequential nature occur, violators are ineligible for penalty relief and other incentives under the Audit Policy. However, this condition does not bar an entity from qualifying for Audit Policy relief solely because the violation involves release of a pollutant to the environment, as such releases do not necessarily result in serious actual harm or an imminent and substantial endangerment. To date, EPA has not invoked the serious actual harm or the imminent and substantial endangerment clauses to deny Audit Policy credit for any disclosure.

Subsection D(8)(b) excludes violations of the specific terms of any order, consent agreement, or plea agreement. Once a consent agreement has been negotiated, there is little incentive to comply if there are no sanctions for violating its specific requirements. The exclusion in this section also applies to violations of the terms of any response, removal or remedial action covered by a written agreement.

9.   COOPERATION

Under Section D(9), the regulated entity must cooperate as required by EPA and provide the Agency with the information it needs to determine Policy applicability. The entity must not hide, destroy or tamper with possible evidence following discovery of potential environmental violations. In order for the Agency to apply the Policy fairly, it must have sufficient information to determine whether its conditions are satisfied in each individual case. In general, EPA requests audit reports to determine the applicability of this Policy only where the information contained in the audit report is not readily available elsewhere and where EPA decides that the information is necessary to determine whether the terms and conditions of the Policy have been met. . . .

Entities that disclose potential criminal violations may expect a more thorough review by the Agency. In criminal cases, entities will be expected to provide, at a minimum, the following: access to all requested documents; access to all employees of the disclosing entity; assistance in investigating the violation, any noncompliance problems related to the disclosure, and any environmental consequences related to the violations; access to all information relevant to the violations disclosed, including that portion of the environmental audit report or documentation from the compliance management system that revealed the violation; and access to the individuals who conducted the audit or review.

F.   Opposition to Audit Privilege and Immunity

The Agency believes that the Audit Policy provides effective incentives for self-policing without impairing law enforcement, putting the environment at risk or hiding environmental compliance information from the public. Although EPA encourages environmental auditing, it must do so without compromising the integrity and enforceability of environmental laws. It is important to distinguish between EPA's Audit Policy and the audit privilege and immunity laws that exist in some States. The Agency remains firmly opposed to statutory and regulatory audit privileges and immunity. Privilege laws shield evidence of wrongdoing and prevent States from investigating even the most serious environmental violations. Immunity laws prevent States from obtaining penalties that are appropriate to the seriousness of the violation, as they are required to do under Federal law. Audit privilege and immunity laws are unnecessary, undermine law enforcement, impair protection of human health and the environment, and interfere with the public's right to know of potential and existing environmental hazards. . . .

3.   "Spotlighting" and "Information Dissemination" Approaches to Improve Compliance

"Spotlighting" as a regulatory strategy to improve performance has become increasingly popular in recent years. Professor Cass Sunstein, for example, has asserted that "informational regulation, or regulation through disclosure, has become one of the most striking developments in the last generation of American law," and that "disclosure of information has become a central part of the American regulatory state—as central, in its way, as command-and-control regulation and economic incentives. . . ." Sunstein, Informational Regulation and Informational Standing: *Akins* and Beyond, 147 U. Pa. L. Rev. 613, 616 (1999). The idea is that information disclosure is a powerful incentive for modifying behavior. The TRI program is the most often cited example of this phenomenon, as we discuss in more detail in Chapter 8, section E.2.c. While spotlighting approaches have been much lauded, see generally Echeverria & Kaplan, Poisonous Procedural "Reform": In Defense of Environmental Right to Know, Georgetown Environmental Law and Policy Institute (2002), questions have been raised about how best to evaluate their effectiveness. U.S. GAO, Program Evaluation: Strategies for Assessing How Information Dissemination Contributes to Agency Goals, GAO-02-923 (Sept. 2002). Some commentators have encouraged increased use of such approaches in the enforcement arena as a way to improve regulated-party performance and also to enhance government accountability. Markell, The Role of Deterrence-Based Enforcement in a "Reinvented" State/Federal Relationship: The Divide between Theory and Reality, 24 Harv. Envtl. L. Rev. 1, 99 (2000).

EPA's Enforcement and Compliance History Online (ECHO) program is an important source of "spotlight" data. ECHO, an online searchable database open to the public, provides enforcement and compliance information covering the previous three years for approximately 800,000 facilities that EPA regulates under the CAA, CWA, and RCRA. EPA considers this an important tool for members of the public to monitor environmental compliance in their communities, for corporations to monitor multiple facilities, and for investors to include environmental performance in investment decisions. The database is available at www.epa.gov/echo/index.html.

4. Performance Track Strategies

EPA has made a number of efforts over the years to create various types of "performance tracks" for regulated parties as a way to "recognize and encourage top environmental performers—those who go beyond compliance . . . to attain levels of environmental performance and management that benefit people, communities, and the environment." EPA, Performance Track Program Guide 2 (September 2005). In September 2005, the Director of Performance Track, Daniel J. Fiorino, issued an updated version of EPA's National Environmental Performance Track Program Guide, http://www.epa.gov/performancetrack/pubs.htm. His cover letter describes the program as follows:

> Performance Track is a voluntary public-private partnership that encourages continuous environmental improvement through the use of environmental management systems, local community involvement, and measurable results. Through Performance Track, EPA recognizes and rewards businesses and public facilities that demonstrate strong environmental performance beyond current requirements. While building a collaborative relationship with EPA, Performance Track participants realize environmental results beyond what could be achieved through regulation and enforcement alone.

EPA's Program Guide establishes five elements for a regulated party to qualify for Performance Track:

- Adopted and implement an environmental management system (EMS)
- Demonstrated "specific past environmental performance achievements"
- Recorded "sustained compliance with environmental requirements"
- Committed to "continued environmental improvement"
- Committed to public outreach and performance reporting

For example, the Program Guide advises that a facility will not be eligible under the "compliance screen" (the fourth element) if it has engaged in criminal activity under federal or state environmental laws or it has had significant violations at its facility.

EPA offers a series of incentives to entities that participate in Performance Track. These include (1) special recognition, (2) networking opportunities, (3) services (such as mentoring), and (4) regulatory incentives in different program areas.*

An April 2006 EPA report, Leading Change: Performance Track Fourth Annual Progress Report, indicates that Performance Track membership has increased dramatically in recent years. As of April 2006, membership had increased to 371 members. EPA indicates that "[s]ince the program's inception [in 2000], Performance Track members have collectively reduced their water use by nearly 1.9 billion gallons, . . . conserved close to 9,000 acres of land[,] and increased their use of recycled materials by nearly 120,000 tons." Id. at 3. EPA has proposed the creation of additional "high-value" incentives for participation in performance-based programs, but some NGOs have urged that EPA study these programs more before doing so.**

NOTES AND QUESTIONS CONCERNING THE ENFORCEMENT POLICY TOOLBOX

1. What are the benefits available to a regulated company that voluntarily discloses to EPA its own violations of environmental statutes or regulations? What conditions must a company meet to qualify for the benefits of EPA's audit policy statement? If a company discovers violations during a compliance audit required as part of a binding settlement agreement, is it eligible for the elimination of gravity-based penalties? What if a violation is identified in a compliance certification required to accompany an application for a Title V Clean Air Act permit? Is EPA bound to adhere to the provisions of the policy statement? In revising the policy in 2000, EPA concluded that it has encouraged voluntary self-policing while preserving fair and effective enforcement, that use of the policy has been widespread, and that users report a high satisfaction rate. EPA lengthened the period during which prompt disclosure must be made from 10 to 21 days. It clarified that a facility in many cases may satisfy the "independent discovery" requirement even where inspections or investigations have commenced at other facilities owned by the same entity.

*EPA's website details these benefits. http://www.epa.gov/performancetrack/benefits/regadmin.htm.
**See, e.g., Voluntary EPA Performance-Based Program Needs More Study before Growth, NRDC Says, Daily Env't Rep. (BNA), June 19, 2006, at A-9; Schaeffer, Data: EPA "Honor System" Leads to More Pollution at 10 out of 13 Industrial Sites Getting Less Oversight (Feb. 8, 2006), www.environmentalintegrity.org/pub360.cfm.

Finally, it indicated that entities that meet all policy conditions except for systematic discovery will not be recommended for criminal prosecution, provided EPA determines that the violation is not part of a pattern or practice of concealment or condoning of environmental violations.

2. One of the most controversial aspects of EPA's audit policy is its failure to provide a privilege for information discovered during an audit and turned over to the government. Why was EPA unwilling to provide such a privilege? Industry has argued that, absent a privilege, a company could be in a worse position after an audit than before, EPA's policy notwithstanding, if the audit reveals information about noncompliance that the government would not have discovered. Absent a privilege, that information may be used as the basis for enforcement proceedings against the company. Many state legislatures have adopted audit protection laws that make available to companies performing an environmental audit the privilege that EPA refused to provide. See, e.g., Alaska Stat. §09.25.450; Ark. Code Ann. §§8-1-301 to 8-1-312; Colo. Rev. Stat. §13-25-126.5; Indiana Code §§13-28-4-1 to 13-28-4-10. Illinois once had the protection, but repealed it in 2005. 415 Ill. Comp. Code Stat. 5/5.22, *repealed by* P.A. 94-580, §10.

Other state audit protection laws go beyond providing privileged status to information submitted to a state environmental agency as a result of an audit by providing immunity from civil or criminal prosecution for any violation voluntarily disclosed to the agency. E.g., Kan. Stat. Ann. §60-3338; Ky. Rev. Stat. Ann. §224.01-040(10); Ohio Rev. Code Ann. §3745.72. EPA has strenuously opposed these immunity laws and has threatened to withdraw or refuse to approve delegations of permitting authority to states that have adopted them. See Beard, The New Environmental Federalism: Can the EPA's Voluntary Audit Policy Survive?, 17 Va. Envtl. L.J. 1, 17-19 (1997). What would be the legal basis for such a withdrawal? See CWA §402(b)(7); CAA §502(b)(5)(E); Inside EPA Weekly Apr. 12, 1996, at 5 (EPA Memo Establishing Criteria for Title V approvals). Some states have amended or repealed their audit protection laws in the face of such threats. Bergeson & Campbell, Carrot or Stick? The Debate over Environmental Auditing, Wash. Law., Sept./Oct. 1997, at 39, 43 (Michigan and Texas); 1997 Mich. Pub. Acts No. 103; Vernon's Ann. Tex. Civ. Stat. Art. 4447cc. For a comprehensive review of state audit privilege laws, see Stensvaag, The Fine Print of State Environmental Audit Privileges, 16 UCLA J. Envtl. L. & Pol'y 69 (1998). For several articles on environmental self-audits, see 5 Hastings W.-Nw. J. Envtl. L. & Pol'y No. 3 (1999).

3. *OSHA's Self-Audit Policy.* The Final Policy Statement Concerning the Occupational Safety and Health Administration's Use of Voluntary Employer Safety and Health Self-Audits, 65 Fed. Reg. 46,498 (2000), commits the agency to treating a voluntary self-audit that identifies a hazardous condition as evidence of good faith as opposed to a willful violation, provided the employer promptly takes corrective measures. The presence or absence of good faith is a relevant factor in assessing penalties for regulatory violations. 29 U.S.C. §666(j).

4. *EPA's Small Business Compliance Policy and Small Local Governments Compliance Assistance Policy.* EPA issued the most recent version of its Small Business Compliance Policy in April 2000, 65 Fed. Reg. 19,630, on the same day that the agency issued its Self-Audit Policy. The Small Business Policy, as its title suggests, is intended to "promote environmental compliance among small businesses by providing incentives for voluntary discovery, prompt disclosure, and prompt correction of violations." The Policy, which implements the Small Business Regulatory

Enforcement Fairness Act of 1996, reduces or waives penalties under certain circumstances for small businesses that disclose and make good faith efforts to correct violations. EPA issued the most recent version of its Small Local Governments Compliance Assistance Policy in 2004. This policy is intended to "promote[ ] comprehensive environmental compliance among small local governments by establishing parameters within which [a] state[] can reduce or waive" a penalty it otherwise would impose on a small local government, so long as the small government, among other things, uses the state's "comprehensive compliance assistance program."

5. EPA's Supplemental Environmental Projects (SEPs) Policy, 63 Fed. Reg. 24,796 (1998), is another compliance incentive policy that has received considerable attention. EPA defines a SEP as an "environmentally beneficial project that a violator voluntarily agrees to perform, in addition to actions required to correct the violation(s), as part of an enforcement settlement." EPA OECA, Beyond Compliance: Supplemental Environmental Projects 4 (January 2001). Thus, a SEP is an action that is "*in addition* to what is required to return to compliance with environmental laws." Id. at 3 (emphasis added). EPA offers to forgo a portion of a civil penalty as an inducement to regulated parties to agree to a SEP in appropriate instances. In other words, as EPA puts it, "[a]ll else being equal, the final settlement penalty will be lower for a violator who agrees to perform an acceptable SEP compared to the violator who does not agree to perform a SEP." Supplemental Environmental Projects Policy, 63 Fed. Reg. 24,796 (1998). EPA has touted the environmental promise of this enforcement tool, and several commentators have encouraged the use of SEPs as well.[*]

EPA does three things in its SEPs policy: (1) identify the types of projects that may qualify as SEPs, (2) explain the "terms and conditions" under which a SEP may become part of a settlement, and (3) address the extent of penalty mitigation appropriate for a specific SEP. The policy lists seven specific types of activities that potentially qualify as SEPs:

1. Pollution Prevention—projects that "involve changes that reduce or eliminate some form of pollution, or that reduce a pollutant's toxicity prior to recycling, treatment, or disposal." EPA OECA beyond Compliance: Supplemental Environmental Projects 4 (Jan. 2001).
2. Pollution Reduction—projects such as improved treatment or reuse of chemicals that "reduce the amount of danger of the pollution which reaches the environment." Id. At 5.
3. Public Health—projects that involve assessments of public health impacts potentially associated with violations.
4. Environmental Restoration and Protection—projects that "improve the condition of the land, air, or water in the area damaged by the violation."
5. Assessments and Audits—audits that explore pollution prevention and similar opportunities.

---

[*]See, e.g., Memorandum from John Suarez, EPA Assistant Administrator, Expanding the Use of Supplemental Environmental Projects (June 11, 2003), available at http://www.epa.gov/compliance/resources/policies/civil/seps/seps-expandinguse.pdf; Lloyd, Supplemental Environmental Projects Have Been Effectively Used in Citizen Suits to Deter Future Violations as Well as to Achieve Significant Additional Environmental Benefits, 10 Widener L. Rev. 413 (2004). For a critical appraisal, see Canales, Supplemental Environmental Projects: The Most Affected Communities Are Not Receiving Satisfactory Benefits (June 2006).

6. Environmental Compliance Promotion—projects that commit the violator to helping other regulated parties achieve compliance and reduce pollution.

7. Emergency Planning and Preparedness—projects in which the violator assists state or local emergency planning and response organizations.

Other projects that do not fit into any of these categories but that "have environmental merit" may be acceptable as SEPs as well. The SEPs Policy contains numerous caveats or conditions on the eligibility of projects that fit into any of these categories (e.g., the SEP project must have "adequate nexus" to the violation and EPA may not be involved in managing funds to be set aside for the SEP).

EPA provides a fairly elaborate methodology for determining how much a penalty should be reduced in exchange for the settling party's agreeing to undertake a SEP. EPA has developed a computer model known as PROJECT to assist in application of the methodology. For a regulated party committing to perform a SEP, the ultimate result in terms of the amount it will be required to pay is that the final settlement penalty must "equal or exceed either: (a) the economic benefit of noncompliance plus 10 percent of the gravity component; or (b) 25 percent of the gravity component only; whichever is greater." 63 Fed. Reg. at 24,801. Thus, like EPA's Self-Audit Policy, excerpted above, the SEPs Policy anticipates that EPA will impose penalties that force the violator to disgorge the economic benefit it gained from the violation; forgiveness or penalty flexibility will come in the "gravity" portion of penalty calculation.

EPA's FY 2005 Compliance & Enforcement Annual Results indicates that EPA has negotiated SEPs for the past five years in the following amounts: 2001, $89 million; 2002, $58 million; 2003, $65 million; 2004, $48 million; and 2005, $57 million.

Many states have adopted SEP programs. For a recent report on these programs, see Bonorris et al., Environmental Enforcement in the Fifty States: The Promise and Pitfalls of Supplemental Environmental Projects, 11 Hastings W.-Nw. J. Envtl. L. & Pol'y 185 (2005). The North Carolina Supreme Court has held that the state's SEP program violates the state constitution. North Carolina Sch. Bds. Ass'n v. Moore, 614 S.E.2d 504 (N.C. 2005).

6. There is considerable debate about the optimal level of enforcement and compliance. Farber, Taking Slippage Seriously: Noncompliance and Creative Compliance in Environmental Law, 23 Harv. Envtl. L. Rev. 297 (1999), presents "an alternative view of environmental law" that focuses on the slippage between adopted regulatory standards and the actual conduct of regulated parties in complying (or not complying) with those standards. Cohen, Empirical Research on the Deterrent Effect of Environmental Monitoring and Enforcement, 30 Envtl. L. Rep. (ELI) 10245 (Apr. 2000), discusses a variety of reasons why increased deterrence may have negative consequences, such as trivializing criminal law and deterring some "good actors" from engaging in regulated activities. A 2005 EPA OIG report indicates that the current reality is that EPA "has not developed effective compliance rates."[*] Continuing gaps in critical data of this sort obviously complicate efforts to apply insights from the debate about optimal levels of compliance to real-world questions concerning the efficacy of EPA compliance promotion approaches.

Figure 10-12 presents data on usage and monetary value of SEPs for 2005.

---

[*]U.S. OIG, EPA Performance Measures Do Not Effectively Track Compliance Outcomes, Report No. 2006-P-00006 3 (Dec. 15, 2005), available at www.epa.gov/oig/reports/2006/20051215-2006-P-00006.pdf.

	Cases with SEPs	$ Value of SEPs
CAA	41	$31,637,689
CERCLA	17	$363,145
CWA	60	$18,427,947
RCRA	18	$3,249,467
Total	136	$53,678,248

Source: EPA, National Enforcement Trends—FY 2005, http://cfpub.epa.gov/compliance/resources/reports/nets/index.cfm.

FIGURE 10-12
FY 2005 Number and Dollar Value of SEPs

7. As this section of the chapter reflects, it is important to monitor agency activities, as well as developments in the law (statutes, regulations, and case law), to understand the direction of, and trends in, environmental enforcement. Two good places to start are EPA's OECA website, www.epa.gov/compliance, and the website of the Environmental Council of the States (ECOS), an institution created in the early 1990s to serve as the voice of state environmental commissioners in Washington, D.C. ECOS has issued reports that focus on enforcement and compliance, such as Success Stories: Enforcement and Compliance, and Ensuring Compliance: State Best Practices (May 30, 2000), and Report to Congress, State Environmental Agency Contributions to Enforcement and Compliance (April 2001). Its State Environmental Agency Contributions to Enforcement and Compliance: 2000-2003 was published in September 2006. See http://www.ecos.org/section/publications. ECOS's journal, ECO*States*, also includes articles on specific strategies for compliance, such as promoting the use of EMSs (environmental management systems).*

---

*See, e.g., Habicht, Environmental Management Systems: Local Resource Centers Launched to Advance Environmental Management Systems within Public Entities, ECO*States* Fall 2002, at 20 (covering EMSs for local governments); Steagall, South Carolina Probes the Relationship between EMSs and Permitting Decisions, ECO*States* Winter 2006, at 25 (addressing the response to EPA's challenge to incorporate EMS options into the permitting and regulatory structure).

INTERNATIONAL ENVIRONMENTAL LAW

In recent years, legitimacy has begun to emerge as an issue ... in international environmental law. ... The growing severity and complexity of international environmental problems has increased the need for institutions with greater legislative, administrative and adjudicatory authority, which can respond flexibly to new problems and information through the development, implementation and enforcement of international norms. Whether the international community is successful in developing such institutions will depend in part on whether they are accepted as legitimate. The issue of legitimacy is thus emerging as a significant factor in the development of international environmental law.

> D. Bodansky, Legitimacy, in Oxford Handbook of International
> Environmental Law (D. Bodansky et al. eds., forthcoming).

International environmental law is now in its adolescence. The hundreds of multilateral environmental agreements adopted since the 1972 Stockholm Conference desperately need implementation. ... Moreover, numerous regional and international efforts have emerged to facilitate the shift from adoption to implementation, compliance, and enforcement.

> Bruch, Growing Up, 23 Envtl. F. 28 (May/June 2006).

This chapter is intended to introduce students to some of the significant aspects of the large, and expanding, field of international environmental law. For an effort to define the concept of international environmental law, see, e.g., P. Birnie & A. Boyle, International Law and the Environment 1-4 (2d ed. 2002). The chapter is also intended to reinforce the approaches to environmental protection embodied in the domestic U.S. environmental laws discussed in the preceding chapters. The two introductory quotes capture some of the challenges contemporary international environmental governance initiatives face. The degree of success (real and perceived) in addressing these challenges is likely to have a significant impact on the future content of international environmental law; it is also likely to influence the identity of the actors who operate as focal points for addressing environmental challenges that have global implications.

Section A focuses on transboundary environmental pollution. Pollution that crosses national boundaries represents a variation of the spillover effects discussed in Chapters 1, 6, and 7. This section provides a brief case study of one of the world's most famous transboundary pollution disputes, involving a trail smelter located on the Canadian side of the U.S.-Canadian border that has received considerable international and domestic attention for its pollution of the U.S. side of the border.

This transboundary pollution problem has its roots in the nineteenth century, and the impacts of the pollution continue to be felt and pose fundamental issues for environmental governance today.

The remaining four sections of the chapter focus on features of the evolving international governance infrastructure that are likely to influence the shape and success of environmental protection initiatives. Section B provides a general overview of multilateral approaches to international environmental governance, with a particular focus on the UN, including some of the international conferences it has helped to convene. Section C turns to treatment of "commons-related" concerns in a global context, with a particular focus on one international environmental agreement developed to address a global commons issue, the Montreal Protocol for the Protection of the Ozone Layer. Section D turns to institutions intended to enhance North American environmental governance, especially the North American Commission for Environmental Cooperation (CEC), the first institution in North America created with a continental focus on environmental issues. Finally, section E provides an overview of the trade/environment debate, a topic that has triggered enormous controversy in recent years.

A.   TRANSBOUNDARY POLLUTION

It is a truism that pollution does not respect political borders. Merrill, Golden Rules for Transboundary Pollution, 46 Duke L.J. 931, 932 (1997). There are numerous examples of air and water pollution traveling across national boundaries. In some cases, the pollution travels hundreds or even thousands of miles. A CEC-sponsored study found that a significant percentage of the dioxin in mothers' breast milk in the Canadian Arctic came from municipal and medical waste incinerators and other sources located outside Canada, in the United States or other countries.* The extraordinarily long borders that the United States shares with Canada (5,525 miles) and Mexico (almost 2,000 miles) create significant opportunities for transboundary disputes in North America in particular.** The United States and Canada are also the world's largest bilateral trading partners, with about $394 billion in goods traded between the two countries in 2003. The lengthy borders and extensive commerce between the United States and its neighbors, and the numerous industrial operations that have set up shop on either side of the border, increase the likelihood of transboundary pollution.*** The *maquiladora* industry, which has expanded rapidly since NAFTA was adopted, for example, is an oft-cited source of pollution on the U.S.-Mexican border.****

*Miller, Tracking Dioxins to the Arctic: CEC Study Tracks Dioxins from Canada, Mexico and United States to the Arctic, TRIO (Fall 2000), available at http://www.cec.org/trio/stories/index.cfm.

**Border 2012: U.S. - Mexico Environmental Program, EPA-160-R-03-001, 4 (2003), available at http://www.epa.gov/usmexicoborder/pdf/2012_english.pdf; Robinson-Dorn, The Trial Smelter: Is What's Past Prologue? EPA Blazes a New Trial for CERCLA, 14 N.Y.U. Envtl. L.J. 233, 237 n.12 (2006).

***Robinson-Dorn, supra, at 237-238 n.13.

****Border 2012, *supra*, at 10; Reblin, Comment, NAFTA and the Environment: Dealing with Abnormally High Birth Defect Rates among Children of Texas-Mexico Border Towns, 27 St. Mary's L.J. 929, 934-940 (1996) (discussing environmental harms resulting from the *maquiladora* program).

Disputes stemming from pollution spillovers are, of course, by no means confined to disputes between countries. In the relatively early days of the United States, on more than one occasion the Supreme Court heard common law cases involving complaints from one state about spillover pollution from another. See, e.g., Georgia v. Tennessee Copper, 206 U.S. 230 (1907); Missouri v. Illinois, 200 U.S. 496 (1906). More recently, Congress has sought to address these issues, and the Supreme Court has had occasion to review Congress's approach. See, e.g., CWA §402(b) and (d); CAA §110(a)(2)(D); Arkansas v. Oklahoma, 503 U.S. 91 (1991) (covered in Chapter 7). Citizens in downstream states have also sought to use the domestic courts to obtain recourse for interstate pollution. See, e.g., International Paper Co. v. Ouellette, 479 U.S. 481 (1987). Intermunicipal border wars are not uncommon either. Courts in New York and in other domestic U.S. jurisdictions "have increasingly been faced with deciding . . . inter-municipal feuds." Zarin, Border Wars and SEQRA, Envtl. Law in N.Y. 89 (May 2006).

Governance approaches for addressing transboundary disputes between countries are generally much less settled than is the case for interstate and intermunicipal disputes in the United States. In his book Environmental Statecraft, Scott Barrett suggests that "[t]ransnational environmental problems are much harder to remedy than the domestic variety because of the principle of sovereignty." S. Barrett, Environmental Statecraft xi (2003). The ongoing saga involving pollution from a substantial industrial operation on the U.S.-Canadian border offers an interesting case study of the challenges involved in addressing significant transboundary pollution.

THE TRAIL SMELTER DISPUTE—THE EARLY YEARS*

The Teck Cominco facility, located on the Columbia River about 10 miles north of the U.S.-Canadian border in Trail, British Columbia, Canada, began processing gold in the late 1800s, and now is one of the world's largest integrated lead and zinc smelters and refining complexes. It has a production capacity of roughly 290,000 tons per year of zinc and 120,000 tons per year of lead, and produces 20 other metal and chemical products. The 1941 Arbitration decision excerpted below describes these background facts, as of that date, as follows:

> In 1896, a smelter was started under American auspices near the locality known as Trail, B.C. In 1908, the Consolidated Mining and Smelting Company of Canada, Limited . . . acquired the smelter plant at Trail as it then existed. Since that time, the Canadian company, without interruption, has operated the Smelter, and from time to time has greatly added to the plant until it has become one of the best and largest equipped smelting plants on the American continent. In 1925 and 1927, two stacks of the plant were erected to 409 feet in height and the Smelter greatly increased its daily smelting of zinc and lead ores. This increased production resulted in more sulphur dioxide fumes and higher concentrations being emitted into the air. In 1916, about 5,000 tons of sulphur per month were emitted; in 1924, about 4,700 tons; in 1926, about 9,000 tons—an amount which rose near to 10,000 tons per month in 1930. In other words, about 300-350 tons of

*Unless otherwise noted, the information in this section concerning the Trail Smelter is taken from Professor Michael Robinson-Dorn's The Trail Smelter: Is What's Past Prologue? EPA Blazes a New Trail for CERCLA, 14 N.Y.U. Envtl. L.J. 233, 237 (2006). The editors are grateful for Professor Robinson-Dorn's review of a draft of this section and for his very helpful and insightful suggestions.

sulphur were being emitted daily in 1930. (It is to be noted that one ton of sulphur is substantially the equivalent of two tons of sulphur dioxide or SO_2.)

The Trail Smelter's operations caused significant damage to air quality, apple orchards, and other parts of the environment in Washington State. Ultimately, this spawned perhaps the most famous transboundary pollution dispute resolution effort ever attempted. In 1928, concerns about this pollution spurred the United States and Canada to submit the matter to the International Joint Commission (IJC), an institution the countries created in 1909 through adoption of the Boundary Waters Treaty. Article IX of the Treaty provided that the nations could submit matters to the IJC for nonbinding investigation and report. The United States was dissatisfied with the IJC report and, after additional discussions, in 1935 Canada and the United States entered into a Convention for Settlement of Difficulties Arising from Operation of Smelter at Trail, B.C. The Convention established a three-person arbitral tribunal to determine post-1932 damages that would be "just to all parties concerned," and to set emission levels. In Article IV it instructed the panel to "apply the law and practice . . . followed in the United States . . . as well as international law and practice" because the government officials at the time did not think there was much available international law that dealt with "international nuisance." They were aware of the U.S. Supreme Court's jurisprudence on interstate transboundary disputes, which they believed to be relatively "evenly balanced in [its] effect on industrial and agricultural enterprise." Read, The Trail Smelter Dispute, 1 Canadian Yearbook of Int'l Law 213, 227 (1963). The tribunal issued a preliminary decision in 1938, and the following final decision in 1941.

TRAIL SMELTER (U.S. v. CANADA) TRAIL SMELTER ARBITRAL TRIBUNAL DECISION REPORTED ON MARCH 11, 1941, TO THE GOVERNMENT OF THE UNITED STATES OF AMERICA AND TO THE GOVERNMENT OF THE DOMINION OF CANADA, UNDER THE CONVENTION SIGNED APRIL 15, 1935
3 R.I.A.A. 1938, 1965 (Trail Smelter Arb. Trib. 1941)

. . . The controversy is between two Governments involving damage occurring, or having occurred, in the territory of one of them (the United States of America) and alleged to be due to an agency situated in the territory of the other (the Dominion of Canada). . . .

As between the two countries involved, each has an equal interest that if a nuisance is proved, the indemnity to damaged parties for proven damage shall be just and adequate and . . . that unproven or unwarranted claims shall not be allowed. For, while the United States' interests may now be claimed to be injured by the operations of a Canadian corporation, it is equally possible that at some time in the future Canadian interests might be claimed to be injured by an American corporation. . . .

[T]he phraseology of the questions submitted to the Tribunal clearly evinces . . . an intention that . . . the Tribunal should endeavor to adjust the conflicting interests by some "just solution" which would allow the continuance of the operation of the Trail Smelter but under such restrictions and limitations as would, as far as foreseeable, prevent damage in the United States, and as would enable indemnity to be obtained, if in spite of such restrictions and limitations, damage should occur in the future in the United States. . . .

The duty imposed upon the Tribunal by the Convention was to "finally decide" the following questions:

(1) Whether damage caused by the Trail Smelter in the State of Washington has occurred since the first day of January, 1932, and, if so, what indemnity should be paid therefor?

(2) In the event of the answer to the first part of the preceding question being in the affirmative, whether the Trail Smelter should be required to refrain from causing damage in the State of Washington in the future and, if so, to what extent?

(3) In the light of the answer to the preceding question, what measures or régime, if any, should be adopted or maintained by the Trail Smelter?

(4) What indemnity or compensation, if any, should be paid on account of any decision or decisions rendered by the Tribunal pursuant to the next two preceding questions? . . .

In conclusion (end of Part Two of the previous decision), the Tribunal answered Question No. 1 as follows:

Damage caused by the Trail Smelter in the State of Washington has occurred since the first day of January, 1932, and up to October 1, 1937. . . . The fact of existence of damage, if any, occurring after October 1, 1937, and the indemnity to be paid therefor, if any, the Tribunal will determine in its final decision. . . .

I

PART THREE

The second question under Article III of the Convention is as follows:

In the event of the answer to the first part of the preceding question being in the affirmative [whether there has been damage], whether the Trail Smelter should be required to refrain from causing damage in the State of Washington in the future and, if so, to what extent? . . .

The first problem which arises is whether the question should be answered on the basis of the law followed in the United States or on the basis of international law. The Tribunal, however, finds that this problem need not be solved here as the law followed in the United States in dealing with the quasi-sovereign rights of the States of the Union, in the matter of air pollution . . . is in conformity with the general rules of international law.

Particularly in reaching its conclusions as regards this question as well as the next, the Tribunal has given consideration to the desire of the high contracting parties "to reach a solution just to all parties concerned."

As Professor Eagleton puts [it] . . . : "A State owes at all times a duty to protect other States against injurious acts by individuals from within its jurisdiction." A great number of such general pronouncements by leading authorities concerning the duty of a State to respect other States and their territory have been presented to the Tribunal. . . . International decisions, in various matters, . . . are based on the same general principle, and, indeed, this principle, as such, has not been questioned by Canada. But the real difficulty often arises rather when it comes to determine what . . . is deemed to constitute an injurious act.

A case concerning . . . territorial relations, decided by the Federal Court of Switzerland between the Cantons of Soleure and Argovia, may serve to illustrate the relativity of the rule. Soleure brought a suit against her sister State to enjoin use of a shooting establishment which endangered her territory. The court, in granting the injunction, said: "This right (sovereignty) excludes . . . not only the usurpation and exercise of sovereign rights (of another State) . . . but also an actual encroachment which might prejudice the natural use of the territory and the free movement of its inhabitants." As a result of the decision, Argovia made plans for the improvement of the existing installations. These, however, were considered as insufficient protection by Soleure. The Canton of Argovia then moved the Federal Court to decree that the shooting be again permitted after completion of the projected improvements. This motion was granted. "The demand of the Government of Soleure," said the court, "that all endangerment be absolutely abolished apparently goes too far." The court found that all risk whatever had not been eliminated, as the region was flat and absolutely safe shooting ranges were only found in mountain valleys; that there was a federal duty for the communes to provide facilities for military target practice and that "no more precautions may be demanded for shooting ranges near the boundaries of two Cantons than are required for shooting ranges in the interior of a Canton." . . .

No case of air pollution dealt with by an international tribunal has been brought to the attention of the Tribunal nor does the Tribunal know of any such case. The nearest analogy is that of water pollution. But, here also, no decision of an international tribunal has been cited or has been found.

There are, however, as regards both air pollution and water pollution, certain decisions of the Supreme Court of the United States which may legitimately be taken as a guide in this field of international law, for it is reasonable to follow by analogy, in international cases, precedents established by that court in dealing with controversies between States of the Union or with other controversies concerning the quasi-sovereign rights of such States, where no contrary rule prevails in international law and no reason for rejecting such precedents can be adduced from the limitations of sovereignty inherent in the Constitution of the United States.

In the suit of the State of Missouri v. the State of Illinois concerning the pollution, within the boundaries of Illinois, of the Illinois River, an affluent of the Mississippi flowing into the latter where it forms the boundary between that State and Missouri, an injunction was refused. "Before this court ought to intervene," said the court, "the case should be of serious magnitude, clearly and fully proved, and the principle to be applied should be one which the court is prepared deliberately to maintain against all considerations on the other side." The court found that the practice complained of was general along the shores of the Mississippi River at that time, that it was followed by Missouri itself and that thus a standard was set up by the defendant which the claimant was entitled to invoke.

As the claims of public health became more exacting and methods for removing impurities from the water were perfected, complaints ceased. It is significant that Missouri sided with Illinois when the other riparians of the Great Lakes' system sought to enjoin it to desist from diverting the waters of that system into that of the Illinois and Mississippi for the very purpose of disposing of the Chicago sewage. . . .

What the Supreme Court says there of its power under the Constitution equally applies to the extraordinary power granted this Tribunal under the Convention. What is true between States of the Union is, at least, equally true concerning the relations between the United States and the Dominion of Canada.

In another recent case concerning water pollution, the complainant was successful. The City of New York was enjoined, at the request of the State of New Jersey, to desist, within a reasonable time limit, from the practice of disposing of sewage by dumping it into the sea, a practice which was injurious to the coastal waters of New Jersey in the vicinity of her bathing resorts.

In the matter of air pollution itself, the leading decisions are those of the Supreme Court in the State of Georgia v. Tennessee Copper Company and Ducktown Sulphur, Copper and Iron Company, Limited. Although dealing with a suit against private companies, the decisions were on questions cognate to those here at issue. Georgia stated that it had in vain sought relief from the State of Tennessee, on whose territory the smelters were located, and the court defined the nature of the suit by saying: "This is a suit by a State for an injury to it in its capacity of quasi-sovereign. In that capacity, the State has an interest independent of and behind the titles of its citizens, in all the earth and air within its domain."

On the question whether an injunction should be granted or not, the court said:

> It (the State) has the last word as to whether its mountains shall be stripped of their forests and its inhabitants shall breathe pure air. . . . It is not lightly to be presumed to give up quasi-sovereign rights for pay and . . . if that be its choice, it may insist that an infraction of them shall be stopped. This court has not quite the same freedom to balance the harm that will be done by an injunction against that of which the plaintiff complains, that it would have in deciding between two subjects of a single political power. Without excluding the considerations that equity always takes into account . . . it is a fair and reasonable demand on the part of a sovereign that the air over its territory should not be polluted on a great scale by sulphurous acid gas, that the forests on its mountains, be they better or worse, and whatever domestic destruction they may have suffered, should not be further destroyed or threatened by the act of persons beyond its control, that the crops and orchards on its hills should not be endangered from the same source. Whether Georgia, by insisting upon this claim, is doing more harm than good to her own citizens is for her to determine. The possible disaster to those outside the State must be accepted as a consequence of her standing upon her extreme rights.

Later on, however, when the court actually framed an injunction, in the case of the Ducktown Company (an agreement on the basis of an annual compensation was reached with the most important of the two smelters, the Tennessee Copper Company), they did not go beyond a decree "adequate to diminish materially the present probability of damage to its (Georgia's) citizens." . . .

The Tribunal, therefore, finds that the above decisions, taken as a whole, constitute an adequate basis for its conclusions, namely, that, under the principles of international law, as well as of the law of the United States, no State has the right to use or permit the use of its territory in such a manner as to cause injury by fumes in or to the territory of another or the properties or persons therein, when the case is of serious consequence and the injury is established by clear and convincing evidence.

The decisions of the Supreme Court of the United States which are the basis of these conclusions are decisions in equity and a solution inspired by them, together with the régime hereinafter prescribed, will, in the opinion of the Tribunal, be "just to all parties concerned," as long, at least, as the present conditions in the Columbia River Valley continue to prevail.

Considering the circumstances of the case, the Tribunal holds that the Dominion of Canada is responsible in international law for the conduct of the Trail Smelter. Apart from the undertakings in the Convention, it is, therefore, the duty of the Government of the Dominion of Canada to see to it that this conduct should be in conformity with the obligation of the Dominion under international law as herein determined.

The Tribunal, therefore, answers Question No. 2 as follows: (2) So long as the present conditions in the Columbia River Valley prevail, the Trail Smelter shall be required to refrain from causing any damage through fumes in the State of Washington; the damage herein referred to and its extent being such as would be recoverable under the decisions of the courts of the United States in suits between private individuals. The indemnity for such damage should be fixed in such manner as the Governments, acting under Article XI of the Convention, should agree upon.

Part Four

The third question under Article III of the Convention is as follows: "In the light of the answer to the preceding question, what measures or régime, if any, should be adopted and maintained by the Trail Smelter?"

[T]he Tribunal . . . decides that a régime or measure of control shall be applied to the operations of the Smelter and shall remain in full force unless and until modified in accordance with the provisions hereinafter set forth [the Tribunal directed the Smelter to implement significant control measures].

Part Five

. . . [I]f any damage as defined under Question No. 2 shall have occurred since October 1, 1940, or shall occur in the future, whether through failure on the part of the Smelter to comply with the regulations herein prescribed or notwithstanding the maintenance of the regime, an indemnity shall be paid for such damage. . . .

THE TRAIL SMELTER IN THE TWENTY-FIRST CENTURY: STILL A SOURCE OF POLLUTION, BUT A DIFFERENT LEGAL APPROACH

Despite this precedent-setting arbitration from more than 60 years ago, and the attendant focus on pollution problems at the Teck facility, the facility's operations have discharged "vast quantities" of pollutants, "including heavy metal-laden slag and mercury, . . . into the Columbia River." EPA estimates that the smelter has discharged more than 13 million tons of slag containing heavy metals into the Columbia. To provide some context, Professor Robinson-Dorn reports that, "as late as 1994 and 1995, the Trail Smelter was discharging more copper and zinc into the Columbia River than the cumulative totals of all permitted U.S. discharges for those materials." In Professor Robinson-Dorn's words, "[b]y any measure, the quantity of hazardous substances discharged from the Trail Smelter is staggering."

EPA has concluded that large amounts of these pollutants have come to rest in Lake Roosevelt, a designated National Recreation Area that is "one of the most popular recreation areas in Washington State" and that also "lies within the ancestral home-lands of the Colville and Spokane Tribes." The lake, which is 135 miles long, extends to about 15 miles from the U.S.-Canadian border. Various environmental studies have shown elevated levels of a wide range of hazardous substances in sediments and fish in Lake Roosevelt, and "that these contaminants pose a risk to aquatic life" and humans. EPA's investigatory efforts, which led the agency to conclude that the lake is severely contaminated and requires attention, were prompted by a Colville Tribes petition to EPA, requesting that it conduct sampling and other, related work.

Rather than pursuing the Arbitral Panel approach used in the earlier Trail Smelter dispute to seek to hold Teck Cominco legally accountable for the discharges from its facility in Canada that were adversely affecting the environment and health in the United States, the United States first engaged the company to discuss its volun-tarily accepting responsibility for the site and, when that effort foundered, the U.S. EPA acted unilaterally to address the contamination by issuing a CERCLA §106 administrative order in which it directed Teck Cominco to undertake an investigation of the site. Even though Teck Cominco refused to comply with the order and EPA declined to pursue this noncompliance legally, the matter did not end there. CER-CLA §310, like provisions in many U.S. environmental statutes (see Chapter 10), gives citizens the right to sue under certain circumstances, and two American citizens, both members of a local Native American tribe, initiated a domestic U.S. citizen suit under CERCLA §310 against Teck Cominco in an effort to enforce EPA's CERCLA §106 order. The State of Washington was supportive of the action, intervening as a plaintiff in the citizen suit. The following quote from then–Washington State Attorney General Christine Gregoire captures the State's perspective: "Teck Cominco can't send highly toxic pollution across the Canadian border and then insist that border protects them from liability. They created one big mess here in the U.S., and they should clean it up, not Washington taxpayers."*

This citizen-driven domestic legal action to enforce the EPA CERCLA §106 order against a Canadian company for contamination that originated at its Canadian facility but that has impacted the U.S. environment has undoubtedly had more legal legs than some anticipated, or wanted. First the U.S. District Court, and then the Court of Appeals, upheld the citizens' right to sue Teck Cominco in U.S. courts to enforce EPA's CERCLA order. These opinions have triggered considerable contro-versy. One scholar argues that the district court opinion "turn[s] . . . principles of sovereignty and international law on their head." Parrish, Trail Smelter Déjà Vu: Extraterritoriality, International Environmental Law, and the Search for Solutions to Canadian-U.S. Transboundary Water Pollution Disputes, 85 B.U. L. Rev. 363, 405 (2005). The Canadian government, the United States and Canadian Chambers of Commerce, the national mining associations for each country, and others filed amicus briefs in the Ninth Circuit in support of Teck Cominco; and a First Nation confederation that represents tribes on both sides of the border, NGOs, and several states similarly supported the plaintiffs. For very different perspectives on this Trail Smelter litigation, see George, Environmental Enforcement across National Borders, 21 Nat. Resources & Env't No. 1, at 3 (Summer 2006), and Du Bey et al., CERCLA and Transboundary Contamination in the Columbia River, id., at 8 (George repre-sented Teck Cominco in the litigation; Du Bey et al. represented the tribes).

---

*Christine Gregoire (then Washington attorney general, now Washington's governor), Press Release, Wash. State Office of the Att'y Gen., Washington State Joins Lawsuit to Force Lake Roosevelt Cleanup (Aug. 31, 2004), www.atg.wa.gov/releases/rel_epa_083104.html.

In short, a very different legal tool (domestic law) has been used this time to address the contamination originating from the Teck Cominco facility, and very different actors have participated in the proceedings (while citizens played an important role in the Arbitration, this time citizens and Native American tribes were formal parties). Following is an excerpt from the Ninth Circuit's recent opinion in the Superfund-related litigation, in which it explains why it believes it has jurisdiction to require Teck Cominco to comply with EPA's order.

PAKOOTAS v. TECK COMINCO METALS, LTD.
452 F.3d 1066 (9th Cir. 2006)

GOULD, Circuit Judge: . . .

I

Teck owns and operates a lead-zinc smelter ("Trail Smelter") in Trail, British Columbia. Between 1906 and 1995, Teck generated and disposed of hazardous materials, in both liquid and solid form, into the Columbia River. These wastes, known as "slag," include the heavy metals arsenic, cadmium, copper, mercury, lead, and zinc, as well as other unspecified hazardous materials. Before mid-1995, the Trail Smelter discharged up to 145,000 tons of slag annually into the Columbia River. . . .

A significant amount of slag has accumulated and adversely affects the surface water, ground water, sediments, and biological resources of the Upper Columbia River and Lake Roosevelt. Technical evidence shows that the Trail Smelter is the predominant source of contamination at the Site. The physical and chemical decay of slag is an ongoing process that releases arsenic, cadmium, copper, zinc, and lead into the environment, causing harm to human health and the environment.

After the EPA determined that the Site was eligible for listing on the NPL, it evaluated proposing the Site for placement on the NPL for the purpose of obtaining federal funding for evaluation and future cleanup. At that time Teck Cominco American, Inc. (TCAI) approached the EPA and expressed a willingness to perform an independent, limited human health study if the EPA would delay proposing the Site for NPL listing. The EPA and TCAI entered into negotiations, which reached a stalemate when the parties could not agree on the scope and extent of the investigation that TCAI would perform. The EPA concluded that TCAI's proposed study would not provide the information necessary for the EPA to select an appropriate remedy for the contamination, and as a result the EPA issued the Order [a CERCLA §106 unilateral administrative order] on December 11, 2003. The Order directed Teck to conduct a RI/FS under CERCLA for the Site. To date Teck has not complied with the Order, and the EPA has not sought to enforce the Order.

Pakootas filed this action in federal district court under the citizen suit provision of CERCLA. §9659(a)(1). Pakootas sought a declaration that Teck has violated the Order, injunctive relief enforcing the Order against Teck, as well as penalties for noncompliance and recovery of costs and fees. Teck moved to dismiss the complaint pursuant to Federal Rule of Civil Procedure 12(b)(1)and 12(b)(6) for failure to state a cause of action under CERCLA and lack of subject matter jurisdiction, on the ground that the district court could not enforce the Order because it was based on activities carried out by Teck in Canada. Teck also moved to dismiss for lack of personal jurisdiction over Teck, a Canadian corporation with no presence in the United States.

In addressing the question of extraterritorial application, the district court acknowledged that "Congress has the authority to enforce its laws beyond the territorial boundaries of the United States," but that it is "a longstanding principle of American law 'that legislation of Congress, unless a contrary intent appears, is meant to apply only within the territorial jurisdiction of the United States.'" However, the district court concluded that the presumption against extraterritoriality was overcome here, because

> there is no doubt that CERCLA affirmatively expresses a clear intent by Congress to remedy 'domestic conditions' within the territorial jurisdiction of the U.S. That clear intent, combined with the well-established principle that the presumption [against extraterritoriality] is not applied where failure to extend the scope of the statute to a foreign setting will result in adverse effects within the United States, leads this court to conclude that extraterritorial application of CERCLA is appropriate in this case. . . .

On this appeal, Teck does not challenge the district court's determination that it had personal jurisdiction over Teck. . . . Teck argues that the district court should have dismissed Pakootas's complaint [because] . . . to apply CERCLA to Teck's activities in Canada would be an impermissible extraterritorial application of United States law. . . .

IV

Teck's primary argument is that, in absence of a clear statement by Congress that it intended CERCLA to apply extraterritorially, the presumption against extraterritorial application of United States law precludes CERCLA from applying to Teck in Canada. We need to address whether the presumption against extraterritoriality applies only if this case involves an extraterritorial application of CERCLA. So a threshold question is whether this case involves a domestic or extraterritorial application of CERCLA.

Unlike other environmental laws such as the Clean Air Act, Clean Water Act, and Resource Conservation and Recovery Act (RCRA), CERCLA is not a regulatory statute. Rather, CERCLA imposes liability for the cleanup of sites where there is a release or threatened release of hazardous substances into the environment. . . .

Here, several events could potentially be characterized as releases. First, there is the discharge of waste from the Trail Smelter into the Columbia River in Canada. Second, there is the discharge or escape of the slag from Canada when the Columbia River enters the United States. And third, there is the leaching of heavy metals and other hazardous substances from the slag into the environment at the Site. Although each of these events can be characterized as a release, CERCLA liability does not attach unless the "release" is from a CERCLA facility.

Here, as noted, the Order describes the facility as the Site. . . . We hold that the leaching of hazardous substances from the slag at the Site is a CERCLA release. That release—a release into the United States from a facility in the United States—is entirely domestic.

The third element of liability under CERCLA is that the party must be a "covered person" under §9607(a). . . . Teck argues that if it is an arranger under §9607(a)(3), then basing CERCLA liability on Teck arranging for disposal of slag in Canada is an impermissible extraterritorial application of CERCLA.

Assuming that Teck is an arranger under §9607(a)(3), we consider whether the fact that the act of arranging in Canada for disposal of the slag makes this an extra-territorial application of CERCLA. Teck argues that because it arranged in Canada for disposal, that is, the act of arranging took place in Canada even though the hazardous substances came to be located in the United States, it cannot be held liable under CERCLA without applying CERCLA extraterritorially.

The text of §9607(a)(3) applies to "any person" who arranged for the disposal of hazardous substances. The term "person" includes, *inter alia*, "an individual, firm, corporation, association, partnership, consortium, joint venture, [or] commercial entity." §9601(21). On its face, this definition includes corporations such as Teck, although the definition does not indicate whether foreign corporations are covered. Teck argues that because the Supreme Court recently held that the term "any court" as used in 18 U.S.C. §922(g)(1) does not include foreign courts, we should interpret the term "any person" so as not to include foreign corporations. See Small v. United States, 544 U.S. 385, 390-91 (2005).

The decision in *Small* was based in part on United States v. Palmer, 16 U.S. (3 Wheat.) 610 (1818), in which Chief Justice Marshall held for the Court that the words "any person or persons," as used in a statute prohibiting piracy on the high seas, "must not only be limited to cases within the jurisdiction of the state, but also to those objects to which the legislature intended to apply them." The Court held that "any person or persons" did not include crimes "committed by a person on the high seas, on board of any ship or vessel belonging exclusively to subjects of a foreign state, on persons within a vessel belonging exclusively to subjects of a foreign state." However, the Court held that even though the statute did not specifically enumerate foreign parties as "persons," the statute did apply to punish piracy committed by foreign parties against vessels belonging to subjects of the United States.

Palmer relied upon two benchmarks for determining whether terms such as "any person" apply to foreign persons: (1) the state must have jurisdiction over the party, and (2) the legislature must intend for the term to apply. Regarding jurisdiction, Teck argued in the district court that there was no personal jurisdiction over it. . . . [W]e agree with the district court that there is specific personal jurisdiction over Teck here.[16] Because there is specific personal jurisdiction over Teck here based on its

---

16. We do not decide whether there is general personal jurisdiction over Teck. Rather, we adopt the district court's conclusion that there is specific personal jurisdiction over Teck here, based on Washington State's long-arm statute, which applies to "the commission of a tortious act" within Washington, and our case law holding that "personal jurisdiction can be predicated on (1) intentional actions (2) expressly aimed at the forum state (3) causing harm, the brunt of which is suffered—and which the defendant knows is likely to be suffered—in the forum state." AT&T v. Compagnie Bruxelles Lambert, 94 F.3d 586 (9th Cir. 1996), is not to the contrary. There, AT&T claimed that Compagnie Bruxelles Lambert was liable under CERCLA because its subsidiary operated a site from which hazardous substances were released. We held that there was no specific jurisdiction over the parent company because (1) the parent company had insufficient independent contacts with the United States to establish personal jurisdiction, and (2) the subsidiary was not acting as the parent company's alter ego. Here, Teck has sufficient independent personal contacts with the forum state to justify specific personal jurisdiction.

allegedly tortious act aimed at the state of Washington, the first *Palmer* benchmark is satisfied, and we can appropriately construe the term "any person" to apply to Teck.

The second *Palmer* benchmark is that the legislature must intend for the statute to apply to the situation. Except for the statutory definition of "any person," CERCLA is silent about *who* is covered by the Act. But CERCLA is clear about what is covered by the Act. CERCLA liability attaches upon release or threatened release of a hazardous substance into the environment. CERCLA defines "environment" to include "any other surface water, ground water, drinking water supply, land surface or subsurface strata, or ambient air *within the United States or under the jurisdiction of the United States.*" §9601(8) (emphasis added). CERCLA's purpose is to promote the cleanup of hazardous waste sites where there is a release or threatened release of hazardous substances into the environment within the United States. Because the legislature intended to hold parties responsible for hazardous waste sites that release or threaten release of hazardous substances into the United States environment, the second *Palmer* benchmark is satisfied here.

Although the *Palmer* analysis supports the proposition that CERCLA applies to Teck, *Palmer* of course does not address the distinction between domestic or extraterritorial application of CERCLA. The *Palmer* analysis, however, in what we have termed its second benchmark, brings to mind the "domestic effects" exception to the presumption against extraterritorial application of United States law. The difference between a domestic application of United States law and a presumptively impermissible extraterritorial application of United States law becomes apparent when we consider the conduct that the law prohibits. . . .

Here, the operative event creating a liability under CERCLA is the release or threatened release of a hazardous substance. Arranging for disposal of such substances, in and of itself, does not trigger CERCLA liability, nor does actual disposal of hazardous substances. A release must occur or be threatened before CERCLA is triggered. A party that "arranged for disposal" of a hazardous substance under §9607(a)(3) does not become liable under CERCLA until there is an actual or threatened release of that substance into the environment. Arranging for disposal of hazardous substances, in itself, is neither regulated under nor prohibited by CERCLA. Further, disposal activities that were legal when conducted can nevertheless give rise to liability under §9607(a)(3) if there is an actual or threatened release of such hazardous substances into the environment.

The location where a party arranged for disposal or disposed of hazardous substances is not controlling for purposes of assessing whether CERCLA is being applied extraterritorially, because CERCLA imposes liability for releases or threatened releases of hazardous substances, and not merely for disposal or arranging for disposal of such substances. Because the actual or threatened release of hazardous substances triggers CERCLA liability, and because the actual or threatened release here, the leaching of hazardous substances from slag that settled at the Site, took place in the United States, this case involves a domestic application of CERCLA.

Our conclusion is reinforced by considering CERCLA's place within the constellation of our country's environmental laws, and contrasting it with RCRA. . . . RCRA regulates the generation and disposal of hazardous waste, whereas CERCLA imposes liability to clean up a site when there are actual or threatened releases of hazardous substances into the environment. It is RCRA, not CERCLA, that governs prospectively how generators of hazardous substances should dispose of those substances, and it is the Canadian equivalent of RCRA, not CERCLA, that regulates how Teck disposes of its waste within Canada.

Here, the district court assumed, but did not decide, that this suit involved extraterritorial application of CERCLA because "[t]o find there is not an extraterritorial application of CERCLA in this case would require reliance on a legal fiction that the 'releases' of hazardous substances into the Upper Columbia River Site and Lake Roosevelt are wholly separable from the discharge of those substances into the Columbia River at the Trail Smelter." However, what the district court dismissed as a "legal fiction" is the foundation of the distinction between RCRA and CERCLA. If the Trail Smelter were in the United States, the discharge of slag from the smelter into the Columbia River would potentially be regulated by RCRA and the Clean Water Act. And that prospective regulation, if any, would be legally distinct from a finding of CERCLA liability for cleanup of actual or threatened releases of the hazardous substances into the environment from the disposal site, here the Upper Columbia River Site. That the Trail Smelter is located in Canada does not change this analysis, as the district court recognized.

CERCLA is only concerned with imposing liability for cleanup of hazardous waste disposal sites where there has been an actual or threatened release of hazardous substances into the environment. CERCLA does not obligate parties (either foreign or domestic) liable for cleanup costs to cease the disposal activities such as those that made them liable for cleanup costs; regulating disposal activities is in the domain of RCRA or other regulatory statutes.

We hold that applying CERCLA here to the release of hazardous substances at the Site is a domestic, rather than an extraterritorial application of CERCLA, even though the original source of the hazardous substances is located in a foreign country.

NOTES AND QUESTIONS RELATING TO TRANSBOUNDARY POLLUTION

1. The Trail Smelter Arbitration has been described as "having laid the foundations of international environmental law, at least regarding transfrontier pollution." A. Kiss & D. Shelton, International Environmental Law 45 (2d ed. 2000). What was the outcome of the Trail Smelter Arbitration? What legal test did it articulate and what law did the panel rely upon in formulating this test? Why did the panel rely on the law it did? What is the precedential effect of the decision given that it was an agreed-upon process under a Convention that identified the issues to be decided?

2. What were the key elements in the analysis of the Ninth Circuit as to why it had jurisdiction to order Teck Cominco to implement the CERCLA §106 order? What differences were there in the analyses of the district court and the court of appeals?

3. While some scholars are likely to favor application of domestic law beyond a state's boundaries as an important mechanism for effective environmental protection, some commentators disagreed strongly with the district court's decision and are likely to disagree with the recent Ninth Circuit decision as well. Some of the concerns raised are that extraterritorial application of domestic environmental statutes may (1) undermine environmental policies of other nations and impinge on their sovereignty; (2) undermine existing diplomatic options for addressing disputes; (3) foster foreign resentment; and (4) be bad for business by inviting retaliatory practices. See, e.g., Abate, Dawn of a New Era in the Extraterritorial Application of U.S. Environmental

Statutes: A Proposal for an Integrated Judicial Standard Based on the Continuum of Context, 31 Colum. J. Envtl. L. 87, 130-137 (2006).

4. Following the citizen suit, EPA and Teck Cominco's U.S. subsidiary, which no one has alleged contributed to the contamination of Lake Roosevelt, entered into a settlement agreement that committed Teck Cominco America to undertake particular investigatory work at the site. Settlement Agreement for Implementation of Remedial Investigation and Feasibility Study at the Upper Columbia River Site (June 2, 2006). EPA has withdrawn its CERCLA §106 unilateral administrator order, and the settlement agreement, by its terms, is not based on that order.

Washington State, interested Native Americans, and some NGOs have expressed concern about the efficacy and adequacy of this settlement, as this excerpt from a Washington Department of Ecology June 2, 2006, news release reflects:

> State officials are concerned that the agreement . . . is unique and untested. There is concern that it may not lead to a cleanup that adequately protects human health and the environment. In addition, the agreement limits state and tribal ability to participate fully in the cleanup process.
>
> This agreement is a private contract between the federal government and an international mining company . . . [t]hat departs from normal settlement and cleanup procedures under both federal and state cleanup laws. Usually, these agreements take the form of a consent order or a consent decree, which is clearly enforceable and reliably requires a polluter to clean up contamination to appropriate standards.

The Confederated Tribes of the Colville Reservation also issued a June 2 statement in which they indicated that they are "uneasy about the settlement because it doesn't follow EPA regulations or U.S. laws."

What is EPA's authority to enter into the Settlement Agreement excerpted above? How and in what forum is the Agreement enforceable? Against what party or parties is the Agreement enforceable? If the Ninth Circuit's decision stands, how would the State and citizens go about enforcing the decision?

5. Are there international processes the citizens could have considered using to try to persuade the Canadian government and Teck Cominco to address the contaminated site? Jutta Brunnée suggests that the common practice to address transboundary disputes has involved "resolution of the concern through diplomatic processes or resort to inter-state dispute settlement." She indicates that the original Trail Smelter case is "the embodiment of that approach" and continues that referral to the IJC is an option—indeed, "[t]he very task of the commission is to address concerns pertaining to boundary waters between the United States and Canada." Brunnée, The United States and International Environmental Law: Living with an Elephant, 15 Eur. J. Int'l L. 617, 633 (2004). What do you think of this suggested approach? What are the implications of the Trail Smelter Arbitration in terms of the interest of either country, or the citizens of each, in pursuing this strategy? To what extent is this mechanism available to citizens? Is the adequacy or legitimacy of this mechanism affected by the extent to which it affords citizens a role? By the powers the IJC possesses, or its accountability to elected officials in each country? Should these types of institutional features matter in considering the legitimacy of an international (or domestic) process? What types of factors are relevant in considering this issue?

What about the CEC's citizen submissions process, discussed below? Submitters have filed a number of submissions that involve transboundary pollution. In August

2006, the CEC Secretariat dismissed the Devil's Lake Submission, SEM-06-002 (30 March 2006), available at www.cec.org, which involved a claim that a North Dakota plan to construct and operate an outlet that would drain water from Devil's Lake in a way that would negatively impact Canadian waters, violated the countries' obligations under the 1909 Boundary Waters Treaty. Article IV of the Boundary Waters Treaty provides that, among other things, boundary waters and waters flowing across the boundary between the United States and Canada shall not be polluted. The submitters alleged that the countries had a duty under the Treaty to resolve the dispute through a reference to the International Joint Commission, and that their failure to make such a reference constituted a violation of their Treaty obligations and a failure to effectively enforce their environmental laws that was actionable under the CEC citizen submissions process. The Secretariat dismissed the submission on the ground that its jurisdiction extends only to failures to enforce "environmental law," which the NAAEC defines to include "any statute or regulation of a Party . . . ," noting that it was "unable to conclude that the anti-pollution provision in Article IV meets the definition of "environmental law." CEC Secretariat Determination for SEM-06-002 (August 21, 2006), available at www.cec.org. The Secretariat indicated it was not clear whether the Boundary Waters Treaty should be considered to be a "statute or regulation" of either party. What are the implications of the CEC Secretariat's action for the viability of a citizen submission to address transboundary pollution of the sort that has contaminated Lake Roosevelt? What are the implications of this action for the domestic enforceability of international agreements?

People to Save Sheyenne v. Department of Health, 697 N.W.2d 319 (N.D. 2005), is a North Dakota Supreme Court decision that also involves the Devil's Lake discharge. Like *Pakootas*, *Save Sheyenne* involved a domestic court considering transboundary impacts. The court in *Save Sheyenne* upheld the North Dakota agency's issuance of a state administrative NPDES permit to discharge water from Devil's Lake into the Sheyenne River, which in turn discharged into the Red River, which flows north across the U.S.-Canadian border into the Canadian province of Manitoba. Manitoba, as well as some U.S. NGOs, opposed the issuance of the permit at the state administrative level, on the ground that the discharge would adversely affect water quality in various ways, and then challenged the permit through the North Dakota court system, up to the North Dakota Supreme Court. The court applied an arbitrary and capricious standard in upholding the state agency's conclusion that the project should be approved despite these concerns.

Assume that the permitted discharge from Devil's Lake does cause harm to waters in Canada, as the permit challengers allege will occur. What recourse would the impacted residents of Canada have? To what extent should the issuance of a permit by the source state serve as a shield to liability or legal responsibility? What would be the analysis if the affected area were in another state in the United States, rather than in Canada? See International Paper Co. v. Ouellette, 479 U.S. 481 (1987).

6. For a thoughtful review of North American environmental cooperation and transboundary issues, see Environmental Management on North America's Borders (R. Kiy & J. Wirth eds., 1998). More recently, Geoffrey Garver, director of the CEC's citizen submissions process, has identified several other transboundary concerns in North America, including the following activities and effects:

- A proposed coal mine in British Columbia on Glacier National Park and the Flathead River system in Montana

- The Tulsequah Chief mine in British Columbia on the transboundary Taku River that flows into Alaska
- The proposed expansion of the Coventry landfill in Vermont on the Lake Memphremagog watershed in Quebec
- Lining the All American Canal in California on wetland ecosystems in Mexico
- Construction of a liquid natural gas terminal in Mexican waters near the Coronado Islands on migratory seabirds listed as endangered in the United States

He notes that smelters near the U.S.-Mexican border have also given rise to international disputes, in particular the Phelps Dodge smelter in Douglas, Arizona, and a copper smelter operated by Grupo Mexico, SA de CV, in Nacozari, Sonora. Garver, CEC Mechanisms and Frameworks for Resolving Disputes over Transboundary Environmental Impacts, CBA-ABA Second Annual National Environmental, Energy and Resources Law Summit (April 28, 2006).

7. There have been numerous bilateral efforts to address transboundary concerns. The CEC has created a database of North American transboundary agreements. It lists approximately 200 agreements and treaties, involving federal, regional, and state/provincial entities.* To provide one example of a transboundary environmental issue, in October 2005, the CEC published a report about opportunities to improve tracking of transboundary hazardous waste shipments in North America. CEC, Crossing the Border: Opportunities to Improve Tracking of Transboundary Hazardous Waste Shipments in North America (October 2005), available at http://www.cec.org/files/pdf/LAWPOLICY/Crossing-the-Border_en.pdf

A FINAL NOTE ABOUT TRANSBOUNDARY ENVIRONMENTAL PROBLEMS: THE POSSIBLE ROLE OF NEPA AND SIMILAR PROSPECTIVE APPROACHES

The United States' NEPA is the classic, and indeed the model, "look before you leap" statute intended to promote the incorporation of environmental issues into the threshold decisionmaking process about whether to authorize different types of activities, including massive projects such as the Teck Cominco facility, and about how to structure their operations to minimize environmental impacts. Many commentators have suggested that the permitting process, including use of NEPA or equivalent state laws, provides a potentially helpful mechanism for addressing transboundary issues. We discuss the extraterritorial application of NEPA in Chapter 4 (pages 263-264). Questions that arise in this context include (1) whether the analysis of the substantive issues associated with the possible project includes impacts on both sides of the border; (2) whether all interested stakeholders (including those on the other side of a border) have an adequate opportunity to participate in the administrative process; and (3) the availability to interested parties of judicial review if they are dissatisfied with the administrative outcome.

In the United States, NEPA itself does not specifically mention transboundary environmental impact assessment (EIA), and there has been considerable debate

*Available at http://www.cec.org/pubs_info_resources/law_treat_agree/transbound_agree/index.cfm?varlan=english.

about whether it should apply extraterritorially. In July 1997, CEQ issued a guidance document on NEPA analysis of transboundary impacts for projects in the United States that addresses these issues to some extent. Council on Environmental Quality Guidance on NEPA Analyses for Transboundary Impacts (July 1, 1997). However, it is not clear whether this guidance has any legal effect since neither the State nor the Defense Department concurred. CEQ's general counsel, Dinah Bear, has summarized the debate concerning the extraterritorial application of NEPA. See Bear, Some Modest Suggestions for Improving Implementation of the National Environmental Policy Act, 43 Nat. Resources J. 931, 949-953 (2003). See also Knox, The Myth and Reality of Transboundary Environmental Impact Assessment, 96 Am. Int'l L. 291, 298, 299 (2002), for a summary of the case law and law review commentary on extraterritorial application of NEPA, and for a discussion of the limited extent to which other countries to date have used their domestic EIA processes to assess and address transboundary impacts.

Professor Knox has offered the following insights concerning the "myth and reality" of transboundary environmental impact assessment, and suggests that it might be helpful to consider TEIAs as a form of "nondiscrimination":

> The dominant story of transboundary environmental impact assessment in international law has the following elements: (1) customary international law prohibits transboundary pollution; (2) according to the classic version of this prohibition, contained in Principle 21 of the 1972 Stockholm Declaration, states must ensure that activities within their territory or under their control do not harm the environment beyond their territory; (3) to ensure that activities within their jurisdiction will not cause transboundary harm, states must assess the potential transboundary effects of the activities; and (4) to that end, states enter into international agreements requiring them to carry out transboundary environmental impact assessment (transboundary EIA) for activities that might cause transboundary harm.
>
> Despite its popularity, this story is not true. It belongs to what Daniel Bodansky has called the "myth system" of international environmental law: a set of ideas that are often considered part of customary international law but do not reflect state practice and, instead, "represent the collective ideals of the international community, which at present have the quality of fictions or half-truths." European and North American countries are adopting regional agreements that provide for transboundary EIA. But these agreements do not require transboundary EIA for all activities that might cause transboundary harm, and they do not link it to any hard substantive prohibition against transboundary harm. In short, these agreements do not much resemble the mythic story of transboundary EIA. At the same time, the agreements are not meaningless. They require EIA for certain types of actions, specify the elements an EIA must include, and provide for significant public participation in the EIA process.
>
> What, then, is going on? If transboundary EIA agreements are not designed to end transboundary pollution in accordance with Principle 21, what are they designed to do? One clue is that the agreements were not written on a clean slate. Most countries in North America and Western Europe have already enacted domestic EIA laws, which are limited in scope and lacking in substantive prohibitions but do contain detailed procedural obligations and provide important avenues for public participation. In large part, the regional EIA agreements reflect these domestic EIA laws. In fact, the main way that the agreements extend beyond the domestic laws is by ensuring that states apply EIA without extraterritorial discrimination—that they take extraterritorial effects into account just as they take domestic effects into account, and that they enable foreign residents to have access to the domestic EIA procedures to the same extent as local

residents. Another principle in international environmental law describes exactly this approach: the principle of nondiscrimination, which says that countries should apply the same environmental protections to potential harm in other countries that they apply to such harm in their own. Examined closely, each regional transboundary EIA agreement is an application of the principle of nondiscrimination.

The nondiscrimination principle has often been overlooked, cast into shadow by the glow surrounding Principle 21, which is generally considered to be the cornerstone of international environmental law. But Principle 21 suffers from serious weaknesses as a cornerstone of international law, not the least of which is that it does not seem to be a law at all. Perhaps it would be more appropriate to think of it as a capstone that has never been set. Despite limitations of its own, the principle of nondiscrimination may provide a better blueprint for the EIA agreements. [Id. at 291-292.]

One of the interesting outstanding questions in the TEIA arena is which approach is likely to prevail, domestically, and internationally—a Principle 21–like approach that purports to prohibit transboundary harm, or a nondiscrimination approach. For a thoughtful analysis of these issues, see Merrill, Golden Rules for Transboundary Pollution, 46 Duke L.J. 931 (1997).

B.   AN OVERVIEW OF THE EMERGING INFRASTRUCTURE OF INTERNATIONAL ENVIRONMENTAL LAW

The 2005 Millennium Ecosystem Assessment, a significant scientific review that UNEP helped to coordinate, offers a stark view of the state of the global environment:

At the heart of this assessment is a stark warning. Human activity is putting such strain on the natural functions of Earth that the ability of the planet's ecosystems to sustain future generations can no longer be taken for granted. . . .

Nearly two thirds of the services provided by nature to humankind are found to be in decline worldwide. In effect, the benefits reaped from our engineering of the planet have been achieved by running down natural capital assets.

In many cases, it is literally a matter of living on borrowed time. By using up supplies of fresh groundwater faster than they can be recharged, for example, we are depleting assets at the expense of our children.*

Some of these environmental stresses on the planet are global in scope. P. Birnie & A. Boyle, International Law and the Environment 6 (2d ed. 2002). The state of the world's fisheries is a good example. The United Nations Food and Agriculture Organization has estimated that roughly one-quarter of marine fish stocks are either fully depleted or overexploited, while another 52 percent of such stocks are fully exploited. United Nations Food and Agriculture Organization, The State of World Fisheries and Aquaculture 2004 32 (2005), available at http://www.fao.org/sof/sofia/index_en.htm. Protection of biodiversity is another issue that transcends state borders that has engendered significant concern. Convention on Biological Diversity, Art. 19,

*Millennium Ecosystem Assessment Board, Living Beyond Our Means: Natural Assets and Human Well-Being 5 (2005), available at http://www.millenniumassessment.org/en/products.aspx.

June 5, 1992, 31 I.L.M. 818 (1992), available at http://www.biodiv.org/doc/legal/cbd-en.pdf. Air pollution concerns, such as destruction of the ozone layer and global climate change (discussed in more detail in Chapter 6 and later in this chapter), are other "commons" issues of global scope that have received extensive public attention.

The perspective that some environmental problems are of a global scale has led many officials and others to conclude that solutions are beyond the capacity of any single country. Instead, if meaningful progress is to be made, countries need to develop ways to work together to increase understanding of the problems and to develop and implement strategies to address them.

From an institutional standpoint, there is no supranational body that has the power to establish binding environmental laws to address global or other environmental concerns. Thus, there is a significant difference between international law and domestic law, which in countries such as the United States is developed through a system in which the legislative and executive branches have power to make laws, subject to constitutional limitations, and the judicial branch has power to interpret such laws and consider their legality. Indeed, some have called for creation of a global environmental organization that would serve as an umbrella (or more) for worldwide environmental governance. A World Trade Organization (WTO) has been created to manage world trade; some have urged that the environment needs a comparable institution. See, e.g., Esty, The Value of Creating a Global Environmental Organization, 6 Env't Matters 13 (2000). To date, however, no such organization has been created, and at least some commentators have concluded that a consensus is emerging that creation of a World Environment Organization is unlikely. K. Von Moltke, On Clustering International Environmental Agreements, in Multilevel Governance of Global Environmental Change, Perspectives from Science, Sociology and the Law (G. Winter ed., 2006).

Briefly, there are several ways in which nation-states may create international law. Treaties are the "most frequent method of creating binding international rules relating to the environment." Birnie & Boyle, supra, at 13. Treaties are generally considered to be analogous to domestic contracts, in which the parties—states—negotiate terms for pursuing agreed-upon objectives. The 1969 Vienna Convention on the Law of Treaties sets out norms that govern the creation and implementation of written treaties.* To provide a brief overview of a few of these principles, the Convention provides that states that have signed a treaty are generally not bound to comply with it until the terms for the treaty's entry into force have been met—for example, the state involved has ratified the treaty and the agreed-upon number of additional ratifications has occurred. As one might imagine, in many instances there is a considerable time lapse between when a treaty is signed and when it goes into effect. Treaties, even when they have come into force, generally do not bind nonparty states. A third general concept: under some circumstances, states may make reservations to treaties in which, for example, they opt out of certain features. While this concept may encourage greater participation in treaties, it also may undermine their effectiveness.

A second source of international law is known as customary international law, which refers to legal norms established by a pattern of state practice over time. Customary international law requires both consistent and observable state practice, and a perceived legal obligation (*opinio juris*) to conform to the pattern. It is defined as

---

*Vienna Convention on the Law of Treaties, May 23, 1969, 1155 U.N.T.S. 331, available at http://untreaty.un.org/ilc/texts/instruments/english/conventions/1_1_1969.pdf.

a "general and consistent practice of states followed by them from a sense of legal obligation." Restatement (Third) of Foreign Relations Law of the United States §102(2) (1987). Given the nature of customary international law, there often is disagreement about whether a particular concept actually constitutes a form of customary law. Further, disagreement may exist concerning the content of such law, if it in fact exists.

While the Westphalian model, which locates states at the heart of international law development and implementation, continues to control much of lawmaking and implementation internationally, other actors are increasingly demanding or taking a seat at the table of international governance. Dean Anne-Marie Slaughter, among other scholars, has suggested that much international governance occurs through a web of "government networks" that extend well beyond federal officials. A. Slaughter, A New World Order (2004). Such other actors include a variety of federal actors, sub-states (U.S. states and local governments, for example), nongovernmental actors (financial institutions and environmental, labor, and other groups), private parties that engage in the activities that are the subject of much international and domestic regulatory effort, and international institutions. Professor John Jackson's overview of international law highlights its fluidity and possible transformation:

> The last decade of the twentieth century and the first of the twenty-first century may not be the most challenging period for the generally accepted assumptions of international law, but this period will certainly rank high on any such list. The growing depth, speed of change, and adjustment required by "globalization," accompanied by striking changes in government institutions, a remarkable increase in nongovernment activity and advocacy, an intense emphasis on market economic ideas, and a backlash against them, have all chipped away at the relatively fragile (perhaps already crumbling) [sic] theoretical foundations of the international legal system as it has been generally accepted for centuries. [J. Jackson, Sovereignty, the WTO, and Changing Fundamentals of International Law 3 (2006).]

Jutta Brunnée suggests that the United States is participating in this evolutionary process. She indicates that, for example, the United States is relying increasingly on approaches to international environmental law and governance that are alternatives to multilateral environmental agreements (MEAs) and customary law. She suggests that the United States is increasingly prepared to take unilateral action to address international environmental concerns. The country's decision not to ratify the Kyoto Protocol and to pursue alternative approaches to address climate change is one example. The *Tuna/Dolphin* dispute, discussed below, in which the United States imposed domestic regulatory standards applicable to its fishing industry on other countries' operations in order to protect dolphins, is another. The U.S. import restrictions were triggered by domestic litigation, through which domestic environmental NGOs influenced rigorous enforcement of domestic U.S. law that required limitations on importation of tuna in order to protect dolphins.

Professor Brunnée further suggests that the United States is placing increasing emphasis on engaging individuals, corporations, and NGOs to foster environmental protection. This includes the notion that the private sector has a critical role to play in fostering sustainable development, through private investment and otherwise. Brunnée, *supra*, 15 Eur. J. Int'l L. at 630, 634. The United States, for example, announced five private-public partnership programs at the 2002 Johannesburg

Summit, involving priorities such as water, energy, health, agricultural production, and biodiversity.*

Another threshold, overarching question about international environmental governance involves its sphere of influence. While the traditional view is that international law is limited to regulating relations among nation-states and excludes matters that fall exclusively within the domestic jurisdiction of any state, Dean Slaughter and some other scholars suggest that the reach of international law needs to expand significantly, into traditionally domestic preserves.

> International law and the international community . . . are . . . coming to have not only the right but in many cases also the obligation to intervene in and influence what were previously the exclusive jurisdiction and political processes of national governments. [Slaughter & Burke-White, The Future of International Law Is Domestic (or, the European Way of Law), 47 Harv. Int'l L.J. 327, 352 (2006).]

Some scholars have questioned the wisdom of extending international law in this way, particularly for "raw international law," that is, international law that has "not been endorsed by our own domestic political process." Some contend that the "democracy deficit" in the formulation of international law undermines its utility. See, e.g., McGinnis and Somin, Should International Law Be Part of Our Law? 59 Stan. L. Rev. (forthcoming 2007).

The rest of this section surveys some of the more significant milestones and actors in the realm of international environmental governance.

THE UN, INTERNATIONAL ENVIRONMENTAL CONFERENCES, AND "FOUNDATIONAL" INTERNATIONAL ENVIRONMENTAL PRINCIPLES

The United Nations has played a significant role in the development and implementation of international environmental law. The 1972 UN Conference on the Human Environment attracted a substantial number of world leaders and produced the Stockholm Declaration. Declaration of the United Nations Conference on the Human Environment (June 16, 1972), reprinted in 11 I.L.M. 1416.

Following the Stockholm Conference, on December 15, 1972, the UN General Assembly adopted Resolution 2997, creating the UN Environment Program (UNEP), the first UN environmental agency. It established the UNEP Secretariat's headquarters in Nairobi, Kenya. While other parts of the UN, such as the UN Development Program (UNDP), also have significant roles relating to environmental protection, UNEP serves as the UN system's "designated entity for addressing environmental issues at the global and regional level."** UNEP defines its mandate to be to "coordinate the development of environmental policy consensus by keeping the global environment under review and bringing emerging issues to the attention of governments and the international community for action." The UN established a UNEP Governing

---

*See Partnership Initiatives Announced at Sustainable Development Summit in Johannesburg: Aim at Priority Issues—Water, Energy, Health, Agricultural Production, Biodiversity, ENV/DEV/J/ 10, 29 August 2002, available at http://www.un.org/events/wssd/summaries/envdevj10.htm.

**United Nations Environmental Programme, Organization Profile 3, http://www.unep.org/ PDF/UNEPOrganizationProfile.pdf [hereinafter UNEP Organization Profile].

Council, comprised of 58 nations that the General Assembly elects for four-year terms, to oversee UNEP.

In the 1980s, the UN "welcomed the establishment of a commission" that would review strategies for sustainable development. This commission, the World Commission on Environment and Development (commonly referred to as the Brundtland Commission after its chair, Gro Harlem Brundtland of Norway), issued Our Common Future in 1987. The Brundtland Commission defined sustainable development as "development that meets the needs of the present without compromising the ability of future generations to meet their own needs." World Commission on the Environment and Development, Our Common Future 43 (1987).

Twenty years after the Stockholm Declaration was adopted and five years after the issuance of Our Common Future, in 1992, the UN convened a Conference on Environment and Development in Rio de Janeiro, Brazil. Often referred to by its popular name, the Earth Summit, this conference attracted an unprecedented number of world leaders and NGOs. The conference generated considerable buzz worldwide, at least in some circles, about a renewed or invigorated commitment to environmental protection on a global scale. It also produced agreement on different conventions to address particular environmental challenges, as well as an overarching set of foundational principles (the Rio Declaration) and a detailed blueprint for implementing these principles, including sustainable development (known as Agenda 21). A UN document captures this perspective:

> The Earth Summit generated a tangible sense of optimism that momentum was at last being created for global change. It gave birth to two major conventions—the UN Framework Convention on Climate Change and the Convention on Biological Diversity—and saw the creation of the UN Commission on Sustainable Development. The Rio Declaration reaffirmed the principles first elaborated in Stockholm twenty years earlier, while Agenda 21 gave the world an action programme for building sustainable development into the 21st century. [UNEP Organizational Profile, *supra*, at 11.]

Ten years later, from August 26 to September 4, 2002, the UN convened a third conference on environmental issues, in Johannesburg, South Africa, entitled the World Summit on Sustainable Development (WSSD). Unlike predecessor conferences such as those in Stockholm and Rio de Janeiro, the Johannesburg conference did not produce any new agreements or establish any new institutions. It did adopt the Johannesburg Declaration on Sustainable Development and a Plan of Implementation of the World Summit on Sustainable Development. The World Summit's signatories reaffirmed their commitment to the Rio principles and to the full implementation of Agenda 21. The World Summit Plan is intended to "promote the integration of the three components of sustainable development—economic development, social development and environmental protection—as interdependent and mutually reinforcing pillars."* Carl Bruch, codirector of international programs for the Environmental Law Institute (ELI) and a legal officer with UNEP from 2003 to 2005, has suggested that the 2002 conference signals a shift in focus, from the design of new agreements to implementation of existing treaties and other arrangements. Bruch, Growing Up, 23 Envtl. F. 28, 30 (May/June 2006). Other commentators have also highlighted the recognition at Johannesburg of a "need to focus on

*World Summit on Sustainable Development, Implementation Plan, para. I. 2 (2002), available at http://www.un.org.

implementation" of promises previously made at Rio and elsewhere. See, e.g., Scherr and Gregg, Johannesburg and Beyond: The 2002 World Summit on Sustainable Development and the Rise of Partnerships, 18 Geo. Int'l Envtl. L. Rev. 425 (2006). UNEP has compiled the following list of milestones in its history.

Milestones 1972-2005

1972 UNEP established after UN Conference on the Human Environment
1973 Convention on International Trade in Endangered Species of Wild Fauna and Flora (CITES)
1975 Mediterranean Action Plan: first of thirteen regional action plans under the UNEP Regional Seas program
1979 Bonn Convention on Migratory Species
1985 Vienna Convention for the Protection of the Ozone Layer
1987 Montreal Protocol on Substances that Deplete the Ozone Layer
1988 Intergovernmental Panel on Climate Change (IPCC) established to assess information related to human-induced climate change
1989 Basel Convention on the Transboundary Movement of Hazardous Wastes
1991 Global Environment Facility established
1992 UN Conference on Environment and Development (Earth Summit) issues Rio Declaration and Agenda 21
1992 Framework Convention on Climate Change
1992 Convention on Biological Diversity
1994 Convention to Combat Desertification
1995 Global Programme of Action (GPA) launched to protect marine environment from land-based sources of pollution
1998 Rotterdam Convention on Prior Informed Consent
1999 UN Global Compact launched
2000 Cartagena Protocol on Biosafety adopted to address issue of genetically modified organisms
2000 Malmö Declaration: a call to action on international environmental governance by the first Global Ministerial Environment Forum
2000 Millennium Declaration: environmental sustainability listed as one of eight Millennium Development Goals
2001 Third IPCC Assessment Report details the extent of human-induced global warming
2001 Stockholm Convention on Persistent Organic Pollutants (POPs)
2002 World Summit on Sustainable Development reaffirms UNEP's central role in international efforts to achieve sustainable development
2005 Kyoto Protocol on climate change enters into force
2005 Bali Strategic Plan for Technology Support and Capacity Building adopted by UNEP Governing Council mandating national level support to developing countries
2005 Millennium Ecosystem Assessment highlights the importance of ecosystems to human well-being, and the extent of ecosystem decline
2005 2005 World Summit agrees to explore a more coherent institutional framework system for international environmental governance [UNEP Organization Profile, *supra*, at 16-17.]

The following excerpt from the 1992 Rio Principles identifies some of the concepts of international environmental governance that many commentators contend serve as foundational principles for such governance. The notion of sustainable development receives particular attention in the Principles. Birnie and Boyle suggest that, "[t]hroughout, the principal concern of the Declaration, and of those who negotiated it, was to integrate the needs of economic development and environmental protection in a single, if not wholly coherent, ensemble. . . . For the first time it is now possible to point to a truly international consensus on some core principles of law and policy concerning environmental protection, sustainable development, and their inter-relationship." Birnie & Boyle, *supra*, at 83. In addition to contending that the importance of the concept of sustainable development for the "resolution of environmental problems is profound and undisputed," Birnie and Boyle observe that sustainable development and environmental protection do not necessarily have identical goals: "[m]ost obviously, sustainable development is as much about economic development as about environmental protection; while these two aspects have to be integrated in order to achieve sustainable development, they remain distinct." Id. at 2-3. Consider this formulation as you review the following excerpt. Be aware that commentators have spilled much ink, and caused the felling of many trees, in efforts to elaborate on the definition of the concept of sustainable development.

UNITED NATIONS CONFERENCE ON ENVIRONMENT AND DEVELOPMENT, DECLARATION OF PRINCIPLES (1992)

Recognizing the integral and interdependent nature of the Earth, our home, Proclaims that:

Principle 1.	Human beings are at the centre of concerns for sustainable development. They are entitled to a healthy and productive life in harmony with nature.
Principle 2.	States have, in accordance with the Charter of the United Nations and the principles of international law, the sovereign right to exploit their own resources pursuant to their own environmental and developmental policies, and the responsibility to ensure that activities within their jurisdiction or control do not cause damage to the environment of other States or of areas beyond the limits of national jurisdiction.
Principle 3.	The right to development must be fulfilled so as to equitably meet developmental and environmental needs of present and future generations.
Principle 4.	In order to achieve sustainable development, environmental protection shall constitute an integral part of the development process and cannot be considered in isolation from it.
Principle 7.	. . . In view of the different contributions to global environmental degradation, States have common but differentiated responsibilities. The developed countries acknowledge the responsibility that they bear in the international pursuit of sustainable development in

view of the pressures their societies place on the global environment and of the technologies and financial resources they command.

Principle 9.   States should cooperate to strengthen endogenous capacity-building for sustainable development by improving scientific understanding through exchanges of scientific and technological knowledge, and by enhancing the development, adaptation, diffusion and transfer of technologies, including new and innovative technologies.

Principle 10.   Environmental issues are best handled with the participation of all concerned citizens, at the relevant level. At the national level, each individual shall have appropriate access to information concerning the environment that is held by public authorities, including information on hazardous materials and activities in their communities, and the opportunity to participate in decision-making processes. States shall facilitate and encourage public awareness and participation by making information widely available. Effective access to judicial and administrative proceedings, including redress and remedy, shall be provided.

Principle 11.   States shall enact effective environmental legislation. Environmental standards, management objectives and priorities should reflect the environmental and developmental context to which they apply. Standards applied by some countries may be inappropriate and of unwarranted economic and social cost to other countries, in particular developing countries.

Principle 12.   States should cooperate to promote a supportive and open international economic system that would lead to economic growth and sustainable development in all countries, to better address the problems of environmental degradation. Trade policy measures for environmental purposes should not constitute a means of arbitrary or unjustifiable discrimination or a disguised restriction on international trade. Unilateral actions to deal with environmental challenges outside the jurisdiction of the importing country should be avoided. Environmental measures addressing transboundary or global environmental problems should, as far as possible, be based on an international consensus.

Principle 13.   States shall develop national law regarding liability and compensation for the victims of pollution and other environmental damage. States shall also cooperate in an expeditious and more determined manner to develop further international law regarding liability and compensation for adverse effects of environmental damage caused by activities within their jurisdiction or control to areas beyond their jurisdiction.

Principle 14.   States should effectively cooperate to discourage or prevent the relocation and transfer to other States of any activities and substances that cause severe environmental degradation or are found to be harmful to human health.

Principle 15.   In order to protect the environment, the precautionary approach shall be widely applied by States according to their capabilities. Where there are threats of serious or irreversible damage, lack of full scientific certainty shall not be used as a reason for postponing cost-effective measures to prevent environmental degradation.

Principle 16. National authorities should endeavour to promote the internalization of environmental costs and the use of economic instruments, taking into account the approach that the polluter should, in principle, bear the cost of pollution, with due regard to the public interest and without distorting international trade and investment.

Principle 17. Environmental impact assessment, as a national instrument, shall be undertaken for proposed activities that are likely to have a significant adverse impact on the environment and are subject to a decision of a competent national authority.

Principle 19. States shall provide prior and timely notification and relevant information to potentially affected States on activities that may have a significant adverse transboundary environmental effect and shall consult with those States at an early stage and in good faith.

As noted above, the notion of sustainable development has won considerable support in many circles, but the challenge has been to define what this term means, and then to determine how to implement it sensibly in specific contexts. The following excerpt, by two officials with the United Nations University Institute of Advanced Studies, considers the challenges for achieving sustainable development.

W. CHAMBERS & J. GREEN, INTRODUCTION: TOWARD AN EFFECTIVE FRAMEWORK FOR SUSTAINABLE DEVELOPMENT
Reforming International Environmental Governance: From Institutional Limits to Innovative Reforms 1, 1-11 (W. Chambers & J. Green eds., 2005)*

Introduction

In 1987, the oft-cited Brundtland Report challenged the international community to achieve "development that meets the needs of the present without compromising the ability of future generations to meet their own needs." Though the Brundtland Report's definition of sustainable development is elegant in its simplicity, the enormous political, academic and policy debates it has spawned suggest that it is insufficient.

Since then, the world of sustainable development has grown unsustainably. New legal instruments, multilateral regimes, institutions and actors continue to appear on the policy-making scene. The research and literature of sustainable development have expanded into a vast multidisciplinary effort, recruiting academics and experts from a wide variety of areas. Even armed with new knowledge and institutions, the international community continues to struggle with the challenges presented by the Brundtland Report.

Nonetheless, progress has been made. Despite the complexity of the issues surrounding sustainable development, we have advanced our understanding of its constituent

---

*W. Bradnee Chambers is a senior program officer and Jessica F. Green is a research associate at the United Nations University Institute of Advanced Studies, Yokohama, Japan.

components. Achieving sustainable development requires recognizing its social, economic and environmental pillars and integrating all three considerations into policy interventions. It requires, as noted in *Agenda 21*, broad consultation with stakeholders. Some would argue that sustainable development demands even larger changes.

To meet these challenges and implement change, international institutions have been created by the handful. Now, there is a growing awareness within the United Nations, and among governments and civil society, that these institutions must be evaluated and governance for sustainable development strengthened. Many have argued that institutions can have a profound effect on policy outcomes. In the case of sustainable development governance, a growing number of studies are linking the failure to make progress to protect the environment and achieve sustainable development to the complexity, inefficiency and weaknesses of current institutions. Major declarations . . . point out the need to streamline and strengthen the system of international sustainable development governance, with the aim of enhancing policy coherence and implementation.

Obstacles to Sustainable Development

These goals, though important, will not be easy to achieve. Governance for sustainable development faces a number of obstacles. The first set of obstacles is procedural— pertaining to the institutional arrangements themselves. The international architecture for sustainable development is highly fragmented, with different institutions focused on different policy aspects. In a sense, this is logical: each of the three pillars of sustainable development has its own priorities, and institutions thus have different organizational missions and goals. Yet the unforeseen consequences of this diffusion are considerable.

The diffuse nature of the system is further fragmented by a lack of strong mechanisms for coordination across institutions. Each of the pillars has its own governing council and member states. . . . [T]here is a hierarchy of priorities within each sector. Thus, the policies of the World Trade Organization (WTO) remain focused on economic growth, while social and environmental measures often take a back seat. Similarly, the policies for sustainable development of the United Nations Environment Programme (UNEP) are environment driven, sometimes to the detriment of economic considerations. Thus, lofty intentions of consistency are overshadowed, not surprisingly, by each institution's mission. This disjuncture between desired and actual policies will persist until a mechanism is created at a level with enough legitimacy and authority to set policy priorities that can and will be adhered to by the institutions of all three pillars of sustainable development.

Lack of coordination across sustainable development institutions gives rise to further problems. Fragmentation becomes self-perpetuating, because policy makers and bureaucrats have difficulty conceptualizing the landscape of sustainable development in its entirety and understanding where individual agencies, bodies and regimes fit into that architecture. It is testimony to this tunnel vision that no in-depth examination has been undertaken of all of the structures and institutions that comprise sustainable development governance. The project that produced this volume, a three-part investigation into the prospects for international environmental governance reform, is one of the first attempts at such a survey.

Fragmentation also gives rise to specialization. Because of the multitude of institutions and their associated legal instruments and processes, policy makers must become experts on one specific issue or policy. As a result, negotiations are narrowly defined and are carried out by experts. Thus, the scope of the problem is constrained by the expertise of the policy makers. Individual international agreements are often negotiated by way of "specific" regimes that are isolated from one another. . . .

Consequently, policy-making for sustainable development remains segregated. The result is twofold. First, the proliferation of agreements and their associated activities causes unnecessary complications at the national level, as signatories struggle to meet their obligations under multiple agreements. . . . Second, isolation of multi-lateral environmental agreements (MEAs) from a larger sustainable development context has resulted in overlapping treaties and even the possibility of conflict.

Underlying these procedural problems that continue to plague sustainable development governance is the substantive complexity of the policy questions at hand. At their core, environmental processes are governed by nature, not international policy. Thus, the current approach to sustainable development governance often results in artificial divisions within ecosystem functioning for the purposes of man-agement. These divisions are further exacerbated by several other characteristics of the interactions between science and policy. First, the scientific uncertainty that surrounds many environmental problems poses additional challenges for policy makers: What decisions can be taken in the face of uncertainty? How much risk is acceptable? What constitutes a precautionary approach? Second, effective solutions to transnational and global problems require collective responses. The incentive to free ride is high, and difficulties in measuring environmental outcomes make compliance a challenge. Finally, the scale of an ecosystem can be local, regional or global. More-over, its well-being may be dependent on specific species or other nearby ecosystems. Institutions for sustainable development must match the scale of the system to ensure maximum effectiveness. Appropriate scales of response can be stymied by the absence of political will or by the artificial division of ecosystems for the purposes of working with units of analysis that are more manageable.

Conclusion

The outcomes of the World Summit on Sustainable Development (WSSD) have reaffirmed the need for institutional reform. The "Plan of Implementation", which details the decisions taken through the course of WSSD process, reiterates that "an effective institutional framework for sustainable development at all levels is key to the full implementation of Agenda 21 . . . and meeting emerging sustainable develop-ment challenges." The "Plan of Implementation" outlines 13 objectives that should govern institutional reform efforts, including integrating the three pillars of sustain-able development in a balanced manner, increasing effectiveness and efficiency through limiting overlap, and strengthening international institutions. . . .

Though changes in the current landscape of international governance are needed, they are not a panacea for achieving the objectives of sustainable develop-ment. The lack of coherence within the formal international institutional architecture reflects a persisting high level of disagreement about what would constitute an effective and appropriate approach to achieving sustainable development. The inabil-ity of the international community to agree upon a common approach to sustainable development governance is largely rooted in disparities between the perspectives and priorities of developed and developing countries. Reducing and overcoming these disparities remain, therefore, critical prerequisites for the creation of an effective, efficient and equitable system of sustainable development governance.

NOTES AND QUESTIONS ON THE RIO PRINCIPLES

1. Several of the concepts embodied in the Rio Principles have been incorporated into one or more multilateral agreements. This excerpt from the Principles is intended to introduce students to some of these ideas. Which Principles support each of the concepts listed below?

    a. State sovereignty
    b. Sustainable development
    c. The responsibility not to cause environmental harm
    d. Intergenerational equity
    e. Common but differentiated responsibility
    f. Polluter pays
    g. The precautionary principle
    h. Duty to evaluate environmental impacts

2. What is your reaction to Oscar Schachter's observation that "[t]o say that a state has no right to injure the environment of another seems quixotic in the face of the great variety of transborder environmental harms that occur every day." Schachter, The Emergence of International Environmental Law, 44 J. Int'l Aff. 457, 463 (1991). What limits would you support with respect to the notion that transboundary harm should be discouraged?

3. What do the Principles have to say about the appropriateness of one-size-fits-all approaches to environmental protection?

4. What strategies do the Principles recommend for pursuing the goal of sustainable development? What do you think was the source of much of the tension that surrounded development of the Principles?

5. The precautionary principle, discussed in Principle 15, has received an enormous amount of attention. In Comparing Precaution in the United States and Europe, J. Risk Res. 5, 317 (2002), Jonathan B. Wiener and Michael D. Rogers find that sometimes the United States is more precautionary while in other cases it is the EU that fills this role.

> A broader analysis reveals that the reality is a complex pattern of relative precaution, both historically and today. Europe appears to be more precautionary than the US about such risks as GMOs, hormones in beef, toxic substances, phthalates, climate change, guns, and antitrust/competition policy. The US appears to be more precautionary than Europe about such risks as new drug approval, the ban on CFCs in aerosol spray cans and the ban on supersonic transport to protect the stratospheric ozone layer, nuclear energy, lead in gasoline, particulate air pollution, highway safety, teenage drinking, cigarette smoking, mad cow disease in blood donations, potentially violent youths, 'right to know' information disclosure requirements, and missile defences.
>
> This broader analysis indicates that neither the US nor the EU is a more precautionary actor across the board, today or in the past. Relative precaution appears to depend more on the particular risk than on the country or the era. This complexity is compounded by the variation within each system: both the US and the EU are federations of subsidiary jurisdictions, with variety in regulatory approaches within each system. Meanwhile, compared to most of the rest of the world, the US and the EU are probably both at the highly precautionary end of the spectrum.

6. How does domestic U.S. regulation address the ideas embodied in Principles 13-17? Which U.S. laws address each of these concepts, and to what extent are the U.S. approaches in harmony with the Rio Principles?

C.   COMMONS ISSUES

As discussed in Chapter 1, one of environmental law's challenges from its inception has been to establish strategies for governance of "commons" areas. This is certainly the case in the international arena. We face significant challenges in protecting a wide variety of commons resources, including our air, water, habitat, and species.

There has been a substantial increase in the number of multilateral environmental agreements (MEAs) over the past 20 years. A 2001 UNEP report identifies 41 "core" environmental conventions of global significance; of these, 31 have been adopted since 1985. Brunnée, The United States and International Environmental Law: Living with an Elephant, 15 Eur. J. Int'l L. 617, 636 (2004). Many of these agreements have been negotiated to address particular issues. These include the Kyoto Protocol to the United Nations Framework Convention on Climate Change, the United Nations Convention on the Law of the Sea, the Convention on Biological Diversity, and the Convention on International Trade in Endangered Species of Wild Flora and Fauna.

The MEAs often have created new institutions to help with their implementation. Professor Jutta Brunnée describes as follows the approach such conventions sometimes use:

> The primary approach to global MEA design today is the "framework-protocol" model. . . . Typically, the initial framework treaty contains only general commitments and establishes information-gathering and decision-making structures. Subsequent protocols to the framework treaty provide binding emission reduction or other environmental protection commitments. [Brunnée, *supra*, at 637.]

This section provides an overview of one such treaty, the Montreal Protocol on Substances that Deplete the Ozone Layer. This Protocol involved a significant environmental development of global dimensions (the emergence of a hole in the ozone layer). Multilateral negotiations led to adoption of a multilateral environmental agreement that the vast majority of countries have now joined, and which has since been refined several times as new evidence has come in. The 1987 Protocol called for a partial phaseout of ozone-depleting chemicals, but subsequent assessments have led to decisions to accelerate the phasing out of different ozone-depleting chemicals.*

The head of the U.S. delegation to the negotiation summarized the significant environmental and financial stakes at issue as follows:

> The Montreal Protocol on Substances That Deplete the Ozone Layer mandated significant reductions in the use of several extremely useful chemicals. At the time of the treaty's negotiation, chlorofluorocarbons (CFCs) and halons were rapidly proliferating

*See Accelerated Phaseout of Ozone-Depleting Chemicals, EPA History, United States Environmental Protection Agency, at http://www.epa.gov/history/topics/montreal/02.htm. Many consider this agreement to be one of the major successes of international environmental cooperation.

compounds with wide applications in thousands of products, including refrigeration, air conditioning, aerosol sprays, solvents, transportation, plastics, insulation, pharmaceuticals, computers, electronics, and fire fighting. Scientists suspected, however, that as these substances were released into the atmosphere and diffused to its upper reaches, they might cause future damage to a remote gas—the stratospheric ozone layer—that shields life on Earth from potentially disastrous levels of ultraviolet radiation.

By their action, the signatory countries sounded the death knell for an important part of the international chemical industry, with implications for billions of dollars in investment and hundreds of thousands of jobs in related sectors. The protocol did not simply prescribe limits on these chemicals based on "best available technology," which had been a traditional way of reconciling environmental goals with economic interests. Rather, the negotiators established target dates for replacing products that had become synonymous with modern standards of living, even though the requisite technologies did not yet exist. . . . [R. Benedick, Ozone Diplomacy: New Directions in Safeguarding the Planet 1-2 (1991).]

Benedick attributed the success of the Protocol to a series of factors, including (1) the role of science, (2) the power of public opinion, (3) UNEP's role as facilitator, and (4) the leadership of the United States. Among other things, the United States was the first to "take regulatory action" and it also "tenaciously campaigned" for international adoption of a "comprehensive global plan for protecting the ozone layer. . . ." Id. at 6.

Benedick concluded that the Protocol

broke new ground in its treatment of long-term risks and in its reconciliation of difficult scientific, economic, and political issues. . . . [T]he Montreal Protocol was achieved with astonishing rapidity. The signing occurred 13 years after the first scientific hypothesis on the ozone layer was published in 1974—and only nine months after formal diplomatic negotiations began in December 1986. . . . [Id. at 8.]

The following is an excerpt from the 1987 Protocol.

THE MONTREAL PROTOCOL ON SUBSTANCES THAT DEPLETE THE OZONE LAYER
Montreal, 16 September 1987

The Parties to this Protocol, . . .

Mindful of their obligation . . . to take appropriate measures to protect human health and the environment against adverse effects resulting or likely to result from human activities which modify or are likely to modify the ozone layer,

Recognizing that world-wide emissions of certain substances can significantly deplete and otherwise modify the ozone layer in a manner that is likely to result in adverse effects on human health and the environment, . . .

Aware that measures taken to protect the ozone layer from depletion should be based on relevant scientific knowledge, taking into account technical and economic considerations,

Determined to protect the ozone layer by taking precautionary measures to control equitably total global emissions of substances that deplete it, with the ultimate objective of their elimination on the basis of developments in scientific knowledge, taking into account technical and economic considerations,

Acknowledging that special provision is required to meet the needs of developing countries for these substances, . . .

Considering the importance of promoting international co-operation in the research and development of science and technology relating to the control and reduction of emissions of substances that deplete the ozone layer, bearing in mind in particular the needs of developing countries,

Have agreed as follows: . . .

Article 2: Control Measures

1. Each Party shall ensure that for the twelve-month period commencing on the first day of the seventh month following the date of the entry into force of this Protocol, and in each twelve-month period thereafter, its calculated level of consumption of the controlled substances in Group I of Annex A does not exceed its calculated level of consumption in 1986. By the end of the same period, each Party producing one or more of these substances shall ensure that its calculated level of production of the substances does not exceed its calculated level of production in 1986, except that such level may have increased by no more than ten per cent based on the 1986 level. Such increase shall be permitted only so as to satisfy the basic domestic needs of the Parties operating under Article 5 and for the purposes of industrial rationalization between Parties. . . .

3. Each Party shall ensure that for the periods 1 July 1993 to 30 June 1994 and in each twelve-month period thereafter, its calculated level of consumption of the controlled substances in Group I of Annex A does not exceed, annually, eighty per cent of its calculated level of consumption in 1986. Each Party producing one or more of these substances shall, for the same periods, ensure that its calculated level of production of the substances does not exceed, annually, eighty per cent of its calculated level of production in 1986. However, in order to satisfy the basic domestic needs of the Parties operating under Article 5 and for the purposes of industrial rationalization between Parties, its calculated level of production may exceed that limit by up to ten per cent of its calculated level of production in 1986.

4. Each Party shall ensure that for the periods 1 July 1998 to 30 June 1999, and in each twelve-month period thereafter, its calculated level of consumption of the controlled substances in Group I of Annex A does not exceed, annually, fifty per cent of its calculated level of consumption in 1986. Each Party producing one or more of these substances shall, for the same periods, ensure that its calculated level of production of the substances does not exceed, annually, fifty per cent of its calculated level of production in 1986. However, in order to satisfy the basic domestic needs of the Parties operating under Article 5 and for the purposes of industrial rationalization between Parties, its calculated level of production may exceed that limit by up to fifteen per cent of its calculated level of production in 1986. This paragraph will apply unless the Parties decide otherwise at a meeting by a two-thirds majority of Parties present and voting, representing at least two-thirds of the total calculated level of consumption of these substances of the Parties. This decision shall be considered and made in the light of the assessments referred to in Article 6. . . .

9. (a) . . . [T]he Parties may decide whether: (i) adjustments to the ozone depleting potentials specified in Annex A should be made and, if so, what the adjustments should be; and (ii) further adjustments and reductions of production or consumption of the controlled substances from 1986 levels should be undertaken and, if so, what the scope, amount and timing of any such adjustments and reductions should be.

(b) Proposals for such adjustments shall be communicated to the Parties by the secretariat at least six months before the meeting of the Parties at which they are proposed for adoption.

(c) In taking such decisions, the Parties shall make every effort to reach agreement by consensus. If all efforts at consensus have been exhausted, and no agreement reached, such decisions shall, as a last resort, be adopted by a two-thirds majority vote of the Parties present and voting representing at least fifty per cent of the total consumption of the controlled substances of the Parties.

(d) The decisions, which shall be binding on all Parties, shall forthwith be communicated to the Parties by the Depositary. Unless otherwise provided in the decisions, they shall enter into force on the expiry of six months from the date of the circulation of the communication by the Depositary. . . .

10. Based on the assessments made pursuant to Article 6 of this Protocol and in accordance with the procedure set out in Article 9 of the Convention [covering Amendments to the Convention or Protocols], the Parties may decide:

(a) whether any substances, and if so which, should be added to or removed from any annex to this Protocol; and (b) the mechanism, scope and timing of the control measures that should apply to those substances. . . .

11. Notwithstanding the provisions contained in this Article, Parties may take more stringent measures than those required by this Article.

Article 4: Control of Trade with Non-Parties

1. Within one year of the entry into force of this Protocol, each Party shall ban the import of controlled substances from any State not party to this Protocol.

2. Beginning on 1 January 1993, no Party operating under paragraph 1 of Article 5 may export any controlled substance to any State not party to this Protocol.

3. Within three years of the date of the entry into force of this Protocol, the Parties shall . . . elaborate in an annex a list of products containing controlled substances. Parties that have not objected to the annex . . . shall ban, within one year of the annex having become effective, the import of those products from any State not party to this Protocol.

4. Within five years of the entry into force of this Protocol, the Parties shall determine the feasibility of banning or restricting, from States not party to this Protocol, the import of products produced with, but not containing, controlled substances. If determined feasible, the Parties shall . . . elaborate in an annex a list of such products. Parties that have not objected to it . . . shall ban or restrict, within one year of the annex having become effective, the import of those products from any State not party to this Protocol.

5. Each Party shall discourage the export, to any State not party to this Protocol, of technology for producing and for utilizing controlled substances.

6. Each Party shall refrain from providing new subsidies, aid, credits, guarantees or insurance programmes for the export to States not party to this Protocol of products, equipment, plants or technology that would facilitate the production of controlled substances.

Article 5: Special Situation of Developing Countries

1. Any Party that is a developing country and whose annual calculated level of consumption of the controlled substances is less than 0.3 kilograms per capita on the date of the entry into force of the Protocol for it, or any time thereafter within ten years of the date of entry into force of the Protocol shall, in order to meet its basic domestic needs, be entitled to delay its compliance with the control measures . . . by ten years after that specified. . . .

2. The Parties undertake to facilitate access to environmentally safe alternative substances and technology for Parties that are developing countries and assist them to make expeditious use of such alternatives.

3. The Parties undertake to facilitate bilaterally or multilaterally the provision of subsidies, aid, credits, guarantees or insurance programmes to Parties that are developing countries for the use of alternative technology and for substitute products.

Article 6: Assessment and Review of Control Measures

Beginning in 1990, and at least every four years thereafter, the Parties shall assess the control measures provided for in Article 2 on the basis of available scientific, environmental, technical and economic information. At least one year before each assessment, the Parties shall convene appropriate panels of experts qualified in the fields mentioned and determine the composition and terms of reference of any such panels. Within one year of being convened, the panels will report their conclusions, through the secretariat, to the Parties. . . .

Article 11: Meetings of the Parties

1. The Parties shall hold meetings at regular intervals. The secretariat shall convene the first meeting of the Parties not later than one year after the date of the entry into force of this Protocol and in conjunction with a meeting of the Conference of the Parties to the Convention, if a meeting of the latter is scheduled within that period. . . .

NOTES AND QUESTIONS

1. What factors does Benedick point to as key to the success of the Montreal Protocol negotiations?

2. Benedick notes that the treaty imposed "substantial short-term economic costs to protect human health and the environment against unproved future dangers. . . . At

Table 11-1
The Montreal Protocol Treaty Regime

1985	Vienna Convention for the Protection of the Ozone Layer
1987	Montreal Protocol to the Vienna Convention
1990	London Amendments and Adjustment to the Montreal Protocol
1992	Copenhagen Amendments and Adjustment to the Montreal Protocol
1994	Vienna Adjustment to the Montreal Protocol
1997	Montreal Amendments and Adjustment to the Montreal Protocol
1999	Beijing Amendments and Adjustment to the Montreal Protocol

the time [when the treaty was created], no measurable evidence of damage existed." What Rio Principle(s) are implicated by this characterization of the facts?

3. How does the Montreal Protocol address the issue of "common but differentiated responsibilities"?

4. The Protocol has been amended and adjusted on multiple occasions since 1987. Adjustments have accelerated phaseouts of already-covered chemicals, while amendments have, *inter alia*, added new substances to be banned or phased out. For example, with respect to main CFCs, the 1987 Montreal Protocol provided for developed countries to achieve a 50 percent reduction in consumption and production by 1998. The London adjustments directed these countries to ban main CFCs by 2000, while the Copenhagen adjustments accelerated this ban to 1996. Similarly, while the Montreal Protocol obligated developing countries to reduce main CFCs by 50 percent by 2008, the London adjustments required that developing countries ban main CFCs by 2010. Table 11-1 shows the development of the Protocol. What procedures does the Protocol establish for adjustments to occur?

5. What incentives does the Protocol create for countries to become parties to it?

6. Recent assessments of the ozone layer suggest significant progress on some fronts. The August 2006 WMO/UNEP Scientific Assessment of Ozone Depletion: 2006, prepared by the Scientific Assessment Panel of the Montreal Protocol on Substances that Deplete the Ozone Layer, provides the following summary of monitoring efforts and the results they have yielded. The Assessment also points out the interrelationship that may exist between seemingly different types of environmental problems—here, the connection between ozone depletion and global warming, a topic we discuss in considerable detail in Chapter 6.

> The provisions of the 1987 Montreal Protocol . . . include the requirement that the Parties . . . base their future decisions on . . . updated . . . information that is assessed through Panels drawn from the worldwide expert communities. . . . Advances in scientific understanding were assessed by the Scientific Assessment Panel in 1989, 1991, 1994, 1998, and 2002. This information . . . led to the subsequent Amendments and Adjustments of the 1987 Protocol. The 2006 Scientific Assessment summarized here is the sixth in that series. . . .
>
> The previous [2002] Assessment presented evidence that the tropospheric abundances of most ozone-depleting substances, as well as of stratospheric chlorine, were stable or decreasing due to actions taken under the Montreal Protocol. Based on these facts, it was stated that "The Montreal Protocol is working, and the ozone-layer depletion from the Protocol's controlled substances is expected to begin to ameliorate within the next decade or so."

The results from over three decades of research have provided a progressively better understanding of the interaction of human activity and the ozone layer. . . .

- The Montreal Protocol is working: There is clear evidence of a decrease in the atmospheric burden of ozone-depleting substances and some early signs of stratospheric ozone recovery. . . .
- Long-term recovery of the ozone layer from the effects of ozone-depleting substances is expected to span much of the 21st century and is estimated to occur later than projected in the previous assessment (2002).
- Understanding the interconnections between ozone depletion and climate change is crucial for projections of future ozone abundances. The ozone-depleting substances and many of their substitutes are also greenhouse gases; changes in ozone affect climate; and changes in climate affect ozone.

[Id. at 1, 20, 21, 24.]

7. In NRDC v. EPA, 464 F.3d 1 (D.C. Cir. 2006), the D.C. Circuit held that "the 'decisions' of the Parties—post-ratification side agreements reached by consensus among 189 nations—are not 'law' within the meaning of the Clean Air Act and are not enforceable in federal court. . . . Without congressional action . . . side agreements reached after a treaty has been ratified are not the law of the land; they are enforceable not through the federal courts, but through international negotiations." What are the possible implications of this decision for implementation of the Montreal Protocol, and for the structure of multilateral agreements more generally?

8. Not all international initiatives in the environmental arena have been as successful as the Montreal Protocol. A comparison of the experience in addressing global warming with ozone depletion provides a good example of this reality. For an interesting analysis of reasons why the Montreal Protocol has been more successful than other multilateral environmental treaties, including the Kyoto Protocol, see S. Barrett, Environment and Statecraft (2003). In his analysis of the Montreal and Kyoto Protocols, Sunstein, Of Montreal and Kyoto: A Tale of Two Protocols, 31 Harv. Envtl. L. Rev. 1 (2007), Professor Sunstein suggests considerable similarities between the two:

Of the world's environmental challenges, the two most significant may well be stratospheric ozone depletion and climate change. At first glance, the problems appear to be closely related. . . . Consider seven similarities between the two problems:

1. Both ozone depletion and climate change have received public recognition on the basis of relatively recent scientific work, theoretical and empirical.
2. Both problems involve the effects of emissions from man-made technologies that come from diverse nations and that threaten to cause large-scale harm.
3. Both ozone-depleting chemicals and greenhouse gases stay in the atmosphere for an extremely long time. Hence the relevant risks are difficult to reverse; even with action that is both immediate and aggressive, the underlying problems will hardly be eliminated all at once. . . .
4. No nation is able to eliminate either problem on its own. Indeed, no nation is even able to make significant progress on either problem on its own, certainly not in the long run. Because of the diversity of contributors, both problems seem to be best handled through international agreements.

5. Both problems involve extremely serious problems of international equity. Wealthy nations have been the principal contributors to both ozone depletion and climate change. . . .
6. Both problems present extremely serious problems of intergenerational equity. Future generations are likely to face greater risks than the current generation, and a key question is how much the present should be willing to sacrifice for the benefit of the future. . . .
7. With respect to both problems, the United States is a crucial actor, probably the most important in the world. The importance of the United States lies not only in its wealth and power; it also lies in the fact that the United States has been an extremely significant source of both ozone-depleting chemicals and greenhouse gases.

Professor Sunstein also notes, however, that the two protocols have had very different degrees of success:

Notwithstanding these similarities, there is one obvious difference between the two problems. An international agreement, originally signed in Montreal and designed to control ozone-depleting chemicals, has been ratified by almost all nations in the world (including the United States, where ratification was unanimous). . . . Nations are complying with their obligations; global emissions of ozone-depleting chemicals have been reduced by over 95%; and atmospheric concentrations of such chemicals have been declining since 1994. By 2050, the ozone layer is expected to return to its natural level. The Montreal Protocol, the foundation for this process, thus stands as an extraordinary and even spectacular success story. Its success owes a great deal to the actions not only of the United States government, which played an exceedingly aggressive role in producing the Protocol, but to American companies as well, which stood in the forefront of technical innovation leading to substitutes for ozone-depleting chemicals.

    With climate change, the situation is altogether different. To be sure, an international agreement, produced in Kyoto in 1997, did go into force in 2005, when Russia ratified it. . . . But numerous nations are not complying with their obligations under the Kyoto Protocol, and the United States firmly rejects the agreement, with unanimous bipartisan opposition to its ratification. Far from leading technical innovation, American companies have sharply opposed efforts to regulate greenhouse gas emissions, and have insisted that the costs of regulation are likely to be prohibitive. Between 1990 and 2004, the United States experienced a decline in emissions of ozone-depleting chemicals, to the point where such emissions are essentially zero. But in the same period, the United States experienced a rapid growth in greenhouse gases. In part as a result, worldwide emissions of greenhouse gases are projected to rise at a rapid rate. An additional complication stems from the fact that developing nations have refused to join the Kyoto Protocol, and it is in those nations that greenhouse gases are increasing most rapidly. In particular, India and China have shown explosive growth in recent years, and China will soon become the leading greenhouse gas emitter in the world.

D.   NORTH AMERICAN ENVIRONMENTAL INSTITUTIONS

Several North American institutions have emerged to foster cooperation on environmental issues between and among the three North American countries and to strengthen the capacity of domestic regimes to promote environmental protection.

This section surveys a few of these institutions, with a particular focus on the Commission for Environmental Cooperation (CEC), the only institution whose focus encompasses the entire North American environment.

1. U.S.-Canadian Cooperation: The International Joint Commission (IJC)

The United States and Canada created the International Joint Commission in the 1909 Boundary Waters Treaty. The countries adopted the Great Lakes Water Quality Agreement (GLWQA) in 1972, added a Protocol to the GLWQA in 1987, and, in 1991, signed the Canada–United States Air Quality Agreement, in which the two governments created an Air Quality Committee to review air contamination–related issues. Stephen Toope and Jutta Brunnée suggest that "the most important role accorded to the IJC has probably been its fact-finding and reporting jurisdiction [in Article IX]. Canada and the United States have jointly referred important issues to the IJC for investigation and comment, including studies of water and air pollution, and water apportionments." They also highlight, on the other hand, the IJC's "lack[] [of] independent powers of enforcement" and the fact that it was "never given the power to shape substantive principles of law." Toope & Brunnée, Freshwater Regimes: The Mandate of the International Joint Commission, 15 Ariz. J. Int'l & Comp. Law 273, 281, 282 (1998).*

2. U.S.-Mexican Coordination: The La Paz Agreement, the BECC, NADBank, and Border 2012

The United States has entered into a series of bilateral arrangements with Mexico to address environmental and other concerns on the U.S.-Mexican border. Some of these concerns stem from the *maquiladora* program, which was established in the mid-1960s to provide financial incentives to plants located in the border region in order to encourage foreign investment on the Mexican side of the border. The number of plants increased dramatically after NAFTA was adopted. By 2001, there were 2,700 *maquiladora* plants in the border states. U.S. EPA and SEMARNAT [Mexico's Secretariat of Environment and Natural Resources], Border 2012: U.S.-Mexico Environmental Program, EPA-160-R-03-001 (2003). Adequate environmental infrastructure has not been put into place to manage the resulting solid waste, sewage, and other needs of the rapidly expanding population. As part of the NAFTA discussions, Mexico and the United States created the Border Environment Cooperation Commission (BECC), which is intended to identify worthwhile environmental infrastructure projects along the border, and a North American Development Bank (NAD Bank), which is intended to help to finance such projects.

In addition to the BECC and NAD Bank, the 1983 La Paz Agreement, formally known as the Agreement on Cooperation for the Protection and Improvement of the Environment in the Border Area, provides the legal basis for an ongoing initiative

---

*For more on the IJC and the scope of its responsibilities, see http://www.ijc.org/en/background/ijc_cmi_nature.htm.

known as the Border 2012 program. Border 2012 is a ten-year environmental program for the border region that has as its mission "protect[ing] the environment and public health in the U.S.-Mexico border region, consistent with the principles of sustainable development." Id. at 6. Key participants include the ten border states (on each side of the border) and the U.S. border tribes, in addition to the U.S. and Mexican governments. The first biennial report of Border 2012 was due in May 2006, but had not been released when this book went to press. The Good Neighbor Environmental Board (GNEB), an independent advisory committee charged with advising the president on environmental relations with Mexico, praised Border 2012's "decentralized process involving the states, municipalities, and tribal governments in the area," while raising concerns about funding and other challenges.*

3.   The North American Commission for Environmental Cooperation (CEC)

The Commission for Environmental Cooperation is the first environmental organization to have a continental reach. The CEC Strategic Plan for 2005 to 2010 captures the regional scope of this institution, noting that the mission of the CEC is "to facilitate cooperation and public participation to foster conservation, protection and enhancement of the North American environment for the benefit of present and future generations, in the context of increasing economic, trade and social links among Canada, Mexico and the United States."**

The following excerpt provides an overview of the origins of this institution. It also reviews the broad scope of the CEC's activities.

KNOX & MARKELL, THE INNOVATIVE NORTH AMERICAN COMMISSION FOR ENVIRONMENTAL COOPERATION
Greening NAFTA 2, 10-12 (D. Markell & J. Knox eds., 2003)

In addition to warning against the pursuit of economic development in disregard of environmental protection, the Rio Conference also highlighted the need for more effective agreements and institutions to address worsening environmental problems. In this light, many saw NAFTA as an opportunity to improve international environmental cooperation among the North American nations.

. . . [T]he NAFTA debate [also] included arguments over, and was itself an example of, the desire of citizens to participate directly in the development and implementation of international policies that affect them. With respect to economic integration and environmental protection, as well as many other areas of international cooperation, nations are struggling over how to respond to the demands for greater public participation in realms that were once the exclusive province of government officials. Increasingly, international institutions are being reshaped to provide greater transparency and access to interested individuals and groups.

*Good Neighbor Environmental Board, Water Resources Management on the U.S.-Mexico Border (Feb. 2005), http://www.epa.gov/ocem/gneb/gneb8threport.pdf. To monitor the Border 2012 initiative, see http://www.epa.gov/usmexicoborder/codocuments.htm.

**CEC Strategic Plan on Trade and Environment, Commission for Environmental Cooperation, available at http://www.cec.org/pubs_docs/documents/index.cfm?varlan=english&ID=1851.

As a result of the NAFTA debate over these issues, the governments produced something significantly different than they had originally envisaged: a supplemental agreement to NAFTA called the North American Agreement on Environmental Cooperation (NAAEC), which established a new trilateral organization, the North American Commission for Environmental Cooperation (the NACEC, or CEC) [the CEC is comprised of three main actors: a council of the Parties' environmental ministers, a permanent Secretariat, and an independent advisory committee]. . . .

Even viewed through the trade/environment prism, . . . the range and creativity of the tools the NAAEC brings to bear on the pollution haven problem are remarkable. . . . [I]t is the first regional environmental organization in North America, with broad mandates to address almost any environmental issue arising anywhere on the continent. . . .

[M]ost of the Council's mandates do not directly concern issues of economic integration. For example, the NAAEC requires the Council to promote and, as appropriate, develop recommendations on public access to environmental information, appropriate limits for specific pollutants, transboundary environmental impact assessment, and reciprocal access to domestic legal remedies for transboundary environmental harm. The NAAEC also gives the Council a long list of topics with respect to which it may make recommendations, including pollution prevention, environmental reporting, scientific research and technology development, long-range transport of air and marine pollutants, wildlife protection, endangered species, and eco-labeling. The list concludes with a catch-all, allowing the Council to consider "other matters as it may decide." The effect of these mandates is to authorize the Council to consider virtually any environmental issue of interest to the Parties.

The mandates of the Secretariat are similarly broad. The NAAEC instructs the Secretariat to provide technical, administrative, and operational support to the Council, and the Council appoints its Executive Director, but the Secretariat also has an important degree of independence from the Parties. The Executive Director appoints the other officials of the Secretariat, and the NAAEC provides that the Secretariat may receive instructions only from the Council, rather than from any individual government or external authority. Moreover, the NAAEC requires the Secretariat to carry out two important types of reporting with limited Council oversight. Article 13 authorizes the Secretariat to prepare a report on any matter within the scope of the annual program without Council authorization and a report on any other environmental matter related to the cooperative functions of the NAAEC unless the Council objects by a two-thirds vote. Since the scope of the annual program has proved to be quite wide, and any environmental matter except a failure to enforce the law can be considered to be related to the cooperative functions of the NAAEC, the effect of Article 13 is to empower the Secretariat to report on almost any aspect of the North American environment that it considers worth exploring. Articles 14 and 15 instruct the Secretariat to administer the citizen submissions procedure—specifically, to decide which submissions meet the threshold requirements of the agreement, which merit a response from the Party at which they are directed, and which warrant preparation of a factual record. The Council decides whether to authorize a factual record, but, once authorized, it is prepared by the Secretariat.

Whether seen as a trade and environment organization or as a regional environmental organization, the CEC provides new avenues of participation to civil society. Three of these avenues are particularly important. First, the NAAEC creates, as one of the constitutive elements of the Commission, a Joint Public Advisory Committee composed of fifteen citizens, five from each Party, and authorizes it to advise the Council on any matter within the scope of the agreement and to provide relevant technical, scientific, or other information to the Secretariat. . . . Second, the NAAEC authorizes the Secretariat to draw upon information submitted by individuals or nongovernmental organizations in its development of a report under Article 13. Third, the Article 14-15 submissions procedure allows any person or nongovernmental organization in any of the three countries to file a complaint alleging that a Party is failing to effectively enforce its environmental law. The NAAEC thus offers two ways that private persons may trigger independent reports on virtually any environmental issue, including sensitive allegations of failure to enforce domestic laws.

The following excerpt discusses the CEC's citizen submissions process, an innovative procedure that allows citizens of any North American country to file complaints with the CEC Secretariat in which the citizens claim that one or more of the three countries is failing to enforce its environmental laws effectively.

G. GARVER, CEC MECHANISMS AND FRAMEWORKS FOR RESOLVING DISPUTES OVER TRANSBOUNDARY ENVIRONMENTAL IMPACTS
CBA-ABA Second Annual National Environmental, Energy and Resources Law Summit (April 28, 2006)

IV.   The Citizen Submission Process

The CEC's citizen submission process gives individual members of the public their most direct means for focusing the CEC's attention on a particular environmental concern—as long as the concern is related to environmental enforcement in one of the three NAFTA countries. Article 14 of the NAAEC provides that any person or nongovernmental organization residing in North America may file a submission with the CEC Secretariat asserting that Canada, Mexico, or the United States is failing to effectively enforce its environmental law. Filing of a submission can lead to the development of a factual record that presents detailed factual information regarding the assertions in the submission. . . .

A.   OVERVIEW OF THE PROCESS

Following receipt of a submission, the Secretariat determines whether the requirements for submissions in NAAEC Article 14(1) are met. The first phrase of Article 14(1) makes clear that a submission must 1) be from a non-governmental organization or person; 2) make assertions regarding enforcement, as opposed to standard-setting or other governmental action not encompassed within the notion of enforcement; and 3) involve enforcement of *environmental* law, as defined in

NAAEC Article 45(2)(a).[20] In addition, to proceed with a submission, the Secretariat must find that it:

(a) Is in writing in a language designated by that Party in a notification to the Secretariat;
(b) Clearly identifies the person or organization making the submission;
(c) Provides sufficient information to allow the Secretariat to review the submission, including any documentary evidence on which the submission may be based;
(d) Appears to be aimed at promoting enforcement rather than at harassing industry;
(e) Indicates that the matter has been communicated in writing to the relevant authorities of the Party and indicates the Party's response, if any; and
(f) Is filed by a person or organization residing or established in the territory of a Party.[21]

Where these requirements are met, the Secretariat may request under Article 14(2) a response from the government Party concerned, taking into account whether:

(a) The submission alleges harm to the person or organization making the submission;
(b) The submission, alone or in combination with other submissions, raises matters whose further study in this process would advance the goals of this Agreement;
(c) Private remedies available under the Party's law have been pursued; and
(d) The submission is drawn exclusively from mass media reports.[22]

Based on the submission and the response, the Secretariat can recommend to the Council under Article 15(1) that a so-called "factual record" be prepared.[23]

If a majority of the Council authorizes preparation of a factual record, the Secretariat, in accordance with NAAEC Articles 15(4) and 21(1)(a), undertakes an in-depth investigation, gathering information from the governments and other sources or developing information itself, often with the assistance of technical or legal experts.

20. According to Article 45(2)(a), "environmental law" means:

[A]ny statute or regulation of a Party, or provision thereof, the primary purpose of which is the protection of the environment, or the prevention of a danger to human life or health, through (i) the prevention, abatement or control of the release, discharge, or emission of pollutants or environmental contaminants, (ii) the control of environmentally hazardous or toxic chemicals, substances, materials and wastes, and the dissemination of information related thereto, or (iii) the protection of wild flora or fauna, including endangered species, their habitat, and specially protected natural areas in the Party's territory, but does not include any statute or regulation, or provision thereof, directly related to worker safety or health.

However, in article 45(2)(b) the agreement excludes from the definition of "environmental law" any law for which "the primary purpose . . . is managing the commercial harvest or exploitation, or subsistence or aboriginal harvesting, of natural resources."

21. NAAEC Article 14(1)(a)-(f).

22. NAAEC Article 14(2)(a)-(d).

23. Under Article 14(3)(a), the Secretariat is barred from proceeding with a submission if the Party notifies it that the subject matter of the submission is the subject of a pending judicial or administrative proceeding, as defined in Article 45(3).

Under Article 15(5), the Secretariat submits draft factual records to the Parties, who then have 45 days to submit comments on the accuracy of the draft. The Secretariat then finalizes the factual record and, if a majority of the Council agrees, publishes it in accordance with Article 15(7) of the NAAEC. Factual records do not reach a conclusion as to whether or not the Party is failing to effectively enforce its environmental law. Instead, they provide information regarding asserted failures to effectively enforce environmental law that may assist submitters, the NAAEC parties, and other interested members of the public in reaching their own conclusions and taking any action they deem appropriate in regard to the matters addressed.[24]

As of March 30, 2006, the Secretariat has received 54 submissions since the CEC's creation, 17 concerning Canada, 27 concerning Mexico, 9 concerning the United States, and one concerning both Canada and the United States. Twelve submissions were pending at the CEC at that time. The CEC has published eleven factual records. . . .

The steady stream of submissions that the CEC has received to date indicates that the community of potential submitters is aware of the submissions process and has begun to test its effectiveness in solving problems of concern to members of the North American public. As one commentator suggests, the value of the citizen submission process may go beyond other available tools in that, among other things, it operates on an international stage and therefore "may attract an audience that other mechanisms will not reach and have a different impact as a result."[26]

At the same time, a potential submitter must take into account the likelihood that a submission will not proceed through the process if the submitters have not pursued private remedies available under the laws of the government whose environmental enforcement is questioned. Article 14(2) guides the Secretariat to consider whether private remedies have been pursued in deciding whether to request a response from the party. Although there is no explicit requirement that private remedies be pursued, let alone exhausted, the NAAEC strongly suggests that a submitter seek domestic relief before filing a submission with the CEC.

Another feature of the process that could affect its suitability to a particular situation is that a factual record cannot impose sanctions or force a party to do anything in regard to the matters addressed. Indeed, as noted above, a factual record does not even reach a conclusion whether the party is failing to effectively enforce its environmental law. As a result, reflecting frustration of some members of the public that factual records are not as effective as they might be, the JPAC and others have advised the Council to commit to some kind of follow-up to a factual record, for example by requiring the party whose enforcement is addressed in a factual record to report periodically to the Council on follow-up actions. To date, the Council

---

24. While the lack of authority to issue sanctions, injunctive relief or even a conclusion on whether there has been a failure to enforce makes the submissions process a relatively soft mechanism, it must be recalled that the citizen submission process touches upon two particularly sensitive areas for national governments: sovereignty and enforcement discretion. Although the governments consistently have expressed their support for the process, Articles 14 and 15 confront them with an inherent tension between their roles as both creators and overseers of the process and as potential targets of it. That the process allows an international organization to present information regarding a country's enforcement of its own laws likely exacerbates this inherent tension. . . . [T]he citizen submission process is at the frontier of North American accountability mechanisms that give an international organization a degree of independence in reviewing the actions of one of the three NAFTA countries.

26. Markell, The Citizen Spotlight Process, 18 Envtl. F. (March/April 2001), at 32.

has deemed follow-up to factual records to be a matter exclusively of domestic concern.

. . . [T]he impact of a submission seems to begin upon its filing. A committee appointed by the Council to review the first ten years of the CEC (the TRAC) noted that as a result of submissions and factual records:

- The proposed Cozumel development was downsized and additional measures introduced to protect a threatened reef. In addition, this case influenced the reform of Mexico's environmental assessment legislation.
- The filing of the submission in the BC Hydro case spurred the resolution of issues that had long been stalled. For its part, the factual record generated ideas for improving the application of the provincial Water Use Planning Process and the federal No Net Loss policy.
- The Secretariat's investigation conducted as a result of the BC Logging submission uncovered deficiencies in the procedures of Fisheries and Oceans Canada that the Department subsequently addressed.
- Fisheries and Oceans Canada increased its presence in the prairie provinces.
- In a letter to BC government authorities, Environment Canada cited the BC Mining submission when it rejected a proposal to adopt a less costly, but less effective, effluent treatment method at the Britannia Mine.
- The submission related to the operation of a shrimp farm in Mexico (Aquanova) encouraged negotiations among the submitters, local and environmental authorities and the developer that led to actions to reduce the impact of the farms' waste water discharge and a mangrove replanting program.[28]

Problem 11-1

CEC Simulation Exercise [Review Articles 14 and 15 of the NAAEC, available at www.cec.org, and then complete this simulation exercise.]

Earthjustice (EJ), an environmental group that litigates Clean Water Act (CWA) and Endangered Species Act (ESA) issues, among others, is concerned about the City of Tallahassee's wastewater treatment operations. In particular, EJ is concerned that the City is operating in a way that results in frequent violations of the CWA and of the ESA—in EJ's view, the discharges from the operations are entering nearby waters in concentrations and amounts that violate the City's CWA permit and that are causing the deaths of various species protected by the federal ESA that depend on the waters.

EJ has asked the federal and state government authorities to take appropriate enforcement action against the City to require it to comply with its environmental responsibilities under the CWA and ESA. The federal government advised EJ that officials from the federal government (from the U.S. Environmental Protection Agency, which is responsible for the CWA, and from the Department of the Interior, which shares responsibility for the ESA) met with City officials to discuss the City's discharges, and the City promised to investigate the alleged violations and to address any violations that it uncovered as soon as possible, subject to its resource constraints. Neither the federal government nor the state government has initiated a

---

28. CEC Ten-Year Review and Assessment Committee, Ten Years of North American Environmental Cooperation (June 15, 2004) [hereinafter TRAC Report], at 46, available at http://www.cec.org/files/PDF/PUBLICATIONS/TRAC-Report2004_en.pdf.

formal enforcement proceeding against the City with respect to the City's alleged violations.

For the EJ attorney, assume EJ has learned about the CEC citizen submissions process and has decided to pursue a submission. Please evaluate this option. In doing so, please consider the criteria and factors that govern whether the CEC's Secretariat would find that the submission warrants further review. Also consider any other factors that you think are relevant to the decision whether to file a submission, such as the recoverability of attorneys' fees, and the possibility of obtaining sanctions or injunctive relief. If there is any additional information that it would be helpful for you to have in determining EJ's position, identify that information as well.

For the Secretariat's attorney, assume the Secretariat has received a submission from EJ. Please evaluate how the Secretariat should respond to EJ's submission. Also assess the appropriateness of developing a factual record. If there is any additional information that it would be helpful for you to have in making this decision, identify that information as well.

For the attorney with the U.S. Department of Justice (DOJ) section that handles complaints filed with the CEC, assume the CEC Secretariat has notified your office that the CEC has received the EJ submission and, further, the CEC Secretariat has issued a Determination under Articles 14(1) and (2) of the NAAEC that the submission warrants a response from the United States. Please evaluate how the United States should respond to the Secretariat's request for a response. If there is any additional information that it would be helpful for you to have in determining the United States' position, identify that as well.

E.   TRADE AND THE ENVIRONMENT

While advocates for reducing trade barriers in order to encourage increased levels of trade claim that such steps lead to greater prosperity, some environmental groups have challenged actions to reduce these barriers because of concerns that the environment will suffer as a result. Riots in Seattle during the 1999 World Trade Organization (WTO) meetings, and similar riots in Cancún in 2003, are symptomatic of the anxiety that efforts to relax trade restrictions engender in some circles. Shaffer, The World Trade Organization under Challenge: Democracy and the Law and Politics of the WTO's Treatment of Trade and Environment Matters, 25 Harv. Envtl. L. Rev. 1, 2, 4 (2001).

The existence and operation of the General Agreement on Tariffs and Trade (GATT), which the WTO administers, and NAFTA have each raised these types of concerns. Environmental groups have raised concerns that, among other things: (1) these trade institutions may operate to undermine or trump international environmental agreements in the event of conflicts, Schultz, The GATT/WTO Committee on Trade and the Environment—Toward Environmental Reform, 89 Am. J. Int'l L. 423, 434 (1995); (2) the trade institutions may similarly operate to supersede domestic environmental laws and thereby undermine domestic environmental governance, Goldman, The Legal Effect of Trade Agreements on Domestic Health and

Environmental Regulation, 7 J. Envtl. L. & Litig. 11, 20 (1992); (3) increased levels of trade may increase the scale of industrial activity and thereby threaten to overwhelm domestic governance capacity that already is stretched to, or beyond, its limits, Ferretti, Innovations in Managing Globalization: Lessons from the American Experience, 15 Geo. Int'l Envtl. L. Rev. 367 (2003); and (4) reductions of trade barriers may lead to a "race-to-the-bottom" and creation of "pollution havens." DeFazio, The Environmental Cost of Free Trade, 7 J. Envtl. L. & Litig. 7, 9 (1992) (suggesting that, for example, NAFTA would result in the importation into the United States of Mexican environmental conditions). Further, from a procedural standpoint, the mechanisms these trade institutions create have been criticized for a variety of reasons, including their lack of accountability and transparency, and their limitations on citizen participation. McRae, Trade and the Environment: The Issue of Transparency, in Greening NAFTA 237 (D. Markell & J. Knox eds., 2003).

The WTO today serves as the primary organization concerned with international trade on a global basis. There are multiple agreements under the auspices of the WTO; probably the most important is the GATT. The GATT and NAFTA each includes provisions intended to limit restrictions on trade, as well as other provisions that allow states unilaterally to interfere with trade in order to protect the environment, under certain circumstances.

One of the major sources of the possible conflict between "free trade" and "environmental protection" policies is intuitively quite easy to grasp. On the one hand, environmental policies frequently seek to regulate activities (such as the manufacture of products) in order to reduce their environmental imprint—their potential adverse effects on human health and the environment. Sometimes environmental regulation establishes performance standards for products, such as the amount of air pollution an automobile may emit. In other cases, environmental regulation imposes restrictions on the processes that can be used to make products, such as limits on how much water pollution a manufacturer may discharge. Indeed, as Professor Sandy Gaines has pointed out, this is frequently what environmental laws are all about; they regulate how products are made. Gaines, Processes and Production Methods: How to Produce Sound Policy for Environmental PPM-Based Trade Measures, 27 Colum. J. Envtl. L. 383 (2002). In either case, environmental regulation may have a significant impact on international trade.

On the other hand, a key purpose of the GATT and other trade regimes is to establish rules that limit a country's ability to impose barriers to trade. One such barrier is to accord more favorable treatment to products from one trading partner than from another. A second is to favor one's own products over the products of other countries. The GATT seeks to eliminate each of these possible barriers in Articles I and III. As Wold et al. put it:

> [T]he most favored nation (MFN) obligation of Article I strives to ensure that an importing country . . . regulates imported products from all countries the same; the national treatment obligation of Article III strives to ensure that national . . . regulatory systems are applied so as not to discriminate between domestic and imported goods of the same type. [Wold et al., Trade and the Environment: Law and Policy 166 (2005).]

The following are excerpts of Articles I and III:

Article I: General Most-Favoured-Nation Treatment

1. With respect to . . . all rules and formalities in connection with importation and exportation, and with respect to all matters referred to in paragraph [ ] . . . 4 of Article III, . . . any advantage, favour, privilege or immunity granted by any contracting party to any product originating in or destined for any other country shall be accorded immediately and unconditionally to the *like product* originating in or destined for the territories of all other contracting parties [emphasis added].

Article III: National Treatment on Internal Taxation and Regulation . . .

4. The products of the territory of any contracting party imported into the territory of any other contracting party shall be accorded treatment no less favourable than that accorded to *like products* of national origin in respect of all laws, regulations and requirements affecting their internal sale, offering for sale, purchase, transportation, distribution or use [emphasis added].

Article XX, the focus of the Appellate Body opinions excerpted below, qualifies the prohibition on environmentally protective practices that otherwise might run afoul of the GATT. The Shrimp-Turtle decisions excerpted in the text focus on two parts of Article XX: its chapeau and XX(g). Article XX(b) also may provide a basis for finding that domestic environmental protection requirements are consistent with the GATT. The relevant text of Article XX reads as follows:

Article XX: General Exceptions

Subject to the requirement that such measures are not applied in a manner which would constitute a means of arbitrary or unjustifiable discrimination between countries where the same conditions prevail, or a disguised restriction on international trade, nothing in this Agreement shall be construed to prevent the adoption or enforcement by any contracting party of measures: . . .

    (b) necessary to protect human, animal or plant life or health;

    . . .

    (g) relating to the conservation of exhaustible natural resources if such measures are made effective in conjunction with restrictions on domestic production or consumption. . . .

So, to bring this brief overview to a close, at a conceptual level the possibilities for conflict between free trade proponents and environment regulatory advocates are substantial. A classic trade position is that, in a case in which tuna, for example, are caught in different ways, the tuna nevertheless are "like products" within the meaning of Articles I and III because they are physically indistinguishable as products. Furthermore, "trade law is hostile to the notion that one WTO member should be allowed to restrict trade in certain goods on the basis of the PPMs [processes and production methods] by which that good was produced in another country." Wold et al., *supra*, at 167. On the other hand, environmentalists may support treating such products differently, because differences in the way the tuna are caught or harvested may have significant environmental effects. At a practical level in terms of WTO jurisprudence, a key question is, how should Article XX be read in tandem with Articles I and III?*

These provisions have been subject to varying interpretations over the years. The 1991 *Tuna/Dolphin* dispute created significant fears in the environmental community that the GATT threatened domestic governments' ability to protect the environment. One casebook suggests that the *Tuna/Dolphin I and II* decisions "launched the trade and environment debate" because of the narrow reading they gave to the permissible scope of product regulation under Article III of the GATT. Wold et al., *supra*, at 203. These decisions raise the following key question: under what circumstances may a government "regulate physically identical or similar products differently because of the environmental conditions under which they were manufactured or harvested?" Id. at 165. In the *Tuna/Dolphin* dispute, the question was whether the GATT's nondiscrimination provisions allowed the United States to regulate tuna caught using "dolphin-friendly" techniques differently from imported tuna caught through harvesting practices that were less "dolphin-friendly."

The dispute involved a U.S. decision to embargo the importation of tuna from Mexico because Mexican tuna boats were not following the dolphin-safe fishing practices the United States had established in the Marine Mammal Protection Act (MMPA). In particular, §101(a)(2) of the MMPA prohibited imports of tuna caught with fishing technology that resulted in incidental kills of ocean mammals (including dolphins) in excess of U.S. standards. Specifically, with respect to the Eastern Tropical Pacific (ETP), an area in which dolphins and tuna sometimes are found in close proximity to each other, the MMPA barred importation of yellowfin tuna harvested with purse-seine nets, which encircle hundreds of thousands of dolphins each year and cause them to drown (dolphins are mammals and breathe air), unless the Secretary of Commerce certified that (1) the government of the harvesting country has a program regulating the taking of marine mammals that is comparable to that of the United States, and (2) the average rate of incidental taking of marine mammals by vessels of the harvesting nation is comparable to, and does not exceed, 1.25 times the average rate of such taking by U.S. vessels during the same period. U.S. environmentalists, concerned that the United States government was ignoring this MMPA direction concerning imports, brought suit to require the United States to enforce the MMPA. A court ordered the government to enforce the statute, and in 1990, the United States imposed an embargo on imports of tuna from Mexico and several other countries. The embargo was to remain in place until the secretary of commerce made the findings summarized above. Mexico challenged the embargo. The GATT Panels concluded that the U.S. embargo was an invalid interference with trade under Article III(4) because the law prevented Mexico from exporting tuna that were "like" U.S.-caught tuna. Products, according to the Panels, are "like" if their characteristics are the same, even if they are produced in different ways.

In more recent decisions, the WTO Appellate Body appears to have been somewhat more receptive to environmental concerns. Professor John Knox has

---

*This chapter does not cover Article XI of the GATT, another provision that is intended to prohibit restrictions on imports in some situations.

suggested that the WTO Appellate Body has "adopted almost every element" of the "moderate environmental proposals" that NGOs have made for reconciling environmental concerns and international trade law. Knox, The Judicial Resolution of Conflicts between Trade and the Environment, 28 Harv. Envtl. L. Rev. 1, 29 (2004).

The following excerpts from the WTO Appellate Body's 1998 and 2001 decisions in the Shrimp-Turtle dispute focus on two of the significant environmental issues in the GATT, the meaning of the Article XX chapeau (opening paragraph) and Article XX(g).

UNITED STATES—IMPORT PROHIBITION OF CERTAIN SHRIMP AND SHRIMP PRODUCTS
AB-1998-4

Report of the Appellate Body

[Malaysia, Thailand, India, and Pakistan filed a complaint with the WTO alleging that a U.S. law, Public L. No. 101-162, §609 (1989), and associated regulations and judicial rulings, operated to limit the United States' importation of certain shrimp and shrimp products in violation of the GATT. Section 609(b)(1) imposed an import ban on shrimp harvested with commercial fishing technology that could adversely affect sea turtles. Section 609(b)(2) provided that the import ban on shrimp would not apply to harvesting nations that are certified. Certifications would be granted to countries with a fishing environment that does not pose a threat of the incidental taking of sea turtles in the course of shrimp harvesting (e.g., because the relevant species of sea turtle are not present or because the harvesting nation harvests shrimp "exclusively by means that do not pose a threat to sea turtles.") In addition, certifications would be granted to harvesting nations that provide documentary evidence of the adoption of a regulatory program governing the incidental taking of sea turtles in the course of shrimp trawling that is comparable to the U.S. program and where the average rate of incidental taking of sea turtles by their vessels is comparable to that of U.S. vessels. The GATT Panel found that §609 is inconsistent with the GATT, among other rulings. The United States appealed part of the Panel opinion to the WTO Appellate Body.]

111. We turn to the second issue raised by the . . . United States, which is whether the Panel erred in finding that the measure at issue [§609 and the implementing Guidelines] constitutes unjustifiable discrimination between countries where the same conditions prevail and, thus, is not within the scope of measures permitted under Article XX of the GATT 1994.

118. In *United States—Gasoline*, we enunciated the appropriate method for applying Article XX of the GATT 1994:

> In order that the justifying protection of Article XX may be extended to it, the measure at issue must not only come under one or another of the particular exceptions—paragraphs (a) to (j)—listed under Article XX; it must also satisfy the requirements imposed by the opening clauses of Article XX. *The analysis is, in other words, two-tiered: first, provisional justification by reason of characterization of the measure under XX(g); second, further appraisal of the same measure under the introductory clauses of Article XX.* (emphasis in original). . . .

A. ARTICLE XX(G): PROVISIONAL JUSTIFICATION OF SECTION 609

125. In claiming justification for its measure, the United States primarily invokes Article XX(g). . . .

126. Paragraph (g) of Article XX covers measures:

relating to the conservation of exhaustible natural resources if such measures are made effective in conjunction with restrictions on domestic production or consumption;

1. "EXHAUSTIBLE NATURAL RESOURCES"

127. We begin with the threshold question of whether Section 609 is a measure concerned with the conservation of "exhaustible natural resources" within the meaning of Article XX(g). . . . In the proceedings before the Panel, . . . the parties to the dispute argued . . . that a "reasonable interpretation" of the term "exhaustible" is that the term refers to "finite resources such as minerals, rather than biological or renewable resources." In their view, such finite resources were exhaustible "because there was a limited supply which could and would be depleted unit for unit as the resources were consumed." . . . For its part, Malaysia added that sea turtles, being living creatures, could only be considered under Article XX(b), since Article XX(g) was meant for "nonliving exhaustible natural resources". It followed, according to Malaysia, that the United States cannot invoke both the Article XX(b) and the Article XX(g) exceptions simultaneously.

128. . . . . Textually, Article XX(g) is *not* limited to the conservation of "mineral" or "non-living" natural resources. The complainants' principal argument is rooted in the notion that "living" natural resources are "renewable" and therefore cannot be "exhaustible" natural resources. We do not believe that "exhaustible" natural resources and "renewable" natural resources are mutually exclusive. One lesson that modern biological sciences teach us is that living species, though in principle, capable of reproduction and, in that sense, "renewable", are in certain circumstances indeed susceptible of depletion, exhaustion and extinction, frequently because of human activities. Living resources are just as "finite" as petroleum, iron ore and other non-living resources.

130. From the perspective embodied in the preamble of the *WTO Agreement*, we note that the generic term "natural resources" in Article XX(g) is not "static" in its content or reference but is rather "by definition, evolutionary." It is, therefore, pertinent to note that modern international conventions and declarations make frequent references to natural resources as embracing both living and non-living resources.

131. Given the recent acknowledgement by the international community of the importance of concerted bilateral or multilateral action to protect living natural resources, and recalling the explicit recognition by WTO Members of the objective of sustainable development in the preamble of the *WTO Agreement*, we believe it is too late in the day to suppose that Article XX(g) of the GATT 1994 may be read as referring only to the conservation of exhaustible mineral or other non-living natural resources. Moreover, two adopted GATT 1947 panel reports previously found fish to be an "exhaustible natural resource" within the meaning of Article XX(g). We hold that, in line with the principle of effectiveness in treaty interpretation, measures to conserve exhaustible natural resources, whether *living* or *non-living*, may fall within Article XX(g).

132. We turn next to the issue of whether the living natural resources sought to be conserved by the measure are "exhaustible" under Article XX(g). That this element is present in respect of the five species of sea turtles here involved appears to be conceded by all the participants and third participants in this case. The exhaustibility of sea turtles would in fact have been very difficult to controvert since all of the seven recognized species of sea turtles are today listed in Appendix 1 of the Convention on International Trade in Endangered Species of Wild Fauna and Flora ("CITES"). The list in Appendix 1 includes "all species *threatened with extinction* which are or may be affected by trade" (emphasis added).

133. Finally, we observe that sea turtles are highly migratory animals, passing in and out of waters subject to the rights of jurisdiction of various coastal states and the high seas. In the Panel Report, the Panel said:

> ... Information brought to the attention of the Panel, including documented statements from the experts, tends to *confirm the fact that sea turtles, in certain circumstances of their lives, migrate through the waters of several countries and the high sea.* ... (emphasis added)

The sea turtle species here at stake, i.e., covered by Section 609, are all known to occur in waters over which the United States exercises jurisdiction. Of course, it is not claimed that *all* populations of these species migrate to, or traverse, at one time or another, waters subject to United States jurisdiction. Neither the appellant nor any of the appellees claims any rights of exclusive ownership over the sea turtles, at least not while they are swimming freely in their natural habitat—the oceans. We do not pass upon the question of whether there is an implied jurisdictional limitation in Article XX(g), and if so, the nature or extent of that limitation. We note only that in the specific circumstances of the case before us, there is a sufficient nexus between the migratory and endangered marine populations involved and the United States for purposes of Article XX(g).

134. For all the foregoing reasons, we find that the sea turtles here involved constitute "exhaustible natural resources" for purposes of Article XX(g) of the GATT 1994.

2. "Relating to the Conservation of [Exhaustible Natural Resources]"

135. Article XX(g) requires that the measure sought to be justified be one which "relat[es] to" the conservation of exhaustible natural resources. In making this determination, the treaty interpreter essentially looks into the relationship between the measure at stake and the legitimate policy of conserving exhaustible natural resources. It is well to bear in mind that the policy of protecting and conserving the endangered sea turtles here involved is shared by all participants and third participants in this appeal, indeed, by the vast majority of the nations of the world. None of the parties to this dispute question the genuineness of the commitment of the others to that policy.

137. In the present case, we must examine the relationship between the general structure and design of the measure here at stake, Section 609, and the policy goal it purports to serve, that is, the conservation of sea turtles.

138. Section 609(b)(1) imposes an import ban on shrimp that have been harvested with commercial fishing technology which may adversely affect sea turtles.

This provision is designed to influence countries to adopt national regulatory programs requiring the use of TEDs by their shrimp fishermen. In this connection, it is important to note that the general structure and design of Section 609 *cum* implementing guidelines is fairly narrowly focused. There are two basic exemptions from the import ban, both of which relate clearly and directly to the policy goal of conserving sea turtles. First, Section 609, as elaborated in the 1996 Guidelines, excludes from the import ban shrimp harvested "under conditions that do not adversely affect sea turtles". Thus, the measure, by its terms, excludes from the import ban: aquaculture shrimp; shrimp species (such as *pandalid* shrimp) harvested in water areas where sea turtles do not normally occur; and shrimp harvested exclusively by artisanal methods, even from non-certified countries. The harvesting of such shrimp clearly does not affect sea turtles. Second, under Section 609(b)(2), the measure exempts from the import ban shrimp caught in waters subject to the jurisdiction of certified countries.

139. There are two types of certification for countries under Section 609(b)(2). First, under Section 609(b)(2)(C), a country may be certified as having a fishing environment that does not pose a threat of incidental taking of sea turtles in the course of commercial shrimp trawl harvesting. There is no risk, or only a negligible risk, that sea turtles will be harmed by shrimp trawling in such an environment.

140. The second type of certification is provided by Section 609(b)(2)(A) and (B). Under these provisions, as further elaborated in the 1996 Guidelines, a country wishing to export shrimp to the United States is required to adopt a regulatory program that is comparable to that of the United States program and to have a rate of incidental take of sea turtles that is comparable to the average rate of United States' vessels. This is, essentially, a requirement that a country adopt a regulatory program requiring the use of TEDs by commercial shrimp trawling vessels in areas where there is a likelihood of intercepting sea turtles. This requirement is, in our view, directly connected with the policy of conservation of sea turtles. It is undisputed among the participants, and recognized by the experts consulted by the Panel, that the harvesting of shrimp by commercial shrimp trawling vessels with mechanical retrieval devices in waters where shrimp and sea turtles coincide is a significant cause of sea turtle mortality. Moreover, the Panel did "not question . . . the fact generally acknowledged by the experts that TEDs, when properly installed and adapted to the local area, would be an effective tool for the preservation of sea turtles."

141. In its general design and structure, therefore, Section 609 is not a simple, blanket prohibition of the importation of shrimp imposed without regard to the consequences (or lack thereof) of the mode of harvesting employed upon the incidental capture and mortality of sea turtles. Focusing on the design of the measure here at stake, it appears to us that Section 609, *cum* implementing guidelines, is not disproportionately wide in its scope and reach in relation to the policy objective of protection and conservation of sea turtle species. The means are, in principle, reasonably related to the ends. The means and ends relationship between Section 609 and the legitimate policy of conserving an exhaustible, and, in fact, endangered species, is observably a close and real one, a relationship that is every bit as substantial as that which we found in *United States—Gasoline* between the EPA baseline establishment rules and the conservation of clean air in the United States.

142. In our view, therefore, Section 609 is a measure "relating to" the conservation of an exhaustible natural resource within the meaning of Article XX(g) of the GATT 1994.

3.   "IF SUCH MEASURES ARE MADE EFFECTIVE IN CONJUNCTION WITH
     RESTRICTIONS ON DOMESTIC PRODUCTION OR CONSUMPTION"

143. In *United States—Gasoline*, we held that the above-captioned clause of
Article XX(g),

> . . . is appropriately read as a requirement that the measures concerned impose restrictions,
> not just in respect of imported gasoline but also with respect to domestic gasoline. The
> clause is a requirement of *even-handedness* in the imposition of restrictions, in the name of
> conservation, upon the production or consumption of exhaustible natural resources.

In this case, we need to examine whether the restrictions imposed by Section 609 with
respect to imported shrimp are also imposed in respect of shrimp caught by United
States shrimp trawl vessels.

144. We earlier noted that Section 609, enacted in 1989, addresses the mode of
harvesting of imported shrimp only. However, two years earlier, in 1987, the United
States issued regulations pursuant to the Endangered Species Act requiring all United
States shrimp trawl vessels to use approved TEDs, or to restrict the duration of tow-
times, in specified areas where there was significant incidental mortality of sea turtles
in shrimp trawls. These regulations became fully effective in 1990 and were later
modified. They now require United States shrimp trawlers to use approved TEDs
"in areas and at times when there is a likelihood of intercepting sea turtles", with
certain limited exceptions. Penalties for violation of the Endangered Species Act, or
the regulations issued thereunder, include civil and criminal sanctions. The United
States government currently relies on monetary sanctions and civil penalties for
enforcement. The government has the ability to seize shrimp catch from trawl vessels
fishing in United States waters and has done so in cases of egregious violations.
We believe that, in principle, Section 609 is an even-handed measure.

145. Accordingly, we hold that Section 609 is a measure made effective in
conjunction with the restrictions on domestic harvesting of shrimp, as required by
Article XX(g).

C.   THE INTRODUCTORY CLAUSES OF ARTICLE XX: CHARACTERIZING
     SECTION 609 UNDER THE CHAPEAU'S STANDARDS

147. Although provisionally justified under Article XX(g), Section 609, if it is
ultimately to be justified as an exception under Article XX, must also satisfy the
requirements of the introductory clauses—the "chapeau"—of Article XX. . . .

The 1998 decision held that the application of the Guidelines was inconsistent
with the chapeau of Article XX because, inter alia, §609 had been applied in a manner
that constituted "unjustifiable discrimination between countries where the same conditions prevail" as well as "arbitrary discrimination." See paragraphs 161-184.
Following this decision, the United States tried to negotiate with several countries
about their practices. In addition, in 1999 the United States made its approach more
flexible, issuing its Revised Guidelines for the Implementation of Section 609 . . . ,
Relating to the Protection of Sea Turtles in Shrimp Trawl Fishing Operations
(Revised Guidelines). 64 Fed. Reg. 36,946 (1999). In 2001 Malaysia complained
about the U.S. practices, and the Appellate Body had occasion to review whether
U.S. law and practices under this revised regime were consistent with Article XX's

chapeau. The following excerpt from the 2001 Appellate Body decision considers this issue.

UNITED STATES—IMPORT PROHIBITION OF CERTAIN SHRIMP AND SHRIMP PRODUCTS
AB-2001-4

Report of the Appellate Body

117. The chapeau of Article XX states:

> Subject to the requirement that such measures are not applied in a manner which would constitute a means of arbitrary or unjustifiable discrimination between countries where the same conditions prevail, or a disguised restriction on international trade, nothing in this Agreement shall be construed to prevent the adoption or enforcement by any contracting party of measures: . . .

118. The chapeau of Article XX establishes three standards regarding the *application* of measures for which justification under Article XX may be sought: first, there must be no "arbitrary" discrimination between countries where the same conditions prevail; second, there must be no "unjustifiable" discrimination between countries where the same conditions prevail; and, third, there must be no "disguised restriction on international trade." The Panel's findings appealed by Malaysia concern the first and second of these three standards.

119. It is clear from the language of the chapeau that these two standards operate to prevent a Member from applying a measure provisionally justified under a sub-paragraph of Article XX in a manner that would result in "arbitrary or unjustifiable discrimination". In *United States—Shrimp*, we stated that the measure at issue there resulted in "unjustifiable discrimination," in part because, as applied, the United States treated WTO Members differently. The United States had adopted a cooperative approach with WTO Members from the Caribbean/Western Atlantic region, with whom it had concluded a multilateral agreement on the protection and conservation of sea turtles, namely the Inter-American Convention. Yet the United States had not, we found, pursued the negotiation of such a multilateral agreement with other exporting Members, including Malaysia and the other complaining WTO Members in that case. . . .

121. . . . We also stated:

> Clearly, the United States negotiated seriously with some, but not with other Members (including the appellees), that export shrimp to the United States. The effect is plainly discriminatory and, in our view, unjustifiable.

123. Under the chapeau of Article XX, an importing Member may not treat its trading partners in a manner that would constitute "arbitrary or unjustifiable discrimination." With respect to this measure, the United States could conceivably respect this obligation, and the conclusion of an international agreement might nevertheless not be possible despite the serious, good faith efforts of the United States. Requiring that a multilateral agreement be *concluded* by the United States in order to avoid

"arbitrary or unjustifiable discrimination" in applying its measure would mean that any country party to the negotiations with the United States, whether a WTO Member or not, would have, in effect, a veto over whether the United States could fulfill its WTO obligations. Such a requirement would not be reasonable. For a variety of reasons, it may be possible to conclude an agreement with one group of countries but not another. The conclusion of a multilateral agreement requires the cooperation and commitment of many countries. In our view, the United States cannot be held to have engaged in "arbitrary or unjustifiable discrimination" under Article XX solely because one international negotiation resulted in an agreement while another did not.

128. . . . [I]n the previous case, in examining the original measure, we relied on the Inter-American Convention [an Agreement the U.S. reached with various countries concerning importation of shrimp] in two ways. First, we used the Inter-American Convention to show that "consensual and multilateral procedures are available and feasible for the establishment of programmes for the conservation of sea turtles." In other words, we saw the Inter-American Convention as evidence that an alternative course of action based on cooperation and consensus was reasonably open to the United States. Second, we used the Inter-American Convention to show the existence of "unjustifiable discrimination." The Inter-American Convention was the result of serious, good faith efforts to negotiate a regional agreement on the protection and conservation of turtles, including efforts made by the United States. In the original proceedings, we saw a clear contrast between the efforts made by the United States to conclude the Inter-American Convention and the absence of serious efforts on the part of the United States to negotiate other similar agreements with other WTO Members. We concluded there that such a disparity in efforts to negotiate an international agreement amounted to "unjustifiable discrimination".

133. We note that the Panel stated that "any effort alleged to be a 'serious good faith effort' must be assessed against the efforts made in relation to the conclusion of the Inter-American Convention." In our view, in assessing the serious, good faith efforts made by the United States, the Panel did not err in using the Inter-American Convention as an *example*. In our view, also, the Panel was correct in proceeding then to an analysis broadly in line with this principle and, ultimately, was correct as well in concluding that the efforts made by the United States in the Indian Ocean and South-East Asia region constitute serious, good faith efforts comparable to those that led to the conclusion of the Inter-American Convention. We find no fault with this analysis.

134. In sum, Malaysia is incorrect in its contention that avoiding "arbitrary and unjustifiable discrimination" under the chapeau of Article XX requires the *conclusion* of an international agreement on the protection and conservation of sea turtles. Therefore, we uphold the Panel's finding that, in view of the serious, good faith efforts made by the United States to negotiate an international agreement, "Section 609 is now applied in a manner that no longer constitutes a means of unjustifiable or arbitrary discrimination, as identified by the Appellate Body in its Report."

B. THE FLEXIBILITY OF THE REVISED GUIDELINES

135. We now turn to Malaysia's arguments relating to the flexibility of the Revised Guidelines. . . .

136. Malaysia disagrees with the Panel that a measure can meet the requirements of the chapeau of Article XX if it is flexible enough, both in design and application, to permit certification of an exporting country with a sea turtle protection and

conservation programme "comparable" to that of the United States. According to Malaysia, even if the measure at issue allows certification of countries having regulatory programs "comparable" to that of the United States, and even if the measure is applied in such a manner, it results in "arbitrary or unjustifiable discrimination" because it conditions access to the United States market on compliance with policies and standards "unilaterally" prescribed by the United States. Thus, Malaysia puts considerable emphasis on the "unilateral" nature of the measure, and Malaysia maintains that our previous Report does not support the conclusion of the Panel on this point.

137. We recall that, in *United States—Shrimp*, we stated:

> It appears to us . . . that *conditioning access to a Member's domestic market on whether exporting Members comply with, or adopt, a policy or policies unilaterally prescribed by the importing Member may, to some degree, be a common aspect of measures falling within the scope of one or another of the exceptions (a) to (j) of Article XX*. Paragraphs (a) to (j) comprise measures that are recognized as *exceptions to substantive obligations* established in the GATT 1994, because the domestic policies embodied in such measures have been recognized as important and legitimate in character. It is not necessary to assume that requiring from exporting countries compliance with, or adoption of, certain policies (although covered in principle by one or another of the exceptions) prescribed by the importing country, renders a measure *a priori* incapable of justification under Article XX. Such an interpretation renders most, if not all, of the specific exceptions of Article XX inutile, a result abhorrent to the principles of interpretation we are bound to apply (emphasis in Appellate Body decision).

138. . . . [I]it appears to us "that conditioning access to a Member's domestic market on whether exporting Members comply with, or adopt, a policy or policies unilaterally prescribed by the importing Member may, to some degree, be a common aspect of measures falling within the scope of one or another of the exceptions (a) to (j) of Article XX." This statement expresses a principle that was central to our ruling in *United States—Shrimp*.

139. A separate question arises, however, when examining, under the chapeau of Article XX, a measure that provides for access to the market of one WTO Member for a product of other WTO Members *conditionally*. Both Malaysia and the United States agree that this is a common aspect of the measure at issue in the original proceedings and the new measure at issue in this dispute.

140. In *United States—Shrimp*, we concluded that the measure at issue there did not meet the requirements of the chapeau of Article XX relating to "arbitrary or unjustifiable discrimination" because, through the application of the measure, the exporting members were faced with "a single, rigid and unbending requirement" to adopt *essentially the same* policies and enforcement practices as those applied to, and enforced on, domestic shrimp trawlers in the United States. In contrast, in this dispute, the Panel found that this new measure is more flexible than the original measure and has been applied more flexibly than was the original measure. In the light of the evidence brought by the United States, the Panel satisfied itself that this new measure, in design and application, does *not* condition access to the United States market on the adoption by an exporting Member of a regulatory programme aimed at the protection and the conservation of sea turtles that is *essentially the same* as that of the United States.

143. Given that the original measure in that dispute required "essentially the same" practices and procedures as those required in the United States, we found it

necessary in that appeal to rule only that Article XX did not allow such inflexibility. Given the Panel's findings with respect to the flexibility of the new measure in this dispute, we find it necessary in this appeal to add to what we ruled in our original Report. The question raised by Malaysia in this appeal is whether the Panel erred in inferring from our previous Report, and thereby finding, that the chapeau of Article XX permits a measure which requires only "comparable effectiveness."

144. In our view, there is an important difference between conditioning market access on the adoption of essentially the same programme, and conditioning market access on the adoption of a programme *comparable in effectiveness*. Authorizing an importing Member to condition market access on exporting Members putting in place regulatory programmes *comparable in effectiveness* to that of the importing Member gives sufficient latitude to the exporting Member with respect to the programme it may adopt to achieve the level of effectiveness required. It allows the exporting Member to adopt a regulatory programme that is suitable to the specific conditions prevailing in its territory. As we see it, the Panel correctly reasoned and concluded that conditioning market access on the adoption of a programme *comparable in effectiveness*, allows for sufficient flexibility in the application of the measure so as to avoid "arbitrary or unjustifiable discrimination." We, therefore, agree with the conclusion of the Panel on "comparable effectiveness."

145. Malaysia also argues that the measure at issue is not flexible enough to meet the requirement of the chapeau of Article XX relating to "unjustifiable or arbitrary discrimination" because the Revised Guidelines do not provide explicitly for the specific conditions prevailing in Malaysia.

146. We note that the Revised Guidelines contain provisions that permit the United States authorities to take into account the specific conditions of Malaysian shrimp production, and of the Malaysian sea turtle conservation programme, should Malaysia decide to apply for certification. The Revised Guidelines explicitly state that "[if] the government of a harvesting nation demonstrates that it has implemented and is enforcing a comparably effective regulatory program to protect sea turtles in the course of shrimp trawl fishing without the use of TEDs, that nation will also be eligible for certification." Likewise, the Revised Guidelines provide that the "Department of State will take fully into account any demonstrated differences between the shrimp fishing conditions in the United States and those in other nations as well as information available from other sources."

147. Further, the Revised Guidelines provide that the import prohibitions that can be imposed under Section 609 do not apply to shrimp or products of shrimp "harvested in any other manner or under any other circumstances that the Department of State may determine, following consultations with the [United States National Marine Fisheries Services], does not pose a threat of the incidental taking of sea turtles." Under Section II.B(c)(iii) of the Revised Guidelines (*Additional Sea Turtle Protection Measures*), the "Department of State recognizes that sea turtles require protection throughout their life-cycle, not only when they are threatened during the course of commercial shrimp trawl harvesting." Additionally, Section II.B(c)(iii) states that "[i]n making certification determinations, the Department shall also take fully into account other measures the harvesting nation undertakes to protect sea turtles, including national programmes to protect nesting beaches and other habitat, prohibitions on the direct take of sea turtles, national enforcement and compliance programmes, and participation in any international agreement for the protection and conservation of sea turtles." With respect to the certification

process, the Revised Guidelines specify that a country that does not appear to qualify for certification will receive a notification that "will explain the reasons for this preliminary assessment, suggest steps that the government of the harvesting nation can take in order to receive a certification, and invite the government of the harvesting nation to provide . . . any further information." Moreover, the Department of State commits itself to "actively consider any additional information that the government of the harvesting nation believes should be considered by the Department in making its determination concerning certification."

148. These provisions of the Revised Guidelines, on their face, permit a degree of flexibility that, in our view, will enable the United States to consider the particular conditions prevailing in Malaysia if, and when, Malaysia applies for certification. As Malaysia has not applied for certification, any consideration of whether Malaysia would be certified would be speculation.

149. We need only say here that, in our view, a measure should be designed in such a manner that there is sufficient flexibility to take into account the specific conditions prevailing in *any* exporting Member, including, of course, Malaysia. Yet this is not the same as saying that there must be specific provisions in the measure aimed at addressing specifically the particular conditions prevailing in *every individual* exporting Member. Article XX of the GATT 1994 does not require a Member to anticipate and provide explicitly for the specific conditions prevailing and evolving in *every individual* Member.

150. We are, therefore, not persuaded by Malaysia's argument that the measure at issue is not flexible enough because the Revised Guidelines do not explicitly address the specific conditions prevailing in Malaysia.

153. For the reasons set out in this Report, the Appellate Body: . . .

(b) *upholds* the finding of the Panel . . . that "Section 609 of Public Law 101-162, as implemented by the Revised Guidelines of 8 July 1999 and as applied so far by the [United States] authorities, is justified under Article XX of the GATT 1994 as long as the conditions stated in the findings of this Report, in particular the ongoing serious good faith efforts to reach a multilateral agreement, remain satisfied."

NOTES AND QUESTIONS

1. What types of changes did the United States make in its regulatory regime between the issuance of the 1998 Appellate Body ruling and the issuance of the 2001 ruling? Why were these changes important to the outcome of each ruling?

2. What were the major arguments Malaysia and others raised to challenge the legality of the United States' domestic efforts to protect turtles? Why was the Appellate Body not persuaded by these claims?

3. Are the tuna/dolphin and shrimp/turtle disputes distinguishable on the facts? Or did the Appellate Body change the law? If the latter, why might a trade institution have become more favorably disposed to environmental concerns?

TABLE OF ACRONYMS

ACM	Asbestos-containing materials
ACRS	Advisory Committee on Reactor Safeguards
AEC	Atomic Energy Commission
AFO	Animal feeding operation
ALJ	Administrative law judge
AMC	American Mining Congress
ANILCA	Alaska National Interest Lands Conservation Act
APA	Administrative Procedure Act
API	American Petroleum Institute
AQCR	Air quality control region
AQRV	Air quality–related value
ARARs	Applicable or relevant and appropriate requirements
BACT	Best available control technology
BART	Best available retrofit technology
BAT	Best available technology
BATEA	Best available technology economically achievable
BCT	Best conventional technology
BLM	Bureau of Land Management
BNA	Bureau of National Affairs
BO	Biological opinion
BOD	Biological oxygen demand
BoR	Bureau of Reclamation
BPCTCA	Best practicable control technology currently available
BPJ	Best professional judgment
BPT	Best practicable technology
CAA	Clean Air Act
CAFO	Combined animal feeding operation
CASAC	Clean Air Scientific Advisory Committee
CATX	Categorical exclusion
CEC	Commission for Environmental Cooperation
CEM	Continuous emission monitoring
CEQ	Council on Environmental Quality
CEQA	California Environmental Quality Act
CERCLA	Comprehensive Environmental Response, Compensation, and Liability Act
CFCs	Chlorofluorocarbons
CFR	Code of Federal Regulations

CITES	Convention on International Trade in Endangered Species
CMA	Chemical Manufacturers Association
CO	Carbon monoxide
CRA	Comparative risk assessment
CRP	Conservation Reserve Program
CRS	Congressional Research Service
CSO	Combined sewer overflow
CV	Contingent valuation
CWA	Clean Water Act
CZMA	Coastal Zone Management Act
DEIS	Draft environmental impact statement
DMA	Diversity maintenance area
DMR	Discharge monitoring report
DO	Dissolved oxygen
DOI	Department of the Interior
DOT	Department of Transportation
DQA	Data Quality Act
DSP	Dominant social paradigm
EA	Environmental assessment
EAJA	Equal Access to Justice Act
ECOS	Environmental Council of the States
ECRA	Environmental Cleanup Responsibility Act
EDF	Environmental Defense Fund
EIP	Economic incentive program
EIS	Environmental impact statement
ELI	Environmental Law Institute
EMS	Environmental management system
ENGO	Environmental nongovernmental organizations
EPA	Environmental Protection Agency
EPCRA	Emergency Planning and Community Right-to-Know Act
ERC	Emission reduction credit
ESA	Endangered Species Act or environmental site assessment
ESD	Environmentally sustainable development
ETS	Environmental tobacco smoke
FAA	Federal Aviation Administration
FACA	Federal Advisory Committee Act
FCCC	Framework Convention on Climate Change
FDA	Food and Drug Administration
FEIS	Final environmental impact statement
FEMAT	Forest Ecosystem Management Team
FFC	Ferric ferrocyanide
FFDCA	Federal Food, Drug, and Cosmetic Act
FHWA	Federal Highway Administration
FIFRA	Federal Insecticide, Fungicide, and Rodenticide Act
FIP	Federal implementation plan

FLPMA	Federal Land Policy and Management Act
FOE	Friends of the Earth
FOIA	Freedom of Information Act
FONSI	Finding of no significant impact
FWPCA	Federal Water Pollution Control Act
FWS	Fish and Wildlife Service
GAO	Government Accountability Office
GATT	General Agreement on Tariffs and Trade
GHG	Greenhouse gases
GIS	Geographic information systems
GPA	Global Programme of Action
GSA	General Services Administration
HC	Hydrocarbons
HCFCs	Hydrochlorofluorocarbons
HCP	Habitat conservation plan
HEW	Department of Health, Education, and Welfare
HHS	Department of Health and Human Services
HMTUSA	Hazardous Materials Transportation Uniform Safety Act
HRS	Hazard Ranking System
HSWA	Hazardous and Solid Waste Amendments
HUD	Department of Housing and Urban Development
I&M	Inspection and maintenance
IPCC	Intergovernmental Panel on Climate Change
ISRA	Industrial Site Recovery Act
ITC	Interagency Testing Committee
LAER	Lowest achievable emission rate
LDR	Land disposal restriction
LEV	Low-emission vehicle
LULU	Locally undesirable land use
MCL	Maximum contaminant level
MCLG	Maximum contaminant level goal
MEA	Multilateral environmental agreement
MGP	Manufactured gas plant
MIS	Management indicator species
MTBE	Methyl tertiary butyl ether
MTD	Maximum tolerated dose
MUSYA	Multiple-Use Sustained Yield Act
MWC	Municipal waste combustor or municipal waste combustion
NAAEC	North American Agreement on Environmental Cooperation
NAAQS	National ambient air quality standard
NAFTA	North American Free Trade Agreement
NAPAP	National Acid Precipitation Assessment Program

NAS	National Academy of Sciences
NCCP	Natural Community Conservation Plan
NCI	National Cancer Institute
NCP	National Contingency Plan
NEP	New environmental paradigm
NEPA	National Environmental Policy Act
NESHAP	National emission standard for hazardous air pollutant
NFMA	National Forest Management Act
NGO	Nongovernmental organization
NIH	National Institutes of Health
NIMBY	Not in my backyard
NIOSH	National Institute for Occupational Safety and Health
NJDEP	New Jersey Department of Environmental Protection
NMFS	National Marine Fisheries Service
NOAA	National Oceanic and Atmospheric Administration
NO_x	Nitrogen oxides
NPDES	National Pollutant Discharge Elimination System
NPDWR	National primary drinking water regulation
NPL	National Priorities List
NPS	Nonpoint source pollution
NRC	National Research Council or Nuclear Regulatory Commission
NRDC	Natural Resources Defense Council
NSPS	New source performance standards
NWF	National Wildlife Federation
O_3	Ozone
O & G	Oil and grease
OECA	Office of Enforcement and Compliance Assurance
OIRA	Office of Information and Regulatory Affairs
OMB	Office of Management and Budget
OSH	Occupational Safety and Health
OSHA	Occupational Safety and Health Administration
OSWR	Office of Solid Waste and Emergency Response
OTA	Office of Technology Assessment
OTAG	Ozone Transport Assessment Group
PAH	Polycyclic aromatic hydrocarbon
PCBs	Polychlorinated biphenyls
PCE	Perchloroethylene
PEL	Permissible exposure limit
PM	Particulate matter
PMN	Premanufacture notification
POPs	Persistent organic pollutants
POTW	Publicly owned treatment works
PPA	Pollution Prevention Act
PPM	Parts per million
PRP	Potentially responsible party
PSD	Prevention of significant deterioration

QA/QC	Quality assurance/quality control
RACM	Reasonably available control measures
RACT	Reasonably available control technology
RCRA	Resource Conservation and Recovery Act
RFA	Regulatory Flexibility Act
RFG	Reformulated gasoline
RI/FS	Remedial investigation and feasibility study
ROD	Record of decision
RPA	Reasonable and prudent alternative
RQ	Reportable quantity
RRRA	Restoration, rehabilitation, replacement, or acquisition
SAB	Scientific Advisory Board
SARA	Superfund Amendments and Reauthorization Act
SDWA	Safe Drinking Water Act
SEC	Securities and Exchange Commission
SEP	Supplemental environmental project
SEPA	State environmental policy act
SFIP	Sector Facility Indexing Project
SIP	State implementation plan
SO$_x$	Sulfur oxides
SPA	Slag processing area
SRF	State Revolving Fund
SWANCC	Solid Waste Agency of Northern Cook County
SWDA	Solid Waste Disposal Act
SWMU	Solid waste management unit
TCLP	Toxicity characteristic leaching procedure
TCM	Transportation control measure
TCP	Transportation control plan
TEIA	Transboundary environmental impact assessment
TMDL	Total maximum daily load
TRI	Toxic Release Inventory
TSCA	Toxic Substances Control Act
TSD	Treatment, storage, and disposal
TSDF	Treatment, storage, and disposal facility
TSP	Total suspended particulates
TSS	Total suspended solids
TTHMs	Total trihalomethanes
TVA	Tennessee Valley Authority
UAO	Unilateral administrative order
UIC	Underground injection control
UNDP	United Nations Development Program
UNEP	United Nations Environment Program
USC	United States Code
USDA	United States Department of Agriculture

USEPA	United States Environmental Protection Agency
USGS	United States Geological Survey
UST	Underground storage tank
VOCs	Volatile organic compounds
WMC	Watershed Management Council
WRP	Wetlands Reserve Program
WTE	Waste-to-energy
WTO	World Trade Organization

TABLE OF CASES

INDEX